Contemporary Literary Criticism

Guide to Gale Literary Criticism Series

For criticism on	Consult these Gale series
Authors now living or who died after December 31, 1959	***CONTEMPORARY LITERARY CRITICISM (CLC)***
Authors who died between 1900 and 1959	***TWENTIETH-CENTURY LITERARY CRITICISM (TCLC)***
Authors who died between 1800 and 1899	***NINETEENTH-CENTURY LITERATURE CRITICISM (NCLC)***
Authors who died between1400 and 1799	***LITERATURE CRITICISM FROM 1400 TO 1800 (LC)*** ***SHAKESPEAREAN CRITICISM (SC)***
Authors who died before 1400	***CLASSICAL AND MEDIEVAL LITERATURE CRITICISM (CMLC)***
Black writers of the past two hundred years	***BLACK LITERATURE CRITICISM (BLC) AND BLACK LITERATURE CRITICISM SUPPLEMENT (BLCS)***
Authors of books for children and young adults	***CHILDREN'S LITERATURE REVIEW (CLR)***
Dramatists	***DRAMA CRITICISM (DC)***
Hispanic writers of the late nineteenth and twentieth centuries	***HISPANIC LITERATURE CRITICISM (HLC)***
Native North American writers and orators of the eighteenth, nineteenth, and twentieth centuries	***NATIVE NORTH AMERICAN LITERATURE (NNAL)***
Poets	***POETRY CRITICISM (PC)***
Short story writers	***SHORT STORY CRITICISM (SSC)***
Major authors from the Renaissance to the present	***WORLD LITERATURE CRITICISM, 1500 TO THE PRESENT (WLC)***
Major authors and works from the Bible to the present	***WORLD LITERATURE CRITICISM SUPPLEMENT (WLCS)***

ISSN 0091-3421

Volume 125

Contemporary Literary Criticism

Criticism of the Works of Today's Novelists, Poets, Playwrights, Short Story Writers, Scriptwriters, and Other Creative Writers

Jeffrey W. Hunter
EDITOR

Jennifer Cromie
ASSOCIATE EDITOR

Rebecca Blanchard
Justin Karr
Linda Pavlovski
ASSISTANT EDITORS

GALE GROUP

Detroit
New York
San Francisco
London
Boston
Woodbridge, CT

STAFF

Library of Congress Catalog Card Number 76-46132
ISBN 0-7876-3200-7
ISSN 0091-3421

Printed in the United States of America
10 9 8 7 6 5 4 3 2 1

Contents

Preface

A Comprehensive Information Source on Contemporary Literature

Named "one of the twenty-five most distinguished reference titles published during the past twenty-five years" by *Reference Quarterly*, the *Contemporary Literary Criticism (CLC)* series provides readers with critical commentary and general information on more than 2,000 authors now living or who died after December 31, 1959. Previous to the publication of the first volume of *CLC* in 1973, there was no ongoing digest monitoring scholarly and popular sources of critical opinion and explication of modern literature. *CLC*, therefore, has fulfilled an essential need, particularly since the complexity and variety of contemporary literature makes the function of criticism especially important to today's reader.

Scope of the Series

CLC presents significant passages from published criticism of works by creative writers. Since many of the authors covered by *CLC* inspire continual critical commentary, writers are often represented in more than one volume. There is, of course, no duplication of reprinted criticism.

Authors are selected for inclusion for a variety of reasons, among them the publication or dramatic production of a critically acclaimed new work, the reception of a major literary award, revival of interest in past writings, or the adaptation of a literary work to film or television.

Attention is also given to several other groups of writers—authors of considerable public interest—about whose work criticism is often difficult to locate. These include mystery and science fiction writers, literary and social critics, foreign writers, and authors who represent particular ethnic groups.

Format of the Book

Each *CLC* volume contains individual essays and reviews taken from hundreds of book review periodicals, general magazines, scholarly journals, monographs, and books. Entries include critical evaluations spanning from the beginning of an author's career to the most current commentary. Interviews, feature articles, and other published writings that offer insight into the author's works are also presented. Students, teachers, librarians, and researchers will find that the generous critical and biographical material in *CLC* provides them with vital information required to write a term paper, analyze a poem, or lead a book discussion group. In addition, complete bibliographical citations note the original source and all of the information necessary for a term paper footnote or bibliography.

Features

A *CLC* author entry consists of the following elements:

- The **Author Heading** cites the author's name in the form under which the author has most commonly published, followed by birth date, and death date when applicable. Uncertainty as to a birth or death date is indicated by a question mark.

- A **Portrait** of the author is included when available.

- A brief **Biographical and Critical Introduction** to the author and his or her work precedes the criticism. The first line of the introduction provides the author's full name, pseudonyms (if applicable), nationality, and a listing of genres in which the author has written. To provide users with easier access to information, the biographical and critical essay included in each author entry is divided into four categories: "Introduction," "Biographical Information," "Major Works," and "Critical Reception." The introductions to single-work entries—entries that focus on well known and frequently studied books, short stories, and poems—are similarly organized to quickly provide readers with information on the plot and major characters of the work being discussed, its major themes, and its critical reception. Previous volumes of *CLC* in which the author has been featured are also listed in the introduction.

- A list of **Principal Works** notes the most important writings by the author. When foreign-language works have been translated into English, the English-language version of the title follows in brackets.

- The **Criticism** represents various kinds of critical writing, ranging in form from the brief review to the scholarly exegesis. Essays are selected by the editors to reflect the spectrum of opinion about a specific work or about an author's literary career in general. The critical and biographical materials are presented chronologically, adding a useful perspective to the entry. All titles by the author featured in the entry are printed in boldface type, which enables the reader to easily identify the works being discussed. Publication information (such as publisher names and book prices) and parenthetical numerical references (such as footnotes or page and line references to specific editions of a work) have been deleted at the editor's discretion to provide smoother reading of the text.

- Critical essays are prefaced by **Explanatory Notes** as an additional aid to readers. These notes may provide several types of valuable information, including: the reputation of the critic, the importance of the work of criticism, the commentator's approach to the author's work, the purpose of the criticism, and changes in critical trends regarding the author.

- A complete **Bibliographical Citation** designed to help the user find the original essay or book precedes each critical piece.

- Whenever possible, a recent **Author Interview** accompanies each entry.

- A concise **Further Reading** section appears at the end of entries on authors for whom a significant amount of criticism exists in addition to the pieces reprinted in *CLC.* Each citation in this section is accompanied by a descriptive annotation describing the content of that article. Materials included in this section are grouped under various headings (e.g., Biography, Bibliography, Criticism, and Interviews) to aid users in their search for additional information. Cross-references to other useful sources published by The Gale Group in which the author has appeared are also included: *Authors in the News, Black Writers, Children's Literature Review, Contemporary Authors, Dictionary of Literary Biography, DISCovering Authors, Drama Criticism, Hispanic Literature Criticism, Hispanic Writers, Native North American Literature, Poetry Criticism, Something about the Author, Short Story Criticism, Contemporary Authors Autobiography Series,* and *Something about the Author Autobiography Series.*

Other Features

CLC also includes the following features:

- An **Acknowledgments** section lists the copyright holders who have granted permission to reprint material in this volume of *CLC.* It does not, however, list every book or periodical reprinted or consulted during the preparation of the volume.

- Each new volume of *CLC* includes a **Cumulative Topic Index,** which lists all literary topics treated in *CLC, NCLC, TCLC,* and *LC 1400-1800.*

- A **Cumulative Author Index** lists all the authors who have appeared in the various literary criticism series published by The Gale Group, with cross-references to Gale's biographical and autobiographical series. A full listing of the series referenced there appears on the first page of the indexes of this volume. Readers will welcome this cumulated author index as a useful tool for locating an author within the various series. The index, which lists birth and death dates when available, will be particularly valuable for those authors who are identified with a certain period but whose death dates cause them to be placed in another, or for those authors whose careers span two periods. For example, Ernest Hemingway is found in *CLC,* yet F. Scott Fitzgerald, a writer often associated with him, is found in *Twentieth-Century Literary Criticism.*

- A **Cumulative Nationality Index** alphabetically lists all authors featured in *CLC* by nationality, followed by numbers corresponding to the volumes in which the authors appear.

- An alphabetical **Title Index** accompanies each volume of *CLC.* Listings are followed by the author's name and the corresponding page numbers where the titles are discussed. English translations of foreign titles and variations of titles are cross-referenced to the title under which a work was originally published. Titles of novels, novellas, dramas, films, record albums, and poetry, short story, and essay collections are printed in italics, while all individual poems, short stories, essays, and songs are printed in roman type within quotation marks; when published separately (e.g., T. S. Eliot's poem *The Waste Land),* the titles of long poems are printed in italics.

- In response to numerous suggestions from librarians, Gale has also produced a **Special Paperbound Edition** of the *CLC* title index. This annual cumulation, which alphabetically lists all titles reviewed in the series, is available to all customers. Additional copies of the index are available upon request. Librarians and patrons will welcome this separate index: it saves shelf space, is easy to use, and is recyclable upon receipt of the next edition.

Citing *Contemporary Literary Criticism*

When writing papers, students who quote directly from any volume in the Literary Criticism Series may use the following general forms to footnote reprinted criticism. The first example pertains to material drawn from periodicals, the second to material reprinted in books:

[1]Alfred Cismaru, "Making the Best of It," *The New Republic,* 207, No. 24, (December 7, 1992), 30, 32; excerpted and reprinted in *Contemporary Literary Criticism,* Vol. 85, ed. Christopher Giroux (Detroit: Gale, 1995), pp. 73-4.

[2]Yvor Winters, *The Post-Symbolist Methods* (Allen Swallow, 1967); excerpted and reprinted in *Contemporary Literary Criticism,* Vol. 85, ed. Christopher Giroux (Detroit: Gale, 1995), pp. 223-26.

Suggestions Are Welcome

The editors hope that readers will find *CLC* a useful reference tool and welcome comments about the work. Send comments and suggestions to: Editors, *Contemporary Literary Criticism,* The Gale Group, 27500 Drake Rd., Farmington Hills, MI 48333-3535.

Acknowledgments

The editors wish to thank the copyright holders of the excerpted criticism included in this volume and the permissions managers of many book and magazine publishing companies for assisting us in securing reproduction rights. We are also grateful to the staffs of the Detroit Public Library, the Library of Congress, the University of Detroit Mercy Library, Wayne State University Purdy/Kresge Library Complex, and the University of Michigan Libraries for making their resources available to us. Following is a list of the copyright holders who have granted us permission to reproduce material in this volume of *CLC*. Every effort has been made to trace copyright, but if omissions have been made, please contact the editors.

COPYRIGHTED MATERIALS IN *CLC*, VOLUME 125, WERE REPRODUCED FROM THE FOLLOWING PERIODICALS:

The Antioch Review, v. 39, Fall, 1981. Copyright © 1981 by the Antioch Review Inc. Reproduced by permission of the editors.—**The Atlantic Monthly,** v. 20, December, 1962. Copyright 1962 by The Atlantic Monthly Company, Boston, MA. Reproduced by permission of the author.—**A Review of English Literature,** v. IV, January, 1963. Reproduced by permission.—**Artforum**, v. 31, November, 1992 for "Who's Afraid of Red Yellow and Blonde?" by Manohla Dargis; v. 33, March, 1995 for Geek Chic" by Gary Indiana; v. 33, March, 1995 for "Minor Magic" by Dennis Cooper; v. 33, March, 1995 for "Slick Shtick" by Robin Wood; v. 33, March, 1995 for Geek Chic" by Gary Indiana; v, 33, March, 1995 for "Slick Shtick" by Robin Wood.©1992, 1995 Artforum International Magazine, Inc. All reprinted by permission of the publisher and the authors.—**AUMLA**, n. 77, May, 1992; n. 81, May, 1994. Both reproduced by permission of the publisher.—**Black American Literature Forum**, v. 24, March, 1990 in a review of 'Blacks.'. Copyright © 1990 by the author. Reproduced by permission of the author—**The Black Scholar**, v. 15, November-December, 1984. Copyright 1984 by **The Black Scholar**. Reproduced by permission.—**Chicago Tribune Books,** July 10, 1994 for "From the Thurber Trove: Good Humor, Good Always" by James Idema. © 1994 Tribune Media Services, Inc. All rights reserved. Reproduced by permission of the author.—**Chicago Tribune,** May 1, 1994 for "Deadly Details and Rules for Living" by Thomas McGonigle. © 1994 Tribune Media Services, Inc. All rights reserved. Reproduced by permission of the author.—**The Christian Century,** November,16, 1994. Copyright 1994 Christian Century Foundation. Reproduced by permission from The Christian Century.—**Christian Science Monitor,** December 14, 1981. © 1981 The Christian Science Publishing Society. All rights reserved. Reproduced by permission from **The Christian Science Monitor**.—**CLA Journal**, v. XXX, March, 1987. Copyright, 1987 by The College Language Association. Used by permission of The College Language Association. —**Commonweal,** v. 24, October 22, 1993; November 18, 1994. Copyright © 1993,1994 Commonweal Publishing Co., Inc. Both reproduced by permission of Commonweal Foundation.—**Concerning Poetry**, v. 10, Fall, 1977. Copyright © 1977, Western Washington University. Reproduced by permission.—**Contemporary Literature,** v. XIII, Summer, 1972; v. XXIV, Spring, 1983; v. 34, Spring, 1993. © 1972, 1983, 1993 by the Board of Regents of the University of Wisconsin System. All reproduced by permission.—**Contemporary Review**, v. 222, February, 1973. Reproduced by permission.—**Critique: Studies in Modern Fiction,** v. XX, 1978; v. XXI, 1980; v. XXXIV, Spring, 1993. Copyright © 1978, 1982, 1993 Helen Dwight Reid Educational Foundation. All reproduced with permission of the Helen Dwight Reid Educational Foundation, published by Heldref Publications, 119 18th Street, N. W., Washington, DC 20036-1802.—**English Studies,** v. 74, October, 1993. © 1993, Swets & Zeitlinger. Reproduced by permission.—**Essays in Literature,** v. 11, Spring, 1984. Copyright 1984 by Western Illinois University. Reproduced by permission.—**The Explicator,** v. 140, Summer, 1982; v. 55, Spring, 1997. Copyright 1982 by Helen Dwight Reid Educational Foundation. Both reproduced with permission of the Helen Dwight Reid Educational Foundation, published by Heldref Publications, 1319 18th Street, NW, Washington, DC 20036-1802.—**Film Comment,** v. 32, January-February. 1996 for "Doing Brando" by Lyall Bush. Copyright © 1996 by Film Comment Publishing Corporation. Reproduced by permission of the author.—**History of European Ideas,** v.11, 1989. Reproduced by permission.—**The Hollins Critic,** v. XXIX, June, 1992. Copyright 1992 by Hollins College. Reproduced by permission.—**The Iowa Review,** v. 5, Winter, 1995. Copyright © 1995 by The University of Iowa. Reproduced by permission of the author.—**Journal of American Culture,** v. 16, Fall, 1993. Copyright © 1993 by Ray B. Browne. Reproduced by permission.—**The Kenyon Review**,

v. XIII, Fall, 1991 for "Gwendolyn Brooks: An Essential Sanity." by Henry Taylor. v. XVII, Winter, 1995 for The Loss of Lyric Space and the Critique of Traditions in Gwendolyn Brooks's In the Mecca" by Cherryl Clarke. Copyright © 1991, 1995 by Kenyon College. Reprinted in a compilation of articles by Henry Taylor in Compulsory Figures, 1992 by the Louisiana State University Press; All rights reserved both reproduced by permission of the Louisiana State University Press and the authors. —**Literature and Film Quarterly**, v. 26, January, 1998. © copyright 1998 Salisbury State College. Reproduced by permission.—**Los Angeles Times Book Review,** February 24, 1985; November 25, 1990; October 23, 1992; September 10, 1993; December 25, 1995; January 19, 1996; February 25, 1996; December 24, 1997. Copyright, 1985, 1990, 1992, 1993, 1995, 1996, 1997 Los Angeles Times. All reproduced by permission. —**Michigan Quarterly Review**, v. 31, summer, 1992 for "The American Sublime, C. 1992: What Clothes Does One Wear?" by Mutlu Konok Blasing. Copyright © The University of Michigan, 1992. All rights reserved. Reproduced by permission of the author.—**Modern Fiction Studies,** v. 37, Winter, 1991. Copyright © by Purdue Research Foundation. All rights reserved. Reproduced by permission.—**Mosiac,** v. XIX, Fall, 1986. © Mosaic 1986. Acknowledgment of previous publication is herewith made. Reproduced by permission.—**The New Criterion,** v. 8, October, 1989. Copyright © 1989 by The Foundation for Cultural Review. Reproduced by permission of the author.—**The New Republic,** v. 47, December 22, 1962; February 25, 1985; January 23, 1989; November 23, 1992; November 14.1994.©1962, 1985 1989,1992 The New Republic, Inc. All reproduced by permission of **The New Republic.**—**New Literary History,** v. 25, Spring, 1994. Copyright © 1994 by New Literary History. Reproduced by permission of The Johns Hopkins University Press.—**New Statesman, & Society,** v. 2, December 15, 1989; January 8, 1993; October 8, 1994. © 1989, 1993, 1994 The Statesman & Nation Publishing Co. Ltd. Reproduced by permission.—**New Statesman,** v. 103, February, 1982. © 1982 The Statesman & Nation Publishing Co. Ltd. Reproduced by permission.—**New York Herald Tribune Books,** v. 5, May 19, 1929; v. 8, March 27, 1932; January 26, 1941; November 25, 1962. Copyright © 1929, 1932, 1941, 1962. by The New York Times Company. Reproduced by permission. —**New York, Magazine,** March 11, 1991; October 3, 1994. Copyright © 1991, 1994 PRIMEDIA Magazine Corporation. All rights reserved. Reproduced with the permission of **New York Magazine.** —**The New York Review of Books,** v. 40, June 24, 1993. Copyright © 1993 Nyrev, Inc. Reproduced with permission from The New York Review of Books. —**The New York Times Book Review**, September 4, 1994; April 21, 1996. Copyright © 1994, 1996 by The New York Times Company. Both reproduced by permission. —**The New York Times Magazine,** November 16, 1993. Copyright © 1993 by The New York Times Company. Reproduced by permission. —**Papers on Language and Literature,** v. 26, Spring, 1990. Copyright © 1990 by The Board of Trustees, Southern Illinois University at Edwardsville. Reproduced by permission.—**Parnassus,** v. 17, Fall, 1992. Copyright © 1992 Poetry in Review Foundation, NY. Reproduced by permission.—**Poetry,** v. 165, October, 1994. © 1994 by the Modern Poetry Association. Both reproduced by permission of the Editor of **Poetry** and the author.—**The Progressive,** v. 46, May, 1982. Copyright © 1982 by The Progressive, Inc. Reproduced by permission of The Progressive, 409 East Main Street, Madison, WI 53703.—**Raritan: A Quarterly Review,** v. 15, Fall; 1995; v. 14, Winter, 1995. Copyright © 1995 by **Raritan: A Quarterly Review.** Both reproduced by permission.—**Renascence: Essays on Value in Literature,** v. 40, Fall, 1987; v. 46, Summer, 1994. © copyright, 1987, 1994 Marquette University Press. Both reproduced by permission.—**Rolling Stone,** October 6, 1994; November 3, 1994; January 22. 1998. © 1994,1998 by Straight Arrow Publishers, Inc. All rights reserved. Both reproduced by permission.—**Sewanee Review**, XCIII, Fall, 1985. © 1985 by Melvin Maddocks. Copyright 1985 by Melvin Maddocks. Reproduced by permission of the editor and author.—**Southern Literary Journal,** v. 27. Spring, 1995. Copyright 1995 by the Department of English, University of North Carolina at Chapel Hill. Reproduced by permission.—**Studies in American Fiction,** v. 22, Spring, 1994. Copyright © 1994 Northeastern University. Reproduced by permission.—**Studies in American Humor,** v. 3, Summer/Fall. 1982. Copyright © 1984 by Southwest Texas State University. Reproduced by permission.—**Studies in Short Fiction**, v. 15, Fall, 1978. Copyright 1978 by Newberry College. Reproduced by permission.—**Studies in the Literary Imagination**, October, 1968. Copyright 1968 Department of English, Georgia State University. Reproduced by permission.—**Studies in the Novel,** v. 24, Spring, 1992. Copyright 1992 by North Texas State University. Reproduced by permission.—**The Southern Review**, v. 27, Autumn, 1991 for "The Uncynical Disillusion of Graham Greene," in **The Southern Review**. Also in his collected works, Martin Lebowitz: His Thoughts and Writing. Reproduced by permission of the author.—**The Spectator,** October 17, 1987; November 5, 1994; April 22, 1995. © 1987, 1994.1995 by **The Spectator.** Reproduced by permission of **The Spectator.**—**Thalia; Studies in Literary Humor**. v. 2, Winter, 1979-1980. Copyright © 1979 by Jacqueline Tavernier-Courbin. Copyright © 1979-1980 by Jacqueline Tavernier-Courbin. Reproduced by **The Threepenny**

Review, v. XV, Fall, 1994. Reproduced by permission.—**Time,** January, 1982; February 11, 1985; October 5, 1987. Copyright 1982,1985,1987 Time Warner Inc. All rights reserved. Both reproduced by permission from Time.—**Times Literary Supplement,** May 16, 1975; December 29, 1989; January 4, 1990; May 24, 1991; November 4, 1994; © The Times Supplements Limited 1975, 1989, 1990, 1991, 1994. All reproduced from **The Times Literary Supplement** by permission.—**Tulsa Studies in Women's Literature,** v. 12, 1993. © 1993, The University of Tulsa. Reproduced by permission.—**Variety,** December 22, 1997. Reproduced by permission.—**Washington Post Book World,** February 7, 1993. © 1993, Washington Post Book World Service/Washington Post Writers Group. Reproduced by permission of the author.

COPYRIGHTED MATERIAL IN *CLC*, VOLUME 125, WERE REPRODUCED FROM THE FOLLOWING BOOKS:

Berman, Russell A. From "Written Right Across Their Faces: Ernst Jünger's Fascist Modernism" in **Modernity and the Text:** Revisions of German Modernism Edited Andreas Huyssen and David Bathrick. Copyright © 1989 Columbia University Press. All rights reserved. Reproduced by permission. —Brownstein, Rachel M. From "The Odd Woman and Literary Feminism," in **American Women Writing Fiction: Memory, Identity, Family, Space.** Edited by Mickey Pearlman. The University of Kentucky Press, 1989. Copyright © 1989 by The University Press of Kentucky. Reproduced by permission.—Christian, Barbara. From **Black Feminist Criticism: Perspectives on Black Women Writers**, (New York: Teachers College, Columbia University. All rights reserved. Reprined by permission of the publisher.—Evans, Arthur R. Jr. From "Ernst Jünger's Auf den Marmorklippen: A Sketch Toward an Interpretation," in **Symbolism and Modern Literature.** Edited by Marcel Tetel. Copyright © 1978 by Duke University Press, Durham, NC. Reproduced by permission.—Flowers, Betty S, From "Wrestling with the Mother and Father: 'His' and 'Her' in Adrienne Rich," in **Private Voices, Public Lives**: Women Speak in the Literary Life. Edited by Nancy Owen Nelson. University of North Texas Press, 1995. © 1995 University of North Texas Press. All rights reserved. Reproduced by permission.—Jones, Suzanne W. From "Dismantling Stereotypes: Interracial Friendships in Meridian and A Mother and Two Daughters," in **The Female Tradition in Southern Literature.** Edited by Carol S. Manning. University of Illinois Press, 1982. © 1993 by the Board of Trustees of the University of Illinois. Reproduced by permission.—Lindberg, Kathryne V. From "Whose Canon? Gwendolyn Brooks: Founder at the Center of the Margins," in **Gendered Modernisms: American Women Poets and Their Readers**. Edited by Margaret Dickie and Thomas Travisano, University of Pennsylvania Press, 1996. Copyright © 1996 by the University of Pennsylvania Press. All rights reserved. Reproduced by permission.—Rhodes, Carolyn. From "Gail Godwin and the Ideal of Southern Womanhood," in **Women Writers of the Contemporary South.** Edited by Peggy Whitman Prenshaw, Copyright © 1984 by The Southern Quarterly. All rights reserved. Reproduced by permission.—Spillers, Hortense J. From "Gwendolyn the Terrible: Propositions on Eleven Poems" in **Shakespeare's Sisters: Feminist Essays on Women Poets.** Edited by Sandra M. Gilbert and Susan Gubar. Copyright © 1979 by Sandra M. Gilbert and Susan Gubar. All rights reserved. Reproduced by permission.—Tate, Claudia, From "Anger So Flat: Gwendolyn Brools' Annie Allen," in **A Life Distilled: Gwendolyn Brooks, Her Poetry and Fiction.** Edited by Maria K. Mootry and Gary Smith. © 1987 by the Board of Trustees of the University of Illinois. Reproduced by permission.

PHOTOGRAPHS AND ILLUSTRATIONS APPEARING IN *CLC* VOLUME 125 WERE RECEIVED FROM THE FOLLOWING SOURCES:

Ashbery, John, photograph. AP/Wide World Photos. Reproduced by permission.

Brooks, Gwendolyn (wearing scarf, dark framed glasses), 1986, photograph. AP/Wide World Photos, Inc. Reproduced by permission.

Godwin, Gail, photograph by Jerry Bauer. Reproduced by permission.

Greene, Graham (wearing dark suit and Medal of Commander of Arts and Letters), Paris, France, 1984, photograph. AP/Wide World Photos, Inc. Reproduced by permission.

Junger, Ernst (close-up, white hair), photograph. Archive Photos/Camera Press. Reproduced by permission.

Powys, John Cowper (wearing a patchwork vest, shawl-collared jacket), age 72, 1945, photograph. AP/Wide World Photos. Reproduced by permission.

Rich, Adrienne (holding certificate of poetry award), Chicago, Illinois, 1986, photograph. AP/Wide World Photos. Reproduced by permission.

Tarantino, Quentin, photograph. AP/Wide World Photos. Reproduced by permission.

John Ashbery

1927-

(Has also written under pseudonym Jonas Berry) American poet, playwright, novelist, critic, editor, and translator.

The following entry presents an overview of Ashbery's career through 1997. For further information on his life and works, see *CLC,* Volumes 2, 3, 4, 6, 9, 13, 15, 25, 41, and 77.

INTRODUCTION

John Ashbery is considered among the most influential and challenging American poets of the postwar period. His highly inventive, often enigmatic verse defies the conventions of logic, linear thought, and realism in an effort to deconstruct language and the paradoxical limits of verbal expression. Drawing attention to the fragmentary quality of unconscious thought and the creative process itself, Ashbery's provocative linguistic experiments, narrative juxtapositions, and improvisational style illustrate the infinite possibility of multidimensional perspective and random experience. Associated with the "New York Poets" during the 1950s and 1960s, Ashbery established his reputation with the award-winning volumes *Some Trees* (1956), *The Tennis Court Oath* (1962), *Three Poems* (1972), and *Self-Portrait in a Convex Mirror* (1975). He received subsequent acclaim with additional volumes such as *A Wave* (1984) and *Flow Chart* (1991). An innovative poet of remarkable intelligence, humor, and originality, Ashbery is recognized as one of the leading poets of his generation.

Biographical Information

Born in Rochester, New York, Ashbery was raised in Sodus, a small upstate New York town near Lake Ontario. His father was a fruit farmer and his mother a former high school biology teacher. Ashbery's maternal grandfather, Henry Lawrence, was a renowned physicist at the University of Rochester whose personal library became a resource for the precocious Ashbery. Though initially interested in painting and later music, Ashbery began writing poetry as a child. Upon graduation from Deerfield Academy in Massachusetts in 1945, Ashbery enrolled at Harvard University, where he majored in English literature, completed a senior thesis on W. H. Auden, and befriended poets Kenneth Koch and Frank O'Hara. After finishing his undergraduate degree at Harvard in 1949, Ashbery moved to New York City to begin study at Columbia University, where he earned a master's degree in French literature in 1951. While in New York, Ashbery entered the booming postwar arts scene with painters Larry Rivers and Jane Freilicher and poets Koch, O'Hara, and James Schuyler—later labelled the "New York Poets" with Ashbery as their foremost representative. Ashbery's first volume of poetry, *Turandot and Other Poems* (1953), was a limited edition publication with illustrations by Freilicher. Between 1951 and 1955, Ashbery worked as copywriter for Oxford University Press and McGraw-Hill. During the early 1950s, Ashbery also wrote two plays—*The Heroes* (1952) and *The Compromise* (1955). A third play, *The Philosopher* (1964), appeared in *Art and Literature* magazine and was later republished with his earlier two in *Three Plays* (1978). The manuscript of Ashbery's second volume of poetry, *Some Trees,* was selected by Auden as the winner of the Yale Series of Younger Poets Prize in 1956 and published the same year. The recipient of two Fulbright scholarships, Ashbery set off for Paris where he lived and worked for the next decade as a poet and art critic for several prominent periodicals, including the *New York Herald Tribune, Art International,* and *ArtNews,* for which he later served as executive editor from 1966 to 1972. While overseas, Ashbery produced *The Tennis Court Oath,* earning him the Harriet Monroe Poetry Award from *Poetry* magazine the next year. Upon his return to New York in 1965, Ashbery published

Rivers and Mountains (1966), a National Book Award nominee, *Sunrise in Suburbia* (1968), *Fragment* (1969), and the novel *A Nest of Ninnies* (1969) with Schuyler. He also received several Guggenheim fellowships, grants from the National Endowment for the Arts, and a National Institute of Arts and Letters Award in 1969. Over the next decade, Ashbery published *The Double Dream of Spring* (1970), *Three Poems* (1972), recipient of a Shelley Memorial Award, and *Self-Portrait in a Convex Mirror,* winner of the Pulitzer Prize, National Book Award, and National Book Critics Circle Award in 1976. He has since published additional volumes of poetry—*Houseboat Days* (1977), *As We Know* (1979), *Shadow Train* (1981), *A Wave* (1984), *April Galleons* (1987), *Flow Chart* (1991), *Hotel Lautreamont* (1992), *And the Stars Were Shining* (1994), and *Can You Hear, Bird* (1995)—and a collection of art criticism, *Reported Sightings* (1989). An art critic for *Newsweek* during the 1980s, Ashbery has also edited numerous anthologies of contemporary poetry, translated several French titles, and taught English and creative writing at Brooklyn College of the City University of New York from 1974 to 1990. He was awarded the Robert Frost medal from the Poetry Society of America in 1995.

Major Works

Ashbery's preoccupation with the indeterminate relationship between language, perception, time, and artistic expression is a prominent feature of his poetry. Influenced by French symbolist writers, modern abstract expressionist art, particularly the action paintings of Jackson Pollack and Robert Motherwell, and the avant-garde music of composer John Cage, Ashbery's poetry derives from the post-logical literary and artistic traditions of the early twentieth century. *Some Trees,* Ashbery's first major publication, displays his technical skill as well as early attempts to articulate multiple levels of reality in flights of imagination and word play. In one poem, "The Instruction Manual," the speaker is a disenchanted technical writer who daydreams about a faraway trip to Guadalajara, suggesting the ironic tension between order and the longing to escape. *The Tennis Court Oath* focuses on the incomprehensible totality of language in disjointed compositions resembling surrealist visual art. The collage poem "Europe," divided into 111 parts with cut-outs from the 1917 British detective novel *Beryl of the Biplane,* revolves around themes of postwar espionage, political paranoia, and the failure of technology and language. In another poem, "They Dream Only of America," Ashbery similarly evokes the disorienting simultaneity of lived experience in a random assemblage of non sequiturs and wide-ranging references to politics, literature, and popular culture. *Rivers and Mountains* is a transitional work that introduces the innovative roving perspective of Ashbery's mature style, particularly as revealed in the poem "Clepsydra," whose title refers to a water clock. This poem, characteristic of many of Ashbery's subsequent compositions, begins mid-thought and contains alternating first and second person observations, exposing the nonverbal interaction between conscious and unconscious reflection. The interchangeable use of first, second, and third person pronouns to portray shifting perspective would become a staple device in Ashbery's work. Another poem from this volume, "The Skaters," suggests the performativity of linguistic displays as a series of dissolving and surfacing activities and entities. *Three Poems* consists of a book length prose meditation divided into three parts. The middle poem, "The System," is among Ashbery's most important linguistic experiments in which he reflects on the living, open-ended qualities of poetry and posits that in the elusive malleability of language inheres the foundation for love, understanding, and interpersonal connectivity. *Self-Portrait in a Convex Mirror* signals the culmination of Ashbery's previous innovations, incorporating fragmentary digressions, crosscuts, irregular syntax, and dreamlike self-examination in evocative language and sensuous phrasing that denies logical comprehension. The title poem, inspired by the self-portrait of sixteenth century Italian painter Francesco Parmigianino, foregrounds the distortions of self-image and sensory perception to explore the limitations of form and the sprawling byways of conscious thought. In a final recital, a recurring feature of Ashbery's poetry, he summarizes the significance and affirmative power of poetry and art as a means to approach the "otherness" of language. "Litany" a notable poem from *As We Know,* further probes the ineffable gap between perception and language. Consisting of two columns of verse, one in roman the other in italic type, Ashbery illustrates the disharmonious intersection of experience, mood, and free association in a cacophony of competing voices. The lengthy title poem of *A Wave,* another significant work, explores the perpetual unfolding of experience and the preconditions for love, particularly as found in epiphany and replenishing moments of speechless withdraw and distraction. Ashbery's investigations into the essence and dimensions of expression is foremost in the book length poem *Flow Chart.* Divided into six sections, the lengthy composition is a pastiche of personal memory, literary allusion, extraneous fragments of daily experience, and internal dialogue that suggest the regenerative nature of language despite its inherent inadequacy and perpetual deconstruction. Subsequent volumes, including *Hotel Lautreamont, And the Stars Where Shining,* and *Can You Hear, Bird,* evince similar efforts to come to terms with the insufficiency and ambivalence of language in Ashbery's trademark amalgamation of meandering ruminations, semantic puzzles, deadpan rhetoric, artful solecisms, and moments of awestruck revelation.

Critical Reception

Ashbery is regarded as one of the most important American poets of the last half century. His demanding, idiosyncratic studies of perception, thought processes, and the mutability of language are consistently praised for their capacity to conjure disquieting verbal landscapes of exceptional depth and resonance. While *Some Trees, The Tennis Court Oath,* and *Three Poems* established Ashbery's reputation as a formidable emerging talent, he is best known for his acclaimed *Self-Portrait in a Convex Mirror,* generally considered his most significant work. Subsequent volumes, particularly *Flow Chart,* have also attracted considerable critical attention and esteem. Though some critics find fault in the opacity of Ashbery's solipsistic poetry, often oblique to the point of impenetrability, most focus on his remarkable ability to evoke the totality of being in accumulations of random observations, incongruous associations, and the fleeting sensations of awareness. Despite the daunting aspirations of his ambitious investigations into the limits of knowledge and expression, as many critics note, Ashbery counters hopelessness with irony, parody, and invigorating language that extracts nascent and residual meanings from seemingly disconnected musings and the mundane minutiae of everyday experience. Distinguished for his linguistic dislocations and capacious vision, critics frequently cite the influence of Wallace Stevens and Walt Whitman in Ashbery's poetry, as well as the aesthetic concerns of avant-garde art and music which informs so much of his work. A highly original and much honored poet, Ashbery is hailed as one of the most significant American poets of the twentieth century.

PRINCIPAL WORKS

The Heroes (drama) 1952
Turandot and Other Poems (poetry) 1953
The Compromise (drama) 1955
Some Trees (poetry) 1960
The Poems (poetry) 1960
The Tennis Court Oath (poetry) 1962
The Philosopher (drama) 1964
Rivers and Mountains (poetry) 1966
Selected Poems (poetry) 1967
Sunrise in Suburbia (poetry) 1968
Three Madigrals (poetry) 1968
Fragment (poetry) 1969
A Nest of Ninnies [with James Schuyler] (novel) 1969
The Double Dream of Spring (poetry) 1970
The New Spirit (poetry) 1970
Three Poems (poetry) 1972
Self-Portrait in a Convex Mirror (poetry) 1975
The Serious Doll (poetry) 1975
The Vermont Notebook [with Joe Brainard] (poetry) 1975
Houseboat Days (poetry) 1977
Three Plays [includes *The Heroes, The Compromise,* and *The Philosopher*] (drama) 1978
As We Know (poetry) 1979
Shadow Train: Fifty Lyrics (poetry) 1981
A Wave (poetry) 1984
Selected Poems (poetry) 1985
April Galleons (poetry) 1987
Reported Sightings: Art Chronicles, 1957-1987 (criticism) 1989
Flow Chart (poetry) 1991
Hotel Lautreamont (poetry) 1992
And the Stars Were Shining (poetry) 1994
Can You Hear, Bird (poetry) 1995
The Mooring of Starting Out: The First Five Books of Poetry (poetry) 1997

CRITICISM

Kevin Clark (essay date Spring 1990)

SOURCE: "John Ashbery's 'A Wave': Privileging the Symbol," in *Papers on Language and Literature,* Vol. 26, No. 2, Spring, 1990, pp. 271-9.

[*In the following essay, Clark offers critical analysis of the poem "The Wave." According to Clark, "Ashbery's poetry is distinguished by an enigmatic style which privileges indeterminacy rather than the traditional symbolist style practiced by most modernist and postmodernist poets."*]

> . . . [long poems] are in a way diaries or logbooks of a continuing experience that continues to provide new reflections and therefore [a long poem] gets to be much closer to a whole reality than the shorter ones do.
>
> John Ashbery
> Interview, *New York Quarterly*

That Ashbery believes long poems are "much closer to a whole reality" than shorter poems is telling. Despite their sometimes inhibiting length and poetics, his own long poems written since 1975 are considerably closer not only to "a whole reality" but to conventional poetic technique, one which few critics acknowledge. One of his most brilliant critics is Marjorie Perloff, who without making a distinction between long and short poems, maintains that Ashbery's poetry is distinguished by an enigmatic style which privileges indeterminacy rather than the traditional symbolist style practiced by most modernist and postmodernist poets. I would like here to refine Perloff's thesis by suggesting that, while Ashbery makes much use of this enigmatic style in his long poems, passages characterized by such a style are blended into and subordinated to a dominant symbolist technique, rendering his later long poems surprisingly conventional and more easily interpretable. A good example is his most recent long poem, **"A Wave"** (1984).

Taken from the book by the same title, **"A Wave"** is characterized by the poet's desire to represent experience as ongoing impression, "the tender blur of the setting." Where most poets write as if meaning can be gathered from distinctly unique or intense episodes, Ashbery—particularly in his more recent long poems—insists that only a sense of meaning can be felt, and this only for short periods.

> And the issue of making sense becomes such a
> far-off one.
> Isn't this "sense"—
> This little dog of my life that I can see—that
> answers me
> Like a dog, and wags its tails, though excitement
> and
> fidelity are
> About all that ever gets expressed?

While his subject here may be the indeterminacy of consciousness, his writing is conventionally referential. By "sense" of meaning he intends the emotional world we inhabit. Since the publication of **"Self-Portrait in a Convex Mirror"** (1975), Ashbery's long poems render this interior world so accurately by transmitting such a multitude of deceptively casual musings, like the one above, that the ideas give way to effect: we retain the impression of a human being continually engaging elementary questions about life more than we retain any of the specific questions or answers. Meaning is not forgotten, but, because Ashbery seems always to doubt but never entirely reject the *possibility* of meaning, we are left with a notion of his continuing uncertainty.

But this is not to say his long poems are afloat, unfixed in a universe of non sequiturs. Most of Ashbery's recent long poems are accessible, though their style can seem at first prohibitively resistant to understanding. Eventually, competent readers can find that the truly enigmatic passages are blended with those of reasonably straightforward language to produce an impression of the conscious mind in alternating periods of perplexity and clarity. And throughout the poem, Ashbery nearly announces his technique as well as his point of view. He is not evasive; he is referential—that is to say, he employs symbolist tools.

Perloff sees symbolist writing as that kind described by Eliot in his call for an objective correlative. In Eliot's words, the "only way of expressing emotion in the form of art is by finding 'an objective correlative'; in other words, a set of objects, a situation, a chain of events which shall be the formula of that *particular* emotion. . . ." Perloff also turns to Auden's claim that a poet may describe the "sacred encounters of his imagination" in terms of something other than the components of that encounter. Surely Perloff is correct in her translation of Eliot's and Auden's poetics, contending that the two High Modernists were committed to a style of writing which renders even the "ineffable" through "concretion of the symbol." Her notion of symbolist writing is nothing new: words signifying discernible referents outside the poem. But focusing on the poet's early verse, Perloff asserts that an Ashbery poem, regardless of length, cuts off "the referential dimension" (266) and that his images usually "have no discernible referents."

For the sake of discussion, then, let us think of the term "symbolist" as nearly synonymous with "referential." Symbolist poetry usually achieves meaning by means of a system of imagery which renders an idea or attitude. In this sense, most poems are symbolist. Those that are not are poems which intentionally sabotage their own grammar in order to call into question conventional poetic processes for communicating. Rimbaud, Stein, Olsen, and even Pound, in certain cantos, practiced variations of such an antisymbolist poetics. Today, while language poets are most actively antisymbolist, their poems are rarely long. (Michael Palmer's "Notes for Echo Lake" [1981] is an exception).

Ashbery's shorter poems are most often antisymbolist in technique, though both long and short have often been incorrectly accused of unnecessary obfuscation, much in the way Gertrude Stein's work was attacked. As Perloff points out, both Stein and Ashbery rise out of the same reformational strain of literature, one which is not primarily symbolist as is most modernist writing. The works of this genre often "seem to have no external referent." The poem is intentionally unclear, "and yet one does keep listening. For the special pleasure of reading a poem like **'These Lacustrine Cities'** [***Rivers and Mountains***] is that disclosure of some special meaning seems perpetually imminent. . . . As readers, we are thus left in a state of expectancy: just at the point where revelation might occur, the curtain suddenly comes down."

"These Lacustrine Cities" is much like the more recent **"Purists Will Object,"** published in ***A Wave.*** The poem's images hint at a logic which continues to evaporate, almost with each subsequent line:

> We have the looks you want:
> The gonzo (musculature seemingly wired to the
> stars)
> Colors like lead, khaki and pomegranate; things
> you
> Put in your hair, with the whole panoply of the
> past:
> Landscape embroidery, complete sets of this and
> that.
> It's bankruptcy, the human haul,
> The shining, bulging nets lifted out of the sea,
> and

always a few refugees
Dropping back into the no-longer-mirthful kingdom
On the day someone else sells an old house
And someone else begins to add on to his: all
In the interests of this pornographic masterpiece,
Variegated, polluted skyscraper to which all gazes are
drawn,
Pleasure we cannot and will not escape.

It seems we were going home.
The smell of blossoming privet
blanketed the narrow avenue.
The traffic lights were green and aqueous.
So this is the subterranean life.
If it can't be conjugated onto us, what good is it?
What need for purists when the demotic is built to last,
To outlast us, and no dialect hears us?

The poem intimates a world of disturbingly radical, almost perverse style, one which privileges the "gonzo," the "pornographic," the "demotic." But beyond the suggestion of this mode of fashion, it is quite difficult to grasp clearly the relationships of images in the poem as well as our own relationship to the poem. How, for instance, does one put "the whole panoply of the past" in one's hair? If the poem is about the innate indecency of civilization or even more particularly about the inhumane aspects of capitalism ("It's bankruptcy . . . / On the day someone sells an old house / And someone else begins to add on to his"), what is the relationship between the mercenary "We" of the first line in the first stanza and the nostalgic "we" of the first line in the second? And how could a dialect "hear"?

And so Perloff borrows a term from critic Roger Cardinal and calls works like this "enigma texts." She contends that all the possibilities of meaning generated by this kind of poem "give way to . . . an 'irreducible ambiguity'—the creation of labyrinths that have no exit." But while we may read one of Ashbery's shorter poems for the pleasurable "state of expectancy" Perloff describes, such a state may not carry us comfortably through all of his longer poems. Indeed, his recent longer poems bring us much closer to "that disclosure of some special meaning" than do his shorter poems. The key is this: in his later long poems Ashbery writes as if he doubts the plausibility of meaning, absolute or relative, and yet he also remains unconvinced about his own doubt. Furthermore, these poems exhibit both nonreferential and referential styles, but clearly privilege the latter, symbolist method. Again, in the long poems of his current phase he favors a symbolist style with which to write about an indeterminate state of existence. His readers must engage his depiction of reality on the chance that it will provide instances of enlightenment and hope. And while Ashbery can seem like an obsessive agnostic, some of his recent long poems, particularly **"A Wave,"** earn a hard won, if temporary, peace of mind in which the questions are either suspended for a time or answers are tentatively proferred.

Before **"Self-Portrait"** Ashbery's long poems were more enigmatic and more nonreferential than those from **"Self-Portrait"** on. His long poems have evolved in three distinct phases, moving from the first radically fractured, Cubist, collagist phase to that of the more prosaic, nonreferential phase. This second phase is marked by a newer elegiac tone and a deceptively unexciting grammar. For all their problems, the poems of this second stage are marvelous attempts at stretching language into a more fruitful zone between utter opacity and conventional symbol.

The first important poem of Ashbery's third and current phase is **"Self-Portrait in a Convex Mirror."** In **"Self-Portrait"** Ashbery uses Francesco Parmagianino's strange painting by the same title as an object of meditation. Here, every gesture, every intellectual position holds it own antithetical possibility; every premise is scrutinized by the poet for its likelihood of falsity. The grammar of the long poems of this phase is not always as intentionally self-sabotaging as that of the shorter. It helps the reader to remember that in these Ashbery is considering the ephemerality of experience while also attempting to render the confusion often brought on by that ephemerality. In most of his shorter, more enigmatic poems, readers are usually set randomly adrift at any given point, referentiality having disintegrated in a chaos of pronouns and lost syllogisms. In **"A Wave"** as in **"Self- Portrait,"** readers oscillate between such a void and a more symbolist terrain with clearer landmarks. In the context of his own canon, Ashbery's suggestion that long poems are "much closer to a whole reality" than shorter poems can be read as an admission that, because of their length, long poems should be grounded by referential, determinate writing—or the reader may simply dismiss the poem as so much endless nonsense. In fact, quantitatively there seems to be far more conventionally discursive writing in these poems than secretive writing. The language virtually achieves what Perloff would have to call "the symbolist."

In **"A Wave"** there exists for the narrator the assumption that there had been an earlier stage in life which was continually fulfilling, when metaphysical anxieties were unnecessary and the spirit was happily replete. But that time of unexamined childlike confidence was abandoned for an adult self-assessment made difficult by a nearly ceaseless skepticism and an equally skeptical approach to that skepticism. The result is the present tentative self-consciousness he describes, a perpetual state of trustlessness. Accordingly,

"A Wave" has two subjects: how to comprehend experience when it seems so ephemeral and how to experience love when it, too, is necessarily evanescent, being only a part of the larger experiential realm.

While **"A Wave"** begins with several difficult passages, the poem grows increasingly philosophical and accessible, though not committing itself to the subject of love until about a quarter of the way through. Here, Ashbery doesn't so much announce his subject, but rather describes it in passing. First, he is discussing a sense of new purpose:

> And no special sense of decline
> ensued
> But perhaps a few moments of music of such
> tact
> and weariness
> That one awakens with a new sense of pur-
> pose. . . .

But, still concerned with this "new sense of purpose," he mentions:

> I am prepared to deal with this
> While putting together notes related to the
> question of love
> For the many, for two people at once, and for
> myself
> In a time of need unlike those that have arisen
> so far.

Thus the poem's intention is declared: the poet will simultaneously discuss twin positives in his life—purpose and love. But of both we can only have some vague understanding. For Ashbery, life occurs, and only rarely are we sensitive to the details of our passing through it, each of us alone in our usual dim state:

> none
> stand with you as you mope and thrash
> your way through time,
> Imagining it as it is, a kind of tragic euphoria
> In which your spirit sprouted.

Because we necessarily must live our lives in the dishevelment of shifting feelings rather than the clarity of confident knowing, we receive life as impression. Each moment continually gives way to the next, being assimilated into a vague supposition based on the past. We cannot constantly compute our positions, and thus Ashbery frequently resorts to the most important word in the poem's lexicon: *sense.* We retain a *sense* of life and of ourselves, and very little more.

Sometimes that sense is, indeed, very vague. During such moments, we gain what Ashbery sees as a "sense" of confusion, which he sometimes illustrates with amusing blocks of bewildering logical connections, very much like the shorter poems. These passages seem to be communicating something about the inevitability of quotidian events. Meaning appears to be real, only hidden or just around the corner.

But again Ashbery does not engage in so indeterminate a style for long, and, just as the quotidian can begin to make some sense at times, his verse becomes increasingly clearer. This is not to say that he believes in belief, so to speak, but that his language resorts once more to dealing with incertitude in a comprehensible manner. Inevitably he shifts back to a more understandable poetic language in order to describe the relationship between attempts at categorizing experience and what that experience will actually come to be. Meaning thus lies not in the "crispness" of rational understanding, but in "a density of . . . opinion" which, because it is not and cannot be carefully calculated, must be a feeling, a "sense" formed of suspended conjecture. The poem consists of a continuing series of Kafkaesque reactions and counterreactions.

> We had, though, a feeling of security
> But we weren't aware of it then: that's
> How secure we were.

Ashbery often uses the words "so" and "and" to propel the poem along against the impediments thrown up by "yet" and "but." Back and forth, the potential contests against the disempowering.

Unlike Stevens, Ashbery is rarely conclusively satisfied; unwilling to forego his "questioning side," he suggests a state of existence in which the processes of the poem continue after the poem's finish until our own demise:

> And so each of us has to remain alone, con-
> scious of
> each other
> Until the day when war absolves us of our
> differences. We'll
> Stay in touch. So they have it, all the time. But
> all was
> strange.

Here Ashbery is not only unwilling to forego his circular doubt, but he is also unwilling to finish the poem on purely symbolist terms. "They" is a sudden, inexplicable intrusion, suggesting perhaps "our differences," or former lovers, or more probably the existence of greater random forces which we cannot control.

The quotations above demonstrate that **"A Wave"** is not a radically fragmented, enigmatic, inaccessible piece of writing. Certainly, many of Ashbery's signature devices appear throughout the poem: the unclear pronoun references, the long sentence fragments, the cleverly misplaced modifiers, the intentional reliance on amorphous, beguiling generalizations. At times, he reverses the process of Eliotic fragmentation by using conventionally logical connectives to link illogically related notions; at other times, he splices nonsensical ideas together by linking them to a single common event. Yet only the opening of the poem is as particularly puzzling as the shorter, purely enigmatic poems. The grammar becomes more conventional and the poem becomes progressively comprehensible as it probes its themes.

Sometime before the publication of **"Self-Portrait,"** Ashbery said that he had been "attempting to keep meaningfulness up to the pace of randomness . . . I really think meaningfulness can't get along without randomness and that they somehow have to be brought together." **"A Wave"** is certainly an attempt to do just that: to grant the poem a symbolist logic while also rendering the sudden moments of confusion and incertitude we often encounter in the course of a day, let alone the course of a lifetime. Generally his writing is symbolist when he *tells* us and enigmatic when he *shows* us. The lasting effect of this blend is to endow the reader with an impression of a consciousness energized by a desire to question while enervated by a propensity to doubt.

Mutlu Konuk Blasing (essay date Summer 1992)

SOURCE: "The American Sublime, C. 1992: What Clothes Does One Wear?," in *Michigan Quarterly Review,* Vol. 31, No. 3, Summer, 1992, pp. 425-41.

[*In the following review, Blasing offers favorable assessment of* Flow Chart. *Drawing parallels to the Romantic poetry of William Wordsworth, Blasing concludes,* "Flow Chart *is a* very *entertaining book, which moves us practically to tears."*]

Flow Chart is John Ashbery's latest experiment; he continues to do his thing, but he knows better than anyone that experimental techniques play differently in 1992 than in 1962, let alone 1912. "One is doomed, / repeating oneself, never to repeat oneself, you know what I mean?" states his predicament. His oversize, long-lined, book-length poem has all the "avant-garde" markings, but he has no illusions that its formal discontinuities represent cultural opposition:

> What right have you to consider yourself
> anything but an enor-
> mously eccentric though
> not too egocentric character, whose sins of
> omission haven't omit-
> ted much,
> whose personal-pronoun lapses may indeed
> have contributed to
> augmenting the hardship
> silently resented among the working classes? If I
> thought that for
> a minute I'd . . . yet,
> remembering how you didn't want to get up
> today, how warm
> the bed was and cozy, you
> couldn't really begin with a proletarian, accus-
> tomed as they are
> to backbreaking
> toil and so (you'd like to think) don't feel it that
> much. Besides
> they never read Henry James' novels.
> Just for the sake of argument let's say I've never
> done an honest
> day's work
> in my life. It's hardly heartbreaking news, not
> a major concern.

This is an experiment without the authorization of either a political agenda or science, the other traditional appeal of the "new": "And as for me, sad to say, / I could never bring myself to offer my experiments the gift of objective, scientific / evaluation." Not only do Ashbery's "experiments" play into the system, but their "newness" is positioned as an anachronism. While the poem takes liberties with notions of "poems," by now that is the norm, and Ashbery actually locates his poet as a wanderer "in the halls of the nineteenth century: its exhibits, / talismans, prejudices, erroneous procedures and doomed expeditions": "I must shade my eyes from the light with my hands, the light of the explosion / of the upcoming twentieth century."

Whether Ashbery's "halls" are meant to hold the echoes of Wordsworth or not, ***Flow Chart*** may be best read alongside *The Prelude.* It is an autobiographical poem, recording "the origin and progress" of the powers of the poet's mind—although Ashbery duly registers appropriate suspicions about "progress," "poet," and "mind." It also reviews his published books: "John's report cards." Wordsworth could well be describing Ashbery's project, beginning with the desire "either to lay up / New stores, or rescue from decay the old / By timely interference"; drawing out "With fond and feeble tongue a tedious tale" in the "hope" that "I might . . . fix the wavering balance of my mind"; and offering the "Song," "which like a lark / I have protracted," to the "Friend" as a "gift," though "prepared" under the "pressure of a private grief, / Keen and enduring," in the confidence that "the history of a Poet's mind / Is labour not unworthy of regard." Both poems give a minute account of subjective responses to events, whether cataclysmic or barely registrable by those less "elevated" sensibilities who lack as large a capability of "being excited without the application of gross and violent stimulants." Ashbery's "egotistical" anti-sublime—consumed with "exquisite nitpicking" and putting "too fine a deconstruction" on everything that may or may not have happened to "me," while days, seasons, and decades roll by "outside"—reaffirms that "we moderns have to 'leave our mark' / on whatever we say and do; we can let nothing pass without a comment / of some kind." In other words, despite Ashbery's unrelenting irony, and despite the ironies that become apparent in juxtaposing him with Wordsworth, reading ***Flow Chart*** is an experience comparable to nothing so much as to reading *The Prelude.*

Wordsworth's assumption that "each man's Mind is to herself / Witness and judge" holds for Ashbery: "Nothing is required of you, yet all must render an accounting." Indeed, legalistic terminology of trials, judges, and sentences abounds in his poem. If there is a "private grief" or a private accounting for some real or imagined failing or guilt, we cannot possibly know it, so that everything registers on a "higher" plane as another attempt, complete with its attendant anxieties, to justify the ways of a "Poet's mind." Certain details—the presence of "John," recurrent plays on "Ashes," and vague references to family, sex, mourning, writing, history, and earlier poems—make for an autobiographical drift, which renders ***Flow Chart*** more compelling than recent Ashbery books, but as usual he denies us the "specifics" and even apologizes for his lapses: "forgive us / our stitch of frivolity in the fabric of eternity if only so that others / can see how shabby the truth isn't and make their depositions accordingly." We are left with the fact that "This is a poem," for it does meet the minimum requirements of allusions and line breaks: "be one of those / on whom nothing is lost. Organize your thoughts in random lines and, later on / down the road, paginate them." Ashbery's "random lines" do add up to "something like / my autobiography": "I say 'I' / because I'm the experimental model of which mankind is still dreaming, though to myself / I'm full of unworked-out bugs and stagefright." More, "I see I am as ever / a terminus of sorts, that is, lots of people arrive in me and switch directions but no one / moves on any farther; this being, in effect, the end of the line, a branch-line / at that."

Not clearly authorized to indulge in a more autobiographical reading, we must resort to a literary reading of such negative millennialism and trace the fortunes of the humanist subject in postmodern times. "Somebody dust these ashes off, open / the curtains, get a little light on the subject: the subject / going off on its own again," Ashbery seems to plead, and we can only agree, but no such luck; he and we are left with "this mound of cold ashes that we call / for want of a better word the past," which "inflect[s] the horizon," "calling attention to shapes / that resemble it and so liberating them into the bloodstream / of our collective memory." As his autobiographical subject dissolves into a universal subject, our reading is deflected to an academic one, and there are enough allusions and meditations on writing to keep us going. Thus personal experience, self-accounting, and private trials are the subjects of the poem, but Ashbery treats them as irrelevant to the reader, who is nevertheless asked to read it—to consume this product.

This product sells "personal experience"—regrettably incommunicable and perhaps not entirely consequential—and "poetry," which is, regrettably, only a luxury for those who can afford such conspicuous consumption: "the coat I wear, / woven of consumer products, asks you to pause and inspect / the still-fertile ground of our once-valid compact / with the ordinary and the true." If we unravel this a bit, we see that we are asked to tailor Ashbery's "coat" to the canonical tradition, never mind the consumer products. Despite the present straits of the "poet," he is "asking" us to reconsider the same "compact" that Wordsworth, for example, invokes to legitimate *Lyrical Ballads:* "It is supposed, that by the act of writing in verse an Author makes a formal engagement that he will gratify certain known habits of association. . . it will undoubtedly appear to many persons that I have not fulfilled the terms of an engagement thus voluntarily contracted. They who have been accustomed to the gaudiness and inane phraseology of many modern writers, if they persist in reading this book to its conclusion, will, no doubt, frequently have to struggle with feelings of strangeness and awkwardness: they will look round for poetry, and will be induced to inquire by what species of courtesy these attempts can be permitted to assume that title." Here is Ashbery: "I can tell you a story about something. The expression will be just right, for it will be adjusted / to the demands of the form, and the form itself shall be timeless though / hitherto unsuspected." Thus

> his literature will have performed its
> duty
> by setting you gently down in a new place and
> then speeding off
> before
> you have a chance to thank it. We've got to find
> a new name for
> him. "Writer" seems
> totally inadequate; yet it is writing, you read it
> before you knew
> it. And besides,
> if it weren't, it wouldn't have done the unex-
> pected and by doing
> so proved that it was quite
> the thing to do, and if it happened all right for
> you, but wasn't
> the way you
> thought it was going to be, why still

that is called fulfilling part of the bargain.

By interweaving Wordsworth and Ashbery at such length, I am suggesting that Ashbery practices his novelties with one eye on tradition. Dressing his "stories" for "the new financial age that offers better reception / to things of the future, like mine," is a marketing strategy, for he is interested in selling: "For a dollar I could put it in the mail to you, / my little tract." *This* might sell better now than Whitman's "I do not say these things for a dollar" of more than a century ago. Indeed, "To the 'newness' then, all subscribe": "So for / sixteen years I dazzled the constituents with sayings of a country I had never seen; they knew I / raved but thought it must always be so when men dreamed, but my darker / purpose never surfaced." "In fact," Ashbery continues, "we never see all there is to see / which is good for business too: keeps the public returning / these days of swiftly eroding brand loyalty": "such / is the interesting climate we live in." If he has a "darker purpose" that is not merely teased into being by his evasive, marketing strategies, it would be the very old-fashioned one of keeping alive, by keeping it in the dark, a private self.

This, for me, is the pathos of Ashbery's project. ***Flow Chart*** confirms the cultural marginalization of "high" poetry by representing itself as a kind of preserve where the subject—*the* endangered species—may be kept alive. No more an "agent" than a cog in the machine, Ashbery's poet attends to "the obscure reveries of the inward gaze," tirelessly registering the rhythms of his inner life and, just as tirelessly, enumerating the difficulties of writing. And his fashionable coat, woven of consumer products, offers camouflage and better protection than the entirely different "enterprise" of going naked. The intractable nature of the poem—as of any Ashbery text—confirms that poetry does not make any difference, unless, perhaps, it markets difference. "The handwriting on the wall" says "return to your abstractions . . . life / has no need of you just yet." This knowledge floods the poet with sudden clarity and reaffirms his charge: "I though I should / sharpen my appearance, for that way lies light, lies life, and yes I am / talking about new clothes as well." One must admire Ashbery's ability to have his cake and eat it, too, in these hard times. *He* keeps telling us that his poem is only about himself and could matter less; but it looks sharp and it pierces. He offers a product, novel in cloth and cut, yet he keeps apologizing that, in substance, it has no cultural function. For the substance he quixotically sets out to preserve comprises the relics of the humanist subject, the "holy remnants of the burnished / mirror in which the Almighty once saw Himself, and wept."

Flow Chart is not merely a parodic simulacrum of a Romantic poem; it has a more serious undercurrent and, I like to think, a real investment in charting the fortunes of the subjective life, public as well as private. Ashbery's poem is how Wordsworth's project sounds today, indistinguishable from the ravings of a mind of "wavering balance." Yet Ashbery is impelled to continue producing it in this way: "I have the feeling my voice is just for me, / that no one else has ever heard it, yet I keep mumbling the litany / of all that has ever happened to me." Similarly, we are impelled to keep reading, not because we expect some ultimate "high" of revelation but for the intermittent "buzz" we get. With no "metaphysical reasons," he goes on doing what he does because he has lost the "formula for stopping," as Jean Baudrillard remarks apropos joggers. After a while we lose the "formula," too, for ***Flow Chart*** is amazingly moving—at least for one given to conspicuous consumption. The poem that deploys an avant-garde style markets, after all, an elitist product, and it attracts us because it shows how "poetry" plays today within the larger cultural discursive economies. In Ashbery's words, "You can't / can it and sell it, that's for sure, but it *is* a commodity, and someday all / will be wiser for it." And, for some "specialists," it plays as a nostalgic preserve, helping alleviate certain anxieties: "I will show you fear in a handful of specialists."

This fearful specialist would like to think, though, that Ashbery remains committed to preserve, "produce," or "enlarge" the capability "of being excited without the application of gross and violent stimulants." That, in Wordsworth's terms, "is one of the best services in which, at any period, a Writer can be engaged; but this service, excellent at all times, is especially so at the present day. For a multitude of causes, unknown to former times, are now acting with a combined force to blunt the discriminating powers of the mind." To keep alive the "discriminating powers of the mind" is, I would argue, Ashbery's "darker purpose," a downright conservative aim that finds models in Wordsworth and James. In other words, I do not buy Ashbery's fashionable "coat"; while ***Flow Chart*** is dressed as a pure product of its culture, it is also a conservative critique, which "darker" and "worthy purpose" gives the author the "right to the name of a Poet."

Or, at least, to the "label" of a poet. "Darkness" in Ashbery, early and late, is associated with the personal, "a darkness of one's own." If his writing is designed to resist the erosion of the very idea of the personal, naturally he can't deliver his "message" or give us the clue to decode it. This is the "quite tiny key to success" he "holds[s] in his hand." He can leave behind only "clues . . . fated not to be found this time," a "trace / of his passing," or a "flicker of ashes in the grate." But here is another irony of his career: "Because in the dark / you knew something and didn't tell it," "the notion / became a battle-cry and soon everybody was trying to disconnect his life and seal it / off, unsuccessfully." He registers an anxiety of influence in reverse, lamenting the appropriation of his stylistic signature—his way of not telling. Since a flow chart diagrams a manufacturing process, ***Flow Chart*** is an appropriate title for the autobiography of a poet who keeps processing his personal experience into a mere signifier of what is most personal, so that it becomes cultural or literary currency, a simulacrum, a "guaranteed . . . label, which lasts forever."

For ***Flow Chart*** is more personal than the personal can ever be, not only because our times are so "interesting" but also because life, as Ashbery often reminds us, is a generic proposition, after all; it's *anybody's* life. So why continue?

> how
> do you keep going next time?
> And I told him for half a dime I'd quit and
> screw
> you too, only that's not done, the very
> pillars of our civilization would crumble . . .
> . . . we the keepers of the trust . . . have to
> somehow find the missing key.

But how? "Where is the one who takes out the ashes, / leaves the key behind"? And who would want to be this "one" anyway? What would there *be* without the ashes? What if "these marginalia . . . are the substance of the text"? "What / if poetry were something else entirely, not this purple weather / with the eye of a god attached, that sees / inward and outward? What if it were only a small, other way of living?" What if "a pleasant, slightly numbed sense of wonderment" were all the reader was vouchsafed? But who could brush off someone who says, "despite my bluster and my swaggering, / [I] have no real home and no one to inhabit it except you"? Plus, "if I am to be cast off, then / *where?* There has to be a space, even a negative one, a slot / for me, or does there?" And "Where are the standard bearers? Why / have our values been lost? Who is going to pay for any of this?" Or "Is it that I'm a sort of jerk?" In short, ***Flow Chart*** is a *very* entertaining book, which moves us practically to tears:

> You get A for effort, but the road to hell is
> paved
> with good intentions. But I'll take the blight,
> thanks. I'm good at working under pressure,
> *as indeed we all must be.*

Harriet Zinnes (essay date June 1992)

SOURCE: "John Ashbery: The Way Time Feels As It Passes," in *The Hollins Critic,* Vol. XXIX, No. 3, June, 1992, pp. 1-13.

[*In the following essay, Zinnes discusses Ashbery's literary career, poetic style, central motifs, and the influence of avant-garde music and art on his work.*]

Writing about John Ashbery is difficult, not because his work is itself difficult or obscure or elusive. It frequently is not. Yet from the beginning he was a puzzle. In a panel on postmodernism as early as December 1979, the poet David Antin could declare, in seemingly contradictory terms, that the poet "brought grandeur to Pop" and that his poems are "sublime claptrap." Yet the puzzle of John Ashbery can be solved—without perhaps totally eliminating contradictory conclusions, and always bearing in mind what the poet wrote in his collected "art chronicles" (***Reported Sightings,*** 1991): "it is impossible to refute a statement made in a poem; poetry is by nature true and affords blanket protection to anything one wishes to say in it." This of course gets Ashbery completely off the disgruntled critic's hook—and the critic too. Do I have carte blanche? Hm. Yet Ashbery's work is not so disjointed in its effects, its surfaces and meaning that one cannot attempt an explanation. The difficulty lies in the fact that the work is more like the ineffable abstractions characteristic of avant-garde contemporary music (at least the music that was important to Ashbery when he began to publish) rather than to contemporary poetry.

"I think I had learned about art from music," Ashbery once told the writer Richard Kostelanetz. His poetry confirms the statement. Wallace Stevens (despite such critics as Harold Bloom) has influenced Ashbery less than has the composer John Cage (and the music of such composers as Anton Webern and Luciano Berio). Often Ashbery's sounds, especially in his early poems, are noises—the words around him in his environment, the words culled at random from books picked up on the quais of Paris, frequently children's books (such as *Beryl and His Biplane*). Such cut-up poems are sound collages. His words therefore in such poems are only secondarily words in the usual sense. Precise meanings are simply not the point. Consider his early poem **"Europe"** that appeared in ***The Tennis Court Oath*** (1962). It begins

> To employ her
> construction ball
> Morning fed on the
> light blue wood
> of the mouth
> cannot understand
> feels deeply)

Richard Howard in an early important essay in his *Alone With America* (1969) summed up the compositional technique that the poet used here as leading to such a "pitch of distraction, of literal eccentricity, that leaves any consecutive or linear reading of his poems out of the question." But in these early poems a "linear reading" was not at all intended because, as Ashbery explained in a 1982 interview, he frequently wrote while listening to classical music on the radio and "occasionally when there are announcements or commercials they get sucked into the poem, as do all kinds of things in my immediate environment; papers that happen to be on my desk at the time, or letters, stray books, magazines." Telephone calls that he will answer while writing may give him an idea. The environment matters. A Cagean mandate. "These things are very important," he said in that interview, "They're the environment that we live in and there's no point in trying to pretend that it's different or should be different." Earlier in 1974 in an interview in the *New York Quarterly* Ashbery confessed that the poem **"Europe,"** "poems of that sort which are really like automatic poetry . . . no longer interest me very much." I'd like to quote the extension of that statement because it not only explains why his early technique is no longer valuable to him (though the 1991 ***Flow Chart*** evidences some return) but reveals a characteristic Ashbery, never arrogant, never pretentious, certainly rarely the romantic bard, always modest and clearly making no superior claims for poetry except expressing his devotion to it. Here are his remarks:

> For instance, the poem **"Europe,"** the long poem in that book, is no longer very close to me. At the time I wrote it I was baffled as to what to do in poetry; I wasn't satisfied with the way my work was going and I felt it was time to just clear my head by writing whatever came into it and that's very much the case with that poem; and I think it helped me along but I don't value it as much as ones I've written since.

It is interesting to see a characteristic example of what Ashbery has written since. Here is a quotation from ***Flow Chart:***

> it looks like a nice day for all this, and I invite
> you to start
>   revving up your VCR:
> who knows what may happen? In the meantime,
> look sharp, and
>   sharply at what is around you; there is
> always the possibility something may come of
> something, and that
>   is our
> fondest wish though it says here I'm supposed
> to say so, not now
>   not
> in this place of wood and sunlight, this stable or
> retiring room
>   or whatever you want to call it.

Here are the long lines of the later Ashbery with their characteristic colloquialisms, their imagery from popular culture, and their Cagean aesthetic, an aesthetic that he began with and is still adhering to. Cage always admonishes composers, artists, poets, listeners, everyone to be attentive. And here is John Ashbery saying: "look sharp, and sharply at what is around you; there is / always the possibility something may come of something."

Obviously, Ashbery himself soon realized that it was disastrous for him to use words as if they were mere sound containers without equivalents of meaning because he was not writing nonsense verse or concrete poetry or Steinian sound structures. He couldn't really transpose the complete Cagean method, only its aesthetic. That is, he couldn't pretend that verbal sound is equivalent to the sounds, let us say, of the digestive tract that Cage used in his composition tapping intestinal organs for his "music." When Ashbery, however, made his auditory imagination a tool of his own inner universe, sounds worked for him, as in such poems as **"Fragment"** from the 1970 volume ***The Double Dream of Spring*** (strange that he did not include in his ***Selected Poems*** of 1985 this mysterious poem that Ashbery calls a love poem,—like all his love poems it probes the imagination and the self). He achieves a similar success in the prose poems in the volume ***Three Poems*** (1972), a volume that to me is truly characteristic of his genius. Sounds then become seductive—siren songs, songs to the "beloved," the absolute, the void in a universe that is inner, that is Zen, that joins sound ultimately to ineffable sense.

Here is a passage from the poem **"Fragment"** that Charles Berger in his essay on the poet in *Beyond Amazement* (1980) describes as a "remarkable stanza of pure lyric energy" illuminating an inwardness in "a blazing candle of artifice." The stanza I should say is unusual for the poet—it is a ten-line stanza that Ashbery may have used, he tells us, because he was reading the sixteenth-century poet Maurice Scève, who wrote in dizaines. Again, here it is:

> Thus your only world is an inside one
> Ironically fashioned out of external phenomena
> Having no rhyme or reason, and yet neither
> An existence independent of foreboding and sly
> grief.
> Nothing anybody says can make a difference;
> inversely
> You are a victim of their lack of consequence
> Buffeted by invisible winds, or yet a flame
> yourself
> Without meaning, yet drawing satisfaction
> From the crevices of that wind, living
> In that flame's idealized shape and duration.

Ashbery's universe, his world, is "an inside one," a daytime that is "never to be defined." Ashbery's center is search, a hope of knowing that is down to zero. His words are "weightless," and time, one of the poet's major themes, is to the poet always ambiguous, particularized in a quotidian that is more like dream ("whispers out of time"). John Ashbery affirms in his work, yes, affirms, "an affirmation that doesn't affirm anything." Such a world in a poem can only be there, within the sounds of the poems. Sounds that are not aleatoric, collages, sound structures, but sounds that are equivalents of this Zen state—affirmative only as they do not reach definition—sounds that evoke a "quiet," absolute time, the void.

Ashbery, therefore, is not trying to name. He gives up on that traditional task of the poet. You cannot "name" what you are doing, he says. Here, he is saying, here it is today, rather perplexing of course, with "crucial" moments experienced but never understood, but somehow all is rather pleasant. Of course there's been a "hitch somewhere," but in a "half-baked kind of way" whatever is out there, all external phenomena, all activity released by and turning again to the self add up to a "cosmic welter of *attractions*" [my italics]. The essentiality of existence is a put-on, not for us to unmask. The "real thing" is "colorless and featureless," Ashbery says over and over again, a belief that accounts for the imprecision of his surfaces, the frequent lack of reference points, his offhand manner, his conscious use of the banal and the cliché. Yet the real thing comes from "primal energy." Still, as Peter Schjedahl once said to me (or did he write this somewhere?) what Ashbery is saying may not be understood but whatever it is it is about growth, spiritual matter, the Zen thing. And that's it. That it cannot be defined yet sensed (in the meaning of sense as that which is denied in the word *nonsense*) becomes the ineffable quality of the verse, the music of Ashbery's lines.

The publication of ***Three Poems*** (1972) was a culmination. Here his disquieting meditations discovered their own music. He had achieved a brilliant success. What he had to say, that is, what he was saying that he could not say, was snugly couched in the music of his prose. Consider the following passage:

> Gazing out at the distraught but inanimate world you feel that you have lapsed back into the normal way things are, that what you were feeling just now was a novelty and hence destined to disappear quickly, its sole purpose if any being to light up the gloom around you sufficiently for you to become aware of its awesome extent, more than the eye and the mind can take in. . . . And you turn away from the window almost with a sense of relief, to bury yourself again in the task of sorting out the jumbled scrap basket of your recent days, without any hope of completing it or even caring whether it gets done or not. . . . At this point a drowsiness overtakes you as of total fatigue and indifference; in this unnatural, dreamy state the objects you have been contemplating take on a life of their own, in and of themselves. It seems to you that you are eavesdropping and can understand their private language. They are not talking about you at all, but are telling each other curious private stories about things you can only half comprehend, and other things that have a meaning only for themselves and are beyond any kind of understanding.

Obviously what Ashbery is saying here—or anywhere else for that matter—is not particularly deep or philosophically rewarding (philosophy is never the task of a poet). Ashbery could say, as John Cage did in *Silence:* "I have nothing to say and I am saying it and that is poetry." The very goal of Zen (but Ashbery's kind of Zen, I believe, is only momentarily assumed and is probably very unorthodox), is inarticulateness, a very special kind of inarticulateness. The world's body of the Zen poet is the animal in the forest. The poet looks up and it is just THERE. Nothing to write home about, but plenty to write poems about: "the major question that revolves around you, your being here." And if Ashbery's poems are about anything, they are about the "permanent now . . . in whatever shape seemed expedient for living the next few crucial moments into a Future without controls." Here is a poet, therefore, whose only controlling belief is in "the next few crucial moments into a Future without controls." Even when the poet uses astrological signs such as the Tarot card figures in **"The New Spirit"** in ***Three Poems*** he is not demonstrating an interest in the occult. With characteristic wit (and Ashbery is so frequently funny) he had explained to the *New York Quarterly* interviewer why he lacked such an interest, "The occult is not mysterious enough."

Ashbery is really very rational. This poet who seems so mysterious as he coolly admits to the unmitigating uncertainties that each moment in life presents (and it is such "crucial moments," whether in the poet's surroundings or in his own mind that provide the substance of the poems—the result of what the critic Marjorie Perloff would call a poetics of indeterminacy) is actually a declarer of the common. Moments can bring anything, after all. But quite simply, as Ashbery writes in ***Flow Chart:***

> Other pleasures are folding the pillow and
> gazing mournfully into
>   the face of the electric clock
> when everything springs apart quite naturally
> and scrawled
>   forms of people are seen pacing the square in
> different
>   directions. . . .

It is all so common! But, of course, says Ashbery, with his usual dry humor: "everything springs apart quite naturally."

Is this cool and rational Ashbery the result of his being brought up on a farm? John Ashbery was born in Rochester, New York, on July 28, 1927, and lived in the small town of Sodus, near Lake Ontario, where his father was a fruit farmer. Dinitia Smith, who managed to have a long interview with the reserved poet, published in the *New York Magazine* of May 20, 1991, was able to elicit characteristic responses from the poet that bear repeating. She writes:

> Ashbery was at first an extroverted child who loved to be with his father on the farm. Then, when Ashbery was four, his brother Richard was born, and Ashbery grew melancholy. Richard became the star of the family, sharing Chester Ashbery's love of the outdoors. "My father was disappointed in me. My father favored him, and I understood."
>
> Ashbery's maternal grandfather, Henry Lawrence, was a distinguished physicist and professor at the University of Rochester. And the poet's mother, unlike many women of her generation, had a college degree. "She had a tremendous reverence for my grandfather," Ashbery says.
>
> "He was a sort of patriarch. He was very cultivated. He knew Greek and Latin. My father was jealous of his ascendancy." From the beginning, Ashbery was caught in a tug-of-war between his father and grandfather, whom he adored.

It is significant that the poet went to live with his grandparents in Rochester when he was a young child and later spent weekends and holidays there. It was his grandfather's library that led to his discovery of literature, and even his interest in painting was encouraged. He was given art lessons. What a "crucial moment," for Ashbery later would become an important international art critic. He was the art critic of the European edition of the *New York Herald Tribune,* Paris, 1960-65, and of the *Art International,* Lugano, Switzerland. He was editor of *Art and Literature,* Paris, from 1963-66, and became executive editor of *Art News* from 1965 until 1972. Later, in 1978, Ashbery became the art critic at *New York Magazine* and later still at *Newsweek.* But Ashbery like his grandfather was also a distinguished professor (of English, of course) at Brooklyn College. Because of a $250,000 five-year grant from the MacArthur Foundation he was able to leave Brooklyn College and teach only once a week at Bard College.

Money early on was a problem. It was for the lack of it that he became an art critic in Paris in 1960, following in the steps of another American poet, Ezra Pound, who, when in London and needing funds, began to write art criticism. Pound, who was an advocate, a propagandist for the new British art, was more strident, more blatantly subjective. Ashbery, on the other hand, was cool, knowledgeable, and generous-minded. When he is unsympathetic to an artist, such as Andy Warhol or Toulouse Lautrec, he never snarls as Pound did but describes the work, considers what makes him "indifferent" to it, all in a very amiable way. This is not to say, by the way, that the art criticism of Pound was not significant. It certainly was. Ashbery had the advantage of writing at the time of such formidable critics as Clement Greenberg, Harold Rosenberg, and the brilliant Meyer Schapiro. It took more than fifty years for Pound's art criticism to be collected, but John Ashbery's appeared in 1991 in a collection called ***Reported Sightings,*** published by Harvard University Press with fine colored reproductions and containing work that appeared as late as 1987.

Both Pound's and Ashbery's art criticism say a great deal about them as poets. Pound, who was the theorist for the Vorticists, the British Cubists, would never have belittled the art of the eccentric poet-painter William Blake as Ashbery does with this wonderful witty remark: Blake's painting, Ashbery said, "is one of the glories of English literature." Pound, who after all lived at a different time, saw parallels between the techniques in painting and poetry and wrote, "I would liken Guido's cadence to nothing less powerful than line in Blake's drawing." Yet clearly cadence is not line. Energy is a different matter. When Ashbery says of Braque's work that "its ambiguity is that of reality," he may be unconsciously explaining his own manipulation of ambiguity in his poetry, but he is not making a parallel of the techniques of the two arts. He is still considering Braque's perception as an artist of his vision of the world.

The more sophisticated relation between the arts that Ashbery observes can be seen in his comment on Jean Hélion (whom he considers "one of the finest painters of any kind today"—i.e., in 1961): "He is a poet's painter, as Ponge (who has written on Hélion) is a painter's writer. Both have invented a new kind of description, poetic without being rhapsodic, which treats the outside of things as though it were their soul, and in which the avoidance of all metaphysical temptations becomes itself a kind of religion." This last statement could be used to describe Ashbery's poetry as well as Hélion's painting. Ashbery looked closely at the objects around him. The "reported sightings" in his poetry were not decorated with the heavy musings of a metaphysician. The mystery lay in the objects just being THERE. What he says about the paintings of his friend and artist, Joan Mitchell, whom he greatly admires, could again be said to apply to the way he works, not with paint of course, but with language. As Ashbery has said in ***Reported Sightings,*** and all poets know: "Poets when they write about other artists always tend to write about themselves." What he says then about Mitchell says a lot about himself:

> A persistent shape, like a helmet or a horse's skull, doesn't give any clue to what the painter intended, except in one painting where it suggests dark masses of trees at the edge of a river. Elsewhere there are antagonisms and sparrings between shapes whose true nature is left unstated, and sudden lashings of caked or viscous pigment whose inspiration is again no longer in nature but in something in the nature of paint, or of the feeling that takes hold of a painter when he attacks it. Yet there is never any sense of transition; we move in and out of these episodes, coherent or enigmatic ones, always with a sense of feeling at home with the painter's language, of understanding what she is saying even when we could not translate it.

This is a passage that is characteristic of the critical prose of John Ashbery. He is never vague; he never hedges. His pen is as sharp as his discerning eye. It is interesting (to turn to the content of the passage) that the poet says nothing about the gestural aspect of the work of this Abstract Expressionist, the unconscious manipulations of the brush so much written about by those who stress the surrealist aspect of the Abstract Expressionists. It was not automatism that Ashbery favored in surrealism. "The automatic gestural painting of Pollock and Klein and their contemporaries looks different from the patient, minute, old-master technique of Tanguy," he notes.

Understandably, then, he loves the work of de Chirico. Is it because objects are so clearly defined even as they are so strangely juxtaposed? I must mention that Ashbery admires another aspect of the painter Joan Mitchell, for like the poet, the painter "does not talk much about her own work, perhaps not out of reticence, but because the paintings *are* meaning and therefore do not have a residue of meaning which can be talked about." Surely that last statement relates to his own poetry. He does not like to talk about what his poetry means. The poetry, to Ashbery, *is* the meaning. Words, after all, to the poet "treat the outside of things as though it were their soul."

This emphasis on the "outside of things" explains his attitude toward Minimal Art and particularly his attitude toward Brice Marden, whose 1975 survey at the Guggenheim Museum led to the artist's international fame. What the artist was showing were his masterly monochrome canvases but even those canvases evoked subtle feelings of color and light. John Ashbery, writing in 1972 about the artist even before the Guggenheim show (and of course before the current show of the "Cold Mountain" paintings of 1988-91 at the Dia Center for the Arts in New York City, through June 21), saw that despite the artist's concentration on the monochrome he was creating not abstractions but luminous objects "for the senses." Ashbery wrote, in part:

> Appearances to the contrary, his art is not negative minimal but positive phenomenal; it is not an abstraction but an object made by and for the senses. . . . Some of his colors can't even be described, let alone paraphrased. . . . Each seems to be the product of every color on Marsden's palette except one; and although these colors have left no visible traces of themselves, they nevertheless burn insidiously in the noncolor that has replaced them. To create a work of art that the critic cannot even begin to talk about ought to be the artist's chief concern; Marsden has achieved it.

Ashbery is indifferent to schools and fashion. He can admire the work of Nell Blaine as well as that of Brice Marden. Early on he praised those fresh, sensuous colors of the lively palette of Blaine, who was an early friend of the poet. He certainly understood the stages in her development. In 1986, he wrote that the painter "long ago moved on from the Constructivist abstraction of her early career, when Hélion and Leger . . . incited her toward a geometrical painting that looks less orthodox and more casual than much American abstract painting of the time. It was only natural, no doubt, that she would eventually move on to figuration, since nature in its liveliness and unpredictability is already latent in her abstractions. Yet the early disciples subsist in her work today, which is never 'impressionistic' even when trying to capture the subtleties of mist-shrouded mountains. . . . The sensuality in these works is backed up by a temperament that is crisp and astringent, which is as it should be, since even at its most poetic, nature doesn't kid around." How Ashberyan that realistic, sharply observed, that unromantic understanding of what's out there: "even at its most poetic, nature doesn't kid around."

What is baffling about John Ashbery is his ability to separate his experience with the visual arts from the content of his poetry. There is very little reference to art in his poems. Even his visual imagery is more metaphor than image. With Ashbery the visual dissipates into the elusive, into faded moments without the dimension of time. Events therefore exist simultaneously. Without time in its usual sense, a demarcation of past, present, and future, Ashbery's events can be occurring all at once—they have been, they are, and they will be. It is all a projection anyway. Nothing is—certainly nothing as static as a visual image. Nothing is, and at the same time, everything is—all at once. In one of his most memorable poems (much anthologized), **"The Instruction Manual,"** in one of his best volumes, ***Some Trees*** (1956) (a volume of the Yale Series of Younger Poets, so casually introduced by W. H. Auden), the poet is enormously local, visual, referential in his treatment though the intention of the particularities is to evoke dream, even romance. The poem contains half a dozen little stories that the persona makes up about "dim Guadalajara, City of rose-colored flowers," as he tries to escape from the "press of having to write the instruction manual"—a manual on the use of a new metal. The description is precise, visual, delicate as the poet conjures up in his revery the city of colored houses, young lovers, an aged mother, fanning herself with a palm leaf fan, yearning for her son, the promenaders, the marketplace, the men selling hats and swatting flies, the delicious public library with its shades of pale green and beige. In a much later poem in his 1975 volume the poet knows that even to arrive in a dream city is to be "wasted with eternal desire and sadness":

> There are still other made-up countries
> Where we can hide forever,
> Wasted with eternal desire and sadness,
> Sucking the sherbets, crooning the tunes,
> naming the names.

A major poem having its source in art is **"Self-Portrait In a Convex Mirror"** in the volume of that title (1975). Yet the poem starts but hardly remains with the portrait by the Renaissance painter Parmigianino. The poem begins:

> As Parmigianino did it, the right hand
> Bigger than the head, thrust at the viewer
> And swerving easily away, as though to protect
> What it advertises.

The poet seems carefully to describe the portrait but because his purposes are tangential, not referential, not descriptive, the portrait almost immediately becomes not object but turning off point toward (as he writes in the poem **"Hopo' My Thumb"** in this same volume) "our selves concaved into view."

So it is "our selves" that is really the subject, but "our selves" with Ashbery is the "I," the "you," the "he"—all forms of the self in these quest poems, for it is always "I" and the other, who are both separate and the same. That strange gesture in the portrait, therefore, "thrust at the viewer / And swerving easily away," is "your gesture"

> . . . which is neither embrace nor warning
> But which holds something of both in pure
> Affirmation that doesn't affirm anything.

This portrait that is Francesco Parmigianino, that is the poet, that is you, that is he, is the mirror into the mirror of "self-reflexiveness," as David Shapiro calls it in his excellent analysis of the poem in his *John Ashbery: An Introduction To The Poetry*. But there is nothing triumphantly narcissistic in this self-reflexiveness. "One would like to stick one's hand / Out of the globe, but its dimension, / What carries it, will not allow it." The portrait is fixed, a stasis. Yet in the experience of the making of it, there was action, in a way a very banal action. Ashbery quotes Vasari's description of the portrait's beginnings:

> . . . Francesco one day set himself
> To take his own portrait, looking at himself for
> that purpose
> In a convex mirror, such as is used by barbers
> . . .
> He accordingly caused a ball of wood to be
> made
> By a turner, and having divided it in half and
> Brought it to the size of the mirror, he set himself
> With great art to copy all that he saw in the
> glass.

But when, as the poet relates it, "in the silence of the studio" Francesco lifted "the pencil to the self-portrait," when even as he drew and "many people came and stayed a certain time," when "those voices in the dusk" became "memories deposited in irregular / Clumps of crystals," what became of those experiences, Ashbery asks the painter, that "became part of you"?

> . . . Whose curved hand controls,
> Francesco, the turning seasons and the
> thoughts
> That peel off and fly away at breathless speeds
> Like the last stubborn leaves ripped
> From wet branches? I see in this only the chaos
> Of your round mirror which organizes every-
> thing
> Around the polestar of your eyes which are
> empty,
> Know nothing, dream but reveal nothing.

Art that began in mundane movements, achieved its mastery, and ended with the artist, having organized everything in his "chamber" for the portrait, knowing and revealing nothing. The artist or the poet creates and then is left with "eyes which are empty." Is art or poetry achieving its fixity, its certainty, only to end in a final uncertainty, in death itself—that land of unknowing, in the portrait, in the poem? Once it was love that "tipped the scales but now is shadowed, invisible / Though mysteriously present, around somewhere." Now even daytime is "nondescript, never-to-be-defined." But we do know something, nothing very startling:

> . . . All we know

Is that we are a little early, that
Today has that special, lapidary
Todayness that the sunlight reproduces
Faithfully in casting twig-shadows on blithe
Sidewalks.

Of course you can't live in a poem, a museum—"And we must get out of it even as the public / Is pushing through the museum now so as to / Be out by closing time. You can't live there." No, you can't merely live in the museum, and even Parmigianino, Ashbery tells us, must have realized that his very portrait never actually achieved what he himself had wanted. What is there then? "Daily activity"? "To be serious about sex / Is perhaps one way," and then there is the philosophy, the ideologies one lives by, but "Each person / Has one big theory to explain the universe / But it doesn't tell the whole story." Whatever is the answer? And it is not Steinian. Ashbery, who now becomes perilously near to being an advocate of suicide (or does he?), in the agony of the predicament, writes:

Therefore I beseech you, withdraw that hand,
Offer it no longer as shield or greeting,
The shield of a greeting, Francesco:
There is room for one bullet in the chamber.

Is the bullet to be in the painted chamber or in the chamber of a gun? Is suicide the answer? The mirror then won't provide a knowing portraiture? The mirror is then transformed, but it is a hideous transformation of the mirror, the major vehicle of the poem. The poet notes that he has seen the city: "it is the gibbous / Mirrored eye of an insect"—so trivial, yet so monstrous, that "gibbous / Mirrored eye of an insect." And all there is left "here and there, in cold pockets / Of remembrance, whispers out of time." So that the poet begins with a portrait painted by a sixteenth-century artist in a convex mirror, places himself in that mirror only to try to break through "that globe," but in the attempt questions the very making of any art. Shapiro considers that "it might be said that the poem finally admits no self-portraiture except the portraiture of a text, a text like a painting." In such a case, the text may remain, but only "here and there, in cold pockets / Of remembrance, whispers out of time."

I have described this poem at some length because, it seems to me, to hold much of what is central to the work of Ashbery. Time, the imagination, poetry, self and the other, loss, love, death,—these are the motifs of Ashbery (and I purposely use a musical term). In the poet's recent interview with Dinitia Smith he admitted that one way to read his poetry is to think of it as "music," as if his words were a musical composition, and he added: "Words in proximity to one another take on another meaning. What you hear at a given moment is a refraction of what's gone before or after." But these surface motifs can only be understood—or heard—in that flow of sound, that movement of the language, the interweaving of vowel and consonant creating a present, a present moment, the only moment in a time that is seductive as it moves musically on and on, as the poet notes momentary experience within time's flow, the only consolation of these "whispers" that are "out of time."

Isn't it likely that the poet named his last book ***Flow Chart*** (1991) because he is so attracted to the flow of time—and to the business and language of contemporary life, for "flow chart" is a contractor's schedule for his painters, electricians, etc., who have to know the sequence of the tasks they have to perform in their jobs. The job requires a certain time. It is a fixed time but because there are always so many contingencies—workers become ill, machinery breaks down, parts are not delivered—the flow chart is interrupted by the random emergency. In his own "flow chart" miscalculations do not merely delay the job of simply getting on, they lead to "the more terrible realization," as the poet had even noted in **"The System"** in ***Three Poems,*** "of reconciling their own ends with the cosmos." But in ***Flow Chart*** Ashbery is much more cynical, his wit is more sharp-edged, but happily there is plenty of it. Beneath his skepticism ("the truth, if there ever could be such a thing") is a deep-seated awareness of the terror of our times.

We live in an age when terror
opens like breadfruit and one must pick and
choose—the seeds
and proverbs just
aren't that numerous. Everybody must vote.
Everybody's vote
be accepted into the
tilting radio tower that is collapsing in one's own
best
interest in one
dark swoop of mingled horror and relaxed
apprehension. . . .

And if there is no horror, there is a "feeling of emptiness" that keeps "turning up like a stranger." Or incessant despair. What to do—"No place to put my despair. Never mind, we'll unpack it later." This kind of black humor is ever present in this series of long poems. The poet always rebounds, however; becomes his usual calm, accepting self. It is because he accepts the contradictions, the simultaneity of horror and pleasure (not necessarily within the experience of the same person). He concedes:

so history constantly dwindles, although one
can still feel
remarkably fit and well-adjusted
to life in an era more decadent than anything
that has preceded
it. . . . that anyone should have to die

so that we may stay on here, sodden but alive,
fortunate
to be able to contemplate our mortality from a
distance
amid kindness
and late imperial emblems, golden dregs of
another civilization
than the one we gulped down just a short time
ago.

Ashbery won't allow the tragic note. Whether it is the threat of death, recognition of brutal imperial wars, personal loss, Ashbery brushes it all off, becomes casual, playfully utters cliches and wonderful one-liners: "Twenty centuries is too much." There is no theological questioning. He goes on with the journey of life, a "journey" that "flows past us like ice chunks." Ice chunks! Not exactly reassuring, but he tells it as he sees it—and endures, ready for the next small pleasure that yields "a pleasant, slightly numbed sense of wonderment."

This is a book that is very New York City. "It seems," he writes as only a realistic, knowledgeable New Yorker can, "only yesterday / that one could find cheap walkup apartments in the East 50s." But what to do about it all? He can only return to his Cagean attentiveness and urge with his usual humor:

. . . Meanwhile, be one of those
on whom nothing is lost. Organize your
thoughts in random lines
and, later on
down the road, paginate them. You'll see
bluebells and cowslips
on every hill; even
dragonflies will have become a thing of wonder,
as long
as you don't get too close, and let water run
through it all. . . .
As long as we're on this planet
the thrill never ceases. Even a garage can be a
propitious place.

And love, what about love? Ashbery says that all his poems are about love. In this volume death certainly seems obtrusive, but in a way here and in all of the volumes the poems are love songs but with the lover absent because the lover and the beloved are one—another aspect of the interchangeability of pronouns in the poet's world.

The "beloved," as Ashbery uses the term, is the universal principle, the cosmic mystery that is there in its essential affections but still eludes us. In the last section of ***Three Poems*** called **"The Recital,"** the poet comments that "emotional happiness blossoms only once," and we are daily fighting "the hydra-headed monster of apathy." It is the stillness that Ashbery is battling or trying to understand because for him it has not yet turned into the true meditator's void. So that in one sense Ashbery has not reached his "beloved," which is apathy, the void, toward which his muted, seductive sounds, his siren songs, are drifting.

Even sex, especially in ***Flow Chart,*** seems beside the point. He says there: "I now . . . / have come belatedly to realize that sex has very little to do with any of it, / that is directly, except insofar as it makes you do something you hadn't thought about / because it brought you to a place you hadn't thought of visiting, / some quiet corner of a garden, unnoticed before, whose perfection of design / no longer seems a threat, / but rather a greeting instead." The absence of the "sensual" lover in the poems (despite Ashbery's occasional welcoming of sensuality in a kind of abstract way) explains much in the poet's work.

There is love of the world, the "other," but since the "you's," the "I's," the "he's" are all forms of the self in these quest poems, there is really no love partner creating fire or tension in the works. As a result, there is little tension, little drama as one ordinarily feels it in a lyric or even in a meditative poem of tradition. In a way, the poems are all love songs with the lover absent because the lover and the beloved are one. Absence, therefore, becomes one of the motifs of the poems. Absence is implied, for example, in his characteristic use of ellipsis, what he calls "this leaving-out business" in **"The Skaters."** Absence is not, however, the lack of presence, for in what Richard Howard has called Ashbery's "poetics of continuity and encirclement" presence is the central ingredient of absence. In **"The Skaters,"** the poet notes:

the carnivorous
Way of these lines is to devour their own nature,
leaving
Nothing but a bitter impression of absence,
which as we know
involves presence, but still
Nevertheless these are fundamental absences,
struggling to
get up and be off themselves.

Absence, therefore, necessarily involving presence, is one of Ashbery's important motifs, another one of the contradictions that the poet memorializes, for it is not the world's ambiguities that the poet responds to but its contradictions existing side by side—a condition in the world which to the poet is equivalent to inevitable failure on every level of life. As he says in ***Flow Chart,*** "Isn't it all going to be a fiction / anyway, and if so, what does it matter where we decide to settle down?"

The contradictions are not Hegelian, not Marxist. There are no opposing forces. Contradictions are—and in being lie still: "Whatever was, is, and must be," Ashbery writes. His quiet music is the poetic equivalence of this stillness. It is in fact the seductive musical element in Ashbery's poetry that makes it live. It is a seduction urged on by an uncanny music, a rhythmical seduction that relates his work to Eros—the only Eros in his work, for, as he says in **"Fantasia on 'The Nut-Brown Maid'"** in ***Houseboat Days,*** even love is no "cause for self-congratulation" and in the "living *picture*" [my italics] that is life,

> You get around this as though
> The eternally revised geography of spring meant
> Something beyond its own sense of exalta-
> tion. . . .

Since essentially all is "stillness," "zero," the flow of time rushing forward and staying still as the Red Queen implied (and Ashbery reminds us), the beloved too is both here and not here, and therefore can be embraced only in memory, or in the moment that has passed: "We were walking / All along toward a door that seemed to recede / In the distance and now is somehow behind us shut," the poet writes in the last named poem. Even sensuality throbs toward what Ashbery calls "nostalgia," and the present moment is all and nothing, is absence as well. Such poetry is flux *and* stasis. Such a poetry has the music of the silence of no time—not the "no time" of the Keatsian persuasion but the "no time" of the Einsteinian revolution. Ashbery knows time is standing still or at least in its rushing forward is rushing backwards head on. "How wonderful the fields are," Ashbery writes. What else is there to say? Is it not all attractive—especially if one knows enough "not to insist, to keep sifting a mountain of detritus / indefinitely in search of tiny yellow blades of grass"?

Evelyn Reilly (review date Fall 1992)

SOURCE: "Afloat," in *Parnassus,* Vol. 17, No. 2, Fall, 1992, pp. 40-51.

[*In the following review, Reilly offers tempered praise for* Flow Chart. *According to Reilly,* Flow Chart *represents "an endless flow of disrupted ruminations, literary fragments, pseudo-conversations, pieces of argument, and other language objects, inviting us to look for patterns but not guaranteeing that there are any."*]

At a time when all the big themes—the gods, the hero, the artist-hero, truth, the imagination, the past redeemed, the utopian dream—are definitely lowercase, it would seem to require a certain hubris to write a very long poem. Yet John Ashbery's new book-length poem, ***Flow Chart,*** fills its 216 pages unabashed. Innocent of themes and unencumbered by the mandates of coherence and unity, this poem can be accused, at most, of the quantitative hubris of a journal kept for decades. It is, in fact, characterized by a qualitative humility, if the Ashberyan refusal to "mean" can be described as such.

Perhaps, as suggested by its title, ***Flow Chart*** is less a long poem than a diagram or chart, a grid laid down over an endless flow of disrupted ruminations, literary fragments, pseudo-conversations, pieces of argument, and other language objects, inviting us to look for patterns but not guaranteeing that there are any. This grid could have been laid down over any segment of the flow, since its boundaries and center are arbitrary. It marks out big squares of language only provisionally, for the purposes of observation.

The flow being charted is distinctly aquatic—sky-reflecting, weather-inflected, and littered with the detritus of daily life on the banks. Bobbing along on this surface, the reader cannot but feel the tug of some of the most ancient (and modern) conceits about time and bodies of water, especially when lines like the following float by:

> Sad grows the river god as he oars past us
> downstream without our knowing him . . .
>
> . . . just as the plaintive sound
> of the harp of the waves is always there as a
> backdrop
> to conversation and conversion . . .

As good postmodern pilgrims, however, we exercise restraint, consider these "appropriations," and do not look to the depths.

Meanwhile, there is an enormous amount of talk going on. Someone has cast a net out into the ambient language and is hauling it all in—truncated tales of childhood incidents, accounts of travels to tropical places, memories of high school, bits of dialogue out of Grade B movies (cowboy movies preferred), self-help platitudes, somebody's legal problems:

> . . . No one can plead ignorance,
> therefore,
> and any other plea-bargain seems out of the
> question, though my
> backers will tell you otherwise. . . .

lyrical expansions inspired by nature:

> Surely the last tragedy will be enough

and the wind must drop, and it does; a single
leaf falls circling,
alights on the water's swiftly moving mirror as
the chorus picks up on hope
in the black promise facing us. . . .

moments of mock epic:

Then the men began to speak in unison: why
not sacrifice something
ordinary, such as a hairnet . . .

Soon all the animals acclaimed the victor, still in
bed with pilgrims,
drunk
with the wine of defeat, and easygoing, like the
hero he never had
the wisdom
to set out to be. And the line of supplicants led
down to some
graceless bushes
on fire, for virtue wears many masks. . . .

literary pastiche:

. . . What is this? A frigid sense
of isolation, tarnished beyond knowledge? Yes,
and the others tell
it differently, and their version too is the truth, or
it is truthful.

. . . I hear America snowing. . . .

As on a darkling strand when the weather
improves a bit,
there was a little more to be seen than was
apparent at first. The
groan of pebbles
lugged back and forth by the undertow, which at
first seemed
temporary and quickly
turned out to be eternal wasn't made to dis-
please me, no more than
were
the hanks of public seaweed deposited at
intervals that might well
have been
predetermined . . .

And, in addition, there are passages of what this reader thinks of as the Ashberyan "high incomprehensible":

but since charm can never
be quite rinsed from these bones it befits us to
go along with it,
congratulate it
at last for having had something to say and not
said it, as torrents
frazzle a canyon

without contributing to its demise unless one
chooses to consider
inexorably
slow processes that score even the cosmic mind
at rarest intervals,
and superficially;

secure in the adding up of all things
into a block of hay from which no strand is
permitted to extrude.

Reading all this is somewhat like engaging in a very long one-sided conversation with a stranger and not being able to decide whether he is the most brilliant person one has ever met, or simply psychotic. (I was reminded of conversations I had in the early 1970s with a physicist-drug dealer, who, I was convinced, was insane, but whose erratic lyricisms about subatomic particles were interspersed with insistences that the properties of the silicon molecule would bring computers into the homes of every American.)

It is, of course, this collagist's taste for discontinuity, exacerbated by the presence of false syntactical connectives, such as the "as" and "unless" in the passage quoted above, that makes for the famous "difficulty" of Ashbery (about whose brilliance *and* sanity I have no doubts). And it is interesting how different it is to negotiate this difficulty in a very long poem than in the shorter ones. For while it might be possible to explicate the shorter poems in some conventional way if one were perversely impelled to do so, the reader of ***Flow Chart*** really has no choice but to give up the struggle for comprehension as we know it and let the flow of language take over. This induces a kind of reading more like drifting than swimming.

Such a shift in poetic initiative from "ideas" in the poet's mind to something generated by the very nature of "language" itself has been one goal of an avant-garde project for poetry traceable at least back to Mallarmé, carried forward by the Dadaists, and embraced today by the language poets as well as by French-influenced academic literary criticism. This shift is also implicit, if less radically demanded, in definitions of poetry that emphasize its density, compression, and thus "opaqueness," relative to the "transparency" of expository prose. In other words, expository prose disappears as you read it, whereas the material presence of poetry and poetic prose cannot (or should not) be escaped. From this point of view, ***Flow Chart*** is exemplary. Scrupulously maintaining its hard, impenetrable surface of language, it provides few openings for a fall into mere comprehension.

Indeed, this extraordinary surface itself becomes the central experience of the poem. The discontinuities that loom so large in Ashbery's shorter poems, each seemingly asking for comprehension, each foiling comprehension in its unique way, in ***Flow Chart*** almost disappear, becoming only a small repeating pattern within a larger seamlessness. Cumulatively created, this paradoxical smoothness is sustained in a masterly exercise of *refus de signifier* or, if one prefers the language of the so-called New York school, of "keeping the surface up."

For all that attention to surface, the invoking and immediate dismantling of images and the incorporation of "anti-artistic" elements invite comparisons of Ashbery's work with that of American painters about whom he has written; for all the hoopla about the word taking on the plasticity of a medium such as paint, and the affinities of the New York poets with the New York school of painting—the visual quality of ***Flow Chart*** is much less important than the aural.

Anyone who has heard Ashbery read his work may wonder how it is that this poet with the charming, but unprepossessing delivery could have been endowed with one of the great ears of our time. Yet it is sound that seduces one into section after section of ***Flow Chart:***

> Hours, years later, we were together.
> The moon unbarred its hold, the thickness of
> brambles was
>   compacted
> just in time to prevent the closing of the door as
> if by magic . . .
>
> I had
> many ties to the region. And yes, life has a way
> of sidling
>   on in rain-slick afternoons
> like this as though nothing were amiss . . .

Ashbery's control over this sound is complete—whether over a mildly ironic passage of rather grand iambics, or the flatnesses of a disjointed vernacular, or the blatant pleasures of a double sestina. There is something of the aging virtuoso here, flourishing skills that have been deliberately abandoned rather than lost.

If Ashbery can be accused of being a tease, it is because of his alternating blandishments of ravishing, "beautiful" music with deliberately deflating, "antiliterary" sounds. His use of the vernacular is particularly interesting because it is so uncontaminated by the wish that this language were other than it is:

> . . . O what awful thing are they
> doing now?
> What make-believe? Idiotic proposals are
> advanced, then they blab
> it,
> it won't work. It doesn't work. Not that anyone
> is what I would
>   call conceited, or
> outgoing either, I güess. . . .

This tone, which can be so annoying because so familiar, embarrasses us because it does not conform to the kind of vernacular we are currently comfortable with in poetry—primarily a sentimentalized ethnic or working-class speech, or a stylized "earnestness." In fact, it is reading Ashbery that enables one to hear how mannered, how "literary," how "high," even, these have become.

The process of exorcising dead "poetic" language requires a particularly vigilant ear. While we may think that Duchamp or the Beats, or whoever, put the notion of "high" art (and language) to bed for good, each generation's "honest" or "vernacular" or "authentic" reencircles itself with the halo of "art" before we know it, becoming a new "high" language that needs to be secularized once again. (This may have been part of what Frank O'Hara had in mind when he warned himself against "nostalgia for the avant guard."

Again and again while reading Ashbery, we confront our own squeamishness about what does not sound "poetic":

> . . . Arts & leisure—80 bucks! As
> quiet as my
> contentment is the voice at my shoulder; make it
> over, Perhaps not
>   a total
> from-the-ground-up rehab, perhaps only a few
> cosmetic touches
> would have an earth-shaking impact, in this
> instance. . . .

In ***Flow Chart,*** this prosaic banality is not even relieved by the frequent line breaks, each with its momentary promise (even if false) of significance, that might make this stuff more palatable. The remarkably long lines just keep rolling in one after another, nonchalantly bringing more litter onto the shore.

> Lately I have this feeling you were avoiding me.
> We could sum it
>   all up as a bunch

> of nerves, little people peeing around, but there
> goes my Dober-
> man's tether, he's off and running,
> not to put too fine a point on it. And the
> cooling-off period ended,
> dirty,
> this time. . . .

However much we may dislike it, this thin sound is the sound of late twentieth-century mass culture. If Auden was right that the job of poetry is to disintoxicate, then we should applaud.

And yet, having said this much, it must be pointed out that the "voices" of this vernacular, this common language, are all oddly the same. As if filtered through a single all-digesting consciousness, they all resolve into a single voice talking to itself, reenacting conversations overheard, remembered, participated in. In fact, the shifting of pronouns that is so characteristic of Ashbery's poetry and that he himself once described as a method of polyphony reveals itself in ***Flow Chart*** as the inner polyphony of ordinary consciousness: the shifts from *I* to *you* during reminiscence, the appearance of *he*'s and *she*'s that remain unnamed because they are known by the ruminating mind we have so intimately entered, the use of the *us* of a generation or of a participant in the larger culture.

But whose consciousness is this? In certain aspects, it is that of John Ashbery, poet. In most aspects, however, its relationship to experience is far removed from anything conventionally thought of as autobiographical. A statement from Henri Michaux, quoted by Ashbery himself in one of the articles he wrote for *ArtNews,* may be helpful here:

> Instead of one vision which excludes others, I would have liked to draw the moments that, placed side by side, go to make up a life. To expose the interior phrase for people to see, the phrase that has no words, a rope which uncoils sinuously, and intimately accompanies everything that impinges from the outside or the inside. I wanted to draw the consciousness of existence and the flow of time. As you would take your pulse.

And an illuminating statement by Roland Barthes, quoted by Marjorie Perloff in her essay on Barthes and Ashbery:

> . . . Barthes wants to create a "novelistic" texture that is no longer "dominated by the superego of continuity, a superego of evolution, history, and filiation."

Adapting these, one might say that Ashbery has created an autobiographical texture that is no longer dominated by the superego of continuity, a superego of personality created by memory and relationship; and in doing so, he has re-created the *experience* of a consciousness. This is consciousness that records the inflow and outflow of ideas, feelings, and sensations with a scientist's dispassion, stepping away from any desire to shape of form. This is a consciousness that is of interest not for its contents or products but for its willingness to exhibit itself simply being in time.

Such is the great honesty and even humility of ***Flow Chart.*** Disabused of grand ideas, Ashbery expresses neither nostalgia for those of the past, nor eagerness to install new ones. This includes ideas about the relationship between language and the world—that there might be a relationship between poetic value and accurate description, for example, or a clear connection between words and moral action, or between words and transcendent meaning:

> . . . what
> if poetry were something else entirely, not this
> purple weather with
> the eye of a god attached, that sees
> inward and outward? What if it were only a
> small, other way of
> living . . .

Another poet, at this intersection, would write antiepiphanies of emptiness or strike a note of grief, but Ashbery, with characteristic quietude, constrains himself to simply reflect this unknowing, in his own way expressing the view that poetry "makes nothing happen":

> . . . and I have this thing
> I must do without knowing what it is or whether
> anyone
> will be helped or offended by it. Should I do it?
> And there, it was
> gone.
> It will never be printed on a banner in a political
> demonstration
> or fed to rabbits first to see whether they die . . .

To write like this must be extremely liberating and yet require great restraint. There is something almost puritanical in the poem's abstentions—from symbolic language, from "high" language unaccompanied by irony, from the search for meaning through memory, from hopes that life might be redeemed through art, and, it also seems, from any notion that existence might be redeemed through love or even affirmed through sex:

> Love that lasts a minute like a filter
> on a faucet . . .

. . . [I] have come belatedly to realize that sex has
very little to do
   with any of it,

Now and then, this refusal to allow language the role of ordering experience into meaning takes on a tinge of affectation:

. . . The massive transcription with
which
he took unforgivable liberties—hell, I'd sooner
join the project
farther ahead, retaining all benefits, but one is
doomed,
repeating oneself, never to repeat oneself, you
know what I mean?

And sometimes it descends to camp (a far less convincing method of dismissing meaning, tainted as it is by disappointment):

. . . Furthermore
the burliest male is but as a handmaiden to the
suspicion of his own
   history:
he's got it right, OK? And so have a few others,
while the waiting's
   been going on. But enough of
this self-congratulation in Aegean sunrises.
Who are we, after all?
   And who needs profundity?

At its worst, the equivalence it grants to all language makes for some ambiguous juxtapositions:

. . . It occurs to me in my home on the
beach
sometimes that others must have experiences
identical to mine
and are also unable to speak of them, that if we
cared
enough to go into each other's psyche and
explore
around, some of the canned white entrepreneur-
ial brain food
could be reproduced in time to save the legions
of the dispossessed, and elephants. . . .

all the porters have shuffled away, under the
erroneous impression
   we haven't the coin
to pay them no doubt, yet it's not true, we would
pay them if we
   could, but just look
how they have left the funhouse mirror clearly
visible for perhaps
   the first time
and we can at last admire our billowing hips and
hourglass
   waists . . .

But at its best, Ashbery's aesthetic offers something rather miraculous—moments of exaltation, available to us even in this sea of unknowing, seemingly as a part of the condition of existence itself:

. . . Sometimes we do
perceive it
this way, like animals that will get up and move
somewhere and
   then drop down
in place again, we hear it and especially we see
it—some whitecap
   curdles
in a leaden expanse of water and we are aware
this moment has
   done its share . . .

So it is surprising to find a more conventionally autobiographical note in ***Flow Chart***—an odd note of personal defensiveness breaking the mandarin calm that pervades most of the poem, as in these lines, selected from an extended argument toward the end:

[some accused me of] making howl-like sounds
at night . . .

. . . Others, recognizing my disinterest, nonethe-
less accused
me of playing mind-games that only the skilled
should ever attempt. My reply, then as always,
was that ignorance
of the law is the law, far from being no excuse,
and we'll see who
   rakes in
the chips come Judgment Day. . . .

. . . I've taken my lumps as well as enjoyed the
good times
now and then, and don't see what difference it
makes to old
   soldiers,
of which I'm proud to count myself one.

. . . chipping away at the noble experiment . . .

. . . set out
on your own at the eleventh hour, into the vast
yawn or cusp . . .

> . . . And when we have succeeded, not know
> what to do with it
> except break it into shards that get more
> ravishing as you keep
> pounding them. . . .

There is something moving about this "old soldier" sharing his doubts and defenses with his readers. And such passages are certainly in keeping with the unwillingness to assert too much that characterizes the entire poem. But sometimes they come close to naming too accurately the very doubts that the reader has been valiantly trying to tamp down. One of these passages jumped out with particular poignancy from page 117 of the poem:

> Anyway, it was life,
> one had to agree, but all the same could have
> been better written,
> with more
> attention to niceties of style and fewer obscure
> references, though
> the concept,
> always, was beyond reproach.

Occurring just when one's bedazzlement was giving way to a kind of numbness from floating in this sea of language for so long, these lines, coyly referring to life instead of art, aroused a doubt that just would not go away. It's not that one would ask that ***Flow Chart*** be better written. No, it's a brilliant piece of writing. The doubt is rather one aroused by so many irreproachable works of "conceptual" art. The shards may be ravishing; the veneer, flawless. But once the concept has been grasped, is there any need to watch it play itself out, more or less repetitively, however glamorous the reiterations?

Is it possible that a poetry so intent on avoiding the frozen "idea" might itself congeal into a "concept"?

Well, yes.

And does ***Flow Chart?***

Almost. Sometimes yes. Sometimes no.

This is the great risk of this kind of experiment—a risk more evident in a very long poem, in which the concept, exposed at such length, loses some of the provocative interest, the engaging shimmer it has in the shorter works.

Yet one does admire ***Flow Chart,*** especially at a time when hardly anyone is risking as much, even if feeling a bit like a soldier for art oneself while reading to the very end. And whatever comes on Judgment Day, one thing is for certain: It will never be "fed to rabbits first to see whether they die."

Martin Kevorkian (essay date Spring 1994)

SOURCE: "John Ashbery's *Flow Chart:* John Ashbery and the Theorists on John Ashbery Against the Critics Against John Ashbery," in *New Literary History,* Vol. 25, No.2, Spring, 1994, pp. 459-76.

[*In the following essay, Kevorkian explores the interactive relationship between Ashbery and his critics. According to Kevorkian, Ashbery's poetry reveals a pattern of "revenge" and "linguistic parasitism" through which he both engages and subtly responds to his critical audience.*]

> That's a phrase I've been saying and hearing for so many years—the people against Nan Patterson—the people against Harry K. Thaw, and now the People against Mary Dugan. I have used that phrase so often that I've almost forgotten its meaning—and, Gentlemen, it has a very deep one.

John Ashbery's poetry asks its Gentlereaders not so much to recover some "deep" significance, but rather to hear its capacity to nudge toward oblivion the ordinary meanings of *almost* ordinary phrases. "One's gone for some grants" carries away the remnants of the expectation that such a one might return from this errand with a bag of deli sandwiches.

> One might say, casually,
> that there was variation in it, that there was
> texture. More, though,
> one still couldn't say.

Flow Chart, a product of John Ashbery's "own genre," lays out a series of speech processes "with communication left out, except in one vital respect. The natural noise of the present hypnotizes the reader and takes him over, or is taken over by him"; so states John Bayley in his review of ***Flow Chart,*** "Richly Flows Contingency." Ashbery's ability to infect us, to get us under the skin of common language where his poetry thrives—this insidious hospitality appears to constitute a "trade secret."

With this general sense of Ashbery's poetic "noise" in the background (for now), the following essay will examine selected instances—some more hospitable than others—of Ashbery's use by the academy, and Ashbery's use of Ashbery's use by the academy. For we will see that Ashbery inhabits not only "natural" noise in his stochastic ramblings, but also exploits the generative power of scholastic chatter. Loosely framed, ***Flow Chart*** claims to convert an early lament, "now the bridge will never be built," into a completed invitation, "It's open: the bridge, that way." Between these endpoints of the bridge's construction, we encounter references to Ashbery's readers and critics, his "onlookers" and "oracles," who appear to have made some unwitting contributions to the building process:

> It was the repeating of them that interested me.
> Repetition makes
>   reputation.
> Besides, it's something you can build with. You
> need no longer
>   inspect the materials
> When you buy them in bulk; they are as a
> territory. What gets built
>   happens
> to be in that territory, though beside it. Your
> reputation as a builder
>   is the one interesting thing

The logic of ***Flow Chart,*** I will argue, offers a descriptive structure for the odd relationship that can evolve between poet and academic readership.

Bayley believes a purely oppositional logic—an even relationship, so to speak—operates between Ashbery and his critical lumberyard: "Ashbery is clearly in revolt against modern academic and deconstructive practices where poetry is concerned: against the whole apparatus of university English departments." One central function of that apparatus comes under obvious attack in ***Flow Chart*** when Ashbery takes as a likeness "a dissertation of some kind. A great deal of thinking went into it and out the other side." Yet mockery does not ensure a poetry that effectively proscribes certain critical responses. Resisting, opposing, assuming the role of a double may even sustain complicated new discourse: even if Bayley is in some sense correct about the attitudes Ashbery expresses, one would still like to resolve the apparent paradox that deconstructive practice has thrived upon Ashbery's poetry.

If repetition interests Ashbery, gives him something to build with, deconstruction has indeed established itself as a familiar tune among Ashbery critics. Ashbery recalls that "Alvin and the chipmunks made nice ambient music for what / I was fussing over"; so, perhaps, did Derrida and the epigones. Jerome McGann testifies from the pages of *Critical Inquiry:* "If Frank O'Hara seems the antithesis of academic work, John Ashbery is, in his own way, its epitome. . . . Ashbery has become the touchstone of deconstructive analysis."

Ashbery voices ambivalence about the institutionalized relationship between poets and the francophilic departments wherein they may reside: "The French still say 'hailstones big as pigeon's / eggs,' and poets are retreating into—or is it out of?—academia." Ashbery himself has gone in one side and, perhaps, out the other of more than one institution of higher learning, yet it is possible that some of the "twaddle" may have stuck. George Steiner has recently commented on the sometimes salutary, sometimes unhealthy relationship between poets and the university: "Observe the semantic duplicity: poets who can be taught are also teachable." In a collection entitled *The Future of Literary Theory,* Alastair Fowler muses on the possible effects of such proximity: "It is sometimes wondered whether new kinds of kinds may be emerging—genres not produced by the usual assemblage, abstraction, modulation, and the like, but instead by novel processes of development. . . . In John Ashbery's poetry . . . abandonment of stable mimetic contexts seems almost to react directly to contemporary literary theory. In fact, one might think of 'theoretic genres,' motivated at least in part by a wish to illustrate (and perhaps validate) some particular theory."

On all such speculation of response to the influence of theory, David Lehman, in "The Pleasures of Poetry," remains more cautionary: "Ashbery's poetry is so richly textured, so replete with allusions and red herrings and complicated rhetorical gestures, that a critic with any degree of ingenuity can easily appeal to [Ashbery's] lines as the support system for a pet critical theory." Along these lines, we might wish to consult some claims from the horse's mouth:

> *John Koethe [Interviewer]: Many of those who are interested in your poetry seem to be interested in it in connection with theoretical ideas, particularly French theoretical ideas, like those of Jacques Derrida. Do you ever read works by such theorists, or do their views influence you secondhand, or do you ever use them in any way?*
>
> Ashbery: No. I think I'm very good subject matter for people who are trying to elaborate new theories of criticism. Perhaps it would be better for me if I didn't know anything about them because then I might consciously try to write stuff that would fit their theories.

Ashbery does not stutter when he says, "No"; Derrida stands denied. Yet the "if . . . then" logic is a bit muddled. And let's look again at that phrase, "perhaps it *would* be better for me *if* I didn't know" (my italics); would it be wrong to infer that Ashbery does know (and may even use) more theory than the absolute denial allows?

We can indeed find Derridean statements in ***Flow Chart,*** some so deliberate as to require almost no ingenuity for the critic to detect: "And these marginalia—what other word is there for them?—are the substance of the text, / by not being allowed to fit in." Or we might find the implied destruction of the hermeneutic space: "only think in terms of surfaces, boundaries." Ashbery, however, takes pains on the same page, "not to put too fine a deconstruction on it." But with conspiratorial sympathy/mockery, he allows that, "Like me / you too chose to put a better construction on these things than perhaps the case warranted."

Clearly, ***Flow Chart*** displays a poet at play with theory. But, other than having revealed evidence of Ashbery's propensity to incorporate "secondary" material into his art, we still have little notion of rules for his game, or of whether stakes exist. Ashbery taunts the reader (and communities of readers) for putting on a "better construction," for seeking

> to unravel ramifications that
> in fact do not exist, but like a gold toothpick are
> merely on hand to
> see that they
> get talked about and maybe some club will invite
> one of them to
> speak.

Ashbery provides a later connection for us to unravel, but any ramification seems little more than the object which constitutes the connection, another gold toothpick of a sort: "The webs intersect at certain points where baubles / are glued to them; readers think this is nice. What else?"

If deconstructive analysis constitutes one major locus of Ashbery criticism, a cultural criticism that would like a serious consideration of the "what else" question emerges as another. Writing on the ethics of literature, Martha Nussbaum explains a personal motivation for seeking a transition (or connection) between playful/deconstructive analysis and the question of the social referent. "After reading Derrida," she comments, "I feel a certain hunger for . . . writing about literature that talks of human lives and choices as if they matter to us at all. . . . We do approach literature for play and delight, for the exhilaration of following the dance form and unraveling webs of textual connection. (Though even here I would not be quick to grant that there is any coherence to an account of aesthetic pleasure that abstracts altogether from our practical human interests and desires. . . . It speaks about us, about our lives and choices and emotions, about our social existence and the totality of our connections)." Along these lines, early in ***Flow Chart,*** Ashbery announces a concern for "What mattered to us":

> Who could have expected a dream like this to go
> away for there are
> some
> that are the web on which our waking life is
> painstakingly elaborated:
> there are real, bustling things there and the
> burgomaster of success
> stalks back and forth, directing everything
> with a small motion of a finger.

Ashbery locates the social referent literally at his fingertips: "My politics shouldn't matter. It's my finger / that should . . . what we are is *digital.*" For Ashbery, evidently, if not precisely the personal, then at least the minutely physiological, *is* the political.

Such direct, if puzzling, citations provide only the first approach to the social referent of Ashbery's poetry. One inventive Marxist critic has found Ashbery to be a deliberate social banalist. In the essay "Ashbery's Dismantling of Bourgeois Discourse," Keith Cohen writes: "In the metaphysical soap opera that is John Ashbery's poetry, a critical scrutiny of language plays a major role. Ashbery aims consistently at the glibness, deceitfulness, and vapidity of bourgeois discourse and in his poems subjects this discourse to a process of disintegration. What some may relegate . . . to the area of language games and gratuitous surrealistic effects is an integral part of a very serious attack." Nevertheless, critics of Ashbery (that is to say those who don't like him) often find an alleged absence of social referent to be Ashbery's weak point. Charles Molesworth in the essay "This Leaving Out Business" finds the "most [notable] . . . hallmark of Ashbery's style" to be "a fear of social reality."

In ***Flow Chart,*** we find Ashbery self-conscious of this discomfort:

> we try to excommunicate everyone including
> ourselves from society:
> even the word "society"
> is something each of us eventually gets a
> stranglehold on, forcing it
> to say "uncle"—there,
> I'm glad I did, and you can go away now.

However, as Ashbery must know, it seems unlikely within the current (po)lit-crit environment that those with social concerns will be so easily dismissed. Molesworth's analysis, along with that of Robert Boyers (the *Salmagundi* editor who published Molesworth's essay), seems the fundament of Ashbery bashing. Defenders of Ashbery, both Marjorie Perloff and David Lehman, for instance, usually start off by immediately taking a defensive stance explicitly against the positions of Molesworth and/or Boyers. In "The Pleasures of Poetry," Lehman notes only that the critical naysayers against Ashbery are in the minority, but in a slightly earlier essay, Lehman has written, "Again and again, by Molesworth and Boyers, . . . Ashbery is seen as part of a cultural movement, a force with wide and allegedly deleterious implications." Lehman says "again and again" but footnotes only the Molesworth attack which I cite here. This particular assault was not only published in *Salmagundi,* but was selected by Boyers to be anthologized in the retrospective *Salmagundi Reader.*

This bit of bibliographic emphasis is all by way of laying the groundwork for a somewhat Kinbotian theory of poetry as counterconspiracy. Though the deconstructive criticism may be purchased "in bulk," so to speak, it is just possible that Ashbery, in the instance of Molesworth, may have stooped to "examine the materials" and built accordingly. "Ashbery eschews the ordinary lyricism of verse, seldom bothering with rhyme or alliteration or strict meter . . . This prose quality goes hand in hand with the flat, affectless tone as well as the diffident, self-questioning attitude. The run of his argument, *the flow of the poem's display of itself* suggests a ruminative impulse at work" (italics mine).

Thus Charles Molesworth gears up for a paragraph in which he enumerates the failings of Ashbery's poetry: it is "illustrative rather than functional . . . hopeless [wearying] chaos . . . Jamesian prose . . . studded with cliches."

Moreover, of Ashbery's collection ***Three Poems,*** Molesworth notes that "no reviewer of this work has had the temerity to suggest it was a good-natured hoax, a jeux d'esprit in which the confessional impulses of contemporary poetry were so gluttonously satisfied that they were simultaneously being scorned. Ashbery stuffed his ['poetry'] with so much mandarin prose, masking such banal content, or at least cultivating a stultifying surface banality, that the modesty of the book's title can be read either as a deadpan joke or a highhanded taunt." It is perhaps ridiculous and maniacal to imagine, not to mention temerarious to suggest, that ***Flow Chart,*** or at least the title (which Ashbery claims usually to pick first), represents a manner of taunt, a deadpan translation of Molesworth's phrase, "the flow of the poem's display of itself."

Whether Molesworth is the specific communicant or not, the reader can hear Ashbery preempting the sort of things that might get said about his poetry. But if we do hypothesize Molesworth, we can spin out a little dialogue.

Molesworth, to conclude his jeremiad, laments the loss of "political fervor in poetry now that the 1960's are past." Ashbery responds, "Oh, stop badgering—where were *you* in the fifties?" (note here again a typical strategy of the Ashbery voice, to inhabit a familiar phrase—where were you in the sixties—and change just one word). Another pertinent decade to this debate might be the thirties, with Ashbery's allusion to the 1930 Vanderbilt/Fugitive/New Agrarian manifesto *I'll Take my Stand.* Again: "My politics shouldn't matter. It's my finger / that should—it's here I'll take my stand."

On the issue of what Molesworth calls Ashbery's "stultifying surface banality," we might note the poet's "banal if agreeable note-spinning" and the even more coy,

> You fuck me, I'll
> fix you. You give me that, and I'll give you this.
> It's all so important
> yet so excruciatingly
> banal, isn't it, darling?

Furthermore, Molesworth accuses Ashbery of "anal retentiveness" and notes Ashbery's lack of "free wheeling humor." Ashbery seems to dispel both claims at once with a line that stands alone: "Excuse me while I fart. There, that's better. I actually feel relieved." To take this all to ludicrous extremes, by a process of elimination we might find within the letters of ***Flow Chart*** the celebration of a sort of "low art." Or, simply, "Fart" (depending on which way you go with the bifurcated F/low).

Perhaps all this has been to make a mountain—or at least a badger's mound—out of a mole's worth of cheap earth. There remains, it seems, the putting of a "better construction" on an already dubious one. To put it rather crassly, can we use some other Theory to talk about my little theory (that Ashbery includes responses to criticism in his poetry)? George Steiner "would define the claim to theory in the humanities as impatience systematized." I fear that I have neither the time nor the conviction to refute him. Ashbery's poetry has led me so thoroughly into the temptations of theory that Steiner's words ring truer than ever: "Parasitic discourse feeds upon living utterance; as in microbiological food-chains, the parasitic in turn feeds upon itself. Criticism, metacriticism, diacriticism, the criticism of criticism, pullulate." My hope and claim is that the very truth of this charge may illuminate the Ashbery phenomenon. Or, rather, that the Ashbery phenomenon may illuminate and revalue a certain reciprocity between the aims of literary study and the aims of contemporary literature being studied.

Two key words which appear in ***Flow Chart*** broadly outline the discussion which follows. Ashbery's poetry will be seen to reveal two related mechanisms: explicitly, the logic of rivalry and "revenge"; and, perhaps more subtly, the cunning logic of the "parasite." "We'd have rivalry at the end, sure, but cunning as well in the abstract."

We might return for a moment to reconsider the implications of Nussbaum's suggestion: that unraveling the web may be an important exercise. Ashbery lets us know that he is aware of one particular issue intimately enmeshed with the web of the world: the issue of revenge. With the flourish of a magician's promise, Ashbery announces:

> Now to expunge
> the revenge-motif, and get it all right for once.
> Life is an embroidery-
> frame, and what you put
> into it gets left there.

But he seems to know the mere declaration won't quite do it, that expunged violence gets reabsorbed into the system: "in this kind of bleached-out crisis- / feeling, the best one can do is remain polite while dreaming of revenge in another key." Such acknowledgement of duplicity, coupled with Ashbery's occasional willingness to be sincerely impolite, seems to function in the mode of revelation, unraveling the problems, the pleasures of revenge. Reneé Girard, probably the most visible "theorist" of the problem of revenge, has repeatedly described the "sacralization" of the destructive cycle of "mimetic desire." Ashbery's language in ***Flow Chart*** at times shadows Girard's—from say, *Deceit, Desire and the Novel* or *Violence and the Sacred*"—up to a point:

Once two were saddled with each other's lies
which became as a
 sacramental trust
for them. They listened, they put forth feelers
pouted on cue, but in
 due
course banshees exploited the situation. And
once the climate of
 trust is destroyed
only lust for vengeance can take its place—or
so *one* would have us
 believe.

The fact that Ashbery emphasizes the "one" implies that he may have a particular theorist (somewhat skeptically) in mind. Girard is one obvious choice, but not the only one. Michael Serres speaks of the epistemology of suspicion, and the drive to destruction mistrust engenders when the gods and goddesses of myth—or the human sciences—enlist Hermes and Argus (Panoptes) to police one another's cheating, and to commit murder: "Tired of these deceitful games, of these tricks, dreaming that our brief lives might escape this monotonous cycle of blood and death, we hope to return to a moment of trust that neither deceives nor cheats." More succinctly, Ashbery reminds us that, "Mercury slew Argus for vulgar reasons."

I find that even as I attempt to deploy theory descriptively from outside the poetry, I am never far from the deranged inkling that Ashbery has already used (and/or defused) said theory from within. However, whereas in the case of Molesworth we could at least posit *some* plausible motive, with the theorists of vengeance we are really stitching with air. But then again, the plausible motive for Ashbery's possible response to Molesworth, if not exactly bloodthirsty, would have to look quite a bit like revenge. That is, if Ashbery's poem responds to a particular critic, the structure of that very response may be described by a theory (to which Ashbery might also be responding).

Ashbery observes that "two were saddled with each other's lies which became as a sacramental trust." In Girard's mimetic system, the critic Molesworth, insofar as he enters into verbal rivalry with the poet, would become the "double" of Ashbery; the reciprocal is true of Ashbery if he picks up the gauntlet. Implicitly, Girard invokes the monadic system of Leibniz to describe the relationship: "In the world of the doubles. . . seen against the comings and goings of the violence that both separates and unites them, the two partners come to be, by turns, the one and only god, who sees everything converge on him and kneel before him, and the puny, speechless, trembling creature . . . a kind of monad . . . at the feet of this god, who has mysteriously taken up residence with the other person, the rival and model for desire." Girard's world of the doubles, to apply it simplistically to the poet versus critic hypothesis, suggests a partnership through which Ashbery's poetry continues to inhabit Molesworth's writing, and Molesworth's critiques make their presence felt in ***Flow Chart.*** In an important respect, however, Ashbery transcends this system, by playing (and seeing) all the positions. Ashbery seems capable of a detached Girardian overview of the system, an insight Girard generally attributes to nonparticipants in the conflict. In Girard's words, "Everyone imitates the other's violence. . . . Uninvolved spectators see this unmistakably." We may recall Ashbery's firm grasp of the violent, predictable quid pro quo of his own relations:

 You fuck me, I'll
fix you. You give me that, and I'll give you this.
It's all so important
 yet so excruciatingly
banal, isn't it, darling?

The work of Michael Serres may serve to help us further describe the relations of exchange discoverable in Ashbery's poetry. Serres does his research on the logical, informational, economical, societal system of "the parasite" by retelling fables and examining their internal structures: "Quite curiously, the manners of this wolf, fox, lion, monkey, cat, or rat are never, or seldom, those of predators; in these stories, they are almost always those of parasites. In the guise of an attack, a theft, a power-play, in the person of these animals, the simple relation of the abusive companion reappears." As described by Serres, the king of the system of Leibniz is the king of uneasy cohabitations, the harmonic master of parasitic polyphony. A network of parasitic relations approaches its "limit," "the system of Leibniz," when the multiplicity of parasites is subsumed into one who controls all exchanges.

Ashbery expresses interest in the fabular world of the parasite and in the beast who plays the parasitic role to the hilt:

It has long been my contention that jackals,

unlike other denizens of the epistemic forest, are
able to predict
the future of metabolizing some kind of parasite
that grows on other
  people's
children and devours them. The eyes are a
profound cobalt blue,
  accepting
of moral dilemmas and sprouting proverbs
slowly, like crystals,
but no, not innocent,
and not lacking in character.

From this rather difficult passage, I gather that Ashbery has noted some harsh wisdom in the jackal's unique speculation: one can go one step better than being a parasite by eating (and "metabolizing") one. The "cobalt blue" eyes linger as the dominant visual image of the passage, but their significance lies not so much in their color as such, but rather in the perceptive power cobalt implies medically—a cobalt blue light is used to diagnose eye and skin infections, which glow tellingly beneath its beam. This perspicuity sets the metabolizer of parasites apart from the other "denizens of the epistemic forest." Serres, writing his animal fabular "epistemology of the parasite," notes, "Quite simply, what is essential is neither the image nor the deep meaning, neither the representations nor its hall of mirrored reflections, but the system of relations. The relation is that of guest to host [*hôte à hôte*]."

Serres's doubling of guest and host recalls J. Hillis Miller's famous demonstration (more difficult in English) that "host" and "guest" are etymologically and semantically interchangeable. Hillis Miller performs this feat in "The Critic as Host," his defense of deconstruction against the charge of Wayne C. Booth and M. H. Abrams that the "deconstructionist reading of a given work is plainly and simply parasitical on the obvious or univocal reading." Gregory Ulmer notes in this context that Serres's "paraliterary text," *The Parasite,* is "a full elaboration (allegory) of the story of deconstruction, of the alien guest in the home." In Hillis Miller's account:

> The poem, in my figure, is that ambiguous gift, food, host in the sense of the victim, sacrifice. It is broken, divided, passed around, consumed by critics canny and uncanny who are in that odd relation to one another of host and parasite. Any poem, however, is parasitical in its turn on earlier poems, or it contains earlier poems within itself as enclosed parasites, in another version of the perpetual reversal of parasite and host. If the poem is food and poison for the critics, it must in its turn have eaten. It must have been a cannibal consumer of earlier poems.

In general resonance with Hillis Miller's imagery, a recurring motif of sacrificial language haunts ***Flow Chart:*** "remonstrance," "sacramental," "sacrifice," "sacrificial wine." This host Ashbery extends to his readers clearly does contain the eaten parasites Hillis Miller mentions, both unaltered pieces of predecessor poems often set off by italics or quotation marks, as well as digested bits of the canon—Shakespeare, the Bible—that fit within the skin of Ashbery's language. And I would further suggest that Ashbery's poetry encloses not only the parasites of earlier poets, but also of earlier critics. If so, Ashbery plays what appears to be the trump (post) card—that is, for this hand—in the allegory of deconstruction. Like the jackal, he metabolizes the parasites.

The deconstructive logic of Hillis Miller incorporates two definitions of the parasite; as we will see, both Serres and Ashbery recognize a third meaning. Hillis Miller provides (from the *American Heritage Dictionary*) the biological and the social definitions: an organism that feeds upon its host, or a person that takes advantage of generosity. Serres calls upon the French language for a third definition, a point his translator, Lawrence Schehr, emphasizes: "the parasite is noise as well, the static in a system or the interference in a channel."

Ashbery plays with both the biological and the social definitions, but also observes the interruptive noise associated with both. Ashbery makes mention of "Noises that bit me, / would-be fanciers skulking around, after an autograph or a piece of your hair, no doubt." "Noises that bit me" appears to combine at least two definitions of the parasite: Serres's included third meaning, noise; and the biological rat or bug that bites. Tagging close behind the noisy nibbling of informational and biological parasitism, Ashbery finds the social parasites, the hangers-on seeking his word and his flesh. "But the last word is always the author's so you might want to dwell a bit / more on the perfections of form adjusted to content, and vice versa too." Dwell well on his poetry while you can, be its *hôte;* for if blue-eyed Ashbery predicts any future in metabolizing your parasitic presence, he will surely find a way for you to dwell in his poetry.

Following his speculation on jackals and parasites, Ashbery ruminates that

                    One very chewy advanced proposi-
tion
seemed to falter, then faded into the background
noise, but—here's
  the thing—
continued, to this day

The parasitic noise persists: "everyone may *bon gré mal gré* ignore it, yet it peaks / and in so doing has its say."

The French expression is the meeting place of ambivalence and ambiguity: "will one or will one not" (an undetermined choice), or "willy-nilly" (an indeterminate state). Serres finds ambiguity to be a necessary ingredient for an information rich system. According to Shannon's equations, ambiguity can provide information precisely because it is ambivalent: on a given level (of, say, one who is transmitting a signal), ambiguity is noise to be filtered out; on the next level up (say, the receiver), however, the very same term—the ambiguity term—changes its sign from negative to positive in the equation describing the total information of the system. "In one case it covers up; in the other case, it expresses." Ashbery's explicit use of ambivalence, and his availability to natural noise, makes for a high degree of ambiguity, but also for "information" (however potentially spurious the handwaving involved in attempting to translate information into "meaning").

The ambiguity function contributes to the poetics of association: "For an observer outside the system, ambiguity must be added, for it increases the system's complexity. . . . Embedded in this process [is] the entire strategy of free association, Freudian slips, jokes and puns. . . . We perceive nothing of the deafening background noise given off by the system, except for interesting pieces of information relating to the general functioning of these transformations or their local breakdown." Ashbery employs both the attention-getting local breakdowns and transformations that send us looking for general patterns: "with as many associations as that," the repeated phrase itself an encoded redundancy, "the whole freight train of associations is set in motion, lumbers gracelessly." One minute transformation causes us to suspect a master plan: the word *perfectibility* misspelled early in the poem—when it was merely an unfulfilled "desire for perfectability"—finds its corrected answer when "human perfectibility" gets "promoted to the first desk." Yet if we check back to the source of the error, we find Ashbery's protestation against "little pieces of the puzzle getting in on the act." Rather than a master plan, perhaps we have detected nothing more than the noise of the typesetting machine: "something like an actual misprint occurs." Perhaps, but such accidental noise can be arranged.

Ashbery acts as a parasite—his poetry derives informational complexity by parasiting, adding bits of noise to, the messages of ordinary language: "thus the message, passing through his hands in the location of the exchanger, is changed. It arrives neither pure nor unvarying nor stable. I am willing to have it improve, but that is a judgment. . . . What is true is that the message is burdened and arrives thus burdened. To speak correctly, it is parasited. The parasite has placed itself in the most profitable positions, at the intersection of relations." Let us return again to Ashbery's phrase "One's gone for some grants." The noise ("sandwiches" scrambled, exchanged for "grants") introduces a complexity that invites the reader to look for a new logic of the message. This new logic might be found to replicate the profitable linguistic parasitism on the signal: the warping of what we might call "office" language points to an academic research-grant-based economy in which sustenance (sandwiches and other forms of bread) is exchanged for words (and words on words).

Bayley concludes his review of ***Flow Chart*** by comparing Ashbery's "noise" to the "fabled" nonsense "dinner table" conversation of Bloomsbury critic Desmond Macarthy: to enrich his description of parasitic noise, Bayley offers the portrait of a famous social parasite. *The Parasite* is full of stories of interrupted meals, and of the art of living by the exchange of fables, information at the dinner table: "the parasite is invited to the *table d'hôte*. . . . [H]e buys his dinner, paying for it in words. It is the oldest profession in the world." The parasite pays with words. Or noise. Or, sometimes, noise interposed on noise's interruption of noise. In our language, the negative connotations of the word *parasite* are difficult to evade; for Serres, the charming art of the parasite may achieve greatness. Ashbery, our "most successful poet," might also be the most thoroughgoing of parasites. Perhaps the best way to live as a parasite (to exchange words for goods) is to be always a parasite (to inhabit the noise of ordinary speech, and to interpose oneself into the discourse of those who have interrupted yours).

Beginning with a "black box" labeled "production," Serres retells a fable while building a cascade of parasites: the tax farmer thrives as "an interrupter" of production, and the rats feast off the farmer's parasitism, until their parasitism is interrupted by a noise. "Yet noise has a subject, the one who makes the noise, in the fable. No doubt it is the farmer, the parasited one. One of the first in the chain, he was thus cheated on behind his back. Awakened by the noise of the rats, cutting and nibbling, he suddenly opens the door. He jumps behind those who were eating behind his back and chases them. The parasited one parasites the parasites. One of the first, he jumps to the last position. But the one in the last position wins this game." We might construct an analogous cascade, beginning with the black box of language, substituting Ashbery for the farmer, and critics (Molesworth, deconstructors, et al.) for the rats.

Like the farmer, Ashbery is both first and last in line at the table of language. Serres notes that the black box of production remains a mystery; though we may explain away Ashbery's strategies as parasitic, he remains very close to our own black box of language. And, according to all observable academic indicators, Ashbery's poetry very nearly approximates the quality of Serres's mysterious genuine source: "Real production is undoubtedly rare, for it attracts parasites that immediately make it something common and banal. Real production is unexpected and improbable; it overflows with information and is always immediately parasited."

Serres observes that "every parasite . . . at the table of a somewhat sumptuous host, soon transforms the table into a theater." A parasitic reading of Ashbery's poetry—an information-rich host—will add complexity and tend to transform the poetry into theater. In this essay, for example, we began to hear a hypothetical dialogue between Ashbery and the subparasite Molesworth. Ashbery's poetry not only invites this manner of theatrical reconstruction, but already plays host to an array of theatrical works: *Lear, Troilus and Cressida, Hamlet, The Trial of Mary Dugan.* This last Ashbery implies is a novel: Ashbery's categorization is perhaps instructive. *The Trial of Mary Dugan* did appear as a novel, but as a parasitic novel, based upon an earlier play. The idea had occurred to you during a performance of a high-school play. / You weren't ashamed to take credit for it—why should you be?"

There is perhaps no need for apology: for a novelist turning a play into a novel, or for a would-be parasitic critic turning poetry into dialogue. According to thermo- and social dynamics, "the parasite was inevitable." Or, less deterministically, "something may come of something." Lear is not heard to argue.

As the reader may have begun to notice, "the parasite doesn't stop. It doesn't stop eating or drinking or yelling or burping or making thousands of noises or filling space with its swarming and din. The parasite is an expansion; it runs and grows. It invades and occupies. It overflows, all of a sudden, from these pages." But it can, for a merciful time, fade "into the background noise." To await, perhaps, a new offering of the host, the host who is always a gracious guest. "Well I see I've not outstayed my welcome." Of such statements, one is apt to feel, the critic remains less assured than does the poet.

Calvin Bedient (review date October 1994)

SOURCE: A review of *And the Stars Were Shining*, in *Poetry*, Vol. 165, No. 1, October, 1994, pp. 44-7.

[*In the following review, Bedient offers tempered praise for* And the Stars Were Shining, *though he notes that this volume is "not one of his strongest."*]

John Ashbery famously has all the humor omitted by Eavan Boland, and then some. As is well known, disappointment leavened by humor, pathos gussied up in tinker-toy hats and cow-belled shoes, is his theme. "The afternoon / will fold you up," he promises in **"Like a Sentence,"** "along with preoccupations / that now seem so important, until only a child / running around on a unicycle occupies center stage." It's part of his charm that he knows we won't believe him, part of his generosity to make the momentarily charming gesture.

"To nail the fizzle," as he put it in the poem **"Joy"** in ***Hotel Lautréamont*** (1992), is his half-serious intent—half-serious because the impossibility of succeeding is clear and a "god-liberating whimsy" is thus required for sanity. Still, despite its high jinks, his poetry is philosophical. He knows as well as Heidegger that the future is the present's fizzle, both its champagne and its expiring tire. But where Heidegger erected a philosophy to it, Ashbery runs around in it like "the emperor's mice" (**"Joy"**). He's a poet of the ontological (and linguistic) blahs.

If the soul begins in a maternally inflected lack, as Lacan and Ashbery seem to agree, Ashbery's distinction is to find amusement as well as pain in this lack, a little room for affectionate fantasy, and to write it into a far more variegated imaginative whirl, and be more congenially companionable about it ("I think we can handle it together," he says in the title poem), than anyone else has done, even Samuel Beckett, for instance.

Compared to Boland, he's never single-stranded about anything, including aging. "It / isn't possible to be young anymore," he says in this most autumnally crumbly of his books. "Yet the tree treats me like a brute friend; / my own shoes have scarred the walk I've taken" (**"Token Resistance"**). This moves brilliantly from "being done to" to "being accepted by" to "having done harm to." It's as deep as it is swift. (The last line, however Lowellian, passes muster.) What saves Ashbery from droopy pathos is a die-hard gratitude for existence, sustained by the mysterious opening of Being to its own future, the exciting quality of that openness, "the blue acquiescence of spring." But of course he's shy about such joy—for, always, and despite the "peace, quiet, a dictionary . . . / It was as if all of it had never happened" (**"And the Stars Were Shining"**). Fizzle.

Still, the new book's not one of his strongest. Its "liberating whimsy" is less inspired than one could wish. The dazzle of, say, ***Houseboat Days*** is scarcely recalled. Partly the autumnal theme discourages it; partly it just isn't there. The focus lacks fierceness. If Ashbery here *performs* a lack of luster ("Okay, but can we have a little luster, / here, please, a little texture," he says in **"Weather and Turtles"**), it's because he's missing it. But that doesn't excuse the frequent silliness, for instance, in **"My Gold Chain,"** "Nobody ever asked me to be a bridesmaid / so maybe I'm a bride?" Such humor is idle, self-flagellation with a rubber duck. "Life is legendary. We're very bullish / on life," he writes in **"World's End."** "Dogs and other lives / convince us life is dog-cheap." This is to beat a dead dog until it whimpers. "Thought I'd ankle over," the poet says in **"In the Meantime, Darling."** "Then the sea rushed past. / Hurricane Charlie and his sister / sure were glad to see us." Who'd have thought that Ashberian comedy would come to this: labored self-pity?

But the Ashbery with a genius for a paradoxically spanking pathos, even for a belated sublime bespattered with banality, is at least enough present in the book to make one want more of him—him exclusively. He's in these lines from **"Like a Sentence,"** for instance:

> I was going to say I had squandered spring
> when summer came along and took it from me
> like a terrier a lady has asked one to hold for a
> moment
> while she adjusts her stocking in the mirror of a
> weighing machine.

Poor little man, the terrier-spring is not ever his to own—
this
is a fine comic conceit. Ashbery the fantastically gifted appears again at the close of the same poem:

> for though we came
> to life as to a school, we must leave it without
> graduating
> even as an ominous wind puffs out the sails
> of proud feluccas who don't know where they're
> headed,
> only that a motion is etched there, shaking to be
> free.

This puffs at the imagination—has a paradigmatic magnificence that the contractions almost guarantee and the exotic "proud feluccas" can't sink (they're not, after all, grand vessels). The moving Ashbery appears again in **"The Improvement":** "I wake up, my face-pressed / in the dewy mess of a dream." This is the "traditional" done right, done over. He's in fine form again in "What's needed is to set us back on the track, having gently peed, and that for some orpheum other than ourselves" (**"What Do You Call It When"**). Boy and old man meld touchingly in the phrases "having gently peed" and "set us back on the track"—and though "orpheum" is not in the Oxford English Dictionary, as the name of some old-style American movie houses, it makes a shelter for the imagination, is the imagination as shelter.

Ashbery is a Renaissance-to-modern humanist of an absolutely minimal kind, which is better than not being one at all—in fact, he's one of the few poets who can still get away with stating humanist sentiments, which he does by getting in the first laugh. Forget big plans to build a world of abundance and justice for all; forget, that is, ambitious humanism. Yet even if "We sure live in a bizarre and furious / galaxy," he says in the title poem,

> now it's up to us to make it
> into an environment for maps to sidle up to,
> as trustingly as leeches. Heck, put us
> on the map, while you're at it.
> That way we can smoke a cigarette, and stay
> and sway,
> shooting the breeze with night and her swift
> promontories.

"Sure" and "Heck" are a tad too anxiously folksy, even if pseudo-folksy, but the casually grand scope, delivered in a shoot-the-breeze idiom, is irresistible.

And now a final example of the splendors of Ashbery from the uneven title poem, the finest yet:

> For we end
> as we are forgiven, with chords the bird prom-
> ised
> caught in our throats, O sweetest song,
> color of berries, that I lied for and extended
> improbably a little distance from the given grave.

Who besides Ashbery can write sublimely about something so dirt-cheap as disappointment with a lying little song the color of berries thrown in at a little distance from the given grave? He has the divine spark.

Joshua Clover (review date Winter 1995)

SOURCE: "In the Act: John Ashbery's *And the Stars Were Shining*," in *Iowa Review*, Vol. 25, No. 1, Winter, 1995, pp. 177-83.

[*In the following review, Clover offers favorable assessment of* And the Stars Were Shining.]

The risk of falling into oneself, of disappearing inside the welter of strategies and signifiers aggregately known as individual style, is endemic among those gifted enough to have such a style in the first place; the more cultural weight that style achieves, the greater the risk. In the case of the greatest poet of our time the risk becomes enormous making the consistency of Mr. Ashbery's poetic achievement since ***Some Trees*** all the more astounding. Almost every book has done something different, has challenged even readers already versed in Ashberiana; each has been dazzlingly full of good stuff. Even ***Hotel Lautreamont,*** which seemed dangerously close to the self-parody and reflexive pastiche of someone who has been famously brilliant—and then brilliantly famous—for too long, can now be seen as a passing through rather than a falling into, the feints and strategies of a mercurial artist in the act of shifting gears. With the exception of the title poem which closes the new collection, ***And The Stars . . .*** is composed exclusively of shorter poems: the majority are less than a page, none longer than two. Within the strictures of this formal space, Ashbery has recontextualized—and regenerated—the poetics his readers are used to encountering in more elaborated circumstances.

Perhaps his most signatory gesture has always been in his transition from line to line: in the words of Louis-Georges Schwartz, "at the beginning of one of Ashbery's canonized works the uninitiated reader expects the slight disjuncture between juxtaposed lines to be patched over by the end, but the space between the lines is slowly revealed as a gaping abyss. The modernist protocol of reading falls off (or in)." Yet against these constructed slippages that keep the reader always *in the act of understanding,* Ashbery's motion is dreamily seamless: line one leads reasonably to line two, and then two to three. . . . However, should lines one and three be introduced at a party they would swear up and down they'd never met. Ashbery though is a master host: his lines, once introduced, always get on famously. This capacity is thematized in **"The Mandrill on the Turnpike,"** which begins, as he so often does, with a casual philosophical proposition: "It's an art, knowing who to put with what." That said, he continues, "and then, while expectations drool, make off with the lodestar / wrapped in a calico handkerchief, in your back pocket." The sinuous, elusive motion here brings to mind the Action Painters who played such a visible role in the New York School from which Ashbery sprang fully grown—but the slyness of this motion is all his. We have been trained to expect certain things from Ashbery: arbitrary detail which does not set the scene (the calico handkerchief), sudden plunges into the lowbrow (the Pythonesque drool)—but aren't these items rather well-wedded? And doesn't this daffy rigor give us the faith to track his ever more fugitive motion? **"Mandrill"** leads us, over the course of the partial page it occupies, through peregrinations beyond what this essay can easily contemplate: "the clock strikes ten, the evening's off and running" and during its passage "every thing and body are getting sorted out," including the speaker, who either is or isn't "Jack"; his brother the spy; "You and Mrs. Molesworth" (a winking nod to Thomas Pynchon, that); and of course "the subjunctive creeps back in, / sits up, begs for a vision, / or a cookie." Well, what's a poem without a speaking part for a (grammatical) mood?

This array of *dramatis personae* and technical measures (and one of Ashbery's tropes has always been the dissolution of the barrier between these categories—the language *is* a character) would sound merely catalogical and frantic from another poet. Ashbery's compositional gift—his unique grace in transitions so fluid they're practically dissociative—has catalyzed his work since the beginning. Such motion in, for example, ***Self-Portrait in a Convex Mirror*** or ***Rivers and Mountains*** served to keep open the possibility of further exploration: the very device for composing longer poems. Returning to such a gesture in a poem of perhaps 25 lines does a different trick entirely, allowing philosophy without conclusion, brevity without the closure he's always rejected. Indeed, Ashbery often does exactly the opposite of that for which he so exalts music: his is a poetry of propositions—philosophical, flirtatious—without resolution. The generous, anti-hegemonic politics of this are rather easy to explicate; the poetics more elusive. Among the few poets who are genuinely moving, most rely on either the carrot of familiar pleasures or the stick of righteousness; Ashbery carries us in his own motion—a motion so often described by both him and his critics in aquatic terms (a wave, the act of looking through a running stream at an intelligence in action) that by now it's second nature to believe it so. But the transits of wave and stream are essentially unidirectional; their endpoints are fixed long in advance; and their motion is, at least in human terms, infinite.

Ashbery's poems defy all three of these qualities. Much has been made of his sudden shifts of direction, and of his explosion of our expectations regarding where (or if) a poem might conclude. However, it's the third quality—his finitude, as it were—which dominates ***And The Stars . . . .*** The concerns of again, or of time's relentless passage, permeate all the integuments of the book, from "Now it's years after that. It / isn't possible to be young anymore" (**"Token Resistance,"** on the first page) to "As children we played at being grownups. / Now there's trouble brewing on the horizon" (part XIII of the title poem, on the final page). Thus it is in concern as well as in construction that the poems of ***And The Stars . . .*** are written under the sign of **"At North Farm,"** which Helen Vendler has read persuasively as a magical token against aging (in which "the dish of milk is set out at night" to propitiate the agents of the afterlife).

In **"Token Resistance,"** age makes its incursions on the speaker over the course of a journey, a descent

> from checkered heights
> that are our friends, needlessly
> rehearsing what we will say
> *as a common light bathes us,*
>
> a common fiction reverberates as we pass
> to the celebration. Originally
> we weren't going to leave home. But made bold
> *by the rain we put our best foot forward.*

The voice of this middle portion of the poem is oddly, amorphously collective in discussing the travels, particularly given how the first line of the poem foregrounds the isolations available to language with excruciatingly awkward syntax: "As one turns to one in a dream." Of course, this "one" is vintage Ashbery, the pronoun which above all suggests French in translation and in turn calls up his beloved Surrealists. If "one" in English is resolutely third-person, in French it's often a formalized displacement of the first person—the linguistic equivalent of holding the self in abeyance which has always charged Ashbery's poetry (as in the similarly phrased passage from **"Self-Portrait,"** the poem which most directly takes up the otherness of the self: "One would like to stick one's hand / Out of the globe, but its dimension / What carries it, will not allow it"). In **"Token Resistance,"** this distanced self comes out the other side of the group passage as the far more defined "me" in the last stanza:

> Now it's years after that. It
> isn't possible to be young anymore.
> Yet the tree treats me like a brute friend;
> *my own shoes have scarred the walk I've taken.*

Before the last two lines there is no individual speaker in the poem aside from the one we know to have caused the poem to exist; the suggestion is that age has concretized the self. But only a sucker would go for that: Ashbery has been dodging such fixity for about as long as Moses was in the desert. The next poem will have only "us" and "them"; when the first person does return, it will be to insist, "Don't look at *me.*"

Yet, at the end of **"Token Resistance,"** something is made tangible, visible, available: "the walk," which has apparently now been made so many times that its course is "scarred" into the ground. This simple transformation crystallizes—with staggering precision—that which has always set Ashbery apart from lesser poets. His poetics have been those of a man with a deeply troubled relationship to the image: he's been—like de Kooning, for example—more gripped by the processes of life than the pictures it provides. The very first line of his ***Selected Poems*** is "We see us as we truly *behave*" [italics mine]. Our view of ourselves is composed of what we do, which begs the question of how such an appearance can be rendered. Frank O'Hara answered the question by exfoliating a genre sometimes dismissed (by fools) as 'I do this, I do that, I go here, I go there' poetry; Ashbery has taxed his and our imaginations by deploying a constellation of solutions, evasions, workarounds, and inventions which become, in the end, what he is. In his way, O'Hara was poet-as-urbanist, tracing the passage of the body through the landscape of industrial modernism; Ashbery in turn traces the passage of the mind through that same landscape. And, having survived the collapse of the modernist project in a way that O'Hara's I-g-centricity couldn't have, he gets the dolorous treat of playing in the rubble.

I don't mean to suggest that Mr. Ashbery *can't* write an image: few poetic visuals match the uncanniness of "In a far recess of summer / Monks are playing soccer" (***Some Trees***), or the hi-def cinematography of this book's "like a terrier a lady has asked one to hold for a moment / while she adjusts her stocking in the mirror of a weighing machine" (**"Like A Sentence"**). It's that he knows that the image, despite its good publicity in writing workshops, is not the sensual core of experience but rather one amongst an array of roughly coeval phenomena passing through the medium of language.

And language is truly the medium Ashbery inhabits, unlike a host of poets who seem to use words only incidentally, because they've been the dominant mode of distributing one's thoughts and feelings for so long. The final line of **"Token Resistance"** is legible as a figuring of legibility itself, as the great reconciliation of language and image: "the walk," the action, the motion, is transmuted into the visible—is *in-scribed* on the world—through the act of its repetition. Repetition, as Berryman reminds us ("What do poets do? They do things *again*"), is the marker of style: in Ashbery, we see style transforming action into image.

John Cage has said that a musical note has four qualities: pitch, timbre, volume, and duration; it's around that final quality that much of his explorations revolved. Ashbery seems to have taken up this gauntlet on poetry's behalf; his theorizing of the effect of style (which is in turn the location of the personal—it's what *one* does) also allows the action—the transit of the self through the language—to elude the transitory, to become a permanent mark. Of course this transformation occurs in the opening poem of ***And The Stars . . .*** as it must: it provides the key which opens (or perhaps unfolds) the entire collection. For not only does it illuminate the relationship amongst the seen, the done, and the said (and this has always been among Ashbery's multifold projects), it supposes an escape from the book's emotional problematic: the sorrow of time's passage. There's a weariness in "My own shoes have scarred the walk I've taken," but also a deeply earned calm moment. If ***And The Stars . . .*** is bound between that rueful "Now" in the first poem and its companion in the last, Ashbery comes within those boundaries to a new sense of the self's duration, of what it means to leave one's mark on the world—and in doing so finds revelation inside the problem of the image.

Twining—or twinning—the internal problem (that of action and image) and the external (the self and time) into a single *topos* also ensures a permeable border between the world and the poem. This becomes a deeply generous gesture, foreclosing on the risk of the hermeticism at which the author has always glanced come-hitherly, without sacrificing the complexity and grand undecidability that he has long owned. It would be a mistake to praise the book's accessibility. Nothing could be less true; in fact, there are ways in which the tracking of Ashbery (and it often feels just like that, like the exulting pursuit of a mind that's departed the familiar maps) is made all the more difficult for the compressed space in which the sudden turns and leaps occur. It's more the case that his grace in providing us with the necessary tools is at its zenith. In **"Like A Sentence"** for example, he takes up the mantle of difficulty—indeed, unknowability—immediately (here again his appropriation of philosophy as a pick-up line): "How little we know / and when we know it!" But having announced epistemology as the topic, he shortly renders it irrelevant:

> It was prettily said that "No man
> hath an abundance of cows on the plain, nor
> shards
> *in his cupboard." Wait! I think I know who said*
> *that! It was . . .*
>
> Never mind, dears, the afternoon
> will fold you up, along with preoccupations
> *that now seem so important . . .*

Having collapsed both the possibility and usefulness of knowing your stuff, the poem (and it's with Ashbery as with no one else that we're tempted to speak of the poem itself as the actant, rather than those two phantasms 'the speaker' and 'the poet') travels by ricochet from "a child / running around on a unicycle" to "where the paths through the elms, the carnivals, begin." This is Ashbery at his most wizardly: shouldn't it be the performing child who is carnivalesque? A small detail, surely, but this virtually aphasic use of language serves to destabilize our faith in knowability as much as the more direct propositions and disclaimers with which the poem opened. And this act required of us, of the readers—the relinquishing of the desire to know—equips us for the poem's final occasion:

> . . . for though we came
> to life as to a school, we must leave it without
> graduating
> even as an ominous wind puffs out the sails
> *of proud feluccas who don't know where*
> *they're headed . . .*

This is the most elegant of hoodwinkings: having persuaded us to abandon knowing where *we're* headed both in the poem's overt rhetoric and covert mechanism (again, his signatorily elusive motion), Ashbery makes us complicit in the spiritual circumstance of the poem: the sorrow of age's procession. This cunningly forced complicity is a gift: we're lured absolutely to that place—that melancholia-suffused lea against time's onslaught—so that we can feel what that is, rather than what it's like. And having gotten us there, he plays one last trick—one which might not have been comprehensible if he hadn't so carefully laid the ground for it in the book's beginning. As we prepare for that mythic water-crossing into the afterworld, we know "only that a motion is etched there, shaking to be free." With such a gesture, returning to the essentiality of time's transformation of action to image, ***And The Stars . . .*** is suddenly apprehensible as a secretly unified whole—and time, like night, "gives more than it takes" (**"As One Put Drunk Into The Packet Boat,"** ***Self-Portrait***): a permanence, something to steer by.

If I mention majestic figures from other disciplines, it's all a way of suggesting what a pure poet Ashbery is, traveling beyond compare. In that same way that we praise a painter for simultaneously laying bare and detonating the possibilities of craft by calling her *malerich* ('painterly'), Ashbery is consummately *dichterich.* If language is a medium we pass through, taking what we think we need (and it is), Ashbery is the poet who *does* give more than he takes: working always to keep the language workable, refusing in the insistence of his motion to allow it to settle into the decrepit fixity of institution.

Steven Meyer (review date Fall 1995)

SOURCE: "Ashbery: Poet for All Seasons," in *Raritan,* Vol. 15, No. 2, Fall, 1995, pp. 144-61.

[*In the following review, Meyer provides critical analysis of* Hotel Lautréamont *and* And the Stars Were Shining.]

For upwards of two decades now, since the acclaim that greeted his 1975 collection ***Self-Portrait in a Convex Mirror,*** John Ashbery has been the United States' preeminent poet, with books selling in the tens of thousands, both at home and abroad. In a recent issue of the British journal *PN Review,* two dozen poets and critics set out to "appraise the mark this American writer" has made and continues to make in Britain—a mark, we are told, that differs appreciably from his influence in the United States. Among the sources of Ashbery's widespread popularity is a feature of his work that he does not share with other contemporary writers and which might therefore account for some of his individual appeal. This is a quite exceptional openness to the influence of earlier writers, especially the first two generations of this century's English-speaking poets. It is this continuity with the poets largely responsible for making modern poetry consequential for readers today that makes Ashbery so recognizably a poet of consequence himself.

Along with his receptivity to the work of other poets,

Ashbery exhibits an equal willingness to draw on the unexpected turns of demotic speech, with which most readers are no doubt more familiar than they are with the tropes of poetry. In poem after poem he demonstrates that everyday usage contains as much grist for poetry as poetry itself does. In adapting the language he finds around him, whether the language of poets or of personal and social life, Ashbery applies a technique that one finds described exactly, if somewhat outrageously, by Isidore Ducasse, the nineteenth-century French writer who called himself the Comte de Lautréamont. "Plagiarism is necessary," Ducasse wrote: "it is implied in the idea of progress. It clasps an author's sentence tight, uses his expressions, eliminates a false idea, replaces it with the right idea." Few writers have been as assiduous, or as unembarrassed, in their pursuit of the *bon mot* as Ashbery, who would have had to look no further than Auden and Stevens and Eliot to find exemplary plagiarists.

Indeed, the title of Ashbery's 1992 collection, ***Hotel Lautréamont***—in deliberate contrast with Rimbaud's "Splendide-Hotel," "erected," as Rimbaud has it, in the splendid isolation "of ice and of polar night"—presents a trope of a man as a hotel where other people stay for a short while and then move on. This permeability of borders, and boarders, is central to Ashbery and his sense of "himself." In a crucial statement, dating from 1976, he observed that "what moves me is the irregular form—the flawed words and stubborn sounds, as Stevens said, that affect us whenever we try to say something that is important to us." It is this sense of a necessary incompleteness in poetry that he insists on, for such "irregular form" is what enables the poetry to survive the circumstances of its own composition—and so make room both for the reader and for the later poet, who is always first a reader.

Perhaps one imagined that Eliot's *Four Quartets* was a paragon of completeness; so Ashbery in ***Hotel Lautréamont*** offers us an additional "Quartet." Similarly, to complement "Ash Wednesday" we are presented with **"Just Wednesday."** (Ashbery, as he often does, plays on his name here, modestly removing it from Eliot's great poem. Now, just how modest is this?) Donne's "A Valediction: Forbidding Mourning" is transformed into **"A Mourning Forbidding Valediction,"** in which the nine quatrains of the original poem, odd and even lines rhyming, are replaced by seven eight-line stanzas, each with the rhyme scheme *abcd cbad.* This magnificent poem alone is worth the purchase of the volume. And what of Stevens, whom Ashbery has called his favorite poet? The 1942 "Notes Toward a Supreme Fiction," surely as great a poem as has been written in this century, consists of three parts: "It Must Be Abstract," "It Must Change," "It Must Give Pleasure." Ashbery, refusing to be silenced by these peremptory judgments, contributes his own obiter dictum: **"It Must Be Sophisticated."** "O what book shall I read now?" he wonders near the end of this truly wonderful poem: "for they are all of them new, and used, / when I write my name on the flyleaf."

Although he never lets one forget that one is reading poetry, not overhearing conversation, Ashbery certainly doesn't want his readers to feel that the concerns which engage him are exclusively literary and merely a matter of reading and responding to books "new, and used." In the same way, he wants his poems to speak to and for as broad a spectrum of his contemporaries as possible. Such ambitions have a precise genealogy. English-language poetry of the last two hundred years—ever since Wordsworth's insistence on using "the real language of men" rather than "the arbitrary and capricious habits of expression . . . frequently substituted for it by Poets"—turns on an ongoing tension between aristocratic and democratic conceptions of the reading public. Is the poetry written for the privileged few or the unexceptional many? Pound and Yeats are perhaps the most powerful modern proponents of a poetic aristocracy, which may account for Ashbery's relative lack of interest in them.

Wordsworth, in calling the volume he coauthored with Coleridge *Lyrical Ballads,* was responding to the late eighteenth-century revival of interest in English and Scottish ballads, a tradition of poetry that predated the Renaissance establishment of a "heightened" English and which seemed to speak for society as a whole in a way that poetry since the Renaissance had not. "Research has shown," the title poem of ***Hotel Lautréamont*** begins, in one of Ashbery's preferred manners, that of the academic spinner of clichés, "that ballads were produced by all of society / working as a team. They didn't just happen. There was no guesswork. / The people, then, knew what they wanted and how to get it. / We see the results in works as diverse as 'Windsor Forest' and 'The Wife of Usher's Well.'" The latter poem is a traditional Scottish ballad, whereas the former, an early production of Alexander Pope's, is composed in his trademark rhymed couplets. As such, it hardly qualifies as a ballad; yet, like "The Wife of Usher's Well," it invites precious little guesswork, and the forest world it portrays is the sort of "golden" world, "harmoniously confused: / Where Order in Variety we see, / And where, tho' all things differ, all agree," that can only be "produced by all of society / working as a team."

"Hotel Lautréamont" is not itself written in traditional ballad stanzas—it is rather a pantoum, an elaborate verse form of Malay origin that was introduced into French early in the nineteenth century and later adapted to English—but it testifies to the increasing importance the ballad has acquired in Ashbery's poetry. The long poem, **"Fantasia on 'The Nut-Brown Maid,'"** for instance, which appeared in the 1977 collection ***Houseboat Days,*** is modeled on the ballad alluded to in the title; and in the 1987 ***April Galleons,*** the poem

"Forgotten Song" begins with variants of lines from several ballads and includes a passage from a third as well. In ***Hotel Lautréamont,*** besides the title poem, Ashbery has included a magical and quite-impossible-to-forget song, **"The Youth's Magic Horn."** Like so much of Ashbery's work of the last decade—after an almost-fatal spinal infection he experienced in 1982—this poem is a "dump" or lament at approaching death. It is divided into two sections of six quatrains each, with the much shorter second and fourth lines of each quatrain repeated throughout each section as a refrain. "First in dreams," the second section begins, "I questioned the casing of the gears the enigma presented / *You're a pain in the ass my beloved* / The twa corbies belched and were gone, song veiled sky that day / *I have to stop in one mile.*" The "twa corbies" are two ravens that, in the Scottish ballad of that name, are overheard discussing the meal they are about to make of "a new-slain knight."

It is not possible in so brief an excerpt to reproduce the beauty that emerges out of this medley of grating language and excruciating pain, since it depends on the song's cumulative effect, but the juxtaposition of dream and ballad in these lines does suggest the significance of Ashbery's concern with ballad form. The same juxtaposition is to be found in W.H. Auden's introduction to Ashbery's first book, ***Some Trees,*** which Auden selected as the 1956 winner of the Yale Series of Younger Poets. Auden suggests that any poet "working with the subjective life"—particularly poets who, like Ashbery, are "concerned with the discovery that in childhood largely, in dreams and daydreams entirely, the imaginative life of the human individual stubbornly continues to live by the old magical notions"—will be "tempted to manufacture calculated oddities, as if the subjectively sacred were necessarily and on all occasions odd." Here Auden is warning Ashbery against another "youth" with a "magic horn" whose influence may readily be discerned in such poems in ***Some Trees*** as the aptly-named **"Popular Songs."** This poet is the younger Auden.

Whenever Ashbery, who wrote an undergraduate honors thesis on Auden, finds himself addressing the importance the older poet had for him, he always makes a point of insisting that it was the early Auden who played the decisive role, the so-called "English" Auden of the 1930s—author, among many other works, of such ballads as "O what is that sound" and "As I walked out one evening." It is not ballads like these, however, that Auden is warning Ashbery against. Rather it is the poet of the 1932 miscellany, *The Orators,* who is to be watched out for; and in an interview with the *Paris Review* in the early 1980s, Ashbery made it quite clear that the message had been received. After noting that Auden "was of two minds about my own work," he added: "You'll remember, though, that he once said in later life that one of his early works, 'The Orators,' must have been written by a madman." It was not the flamboyant discontinuities of the work, the "calculated oddities," that demonstrated the writer's madness, but the fact that in this remarkable anthology of verse and prose forms the twenty-four-year-old Auden had tried to combine the dreamlike rhetoric of "an inner mythological life" with the public formats of the ode and the ballad, or, as he titled two sections of the work, the "journal of an airman" with an "address for a prize-day."

"The problem for the modern poet, as for everyone else today," Auden suggested in 1938, shortly before he left Europe for America, "is how to find or form a genuine community." As Ashbery puts it in **"Hotel Lautréamont":** "It remains for us to come to terms with *our* commonality." The traditional ballad represents for Ashbery, as it did for Auden, the poetry of "a community united in sympathy." The central task for the modern poet, then, is to try to create works that function the way ballads do, only for a community in which the shared experience is the feeling, as Ashbery described it in 1972, of everything "slipping away from me as I'm trying to talk about it." "A sense of permanent unraveling," he has also called it. One consequence of the resulting "simultaneity of conflicting states of being" is that for the poet, attentive above all to the play of language about him, the composition of modern life takes the form of an indefinitely extended "mix" of discourses: high, low, middle, whatever.

In the summer of 1955, shortly after being notified of his selection by Auden for the Yale Series, Ashbery left New York, where he had been living since his graduation from Harvard in 1949, to spend a year in France on a Fulbright. Between 1955 and late 1965 he lived continuously in France except for the 1957-58 school year which he spent back in New York as a graduate student in French literature at N.Y.U. If, as Ashbery has suggested, French writing played a relatively small role in his "experimenting with language" during these years, this was because the major role was performed by another American who half a century earlier had made Paris her home: Gertrude Stein. Thus he observes of novelist and former *Paris Match* columnist Pierre Martory—whose first collection of poetry, *The Landscape Is Behind The Door,* translated and introduced by Ashbery, was published last year—that "his take on [things French] has something distinctly and irreverently American about it." When they met, Martory, with whom Ashbery lived during much of the decade, "was reading Emily Dickinson, Eliot and Gertrude Stein."

In a 1957 review of Stein's posthumously published *Stanzas in Meditation,* Ashbery described the poetry he would come to write. Only he did so by describing Stein's work:

> Like people, Miss Stein's lines are comforting or annoying or brilliant or tedious. Like people, they sometimes make no sense and sometimes make

> perfect sense or they stop short in the middle of a sentence and wander away, leaving us alone for awhile in the physical world, that collection of thoughts, flowers, weather, and proper names. And, just as with people, there is no real escape from them. . . . Sometimes the story has the logic of a dream . . . while at other times it becomes startlingly clear for a moment, as though a change in the wind had suddenly enabled us to hear a conversation that was taking place some distance away. . . . In its profound originality, its original profundity, this poem that is always threatening to become a novel reminds us of the late novels of James . . . which seem to strain with a superhuman force toward "the condition of music."

There is no better, no more concise, description of Ashbery's subsequent poetry—despite the tremendous stylistic differences that one encounters in the thirty years of writing between his second book, ***The Tennis Court Oath,*** and ***Hotel Lautréamont.*** Ashbery includes here all the figures that he will use again and again in describing his own work: the everyday discontinuities of meaning and sentence structure, the dream-logic, the snatches of conversation, the music. These are all extrapoetic experiences that seem particularly suited to describing what he called in 1972 "the movement of experiencing" or "the experience of experience," and it was precisely this general sense of experience that he suggested fifteen years earlier was Stein's primary concern in *Stanzas in Meditation.* "It is usually not events which interest Miss Stein, rather it is their 'way of happening,' and the story of *Stanzas in Meditation* is a general, all-purpose model which each reader can adapt to fit his own set of particulars." Stein's work offered Ashbery a way of accommodating Auden's warning about confusing private dream and public ballad. Ashbery's poetry would henceforth be "about the privacy of everyone," the way experience feels to anyone.

The poems collected in ***The Tennis Court Oath,*** which like ***Hotel Lautréamont*** is dedicated to Martory, represent Ashbery's first attempts to think Stein through on his own terms, that is, in his own terms. Indeed, it is the nature of his terminology that most clearly distinguishes Ashbery from Stein. Whereas Stein, at least in *Stanzas in Meditation,* confined herself to "colorless connecting words such as 'where,' 'which,' 'these,' 'of,' 'not,' 'have,' 'about,' and so on" ("though now and then Miss Stein throws in an orange, a lilac, or an Albert to remind us that it really is the world, our world, that she is talking about"), Ashbery includes everything—every word and sequence of words—he can find. If Stein entertains the same range of events in her work, nonetheless she insists on using her own language: making over the received words, and in the process making the particular events as hard to discern as possible. What defines Ashbery's language as his own, by contrast, is its openness to the language of others. This is his signature. The poems are "his" because the lines are everybody's.

"Back from his breakfast, thirty-five years ago, / he stumbles, finds in the sun a nod that's new." So begins the exquisite **"And Socializing"**—and it is back to this era of "future memories," with its potent combination of party-going and poetry-writing, that Ashbery returns again and again in ***Hotel Lautréamont.*** The American original for this blending of the social and the poetic is, of course, the author of "Song of Myself," and on several occasions in the 1992 collection Ashbery takes the work of Whitman as his starting-point. He even stages an encounter, in **"A Driftwood Altar,"** with the writer who so memorably identified himself as "a trail of drift and debris": "Of all those who came near him at this stage, only / a few can describe him with any certainty: a drifter / was the consensus, polite with old people, indifferent to children, extremely interested in young adults, / but so far, why remember him? And few did, / that much is certain. I caught up with him / on a back porch in Culver City, exchanged the requisite nod, / shirt biting the neck . . ." Whitman, it will be recalled, concluded his epoch-defining "Song" by leaving everything up in the air: "Failing to fetch me at first keep encouraged, / Missing me one place search another, / I stop somewhere waiting for you."

Ashbery's references to past poetry are frequent, but they are rarely obscure. Unlike Eliot or Pound, he is not interested in impressing the reader with a vast range of esoteric knowledge. On the contrary, it is his range of common usage, the way he joins idioms that too often appear mutually exclusive, which is so impressive. He prefers to use language he can expect the reader to be relatively familiar with, so that the transformations worked on it will be recognizable. Hence the high proportion of titles and first lines in his literary allusions. The two most familiar titles in Whitman's oeuvre, for instance—*Leaves of Grass,* the name of the collected poems, and "When Lilacs Last in the Dooryard Bloom'd," the elegy for Lincoln—are all that a reader needs in order to grasp what Ashbery is after when, in **"Notes From the Air,"** reference is made to "some stranger's casual words" that concern "the square of barren grass that adjoins your doorstep." Similarly, in the superb **"Wild Boys of the Road,"** one passes directly from "the tin / posy in the doorjamb," wonderfully characterized as being "as unconcerned as if this were a hundred and fifty years ago"—as if Whitman's "poesy" had yet to be written—to the poem's final sentence which, seventy-five words long, begins "The leaves are too little at the top" and ends on the sobering note of "stone plinths with fringe of grass." The enumerative and almost infinitely expandable sentence quite literally frames the "stone plinths"—the gravestones of those Ashbery is elegizing, including himself—with perhaps the most resonant phrase in American literature: "leaves . . . of grass."

In speaking of the long prose poems gathered in the 1972 ***Three Poems,*** Ashbery has observed that "I would be able to write just a couple of pages at a time. I would be left with an overwhelming anxiety, not knowing whether I was ever going to be able to finish this thing or what on earth I was going to put in it." If Ashbery's poetry avoids, in Richard Howard's words, "the invoked anxiety of a closed form," there still remains the need to come up with an ending for the "open" work. Moreover, as Ashbery suggests, how to end is only half the problem; the other half is the perplexing business of just "how to continue"—which, as it happens, is the title of the final poem in ***Hotel Lautréamont.***

"Oh there once was a woman / and she kept a shop / selling trinkets to tourists / not far from a dock / who came to see what life could be / far back on the island." So unfolds the first of the five stanzas of this song, with its parties and friends and lovers, "a marvel of poetry / and irony." The simplicity of the language, the generalized model it presents, the explicit concern with unity as well as with the contradictions of "our commonality," all these mark the poem as a contemporary ballad. As such, it is a fitting companion piece to a work like Elizabeth Bishop's "The Burglar of Babylon." Written in traditional ballad stanzas, Bishop's poem takes as its subject "the death of a Brazilian bandit in which emotionally charged ellipses build up to a tragic grandeur"—as Ashbery has put it—beginning and ending with the lines, "On the fair green hills of Rio / There grows a fearful stain: / The poor who come to Rio / And can't go home again." In the modern world the country has become part of the city, and with it has come a pressing need for something resembling the traditional ballad.

Ashbery, like Bishop, seeks to reintroduce us in his "general, all-purpose" poem to this new world in which we are all living and dying—poets and party-goers as well as the poor in the "fair green hills"—and hence to reintroduce us to one another. That is all. There is no particular message. But the poetry does have something to tell us, all the same. By its own example, it demonstrates "how to continue" much as **"The Instruction Manual,"** in ***Some Trees,*** had done. ("As is my way, I begin to dream, resting my elbows on the desk and leaning out of the window a little, / Of dim Guadalajaral City of rose-colored flowers! / City I wanted most to see, and most did not see, in Mexico!") This is a poetry that not only instructs us to continue but shows how we may do so, even when it seems that "we are in the departure / mode": how to continue, that is, as inhabitants of what Ashbery, in a phrase entered twice in this *Hotel's register,* calls "our example, earth."

In his most recent collection, published last winter, Ashbery seems to have removed his attention from the earth to the stars—beginning with the title, ***And the Stars Were Shining.*** Does this mean that he has gone transcendental? I have to confess that when I first read these poems I thought that the poet, after more than forty years of gentle rigor, was finally showing signs of fatigue. The poems really did seem mechanical, as they have so often been accused of being: automatic, insubstantial, forced. I was especially confused by the twenty-four-page title poem, which consists of thirteen sections of varying lengths. These are sufficiently various that I wondered what difference it would make if they were treated as separate poems and given individual titles instead of being numbered—hence instead of being parts of the poem, **"And the Stars Were Shining,"** merely parts of the book ***And the Stars Were Shining.***

I mention this initial response because I suspect that it is the sort of experience which readers who distrust—and more, *dislike*—Ashbery's writing typically have. Needless to say, the first impression was mistaken. The writing is exactly the kind that one should, by now, have come to expect from this poet: whatever's not expected. The problem is that having learned to expect the unexpected doesn't necessarily make it any easier to accept. In the latest poems, it is the halfhearted, almost blasé, gestures that Ashbery seems intent on making which prove so deceptive, the recycled imagery of a "middle" state between life and death (stars, sea, island, dream, night). Instead of ***Hotel Lautréamont***'s fierce meditations on death—mixing acceptance and disbelief, indelicacy and despair—these poems seem merely to offer token resistance. No "purgatory of words," such as one finds in the 1991 book length poem ***Flow Chart,*** just a couple of shining stars resting on their laurels, drinking beers and, as one is informed late in the new collection, "shooting the breeze with night and her swift promontories."

Yet "token resistance" is Ashbery's own phrase, the title of the opening poem. In his relaxed way, he's pursuing what animates the ordinary, not its elevation—in effect, bringing the stars down to earth. In a recent interview he thus observed, concerning the collection's title (which directly translates *E lucevan le stella,* the aria that Cavaradossi, the painter and lover of Tosca in Puccini's opera *Tosca,* sings before his execution), that "one day" he had "thought of the title in Italian and thought of it being translated into English and it was kind of funny in English . . . a sort of unnecessary bit of information. The fact that they were shining." In Ashbery's new poetry, as in all successful poetry, the poet concentrates on what the mind hungry for information, especially information about which it can be certain, supposes to be unnecessary bits of info. The "present, with its noodle parlors / and token resistance" is still life; and to deny, or resist, this embarrassing fact is to place oneself above life, which is what Ashbery—stars and all—won't do, if he has any say in the matter.

"So must one descend from the checkered heights / that are

our friends," Ashbery's poem of "token resistance" concludes: "needlessly / rehearsing what we will say / as a common light bathes us, // a common fiction reverberates as we pass / to the celebration. Originally / we weren't going to leave home. But made bold / somehow by the rain we put our best foot forward. // Now it's years after that. It / isn't possible to be young anymore. / Yet the tree treats me like a brute friend; / my own shoes have scarred the walk I've taken." It's not just Ashbery's shoes that have scarred this particular walk, however. "There was a time," Wordsworth's immortal Ode begins, "when meadow, grove, and stream, / The earth, and every common sight / To me did seem / Apparelled in celestial light . . . The Youth, who daily farther from the East / Must travel, still is Nature's Priest, / And by the vision splendid / Is on his way attended; / At length the Man perceives it die away, / And fade into the light of common day." Against Wordsworth's opposition of "common" and "celestial" Ashbery offers his token (that is to say, exemplary) resistance—collapsing the distinction in a "common light" that still leaves room for Wordsworth's "common fiction" of uncommon splendor.

Originally we weren't going to leave home. But made bold somehow by the rain we put our best foot forward. Now it's years after that. It isn't possible to be young anymore. This is Wordsworth's and Ashbery's common predicament. Where they part company is in their responses, as witnessed in the divergent perceptions of a "single" tree. First, Wordsworth: "But there's a Tree, of many one, / A single Field which I have looked upon, / Both of them speak of something that is gone." Then Ashbery, two hundred years later: "Yet the tree treats me like a brute friend." With his brutal honesty, Ashbery obliges one to attend to the present moment instead of the Wordsworthian life at a remove. "Our life is but a sleep and a forgetting," Wordsworth sometimes imagines. And Ashbery? "It was as if all of it had never happened, / my shoelaces were untied, and—am I forgetting anything?" Bringing to a close both ***And the Stars Were Shining*** and **"And the Stars Were Shining,"** these lines testify to Ashbery's extraordinarily surefooted appropriation of Wordsworth in the volume, for it is as if Wordsworth were speaking, yet the words come out Ashbery's.

Ashbery grew up on a farm outside Rochester—spending many weekends in town, where his grandfather was chairman of the University of Rochester physics department—and he has said that "the one thing I wanted to do was get the hell out of where I was and go to a city, preferably New York, and that's what I ended up doing." In a nostalgic frame of mind he muses not on "the growing Boy," as Wordsworth did or like the more conventionally Romantic Martory, but on his years as a "young adult." The poet's state of mind isn't exactly nostalgic, however, because it doesn't face in just one direction. The young adult he remembers is the young adult whom, as a child, he imagined he would become. This complex, Janus-faced temporality is probably the most distinctive feature of Ashbery's poetry, much more so than the often-commented-upon play with personal pronouns. At different points in his career the play of time (in the sense that one speaks of the play of light) has itself taken distinctive forms, as it does again in ***And the Stars Were Shining.***

Ashbery's relation with Martory plays an exemplary role here. Martory has said that when they lived together he showed Ashbery his poems "without putting any pressure on him, and he didn't seem to pay any attention. . . . He did do that later, much later . . . [and] seems to have discovered suddenly that I am a poet." This new attention to Martory's poetry is one aspect of the renewed attention that, in the writing of the last decade, Ashbery has directed toward the period of his youth. This extended period may be characterized as a time of schooling, and further divided into three parts: first, the years that Ashbery's grandfather, as he has put it, "took over my education"; second, his formal training at Deerfield Academy, Harvard, and Columbia; third, the self-reeducation that occurred during the years in Paris.

It is in his schooling, in fact, that Ashbery's differences with Wordsworth can most clearly be observed. For whether one takes the Ode as one's touchstone, with Nature understood as "that immortal sea / Which brought us hither," or earlier poems in which Wordsworth describes "the growth of mental power" as a consequence of his schooling in a difficult and glorious Nature, he always insists that it is to Nature that one owes one's imaginative capabilities and hence capacity for heightened ("poetic") consciousness. Wordsworth's Nature—embodied if not fully realized in a countryside that exists beyond the reach of an unsympathetic and unsympathetically portrayed city—is precisely where Ashbery feels least at home. Concerning his own country home, a Victorian mansion he has been restoring for the past fifteen years to resemble his grandfather's house in Rochester, he has said: "I kind of like the fact that I have a house in upstate New York and I have the advantage of no longer being a child and also of being able to get to New York City whenever I want and very easily."

In this way Ashbery is able, even outside his poetry, to resolve the conflict he experienced so strongly as a child between country and city, a divide that Wordsworth wished, if anything, to widen. As I suggested earlier, the decisive collapse of this distinction, with country moving in on the city and city moving out into the countryside, serves as a defining characteristic of modern life and modern poetry. The sun now rises, as Ashbery observed two decades ago, in a suburbia that stretches beyond the horizon, "the morning holocaust become one vast furnace." Still, the true site of exile for Ashbery—and in this he stands opposed to all forms of primitivism, Romantic or Modernist—is the cityless country. What sets his work off from most poetry written today is that in it country and city are accompanied by temporal cousins that are inseparable not only from the two intersecting spatial grids but also from each other. When city and country meet, two distinct forms of temporality collide, linear and cyclical; time that's organized minute by minute—day to day, week to week, month to month—or by season ("Next thing you know it's winter"). Filofax vs. *Farmer's Almanac.* The unyielding movement of *then and now* and the turning back on itself of *then is now.*

Ashbery's poetry serves as an extreme yet nonetheless composed form of reverie, something along the lines of Keats's "Was it a vision, or a waking dream? . . . Do I wake or sleep?" One consequence is that the seasons and cycles of the pastoral city receive the attention due them. The soul "isn't engaged in trade," Ashbery attests in the superb **"Not Planning a Trip Back":** "it's woven of sleep and the weather / Of sleep." Yet neither is it absolutely disengaged. Day-to-day rhythms are conjoined with the very differently patterned day-to-night-to-day rhythms. As he proposes in **"Just For Starters,"** effectively setting the stage for Keats: "I don't know what got me to write this poem / or any other (I mean why does one write?), / unless you spoke to me in my dream / and I replied to your waking / and the affair of sleeping and waking began."

The "inhabited landscapes" of Martory's poetry are alternately foreign and local, rural and urban, actual place and painted (or filmed) representation. It's much more difficult to specify the exact nature of Ashbery's settings; still, one can assert that, like Baudelaire's "Landscape," a ravishing translation of which is included in Ashbery's 1984 collection, ***A Wave,*** every landscape in ***And the Stars Were Shining*** is cityscape. What distinguishes Ashbery's poetry from both Martory's and Baudelaire's is not the subject matter but the quantity and range of his unsettling juxtapositions, the "motion" with which the riddling **"Like a Sentence"** concludes, "etched there, shaking to be free."

A sort of informal formality has always characterized Ashbery's poetry—the way, for instance, his longer poems incorporate seemingly arbitrary formal schemes, whether the length of the line, the number of lines per stanza, or even, as in a work like the 313-line **"Clepsydra,"** the sheer absence of stanzas or strophes. The form remains recognizably arbitrary, artificial, yet it becomes integral to the particular work. It's this *in*formalism that Ashbery stretches almost to the breaking point in **"And the Stars Were Shining."** In formal terms nothing holds this baker's dozen of sections together, which range from twelve lines to a hundred and thirty, divided into strophes of varying lengths, with even a rhymed quatrain—a variant on the common measure of hymns—thrown in for good measure: "where not too much ever happens, // *except growing up, hook by hook, / year after tethered year. / And in the basement, that book, / just another thing to fear.*"

"I've never really done this before," Ashbery acknowledges at the beginning of section 8. "See, I couldn't do it . . . See, I can try again." "There is still another thing I have to do," section 11 opens: "*I've* never *been able to do this*" (Ashbery's italics). Just what *this* is—"this icon. That walks and jabbers / fortuitously or not"—becomes clearer in the next-to-last section, which concludes: "the hothouse beckons. / I've told you before how afraid this makes me, / but I think we can handle it together, / and this is as good a place as any / to unseal my last surprise: you, as you go, / diffident, indifferent, but with the sky for an awning / for as many days as it pleases it to cover you. / That's what I meant by 'get a handle,' and as I say it, / both surface and subtext subside quintessentially / and the dead-letter office dissolves in the blue acquiescence of spring."

The "you" in these lines may refer to the reader or to some unidentified third party, but surely it's addressed "quintessentially" to the words on the page, "my last surprise," dead letters dissolving in "blue acquiescence." This poem, and the entire volume, is composed under the sign of Death, "a life of afterwords," its presiding spirit the still scandalously underappreciated American poet Laura Riding, whose writing Ashbery has worked diligently to publicize. Riding, who died at the age of ninety in 1991, was the author of such important poems as "The Judgement," "The Life of the Dead," and "Death as Death." In the early 1940s she stopped writing poetry when she concluded that it was impossible to remove the poet, who never means exactly what the words seem to say, from the poetry. Two of Ashbery's poems in the present volume, **"World's End"** and **"Footfalls,"** complement poems of Riding's with identical or nearly identical titles ("World's End," "Footfalling"). Behind the four-stanza pantoum **"Seasonal"** in ***Hotel Lautréamont,*** in which Ashbery contemplates "what a lying writer knows," can be discerned the harsh truths of Riding's withering prose poem, "Poet: A Lying Word."

Now, in **"And the Stars Were Shining,"** Ashbery keeps pace with Winter. "It was the solstice," the poem opens, "and it was jumping on you like a friendly dog." The sun, and with it the passage of time, does not stand still, despite the fact that that is what "solstice" literally means. During the first eleven sections of the poem the season remains constant; this is a poem of winter, of *undoing,* but not, like the more insistently analytic poetry of the late fifties, with the objective of "taking poetry apart." In contrast to Eliot in "The Waste Land" ("I had not thought death had undone so many"), Ashbery stands firmly on the side of life and the life of poetry. "It was their / funeral, and they should have had a say in its undoing."

When, at the end of the poem's penultimate section, Spring is observed to "acquiesce"—presumably to anything one wants, hope springing eternal—and then in the last section, thirteenth month of a long winter, the interlocutor is told that "Summer won't end in your lap" (meaning both *Summer won't come to an end with you* and *you won't be settling down with Summer*), these are *prospective* seasons. The speaker stands outside their orbit even if his writing may not: "So—if you want to come with me. . . ." He remains in his poetry and yet can envision, *pace* Riding, the poetry surviving his death. Here, "at the end," Ashbery composes himself in the face of his own death, and not, as in so many of his previous poems, in confronting the deaths of others. On this occasion time is neither cyclical (it remains winter, never quite making it to spring) nor linear (it remains winter, after all). It's time to end, unless the poet has forgotten something, in which case it's time to move on.

FURTHER READING

Criticism

Costello, Bonnie. "John Ashbery and the Idea of the Reader." *Contemporary Literature* XXIII, No. 4 (Fall 1982): 493-514.

Examines strategies for establishing meaningful communication between writer and reader in Ashbery's poetry.

Edelman, Lee. "The Pose of Imposture: Ashbery's 'Self-Portrait in a Convex Mirror.'" *Twentieth Century Literature* 32, No. 1 (Spring 1986): 95-114.

Discusses problematic aspects of self-reflexivity and representation in "Self-Portrait in a Convex Mirror."

Fink, Thomas A. "The Comic Thrust of Ashbery's Poetry." *Twentieth Century Literature* 30, No. 1 (Spring 1984): 1-14.

Examines the function of humor in Ashbery's poetry, especially as evident in elements of hyperbole, absurdity, and linguistic playfulness.

Gregerson, Linda. "Among the Wordstruck." *The New York Times Book Review* (23 October 1994): 3.

A favorable review of *And the Stars Were Shining.*

Imbriglio, Catherine. "'Our Days Put on Such Reticence': The Rhetoric of the Closet in John Ashbery's *Some Trees.*" *Contemporary Literature* XXXVI, No. 2 (Summer 1995): 249-88.

Explores the significance of repressed sexuality and homoeroticism in *Some Trees.*

Longenbach, James. "Ashbery and Individual Talent." *American Literary History* 9, No. 1 (Spring 1997): 103-27.

Offers analysis of Ashbery's critical views, poetic style, and assumptions about the relationship between poetry and political protest.

Lundquist, Sara L. "Légèreté et richesse: John Ashbery's English 'French Poems.'" *Contemporary Literature* XXXII, No. 3 (Fall 1991): 403-21.

Examines the significance of French literary influence and Ashbery's linguistic preoccupations in "French Poems."

Mohanty, S. P. and Jonathan Monroe. "John Ashbery and the Articulation of the Social." *Diacritics* 17, No. 2 (Summer 1987): 37-63.

Examines the social voice in Ashbery's poetry through analysis of "A Wave" and *John Ashbery,* a volume of critical essays edited by Harold Bloom.

Norton, Jody. "'Whispers Out of Time': The Syntax of Being in the Poetry of John Ashbery." *Twentieth Century Literature* 41, No. 3 (Fall 1995): 281-305.

Explores aspects of subjectivity and temporality in Ashbery's poetry in the context of philosophical writings by Martin Heidegger, Ludwig Wittgenstein, and Jacques Derrida.

Additional coverage of Ashbery's life and career is contained in the following sources published by Gale: *Contemporary Authors,* Vol. 5-8R; *Contemporary Authors New Revision Series,* Vols. 9, 37; *Dictionary of Literary Biography,* Vols. 5, 165; *Dictionary of Literary Biography Yearbook,* Vol. 81; *DISCovering Authors Module: Poets;* and *Major Twentieth-Century Writers.*

Gwendolyn Brooks

1917-

American poet, novelist, children's writer, editor, and autobiographer.

The following entry presents an overview of Brooks's career through 1996. For further information on her life and works, see *CLC,* Volumes 1, 2, 4, 5, 15, and 49.

INTRODUCTION

A powerful voice of black consciousness and social protest in mid-century America, Gwendolyn Brooks is among the most distinguished African-American poets of the twentieth century. With the publication of her second volume of poetry, *Annie Allen* (1949), she became the first black American writer to win a Pulitzer Prize. Noted for her mastery of traditional forms and poignant evocation of urban black experience, Brooks emerged as a leading black literary figure during the 1950s and 1960s. Drawing upon both European models and African-American folk tradition, her lyrical poetry addresses racial injustice, poverty, and the private struggles of young black women with exceptional precision, psychological depth, and authenticity. In addition to *Annie Allen,* Brooks is best known for *A Street in Bronzeville* (1945), *The Bean Eaters* (1960), *In the Mecca* (1968), and her only novel, *Maud Martha* (1953). During the late 1960s, Brooks embraced the Black Power and Black Arts movements, marking a dramatic shift in her poetry toward increasingly polemical declarations of black pride and African cultural nationalism.

Biographical Information

Born in Topeka, Kansas, Brooks was raised in the poor South Side section of Chicago by devoted parents; her mother abandoned teaching for marriage and motherhood and her father, the son of a runaway slave who fought in the Civil War, gave up his ambition to attend medical school to work as a janitor. Out of the loving security of her home, Brooks early experienced racial prejudice in grade school, where other black students ridiculed her for her dark skin and lack of social or athletic abilities. Brooks found solace in reading and writing, which her parents enthusiastically encouraged; after reading her seven-year-old daughter's precocious poetry, Brooks's mother proclaimed to her, "You are going to be a poet." Brooks published her first poem at age thirteen in *American Childhood* magazine. At age sixteen she met Langston Hughes, who read her poems and offered encouragement after a poetry reading. Brooks's early poetry reflects her interest in William Wordsworth, John Keats, Emily Dickinson, William Cullen Bryant, and Percy Bysshe Shelly. After graduating from an integrated high school in 1934, Brooks continued to devote herself to writing and even corresponded with Harlem Renaissance poet James Weldon Johnson, who commented favorably on her poetry and suggested that she read modern poets. Brooks was a regular poetry contributor to the *Chicago Defender* beginning in 1934. After graduating from Wilson Junior College in 1936, she briefly worked as a maid and as a secretary for a spiritual charlatan who managed a massive slum tenement known as the Mecca. Brooks later recalled both of these painfully degrading job experiences in her poetry. In 1938 Brooks joined the NAACP Youth Council, where she met her husband, Henry Lowington Blakely II, whom she married the next year; their son was born in 1940, and daughter in 1951. From 1941 to 1942 Brooks attended a poetry workshop with Inez Cunningham Stark, who helped hone her technical skills. Brooks won the Midwestern Writers Conference prize in 1944 with the "Gay Chaps at the Bar," and again in 1945 with "the progress." Both poems appeared in her first volume of poetry *A Street in Bronzeville.* Brooks was named one of the ten most outstanding women of the year by *Mademoiselle* magazine in 1945 and received several prestigious honors, including a National Institute of Arts and Letters grant in 1946, an American Academy of Arts and Letters Award in 1946, and Guggenheim fellowships in 1946 and 1947. Brooks's next volume of poetry, *Annie Allen,* won a Eunice Tietjens Memorial Prize from *Poetry* magazine in 1949 and a Pulitzer Prize in 1950. During the 1950s, Brooks published her only novel, *Maud Martha,* and a book of children's verse, *Bronzeville Boys and Girls* (1956). Her third volume of poetry, *The Bean Eaters,* heralded Brooks's growing social and racial consciousness at the height of the civil rights movement. Her *Selected Poems* (1963) received a Robert F. Ferguson Memorial Award and Thormod Monsen Literature Award in 1964. In 1967 Brooks attended the Second Fisk Writers Conference, where she was captivated by younger black writers such as LeRoi Jones (Amiri Baraka) and Don L. Jones (Haki Madhubuti), whose message of black solidarity Brooks embraced as her own, marking a decisive turning point in her career. Brooks hosted poetry workshops for members of the Chicago gang the Blackstone Rangers, traveled to Africa twice in the early 1970s, and supported black publishing ventures by having her subsequent work published by Broadside Press in Detroit and Third World Press in Chicago. She also served as editor of several Broadside Press anthologies. In 1968 Brooks received a National Book Award nomination for *In the Mecca* and succeeded Carl Sandburg as poet laureate of Illinois. In 1971 she received the Black Academy of Arts and Letters Award. During the 1970s and 1980s Brooks published additional small volumes of poetry, her autobiography *Report from Part One* (1972), children's verse in *The Tiger Who Wore White Gloves* (1974), and the writing manuals *Young Poet's Primer* (1980), *A Capsule Course in Black Poetry Writing* (1975), and *Very Young Poets* (1983). A noted teacher and mentor for young poets, Brooks has sponsored numerous poetry contests and workshops, often financed at her own expense, and taught at many colleges and universities since the early 1960s. In 1985 Brooks was appointed poetry consultant for the Library of Congress. She has received numerous additional honors, including the Frost Medal from the Poetry Society of America and a Lifetime Achievement Award from the National Endowment for the Arts in 1989, and a National Book Foundation medal for lifetime achievement in 1994.

Major Works

Brooks's poetry in *A Street in Bronzeville* reveals the formal accomplishment, colloquial rhythms, and social concerns that characterize most of her work. The first section of the volume presents a realistic montage of everyday episodes and scenes in Bronzeville, the poor Chicago neighborhood of her childhood and early marriage. Drawing upon a variety of poetic styles, including the sonnet, ballad, blank verse, and blues, Brooks relates the frustrated hopes, economic deprivation, violence, and racial prejudice experienced by ordinary Bronzeville men, women, and children. In "The Ballad of Chocolate Mabbie" the title character is jilted by her boyfriend for a light-skinned girl; "The Sundays of Satin Legs Smith" depicts one man's futile effort to escape poverty and racism through flamboyant dress and sex. The second section of the volume, consisting of the sonnet series "Gay Chaps at the Bar," deals with the unsung heroism of black soldiers during the Second World War. Brooks continued these social themes in *Annie Allen,* which focuses upon the maturation of its young, black female protagonist. Divided into several sections, including "Notes from the Childhood and Girlhood," "The Anniad," "Appendix to the Anniad," and "The Womanhood," Brooks chronicles Annie's home life, youthful innocence, growing self-awareness, and romantic relationships amid the same grim, poverty-stricken setting of *A Street in Bronzeville.* The centerpiece of the volume is "The Anniad," a long mock-heroic epic whose title alludes to Homer's *The Iliad.* This complex poem juxtaposes Annie's idealism with the stark reality of her limited circumstances as a black woman, wife, and mother. Brooks elaborated upon similar themes in *Maud Martha,* an autobiographic novel comprised of thirty-four vignettes that chronicles the childhood and emotional development of an unhappy, self-conscious black woman who struggles to find dignity and confidence despite poverty and racial discrimination from both blacks and whites. In *The Bean Eaters* Brooks moved away from personal subjects to address the mounting alienation and despair of African-Americans during the late 1950s. The title of the collection alludes to Vincent van Gogh's painting *The Potato Eaters.* Many of these poems relate the failed efforts of those in the black community to escape hopelessness through materialism, religion, racial integration, and reckless living. This volume includes Brooks's much anthologized poem "We So Cool," which mimics the self-defeating defiance of pool hall drop-outs. In another poem, "Ballad of Rudolph Reed," Brooks describes the tragic result of a black man's attempt to move his family into a white neighborhood. Brooks also linked the experiences of Chicagoans with national events in several poems, including "A Bronzeville Mother Loiters in Mississippi. Meanwhile, a Mississippi Mother Burns Bacon," which deals with the 1955 murder of Emmett Till, a black teenager killed for allegedly whistling at a white girl. Brooks's *Selected Poems* contains several new poems which further evince her commitment to social causes. In one poem, "Riders to the Blood-Red Wrath," Brooks extols the activities of the Freedom Riders and others involved in the civil rights movement. *In the Mecca* marks a transition in Brooks's poetry, reflecting a turn away from the humor and irony of earlier volumes toward the overt political tone and subjects of her subsequent work. The long title poem, written in free verse and replete with literary and biblical allusions, is set in the dilapidated Mecca apartment complex of Brooks's earlier employment. The narrative revolves around Mrs. Sallie, a single mother of nine children, and her frantic search to locate her missing child, Pepita, within the sprawling residence. While searching for Pepita with the police, Mrs. Sallie encounters other inhabitants of the Mecca, most of whom are too preoccupied with their own obsessions to offer assistance or compassion. Pepita's body is eventually discovered under the roach infested cot of Jamaican Edward, who has raped and murdered the young girl. *In the Mecca* also contains an elegy for Malcolm X and slain civil rights activist Medgar Evers. The evolution of Brooks's political and racial consciousness is documented in *Report from Part One,* an assemblage of interviews, reviews, and autobiographic prose that recounts her visits to Africa and new black aesthetic. Brooks's poetry in *Riot* (1969), *Family Pictures* (1970), *Aloneness* (1971) and *Beckonings* (1975) reflects her revolutionary perspective and black pride. For example, "The Third Sermon of the Warpland" in *Riot* deals with Chicago street disturbances after the assassination of Martin Luther King, Jr., and "The Life of Lincoln West" in *Family Pictures* presents a white man's derisive view of dark-skinned blacks. Brooks collected and republished many of these poems in *to disembark* (1981).

Critical Reception

Brooks is highly regarded as a major contemporary American poet and preeminent African-American literary figure. Consistently praised for her technical skill and intimate portraits of black personalities and urban life, she has won both critical and popular admiration among her readers. As many critics note, Brooks possesses an uncanny ability to transmute commonplace subjects into the extraordinary, especially those seemingly insignificant events in the lives of the poor and dispossessed in her native Chicago. According to Cheryl Clarke, "Brooks's entire oeuvre has been studies of black subjectivity, of African-American oral and written traditions, sources of knowledge and faith systems; of the psychic and physical effects of racism on the lives of black and white people; and of the richness of the lyric." Critical analysis of Brooks's work is focused primarily upon her poetry in *A Street in Bronzeville, Annie Allen, The Bean Eaters, In the Mecca,* and her novel *Maud Martha,* together considered her most accomplished works. Brooks's poetry after her 1967 racial awakening has received mixed reaction. While some critics disapprove of the ideology and polemical tone of her poetry from *In the Mecca* forward, others continue to appreciate the impressive force and universal appeal of her work. Brooks has also received both praise and criticism for the complexity and ambitious themes of her work. Despite her identity as a "New Black" poet during the late 1960s and 1970s, Brooks is recognized as a prescient commentator on race and female oppression for her work that predates the civil rights, Black Power, and women's movements. As Kathryne V. Lindberg writes, "Brooks has always addressed and continues to address difficult issues, including those often decorously silent intimate traumas of abortion, color caste, domestic abuse, alienation, and motherhood in poverty. Defiant in the face of a painful history of racist lies and false consciousness that refuses to yield a 'useable past,' she has actively fashioned models of personal and communal dignity as poetic blueprints for 'cultural survival.'"

PRINCIPAL WORKS

A Street in Bronzeville (poetry) 1945
Annie Allen (poetry) 1949
Maud Martha (novel) 1953
Bronzeville Boys and Girls (juvenilia) 1956
The Bean Eaters (poetry) 1960
Selected Poems (poetry) 1963
In the Mecca (poetry) 1968
Riot (poetry) 1969
Family Pictures (poetry) 1970
Aloneness (poetry) 1971
A Broadside Treasury [editor] (poetry) 1971
Jump Bad: A New Chicago Anthology [editor] (poetry) 1971
The World of Gwendolyn Brooks [includes *A Street in Bronzeville, Annie Allen, Maud Martha, The Bean Eaters,* and *In the Mecca*] (poetry and novel) 1971
Report from Part One (autobiography) 1972
The Tiger Who Wore White Gloves: Or, What You Are You Are (juvenilia) 1974
Beckonings (poetry) 1975
A Capsule Course in Black Poetry Writing [with others] (nonfiction) 1975
Primer for Blacks (poetry) 1980
Young Poet's Primer (nonfiction) 1980
Black Love (poetry) 1981
to disembark (poetry) 1981
Mayor Harold Washington and Chicago, the "I Will" City (poetry) 1983
Very Young Poets (nonfiction) 1983
The Near-Johannesburg Boy, and Other Poems (poetry) 1986
Blacks [includes *A Street in Bronzeville, Annie Allen, The Bean Eaters, Maud Martha, A Catch of Shy of Fish, Riot, In the Mecca,* and most of *Family Pictures*] (poetry and novel) 1987
Gottschalk and the Grande Tarantelle (poetry) 1988
Winnie (poetry) 1988
Children Coming Home (poetry) 1991

CRITICISM

William H. Hansell (essay date Fall 1977)

SOURCE: "The Poet-Militant and Foreshadowings of a Black Mystique: Poems in the Second Period of Gwendolyn Brooks," in *Concerning Poetry*, Vol. 10, Fall, 1977, pp. 37-45.

[*In the following essay, Hansell examines political themes and aspirations in the "second period" of Brooks's poetry. According to Hansell, Brooks "dramatically portrays the black poet's role in the revolution which is intended to bring about a rededication to American ideals."*]

Gwendolyn Brooks, in a 1976 interview at the University of Wisconsin-La Crosse, said that her work falls into three periods which correspond to "changes" in her perspective. A study of her work seems to reveal strong grounds for agreement with her. My criteria for making the division derive from changes in her portrayal of the role of the poet and of the function of art, and her gradual adoption, beginning in the poems of the second period, of attitudes which foreshadow a mystique of blackness. Works of the first period are ***A Street in Bronzeville*** (1945), ***Annie Allen*** (1949), and ***The Bean Eaters*** (1960). The second period is represented by the "New Poems" section of ***Selected Poems*** (1963) and by two uncollected poems, **"The Sight of the Horizon"** (1963), and **"In the Time of Detachment, in the Time of Cold"** (1965). Her most recent collections mark the third phase in her development; they are ***In the Mecca*** (1969) and ***Riot*** (1969/1970), ***Family Pictures*** (1970), and ***Beckonings*** (1975).

In the second period, which finds the author wholly committed to the idea that art has a political function, Miss Brooks advocates militancy for both poet and layman. She dramatically portrays the black poet's role in the revolution which is intended to bring about a rededication to American ideals. In this period also appears the first definite signs of a black mystique.

A significant theme in poems of the second period is Miss Brooks's explicit declaration of the political function of art, an attitude consistent with her belief that the immediate environment is what the artist knows best and must deal with if he is to retain his integrity and authenticity, and more especially with her belief that the most valid and meaningful art has direct relevance to the lives of the people from which it arises. Since Afro-Americans everywhere in this country, as much in urban ghettoes as in Southern farm communities, were in a ferment of political activity, Miss Brooks, in response to this influence on her milieu, increasingly introduced politics into her work. Events, as Miss Brooks said herself in 1969, caused her to see new things: "Many things I'm seeing now I was absolutely blind to before. . . ."

The "New Poems" section of ***Selected Poems*** (1963) is truly transitional in that it contains poems in her earlier manner and poems which forcefully state her new concern with the artist as political militant; and for the purposes of this discussion as well as to sharpen the contrast, I have grouped the poems accordingly. Poems typical of her earlier work are discussed first. **"Old People Working,"** for example, is closer to her earlier concern with the personal experiences of her characters. It portrays an elderly couple who have only very slight awareness of anything beyond their immediate concerns. These two preserve their dignity, despite the trivial tasks required of them, by making their labor an expression of their love and gesture of defiance:

> Old people working. Making a gift of garden.
> Or washing a car, so some one else may ride.
> A note of alliance, an eloquence of pride.
> A way of greeting or sally to the world.

Their "garden," their "gift" of beauty and love, is their welcome or challenge to the world. The couple have little enough to work with, and the physical product of their work is for "some one else"; but the spiritual capacity which generated the work and is sustained by it belongs to the couple alone. Other "New Poems" dealing with subjects and themes similar to her earlier work are **"To Be in Love"** and several very short poems in the sub-section entitled "A Catch of Shy Fish."

A somewhat ambiguous poem about two artists, **"Spaulding and Francois,"** contrasts the "Art-loves" of artists to the demands of their audience. The artists who speak in the poem long to portray "Things Ethereal," "spiritual laughter," "the happiness / Of angels," but, as the final section states,

> the People
> Will not let us alone; will not, credit, condone
> Art-loves that shun
> Them (moderate Christians rotting in the sun.)

Obviously, from the point of view of the artists, what the people want seems contemptible, as "moderate Christians rotting in the sun" is a description full of contempt. Taken on its own, **"Spaulding and Francois"** seems a conventional artistic outcry against the demands of an insensitive, unimaginative, even materialistic audience. Yet, in view of Miss Brooks's constant concern with commonplace individuals and experience, it is difficult to reject the feeling that the artists, in their abstraction and otherworldliness, are also being mocked. In any case it is certain from other poems in the "New Poems" section that Miss Brooks remains very much committed to the idea that the commonplace and practical are legitimate, and perhaps necessary concerns of the artist.

"Big Bessie Throws Her Son into the Street" seems to have as its primary theme the necessity of dealing with reality, with actual conditions, as opposed to indulging oneself in the contemplation of beauty. The mother, "Big Bessie," commands her son to give up his "beautiful disease," which seems to be like the desire of **"Spaulding and Francois"** to contemplate "the happiness / Of angels." Big Bessie's son is not told he must totally abandon all concern with beauty and with dreams ("candles in the eyes"); he is told those things "are not enough." Her command to him, therefore, is to engage life directly, to "Go down the street." As Miss Brooks portrays the situation, the son could represent an individual who would prefer to remain aloof from practical affairs. His mother's urging is that he must participate. By extension, Miss Brooks affirms in this poem her belief that individuals must take a vital and direct role in affairs.

Poems dedicated to Robert Frost and Langston Hughes imply a similar artistic attitude. In **"Robert Frost"** she stresses his capacity for balancing the desire, to borrow from another poem, for "Things Ethereal" with the demands of "the common blood." More abstractly stated, her comment on Frost seems to emphasize his success at balancing contraries. Her tribute to Langston Hughes stresses different qualities. She celebrates his love of life and his contribution to racial pride; but she also stresses Hughes's apparent belief that art should not be an end in itself when the times demanded a different kind of activity. Rather, as Miss Brooks describes those times in the final lines of the poem, it is clear that the function of a poet like Hughes, as "helmsman, hatchet, headlight," is to direct events and provide whatever weapons are necessary.

"Riders to the Blood-Red Wrath" is perhaps the most explicit portrayal of Miss Brooks's new sense that the political militant and the poet who writes about militant themes share identical roles. Each brings closer the time when authentic "Democracy and Christianity" will prevail. The poet seems as much an actor, a participant, as the militant in the street. In this longest of the "New Poems," a woman narrator declares that her illicit sexual relations with a man show that she is "waiving all witness" with conventional attitudes toward love. She dismisses objections of the tradition-minded; for she evidently believes her own behavior is appropriate. By breaking with "ancestral seemliness" and shamelessly believing in this new "excess," she affirms a new style of life, which cuts her and her lover off from those who dwell in the past and who fear the future. The girl's new allegiance is to those who confront reality and who militantly participate in the effort to bring about the Afro-American's full participation in American life. The newness of the narrator's values, I believe, lies primarily in her belief that authentic American ideals have never significantly determined behavior. There has been only pretense both on the part of whites and of blacks.

The second section of **"Riders"** makes it immediately evident that this "renegade" behavior is not simply a rejection of conventional sexual mores. The narrator announces:

> The National Anthem vampires at the blood.
> I am a uniform. Not brusque. I bray
> Through blur and blunder in a little
> voice!

Metaphorically the narrator states that it is American ideals which have permeated her being and now drive her to protest against national practices. Her protest, although seemingly insignificant, is nonetheless "a tender grandeur," which must no longer be concealed:

> Under macabres, stratagem and fair
> Fine smiles upon the face of holocaust,
> My scream! unedited, unfrivolous.

We are told that the woman has suffered intensely from the suppression of the desire for vengeance, and that her self-control prevented her from accepting rewards she felt deserving of:

> . . . meriting the gold, I
> Have sewn my guns inside my burning lips.

In the third section of the poem it would appear that despite her restraint, the narrator suspects her pain and rage may have been prematurely detected. "Did they detect my parleys and replies?" she asks, and then relates the events which might have revealed her true feelings:

> My Revolution pushed his twin the mare,
> The she-thing with the soft eyes that conspire
> To lull off men, before him everywhere.

Apparently personifying overt actions as male and the necessary disguises she has employed as female, the narrator tells us that the "she-thing" (black submissiveness as well as the narrator's feminine submissiveness?) has beguiled "them," beguiled and misled those she is rebelling against. Her disguise "in mottles of submission" has both concealed her true nature and uncovered "sedition" in the enemy.

The narrator remains confident, moreover, that the enemies are ignorant of certain qualities in her character, as of her ability to endure and to contain her rage but not to feed on it.

> They do not see how deftly I endure.
> Deep down the whirlwind of good rage I store
> Commemorations in an utter thrall.
> Although I need not eat them any more.

The narrator, and Afro-Americans generally have not been

reduced to feeding only on their grief and rage, literally, are not consumed with bitterness. The lines also state that the rage is good, because justifiable; it is rage aroused by undemocratic and un-Christian practices which violate American ideals.

With section five and the explicit references to the African and slave heritage, the narrator clearly begins to speak for the entire race and reveals a major inspirational source for the decision to break with discredited practices. She is sustained by an ancient tradition neither passive nor pacific. Africa provides a testimony to a rich cultural past of wealth and power, a testimony to a warlike heritage.

After Africa, the narrative introduces events which led to enslavement in America, especially the "middle passage," during which the captors and captives established inextricable bonds. Then the period of slavery is recalled, and memories of the cruelty and labor revived. The Afro-American's entire condition, the narrator states, was the artifice, the creation of the master.

Continuing, the narrator reads in the racial experience a lesson of international significance:

> But my detention and my massive stain,
> And my distortion and my Calvary
> I grind into a little light lorgnette
> Most sly: to read man's inhumanity.

The "little light lorgnette" seems to be the poet-narrator's phrase for her poetry, which disguises its true revolutionary intentions. She goes on to reveal her awareness that "she" (her race) has not been the only victim of war and injustice:

> And I remark my Matter is not all.
> Man's chopped in China, in India indented.
> From Israel what's Arab is resented.
> Europe candies custody and war.

Recognizing that suffering and persecution observe no racial or national boundaries, the narrator announces her love and her duty to "esteem" all men:

> Behind my expose
> I formalize my pity: "*I* shall cite,
> Star, and esteem all that which is of woman,
> Human and hardly human."

Hardly here seems to mean "inhuman" rather than "barely"; but Miss Brooks seems to have meant that she loves even those responsible for slavery and other inhumanities.

Having pledged her faith in all mankind, the narrator now announces her mission. Her rejection of past evils and her affirmation of universal ideals which have failed to sufficiently effect practices, mark her effort as a rebirth and rededication:

> Democracy and Christianity
> Recommence with me.

Although the black experience is the immediate provocation, and its relationship to inhumanities everywhere the general one responsible for inspiring the narrator to a rededication, it is important to observe that the ideals are "American ideals." In later poems, for example, in all three **"Sermons," "In the Mecca,"** and ***Riot,*** the rededication will be to "blackness" or "black integrity," rather than, as explicitly stated here, "Democracy and Christianity." The Afro-American's "continuing Calvary," in any event, is no longer to be a passive victim, or object of charity or good intentions, but to be the militant, perhaps violent, agent in the attempt to achieve liberty and love for all:

> And I ride ride I ride on to the end—
> Where glowers my continuing Calvary.
> I,
> My fellows, and those canny consorts of
> Our spread hands in this contretemps—for—
> love
> Ride into wrath, wraith and menagerie [.]

Those who are fully dedicated to "this contretemps—for—love" and those who are simply "canny consorts," perhaps meaning the opportunists, nonetheless contribute.

The positive significance of black militancy as here portrayed cannot be overstressed. Brotherhood, equality, and love are the impelling forces. Despite whatever furious resistance, and without confidence of victory, as the final lines state, the black man is dedicated to his mission of truly initiating the rule of democracy and Christianity:

> To fail, to flourish, to wither or to win.
> We lurch, distribute, we extend, begin.

Therefore, beyond "Good rage," the Afro-American is sustained by the African heritage, by the acknowledgment, however painful, that the fate of the white and black races is irrevocably linked, by the recognition that blacks have ties with all peoples subjected to persecution and oppression—thus are linked to all men—by the realization that the black preserves the highest values and ideals, which in this poem are combined under the rubric "Democracy and Christianity," and, finally, by the conviction that it is the Afro-American's mission to try, with whatever allies he finds, to bring these ideals into practice. Although **"Riders"** portrays a black militant dedicated to American ideals, the importance Miss Brooks ascribes to the "warrior" heritage, to the strength and former greatness of African forebears, and to the lessons learned during slavery and afterwards foreshadows a black mystique.

Two uncollected poems of Gwendolyn Brooks, which were published in a period between the ***Selected Poems*** (1963) and ***In the Mecca*** (1968), further illustrate developments already noted in **"Riders to the Blood-Red Wrath"** and can be included with work of her second period.

"The Sight of the Horizon" (1963) repeats the determination and qualified optimism of **"Riders to the Blood-Red Wrath,"** but there is much less emphasis on the potential for violence in the struggle. In fact, the poem seems primarily concerned to ask what course can be trusted to carry blacks most directly to the long-denied goal. Miss Brooks does not appear to advocate any particular strategy; her insistence is that the effort be predicated on achieving total participation. It is the only "Horizon," the only "Garden," which will at the same time redeem both blacks and America.

Alluding broadly to the history of postponed equality, the first stanza states the continuing uncertainty as to the course to be taken.

> After such mocks—what Motive?
> What certain Spur? (To find
> Among all nervous rebels that bewitch
> The melancholy capitals of the mind.)

But if the strategy to follow is doubtful, shadowed by "melancholy" possibilities, the goals seem attainable and fairly certain. These are the fulfillment of an ideal and the attainment of a vital necessity for life. There is something more, too. I believe the third and fourth lines just quoted state the narrator's awareness that traditional attitudes must change. The black man, in this sense, can no longer accept the identity and role determined by "white" society.

> The Sight of the Horizon.
> Possession of our breath:
> Possession of our vagrant vision; even
> The legendary mammoth of our death.

Of course, the lines might also suggest her awareness that if "possession" of the vision is demanded, the consequence could be fatal reprisals. Just as in **"Riders,"** however, the imperative seems to be "To wither or to win."

The last two stanzas state clearly that nothing short of full achievement of their vision will satisfy Afro-Americans. An America free of racism and oppression, therefore a society for the first time fully American in practice, is the goal. The twofold aspect of the black man's mission is thus carried over from **"Riders,"** for as blacks enter fully into their proper share, America for the first time fulfills its ideals.

> We seek no clue of green.
> We seek a Garden: trees,
> The light, the cry, the conscience of the grass.
> In this most social of all centuries.
>
> We seek informal sun.
> A harvest of hurrah.
> We seek our center and our radius.
> Profound redemption. And America.

The second uncollected poem from the middle period comes the closest to accepting the necessity of violence to "repair . . . a ripped, revolted land" and make possible love and unity between men in this country. **"In the Time of Detachment, in the Time of Cold"** (1965) is a tributary poem to Abraham Lincoln and was included as the first of seven dedicatory pieces by various authors in *A Portion of That Field.* In tone and theme it is closer to **"Riders to the Blood-Red Wrath"** than to **"The Sight of the Horizon."** Lincoln is addressed as the only one who can lead the way in a gravely troubled time.

The opening lines invoke "the good man" who could still act as the "renouncer" of the present time's "Grave grave legalities of hate. . . ." The narrator describing the contemporary situation, with its betrayals ("bogus roses") and violence against advocates of equality and justice ("demondom") speaks not for a race but for all Americans. Lincoln is beseeched to restore the unity and love in a "ripped, revolted land." But because the unity may not easily be achieved, Lincoln's spirit is invoked, finally, as the possible inspiration for violent changes in ideas and attitudes:

> Singe! smite! beguile our own bewilderments
> away.
> Teach barterers the money of your star!
> Or
> Retrieve our trade from out the bad bazaar.
>
> In the time of detachment, in the time of cold, in
> this time
> Tutor our difficult sunlight. Rouse our rhyme.

The allusion to the biblical episode in which Christ performed the single act of violence in his recorded life is very appropriate in this context. He drove money-lenders from the Temple, charging they corrupted the law and holy places; and Lincoln, of course, accepted the use of violent means to halt what he believed was an erroneous and harmful misinterpretation of the Constitution. It is also interesting to note that the final phrase, "Rouse our rhyme," seems intended to imply that "rhyme," poetry, is an appropriate form for the expression of militant and idealistic political attitudes. Rhyme is here the proper accompaniment of whatever actions are necessary to restore America to its ideals. The poet, then, complements the work of the politician-statesman.

The "New Poems" in ***Selected Poems,*** therefore, are most notable for their portrayal of black artists as the militant leaders in the effort to accomplish a revolution in white attitudes toward blacks. The tribute to Hughes, to the courage of Big Bessie, and to the narrator of **"Riders to the Blood-Red Wrath"**—these essentially resolve the conflict of the artist in choosing between abstract beauty and practical good in favor of the latter. The first evidence of Miss Brooks's acceptance of a mystique of blackness is revealed, I believe, in her portrayal of the black artist's special role as literally that of remaking America in the image of what formerly had been merely professed ideals. Perhaps Miss Brooks is saying that the black artist is suited to his apocalyptic function because he—his people—has chiefly been the victim and seldom the offender. For example, the narrator of **"Riders"** states that the Afro-American's cooperation in the distortion of American ideals has been a disguise, a self-protective mask. The works of the second period announce that the masks, which were often as destructive as they were protective, are coming off in order to end tacit cooperation in "demondom" and to allow Afro-Americans full participation, even leadership, in the work of taking America closer to its ideals.

Hortense J. Spillers (essay date 1979)

SOURCE: "Gwendolyn the Terrible: Propositions on Eleven Poems," in *Shakespeare's Sisters: Feminist Essays on Women Poets,* edited by Sandra M. Gilbert and Susan Gubar, Indiana University Press, 1979, pp. 233-44.

[*In the following essay, Spillers examines the form, language, and unassuming subjects of Brooks's poetry. "The style of Brooks's poetry," writes Spillers, "gives us by implication and example a model of power, control, and subtlety."*]

For over three decades now, Gwendolyn Brooks has been writing poetry which reflects a particular historical order, often close to the heart of the public event, but the dialectic that is engendered between the event and her reception of it is, perhaps, one of the more subtle confrontations of criticism. We cannot always say with grace or ease that there is a direct correspondence between the issues of her poetry and her race and sex, nor does she make the assertion necessary at every step of our reading. Black and female are basic and inherent in her poetry. The critical question is *how* they are said. Here is what the poet has to say about her own work:

> My aim, in my next future, is to write poems that will somehow successfully "call" all black people: black people in taverns, black people in alleys, black people in gutters, schools, offices, factories, prisons, the consulate; I wish to reach black people in mines, on farms, on thrones; *not* always to "teach"—I shall wish often to entertain, to illumine [Emphasis Brooks]. My newish voice will not be an imitation of the contemporary young black voice, which I so admire, but an extending adaptation of today's G. B. voice.

Today's G. B. voice is one of the most complex on the American scene precisely because Brooks refuses to make easy judgments. In fact, her disposition to preserve judgment is directly mirrored in a poetry of cunning, laconic surprise. Any descriptive catalog can be stretched and strained in her case: I have tried "uncluttered," "clean," "robust," "ingenious," "unorthodox," and in each case a handful of poems will fit. This method of grading and cataloguing, however, is essentially busywork, and we are still left with the main business: What in this poetry is stunning and evasive?

To begin with, one of Brooks's most faithfully anthologized poems, **"We Real Cool,"** illustrates the wealth of implication that the poet can achieve in a very spare poem:

> We real cool. We
> Left school. We
> Lurk late. We
> Strike straight. We
> Sing sin. We
> Thin gin. We
> Jazz june. We
> Die soon.

The simplicity of the poem is stark to the point of elaborateness. Less than lean, it is virtually coded. Made up entirely of monosyllables and end-stops, the poem is no non-sense at all. Gathered in eight units of three-beat lines, it does not necessarily invite inflection, but its persistent bump on "we" suggests waltz time to my ear. If the reader chooses to render the poem that way, she runs out of breath, or trips her tongue, but it seems that such "breathlessness" is exactly required of dudes hastening toward their death. Deliberately subverting the romance of sociological pathos, Brooks presents the pool players—"seven in the golden shovel"—in their own words and time. They make no excuse for themselves and apparently invite no one else to do so. The poem is their situation as *they* see it. In eight (could be nonstop) lines, here is their total destiny. Perhaps comic geniuses, they could well drink to this poem, making it a drinking/revelry song.

Brooks's poetry, then, is not weighed down by egoistic debris, nor is her world one of private symbolisms alone, or even foremost; rather, she presents a range of temperaments and situations articulated by three narrative voices: a first-person voice, as in **"Gay Chaps at the Bar."**

> We knew how to order. Just the dash
> Necessary. The length of gaiety in good taste.
> Whether the raillery should be slightly iced
> And given green, or served up hot and lush.
> And we knew beautifully how to give to women
> The summer spread, the tropics of our love.
> When to persist, or hold a hunger off.
> Knew white speech. How to make a look an
> omen. . . .

an omniscient narrator for the ballads:

> It was Mabbie without the grammar school gates
> And Mabbie was all of seven
> And Mabbie was cut from a chocolate bar
> And Mabbie thought life was heaven. . . .

And then a concealed narrator, looking at the situation through a double focus. In other words, the narrator ironically translates her subject's ingenuousness. To this last group of poems belongs **"The Anniad,"** perhaps one of the liveliest demonstrations of the uses to which irony can be put.

A pun on *The Aeneid or The Iliad,* the title of this piece prepares us for a mock heroic journey of a particular female soul as she attempts to gain self-knowledge against an unresponsive social backdrop. At the same time, the poem's ironic point of view is a weapon wielded by a concealed narrator who mocks the ritualistic attitudes of love's ceremony. The poem is initially interesting for its wit and ingenuity, but eventually G. B.'s dazzling acrobatics force a "shock of recognition." Annie, in her lofty naiveté, has been her own undoing, transforming mundane love into mystical love, insisting on knights when there are, truly, only men in this world. Annie obviously misses the point, and what we confront in her tale is a riot of humor—her dreams working against reality as it is. We protest in Annie's behalf. We want the dream to come true, but Brooks does not concede, and that she does not confirms the intent of the poem: a parodic portrayal of sexual pursuit and disaster.

Shaped by various elements of surprise, **"The Anniad"** is a funny poem, but its comedy proceeds from self-recognition. Brooks gives this explanation:

> Well, the girl's name was Annie, and it was my pompous pleasure to raise her to a height that she probably did not have. I thought of *The Iliad* and said: 'I'll call this "The Anniad."' At first, interestingly enough, I called her Hester Allen, and I wanted then to say "The Hesteriad," but I forgot why I changed it to Annie . . . I was fascinated by what words might do there in the poem. You can tell that it's labored, a poem that's very interested in the mysteries and magic of technique. . . .

From the 1949 Pulitzer Prize winning volume, ***Annie Allen,*** **"The Anniad"** may be read as a workshop in G. B.'s poetry. Its strategies are echoed in certain shorter poems from ***A Street in Bronzeville*** and ***The Bean Eaters,*** particularly the effective use of slurred rime and jarring locution in **"Patent Leather"** and **"The Sundays of Satin-Legs Smith."** In narrative scope and dramatic ambition, **"The Anniad"** anticipates ***In the Mecca,*** written some twenty years later.

Forty-three stanzas long, **"The Anniad"** is built on contradictions. Locating their "answer" or meaning constitutes the poem's puzzle and reward. Here are the two opening stanzas:

> Think of sweet and chocolate,
> Left to folly or to fate.
> Whom the higher gods forgot
> Whom the lower gods berate;
> Fancying on the featherbed
> What was never and is not.
>
> What is ever and is not.
> Pretty tatters blue and red,
> Buxom berries beyond rot,
> Western clouds and quarter stars,
> Fairy sweet of old guitars
> Littering the little head
> Light upon the featherbed. . . .

After saying all we can about the formal qualities of these stanzas, we are still not certain about the subject of the poem. By means of slurs and puzzles of language, the action is hustled on, and circumlocution—"tell all the truth, but tell it slant"—becames a decisive aspect of the work's style. This Song of Ann is a puzzle to be unraveled, and the catalog of physical and mental traits deployed in the first fifteen stanzas becomes a set of clues. Not unlike games or riddles played by children, the poem gathers its clues in stanzas, and just as the questioner in the child's game withholds the solution, the speaker here does the same thing, often to the reader's dismay. However, once we know the answer, the game becomes a ritual where feigned puzzlement is part of the ceremony. In a discussion of Emily Dickinson's poetry, Northrop Frye points out that the "riddle or oblique description of some object" is one of the oldest and most primitive forms of poetry. In **"The Anniad"** the form gains a level of sophistication that is altogether stunning.

The dilemma of Annie is also that of "Chocolate Mabbie": the black-skinned female's rejection by black males. The lesson begins early for the black woman, as it does for young Mabbie. A too well-known theme of black life, this idea is the subject of several G. B. poems, but usually disguised to blunt its edge of madness and pain. With Mabbie's experience in mind, then, we are prepared for the opening lines of **"The Anniad"** and their peculiar mode of indirection.

The color theme is a crucial aspect of the poem's proposition and procedure, posing light skin and dark skin as antagonists. The question is not merely cosmetic, since hot combs and bleaching creams were once thought to be wonder workers, but it penetrates far and sharp into the psychic and spiritual reaches of the black woman's soul. I know of no modern poet before Brooks to address this subject, and as she does so, she offers the female a way out not only by awaking the phobia, but also by regarding it as yet another style of absurdity. The point is to bury inverted racism in ridicule and obscure reference, but not before contemplating its effects.

In **"The Ballad of Chocolate Mabbie,"** the situation goes this way:

> Out came the saucily bold Willie Boone.
> It was woe for our Mabbie now.
> He wore like a jewel a lemon-hued lynx
> With sandwaves loving her brow.
>
> It was Mabbie alone by the grammar-school
>   gates.
> Yet chocolate companions had she:
> Mabbie on Mabbie with hush in the heart.
> Mabbie on Mabbie to be.

An interesting contrast to Mabbie's ballad is **"Stand Off, Daughter of the Dusk":**

> And do not wince when bronzy lads
> Hurry to cream-yellow shining.
> It is plausible. The sun is a lode.
>
> True, there is silver under
> The veils of the darkness
> But few care to dig in the night
> For the possible treasure of stars.

If metaphor is a way to utter the unutterable, then "cream-yellow shining" and "veils of darkness"
hint at It, but both are needlessly quaint, drawing attention away from the subject. Not one of her best or most interesting poems, it does articulate the notion of rejection without preaching a sermon about it. In **"The Anniad,"** by contrast, the mood is sardonic and words are ablaze with a passion to kill, both the situation and one's tendency to be undone by it.

The male lover's ultimate choice to betray "sweet and chocolate" leads Annie's "tan man" to what he would consider the better stuff:

> . . . Gets a maple banshee. Gets
> A sleek-eyed gypsy moan.
> Oh those violent vinaigrettes!
> Oh bad honey that can hone
> Oilily the bluntest stone!
> Oh mad bacchanalian lass
> That his random passion has!

Clever synecdoche works here for the poet rather than against her, as it does in **"Stand Off,"** and its comic distortions are reinforced by slant rhyme in the last two lines of the stanza. "Bad" honey is the best kind in colloquial parlance, "bad" having appropriated its antonym, and in the midst of "vinaigrettes" and "bacchanalian lasses," it is a sharp surprise.

"Tan man" himself gets similar treatment:

> . . . And a man of tan engages
> For the springtime of her pride,
> Eats the green by easy stages,
> Nibbles at the root beneath
> With intimidating teeth
> But no ravishment enrages.
> No dominion is defied.
>
> Narrow-master master calls;
> And the godhead glitters now
> Cavalierly on his brow.
> What a hot theopathy
> Roisters through her, gnaws her walls,
> And consumes her where she falls
> In her gilt humility.
>
> How he postures at his height;
> Unfamiliar, to be sure,
> With celestial furniture.
> Contemplating by cloud-light
> His bejewelled diadem;
> As for jewels, counting them,
> Trying if the pomp be pure. . . .

Rodent, knight, god, by turn, "Tan man" is seen from a triple exposure: his own exaggerated sense of self-worth, the woman's complicity with it, and the poet's assessment, elaborated in the imaginative terms implied by the woman's behavior. Given the poem's logic, the woman and the man are deluded on opposing ends of the axis of self-delusion. As it turns out, he is not the hot lover "theopathy" would make him out to be, but Annie denies it, fearing that to say so would be to evoke an already imminent betrayal:

> . . . Doomer, though, crescendo-comes
> Prophesying hecatombs.
> Surrealist and cynical.
> Garrulous and guttural.
> Spits upon the silver leaves
> Denigrates the dainty eves
> Dear dexterity achieves . . .
>
> Vaunting hands are now devoid
> Hieroglyphics of her eyes
> Blink upon a paradise
> Paralyzed and paranoid.
> But idea and body too
> Clamor "Skirmishes can do.
> Then he will come back to you."

This scene of "ruin," brought on by sexual impotence, gains a dimension of pathos because it anticipates the woman's ultimate loneliness, but this judgment is undercut by the caricature of the male.

In order to fully appreciate the very pronounced contrast between other G. B. poems and this one, we should note the quality of images in **"The Anniad."** The dominant function of imagery here is auditory rather than visual, because Brooks, as well as the reader, is so thoroughly fascinated with the sound of words: for example, "Doomer, though, crescendo-comes / Prophesying hecatombs." This heavy word-motion is sustained by the most unlikely combinations—"surrealist and cynical," "garrulous and guttural," etc. The combinations are designed to strike with such forceful contrariness that trying to visualize them would propel us toward astigmatism. We confront a situation where the simple image has been replaced by its terministic equivalent, or by words which describe other words in the poem.

Brooks's intensely cultivated language in **"The Anniad"** appears to rely heavily on the cross-reference of dictionaries and thesauri. *Lexis* here is dazzling to the point of distraction, but it is probably a feature of the poem's moral ferocity. It is clear that the poet, like others, has her eye on the peculiar neurosis that often prevails in sexual relationships. Rather than dignify it, she mocks its vaunted importance, exaggerating its claims nearly beyond endurance. In effect, exaggeration destroys its force, desanctifying hyperbolean phallic status. At the same time, it appears that a secondary motivation shadows the primary one—the poet's desire to suggest a strategy for destroying motives of inferiority in the self. This psychological motif in Brooks's early poetry is disturbing. At times it appears to verge on self-hatred, but style conceals it. **"Men of Careful Turns"** offers an example, I think, by depicting an interracial love affair corrupted by racism and certain intervening class loyalties. To conceal her disappointment, the black female narrator claims moral superiority over the white male, but in this case, as in **"The Anniad,"** the literal situation is carefully disguised.

In the hands of a lesser poet Brooks's pyrotechnics would likely be disastrous, but G. B. achieves her aim by calibrating the narrative situation of the poem to its counterpart in the "real" world. Grounded in solidly social and human content, the poem is saved from sliding off into mere strangeness. The mischievous, brilliantly ridiculous juxtapositions achieve a perspective, and we gain thereby a taste for, rather than a surfeit of, exaggeration toward a specific end: to expose the sadness and comedy of self-delusion in an equally deluded world.

By contrast, a poem whose principle of composition is based on continuity of diction is another of the sonnets, **"Still Do I Keep My Look, My Identity."** A model of precision, the poem reworks a single sentence to elaborate its message:

> Each body has its art, its precious prescribed
> Pose, that even in passion's droll contortions,
> waltzes,
> Or push of pain—is its, and nothing else's.
> Each body has its pose. No other stock
> That is irrevocable, perpetual
> And its to keep. In castle, or in shack.
> With rags or robes. Through good, nothing, or
> ill.
> And even in death, a body, like no other
> On any hill or plain or crawling cot
> Or gentle for the lilyless hasty pall
> (Having twisted, gagged, and then sweet-ceased
> to bother),
> Shows the old personal art, the look. Shows what
> It showed at baseball. What it showed in school.

This concentration on a single notion is essential to the working out of the poem, and the qualifying phrases, which establish momentum, create the effect of the poem's being made in front of us. The careful structuring of the body's lines, imitated in time and space, is inherently strategic.

In its directness of presentation, **"Still Do I Keep My Look"** (like **"Gay Chaps at the Bar"**) may be relegated to the category of what might be called G. B.'s "pretty" poems: the sword has been blunted by a closer concession to the expected. An excerpt from **"The Old Marrieds"** provides another example:

> But in the crowding darkness not a word did
> they say
> Though the pretty-coated birds had piped so lightly
> all the day.
> And he had seen the lovers in the little side streets.
> And she had heard the morning stories clogged with
> sweets. . . .

The opening poem of ***A Street in Bronzeville,*** **"The Old Marrieds"** belongs to G. B.'s early career. Its tender insistence is matched elsewhere: for instance, **"In Honor of David Anderson Brooks, My Father"** and **"The Bean Eaters,"** both from the volume ***The Bean Eaters.*** An aspect of the poet's reality, this compassionate response to the lives of old people has its complement in her version of the heroic. Two poems from ***In the Mecca,*** **"Medgar Evers"** and **"Malcolm X,"** are celebratory:

> The man whose height his fear improved he
> arranged to fear no further. The raw
> intoxicated time was time for better birth or
> a final death.
>
> Old styles, old tempos, all the engagement of
> the day—the sedate, the regulated fray—
> the antique light, the Moral Rose, old gusts,
> tight whistlings from the past, the mothballs
> in the love at last our man forswore.
>
> Medgar Evers annoyed confetti and assorted
> brands of businessmen's eyes.
>
> The shows came down: to maxims and surprise
> and palsy.
>
> Roaring no rapt arise-ye to the dead, he
> leaned across tomorrow. People said that
> he was holding clean globes in his hands.

A poem for the slain civil-rights leader of Mississippi, **"Medgar Evers"** reconciles celebration and surprise. G. B. has not exaggerated a feature of reality—Evers' heroism—but has invested that reality with unique significance. A similar notion works for **"Malcolm X,"** with a touch of the whimsical added:

> Original
> Ragged-round.
> Rich-robust.
> He had the hawk-man's eyes.
> We gasped. We saw the maleness.
> The maleness raking out and making guttural the air
> And pushing us to walls.
>
> And in a soft and fundamental hour
> A sorcery devout and vertical
> beguiled the world.
>
> He opened us—
> who was a key,
>
> who was a man.

In these two poems, as well as others from the later volumes, Brooks explores various kinds of heroism by means of a shrewd opposition of under-statement and exaggeration. From ***The Bean Eaters,*** **"Strong Men Riding Horses"** provides a final example:

> Strong men riding horses. In the West
> On a range five hundred miles. A thousand.
> Reaching
> From dawn to sunset.
> Rested blue to orange.
> From hope to crying. Except that strong men are
> Desert-eyed. Except that strong men are
> Pasted to cars already. Have their cars
> Beneath them. Rentless too. Too broad of chest
> To shrink when the Rough man hails
> Too flailing
> To redirect the challenger, when the Challenge
> Nicks; slams; buttonholes. Too saddled.
>
> I am not like that. I pay rent, am addled
> By illegible landlords, run, if robbers call.
> What mannerisms I present, employ,
> Are camouflage, and what my mouths remark
> To word-wall off the broadness of the dark
> Is pitiful.
> I am not brave at all.

This brilliant use of familiar symbols recalls the staccato message of movie advertisements. It conjures up heroes of the Western courtly love tradition from Charlemagne to Gawain to John Wayne and Superman. Counterpoised against this implied pantheon of superstars is a simple shrunken confessional, the only complete declaratives in the poem. That the speaker pits herself against the contrived heroes of a public imagination suggests that the comparison is not to be taken seriously. It is sham exactly because of the disparity between public idealism and the private condition, but the comic play-off between the poet's open, self-mocking language (a pose of humility) and the glittering, delirious "dig-me-brag" of the "strong men" is the demonstration, more precisely, of the opposing poles of reality—exaggeration and under-statement. In the world of

Gwendolyn Brooks, the sword is double-edged, constantly turning.

Only a fraction of the canon, the poems discussed in this essay represent the poet's range of strategies and demonstrate her linguistic vitality and her ability to allow language to penetrate to the core of neutral events. The titles of Brook's volumes, from ***A Street in Bronzeville*** to ***In the Mecca,*** suggest her commitment to life in its unextraordinary aspects. Reworking items of common life, Brooks reminds us that creative experience can be mined from this vast store of unshaped material. To see reality through the eyes of the clichéd or the expected, however, is not to revisit it but to hasten the advance of snobbery and exclusion. In her insistence that common life is not as common as we sometimes suspect, G. B. is probably the democratic poet of our time. That she neither condescends nor insists on preciousness is rewarding, but, above all, her detachment from poetry as cult and cant gives her access to lived experience, which always invigorates her lines. By displacing the familiar with the unfamiliar word, Brooks employs a vocabulary that redefines what we know already in a way we have not known it before. The heightened awareness that results brings to our consciousness an interpenetration of events which lends them a new significance.

Some of Brooks's poems speak directly to situations for which black women need names, but this specificity may be broadened to define situations that speak for other women as well. The magic of irony and humor can be brought to bear by any female in her most dangerous life-encounter—the sexual/emotional entanglement. Against that entanglement, her rage and disappointment are poised, but often impotently, unless channeled by positive force. For women writers, decorum, irony, and style itself are often mobilized against chaos. Thus, women don't cry in Brooks's poetry nor does she cry over them, but the poet is remarkably alive and questioning in the dialectical relationship she poses between feeling and thinking. Hers is a tough choice of weapons because it has little use for the traditional status of woman—connubial, man-obsessed. The style of Brooks's poetry, then, gives us by implication and example a model of power, control, and subtlety. No idealogue, Brooks does not have to be. Enough woman and poet, she merges both realities into a single achievement. Comedy and pathos, compassion and criticism are not estranged integers in this poetry, but a tangled skein of feeling, both vital and abstract, imposed on a particular historical order. With a taste for the city and an ear for change, Gwendolyn Brooks restores the tradition of citizen-poet.

Mary Helen Washington (essay date Summer 1983)

SOURCE: "'Taming All That Anger Down': Rage and Silence in Gwendolyn Brooks' *Maud Martha,*" in *Massachusetts Review,* Vol. XXIV, No. 2, Summer, 1983, pp. 453-66.

[*In the following essay, Washington discusses the critical reception of* Maud Martha *and the suppressed rage, self-loathing, and reticence displayed by Brooks's autobiographic heroine.*]

> Then emotionally aware
> Of the black and boisterous hair,
> Taming all that anger down.
>
> *Gwendolyn Brooks*

When Gwendolyn Brooks' autobiographical first novel, ***Maud Martha,*** was published in 1953 it was given the kind of ladylike treatment that assured its dismissal. Reviewers invariably chose to describe the novel in words that reflected what they considered the novel's appropriate feminine values. The young black woman heroine was called a "spunky Negro girl" as though the novel were a piece of juvenile fiction. Reviewers, in brief notices of the novel, insisted on its optimism and faith: Maud's life is made up of "moments she loved," she has "disturbances," but she "struggles against jealousy" for the sake of her marriage; there is, of course, "the delicate pressure of the color line," but Maud has the remarkable "ability to turn unhappiness and anger into a joke." Brooks' style was likened to the exquisite delicacy of a lyric poem. The *New York Times* reviewer said the novel reminded him of Imagist poems, of "clusters of ideograms from which one recreates connected experience."

In 1953 no one seemed prepared to call ***Maud Martha*** a novel about bitterness, rage, self-hatred and the silence that results from suppressed anger. No one recognized it as a novel dealing with the very sexism and racism that these reviews enshrined. What the reviewers saw as exquisite lyricism was actually the truncated stuttering of a woman whose rage makes her literally unable to speak.

This autobiographical novel is about silences. Maud Martha rarely speaks aloud to anyone else. She has learned to conceal her feelings behind a mask of gentility, to make her hate silent and cold, expressed only in the most manipulative and deceptive ways. When she is irritated with her husband, Paul, who pinches her on the buttocks, trying to interest her in the activities of the book he is reading, *Sex in the Married Life,* she rises from the bed, as though she is at a garden party, and says "pleasantly", "'Shall I make some cocoa?' . . . 'And toast some sandwiches?'" That she is aware of this pattern and its destructiveness and of her need to change is clearly part of the novel's design:

> There were these scraps of baffled hate in her, hate

> with no eyes, no smile and—this she especially regretted, called her hungriest lack—not much voice.

But the silences of ***Maud Martha*** are also Brooks' silences. The short vignetted chapters enact Maud Martha's silence. Ranging in length from one and a half pages to eighteen pages, these tightly controlled chapters withhold information about Maud just as she withholds her feelings; they leave her frozen in an arrested moment so that we are left without the reactions that are crucial to our understanding of her. With no continuity between one chapter and the next, the flow of Maud's life is checked just as powerfully as she checks her own anger. The short, declarative sentences, with few modifiers and little elaboration, are as stiff, unyielding and tight-lipped as Maud Martha herself.

An example of Brooks' tendency to check Maud's activity (and thus her growth) is chapter five, ironically entitled, "you're being so good so kind." As the teen-aged Maud awaits a visit from a white schoolmate named Charles, she begins to feel embarrassed by the shabbiness of her home and worried that her house may have the unpleasant smell that "colored people's houses necessarily had." It is a moment of pure terror. She is the whole "colored" race and "Charles was the personalization of the entire Caucasian plan" about to sit in judgment on her. Charles never actually materializes. The chapter ends with a freeze frame of Maud hiding in the bathroom, experiencing an emotion worse than fear:

> What was this she was feeling now? Not fear, not fear. A sort of gratitude! It sickened her to realize it. As though Charles in coming gave her a gift. Recipient and benefactor. It's so good of you. You're being so good.

These last three lines, set off from the rest of the text, are a commentary by a black consciousness more aware and more removed from the event than the teen-aged Maud. While the commentator's indignation is reassuring, we can only imagine how the visit would have affected Maud: whether Charles continues to have such power when he appears, or whether Maud is as truly defeated in the encounter as her position behind closed doors intimates.

In all the chapters covering Maud's girlhood on the south side of Chicago in the 1930s and 40s, there are powerful oppositions to her freedom. In chapter one, for example, "description of Maud Martha," she decides on a personal metaphor for herself: she is a dandelion, a sturdy flower of demure prettiness, but just as a puff of wind can destroy it, so her belief in its—and her—power to allure is easily shaken, for,

> it was hard to believe that a thing of only ordinary allurements—if the allurements of any flower could be said to be ordinary—was as easy to love as a thing of heart-catching beauty.

Maud's wish to be alluring is dashed in the last two sentences of this chapter by a sudden shift to a description of her prettier sister, Helen, who is described in a gasp of pure pleasure at the thought:

> . . . her sister Helen! who was only two years past her own age of seven, and was almost her own height and weight and thickness. But oh, the long lashes, the grace, the little ways with the hands and feet.

Once, at age ten, when she is trying to appear more daring than she feels, she calls out "'Hi handsome'" to the little boy Emmanuel riding by in his wagon. He scowls back, "'I don't mean you, old black gal'" and he offers the ride to her sister Helen. In this chapter Maud tries to account for the mysterious, implacable design which has determined her inferior status and the greater worthiness of light-skinned beauties like Helen. In the short, staccato sentences that characterize much of the novel's narration, she tries to be nobly superior about her family's preference for Helen:

> It was not their fault. She understood. They could not help it. They were enslaved, were fascinated, and they were not at all to blame.

Yet is not her nobleness we feel in these sentences, but her anger. These broken utterances, as Anna Julia Cooper called them, are evidence of a woman denied expression of powerful feelings.

The painful awareness of herself as an undesirable object whose worth cannot be gauged by eyes accustomed to dismissing the commonplace mystifies the child Maud. She is disdainful of her family's failure to see that she is smarter than Helen, that she reads more, that old folks like to talk to her, that she washes as much and has longer and thicker (if nappier) hair. But from the age of seventeen to the birth of her first child (chapters ten through nineteen) her own self-perception is dismissed while she abandons herself to the obligatory quest for a man. When she is finally chosen by one of "them," or, in her words, when she "hooks" Paul, her language and attitude shift. She now sees herself entirely through Paul's eyes. In the chapter called "low yellow," Maud engages in a grotesque act of double consciousness in which she fantasizes about Paul's negative view of her:

> He wonders as we walk in the street, about the thoughts of the people who look at us. Are they thinking that he could do no better than—me?

> Then he thinks, Well, hmp! All the little good-lookin' dolls that have wanted *him*—all the little sweet high yellows that have ambled slowly past *his* front door—What he would like to tell those secretly snickering ones!—That any day out of the week he can do better than this black gal.

Rewarded for her pains with marriage, Maud settles down to "being wife to *him,* salving him, in every way considering and replenishing him." In chapter sixteen "the young couple at home" we perceive how Maud is the one who's been "hooked," who feels hemmed in, cramped, and "unexpressed" in this marriage. Though she is as disappointed as he in their life together, she evades her feelings. Once, in a classic example of self-abnegation, she worries that *he* is tired of *her:*

> She knew that he was tired of his wife, tired of his living quarters, tired of working at Sam's, tired of his two suits. . . . He had no money, no car, no clothes, and he had not been put up for membership in the Foxy Cats Club. . . . He was not on show. . . . Something should happen. . . . She knew that he believed he had been born to invade, to occur, to confront, to inspire the flapping of flags, to panic people.

Maud's lack of voice and indirection become more troubling for us when, as a grown woman confined to a small apartment and to being Mrs. Paul Phillips, she seems to have become an accomplice to her own impotence. Maud's passivity in the face of the persecutory actions of others inhibits her growth and reflects her resistance to facing her anger. When Maud and Paul are invited to the Foxy Cats Club Ball, where acceptance requires sophistication and good looks, Maud is once again up against the image of the "little yellow dream girl." Thinking about how she will forestall her old feelings of inferiority, she prepares for the event in language we know will defeat her:

> "I'll settle," decided Maud Martha, "on a plain white princess-style thing and some blue and black satin ribbon. I'll go to my mother's. I'll work miracles at the sewing machine."
>
> "On that night, I'll wave my hair. I'll smell faintly of lily of the valley."

The words she uses to refashion herself—*white, princess, wavy, lily*—all suggest how complete a transformation she imagines she needs in order to be accepted. At the club, Paul goes off with the beautiful, "white-looking" curvy Maella, leaving Maud on a bench by the wall. Maud imagines how she might handle the interloper:

> I could . . . go over there and scratch her upsweep down. I could spit on her back. I could scream. "Listen," I could scream, "I'm making a baby for this man and I mean to do it in peace."

Instead of asserting herself, however, Maud chooses to say nothing. The scraps of rage and baffled hate accumulate while she resists the words of power as though she has subjected her language to the same perverted standards by which she judges her physical beauty. In one of the early chapters she describes the "graceful" life as one where people glide over floors in softly glowing rooms, smile correctly over trays of silver, cinnamon and cream, and retire in quiet elegance. She imagines herself happy and caressed in these cool, elegant (white) places, and she aspires to the jeweled, polished, calm lives the people live there. This life, as she imagines it, is like a piece of silver, silent and remote and behind bright glass. The black world, as symbolized by the Foxy Cats Ball, is, by comparison, hot, steamy, sweaty and crowded. Far from caressing her, this real world batters her until she retreats into her imagination, refusing to speak in it because it does not match the world of her fantasies. She conceals her real self behind the bright glass of her strained gentility.

All of this pretense, this muted rage, this determination to achieve housewifely eminence—the feminine mystique of the 1950s—the desire to protect herself, "to keep herself to herself," masks so much of Maud's real feelings that we are compelled to consider what is missing in ***Maud Martha.*** Are there places in the novel where the real meaning of the character's quest is disguised? Are there "hollows, centers, caverns within the work—places where activity that one might expect is missing . . . or deceptively coded"?

Something *is* missing in ***Maud Martha,*** something besides the opportunity to speak, something we have the right to expect in Maud's life because Maud herself expects it. She has already—in the first chapters—begun to chafe at the domestic role, and yet Brooks suggests that Maud has no aspirations beyond it. When Maud asks in the last chapter, "'What, *what,* am I to do with all this life?'" she is expressing the same sense of perplexity her readers have been feeling throughout the novel. How is this extraordinary woman going to express herself? She claims not to want to be a star because she once saw a singer named Howie Joe Jones parade himself before an audience foolishly "exhibiting his precious private identity" and she has vowed that she will never be like that: "she was going to keep herself to herself." The artist's role, she says, is not for her. But the fact that she has considered and dismissed the possibility is revealing:

> To create—a role, a poem, a picture, music, a rapture in stone: great. But not for her.

> What she wanted was to donate to the world a good Maud Martha. That was the offering, the bit of art, that could not come from any other. She would polish and hone that.

Everywhere in the novel, however, Maud's artistic intentions are indirectly revealed. She perceives the world sensuously, she responds to the complexity of beauty.

> What she wanted to dream, and dreamed, was her affair. It pleased her to dwell upon color and soft bready textures and light, on a complex beauty, on gem-like surfaces. *What was the matter with that?* (italics mine)

What indeed is the matter with a woman having such subversive ideas? In an article on the sexist images of woman in modernist texts, Joyce Carol Oates maintains that by aspiring to art women violate the deeply conservative and stereotypical images of men. The autonomy of the artist is considered unnatural for women, unfeminine, and threatening. Maud uses the language of the artist as she surrenders her claim to be an artist; her language betrays her. Maud's gifts are words, insight, imagination. She has the artist's eye, the writer's memory, that unsparing honesty which does not put a light gauze across little miseries and monotonies but exposes them, leaving the audience as ungauzed as the creator.

It is natural to wonder why Brooks, in her "autobiographical novel," did not allow Maud the same independence and creative expression that she herself had as a writer. After all, Brooks was her own model of a black woman artist in the 1950s. In her autobiography, ***Report From Part One,*** she describes the exuberance she felt as she waited for books she would review to arrive in the mail, the "sassy brass" that enabled her to chide Richard Wright for his clumsy prose, and her eager sense of taking on the responsibility of a writer. But Maud, who *craves* something "elaborate, immutable, and sacred," who wants to express herself in "shimmering form," "warm, but hard as stone and as difficult to break," is never allowed to fulfill these cravings.

Novelist Paule Marshall has pointed out that women writers often make their first woman protagonist a homebody, as if to expiate for their own "deviance" in succeeding in the world of men. There is, she says, some need to satisfy the domestic role, and so they let their characters live it. ***Maud Martha*** ends with a pregnancy, not a poem; but if Maud has no life outside of marriage, she has a child, through whom she begins to hear her own voice.

The pregnancy actually becomes a form of rebellion against the dominance of both her mother and her husband. She screams at Paul in the midst of her labor pains, "DON'T YOU GO OUT OF HERE AND LEAVE ME ALONE! Damn! Damn!" When her mother, who is prone to faint over blood, comes in the door, Maud sets her straight about who's important in this drama: "'Listen, if you're going to make a fuss, go on out. I'm having enough trouble without you making a fuss over everything.'" In that one vital moment of pulling life out of herself, Maud experiences her own birth and she hears in the cries of her daughter Paulette something of her own voice:

> a bright delight had flooded through her upon first hearing that part of Maud Martha Brown Phillips expressing herself *with a voice of its own.* (italics mine)

Shortly after the birth of her child, Maud speaks aloud the longest set of consecutive sentences she has so far uttered. For a woman who has hardly said more than a dozen words at one time, this is quite a speech:

> "Hello, Mrs. Barksdale!" she hailed. "Did you hear the news? I just had a baby, and I feel strong enough to go out and shovel coal! Having a baby is *nothing,* Mrs. Barksdale. Nothing at all."

Pregnancy and the birth of a child connect Maud to some power in herself, some power to speak, to be heard, to articulate feelings.

Yet however powerful the reproductive act is, it is not the same as the creative process: a child is a separate, independent human being, not a sample of one's creative work. Without the means to satisfy her deeper cravings for her own inner life, Maud's life remains painfully ambiguous. Brooks must have felt this ambiguity in Maud's life, for when she imagined a sequel to ***Maud Martha,*** she immediately secured some important work for Maud and dispensed with the role of housewife. In a 1975 interview, Brooks was asked to bring ***Maud Martha*** up to the present day. With obvious relish, Brooks eliminates Maud's husband:

> Well, she has that child, and she has another child and then her husband dies in the bus fire that happened in Chicago in the fifties. One of those flammable trucks with a load of oil ran into a street car and about thirty-six people burned right out on Sixty-third and State Streets. *So I put her husband in that fire.* (italics mine) Wasn't that nice of me? I had taken him as far as I could. He certainly wasn't going to change. I could see that.

Brooks insists that Maud feels some regret at the loss of her husband, but returning from the funeral Maud is "thinking passionately about the cake that's going to be at the wake and how good it's going to be." Having safely buried

Paul, Brooks proceeds to explain how Maud Martha will get on with her own adventures. She will be chosen as a guide to accompany some children on a trip to Africa, and will use her slender resources to help them. She will live her life with herself at its center.

Brooks' tone as she describes the sequel to ***Maud Martha***—so freewheeling and aggressive and self-assured—reveals by comparison the uncertainties and the tensions of the 1953 version. Maud needs a language powerful enough to confront life's abuses. Maud's polite, precious and prim little rhetoric is no match for the uncouth realities she faces as a poor black woman. Rhetoric and setting seem to be at odds with each other just as they are in Brooks' 1949 epic poem ***Annie Allen*** in which, using the language of the tradition of courtly love, she tries to tell the tragic love story of a poor black woman named Annie Allen. There is power in yoking together the diction of chivalric, religious, and classical traditions and that of a woman born into a world of "old peach cans and old jelly jars," but the power of ***Annie Allen*** derives from the poet's ironic perspective. Maud's life is told in her own words and thoughts and so the poet's perspective is not available. Maud needs more access to the vernacular.

One wonders if Brooks also denies Maud a more dynamic role in the novel because of her own ambivalence (understandable in terms of the restrictions on women in the 1950s) toward women as heroic figures. In her poetry all the heroes are men, from the dapper hustler Satin-Legs Smith to the renegade Way-out Morgan or the soldier in **"Negro Hero"** or the armed man defending his family against a white mob, Brooks selects the heroic strategies of men and the ritual grounds on which men typically perform. Even a plain man like Rudolph Reed has a moment of glory as he runs out into the street "with a thirty-four / And a beastly butcher knife." He dies in defense of his family, while his wife, who has been passive throughout the entire ballad, stands by mutely and does nothing "But change the bloody gauze."

Brooks, in her poetry, seldom endows women with the power, integrity, or magnificence of her male figures. The passive and vulnerable Annie Allen, the heroine of her Pulitzer Prize winning poem, is deserted by her soldier husband and left pathetically mourning her fate in her little kitchenette, "thoroughly / Derelict and dim and done." Sometimes Brooks' women manage to be "decently wild" as girls, but they grow up to be worried and fearful, or fretful over the loss of a man. They wither in back yards, afraid to tackle life, they are done in by dark skin; and like "estimable Mable," they are often incapable of estimating their worth without the tape measure of a man's interest in them.

Brooks does allow Maud to grow in some ways, to become more in control of her life and to speak out against the racist violence of her life. When Maud moves away from the domestic sphere of her little kitchenette apartment and out into a larger social and political world she feels more urgently the need to speak. There are three racial encounters leading up to Maud's self-affirmation. Each encounter involves a change in the language Maud has available to her; each moves her closer to experiencing and expressing her rage. In the last of these three encounters Maud makes the longest speech of the novel: she tries to explain to her child, Paulette, that Santa Claus loves her as much as any white child.

A large downtown department store in the 1940s, a place where black women were generally allowed to work only as "stock girls" or kitchen help, is fundamentally alien territory for Maud, and yet it is on this hostile ground that she finally asserts herself. On the traditional Christmas visit to see Santa Claus with Paulette, Maud notices that Santa is merry and affectionate with the white children but distant and unresponsive with Paulette, looking vaguely away from her as though she is not there. As Maud sees her own child learning the lessons of inferiority and invisibility she speaks up to him in a clear and uncompromising statement that forces him to recognize Paulette:

> "Mister," said Maud Martha, "my little girl is talking to you."

Maud suddenly experiences her anger as powerful enough to lead to physical violence. She yearns to "jerk trimming scissors from purse and jab jab jab that evading eye." Now there is no desire to cover up her rage, to feign cold indifference:

> She could neither resolve nor dismiss. There were these scraps of baffled hate in her, hate with no eyes, no smile, and—this she especially regretted, called her hungriest lack—not much voice.

Ironically this chapter, where Maud regrets her lack of voice, is the one where she does the most talking. In the longest speech of the entire novel she tries to make Paulette believe that Santa Claus did like her:

> "Listen, child. People don't have to kiss you to show they like you. Now you know Santa Claus liked you. What have I been telling you? Santa Claus loves every child, and on the night before Christmas he brings them swell presents. Don't you remember, when you told Santa Claus you wanted the ball and bear and tricycle and doll he said 'Um-hm?' That meant he's going to bring you all those. You watch and see. Christmas'll be here in a few days. You'll wake up Christmas morning and find them and then you'll know Santa Claus loved *you too.*"

From Maud Martha, this is a veritable torrent of words, but the problem with her words is that they are still part of her subterfuge: She denies Santa Claus' rejection of Paulette and insists that Paulette deny her own perception of Santa's cold indifference.

The honest voice in this chapter is Paulette's. She persists:

> "Why didn't Santa Claus like me?"
>
> "Baby, of course he liked you."
>
> "He didn't like me. Why didn't he like me!"
>
> "It maybe seemed that way to you. He has alot on his mind, of course."
>
> "He liked the other children. He smiled at them and shook their hands."
>
> "He maybe got tired of smiling. Sometimes even I get—"
>
> "He didn't look at me, he didn't shake *my* hand."

In the chapter "a birth" Maud has said that her daughter's voice is part of her own. Mother and child are locked in a conversation that forces Maud out from behind the bright glass of her pretense. Now Maud admits rage, laments her lack of voice, speaks aloud, and bites back the tears as she looks down at her child's trusting face, knowing she cannot keep for her a fairy tale land where no Santa Claus ever hates a black child. Brooks does not leave Maud frozen in this chapter; we do see her acting and speaking. But perhaps the most important change is that Maud is given her most aggressive role when she confronts the racism of that cool, elegant, white, fantasy world.

If Brooks' novel seems fragmentary and incomplete, undoubtedly it is because the knowledge of one's self as a black woman was fragmented by a society which cannot imagine her. I am thinking specifically of the 1940s and 50s, those post World War decades which enshrined the Great American Domestic Dream of a housewife and a Hoover in every home. If the housewife in that dream was a white woman, the servant was always a black woman—simple and unsophisticated, as the reviews called Maud Martha. The leading black magazines of those years—*Ebony, Negro Digest, Crisis*—contributed their share of images of black women as idealized child-like creatures and assumed that their basic role was to satisfy the male imagination. The magazine *Crisis* alternated pictures of cute babies and "cute" women on its covers, while the covers of *Negro Digest* featured bathing beauties, tennis beauties, homecoming queens, and pin-ups in various stages of undress. In contrast to these pictures of black women, the back page of the *Digest* spotlighted "Men of Achievement," so that back to back with the smiling faces and exposed bodies of black women were mini-stories about the first black man to enter a prestigious college, to excel in athletics or to perform valiantly in some war. The August 1947 issue of the *Digest* featured on its back page the bravery of Negro volunteers (all men) during the Civil War; on the cover there is a picture of a fan "girl" whose partially nude body is coyly hidden behind a polka dot umbrella. Beneath the fan girl's picture is the title of the opening article by Era Bell Thompson, "What's Wonderful About Negro Men."

The articles about black women in these magazines range from condescending to obscene. The titles themselves reveal extreme hostility: "What's Wrong With Negro Women?", "Are Black Women Beautiful?", "The Care and Feeding of the Negro Woman." This last article, based on the metaphor of cultivating a really fine pet, claims that a properly trained female will develop the loyalty of a German Shepherd and the cleverness of a Siamese cat and will provide many hours of diversion and relaxation for her owner. The article "What's Wrong With Negro Women?" lists among the many shortcomings of black women their lack of cultural interests, their sense of inferiority to white women and their lack of militancy: "Where are the Negro women of self-sacrifice and courage in the cause of the race?" the writer Roi Ottley wonders. "There is not one woman to rank with the distinguished Harriet Tubman."

If we consider the way ***Maud Martha*** was received in 1953 by the literary community (black and white males), then we can clearly see another example of how black women were silenced in the 1950s. Despite Brooks' stature as a Pulitzer Prize winning poet, no one in 1953 had more than 600 words to say about the novel. The reviewers of Ellison's *Invisible Man,* (published just the year before, when Ellison was relatively unknown), suffering no such taciturnity, devoted as many as 2,100 words to Ellison's novel. *The New Republic, The Nation, The New Yorker,* and *The Atlantic* contained lengthy and signed reviews of *Invisible Man.* Wright Morris and Irving Howe were called in to write serious critical assessments of Ellison's book for *The New York Times* and *The Nation.* In contrast, *The New Yorker* review of ***Maud Martha*** was unsigned, suggesting that the real "invisible man" of the 1950s was the black woman. Brooks' character was never held up for comparison to any other literary character. Ellison's nameless hero was not only considered "the embodiment of the Negro race" but the "conscience of all races;" the titles of the reviews—"Black & Blue," "Underground Notes," "A Brother Betrayed," "Black Man's Burden"—indicated the universality of the invisible man's struggles. The titles of Brooks' reviews—"Young Girl Growing Up" and "Daydreams in Flight"—deny any relationship between the protagonist's personal experiences and the historical experiences of her people. Ellison himself was compared to Richard Wright, Dostoevsky and Faulkner; Brooks only to the unspecified "Imagists." Questions about narrative strategy, voice, and methods of characterization that were asked of *Invisible Man* were obviously considered irrelevant to an understanding of ***Maud Martha*** since they were not posed. Most critically, Ellison's work was placed in a tradition; it was described as an example of the "Picaresque" tradition and the pilgrim/journey tradition by all reviews. ***Maud Martha,*** the reviewers said, "stood alone." Not one of these reviewers could place ***Maud Martha*** in the tradition of Zora Neale Hurston's *Their Eyes Were Watching God* (1937), Dorothy West's *The Living Is Easy* (1948), or Nella Larsen's *Quicksand* (1928). Is this because no one in 1953 could picture the questing figure, the hero with a thousand faces, the powerful, articulate voice, as a plain dark-skinned woman living in a kitchenette building on the south side of Chicago?

The supreme confidence of Ellison's text—its epic sweep, its eloquent flow of words, its historical significance—invites its greater critical acceptance. By comparison the ***Maud Martha*** text is hesitant, self-doubting, mute, retentive. Maud is restricted, for the most part, to a domestic life that seems limited and narrow. At the end of the novel, poised on the edge of self-creation, at the moment we expect the "illumination of her gold," she announces that she is pregnant again, and happy.

My initial reaction to this ending was critical of Brooks for precluding any growth beyond the domestic life. But that disappointment ignores the novel's insistence that we read Maud's life in tone, in images, and in gestures. Released from an incapacitating anger, Maud becomes exhilarated and full of energy. In the last chapter she is out of doors with her daughter on a glorious day. She is outside of all the spaces that have enclosed her—the bedrooms, the kitchens, the male clubs, the doctors' offices, the movie theatres, the white women's houses, the dress shops, the beauty parlors; out of the psychic confines which left her preoccupied with her "allurements" and presumed deficiencies. Free from destructive self-concern, Maud thinks of the people around her, of the glory and bravery in their ability to continue life amid the reality of city streets, lynchings in Mississippi and Georgia, and the grim reminder of death as the soldiers, back from war, march by with arms, legs, and parts of faces missing. Maud says she is ready for anything. So this catalog of evils (include the Negro press' preoccupation with pale and pompadoured beauties) has to be seen as Maud's growing sense of relation to the social and political problems of her world. Even Maud's pregnancy can be seen as a powerful way-of-being in the world. For, in the midst of destruction and death, she will bring forth life.

Brooks then re-introduces the raised arm image of the first chapter, when Maud at age seven longed to fling her arms rapturously up to the sky. In the final chapter the raised arms are like "wings cutting away all the higher layers of air." There is the suggestion of flight and transcendence; her arms, purposeful and powerful, directing her up out of a dark valley. In sharp contrast to the child whose dearest wish was "to be cherished" as a yellow-jewelled, demurely pretty dandelion, this Maud thinks of the common flower as an image of survival and self-possession:

> for would its kind (like her) come up again in the spring? come up, if necessary, among, between, or out of—the smashed corpses lying in strict composures, in that hush infallible and sincere. . . .

Still, in spite of all the victorious imagery in this last chapter, there is a sense of incompleteness about Maud's quest; some exploration not undertaken, some constriction of the blood. Brooks does not solve the problem of Maud's anger or of her silence. Part of this lies in the privateness of Maud's story. Her constant self-analysis and self-consciousness emphasize her solitariness. She lives alienated from the two blood-related women in her life—the fussy, domineering mother and the vain sister. She has no women friends. Though she succeeds through heroic individual effort in rejecting others' definitions of her, she is still unable to express the full meaning of her growth. True, the presence of another "woman-in-embryo" allows her a first move towards freedom, but she does not have the advantage of Zora Hurston's Janie who can tell her story to an eager, loving listener whose life is changed by hearing the tale. I only wish Brooks had found a way for Maud to know that someone in the community had grown ten feet higher from listening to her story.

Beth Brown (review date November-December 1984)

SOURCE: A review of *Beckonings,* in *Black Scholar,* Vol. 15, no. 6, November-December, 1984, pp. 63-4.

[*In the following review, Brown offers positive evaluation of* Beckonings.]

This special edition of Gwendolyn Brook's ***Beckonings*** can be found on the local library shelf in a beige and chocolate cover. The poems will have private meanings for most poets. In 1975, I was writing the poems which were published in *Lightyears.* Gwendolyn Brooks was one of those distant ethereal figures whose works I stood in line to buy at bookstores. Her volumes were curiously hard to obtain. Fortunately, for me and about twenty-five other people, the Poet

Laureate of Illinois and recipient of the Pulitzer Prize read at the Museum of the University of Pennsylvania on April 26, 1983. Her reading was sponsored by Dr. Houston A. Baker, Jr., Albert M. Greenfield Professor of Human Relations as well as the President and Provost of the University. Before the reading, the endowers of Dr. Baker's chair were introduced, and the establishment of the Albert I. Greenfield Intercultural Center on the campus. This was truly an auspicious occasion!

Ms. Brooks' reading marked a turning point in several careers. In fact, she seemed to charm everyone who came into her presence. She spoke slowly and patiently. In fact she is the most cautious public, reader of the Afro-American poets, perhaps, of all poets. She read from a spectrum of her works, pausing to explain the legal controversies and critical battles that have surrounded her publication. Gwendolyn Brooks is not now associated with poetic licenses, yet it is difficult to imagine how closely her legacy parallels that of our outstanding political leaders. Present at the reading was Daniel Hoffman, an expert on Carl Sandburg, whose job Ms. Brooks now holds.

The reissue of ***Beckonings*** features a pencil drawing of the poet by her brother, Raymond Brooks, on the back cover—her broad nose, set grimace, soft eyes. The critical comment is by the late Hoyt Fuller: "The aching loveliness of these poems is sometimes close to unbearable. Through the magic of Gwendolyn Brooks' words, we hold in our souls' eye a vivid image of our beauty, we glimpse what we might yet be. An incredible woman, this poet: she would urge us into our ultimate, our transcendent humanity, with her love."

A dozen poems begin with a tribute to her brother's memory, **"Raymond Melvin Brooks":** "He knew how to put paint to paper— / made the paper speak and sing. / But he was chiefly a painter of days and the daily, / with a talent for life color, life pattern: / a talent for jeweling use and the usual, / a talent for practical style." The ordinariness which she brings to the extraordinary rescues the simplicity seen in the ornamentation of objects and events. It is with no small solemnity one reflects on the eight years that have passed since the publication of the poems, with their nuances of swagger in speech, the acknowledgment, abruptly, as poetry tends to do, of more awesome horizons. For example, this poem, **"To John Oliver Killens in 1975":**

> John,
> look at our mercy, the massiveness that it is not.
> Look at our "unity," look at our
> "black solidarity."
> Dim, dull and dainty.
> Ragged. And we
> grow colder; we
> grow colder.
>
> See our
> tatter-time.
>
> You were a mender.
>
> You were a sealer of tremblings and long
> trepidations.
> And always, with you, the word kindness was
> not
> a jingling thing but an
> eye-tenderizer, a
> heart-honeyer.
>
> Therefore, we turn, John, to you.
> Interrupting self-raiding. We pause in our falling.
> To ask another question of your daylight.

These poems have an amazing informality, not at all like the preachments of epic ***Annie Allen*** or the looming sermons of ***In the Mecca.*** They pop with humor, invade the speech with warning, paint a too familiar horror. Gwendolyn Brooks has become, in some sense, unbelievable. Her poems stand at the crossroads between "we live" and "we used to live." She has always spoken with a kind of musical understatement. In ***Beckonings,*** she blends the Homeric meter which qualifies her heir to the throne of Carl Sandburg with the bending, flattering tones of a Duke Ellington trumpet.

After her reading at Pennsylvania, Ms. Brooks shook hands, autographed books, and gave advice. Surrounded by benefactors, professors, filmmakers, poets, and the ever-present admiration of youth, she appeared to carry the responsibility of her position in the world of poetry with a bowed, respectful mien.

Barbara Christian (essay date 1985)

SOURCE: "Nuance and the Novella: A Study of Gwendolyn Brooks's *Maud Martha,*" in *Black Feminist Criticism: Perspectives on Black Women Writers,* Pergamon Press, 1985, pp. 127-41.

[*In the following essay, Christian examines the social context and presentation of* Maud Martha. *According to Christian, Brooks's "emphasis on the black girl within the community is a prefiguring of black women's novels of the sixties and seventies, which looked at the relationship between the role of women in society and the racism that embattled the black community."*]

Maud Martha, Gwendolyn Brooks's only novel, appeared in 1953, the same year that *Go Tell It On The Mountain,* James Baldwin's first novel, was published. By that time,

Brooks had already published two books of poetry, ***A Street in Bronzeville*** (1945) and ***Annie Allen*** (1949), for which she won the Pulitzer Prize. But although she was an established poet, Brooks's novel quietly went out of print while Baldwin's first publication was to become known as a major Afro-American novel. Brooks's novel, like Baldwin's, presents the development of a young urban black into an adult, albeit Brooks's major character is female and Baldwin's is male. Her understated rendition of a black American girl's development into womanhood did not arouse in the reading public the intense reaction that Baldwin's dramatic portrayal of the black male did. Yet Paule Marshall (whose novel, *Browngirl, Brownstones* (1959) is considered by many critics to be the forerunner of the Afro-American woman's literary explosion of the 1970s, would, in 1968, point to ***Maud Martha*** as the finest portrayal of an Afro-American woman in the novel, to date, and as a decided influence on her work. To Marshall, Brooks's contribution was a turning point in Afro-American fiction, for it presented for the first time a black woman not as a mammy, wench, mulatto, or downtrodden heroine, but as an ordinary human being in all the wonder of her complexity.

Why is it that ***Maud Martha*** never received some portion of the exposure that Baldwin's novel did, or why is it still, to this date, out of print, virtually unknown except to writers like Marshall and a small but growing number of black literary critics? Even within the context of Black Studies or Women's Studies, Brooks's novel is unknown or dismissed as "exquisite," but somehow not particularly worthy of comment. One could say, of course, that ***Maud Martha*** was not significant enough to receive such attention. However, comments such as Marshall's tend to nullify that argument. Or one could say that Brooks's accomplishment as a poet overshadowed, perhaps eclipsed, her only novel, although the novel shares so many of her poetic characteristics that one would think that it would attract a similar audience. I am inclined to believe that, ironically, the fate of the novel has precisely to do with its poetic qualities, with the compressed ritualized style that is its hallmark, and as importantly, with the period when it was published.

George Kent tells us in his essay "The Aesthetic Values in the Poetry of Gwendolyn Brooks," that her pre-sixties poetry was published at a time when the small number of blacks reading poetry expected that it be "the expression of interest in the universal, but without the qualifications or unstated premises or doubts regarding Blacks' humanity." And that the larger white audience "reflected happiness when they could assure the reading public that the artistic construct transcended racial categories and racial protest . . . and yet paradoxically insisted upon the art construct's informative role, by asserting that the Black artist was telling us what it meant to be a Negro." These observations would, I believe, also apply to the anticipated reading audience of ***Maud Martha,*** a poetic novel of the 1950s without any of the sensationalism that characterized popular novels about blacks—a novel that would be considered art. But although ***Maud Martha*** certainly does have these perspectives, it provides another dimension, in that it focuses on a young black girl growing into womanhood without the employment of Afro-American female stereotypes found previously in the novel. While poetry was expected to transcend racial boundaries and aspire toward universality, the novel, by definition, dealt with a specific individual's interaction with her society. The type of interaction that even this small literate audience was used to in the "Negro Novel" was not at all present in ***Maud Martha.***

In the novels written by black women in the first half of the century, most featured tragic or not so tragic mulattas, as in the Harlem Renaissance novels of Nella Larsen and Jessie Fauset, or the oppressed and finally tragic heroine, as in protest novels like Ann Petry's *The Street* (1945). Dorothy West's *The Living Is Easy* (1949), the closest in time to Brooks's ***Maud Martha,*** focuses on a central protagonist who resembles the heroines of the Renaissance period, in that an almost histrionic investment in social mobility and decorum is her principal value. And even in that innovative novel of the 1930s *Their Eyes Were Watching God* (1937), Zora Neale Hurston imbues her major character with an extraordinary life. However, Brooks's major character is neither an aspiring lady, the Major's wife, nor a necessarily beautiful and doomed heroic figure. She lives, like so many of us, an ordinary life, at least on the surface. An excerpt from the novel distinguishes its stance from its predecessors.

> On the whole, she felt life was more comedy than tragedy. . . . The truth was, if you got a good Tragedy out of a lifetime, one good ripping tragedy, thorough, unridiculous, bottom-scraping, *not* the issue of human stupidity, you were doing, she thought, very well, you were doing well.

In its insistence on examining the supposed "trivia" that makes up the lives of most black women, their small tragedies and fears notwithstanding, ***Maud Martha*** ran counter to the tone of "the Negro Novel" that both blacks and whites would have expected in 1953. For Brooks replaced intense drama or pedestrian portrayal of character with a careful rendering of the rituals, the patterns of the ordinary life, where racism is experienced in sharp nibbles rather than screams and where making do is continually juxtaposed to small but significant dreams.

Brooks's portrayal of a black woman whose life is not characterized as "tragic" was perhaps due partly, to two overlapping trends in Afro-American life and thought of the 1950s. One was the integrationist thrust, which culminated in the Supreme Court Decision of 1954. Arthur P. Davis points out the complexity of this thrust in *From the Dark Tower.* On the one hand, black writers like Wright, Hughes, Himes, and Brooks had participated through their literature in the protest movement of the 1940s against racism and poverty, especially its manifestations in the urban ghetto. To some extent, the effect of the literature was the development of an *apparent* climate in the country out of which full integration could develop. Emphasis on the overall black protest movement of that period had been on securing equality through the law, thus the significance of the 1954 Supreme Court decision. On the other hand, "there was surface and token integration in many areas, but the everyday pattern of life for the overwhelming majority remained unchanged. In the meantime he [the Negro literary artist] had to live between two worlds and that for any artist is a disturbing experience.

In the 1940s, black writers like Richard Wright had presented the everyday pattern of life for the overwhelming majority of blacks in as dramatically tragic a form as possible in an attempt to affect the philosophical underpinnings of America toward its black native sons. One unwanted result of this dramatization was white America's tendency to stereotype blacks as creatures entirely determined by their oppression, a tendency that undermined blacks' humanity as much as the previous attitude that they were genetically inferior. Many black intellectuals' reaction to this "protest" stereotype was to emphasize those qualities blacks shared with all other human beings. Thus, the "expression of interest in the universal" could be seen in the major books of the 1950s published by already established writers: e.g., Wright's *The Outsider* (1953), in which he attempted to weave together the impact of racism on the black man with philosophical issues about the existential nature of all men, or Ann Petry's, *The Narrows* (1953), which is set not in the urban ghetto of *The Street* (1945), but in a small New England city and focuses on the relationship between a black man and his white mistress. *Invisible Man* (1952), perhaps the most influential Afro-American novel of the period, emphasizes this double-pronged approach among blacks, for Ralph Ellison consciously weaves together motifs of both Afro- and Euro-American culture as the foundation of the novel's structure. Afro-American writers, in other words, were trying out new settings, approaching new subjects. In general, these new approaches attempted to break the image of the black person as an essentially controlled and tragic individual, as well as to dramatize the variety of his or her experience. The political tone of integration and literary striving to portray black people's many-sided experiences went hand in hand.

One aspect of these strivings was a return to the chronicle of the black family that was apparent in some of the Renaissance novels of Jessie Fauset. But while her novels were entirely about the upper middle class, whose conventions supposedly mirrored those of their white counterparts, the novels of the 1950s featured lower middle-class folk set against the background of coherent, specifically black communities. Unlike the conventional novel of the 1920s or the protest novels of the 1930s and 1940s, the novel of the 1950s put more and more stress on the black community as community. Still there were novels like Himes's *The Third Generation* (1954), which traced the maturation of a black boy within a family that attempts to restrict his growth.

In fact many of the novels of the late 1940s and the 1950s put some portion of the blame for the conflicts of the main characters on the black wife and/or mother, who is depicted as a powerful embodiment of white middle-class values. Variations on this theme appear not only in Himes's *Third Generation* but in West's *The Living is Easy* and *The Outsider,* novels that precede the infamous Moynihan Report (1966). In the popular arena, the image of the aggressive, castrating black female who is bent on making the male tow the line was made popular through Sapphire, a major character in the Amos n' Andy radio programs of the late 1940s and 1950s.

Interestingly, this image, a variant of the old plantation mammy, became current at a time when sociology, one of the major image makers of blacks, paid little attention to the black family. As Billingsley points out in *Black Families in White America* (1966), sociology did not discover the black family until the 1930s and by the 1950s had virtually abandoned it. The academic view of the black family, the context within which most studies of black woman were initially conducted, was, during the 1940s and 1950s represented by Frazier's *The Negro Family in the U.S.* (1948) and Cayton and Drake's *Black Metropolis* (1948). Both studies emphasized the strength of the black mother, her coping with poverty, poor housing, and desertion, which, ironically, was interpreted by many to mean that she was more powerful than the black man and therefore too powerful. And though this attitude would not be fully developed or officially authorized until the Moynihan Report, one can in hindsight see the process by which this view gained currency during the 1950s.

But just as Brooks's Maud Martha is not a tragic figure, neither is she a domineering personality. As daughter and then as a mother, she exhibits little of the willfulness associated with Sapphire or even Cleo, the major character of *The Living is Easy.* Her strength is a quiet one, rooted in a keen sensitivity that both appreciates, and critiques her family and culture. Brooks's portrayal of an ordinary black girl who cherishes the rituals of her community even as she suffers from some of its mores both conformed to and deviated from the family chronicles of the 1940s and 1950s. Her emphasis on the black girl within the community is a prefiguring of black women's novels of the sixties and seventies, which looked at the relationship between the role of woman in society and the racism that embattled the black community.

Yet a description of ***Maud Martha*** as a work of such grand intentions would undercut its peculiar quality. In keeping with it smallness, more precisely its virtual dismissal of the grand or the heroic, ***Maud Martha*** is a short novel. Properly speaking, it should be called a novella, not only because of its length but more importantly, because of its intention. Brooks is not interested in recreating the broad sweep of a society, a totality of social interaction, but rather in painting a portrait in fine but indelible strokes of a Maud Martha. In an interview in 1969 with George Stavros, editor of *Contemporary Literature,* Brooks says of her process:

> I had first written a few tiny stories and I felt that they would mesh, and I centered them and the others around one character. If there is a form I would say it was imposed at least in the beginning when I started with those segments or vignettes.

And Brooks goes on to agree with her interviewer when he says that "the unity of the novel is simply the central point of view of Maud Martha herself as she grows up."

Brooks's comments emphasize two points: the centrality of Maud Martha's inner life, for the novella is a revelation of her thoughts, and her reflections on her limited world. Unlike her predecessors, with the exception of Hurston's Janie Stark, Maud Martha is not just a creation of her external world; She helps to create her own world by transforming externals through her thoughts and imaginings. This is a quality seldom attributed to ordinary folk in previous black women's novels. And yet, in illuminating Maud Martha's specific individuality, Brooks must necessarily show her in relation to other people and her physical environment, the basis for the world she knows, imagines, even extends. The other point of emphasis in Brooks's description is her use of the word *tiny* and how diminution affects the form of this novella, the use of segments or vignettes. In all, the 170-page novella is divided into 34 chapters, many of which are three or four pages long, few longer than ten pages, "the small prose sections fitting together like a mosaic." This double emphasis of the novella is introduced in the first vignette, the "description of Maud Martha." Immediately we are in the midst of Maud Martha's images of fancy and her sense of her own ordinariness and diminutiveness.

> What she liked was candy buttons, and books, and painted music (deep blue or delicate silver) and the west sky altering, viewed from the steps of the back porch; and dandelions. . . . dandelions were what she chiefly saw. Yellow jewels for everyday studding the patched green dress of her back yard. She liked their demure prettiness second to their everydayness; for in that latter quality she thought she saw a picture of herself, and it was comforting to find that what was common could also be a flower.

As a prose piece, ***Maud Martha*** is a fusion of these two qualities, the sensitive and the ordinary, not only in its characterization of its protagonist, but also in the moments the writer chooses to include in her compressed rendition of an urban black woman's life. Yet these moments, as they form a whole, both look back to the novels of the 1940s and toward black women's novels of the 1960s and 1970s. Since the time period of ***Maud Martha*** is the thirties and the forties, it is not surprising that the impact of the Depression on black family life (e.g., in "home" and "at the Burns-Coopers") are some of the moments Brooks chooses to telescope. But there are also vignettes about a dark girl's feeling of being rejected by her own community ("low yellow" and "if you're light and have long hair"), a theme that Toni Morrison would use as the basis for her complex analyses of cultural mutilation in *The Bluest Eye* (1970). There are segments about the relationship between the rituals of a black culture and the development of character ("kitchenette folks" and "tradition and Maud Martha"), a structural technique that Paule Marshall would expand and refine in her novels. There are moments that are particularly female ("a birth," "Helen," "Mother comes to call"), themes that would become increasingly important to black women novelists of the seventies. And there are "universal" moments, in that human beings, whatever their race, sex, or class, muse about the meaning of existence and the degree of responsibility they must take to shape their own lives ("posts," "on 34th Street"), an underlying theme in Walker's *The Third Life of Grange Copeland* (1970).

Maud Martha, then, is a work that both expresses the mores of a time passing and prefigures the preoccupations to come. Georg Lukas in his analysis of another novella, Solzhenitsyn's *One Day in the Life of Ivan Denisovich* (1953), points out that novellas often appear at the end of a historical period or at the beginning of a new period, that often they are "either in the phase of a not yet (noch nicht) in the artistically universal mastery of the given social world, or in the phase of the no longer (nichtmehr)." His analysis of the genre is one way of locating the elusive significance of this "exquisite" novella. For in its focus on a single character or situation rather than the totality of a society and in its economy of presentation, the novella may summarize the essentials of a period that has just ended and be an initial exploration into attitudes that are just forming. Though not consciously intending to write a novella, the writer may find that in trying to express the moment of transition from one mode of interpreting reality to another, the present cannot be expressed in the novels of the past, nor is the totality of the new reality understood enough to transform it.

I think that it is important to note that the period of the 1930s and 1940s had been written about in many black novels. Wright's *Native Son* (1941) is set in that period as is Petry's *The Street* (1945). What Brooks does is to present another version of black life of that time, as she may have experienced it, but also as she could interpret it through the integrationist thrust of the 1950s. Yet she also pointed to future emphases: the sense of the black community as community and the black reaction to impose white notions of beauty, cultural nationalist concepts of the 1960s; as well as the sensitivity and specificity of the black women's experience as woman, a pervasive theme of the seventies. In effect, the seeds of these themes were sowed in the thwarted expectations of the integrationist thrust. And though Brooks could hardly foresee the Civil Rights Movement, the Black Power Movement, or the Women's Movement and their impact on American literature, her experience as she described it in ***Maud Martha*** was the outline of some of the reasons for the desires and goals of these movements. When Maud Martha's little daughter, Paulette, is rejected by a white Santa Claus and asks "why didn't Santa Claus like me?" and Maud Martha must try to explain why without saying why, we are witnessing one of the "trivial" but significant reasons for the 1960s black search for nationhood. When Helen, Maud Martha's sister, proclaims to her, "you'll never get a boyfriend, if you don't stop reading those books," we hear in Maud Martha's sighs the rumblings of the redefinition of woman that would be attempted in the 1970s. Perhaps, as Arthur P. Davis pointed out, because there was an apparent climate of change but little actual change, and the Negro artist of the 1950s was living between two worlds, Brooks's rendition of Maud Martha's life would have to look backward and forward.

Yet Brooks's overt intention in writing ***Maud Martha*** was not to reinterpret the past or prefigure the future. She tells us that she "wanted to give a picture of a girl growing up—a black girl growing up in Chicago, and of course much of it is wrenched from my own life and twisted." In ***Report from Part I*** she provides us with a partial list of some of those "twists," how she used her knowledge of her specific community and her perception of her own life and culled from it the essence of "a black girl growing up in Chicago." She also tells us that the first passage she wrote for the novella became the opening of the last chapter. That passage emphasizes Maud Martha's awareness of the bursting life within her and without her; the result of which is her whisper, "What, *what* am I to do with all of this life?" That question, which permeates the entire novella, is both its theme and nuance, both the question of all persons in all times and the question of that specific individual in that specific time. Life was drastically limited for an ordinary black girl in the Chicagos of the 1940s, as it was for most ordinary people. And yet, like most ordinary people, there is so much life in Maud Martha. *Whispering* the question emphasizes its ironic truth, for to most institutions, most authorized social processes, even most literature, neither Maud Martha nor her question is at all important.

In a sense, then, the conflict of the novella is contained in its subject—that such a person as Maud Martha is seldom seen as imbued with importance. Thus, the question that permeates the entire novella is based not so much on the usual "character in a conflict" motif, but in the gradual unraveling of the life that is in Maud Martha, this ordinary, unheroic girl. The novella does not have intense dramatic rises and falls, so much as it presents a typical life as not at all typical in the flat meaning of the word. Concurrently, the novella is the embodiment of the idea that a slice of anybody's life has elements of wonder and farce, wry irony and joy. No fire and brimstone need fly. But since the hero or heroine, the exceptional person, has been extolled in most societies, Brooks's orientation is in itself a challenge to a venerated "universal" idea. In framing her intention as she did and in carrying it through in her "tiny" novel, Brooks articulated the value of the invisible Many. The social and literary black movements of the 1960s and 1970s would emerge precisely because these Many would insist on the value of their "little" lives and would ask the question: "What, *what* am I to do with all of this life?"

(2)

That ***Maud Martha*** is partially based on Brooks's own experience as a young black girl growing up in the Chicago of the 1930s and 1940s contributes to the authenticity one feels while reading the novel. In other words, ***Maud Martha*** is not merely a response to the social images of blacks that were current in the 1950s, but it is also a manifestation of Brooks's own philosophy about the relationship between life and aesthetics. She distinguishes a memoir from an autobiographical novel by calling the former "a 'factual' account," while the latter is "nuanceful, allowing." As is true of many novellas, ***Maud Martha,*** is economical in its presentation, but there are many styles of economic writing. What characterizes this novella is not only its precision, but its nuance, and how these stylistic elements are organic to its underlying theme: the wonderfulness of a Maud Martha.

As a poet, Brooks is known for her precision of language, for the care with which she chooses every word and that "concentration, that crush" in her work. It is not surprising, then, that ***Maud Martha*** also shares this characteristic. Brooks says of the poet's unique relationship to language that:

> the poet deals in words with which everyone is familiar. We all handle words. And I think the poet, if he wants to speak to anyone is constrained to do something with these words so that they will "mean something," will be something that a reader may touch.

Her emphasis on the word as being, not as abstraction, but as sensory and concrete, underlines her choice of words in her novella as well as her poetry. ***Maud Martha*** is a compression of images from which the prose radiates. So that in the chapter "spring landscape: detail," Brooks's description of Maud Martha's school is concrete, sensory:

> The school looked solid. Brownish-red brick, dirty cream stone trim. Massive chimney, candid, serious.

Most of Brooks's adjectives are certainly concrete. But look at how they move to the words, *candid, serious,* words that are usually abstract but have now become concrete, something you can touch in this spring landscape. And when her description of the solid school is contrasted with the school children whom she describes as "bits of pink, of blue, white, yellow, green, purple, black carried by jerky little stems of brown or yellow or brownblack," who blow into the schoolyard, Brooks shows us more than the color or line of this landscape. She evokes the touch, the feel of a configuration of attitudes represented by the solid dullness of the school, as opposed to the vibrant playfulness of the children. Hence the words that the reader may touch moves him/her toward the nuances he/she cannot touch. The precision and the nuance work hand in hand.

Not only can one touch Brooks's words, one can hear them. Rhythm and sound are not as important to the quality of prose as they are to poetry. But even though ***Maud Martha*** is written in the form of prose narrative, Brooks employs many of the techniques she uses in her poetry. The pacing of words through her adroit use of juxtaposition, the alternation of short and longer units, the creation of emphasis through alliteration and imagery, the selection of specific sounds to evoke a certain quality—all these elements are characteristic of the prose of ***Maud Martha*** and contribute to its quality of nuance. Maud Martha's assessment of her first beau is typical of Brooks's use of rhythm and sound to advance the prose narrative:

> For Russell lacked—What? He was—nice. He was fun to go about with. He was decorated inside and out. He did things, said things with a flourish. That was what he was. He was a flourish. He was a dazzling, long and sleepily swishing flourish.

The emphasis in this two-page chapter is on Maud Martha's recognition of her first beau's grand superficiality, a quality that is not enough to absorb her, though it had vanquished so many others. So that the passage quoted above is not just a description of Russell, but a process of insight for Maud Martha as well as for the reader from which we learn much about her character by feeling her reaction to Russell. Brooks gives us the nuance of Maud Martha's insight as well as the factual through her choice of words, imagery, and sounds. The dashes indicate reflection, the slowing of the pace, as Maud Martha begins her assessment. "He was fun to go about with" is followed by equally short sentences that use repetition to create a gradual quickening of pace—*He* was, *he did things,* said *things, he was*—until the pace slows down to the moment of recognition "That was what he was." Finally, various elements of language, repetition, imagery, alliteration, assonance, combine in the long sentence that summarizes his essence: "He was a dazzling, long and sleepily swishing flourish," in which the z's, s's, l's and i's evoke Russell as much as the meaning of the words themselves.

Because of her careful use of these poetic devices, Brooks is able to compress the prose narrative, drawing fine outlines of mood, emotions, thought, and events without having to fill in many details. By eliminating the nonessential fact, by creating nuance, we touch, see, and hear the whole much in the same way a few deft lines by an accomplished artist can suggest the entire human body. Abstraction of form is only possible because we recognize, know, *what* is being suggested. But even more than recognizing the mood, emotion, event, we can concentrate on its essence, without the distraction of superfluous details that can sometimes obscure rather than reveal. And because of Brooks's distillation, our experience is more focused, more intense.

But poetic devices are not enough to make a novella. The form, by definition, involves some kind of narrative, some reflection of external as well as internal reality, some development of character, as well as a structure that shows the organic relationship between these elements. So while Brooks employed poetic devices to advantage in ***Maud Martha,*** she also had to utilize the techniques of fiction. Yet the line between her poetic and prose techniques is not a hard one, for her creation of nuance is especially critical to the overall design of the novella. Not only does each vignette evoke the essence of a specific mood, emotion, thought or event, it contributes to a composition that suggests the essence of Maud Martha's character and the pattern that is her life. Brooks's poetic sensitivity is especially apparent in the novella's structure, for she usually selects only those moments that accomplish two things: reinforce the outline of a pattern that is repeated in many other lives and is being reenacted here, while paradoxically focusing on Maud Martha's individuality. The effect is that of a ritual performed for time immemorial by different actors, who can vary the pattern only slightly—the actor this time being an ordinary girl from Chicago. The tension between these two elements, a pattern that seems prescribed and Maud Martha's transformation of it, moves the narrative.

The pattern of Maud Martha's life is presented in extremely short, condensed chapters, thirty-four in all, which are loosely divided into six phases. While Brooks's creation of nuance suggests Maud Martha's inner life, the chapter divisions are the external structure of the novel. These divisions are stages in the universal process of becoming an adult and therefore an outline of societal configurations of custom, culture, and historical forces which help to shape that individual. Thus the phases of early childhood and school, adolescence, courtship, work, marriage, the beginning of a family, the impact of the Depression of the 1930s and the war in the 1940s are a general outline of life for a young American girl growing up in the 1930s and 1940s. The moments Brooks selects to focus on in these divisions, however, are to a large extent a reflection of her view of that external reality. In concretizing the universal outline, she stresses both the rituals of a black family and community. She outlines the individuality of the girl-woman Maud Martha while emphasizing the impact of the particular concept of beauty, as well as the societal limits of being a woman, upheld by her community, on her personality. She focuses on the ordinary tone of Maud Martha's life while stressing the complexity of her inner character. Because we know, in general, the universal concept of growing up, because we know, in general, about family life and community, because we know, in general, the way that girls and women should be, she can evoke these configurations through nuance while emphasizing the uniqueness of Maud Martha's character and context. Thus, the "racial element is organic not imposed." So is her portrayal of womanhood and of the ordinary person.

At the crux of Brooks's composition is the development of her central actor. Of course; the chronology of the novella is its outer movement, but it is Maud Martha's sensibility, her perception of the world, that enlivens the narration. Yet Brooks does not use the "I," the first person point of view. As is her custom in many of her poems (e.g., **"The Rites for Cousin Vit," "Mrs. Small"**), the author creates a character for whom she cares intensely, but from whom she is clearly detached. And though the substance of the novel is told through Maud Martha's eyes, Brooks suggests, by her use of the objective third person, that other eyes see what hers see. While the reader feels intimately connected to Maud Martha he/she is constantly a ware of the world around Maud Martha as separate from and yet connected to her. Brooks use of an omniscient narrator who sees through Maud Martha's eyes emphasizes the sensibility of her central actor solidly located in a world of many others. The beginning of the vignette "Tim" illustrates how effective this technique is as a means of establishing Maud Martha's relationship to the outer world:

> Oh, how he used to wiggle!—do little mean things! do great big wonderful things! and laugh laugh laugh.
>
> He had shaved and he had scratched himself through the pants. He had lain down and ached for want of a woman. He had married. He had wiped out his nostrils with bits of tissue paper in the presence of his wife and his wife had turned her head, quickly, but politely, to avoid seeing them as they dropped softly into the toilet, and floated. He had a big stomach and an alarmingly loud laugh. He had been easy with the ain'ts and sho-nuffs. He had been drunk one time, only one time, and on that occasion had done the Charleston in the middle of what was then Grand Boulevard and is now South Park, at four in the morning. Here was a man who had absorbed the headlines in the Tribune, studied the cartoons in Collier's and the Saturday Evening Post.
>
> These facts she had known about her Uncle Tim. And she had known that he liked sweet potato pie. But what were the facts that she had not known, that his wife, her father's sister Nannie, had not known? The things that nobody had known.

Clearly, Tim and his life exist outside of Maud Martha's head, but it is her language that articulates his individuality. And it is also her language that indicates that she is a woman, is black, and lives in a certain section of Chicago. The way she chooses details that appear trivial on the surface but cumulatively communicate a feeling for and a knowledge of this man, the way she focuses on intimate details that emphasize his relationships with others, are styles of speaking that often indicate a woman's voice. The content of these details tells us that he is a working-class black man who lives in Chicago and is somewhat interested in the world beyond him. And it is typical of Maud Martha's personality that she would ask what was beneath the surface—What were "the things that nobody had known?"

The qualities of Maud Martha's language is, in fact, of considerable importance to the major theme of the novella. Brooks carefully constructs Maud Martha's voice as that of a woman. The images she uses throughout the book are often derived from the world of the home, the world of cooking, of flowers, ferns and furniture, the world of emotional relationships—worlds that have traditionally been seen as woman's domain. And much of what Maud Martha says is not said aloud; it is usually her internal conversation with herself, since her observations, critiques, and musings are not considered important. There is also a way in which her persistent attention to size (which sometimes stems from her own feeling of littleness) connotes "the smaller sex," as well as the ordinary person, a scale that is reflected in the tinyness of the novel itself. And it is often because she understands that there is sometimes so much in what appears to be so little that she gleans many insights about herself and her world.

In fact, the critical aspects of Maud Martha's sensibility are her ability to see beneath the mundane surface of things and to transform the little that is allowed her into so much more than it originally was. As Paule Marshall puts it, "In her daily life, Maud Martha functions as an artist. In that way this novel carries on the African tradition that the ordinary rituals of daily life are what must be made into art." In her adolescence, Maud Martha is able to put this insight into words in the vignette, "At the Regal."

> To create—a role, a poem, picture, music a rapture in stone: great. But not for her.
>
> What she wanted was to donate to the world a good Maud Martha. That was the offering, the bit of art, that could not come from any other.
>
> She would polish and hone that.

That awareness of her own being, as valuable, unique, as created by herself yet connected to those around her, marks her personal development. So that she can refuse to be devalued by her potential employer, Mrs. Burns-Cooper, though there is only "a pear in her ice box and one end of rye bread." She can be hurt by her husband's desire to be a social somebody, understand how that is linked to his hidden dislike of her dark skin and heavy hair and yet maintain her own sense of worth, precisely because she has developed her own standards, her own concept of the valuable.

It is the articulation of this value in Brooks's unheroic ordinary black girl from Chicago, a value that is almost always celebrated in the heroic, the extraordinary, the male, that marks the distinctive language, movement, substance of ***Maud Martha.*** Through her use of nuance, Brooks is able to present this celebration in its essential form, suggesting that Maud Martha is one of any number of ordinary people, who, against the limits of the mundane life, continue to create themselves.

R. Baxter Miller (essay date 1986)

SOURCE: "'Define . . . the Whirlwind': Gwendolyn Brooks' Epic Sign for a Generation," in *Black American Poets Between Worlds, 1940-1960,* edited by R. Baxter Miller, University of Tennessee Press, 1986, pp. 160-73.

[In the following essay, Miller examines the major themes and structure of In the Mecca. *According to Miller, Brooks draws upon Anglo-American poetry, Judeo-Christian myth, and folklore to explore the paradox of the American Dream within the context of African-American experience.]*

For twenty-three years, Gwendolyn Brooks tried to write her epic ***In the Mecca*** (1968). Her portraits of the Black community began with ***Street in Bronzeville*** (1945) and continued with ***Annie Allen*** (1949), ***Maud Martha*** (1953), and ***Bean Eaters*** (1960). But these books did not fulfill her ambition to write in the heroic genre. An epic should rank with the classics; it should portray the narrator's journey, the obstacles encountered, and the final vision of victory.

Brooks tried to write a Black epic in the title poem of ***Annie Allen*** but failed. Because the style was too lofty for the theme, an unintentional mock epic resulted. She had heeded the critics too carefully; their requests had led her to substitute Germanic mythology for the Black folk life that she knew. If Latin and Greek diction replaced the Black vernacular, the folk voice would not be evident.

Before Brooks attempted an epic again, she wrote ***Maud Martha.*** In this autobiographical novel, she practiced the technique of focusing upon the life of one woman and the characters and problems come upon. Brooks tested, too, her skill for creating an undramatized narrator, the fictional self conceived in the work, who can enter characters' minds or withdraw into objectivity. Her next book, ***The Bean Eaters*** (1960), continued some good poems, especially those concerning the fifties, yet few of these verses demonstrated majestic finish and thematic depth. The poems did not rival the fine sequences of sonnets that end her first two volumes. Once again she wanted to attempt a long poem. Could free verse and ballad succeed where rhyme royal and sonnet had not? The next book would tell. A year after its publication (1969), George Starvros, an interviewer for *Contemporary Literature,* would question: "Let me ask you about the character in your poetry and in your novel ***Maud Martha. In the Mecca,*** your most recent volume, portrays life in a large city building. ***A Street in Bronzeville*** gave similar vignettes of people in the city. The same, I think, can be said of all your work." Brooks replied, "It's a fascination of mine to write about ghetto people there." One can evaluate her success in this effort, first in light of the Anglo-American tradition of poetry, next in the paradox of the American Dream, and finally in some skillful use of techniques such as Christian myth, parody, and narrative distancing. ***In the Mecca*** is a most complex and intriguing book; it seeks to balance the sordid realities of urban life with an imaginative process of reconciliation and redemption.

Before an explication of the title poem, one needs to know some background. In her interview with Starvros, Brooks comments:

> . . . when I was nineteen and had just gotten out of junior college, I went to the Illinois State Employment service to get a job. They sent me to the Mecca building to a spiritual advisor, and he had a fantastic practice; lucrative. He had us bottling up medicine as well as answering letters. Not real medicine but love charms and stuff like that he called it, and delivered it through the building . . .

Brooks's explanation here closely correlates with the description of Mecca that appears on the back of her title page:

> . . . a great gray hulk of brick, four stories high, topped by an ungainly smokestack, ancient and enormous, filling half of the block north of Thirty-Fourth Street between State and Dearborn . . . the Mecca building is U-shaped. The dirt court-yard is littered with newspapers and tin cans, milk cartons and broken glass. . . . Iron fire escapes run up the building's face and ladders reach from them to the roof. There are four main entrances, two on Dearborn and two on State Street. At each is a gray stone and threshold and over each is carved "The Mecca." (The Mecca was constructed in 1891, a splendid palace, or showplace of Chicago).

The date of 1891 is significant because it designates the post-Darwinian world. In American history, industrialization had ended the dream of an agrarian world. The Chicago Mecca, in this light, becomes ironic when one considers the other Mecca, the holiest city of Islam and birthplace of Mohammed. Having wanted to write two thousand lines, Brooks settles for slightly more than eight hundred. She says: "This poem will not be a statistical report. I'm interested in a certain detachment, incisiveness. I wish to present a large variety of personalities against a mosaic of clarity, affairs, recognizing that the *grimmest* of these is likely to have a streak or two streaks of sun." The intention is to expand a dramatization of individual scene into universal type so as "to touch every note in the life of this block-long block-wide building would be to capsulize the gist of black humanity in general."

The simple plot and structure of **"In the Mecca"** (the poem) present an urban setting. For convenience one can divide the narrative into three sections. Part I sets forth the return home from work of Mrs. Sallie Smith, mother of nine. The focus here is on the neighbors that she encounters and on the characterizations of her children. In the second part, the shortest, the woman notices that Pepita, one of her girls, is missing. This prompts the first search through the tenement and allows for further characterization and biblical parody. Part II also concerns the paradox of American myth. The longest section is Part III, which constitutes almost half of the verse. Here the police retrace the Smiths's search. Because of its themes and styles, Part III is probably the richest. The following contribute to its power: militant declarations, interracial lovemaking, rhetorical questions, and Christian myth. The poem ends with the discovery of Pepita's corpse under the bed of Jamaican Edward.

"In the Mecca" represents opposite strains of the Anglo-American tradition. One finds a naturalistic version of Walt Whitman, by way of the industrial age, and the redemptive, if frustrated, potential that characterizes the world of T. S. Eliot. But these influences work so that the peculiarities of the Black American experience transform them into a new and creative vision. By adapting to the social forces of the sixties, the poet uses a new milieu. Her canvas is a most demanding time in American history. For this and other times, Gwendolyn Brooks holds to light the soundness of body and mind against the decline of courage and assurance, a lapse which emerged with modernity and the shadow of the holocaust. She continues to believe that imaginative and verbal power challenge and balance finally the danger which posits the insignificance of human life and the indifference to human extinction. For her generation, the defining emblem is ultimately the whirlwind, the collapse of self-confidence, the failure to transform social ill once more into epic victory and to reclaim from the time before the holocaust, and the later accusation of "reverse discrimination" in the United States, the heroic and blues-esque will of Black hope. Whereas for Margaret Walker, cleansing has been the metaphor for the perspective which woman takes on historical and cosmic evil, the depth here every bit as great as Melville's "mystery of iniquity," for Brooks the sign is medication. The artistic process itself plays out the action of healing, while the poem serves as both epic quest and sacramental liberation.

Mary Melodie, one of Mrs. Sallie's daughters, shows this turmoil. She likes "roaches, / and pities the gray rat." To her, headlines are "secondary," even though she knows that "blood runs like a ragged wound through the ancient flesh of the land." The imagery implies the naturalism of Richard Wright and others, for to such writers people are manipulated by forces beyond their control. Yet Brooks's point is not that life is crushed inevitably, it is, rather, that even the most lowly insect is sacred. Such a proposition returns a reader to Emerson's belief that each individual reflects all Being. It leads similarly to Whitman's indebted idea that a leaf of grass indicates Eternal Reality. In her description of Mary Melodie, the narrator disorients the reader. Although the imagery indicates naturalism, the statement suggests transcendentalism. To Mary, the deaths of roaches signify what pervades all Life. The naturalism after 1850 tempers the romantic vision, when the undramatized narrator withdraws from Mary's mind:

> Trapped in his privacy of pain
> the worried rat expires,
> and smashed in the grind of a rapid heel
> last night's roaches lie.

This suggestion of the post-Darwinian universe reinforces the date of 1891 on the copyright page. Similarly it recalls the imagery that helps depict Prophet Williams, an "engine / of candid steel hugging combustibles." Mrs. Sallie describes three of her children—Emmett, Cap, and Casey:

> skin wiped over bones
> for lack of chub and chocolate
> and ice-cream cones,
> for lack of English muffins
> and boysenberry jam.

The ensuing question is a twentieth-century one and could suit well the wasteland: "What shall their redeemer be"? That Brooks' version has a concrete setting in Chicago adds to the intensity of her effect.

The poverty of the three children mentioned above is as real in the second part as in the first. The levels of the narrator's dramatization in verse in the second part move from the particular to the general: personal, racial, urban, and human. By giving a setting of the city, the narrator implies a need for the pastoral, since the human mind conceives by contrasts. It is striking, indeed, to find in her compressed style, resembling that of Pound and Eliot, the truth of Thomas Gray. Still it was this eighteenth-century poet of graveyards who wrote once on the same theme of death concerning the human potential and the genius that can redeem reality.

> And they [the children] are constrained . . .
> upon fright and remorse and their stomachs . . .
> are rags of grit.
> . . . .
> many flowers start, choke, reach up,
> want help, get it, do not get it,
> rally bloom, or die on the wasting vine.

From the narrator's observation, the plot reverts to a drama of poetry, where Mrs. Sallie still performs the lead. The image and tone suggest both the Old Testament and the folk ballad. "No More Auction Block." In the first part, one finds an emphasis on lost children; in the second, there is an implication of Black death, which is archetypal. The present only foreshadows Pepita's end: "One of my children is gone."

That Don Lee, a poet of the sixties, appears in **"In the Mecca"** recreates him as a man of its imaginative world as well as a man of history. The Lee in the poem lives at the midpoint between mimesis and reality. He wants "not a various America . . . a new nation / under nothing." One must remember that this Lee is a tenant in the building described, as are all of the other characters. Should the reader elect to jump from the mimetic world to the historical one, he may get into trouble. Like the real Lee (Madhubuti), he may find that only one portrait in the poem is truly distinguished:

> Way-Out Morgan is collecting guns
> in a tiny fourth-floor rooms.
> He is not hungry, even, though skillfully lean.
> He flourishes, ever, on porridge or pat bean
> pudding or wiener soup—fills fearsomely
> on visions of Death to-the-Hordes-of-the White
> Man.

Madhubuti, of course, has his own followers and his ideology. Here, however, the latter spoils his opportunity to appreciate fully the range of Gwendolyn Brooks. She does depict Morgan with the imagery and power necessary to make him real. But she portrays John Tom, too (no incidental name), St. Julia Jones, and others who have different beliefs. All live in this decaying city; only through imagination can the reader constantly sustain their opposing visions. But in ***Mecca*** sustentation is all.

The final two hundred lines show once more the influence of Eliot. The refrain, in particular, indicates a sordid world that has profaned what once was sacred: "How many care Pepita?" The prostitutes and harlots are unconcerned, as the phallic imagery shows: "the obscene gruntings / the dull outwittings / the flabby semi-rhythmic shufflings." Equally obscene are those people, young or old, who make vulgar love. Preoccupied with their own lives, past and present, the characters lack any answers, and the narrator will have to give her own. These inhabitants of the city can no more acknowledge the sacredness of procreation than Alfred, the confused poet, can see that divinity is already within him:

> Hush.
> An agitation in the bush.
> Occulded trees.
> Mad life heralding the blue heat of God
> snickers in a corner of the west windowsill.

Other characters inhabit this Mecca, Brooks's wasteland, though they number too many to receive more than passing attention. Among them are Dakara, the reader of *Vogue;*

Aunt Tippie and Zombie Bell, who are undramatized; Mr. Kelly, the beggar with long gray hair; Gas Cady, a grave robber; the janitor, a political person; Queenie King, an "old poem silvering in the noise"; and Wallace Williams, proclaimer of his virility. To all, the narrator's answer to the rhetorical question applies equally: "these little care, Pepita, what befalls a / nullified saint or forfeiture (or child)."

Set against this background, the description of Alfred becomes particularly significant, for it suggests that the world has passed from hope to hopelessness. For his authorities, Alfred cites Baudelaire, Browning, and Neruda, but his best trick is to parody Whitman. To affirm the redemptive potential of the human spirit, the nineteenth-century poet wrote: "Good-bye and hail! my fancy." To deprive humankind of such belief, Alfred expresses the opposite: *"Farewell, and Hail!* Until farewell again." Tension separates the literary vision of the past from that of the present.

Other observations show that this is less the world of Thomas Gray and Walt Whitman than that of T. S. Eliot. Consider Aunt Dill, who wears "Tabu" perfume. Little Papa, probably her husband, has been dead for nine years, and all of her children were still-births. As a woman who loves God, she reminds the reader of St. Julia. More importantly, she illustrates the paradox that Pepita faced: to grow into a woman who should be shunned or to die in the innocence of youth. Dill

> Is not
> true-child-of God for are we ever to
> be children? are we never to mature,
> be lovely lovely? be soft Woman
> rounded and darling . . . almost caressable . . .
> and certainly wearing *Tabu* in the name of the
> Lord.

Usually ambivalent in attitude, Alfred hates Mecca, when he confesses,

> something, something in Mecca
> continues to call! Substanceless
> . . . .
> an essential sanity black and electric
> builds to a reportage and
> redemption
> . . . .
> A material collapse
> that is Construction.

From Alfred, however, one will hardly get the opinion of the undramatized narrator or the implied author. Since the beginning, Brooks has portrayed him as a weak man and an inadequate intellectual. Pepita, on the contrary, is a true poet, just as Alfred is a false one. Despite her youth, she responded to life with sincerity and sensitivity: "'I touch'—she said once—'petals of a rose. / A silky feeling through me goes.'" For a brief moment the reader receives an alternative vision set against the urban chaos of squalor and hopelessness.

The urban setting reveals the paradox of the American dream. At the beginning, the narrator shifts the focus from her reader to a persona. By combining the imperative and the expository, the verse commences: "Sit where the light corrupts your face. / Mïes Van der Rohe retires from grace. / And the fair fables fall." Thomas Earl, one of Mrs. Sallie's children, loves an American folk figure. In tone, however, the narrator questions the validity of John Chapman, now transformed into American legend. She does not mention Mecca, Saudi Arabia, but its reputation for uncultivability suits well the imagery and myth:

> It is hard to be Johnny Appleseed.
> The ground shudders.
> The ground springs up;
> hits you with gnarls and rust,
> derangement and fever, or blare and clerical
> treasons.

Characterizations in the narrative parody American myth. Melody Mary, Thomas Earl, and Briggs have "gangs rats appleseed." Examine each word within the quotation mark, first as an entity and then as a whole. Each of the first two images implies the urban experience, but the last suggests the frontier. The collectivity of the line leaves the reader with two questions. Is the idea that "gangs" or "rats," as social reality, corrupt myth and dream, "appleseed," beyond recognition? Or can myth, "Appleseed," redeem the ghetto from "gangs" and "rats"? By their very disjunction such inquiries mislead, for the purpose here is to create not a separation of perspectives but a unity composed of alternative points of view.

One must measure American ideals against the social reality of Mecca. In one scene Emmett, a daughter of Mrs. Sallie, seizes the telephone from John Tom. Considered on various levels of meaning, this incident becomes complex. In a fine wordplay on time and the American Dream, the narrator recreates the folk legend of the submissive Black: "Despite the terror and the derivation, / despite the not *avuncular* frontier, / John Tom, twice forty in 420, claims / Life sits or blazes in this Mecca." When the narrator intervenes, Tom has provoked already the "calm and dalliance" of law. On a second level, the narrator becomes unintentionally ambiguous. An exclamation that concerns the size of Pepita results in the American Dream ironically rendered. The twist is that one can be small in thoughts as well as in dimensions: "How shall the Law allow for *littleness!* / How shall the Law enchief the chapters of / wee brownblack chime, we brown-black chastity." With the arrival of the impersonal policemen begins a second trip through the Mecca, one which ends in the discovery of the dead child. The officers and the character Amos have different ideologies, since the latter is a bitter militant. He says of a personified America: "Bathe her in her beautiful blood."

"In the Mecca," the title poem, portrays the urban scene through a straight or ironic use of Christian myth and through parody. Throughout the plot, the verse changes the point of view between the narrator and her characters. The situation of Briggs, another of Mrs. Sallie's children, reworks a central motif in ***Maud Martha:*** at some point human concern passes from social reality—a difficult concept with which to deal—to religion and forgetfulness. The narrator first enters into the character's mind and then withdraws. In the initial description of the young man there comes ironic detachment, but after the reader learns about his problems with the gangs in his neighborhood, the vision comes from within: "Immunity is forfeit, love / is luggage, hope is heresy." The narrator, nevertheless, can step back from the character and speak directly; she can explain human psychology brilliantly: "there is a central height in pity / past which man's hand and sympathy cannot go."

Reviewing the first 254 lines of the poem shows that they have described, first, Mrs. Sallie's return home; second, her children; and third, Alfred, the neurotic artist. But line 255 begins the inciting incident, which both the poem and its reader must resolve. Where is Pepita, Sallie's ninth and missing child? The abrupt shift from the narrator's heightened style shocks when Sallie's children reply emphatically in the Black vernacular: "*Ain seen er I ain seen er I ain seen er / Ain seen er I ain seen er I ain seen er.*"

Like most characters in Mecca, Loam Norton worries more about his own concerns than about Mrs. Sallie's daughter. He remembers Belsen and Dachau, the prison camps of World War II, and possibly his own children. But in a parody of the Twenty-third Psalm the narrator interrupts and holds the stage:

> The Lord was their shepherd
> Yet did they want.
> Joyfully, would they have lain in jungles or pastures,
> walked beside waters. Their gaunt
> souls were not restored, their souls were banished.
> . . . .
> Goodness and mercy should follow them
> all the days of their death.

For her character St. Julia Jones, the narrator parodies with equal fidelity the same passage. There the effect was less a religious cynicism than a folk joy. Sallie Smith saw Julia, who asked:

> "Isn't our Lord the greatest to the brim?
> The light of my life. And I lie late
> past the still pastures. And meadows. He's the comfort
> and wine and piccalilli for my soul.
> He hunts me up the coffee for my cup.
> Oh how I love that Lord."

When Alfred dreams of being a red bush "In the West Virginia autumn," the image implies the appearance of the Lord to Moses (Exodus 2:3). The narrator knows that man, by being alive, is already divine; Alfred doubts: "the bush does not know that it flames." The force of the ending comes from a repetition of this tone. Jamaican Edward "thrice denies any involvement with Pepita," just as the Peter of the New Testament (St. Matthew 26:4) refuses to acknowledge Christ. The girl lies beneath Edward's cot in the dust. Despite differences in sex and age, she resembles Jesus.

If the title poem, Part I of ***In the Mecca,*** shows the callousness of the people in the ghetto, Part II, "After Mecca," offers a corrective or redeeming vision. Here Brooks takes historical figures from the sixties and elevates them to a level of myth where they transcend life. First she describes Medgar Evers, the Civil Rights leader assassinated in 1963. Never settling for a mere recording of history, she transforms fact into a tercet of prophecy: "Roaring no rapt arise-ye to the dead, he / leaned across tomorrow. People said that / he was holding clean globes in his hands." In this section, Brooks goes beyond description to symbolism. She reshapes history to make it reflect social vision, created form, and human imagination. Next she portrays Malcolm X, the Black leader slain in 1965. The emphasis, however, should fall not upon history alone but upon Malcolm's role as a political magician. Since the beginning of the volume, such a type of human being has evolved. An artist, like a magician, seeks to create a new order of reality, although the former wants to change the physical world and the latter to institute an imaginative one. By the power of words, the writer seeks to mesmerize her reader with the spell of form. Alfred was a poet, if not a great one; by her life and death, Pepita was more exemplary. The narrator of the verse in **"In the Mecca"** was, too, for only in her role as seer and harmonizer could she find irony and avoid despair. To envision Malcolm means to reconstruct the many types that precede, as word-maker, ironist, visionary, and prophet:

> in a soft and fundamental hour
> a sorcery devout and vertical
> beguiled the world.

He opened us—
Who was a key
who was a man.

At the end of ***In the Mecca*** redemptive vision depends upon two poems: **"The Sermon on the Warpland"** and **"The Second Sermon on the Warpland"** (hereafter **"Second Sermon"**). The first demonstrates Brooks's ability to portray reality initially from one point of view and then from another, which clarifies the original. The poet reverts to her habit of coining words, as necessary. What does "Warpland" mean? If the word "Sermon" parodies Christ's speech on the Mount, "Warpland" implies not geographical place but military design—a "war planned"—and the problem of distortion, the "warpland." Yet the several strengths, the speakers in the verse, express the opposite yearnings of the human spirit: "Say that our Something is doublepod contains / seeds for the coming hell and health together." The voice of a Black militant, shortly afterward, recalls Amos or Way-Out-Morgan in the title poem. But in this world of pervasive irony and contradiction, speech must end in an oxymoron.

Prepare to meet
(sisters brothers) the harsh and terrible weather;
the pains;
the bruising; the collapse of bestials, idols.
. . . .
the seasoning of the perilously sweet!
the health, the heralding of the *clear obscure!*
[emphasis mine]

To this voice, Brooks adds a corrective or balancing resonance. Perhaps her greatest gift is a talent for creating opposite viewpoints within the same poetic world. With equal adeptness she can imagine the militant and renew the meaning of Christ's words to His disciple, Peter (St. Matthew 16:18). In both instances she stresses universality within the framework of the Black American experience. To one who has read ***In the Mecca*** as an objective correlative, the narrator here becomes Pepita, resurrected and grown into womanhood. The figure is older and maternal:

"Build now your church, my brothers, sisters.
Build.
. . . .
Build with lithe love. With love like lion eyes.
With love like morningrise.
With love like black, our black—
luminously indiscreet;
complete; continuous."

Immediately following this poem, **"Second Sermon"** results in a final triumph for the human imagination: "This is the urgency Live: / and have your blooming in the noise of the whirlwind." The verse has four parts. The first gives the theme quoted last; the second emphasizes the need to give form, to "stylize the flawed utility." In the third division one discovers the chaos against which the imagination conceives. At the end (IV), comes a description of Big Bessie, who stands in the wild weed.

What a metaphor that whirlwind is. From it, one can look at various angles and see diverse personalities, including the arrogantly indifferent, inhumanely callous, and hopelessly contemplative. The narrator's voice reaches back to the end of ***Annie Allen.*** There, for the first time in Brooks's verse, a speaker possessed some intuitive truth which neither the characters in the poem nor the readers outside fully understood. The observer here is not a well-rounded character; she is, rather, the Imaginative Mind that resolves disparities:

Not the easy man, who rides above them all,
not the jumbo brigand,
not the pet bird of poets, that sweetest sonnet,
shall straddle the whirlwind.
Nevertheless, live.

The third and fourth parts show that imaginative vision can save the listeners in the world of Mecca. By perceiving this world, in its contradictions and ironies, the observer has ordered chaos. Is this the final paradox?

All about are cold places,
all about are the pushmen, and jeopardy, theft—
all about are the stormers and scramblers but
. . . .
Live and go out
Define and
Medicate the whirlwind.

The noblest virtue of Big Bessie, the woman who concludes the volume, is imagination. Without disillusionment, she can look at life and survive. Brooks owes part of the imagery to Langston Hughes' Semple: "Big Bessie's *feet* hurt like nobody's business / but she stands—bigly—under the unruly scrutiny, stands in the / wild weed (emphasis added). By vision and endurance, the Big Bessies redeem the city in which the Pepitas are slain.

For twenty-three years, Gwendolyn Brooks had sought this balance of vision. In ***Street in Bronzeville,*** she had been a poet of the unheroic, but the folk religion lingered. It manifested itself at the end of ***Annie Allen*** and subsided in ***Maud Martha*** and ***Bean Eaters*** only to reappear more intensely in ***Mecca.*** By then Brooks had practiced ironic detachment and varying distance of narration. Drawing upon Christian myth and different strains of Anglo-American poetry helped her to enrich an epic in which the narrator is heroine. From a certain vision of Chicago as wasteland, Brooks moved to a double perspective of destruction and creation; from Pound and Eliot, her journey led back to Whitman. But the reason is not that Whitman is especially important. It is only that he is romantic in some way that Black folk are: rebelling against constraint, hoping for natural redemption from the depths of an industrial age. If the city corrupts the romantic vision, does it matter? Revealing the paradox of the American Dream suffices, for to show one's reader paradise is not the only way to save his soul.

In the aesthetic formulations, Gwendolyn Brooks remains the talented poet. She imposes the personal voice upon the sources and archetypes of the literary generation. Through the quest for epic form, she combines the impulse toward architectonic space with prophetic invocation, fusing at once the written and the spoken word. Often when she draws upon Judaeo-Christian, historical, and folk sources, through the ornate style or through the vernacular, she opposes the id to the superego, balancing the contradictory tensions which inform human existence. With metaphoric power and intellectual depth, she reconfigures the events of modern history into complex symbol. Whatever her invaluable contributions to the current era, especially from 1945 to 1986, her poetry still signifies two generations past. Yet her language subsumes and transcends historicity.

Claudia Tate (essay date 1987)

SOURCE: "Anger So Flat: Gwendolyn's Brooks's *Annie Allen*," in *A Life Distilled: Gwendolyn Brooks, Her Poetry and Fiction,* edited by Maria K. Mootry and Gary Smith, University of Illinois Press, 1987, pp. 140-52.

[*In the following essay, Tate examines the form, structure, and heroine of* Annie Allen. *As Tate notes, Brooks presents "an emotionally charged satirical comment about the tragedy of a woman's inactive life, a tragedy compounded by racial prejudice."*]

In 1950 Gwendolyn Brooks became the first black American to receive a Pulitzer Prize for literature for ***Annie Allen*** (1949), a collection of rigorously technical poems, replete with lofty diction, intricate word play, and complicated concatenations of phrases. One particular poem, **"The Anniad,"** which constitutes the second of three sections in the collection, is especially characteristic of Brooks's fascination with "the mysteries and magic of technique." In fact, **"The Anniad"** seems to possess an inordinate amount of word mystery and magic. Brooks readily admits that **"The Anniad"** is a "labored" poem, although she also says that she derived a great deal of satisfaction from writing it: "What a pleasure it was to write that poem! . . . I was just very conscious of every word; I wanted every phrase to be beautiful, and yet to contribute to the whole . . . effect."

Perhaps the delight she took in creating **"The Anniad"** was responsible for her indulgence in the complicated techniques that densely pattern the poem's texture, as well as those in the other two sections of the book, "Notes from the Childhood and the Girlhood" and "The Womanhood."

The complicated techniques in ***Annie Allen*** produce virtual curiosity pieces of intellectual verse, which her critics consistently mention as prize-worthy. But by the same token, these critics seldom focus full critical attention on this book; instead, they discuss those collections that employ subtle social commentary and realistic depictions of urban settings. As a result, ***A Street in Bronzeville*** (1945), ***The Bean Eaters*** (1960), ***Selected Poems*** (1963), and ***In the Mecca*** (1968) receive the lion's share of critical coverage. By contrast, ***Annie Allen*** seems peculiarly abstract and extremely esoteric. These characteristics are responsible for that collection being labeled "intellectual" and "academic," and they are also responsible for its smaller allotment of critical attention.

When we examine the surface texture of the poems that map out the events in the poetic life of Annie Allen, the imaginary focal character who is the namesake for this collection, we find no explicit social statement regarding race, caste, or gender. These poems are found in the first two sections of the book, "Notes from the Childhood and the Girlhood" and "The Anniad," and specifically include **"the birth in a narrow room," "Maxie Allen," "the parents: people like our marriage Maxie and Andrew," "Sunday Chicken," "the relative," "downtown vaudeville," "the ballad of late Annie," "do not be afraid of no," "my own sweet good," "The Anniad,"** and "Appendix to the Anniad." Moreover, the verbal complexity of these poems seems to work at cross-purposes with the simplicity and habitual passivity of Annie's life, in that her life reflects a virtual absence of acts of conscious volition and emotional complexity. In fact, her life seems to be comprised of her deliberate refusal both to act decisively and to reveal her emotional responses. Events in her life seem only to happen to her; seldom does she appear to be an active agent, precipitating them. Moreover, the methods used to communicate the series of incidents themselves are extremely commonplace. Hence, there is a marked disparity between the elaborate structural techniques that create the poem and the content of Annie's life that the poem depicts. This discordance constitutes curious features in the text of the poem, which compels me to ask whether the poem is simply veneered in artifice or whether the elaborate techniques that texture the poem contain interpretative significance in their own right.

I suggest that **"The Anniad,"** as well as the poems in "Notes from the Childhood and the Girlhood," are not merely cloaked in elaborate surface design, but rather, that the structural formats for the poems, in and of themselves, communicate discursive content about Annie's life, specifically her emotional response to the series of events that constitute her life. Moreover, formal devices such as diction, imagery, and meter, create the mood and atmosphere for the poems. These techniques express the author's attitude toward her subject in place of her explicit comment. Brooks combines these devices with conventional forms of satirical verse. These verse forms inherently dictate how the subject is to be regarded, that is, whether the subject is to be viewed sympathetically or critically. She further blends this technique with another source of tension found between what is said and how it is said. In literary terms, she combines satirical format with the tension created between content and its communicative image. This duality between content and its corresponding imagery converges, does not fully synthesize, into a unified interpretation. The content seems to be consistently at odds with its expression, and the resulting tension contours and concatenates each poem.

For example, we frequently find that Brooks seems to be ridiculing aspects of Annie's life, but Brooks does not do so by employing explicitly critical, descriptive language. To the contrary, she employs conventional, formal, satirical techniques for expressing her attitude toward her subject. Instead of outwardly criticizing Annie's mother, we find the mother-daughter relationship depicted in **"Maxie Allen"** rendered in doggerel. Doggerel is a satirical form that inherently suggests ridicule independent of content. Thus, the loose meter itself informs us that Brooks is censuring the poem's narrative content. This technique of using form to communicate content is repeatedly employed in both "Notes from the Childhood and the Girlhood" and **"The Anniad."** In fact, this tension climaxes in **"The Anniad,"** where Brooks relies on mock-heroic conventions in order to underscore the gravity of her criticism of Annie's adult life.

On first meeting Annie Allen, we find her described as an ordinary black girl, born in an urban ghetto in the early 1900s. Her parents, Maxie and Andrew Allen, are hardworking, decent, very moralistic people, who believe that their kindness, simplicity, and humility will merit them their just rewards. All they need to do is wait patiently for their receipt. Annie is the necessary product of such a union. She is a docile, well-behaved child, whose total dependence on her mother's dispensation of approval and subsequent affection shapes her life. Maxie has suppressed the possibility of disobedience in her daughter. Maxie has also eliminated the outward expression of Annie's longings in the process by insisting that she be thankful for what she has instead of yearning for what she does not possess. In most social circles Maxie would be credited with having successfully raised a daughter; however, on close observation, we notice that her maternal wisdom has stifled Annie's willfulness and driven her imagination underground.

Brooks expresses her criticism for Maxie's ultimate failure as a mother by rendering the poem in doggerel. Here, technique, rather than merely explicit comment, is the vehicle for censuring, even ridiculing the mother's inability to nurture Annie's emerging imaginative spirit:

> Maxie Allen always taught her
> Stipendiary little daughter
> To thank her Lord and lucky star
> For eye that let her see so far,
> For throat enabling her to eat
> Her Quaker Oats and Cream-of-Wheat,
> For tongue to tantrum for the penny,
> For ear to hear the haven't-any,
> For arm to toss, for leg to chance,
> For heart to hanker for romance.

Brooks reduces all the lessons that this mother must teach her daughter in order to promote her survival and happiness to lessons in gratitude for possessions that are not adequate to nurture Annie's emotional development—Quaker Oats, Cream-of-Wheat, and a penny. In this manner the subject is trivialized and combined with the monotonous doggerel meter. These techniques communicate Brooks's criticism of Annie's mother. Moreover, whenever desire surfaces in Annie's consciousness, her response is to suppress this desire. As a result, her anger, resentment, and guilt arise, but these emotions cannot be revealed as well. Consequently, Annie represses all of her emotional responses and denies them expression by flattening them out until only her gratitude is perceptible. These repressed emotions only resurface in her daydreams. But in this imaginary realm, her desire for adventure is transformed into the wish for someone else to enact her plans. Someone else must engage her wish, and this person, we are told, is a husband.

Brooks also describes Annie as an "unembroidered," "chocolate" brown-skin girl, who is plain in appearance and excessively complaint. Yet in the place where surface pattern would be if she were pretty or spirited is her wondrous and "stupendous" imagination that fancies a private life for which she has no outward expression:

> Sweet Annie tried to teach her mother
> There was somewhat of something other. . . .
> . . .
> She did not know; but tried to tell.

Rather than try unsuccessfully to explain the life of her imagination and her longings to her mother, she conceals them within herself, again by flattening them out and, thereby, denying them visible surface expression. But no matter how hard she tries to suppress her imaginary world, it inevitably confronts the real circumstances of her life, and this confrontation creates a sense of vague dissatisfaction.

When we recall the first poem in ***Annie Allen,* "the birth in a narrow room,"** not only do we note Annie's humility, reflected in the lower case letters of the title, but we also see that this poem foreshadows the inevitable conflict between the real circumstances of her submissive life and her imaginary projections of adventure:

> "I am not anything and I have got
> Not anything, or anything to do!"—
> But prances nevertheless with gods and fairies
> Blithely about the pump and then beneath
> The elms and grapevines, then in darling
> endeavor
> By privy foyer, where the screenings stand
> And where the bugs buzz by in private cars
> Across old peach cans and old jelly jars.

Annie's admission of her feelings of personal inadequacies do not incite physical activity, but they do cause her to frolic with imaginary sprites. In this way she finds adventure among embellished commonplace objects, in the recesses of her mind. Hence, the first poem in the collection foreshadows the emerging duality in Annie's character, which is composite of her outward expression of inactivity, acquiescence, and resignation (a role prescribed for her by her mother as well as by society at large) and her inner life of fantastic, willful adventure. This type of duality develops throughout the collection to poem XV in "The Motherhood," where imaginative and suppressed longings verge upon conscious assertion, ultimately to become new directives for living.

But until that time, the only occasion when Annie demonstrates filial rebellion occurs at the funeral of a relative. Here, she displays her contrary feelings, but only when no one can witness her transgression:

> She went in there to muse on being rid
> Of relative beneath the coffin lid.
> No one was by. She stuck her tongue out; slid.
>
> Since for a week she must not play "Charmaine"
> Or "Honey Bunch," or "Singing in the Rain."

Her resentment is hidden beyond the sight of disapproval. Rather than face parental rejection for impudence, she squeezes herself into that "pinchy" space, where "[her] own sweet good[ness]" dominates her personality, and where her rebelliousness cannot be observed. Annie's behavior demonstrates that she is acutely aware of the struggle between the dual sides of her character—her external, exaggerated "sweet good[ness]" and her internal desire to create a "stupendous," autonomous self. But in order to make her dreams real, she knows she must exercise a "darling endeavor" and cast off others' expectations with the adamantly audible "no."

Brooks records Annie's attempt to say no in **"do not be afraid of no."** In this poem Annie admits that

> To say yes is to die
> A lot or a little. . . .
> . . .
> It is brave to be involved,
> To be not fearful to be unresolved.

But instead of enacting her decision to say "no" and live, she elects another way to say what she thinks is "no," although she does not realize the implications of her choice. Hence, not only does she not say "no," but she does not elect to be either involved or resolved in any course of action. She merely continues essentially as she had before. But instead of enacting her decision to say no and live, that is, to utter the word and externalize her internal life, she elects a new wish that is merely another way of saying yes: "Her new wish was to smile / When answers took no airships, walked a while." Rather than reply with the audible no, she smiles sweetly and sighs with the hope that her reluctance to speak would be perceived as the unuttered "no." But her choice of action is not effective. She forfeits the possibility of independence and continues to spin bits of an imaginary life in her daydreams, described as "spilling pretty cherries."

For Annie, there is only one acceptable way to escape from saying yes to her mother and to grasp a life of her own. That course is outlined in **"the ballad of late Annie":**

> Late Annie in her bower lay,
> Though sun was up and spinning.
> The blush-brown shoulder was so bare,
> Blush-brown lip was winning.
>
> Out then shrieked the mother-dear,
> "Be I to fetch and carry?
> Get a broom to whish the doors
> Or get a man to marry."

Annie's mother literally tells her to obey her orders or to get married (which is the only proper course to freedom beyond a mother's reign for a young woman in Annie's day). Because Annie cannot say "no" in an audible voice, her choice is to use her "own sweet good[ness]" in order to secure a man worthy of her fancying spirit. In this manner, she plans to flee her mother's dominion and establish her own kingdom with the help of a suitable mate. Moreover, the text of the poem itself is veiled in coded meaning, which can be explained by examining the act of sleeping, which is both the dominant event and the unifying, figurative motif in the poem. Here, the act of sleeping underscores Annie's languid, dormant, and unresisting character. The events described in this poem—her oversleeping and the resulting chastisement—both serve as a paradigm for Annie's thwarted emotional development and foreshadow the events described in the poetic discourse of **"The Anniad."**

We recall that Annie has not learned to say "no," but instead says nothing with a smile and a sigh. We surmise that this behavior is repeatedly misunderstood as an expression for "yes," which she has already equated with death. Then when we recall the multiple meanings of the word "late" in **"the ballad of late Annie,"** we note that not only has Annie overslept, but also that the entire poem addresses her as if she were deceased, that is as if the poem were an elegy for the unresisting Annie. Although Annie is not, in fact, dead, her defeat is clearly predicted, and this ominous shadow of defeat falls across Annie's effort to establish her domestic kingdom in **"The Anniad."**

"The Anniad" is a long poem which Brooks says deliberately alludes to Homer's *Iliad.* Although **"The Anniad"** is not of book-length proportions, like its analogue, it is an episodic, narrative poem that is long by contemporary standards. Although **"The Anniad"** does not employ a setting that is remote in time and place, and the major character does not possess heroic stature, **"The Anniad"** does conform to other epic conventions. The poem focuses on a universal problem, the deteriorating relationship between men and women. Furthermore, the poem reveals the consequences of the intervention of fate, in the form of world war, on these relationships. In addition, when we refer to *The Iliad,* we are mindful that both poems concentrate on the activity of brooding. *The Iliad* depicts Achilles' physical inactivity while he externalizes his anger and refuses to fight. **"The Anniad,"** on the other hand, depicts Annie's deliberate refusal to act with conscious volition, while she simultaneously suppresses the outward show of both her emotions and desires by relegating them to the internal region of her daydreams. The very complicated **"Anniad"** also recalls the somewhat legendary events surrounding the marriage ritual. The poem records Annie's anticipated courtship, its actuality, her marriage, separation because of war, her husband's return, his temporary infidelity, their reconciliation, followed by his permanent desertion. In other words, the poem recounts a series of girl wins boy episodes, and her ultimate loss.

Throughout these domestic crises, Annie remains sweet, good, and polite, believing that these virtues alone will ultimately merit her happiness. Therefore, in the face of turbulent domestic activity, Annie remains virtually inert and exhibits no perceivable emotional response. In fact, the absence of her emotions seems to work at cross-purposes with the complex expression that gives the details of her life their expression. Her life, although particularly eventful, seems peculiarly emotionally static. Moreover, her inability to say "no" seems to exaggerate the passivity of her inactive life. Events seem to happen to her, and her only response is to wait for these events to have occurred.

At the beginning of **"The Anniad,"** Annie is described as a brown-skin girl, reclining on her bed, daydreaming about her virgin knight. He represents freedom from her parental abode:

> Think of sweet and chocolate,
> Left to folly or to fate,
> Whom the higher gods forgot,
> Whom the lower gods berate;
> Physical and underfed
> Fancying on the featherbed
> What was never and is not.
> . . .
> Watching for the paladin
> Which no woman ever had, . . .

Annie endows her knight with fullness of character and the will to act, aspects that she is aware of but does not possess or seem to desire herself. Her imagined suitor is "paradisiacal and sad"; thus, he has broad expanses of emotions and intellect. In addition, he has height, breadth, and depth of moral as well as physical vigor. He is "Ruralist and rather bad / Cosmopolitan and kind." Hence, her potential mate possesses a full 360 degrees of character. He can say both "yes" and "no," whereas she is a flat 180 degrees of "yes," or silence with a sighing smile. She is described as a "thaumaturgic lass", her brilliance has been dulled, her height has been leveled, and her will has been rendered inactive by conventional codes of decorum. The only way she can hold onto some bit of her former thaumaturgy, brilliance, "stupendous" self, is by "Printing bastard roses [her ill-conceived daydreams] there" on her image in the looking glass. The anger and resentment she feels, because she cannot reveal the vitality of her internal life, is patted down, suppressed, and flattened like her unruly hair:

> Then emotionally aware
> Of the black and boisterous hair,
> Taming all that anger down.

Again, flattening and silencing her displeasure are the ways in which she responds to the circumstances of her life. Such responses function to inhibit the possibility of her resolving to act decisively with full conscious volition.

Annie's emotional and intellectual lives, therefore, neither synthesize nor achieve autonomy. As a result these aspects of her character retain their duality. One side surfaces as contortions of virtual physical inertia, while the other side is dynamic but remains submerged in her internal life. She counteracts the possibility of the latter surfacing by tensing her face in a hard, tight smile and by flattening the unruly volume of her "boisterous" hair. In other words, she flattens the angry contours of her face into a sighing smile, and smooths the expanding height of her rebellious, voluminous hair into a composed, compressed, and compliant style.

Our expectations for the conventional, heroic character conflict with the submissiveness of Annie's life. **"The Anniad"**'s impelling form and erudite diction seem peculiarly inappropriate for describing her inert life. Moreover, the missing expression or exalted emotions, typically found in the epic, are startling in their absence. These aspects, in juxtaposition, function to accentuate one another, disturbing us as we try to make form and content synthesize into a unified structure. As a result, first, we are forced to look beyond the description of Annie's submissive life, as seen in the narrative content of the poem, in order to determine if her emotional life is given expression in other ways. And second, we are compelled to look beyond the surface texture of the poem in order to reevaluate the suitability of epic format for the poem.

During this reevaluation process, we recall that there has consistently been a clear separation between Annie's two selves in all of the poems in the first two sections. On one hand, Annie's internal emotional complexity appears in the textual activity in the poems that depict her life; on the other hand, her external, inert life is depicted in the narrative content of **"The Anniad."** Thus, a system of reversals operates throughout the poem relating to the conflict between the content and the manner of its expression. In this context, Annie is much like a landscape of fertile hills and valleys that has been leveled to ordinary starkness. Whereas she once possessed contours of character, she has now been flattened out into a smooth plane. Whereas she was once a "stupendous" being, she has now been squeezed into a too-small, restricted space. As a result her splendor has literally been choked out of her:

> Now, weeks and years will go before she thinks
> "How pinchy is my room! how can I breathe!
> I am not anything and I have got
> Not anything, or anything to do!"—

When the reader understands the results of Annie's careful maternal and social nurturing, which are described above, the anger that Annie suppresses is located. It originates in Brooks and is transferred to the reader. Brooks incites our response not only by revealing Annie's fate of unhappiness and loneliness, but Brooks also compounds our disturbance by inciting our impatience with the poem's extreme artifice and with the seeming inappropriateness of the epic format. Thus, the erudite descriptions are, in themselves, indirect expressions of Brooks's anger, which has been suppressed and flattened out into complex, static language. In this manner, Brooks supplies Annie and her readers with the missing anger. The anger, therefore, is simply not in the narrative of the poem but in the work at large, which is the product of "the convergence of the text and the reader's response."

When we read **"The Anniad"** in this manner, the poem cannot be regarded as an epic poem, as the allusion to *The Iliad* might suggest. **"The Anniad"** is not a poem that depicts heroic character or events. To the contrary, I contend that **"The Anniad"** is a mock-heroic satire, in that commonplace characters and events have been elevated in a ceremonious manner by using lofty diction and complicated techniques. It bears repeating that this literary form is, in itself, also the embodiment of Brooks's indirect expression for anger. Hence, Brooks deliberately cloaks her own anger, arising from the events she represents in the poem, in satire as the vehicle for expressing Annie's suppressed anger. By using satire, Brooks does not have to engage in a severely direct and explicit form of censorship. The form inherently ridicules; it ridicules the destructive domestic forces in the life of a young black woman as well as those in the lives of most women. By relying on this literary form, Brooks uses it to communicate not only emotional content, but also social and moral criticism.

Although marriage, in and of itself, is not described as a destructive force in the poem, it can become the site on which the fullness of a woman's evolving character and ambitions are sacrificed. In this manner, maturity and ambitions are often exchanged for "domestic bliss." And domestic bliss is often nothing more than one spouse electing either to say "yes" or to smile in silence with a sigh. This tragic scenario is both recorded and severely ridiculed by relying on the literary form of mock-heroic satire.

The text of **"The Anniad,"** when seen as a literary work, becomes a powerful statement about the cost of extreme forms of role-playing. Consequently, the work becomes an emotionally charged satirical comment about the tragedy of a woman's inactive life, a tragedy compounded by racial prejudice. In fact, the high epic allusion is nothing more than an inversion of the epic form, and although mock-heroic satire is normally associated with a burlesque or comic presentation of its subject, here the mockery is bitter, that is, Juvenalian, in nature. This satire operates by not only relying on the narrative content of the poem, but also and more importantly by using a literary form as a vehicle for communicating both emotional and factual content.

When **"The Anniad"** is seen as a literary work that must be responded to in order to attain its interpretative significance, the work becomes a powerful statement about the cost of subscribing to extreme forms of role-definition. In this way, the poem ceases merely to be a complex, intellectual exercise, but becomes a serious statement about the destructive social and domestic rituals that are unquestioningly followed. Moreover, when we heed the color codes interwoven throughout the poem, we discern that Brooks is also criticizing the color caste system that further circumscribes Annie's life within barriers of racial prejudice. The reader's response to this woman—and to the social contingencies that design her life—is anger; this anger converges with Brooks's own, and both forms occupy the place where Annie's absent emotional response should be.

When we regard **"The Anniad"** as a satire, not only do we see the poem as an expression of cloaked anger, but we also understand how the other poems in the collection are to be read. We see that Brooks has crowded Annie's anger back into "pinchy" obscurity of form in poem after poem, where she contends it takes a little bit of patience to see the rage.

Once we have located the rage, encoded on Annie's tightly smiling face and patted-down hair, Brooks does not abandon us. She suggests a route for her sisters in spirit to take in order to escape Annie's fate and cross the "screaming weed" of desperation, referred to in the last poem of the collection, XV in "Womanhood." Here, the unidentified speaker declares that it is all right to acknowledge openly her pain:

> Men of careful turns, haters of forks in the road,
> . . .
> Grant me that I am human, that I hurt,
> That I can cry.

She contends that after the pain has been acknowledged, she must celebrate by affirming her life in the presence of other women, despite the fact that she has arrived late both to this level of self-awareness (an internal region) and to this party of women (an external event):

> Open my rooms, let in the light and air.
> . . .
> And let the joy continue. Do not hoard silence
> For the moment when I enter, tardily,
> To enjoy my height among you. And to love
> you.
> . . .

When she is asked to sit down and be quiet, she is compelled to demand "a chair, but the one with broken straw," so that she might sit, but sit uncomfortably in order to be compelled to stand. When she is told "intelligence / Can sugar up our prejudice with politeness . . .," she remembers to "extend [her] hand and teeth" in a tight, sighing smile, which is an indirect expression of anger. And finally, Brooks has her speaker demand that her sisters stand and join hands to map out new expectations:

> . . . Rise.
> Let us combine. There are no magics or elves
> Or timely godmothers to guide us. We are lost,
> must
> Wizard a track through our own screaming weed.

The word "wizard" of Gwendolyn Brooks's ***Annie Allen*** maps out the route for Annie's sisters not to take and points, instead, to another. In "wizard[ing] a track through [their] own screaming weed," they locate the untrodden course, which leads to discovering and learning how to nurture themselves.

Maria K. Mootry (essay date March 1987)

SOURCE: "'Chocolate Mabbie' and 'Pearl May Lee': Gwendolyn Brooks and the Ballad Tradition," in *CLA Journal,* Vol. XXX, No. 3, March, 1987, pp. 278-93.

[*In the following essay, Mootry discusses the appropriation of folk ballad and blues conventions in Brooks's poetry. "While, on the surface, these folk elements make her poetry more accessible to the reader," writes Mootry, "a closer examination reveals insinuations and refinements of technique that augment the complexity so characteristic of her work."*]

Among the five major volumes of Gwendolyn Brooks' poetry, one of the notably recurring poetic forms is the ballad. From **"The Ballad of Chocolate Mabbie,"** in her first volume, to **"The Ballad of Edie Barrow"** in her last major book, Brooks shows a continued interest in this popular or folk art form. Brooks' attraction to ballads is not unique. In their revolt against the artifice, formalism, and abstraction of eighteenth-century classicist poetry, romantic poets like Coleridge and Wordsworth often turned to folk ballads for subjects and techniques. They liked the fact that the ballad, as a folk form, focused on the outcasts of society, including abandoned mothers, prisoners, and beggars. At the same time, they valued the ballad's language and structure because it seemed to avoid the pretensions of eighteenth-century classicist poetry. In his famous preface to the second edition of *Lyrical Ballads,* Wordsworth maintains that the language of all poetry, like the language of the ballad, should be neutral, simple, and essentially the same as everyday speech. Coleridge and Wordsworth, however, aimed merely to *imitate* the ballad form in order to demonstrate the value of their new theory of poetics. Brooks' use of the ballad reflects a similar desire to recover a simpler, more direct, poetic form; it also reflects her belief that the poet should "vivify the commonplace."

However, Brooks goes beyond the mere imitation of ballad themes and techniques to create more varied and complex structures. The result is that while on one level her ballads are simple and direct, on another level they are deeply ironic and complex, both in theme and technique. Thus through her use of ballads, Brooks meets the demands of two ostensibly disparate audiences: the "art for art's sake" audience with its emphasis on the poem as its own excuse for being and the "common" audience who looks for familiar structures and social or moral messages. In the process, Brooks recovers the ballad tradition by using its themes and techniques; she reinvigorates that tradition by infusing it with new themes and variations; and finally, she critiques the tradition by using parodic techniques. The overall effect, however, is the revelation of contemporary, often unpleasant, truths about Afro-American and American society.

In this essay, observations of Brooks' use of the Western folk ballad tradition in her poetry will be based on the analysis of the poems **"The Ballad of Chocolate Mabbie"** and **"Ballad of Pearl May Lee,"** which appeared in her first volume, ***A Street in Bronzeville*** (1945). These poems were selected not only because they are literary ballads, but because, as their titles suggest, each is Brooksian in its emphasis on a "woman-identified" vision. Gordon Hall Gerould, in his study of the European folk ballad, notes that "the sorrows peculiar to women serve the ballad poets . . . for some of their most poignant moments." Brooks continues this thematic aspect of the European folk ballad tradition, often infusing into her own literary ballads the complex use of additional folk elements from the Afro-American spirituals and blues (sacred and secular) traditions. Before analyzing the poems, however, it may be useful to review briefly the major folk ballad conventions.

I. The Ballad Tradition

The original popular (or folk) ballad is anonymous, transmitted by oral tradition, and tells a story, often about events well known to its audience. Whatever affects the thoughts and emotions of a community may become the subject of a ballad, but the most frequent themes are unfaithful lovers, shocking murders, mysterious happenings, and political oppression. For example, the latter theme is expressed in the English ballads of Robin Hood, who defended the rights of the common people against the predatory rich. Perhaps because the story is usually well known to the audience, the ballad poet tends to present his narrative in a series of dramatically striking episodes. The audience is left to fill out the complete narrative since characterization is brief, transitions are abrupt, and action is often developed through dialogue.

The language of folk ballads is usually simple in diction and meter. However, because many ballads have been handed down from generation to generation, the diction often ranges from the Scottish or Anglo-Saxon vernacular to archaisms reflecting past poetic oral conventions or everyday usage. Inversions of syntactical structures are also common, perhaps to maintain earlier narrative conventions. Regarding stanzaic form, the typical folk ballad uses the ballad stanza, an *abcb* four-line stanza with alternating four-stress and three-stress lines. However, even where the ballad stanza is not employed, there tends to be the use of refrains and repetition of phrases or parallel phrasing. Often a refrain is repeated with only a slight change, creating what is called an incremental refrain.

Although many ballads begin *in medias res,* just as frequently the ballad employs stock opening phrases to establish its narrative structure. In any event, because of its elliptical episodic structure, colors, actions, and even dialogue are often metonymic and multifunctional. Finally, ballads often also close with some kind of summary stanza. This final stanza often continues the incremental nature of ballad repetition, as well as the simplicity with which tragic situations are presented.

These are some of the major features of the Western European folk ballad. Of course, there are many variations and exceptions to these rules, but for the purpose of this essay, these core conventions may serve as a guide in assessing how Brooks uses the folk ballad tradition and how she departs from it in two of her most powerful literary ballads.

II. **"The Ballad of Chocolate Mabbie"** and the Afro-American Sacred Tradition

In **"The Ballad of Chocolate Mabbie,"** Brooks deals with the pathos of intraracial discrimination, one of her recurring themes. Seven-year-old Mabbie falls in love with her classmate, Willie Boone, moons over him in history class, and waits for him outside the grammar school gates. In an epiphanic scene, Mabbie's erstwhile "lover" appears insouciantly in the company of a light-skinned, long-haired beauty. At the poem's conclusion, Mabbie is left to "chocolate companions" and to her own resources.

In **"The Ballad of Chocolate Mabbie,"** Brooks uses many of the European ballad conventions mentioned above. For instance, the poem begins with an opening phrase which establishes its narrative character: "*It was* Mabbie without the grammar school gates. . . ." The use of the connective "and" reinforces both the poem's plot structure and its apparent simplicity. An almost childlike progression of sentences makes up this first stanza:

> *It was Mabbie* without the grammar school
> gates.
> *And* Mabbie was all of seven.
> *And* Mabbie was cut from a chocolate bar.
> *And* Mabbie thought life was heaven. (emphasis
> mine)

Repetition appears in the phrasing, "It was Mabbie . . . / And Mabbie was . . . / And Mabbie thought. . . ." This parallel repetition recurs in the third stanza, which repeats the opening line: "It was Mabbie without the grammar school gates." The repetition becomes incremental with the closing stanza, where the opening line is again repeated with the meaningful change of one word, "without," to the word "alone," i.e., "It was Mabbie *without* the grammar school gates" (first stanza) becomes "It was Mabbie *alone* by the grammar school gates" (sixth and last stanza—emphasis mine).

Archaic or somewhat outdated usages appear unobtrusively in **"Chocolate Mabbie."** The word "without" in the poem's first line is clearly archaic; and certain words have an archaic aura, e.g., "saucily," "woe," and "lemon-*hued*" in the fifth stanza. To this suggestion of the old ballad tradition, Brooks juxtaposes modern vernacular language, particularly in the key phrase, "cut from a chocolate bar." Also noteworthy is Brook's use of predominantly Anglo-Saxon words. Often monosyllabic, often with hard consonants, and often used alliteratively, these words with Anglo-Saxon roots create a harsh if vigorous tone and reinforce Brooks' debt to the European (English) folk tradition. Examples of these key words occurring in **"Chocolate Mabbie"** include "without," "gates," "seven," "cut," "thought," "heaven," "school," "cool," "soon," "brow," and "alone." Also, the preponderance of "to be" verbs and pronouns reflects an Anglo-Saxon linguistic base. One of the few interpolations of an Afro-American vernacular phrasing in the poem occurs in the fourth line of the second stanza where Brooks describes Mabbie's ardor for Willie: "Was only her eyes were cool" is at once a balladic inversion and a Black English construction. The very absence of sustained Black English in the poem accentuates this line, which interestingly anticipates the masterful title of one of Brooks' most famous poems, **"We Real Cool."**

Turning to its stanzaic form, **"Chocolate Mabbie,"** like the traditional ballad, uses the *abcb* rhyme scheme with rhythmic alternating four-stress and three-stress lines. For instance, the first stanza of the poem scans as follows:

> It was, Mabbie without the grammar school
> gates.
> And Mabbie was all of seven.
> And Mabbie was cut from a chocolate bar.
> And Mabbie thought life was heaven.

Further balladic elements include the repetition of phrases and the use of parallelisms mentioned above, particularly the incrementally juxtaposed line which opens the first and last stanzas:

> It was Mabbie *without* the grammar school
> gates.
> . . . .
> It was Mabbie *alone* by the grammar school
> gates.

Balladic epithets also appear in such phrases as "the pearly gates," "bold Willie Boone," "lemon-hued lynx" and "sandwaves." Yet while these epithets merely *adorn* the traditional ballad, in **"Chocolate Mabbie"** they become hyperbolic, a mockery within a mock-tragedy. "Bold Willie Boone" and his "lemon-hued lynx" are inflated references to school children which infuse **"Chocolate Mabbie"** with a satiric tone. The foreshadowing voice of the narrator deepens the sense of satire when describing Mabbie's school gate vigil in the fourth stanza:

> Oh, warm is the waiting for joys, my dears,
> And it cannot be too long.
> Oh, pity the little poor chocolate lips
> That carry the bubble of song!

If exaggerated language in **"Chocolate Mabbie"** mocks the ballad tradition when it is applied to these prepubescent ordinary characters, the poem's understated plot similarly burlesques another major ballad feature, the episodic, sensationalist plot. While the plot of **"Chocolate Mabbie"** is "cinematic" in that it offers a montage-like series of images, in actuality the story is minimal. The reader observes a love-sick Mabbie outside the gates, observes Mabbie in the history class, and observes Mabbie desolately watching Willie leave with his "lemon-hued lynx." These everyday "events" in **"Chocolate Mabbie"** pale before the far more shocking events of such traditional ballads as "Sir Patrick Spence," in which a heroic sailor is involuntarily sent to his death, or "Child-Waters," where a young woman's consuming love ends in an illegitimate baby and public humiliation.

In spite of her occasional parodic stance, Brooks adds to the traditional ballad conventions a theme that is at once universal and particularlized. **"Chocolate Mabbie,"** at its core, is a poem about unrequited love. To the theme of unrequited love is added the theme of intraracial discrimination within the black community. As Arthur P. Davis has noted, this is a recurring issue in Brooks' poetry. When this theme is linked to the theme of a female child's developing identity the black community. As Arthur P. Davis has noted, this is a recurring issue in Brooks' poetry. When this theme is linked to the theme of a female child's developing identity within the black community, it may not be sensationalist, but it does take on the power of harsh revelation. The result, ultimately, is that **"Chocolate Mabbie"** is not only about the loss of love, but even more so, it is about the loss of innocence.

It is in addressing the theme of "innocence versus experience" that Brooks further modifies her use of the European ballad tradition by drawing on subjects and themes common to the Afro-American sacred folk tradition. The opening lines of **"Chocolate Mabbie"** express Mabbie's delusions of love in quasi-religious terms. To Mabbie, who "thought life was heaven," the grammar school gates have become "the pearly gates." References to "pearly gates" recur frequently in Afro-American spirituals, usually when linked to the theme of the Second Coming. This messianic theme and its attendant imagery are parodically and mockingly reconstructed in the third stanza, where Mabbie's hopes for Willie's attention are expressed in the final line: "He would surely be coming soon." Thus, in another hyperbolic strategy, Mabbie is shown as having made a religion of love. Yet, from another perspective, the folk spirituals or sacred tradition is not so much mocked as used as an analogue of secular dilemma. In a further analogy to the biblical tradition, Mabbie, like Adam and Eve, is banished from her prelapsarian state. Thus if the imagery suggests apocalyptic visions, it also looks backward to the Fall. Mabbie's "guilt" is a moot point because she, like all humans, is original sin personified, being "graven by a hand less than angelic." However, the implications are twofold. Brooks is not only speaking of original sin in a Calvinistic sense, but primarily of the social "sin" of being born black and female. In addressing this theme of loss of innocence, Brooks resorts neither to a sense of predestined fate nor to the romantic transcendence of ideal black womanhood so common to her predecessors during the Harlem Renaissance. Rather, the bitterness of Mabbie's rejection by Willie and the collapse of Mabbie's naive worldview is balanced by the implied possibility of the reconstruction of self in society. Mabbie must learn to use her personal resources, to cherish her "chocolate companions" and not to waste her personal resources, to cherish her "chocolate companions" and not to waste her time brooding over male "betrayal." As Brooks advised in her autobiography,

> [b]lack women must remember . . . [t]hat her [sic] personhood precedes her femalehood, that, sweet as sex may be, she cannot endlessly brood on Black man's blondes, blues and blunders. She is a person in the world—with wrongs to right, stupidities to outwit, *with* her man when possible, on her own when not. . . . Therefore she must, in the midst of tragedy and hatred and neglect . . . mightily enjoy the readily available: sunshine and pets and children and conversation and games and travel (tiny or large) and books and walks and chocolate cake. . . .

By infusing satire and parody into **"Chocolate Mabbie"** Brooks establishes the poem's distance from the simple folk ballad tradition. Despite the ballad conventions and sacred imagery, the poem has a mocking quality which gives it a complex cutting edge and reinforces its ideas. The childlike syntax of the opening stanza goes beyond balladic simplicity to a primerlike quality. It is as if an elementary school child is adding sentence to sentence with no sense of subordination. This simplicity underscores the fact that on one level Brooks is writing about "puppy-love" and humorously focusing on a transitory childish crush and its inevitable demise. Yet, in the final stanza the narrator loses her sardonic tone. Thus the reader is reminded that if this is, from one perspective, childish subject matter, ultimately it is a serious poetic statement about the dilemma of growing up black and female in America.

III. **"The Ballad of Pearl May Lee"** and the Afro-American Blues Tradition

"The Ballad of Pearl May Lee" shows Brooks at her grittiest—blackening and womanizing the ballad form. Through her focus on a black woman narrator, her stark descriptions of grim, racially based sexual drives and her linkage of the theme of revenge with the brutal racist act of lynching, Brooks achieves remarkable complexity both in the poem's structure and in its poetic statement.

The theme of this second, longer poem, like the subject of **"Chocolate Mabbie,"** is the common folk ballad theme of unrequited love. **"Pearl May Lee,"** however, is a sensational story about a lynching, told through a dramatic episodic narrative which includes several shifts in scene and the use of dialogue in its rhetorical strategy. True to folk balladry, the tale opens at a crucial point in the progression of events. The reader/listener overhears Pearl the narrator retelling her story *in medias res:*

> Then off they took you, off to the jail,
> A hundred hooting after. . . .

Thus, in the **"Ballad of Pearl May Lee"** Brooks changes from the third-person narrator of the European ballad to the immediacy of a highly involved first-person speaker, which is characteristic of the Afro-American blues tradition. Pearl May, the poem's opening speaker, addresses her once derelict and now murdered lover, Sammy, and retells the gory details of his lynching. In the process, however, Pearl May becomes herself the subject of the poem; it is her emotional reactions to events and not the events themselves that Brooks brings into focus. The narrative stance in the poem fluctuates. At times Pearl is almost an objective chronicler of events, as when she recounts in the thirteenth stanza: "They wrapped you around a cottonwood tree." At other times she acts as a judgmental choric voice, as when she remarks, "You had it coming surely." But hers is primarily a lyrical voice, reflecting on her own dilemma and feelings, as when she soliloquizes; "Though never was a poor gal lorner."

As with the traditional ballad, **"Pearl May Lee"** contains several episodic shifts in scene. The poem opens with the speaker in her home; then the speaker dramatizes the jail cell scene following Sammy's arrest; next, in a kind of flashback, Sammy and Pearl's school days are recalled; subsequently Pearl May imagines Sammy's seduction scene on the fringe of town in the back of a Buick; next she imagines the lynching scene; and finally, she returns to her present state of mind. These abrupt shifts in scene are simultaneously balladic and also reflective of blues techniques. Sammy's incarceration recalls many "jailhouse" blues songs. Ironically, while he is held behind cell bars, Pearl May, like so many blues women, is imprisoned by her confusion and despair. She literally begs to be dug out of her depression and loneliness when she cries: "Oh, dig me out of my don't despair / Oh, pull me out of my poor-me." In so doing she echoes the paralysis expressed by Ma Rainey, the great classic blues songwriter and singer, in "Deep Moaning Blues:"

> My bell rang this morning, didn't know which-a-way
> to go,
> I had the blues so bad, I sit right down on my
> flo.

At the same time, structurally, Pearl's lines recall the traditional ballad lament, as seen in this concluding stanza from "Bonny Barbara Allen:"

> "O mother, mother, make my bed!
> O make it safe and narrow!"

This lament parallels the concluding stanza of **"Pearl May Lee"**:

> "Oh, dig me out of my don't despair.
> Oh, pull me out of my poor-me.
> Oh, get me a garment of red to wear. . . ."

Both of these laments contrast with the similarly structured mock-lament in the sixth stanza of **"Chocolate Mabbie"**:

> Oh, warm is the waiting for joys, my dears!
> And it cannot be too long.
> Oh, pity the little poor chocolate lips
> That carry the bubble of song.

In the presentation of episodes the language of **"Pearl May Lee"** is, like ballad language, simple, idiomatic, sometimes harshly direct. Pearl May's reaction to Sammy's lamented death is to "cut [her] lungs with . . . laughter," but she realizes paradoxically that "never was a poor gal [herself] lorner." Many blues idioms infuse the vernacular language of this poem with a particularly Afro-American blues realism. For instance, Sammy's rejection of Pearl is phrased as the inability to "abide dark meat." Yet Brooks juxtaposes this stark sexual reference with the romantic ballad language Pearl uses when she tries to imagine Sammy at his fatal lover's tryst. In this narrative-within-the-narrative, balladic phrases appear in such lines as "*The moon an owl's eye minding*; / The sweet and thick of the *cricket-ballad dark*" (emphasis mine).

Dialogue in **"Pearl May Lee"** is similarly varied. It is usually simple, even crude, as when the white woman turns against Sammy with the accusation: "You raped me, nigger." However, at times the poem's diction includes balladic phrasing, as when Pearl May begs, "Oh, get me a garment of red to wear." The structure and semantics of this request are not a part of contemporary American or Afro-American language, particularly the usage of "garment" instead of "dress." The use of the word "garment" fits into the poem's patterning of words with Middle English etymology, both within and outside dialogue. Such words, which often begin with hard sounds and are often used alliteratively, recreate the forceful balladic tone of many English ballads. Other examples in **"Pearl May Lee"** are "cut," "laugh," "dig," and "pull."

In addition to its balladic language conventions, **"Pearl May Lee"** is composed of variations on the ballad stanza. While much of its phrasing comes from the blues, and while its dramatic situation is a blues dilemma, stanzaically it departs from classic blues verse form of three lines with an *aab* rhyme scheme. Instead, its variation on the ballad stanza relies heavily on the use of three devices: repetition, rhyme, and refrains. For example, the first stanza sets a pattern for stanzas two through five, stanzas eight and nine, and stanzas eleven through sixteen. In each, three lines are followed by a refrain which repeats the rhyme of the second line. The entire first stanza reads:

> Then they took you off to the jail,
> A hundred hooting after.
> And you should have heard me at my house.
> I cut my lungs with my laughter.
>   Laughter,

Laughter,
I cut my lungs with my laughter.

Stanzas six, seven, and ten, however, consist of six lines, with the opening two lines being followed by a repeated set of lines. For example, the sixth stanza reads:

At school, your girls were the bright little girls.
(*a*)
You couldn't abide dark meat. (*b*)
Yellow was for to look at. (*c*)
Black for the famished to eat. (*b*)
Yellow was for to look at. (*c*)
Black for the famished to eat.(*b*)

Not only are phrases and refrains repeated within stanzas, but in a complex patterning of parallel structures, entire stanzas are repeated for incremental emphasis. Thus, the fourth and fifth stanzas are repeated as stanzas fifteen and sixteen. Only one line is altered in the process: "But you paid for your white arms, Sammy boy," in the fourth stanza, becomes "You paid for your dinner, Sammy boy," in the fifteenth stanza. However, Brooks cleverly varies her stanzaic rhymes and repetition throughout the poem by using off rhymes, hyphenated word rhymes, and even coinages, e.g., the word "lorner" in stanza two, which is a comparative of the obsolete Middle English word "lorn."

In addition to coinages reminiscent of European ballads, phrases like "white arms" and "pink and white honey" form part of the many balladic epithets used in **"Pearl May Lee."** Some of these epithets come from the romantic ballad tradition, such as the "cricket-belled dark" mentioned above; others from American and Afro-American vernacular. The sheriff, for instance, is "the red old thing," while Sammy hates "dark meat."

Colors in **"Pearl May Lee"** are used metonymically in both the balladic and Afro-American vernacular sense. References to white, red, and black thread the poem, creating multiple associations with racial hegemony (the white Southern oppressors), violence (the angry sheriff is described as a "*red* old thing"), life ("garment of *red*"), and the reality of intraracial color discrimination ("*Black* for the famished to eat; *yellow* to . . . . look at").

The use of dialogue as a foreshadowing device as well as a dramatic element is another balladic technique in **"Pearl May Lee."** For example, the sheriff predicts to Sammy: "You son of a bitch, you're going to hell!." And the white woman, his erstwhile lover, promises: "My body tonight, niggerboy. I'll get your body tomorrow."

Ultimately, all of the personae in **"The Ballad of Pearl May Lee"** are actors in a dramatic tragedy that is at once universal in its linkage of the great themes of desire and death, but particular in its peculiarly American and Afro-American nuances. The "red old" sheriff and the "hundreds hooting after" reflect a racist Southern communal history of vigilante justice based on the principle of unadulterated Southern womanhood. While their actions parallel the actions of the seven foresters in "Johnie Cock" who gleefully dismember a virile youth for the brash "crime" of poaching, the racial motivation for the lynching of Sammy is uniquely American. Similarly, while the white woman betrayer-lover parallels the old palmer who sneaks away to tell the foresters of Johnie's crime, again the peculiar mixture of desire, shame, and racial hatred reflects a special American dilemma. Pearl May's cutting laughter and sense of justification ("You had it coming surely") reflects the painful but prescient "I told you so" attitude of characters like Johnie Cock's mother, who begged him to "stay at hame." But the fury and brutal sense of revenge felt by Pearl May is perhaps more akin to that of Lady Erskine, who, in the ballad "Child-Owlet," has her nephew dismembered because he refused her advances. Even if Pearl's ambivalence, the ambiguity of her final state of mind ("Oh, dig me out of my don't despair . . . Oh get me a garment of red to wear"), parallels the convention of remorse following revenge common to the ballad convention, it also parallels the Afro-American blues mixture of "meanness" and regret as reflected in these lines:

Too sad to worry, too mean to cry,
too slow to hurry, too good to lie, ... (Ma Rainey, "Victim of the Blues")

Thus, both the ballad tradition and the blues tradition are reflected in **"Pearl May Lee"**'s structure, in its imagery, and in its core theme of the interrelation between sex, violence, and death. By making her speaker-heroine a semi-omniscient first-person narrator, Brooks was able to use the conventions of these two traditions to enhance her "woman-identified" stance and her art.

In conclusion, Brooks' use of folk traditions varies considerably. At times, it is straightforward, at other times parodic; and often it is a complex mixture of both. Further analysis of her use of the traditions of ballads, blues, and spirituals needs to be made before any full understanding of her art can be achieved. The relationship between the blues tradition and the ballad tradition, for instance, needs further exploration. At this point, based on two powerful examples, it can be argued that Brooks turned to folk forms—ballad, blues, and spirituals—not out of any sentimental attachment to a given tradition but to deepen her poetic structure. While, on the surface, these folk elements make her poetry more accessible to the reader, a closer examination reveals insinuations and refinements of technique that augment the complexity so characteristic of her work. In so doing, Brooks has met her own criteria expressed in this early statement for an effective black poet:

> The Negro poet's most urgent duty, at present, is to polish his technique, his way of presenting his truths and his beauties, that these may be more insinuating, and therefore, more overwhelming.

Houston A. Baker, Jr. (review date Fall 1990)

SOURCE: A review of *Blacks*, in *Black American Literature Forum*, Vol. 24, No. 3, Fall, 1990, pp. 567-73.

[*In the following review, Baker offers an overview of Brooks's poetry and favorable evaluation of* Blacks.]

When a compendium of her poetry entitled ***The World of Gwendolyn Brooks*** appeared in the 1970s, the Poet Laureate of Illinois seemed fitly rewarded for a life of creative labor. The collection represented more than three decades. And its very name seemed proper and patently personal—a tribute to the genius behind its assembled offerings. "The world of Gwendolyn Brooks," one thought. "Yes, that is certainly appropriate for a Pulitzer Prize winner, a Poet Laureate, a guardian, model, and mentor in the world of American and Afro-American letters."

Yet, in 1987, with less than exultant fanfare, "the world of Gwendolyn Brooks" gave way to the unadorned, firmly bound, and privately published compendium ***BLACKS.*** Issued under her own publishing imprimatur, The David Company, the new collection bears strikingly large gold letters on its cover which spell ***BLACKS.*** Beneath, and in smaller type, the poet's name appears. From the proper "world" of Gwendolyn Brooks, we move to the common denomination BLACKS. A reading of ***BLACKS*** reveals the striking appropriateness of the retitling.

To read the new volume is to be struck once more by Brooks's genius at portraiture. ***A Street in Bronzeville*** (1945) is a series of vignettes, pithy character studies, and portraits of people who in a later volume are called ***The Bean Eaters*** (1960). Like ***Annie Allen*** (1949), for which she received the Pulitzer Prize, Brooks's novella ***Maud Martha*** (1953) is an extended portrait, a lyrical evocation of days, years, people, and events in the everyday lives of Afro-American women. These early works are a kind of apprenticeship for the energetic portraits that appear in ***In the Mecca*** (1968).

What appreciative reader of Brooks's poetry can soon forget the exquisite yellow youth of Jessie Mitchell's mother; the glories of De Witt Williams on his way to Lincoln Cemetery; the sartorial aesthetics of Satin Legs Smith; the wonders of Hattie Scott; a venomous eulogy by Pearl May Lee; the loiterings of a Bronzeville Mother in Mississippi; Kid Bruin, Mrs. Small, Sallie Smith, or a stunning Bronzeville Woman in a Red Hat? Or who can fail to recall an encounter with poetical sections such as "A Catch of Shy Fish" or "Young Heroes?"

The impression left by Brooks's portraits is that of a universe crafted by an inventive artist. No, perhaps it is better described as a gallery of originals midwived into language. In **"To Keorapetse Kgositsile"** Brooks writes: "Art is life worked with: is life / wheeled, or whelmed: / assessed: / clandestine, but evoked." Rather than paint or clay, her own medium is a mind that evokes, names, provides common denominations in language that is clean, often spare, and wondrously economical.

> We real cool. We
> Left school. We
> Lurk late. We
> Strike straight. We
> Sing sin. We
> Thin gin. We
> Jazz June. We
> Die soon.

What strikes a reader about Brooks's seven "real cool" pool players at the Golden Shovel, or her pragmatic "Old Mary," or a "Bronzeville Man with a Belt in the Back" is their utter commonness. Named by the poet, they are felt always to have existed as BLACKS—as occupants of a common street—sharers of a common lean cuisine of beans.

But to see Brooks merely as a creator of portraits is scarcely to distinguish her from a host of other American writers. For the portrait, as an emergent form of Enlightenment individualism, has enjoyed a ruggedly individualistic poetic heyday in American letters. From Theodore Ward's *Simple Cobler of Aggawam,* through Lowell's Hosea Biglow, Whitman's democratic vistas, Edgar Lee Masters's Spoon River people, Sandburg's Bunk Shooter and other denizens of Chicago, to Sherwood Anderson's Winesburg gallery, portraiture marks a vernacular tradition. As Brooks works the tradition, it descends directly from Sandburg and Masters. It is entirely correct to add, however, that the poet's Afro-American predecessors such as Langston Hughes and Sterling Brown were also within her general field of influences. A survey of Hughes's myriad volumes reveals a veritable cornucopia of urban, Afro-American portraits. And Brown's *Southern Road,* with its stirring pictures of Maumee Ruth, Big Boy Davis, Sister Lou, Sam Smiley, and others, offers a rural counterpart to Brooks's urban gallery.

If the poetic staple of her work is so familiar to American

letters, no critical account can claim to have defined the poet simply by labeling her a portraitist. We might supplement the claim by noting that Brooks's people are of African descent and can thus be said to add a unique racial and cultural mixture to the general gallery. But this addendum runs head on into the reality of her black predecessors. Fenton Johnson, Countée Cullen, Hughes, and Brown had all provided distinctively African American portraits in advance of Brooks.

The poet's uniqueness does not reside, then, simply in her portrayal of the commonplace. It resides most decisively in another feature of her poetical world—namely, her clear rejection of glorifying ideologies of the common man. Her people have neither the blues temperateness of Sterling Brown's strong men getting stronger, nor the *joie de vivre* of Langston Hughes's black urbanites, who want to dig and be dug in return. They are not proponents or exemplars of obtainable egalitarian goals. They are not blessed with a consciousness of mission—a sense of manifest destiny or a surety of predestined roles in the unfolding of a mighty national enterprise. They live always at the limits of a bitterly tested tolerance. Old Mary acknowledges:

My last defense
Is the present tense.
It little hurts me now to know
I shall not go
Cathedral-hunting in Spain
Nor cherrying in Michigan or Maine.

Lester laments in **"Strong Men, Riding Horses":**

What mannerisms I present, employ,
Are camouflage, and what my mouths remark
To word-wall off that broadness of the dark
Is pitiful.
I am not brave at all.

So much for barbaric yawps. Whimpers are the stuff of Bronzeville, not big bangs.

The jazz singer Mose Allison intones: "It's just as well the world ended / Things weren't going that well anyway." His assessment defines the universe of Brooks's common folks. Implicit in the poet's portrayals, in fact, is a grammar of dissent. Frontal irony and subtle antagonism are directed against all romantic ideologies of progress and metaphysical salvation. Race, class, gender, and nationality are the grounds of divisiveness and conflict that put such ideologies to shame. Skin color as a sign of race in America, for example, can cause unappeasable anguish. Maud Martha thinks: ". . . it's my color that makes h[er husband] mad. . . . What I am inside, what is really me, he likes okay. But he keeps looking at my color, which is like a wall. He has to jump over it in order to meet and touch what I've got for him." Class causes white women who are putative "lovers of the poor" to grow sick with fear and disgust. Philanthropically entering narrow halls of poverty, they are overcome by sights, sounds, and smells of the lower class. Nationality fosters crescendos of "Doomer"—unending war with unending destruction of "gay chaps" who serve as cannon fodder. Gender confines women to agonizing spaces; they are locked in gray rooms filled with heavy-diapered children . . . and vermin. One of the most sickening gender images in Brooks's poetry occurs in ***Maud Martha:*** "She could only stand helpless, frozen, and watch the slick movement [of a roach] suddenly appear and slither, looking doubly evil, across the mirror, before which she had been calmly brushing her hair." Possibilities for heroism are few in a world overdetermined by race, class, gender, and nationality. The bleakness of this universe is in part a function of Brooks's modernism. Commencing her career during "The Great War," she seems to have absorbed a healthy dose of the artistic malaise that prompted somber reveries of a Godless and irreversible universe of atomic fission. But her grammar of dissent is not entirely a by-product of the era in which she began her career.

Her antagonism to glorifying ideologies is also a product of a distinctive artistic credo—a signal aesthetics. Her creative orientation is designed, in fact, to match a world that guarantees the "commonness" of blacks through its restrictive codes of race, class, nationality, and gender. Adornment, embellishment, flamboyance, and proclamations of heroism are as anomalous in such a world as (to summon the poet's own image) "a rose in a whiskey glass." Stability, sanity, physical and mental development, and day-to-day safety survival depend upon an almost brutal refusal of self-deception and artistic idealism.

What insures and guards the day in Bronzeville is not the exalted proper name, but a common denomination. Mrs. Sallie Smith of ***In the Mecca*** instructs us: "First comes correctness, *then* embellishment! / And music, mode, and mixed philosophy / may follow fitly on propriety / to tame the whiskey of our discontent!" What is common is, also, proper or appropriate in the world of the Mecca. Similarly, in the world of "the children of the poor," it is necessary first to "civilize a space"—to claim and *name* a territory of one's own—before embellishing the air with notes of "hurting love." Again, Satin Legs Smith is the very bewitcher and bewilderer of what Brooks calls "flowers" and harmonies of a "Western field"; his is a common (communally accepted) splendor.

Two poems resonantly define Brooks's aesthetics. The first, entitled **"The Egg Boiler,"** reads:

Being you, you cut your poetry from wood.

The boiling of an egg is heavy art.
You come upon it as an artist should,
With rich-eyed passion, and with straining heart.
We fools, we cut our poems out of air,
Night color, wind soprano, and such stuff.
And sometimes weightlessness is much to bear.
You mock it, though, you name it Not Enough.
The egg, spooned gently to the avid pan,
And left the strict three minutes, or the four,
Is your Enough and art for any man.
We fools give courteous ear—then cut some more,
Shaping a gorgeous Nothingness from cloud.
You watch us, eat your egg, and laugh aloud.

The "egg boiler" is not like Hawthorne's artist of the beautiful. He is a craftsperson of the ordinary. Rather than delicacy of inscription or grace beyond the reach of art, he longs for a weighty and nourishing creativity. As he defines the world, traditional idealistic aesthetics are laughable. While there is, surely, more than a little irony intended by the poem's speaker (after all, she *is* the cloudland aesthetician and creator of the "you" who mocks her), there is also a sharp critique of idealistic art. And it is the egg boiler who finally emerges as sympathetic. He (or she) is an artist of the commonplace with whom we can identify in his (or her) conversion of everyday rituals into poetry "Enough."

To bestow a common denomination within restricted economies of class, race, nation, and gender in the United States is to seize a nourishing poetic initiative. Common things commonly named have a way of surviving even the grossest human follies. The conclusion of ***Maud Martha*** reads: ". . . and it was doubtful whether the ridiculousness of man would ever completely succeed in destroying the world—or, in fact, the basic equanimity of the least and commonest flower: for would its kind not come up again in the spring? come up, if necessary, among, between, or out of—beastly inconvenient!—the smashed corpses lying in strict composure, in that hush infallible and sincere." These lines seem to contradict my earlier claim about the absence of celebratory ideologies in Brooks's work. Their optimism about the essentiality of the "common" is, however, intriguingly qualified by a second poem about naming and the commonplace.

Immediately preceding **"The Egg Boiler"** in ***The Bean Eaters*** is a poem called **"The Artists' and Models' Ball"**:

Wonders do not confuse. We call them that
And close the matter there. But common things
Surprise us. They accept the names we give
With calm, and keep them. Easy-breathing then
We brave our next small business. Well, behind
Our backs they alter. How were we to know.

Grand occasions such as artists' and models' balls may appear as wondrous events staged by people self-defined as wondrous. These occasions sustain their wonder because they are framed as "balls," as ritual events. It is, in fact, their very separateness from everyday life that provides stability.

Items of everyday use, by contrast, are not so accommodating. Framed only by hastily uttered names and subject always to continuous exchange in the social and verbal world of common folks, they are always in circulation and never separate from hourly commerce. Hence they are the most elusive things of all. They cannot be fixed and held permanent by an ethics and aesthetics of wonder. Like the egg for boiling, the space for civilizing, or the wardrobe and Sunday seductions of Satin Legs Smith, such things are given moment only by a name. But their moment is precariously fragile. Any extension brings another name and alters their "thingness" through parlance and use.

Let me add here, however, that Brooks's own poetical naming often *situates* itself within a common order rather than employing the vocabularies of such an order for names. Her polysyllabic verse with its taut syntax and her grammatical substitutions of adjectives and adverbs for nouns often make her poems anything but idiomatic. Her grammatical acrobatics produce memorability and subversion. It is difficult to forget a "thaumaturgic lass," a vaudevillean of "magnificent, heirloom, and deft," or a hipster whose title is bestowed by "inamoratas, with an approbation." Subversion results from the appropriation of the full weight and heft of the King's English to portray lives of common subjects. (Classical genre watchers and style setters such as Aristotle and Boileau must cringe each time Brooks unhinges the standard in order to portray the common.)

To return to the question of alteration and the commonplace, it seems fair to say that essentialism—the belief that each "thing" has an enduring essence—has no part in Brooks's aesthetics. The speaker of **"The Artists' and Models' Ball"** knows, for example, that common names do not capture essence. They exist, as previously noted, as survival strategies. Against the chaos perpetuated by race, gender, class, and national ideologies they offer possibilities for a human and humane—if temporary—ordering of restrictive spaces.

A notion of the ever altering thingness of the commonplace—a shiftiness that requires and is a function of ceaseless naming—is the truly distinguishing notion of Gwendolyn Brooks's art. Her poetical portraits alter each time we call their names. They assume a different thingness each time she, as a brilliant and accomplished public reader, sets them eloquently before us. Their alteration, however, is not merely a result of our willed and continuous naming. An elusive and always expanding space called "context" also causes them to shift—to change in unaccountable ways "behind our backs."

For example, the lackluster and whimpering populace of Bronzeville that was "not brave at all" in the 1940s transformed itself, quite miraculously, in the United States during the 1960s and assumed the common name BLACKS. Thunderstruck as she was by this behind-the-back evolution of her bean eaters and garbagemen dignified as any diplomat, Brooks maintained her aesthetics of two decades' standing. She assumed that her task was to provide a common ground and denomination for these new BLACKS. "Common," of course, as Mrs. Sallie Smith has taught us, can signify *appropriate.* When BLACKS became bold, heroic rioters jerking the times out of joint, Brooks energetically relinquished her direct and implicit condemnations of nationalistic grandeur. She became a namer of the militant struggle that not so long ago comprised a common ground and cause for BLACKS in the United States. She came to know in her own life what she had always claimed in her aesthetics: Common denomination can sometimes be a matter of dramatic alterations. The job for the poet facing this continuing drama of transformation is to:

> Live not for battles won.
> Live not for the-end-of-song.
> Live in the along.

To live in "the along" is to inhabit the everyday. It is to confront race, class, national, and gender restrictions with a common lexicon. For Brooks it is to do exactly what she has done in offering a newly retitled volume of her work; it is to provide and share in the common denomination of BLACKS.

Henry Taylor (essay date Fall 1991)

SOURCE: "Gwendolyn Brooks: An Essential Sanity," in *Kenyon Review,* XIII, No. 4, Fall, 1991, pp. 115-31.

[*In the following essay, Taylor offers an overview of Brooks's poetry, artistic development, and critical interpretation.*]

Gwendolyn Brooks's emergence as an important poet has been less schematic, but not less impressive, than commentary upon it has suggested. It is difficult to isolate the poems themselves from the variety of reactions to them; these have been governed as much by prevailing or individual attitudes toward issues of race, class, and gender, as by serious attempts at dispassionate examination and evaluation. Furthermore, Brooks's activities in behalf of younger writers have demonstrated her generosity and largeness of spirit, and wide recognition of these qualities has led some critics away from the controlled but genuine anger in many of the poems. Brooks has contributed to this process; in interviews, and in her autobiographical ***Report from Part One*** (1972), she speaks engagingly and with apparent authority about her own work, and many of her judgments have become part of the majority view of her career. Nevertheless, it is worthwhile to consider whether there might be more unity in the body of her work than conventional divisions of her career suggest.

Brooks herself, as William H. Hansell has noted, indicated the divisions when, "in a 1976 interview at the University of Wisconsin-La Crosse,[she] said that her work falls into three periods that correspond to 'changes' in her perspective." Hansell's note: "Works of the first period are ***A Street in Bronzeville*** (1945), ***Annie Allen*** (1949) and ***The Bean Eaters*** (1960). The second period is represented by the "New Poems" section of ***Selected Poems*** (1963) and by two uncollected poems, **'The Sight of the Horizon'** (1963) and **'In the Time of Detachment, in the Time of Cold'** (1965). The third phase of her development is marked by her most recent collections: ***In the Mecca*** (1969) [1968], ***Riot*** (1969), ***Family Pictures*** (1970) and ***Beckonings*** (1975)."

Whether a writer's development involves improvement is highly questionable, but writers often think they are improving, because they are usually more interested in work in progress than they are in work long since completed. Since the mid-1960s, Brooks has revealed these attitudes in numerous comments on her awakening to the situation of the Black writer in America. On the other hand, when she ended her association with Harper & Row, and began to place her work with Black publishers, she retained the rights in her early work, and reprinted the bulk of it in a collected volume entitled ***Blacks*** (1987). The stark inclusiveness of that one-word title suggests that Brooks perceives unity as well as variety in the range of her concerns and voices.

Report from Part One and, more recently, the late George Kent's *A Life of Gwendolyn Brooks* (1990), provide generous insight into the origins of Brooks's art. Her own work provides a livelier evocation of her early years than Kent manages in his first two chapters, but he has made a thorough examination of the young girl's notebooks, which she kept industriously. The child appears to have taken seriously her mother's prediction that she would grow up to be the "lady Paul Laurence Dunbar." Kent finds that she was a victim of an intraracial prejudice which put very dark girls at a social disadvantage among Black people of her age. (This theme recurs in Brooks's poetry through ***In the Mecca.***) The energy which might have gone into a more active social life was instead poured into poems and stories which show promise more in their profusion than in their accomplishment.

Though she had been publishing poems in the *Chicago De-*

fender since her high school days, she was twenty-eight when ***A Street in Bronzeville*** (1945) appeared. Concerning what was "new" about it, Kent writes:

> The poet had rejected the exotic vein of the Harlem Renaissance—the celebration of unique racial values, such as defiance of social proscription through emphasis upon joy and soul. A few poems in ***A Street*** work close to this vein, allowing the reader the enjoyment of the old colorful images, but use one device or another to bring them to the court of critical intelligence. Thus "patent leather" and other poems devalue the "hipness" that the Harlem Renaissance would have celebrated.

As have all American poets, Brooks inherited the old problem of language, which in the nineteenth century divided poets into rebels and loyalists—those who knew that the central problem was to establish independence in the language of the colonizing country, and those who were content with the poetic tradition of the colonizers. This dilemma is exponentially more difficult for a Black woman; a term like "the lady Paul Laurence Dunbar" hardly needs comment on the forms of oppression it implies and, implicitly, accepts.

Still, Brooks had applied herself assiduously to the absorption of a largely white male tradition, in the apparent belief that all great poetry in English had something of value to teach her. ***A Street in Bronzeville*** introduced a poet of more technical accomplishment than was usual even in the mid-1940s. Forty-five years later, the variety of forms and tones in the collection remains impressive; Donne, Robinson, Frost, Dickinson, and even Ogden Nash seem to have left occasional marks, as well as Hughes and the blues.

But what strikes most forcibly now is the sophistication, and the Dickinsonian way in which sophistication sometimes becomes a shield, from behind which almost invisible darts fly often and accurately. Throughout Brooks's poetry, delicate satire regularly breaks through a surface which is pretending in some way to be well-behaved.

In twelve lines, for example, **"the vacant lot"** provides a richly populated scene, in tones modulating from apparent nostalgia and regret through sarcasm to controlled, satiric flatness:

> Mrs. Coley's three-flat brick
> Isn't here any more.
> All done with seeing her fat little form
> Burst out of the basement door;
> And with seeing her African son-in-law
> (Rightful heir to the throne)
> With his great white strong cold squares of teeth
> And his little eyes of stone;
> And with seeing the squat fat daughter
> Letting in the men
> When majesty has gone for the day—
> And letting them out again.

Throughout ***A Street,*** individual poems have lowercase titles when they are grouped under a larger heading. Despite this consistency, however, the device occasionally creates a local effect; here the suggested insignificance of the lot is emphasized by an immediate and energetic portrayal of what is not there. Among the departures is the mysterious African son-in-law, who briefly dominates the poem, his teeth packing the seventh line with stressed monosyllables, but whose "majesty," by the end of the poem, is cruelly diminished.

The gulf between imagined majesty and hard reality is a frequent theme in ***A Street.*** Its most ambitious treatment is **"The Sundays of Satin-Legs Smith,"** a narrative of just over 150 lines in which satire is deepened by compassion. The ironic contrasts begin with the title; the protagonist's name yokes the exotic and the ordinary. The polysyllabic opening introduces a narrator whose self-consciously elegant language is mock-heroic:

> Inamoratas, with an approbation,
> Bestowed his title. Blessed his inclination.
>
> He wakes, unwinds, elaborately: a cat
> Tawny, reluctant, royal. He is fat
> And fine this morning. Definite. Reimbursed.

As Satin-Legs commences his morning ablutions, the speaker becomes an ironically patient lecturer, addressing a "you" who is presumed innocent of the life being unfolded here, and who may therefore be taken as white. In the following excerpt, the sentence "Maybe so" ends a passage of fourteen lines, concerning the appropriateness of Satin-Legs's choice of scents and oils, which both recalls and quietly subverts the sonnet tradition:

> . . . might his happiest
> Alternative (you muse) be, after all,
> A bit of gentle garden in the best
> Of taste and straight tradition? Maybe so.
> But you forget, or did you ever know,
> His heritage of cabbage and pigtails,
> Old intimacy with alleys, garbage pails,
> Down in the deep (but always beautiful) South
> Where roses blush their blithest (it is said)
> And sweet magnolias put Chanel to shame.

Satin-Legs has only an artificial flower, made of feathers, for his lapel; in the first of two brief asides, the speaker says, "Ah, there is little hope." Satin-Legs will have "his lotion, lavender, and oil"

> Unless you care to set the world a-boil
> And do a lot of equalizing things,
> Remove a little ermine, say, from kings,
> Shake hands with paupers and appoint them
> men. . . .

But the speaker decisively returns to an inspection of "The innards of this closet." More strongly than "Maybe so" above, "innards" underscores the speaker's dualistic sense of language and class; if Satin-Legs is being satirized, so is the addressee, whose ignorance is more broadly satirized in such later poems as **"I love those little booths at Benvenuti's," "The Lovers of the Poor,"** and **"Bronzeville Woman in a Red Hat."**

The closet contains the gaudy accoutrements of such a dandy as Satin-Legs is, or aspires to be; colors are "sarcastic," tailoring is "cocky," ties are "hysterical." Following this exposition of his tastes, two lines in a second brief aside hover between solemnity and humor:

> People are so in need, in need of help.
> People want so much that they do not know.

True enough; but the idea is complicated by its placement, which suggests that Satin-Legs needs advice from a refined haberdasher. Creating himself "is all his sculpture and his art." However, after he enters the street, halfway through the poem, there is no further description of his appearance; instead, we see how things appear to him. Through the narrator, we experience his surroundings more vividly than he does. "He hears and does not hear" an alarm clock, children, a plane, voices, and the elevated train. "He sees and does not see" broken windows patched with newspaper, children in worn but decently patched clothes, and

> men estranged
> From music and from wonder and from joy
> But far familiar with the guiding awe
> Of foodlessness.

The music he hears is popular blues; the narrator notes the absence of strains by Saint-Saëns, Grieg, Tschaikovsky, Brahms, and questions whether he could love them if they were audible; one brings to music what one is:

> The pasts of his ancestors lean against
> Him. Crowd him. Fog out his identity.
> Hundreds of hungers mingle with his own. . . .

From a movie, where he is reminded that "it is sin for his eye to eat of" the heroine's "ivory and yellow," he proceeds toward the goal of all his efforts. In a line that tumbles anticlimactically from faint echoes of the courtly tradition to a place where main courses are served on meat platters, he "Squires his lady to dinner at Joe's Eats." The "lady" is different every Sunday, but there are constant characteristics, most of them supplied by the overstated dress and makeup that Satin-Legs could be expected to admire. The ending of the poem subtly suggests that this is a kind of death-in-life. Remarking that the food is plentiful at Joe's Eats, the narrator interjects: "(The end is—isn't it?—all that really matters.)" The poem concludes with the achievement of Satin-Legs's objective:

> Her body is like new brown bread
> Under the Woolworth mignonette.
> Her body is a honey bowl
> Whose waiting honey is deep and hot.
> Her body is like summer earth,
> Receptive, soft, and absolute . . .

The slant rhymes undercut the directness of the statements, and draw attention to the "absolute" nature of receptive earth, where, in the old courtly usage, Satin-Legs Smith is about to die. Unlike the pool players in **"We Real Cool,"** who "die soon" in many senses, Satin-Legs will survive; this Don Juan's version of Hell is to repeat this cycle indefinitely, with "little hope" of redemption. The ignorant white observer is presumed to accept this ending as all that really matters.

Brooks wrote this accomplished poem toward the end of her work on ***A Street,*** probably in response to Richard Wright's evaluation of the manuscript she had sent to Harper & Brothers; he praised her skill and genuineness, but added that "most volumes of poems usually have one really long fine poem around which shorter ones are added or grouped."

A Street concludes with a sequence of twelve sonnets, **"Gay Chaps at the Bar,"** which is close enough to what Wright was asking for. **"Gay Chaps"** is among the stronger poetic responses we have to World War II, and deserves inclusion in anthologies devoted to that subject, along with **"Negro Hero,"** the monologue of a Black mess attendant who took up a machine gun and used it effectively when his ship was attacked at Pearl Harbor, despite regulations of the strictly segregated Navy of that era, in which Black personnel did not handle firearms.

Brooks adopts several points of view throughout **"Gay Chaps at the Bar"**—omniscient, first person singular, first person plural—and her speakers demonstrate that Black soldiers suffered the same terrors and hopes as any other soldiers. But she is equally concerned to present the injustices of the Black warriors' situation, and reasonable doubts about what they might have been fighting for. The sonnets submit to convention in several ways, but Brooks uses slant rhyme in them more often than she had earlier; they extend the range of sonic choices, and help to emphasize the paradox that these men were fighting for a country which in many ways refused to claim them.

Brooks's interest in traditional technical virtuosity reaches an apex in ***Annie Allen,*** the collection for which she received the 1950 Pulitzer Prize. The book is arranged in three sections: "Notes from the Childhood and the Girlhood," "The Anniad" (which includes the long poem of that title and two short pieces as "Appendix to The Anniad"), and "The Womanhood." The eleven short poems in the first section establish Annie as a daydreamer, resentful of restrictions imposed by her parents and society, hopeful of some idealized rescuer.

"The Anniad" is a technical tour de force: 301 lines in forty-three seven-line stanzas, employing thirty different rhyme schemes, a compelling meter (trochaic tetrameter catalectic), and a diction that is elaborate, dense, and compressed. Paraphrase is often difficult, and it is also difficult to resist being carried along on the sound waves, heedless of incomprehension. There is a definite narrative; some of the details are obscure, though the poems in the first section of ***Annie Allen*** provide background for the entrance to the poem:

Think of sweet and chocolate,
Left to folly or to fate,
Whom the higher gods forgot,
Whom the lower gods berate;
Physical and underfed
Fancying on the featherbed
What was never and is not.

What is ever and is not.
Pretty tatters blue and red,
Buxom berries beyond rot,
Western clouds and quarter-stars,
Fairy-sweet of old guitars
Littering the little head
Light upon the featherbed.

Watching for the paladin
Which no woman ever had,
Paradisiacal and sad
With a dimple in his chin
And the mountains in the mind;
Ruralist and rather bad,
Cosmopolitan and kind.

The imperative of the first line, repeated six more times throughout the poem, implies a reader or listener. This strategy, not as fully developed as in **"The Sundays of Satin-Legs Smith,"** still gives the speaker awareness of an audience, and an inclination to perform. In various tones—affectionate tolerance, adult amusement, or sadness and anger—the speaker shows us the impossible romantic aspirations that fill Annie's "light" and "little" head. The paladin's virtues are impossibly contradictory; that he is not a person, but an imaginary being, is obvious enough, but emphasis is provided in the relative pronoun: "Which no woman ever had."

As she grows older, a "man of tan" courts Annie, and his qualities and her predilections arouse her:

What a hot theopathy
Roisters through her, gnaws the walls,
And consumes her where she falls
In her gilt humility.

They move to a "lowly room" which she tries to transform into a lovely love nest. There follows a passage which has been subject to more than one critical bias:

Doomer, though, crescendo-comes
Prophesying hecatombs.
Surrealist and cynical.
Garrulous and guttural.
Spits upon the silver leaves.
Denigrates the dainty eves
Dear dexterity achieves.

Names him. Tames him. Takes him off,
Throws to columns row on row.
Where he makes the rifles cough,
Stutter. Where the reveille
Is staccato majesty.
Then to marches. Then to know
The hunched hells across the sea.

Vaunting hands are now devoid.
Hieroglyphics of her eyes
Blink upon a paradise
Paralyzed and paranoid.
But idea and body too
Clamor "Skirmishes can do.
Then he will come back to you."

To the reader biased toward a belief in the occasional usefulness of paraphrase, "Doomer" presents difficulties; but the second of these three stanzas helps to identify it as a power suggestive of Uncle Sam, the draft, and the intrusion of war. Noisily, prophesying slaughter, speaking almost bestially, it attacks the little home life Annie has with difficulty achieved. It calls "tan man's" name, inducts him into armed service, sets him to drill with guns, reveille, and marches, and ships him overseas. Annie, bereft, looks blankly on her altered life, but wants to believe he will not be killed.

Hortense J. Spillers, on the other hand, offers a feminist reading of the passage in "Gwendolyn the Terrible: Propositions on Eleven Poems": "As it turns out, he is not the hot lover 'theopathy' would make him out to be, but Annie denies it, fearing that to say so would be to evoke an already imminent betrayal: [quotes first and third of above stanzas]. This scene of 'ruin', brought on by sexual impotence, gains a dimension of pathos because it anticipates the woman's ultimate loneliness, but this judgment is undercut by the caricature of the male."

This may constitute misreading for the sake of an overriding theme, but Spillers characterizes, with justice and unintended irony, the poem's "specific end: to expose the sadness and comedy of self-delusion in an equally deluded world."

Upon his return, troubled by conflicting recollections of horror and of power, and by predilections imposed on him in a white-dominated society, "tan man" finds a mistress whose color is more honey than chocolate. The twenty-third stanza begins by repeating the first line of the poem, and launches an account of Annie's life alone, from winter through the following fall; she attempts social gaiety, esoteric learning, the high life, and then tries to settle toward her husband's return. The speaker turns to "tan man" and chastises him:

> Hence from scenic bacchanal,
> Preshrunk and droll prodigal!
> Smallness that you had to spend,
> Spent. Wench, whiskey and tail-end
> Of your overseas disease
> Rot and rout you by degrees.

At home again, he wastes away, and at last leaves the world, and the two women, who are contrasted harshly in successive stanzas:

> Leaves his mistress to dismiss
> Memories of his kick and kiss,
> Grant her lips another smear,
> Adjust the posies at her ear,
> Quaff an extra pint of beer,
> Cross her legs upon the stool,
> Slit her eyes and find her fool.

> Leaves his devotee to bear
> Weight of passing by his chair
> And his tavern. Telephone
> Hoists her stomach to the air.
> Who is starch or who is stone
> Washes coffee-cups and hair,
> Sweeps, determines what to wear.

The second of these stanzas, the fortieth in the poem, reflects Annie's static helplessness; it is the only one with two rhymes instead of three. She becomes the victim of nightmares and a harried resignation, but the final stanza mutes the verbal flash:

> Think of almost thoroughly
> Derelict and dim and done.
> Stroking swallows from the sweat.
> Fingering faint violet.
> Hugging old and Sunday sun.
> Kissing in her kitchenette
> The minutes of memory.

Though much of the satire in this poem seems to be directed at Annie's innocent romanticism, and at the circumstances which have nourished it, the tone of the last stanza turns toward sympathy. Annie's pathetic stillness, the amatory participles describing small aimless gestures, are mitigated by the "almost" in the first line, and by the iambic fullness of the last. Annie is now twenty-four, and has endured a series of disillusionments and bereavements. If she is to blame for some of them, so is the world.

Whereas the poems of the first two sections of ***Annie Allen*** speak of Annie in the third person, the third section opens with a sequence of five sonnets, "the children of the poor," in which the mother speaks in the first person. The sequence quickly ranges over several questions arising from the profoundly mixed blessings and curses of disadvantaged parenthood—how to protect children, teach them, prepare them for the fact of death. The fourth sonnet is a complex variation on the persistent American theme that art could not flourish in the period when people of ability were occupied with settling the country. Its punctilious adherence to Petrarchan conventions of structure momentarily withholds the sarcasm that bursts through in the sestet. It begins with two short sentences occupying exactly half a line: "First flight. Then fiddle." The remainder of the octave describes the fiddling, fraught with "feathery sorcery" and "silks and honey," yet covertly rebellious:

> muzzle the note
> With hurting love; the music that they wrote
> Bewitch, bewilder.

The sestet returns to the fighting:

> But first to arms, to armor. Carry hate
> In front of you and harmony behind.
> Be deaf to music and to beauty blind.

Win war. Rise bloody, maybe not too late
For having first to civilize a space
Wherein to play your violin with grace.

Enjambment and shifting caesuras lend energy to much of the poem, but in the final couplet the energy is "civilized" to excessive tameness, reinforcing the "maybe" in the preceding line. The poem hovers between satire and direct polemic, both attacking and appropriating the notion behind it.

The inclusive vision that results in such a poem finds a variety of more single- minded expressions in the remainder of the book; this section of ***Annie Allen*** contains a few underachieved poems, but on the whole it is a sustained illustration of Brooks's many virtues. There are straightforwardly affectionate sketches, satiric portrayals of Black characters and of ignorant or sheltered whites, seized moments in the manner of Emily Dickinson, love poems, polemical addresses. The book concludes with an untitled poem of considerable power, addressing "Men of careful turns, haters of forks in the road," and declaring the speaker's full humanity. Its characterization of establishment caution is icily exact:

"What
We are to hope is that intelligence
Can sugar up our prejudice with politeness.
Politeness will take care of what needs caring.
For the line is there.
And has a meaning. So our fathers said—
And they were wise—we think—at any rate,
They were older than ourselves. And the report is
What's old is wise. At any rate, the line is
Long and electric. Lean beyond and nod.
Be sprightly. Wave. Extend your hand and teeth.
But never forget it stretches there beneath."

The poem ends with a chilling recognition that things will not soon change, especially if polite requests are depended on. The last line memorably combines determination and pessimism:

Let us combine. There are no magics or elves
Or timely godmothers to guide us. We are lost, must
Wizard a track through our own screaming weed.

If there are sharp divisions in Brooks's career, one of them comes at this point. As George Kent puts it, "For both whites and Blacks, Gwendolyn would from now on be tagged 'the first Negro to win a Pulitzer Prize,' and with that label would come the roles of spokeswoman and arbiter in the upper realms of her city's and her nation's cultural affairs." We may be able to see whether Brooks's work changed noticeably after this, but the question is obfuscated by the churning assortment of critical responses to her new status. The problem of Brooks's place in a white literary establishment had in fact been thrown into relief by Paul Engle's August 26, 1945, review in the *Chicago Tribune,* of ***A Street in Bronzeville.*** Especially in the 1940s, trying to declare Brooks's transcendence of racial differences was to fall into the nearly inescapable trap of simultaneously affirming and denying the importance of race in her work: ". . . Miss Brooks is the first Negro poet to write wholly out of a deep and imaginative talent, without relying on the fact of color to draw sympathy and interest. . . . The finest praise that can be given to the book is that it would be a superb volume of poetry in any year by a person of any color."

There is no reason to doubt Engle's sincere admiration of Brooks's work, or the honesty of his conviction that race should not be the issue that it is; but it is hard to get away from the hint of exclusiveness, the suggestion that Brooks is a fine poet, not regardless of her color, but despite it. In later years, increasing numbers of Black writers would question the extent of Brooks's commitment to Blackness; but there were confusing earlier questions by less militant writers. J. Saunders Redding, for example, in a generally favorable review of ***Annie Allen*** in the *Saturday Review,* found references to intraracial color preferences too esoteric: "Who but another Negro can get the intimate feeling, the racially-particular acceptance and rejection, and the oblique bitterness of this? . . . The question is . . . whether it is not this penchant for coterie stuff—the special allusions, the highly special feeling derived from an even more special experience—that has brought poetry from the most highly regarded form of communication to the least regarded."

Redding and Engle were saying remarkably similar things, and missing an important element of Brooks's art. She sought to make her Black characters as rounded as poetry permits; this necessarily involved treating aspects of the Black experience which are imposed by white society. Through her first two books, her anger at injustice is comparatively restrained, but several poems in ***The Bean Eaters*** greatly increase the pressure of rage against the control of mature technique.

In one or two instances, the pressure overcomes control. **"A Bronzeville Mother Loiters in Mississippi. Meanwhile, a Mississippi Mother Burns Bacon"** is a daring response to the murder of Emmett Till, a Chicago teenager who was beaten and killed in 1955, during a visit to Mississippi. Brooks adopts the point of view of the young white woman who accused the youth of making sexual advances toward her. The sympathetic portrayal of the woman is striking; the husband, however, is a flat symbol of murderous white male oppression. He deserves that status, but in the poem he fails to earn it; instead of a plausible and therefore frightening and disgusting human, we have something too much like a cartoonist's drawing of Bull Connor. On the other hand, the woman's romantic vision of southern womanhood collapses convincingly before her growing knowledge of the Dark Villain's innocent youth:

> Had *she* been worth the blood, the cramped
> cries, the little
> stuttering bravado,
> The gradual dulling of those Negro eyes,
> The sudden, overwhelming *little-boyness* in that
> barn?

Flat portrayal of white characters is more effective in such satirical poems as **"The Lovers of the Poor"** and **"Bronzeville Woman in a Red Hat,"** where reduction of characters to cartoons serves a dual function: it permits broad sarcasm and indulgence in playful diction, and it invites the white reader to feel excluded from the portrait until it is too late to escape inclusion in it. Both poems portray whites in the act of dehumanizing Blacks, though **"Bronzeville Woman"** is heavy-handed in this respect. A rich and overbearing woman has had to replace her Irish housemaid, and the agency has sent a Black woman, whom the employer calls "it" throughout the poem. The portrayal becomes more effective, if nearly sentimental, in contrasting the reactions of the employer and the employer's child, "Not wise enough to freeze or be afraid."

The other major treatment of racial violence is **"The Ballad of Rudolph Reed,"** a fiercely ironic narrative of the violence that follows a Black family's purchase of a house in a white neighborhood. Traditional ballad meter and language give the poem a strange atmosphere of remoteness:

> Rudolph Reed was oaken.
> His wife was oaken too.
> And his two good girls and his good little man
> Oakened as they grew.

Contemporary racist brutality breaks with great force into such a setting, but the poem is strong enough to contain the atrocity of Reed's death, which comes as he is defending his house against rock-throwers who have wounded one of his daughters. The end of the poem is a powerful tableau of grief and strength:

> By the time he had hurt his fourth white man
> Rudolph Reed was dead.
> His neighbors gathered and kicked his corpse.
> "Nigger—" his neighbors said.
>
> Small Mabel whimpered all night long,
> For calling herself the cause.
> Her oak-eyed mother did no thing
> But change the bloody gauze.

These somewhat extended poems concerned with racial injustice, white insensitivity, and violence, are scattered through an unusually varied collection of shorter poems, from the brilliant miniature **"We Real Cool"** to such humorous pieces as **"On the Occasion of the Open-Air Formation of the Olde Tymer's Walking and Nature Club."** It is this mixture, perhaps, more than the presence of the longer poems, which led some readers to regret the increased emphasis on social issues in ***The Bean Eaters***—as if social issues were making their first appearance in Brooks's work. It is true that these longer poems are more explicit, and reveal anger more openly, than do most of Brooks's earlier poems; but most of the shorter poems aroused regret that Brooks could not be consistently polite.

The new poems in ***Selected Poems*** (1963) did little to change these impressions; **"Riders to the Blood-Red Wrath,"** with its evocations of African majesty, the squalor of slave ships, and the commitment of Freedom Riders, both extends and rejects the polemical manner. Its content is occasion for celebration and exhortation, but in style it reverts to a density Brooks had not used at length since **"The Anniad."** It crams a racial history into a single consciousness, which ranges without transition between individual and collective recollection, and gathers momentum toward the polemical ending: "To fail, to flourish, to wither or to win. / We lurch, distribute, we extend, begin."

On the other hand, a number of the new poems are brief character sketches; these presage the ambitious and thickly populated ***In the Mecca*** (1968), the book which has been said to initiate the third period in Brooks's career. If it does mark a significant shift in Brooks's way of writing and of thinking about what she is doing, this is more evident in the shorter poems that follow the title poem. **"In the Mecca"** is, at just over 800 lines, Brooks's most ambitious single poem; but in strategy and style it is an extension, not a repudiation, of her earlier excellences.

Epigraphs provide the information that the Mecca building, an extravagant apartment complex erected in Chicago in 1891, degenerated into an overcrowded tenement. Kenny J. Williams adds the important fact that the building was razed in 1952.

In bare outline, the narrative is grim: Mrs. Sallie Smith returns to her apartment from hard domestic labor, and begins to prepare dinner for her family of nine children; she notices suddenly that the youngest, Pepita, is missing. There is a fruitless search, police are called, and at last the child is found murdered.

The poem begins with a single line on a page by itself:

"Now the way of the Mecca was on this wise." It remains for the poem to unfold the wrathful irony in this echo of Matthew 1:18 ("Now the birth of Jesus Christ was on this wise"). The rest of the poem is based in the present tense; Mrs. Smith encounters four neighbors on the way to her apartment, and each is sketched briefly; Alfred, an English teacher and untalented would-be writer, comes to act as a choral commentator as the poem develops. The children have their distinctive ways of trying to defend themselves against the reality of their lives; Melodie Mary, for example, "likes roaches, / and pities the gray rat." She is dimly aware of headlines announcing strife and suffering in China, but

> What if they drop like the tumbling tears
> of the old and intelligent sky?
> Where are the frantic bulletins
> when other importances die?
> Trapped in his privacy of pain
> the worried rat expires,
> and smashed in the grind of a rapid heel
> last night's roaches lie.

When the family goes in search of Pepita, they inquire of several neighbors, each of whom is given several lines of characterization. Great-great Gram, who recalls her childhood in slavery, reverts to childhood as she recalls popping little creatures that "creebled" in the dirt of the cabin floor, thus inverting Melodie Mary's treatment of the same subject. Aunt Dill, reveling in her report of a child's rape and murder the previous week, is a gruesome parody of unfeeling self-satisfaction.

Toward the end of this section, there are three portraits without reference to Pepita or her whereabouts. The first, concerning Don Lee, is similar to several other poems Brooks has written about notable Blacks; even in the context of this poem, it appears to portray the poet and activist now named Haki R. Madhubuti. Along with Alfred's references to Léopold Sédar Senghor, "Poet, muller, President of Senegal," this constitutes unobtrusive anachronism. **"In the Mecca"** contains few references which can be dated precisely, but some of them, such as Senghor's presidency of Senegal (1960-1980), convey the impression that the Mecca existed in the 1960s. This effect is only slightly complicated for the reader in possession of such arcana as the year of its demolition; the building itself may have been infamous, but its destruction did not significantly change the lives with which the poem is concerned. Brooks's Mecca outlives its namesake, and becomes a perceptible metaphor as well as a symbol.

The increasing desperation of the search for Pepita is reflected in the rapidity with which new characters are introduced from this point on. In the whole poem, over fifty people are mentioned by name or characteristic label; more than half of them appear in the last 200 lines. Because this large cast moves in quickly, sometimes at the rate of four people per line, there is room near the end of the poem for four strophes of between a dozen and two dozen lines each, the first two introducing new characters, the third and fourth returning to Aunt Dill and Alfred, respectively. The two new characters reinforce the balanced vision of the whole poem: Way-Out Morgan is collecting guns, imagining "Death-to-the-Hordes-of-the-White-Men!"; Marian is ironing, wishing for some disaster to befall her so she may be noticeable. Absorbed in their visions, they have no time to wonder where Pepita is. Aunt Dill reappears in a gooey cloud of self-satisfaction; the narrator calls her

> the kind of woman you
> peek at in passing and thank your God or zodiac
> you
> may never have to know. . . .

In this welter of selfishness, Alfred makes a final appearance, allowing Brooks a sly reference to the temporal limbo in which she has erected this cosmos:

> I hate it.
> Yet, murmurs Alfred—
> who is lean at the balcony, leaning—
> something, something in Mecca
> continues to call! Substanceless; yet like mountains,
> like rivers and oceans too; and like trees
> with wind whistling through them. And steadily
> an essential sanity, black and electric,
> builds to a reportage and redemption.
> A hot estrangement
> A material collapse
> that is Construction.

The next strophe begins with two lines that look back toward this reverie, and forward to the discovery of Pepita's body:

> Hateful things sometimes befall the hateful
> but the hateful are not rendered lovable thereby.
> The murderer of Pepita
> looks at the Law unlovably.

Beneath Jamaican Edward's bed lies the body of Pepita, who "never learned that Black is not beloved." Remembering a rhyme the child once made with "rose," her mother decides to "try for roses." The final four lines of the poem revert to what only Jamaican Edward could have seen, but the powerful image of horror is rendered in a style that can only be the narrator's:

> She whose little stomach fought the world had

wriggled, like a robin!
Odd were the little wrigglings
and the chopped chirpings oddly rising.

"In the Mecca" is a large and largely successful poem, a benchmark in Brooks's career. The poem draws its strength both from her increasing interest in the possibilities for polemic in poetry, and from her broad and deep familiarity with poetry's technical resources. Except in scope and achievement, it is not a radical departure from the work which preceded it. However, it was completed during a time of upheaval in Brooks's sense of herself as a poet, and the shorter poems collected with it are evidence of a major division in Brooks's career.

Much has already been made of the external forces that wrought important changes in Brooks's thinking about her life and work. At the Fisk University Writers' Conference in 1967, she encountered, more forcibly than she had before, the power of young Black writers committed to making a literature for Black people, and to liberating themselves and their people from white oppression. The experience energized her in new ways. She also worked briefly with the Blackstone Rangers, a street gang whose younger mentors, especially Walter Bradford and Don L. Lee, provided encouragement as she sought her "newish voice."

"After Mecca" is a coherent sequence of separate poems; it gathers force by proceeding from individual portraits, through two "public occasion" poems and the three-part **"Blackstone Rangers,"** to **"The Sermon on the Warpland"** and **"The Second Sermon on the Warpland."** As the field of vision expands from one poem to the next, the formal scope extends from brief and nearly metrical to more widely various free-verse lines. The diction, however, remains characteristically Brooksian, as in this conclusion to "The Leaders," the second part of **"The Blackstone Rangers":**

The Blackstone bitter bureaus
(bureaucracy is footloose) edit, fuse
unfashionable damnations and descent;
and exulting, monstrous hand on monstrous
hand,
construct, strangely, a monstrous pearl or grace.

But along with certainly that she had much to learn from younger Black writers, there came a desire to reach audiences unaccustomed to hearing or reading poetry. This arose partly from increasing doubt about dependence on the Eurocentric tradition she had so thoroughly commanded for most of her career; at this point, the language problem referred to early in this essay becomes extremely difficult, despite Anglo-American's flexibility and relative openness to other traditions. With a few notable exceptions such as **"We Real Cool,"** Brooks's poetry has depended not only on fresh and unusual language, but on the varying degrees of surface difficulty that such wordplay often creates. Her attempts at a more accessible style have sometimes resulted in oversimplified moralizing, and in indecision about which poems or versions of poems to reprint.

Of the roughly fifty poems Brooks published between 1968 and 1987, a few have appeared only in periodicals, and only nineteen are collected in ***Blacks.*** A white reader might be tempted to think that some of this indecision arises from Brooks's having accepted, in 1985, her second major accolade from the literary establishment, when she became Poetry Consultant to the Library of Congress; but in interviews over the past twenty years, and in her tireless work for Black writers during her tenure at the Library, she has demonstrated unwavering commitment to the cause of freedom for oppressed people.

Brooks's wavering over certain poems is evidence of crisis, but it is important to remember that crisis is usually much more rewarding for artists than for politicians. In adjusting her accustomed tools to her new tasks, she has taken some directions which she seems later to have reconsidered, but occasional frustrations have not sent her back to techniques in which she has long been adept. Her most recent collection, ***Gottschalk and the Grande Tarantelle*** (1988), is cause for gratitude that she has not retreated from trying to perfect her new ways of working.

This handsome chapbook contains only four poems, but one of them is **"Wine,"** some 375 lines spoken by Wine Mandrel. The character is of course a literary creation, partaking of what Brooks knows of Mrs. Mandrel, and of what she knows of herself and the world. There are passages where one might wish that more memorable language had been found for the urgent messages:

we are all vulnerable—
the midget, the Mighty,
the richest, the poor.

But Brooks has hold of something here. In her early work, personal history (not necessarily her own) was a dependable provider of material. She began to merge social and political history with that strain in poems like **"The Ballad of Rudolph Reed"** and **"A Bronzeville Mother Loiters,"** and perfected that merging in **"In the Mecca."** Now, she is after larger historical scope, and appears to be on the brink of finding the means to achieve it without surrendering particularity. As she has Wine Mandrel say,

This is the time for Big Poems,
roaring up out of sleaze,

poems from ice, from vomit, and from tainted blood.

Cheryl Clarke (essay date Winter 1995)

SOURCE: "The Loss of Lyric Space and the Critique of Traditions in Gwendolyn Brooks's *In the Mecca,*" in *Kenyon Review,* XVII, No. 1, Winter, 1995, pp. 136-47.

[In the following essay, Clarke examines the significance of ambiguity, indeterminacy, and postmodern subjectivity in In the Mecca. *According to Clarke, "'In the Mecca' is an enunciation of place, fragmentation, despair, death, and a frantic splitting of the narrative strategies of showing and telling."]*

What else is there to say but everything?

In the Mecca

The 1952 razing of Chicago's once magnificent showplace, the Mecca, was an act of erasure, causing Gwendolyn Brooks, by the late 1960s, to reconsider her own location in the tradition of African-American literature. Designed by George Edbrooke, "famous for his ability to utilize aesthetically large spaces," and built by the D. H. Burnham Company in 1891 for the white wealthy of Chicago, the Mecca became one of the early examples of a multifamily dwelling:

> . . . During the Columbian Exposition of 1893 it was one of the places in the city that visitors wanted to see. (Later it was still a tourist attraction, but not because of its beauty.)

By 1912, the Mecca housed the black elite of Chicago. After World War I, the building began its decline. By the Great Depression the once elaborate showplace and tourist attraction had become a crowded slum for poor black people and a symbol of encroaching urban blight—a great hulk of modernity confining thousands of expendable people to the bowels of the city.

The Mecca was girded by three balconies and guarded by ornate wrought iron grillwork. Off these balconies, doors opened to the apartments, "like tiers of cells in a prison cellblock." Hard wood floors splintered, and beneath the balconies the tile was broken in many pieces. The Mecca contained 176 units. Some apartments had seven rooms. After the Depression, no one ever knew how many people lived there at any one time. Estimates of three thousand to nine thousand people have been given. "'You'll find them sleeping in the kitchen under the sink, anywhere they can sleep,'" one tenant is quoted as revealing to a journalist.

Gwendolyn Brooks began to write ***In the Mecca*** as a "teenage novel" in 1954. Brooks drew upon her firsthand experience as secretary to "a patent medicine purveyor" during the 1940s. She had walked through its U-shaped great gray hulk, its littered atria; passed by the once-beautiful marble walls and the once plushly carpeted floors; looked up to see the accumulated dirt and grime on the glass of its skylights emitting a kind of unreal light; passed her hand along its rusted wrought iron; mused over what remained of its useless fountains.

Her editors were never enthusiastic about the manuscript, counseled that her training in poetry had ill-prepared her for the "freer area of prose" and discouraged her. Harper's would publish the novella, ***Maud Martha*** in 1953, the polemical ***Bean Eaters*** in 1960, and the noted ***Selected Poems*** in 1963, before Brooks would turn her attention again to ***In the Mecca***—this time conceived as a book-length poem, "2,000 lines or more."

Brooks's entire oeuvre has been studies of black subjectivity, of African-American oral and written traditions, sources of knowledge and faith systems; of the psychic and physical effects of racism on the lives of black and white people; and of the richness of the lyric. Brooks is a strong reader of blackness, a strong poet of place and region (the south side of Chicago), and a strong interpreter.

In the Mecca is Brooks's last book published by Harper's, her publisher of twenty-five years. In many ways ***In the Mecca*** marks Brooks's rejection of a safe subject position inside the American literary tradition. Indeed, the Pulitzer Prize winner announced in 1969 that Broadside Press, run by poet and promoter of the new black poetry Dudley Randall, would publish her next book, ***Riot*** (1969).

When the collection ***In the Mecca*** was published in 1968, the Mecca building had been razed for sixteen years. The poem **"In the Mecca"** does not attempt to historicize the action within the 1940s or 1950s nor is there any over attempt to inscribe within the narration or the narratives the real history of the 1960s. The poem sits as a gate to the text as if the real Mecca's great gray hulk of brick still filled half the block north of Thirty-fourth Street between State and Dearborn. As "perceptible" metaphor and symbol, the Mecca is a lesson on the spiritual and psychic condition of urban black people in post-modernity.

Brooks had been transformed by the apocalyptic decade of witness and the ringing testimony of the new black consciousness articulated by militant young black poets of the sixties, and sought a place among them. The narrator's authority in the poem parallels Brooks's own subject position as poet and soon-to-be arbiter of the new black arts movement in the Midwest. No longer Hyena, "[t]he striking debutante. / A fancier of firsts," but Esu, perhaps, the androgynous Yoruba god of chance who lurks at gateways, on highways, and at crossroads. Brooks moved her witness out of "her dusty threshold." Like her narrator, Brooks arrives in the wake of destruction; signifying indeterminacy, ambiguity, fluidity, unpredictability, and liminality. Uncertain, ironizing, and critiquing traditions and texts—Brooks's own and others—the poem extends a provisional hope—outside the Mecca. Brooks writes in her notes, "Work Proposed for 'In the Mecca'":

> . . .I wish to present a large variety of personalities against a mosaic of daily affairs, recognizing that the *grimmest* of these is likely to have a streak or two streaks of sun.

In **"In the Mecca,"** Brooks locates her narrator within a more transgressive space and creates a "speakerly text." **"In the Mecca"** is an enunciation of place, fragmentation, despair, death, and a frantic splitting of the narrative strategies of showing and telling. **"In the Mecca"** is a text which "Signifies" on the rich resources of African-American narrative and English poetry.

The movement of the poem's 807 lines winds narrowly with the movement of the narrator/witness/interpreter and the reader (who is reluctant) as if through the corridors of the once splendid dwelling. The poem will be encountered as a text of texts, in which race, sexuality, and gender are deeply implicated. Through a chronological reading of select narrations and narratives, I will also examine Brooks's narrative and rhetorical strategies as a turning to new space. I also read this poem as a post-modern elegy on the place of the lyric in African-American poetry.

As much as they Signify on antecedent texts, Brooks's strategies of shifting subjectivity, dispersed narration, and polyvocality look forward to Toni Morrison's strategies in her revised slave narrative, *Beloved.* As the enunciated story/mystery of Sethe's murder of her daughter tells itself, the reader must encounter the slave stories of Paul D., Baby Suggs, Stamp Paid, Sethe herself, and numerous other liminal and marginal characters whose accounts of atrocities committed against them are as horrific or more horrific than the ones committed against Sethe or the one Sethe committed against her young daughter. Morrison, nearly twenty years after Brooks's revisionary work, critiques historians—white and black—and undertakes to revise antecedent black (and white) texts in *Beloved.*

The action of Brooks's poem, on the surface, revolves around the search of Mrs. Sallie Smith, "this low brown butterball," for her missing daughter, Pepita, whom she and the reader ultimately discover is murdered. The reader is confronted with a relentless narrator who compels the reader to hear the stories—in multivoice and multivernacular irony—of characters speaking their own atrocities and failings contextualized/framed by a fictional Mecca, infusing the poem with a Gothic dread.

Full of temporal inversions, **"In the Mecca"** functions as a mystery, a "narrative-within-a-narrative." The modes of narration split sharply between its "showing" of Mrs. Sallie's desperate, passive search for her missing child, Pepita, and the frantic deployment of polyvocal and multidiscourse tellings. In each mode of narration, the narrator causes in the reader crises of witness, "an anxiety of fragmentation," a cut-off-ness, an isolation which in the poem is enhanced by the indifference of the other characters/subjects to the fate of the missing child and the distancing, elevated rhetoric and speech acts of the narrator, who knows, of course, the outcome of the search for Pepita.

Additionally, the play among narrative modes in the poem critiques and pays homage to the lyric, the ballad, the sermon, the slave narrative, the proverb, the psalm. The narrator enunciates these strategies and they are dispersed throughout the modes of discourse adopted by the other telling subjects. Through the deployment of end rhyme, the location of the lyric passages, the satirizing of the vernacular speech, the revising of African-American storytelling traditions, the poem acknowledges Brooks's "deep and broad familiarity with poetry's technical resources," and embraces and extends the formal, metric, and lyric proficiency of her antecedent texts.

Much of what Gates has said about Ishmael Reed's *Mumbo Jumbo* as "a book about texts and a book of texts, a composite narrative composed of subtexts, pre-texts, post-texts, and narratives-within-narratives," most certainly be said of **"In the Mecca."** The narrative is a book of texts, and each of the subjects is a text of itself. The narrator—and perhaps Brooks—functions as Esu and is the interpreter of black subjectivity in the poem. The poem is profoundly post-modern.

The movement of the poem, the space it takes on the page, the way it makes the reader go on the search is both telescopic and documentary. The poem evokes hallways, in an almost concrete fashion. The narrator is a film director, commanding attention to her epic production with its epigraph of biblical revision: "Now the way of the Mecca was on this wise."

The reader, like a reluctant viewer, is directed and commanded to "Sit where the light corrupts your face" and to follow the poem's constricted lineation down the corridors of the place to capture a perverse "social panorama." A mediating but unconscious subject led by the narrator, Mrs. Sallie leads the reader through a desolate space ringing with different languages: first as she, home from work, "ascends the sick and influential stair" to her fourth-floor apartment, and then as she winds back through the place in search of Pepita. Through Mrs. Sallie's subjectivity, the reader witnesses the other subjects. Ultimately the narrator, and not Mrs. Sallie, is the one who brings the reader to witness the truth of Pepita's murder.

At the third line of the poem, "the fair fables fall," the narrator tells the reader that this will be no predictable narrative—not ***Annie Allen*** nor even ***Maud Martha.*** As transgressive as they were, Annie and Maud were the centers. Subjectivity shifts in **"In the Mecca."**

Indirect discourse predominates and is a function of the narrator's control of the display of language and the more sympathetic subjects. Direct discourse is allowed more sparingly to evoke humor, sarcasm, irony, and realism; and the narrator's distance from the enounced. Free indirect discourse is employed to communicate the more authentic historical horrors and the subjects' interiority—and perhaps the narrator's empathy. Christian devotion, as practiced in the Mecca, is called into question through St. Julia Jones's direct and ostentatious expression of religiosity in her farcical exuberance: "'He hunts up the coffee for my cup. / Oh how I love that Lord.'" The narrator retrieves control to *show* Prophet Williams, the religious charlatan, "rich with Bible" but whose wife, Ida, "was a skeleton / was a bone" and "died in self-defense" and alone. The narrator's interior eruption. "(Kinswomen! / Kinswomen!)," "Signifies" on the speaker's appeal, "Oh, Kinsmen, we must meet the common foe," in Claude McKay's famous poem, "If We Must Die" and laments the sacrifices of black women's lives, indeed of women's lives (and bodies), and signals further sacrifices to be revealed "on this wise." This eruption is perhaps the only place where the narrator reveals a gender identity and empathy.

There is irreparable damage in this place, and Alfred, an unreliable witness whose subjectivity is conveyed primarily through indirect discourse, contends with the narrator for presence. He is much less reluctant than the reader, is persistent, reappears five times—more than any of the other more than fifty subjects. At times his relationship to the narrator evokes younger black poets' relationship to Brooks; at other times Alfred seems to be a persona for Brooks, apprenticing herself to the younger (male) poets. Alfred has not the narrator's language nor rhetorical power. He has too many masters and is distracted by too many pretenders: "Shakespeare . . . Joyce or James or Horace, Huxley, Hemingway," "pretty hair," "that golden girl," respectively. Yet he is relentless in his witnessing and will grow from the experience. Will he be able to take the story beyond the Mecca?

Such hope cannot be extended to Mrs. Sallie and eight of her nine children. The narrator shifts her attention from the reader to Yvonne, Melodie Mary, Cap, Casey, Thomas Earl, Tennessee, Emmett, Briggs—all except Pepita. Each child's world is as restricted and dangerous as their names are ambitious and imaginative. Explanatory narratives of impoverishment, sexual exploitation, potential crime and violence, hunger, and isolation interpret each child's psychic and physical space. Yvonne, Mrs. Sallie's oldest, offers a more extended lyric moment as she "prepares for her lover" and ponders and plans a subversive sexuality:

> It is not necessary. . . .
> to have every day him whom
> to the end thereof you will love.

And Mrs. Sallie muses over the space she occupies in two disparate worlds—that of the Mecca where her daughter, "Melody Mary likes roaches" and that of her "Lady's pink convulsion, toy-child . . . under a shiny tended warp of gold." In lyric parody, in sing-song, slant-rhyme cadence, Mrs. Sallie wishes for a reversal of fortunes:

> "And that would be my baby be my baby. . . .
> And I would be my lady I my lady. . . ."

The lyric cannot exist in the Mecca; neither can the reversal of class and race locations.

The narrator's paradoxical rhetorical gesture, "What else is there to say but everything?" alerts the reader that language will not be impoverished in the showing and the telling. The focus shifts back to Mrs. Sallie as she, "counting noses," asks, in the vernacular, 'WHERE PEPITA BE?' This and variations of it become the strophe for the duration of the poem and extend beyond the question of Pepita's whereabouts to each character's telling of his/her own psychic location/place. Pepita is not the only tragedy here:

> In twos!
> In threes! Knock-knocking down the martyred
> halls
> at doors behind whose yelling oak or pine
>   many flowers start, choke, reach up,
>   want help, get it, do not get it,
>   rally, bloom, or die on the wasting vine.

Paying homage to and parodying the origins of black narrative traditions, Brooks inverts "space and time" by confronting Mrs. Sallie with "Great-great Gram," her first encounter in the search. Great-great Gram, an ex-slave, renders her testimony, a slave narrative. The performative quality of Great-great Gram's enouncement is unsettling. Though she uses the vernacular minimally, Great-great Gram's rhetorical directness is nearly as caricaturist as St. Julia Jones. On the other hand, conveying Great-great Gram's nostalgic yet realistic recollections of slavery through direct address, Brooks parodies our notion of the conventional, mediated slave narrative. The missing Pepita does not concern Great-great Gram as much as it stirs a childhood memory of younger sister, "Pernie May," who was the "best popper" of that "something that creebled" in the dirt; or the more eloquent reflection:

> . . . Some slaves had beds of hay
> or straw, with cover-cloth. We six-uns curled
> in corners of the dirt, and closed our eyes,
> and went to sleep—or listened to the rain
> fall inside, felt the drop
> big on our noses, bummies and tum-tums. . . .

This narration is particularly rich as it recalls for the reader the great migrations of the slaves descendants from the South to the North to cities like Chicago, Detroit, New York, Washington, D.C.; and of the real Mecca's history as one of the sites where that history and memory reside. Finally, Brooks collapses historical and present time as Great-great Gram's story of Pernie May refers the reader to Mrs. Sallie's younger daughter, Melodie Mary, who smashes roaches, "in the grind of her rapid heel."

Loam Norton, Mrs. Sallie's next encounter, also a very rich enouncement, has not seen Pepita either. He is preoccupied like Great-great Gram, with a correlative atrocity, "Belsen and Dachau." Using free indirect discourse for the first time, the poem presents Loam. The narrator reads Loam's thoughts, in a cynical revision of the Twenty-third Psalm. The past and present histories of the victims of slavery and the victims of the Holocaust are linked in time-worn signs: "jungles and pastures":

> . . . The Lord was their shepherd.
> yet they did want.
>
> Joyfully would they have lain in jungles or
> pastures
> . . . . Their gaunt
> souls were not restored, their souls were
> banished.
> In the shadow valley
> they feared the evil, whether with or without
> God.
> They were comforted by no Rod,
> no Staff, but flayed by, O besieged by, shot a-
> plenty.
> . . . .
> Goodness and mercy should follow them
> all the days of their death.

Enhancing the "speakerliness" of the text, the revised Psalm exemplifies the narrator's critical and interpretive functions as Great-great Gram's narrative shows the distance the narrator/interpreter must observe between subject and self. Also, Loam's monologue on the failure of faith calls upon the reader to revisit St. Julia Jones's libidinous exhorting of the Twenty-third Psalm at the beginning of the poem ". . . And I lie late in the still pastures. And meadows. . . ." Loam asserts to the reader, "I am not remote, / not unconcerned" as if to vindicate himself (and Great-great Gram) for his preoccupation with his own horror.

Even the door becomes a speaker and a witness, questioning Mrs. Sallie's and her children's return: "What are you doing here? and where is Pepita the puny—the halted, glad-sad child?" The speaking door is an odd moment and a parodic comment on the Gothic urges of this mysterious poem; yet this is a place of "martyred halls" and "yelling oak and pine," rife with death and history. As the reader follows the Smiths back into their apartment, the poem breaks and constricts into eight narrow, slant-rhymed lines, mirroring their reentry into the apartment, as they try to "subdue / the legislation of their yoke and devils" with a false lyricality:

> Has just wandered!
> Has just blundered
> away
> from her own.
> And there's no worry
> that's necessary.
> She
> comes soon alone.

But their hope for Pepita is fractured as they consider how endangered young girls are in the Mecca, a place of female violation/exploitation:

> And that lank fellow looking furtive.
> What
> cold poison could he spew, what stench commit
> upon a little girl, a little lost girl. . . .

The reader's hope is not recuperated either as she witnesses Mrs. Sallie's encounter with "The Law," to whom a missing "Female of the Negro Race" is of less concern than a "paper doll" or a "southern belle." They constrain Mrs. Sallie with "a lariat of questions." The Law leaves. Aunt Dill, a sinister witness, forecasts the accident, the murder of Pepita, as she arrives to give false comfort to the Smiths: "Little gal got / raped and choked to death last week."

Aunt Dill's gratuitous monologue hardly prepares the reader for one of the major crises of fragmentation in the poem: Mrs. Sallie's withdrawal from her subject position and from the narrative. The reader sees Mrs. Sallie and her children no more. The Law returns, and thus begins the second principal part of the poem. The Law proceeds through the place to ultimately uncover the "accident." The narrator has full control of the showing and most of the telling. Introduced to many more language users, whose baffling testimonies are relayed through the narrator, the reader is confronted with unmediated testimonies and interpretations. The reader must bear witness to subjects previously encountered as well as new ones, even more isolated from one another and fragmented by their atrocities and failings.

Alfred appears again—and has not seen Pepita—but offers a paean, in free indirect discourse, to Senghor, "negritude needing" which signals movement beyond his own mediocrity and Western derivativeness. Enhanced by the alliteration in the eighth line, Mazola's interior narration meditates on how easy death is in this place. This passage perhaps also laments the death of lyric within the tradition:

> . . . the strangest thing is when the stretcher
> goes!—
> the elegant hucksters bearing the body when the body
> leaves its late lair the last time leaves.
> With no plans for return.

Alfred's paean to Senghor—the major exponent of negritude—is countered by the narrator's competitive paean to Don L. Lee—the eminent black nationalist poet—and reinforces the loss of lyric. This latter enunciation about Lee signifies a turning to new space in the present, the possibility of a new world-view and creative production. The Don Lee exhortation may hold out the prospect of reclamation beyond the "art-lines" of Senghor and also beyond the lyric:

> Don Lee wants . . .
> new art and anthem: will
> want a new music screaming in the sun.

Now the poem begins to more overtly reflect the black political climate of the sixties, its apocalyptic nature, the turning of blacks toward themselves and against white sanction, acceptance, tutelage, the violent wrenching of an enduring symbiosis.

In the poem's first dialogue, Amos argues with the "gradualist," who says, "Takes time." Amos prays for the purgation of a feminized America. America must be slapped, kicked prostrate, heel ground into "that soft breast" in order that *she* can rise, recover. "Never to forget." America must be gendered female to be conquered and therefore rehabilitated, "recover[ed]."

"The ballad of Edie Barrow," an intensely formalist moment, announces itself to the reader, and is a "surface divergence." On one level this is Edie's story of how she gives herself to a gentile boy and is rejected by him when he marries one of his own kind. On another level, Brooks is Signifying on her copious use of the ballad form in her earlier poetry. Brooks offers Edie's ballad as a counterpoint to Amos's prayer, and inverts it. The lyricality and alternating end rhyme disguise the cynicism of its narrative. Also, Edie's metonymic lament that her situation as compromised woman will be as a "hungry tooth in my breast" is juxtaposed to Amos's vengeful prayer that "Great-nailed boots . . . heel-grind that soft breast" of America, the metaphorical woman. Edie's cynical lyric of sex also recalls Yvonne's more naive lyrical moment. Edie, as one of several sexual females, illuminates how the feminine is constructed, remade, and degraded in the Mecca—both as place and as poem. The few lyric moments in the poem are sustained by the female subjects. **"The ballad of Edie Barrow"** represents more than any other passage the loss of lyric space. Sexuality, throughout this poem, is configured in male and female subjects as a corrupted heterosexuality. This corrupted sexuality is humorously and more cynically revealed when Prophet Williams, that signifier of inauthentic religion, is revisited, but this time as a purveyor of potions and elixirs who has:

> Drawing and Holding Powder, Attraction
> Powder, Black
> Cat Powder, Powerful Serum,
> "Marvelous Potency Number Ninety-one"
> (which stoppeth husbands and lovers from dastardy)

As she continues the frantic pace, through the fragmented community of language- users, the narrator, for the first time, addresses the missing girl, Pepita, directly: "How many care, Pepita?" Not Staley and Lara, Simpson, Bixby and June, "these three Maries," Great-uncle Beer, Wezlyn, Insane Sophie. "How many care, Pepita? . . . these little care, Pepita, what befalls a / nullified saint or forfeiture (or child)." Who does Pepita become in this moment—without the mediation of Mrs. Sallie? Perhaps she becomes a symbol of Brooks's antecedent texts, her loss of lyric autonomy.

Alfred, having found his own voice, returns and, for the first time, in a direct testimony rejects the tutelage of his white masters, "Not Baudelaire, Bob Browning, no Neruda" and muses aloud:

> "A violent reverse.
> We part from all we thought we knew of love
> and of dismay-with-flags-on. What we know
> is that there are confusion and conclusion.
> Rending.
> Even the hardest parting is a contribution. . . .
> What shall we say?
>
> Farewell. And Hail! Until Farewell again."

"We part from all we thought we knew of love" signals the painful parting with the lyric testament—at least in the Mecca. Lyric is sex, lyric is female, lyric is Western contamination—racial as well as artistic. Again the question of what is there to say, what is the language beyond the ending, beyond "Farewell"? What can be reclaimed or recuperated? Certainly not Pepita—and perhaps not anyone else in the Mecca. There is damage here, irrevocable, as the narrator takes the reader closer to the reality of the "accident."

The narrator reemerges with the startlingly sarcastic narrative of the "sixtyish sisters, the twins with floured faces," who "muffle their Mahler, finish their tea, / stare at the lips of the Law." The sisters exemplify bourgeois intransigence and indifference to the fate of Pepita. They are sharply juxtaposed to an equally satiric narration of Way-out Morgan, a bitter black militant collecting guns, "sinfully lean . . . fills fearsomely / on visions of Death-to-the-Hordes-of-the-White-Men! Death!" He envisions, like Amos, a vengeful sacrifice. But as an inversion of Amos, for whom sex is a metaphor for conquest, Way-Out "postpones" the real thing, "a yellow woman in his bed . . . to consider" his vision of "Ruin."

However, the final depiction of Alfred, "lean at the balcony leaning" posits sacrifice and offers hope, and perhaps resurrection.

> . . . something in Mecca
> continues to call! Substanceless; yet like mountains. .
> .
> . . . . And steadily
> an essential sanity, black and electric,
> builds to a reportage and redemption
>   A hot estrangement.
>   A material collapse that is Construction.

Finally dwarfed by Alfred's commanding rhetoric, the narrator presents the body of the murdered Pepita, "beneath the cot" of her murderer, Jamaican Edward. Pepita's body and Jamaican Edward are the last of the more than fifty characters/subjects/witnesses the narrator shows us. Though the reader has never known Pepita, her body provides that "essential sanity," some relief, and a grounding in chaotic space. The narrator quotes Pepita's own childishly lyrical words and rhyming couplet to the reader: "'I touch'—she said once—'petals of a rose. / A silky feeling through me goes!'" The reader, as Alfred in the passage above, must see construction from material collapse, must, in seeking reality, "explore the injury inflicted by it," must find the language ("reportage") to reemerge from the paralysis induced by it, must "move on." It is uncertain the reader can move on.

And finally, Mecca, with all of its historical, metaphorical, cultural, political resonances for African-Americans, is a place/space of dissolution and desolation—a dystopic space despite Malcolm X. The modes of narration remain split, which signify the impossibility of reconciliation. There is a possibility of renascence—outside the Mecca—the possibility of something "black and electric" rising out of the rubble, perhaps even out of the dead Pepita's "chopped chirpings oddly rising." However, the possibility of new space, new speech, and new agency become more realized in "After Mecca," the male-focused space of occasional, exhortatory, eulogistic poems of the second section of the book.

Kathryne V. Lindberg (essay date 1996)

SOURCE: "Whose Canon? Gwendolyn Brooks: Founder at the Center of the 'Margins,'" in *Gendered Modernisms: American Women Poets and Their Readers,* edited by Margaret Dickie and Thomas Travisano, University of Pennsylvania Press, 1996, pp. 283-311.

[In the following essay, Lindberg discusses Brooks's artistic development, critical reception, and identity as a spokesperson for African-American women. According to Lindberg, Brooks sought to overcome "the double bind of a black woman artist who would be heard as something other than victim of or exile from her race and class."]

> Black Poet, White Critic
>
> A critic advises
> not to write on controversial subjects
> like freedom or murder
> but to treat universal themes
> and timeless symbols
> like the white unicorn.
> A white unicorn?—Dudley Randall,
>
> *"You can say anything you want about black women"*—

or so said a poet-critic colleague of mine when I mentioned that I was writing an essay on Gwendolyn Brooks. This could be a green light or a roadblock. Except for the solipsist or the most *entitled,* either by unexamined literary expertise or a valid license, as it were, to represent *the* BLACK WOMAN, it is not a simple declaration of fact. Let us not quibble—but mustn't we profoundly quibble?—over "can" and "may," over competence and permission. Depending on the race, gender, and politics of speaker and auditor, the force and function of the irony of my colleague's statement cut in rather different directions. Did s/he mean "go right ahead, *you* can be trusted?"—issuing, as it were, a *carte blanche.* Did he/she mean that black women poets are fair game, while black male critics remain untouchable? Did s/he mean that, given the spread of interest and jaggedness of identity politics, the playing field is level enough for even a professional (can't one, in these days of overidentification, silently assume the modifiers "white" and "androcentric" if not "male"?) reader of, say, Ezra Pound to cross gender or color lines? Or did s/he mean, rather as Gwendolyn Brooks might have coached, to finish that half sentence with a resounding, "but *we* don't have to listen!!!"

Putting aside my own double or treble academic (dis-)qualifications, is Gwendolyn Brooks's own license to represent *the* BLACK WOMAN current and negotiable? Some, including most black feminist literary academicians, who, not without evidence, find her critical comrades and male-defined position troubling, would say "no" or "no longer." While such issues will dance around the margins of my text, I do not presume to choose or deny representativeness, acceptable blackness or whiteness, and/or proper feminism. Instead, guided by the later poetry and programmatic statements of Gwendolyn Brooks, I hope to open certain issues that seem confused, yet hardly muted by recent academic appropriations of black women's writing and the legitimation routines that authorize such de- and recanonizations. I *set up* this essay, not assertively to apologize for what may be deduced as/reduced to my whiteness or womanhood, but with the hope that I am a better ironist than those who would mark the limits of (my) authority with the same assurance as they/we (the old New Critics of poetry and culture) were wont to remark its limitlessness. Instead, I wish to open, in what I hope will be a challenging way, issues of the poetics and reception of Gwendolyn Brooks since her 1967 turn away from white literary mainstream values and publication.

From the beginning of her poetic career, Brooks has shown an acute consciousness of and responsibility regarding issues of representation, audience, and authority. The first black woman to receive a Pulitzer Prize, trumpeted for the longest time by the white liberal establishment as a prodigy for adding just enough political correctness while observing strictures of form, she has always addressed and never easily hierarchized the treble joy/oppression of womanhood, poverty, and blackness. While it should be noted that adoption and emphasis of this last category, "blackness," as against Negro-ness, marks a momentous shift in Brooks's work, it is somewhat inaccurate to rend her corpus in two or three: into a before, during, or after the Black Power and Black Arts moment(s), or, for that matter, a complete shift in focus from the oppression of women to support for what looks to some like the simply misogynist and nationalist Black Arts tradition. Brooks, I contend, did not radically change her poetic themes. Even obvious modulations in her line and other organizing musical techniques are, on the whole, unremarkable. After having cut a figure in several strict verse forms, she took a typically modern and American turn to free verse, and moved closer to the ordinary language of her elected community. Certainly the texture of her poems, her palette of allusions and affiliations, has shifted from the white Anglo-American canon, but ***In the Mecca*** (1968), which Haki Madhubuti plausibly claims "'blacked' its way out of the National Book Award," is as remarkable for its range of verse forms as for its direct treatment of race and class oppression. Nevertheless, black and/or feminist critics have tended to narrow her politics to one aspect of the struggle, while white mainstream poetry reviewers have dismissed her apparently less artful later style as flat and too political. There is no reason to assume that a particular political commitment must turn one toward or away from artistic experiment or accomplishment; but, perhaps in part because (white, mostly male, academic) critics have been so busy excusing or obscuring (bad) politics in the name of high art, they have not trained themselves or prepared us to hear music in the heteroglossia that assaults the urban eye and ear. Questions about Brooks's abandonment of artistry persist, framed as the opposition between craft and commitment. In a 1969 interview by George Stavros for *Contemporary Literature,* Brooks answers charges about having "abandoned lyric simplicity for an angrier, more polemical voice" with

> Those are the things that people say who have absolutely no understanding of what's going on and no desire to understand. No, I have not abandoned beauty, or lyricism, and I don't consider myself a polemical poet. I'm a black poet, and I write about what I see, what interests me, and I'm seeing new things.

Brooks has always questioned, and, in the mid-sixties, she articulately and consistently refused the limits placed on the reputed natural "clowning" or super respectability of "colored people." If only by implication later made explicit, her earliest work also questioned the exceptional "race" and "gender" writers—artists, musicians, sports figures, politicians, or "exception Negroes" in general—when she literalized the politics and epistemology of *representation.* As teacher, critic, and inspirational speaker, Brooks increasingly began to use her position as respected artist to give voice to a solidarity that begins to resolve the double bind of a black woman artist who would be heard as something other than victim of or exile from her race and class. Awareness of divided and divisive loyalties to a conventional (white, European, Aristotelian, or simply "decorous") notion of art and to a constricted notion of her "People" was hardly born with the sixties. It is fitting that Brooks's most significant mentor, Langston Hughes (whom she first heard in the church where she also first heard and met James Weldon

Johnson), gave such clear voice to his own dilemma as a Negro artist. In "The Negro Artist and the Racial Mountain," Hughes, whose own metaphors are underwritten by W. E. B. Du Bois's "double consciousness" as well as by the strictures of *The Crisis* against which the poet rebels, sounds a condition that Brooks would almost of necessity turn into a poetic theme:

> The road for the serious black artist, then, who would produce a racial art is most certainly rocky and the mountain is high. Until recently he received almost no encouragement for his work from either white or colored people. . . .
>
> The Negro artist works against an undertow of sharp criticism and misunderstanding from his own group and unintentional bribes from the whites. "O, be respectable, write about nice people, show how good we are," say the Negroes. "Be stereotyped, don't go too far, don't shatter our illusions about you, don't amuse us too seriously. We will pay you," say the whites.

With full knowledge that, as a mainstream Negro writer, her representations were going to be (designated) more representative—if not more "equal"—than others, Brooks worried both how blacks (then *Negroes*) should be represented in literature, and how whites misread, cruised, or otherwise misused *the* black experience—which was hardly monolithic. ***Annie Allen,*** the 1949 collection that secured her the Pulitzer, shows Brooks's manifold concern about how blackness is constructed and perceived from outside. Even if she sometimes too-much-protests a bourgeois respectability she would later dismiss, a poem like **"I love those little booths at Benvenuti's"** assaults certain images and expectations of "Bronzeville" in the minds of white readers and spectators. Brooks exposes and returns the oppressive (white male) gaze of outsiders, and she does so by temporarily adopting the outsider's or suburbanite's perspective. In this way, she more than slightly confuses subject looking and object seen, "they" and "one." But by the same token, we get a clear sense of "us *versus* them":

> They get to Benvenuti's. There are booths
> To hide in while observing tropical truths
> About this—dusky folk, so clamorous!
> So amorous,
> So flatly brave!
> Boothed-in, one can detect,
> Dissect.
> . . . .
> But how shall they tell people they have been
> Out Bronzeville way? For all the nickels I
> Have not bought savagery or defined a "folk."
>
> The colored people will not "clown."
>
> The colored people arrive, sit firmly down.
> Eat their Express Spaghetti, their T-bone steak.
> Handling their steel and crockery with no clatter,
> Laugh punily, rise, go firmly out of the door.

Maud Martha (1953), Brooks's lyric novel and her only published long fiction, not only focused on what it means to be black Maud (as against golden Helen, her sister), but it also turns the tables on what it means to be reduced—or is it inflated?—to a synecdoche for one's race. By making one white visitor to the black community representative of his race, Brooks again makes the reader look at the spectator who, because he cannot step outside his whiteness, does not recognize himself as an intruder. We don't get inside the head of the visitor, any more than we are exactly in the booth with the "good view" at Benvenuti's, but Maud fixes the visiting white man by fully elaborating the ways she protects her personal space. Long before Black Power declarations of racial self-definition, Brooks more than once subtly makes visible the assumptions that underwrite white control over the figurative power of racial interaction. Maud Martha refuses simply, as Brooks would later say, to worship whiteness or whine about race. If blackness and femaleness can be essentialized, whiteness still demands individuation: when was the last time a white man was allowed to speak for all white men, or even all American white men? Yet long since *we* ceased giving over the power of voicing the body politic to king or president, there persists a disturbance in representation/representativeness by which black people—*the* racial and, I would add, sexual other(s)—are somehow fixed as slates upon which "whiteness" (an absent or *understood* adjective for American individualism) can be written in almost invisible chalk. Here one of Brooks's formulas, from ***Primer for Blacks,*** intervenes to help us read ***Maud Martha:***

> The conscious shout
> of all that is white is
> "It's Great to be white."
> The conscious shout
> of the slack in Black is
> "Its Great to be white."
> Thus all that is white
> has white strength and yours.

In a discussion of the "Great" or Emersonian tradition of American literature and scholarship (exemplified by "The American Scholar"), Toni Morrison hints something of the threat that African American (read Brooks's BLACK?) questioning or wrenching of individualism and self-determination, the very lynchpins of American man-or personhood, can have, Morrison says:

> [A]utonomy, authority, newness and difference, absolute power not only become the major themes and presumptions of American literature, but . . . each one is made possible by, shaped by, activated by a complex awareness and employment of a constituted savagery, that provided the staging ground and arena for the elaboration of the quintessential American identity.

The self constituted as and by Maud Martha, one of the ordinary "kitchenette people," is made—and assertively remakes herself—not from savagery but from (black) submission and other undistinguished maternal and female matter. Here and in other instances, Brooks manages at least to tweak the system to which Morrison refers—and, further, one might add, to work this revolution surgically within tight lyric confines. At moments, her destructive meditations are not wholly unlike Dickinson's persistently private explosions. But Brooks is always aware of "the People" and her public; that is, of race, of being racialized, and of the need to seize the power and tools of representation.

It is, I should think, customary enough for black academics and poets to be called upon—usually from "above"—to represent *their* race. Brooks reassigns this honor, or curse, to Maud Martha. Her novelistic/autobiographical answer, painted in miniature from the inside of Maud Martha's experience as this very difference in persona, at once recalls Du Bois's prerogative (setting aside for work his cultivated representative status) of determining the level of his social interactions with whites. But Brooks also subtly undresses and redresses the dynamics of rhetorical power differentials by making a young white male classmate who calls on Maud intrude into a community that, he is made to assume, can only feel blessed by his presence and/or whiteness. We readers are thus ironically privy to—and, in some cases, the butt of the dramatic irony of—Maud Martha's educated perspective on race matters:

> though she liked Charles, though she admired Charles, it was only at the high school that she wanted to see Charles.
>
> This was no Willie or Richard or Sylvester coming to call on her. Neither was she Charles's Sally or Joan. She was the whole "colored" race, and Charles was the personalization of the entire Caucasian plan. . . .
>
> What was this she was feeling now? Not fear, not fear. A sort of gratitude! It sickened her to realize it. As though Charles, in coming, gave her a gift.
>
> Recipient and benefactor.
>
> It's so good of you.
>
> You're being so good.

If one can safely assume that the readership of ***Maud Martha*** included a large number of white integrationists of several stripes, Brooks has brilliantly diagnosed, announced, and reversed a disturbance in representation by which white folks are accustomed, as discrete individuals, to identifying individuals who can stand for the group—of colored, Negro, black, other folk(s). Brooks stages, with ironic equanimity (as against Maud's expected Negro gratitude or feminine reserve) a practical encounter that tests liberal notions of accommodation: "Here was the theory of racial equality about to be put into practice, and she only hoped she would be equal to being equal."

If in 1953 Brooks was content to have Maud Martha analytically voice the options open to an ordinary woman—even an "old black gal"—she was audacious enough to create a character who could create herself within the limits of her male-identified world of marital banality:

> To create—a role, a poem, picture, music, a rapture in stone: great but not for her.
>
> What was wanted was to donate to the world a good Maud Martha. That was the offering, the bit of art, that could not come from any other.
>
> She would polish and hone that.

Brooks's 1967 announcement of a different public role for herself as poet, along with her embrace of the evolving role of New Black, might have been impossible and surely would not have been very forceful if she had not threaded a consistent meditation on racial and artistic self-construction—and reconstructions of racial and sexual otherness—through her work.

Brooks has always addressed and continues to address difficult issues, including those often decorously silent intimate traumas of abortion, color caste, domestic abuse, alienation, and motherhood in poverty. Defiant in the face of a painful history of racist lies and false consciousness that refuses to yield a "useable past," she has actively fashioned models of personal and communal dignity as poetic blueprints for cultural survival. An early poem like "the mother" (***A Street in Bronzeville,*** 1945) adumbrates her later focus on rejected, imperiled, and criminalized urban youth, even as it admits of wildly different ethos and messages: from an anti-abortion plea to a manifesto of women's choice and self-determination. This poem in particular continues to garner classroom and critical response for its complex deconstruction(s) of subjectivity and/or the androcentric lyric tradition. As Barbara Johnson has noted, Brooks bends the genre of apostrophe by addressing the literally doubly victimized, the imaginatively doubly redeemed, and inextricably compounds nonmother and unborn as agent and object of abortion. Brooks manages to convey the force of desire, regret and affirmation without sentimentalizing the role of mother or erasing the horrors of unrealized pasts and futures:

> ABORTIONS will not let you forget.
> You remember the children you got that you did not get,
> The damp small pulps with a little or with no hair,
> The singers and workers that never handled the air.
> You will never neglect or beat
> Them, or silence or buy with a sweet.

After that first stanza, which complicates the ontological and epistemological categories generically fixed by personal lyric and the address of apostrophe, the subject—and here both positions of aborted relationships share objecthood and agency—switches from the general or colloquial "you" to an only more apparently fixed "I" that promises but fails to represent a single point of view or viable position, if only because it is addressed both to the unborn and the unknowing audience. Characteristically, Brooks both invites and inhibits identification as well as easy judgment from above and outside:

> Believe that even in my deliberateness I was not deliberate.
> Though why should I whine,
> Whine that the crime was other than mine?
> Since anyhow you are dead.
> Or rather, or instead,
> You were never made.

If Brooks there achieves in an exemplary fashion the virtually impossible task of at once humanizing and equivocating over victim and agent—of making present, speaking as and to, those who definitively never were—she elsewhere works a similarly undecidable agency into the public arena of city streets and community. In fundamental ways, she has come increasingly to violate fixed definitions of gender and race roles as well as systems of representation and cultural reproduction. Perhaps an extreme case, ***Riot: A Poem in Three Parts*** (1969), gives life to the humor and horror of needs denied and escape routes blocked. I can only skim the first poem, which is, granted, a long cry from the second, **"The Third Sermon on the Warpland,"** with its phoenix rise of "A woman is dead. / Motherwoman. / She lies among the boxes. . . . " Still, the sequence's beginning, beginning with the source and thrust of its epigraph, indicates the range of Brooks's irony and her complex identification with the rioters:

> A riot is the language of the unheard.
>
> —Martin Luther King, Jr.

> John Cabot, out of Wilma, once a Wycliffe,
> all whitebluerose below his golden hair,
> wrapped richly in right linen and right wool,
> almost forgot his Jaguar and Lake Bluff;
> . . . .
> Because the "Negroes" were coming down the street.
>
> Because the Poor were sweaty and unpretty
> (not like Two Dainty Negroes in Winnetka)
> and they were coming toward him in rough ranks.
> In seas. In windsweep. They were black and loud.
> And not detainable. And not discreet.
> . . . .
> John Cabot went down in the smoke and fire
> and broken glass and blood, and he cried "Lord!
> Forgive these nigguhs that know now that they do."

Long before ***Riot,*** and before the events therein ironically recorded from within and without the virtual reality of an old negritude, which marks its fall from grace by its dialect apostrophe to "nigguhs," was swept over by a wave of unaccommodating black victims-turned-agents of potentially constructive destruction, Brooks's poetry had italicized and complicated b/Blackness. She had always been hard on Negroes with class pretensions, those who would marry or buy their way into whiteness. She did not abandon the intellectual or literal neighborhood of working-class blacks for the suburbs of academic or other prestige. And beyond the empirics of such community identification, her works explicitly warn of the various temptations to escape or explain away the racism that some black bourgeois, not to mention the intellectuals, refuse to acknowledge. Again, a set piece from ***Maud Martha*** is particularly revelatory. Maud, at the beauty parlor, thinks she has heard Miss Ingram, a cosmetics saleswoman (about whom Maud "wondered if . . . she knew that in the 'Negro group' there were complexions whiter than her own"), say, "I work like a nigger to earn a few pennies." Seeing no reaction, Maud thinks she must have been wrong. As it turns out, Sonia Johnson, the beautician, failed to react because *she* was certainly not a "nigger," and *she* knew what the word meant:

> these words like "nigger" don't mean to some of these here white people what our people *think* they mean. Now, "nigger," for instance, means to them something bad, or slavey-like, or low. They don't mean anything against me. I'm a Negro, not a "nigger." Now, a white man can be a "nigger," according to their meaning for

the word, just like a colored man can. So why should
I go getting all stepped up about a thing like that?

Therein, Brooks not only underscores the sometimes illusory power of renaming, she insists on a solidarity that will later manifest itself in a refusal to condemn the New Blackness of the sixties that the author behind Maud—who was, after all, a "plain ol' black gal"—might have been expected to reject. But, really only those who failed to read the bold code could have expected that!

Before the 1967 official D Day—or *b/B*lack day—her poetry had more than once occasioned the negative commentary of white critics and, in at least one hilarious—or is it scary?—case, broadcasters, who found her language assaultive and her subject matter too frank. Indeed, Brooks's famed "ordinary Negroes" were extraordinarily aware of being positioned within and without their poetic sketches and larger historical and literary traditions. One incident on the road to her ultimate declaration of independence from mainstream aesthetic strictures and white bourgeois values is worth nothing. It too is a reflection and public opening on her earlier work. I have in mind the controversial half-life and musical resurrection of "of De Witt Williams on his way to Lincoln Cemetery" (***A Street in Bronzeville,*** 1945).

In 1962 a Chicago radio station, WNEW, on which Brooks had decades earlier read her poem, banned Oscar Brown Jr.'s musical rendering of **"Elegy of a Plain Black Boy"** on the grounds that the recurrent phrase "a plain black boy," echoed in and from Brooks's poem, would offend Negroes and violate strictures against mixing politics into art. Of her twenty-year-old poem, updated with a direct address to the new ban on "black," she submitted the assaultive defense that explains her repositioned writing Subject and subject matter; thus: "'the life and death of a pitiful yet proud and lip-out-thrusting, chest announcing youth.'" Recall for a moment De Witt Williams, as he visits in death the haunts of a youth that, after Brooks's treatment cannot remain simply ill-spent. There is no small freight of literariness in the parody of the interstate journey of Lincoln's bier recorded in Whitman's "When Lilacs Last in the Dooryard Bloomed" and the skewed identification effected by the substitution of "Nothing but a plain black boy" for "Coming for to carry *me* home" of the spiritual's second line:

He was born in Alabama.
He was bred in Illinois.
He was nothing but a
Plain black boy.

Swing low swing low sweet sweet chariot.
Nothing but a plain black boy.

Drive him past the Pool Hall.
Drive him past the Show.
Blind within his casket,
But maybe he will know.

I do not mean to diminish the history and changes of political position and identification that intervene between the Brooks(es) of the forties, early sixties, and the near past; surely her poetry and programmatic prose would not permit such easy moves. Nevertheless, her interrogations of race, class, and gender remain both complex and in revisionary conversation with several traditions of which she has become part. At one point, Brooks characterizes her post-1967 work as a change of ethos and attitude, from supplication to self-possession:

> Much of the work that preceded the days of considerable black fire belongs in a category I call "condition literature." You remember, in "Song of Myself," Walt Whitman loves animals because they do not tirelessly "whine about their condition." A good many of us who preceded the pioneering influence of Baraka did a lot of poetic, dramatic, and fictional whining. And a lot of that was addressed to white people. We sensed ourselves crying "UP" to them. "Help us," we seemed to cry. We were fascinated by the sickness of the black condition.

I would qualify Brooks's self-corrective dismissal, in that a great deal of what she did involved more than whining or satisfying the guilt, curiosity, imagination of a white audience. But, she does not need me to save or choose her most effective work. It has had impact and influence, and she herself has revisited it in later poems and anthologies.

Even in the most declarative or rhetorical mood, her poems remain, according to her announced non-Western poetics of change and ad hoc utility, in-process and revisionary in their focus on youth and popular misconceptions about inner-city blight. Perhaps the occasional or instructive poems titled or subtitled "Sermon," "Dedication," "Preachment" do not so much conceal as proclaim the irony and distance out of which she configures an identification with, and encouragement of, what are now generations of energetically self-destructive but infinitely promising inner-city young people. If literary allusions and artful oscillations between third-person narrative and internal monologue are more pronounced in ***Annie Allen, Maud Martha,*** and peak in ***In the Mecca,*** such poems as **"Primer for Blacks"** and **"To Those of My Sisters Who Kept Their Naturals"** (***Primer for Blacks—Three Preachments,*** 1991) and the pair **"The Chicago Picasso"** (one of ***Two Dedications,*** 1967) and **"The Chicago Picasso, 1986"** at once recall her earlier performances (sometimes directly citing and renewing earlier poems) and bear witness to New Black consciousness. **"Requiem Before Renewal,"** the Third Preachment in ***Primer for Blacks,*** names her prospective yet revisionary strategy. In this vein, **"The Black Stone Rangers, I, As Seen by Disciplines"** [not disciples] (1968) asserts faith in black self-determination:

There they are.
Thirty at the corner.
Black, raw, ready.
Sores in the city
that do not want to heal.

If the Blackstone Rangers were her special link to an allegedly "sick" or stagnant pool of alienated youth talent, the occasional poems Brooks has written as poet laureate of Illinois (named so after Carl Sandburg, in 1968) and for Mayor Harold Washington and Chicago elaborate the general empowerment that comes from an unblinking recognition of potential behind the bleakest facades. **"A Hymn to Chicago,"** in the self-published pamphlet ***Mayor Harold Washington and Chicago the "I Will" City*** (1983), locates strength and beauty even as it "italicizes" a harsher truth:

This city mixes garbage and stars. This city seems
able
to make a carol out of what has been obscure. . .

. . . This city,
for all its age, is alive with youth-music and youth-
fragrance,
the music and green and fragrance youth knows
how to
manufacture for itself, cannot give to others,
cannot describe.
Need I italicize our truth
that this city
is imperfect, that within it
crime, race injustice, and cunning prowl and
have prowled
. . . .
Italics emphasize. They do not commend
rejection of all that surrounds

Indeed, it seems to me—*pace* editors like Haki Madhubuti who would make her post-1967 position univocally freeze in heroic portraits of male revolutionary race heroes (including his former self, Don L. Lee, and the Rangers who made up her first workshop gang) and mostly feminist critics who lament this alleged fixity—that Brooks remains open to change and self-re-creation. Haki Madhubuti's Third World Press, which recently reissued the out-of-print ***Maud Martha,*** publishes an extensive and somewhat self-duplicating list of Brooks's poems, whose reprints are often subtle recastings, to which I refer you for proof of Brooks's range and coherence of vision. Perhaps her consciousness, evident in her poetic penetration of the more-than-victim *versus* assailant attitude of young gangsters and other marginalized black urban youth, is not the unification or overcoming of Du Bois's "double consciousness" in a monolithic and potentially obsolete Black Power pose, but a long unfolding of the contradictory interpellation of blackness, an open call, if you will, from poet to people that continues to mark internal differences, mock the mastering white (if not also the male) gaze, and celebrate the ironies that empower the disempowered by a chiding celebration of the honorific name, the Black Magic, that used to be a curse. Again, I will not quote, but I suggest you read, the full text of this short "Preachment"; the following excerpt from the first, third, and eighth (final) stanzas of **"Primer for Blacks"** suggests Brooks's inclusiveness and her strategic separatism:

Blackness
is a title,
is a preoccupation,
is a commitment Blacks
are to comprehend—
and in which you are
to perceive your Glory.
. . . .
The word Black
has geographic power,
pulls everybody in:
Blacks here—
Blacks there—
Blacks wherever they may be.
And remember, you Blacks, what they told
you—
remember your Education:
"one Drop—one Drop
maketh a brand new Black."
Oh mighty Drop.
—And because they have given us kindly
so many more of our people
. . . .
All of you—
you COLORED ones,
you NEGRO ones,
those of you who proudly cry
"I'm half Indian"—
those of you who proudly screech
"I'VE got the blood of George WASHington in
MY veins—
ALL of you—
you proper Blacks,
you half-Blacks,
you wish-I-weren't Blacks,
Niggeroes and Niggerenes.

You.

As we shall see, more than her verse form or topics,

Brooks decisively changed the force of her irony against the political and cultural status quo that quite systematically dictates standards and undervalues black accomplishment—except when the "natural," blues, rap, or Harlem enjoy temporary renaissance. Consonant with the changing literary and literal politics of the young writers and activists of the Blacks Arts Movement, in particular the position expressed and the scene captured in Larry Neal's and LeRoi Jones's *Black Fire* (1968), Brooks deliberately changed the composition, site and invited response of her audience. After the uprisings of the mid-sixties and in the wake of an increasingly elitist or accommodationist civil rights movement, Brooks adopted certain practices and principles from her younger radical colleagues; she also began publishing at small black presses and working with groups of younger and almost exclusively black inner-city young people. Exemplary here is ***Jump Bad: A New Chicago Anthology*** (Broadside Press, 1971), the anthology of poetry, short prose pieces, and programmatic criticism edited or "presented" by Brooks. This book grew out of the community poetry workshops, formal and informal, Brooks *led*—a word she avers in this context—in Chicago beginning in 1967. Brooks's introduction tells something of her own conversion experience as well as the composition of her audience. Again, though, "audience" is also not quite right, since she is auditor as much as speaker; pupil as well as teacher of a group of young poets and performers from the "literary-minded among the Blackstone Rangers," "teen 'Gangsters,'" whom she met at "the First Presbyterian Church on the South Side." None of the irony of her position is lost on Brooks: middle-aged Lady Pulitzer up against the first members of Kuumba (founded by Val Gray Ward), who were some *Baaad* young folks, including Don L. Lee, "who had already published 'Think Black,'" and Sonia Sanchez, whose poem "We a BadDDD People" and anthology *We Be Word Sorcerers* (1973) intertextually and nominally honor Brooks's first broadside for Broadside Press, **"We Real Cool,"** a poem to which we shall return.

It is with an understanding of her own story, even here subsumed to black *his*tory, that Brooks delineates the position, predisposition, and even the grammatical prepositions that define her "New Black" poets, and herself as a (new) black poet:

> With the arrival of these people my neatly-paced life altered almost with a jerk. Never did they tell me to "change" my hair to "natural." But soon I did. Never did they tell me to open my eyes to look about me. But soon I did. Never did they tell me to find them sane, serious, substantial, superseding. But soon I did. . . .
>
> Incidentally, the question of my status, my position, (was I or was I not a Teacher, a Workshop Ruler?) was soon a gentle joke. I "taught" nothing. I told them, almost timidly, what I knew, what I had learned from European models (well, Langston Hughes too!) And they told me without telling me that the European "thing" was not what they were about. . . .
>
> Many of these black writers are now involved in an exciting labor, a challenging labor. . . . They are blackening English. Some of the results are effective and stirring. Watch for them.
>
> True black writers speak *as* blacks, *about* blacks, *to* blacks.

Brooks describes her first encounter with the "New Black[ness]" of such young black poets and playwrights as LeRoi Jones and Ron Milner at the Writers' Conference at Fisk University in 1967 as her full public transformation from Negro to a Black: "It frightens me to realize that, if I had died before the age of fifty, I would have died a 'Negro' fraction." Rather than gloat or despair about her distance and irrelevance from the young who would just barely respect anyone's mainstream credentials, she listened and began bridging the "generation gap," which, Brooks came to insist, never (should have) existed among blacks. Her account of this event is worth revisiting at some length, if only because *we* might wish to heed her cautionary note about appropriation embedded in her own self-effacing enthusiasm for the male revolutionary poet-heroes performing in Nashville:

> Until 1967 my own blackness did not confront me with a shrill spelling of itself. I knew that I was what most people were still calling a "Negro.". . .
>
> Suddenly there was New Black to meet. . . . I had been "loved" at South Dakota State College. Here I was coldly Respected. . . . Imamu Amiri Baraka, then "LeRoi Jones," was expected. He arrived in the middle of my own offering, and when I called attention to his presence there was jubilee in Jubilee Hall. . . .
>
> Up against the wall, white man! was the substance of the Baraka shout, at the evening reading he shared with fierce Ron Milner among intoxicating drumbeats, heady incense and organic underhumming. Up against the wall! And a pensive (until that moment) white man of thirty or thirty three abruptly shot himself into the heavy air, screaming "Yeah! *Yeah*! Up against the wall, Brother! KILL 'EM ALL! KILL 'EM ALL!"
>
> I thought that was interesting.
>
> There is indeed a new black today. He is differ-

> ent from any the world has known. He's tall-walker. Almost firm. By many of his own *brothers* he is not understood. And he is understood by *no* white. Not the wise white; not the Schooled white; not the Kind white. Your *least* pre-requisite toward an understanding of the new black is an exceptional Doctorate which can be conferred only upon those with the proper properties of bitter birth and intrinsic sorrow. I know this is infuriating, especially to those professional Negro-understanders.

Brooks's poems as well as their means of publication and distribution changed from styles acceptable to the big New York commercial houses to those possible only in workshops, readings, and small press anthologies. In the sixties, the lines of black (and perhaps not only b/Black) poetic communication were strong and strongly interwoven among many community and political organizations and movements. The circuit Brooks entered was at least circumjacent to the work and workers of SNCC (Student Nonviolent Coordinating Committee), SCLC (Southern Christian Leadership Conference), the Black Panther Party, and other groups that had been literal and figurative fellow travelers on freedom marches and voter registration drives. I do not mean to project sixties nostalgia onto a complex scene whose coalitions were sometimes rather costly, but black and/or revolutionary unity during that period has been nearly erased by interested revisionary histories from several sides. Further, not to expose any secrets that Brooks and more than one black public intellectual continue to reveal, the easy flow of artists and information from performance venues as varied as black colleges (whether traditionally Negro Southern colleges or inner-city state community colleges and universities), organized or informal youth groups (even "gangs"), churches and prisons, and public commemorative occasions (especially in cities with black leaders) continues. Such networks are always somewhat fragile, as capable of excluding members on account of revolutionary purity or Puritanism as being co-opted by critics in search of authenticity, the academic descendants, perhaps, of "professional Negro-understanders."

In any case, consistent with Brooks's 1967 embrace of "New Black," she offered ***Report from Part One,*** her autobiography-in-process, long awaited by Harper and Row, to Dudley Randall's Broadside Press. In *Broadside Memories: Poets I Have Known* (1975), his memoir and celebratory program of the press's first ten years, Dudley Randall's account of her association with Broadside Press neatly indicates the range and redirection of her work enabled by this change of publisher and audience:

> After the assassination of Martin Luther King, she told me she was doing a little book and wished to donate it to Broadside Press. Titled ***Riot,*** it was published in 1969. All proceeds from the book go to Broadside. It was followed by ***Family Pictures,*** and ***Aloneness,*** a children's book.
>
> One day she called me and said she wanted her autobiography to be published by Broadside. Thinking of her welfare, I declined. . . . Upon publication ***Report From Part One*** was greeted with an enthusiastic review by Toni Cade Bambara on page one of the *New York Times Book Review.*
>
> Her latest book is ***Beckonings,*** where she tries a style simple and direct enough to reach all Black people, yet rich and deep.

Broadside began by issuing famous poets' broadside poems with original art but soon moved to single book and group anthology publications of new poets. Created by Dudley Randall's vision and with little funding, publishing an impressive roster of black poets and scholars, Broadside surely needed Brooks's prominence and sales potential. But there was much more than that, for Brooks had found both herself and/or a new role as an activist artist, even as she was helping to found a community of poets. Brooks's first Broadside broadside, **"We Real Cool,"** whose title and refrain, borrowed from black English street argot, became something of an anthem, has an interesting history that makes Brooks a leader *avant la révolution,* if you will. Dudley Randall tells it, thus:

> In May 1966, I attended the first Writers' Conference at Fisk University, and obtained permission from Robert Hayden, Melvin B. Tolson, and Margaret Walker, who were there, to use their poems. . . . I wrote to Gwendolyn Brooks and obtained her permission to use **"We Real Cool."** This first group of six Broadsides [is] called "Poems of the Negro Revolt."

Differently presented and received seven years after its publication in the collection ***The Bean Eaters*** (1960), Randall's broadside of Brooks's **"We Real Cool"** "was lettered white on black by Cledie Taylor to simulate scrawls on a blackboard," in keeping with the care he took to "harmonize . . . the poem, in paper, color, and typography." This is to say that Brooks's poem was afforded a place of distinction, if not literally a space on many a wall. This poem continues to generate interest, and, if only because I was at least surprised to see it treated to an apparently gratuitous dismissal in a recent issue of *Callaloo,* I would like to spend a few moments over it. Before rival readings, the poem, unfortunately sans graphics:

"We Real Cool"

The Pool Players.
Seven at the Golden Shovel.

We real cool. We
Left school. We

Lurk late. We
Strike straight. We

Sing sin. We
Thin gin. We

Jazz June. We
Die soon.

Of this poem Hortense Spillers, praising the "wealth of implication" in this "[l]ess than lean poem," says it is "no nonsense at all." Finding original artistry, in-crowd and in-race code, and a full range of traditional poetic techniques in Brook's poem, Spillers say that Brook's players "subvert the romance of sociological pathos" and, quite comfortably, she has them read Brooks's lines, thus:

> They make no excuse for themselves and apparently invite no one else to do so. The poem is their situation as *they* see it. In eight [could be nonstop] lines, here is their total destiny. Perhaps comic geniuses, they could well drink to this poem, making it a drinking/revelry song.

I would like to bring Helen Vendler's recent mention of Brooks into conversation with Spillers's earlier tribute. Speaking with the well-earned authority of her position as a major reader of *the* Western cannon and an influential critic of new poet candidates to that tradition, Vendler writes about the new national poet laureate in *Callaloo,* the most important wider-than-academic journal of black and Third World poetry. She generously praises and candidly corrects (explicitly *not* in the sense of "political correctness") the "Identity Markers" Rita Dove marshals to "confront . . . the enraging fact that the inescapable accusation of blackness becomes, too early for the child to resist it, a strong element of inner self-definition." At one point, Vendler economically dismisses Brooks in questioning one of Dove's "relatively unsuccessful historical excursions in a lyric time-machine." Not to make too much of a few lines, I quote her dismissal in full: "This [Dove's early 'odyssey'] may owe something to Gwendolyn Brooks's **'We Real Cool,'** but it avoids the prudishness of Brooks's judgmental monologue, which though it is ostensibly spoken by adolescents, barely conceals its adult reproach of their behavior.

Even though Vendler indicates that Brooks's poem is not properly addressed to the white critical tradition, her response does not fail to register, however unwittingly, Brooks's double movement at once to narrow and to expand the usual distance readers of poetry traverse in becoming—or resisting becoming—"We," whether *real cool* or not. By making Brooks admonish the adolescents, Vendler makes pretty clear who isn't *We*—not to say who "We" isn't. It seems that, however fallen, Brooks, the poet, simply must share the critic's position above those pool players. Curiously, from their different aesthetic and experiential positions, Vendler and Spillers both give valid readings of the poem, and it is no accident that they fix on the pronoun that hangs out there like the prepositions from William Carlos Williams's famous wheelbarrow.

Not to dwell overlong on the ethos or impact of the very different constructions invited by Brooks's "We," I add Brooks's own commentary on the poem, which is delivered as stage directions for her public readings:

> First of all, let me tell you how that's [**"We Real Cool"**] supposed to be said, because there's a reason why I set it out as I did. These are people who are essentially saying, "Kilroy is here. We *are.*" But they're a little uncertain of the strength of their identity. The "We"—you're supposed to stop after the "we" and think about *validity,* of course, there's no way for you to tell whether it should be said softly or not, I suppose, but I say it rather softly because I want to represent their basic uncertainty.

Characteristically, Brooks invites both identification with and objectification of the young men—depending, perhaps on such categories as the race, gender, age of her/their audience. There is something cunning and deceptive both about the openness of Brooks's "We" and her variable distance from both the pool players to whom it refers and the people—at least since its Broadside republication—it seems to rename. Rather like the young white man who, in Brooks's story about Baraka, heeded a call not intended for him, or the "You" of **"Primer for Blacks,"** that shifty pronoun works a critique on audience overidentification and poet's supposed representativeness. After all, isn't *she* supposed to correct the young punks, not to follow them as new leaders? But which *she*? The writer of **"We Real Cool,"** ***The Bean Eaters*** (1960)? Or the writer of the 1967 broadside, **"We Real Cool"?** And should the differences of context and thus of content be *fixed*—either in the sense of "healed" or "halted"? Brooks put(s) her readers, specifically a black audience that is not limited to the no-longer-New Blacks of the sixties, to work on such questions.

Rather than stand as the highly decorated, proper, and representative lady and/or poet for her race (the "lady 'negro poet'"), Brooks chose to transform a black audience into poets or, as William Blake might say, prophets. Brooks's address is wider than Whitman's mutual embrace of writer and his people. More literal, literary, and liberating are her encouragement and publicity in favor of young poets than the hope that one day, perhaps crossing to Brooklyn on a ferry, one might think her thoughts. Indeed, it might be that her greatest offense against the literary and academic establishment(s)—the refusal to rest on her (canonical) laurels and apparent dismissal of the capital "P" of Poetry, which is also her refusal to repeat the talented-tenth or exclusive single, sanctioned post of (non-)representative poet, such as Hughes in the Harlem Renaissance—encrypts her most direct engagement of literary history.

Despite a fair amount of thunder and fire, her statement is no "No in thunder," but a generous "Yes" to those systematically excluded from the academic and elitist poetic apparatus. Let me digress for a moment, moving from black to Blake, if you will. Indeed, there is something Blakean, revolutionary yet (re-)visionary, in Brooks's poetic address or ethos that jibes with Blake's ironic assault on Milton and literary canonizations that would create and define both "a fit audience though few" and "justify the ways of God to Man"—not to mention Western Truth for all time readable in a certain poetic genealogy and line. Let me remind you just how economical Blake can be, when he quotes a few words of the biblical Moses at the end of his preface to *Milton*. Moses prevented his servant from forbidding unsanctioned competing men from prophesying with the words "Would to God that all the Lord's people were prophets" (Numbers 11:29). With this epigraph, standing as it does at the beginning of his poem against limits placed on the religion and politics of his time, Blake takes aim against the one Holy and Apostolic Church that English poetry was becoming—ironically, under the name of Milton, erstwhile radical Protestant.

Like Blake, Brooks subsumes and revises the conventional role of poet. Sometimes she critiques the old by celebrating and enacting her new position within poems. **"The Wall,"** for instance, records and comprises Brooks's poetic dedication of "the mural of black dignity" painted on a slum wall at Forty-third and Langley in Chicago. In a *mise-en-scène* that depicts the poet—"She our sister is"—who rises to the podium in order to celebrate and, with the other "Women in wool hair chant their poetry," to take poetry from off shelves and paintings down from walls to this Wall. She is but one of the celebrants, one with the graffiti artists, also an organic cultural critic, celebrating her own history and promise. With one stroke, she helps deface the ugliness of the slum, while together poet and multimedia artists worship, make "yea" and "announcement," "chant," and "sing." Thus, with the African ornaments of sixties costumes and the figures of high art, Brooks at once very precisely locates in time, space, and with the proper names of some participants, the occasion of this celebration of perpetual movement as an assertion of human dignity:

> "THE WALL"
> August 27, 1967. . . .
>
> A drumdrumdrum.
> Humbly we come.
> South of success and east of gloss and glass are sandals;
> flowercloth;
> grave hoops of wood or gold, pendant
> from black ears, brown ears, reddish brown
> and ivory ears
> . . . .
> . . . In front of me
> hundreds of faces, red-brown, brown, black, ivory,
> yield me hot trust, their yea and their Announcement
> that they are ready to rile the high-flung ground.
> Behind me, Paint.
> Heroes.
> No child has defiled
>
> The Heroes of this Wall this serious Appointment
> this still Wing
> this Scald this Flute this heavy Light this Hinge.
>
> An emphasis is paroled.
> The old decapitations are revised,
> The dispossessions beakless.
>
> And we sing.

In order to sing prophetic poetry with her young people, Brooks had further to go than Blake, since she had not only to reject and replace one precursor, but she had also to renounce the monumentalization of Western art and her own assigned position(s) therein: "First," "Negro," "Woman," "Poet(ess)," and so on. Just so, with reference to Larry Neal and LeRoi Jones's *Black Fire* (1968), her own contribution to ***A Capsule Course in Black Poetry Writing*** (1975) prizes the utility as well as the perpetual revolution and resistance of the Black Art she had first embraced, as such and by her own account, in 1967 at the Second Black Writers' Conference at Fisk. In her "Course" she is, again, pupil of the young and poet-in-process; thus:

> The new feeling, among the *earnest* new young black creators, was that concern for the long-lastingness was western and was wrong. One created a piece of art for the enrichment, the instruction, the extension of one's own people. Its usefulness may or may not be exhausted in a day, a week, a month, a year. There was no prayerful compulsion—*among the earnest*—for its idle survival into the centuries. The word went down: we must chase out Western measures, rules, models.

Directly, as a poet consciously and publicly revising both her own image and the poet's representative function, Brooks, in the appendix/marginalia to ***Report from Part One,*** opens both person and category "Poet and/or G. B." to change and public interaction and construction. She is conscious of writing at, to, within the limits of a topical tribute to the changes wrought in her by—young and mostly male—revolutionary heroes. She is conscious, too, of future (r)evolutions from poets, prophets, and just plain people she will address and support. Ironically, her secure fame and position enable her to renounce the poet's traditional aesthetic distance:

> My aim, in my next future, is to write poems that will somehow successfully "call" (see Imamu Baraka's "SOS" [*Black Fire*]) all black people: black people in taverns, black people in gutters, schools, offices, factories, prisons, the consulate; I wish to reach black people in pulpits, black people in mines, on farms, on thrones, *not* always to "teach"—I shall wish often to entertain, to illumine. My newish voice will not be an imitation of the contemporary young black voice, which I so admire, but an extending adaptation of today's G. B. voice.

Let me make clear that Brooks does not see what I am calling her shift in intended audience (also a shift from general poetic and academic to specifically black community venues) as renunciation of, say, prestige for virtue. She announces a new, provisional yet prophetic writing in the terms of a new (black) consciousness and the affirmation of the beauty of her own dark skin; from the first, we might remember, her poems remarked the self-hatred imposed by color caste and versions of white beauty. And, while her apparent adoption of such roles as queen and mother to poets might seem, from a certain perspective, to recapitulate the old virgin-whore construction, Brooks doesn't end with that rebeginning:

> I—who have "gone the gamut" from an almost angry rejection of my dark skin by some of my brainwashed brothers and sisters to a surprised queenhood in the black sun—am qualified to enter at least the kindergarten of new consciousness now. New consciousness and trudge-toward-progress.
>
> I have hopes for myself.

FURTHER READING

Criticism

Hughes, Gertrude Reif. "Making It *Really* New: Hilda Doolittle, Gwendolyn Brooks, and the Feminist Potential of Modern Poetry." *American Quarterly* 42, No. 3 (September 1990): 375-401.

Examines the appropriation of modernist literary strategies and anti-heroism in the poetry of Doolittle and Brooks.

Kent, George E. "Aesthetic Values in the Poetry of Gwendolyn Brooks." In *Black Literature and Humanism,* edited by R. Baxter Miller, pp. 75-94. Lexington: University Press of Kentucky, 1981.

Discusses elements of existential despair and the social alienation of African-Americans in Brooks's poetry.

Miller, R. Baxter. "'Does Man Love Art?': The Humanistic Aesthetic of Gwendolyn Brooks." In *Black Literature and Humanism,* edited by R. Baxter Miller, pp. 95-112. Lexington: University Press of Kentucky, 1981.

Explores Brooks's humanistic perspective and universal artistic concerns in her poetry.

Park, Clara Claiborne. "First Fight, Then Fiddle." *The Nation* (26 September 1987): 308-12.

Provides an overview of Brooks's life and work through review of D. H. Melham's *Gwendolyn Brooks: Poetry and the Heroic Voice* and Maria K. Mootry and Gary Smith's *A Life Distilled: Gwendolyn Brooks, Her Poetry and Fiction.*

Shaw, Harry B. "Perceptions of Men in the Early Works of Gwendolyn Brooks," in *Black American Poets Between Worlds, 1940-1960,* edited by R. Baxter Miller, pp. 136-59. Knoxville: University of Tennessee Press, 1986.

Examines Brooks's presentation of black male figures in *A Street in Bronzeville, Annie Allen, Maud Martha,* and *The Bean Eaters.*

Interviews

Stavros, George. "An Interview with Gwendolyn Brooks." *Contemporary Literature* XI, No. 1 (Winter 1970): 1-20.

Brooks discusses contemporary black poetry, her artistic influences, major themes and technical aspects of her work, and changes in her political consciousness and perspective.

Tate, Claudia. "Gwendolyn Brooks." In *Black Women Writers at Work,* edited by Claudia Tate, pp. 39-48. New York: Continuum, 1985.

Brooks discusses the emergence of her new black consciousness during the late 1960s and her artistic aims and political perspective as a black writer.

Additional coverage of Brooks's life and career is contained in the following sources published by Gale: ***Authors in the News,*** **Vol. 1;** ***Black Literature Criticism; Black Writers,*** **Vol. 2;** ***Concise Dictionary of American Literary Biography,*** **1941-1968;** ***Contemporary Authors,*** **Vols. 1-4R;** ***Contemporary Authors New Revision Series,*** **Vols. 1, 27, 52;** ***Children's Literature Review,*** **Vol. 27;** ***Dictionary of Literary Biography,*** **Vols. 5, 76, and 165;** ***DISCovering Authors; DISCovering Authors: Canadian; DISCovering Authors Modules: Most-Studied, Multicultural, and Poets; Major Twentieth Century Writers; Poetry Criticism,*** **Vol. 7;** ***Something About the Author,*** **Vol. 6; and** ***World Literature Criticism.***

Gail Godwin

1937-

(Full name Gail Kathleen Godwin) American novelist, short story writer, essayist, and librettist.

The following entry presents an overview of Godwin's career. For further information on her life and works, see *CLC,* Volumes 5, 8, 22, 31, and 69.

INTRODUCTION

Gail Godwin is a gifted popular writer whose work has been praised for its convincing development of characters. With story lines closely paralleling her own life experiences, she writes about issues pertaining to women—male-female roles, marriage, family, personal freedom, self-concept, and self-actualization. Often her characters define themselves through the art or literature they create or study, graying the line between reality and fiction. She has based many of her characters on her own family members and tragic incidents in their lives that have affected her. Thus, Godwin's narratives can be perceived as analyses of her life. While not all of her novels are set in the South, her southern upbringing pervades each work through settings, events, cultural references, or characters struggling with Southern traditions and stereotypes. *A Mother and Two Daughters* (1982) launched Godwin into the ranks of best-selling authors.

Biographical Information

Godwin was born in Birmingham, Alabama, and raised in a "manless little family" by her mother and grandmother until she was an adolescent. They were dissimilar role models. Her grandmother was a traditional Southern woman who ran the household and set aside her interests for others. She is represented by Edith in *The Odd Woman* (1974). Her mother, Kathleen Godwin, was a reporter for the local paper, a junior college teacher, and weekend romance writer. She imbued Godwin with a love of storytelling. Kathleen would become Kate in the *Glass People* (1972) and Kitty in *The Odd Woman.* When Godwin was eleven years old, her mother married Frank Cole, with whom she never developed a close relationship. He figures as the stepfather Ray in *The Odd Woman.* Godwin finally met her charismatic father, Mose Godwin, who had left the family shortly after her birth, at her high school graduation. She lived with him briefly while attending Pearce Junior College in Raleigh, North Carolina; later he would commit suicide. The lovable Uncle Ambrose who kills himself in *Violet Clay* (1978) and the disconsolate Walter Gowan in *Father Melancholy's Daughter* (1991) are patterned after Mose. Godwin's uncle and half-brother also committed suicide; the latter's story was retold in *A Southern Family* (1987). After graduating from the University of North Carolina, Godwin took a job as a reporter with the *Miami Herald.* She was fired a year later because she persisted in infusing her stories with human-interest details rather than just presenting the facts. During the same year, she was married for three months to newspaper photographer Douglas Kennedy. This union would be fodder for Godwin's first novel, "Gull Key." This novel, however, was never published because she sent the only manuscript copy to a publisher whom later she could never track down. In 1962 she went to London, where she worked for the U.S. Travel Service at the American embassy, traveled, and took writing classes. She met her second husband, British psychiatrist Ian Marshall, in one of her classes. Her first published novel, *The Perfectionists* (1970), is based on her second, also very brief, marriage. Upon her return to the United States, Godwin studied writing and pursued her postgraduate degrees at the University of Iowa, earning her M.A. degree in 1968 and her Ph.D. degree in English in 1971. Her thesis was the novel *The Perfectionists.* While in the Iowa Writers' Workshop, she studied under Kurt Vonnegut along with fellow student John Irving. Later, as Irving was writing *The World According to Garp* and she was writing *Violet Clay*, they exchanged chapters as they wrote them. Besides novels, Godwin has written short stories and essays and has been the librettist of musical works by her companion, Robert Starer. She has garnered many honors, including a National Book Award nomination for *The Odd Woman*, American Book Award nominations for *Violet Clay* and for *A Mother and Two Daughters*, a Janet Kafka award and Thomas Wolfe Memorial award for *A Southern Family*, an Alabama Library Association Best Fiction award for *Father Melancholy's Daughter*, as well as National Endowment for the Arts grants in creative writing and for librettists, and a Guggenheim fellowship.

Major Works

Godwin forces her protagonists, who are nearly without exception women, to reevaluate their lives and desires when confronted with an adversity, be it a sudden death in the family, a breakdown in a marriage, or some other incident. In *The Perfectionists* Godwin describes the disintegration of American Dane Empson's "perfect but unhappy marriage" to a British psychiatrist while on vacation with his sullen three-year-old son and a patient. Dane struggles to understand what she wants from the marriage and what her role is in it. Another unhappily married woman, grappling with the same questions of self-abnegation and resolution, is the protagonist of the *Glass People*. Cameron Bolt adores and pampers his wife, Francesca, but stifles her personal growth until she literally bolts for freedom. Freedom brings complications for which she is unprepared, and she ultimately returns to her welcoming husband, although she is pregnant by another man. The book confirmed Godwin's talent, but *The Odd Woman* demonstrated a significant advance in her development. In the novel an unmarried literature professor, Jane Clifford, engaged in a love affair with a married man, Gabriel Weeks, mulls over freedom, identity, and self-fulfillment by examining the lives of real and literary women. Following the death her grandmother, she analyzes the roles of her mother (a romantic, accommodating wife), her grandmother (a traditional Southern lady), friend (a militant feminist), and colleague (a successful, married career woman) and reflects on how she twines literary fantasies into her life, especially in her relationship with Gabriel. This novel is twice as long as Godwin's previous ones because of her inclusion of more flashback, fantasy, and actual incidents and of the characterizations of several women. In *Violet Clay* Godwin explores the relationship of the artist and her art, as the title character seeks to establish her self-identity. Violet is a Southern woman who goes to New York to become an artist, but settles for being an illustrator of romance novel covers. Shaken by losing her job and her lover, then her Uncle Ambrose's suicide, she moves into her uncle's cabin to gain insight into his stagnated writing career and to rediscover her artistic self. The narrative of Godwin's next two novels, *A Mother and Two Daughters* and *The Finishing School* (1985) also evolves from death. In *A Mother and Two Daughters* Godwin explores relationships, Southern stereotypes, the New South, and such issues as abortion as the central characters aspire to selfhood after the death of the father. It is the first book in which Godwin tells a story from the perspective of more than one character. These characters include the recently widowed mother, Nell Strickland, and her thirty-something daughters Cate, a twice-divorced college professor, and Lydia, a mother who has left her husband. In *The Finishing School* a middle-aged actress recalls the summer she was fourteen and she and her mother stayed at her aunt's home following the death of her grandparents and father and she became the protégé of a failed actress. The book presents a good portrait of adolescence using a style that is both mythic and folkloric. *A Southern Family* is based on the suicide of Godwin's half-brother. In the novel, author Clare Quick is visiting her family in North Carolina when her brother, a divorced father, kills his girlfriend and himself. The book delves into the reactions of the survivors (the family and the community) and the family history and relationships that might shed light on such an unpredictable event. Godwin derived the despondent father in *Father Melancholy's Daughter* (which focuses on role reversal) from her own father's experience with depression. After her mother runs off when she is six, Margaret Gower assumes the role of nurturer as her Episcopal priest father is unable to overcome his heartbrokenness. This book is a combination of domestic fiction, mystery, and religious novel. Godwin returns to the theme of matrimony and its complexities in *The Good Husband* (1994). The story involves four characters undergoing profound changes. Alice Henry, who recently had a miscarriage, is contemplating divorcing her eccentric, Southern novelist husband, Hugo, and is becoming interested in her friend Magna Dowers' husband, Francis Lake. Caring and steadfast Francis, who is ten years younger than Magna, left the priesthood to marry her. But now as she is dying, Magna encourages Alice's interest in him.

Critical Reception

Although she produces a new novel every few years, and has experimented with various literary modes and techniques, Godwin has consistently won the respect of reviewers. As Mary Ann Wimsatt noted, "During slightly more than twenty years of an active career, Gail Godwin has established herself as one of the most gifted, prolific, and popular late twentieth-century Southern novelists." Most of her books are characterized as well written, well executed, readable, witty, and having vivid, believable characters. "Her meticulously controlled fiction," wrote Paul Gray, "creates the illusion of life unpredictably unfolding and of characters trying to make moral sense out of experiences that overwhelm thought." *The Odd Woman, The Finishing School,* and *A Southern Family* attracted favorable reviews and a large popular audience. However, *Violet Clay* and *The Good Husband* were less appreciated by reviewers, the former for being too intelligent, the latter for being overambitious and too symbolic. Despite such criticism, Godwin remains highly regarded for her depiction of authentic female protagonists whose private struggles and insecurities reflect those of many modern women. Wimsatt added, "All Godwin's novels, from *The Perfectionists* in 1970 to *Father Melancholy's Daughter* in 1991, center upon young women struggling to attain their independence, establish their identity, and successfully pursue their work despite the restraints of male-dominated culture and with or without the companionship or support of men." In a review of *A Southern Family,* Gray concluded, "Born in the South, Godwin appears to be one of those writers who inherited a subject for life; then she developed the wisdom and talent to make her birthright seem constantly fresh and enthralling."

PRINCIPAL WORKS

The Perfectionists (novel) 1970
Glass People (novel) 1972
The Odd Woman (novel) 1974
Dream Children (short stories) 1976
Violet Clay (novel) 1978
A Mother and Two Daughters (novel) 1982
Mr. Bedford and the Muses (short stories) 1983
The Finishing School (novel) 1985
A Southern Family (novel) 1987
Father Melancholy's Daughter (novel) 1991
The Good Husband (novel) 1994

CRITICISM

Susan E. Lorsch (essay date 1978)

SOURCE: "Gail Godwin's *The Odd Woman:* Literature and the Retreat from Life," in *Critique: Studies in Modern Fiction,* Vol. XX, No. 2, 1978, pp. 21-32.

[*In the following essay, Lorsch examines the significance of literature and imaginative thought for the female protagonist of* The Odd Woman. *According to Lorsch,* "The Odd Woman *centers on the relation between literature and life, especially on the effect that literature—and the lies it often tells—has on those who believe it.*"]

Gail Godwin's ***The Odd Woman*** (1974) does not at first glance seem to be in the currently popular mode of self-conscious fiction—and perhaps for this reason has not attracted the critical attention it deserves. Neither a work as involuted as one by Borges nor a *Kuenstlerroman,* ***The Odd Woman*** centers on the relation between literature and life, especially on the effect that literature—and the lies it often tells—has on those who believe it. Of special interest is the novel's focus on fiction's traditional portrayal of women and its effect on women's relations with and reactions to men.

For Jane Clifford, the protagonist of ***The Odd Woman,*** words possess an almost magical quality. The novel opens with Jane lying in bed trying to overcome her usual insomnia by pondering the written records of sleeplessness left by other insomniacs. To Jane, words seem imbued with the power to heal, the power to influence life:

> she believed in them deeply. The articulation, interpretation, appreciation, and preservation of good words. She believed in their power. If you truly named something, you had that degree of control over it. . . . The right word or the wrong word could change a person's life, the course of the world.

As Jane admits to herself, "everything for her is measured in words."

To Jane, a professor of English literature serves as far more than simply vocation or avocation. It is not just an object of perception but conditions her very mode of seeing. She views her own life through the refracting filter of literature. Jane's mother, Kitty, oversimplifies matters when she accuses Jane of looking up her life in books, but Jane interweaves her life with books; she experiences her life through literature, through the books she has so entirely assimilated. A teacher of Romantic and Victorian literature, Jane has lived since graduate school "more in the nineteenth century than in her own." For Jane the worlds of fiction and the "real" world are one: she admits to a student that, gazing at the moon, she might perhaps perceive it through Coleridge's poetry. Climbing off this student's motorcycle, she "made a point of thanking him with the formality of a Jane Austen heroine climbing decorously from a carriage."

Jane not only experiences literary worlds as real, she treats the actual world as if it were an aesthetic creation. The anecdotes of her family history become the formative stories of Jane's present as well as her past, serving as simply so much more fiction for her to analyze and interpret. Jane dwells, for example, on "Kitty's train story," Edith's fainting story, and Cleva's escape story. Her astute friend Gerda, criticizing Jane's conception of her family history, asserts that Jane transforms her relatives into symbols and their stories into myths. Jane creates her own personal yet widely allusive fictions.

Central to the plot of ***The Odd Woman*** and to Jane's conception of art and life is her relationship with Gabriel Weeks. We might expect Jane's affair with Gabriel to represent her life in the "real" physical world in contrast to her life in the world of her literary imagination. A rather silent man, Gabriel denies the importance of words, and Jane's encounters with him center around sexual rendezvous, non-verbal meetings. Such an estimate of the relationship, however, is misleading, for Jane's affair with Gabriel is but one more expression of her overwhelming immersion in words. Gabriel is a product of Jane's very literary imagination: having heard him speak at a Modern Language Association seminar, Jane *dreams* him as a lover. Even long after their sexual relationship has begun, she admits to herself that he "represented a dream." Her affair with Gabriel begins with her researching him, tracking him down through her imagination with the aid of the *Oxford English Dictionary,* various indexes and catalogues, and Gabriel's monograph.

Jane's prefabricated fantasy affair with Gabriel, she tells us that "with Gabriel—she often planned her conversations, sometimes weeks in advance"—reveals and reflects an attitude which underlies her concern with literature. Godwin links Jane's interest in fictions with the wish to avoid sexuality, to ignore or de-emphasize the physical world in favor of the world of the imagination. Note that the motivations behind Jane's previous affair (and near marriage) were the literary discussions and intellectual rapport Jane enjoyed with her lover's mother. Gabriel represents for Jane not immersion in but escape from the physical world. Jane's relationship with Gabriel proves almost a denial of sexuality and of physicality. After being with Gabriel, Jane finds herself constipated: "They had shared the same hotel room, and the result was that she had been unable to go to the bathroom for three mornings because she could not bear to make the noises necessary to these functions."

Gabriel, in turn, proves a suitable match for Jane. His interest in love seems equally intellectual and hypothetical: the topic of his monograph is "Lessons on Love by Three Pre-Raphaelite Painters." Along with Jane, one feels Gabriel's presence as intellectual rather than physical: the novel, narrated so completely from Jane's point of view, gives scant description of Jane and Gabriel's lovemaking. Gerda tells Jane that Gabriel must be Jane's perfect lover—that is, "*a perfect blur,*" someone only remotely physical. Gabriel, the intellectual lover derived from dreams and words and paper research, is indeed Gabriel the angel.

Interestingly, in an earlier novel Godwin's main character wonders what it would be like to make love with an angel. In ***The Odd Woman,*** Jane Clifford finds out. The only way she can physically fulfill herself in bed with an angel is to escape into a fantasy; an angel cannot by his very nature be a satisfactory lover, and a satisfactory lover seems not to be what Jane seeks. Such sexual failure and the falsification implied by dreaming for oneself and angel as a lover is foreshadowed by the poem which Jane discusses with her students.

Early in ***The Odd Woman*** we are told that Jane teaches Blake's "The Angel" to her class and surely the speaker of the poem represents Jane: "I dreamt a Dream! what can it mean? / And that I was a maiden Queen, / Guarded by an Angel mild." Just as Jane dreams up Gabriel, her "Angel mild," she envisions herself most comfortably as a "maiden Queen," virginal and pure, whose only safe object of physical affection might be an Angel mild. For Jane, angels have the innocence she had before puberty and before Kitty's remarriage forced sexual knowledge on her:

> "Little Jane has *Engelshaar.* . . . The hair of an angel. It will soon turn dark. Yes, my dear, as the soul loses its purity, the *Engelshaar* must go dark." Within months, Jane had witnessed, horrified, the old nun's prophecy fulfill itself. Her hair became dark the winter she was in the fourth grade, the first winter she spent her weekends with the newly married Kitty and Ray. And there was worse to come. Soon, on other parts of her body, dark hair began to grow as well. She was alarmed and shaved herself with a razor and got down on her knees at night and prayed it would not come back. It came back. Darker and thicker than before. Her guilt pressed upon her.

The happiest time of Jane's adult life is the period in which she retreats from the physical world into the world of the mind and writes her dissertation:

> She withdrew into her carrel in the quiet of the library; she withdrew, without embarrassment, into the utter earnestness of her mind. Here she was pure and light, stripped of her usual fears about her own inadequacies, about the uncertainties of the future. . . . Outside, it snowed constantly. One snow followed another. The campus was white and silent. Outside and inside her, all was cold, white, pure. She looked in the mirror of the library's women's room and saw a clear-eyed being with nothing about her wasted, no excess skin or energy which was not in use. Her skin, it seemed to her, glowed with a mental and spiritual electricity, like a saint's skin.

Clearly, Jane's immersion in her work and the chaste frozen environment in which she thrives reflect her fears of and retreat from sexuality and the world around her.

Jane's attitude toward sexuality, that she can only allow herself to make love to an angel ethereal and mild, derives from the influence of her grandmother. Edith, who raised her. Edith tells the young and impressionable Jane that "There are certain duties in marriage. . . . There are certain things one has to go through with because the man needs them, you see." Central to Jane's familial mythology is the episode bringing Edith together with her husband-to-be. Jane "had always liked that story; something in it was very close to her, very close to her own feelings about the human race."

> "Life is a disease," [Edith] moaned, and fell forthwith in a slender heap of white lawn at the feet of a young German immigrant named Hans Barnstorff, who adored her on sight. When she woke from the fever, on her daddy's farm, all her hair fallen out, there was Hans, who still saw the most beautiful woman in the world. "Let me protect you from it," he said.

Edith's marriage, then, becomes a retreat from life. Godwin uses Jane's strong identification with Edith and with the view that life is a disease to explain Jane's interest in the angel Gabriel which she connects with Jane's dependence on literature. In a love affair with Gabriel, Jane hopes to recapture her innocence and be the maiden Queen of Blake's Song of Experience. As in Blake's poem, life's romantic dreams of innocence end in experience, with the morning dawning and the angel gone.

Gabriel and Edith are not the only characters Godwin uses to underscore Jane's problems. In contrast with Jane, characters as different as Ray and Howard disclose that not only is Jane's interest in literature symptomatic of her problems with sexuality but such interest itself causes problems for Jane. Both Ray and Howard symbolize and embody sexual energy in Jane's world. The man who took Kitty away from Jane and Edith and who nightly attracts Kitty away from her jealous daughters has the apt surname "Sparks" (compared with the weak Gabriel *Weeks*). To Jane, Ray represents a threatening physicality.

Her student, Howard Cecil, also confronts Jane with her fears of the body. While Jane wants to relate to Howard through ideas, unemotionally and intellectually, "Howard spoke in terms of 'feeling' always." Jane, on the other hand, tries to be what Kitty's apt typographical error describes her as: "a good think." When Howard challenges Jane to join him on his motorcycle, she primly climbs aboard and that night dreams of making love with him—Jane's repressed sexuality bursts forth even more obviously in her orgy of drawing pornographic pictures, pictures which she characteristically flushes down the toilet the following morning.

Just as Ray was Kitty's student, Howard is Jane's, and Jane notices the symmetry. Although both attend a literature class, Ray and Howard are anomalies in such a group. Ray's "all-time favorite book" is *The Fountainhead,* and Howard disagrees with Jane about the power and importance of words: "I don't think certain things can be named. . . . I think a poem just *is.*" The similarity between Ray and Howard forces itself upon Jane's consciousness when Ray echoes the question Howard had posed to Jane: "Don't you want to be happy?" These two sexual representatives of the non-literary world, Ray and Howard, become spokesmen, then, for the happiness which they have found and which Jane cannot seem to find. Linking these two unlikely men together, Godwin implies that Jane's interest in words, her literary imagination, stands in the way of her happiness, or perhaps even causes her unhappiness.

By comparing Jane and Gerda we can begin to see exactly how and why Jane's immersion in literature prevents her from being happy. Gerda represents the "real" world as opposed to the inner life of the imagination represented by Jane. Gerda labels Jane a romantic and sees herself as a realist. When Gerda decides to marry Bobby Mulvaney, she takes practical matters rather than love into consideration, for she is not an English major but an economics major: "I would be bringing him something and he would be bringing me something. . . . I believe marriage is an economic proposition: the whole world did, until literature confused the issue." Gerda's marriage does not survive, but then neither does Jane's romantic engagement to James, or James's mother.

In the present of Godwin's novel, Gerda manages *Feme Sole,* a feminist magazine which she aggressively and affirmatively, as well as humorously, refers to as her new organ. In contrast, Jane is about to teach George Gissing's *The Odd Women.* The expression "feme sole" is "derived from the Old French 'woman alone.' In legal terms . . . it means an unmarried woman, divorcee, or widow." In contrast to the rubric "feme sole," "odd woman" connotes, as Gissing tells us, a state of incompleteness: "So many *odd* women—no making a pair with them. The pessimists call them useless, lost, futile lives." Jane herself admits that she sees herself as fitting into Gissing's definition. In the essential difference between "feme sole" and "odd woman" lies the difference between Gerda and Jane which results from their differing orientations. Jane becomes an "odd woman" rather than a "feme sole" precisely because, as Gerda tells her, she is a "novel-reader," a "starry-eyed romantic."

As a small child, Jane waited for her life to begin, believing that literacy would be the key to open life for her: "When is my life going to start, she had thought—even then, at age five. And she was sure it would start when she began going to school and learned how to read and write." Once she learns to read and write, Jane conceives a new notion of when life will begin, believing it will come when she finds a man and falls in love. Being engaged to James, she finally thinks "about how softly she had slipped into her destiny, how unobtrusively her 'real life' had begun." While Gerda, feme sole, vows no longer to "ask or expect to be fulfilled or emotionally completed by a member of the opposite sex," Jane, the odd woman (her relationship with James having failed), believes she must keep herself "open and alert. I have to keep ready for my other half." Such a notion with its disturbing sense of insufficiency and incompleteness derives directly from literature—from novel reading.

The very title of Godwin's novel testifies to the importance of literature's harmful effect on women. Jane turns to a significant passage from Gissing's *The Odd Women* and quotes an excerpt from it. The entire passage proves central to Jane's problem and Godwin's purpose. Under discussion is a woman's love affair with a man who, it turned out, was not to be trusted. Rhoda Nunn, the central figure in Gissing's novel, has little sympathy for the woman but does not directly blame her for her lack of judgment:

> All her spare time was given to novel-reading. If every novelist could be strangled and thrown into the sea should have some chance of reforming women. The girl's nature was corrupted with sentimentality, like that of all but every woman who is intelligent enough to read what is called the best fiction, but not intelligent enough to understand its vice. Love—love—love; a sickening sameness of vulgarity. What is more vulgar than the ideal of novelists? They won't represent the actual world; it would be too dull for their readers. In real life, how many men and women *fall in love?* Not one in every ten thousand, I am convinced. Not one married pair in ten thousand have felt for each other as two or three couples do in every novel.

Literature fosters certain expectations in its readers, and Jane proves a prime example.

Reading *The Odd Women,* Jane sympathizes with the romantics of the novel who have fallen prey to literature's lying promises: "When Monica Madden, who was still young and pretty, met the older Widdowson, a bachelor with money, in Battersea Park, Jane thought furtively, as she had thought the last time she read this novel: Oh, go ahead and marry him. Why not? Maybe in this reading it will come out better." To be happy Jane feels she must have the love literature promises her; but Gissing tells us—and Godwin's title endorses the belief—that such love is not to be had in the actual world. The blanket indictment of writers and readers seems, however, belied in Godwin's novel by the example of Kitty, both a writer and a reader, satisfied in her marriage to Ray Sparks. We must ask how Kitty, unlike Jane, escapes the harmful effect of literature.

Literature seems to operate in Kitty's life much as it does in Jane's. An insomniac like Jane, Kitty also relies on reading as a cure. Kitty now teaches Medieval History—one kind of story-telling—and at one time, like Jane, taught Romantic Poetry. Moreover, Kitty has authored what would be the very worst kind of fiction according to Gissing and Godwin, the romantic fiction so harmful to women because of the expectations it nurtures. Kitty wrote stories for *Love Short Stories,* love stories which "repeat the same old plot again and again; the plot of a girl, give or take the color of her hair, who threw everything out the window to get her man."

Unlike Jane, however, Kitty manages to balance the outer with the inner life, to live both in the actual world and in the world of the imagination. While Jane joins Edith in endorsing the view that "life is a disease," Kitty joins Cleva, Jane's great aunt who ran away with a man only to return in a coffin, in embracing life and running away with her unbridled impulses:

> Edith recognized in Jane a similarity to herself, another similarity Kitty did not have. . . . Perhaps Edith saw in Jane her own tendency to imagine the worst. For when Edith said to Kitty, who was embarking on a date with an Undesirable, "You know what happened to Cleva," Kitty (as she reported to Jane, years later) simply said, "Oh, pooh." Not so with Jane.

Kitty runs off with two men, first Jane's father and later the non-literary Ray Sparks. Although Kitty carries on an affair of the imagination mostly via telephone calls in public booths with a professor of English, an affair reminiscent of Jane's relationship with Gabriel, Kitty eventually gives the man up in favor of Ray. She offers the wry and pragmatic explanation: "I was so sick of always having to clutter up my purse with all that heavy loose change."

Despite Gissing's and Godwin's warning of the dangers of literature, of the harm the fantasy world of fiction can exert on a woman's "real" life, Kitty mediates between the two worlds. She manages the balance because she has practical insight into the relationship between the literary world and the actual one:

> One day Jane, who was four or five at the time, asked Kitty "Why don't you write a story about a woman who teaches school at the college and writes love stories on the weekend and has a little girl like me?"
>
> "It wouldn't sell, that's why," replied Kitty.

> "Oh, I think it would be very interesting to read," said Jane.
>
> "It would be interesting to people like you and me," Kitty said, "but I can assure you, *Love Short Stories* wouldn't buy it. My girls have to have respectable, slightly glamorous jobs, but nothing too important. There must be nothing too permanent or heavy in their lives, because they have to throw it all out the window when the man comes along."

Kitty distinguishes between what we find in books which is subject to economic necessities and what we find in life. She tries to explain to five-year-old Jane that life and art differ. More than twenty-five years later we find Kitty still trying to impress the lesson on Jane:

> You are such a child in some ways, darling. You're such a good little *student.* You've always been one to look up your life in books and develop crushes on teachers who would tell you "answers." So [George Eliot] was happy, "outrageously happy," for twenty-five years with [Lewes]. Can anyone *living* look me in the eye and tell me they have lived with a man for twenty-five years and been *outrageously happy?* You're living in myths, Jane, to expect such things. . . . The trouble with myths . . . is that they leave out so much. They leave out all the loose ends, all those messy, practical details that make living less than idyllic. That's why myths can remain beautiful.

Like Rhoda Nunn of *The Odd Women,* Kitty understands that the worlds of literature and everyday life are discontinuous, separate, and that she cannot carry expectations from the one to the other.

Jane, on the other hand, lives according to the belief that life and art can indeed be one. When Edith forces a tour of Europe on Jane, Jane finds herself uncomfortable and unhappy travelling:

> But London was different. Jane recognized it at once. She knew it intimately. It was like coming home, to your soul's home. She never got lost—not once. It was as though she carried a map of the city inside her head. If she wanted to see the courtroom when the case of *Jarndyce v. Jarndyce* was heard in *Bleak House,* she took a bus or a tube and went to Lincoln's Inn. If she wanted to sit in the church of Saint-Dunstan-in-the-West, where a vicar named Donne had preached every Sunday, she went to Fleet Street. . . . London was Jane's city. . . . Yes, London was safe. It was like wandering around in your own imagination. . . . Nothing was difficult for her here. The printed word transformed itself obediently into reality whenever she called upon it.

Jane finds a haven in England because here literature and life are one; her expectations are fulfilled. Returning to America, she continues to seek such fulfillment. She "ransacked novels for answers to life," believes that "once she had truly named her insomnia . . . she could befriend it," intends to rely on words to dissuade potential criminals from harming her, and yearns for the true love her favorite fictions have conditioned her to expect.

At one point early in ***The Odd Woman*** Jane admits to herself that she reads too much for her own good and she goes on to realize that

> stories were all right, as long as you read them as what they were: single visions, one person's way of interpreting something. You could learn from stories, be warned by stories. But stories, by their very nature, were Procrustean. Even the longest of them had to end somewhere. If a living human being tried to squeeze himself into a particular story, he might find vital parts of himself lopped off. Even worse, he might find himself unable to get out again.

Jane does not heed her own warning, and Godwin underscores the fact. She prepares us for the above passage with the statement that Jane "had an insight—*the beginning of one, rather*—about stories" (emphasis added). Jane fully learns the lesson, Kitty's lesson, and completes her insight in the final pages of the novel; indeed, the entire book moves toward the climax and the completion of Jane's perception that the worlds of life and art are far from identical.

In addition to the story of Edith fainting away at the feet of her husband-to-be, Hans, with the words "life is a disease," and the story of Kitty's decision finally to rid herself of all that loose change, the story of Cleva's elopement and subsequent death influences Jane tremendously. In 1905 Cleva ran off with an actor in a melodrama passing through town, had an illegitimate child, and

> returned ten months later, in a coffin. Her death remained a mystery. Hans had gone to New York on the night train and returned with the coffin and the infant girl, after Edith had received a note from Cleva, scrawled in pencil on the back of a torn theatre program: "*Sister I am in grave trouble please can somebody come the villain has left me,*" and an address.

The force of the story for Jane issues in part from the fact that she has a tangible written relic of the episode over which she can and does ruminate at length: the note from Cleva to Edith. In support of Jane's belief that life and art are indeed continuous, the melodrama in which Cleva's "villain" acted is aptly *The Fatal Wedding*. Taking off from the title and comparing Cleva's story to Edith's life, Jane agrees with Edith in concluding that "You had your choice: a disastrous ending with a Villain; a satisfactory ending with a Good Man. The message was simple." Jane believes that, like art, the actual world is composed of heroes and villains, and she casts her life accordingly. Ray Sparks acts the part of a villain along with two of Jane's elementary school teachers. At a Modern Language Association seminar, Gabriel and Zimmer play hero and villain respectively.

At the end of ***The Odd Woman*** Jane tracks down and visits Von Vorst, the villain of *The Fatal Wedding* and the man with whom, she has supposed all her life, Cleva ran off. Contrary to all Jane's expectations and the scenario she had prepared herself for, Von Vorst does not act the part of the villain. When Jane returns home, the truth of the encounter hits her in a shocking revelation: the villain in life, the man who carried Cleva off, may not have been the villain of the play in which he acted; Cleva's lover may not have been Von Vorst: "Did 'villain' in 1906 simply mean the person you hated because he had hurt you—as 'son of a bitch,' 'prick,' 'bastard' meant today regardless of what mild creature played Villain or Man About I own on the stage?" The man with whom Cleva ran off may well have been Edwin Merchant, who played the part of the hero and "happy husband" in the melodrama.

Finally, the full insight that the literary world has no necessary correlation with the actual world bursts on Jane. Villains in art need not be villains in life. Moreover, her insight confirms the truth of Jane's early wondering whether or not the concept of the self is itself a myth—"Characters were not so wholly good or bad, heroes or villains, anymore," whether or not the very notion of personality—the staple of fiction—is itself false. As the concepts of personality and of heroes and villains die, so does "all the stuff of novels" on which Jane depends to give meaning to her life.

Unfortunately, ***The Odd Woman*** does not end on an optimistic note of lessons learned. Jane will try to incorporate Edwin Merchant as villain into a new mythology rather than give up the belief, so central to her, that art accurately reflects and comments on life. The revelation comes too late for thirty-two-year-old Jane Clifford. Even though she has—however half-heartedly—managed to break off her unhealthy relationship with Gabriel, she remains an "odd woman" still. The novel closes with the snow falling, reminding us of Jane's retreat when writing her dissertation, and pointing to another such frozen retreat from the actual world. Godwin seems to offer a forceful indictment of literature and the harmful effects it can have on its readers. Jane can never be happy except, perhaps, in the safe world of the imagination, the only world which can begin to fulfill the expectations literature has fostered in her. We must go on to ask how Godwin can escape her own indictment of literature, whether her message does not undermine the very novel in which it is embodied. Gissing's novel first gives voice to the charge against fiction and the lies it tells to women, and he would probably defend his own novel against the charge by asserting that it counteracts those lies, offering women bleak truth instead. As Jane notes, Gissing's novel displays his "unrelenting pessimism. It was one of the few nineteenth-century novels she could think of in which every main female character who was allowed to live through the last page had to do so alone. The book's ending depressed her utterly." Godwin might find her defense against the charge she, too, levels against literature in pointing to the pessimistic ending of Jane's story as an example of the truth-telling that we must require from contemporary fiction. Godwin, however, has some of the Jane Clifford in her, and her novel still embodies some of the old attractive lies.

In Sonia Marks we have a fairy-tale figure, the woman who represents something special to Jane, who is a "winner." Not only the mistress of an attractive and interesting man (unlike Ray Sparks) who manages to become his wife and a mother, Sonia proves a popular and spell-binding professor of literature who never had to sell out like Kitty and write *Love Short Stories* or give up her dreams. According to Jane, Sonia has it all. Here we have the woman in "real" life who fulfills all the promises fiction offers, and Godwin does not undercut or deny Jane's vision of Sonia. Perhaps, she admits, we *can* have it all; Godwin yearns to believe the conventional fictions that tell us that men and women do fall in love and live happily ever after. Gerda's pragmatic economic point of view may be right, but we still join Godwin in favoring Jane, the "heroine" of ***The Odd Woman*** and the focus of our sympathies, who has not given up love like Gerda.

Finally, Godwin proves unwilling to choose the outer life over the life of the imagination in a decision that her novel—Sonia Marks notwithstanding—argues will prove necessary. Like Jane, Godwin's narrator prefers "building your own interior castle" to living in the actual world. Godwin's novel closes not with Jane Clifford, a hopeless, albeit sympathetic case, but with her neighbor, a man (interestingly) who, more than anyone else in the novel, represents the escape from life and the immersion in art and the world of the imagination:

> He kept bird-feeders. A modern-day hermit if there ever was one, he worked in the library's Special Collections and kept to himself. [Jane] had watched him often from her window, frail, ner-

vously alert, refilling those feeders. At night, after the rest of the street was long asleep, she heard him playing Mozart.

Despite her convincing quarrel with the literary imagination, Godwin ends ***The Odd Woman*** with the beautiful and simple image of Jane lying in bed listening to this man take elements of the actual world and transform them into something far more precious—art:

> All was silent, safe and still. [Jane's] heartbeat slowed from melodramatic terror to its usual insomniac tick. From the little concrete house behind came the barely audible tinkle of a soul at the piano, trying to organize the loneliness and the weather and the long night into something of abiding shape and beauty.

Marilynn J. Smith (essay date 1980)

SOURCE: "The Role of the South in the Novels of Gail Godwin," in *Critique: Studies in Modern Fiction,* Vol. XXI, No. 3, 1980, pp. 103-10.

[*In the following essay, Smith discusses the influence of Southern culture and values on the protagonists of Godwin's fiction. According to Smith, "Beyond family ties and soft accents, the most significant positive trait is the willingness to dream, which Godwin seems to attribute to Southerners."*]

Gail Godwin, who was born in Alabama and raised in North Carolina but has lived in the Midwest and New York, is a novelist and short story writer concerned with the problems of developing self-identity and seeking the "best life." Many of Godwin's characters attempt to counteract their inclination to dream, or to retreat from life, by finding solutions to their problems by compromising their dream in life. When a character cannot find true love, when one wants to write the perfect book or article, or when one is searching for the perfect visual theme, these characters at last, after considerable brooding, act in order to cease the inactivity of dreaming: cutting off the love affair, committing suicide, or actually working. While perhaps not true in fact, the myth surrounding Southerners is that they are dreamers of an illusive reality based on unattainable absolute ideals. The role of the South in Godwin's novels is best seen as a welcome retreat from the harsh realities, sometimes from the North itself, but also as the root of an ambivalent perception of an illusive world of artificial conventions which prevents one's happiness.

The process of self-realization, of finding the "best life," often requires a comparison of what we are now with what we were and what we were raised to anticipate being. In times of broadening sex roles, such comparison leads us to reject or at least to question the ideals of childhood. In most of Godwin's novels the childhood is a Southern, genteel one which, although rejected by fleeing North, is not easily forgotten. In the novels considered here we are first introduced to the main characters, all women, after they have already left home, although they either return home for a visit or return through memory to re-create the period of growing up. Furthermore, even though they reject the models of their grandmothers, certain Southern traits stay with them. Although they philosophically reject the ways of the Old South, they are not emotionally ready or able to cut the tie totally. Beyond family ties and soft accents, the most significant positive trait is the willingness to dream, which Godwin seems to attribute to Southerners. When in ***Violet Clay*** (1978), for example, Violet imagines an interview she will hold after she becomes a famous artist, she anticipates the answer to the question, "Do you think yourself a Southern Painter?" Significantly, she does not answer either way: "—Well. I'm proud to share my birthplace with Allston. I was influenced by his 'Moonlit Landscape' when I was a young painter. But I was also influenced by Ryder, Inness, the Swiss Fuseli. I like the way they have of catching the mundane off guard, getting out of the preconceived everyday vision. Perhaps Southerners aren't as ashamed of being dreamers. But these painters were all dreamers." Allston, by the way, was born in South Carolina but later moved to Boston.

Many of Godwin's characters are raised in the South, the Carolinas, more specifically. Some works, such as ***Glass People*** (1972) and a few stories, only hint at the North Carolinian mountains and general geographical area. Others, such as ***Violet Clay*** and ***The Odd Woman*** (1974), are clearly Southern in origin. While ***Glass People*** presents the cosmopolitan present in conflict with a Southern past, the more recent novels, coincidentally more feminist, are clearly concerned with the effects of a genteel Southern upbringing. Such effects are not totally rejected since the heroines nostalgically look to the place and people of their origins. Interestingly, a progressive localizing has taken place in the six years between ***Glass People*** and ***Violet Clay***: in the earlier novel Francesca's home, somewhere near Claretown, is not exactly stated; in ***The Odd Woman*** Jane Clifford returns to a non-specified Southern town which from the clues is Asheville; and Violet is raised on the Battery in Charleston.

In ***Glass People***, although it has a Southern flavor, few obvious clues link Francesca to anything South. Before moving to California with her new husband, Cameron, and a brief separation in New York, Francesca has lived in an area that is mountainous and in the eastern half of the country. Since the crux of the novel appears to center on the interrelationships of the couple, and since Francesca herself does not perceive her difficulties to be associated with her upbringing entirely, the South plays a minor role in the workings of the novel.

The odd woman, Jane Clifford, on the other hand, generally localizes part of her conflicts in her Southernness. Jane feels odd not only because she is a Southerner out of her element but because even at home she does not accept or fit into the old ways. Jane, young and unmarried, is teaching literature at a large Midwestern university, much like Urbana, Illinois, where Godwin herself was teaching the year she wrote the novel. During the semester break Jane leaves the wintery North to "go South" to attend her grandmother's funeral. While the town is unspecified, allusions to Thomas Wolfe, the French Broad River, and the mountains suggest that she went to Asheville. There, she is reminded of her oddity in her family of at least somewhat conservative Southerners. The major source of contemplation, however, is the death of Edith, Jane's grandmother.

Edith, epitomizing the refined Southern matriarch, presents a source of conflict for Jane, who is constantly searching for the best and uncompromised in life. Proper, prone to fainting spells in stressful situations, taste in elegantly distinctive clothes, vain, and a bit deceitful, Jane's grandmother left fifteen pairs of white gloves and a "bottle of Harvey's Bristol Cream behind a stack of dishes." Jane had been very close to her grandmother, often preferring her company to her stepfather's. Closely connected in memory is the story the grandmother often related about her sister, who ran off on the Northbound train to follow a traveling acting group. Great Aunt Cleva left with an actor and died ten months later, leaving a baby and a note on a theater program saying that the villain had left her and she was in grave trouble: "It was never too early, said Edith, to begin warning a girl of the price to be paid for certain kinds of folly. . . . You had your choice: a disastrous ending with a Villain; a satisfactory ending with a Good Man. The message was simple, according to Edith." She was to Jane an admirable old Southern lady who knew about refinement but who put all stock in propriety and happiness. She was, too, the source of conflict for Jane, who spends the entire novel contemplating the existence of eternal love. Ironically, Jane later discovers that Cleva had not run off with the actor who played the villain in the traveling melodrama, but the good man. Edith did not provide the answer Jane sought.

In ***Violet Clay*** the setting of Violet's early years is the South, primarily Charleston and her unspecified school in North Carolina. Violet's Charleston is romanticized only by her Uncle Ambrose's novel: otherwise, it is a place to remember, to be haunted by, to flee. The place is described in a negative light, an "inbred hothouse of a city," where the Library Society does not have *Uncle Tom's Cabin,* and where her mother drowned herself in the yacht basin when she learned of Violet's father's death in World War II. Violet's grandmother is a widow living in an antebellum mansion on the Battery, one of the most prestigious sections of Charleston, who must continually sell antiques as her resources diminish. When she dies, the house goes to the bank. Granny, too, is a strong matriarch much concerned about propriety. Although she adheres to the same concerns for gentility and tradition, she is not the same refined Edith; she allows much more reality to creep into her drunken conversations. Unlike Edith, who had no special talents, Violet's grandmother was a pianist trained to play professionally. Instead of auditioning in New York, however, she left Burnsville, North Carolina, to marry Mr. Clay from Charleston, raised their sons alone when he died, then had regrets when her fingers were no longer flexible. Granny felt she had wasted her talents on an antique-poor lawyer who did not provide for her as grandly as she had envisioned. Although a Southerner herself, she viewed herself as an "imported bride" in Charleston and was attracted to another outsider, a "large Yankee-voiced . . . disturber of the local mores," Violet's namesake. This woman who was brought to Charleston because of her husband's harbor work in 1920 was a dear friend of Granny's but was scorned by Violet. The "Big V.," as Violet called her grandmother's friend, was the opposite of refined Granny, who thought the same way as the large husky-voiced newcomer but would never remove the illusion of gentility and grace to demonstrate it. The young Violet wanted to be totally separate from the power and image of her godmother. We know that the Big V. taught Granny how to smoke, but we do not know when or how Granny started her large daily intake of gin, equally under cover. The first of many excuses Violet offers for not producing her "picture" is that she spent the summer between graduation and what was to have been her art career as an errand girl to the liquor store:

> If only I didn't have to do errands for Granny, I would tell myself, I could get a head start on "the picture" this afternoon. But duty was duty, which was to go upstairs after lunch but never before one, by which time Granny was dressed and made up and regarded me with playful nonchalance, as though I'd been another one of the ghosts who inhabited her house. She would dole out some cash from a little enameled box meant for playing cards, which contained our weekly food and drink allowance. "Tell Mr. Dinwiddie we're expecting some people in, why don't you?" she would muse, on the days I went for the quart of gin.

In Violet's attempt to find out about her dead parents and fleeting heritage, gradually being sold to the antique dealers, she tries to find out more from her grandmother that summer. The alcoholic widow had a three-part story routine: one about sacrificing her music to marriage, another as a "warning against men—especially lawyers—and all their tricks," and then funny memories of her old friend, the Big V. Clearly Violet did not trust the advice coming from a gin-loosed mind because she ends the summer by marrying Lewis, the godmother's lawyer nephew. The last image of Granny is as the liquor store keeper found her: a year after Violet leaves, Mr. Dinwiddie misses Granny's regular stops, so he climbs in a window and discovers her body. She was able to maintain the illusion of decorum: "She was fully dressed, lying on her bed. Both bottle and glass were concealed in the flowered slop jar of an eighteenth-century commode beside the bed. Her face wore a mocking, triumphant little smile."

Violet's relationship with her grandmother and godmother, of course, is a further example of ambivalent Southern living. Young Violet, Southern by birth, is repulsed by the Yankee coarseness of her godmother. Interestingly, the matriarch, who on the outside always exhibited refined, cultured manners, thoroughly enjoyed the outgoing, nearly improper personality of her old friend. Although young Violet said she resented her godmother, perhaps out of jealousy but probably from lack of self-knowledge, she followed the actions of her grandmother and not her advice.

In most of Godwin's stories and novels, the heroines are to some extent at odds with the desire for fulfilling their lives and yet maintaining the security of old traditions which are forever changing but nevertheless provide ready answers. The old tradition for these women and for some of the men—is one of illusions: fashion, refinement, correctness, and perfection. The reason that the heroines literally flee and try to reject the notion of old Southern womanhood is that, when the grandmothers die, they take the last remnants of an institution that was already disintegrating. What even the next generation, the heroines' mothers, are unwilling to do is to believe or accept the older generation's idea of idealized social commitment or convention. Violet's own mother, a lower-class Southerner, committed suicide when her husband died, leaving her with a baby in his old Charleston home with Granny. Jane's mother ran off and married a reckless lover who died in the same war that killed Clay. She eventually married Edith's idea of a "good man," a conservative Southerner, because she gave up on the dream of finding the perfect combination: "I wanted a kind of marriage I knew my parents had not had: a marriage of passion *and* esteem. I wanted so many things it makes me sick to remember." In essence, Kitty, Jane's mother, tells her that she is living in a myth to be looking for perfect love. Gerda, an old friend whom Jane sees in Chicago on her way back to the Midwestern university town, tells her the same thing with less tact. Gerda, also Southern-fled, is now an active feminist and has rejected all ideas associated with the conventions and dreams of the South. The two women are at opposite ends of the visionary pole: dreamy idealization and bitter realism. Gerda, who has been burned in love, asks her friend, "Do you feel yourself trapped, Jane, when you least expect it, in all that old myth they sold us about Southern womanhood, having to be 'soft and feminine,' and all that crap? I do." She also feels disillusioned and spiteful, at the other end of the romantic spectrum: "God," she shouts at Jane, who rejects terming love "crap," "you're such a fence-sitting Southern bitch! . . . You can't bear the smell of reality." Jane, the dreamer of eternal happiness, is still sitting on the fence at the end of the novel. She imagines that Urbana's notorious "Enema Bandit" is about to break into her duplex apartment. She envisions being able to talk him out of victimizing her by telling him to take on her identity and to go South and find his "best life":

> In a way I really feel for you. . . . Take my advice and get out of here. Go in my closet and dress yourself in my warmest clothes; take my purse . . . and start walking . . . to the bus station and take the first bus out and don't get off till you've reached the place where the snow melts away and you think you can turn your oddities inside out like a sock and find your own best life by making them work for you instead of being driven by them. That's the best advice I have to offer.

Even Violet, who has less illusion about the South, cannot break away entirely. She is willing to leave her husband in Greenville, go to New York to try to be a famous painter, get involved in private love affairs, but is still prevented from publicly being unladylike. One evening she is lonely and considers sitting at the piano bar where her Uncle Ambrose spent his leisure time, "But the ideals of Southern womanhood were still too strongly ingrained in me." When Violet is trying to meet people important to her career or personal interests, she is conscious of turning on her "Southern charm." Her Uncle Ambrose, himself the old Southern gentleman, long ago removed from Charleston, presented to Violet a graphic object lesson of procrastination, lethargy, and the ultimate despondence—suicide. Violet worries that his wife would compare him and her as dreamers, that she herself "shared some portion of Ambrose's swerving temperament," and that the wife "condemned the pair . . . as two indolent, capricious Southerners unable to stick to any project or relationship for long." Nevertheless, Violet may not perceive her inability to find the visual theme to get good work done so much a Southern problem as a personal one, unless it was the summer she stayed with Granny in Charleston and could not get work done for the heat and the errands to the liquor store. Uncle Ambrose's suicide, however, helps to jolt Violet into serious artistic activity which finally succeeds. We may not be aware of many Southern-based conflicts, however, since the story is told by Violet herself, who has not entirely cut off the years connected with her Southern experience. She is so much haunted by the Charleston ghosts that she seems to have taken the summer heat with her to New York and then is unable to move. When Violet leaves the South, her grandmother has already died; she deserts her husband and is cut from her namesake's will. She cuts physical ties but cannot entirely forget them; she, too, is on the fence and, like Jane, is only semi-liberated from her illusions.

So the conflict between self-fulfillment and the security of compromised conventions associated with old Southern convention is not entirely resolved in Godwin's novels. Like Violet's first successful painting, titled "Suspended Woman," these woman are suspended. In their own way they are searching for happiness, but as Jane's mother told her, outrageous happiness is a myth. Whether or not searching for perfect love and happiness is a typical Southern myth is moot; the real point is that the heroines feel part of being a Southerner involves such a search. Godwin's characters search for happiness through self-fulfillment and dreaming of absolutes. As in dreams, waking up sometimes brings fulfillment, failure, or continued search.

Paul Gray (review date 25 January 1982)

SOURCE: "Romance Turned Upside Down," in *Time*, January 25, 1982, p. 72.

[*In the following review, Gray offers praise for* A Mother and Two Daughters.]

In simpler times, happy stories ended with a marriage proposal or a wedding. ***A Mother and Two Daughters*** is decidedly cheerful: but living happily ever after, in the old-fashioned sense, is the very fate its heroines struggle to escape. They find themselves in a romance turned upside down: girl meets boy, boy offers her his hand, she shakes it and marches on.

In four earlier novels and a collection of short stories, Author Gail Godwin, 44, has presented a distinctive gallery of rogues, female, troubled and courageous. They tend to have Southern backgrounds, with all the accompanying luggage of traditions and social forms, and an unsettling inclination to think and act on their own (Godwin was raised in Asheville, N.C., and has taught English and creative writing at Vassar and Columbia, among other places). The author's fifth novel repeats previous patterns on a grander scale: more main characters, broader swatches of life to dazzle and puzzle them.

The catalyst for all that follows is the fatal heart attack of Leonard Strickland, a gentle North Carolina lawyer fond of Montaigne and Cicero. After 40 years of his benign companionship, his widow Nell doubts her ability to go it alone: "He protected me from so much . . . from my harshest judgments of myself as well as of others." Strickland's death also catches his two daughters at awkward points in their lives. Cate, headstrong and twice divorced, is approaching her 40th birthday and teaching English at a small college in Iowa: like her previous school in New Hampshire, this one too seems on the verge of closing for lack of funds. And Lydia, the prim younger daughter and mother of two teen-age sons, has just walked out on her banker husband after 18 years of marriage.

None of these problems is unique, of course, in fact or fiction, and Godwin never claims otherwise. She does make the three women who face them singularly interesting. They are all intelligent enough to wish, sometimes, that they were less so. Nell would like to blend comfortably into the extending circle of Southern widows in her town, but her acerbic side keeps her at a slight, disquieting remove. Cate periodically feels the urge to "lapse wearily" into a man's care and then bristles angrily at her own weakness. Lydia tries to organize herself into happiness, knowing that each new accomplishment will set the stage for another bout of worry and planning. Stubbornly, she pursues the dream: "It really did seem to her that she had a chance of getting it all in."

Characters who believe that usually get a rude comeuppance. But Godwin places her women in an extremely amiable world. Their wills are not thwarted, their plans are not crushed by reality. They do not face discrimination or sexism but rather an excess of love from those around them. Cate meets the father of one of her students: he turns out to be a millionaire industrialist who lives in a castle on the banks of the Mississippi River. Before long, he asks her to marry him: "Oh hell, she thought, why couldn't this be the thirteenth century? Then it would all be decided for me." Lydia's tender trap appears in the form of a handsome podiatrist in Winston-Salem. Their lovemaking inspires her to write a term paper on Eros for one of the college courses she is now taking. Lydia discusses the topic with her professor, a Harvard-educated black woman: "I don't know where this sort of thing *fits* in my life, or whether I can make it fit, or whether I even want it to fit. That's why I'd like to get to the bottom of whatever this thing is."

The notion of winnowing out the dark secret of sex through a college composition is comic. It is also, coming from Lydia at this point, endearing. Godwin's long, leisurely narrative is too inclusive and ingratiating to encourage snap judgments or condemnations. She allows her women to be as naive or foolish as they wish, but she also weighs in the balance the fact that they are striving toward a vision, however unclear. Near the end, she lets them realize most of it.

A coda assembles all the surviving characters for a reunion on a North Carolina mountain in the fall of 1984. Nell, Cate and Lydia are happy in ways that they would have chosen, and did in fact choose. The hills are alive with the sound of music.

This idyllic conclusion seems inevitable, given the events that have preceded it. Spurned suitors do not stalk off but remain on call, ready to be helpful whenever the women they love need them. Lydia's sons do not resent the disruptions their mother has imposed on their lives; they remain obedient and promising. When Cate needs a job and a place to live, both appear. Thanks to the dead father and the abandoned banker and the rejected millionaire, there is enough money on tap to keep Nell, Cate and Lydia as comfortable and restless as they could wish.

Such behavior is preposterous, and why not? Despite its abundance of realistic details, ***A Mother and Two Daughters*** is at heart an old story in brand-new clothes. This time around, Rochester does not get Jane Eyre; she tells him to keep his distance while she manages the estate. Godwin's version of this turnabout is entertaining and stereoscopic. Her novel can be read as a straightforward account of three plucky women imposing their wills on a receptive world; it can also be seen as a gentle comedy of the unfettered consciousness. Viewed both ways at once, it is engrossing and deep.

Wendy Schwartz (review date May 1982)

SOURCE: "With Men and Without," in *Progressive,* Vol. 46, May, 1982, p. 59.

[*In the following review, Schwartz offers positive assessment of* A Mother and Two Daughters.]

Historically, novels by and about women have been taken less seriously than novels by men. This pattern is changing, however, as publishers seek to capitalize on the feminist market. A good many feminist writers deserve this new attention, and it is no longer possible to count on the bones of a single corset the women who write fiction of quality about women. Gail Godwin is one such writer, and in ***A Mother and Two Daughters*** she continues to explore the concept of independence from men, the theme of her previous novels.

The women of the title are educated Southerners. Nell Strickland, the mother, is adjusting to the loss of her well-to-do and devoted husband and experiencing independence for the first time in her life. She savors life on her own for a few years but then commits herself to a man unworthy of her and inferior to her first husband. Cate, the elder daughter, is known as the family radical for having married twice and engaging in the mildest of 1960s-style protests. A professor and a romantic, she pursues her quests for a university appointment and a perfect lover. Her sister Lydia, the mother of two sons, leaves her stodgy husband in search of the greater fulfillment she has heard is available to women willing to take risks. She completes her education, becomes the star of a television cooking program, and settles in with a bland Jewish podiatrist, whom she refuses to marry as a matter of principle.

Each of these women, like the novel's other female characters, feels the tug of autonomy. For most, however, the love of a man proves the greater need, and the women trade off at least part of their independence for a warm, attractive body with an authoritative voice. The remainder, like Cate, have a rougher time of it in their younger years—while their married peers take direction from self-assured men—but finally they succeed, unsoured by the compromises endured by the wives. Godwin's skill in portraying such varied women's attitudes toward life with and without men is remarkable.

Because Cate defines herself by her politics, hers is the more unusual story. Her socialism, however, makes her only a slightly more sympathetic character than Lydia, whose mean-spiritedness and greed have been codified into neoconservatism. Cate has neither time nor respect for people's feelings; like other well-born leftwingers, she fails to realize her sacrifices will not be appreciated or emulated by the less fortunate. Similarly, her public championing of individual "underdogs" both patronizes them and discomfits others whose lesser generosity she means to expose.

Godwin's knowledge covers a wide range of subjects, from investment banking to preparing the dead for the mortuary. It is a rich, if cluttered, book. There are too many extraneous figures and flashbacks, included at the expense of more telling portraits of the principals. In this, her most ambitious work, Godwin has for the first time left us without a truly memorable heroine. She has, for the first time as well, neatly tied up all the plots and subplots. In the 1984 epilogue, each character has not only found personal happiness but has done so in a way that benefits others.

The book might well have been issued as two or more novels, so complete and interesting is each of its tales. Nevertheless—or perhaps because of this—I found ***A Mother and Two Daughters*** nearly impossible to put down.

Joanne S. Frye (essay date Spring 1983)

SOURCE: "Narrating the Self: The Autonomous Heroine in Gail Godwin's *Violet Clay*," in *Contemporary Literature*, Vol. XXIV, No. 1, Spring, 1983, pp. 66-85.

[*In the following essay, Frye examines the relationship between narrative design and self-creation in* Violet Clay. *"By granting Violet the power of the narrative process to explore possibilities and to assess patterns," writes Frye, "Godwin has given her heroine the capacity to be 'the subject of her own destiny,' a destiny created and renewed with each new choice."*]

Though both contemporary fiction and current literary theory are often concerned to tell us that plot is passé, few of us are actually prepared to relinquish the idea of narrative pattern: the process of narration is too closely bound into our sense of humanity. Even from an existentialist perspective, which accurately identifies the reliance on stories with bad faith and inauthentic living, stories remain a human necessity: fiction is "deeply distrusted and yet humanly indispensable" or "'fiction' designates an apparently *unavoidable* tendency to reconstitute the self in more comfortable categories." We know, of course, that we cannot expect our lives to respond to easy plotting, but we nevertheless feel a recurrent need to narrate the events of our lives to ourselves and to each other, to give shape to the disorder of lived experience. We use narration to identify possible patterns, to assess causality, to hold onto a self-definition, to make connections between our own lives and the lives of other people. We even, I would argue, feel an individual human need for the closure that our literary texts ostensibly withhold: that is, for the sense of some affirmed destiny which governs and makes sense of the contingency of daily lives, what Frank Kermode has called "a need in the moment of existence, to belong, to be related to a beginning and to an end."

To view human activity through narrative pattern, however, causes obvious difficulties, particularly if we rely on those plots that are ingrained in our sense of Western culture. Familiar plots create expectations which may interfere with less familiar outcomes: human lives become truncated, misshapen by reliance on the known in lieu of exploration of the unknown. The desire for a sense of destiny may yield an urge toward premature closure which grants the past too much control over the future or which precludes full exploration of human capacity. People risk becoming trapped in the plot patterns of the old stories, the old conclusions.

The problem, then, is to minimize the negations and denials implicit in story-telling, without destroying the interpretive powers which the process of narration can give to us in the assessment of our individual experience. The problem is particularly acute for individual human beings searching for new ways to structure their lives, and for novelists attempting to interpret relatively new areas of human experience.

It is in this context that Gail Godwin's ***Violet Clay*** takes on particular interest: its concern is with a relatively unexplored area of human experience, and its response to the problem gives new insights into the dangers and values of narration itself. Its opening sentence is the assertive self-definition of its protagonist—"I am a painter"—but its narrative commitment is to a complex exploration of the significance of narrative design in the full claiming of selfhood. Though Godwin is writing through the voice of her painter-protagonist, she has cast the dominant problem of human perception and human choice not as a visual problem but as a problem of narrative design.

When ***Violet Clay*** was published in 1978, it seemed a disappointment to a number of Godwin's admirers. One reviewer attributed to it "the pep-talk quality of so many recent novels in which the heroine strides off the last page, her own woman at last." The same review explicitly contrasted Godwin's previous novel, ***The Odd Woman,*** with the "narrow conception and general thinness" of ***Violet Clay.*** Such a contrast has some validity but I do not think it does justice to the actual complexity of Godwin's task in ***Violet Clay:*** with few literary paradigms, Godwin is attempting the creation of an autonomous heroine who defines herself by her relationship to her work without relinquishing her identity as a woman. For both Godwin and her protagonist, this process evolves through a complex analysis of the power of narrative structures.

Concern with the power of narration is scarcely new in Godwin's novels. Although her first two novels are less overtly concerned with narrative problems, both obliquely address the significance of narrating for the definition of self. ***The Perfectionists*** frequently considers the stories people tell one another about their lives, and its own rather chilling story ends with Dane's projected narrating of her "cosmic" experience to her psychotherapist husband, thereby finding some way to label and control what has been a violent loss of control in relation to her intransigent stepson. In a very different context, ***Glass People*** also affirms the significance of narrated self-definition: Francesca relinquishes her minimal bid for freedom and autonomy when she relinquishes her power to narrate for herself in order to return to the role and the self-definition assigned to her by her husband. Without his confirmation, she seems unable to assess the reality of her own existence; even when she is away, she writes him a letter through which "by imagining an audience, even if it was only Cameron, she was able to document herself."

Godwin's third novel, ***The Odd Woman,*** goes much further in its concern with the significance of narrative pattern for arriving at a satisfactory self-definition: its protagonist is Jane Clifford, professor of literature, whose dominant mode of perception is through the identification of a literary parallel or a relevant narrative pattern in her own personal family history. There are clear dangers for Jane in this reliance on literary precedent, as Susan Lorsch has pointed out in her discussion of ***The Odd Woman*** and "the effect that literature—and the lies it often tells—has on those who believe it." But even for Jane, those dangers can be averted by remembering that though stories do provide a significant pattern, they have only limited explanatory power:

> Stories were all right, as long as you read them as what they were: single visions, one person's way of interpreting something. You could learn from stories, be warned by stories. But stories, by their very nature, were Procrustean. Even the longest of them had to end somewhere. If a living human being tried to squeeze himself into a particular story, he might find vital parts of himself lopped off. Even worse, he might find himself unable to get out again.

By the writing of ***Violet Clay,*** then, Godwin has given new emphasis to these concerns with both the crucial defining power of narrative and its destructive self-limiting capacity. Through her central focus on considerations of narrative design, Godwin reassesses the need to hold on to possibilities while still making commitments, to have a defined selfhood without capitulating to the kinds of external, self-denying self-definitions that Dane and Francesca do in the first two novels and that Jane is struggling against in the third novel. Violet Clay, the first of Godwin's protagonists to tell her own story, is both agent and recipient of the narrative process as she uses narrative patterns to gauge patterns in her own behavior, trying always to arrive at a self-definition continuous with the past and appropriate for the future and to work out patterns for her own sense of autonomous selfhood.

As Ian Watt has pointed out, the specification of the individual and the human understanding of causation are not only the central structuring elements of the novel but also the general human effects of memory. Certainly memory serves these purposes in Violet Clay's uses of narrative toward self-definition and causal analysis. Much of the novel is concerned with her sorting out and discarding old self-limiting plots. She remembers and reevaluates the stories she has told herself all her life, and, in the process, she formulates another umbrella plot, looser and less familiar but nonetheless committed to the analysis of individuality and causation through the probing of memory.

This process of claiming and reclaiming past selves is never simple, particularly because a person may often wish to deny previous selves or to dissociate past actions from present self-awareness. Some of this confusion of continuity and discontinuity marks Violet's sense of herself and her structuring of her narrative. The core of the narrative time—a few short months of present time from an August day in New York to a mid-October day in Plommet Falls—provides the defining self-concept through which Violet probes past contributions to that self-concept and future implications of the changes it is undergoing. As she moves backward in time through her memories, she is exhuming her past selves and seeking areas of congruity between past and present; but as she is attempting to identify who she was in the past and who she is in the narrative present, she is also seeking the crevices in those apparently fixed self-definitions in order that she may simultaneously hold on to a continuous selfhood and understand the process by which she has broken free of those falsely constrained selves. As she strips away the various false labels and story lines that she had previously imposed on herself, she moves closer to formulating a self which meshes with her narrating self without denying her past experiences.

The narrative opens on a day which comes to be defined as Violet's "Day of Lost Options." Its significance cannot, of course, be evident to her or to us as we are embedded in her sense of present reality. But its events become the focus for her restructuring of her self-definition and as such they obtain a significance not present in the events themselves. Like lived reality, in other words, the day has no inherent pattern but assumes a pattern because Violet chooses it as the lens for her self-analysis. It is the day on which she loses her job and learns of her uncle's suicide, but more significantly it is the day on which she begins to shift responsibility for her life away from external forces and toward her own controlling sense of agency. Her assessment of her situation at that time—even before she has learned of her uncle's death—indicates how far she has to go in her redefining narrative: "I felt as though someone had canceled out all my own hope as well, taken away everything: my man, my livelihood, my youth, my promise, what looks I had, the roof over my head." In the midst of that day, she seeks pattern not in her own assessment but in the attribution of blame to external forces.

Nonetheless, that is the day on which, as she says in the opening paragraph, "my story begins in earnest"—the day through which she begins to view and review her own experiences. From the beginning, it is clear that while she has much to learn, she also has much she can retain from that self. The first evidence of continuity is present in her careful interlacing of present tense with past tense as a way of identifying qualities that remain central to her: "I *am* a painter. I *like* to listen to music while I work" (my italics). And then: "Even though I was doing hard work, I was in that rarefied state of consciousness I *like* best: submerged to a sensuous degree in my subject, yet allowing my thoughts to roam free. Today, they were striking out in many different directions, yet weaving a pattern, too. I was thinking of death and love and ambition" (my italics). The self-definition she is formulating through her new narrative construct opens out from her continuous commitment to her work and from the developing need for a new pattern which can interweave her thoughts of death, love, and ambition.

As we proceed through this opening day, we identify additional techniques through which the narrative process addresses simultaneously the congruence and the alteration in Violet's selves. We become conscious not only of precise verb tense, but also of narrative superimposition of a past Violet on the present Violet. Consider, for example, the beginning of chapter 3: as Violet walks toward her interview with Doris Kolb—which brings the loss of her job—she is discomfited by memories of a younger self: "I looked at my reflection in each plate-glass window I passed and recalled every detail of that younger version, getting dressed in a room by herself in the Martha Washington Hotel." It is significant that the present reflection is directly superimposed upon the physical self-image of the past, but it is also significant that the past self, in this instance, is recalled in the third person: her present self seems cut off from that younger, hopeful self. The jarring of the sense of connection against the sense of disconnection establishes the necessity of the circuitous narrative, for only in this manner can she safely acknowledge her past self and begin to seek out the appropriate continuities and establish narrative links.

We become increasingly aware that the narrative progression, in fact, is operating in three time schemes: not only in the narrative present and the remembered past but also in the narrative future. That is, we begin to recognize that our perspective is not submerged in the Violet of the present moment but is rather meshed with the perspective of the Violet who has lived through all of these experiences, past and present, and is assessing *both* from yet another temporal distance. Though we believe that the Violet walking towards Doris Kolb's office does indeed remember her younger self setting out to the galleries, we also begin to recognize the narrative implications of the juxtaposition: the false optimism of the one self and the jaded cynicism of the other reflect not only each other in inversion but also a continuous thread of self-observation and need for external confirmation in her sense of destiny.

Though the narrating self is not explicitly present in these juxtapositions, Violet implicitly suggests narrative selection and judgment here, just as she did in her opening use of present tense. In a later juxtaposition, she more sharply focuses the narrative lens through her present self toward a past self and thus emphasizes the concept of a continuous selfhood:

> But now, looking across the space of nine years at that evening, I understood its essence. There I had crouched in the shadows of my own potential. I had my feelings and I had my materials, but I didn't know how to make one work for the other. There I sat, waiting for something to happen, for the phone to ring, for help to come from outside. That something was happening inside, I never considered. That certain equations were being made, certain colors and tonal values being locked away in my visual memory which could later be opened by the right combination of accumulated experience, I never dreamed. And if I had been told, I would have replied impatiently, "But I want something tonight!"
>
> Now I saw the painting that might come out of all this. It would come out of that evening, but balanced by this one. "Violet in Blue" was how I thought of it.

Such memories are accumulated into coherent narrative not by the chronology of a past self yielding a present self, but by the constructed story of a present self growing into recognition of the future narrating self. Each juxtaposition aids in the gradual trust in a genuine sense of destiny, a destiny in the form of a goal to be grasped and shaped rather than a fate to be passively awaited. Thus when Violet feels early in her stay at Plommet Falls that she is replaying "that same sense of destiny waiting in the wings" which she had felt the summer after graduation from college, we can recognize with the narrator that this belief is fraught with the dangers of past selves, but also pregnant with the possibilities of the future self. By this time in the narrative, we are increasingly aware that the shaping force for Violet's narrative is not mere casual memory but rather a conscious search for the defining coherence of a selfhood.

The narrative in which we actually share, then, is a different sort of narrative from the old story lines which had continually falsified Violet's past self. This narrative refuses to be contained by paradigmatic plot and seeks instead the possibility of explanation and coherence without "lopping off" significant parts of the self. In the final chapter, Violet speaks directly in the voice of her future self, remembering the closing episode of this part of her story:

> I like to remember that October morning. I like to go back into it from the "future," where I now live, and retrospectively paint into it all the prescient signs of my belated emergence. For years of my life I developed my negative propensity for

> time travel. At a moment's notice I could plunge into some awful moment of the past (or some awfuler fantasy about the future) and come back with enough material to take a lugubrious bath in. Now I am becoming adept in making the positive trip as well. I send my mental spaceships to points past or future and it frequently comes back with old buds of present blossomings (like that October morning); or sometimes a bold design for fruits to come.

The "buds," of course, were only there because they have yielded blossoms: she would not otherwise recognize their generative possibilities. What she is narrating for us is not a simple linear success story but rather the process by which she has reclaimed and redefined herself toward the possibility of success. As a process of selection, narration has provided her with a continuous selfhood founded on those past choices and past identities that she wishes to claim rather than on those that preclude the possibility of change and of committed work. Her opening label of herself as "a painter" thus becomes the defining thread for her continuous effort towards a destiny that is process rather than closure.

This overarching narrative pattern is very different from a rigid sense of plot: it indicates and identifies continuous patterns of choice rather than imprisoned self-limitation. But much of Violet's effort in her narration must be to remove the props of inauthentic use of plot to structure her selfhood, as is especially evident in her relationship to her work as illustrator of gothic romances. Because she is careful always to read the novel she will illustrate—a sign of the latent integrity of her relationship to her work—she has a large store of plots which function in her thought processes. From these plots she has abstracted the obvious formula pattern which dominates essentially all of her cover illustrations: the heroine flees from the sinister-looking mansion, but eventually is retrieved by the villain who turns hero and comfortably ensconces her in the mansion turned benevolent. At the novel's opening, the formula has become a dangerously available self-defining pattern for Violet, who too clearly identifies with the heroines of these stories: indeed, in the first chapter, she is using a photograph of herself as model for the current illustration.

Even at the beginning of the novel, Violet displays a reasonable skepticism about this formula plot, particularly as she questions its conclusion—"we would belong to each other now and always"—and its failure to acknowledge any story beyond the "always." But her early skepticism is partial; as she goes on to create the story beyond the end of the story, she manages only to invert the gothic formula by a series of questions and possibilities all couched in the need for formula definitions. The bemused cynicism of her projected story is very clearly linked to the fact that this is a thinly disguised version of her own marriage and divorce, which she then narrates for us undisguised in the second chapter. But her evident relish for the pattern of gothic romance is clear enough in the conclusion of the inverted pattern, in which she gives the hero a new bride who loves to listen to the story of the first wife, enjoying the "piquant" pleasure of sitting "in a warm, well-appointed place, listening in comfort and security to the tale of the wild ungrateful woman fleeing into the outside world, toward some sharp, shivery destiny of her own." Through such a transformation, Violet can simultaneously invoke the comfort of a defined pattern for her life and hold on to the apparent claim to freedom of movement, without taking genuine responsibility for her own "destiny." She can, even in the "freedom" of her role as artist rather than wife, continue to be an appropriate gothic heroine.

At this point in the narrative, the dangers of a fixed plot are evident. She has chosen a label rather than making a genuine causal connection, as she will later learn to do. At present, her dominant self-perception is that of victim, a label obviously related to her identification with the gothic heroine. She particularly likes to think of herself as "The Orphan" and thereby make herself eligible for "the currency of sympathy." True to this early pattern, her reaction after having lost her job is to wallow in self-pity and gin because the "grooves of my mind were more accustomed to the concept of Violet Clay as victim than as victress." Like her earlier attempt, her attempt to deal with the latest trouble is to develop a narrative line according to the false semblance of significant pattern. First she rejects the narrative line someone else might have followed: "In someone else's story, the heroine would have embraced her setback." Then, she defines her own contrasting personal conclusion, through her integration of the gothic formula: "With the names and faces bobbed up phrases, fully formed and with an incontestable rhythm, like certain worn-smooth sentences that recurred predictably in the gothics I had illustrated: 'And then I knew that someone in that house wanted me dead.'" After identifying the appropriate despairing refrains for her life as victim, she weaves her "own weird patterns of cause and effect" and defines the pattern once more as one of victimization, the fault of external circumstances beyond her control.

Though Violet claims to be doing only survival work in her job as illustrator, she has a decided emotional commitment to the gothic romance. So long as she can pretend to herself that she is responding to economic exigencies, she need not confront the realities or falsities of her own earlier ambitions to be a serious artist; further, in her work she is continually rehearsing her plot for her own life: the urgency to have an external destiny confirm her own identity, her own reality, as part of a pattern. In another context, she identifies as the "perfect adolescent dream: freedom within safety."

Similarly, what she wishes at this point from the externals of her life are excitement, validation and achievement without risk, "that ecstatic sense of being dragged screaming toward one's destiny." In her commitment to the gothic formula and its implications for her own self-perception, she obviously runs the risks identified in Jane Clifford's thoughts: having "vital parts of [her] self lopped off" and becoming "unable to get out again" from the imposed self-definition which the narrative line brings. And with her commitment to formula plots comes a commitment to premature closure: a clear indication of the way in which she must learn new uses of narrative before she can reach an autonomous selfhood.

In part, Violet minimizes her risk by denying herself total commitment to any single plot: she simultaneously gauges her life by life patterns she attributes to people around her and creates at least the possibility for expanded interlocking life patterns. She has made a story out of her mother's suicide as a young grief-ridden widow—and she has had this fascination further emphasized by her uncle's fictional transformation of that suicide in his first novel. Similarly, she listens attentively and makes subsequent mental reference to her grandmother's narrative of her life story: the tale of the gifted young pianist who is subverted into marriage by the "tempting picture" of the "accomplished wife and mother who turns her gifts to the enhancement of Home"—the very image of "the safe and rich and beautiful." She creates a myth from her uncle Ambrose's life—as I will discuss later at length—and she hears the life tales of Milo and finally of Sam with the relish of a story-lover searching out the patterns in another person's life. The risks in each of these patterns are less because no single pattern dominates: each would seem to bring with it a different sense of her own appropriate destiny and each can make some contribution to the larger flexible narrative so long as she refrains from making these lives into paradigms for her own. But it is only a fine line between narrative gauges and narrative models; she continually risks denying what the imposed narrative coherence inevitably leaves out. Hence she must learn not to make the implicit assumption that each story has an "ending," that each protagonist has a fixed, defining destiny.

Each of the life stories that has particular appeal to Violet is founded on one or the other of her two major self-definitions: the artist and the woman. Indeed, the greatest conflict she faces in her application of external narrative lines to her own life is the conflict between these two dominant modes of self-perception. This conflict is evident from the beginning in her inversions of the gothic formula, but it becomes even more sharply defined as she reconstructs her personal past. Her memory of the decisive summer in Charleston yields the seeds of the conflict: she has just graduated from college and returned to her grandmother's for a summer's respite before taking on the art world in New York. But her stay is dominated by two stories: her grandmother's story of capitulation to femininity and her own projected story of "The Young Woman as Artist." Though she paints regularly and congratulates herself "for having achieved a modern girl's sexual rights without having to marry and ruin my career," she is also magnetized by her grandmother's repeated narrative: "some deeply feminine side of me loved this story of how the talented young Georgette had succumbed to a blitzkrieg assault on her vanity."

Her own abrupt capitulation to Lewis Lanier that very summer does not come as a surprise but neither does it resolve the conflict. She perceives her marriage as "captivity," but, worse, she values it as precisely that: "There was something sexy about having been captured, having been forced . . . to lie down in the sweet juices of traditional womanhood and abandon the hubris of an edgy, lonely struggle." She is particularly aroused by the perception of herself as a helpless "girl," and can even be brought to sexual climax by hearing Lewis murmur, "Poor little girl, I'll take care of you now." The false urge toward self-definition is easily satisfied on one level: all she has to do is think, "I am now a wife" and give herself up to her "senses, to Womanhood."

Even so, her abdication is incomplete because the story and the self-definition are only partial: in adopting the story of the wife, she has denied the story of the artist. Again, her abrupt rejection of one mode for another is neither surprising nor absolute. When she suddenly departs on the bus for New York, wishing to leave behind her self-definition as wife, she takes with her the possibility of pregnancy; in her final days with Lewis she adds to her sexual stimulants the chanted phrase: "Would you like a baby?"

The most direct confrontation between the two narrative patterns, then, comes after she has arrived in New York: graphically it takes the form of menstrual blood, the release from the possibility of pregnancy. But even then she does not know which pattern she wishes to define her. She recognizes that her departure had been tentative: "One foot in the door of the Unknown, the other still holding open its place in the Book of Old Plots." More, she half wishes she could have followed the plot of the "return of the prodigal wife":

> Safe again within the bounds of just enough approval, I would have painted my way complacently through all the violets, then the roses and the lilacs, and finally become my very own Still Life with Lilies. My grandchildren would fight over my best paintings after the funeral. They would hang them in their homes and get busy tending the Legend. How She of the Untamed Spirit had once flown the coop but returned in

> plenty of time to cultivate her own garden—and make their lives possible.
>
> Now here I was, in a run-down women's residence hotel, trapped in the chilly pink waters of my new freedom. And with no prospects—not even a biological one—of any legend to commemorate the fact that I had walked the earth, that I had once been special.

I recapitulate this section of Violet's memories at such length because it so clearly emphasizes both her need to fit into a narrative and her difficulties in doing so because she must inevitably deny some part of her own reality. The problem, of course, derives from the falseness of the plots themselves, particularly from their insistence that as a woman she must make an either/or choice between her femaleness and her ambition. She has no available pattern for narrative connections that include both work and womanhood. It is not a problem that disappears even after she has ostensibly chosen her work; she continues to debate, in various forms, "the merits of perilous freedom versus stifling security." Her whole adoption of the gothic romance as a means of self-definition is merely a continuation of the same conflict: the urge to relinquish self-definition to the responsibility of someone else, if not a man, then at least an externally imposed destiny and self-definition. Having chosen art, she still refrains from actively pursuing it. For the moment, she continues to find it easier to remain within the confining but safe story line of the victim.

But that is to oversimplify both the choices that Violet makes and the implications of narrative structures for her self-definition. While she does not actually begin to take control of her own destiny until the day her story begins "in earnest"—i.e., nine years after she arrived in New York—she has worked out ways of preventing total self-victimization. And while her reliance on narrative patterns is certainly full of self-falsifications, it also provides her with her tentative tools of survival. The story of the young artist has to be altered and compromised, but it provides her with partial sustenance until she learns to make a more complex use of her need for pattern.

This story of the young artist—as both sustenance and foreclosure—is most fully explored through her relationship with her uncle Ambrose. As a novelist and a family member, Ambrose provides a model touching upon two of the most significant needs in her own search for narrative integration: the connection with a personal heritage and the idea of the successful artist. Through these connections she maintains a link to her own past and to her desired future; but simultaneously she uses that link to deny responsibility for herself. When she first arrives in New York—as we are told in additional extended memory sequences—she has a naïve faith in his capacities and his commitment to Art. As the years pass, she is given ample reason for skepticism about this vision of him, but her need is too powerful: she requires his "story" as a model for her own and so she retains her personal myth about Ambrose the novelist as a base for her own personal myth about Violet the artist. When she risks confronting stray fragments of contradictory reality, she merely bypasses them: the fictitious narrative line which she and he have colluded in developing to explain his life is far too important in their mutual self-perceptions for either of them to risk the loss of its coherence. When he verges on admitting failure to her, she refuses even to acknowledge the admission and instead pushes him on with what he takes as a "recipe for salvation." Her superficial response is founded in her own necessity to believe his success story: "I wanted both to reassure him and be gone. To set him back on the road ahead of me in order to give myself a little more time." So long as he has not yet given up his destiny, she can feel secure in the future reality of her own. While she does not thereby gain an impetus toward her own achievement, she does at least hold on to the possibility of a future.

Even later, when she has begun to realize that her image of Ambrose is distorted, she refuses to give up her sense that his life is a model for her own: regardless of his failings, he provides her with some sense of shared reality, a mutual commitment to a goal. As she tells Milo the night of Ambrose's suicide:

> "I felt he was there for me to refer to, living his life a little ahead of mine, wanting the things I wanted. Even his flaws and mistakes have given me a certain comfort. I could sort of measure myself, judge myself, by him. I can't imagine not having someone between me and . . . I'm not sure what. Darkness? Hopelessness? Where he has been for so long is it going to be just dark, hopeless space? I mean, you can't refer to a void, can you?"

Because his story has been so central in sustaining her, his death, particularly the death of his paradigmatic story, is very threatening to Violet: she is forced to confront a chaotic reality or a reality with an intolerable shape. Or she must finally arrive at a new definition of shape, a new assessment of her own self-definition.

Ambrose, of course, had experienced a similar confrontation himself; because he could not alter his own rigid story line or live with a recognition of chaotic reality, his suicide was the only possible ending to his story. As he had made his entire life into a fiction, so he had an obligation to his sense of an appropriate ending. But more than that, the fiction he had made of his life was increasingly multiple and so risked having no appropriate ending at all. His "shape-shifting" novel finally seems to have no shape at all; based on the vision of "modern man awash in the flux of too many complexities and possibilities," it loses all possibility of narrative design and eventually disintegrates into the three speculative "outlines" of his own last memory-fantasy constructions. In these, he seems to have fused reality and fiction in a final effort to construct himself, to establish a sense of coherence. Near the end of the third outline, he writes: "Now at this juncture a resounding *dénouement* is needed, a deep twist which would connect all the levels of his tale and free him from his dilemma." Though he claims the protagonist is interested only in living it, not in writing it, he ends the outline with a direct address which merges not only his own identity and the protagonist's, but also his sense of the fiction and the life: "How to end such a tale of unaccomplished desires? You bankrupt rascal, this has been your biggest caprice of all."

His suicide, then, is his final acknowledgement of the importance of a shape. As such, it is extremely unsettling to Violet, not only because she cared about him, but also because she too believes in the power of narrative design and has believed in the design of his life as a model for her own. She does not ever fully comprehend the reasons for his death, but through it she is forced to acknowledge that his life had a reality beyond her own uses of it: "Angels, prods, warnings, models, demons. With what variations we occupied one another's thoughts!"

In forcing herself to recognize that Ambrose existed apart from her own uses of him, Violet finally begins to come to terms with the major weakness in her use of other people's stories to help formulate her own: she has created fixed myths rather than allowing for the fictitiousness and resulting instability of all narrative coherences. Stories do not become entrapments of the self if they are temporary and explanatory, agents for change instead of specious attempts to capture reality. What Frank Kermode has said of cultural uses of fiction and myth holds true for individual uses as well: "Fictions are for finding things out, and they change as the needs of sense-making change. Myths are the agents of stability, fictions the agents of change. Myths call for absolute, fictions for conditional assent . . ."

Violet has an extremely powerful need for sense-making but for most of her life she has attempted to satisfy that need through myth rather than through story. In her urgency to contain and define reality and her selfhood, she has relied upon false connections and epigrammatic labels which satisfy the explanatory urge but enforce a fixed identity rather than enabling change. As she has conspired in Ambrose's mythologizing of his life, so she has risked mythologizing her own: "My life as I saw it then took on the aura of myth. I was not Violet Clay so much as I was the Penitent Who Still Dared to Aspire. In my solitary cabin I seemed to be always under the probationary gaze of someone who would not let me get away with a thing." Though she is by this time much closer to implementing her genuine commitment to her work, she has not yet assumed responsibility for herself nor learned the limitations of narrative coherence. The mythologizing, the labelling—these are remnants of the self-falsification in which she implicated her uncle Ambrose during his life and in which she continues to implicate him after his death. But like most of her narrative patterns, these falsifications provide partial sustenance and continuity as well as denial of full responsibility for herself.

So too with her need for external confirmation. Like fictions themselves, the human desire to be observed and validated by an external perspective—a desire implicit in the creation of stories—indicates a pattern of inauthentic living and yet is also central to the individual desire to overcome isolation. The reliance on the "probationary gaze" is an indication of Violet's continuing need for such confirmation. In her insecurity, she has often projected or sought out an external perspective as one way of shaping and validating her selfhood: playing out lovers' quarrels "while my cool self watched," externalizing her present activity "as though we were on a movie set," returning to the same place for a haircut "out of sheer need to be recognized for myself," and recurrently projecting the comments of future art critics upon her life and work. In their extreme form, these attempts are completely debilitating, as in her early days in New York when she seems unable to move without external guidance: "waiting for it to happen, waiting for my fate to begin shaping itself. I waited mostly for the phone to ring, . . . for some outside voice to explain to me what I was doing there and where I was to go next." Even in their less extreme form, her attempts risk being inauthentic denials of her own isolation: in Plommet Falls, she softens her self-imposed solitude by doing her work before "some invisible audience." As she seeks confirmation and explanation, she relies on the audience, the "probationary gaze," the long-awaited voice of fate to provide a gauge for the self, a shape and purpose for an insecure identity.

But, though dangerous, these efforts—like the other patterns of her story-telling urges—are not entirely false. They are an immature manifestation of the genuine need that gives impetus to the larger narrative itself: the protagonist's need to step back from herself and identify patterns of selfhood, meaningful definitions of her own actions. As a personal assessment of her own past, her story inevitably requires a high degree of self-consciousness: she observes her own activities as she tries to link them together. But more, she invokes an immediate audience in the reader to help her define and assess her own patterns of selfhood: "you," she says repeatedly, as when she identifies "the morning on which I invite you to enter my life" or says, "In case you're worrying" and "perhaps you remember it, too." The effect of such reminders is complicated: the reader is drawn into the immediate process of the narrative and is even implicated as a participant in the structuring process. The narrator-protagonist is not telling us a finished tale but is rather requiring of us a recognition of her own sense of self, a validation which refuses to be a self-entrapment.

This need for recognition is closely linked to another of the human needs which the process of narrating addresses: the need to set one's own potentially solipsistic experience in a larger human context, the need to be not only unique but also similar to other people. This, of course, leads to one of the powerful risks Violet faces in comparing her own life to the stories she has made out of other people's lives: the risk of merging her own identity into the paradigmatic tale as a way of generalizing human experience. The story of her own marriage verges too closely on matching her grandmother's, and her own escape from that marriage is easily seen as an escape from her grandmother's fate, her grandmother's story. The drastic revision in Ambrose's story which his suicide requires similarly threatens her story and forces her to re-write both his and her own selfhoods. But despite such risks, the need remains and must be met in other, less confining ways. In part, this need is served by the direct address to the audience, the involvement of readers in shaping and expanding the personal base of Violet's own narrative, particularly when she makes generalizations that deliberately embrace protagonist and reader: "As any of you know who have been there, there is a certain point on the road downward from your hopes. . . ." The effect of such inclusion is a focused version of the entire narrative: my story is in significant ways congruent with your own; telling the story itself enables the sense of human connection without automatically denying the sense of individual identity. In the chapter titled "A Reverie"—which is a sort of "spiritual retreat," a brief but decisive preparation for her later retreat at Plommet Falls—one of Violet's clarifying insights prepares her for the possibility of fruitful generalization: "Weren't we all involved in the same contest between living and dying, between doing what we wanted and needed to do and not doing it?" Her further exposition of this question invokes the sense of narrative coherence she has created for paradigmatic lives, but it shows a greater sense of open-endedness, a willingness to gauge the need for coherent individual stories against the possibility of altering the story line: she can accept her own conflicting urges as her individual responsibility and yet as part of a larger pattern of human need.

What Violet has begun to learn in the months following her "Day of Lost Options" is that she cannot rely upon the false shaping of narrative pattern. Order remains crucial to her. But she is learning to distinguish between order that falsifies and denies reality and order that helps to shape and give meaning to reality. The complexity of the total narrative design, then, is her way—and Godwin's—of retaining and validating her need for narrative coherence while still resisting its falsifications. She finally recognizes that the process of narration is closely linked to the process of self-victimization—both through the use of gothic patterns and through the reliance on external labels and definitions of self. Similarly, she recognizes that in both processes, she risks avoiding responsibility for her own actions: on the one hand by requiring external confirmation and on the other by blaming external circumstances. The narrating Violet has at last acknowledged these processes to be specious in the forms invoked by her younger self; at the same time, from her retrospective assessment of her own development, she knows how crucial the need is. Her final plunge into solitude marks the impossibility of living without some external context, and her entire narrative represents the healing of a self-defined selfhood through creating the narrative links for an audience and for her own self looking backward. The problem in seeking external confirmation evolves not from needing the involvement of some audience but from relying on that audience to define oneself—relinquishing the process of self-definition rather than claiming it. In using the narrative process simultaneously to claim her past self and to achieve a distance on it, Violet has renewed the process of external confirmation while retaining her obligation to self-definition.

In the course of structuring her life, narrating through the defining focus of her Day of Lost Options, Violet Clay has found a way of balancing existential reality against narrative form. Her predecessor in ***The Odd Woman,*** Jane Clifford, was obsessed with the Aristotelian concept of plot, moving "from possibility to probability to necessity"; at the same time she was very conscious that "you had to write yourself as you went along." For Violet, the Day of Lost Options forces the knowledge that she must forego the sense of a necessary ending, forego a confirmed destiny—forces the knowledge, in fact, that her lost options were in some sense only "escape clauses" which prevented her from ever forging her possibilities toward a future. In formulating her new plot, stripped of escape clauses and shaped through a new knowledge of responsibility for herself, Violet avoids the premature closure of false destiny and establishes a new sense of destiny which keeps her always at the point of possibility and yet defined by a commitment that integrates past decisions. She does not, as Ambrose does, become "obsessed by the *other* ways things could have gone in life"; rather, she acknowledges the way things have gone and uses the narrative process to prepare herself for the future.

Her first major painting is in some sense the visual manifestation of this narrative process. The painting is a depersonalized portrait of Sam (Samantha), who comes closest to being an appropriate narrative model for Violet, not because

Sam's life itself is paradigmatic but because she has learned ways not to deny the past—which for her has been particularly horrible—and yet still to claim the future: "She was like some hybrid woman, a composite of what had always been and what could be." The thematic focus of the painting is thus a new version of the old conception for "Violet in Blue," whose challenge Violet had defined as "how well I could capture that state of *precariousness,* how well I could evoke, through paint, choices hanging in the balance, the way different thicknesses (like different individuals) strove to impose their color against all that would go on anyway." This old challenge is refocused and renewed in Sam, "a subject that could be a match for my inner necessities." Violet realizes that Sam represents a refusal of the old gothic picture, a refusal of victimization, and a refocusing of the old questions for Violet herself: "There was something about her picture that intrigued me also. Sam had built her own house and was running in a different direction. Was there a choice to be made between these pictures or was it a matter of finding a new composition that could sustain a balance between them?"

Titled "Suspended Woman," the resultant painting becomes the affirmation of destiny that refuses closure: a reflection of Violet's own "inner necessities," a restoration of her commitment to her work, a renewal of an old conception, a claiming of herself as woman. The final two paragraphs of the novel give verbal play to the conception that takes visual form in the painting:

> And there she is, and will remain, securely netted in layers of light.
>
> Meanwhile that limitless radiance which eludes us all spins on, taking our day with it, teasing and turning us for a time in its vibrant dimensions, continuing to spread its blind effulgence when we have gone.

Its excessive language in part undermines the effectiveness of the statement, but at the same time it also mocks the possibility of concluding at all. Like the painting, the conclusion of the narrative pattern is fixed and yet resists conclusiveness.

Nearly five years before the publication of ***Violet Clay,*** Godwin wrote some notes on the concept of "a fully human heroine." In the concluding section, she indicates some defining characteristics that are clearly a part of her thinking in ***Violet Clay.*** A fully human heroine would be, she says, "the subject of her own destiny, not the object of 'Blind Destiny' nor a character in someone else's destiny." Such a heroine would also have a commitment to work and to growth and a sense of claiming her own identity and place. Having cited Jung's statement that "the larger problems of life are by their very nature insoluble," Godwin adds, "My heroine would not *solve* these problems, then, but she would be worthy of them."

Violet Clay has not solved the problems of life nor has she found a way to resolve the conflicts between her sense of self as artist and her sense of self as woman. But in steadily addressing these problems, she has learned to use the process of narration itself to open the future and to affirm her autonomy and her self-definition rather than to deny and confine her. By granting Violet the power of the narrative process to explore possibilities and to assess patterns, Godwin has given her heroine the capacity to be "the subject of her own destiny," a destiny recreated and renewed with each new choice. Violet Clay has learned not so much the art of painting as the art of narrating the self and acting towards an ever-changing destiny.

Carolyn Rhodes (essay date 1984)

SOURCE: "Gail Godwin and the Ideal of Southern Womanhood," in *Women Writers of the Contemporary South,* edited by Peggy Whitman Prenshaw, University Press of Mississippi, 1984, pp. 55-66.

[*In the following essay, Rhodes explores Godwin's treatment of Southern values concerning motherhood and female duty in her novels. According to Rhodes, "Godwin's writings dissect the conservative feminine myth of the South not just to expose its debilitating central demand for a selflessness that precludes self-discovery, but also to present remedies."*]

Gail Godwin's fiction has reflected many of the myths and manners of the South. Some of her most sympathetic characters have been Southern women whose struggles toward self-discovery required them to reject traits demanded by the traditional ideal of Southern womanhood. In her novels published during the 1970s, Godwin often depicted that ideal as alive and deadly: it entailed a set of values bent toward restraining Southern belles to narrow notions of grace and duty. In her social criticism, Godwin spoke even more explicitly of the dangers of the old ideal of "Southern Womanhood," with its constricting effects on the docile daughters of the misguided mother who tried to model and impose the tradition of shallow ladyhood. Only in her latest novel have the three featured Southern women attained the balance that Godwin admires: without fleeing the South, they manage to achieve autonomy and to define grace and duty in their own ways.

All five of Godwin's novels feature the quests for identity of women who fear failure, and who are distracted by differing notions of what their best selves might be and become. In her three longer novels, those published in 1974, 1978, and 1982, the protagonists are Southern-born, Southern-bred, and aware of the ambiguities of their heritage. Similar characters appear in some of her short stories. Godwin has also discussed the stereotypes of Southern Womanhood in journalistic commentary. This author's writing, then, conveys her explicit and implicit views on the Southern heritage as a shaping factor in the lives of certain women of the twentieth century, groups identified carefully by class and age and attitude toward an ideal of womanhood. In both article and fiction, she distinguishes the stereotype from the individual, and she often depicts Southern women in the context of the traits she attributes to heritage-bound Southern mothers and their fleeing daughters. Godwin also focuses upon the confrontations which set women free, which she describes directly as social critic and dramatically in fiction when her protagonists confront their Southern constrictions and attempt to break out of them.

In her article, **"The Southern Belle,"** on the ideal of Southern womanhood in *Ms.* in 1975, Godwin analyzed two contemporary generations of women and their responses to each other and to the typical expectations set up for them as Southern Belle and Southern Lady. She begins by insisting that only the Southern region of the United States places such an explicit list of ladylike goals before its young women. And although they may be directed primarily toward white women of the would-be-leisured classes, the distinctive traits are known not only to other Southerners but to others throughout the nation. Only in the South does a growing girl find "an image of womanhood already cut out for her, stitched securely by the practiced hands of tradition, available for her to slip into, ready-made, and hence-forward 'pass' as a 'lovely person.'"

Demands imposed on females by the idealized image have changed little in two hundred years, whether glorified as archetypal or satirized as banal. Many Southern women still seek to merge into the myth and to lure their daughters toward embodying its traditions. Godwin finds their ardor for the past admirable when it encourages grace and courtesy, yet dangerous in its refusal to recognize reality. As she lists the "trademarks of the tradition," she prepares readers for her conclusion that loveliness may not fully compensate for the shallowness and evasion inherent in them:

> . . . soft hands and soft voices; first concern for others, not self; refusal to dwell on subjects of ugliness, unpleasantness, violence, tension, strife: sauve short-circuiting of all "embarrassing questions"; cultivation and veneration of tradition and beautiful things; impeccable manners; spotless "reputation."

Throughout the essay, Godwin dramatizes with piercing anecdotes the small daily traumas that beset a wife and mother who strives to live in the Southern ideal, who must appear always hospitable, congenial, and charming while resorting to deceptions and avoidances so as to keep the surface of her life looking smooth. She will "minister, forestall, deflect, prevaricate, suffer martyrdoms" rather than allow any scene to occur. Godwin points out that the Southern Lady has to take hypocritical and ultimately self-deceptive stances to preserve the semblance of fulfillment in her limited life: she avoids all, honest recognitions of sexuality, politics (especially racial relations), and violence (so that she shudders away from much of current history). To her tractable daughters, she can overtly teach the skills of a hostess and home manager, while covertly conveying subtle methods for the management of men, particularly how to win "maximum benefits . . . without threatening masculinity." While never seeming rude, she can show those docile daughters the use of indirect remarks so that they too can snub, demean, or evade unwelcome topics or unacceptable people.

Godwin perceives, and illustrates with sometimes tender humor, that the mother who devotes her life to indoctrinating the Ideal of Southern Womanhood, dutiful to *her* mother's model, sadly misses a most significant aspect of selfhood. Godwin explains the vagueness, the elusiveness, of such a woman, lacking opinions or goals beyond her domestic sphere, becoming blank because she is dedicated to others in that small world. Accepting the boundaries of the Southern heritage, she has dutifully found ways to count her blessings but has never turned inward to assess her uniqueness:

> Many a Southern woman has died, and more will die, without ever having once strained toward what Jung called "the task of personality," without ever having once confronted her true reflection beyond the quicksilver image of what her heritage has prepared her to be.

Godwin's explicit, journalistic, portrait of Southern motherhood in service to the old ideal is certainly a sorry picture.

No such dismal stereotype is developed at length among Godwin's characters who are Southern mothers. And yet, ticking off the stereotypical traits one by one, readers will find most of them in the two mothering women who represent the ancestry of Godwin's best known heroine, Jane Clifford, the protagonist of ***The Odd Woman.*** Transmuted by love and eased with wit, the Southern foibles of her mother and grandmother have charm for Jane and for the reader. Moreover, they are richly self-aware as personalities and thus they escape the last damning accusation that Godwin directs at the stereotypical Southern mother. Yet their taboos and withdrawals constrict them and narrow their worlds.

Edith Dewar Barnstorff, Jane Clifford's grandmother, epitomizes the "original Southern lady." Born in the 1890s, living until the 1970s, she ardently tries to shape both her daughter Kitty and her granddaughter Jane by her standards of purity and gentility. Purity for Edith means enduring, not enjoying, sex within marriage, and knowing that other sexuality is wicked and will probably bring doom to women who indulge in it. Gentility's ramifications involve pride and propriety, the pride of knowing who we were, long after the old landholdings are gone, and the propriety of fine manners, carriage, and dress. Jane recalls that Edith's favorite disciplinary sentence was "Nice people don't act that way." In her youth, Edith succeeded as a belle, fainting into the arms of the doting man who would be, for her, the perfect husband—awed, protective, considerate of her delicate sensibilities, and away from home often. She has carried intact through the murky twentieth century the clear standards of her nineteenth-century Southern heritage. While Jane can envy the certainty of Edith's choices, she perceives that the decisions are easy because they are dictated by formulas, "based simply on what tradition expected of her . . . written out in some etiquette book copyrighted about 1890."

Kitty, Edith's daughter and Jane's mother, was a flamboyant belle, unwilling to forego the sensual when young, but converted by her matronhood to a philosophy of renunciation. She enjoyed her heyday as enchantress, beset by suitors, though none of them were quite the flawless gentleman her mother wished. Kitty has in her middle years become a searching person, deeply religious and considerably more complex than the hollow stereotype of the Southern Lady as Indoctrinating Mother. However, Kitty can be as crafty as the shallowest woman. She tosses coy catch phrases to her daughters in efforts to mend their manners, and she manipulates her adoring husband, resorting even to tears—shamelessly, Jane thinks. Worse, she tends to reject her own self as "silly." The subjects that Kitty shared with Jane, then later dismissed as silly to recall, were her young dreams and her uneasiness about her later place in the moving world. She tries to tell her daughter how encompassing her yearnings had been: "I wanted it all. I wanted love. I wanted a career . . . everything eternally beautiful, with no compromise." And she wanted a marriage, not just of esteem, like her parents, but of passion, too. She confesses to Jane that she is "sick to remember" the power of her desires, and advises her daughter to dream more sanely, not to ache for the impossible. Such cautions may be universal, since older generations, male as well as female, repeatedly warn the young to try not to care too much. But Kitty's comments on the way dreams must be limited place her views on delusive hope in a very Southern context. "I was brought up," she says, "to believe woman's best virtue was that of renouncing herself." So she was torn between the love of others (husband, babies) and wishes for herself that she had to call selfish and try to dismiss as "silly." Kitty believes herself born too late to find the old Southern certainties that had guided her mother; yet she feels that she and her daughter Jane have been born too soon to take part in the coming time of the new settled patterns.

As Kitty compares herself with her mother, so does Jane measure herself by contrast with both her mother and grandmother. Jane sometimes wishes she could learn the social deftness of her woman forbears, and she admires the serenity of their acceptance of roles. Yet she can feel only disdain for many mannerisms of typical Southern women. For instance, she is glad that she and her best friend Gerda have never exchanged "those insincere little kisses and hugs" which Southern women "lavish on each other in public," even women "who detest each other." The ideal of Southern Womanhood, the full panoply of traits, horrifies Jane. The perfect Southern lady of her mother's generation appears in ***The Odd Woman*** as the dull and proper Cousin Frances, Edith's niece. She embodies traits that Jane has fled from, even though they are the exact trademarks that pass for gentility. Frances is correct, solicitous, well-kept in every sense. Smooth routines structure her life: entertaining, shopping, her country club and women's clubs—she takes pride in belonging to both the United Daughters of the Confederacy and the Daughters of the American Revolution. Her clothes are in the best taste and her hair and hands show that she is frequently groomed by "some respectful slave at the beauty parlor." Jane asks herself if she would have enjoyed being Frances, "safe and secure on my husband's thousand acres." Her answer is "Perhaps. If I had . . . a lobotomy first."

In her *Ms.* article, **"The Southern Belle,"** Godwin writes of Southern daughters—those who stay and those who flee. She emphasizes the difficulty for any woman who questions her Southern heritage but would like to stay in the South without taking some traditional role; her peers will gently, firmly ostracize her, pulling her "back onto the beaten path." Thus, the rebellious woman, if she "begins to succeed" in her search for new images of selfhood, is likely to be made so uncomfortable that she must flee the South—"depriving future generations of girls of her example." Moreover, the fleeing rebel leaves the land to the spiritual clones of their Southern mothers, clones shaped with a "repertoire" of superficial graces known to be attractive to the "right" sort of man for the production of still other generations of spiritual clones.

The author's comments parallel her handling of Southern protagonists in her novels up until ***A Mother and Two Daughters.*** Venturesome, questioning daughters flee the South, yet they cannot fully escape it. In Kitty and in Jane,

Godwin conveys the truth that every mother had a mother. Many of Edith's graces live on in Kitty. And Jane is spiritually the daughter of both. She partly inherits, along with their Southern accents, not a few of their Southern values and qualms, transmuted because she does question them, yet still haunting her.

The title character in ***Violet Clay*** is another Southerner, born and bred in Charleston, who reacts to Southernness by fleeing from it. Fatherless before birth, and motherless since infancy, she is still the daughter of an insistent heritage of the South. She compulsively measures herself with reference to those who reared her, the grandmother and uncle who instilled dear old lies, or perhaps half-truths, of the family's heritage. These lady and gentleman kindred, rather than her motherline, provide her models. She has little contact with her mother's people, simply mill-country folks. Ironically, these proud Charlestonians who molded Violet's sense of the South have wasted their lives, perhaps not without a certain pride in being as doomed as their homeland. Pride is even more evident in the energy both find to support keeping up appearances of decorum while glossing over their failures. Grandmother, as everyone knows, is a secret alcoholic, skillful in using gracious manners to enchant the world into sharing her pretenses of dignity. She confides in her granddaughter that she succumbed to her beau because of secret fears of failure in her potential career as a pianist and because of her pride as a belle who could capture the 32-year-old who had rejected so many other belles. She was totally won at last by the myth, the "subversive, tempting picture" which could lead even an ambitious woman of 1919 from dreams of self-fulfillment to dreams of traditional glory:

> The picture was of that lady so feted in our day—her praises were sung in every women's magazine—the accomplished wife and mother who turns her gifts to the enhancement of Home. I saw myself, safe and rich and beautiful, seated at a nine-foot grand in Charles's ancestral home.

Violet leaves the South and succeeds in New York as a commercial artist, yet plays variations on the ancestral tensions. She cannot respect her own work, a craft that usually is crass. She sells romantic covers for Gothic novels, depicting women running away from houses. And her deepest fears are fears of failing if she should dare to aspire to higher art.

Violet also compares her life to her Uncle Ambrose's, whose role as Failed Southern Gentleman is relevant because he served as surrogate parent, modeling self-deceit and ultimate hollowness. After publishing a promising, though excessively romantic first novel, he then lived on for decades as a writer of fading promise. His Southern charms serve mainly to seduce a series of women into supporting him emotionally, even to an extent economically. Finally, he commits suicide. Even that gesture fails in one way; he does not carry it off as gracefully as intended. Violet lingers over her recurring sense of descent from a line of failed artists, sometimes finding wry consolation in her intent to fail with grace. She thinks she could go down as "a dignified loser . . . if it came to that" reminding herself that her part of the country "had made its biggest loss into a sort of debonair victory."

Women in most societies may find it more difficult than men to rebel from the demands of tradition, since they are expected to transmit received truisms as unquestioned truths. They have fewer chances to test socially-accepted rules, fewer chances to gain varied experiences which help a searcher to tell truth from tradition. During the 1970s what Godwin wrote about the American South shows her concern with the customs and taboos which make the traditional roles of women even more inflexible. Southerners who believe in the heritage of the old South try harder to turn women into exemplars and transmitters of its old virtues. When those are shallowly defined, and Godwin sees how often they are mere forms, the most admired mothers perpetuate falseness. Dutiful daughters replicate their mothers, and questing daughters "flee for their lives." Even after their flights, they are hampered in their searching for honesty and autonomy because of lingering fear of all that is disruptive. Raised voices, the threat of a scene, whatever her mother would call ugly or strident, will tend to disgust even the expatriate daughters, will often send them into trembling retreat. Away from home, they do have the courage of some quite liberated convictions about sexuality. Nonetheless, they often think of "what people will say," and sometimes trim their behavior accordingly. Their shudders over "scenes" make particularly interesting the processes depicted by Godwin as essential to growth. They often achieve breakthrough insights by means of intense, even angry and loud, confrontations with their friends.

Until her latest book, ***A Mother and Two Daughters,*** Godwin held out little hope for daughters who stayed at home. They simply relived the Southern fallacies. She presented dramas of psychological progress featuring the growth of the venturesome ones who abandoned the South. As social critic, she wrote of the typical ex-Southerner Carter Stephens having a chance to grow, to break out of the "vicious circle" of heritage-bound continuity. Breaking the old spell depends, for Carter, upon getting in touch with the reality of a black woman, that home-bred alien who abhors the heritage. Marianne, her black acquaintance, and Carter have met as women with careers in the North. Both are eager to "work hard at being friends" and know how much they have in common, such as their love of books and their strains with men and the larger problem of designing their lives. Both take pride in broadmindedness: they intend not to be "petty nor isolationist nor heritage-handicapped" both "like being women" but find "being human more important." Their friendship meets its test when Carter defends the Southern habit of false-sweet pretendings; she likes making things nicer. Marianne challenges not just her social values but her maturity by asking, "Don't you think it's time you outgrew all these meaningless trappings of the privileged elite?"

Before Godwin lets Carter reply, the writer comments pointedly that a "portion of social history hangs in the balance" while Carter weighs her choices. She can take the old-Southern condescending option of avoiding a scene, feeling smug because Marianne hadn't had the advantages which would have taught her not to be rude and critical. Then Carter considers being honest, recognizes her anger and her need "to challenge . . . and be challenged in return," to have the furious encounter that "only friends and equals can have."

Do they win an open, lasting, taboo-free friendship by letting all hell break loose, airing out their particular hell-bent heritages? Godwin asks the cogent question: Can either of them get beyond her particular identity, blackness for one and Southern breeding for the other? Do they really want to outgrow their pasts, either of them?

> If they do, they may stay up shouting at each other all night, asking and answering the kinds of embarrassing questions that would rock the traditional Southern home on its foundations. Marianne will explode into flames of rage at the injustice of centuries and Carter will dissolve backward into tears of nostalgia for that life of her mother's, where no dangerous questions are broached and the troublesome self is negated.

Godwin chooses to let her readers decide whether the two women work through their furies, and survive the long night of rage and nostalgia. But she praises the benefits of such confrontation: when women keep trusting each other, articulating and sharing their versions of their pasts, individual and cultural, painful yet necessary, maturity will evolve. This 1975 article reaches the conclusion that only after such sharing can we "be one day nearer" to the happy time "when all constricting, debilitating stereotypes," including those of traditional Southern Womanhood, will be "relegated to the archives of human evolution."

In ***A Mother and Two Daughters,*** Godwin's three protagonists do not succumb to the debilitating stereotype of Southern Womanhood in the least. Most of the traits of the Southern Lady seem to them amusing anachronisms. The novel suggests that Godwin can foresee prospects for the best hopes of her 1975 analysis coming true. Yet faint variations of the types she noted do appear in the form of a rebel daughter and a docile daughter. Cate, the rebellious troublemaker, questions all injustices, worries her family with her protestings, and seems to be bound to flee forever from the South. But she returns at the end to her roots in the hills of North Carolina, as a base from which she travels to earn her venturesome living. Lydia, the docile daughter, and Nell, the mother, preserve the graces of Southern ladies while avoiding the pitfalls of hypocrisy and shallowness. All three women relish "the task of personality" and each in her own way is both sensual and self-determining.

The novel is a comedy. Witty talk and wry perceptions pervade it, and it is also comic in that larger sense of happy endings—prizes are distributed and journeys lead to lovers meeting. Some of the humorous moments feature old concepts of Southern Womanhood. Throughout her life Nell has taken pride in keeping a critical distance from traditional Southerness, remaining an observer who "masqueraded adequately . . . as a 'Southern Lady.'" Yet Godwin juxtaposes this conscious pride in her freedom from the stereotype with a lasting distress at Cate's greater freedom from it, Cate's disordered life: Nell cannot forgive her rebel daughter "for not making more of an effort to blend gracefully into the landscape." Lydia, the second daughter, indoctrinated in docility by her traditional father, only gradually breaks away from the formulaic successes of the Southern belle. As stages in her awakening to the task of personality, she leaves her husband and home, studies sociology and feminism, develops a true sisterly friendship with a black woman, and takes a lover. Lydia tries to envision her life in neatly labeled compartments, and even after her unconventional independence has been attained, one of these compartments reads "STILL A LADY." Lydia's discovery of a career depends upon her ladylike air and her absorption with Southern life. She becomes a TV celebrity, charming her audiences with visits to the sites of gracious living.

Light touches, then, play upon the manners and graces of the South, while debilitating flaws are mostly "relegated to the archives of human evolution," as Godwin wished in her *Ms.* article. Racial bigotry, for example, has been transcended by all of the featured characters, even though the off-stage activities of realistically vicious bigots have cruelly changed the course of the lives of the two major black characters before the close of the novel. On stage, more hopeful trends are dramatized. Crucial to Lydia's development was her friendship with Renee Peverell-Watson and her guidance from Calvin Edwards. In the novel's epilog, set five years after its major events, Renee's daughter has married Lydia's son. The only members of either family who feel strain about this interracial marriage are blacks: on the bride's side, Renee's brother, the patriarch of the Peverells, and on the groom's side, Azalea, Aunt Theodora's maid-companion, who opposes "mixing" on principle. Amusingly, the concept of the lady in the South of 1984 (the date of the epilog) has been quite detached from concern with color, although not from beauty and grace and demeanor. Camilla, the bride, impresses her white mother-in-law as "a perfect lady" and the matriarchal Aunt Theodora agrees.

In summary, Godwin's writings dissect the conservative feminine myth of the South not just to expose its debilitating central demand for a selflessness that precludes self-discovery, but also to present remedies. This author recognizes the beauty of ordered lives, and clings to hopes that Southern grace in its best sense can be cherished, can still enhance the old South's new daughters. But more emphatically she cautions that traditional roles when merely traditionally fulfilled endanger the spiritual lives of two generations: both the Southern mothers who model such roles and the daughters whom they dutifully try to mold toward the confining Ideal of Southern Womanhood. Women reared to reenact the traditional values must learn, Gail Godwin insists, to see their fallacies, explore them openly among critical friends and find new ways to be themselves, continually self-creating. And the three Southern women delineated in Godwin's latest work, ***A Mother and Two Daughters,*** all manage to sustain their self-creativity without permanent flights from the South and without romantic denials of contemporary realities; as a result they can be shown moving into a wholesome future, not problem-free by any means but free of the problems imposed by the rigid model of constraining Southern Ladyhood.

Paul Gray (review date 11 February 1985)

SOURCE: "Deliberate Speed, Stunning Effect," in *Time,* February 11, 1985, p. 87.

[*In the following review, Gray asserts that* The Finishing School *is Godwin's "most artful and accomplished novel and an old-fashioned, irresistible page turner."*]

With ***A Mother and Two Daughters*** (1982), her fifth novel, Gail Godwin joined that select circle of critically praised authors who have also produced best-sellers. This happy event entitled her longtime admirers to mixed emotions. While it is pleasurable to see a favored writer receive the success she deserves, it is irksome to realize that membership in a small club of discriminating readers has suddenly been thrown open to multitudes. If so many people, the reasoning follows, liked Godwin's loose, loving chronicle of three plucky females, then maybe we should find it disappointing. And whom will she write for next time, all of them or us?

The Finishing School should thoroughly satisfy both of Godwin's constituencies. It is at once her most artful and accomplished novel and an old-fashioned, irresistible page turner. The plot, like that of ***A Mother and Two Daughters,*** is set in motion by the death of a father and the adjustments demanded of the women he protected. But this time Godwin has made things harder on the survivors, particularly a young daughter who must endure a brief but harrowing rite of passage toward maturity.

Justin Stokes, 40, a successful stage actress, looks back on the summer she turned 14 and staked her claim on a future. In the beginning, the teen-age girl feels doomed by fate, with fair reason. Within the past two years, her mother's patrician parents, who helped raise her in a grand Virginia house, have both died. Then her father is killed in a car accident. Justin's mother must transplant her and her younger brother to a village in upstate New York, to the tidy, stultifying suburban home of Aunt Mona, the late husband's sister. Stunned by her losses and longing for the old days "before everybody started dying," Justin mopes and takes solitary bike rides through this alien Yankee territory. On one such foray, she discovers a tumbledown hut by the side of a pond and decides to investigate. When she sees a woman inside, lying on a blanket and reading a book, Justin screams.

She will scream again, as it happens, by this same hut, near the end of her story; Justin's creator endows memory with intricate patterns of repetition. Between these two outbursts, the girl finds herself "enchanted" and "bewitched" by the woman she has stumbled across. Ursula DeVane, 44, lives in a stone house her ancestors put up two centuries earlier; she shares the place with her younger brother Julian, a melancholy piano teacher whom Ursula is determined to force into fulfilling his early promise as a concert performer. To this end, she has sacrificed her own career as an actress and successive parcels of the family's properties.

Or so she tells Justin. The growing friendship between the uprooted girl and the landlocked aristocrat shimmers with ambiguities and half-truths. Justin is flattered that a woman as haughty as Ursula seems genuinely interested in her and her disrupted perceptions. To find such a confidante in an alien place seems an answered prayer: "She lived the kind of life that reminded me a lot of the one we had lost." For her part, Ursula appears to take on this fledgling out of a mixture of kindness, boredom and the desire to create: "She's a clean slate. When she meets new people, or new challenges, she is free to respond to the unique demands of the moment." Ursula starts calling the hut where they first met, on the dwindling DeVane estate, Justin's "finishing school," the place where example will groom youth for the trials that await it.

This description proves accurate, but in ways neither of the friends could have imagined. Justin learns much from her mentor, including the necessity of betraying and abandoning her, of finishing an evil that Ursula's school had hidden from its inception. The vague outlines of this conclusion are visible in the first few pages of Justin's narrative; the hows and whys appear with deliberate speed and stunning effect. Godwin's account of the making of a forcibly modern heroine (career, two failed marriages) uses nearly every trick in the book, circa the 19th century. Good Dickensian fun is had with Justin's Aunt Mona, a kind but stereotyped soul who cannot resist mentioning, regardless of context, the advantages that life has failed to bestow upon her. But Mona's idiosyncrasy serves more than comic relief. She emerges as exactly the sort of woman who would marry, and then separate from, the kind of man who would naturally feel obliged to assist Justin—at just the moment when his kindness can do the most harm.

Nothing, ultimately, is wasted in ***The Finishing School.*** Every character and scene leads somehow toward an inexorable crisis. Simply coasting on the surface of this tale, while waiting for the crash, is most enjoyable. Those readers who want to know why they are having such a good time can stand back and appreciate Godwin's skill. She has taken some timeworn contrivances and shown, by example, why storytellers invented them in the first place: to heighten life into story, to funnel random experience into manners, morals and destiny.

Lisa Mitchell (review date 24 February 1985)

SOURCE: A review of *The Finishing School,* in *Los Angeles Times Book Review,* February 24, 1985, pp. 2, 10.

[*In the following review, Mitchell offers qualified praise for* The Finishing School, *while pointing out some of the novel's technical flaws.*]

What do actors do to survive between plays? Not as in how do they pay their rent, but in where do they live out their dramas? With and for whom can they perform? What do they do to avoid the dreaded "ordinariness"? For 40-year-old Justin Stokes, with successful New York plays to her credit, she becomes obsessed with a desire she had during the summer that she turned 14.

An appealing subject, since we all probably have had a summer that became *the* summer; one special section of intense joy and pain that remains forever roped off in enchantment from the rest of our lives. It may have involved a first job, a memorable trip, a change in family circumstances, but, inevitably, if there was real magic, it involved a person. For young Justin, it was Ursula De Vane, a dynamic, unconventional 44-year-old woman with "a flair for improvisations," an actress *manque* with her own need for an audience. That need is at least one explanation for the sophisticated Ursula to encourage so young a girl into such an intense friendship. There is no wonder at all for the girl's infatuation with her.

Justin is a stranger in a strange land, having recently been uprooted from her Virginia home where, within a year, her father and the grandparents who raised her all died. Against Justin's protests and pleadings, her mother moves their remaining family north to the rural township of Clove, in Upstate New York. Here, Justin, her displaced mother and 6-year-old brother come to live in a characterless house with their bourgeois Aunt Mona and her surly, spoiled daughter.

Then one day, Aunt Mona's deadly plastic runners over her sea-foam green carpets and Clove's look-alike houses with no history and school bus rides of harsh Yankee accents are no longer the sole borders of Justin's life. For Justin has happened upon an old stone hut in a pine forest, and in it, a woman who makes the sun come out. The stone hut stands on what is left of the once vast De Vane property. It is Ursula's retreat; the place where Ursula comes to be "re-reading Proust" until her brother Julian's robotish piano students finish their lessons up in the big main house. The stone hut, nicknamed "The Finishing School," is a key spot for Ursula, who once taught at a real finishing school, to expound her theories on life and art to Justin. It is also the site of pain and betrayals that are hinted at all through the book.

Gail Godwin gives us the adult Justin as narrator—opening the novel after Justin has had an exceptionally vivid dream about Ursula, and "when Ursula appears in a dream, it is usually to stir things up." So Justin stokes her memories, and, in reviewing the old situation, brings her 14-year-old self to us in flashback.

The time we spend with this sharp, sensitive adolescent girl is delightful. Every emotion rings true: her self-consciousness over being so mesmerized by a woman; her conflicts of loyalties between her mother—now a disappointment—and her dazzling new mentor/friend. We can ache for this Justin so chagrined over her dependence on Ursula's approval, meticulously pacing her visits to the De Vane house, lest a teen-ager wear out her welcome. We can relish this girl with a need for magic, who goes off to "meditate" or "become" Ursula when she is alone; this wise person in that funny country between child and woman, sitting there trying to sort out feelings that cannot be labeled and may never really be fully understood.

Unfortunately, the time we spend in her engaging company is interrupted again and again by the adult Justin's digressions of hindsight and omniscient teases of what is to come—which is all the more an awkward device when narrator apologizes to reader for having digressed, then continues to do so.

I certainly quarrel with Godwin allowing constant hints of the "betrayals" and "tragedy" that lie ahead. If they're meant as appetite whetters, more's the letdown when the outcome finally arrives. There's also a maddening repetition of scenes and dialogue as Justin first tells us about something Ursula said and did, then, chapters later, plays the actual scene—*word for word*—so you keep shuffling pages back and forth, thinking scene transpositions from earlier drafts somehow weren't ironed out in the published edition. There are other narrative repetitions (and must we be told how Aunt Mona's "feathercut quivers" every time she appears?). There are heavy-handed expositions, collaring us to make sure we *get* something that was quite clear in the first place. This is all the more dumbfounding among so many lovely, subtle thoughts, clever ironies and well-crafted passages; all the more bizarre in a novel by a talented and critically acclaimed writer as Gail Godwin surely is.

But I loved the basic subject so much, I wanted to look away from the technical flaws the way you do when you discover that your new Big Crush has dandruff. The point is, I had a good time, anyway. I loved dramatic, eccentric Ursula and her fierce twin beliefs of avoiding ordinariness and staving off "jellification," i.e., the dangerous state of not changing. And I loved the adult Justin's need to stir up drama, to connect 26 years ago with today. "For what it's worth," she says to the Ursula in her head, "I have absorbed you. As long as I live, you live in me." For what it's worth, ***The Finishing School*** says full speed ahead to honoring our old obsessions—and that's worth a lot.

William H. Pritchard (review date 25 February 1985)

SOURCE: "Maiden Voyage," in *New Republic,* February 25, 1985, pp. 31-2.

[*In the following review, Pritchard offers praise for* The Finishing School, *which he concludes is Godwin's "best novel."*]

The "finishing school" is in fact an old stone hut by a pond in Clove township, upstate New York, where at the beginning of her 15th year and over the course of an extraordinary summer, Justin Stokes comes of age. The agent who plants formative aspirations within her is Ursula DeVane, an unmarried woman of 44 who—with her reclusive brother Julian, a talented concert pianist reduced to giving lessons to neighborhood children—lives in her father's old house and grounds, selling off his acres as economic necessity directs. By contrast with Ursula's rootedness, Justin has been painfully uprooted. Her own father recently dead, she has been wrenched from the established routines of a comfortable home in Virginia and relocated in the unfamiliar and largely unappealing confines of Lucas Meadows—a small community most of whose members work for IBM, eight miles away in Kingston, New York.

Justin, her mother, and younger brother live with her aunt Mona and cousin Becky in a house which is, alas, everything Ursula DeVane's is not (it has seafoam wall-to-wall carpeting in the living room, protected by clear plastic runners leading to the various sitting places). Aunt Mona has redone Justin's room for her in what the girl, with a sense of the aesthetically trashy, has intolerantly dubbed "Raspberry Ice." Within its confines, lonely and yearning for her lost past and her as yet uncertain future, Justin reaches out in imagination to the freedom, the cultural style, which Ursula comes increasingly to embody.

These are some of the materials which Gail Godwin in her sixth novel (she has also published two collections of shorter fiction) has woven into an engaging, shapely narrative of cumulative power. There is nothing unfamiliar in her material. At least since Lawrence's *The Rainbow,* in the relationship of that other Ursula with her "beloved, subtly-intimate teacher" Winifred Inger, we have had literary treatments of the love between aspiring girl and mature, "advanced" woman (Winifred Inger is interested in the "Women's Movement"). Gail Godwin writes with none of the steamy abandon Lawrence lavishes on Ursula and Winifred's nocturnal swim together (although her Ursula does attempt, without success, to get Justin to swim with her in "their" pond), and her narrative voice is much more carefully modulated than Lawrence's eventually monotonous and rather external presentation. Godwin creates nuance and variety by making Justin speak through different voices: the fulfilled actress she has become, now haunted by a moment from her past and meditating upon it; but also the young Justin, speaking to us from present urgency, having fallen under the spell of a powerful woman. Yet this young Justin also recalls a younger one, as events from her previous life in Virginia with grandparents, father, and mother are reviewed. Some words of hers from the novel describe well its technique:

> In following the natural flow of my memories as they leap forward, then draw back, then leap forward again, I am digressing from what I want to do most. I want to go back and claim the girl I was—the girl Ursula DeVane chose for her special friend, that summer in Clove. I want to take myself through the summer as it unfolded, no

> conscious lies or glossings-over, but only the wisdom of retrospect.

But interestingly enough such wisdom is exactly what the novel shows to be impossible, or at least emptily abstract and pious in character. To believe in its secure attainment is to exhibit a naiveté comparable to that revealed at one moment in the book when Justin, looking at her youthful face and body in the mirror, and with a sense of her whole life ahead, tells us that

> it seemed perfectly possible to me . . . that with resolution and a little prudent foresight—and from learning from the example of people like Ursula—I could get through life without ever committing any act that would haunt me later.

This delusory hope the novel exposes, yet does so in a way that is free from gloating or heavy-handed irony. John Updike says in his memoir, *The Dogwood Tree,* that in maturity he found no certain substitutes for the misguided assumptions of childhood. In a similar manner, ***The Finishing School*** shows the wisdom of retrospect to be no more sustaining or invulnerable to attack than the "prudent foresight" of youth.

There are various stylistic means by which Gail Godwin refuses to over-invest in any single, "true" point of view or nugget of meaning. As the narrative leaps forward and draws back, as the narrator shifts from one age-perspective to another, events recur and are retold with different emphasis, and by way of making our awareness more complicated. Rather than presenting the young Justin's experience in a relatively direct way, her older self overlays it with all the qualifications and hesitations of alternative ways of talking:

> As I review these memories in painstaking detail, trying to see what was true and not flinch from those truths, I've even speculated whether my "possessed" behavior toward Ursula was a semiconsciously contrived ploy on my part to make my mother see that she ought to have taken me away from Clove. But no, that's going too far; that would make me a monster, like little Mary Tilford in *The Children's Hour* who wrecks a school and the lives of two women in order to keep from being sent back to the school. I was not a monster—not that kind of monster, anyway. I told no lies: I even kept from my mother the extent of my preoccupation with Ursula. I loved Ursula more than my mother that summer, and I didn't want my mother to know it.

And so on, giving somewhat the effect of Eliot's notion of ironic wit as "a recognition, implicit in the expression of every experience, of other kinds of experience which are possible."

Yet it would be wrong to overstress the complications and difficulty of this novel, since it is distinguished throughout by a lucid and unpretentious gravity of speech, its narrative voice giving us confidence as it conveys—in Lionel Trilling's useful formulation—"both the modulation and the living form of what is being said." This is, quite simply, a voice one likes and trusts, and it lives just as convincingly in the incidental details of place and person as in larger and more thematic concerns. For example, the voice is filled with IBM lore ("I've Been Moved" as the quip has it), attaching itself to the Kingston and Poughkeepsie operations of that company. (One instance: Thomas J. Watson Sr., visiting the men's room at the Poughkeepsie site, found an employee disregarding the "Please Wash Hands Before Returning To Work" sign. When the founder of IBM asked the employee why he ignored the sign, the man explained that "I'm not going back to work, I'm going to lunch.") The portrait of Justin's fat friend Joan, who invites her for a swim in her swimming pool but declines to participate herself ("You just swim all you want," she said in her mild, uninflected voice, "and I'll sit up here under the umbrella and watch you"—and so she does, in her "jumbo-sized suit"), is humorous and even poignant, without a trace of clever "satiric" narrative showing-off. So is the portrait of "Mott"—Justin's aunt's ex-spouse (and an IBMer), who unknowingly precipitates the book's painful denouement. There is a thoroughly believable and sympathetic account of Justin's first Broadway show, which turns out to be, luckily for her, *My Fair Lady.* And, appropriate to a book the sound of whose narrative voice is crucial, there are delicately noted bits of music, played splendidly (or butchered) by Ursula's brother (or his pupils): Beethoven's "Moonlight" Sonata; Liszt's "Mephisto Waltz"; Chopin's B Flat Scherzo; "Happy Birthday to You" and "Dixie."

"That is the power of the artist, you see," says Ursula to the young Justin: "If you are an artist you learn how to trap the yearning and put it where you want it, put it where it goes. That's the secret all true artists come to know." Gail Godwin has learned the secret and trapped it in this, her best novel. Shorter and more tightly controlled than the overlong though often absorbing ***A Mother and Two Daughters, The Finishing School*** develops the first person voice used in her novella **"Mr. Bedford"** (in ***Mr. Bedford and the Muses***) into a narrative of humanly impressive energies, as happy-sad in its texture as life itself may be said to be. Its sympathies and ironies are equally directed at all, irrespective of age or sex, and it is wholly empty of rancor or shrillness or mean-mindedness. For those reasons it helps us, as Wallace Stevens said poetry should do, to live our lives.

Paul Gray (review date 5 October 1987)

SOURCE: "Polite Forms of Aggression," in *Time*, October 5, 1987, p. 82.

[*In the following review, Gray asserts that in* A Southern Family *"Gail Godwin again displays the narrative verve and generosity that won critical praise for her early works. . . . "*]

Clare Campion, 42, a successful novelist living in New York City, pays one of her infrequent visits home to Mountain City in western North Carolina. There she finds her mother Lily, her stepfather Ralph Quick and her two half brothers, Theo, 28, and Rafe, 26, all of them behaving incorrigibly in character and thereby reminding Clare of why she had left them and the South in the first place. Her only respite from what she calls "the ongoing theatricals of the family" is the companionship of her childhood friend Julia Richardson. Years earlier, Julia gave up a promising career as a historian and returned to Mountain City to teach in the local college, take care of her dying mother and then look after her father. These two women manifest the attraction of opposites. Clare has apparently broken free of her past and asserted her talent in the world at large; Julia has surrendered her future to duty. Each regards the other as a path not taken.

All the elements seem to have been assembled for a spirited feminist parable about the oppressive choices that society forces on women. Indeed, that story can be found within ***A Southern Family,*** but so can many others. In her seventh novel, Gail Godwin again displays the narrative verve and generosity that won critical praise for her early works and then popular, best-selling acclaim for ***A Mother and Two Daughters*** (1982) and ***The Finishing School*** (1985). Her meticulously controlled fiction creates the illusion of life unpredictably unfolding and of characters trying to make moral sense out of experiences that overwhelm thought.

Hence Clare's discomfiture over her latest trip home is suddenly dwarfed by tragedy: Theo, whose wife has left him with custody of their young son, goes off one Sunday afternoon to see his current girlfriend, a nurse who is trying to disentangle herself from their affair. Within hours, both are dead of gunshot wounds, apparently administered by Theo in a murder-suicide. This event throws the members of the Quick family, their friends and the close-knit society of Mountain City into paroxysms of confusion and self-reproach. What made Theo do it? Could he have been saved, and, if so, who failed him?

As each character looks back at Theo and searches for clues to explain his fate, a complex portrait slowly emerges, not only of a troubled young man but of an entire community losing its ideals and energies. Theo's marriage to Snow Mullins, a red-neck girl with a ninth-grade education, was a gauntlet thrown down at the Quicks' precarious sense of stature, indeed at Mountain City's communal illusion of social propriety. Theo's younger brother Rafe remembers, "I mean, it was embarrassing at the wedding, seeing how Mom's friends tried to keep their faces from showing how horrified they were when the bride's side of the church started filling up."

Theo's father Ralph cannot share in this outrage because he is not entitled to it by birth: "If social class could be measured on a ruler—and lots of people sure as hell acted as if it could—he would estimate that both he and Snow had married up about four inches, he going from about the five- to the nine-inch measure on a ruler, Snow from about the three- to the seven-inch one; he figured he had brought Lily and their children back down to a seven." Lily thinks so too, and her resentment is an important factor in the simmering deterioration of their marriage. One character recalls Theo's comment on the elaborate manners of his fellow Southerners: "Their politeness is a very effective form of aggression."

Along with her grief and guilt at not having paid more attention to a half brother 14 years her junior, Clare is haunted by something Theo said to her the day before his death: "I was thinking how nice it would be to be a character in one of your novels." Assuming that she was about to be flattered, she had asked him why. His reply: "Because you take care of them so nicely. You let them suffer a little, just enough to improve their characters, but you always rescue them from the abyss at the last minute and reward them with love or money or the perfect job—or sometimes all three."

A daring irony is at work here, for the same thing could be said about some of Godwin's novels, especially ***A Mother and Two Daughters.*** As a stand-in for her creator, Clare must wrestle with the question of whether all fiction, including ***A Southern Family,*** necessarily lies about reality by giving it the coherence of beginnings, middles and ends. Furthermore, before Theo's death, Clare had been working on a novel that would signal a breakthrough in her career, one that "was going to *get beyond* family life and the South and independent youngish women wriggling out of the deadly twin-embrace." Instead of finishing that book, she is forced to live through the old stories all over again.

Clare's predicament can be read as Godwin's veiled explanation for returning to the same themes and materials she has worked on so thoroughly in the past. If so, the gesture is considerate but unnecessary. Born in the South, Godwin appears to be one of those writers who inherited a subject for life; then she developed the wisdom and talent to make her birthright seem constantly fresh and enthralling.

Anita Brookner (review date 17 October 1987)

SOURCE: "Time and the Single Girl," in *Spectator*, October 17, 1987, pp. 36-7.

[*In the following review, Brookner offers positive evaluation of* A Southern Family.]

Thirteen years ago Gail Godwin wrote an extraordinarily capacious and sympathetic novel entitled ***The Odd Woman.*** Both the title and the theme were taken from George Gissing's novel, *The Odd Women,* a bleak and chilling account of what happens to women who are not married. According to Gissing they are forced into menial work and end up in institutions, drunk or mad or both. The shame of spinsterhood was apparently at its peak in the sunset years of Victorian values. Gail Godwin took over the burden of this lament, but by 1974 that shame had mutated into mere uncertainty of status: the unmarried woman, honourably furnished with a lover and a university career, overcame her disadvantages but felt lonely, unprotected. This was before the days of networking, assertiveness training, and power dressing. Spinsters today manage better, may have babies, can achieve solvency and viability. At some point they may even soar over the top into triumphalism, surveying their good fortune at doing without the tedium or the torment of a man and comparing themselves favorably with their exhausted married sisters.

All this is illusion, of course, as Gail Godwin's Jane, the Odd Woman of the title, knew in her heart even in 1974. For Jane's heart was where all the arguments took place, and the novel assumed an almost 19th-century substantiality as a result of it. There is not much heart in the beadier woman's novel of the 1980s, and that is why so many women, looking secretly for a literature that will connect with their own desires, turn to more leisurely representations. Jane, a teacher at a midwestern college, flies home for a family funeral. The weather is bad; snow interrupts communications; there is plenty of time for reflection. Home is in hillbilly country, innocent and cunning territory, backward and contemporary in alarming alternations of mood. Discomfort, displacement lie in wait.

Jane's pretty mother has married a redneck building contractor as her second husband, and there are younger children of the second marriage. Aches and resentment are activated as soon as Jane walks in the door, but the beauty of the novel—and it has a certain real beauty—lies in the thoughtfulness with which these are tackled. Jane is noble, vulnerable, loving, and regretful, all to a very recognisable extent, and the message seems to be that these values are still a woman's best attributes, for they bring Jane safely through to the end, sadder, wiser, but vindicated.

The virtues of small town living—that old American dream—are celebrated here, as well as a refusal to embrace metropolitan corruption. The scene in which Jane, in New York to meet her lover, goes frantically shopping for a new dress, buys one she hates because the assistant is elderly and looks unwell, and then accidentally leaves it in a taxi on her way back to the hotel, will probably awaken an echo in many a woman's memory. The absorbing quality of the novel perhaps resides in its innate domesticity, as if a woman's loyalties still lie close to home, no matter where her other activities might lead her.

Gail Godwin is also known in this country for her collection of stories entitled ***Mr Bedford and the Muses*** and the novel called ***Violet Clay.*** All three are published in paperback by Pavanne. In ***Violet Clay*** a violent and mysterious death, that of Uncle Ambrose, sets the heroine off on her journey of discovery, a journey that takes her to a cabin in the woods in an attempt to repossess the lost dead man, with his secrets still undiscovered. Godwin is an old-fashioned novelist who evidently believes that the family will furnish all the material she needs for her long chronicles, which are in themselves journeys of emotional as well as physical discovery.

Now she has produced her longest chronicle to date. ***A Southern Family*** runs to 530 pages and although noticeably flawed is mesmerically absorbing. It should be said at the outset that its themes have been tackled before: a violent death in the family, mysterious and unexplained, has all the other members spinning like tops in their efforts to get to the bottom of it. Reunited for the funeral, they then go off again in their divergent directions to question their consciences. We are in hillbilly country again, and the pretty mother, Lily, has married a redneck building contractor as her second husband . . .

The status of the novel's unmarried woman has been lifted a notch higher, as befits the ideology of the day: Clare is a novelist and Julia a college instructor. They have a certain dignity, these women, and all the time in the world to talk in page-long paragraphs. No detail is too minute for them, or immaterial. The men also reflect the spirit of the age in that they are becoming more noticeably unheroic. It seems to be the odd woman's awkward privilege to point this out, at least so Lily, Julia and Clare would appear to tell us. Lily, the wife, is seen to have deteriorated with marriage. Clare, living in concubinage, is torn with anxiety. Only Julia, celibate, but with a face-saving George in the background, is her own woman.

I enjoyed it. It had the reassuring solidity of a novel by Mrs Gaskell for me as I ploughed through its thickening and repetitive preoccupations. It is not smart: that is its virtue. It is probably, no, almost certainly, not as good as ***The Odd Woman.*** But is seems likely that it will speak to women who still have a desire to be old-fashioned, and who like a fiction that reflects their major concerns. Not only odd women need apply, even though for once they come out on top.

Rachel M. Brownstein (essay date 1989)

SOURCE: "*The Odd Woman* and Literary Feminism," in *American Women Writing Fiction: Memory, Identity, Family, Space,* edited by Mickey Pearlman, University Press of Kentucky, 1989, pp. 173-84.

[*In the following essay, Brownstein explores literary feminist themes in* The Odd Woman *and Godwin's opposition to "feminist categorization" among contemporary critics. According to Brownstein,* "The Odd Woman *suggests that real, interesting women must imagine and construct their identities in the terms of traditional fiction, so as to revise them."*]

At the age of four or five, Jane Clifford, the protagonist of Gail Godwin's ***The Odd Woman,*** was already concerned with the representation of women in fiction. She asked her mother, Kitty, a college teacher who wrote love stories on weekends:

"Why don't you write a story about a woman who teaches school at the college and writes love stories on the weekend and has a little girl like me?"

> "It wouldn't sell, that's why." replied Kitty.
>
> "Oh, I think it would be very interesting to read," said Jane.
>
> "It would be interesting to people like you and me," Kitty said, "but I can assure you, *Love Short Stories* wouldn't buy it."

In an article about writing fiction, the author of ***The Odd Woman*** recalled that her own mother, like Jane's, wrote on week-ends for magazines called something like *Love Short Stories.* Her "specialty was the representative heroine, not the singular, the 'passing strange,'" Godwin explained; she edited "the most interesting parts of herself out of the heroines she sent to New York. . . . For practical reasons, for reasons of sanity as well." Grown-up daughters of romance-writing mothers, having been raised on the profits from *Love Short Stories,* and not on the stories themselves, are shrewd about the lure and the lie of romantic fiction. And they remain preoccupied by it. How fictions and stereotypes of the romantic heroine function in complex real women's minds and lives is a theme of all Gail Godwin's novels. It is articulated most pointedly in ***The Odd Woman*** (1974). The heroine, Jane Clifford, is defined to begin with as odd first of all—as not representative, singular, "passing strange." In this, Godwin persuasively shows, she is, precisely, representative—of "people like you and me," that is, women who see themselves as more interesting than standard representations of women in fiction. ***The Odd Woman*** suggests that real, interesting women must imagine and construct their identities in the terms of traditional fiction, so as to revise them.

Like her mother, Jane Clifford thinks about heroines and love stories in the way of business. A thirty-two-year-old single (unmatched, odd) professor of English, she reflects on commercial romances like the ones her mother used to write and also on the kind written by Jane Austen and George Eliot that educated women read; she measures herself against both novel heroines and their female creators. Her own life feels like a fiction. So much, and so literally, does Jane think about the love writ large in novels that she suspects herself of having dreamed her current affair with a married man, the remote, too perfectly named Gabriel Weeks, a comically parodic version of an angel (as opposed to a Romantic demon?) lover. He is a professor, too, of (for a slight change) art history. The love of Jane's mother's life was an English professor; with the exception of her dashing oldest friend, Gerda Mulvaney, the publisher of a radical feminist newspaper, all of Jane's best friends are academics. Pedantic Gabriel aims to catalog the kinds of love—according to him, there are just six—while the women professors tend to think about it novelistically, as story. For them the boundaries between fiction and daily life are transparent and permeable. When her colleague Sonia Marks tells Jane she's trying to imagine the man who'd be just right for her, she means she's trying to decide between Heathcliff and Mr. Knightley. For Jane the twenty-five years George Eliot spent with G. H. Lewes are as personally significant as the twenty-five years of her mother's second marriage to coarse Ray Sparks (Kitty's former student, who courted her by calling her his "Belle Dame Sans Merci" at the end of an exam paper). Nearly as significant as the twenty-five years Gabriel Weeks has been married to Ann, whom he has no plans to leave. Jane is a literary academic to the core: in her fantasy about being attacked by a pervert, she talks the man out of his vile intention and then suggests, hilariously, "Perhaps you ought to apply for a Guggenheim." A pretentious piece of pornographic fiction by one of her colleagues infuriates her because it records its author's passage through a fashionable life stage and also because it fails to give its readers credit for identifying its literary analogue. It is called *The Country Husband;* discreetly, we are told we recognize Wycherley, the Restoration precedent. (Is there also a shy misjudged poke here at John Cheever?) The line between comradely familiarity with academics and satirical contempt of them is very fine.

Godwin's own title echoes the title of a novel by George Gissing (another G. G.), *The Odd Women,* which Jane Clifford is planning to teach (we get her reading notes) in a course called Women in Literature. Jane the professor, like Godwin the novelist, is preoccupied with women's lives, their differences and samenesses, and inevitabilities, the apparently urgent necessity to choose one kind from a finite, already published list. It is her habit to contrast the fullness and pointedness of words, the clarity of roles, and the conclusiveness of finished plots, with the mixed motives, multiple selves, and meaningless accidents and impulses that govern actual selves and experiences. As she fantasizes and thinks and talks and reads about literature and women, a.k.a. art and love, Jane is working at critically understanding and artistically shaping her own character and destiny as if they were in a novel. The personal, for her, is the professional. When she thinks about the taken-for-granted "romantic" pattern of love-then-marriage women's lives are expected to conform to, it is important to her that serious English fiction—by Jane Austen and George Eliot—has given this pattern moral and aesthetic weight: the authority of fiction makes the pattern weigh heavily on her.

The thoroughgoing literariness of its protagonist is a clue to ***The Odd Woman***'s historical moment. In the mid-seventies real and fictional literary women like Jane Clifford were fascinating to themselves and others as never before—or perhaps since. One early result of the feminist movement, which was criticizing the accepted images of women as fictions, was to make women writers, of and about fiction, oddly glamorous figures. Bluestockings had been forbidding and schoolteachers notoriously sexless, but the new literary women were something else. Ellen Moer's phrase, the title of her 1976 book, was itself inspiriting; it put women professors and readers in the same category as Jane Austen and George Eliot—and their heroines. Reading and writing, readers and writers, were sexy. A conspicuous literary legacy of the women's movement in the second half of the twentieth century is fiction about English majors by English majors, who set about deliberately to revise the standard heroine's character and life story. Margaret Drabble's novels and Godwin's are the obvious examples, but the protagonist of *Fear of Flying* (1973) is also, remember, a graduate student of literature.

Even when they remained chastely professional, in print, what women professors had to say was in the mid-seventies interesting to an unprecedentedly wide public. They themselves seemed attractive role models, professional women who thought professionally about love and its images and stories, achieving, as they did so, an enviable integration of love and work. In ***The Odd Woman*** Jane Clifford feels a familiar old-fashioned pang when a New York City cab driver, hearing she's a teacher, says, "That explains it," meaning her frumpy unmarriedness; but Jane's classy friend Sonia Marks, with her children, the already-married lover she got to marry her, her intellectual intensity, her charismatic classroom style, her long list of publications, and her tendency to blush endearingly to the roots of her beautiful hair, is a bright female college student's ego ideal. Jane and Sonia share passionate conversations about literature, taking off from fiction, they enter an empyrean where desire, speculation, and imagination come together, as they, together, commune with a third person, the writer. Jane tells a student that literature is valuable for allowing us to share someone else's consciousness; Godwin shows that it also, importantly, provides an occasion for sharing intimate thoughts with an equally literary friend. As they chew the fat frontier between literature and life, Jane and Sonia embark on an ecstatic shared flight into a heady realm where forgetfulness of the small, confining self becomes a sense that that self has been enlarged to include sister selves, of women writers and of women who have been written about. The postcoital talk Jane ekes out of her lover, Gabriel, is careful and dull, in dramatic comparison. The literary women's talk is a model for the reader's response.

The Odd Woman is a novel of an odd moment—one that was perhaps not so decisive as the moment when the literate women of England picked up Samuel Richardson's *Pamela* (1742), but that is now as interesting to reflect on. When it first appeared, the new wave of feminist literary criticism was just cresting: Mary Ellman's *Thinking about Women* (1968), Kate Millett's *Sexual Politics* (1969), and Elaine Showalter's *A Literature of Their Own* (1973) had already been published, along with several influential essays on women and art; Patricia Spacks's *The Female Imagination* (1975—the year of *Time*'s "Women of the Year" cover), Ellen Moers's *Literary Women* (1976), and Sandra M. Gilbert and Susan Gubar's *The Madwoman in the Attic* (1979) would round out the decade. Like these books Godwin's addresses the question of how literature and the values a woman reader derives from it reflect and determine women's lives. Although ***The Odd Woman*** takes pains to distinguish its protagonist (and itself?) from the excesses of man-hating feminists, Gerda Mulvaney and her basement-full of unattractive staff members of *Feme Sole,* it is hard not to read the novel today as an expression of the feminism of the seventies. The conclusion Jane Clifford comes to, about going with or through one's own oddnesses so as to transcend them, asserts the importance of personal liberation rather than the liberation of a group; still, the problems and specificities of women as a group are what the novel most closely attends to.

Reviewing it in 1974 in *The New York Times Book Review,* Lore Dickstein compared ***The Odd Woman*** to "the best of Doris Lessing and Margaret Drabble" and went on to identify them parenthetically as "two writers who have vociferously rejected the feminist categorization of their work." By now others have joined them and Godwin in insisting not only that they were not feminist writers but also that as they are writers first and only incidentally women they dislike being called "women writers." The question of "feminist categorization" is problematic; there are nearly as many ways of being a feminist as there are of being a Jew. As the South African Lessing and the English Drabble were doing in the seventies, Godwin was writing primarily about women who counted the ways they were like and unlike other women, in fact and in fiction. She would continue to do so, in ***Violet Clay*** (1978), ***A Mother and Two Daughters*** (1982), ***The Finishing School*** (1984), and ***A Southern Family*** (1987). Godwin's women are not feminist rebels any more than they are a romance writer's stereotyped creatures; they no more attack the establishment than they fall in love with sexy men, period, or concern themselves only with the women's-magazine work of childbearing, child rearing, cooking, and homemaking. But they do share a characteristic which is imagined as distinctively womanly. Women as Godwin sees them (along with Drabble and perhaps Lessing, too) are distinct from men in the kind of self-consciousness they have and in the way images of women compulsively inform their identity. To discover who they are, Godwin's heroines measure themselves against one another and against conceptions of "woman"; they experience other women's characters and destinies (or stories) as eerily mirroring, prefiguring, determining their own. Even when they are artists and actresses, Godwin's protagonists have the souls of novelists. They are literary women who think of themselves as burdened by women's stories, by female character and destiny as it has been imagined; a literary conception of character and destiny compels them to contemplate the selves and lives of other women as if they were reading them. Violet Clay, a painter, earns her living by painting covers for gothic novels, whose heroines suffer agonies that grotesquely parallel her own; Justin, the young protagonist of ***The Finishing School,*** becomes an actress after making her first connection to art and performance through an older woman she loves as the living image of culture and fine feeling. The author of ***A Mother and Two Daughters*** confesses that she was interested in the ways each of three women in a family "had shaped and been shaped by the other two heroines"; in ***The Finishing School,*** Godwin went on to explore a girl's formative relationship with a fascinating older woman who seems to represent what she wants to be. Showing her heroine rejecting her own mother and aunt, suggesting how the young girl's unspoken fantasy about her reflects and reinforces the older woman's fantasy image of herself, Godwin writes evocatively and tactfully there about a familiar element of women's lives that feminist discourses about mother-daughter bonds and lesbian relationships do not quite get at.

The life realistically portrayed in ***The Odd Woman*** is dense with details especially familiar to literary women: less educated women need to muster more imagination to identify with the heroines of gothics. But now that it is nearly fifteen years after its publication, the feminist critic—a professionalized category that has replaced "literary woman"—will be (depending on her age) startled or made nostalgic by aspects of the action. One is awed by the evidence of the women's movement's intensest moment, when it seemed plausible for an exhausted professor, accidentally trapped in a hotel room with another woman and longing to be alone, to launch indefatigably into a discussion of literary prototypes for women's lives, as Jane Clifford does. It is hard to believe that in 1974 it was credible that two women faculty members in their early thirties would exchange notes like these:

> Tomorrow in class I'm doing a pop woman's fiction book published in the 1860s, and the thought of the soap opera is much on my mind. *Jane Eyre* is a great soap opera! Too many women's lives conform to its pattern. Do you think the soap opera follows life or do we pattern our lives with their innumerable crises and catastrophes and shifting casts of characters after this model? Have a good week. Sonia.
>
> Dear Sonia: Today when we were talking about Hawthorne again, you said that for him the women represented all the qualities which the man has self-destructively despised in himself and thus projected onto, or "stored" in the woman for safekeeping. You said that (according to Hawthorne) the man needs union with her to restore into himself the sundered parts which would make him a whole human being. *Now* I can't get out of my mind the possibility that over the centuries we may have abandoned certain human qualities, too: "left them to the men," so to speak, as we leave the garbage and the storm windows to men. I wonder what are these qualities we have given up? Have you any ideas?

Ah, even if they did write in jargon, there were giantesses on the earth, in those days; bliss was it in that dawn to be alive!

The literary feminism of the seventies, personal, passionate, and unmediated by schisms or outside alliances, was perhaps naive but enviably enlivening. Godwin's 1974 portrait of academic literary women enjoying scholarly/personal sympathy contrasts sharply with her 1985 row with a number of them, provoked by her review, in *The New York Times Book Review,* of *The Norton Anthology of Literature by Women: The Tradition in English,* edited by Sandra M. Gilbert and Susan Gubar. For all that she had created a successful novel about a woman who was excitedly rereading literature from a woman's point of view, teaching a course in Women in Literature, and delighting in the covers of novels of Gissing and Wharton reissued in the enthusiasm of the literary feminist moment, Godwin came out strongly against "feminist categorization," in theory and, especially, in these anthologists' practice. And by attacking Gilbert and Gubar's anthology, she brought down upon herself the wrath of the best-placed feminist literary critics, sisterhood being by 1985 a literary power to reckon with. Because it involves the question of canons—what students should read, what values are represented by traditional as compared with revisionist syllabi—, the controversy has unfortunately been interpreted as an argument about reading literature for "narrow" feminist ideological purposes vs. reading for more "purely" "literary" values. But Godwin's novels, which imagine women's lives in terms of their reading and writing, make it clear that such an opposition is less than useful.

Although Jane Clifford would probably have found an anthology of women's writing helpful, however flawed, she might have been annoyed, as Godwin was, by the Norton. Godwin quibbled, as any critic of an anthology can hardly help doing, with the choice and range of the selections; she quarreled, more significantly, with the very idea of an anthology based on Gilbert and Gubar's feminist theory of women's literature. It resulted, she wrote, in a "leveling of artists and their art, . . . forcing the individual female talent to lie on the Procrustean fainting-couch of a 'dis-eased' tradition." Her most serious criticisms of Gilbert and Gubar are (1) that their anthology "is organized to bear out Virginia Woolf's opinion that women's books 'continue each other,'" and (2) that it is dominated by the thesis they set forth in *The Madwoman in the Attic,* that women writers are preoccupied with gender and afflicted by an "anxiety of authorship." In the first instance, as Nancy K. Miller has observed, Godwin makes a symptomatic mistake: Virginia Woolf in fact wrote simply that books, not women's books, "continue each other." With this statement Godwin surely would agree: ***The Odd Woman,*** like its protagonist, is haunted by intertextuality or literary ancestor-regard, recollections of books about women, and of women writers. The quarrel with Gilbert and Gubar here is a minor one which depends on a definition of terms: "women's books," as Godwin's reference to Gissing dramatically makes clear, are, for her, books written for women to read, books about women's lives—which may have been written by men. Defining the term is something about which reasonable feminists may easily disagree.

Godwin's second objection to Gilbert and Gubar's anthology is more serious, and it is persuasive. The authors of *The Madwoman in the Attic,* eager to establish the legitimacy of feminist literary criticism and theory, accepted a theory of writing as assuming and discoursing with authority. Women, they argued, have traditionally been deprived of authority and therefore suffer anxiety about undertaking authorship. Understandably, Godwin disagrees. Writing in a tradition of literature dominated by women, she rejects the idea that "an anxiety of authorship" besets and cripples writers of her sex. If one is haunted by the example of George Eliot, if one's own mother was a writer, one naturally believes that, on the contrary, women and literature have a special connection—that women have a stake in literature, that it is their birthright to be writers.

The Odd Woman suggests that as Godwin sees it the authority of women writers is both burdensome and real. Godwin's example would serve to support Gilbert and Gubar's thesis that women writers have made peculiar and significant contributions to the discourse on gender, and that their having written—as women or not—has affected the lives of women in general. ***The Odd Woman*** is about women who imagine their lives as fictions, and about fictions women live by; its heroine sees her life as a plot. Jane Clifford's Great-aunt Cleva, who ran away with a villain (or was it a hero?) of a melodrama, was as moved by literary example as Jane the professor is; and the influences on Jane, for whom Cleva's life is story, are also a mix of real and imaginary people. Desperately seeking idyllic romantic love on which to base a life as perfectly shaped and finished as literary character or literary form, haunted by the contrasting examples of women in her family—her coaxing compliant mother, her delicate lady grandmother, and long-dead Cleva—Jane Clifford is beset by representations of women, that is, by the idea of other women as representations of what a woman's life might be. Her oddness—as opposed to the predictability of her mother's romance heroines—is ultimately ironic; in perceiving other women as images she resembles the heroines of the great tradition of women's fiction in English, Emma Woodhouse, Lucy Snowe, Dorothea Brooke. From a feminist point of view, one might condemn such characters' pride in their superiority to other, simpler women. Or one might, more profitably, study such images beset by images in order to analyze how gender has been constructed in culture, and how it figures in women's subjectivity. Novelists like Godwin, who write in and of the traditional self-reflexive women's novel, are working along lines that run parallel to those of many feminist theorists.

The death of Jane's grandmother provokes the action of ***The Odd Woman;*** it precipitates the heroine out of the bed in which she has been unable to sleep and into a series of encounters with the significant people in her life. One of those is the dead Edith herself. Looking down at the old lady in her coffin, Jane thinks: "This figure was ageless, queenly, invulnerable. Completed. The expression on the face of this woman who had lived out her life beset with fears about things that never happened was an expression which scorned fears. Fears were for those who had something left to lose. The dead face of Edith . . . was a detached, cool comment on a completed existence. It was a face neither masculine nor feminine, simply regal; a face that had transcended pain, uncertainty, sex. Achieving death, Edith had rid herself at last of troublesome womanhood." Having transcended her womanhood, Edith is, precisely, dead, as a sublimely transcendent "art" unmarked by the particularities of experience would be. As Gilbert and Gubar have argued, identification with ideal transcendent art—the "perfect woman, nobly planned," the "Angel in the House," perhaps, the "Love Goddess," the "ewig Weibliche"—has been projected onto women, to haunt and to cripple them, throughout the centuries. In the nineteenth century—Jane Clifford's specialty—, the idea of woman-as-art became especially complex, especially confining, especially fascinating. As Gilbert and Gubar have shown, woman contained, mirrored, and framed, transformed into a symbol of art, an artifact stripped of desire and vitality, has been a persistent image of transcendence, which has lodged with complex consequences in women's minds. When Jane Clifford looks down at her grandmother's body, she experiences the pull of the image of women as art, which haunts her professional and private life. But she also recognizes that this transcendent, completed Edith is unwomanly and dead—that transcendence as art, for living women, is unacceptable.

For all its regard for nineteenth-century English literature, ***The Odd Woman*** is inspired by revisionist energy. Its best, most original moments are modern ones: Jane's all-night orgy of self-expression, making pornographic drawings; the half-a-chapter in which she packs her bags, deciding and undeciding to leave Gabriel, in a hotel room filled with cheering, jeering spectral selves. And Jane Clifford's preoccupation with nineteenth-century English novels is distinctively American, the way Henry James in his preoccupation with European culture was American. There is a little absurd snobbishness in this novel about old family noses and heirloom silver, a little too much eagerness to dispatch uncultured close relatives by caricature. One is tempted to venture that Godwin's very earnestness about art as transcendence—like Gilbert and Gubar's—is also oddly American, in the tradition of Edith Wharton and James. (Surprising, in this context, to find some odd infelicities of observation and language: the "tendrils" of an avocado plant get "twined" up grocery string, a "package store" is situated in New York City, and "courtesy phones" are called on without irony.) The most dramatic difference between ***The Odd Woman*** and the nineteenth-century predecessors that preoccupy it is the vividness with which this novel presents the female body. Created by a novelist concerned with form and frames, Jane Clifford's body is not so much the locus of desire (which seems to be localized in the brain) as a container—not, as traditional imagery has it, for a male organ or a child, but for a distinctive identity.

The female body as Godwin portrays it is not an instrument for pleasure or reproduction but, rather, an enclosure for the self, mortal and vulnerable. The genitalia are less important than other organs. Prominent among these others are the female brain, which keeps Jane up night harboring erotic fantasies and thoughts of insomniac female relatives. But even more important are the viscera. Jane's psychic demons tend to haunt the gut; she suffers constipation for fear of her lover's hearing her shit, and indulges in self-destructive and self-indulgent overeating and drinking, then vomiting. The dark side of both her fantasy life and the town she lives in are menaced by the grotesque and ludicrous Enema Bandit who wears a woman's stocking over his head; she hears about him on the radio and imagines he is just outside her house. When too much pressure to conform to alien standards makes her faint, like her southern grandmother before her and any delicate Victorian heroine, Jane notes her symptoms with a clinician's eye: "She knew the first signs all too well: the cold dampness on the surface of the skin, the queasiness, the rising horror at the prospect of having the self she knew and kept track of dissolve into nothing." Jane's self-consciousness is devoted to keeping track of herself, preventing it from dissolving. She experiences conflicting fluid selves inside her that she seeks to contain; she also wants release from the confines of the body, the family, the limited identity that keep her small and personal. The sense of the body as a fragile, vulnerable container of a self or selves problematically female is what ***The Odd Woman*** most convincingly conveys. Godwin is good on the body loathsome in dressing rooms and at odds with its digestive tract. Her concern with the containing body neatly parallels Jane's preoccupation with literary role models and also parodies it. The literary idea of the finished, meaningful life, of the self named, shaped, and realized the way a literary character or work is, haunts traditional English novels; novels like Gissing's and Godwin's seek to demystify it. But to grapple with it is, of course, to acknowledge the idea's force, as ***The Odd Woman*** does, and to testify to its continuing strength. The identification of women and art has lodged persistently in female self-consciousness. It has imprisoned but also enriched and enabled women in a range of ways, by giving Kitty (and Gail Godwin's mother), for instance, a Gothic formula for limited success, by presenting more sophisticated writers like Godwin herself with a complex situation for revision. Perhaps women's real lives are—as Godwin suggests—stranger than women's fiction because the one contains the other, which shapes it.

Godwin continues to explore literary-feminist themes. In her most recent novel, as in ***A Mother and Two Daughters,*** she writes about a whole family, but as ever she writes best about the writing women in it. The protagonist of ***A Southern Family*** (1987) is a novelist, alliteratively named Clare Campion; pointing to her autobiographical model, she reflects that she has achieved "an enviable combination of artistic and popular success" through her work. It is not only of biographical interest that Godwin's best characters are women engaged in writing their lives: Clare, who wrote a novel based on the family life of her best friend, Julia; Julia, who writes doggerel to express herself in secret; Clare's sadly unfulfilled mother, the author of an unfinished novel that would have blown the lid off her town; and the lower-class Snow Mullins, who reveals a startlingly high level of literacy and insight in her letters. As the novelist-protagonist, who turned her best friend into fiction, ponders the question of how to avoid the novelist's lie of making too tidy sense of real people and real life, Godwin, behind her, confronts her theme, women's literary self-imaging.

Self-reflexive traditional fiction like Godwin's continues usefully to map literary-feminist concerns. Although feminism and attitudes toward gender have both changed since the mid-seventies, Jane Clifford's work still remains to be done: sorting out *Jane Eyre,* soap opera, and real women's lives; tracing ways men's and women's ideas of the masculine and feminine shape both the literature and the lives they make. Writing novels is one way to do such work. Identifying women with romantic fictions of perfection and transcendence is an old, seductive trick of patriarchy that thoughtful women novelists have long worked together toward deconstructing. It is false and impoverishing; so is polarizing life and art, feminist and literary values.

Rhoda Koenig (review date 11 March 1991)

SOURCE: A review of *Father Melancholy's Daughter,* in *New York,* March 11, 1991, pp. 86-7.

[*In the following review, Koenig offers negative assessment of* Father Melancholy's Daughter.]

An upbeat novel about depression, an inquiry into the meaning of the Passion and the Resurrection—***Father Melancholy's Daughter*** goes into some strange territory for mainstream fiction. The trouble is, it goes in there with all the old paraphernalia of not only mainstream but women's fiction, all those cleft sticks and hip boots of romantic yearnings, endearing twinkliness, and recipes to try in your own home.

The daughter of an Episcopal rector, Margaret Gower has devoted most of her twenty-year-old life to looking after him. When Margaret was six, her mother left their insistently nice Virginia town one day with an old schoolmate (female) to Find Herself in the art world of New York. Some months later, Mrs. Gower died in an accident, her legacy a husband who is continually drawn behind the "black curtain" of depression and whose religious beliefs prevent him from relying on drugs.

As well as tending to a gloomy man who is useless around the house, Margaret tries to make sense of her mother's departure, to imagine why a woman would desert the husband and daughter she always said she loved. She protests to a friend that her parents never fought; the girl suggests, "It could have been a more subtle thing, like walking pneumonia."

When Gail Godwin shows the abandoned father and daughter being aware of the presence of God in their lives and trying to understand how His suffering can help them, ***Father Melancholy's Daughter*** can be insightful and moving. Struck by his daughter's resemblance to his dead wife, and her greater maturity, Walter Gower says, "Margaret, I think you're your mother *redeemed* somehow." If her father feels exalted by this, Margaret feels angry: "If my personality had been built upon her leavings, who might I have been if she hadn't left?" Original sin, the rector later concludes, may be repeating your parents' mistakes.

Much of the book, however, suffers from its own case of walking pneumonia. Coming to Terms With Life isn't much of a plot—an awful lot of cocoa-making and hand-holding goes on in this novel, which, though set in the seventies and eighties, sounds too often as if we're back in the gingham-covered fifties. There is a cloying would-be romance with a young clergyman ("Adrian said he had never known chicken could taste like this; and the broccoli!") and a general attitude of niceness-is-all.

Margaret's father praises her lack of malice, but a bit of that, or wildness or neurosis, wouldn't be amiss in a girl so prim ("Oh, bother" is how she curses). There is also a great deal of sloppy writing ("womanish" for "womanly"; "the reason . . . was because"; "disinterest" for "indifference") that seems to be part of the character at first, but is so pervasive and uninflected it must be the carelessness of the author. I realize that Godwin may be trying to show us the grace of the ordinary, but she has, for me, only confirmed its ordinariness and made me wish this novel had been written by John Updike.

Isobel Armstrong (review date 24 May 1991)

SOURCE: "The Secrets of St. Cuthbert's," in *Times Literary Supplement,* May 24, 1991, p. 21.

[*In the following review, Armstrong lauds Godwin's* Father Melancholy's Daughter.]

Early in Gail Godwin's new novel [***Father Melancholy's Daughter***], Daddy, the "Father Melancholy," of the title, Episcopal Rector of St Cuthbert's and its contracting Virginian congregation of the early 1970s, holds hands with his guest and family to say Grace at dinner. The reaction of incredulous cynicism from his wife's friend, Madelyn, his wife Ruth's embarrassment, his six-year-old only daughter's fury at the sophisticated stranger's intrusion, and Daddy's always slightly exasperating goodness, are caught in the unassuming virtuosity of Godwin's writing. A complex interaction between the members of this linked circle is registered in the briefest of episodes.

The making, breaking and re-making of relationships among these characters form the inner circle of this narrative. It is as subtly restricted by the boundaries of a small-town Southern church and its parishioners as the life of Margaret, daughter of the depressive Rector, is circumscribed by her duty to him. The efforts of father and daughter to understand Ruth's betrayal of them after she has been carried away by Madelyn, a director of blasphemous avant-garde plays in New York, is the main theme of the book. Their obsession is the more poignant because it takes place among the mild, recurrent and often comic details of parish life: in the responses to Psalm 118, "Some voices sounded more convinced than others. During the beat of silence between the verses, Miriam Stacy's sinuses began to drain."

Godwin has always been fascinated by "unrequited daughters": daughters, that is, growing up without one or both parents; and their attempt to compensate for the incompleteness or one-sidedness of the family becomes the dynamic of her plots. Here, both father and daughter, locked into dependence, are forced into an addictive hermeneutics of the past. The exhaustive search for explanation becomes compulsive. Narrative tension builds up because the facts of Ruth's desertion, her mysterious source of income, her death in a car crash in England, and Madelyn's true relation to her, continue to be discovered right up to the end of the book.

The novel closes where it begins, repeating the idea of the circle, as we realize that it is actually the daughter, Margaret's, autobiography, still in the act of being written. Yet because the "novel" is still being written, the satisfyingly shaped closure of the story—containing a number of surprises—actually opens out Margaret's life again. She stops being a voyeur of her past. In an arresting memory of avid curiosity she recognizes her double in a strange woman churchgoer she once found trespassing, searching the closet for secrets.

Is she liberated by the death of her father? He, overwhelmed by local politics and struggles against a property developer, dies of a heart attack in the act of reconsecrating a vandalized statue of Christ. But while she ironizes and exposes the tensions of the father-daughter relationship. Godwin never offers an easy oedipal judgment. Indeed, superficial Freudianizing is covertly criticized. The relationship, despite its classic psychoanalytical features, is nourishing.

It is this scrupulousness, perhaps, which enables the book to be mystery story, domestic fiction and religious novel all at once. The narrative takes in different genres, just as it approaches sex, worship, cooking, reading a book and dressing, with immediacy and delicacy of detail. The same honesty pits simpler "Southern" values against New York sophistication—against Madelyn's aggressive theatrical travesty, *Pas de Dieux*, or against a wildly bizarre telephone quiz, offering phantasmal Buicks and sapphire pendants, which is described with a mixture of hysteria and hilarity at the moment of Father Melancholy's death. At the same time, the novel recognizes Southern conservatism and the sheer tedium of being the Rector's daughter. "Do-gooder Dishes. . . . Sanctimonious Cuisine", she mutters, throwing out a decade's worth of foil cartons, relics of a congregation's goodwill.

Skilfully written, accessible, funny, discriminating, Gail Godwin's novels are unusual in being readable and thoughtful. But her publishers need to be more efficient. At the time of writing this is the only one of her novels which is currently available in Britain.

Suzanne W. Jones (essay date 1993)

SOURCE: "Dismantling Stereotypes: Interracial Friendships in *Meridian* and *A Mother and Two Daughters*," in *The Female Tradition in Southern Literature,* edited by Carol S. Manning, University of Illinois Press, 1993, pp. 140-57.

[*In the following excerpt, Jones examines Godwin's presentation of an interracial friendship and Southern racial dynamics in* A Mother and Two Daughters. *"Stereotypical thinking exists in Gail Godwin's world," writes Jones, "but not between blacks and whites who know each other personally."*]

> For various reasons, the average, struggling, nonmorbid Negro is the best-kept secret in America. His revelation to the public is the thing needed to do away with that feeling of difference which inspires fear and which ever expresses itself in dislike.
>
> —Zora Neale Hurston, "What White Publishers Won't Print"
>
> We must recognize differences among women who are our equals, neither inferior nor superior,

and devise ways to use each other's difference
to enrich our vision and our joint struggles.

—Audre Lorde, "Age, Race, Class, and Sex"

When pondered together, these meditations on difference raise some perplexing questions. How do we discover a shared humanity without erasing difference? How do we use difference to enrich our vision if we fear it? How can we come to understand difference differently? When Zora Neale Hurston wrote "What White Publishers Won't Print" in 1950 before the civil rights movement began, she believed literature could help reduce white prejudice by proving blacks to be "just like everybody else." When Audre Lorde called for new patterns of relating across differences at Amherst College in 1980, she ended her powerful plea with lines from an unpublished poem, "we seek beyond history / for a new and more possible meaning," lines that suggest the power and importance of imaginative literature in producing change. Currently Henry Louis Gates, Jr., writing when racism is once again on the rise, continues to insist on the power of language to shape perception: "Race has become a trope of ultimate, irreducible difference . . . we carelessly use language in such a way as to *will* this sense of *natural* difference into our formulations. To do so is to engage in a pernicious act of language, one which exacerbates the complex problem of cultural or ethnic difference, rather than to assuage it or redress it." Several contemporary Southern novelists are attempting to assuage and redress this complex problem in their fiction, to deal with difference in the way Audre Lorde calls for. I am limiting my discussion to two novels written by Southern women after it was obvious that desegregation, in and of itself, would not eliminate prejudice—*Meridian* (1976), by Alice Walker, and ***A Mother and Two Daughters*** (1982), by Gail Godwin. I am interested in the literary techniques they employ to dismantle the stereotypes of Southern womanhood produced by the patriarchy of the Old South—stereotypes that persisted after the Civil War ended slavery and after the civil rights movement ended legal segregation. Both Walker and Godwin imagine shared experiences for their black and white characters, calling attention not only to their common interests and common humanity but also to other similarities that the South's preoccupation with racial differences overshadowed: gender and class. Walker and Godwin do not attempt to erase difference so much as to assure that difference is not misread or misnamed, to show that it is not biologically determined but culturally conditioned.

Recognition of any similarities between black and white women has been rendered difficult in the South by a history of slavery and segregation, which caused blacks and whites to define themselves in opposition to each other, to see difference as innate rather than socially constructed. Though not representative of the majority of Southerners, the white plantation society, because of its economic and social dominance, established conventions of behavior for women, both white and black. The white woman was expected to be a "lady"—physically pure, socially correct, culturally refined, and dutiful to family. Lower-class white women were less-refined, more hardworking versions of this same ideal of the dutiful wife. In contrast, plantation society defined black women as promiscuous wenches, prolific breeders, hardworking mules, or nurturing mammies. Irving H. Bartlett and C. Glenn Cambor contend that "each image was paradoxical and something far less than that of a mature, autonomous, and well-integrated woman." The white "lady" was deprived of her full sexual and maternal identity while the black woman was deprived of her equality and her humanity. Literary critic Minrose Gwin argues that "just as black women were forced to be strong, white southern women often were compelled to appear weak." Even though these racial stereotypes were inaccurate, as historians Catherine Clinton, Paula Giddings, and Anne Firor Scott have shown, they have affected black and white women's images of themselves as well as their images of each other. Psychologist Mark Snyder has observed the power of stereotypes to become self-fulfilling: "In interracial encounters, racial stereotypes may constrain behavior in ways to cause both blacks and whites to behave in accordance with those stereotypes." He also points out that when people have adopted stereotypical ways of thinking about another person, they "tend to notice and remember the ways in which that person seems to fit the stereotype while resisting evidence that contradicts the stereotype."

The difficulty of realizing that racial differences are socially constructed rather than biologically determined is evident from the following passage of Mary Chestnut's Civil War diary. An aristocratic white woman, Chestnut can see the brutality of slavery, but the ideology of plantation society blinds her to the fact that it is the system that degrades the female slave, rather than the female slave who is naturally inferior:

> Under slavery we live surrounded by prostitutes, yet an abandoned woman is sent out of any decent house. Who thinks any worse of a Negro or mulatto woman for being a thing we can't name? God forgive us, but ours is a monstrous system, a wrong and an iniquity! Like the patriarchs of old, our men live all in one house with their wives and their concubines; and the mulattoes one sees in every family partly resemble the white children. . . . My disgust sometimes is boiling over. Thank God for my country women, but also for the men! They are probably no worse than men everywhere, but the lower their mistresses the more degraded they must be.

Such reasoning, the literary critic Hazel Carby argues, was part of the nineteenth-century ideology of Southern womanhood, which held that the white man was "merely prey to the rampant sexuality of his female slaves." This dichotomous thinking shows not only that stereotypes falsify the causes of behavior but that they are also used to bolster self-esteem.

For years white women have defined themselves in opposition to their black sisters, but black women have done the same. One hundred years after Chestnut confessed these strong feelings, Toni Morrison wrote an article for the *New York Times Magazine* rightly questioning the relevance of the women's liberation movement for black women and proudly affirming her identity as a black woman by delineating the differences between the races. She reminisces about a trip to Charlotte, North Carolina, where she was struck by the "accuracy and fine distinctions" of the labels "White Ladies" and "Colored Women" on bathroom doors: "The difference between white and black females seemed to me an eminently satisfactory one. White females were *ladies,* said the sign maker, worthy of respect. And the quality that made ladyhood worthy? Softness, willingness to let others do their labor and their thinking. Colored females, on the other hand, were *women*—unworthy of respect because they were tough, capable, independent and immodest." Morrison's perspective allows her to question the ideology of Southern womanhood and to reverse its positive and negative attributes. The following description, however, still bears evidence of stereotypical thinking:

> Black women have always considered themselves superior to white women. Not racially superior, just superior in terms of their ability to function healthily in the world. . . . Black women have no abiding admiration of white women as competent, complete people. Whether vying with them for the few professional slots available to women in general, or moving their dirt from one place to another, they regarded them as willful children, pretty children, but never as real adults capable of handling the real problems of the world.
>
> White women were ignorant of the facts of life—perhaps by choice, perhaps with the assistance of men, but ignorant anyway. They were totally dependent on marriage for male support (emotionally or economically). They confronted their sexuality with furtiveness, complete abandon or repression.

While Morrison emphasizes significant differences in the social experiences of the races, she does not take into account the differences between white individuals, based on other factors such as class.

Throughout this one hundred-year period, some Southern women writers, both black and white, have attempted to undermine racial stereotypes by depicting a common bond between black and white women. In *Black and White Women of the Old South* Gwin has pointed out that this bond was often based "on an acknowledgement of common womanhood and common humanistic values." This bond, however, was never depicted as one of friendship and equality. Because of the times in which Alice Walker and Gail Godwin live, they are able to push further than their literary foremothers in imagining relationships between black and white women. Each creates a protagonist who discovers not only some similarity but the individuality in a woman of a different race. Then, each becomes better able to understand the other's difference. In Walker's *Meridian,* a Southern black civil rights worker, Meridian, discovers that a Northern white coworker, Lynne, is not simply a superficial white girl looking for adventure but a hard worker, just as committed to the movement as Meridian is. In Godwin's ***A Mother and Two Daughters,*** Lydia, a genteel young white "lady," enrolls in a women's studies class at the University of North Carolina at Greensboro and discovers that her black sociology professor, Harvard-graduate Renee, shares her own tastes and interests. The black writer, then, has her black protagonist realize that racial difference is not a matter of simplistic opposition, and the white writer has her white protagonist make the same realization. Thus the struggle that each main character has in overcoming racial stereotypes reflects the struggle that each writer imagines is the experience of readers of her own race. But readers whose race is not the same as the author's also gain knowledge about the complex functioning of racial stereotypes. For example, in reading *Meridian* many of my white female students were surprised by Meridian's biased opinions about white women, a discovery that made them think differently about themselves and their interactions with black women. . . .

Gail Godwin sets her novel, ***A Mother and Two Daughters,*** in North Carolina about fifteen years after the 1960s civil rights movement. Lydia, one of the two daughters of the title, is a 1980s version of the nineteenth-century Southern lady. Graceful, modest, refined, and well-mannered, she has devoted her life to her husband and children. When the novel opens, Lydia fits the stereotype that Godwin described in her 1975 *Ms.* article, **"The Southern Belle":** "soft hands and soft voices; first concern for others, not self; refusal to dwell on subjects of ugliness, unpleasantness, violence, tension, strife; suave short-circuiting of all 'embarrassing questions'; cultivation and veneration of traditional and beautiful things; impeccable manners; 'spotless reputation.'" But in fulfilling this role, Lydia has not been fulfilled. To find another self hidden behind the social mask, Lydia leaves her husband and her home and returns to college, where she discovers sociology, feminism, and a black friend, Renee.

Establishing a friendship with Renee plays a central role in Lydia's break with traditional Southern values and in her emerging sense of self, although the interracial friendship is not as prominent in Godwin's novel as it is in Walker's. Lydia's thrill in telling her sister Cate about her new friend comes as much from the fact that Renee is highly educated as from the fact that she is black. Cate, an English professor, has mercilessly criticized Lydia's country-club friends as superficial and her suburban life as trivial. But Lydia considers her new friend as evidence of the reverse—of her widening horizons and of her growing interest in a life of the mind. When she explains the impact her friendship with Renee and Renee's friend Calvin have had on her life, Lydia reveals her previous racial prejudice. She says she used to assume that all robbers and muggers were black and that all victims were white. Now she resents the "bad publicity" that an individual black criminal brings to the race. While Lydia has yet to realize that the "bad publicity" comes not from individual blacks who commit crimes but from whites who see such behavior as a sign of racial inferiority, she is learning that all blacks are not alike by getting to know two black individuals.

In contrast to the relationship between Lynne and Meridian, which emerges after a long struggle, there is little conflict between, or within, Lydia and Renee as they become friends. In part the ease of developing their friendship, despite Lydia's racial prejudice, has to do with their positions in life. Lydia, newly separated from her husband, is eager to prepare for a career; Renee, a Harvard graduate about to have her first book published, has a successful career. So Lydia sees Renee, who is also younger than she is, as a role model, a woman to admire: "Renee's office door was open. She was sitting at her desk, reading an aerogram with an English stamp and smoking a little brown cigar. Framed by shelves full of glossy books and wearing a twill pantsuit with a low-necked cerise silk blouse, she was the advertiser's dream-image of the woman who has 'made it.'" Godwin chooses the details carefully here. They not only reflect the worldly working woman dressed for success but also counter the Southern white stereotype of the black woman. The books, aerogram, and slim cigar indicate that Renee is hardworking, educated, and sophisticated. Lydia is fascinated by Renee because she has never met an upper middle-class black woman. Indeed, Lydia acknowledges Renee's "superiority over her in many of the areas the world values." In this pairing of white and black women, Godwin inverts the traditional Southern racial hierarchy by making the black character superior to the white.

A more significant factor in establishing their friendship as well as in emphasizing similarities between the two women is that their tastes and values are alike, something Lydia discovers when Renee asks her home to lunch. In Renee's home Lydia finds a similarity in tastes: a gray frame house on a "genteel old street," rooms filled with plants and antiques, damask napkins and cut glass. In Renee's conversation Lydia discovers, to their mutual delight, a similarity in interests: French cuisine, sociology, children, the nature of love, the significance of social classes, snobbery. Race is not an issue in their friendship, though social class certainly is. Lydia feels neither hidden guilt, as Walker's Lynne does, nor a desire to confirm liberal views, either of which might cause her, as a white woman, to seek a friendship with Renee *because* she is black.

Godwin uses the relationship between Lydia's mother's friend Theodora and her black maid, Azalea, as a contrast to the friendship between Lydia and Renee. Godwin underlines the generational change in Southern race relations by juxtaposing Lydia and Renee's lunch with a luncheon Theodora gives the same day. Lydia's mother Nell describes it this way: "'There the three of us sat around the dining table, me and Theodora and Wickie Lee. And Azalea sat in the kitchen having *her* lunch. Theodora spent most of the time hollering back and forth with Azalea, and Wickie Lee and I sat in silence, picking at our shrimp salad.'" This brief scene depicts both the inequality and the irony of relationships between black maids and their white employers in the South. The conversation between Theodora and Azalea reveals that they have more to talk about than Theodora and her two white friends. When Wickie Lee deserts Theodora, it is Azalea, and not her white friend Nell, whom Theodora goes to for comfort. Yet Godwin makes her readers painfully aware that Theodora's relationship with Azalea is patronizing and self-centered. In giving Azalea her old clothes and jewelry and having her move into the house with her, Theodora appears generous. But such gestures are easy to make; they do not signify friendship, as Azalea understands:

> [Theodora] said to Azalea, "The old order changes, Azalea. Why, look at us. Who would ever have thought you and I'd be coughing each other to sleep on the opposite sides of our wall?"
>
> Azalea gave Theodora a level look. "You perfectly capable of winning any argument all by yourself, Miss Thea, but you know and I know there's still that wall." She settled back in her chair with a dark smile, looking for all the world as if *she* had won.

Unlike Theodora, Lydia is conscious of the racism that still exists in the interracial relationships in Southern society. Thus she is proud of the difference between her relationship with Renee and Theodora's relationship with Azalea. And yet for Lydia, the only embarrassing moments in their friendship come when she is reminded that Renee is black, a difference she no longer thinks about. Godwin indicates that similarities in feminist politics and social class have made Lydia forget about racial difference. But Godwin has Renee remind Lydia of this difference. Renee uses the word *nigger* in class, and she frequently drops her refined Southern drawing-room drawl and turns on her down-home Southern black dialect. Renee enjoys slipping into black dialect because the use of the two languages allows her to assert both similarity and difference. Lydia can only equate such language with Azalea, and yet at first Lydia cannot equate Renee with Azalea, even though they have the same skin color. However, Renee's continued use of Azalea's language makes Lydia conscious of the difference in skin color and therefore heritage between herself and her friend, at the same time that Lydia has decided there is no difference.

At first Lydia avoids this issue. Seeing class similarities between blacks and whites has allowed her to move beyond racial stereotypes. She does not want to consider racial differences. Eventually Renee's language switch catches Lydia off guard, and she giggles at the contrast. Like Meridian and Lynne, Lydia and Renee end up laughing together. But they indirectly acknowledge difference rather than directly confront it the way Meridian and Lynne do. There is a mannerliness about their relationship that does not exist in the relationship between Lydia and her sister Cate or between Meridian and Lynne. Lydia and Renee's friendship is much like the one Godwin imagines in her essay **"The Southern Belle"** between a black woman and her white friend who would probably hesitate to ask "embarrassing questions." Lydia remains too much of a polite Southern lady to ask Renee embarrassing questions. However, as Lydia becomes more at ease with difference, she becomes more comfortable with Renee, and she expresses an interest in Renee's family history. Godwin implies that only after black and white Southern women discover some similarities will they be able to begin to understand racial differences, not as innate or uniform, but as variably conditioned by a variety of social and cultural experiences.

Even though Renee may dress and act a part that previously few black women had filled, she transcends any stereotype, white or black, as Lydia's observation shows: "There was something wickedly arrogant about it, when Renee did it [drop into black dialect], as if she were showing her listeners that, though she was equally at home in both worlds, she was actually above both." Godwin does not want readers to mistake Renee for a black woman trying to act white, a mistake Lydia's sister Cate makes when Lydia first tells her about Renee and Calvin. Cate too easily equates their upward mobility with insensitivity to racism and to the plight of their own race. Renee's teaching techniques and her decision to become a civil rights lawyer prove Cate's view false.

In the course of the novel, Godwin further dismantles racial stereotypes by having Lydia discover that in addition to Renee's having traits Lydia has thought of as "white," Lydia herself has characteristics she has attributed only to blacks. Her marriage to Max has lacked sexual passion, a characteristic she has stereotypically equated with the black race. On a vacation to New Orleans with Max the year before, she had hoped they would be freed from their "tight, civilized" lives by "some Negro playing a saxophone," but "not the faintest throb of the jungle drum beat in their veins." After her separation from Max, Lydia finds sexual passion with a podiatrist named Stanley, but she has difficulty integrating this newly discovered part of her self into the old definition of the Southern lady. To Lydia a lady is not a lover; she is an "amiable bed partner." For a while Lydia tries to compartmentalize her life (mother, student, respected friend of Max, secret lover of Stanley), deciding that if she is a lover in private, she can still be a lady in public. Eventually though, the contents of one compartment of her life spill into another, and she is forced to come to terms with all parts of her self. She discovers that the passion of "the other" is in some respects a repressed part of her self.

In *Black and White Women of the Old South,* Gwin argues that in the nineteenth century women of both races, bound by dualistic thinking, "often viewed one another as missing pieces of a female identity denied them by the patriarchal culture. Female narrators of the slave narratives reveal their yearning for the chaste respectability of their white sisters, while the diaries and memoirs of the white women show their intense jealousy of the stereotypical sexuality of the slave woman. Each is only one half of a self." In ***A Mother and Two Daughters,*** Gail Godwin brings these two halves together in both Lydia and Renee. At the same time that Godwin confers sexuality on Lydia, she gives Renee upper middle-class respectability with all its virtues and flaws. When Renee speaks derisively of the lower class whites who could not appreciate the weimaraner that she bought from them, Renee shows that upper middle-class blacks can be as snobbish as upper middle-class whites.

By the conclusion of ***A Mother and Two Daughters***, Lydia feels in some ways "closer to Renee than to her own sister." As testimony to this friendship, Godwin ends the novel with a symbolic marriage. Lydia's son Leo marries Renee's daughter Camilla, who Cate says is just like Lydia. At first, despite her new racial awareness, Lydia is shocked by the prospect of an interracial marriage in her own family, but she quickly acquiesces when she forces herself to think of Camilla as an individual. For as Carolyn Rhodes has noted, "The concept of the lady in the south of 1984 (the date of the epilog) has been quite detached from concern with color, although not from beauty and grace and demeanor. Camilla, the bride, impresses her white mother-in-law as 'a perfect lady' and the matriarchal Aunt Theodora agrees."

If Gail Godwin's ending seems too pat and idealized, it does not totally depart from realism. In a traditional comedic resolution the harmony between a man and a woman symbolizes a larger harmony within the society. In Godwin's novel, however, the harmony that exists between black and white individuals is not extended to racial groups. Racism still exists in her fictional Southern world, though it is relegated to the background: a woman in a supermarket says she pities the children that Leo and Camilla will have, the Klan still marches in Greensboro, Calvin's life is threatened and he heads north, and the prejudiced white father of a "D" student in Renee's class firebombs her house and kills her dog. And yet the reader is not left without hope. Stereotypical thinking exists in Gail Godwin's world but not between blacks and whites who know each other personally.

Neither Godwin nor Walker suggests that interracial friendships will eliminate prejudice between groups, nor do they subscribe to "the mystical belief that the category 'woman' is the most natural and basic of all human groupings and can therefore transcend race division," a phenomenon that Gloria Joseph and Jill Lewis warn against in *Common Differences.* Although Godwin's portrait of the dynamics of interracial friendships is not as satisfyingly complex as Walker's, both writers suggest that if black and white women would only listen to each other's stories and find out about each other's lives, perhaps we would discover similarities that might allow us to better understand differences, as well as give us common goals. Both Gail Godwin and Alice Walker try to provide readers with such an experience through these novels. They make what we felt was strange about "the other" more familiar at the same time that they challenge our own sense of self. By imagining, as Audre Lorde calls for, some new "patterns for relating across our human differences as equals," Alice Walker and Gail Godwin enable us to see that unity need not depend on homogeneity nor difference mean separation or simplistic opposition.

Linda C. Pelzer (essay date Spring 1993)

SOURCE: "Visions and Versions of Self: The Other/Women in *A Mother and Two Daughters,*" in *Critique: Studies in Modern Fiction,* Vol. XXXIV, No. 3, Spring, 1993, pp. 155-63.

[*In the following essay, Pelzer examines the quest for self-identity among the female protagonists of* A Mother and Two Daughters. *According to Pelzer, "Visions and versions of other women, other selves, always, inevitably, and necessarily lie behind the identities of Godwin's heroines, for as* A Mother and Two Daughters *attests, women become and are in relation to each other."*]

Gail Godwin's novel ***A Mother and Two Daughters*** (1982) charts the struggle to selfhood of three women bound by the inextricable ties of family relationship. To define their selves and to achieve their own identities, Godwin's heroines confront community, family, and their own opposing other selves to achieve their own sense of individuality and self-worth. Their successes and failures are measured against the visions and versions of self that people the novel.

Like the novels that precede it, ***A Mother and Two Daughters*** reflects Godwin's ongoing concern with women in the process of self-creation and her examination of the fictions by which they define themselves. Self-aware and self-questioning, her heroines, as Carolyn Rhodes characterizes them, are "women who fear failure, and who are distracted by differing notions of what their best selves might be." The titular heroine of ***Violet Clay*** (1978), for instance, measures herself against a grandmother and uncle who provide her with models of being, and Jane Clifford, the protagonist of ***The Odd Woman*** (1974), finds her models of self in the stories of women, both real and literary, that shape her consciousness.

Godwin places her mother and two daughters within a similar context. She pairs them all with other women, including each other, who represent possibilities for their own self-definition. In some cases, these others are ideal selves, freely chosen and providing models toward which each character strives. In other instances, they are omens of the underside of self, of self-assertion gone wrong. Whatever the case, Godwin's heroines learn much from these visions and versions of self, for they provide touchstones of value and meaning that mark the way toward full selfhood. At the same time, they function as a narrative device that allows Godwin to explore the complexity and ambivalence of relationships between women, relationships that are crucial to the development of self.

Establishing the boundary between self and the person of the (m)other constitutes the primary challenge to self-definition; and social scientists such as Nancy Chodorow, Signe Hammer, and Carol Gilligan have written eloquently of this complex mother-daughter relationship. ***A Mother and Two Daughters*** testifies as well to its primacy and its complexity. On the one hand, each daughter feels the strong pull of the mother's identity, providing as it does a preconceived shape for her own inchoate self. On the other, each struggles against what Hammer describes as the expectation that daughters will "assume the identity of their mothers" and therefore have no reason "to achieve a sense of separate self." If the family is, as Nina Auerbach asserts, "the first community we know, and it takes the shape of Mother," whose "power is seen as all-suffusing," then daughters clearly have the difficult task of defining a self in relation to that community, to their mothers.

Complicating the mother-daughter relationship, moreover, is the sibling relationship. On the one hand, sisters are rivals, each child vying with the other for their parents' love and approval of her separate self. On the other, sisters are, as Toni McNaron notes, "a special kind of double": a sister, according to McNaron, is "both ourselves and very much not ourselves." Although sisters may find comfort in the familiarity of similarity, they inevitably experience the tug of independence, responding to what Elizabeth Fishel describes as the "deep-rooted need to be different." As Fishel notes, "From the years of psychological jousting between sisters in the early family arena emerge the first tentative boundaries of their personalities."

Godwin's concern is with both types of familial relationships; she does not privilege one over the other. In fact, in **"Becoming the Characters in Your Novel,"** an essay written shortly after the publication of the novel, Godwin noted that her challenge had been to show "the subjective reality" of "three strong and different women bound by the closest of ties" and to convey "the mysterious way in which [each] had shaped and been shaped by the other two heroines." As Godwin's observation suggests, Nell Strickland and her two daughters, Cate Galitsky and Lydia Mansfield, find in each other their most complicated visions and versions of self, for the family relationship is part of the baggage that each must carry on the journey to selfhood.

Late in the novel, on the occasion of her first-born's fortieth birthday, Nell Strickland confesses to Cate her initial fear of motherhood, her sense of inadequacy about coping with "a seven-pound bundle of aching, miserable *questions*":

> "But I'll never forget that awesome helplessness. You were . . . completely beyond me. With Lydia, it was so easy. They brought her in, she was crying: I held her and I knew that was all I was expected to do. And she seemed to accept it, and stopped crying at once. It was as if I had conveyed my certainty to her, the certainty I didn't have with you. You missed the certainty, but in a way, Lydia got shortchanged too. I was so busy doing what I knew to do that I skipped over the awe."

Nell's confession cuts to the heart of the differences between her daughters: In Cate, Nell's awe breeds a profound and provocative assertion of difference; in Lydia, Nell's certainty yields a deliberate but anxious statement of connection. Both daughters mirror their mother, but different aspects of her. Cate is the assertive Nell, the bold and efficient woman who rules their family by day. Lydia is the genteel Nell, the perfect wife and mother who appears at night, when Leonard, husband and father, returns from work. The "old family configuration," as Cate remembers it, Nell and Lydia "'tamed'" by Leonard's presence, Cate assuming "the more ferocious properties of the vanished mother," underlies the relationship between mother and daughters, even unto adulthood.

Underlying the relationship as well is the relationship between the sisters. Lydia wants "to love and admire her sister," and Cate admits "affection" for Lydia, "even a certain *attraction* to her, up to a point." Neither, however, models herself on the other. In fact, each stands opposed to the other's self—in part because she fears the part of herself that she sees in the other; in part because old grievances and hurts live long in memory. As much as Cate fears "'the loss of [her] will to resist,'" for example, she is tempted by a desire to be taken care of that reminds her of Lydia. Moreover, she cannot forget that her sister was the good and proper daughter and that "Nell would have liked her [eldest child] to be a different daughter." For her part, Lydia, a "great sleeper," for all her practical efficiency and seeming complacency, asks herself a question that in its challenge to her status quo sounds mildly of Cate: "what kind of life would make one want to stay awake." She nurses a childhood hurt, however, a feeling that Cate, "the squeaky wheel," usurped all their parents' attention and concern, that Lydia was punished, in effect, for being what their parents expected her to be.

Clearly, the family relationships are central to the characters' self-definition. Mother, daughter, sister, each relation shapes the self, but it also threatens at times to engulf it. As Cate, following her bitter argument with Lydia, declaims, "nobody who is, first and foremost, a 'family member' has a hope in hell of becoming a whole person."

The conflict between identification and autonomy within the family relationship is so wrenching that it leads almost inevitably to the search for an ideal self beyond the bounds of family. As Hammer explains,

> The search for an ideal mother [and I would add sister] is part of the search for an ideal self, one who has already "arrived." It is fantasy of a readymade, grown-up self who no longer has to be a daughter to her mother, but can be a friend. Trying out an ideal self, or various ideal selves, is a way of reaching out toward adulthood, another way of separating. . . . In looking for ideal mothers elsewhere, and in trying to construct ideal selves, daughters are testing reality.

Godwin's protagonists certainly illustrate the truth of Hammer's assertion. They form friendships with other women who embody the lives and stories they seek as models, and their friendships with or connections to these other women are crucial to their efforts to create selves. In fact, these relationships provide further evidence of Elizabeth Abel's observation that "friendship becomes a vehicle of self-definition for women, clarifying an identity through relation to an other who embodies and reflects an essential aspect of self."

Lydia Mansfield, the daughter most in need of an ideal self, finds it in Renee Peverell-Watson, professor of sociology and instructor of Lydia's university course on the History of Female Consciousness. For the first thirty-six years of her life, Lydia has settled rather complacently into the roles of wife and mother expected of her. If she has been unhappy, few would guess it, and even Lydia herself is startled out of her sleeping life by the childish wisdom in her son's matter-of-fact response to a school friend's question "Is your mother an invalid or something?": "'Oh, no,' said Dickie airily, 'she just likes to sleep a lot.'" Her decision to leave her husband and to complete the college degree she had forsaken for marriage and motherhood is surprising, even to herself initially; but once she makes it, Lydia will not retreat from her course. In Lydia, Godwin creates a "proper younger daughter," as she says, "so nervous with her sense of responsibility, so aching with her need to accomplish something for herself," a young woman set "on her course of cautious, but ardent, self-emancipation."

When she meets Renee, Lydia has already taken her first tentative steps toward self-emancipation. Her friendship with her instructor, whose exotic black beauty and "wicked" arrogance fascinate Lydia, helps her to develop her own stride. Lydia fantasizes, for instance, about "how she and Renee would become friends after she had proved her mind to her teacher," and this desire to be worthy of her teacher drives her to explore worlds of ideas and possibilities that she had never known or even imagined to exist. (Ironically, Lydia chooses as her ideal self a surrogate for her sister, also a college professor. Her choice suggests her desire to be worthy of and equal to Cate, at least intellectually, and further demonstrates the curious bond between sisters.) Renee, as Lydia confides to Cate in a rare moment of sisterly confidences that erupts into hurtful accusations precipitating an almost irreparable breach between them, is a model of achievement and accomplishment, the kind of woman she intends to be.

In finding her ideal self in Renee, Lydia reveals much about the nature of the self she is defining, for both women want not so much to change the world as to create a self capable of appropriating the things of their world. Certainly, Cate's criticism of Renee applies to Lydia as well, for both women are striving "'to create themselves afresh, out of the ruins of that old oppressive society.'" Each, in other words, wants a self powerful enough to acquire what she has been denied. Because neither has actually been part of that "old oppressive society," disenfranchised on the basis of sex or race or both, Lydia and Renee share a desire to belong, to take their places as fully realized selves within the world as it exists.

Lydia's selection of Renee Peverell-Watson as an ideal self also says much about the relationship between self and other, for Lydia chooses a version of self that does not threaten to usurp her self, always the danger inherent in identification with an other who is perceived as superior to the self. In spite of her accomplishments, Renee holds no more power than Lydia, for she herself is striving to exceed traditional expectations, not just of gender but also of race. Lydia, however, struggles only against expectations of gender, a fact that equalizes their relationship. As Lydia herself recognizes,

> Renee's life intrigued Lydia; her progress pricked sharply at Lydia's competitive spirit. Lydia ticked off what Renee had against what she herself had; and what she had that Renee hadn't. She looked forward to learning all she could from her new friend. But though she acknowledged Renee's superiority over her in many areas the world values, Lydia felt, at bottom, a sweet, secret security in being who she was that all the striving, achieving Renees in the world could not topple. Lydia knew she could and would learn a great deal from Renee, but without the humiliation of Renee's ever being a threat.

To avoid the tyranny of the other, the loss of self inherent in identification with the other, there must be some equality between self and other, a delicate balance that allows each its integrity. Lydia and Renee share just such a relationship. In fact, their friendship exemplifies the "self-reflexive enterprise" that Abel identifies as "a means to mutual recognition instead of an obstacle to objectivity" in the process of self-creation.

Unlike her sister, Cate Galitsky needs no ideal self to guide her toward self-definition, for her sense of self is strong. Convinced that "one of the best ways to keep from atrophying was to move forward continually to meet the advance of the unpredictable," Cate charges through life, challenging anyone and anything that impede her progress. Cate's sense of self is so strong, however, that it threatens to alienate her from what Godwin's novel suggests are necessary relationships with other people. Her tendency, as Godwin notes, "to rail against complacency and rebel against the status quo" frequently places her at odds with even those who love her—mother, sister, godmother, lover—and Lydia sees her sister "[move] each year a bit closer to the precarious edge." Cate herself worries about and even a little fears such a future.

Because Cate defines her self in opposition to others, Godwin identifies her with the novel's misfits and outcasts, those who have placed themselves on the periphery of human relationships and are attempting to sustain themselves alone. Theodora Blount, for instance, the "Maiden Queen" who alienates others by her attempts to rule their lives, is Cate's estranged godmother, and Cate's Uncle Osgood, a horribly disfigured recluse who carves wooden animals (a talent that suggests an artistic sensibility generally associated with the feminine), is her "personal talisman." Most ominous of these visions of self, however, is Taggart McCord, the "town's wildwoman" and a suicide.

As a child, Cate had been fascinated by the "glamorous" woman who dressed like a gypsy and teased the soda jerk about the eroticism of the architecture of the Baptist Church on the day that she treated both Lydia and Cate to a "Pig's Dinner," "a forbidden treat on the menu" at the drugstore soda fountain. Now Cate is shocked to learn that this independent and rebellious woman of high intelligence and fine sensibility, this woman so very like herself, has died by her own hand and so alone that nobody had discovered her body until three weeks after her final act. Cate feels "slightly betrayed" by Taggart's suicide, "as though Taggart had let the team down. And then she had worried that she considered *herself* on Taggart's team." If Taggart's is the fate of the separate and isolated self, then perhaps Cate is right in thinking that "maybe there are people whose patterns are meant to provide warning to others."

Certainly this is the use to which Godwin puts her novel's misfits and outcasts. They serve as omens of the self gone wrong. They represent the dangers of living only in opposition. The self alone, they suggest, is ever in danger of plummeting into the abyss of solipsism, of being cut off by itself in itself, and therein lies despair and death. In Taggart's tragic fate, Godwin suggests the need for both self and other to achieve full identity, for only in relation to others does the ego discover and assert itself and live.

Certainly that is the point of Taggart's suicide, but it is also the point of the transformations in Cate's other omens of self, Theodora and Uncle Osgood. By the novel's end, both have expanded their selves to include others, and both are enriched for doing so. Theodora, for instance, by allowing Wickie Lee, her protégée, to preserve her integrity of being, acquires a family to fill the void of her existence, and Uncle Osgood, who is sharing his mountain retreat with two young student-apprentices of Appalachian folk people and crafts, is genuinely at peace with himself and his world when he dies. By the novel's end, these omens of self have become versions of self. No longer outcasts or misfits, they find happiness and satisfaction by including other in self. They also prefigure the change in Cate, who, like them, opens herself to another, Heather, the idealistic country doctor who shares the mountain aerie Cate has inherited from her Uncle Osgood, and finds no concomitant loss of self in doing so. Cate avoids Taggart's fate as well as the alienating eccentricity of the solitary beach walker from whom she had once fled by connecting herself to someone other than her self.

Godwin's two daughters are not alone in their quests for self-definition. They are joined, perhaps rather surprisingly to some, given the sense of completeness generally ascribed in cultural stereotypes to most mature women, and especially to mothers, by their mother, Nell Strickland, who suddenly finds it necessary following the unexpected death of her husband to create herself anew. A private woman, Nell has "excluded the innermost kernel of herself" from others and has "masqueraded" as a "'Southern Lady'" for most of her life. She has also "lived in Leonard's story until it became more true than her own suppressed version," so at her husband's death, she can only wonder what she will be without him.

In focusing upon Nell, Godwin grants this mother an integrity, a subjectivity, generally denied her type. As Marianne Hirsch has observed,

> The multiplicity of "women" is nowhere more obvious than for the figure of the mother, who is always both mother and daughter Her representation is controlled by her object status, but her discourse, when it is voiced, moves her from object to subject. But, as long as she speaks as mother, she must always remain the object of her child's process of subject-formation; she is never fully a subject.

Nell Strickland, however, is certainly a subject in ***A Mother and Two Daughters;*** and in telling Nell's story (or, more accurately, in allowing Nell to fashion another story for herself), Godwin asserts the continuous process of self-creation.

Nell's first response to her new situation is to savor the luxury of being "nobody." She treasures what Godwin terms her "aloneness" because it allows her the freedom to be nobody but herself. As Nell herself explains it,

> When the struggle to "be yourself," and "hold your own"—and hold on to the people you thought you could not lose and still live without—was over, you could actually find pleasure in being nobody. Or you could *be* yourself, but without all that unnecessary pain of assertion.

Such a response, however, is not without its dangers, for it can lead to the isolation and alienation that eventually threaten selfhood. Nell, however, avoids this fate by searching for yet another self.

To create herself anew, Nell studies the visions and versions of self offered as models to her, chief among which are her contemporaries and fellow members of the Mountain City Book Club, but in nearly every case, she finds them lacking. Unlike Nell, they are no longer striving to be; instead they have settled for what they have become. As Nell reflects, "There's Theodora trying to amuse herself with a stray hillbilly girl; and Grace Hill with her imaginary ailments . . . ; and Sicca Dowling drinks, her face is a shambles; and Gertrude Jones makes a pilgrimage to Europe every year and affects a lively interest in all things architectural." To Nell, none of these women represents possibility, so she cannot find an ideal self in them.

Nell's quest is complicated, moreover, to an extent that her daughters' quests never quite are, by a need to reconcile her future self and her past self, for the young woman that she was haunts Nell now like never before. To Nell, "the lonely, self-defensive, sharp-tongued nurse with her young appetites all ajangle seemed like a younger sister" rather than a former self. Yet Nell is aware that "the young woman had not passed out of existence, but she had become encased in a smoother, wiser, rounder version of herself." This former self is an other self sharing the present self and shaping the future self, and all are Nell Strickland.

Nell faces her former self in the presence of her childhood friend Merle Chapin, who, as Nell reflects, "connects me with feelings I thought I was rid of for good." Merle has the power to remind Nell of "a fear of some insufficiency" in herself, a fear that Nell had managed to suppress but never conquer. Merle, however, helps Nell to conquer her fear of her former self by making her see that she has been reconciled to it for some time. As she says to Nell, "'You've changed so much since our Farragut Pines days. . . . back then you had a shell around you a foot thick. . . . And now you're just as warm and loving and natural as can be. . . . You love yourself more now, Nell, and it's just beautiful on you.'" Merle's assessment helps Nell to see that she is another self and that it is still possible to become yet another. In conquering her fear of her old opposing other self, coming to her in the guise of her old friend, Nell embraces both self and other.

Nell's confrontation with her own opposing other self also suggests that self-definition frequently depends upon self-image, an imaginative vision of self as "real" as any other; and Godwin uses a series of mirror scenes to illustrate this point. Each of her heroines confronts her self as other in a mirror, examining her physical image and comparing it to her mental image of herself as a way of gauging her identity. Cate, for instance, is generally surprised by her mirror image, for it reflects an unfamiliar self. On one occasion, she is amazed when she unexpectedly catches her self "frowning in the mirror" and muses, "So that's how she looked when she thought." Coming upon her reflection in a mirror or window on other occasions, Cate is "startled" to find that her self and her vision of self seem not to coincide:

> Who was this blond young woman in jeans striding fiercely along, her chin stuck out against the wind? Where was that wise, mellowed person of middle years who had outlived the treacheries of her body and was loved and admired for herself? She was almost disappointed to have lost touch with this reassuring future self.

Inevitably, Cate's self is at odds with her own self-image, just as she is with everyone else; and she must struggle throughout the novel to reconcile this opposition.

Lydia and Nell also confront self and self-image as they redefine their identities. Lydia, for instance, catching her reflection in the mirror at her childhood home, "admired herself glide by." "Completely centered" in the mirror that once reflected only the top of her young girl's head, Lydia smugly approves of the self she is creating, for it coincides with her imaginative self: "She had to admit she was better-looking now than at any previous time in her life. These were her peak years." Nell also accepts her vision of self, for she recognizes its connection to her self-image. Trying on a bathing suit, Nell comprehends past, present, and future in one glance: "I'm not nineteen, thought Nell, observing her angles in the three-way mirror, but I'm not disgusting. . . . And to think, mused Nell, trying on her second-favorite suit, these very looks that have served me well used to give me such pain." In every instance, Godwin's heroines must confront self-image if they are to understand self, for it, too, is a vision that shapes an identity.

A Mother and Two Daughters is filled with these alternate visions and versions of its heroines' selves, and that fact testifies to the importance of the other to self-definition and self-creation. The other may be opposed to self. It may be an ideal self. It may even be the self. Whatever the other's form, however, Godwin's heroines achieve their selfhood in relation to it. As Rachel M. Brownstein observes, "To discover who they are, Godwin's heroines measure themselves against one another and against conceptions of 'woman'; they experience other women's characters and destinies (or stories) as eerily mirroring, prefiguring, determining their own." Visions and versions of other women, other selves, always, inevitably, and necessarily lie behind the identities of Godwin's heroines, for as ***A Mother and Two Daughters*** attests, women become and are in relation to the other.

Sara Maitland (review date 4 September 1994)

SOURCE: "The Wife Every Woman Wants," in *New York Times Book Review*, September 4, 1994, p. 5.

[*In the following review, Maitland complains that Godwin's* The Good Husband *"is overloaded with attempts to make it a larger scale book that it is."*]

Gail Godwin is a good writer, but ***The Good Husband*** is not a good novel. This is both sad and slightly puzzling, because it ought to be. Certainly all the right ingredients seem to be in place. The four main characters are interesting and convincing; their difficulties are real and persuasive; the principal plot is well constructed and involving. Most important, Ms. Godwin has a remarkable capacity for the subtle presentation of real insight. The novel includes a stillbirth, the description of which is brilliantly delayed until the effects of that death and the personal needs of both parents are established; it moved me to tears with its sensitivity. And this is no solitary instance of the novel's superb writing.

The central theme—a dying woman reflecting on her life and having a profound effect on those who travel that last journey with her—is not new. But in Magda Danvers, who has decided against any heroic measures as she enters the last stages of ovarian cancer, Ms. Godwin has created a character well equipped to explore the meaning of her own death, and with a complex enough history to create convincing questions in other people's minds. Magda has moved from being a brilliant, iconoclastic scholar to becoming one of those teachers that students deserve to have more of. In her 30's she married Francis Lake, 12 years her junior, whom she "stole" from a Roman Catholic seminary. Through nearly 25 years of marriage, Francis's devoted service to Magda has made her style of life, and now her chosen style of dying, possible; he is the "good husband" of the title, the male wife so much longed for by so many women.

The process of dying and its disintegrations, the strains it puts particularly on loving partners, are not shirked here: Francis's pain and exhaustion are beautifully presented. So too are the uses that other characters find for the long period of waiting; while some people avoid the dying, others deliberately expose themselves to the privileged honesty and the patient stillnesses of terminal illness. While Magda struggles to do her dying properly and Francis struggles just to get through it, Magda's colleague, the novelist Hugo Henry, and his editor and wife, Alice, the parents of the dead baby, use the emotional space their friends are involuntarily creating to reassess their own lives, their own needs and losses.

All four of these characters have enough universality and enough specificity to make the novel both emotionally and intellectually gripping. So what has gone awry? Some of Ms. Godwin's problems are relatively minor: around the main characters are a large number of unrealized (indeed, too frequently, caricatured) personalities, like the unspeakable college president and his wife who, though funny, do not seem to belong in this book at all. Nor can Ms. Godwin really think of anything plausible for her characters to do once Magda is dead; the end of the novel is sadly weak.

But the real problem is that ***The Good Husband*** is overloaded with attempts to make it a larger scale book than it is. The novel is overambitious, too full of unnecessarily "meaningful" symbolism. Magda's life work—including her controversial first publication, "The Book of Hell"—was concentrated on "visionary" writers, including Blake, Dante and assorted medieval mystics. Magda is presented, too heavy-handedly, in this prophetic mode. She consciously seeks for significance, and Ms. Godwin follows her; but Ms. Godwin seeks without much irony or subtlety.

Magda—echoing, I suspect, Ms. Godwin—believes that "we live in and by our symbols, they bind up mundane reality for us . . . make our mundane life cohere and coinhere." In consequence, a great deal of energy goes into finding these symbols. A central one, for instance, is the medieval misericord, a type of monastic seat. Monks were meant to stand for the whole of their liturgical office, which could last for 10 hours in a day. During the Middle Ages, a measure of relief came with the invention of tip-up seats, designed so as to provide a ledge on which a weary monk could prop his backside while appearing to be properly standing up. On the underside of this misericord, or "pity seat," there was usually a woodcarving, very often depicting everyday subjects (cooking, gardening, family scenes) or rendering spiritual and mythical subjects (biblical scenes, legendary monsters) in a domestic, everyday mode. Because of the tipping nature of the seats, they were "secret" carvings, not easily seen. Thus, in European cathedrals and monasteries, the ordinary and commonplace literally propped up the divine, visionary work of the monastic orders. Francis, whose mundanity underpins Magda's visionary work, photographs and studies and, after his wife's death, lectures on misericords.

Like Magda and Ms. Godwin, I believe in the symbolic and want fiction to explore it. But it is extremely difficult to do this sort of writing within the structures of the conventional social realist novel. Dostoyevsky abandoned the attempt. In the English-language tradition, George Eliot and, occasionally, E. M. Forster managed it, but both were writing when the omniscient narrator still reigned unchallenged. Successful contemporary writers have sought out different genres and structures (magic realism, science fiction, poetry) when they wanted to tackle these sorts of questions. It is interesting that Ms. Godwin never has Magda even mention a contemporary "visionary" writer: one thinks of William Golding or Annie Dillard, Patrick White, Margaret

Atwood or Ursula Le Guin, as well as many contemporary South American and Italian writers. Given that Hugo, one of the central characters of ***The Good Husband,*** is himself a novelist, with writer's block and huge intellectual ambition, this omission strikes me as odd and evasive, but it is probably wise. Such writers, by contrast, show precisely the problems in Ms. Godwin's own work.

As a writer and a reader, I would like it to be possible to reinfuse the social novel, the domestic novel of manners, at which Gail Godwin is clearly an expert, with mythic significance. I am not certain that it can be done, but, in any case, perhaps Ms. Godwin is not the writer to do it. It needs a bolder approach, and probably a greater rigor and a more highly developed self-irony than she shows signs of here. Instead, she gives us a perceptive domestic novel heavy with pretension.

Juliet Fleming (review date 4 November 1994)

SOURCE: "Facing a Grim Future," in *Times Literary Supplement,* November 4, 1994, p. 22.

[*In the following review, Fleming offers unfavorable assessment of* The Good Husband.]

Gail Godwin's ninth novel [***The Good Husband***], set in an imaginary college in upstate New York, is a meditation on paths not taken: on early death, vocations abandoned, careers not realized, marriages fractured, a child strangled in the womb. Its melancholy sweetness results from the fact that each of its four protagonists learns to abandon his or her early certainties and aspirations in favour of a grimmer, sternly tentative future.

The courage to accept the drastic re-routing of life is exemplified by Magda Danvers, a university professor who, dying of ovarian cancer at the age of fifty-eight, is famous in her community for the courage with which she announced her illness: "Well, I was always a good student; now I must see what I can learn from my final teacher." But cancer increasingly shatters her body, dignity, memory and mind; and the novel closes on Magda's realization that even the will to learn from experience must ultimately be given up: "Let it go, let it all go. How foolish and arrogant of me to expect that my *mind* would somehow to the very end be exempt. . . . Let it all break up in pieces and find its way into the dark stream."

Magda's husband, Francis, is an anomaly in the novel in that he has no desires of his own. Training for the priesthood for the sake of his mother; cleaning a fanlight at the top of a ladder in a chill October breeze; packing lunches for Magda; or changing her soiled sheets, Francis Lake finds himself happy. As he explains, "It suits me to serve other people's needs." Having left the priesthood to marry, Francis retains an aura of quiet other-worldliness that makes him oddly compelling, especially to women. He can also be frustrating company. For years, Magda has wanted to know why, having heard her lecture, he left the seminary in search of her: she is at last driven to warn him: "Its *sinful* not to keep track of who you are. You'll suffer for it yet, mark my words." Francis is too good and has too little sense of narrative to suffer much, but Hugo's wife, Alice, who is also good but has fallen in love with Francis, suffers precisely from his obliviousness to what is going on between them.

The Good Husband is peopled by practioners and critics of writing. Hugo Henry, the novel's curmudgeonly novelist, is, like Godwin herself, the author of light books and is currently writer-in-residence at Aurelia; Alice works intermittently as an editor; Magda is the author of *The Book of Hell: An introduction to the visionary mode,* and the star of Aurelia's English department. Godwin's self-serving fantasy that the academic study of literature comprises the simple celebration of its mystical powers to make us all better people, and her touching belief that English academics speak in brilliant witticisms, even when they are at home on their death beds, makes for some serious nonsense, and renders Magda an unconvincing character.

Godwin regularly subjects her readers to long disquisitions on the novelist's craft, usually in the form of lectures by Alice or Hugo, and always culminating in the claim that, in the words of Hugo's patron, "reading and writing can actually save somebody". The politics of this claim aside, its endless reiteration begins to make us feel embarrassed for Godwin. It also matters that she seems not to have noticed just how disagreeable Hugo Henry is. Godwin often uses "indirect free discourse", which conflates a character's thoughts with a more objective description of what is going on around them. As a result, the reader spends a lot of time in uncomfortable proximity to class-conscious, homophobic, misogynist Hugo: "wherever he lived, whatever he achieved, the enemy would always be in town, devaluing, snickering, cramping his space, spoiling his glories. Such as they were." It is almost as bad to be cooped up with Francis's baffling naivety; indeed, the episode where Alice, Hugo and Francis fly to Shannon is the best evocation of a transatlantic flight that I have ever read, its twenty-five pages having much the same effect as six hours on Virgin.

Anita Brookner (review date 5 November 1994)

SOURCE: "A Servant or a Saint," in *Spectator,* November 5, 1994, pp. 51-2.

[*In the following review, Brookner offers positive evaluation of* The Good Husband.]

Here is a capacious and substantial novel which will impress its readers as either extremely moving or extremely sentimental. The charge of sentimentality will arise from the fact that all the characters are virtuous, even the baroque and self-aggrandising woman professor, even the redneck novelist with writer's block and an attitude problem.

Gail Godwin has made something of a speciality of writing about unsuitable attachments, which neither her heroine, nor perhaps the author herself, perceive to be unsuitable. In Godwin's fine novel of 1974, ***The Odd Woman,*** Jane goes to meet her married lover, or rather tries to meet him, in New York: she has been harried into buying an unsuitable dress, the weather is unsuitable, her lover is unsuitable, and the cast of her mind is unsuitable, all of these factors unfitting her for her unsuitable relationship. In ***Violet Clay*** the heroine is devoted to a lachrymose uncle, whom she supports with vast and undeserved quantities of encouragement. In ***Father Melancholy's Daughter*** the daughter of the title wastes her life in devotion to two priests, neither of whom is worthy of her attentions. And in the present novel the good husband renounces his priestly vocation to love and nurse a petty tyrant of a wife whose fatal illness demands every minute of his care, so that he becomes either a servant or a saint. The interpretation is left open, yet one has no hesitation in assuming that Gail Godwin is on the side of the angels.

Francis Lake, the good husband, is the satellite of Magda Danvers, his academic diva of a wife. Magda's fame and authority, one might say her grandiosity, stem from her bestseller, *The Book of Hell: An Introduction to the Visionary Mode,* and her status as an all-star lecturer on various visionary modes in various unpromising venues. In one of these, a seminary, she notices a young novice cleaning windows; he drives her to the airport the following morning and turns up on her doorstep some time later just in time to nurse her through the 'flu. This is prophetic; when Magda succumbs to cancer it is her husband who tends her until her death, a process described in appropriately agonising detail. Francis has no other function than to serve this harpy, whom the reader mistrusts but whom the author respects. He has, however, an interest in misericords which will eventually provide him with the means to escape Aurelia College, and another of its complications, the ladylike Alice Henry, also virtuous, also unfortunate, also the embodiment of unsuitability, inasmuch as she is married to half-baked writer Hugo with his one success and his inability to follow it up.

As always in Gail Godwin's calm and unassuming but curiously impressive fiction there are theological overtones. These never become overt, but are used as a corrective to the worldliness of the overall design. For small towns, even very small campuses, can be worldly: there is money to be solicited, potential donors to be courted, prestige publications to be extracted from high profile instructors. There are also matters of class and family to be investigated, and in many cases these prove to be intractable. Why, for instance, should Alice Henry retreat into frigidity, although the loss of her baby would seem to be a sufficient cause? Surely the death of her brother and confidant, many years earlier, and the feeling of loss that this death engenders, constitute a rather more potent explanation? And if her husband, self-obsessed Hugo, cannot write another novel, might this not be due to the memory of his illiterate father which intrudes obsessively, and always on occasions when he is being entertained by the wealthy and the gracious?

Thus we have enough material for an absorbing novel, even without the troubling matter of virtue to contend with. I succumbed completely to Aurelia College and to its densely populated hinterland: I recognised, an unavoidable necessity, the fund-raising president, and I grew to detest the prestigious dying professor with her passion for visionaries who cannot even detect the visionary capacities of her good husband. But Alice Henry can. And Alice is unhappily married. To reveal more would be to spoil this grave, simple and comforting novel for potential readers. These readers are likely to be women. But the old-fashioned morality of the story, with its domestic detail and its sense of duty, will have a more universal appeal and deserves indulgence, an indulgence which will at the end have become transformed into respect.

In the acknowledgments the author mentions the lessons she learned from the death of a friend, and her debt to the behaviour of another friend who revealed 'grace' and 'dedication' in his daily living. Perhaps she is fortunate in her choice of friends. Undoubtedly they have a friend in Gail Godwin, who seems to possess an unusual patience and an ability to learn which are visible, again, in her 'good' characters and are markedly absent in those to whom she denies grace. Her novel takes its time, has reproductions of misericords on its title pages, and is nearly a blockbuster in length. It is the ideal antidote to those aspects of contemporary fiction which have become affectless and formulaic. Even its naivete is acceptable. I found it guileless, dignified, and ultimately persuasive.

Trudy Bush (review date 16 November 1994)

SOURCE: "A Modern Death," in *Christian Century*, November 16, 1994, pp. 1088-91.

[*In the following review, Bush offers tempered criticism of* The Good Husband.]

Deathbed scenes were a staple of novels in the 19th century, when writers could only hint at sex. In this century, as the novel has dealt more and more explicitly with sex, death has been the taboo. But recently some authors have again considered the process of dying as a fit subject for literature. In Gail Godwin's novel, the main character attempts to order her life and to find the meaning of that life as she prepares for death.

Magda Danvers, a brilliant 58-year-old academic, is dying of ovarian cancer. Refusing treatments that can do little to prolong her life, she decides that she will spend her remaining months learning all she can from our last great teacher, death. In her dying, as in her living, Magda is cared for by her husband, Francis, an ex-seminarian 12 years her junior who provides loving, self-effacing service.

As Magda declines, many of her friends stop coming to visit. The few who continue to do so are helped by her example to work out troubling issues of their own lives. Foremost among these is Alice Henry, who is trying to recover from the loss of her baby and to cope with the emptiness of her marriage. Meanwhile, her husband, Hugo, a renowned southern novelist, regains his sense of vocation and finds the subject for his next book through the aid of another courageous dying woman he meets on a lecture tour.

Like Tolstoy's Ivan Ilyich, Magda struggles to gain clarity about the patterns of her life. But in Godwin's novel that quest is not moral or religious. For Magda, preparing to die requires "ordering her loves" by discovering what people, accomplishments and ideas were really hers. Though she has been a brilliant teacher, she has not lived up to her early promise as a scholar. After writing a spectacularly successful first book about visionary writers, published when she was still a graduate student, she has worked sporadically on its successor for 25 years.

Now she will never finish the volume. Determining why she was so unproductive is one of the tasks she must accomplish. She must determine what her gift and contribution have been. And she must clarify what Francis has meant to her. For Magda, then, dying well requires resolving personal, therapeutic and social issues. The issues are not religious ones of repentance, atonement or reconciliation, but issues of self-knowledge and wholeness.

Godwin gives no indication that we are to read Magda as anything other than an admirable character. As she nears death she becomes more and more of a Jungian archetype, a wise crone. I found Magda fascinating, but I also found her pretentious and flawed, and her example less than adequate. She is uncritically presented as a model of heroic individualism, a woman who has chosen for herself everything from her name to her profession to her hair color. Magda's story lacks the sense that life is sometimes out of our control, that we cry out against the suffering thrust upon us, that we are sometimes forced to grow entirely against our will. Though it may sometimes be possible to master our fate by assenting to those things we cannot avoid, the process is not likely to be as uncomplicated as Godwin presents it.

Emptying oneself, subduing one's ego so that one can see clearly, are admirable goals, and this is what Magda succeeds in doing. Because the dying woman no longer wants anything from others, the novel tells us, she could see what people "wanted and were scheming to get, what they were afraid they wouldn't get, and whom they loved and didn't love. She could see even those things they didn't know about themselves. She saw what would be good for them and what would be bad for them. Only she was no longer able to communicate any of this." Magda is ready to die when her consciousness has become emptied and thus ready for whatever new thing awaits us after death. The novel gives no hint of what that might be.

Godwin's story seems to be governed by Socrates's dictum that the unexamined life is not worth living, but it doesn't convincingly develop that idea. Magda's one unhappiness with Francis, who devotes his life to faithfully caring for her, is that he is so unreflective. He denies her the one thing she longs to have: some knowledge of his inner life. Indeed, Francis claims not to have one. Though Magda tells him that he will one day suffer for his refusal to take stock of himself, this prediction does not come true. Magda examines her life and gains clarity and power. Francis does not, but remains happy. The author gives us no direction for how to interpret this.

Equally unsatisfying is Godwin's portrayal of Francis. His goodness is presented as instinctive. He has always wanted to serve others and has done so apparently without conflict. "You know, Francis, just as the monks kept learning alive in the Dark Ages, it's going to be people like you who keep human kindness and charity alive in ours," the old priest who has been Francis's mentor tells him. Godwin complicates our reading of Francis through Magda's negative reactions to him. Her term of endearment has always been "sweet fellow," but as she nears death, increasingly angry at his refusal to help her analyze their life together, she calls him "dummy" or "Prince Humdrum."

In her last thoughts, Magda speculates that Francis is so

attractive to women because, not having claimed his own interior life, he is a cipher on whom women can inscribe their fantasies. She wonders if it is easier for the obtuse than the self-aware to be good, and she sums up Francis as a good husband, "as husbands go." The novel ends with Magda's posthumous letter to Francis, declaring her love for him and her gratitude for his goodness and service. Alice Henry, presented as a sympathetic and discerning character throughout the novel, finds him admirable and falls in love with him. Francis and his goodness remain a puzzle.

While praising the novel for its witty dialogue, well-paced plot and bright, successful characters, critics have also found the novel unsatisfactory. *The New York Times* found it pretentious and said it lacked boldness and a sense of irony. That problem similarly mars Godwin's exploration of the meaning of goodness and of a good death.

Mary Ann Wimsatt (essay date Spring 1995)

SOURCE: "Gail Godwin, the South, and the Canons," in *Southern Literary Journal,* Vol. 27, No. 2, Spring, 1995, pp. 86-95.

[*In the following essay, Wimsatt examines Godwin's critical reception and elements of autobiography, Southern culture, and feminism in her fiction. According to Wimsatt, "Any suspicions that Godwin's popularity has diminished her artistic achievement may by be silenced . . . by a glance at her skill in various literary modes and her persistent experimentation with technique."*]

During slightly more than twenty years of an active career, Gail Godwin has established herself as one of the most gifted, prolific, and popular late twentieth-century Southern novelists. She has published eight substantial novels, two collections of short stories, numerous perceptive reviews of books by fellow writers, and several long essays setting forth the connections between her life and writing. Indicating her increasing prestige within the literary community are her long-time residence at the artists' colony in Woodstock, New York, the commendations of her work by such established authors as Joyce Carol Oates, John Fowles, and Kurt Vonnegut, and the claims of reviewers that—in a typical though trite observation—she carries forward "the Southern tradition of Flannery O'Connor and Eudora Welty."

As Godwin herself has repeatedly said, much of her fiction is autobiographical in nature. Recognition of this fact is fundamental to an enlightened understanding of her novels. They are grounded in the circumstances of her early life. Her mother and father were divorced shortly after she was born, and she was reared by her mother and grandmother; during her teens and young adulthood her mother remarried, in Godwin's eyes unhappily, and Godwin had unpleasant, embittering experiences with her stepfather. Also during this period, Godwin moved from two unsuccessful early marriages through insecurity and doubts about her abilities as an author to increasing confidence and success in her work. Drawing on these and related matters, Godwin in her fiction of the early 1970s explores the situation of women trapped in unhappy marriages or love affairs: Dane Empson in ***The Perfectionists*** (1970), Francesca Bolt in ***Glass People*** (1972), Kitty Sparks and Jane Clifford in ***The Odd Woman*** (1973), and similar figures. In her later work, continuing to draw on personal experience, Godwin depicts, with ever surer hand, the careers of independent, successful women who are usually connected, as she is, with writing or the arts. Among these women are painter Violet Clay in ***Violet Clay*** (1978), actress Justin Stokes in ***The Finishing School*** (1985), and author Clare Campion in ***A Southern Family*** (1987).

Aesthetically, Godwin has employed and mastered several established strains in literature, among them realism, fantasy, allegory, folktale, and myth, using personal experience as the basis for excursions into highly imaginative material. Yet despite her achievements in literary art, unlike other postmodern writers like Anne Tyler, whom in range and productivity she resembles, Godwin has not yet been fully assimilated into Southern literary canons. In this essay I propose to examine briefly what I see as the major reasons for her exclusion, and then to argue for her inclusion by looking at her dexterity in mode and technique, her sensitive portrayals of women who struggle with the kinds of problems she herself has had to contend with, and the shifts in the personal and social circumstances of a various characters in her fiction that originate in the difficulties caused by family, race, and class relationships in the late twentieth-century South.

The two main reasons for Godwin's exclusion from the canon are probably her consistent appearance on best-seller lists, which undermines her claim to be considered a serious writer, and her feminism—or, perhaps more accurately, the standard perception of how she handles feminist issues in her work. In regard to her popularity, the situation may be generally described as follows. Because education in America has historically been the domain of the privileged classes, both makers of canons and so-called canonized authors have been suspicious of popular writers, particularly of popular women writers—as, in different ways, Hawthorne's complaint about the "d——d mob of scribbling women" and Thomas Wolfe's description of *Gone With The Wind* as an "immortal piece of bilge" make clear. From Frank Yerby to Gail Godwin, the popularity of an author has diminished his or her chances for inclusion in a canon that traditionally has been shaped by often elitist academics as well as by critics, publishers, and authors intent on protecting their own dominions, even though the majority of canonical authors—Hawthorne, Henry James, and Wolfe among others—were widely read and influential during their lifetimes.

But the charge occasionally made by critics that Godwin's work stands halfway between serious and popular writing must be dealt with, because it is also true that persistent popularity may lead a writer who is responsive to the demands of her public to cheapen or diminish, however unwittingly, her art. Any suspicions that Godwin's popularity has diminished her artistic achievement may be silenced, I believe, by a glance at her skill in various literary modes and her persistent experimentation with technique. Godwin has worked, with impressive range and virtuosity, in diverse, even divergent, strains in literature—with realism in ***A Mother and Two Daughters*** (1982), with fantasy in the title story of her first short story collection, ***Dream Children*** (1976), with allegory in the widely taught story from ***Dream Children,* "A Sorrowful Woman,"** and with mythic or folkloric structures in ***The Finishing School.*** Godwin's talent in technical experimentation is shown at its best, perhaps, in ***A Southern Family*** (1987), one of her most impressive novels to date. In this long, complicated book centering on three generations of a western North Carolina family with ties through marriage both to city life and to the mountains, Godwin experiments, in a manner recalling such modernist authors as Faulkner, with structural elements involving disruption of chronological time and multiple points of view.

The issue of Godwin's feminism may be dealt with fairly briefly. To my knowledge her stand on broadly feminist issues has not, thus far at any rate, been seriously criticized, but then neither has the kind of feminism she displays in her writing been fully understood or explored. The author of an essay published in 1980 alleges, for example, that the nature of Godwin's feminist concerns, and her method of presenting them, ally her more closely with such writers as Jane Austen and George Eliot than with more recent, more radical feminist authors—a claim perhaps fueled by Godwin's slightly acerbic review of *The Norton Anthology of Literature by Women* (**"One Woman Leads to Another"**). That such a statement in an otherwise perceptive essay does less than justice to Godwin's writing is made evident by the following fact. All Godwin's novels, from ***The Perfectionists*** in 1970 to ***Father Melancholy's Daughter*** in 1991, center upon young women struggling to attain their independence, establish their identity, and successfully pursue their work despite the restraints of male-dominated culture and with or without the companionship or support of men.

Many aspects of Godwin's work connect it with the historical conditions of Southern culture and literature, and render it worthy of inclusion in the canons. In her most important novels, Godwin treats from one or another angle several elements that over time have characterized Southern civilization, especially the persistently thorny issues of family, race, and social class. Her methods of dealing with these issues reflect her knowledge of Anglo-American literary traditions, to which she gives a recognizably Southern slant, and they also reflect her awareness of both Renascence and postmodern cultural attitudes toward class and race as conveyed in Southern literature. Throughout her long fiction, she explores the central concerns of her protagonists within the context of carefully wrought, finely nuanced depictions of Southern society that make plain the continuing struggles in the region involving family, class, and race.

As already indicated, Godwin filters transformed aspects of personal experience into increasingly complex novels that depict the struggles of ambitious, talented women in late twentieth-century America, sometimes contrasting their problems with those faced by women of earlier generations. In these novels she examines several related concerns, notably those of young women needing the companionship of both women and men, and the relationship among independence, love, marriage, creativity, and freedom. These concerns frequently intersect, with predictably problematic results. Dane Empson and Francesca Bolt, the central figures in ***The Perfectionists*** and ***Glass People*** respectively, are unhappily married, and neither is able to be creative or productive in her work. Jane Clifford, a university professor in ***The Odd Woman*** (1974), seems at first glance better situated than Dane and Francesca because she is educated, single, and self-supporting. Throughout much of the narrative, however, she vacillates between establishing an independent career and adjusting her plans to those of her lover, Gabriel Weeks. Central characters in ***A Mother and Two Daughters*** and ***A Southern Family***—notably Cate Galitsky, Lydia Mansfield, and Julia Lowndes—have each been married. But in the present time of these books each is single, with Cate and Lydia having abandoned the security offered by marriage in order to embark on a search for a rewarding type of work. When studied as a group, Godwin's novels tell a single story, that of a woman's difficult but ultimately successful quest for self-definition and a satisfying career with or without the support of other people, especially men.

Connected to the fortunes of these and other figures in Godwin's novels are the changing nature and role of the twentieth-century South. In Godwin's most substantial fiction the South is a region participating in the mainstream of contemporary American life while experiencing the upheavals of sunbelt explosion. But it is also a region that exhibits distinctive cultural traditions expressed through the conflicts among different generations, races, and social classes. In her early novels, Godwin is more interested in exploring the problems that marriage causes her protagonists than she is in elaborating upon Southern social and racial experience. But as she moves in her later work toward depicting heroines who, whether married or not, are established in successful careers, she also moves from Southern settings that are only briefly sketched to full, thoughtful examinations within the context of Southern culture of the apparently perennial human issues of family, race, and class.

Godwin uses Southern settings in each of her novels after ***The Perfectionists.*** But in ***Glass People, The Odd Woman, Violet Clay,*** and ***The Finishing School,*** she depicts the region chiefly in sections of the novels that occur in the past, and hence it functions as a background for the main action rather than as an important influence upon it. Perhaps as a consequence, Godwin's descriptions of the South in these books are short and lightly parodic. The widowed mother of young Justin Stokes in ***The Finishing School,*** for instance, eventually marries a suitor from South Carolina who bears an honored patronymic in the state, that of Ravenel. And Violet Clay in the novel of that title spends a summer in Charleston, a fact that enables Godwin to play with old Charleston pedigrees, evoke the charm of historic customs like the St. Cecilia Ball, and invent distinctive regional names like that of the old "Fortescue-Clay House," a designation that evokes the names of such venerable Charleston dwellings as the Heyward-Washington house.

In the books that constitute perhaps her most impressive work to date, ***A Mother and Two Daughters*** and ***A Southern Family,*** Godwin gives the South extended and thoughtful treatment. As a postmodern Southern author, she is not involved in the probing inquiry into the historical conditions of Southern culture that fueled the writing of the Renascence; and she often exhibits little sympathy with outmoded aristocratic customs. But she is obviously concerned with the problems that time, change, industrialization, and ostensible progress have caused inhabitants of the late twentieth-century South. With deft satire, for instance, she comments through Julia Lowndes in ***A Southern Family*** upon the triumph of unenlightened egalitarian developments over gracious patrician customs in North Carolina. While driving her father to a friend's home, Julia notes that "the Van Camps' vast meadowland, where their show horses used to romp and graze, had become a private golf course for a community of mansard-roofed dwellings called "'Townhouse Acres.'" Julia's elderly father, who is "never more lively than when he [has] things to sneer at," deplores "the nailed-down shag carpeting, the democratically identical balconies overlooking the picture-postcard views," the "cupids in a fountain surrounded by too many colors of impatiens," and the "'color-coordinated'" bathrooms and kitchens." "If it's all the same to you," he tells Julia, "I'd prefer to finish out my days in that old-fashioned thing called a *house,* even if I do have a stroke while mowing my lawn."

One of the most striking elements in Godwin's fiction—yet one that even the best of her critics has overlooked—is her portrayal of the changes in several generations of Southern families as they confront class and race divisions in the late twentieth-century South. In her novels Godwin depicts a full range of social classes, represented by patricians Neville Richardson, Anthony Gallant, and Alicia Gallant in ***A Southern Family;*** by members of the middle, upper-middle, or professional classes such as Sonia Marks in ***The Odd Woman*** or Justin Stokes in ***The Finishing School;*** and by women from the rural or mountain classes like Wickie Lee Blount in ***A Mother and Two Daughters*** and Snow Mullins Quick, together with her Appalachian mountain relatives, in ***A Southern Family.*** Particularly in her fiction of the 1980s, Godwin is intent on showing the rejection or partial rejection of older aristocratic traditions by middle-class Southern women and men—as well as their efforts, which meet with only partial success, to establish connections with members of the rural class.

In ***A Mother and Two Daughters,*** for instance, *grande dame* Theodora Blount of Mountain City—Godwin's fictionalized version of Asheville—befriends the unwed, pregnant mountain girl Wickie Lee. Wickie Lee establishes herself financially by making exquisite little dolls, pulls herself up the social scale by contracting a successful marriage to a Mountain City widower, and, in a satisfying ironic stroke, is eventually revealed to be a distant relative of the snobbish Blount clan. In ***A Southern Family*** elegant Alicia Gallant befriends confused, unhappy Ralph Quick, a Mountain City man with a smattering of Cherokee Indian blood who is descended from an Appalachian family, and who is also Godwin's first partially sympathetic portrait of a character based upon her stepfather (she had earlier portrayed such a figure, much less favorably, as Ray Sparks in ***The Odd Woman***). In ***A Southern Family*** Godwin explores the connections between the middle-class South and Appalachia through the marriage of Ralph's son Theo Quick to the young mountain woman Snow Mullins, examining these connections in detail after Theo's sudden suicide brings the Quick and Mullins families into contact. The relationship between the families enables Godwin to dwell upon the independence, self-sufficiency, and solidarity of the Mullins family and to emphasize—in a brilliant section of the novel narrated by Snow—the intelligence, shrewdness, self-sufficiency, and pride of Theo's widow, as well as the contempt Snow naturally feels for what she sees as the affectations and the overly refined manners of the Quick family. Such sections also enable Godwin to describe, in passages connecting nineteenth- and twentieth-century Southern history, the "striking aesthetic deterioration" of the Appalachian landscape caused by sunbelt explosion resulting in careless deforestation and mining. Moreover, these sections indicate Godwin's informed historical awareness of Northern misunderstanding of the South, of ethnic prejudice, and of indigenous Southern sociocultural criticism:

> The lumber mills had raped and pillaged, mining operations had heaped gigantic gray and yellow piles of the earth's innards along the road; new roads crisscrossed indiscriminately, trapping solitary old buildings, or parts of towns, in culs-de-sac; sleek modern brick-and-glass factories with turf lawns and nursery trees shared the same hills with tar-papered shacks and dirt yards. The people in the tar-papered shacks probably worked in the factories. Come South, said the old advertisements in Northeastern newspapers and trade journals, and take advantage of the "cheap and contented, 99 percent pure Anglo-Saxon labor." W. J. Cash had quoted such advertisements. And who had put them in those Northern papers? Who had invited the Yankee owners down, offering them inducements of free sites and tax exemptions? Impoverished Southerners who were too hungry to realize, or to care about, the irony: Yankees went to war with the South to free the enslaved blacks; then the conquered South invited them back to enslave the "cheap, contented, 99 percent pure Anglo-Saxons."

That Godwin in her fiction of the late 1980s is intent on depicting historic changes in American social patterns is shown by her emphasis upon racial tensions and interracial friendships in contemporary Southern settings. As in all her most substantial writing, the situations she portrays have a generational as well as a racial and social aspect. In ***A Mother and Two Daughters,*** for instance, she delineates important Southern social advances through a series of representative characters and actions. In the oldest generation portrayed in the novel, that of women and men in their sixties and seventies, she explores the intricacies of the racially inflected but deeply loving relationship of Theodora Blount and her long-time housekeeper Azalea—two old friends who by the end of the novel dress almost exactly alike, with Azalea wearing "a brooch Theodora had given her exactly as Theodora wore *her* brooch: pinned dead center in the decolletage."

In the second generation of ***A Mother and Two Daughters,*** represented by women and men in their thirties and forties, racial and social circumstances take a different, more serious, and also more heartening turn. Toward the end of the book, the Ku Klux Klan appears in Greensboro, and Klan members threaten the life of black television producer Calvin Edwards in Winston-Salem. These and similar incidents prompt one of the most interesting characters in the novel, Calvin's friend the sociology professor Renee Peverell-Watson—who is descended from a slave and an antebellum slaveholding minister—to enroll in law school in order to train herself to fight the growth of prejudice and racial injustice in the state. Stressing cultural progress, through deliberately symbolic literary procedures, Godwin shows how younger Southerners are breaking down traditional racial barriers by emphasizing the close bond between Renee and her white student Lydia, a housewife-turned-television-cook-show hostess, as well as the even closer ties between Lydia's son Leo and Renee's daughter Camilla, an elegant, accomplished young woman educated in England. In a long epilogue set five years after the main action of the novel, Godwin depicts the courtship and happy marriage of Leo and Camilla in an action designed to symbolize the ties among enlightened people of each race.

Reviewing Godwin's work, and also reviewing the issues explored in this essay, I believe several points need reemphasizing. Developments in theory and criticism during the last several decades have enabled scholars and readers to move beyond the strictures of the New Critics against autobiographical interpretations of literature and hence to explore in reasonably enlightened fashion the variegated, complex, and shifting relationships between an author's life and work. Such an approach seems particularly fruitful for investigations of the wellsprings of Godwin's writing. Like authors before her, Godwin appears to have mastered various technical aspects of her craft before she achieved a mature understanding or control of the autobiographical material underlying it. As her work has evolved, she has handled with growing dexterity the difficulties caused by her two broken marriages, her mother's remarriage, and her unhappy relationship with her stepfather—subjects that she explores with mature aesthetic rendition but not with mature understanding in such early books as ***The Perfectionists*** and ***The Odd Woman.*** She renders a thoughtful, sensitive reappraisal of the same subjects in the finely crafted, intricately constructed novel ***A Southern Family.*** As for the other issues considered in this essay, it seems clear that Godwin possesses a sensitive comprehension of the elements in Western, American, and Southern civilization that have affected and continue to affect Southern—as well as Western and American—class, race, and gender relationships. She understands and adroitly portrays the complications inherent in the interrelationships among several generations of family and community members as these interrelationships are influenced by the changes in late twentieth-century society, changes precipitated by the sunbelt explosion and, more generally, by the continuing rapid alterations in the social institutions that for millennia have characterized Western culture.

How these observations may finally be summarized in surveying Godwin's development as an author and the relationship, still imperfectly understood, between so-called popular writing and high, serious, or canonical writing runs more or less as follows. A reviewer whose name at present escapes me once remarked that popular and serious literature treat many of the same subjects, albeit in different manners necessitated by different markets and readers. Georg Lukacs, Northrop Frye, Fredric Jameson, and other theorists who have investigated the similarities between popular and serious—or academically respectable, or institutionally canonized—writing would almost certainly agree. But as the beneficiaries of these and other theorists, and also as late twentieth-century students of various types of narrative, we do not need, I suspect, official assurance to convince us that the talented and productive Gail Godwin deserves a place in Southern and American literary canons.

FURTHER READING

Criticism

Cheney, Anne. "A Hut and Three Houses: Gail Godwin, Carl Jung, and *The Finishing School.*" *Southern Literary Journal* 21, No. 2 (Spring 1989): 64-71.

Examines the significance of Jungian psychology and the archetypal symbolism of the house in *The Finishing School.*

Cheney, Anne. "Gail Godwin and Her Novels." In *Southern Women Writers: The New Generation,* edited by Tonette Bond Inge, pp. 204-35. Tuscaloosa: University of Alabama Press, 1990.

Provides an overview of Godwin's life and an analysis of her novels.

Clemons, Walter. "Three Women." *Newsweek* (11 January 1982): 62, 64.

A tempered review of *A Mother and Two Daughters.*

Davenport, Gary. "Styles of Recent American Fiction." *Sewanee Review* XCIV, No. 2 (Spring 1986): 296-302.

Offers positive evaluation of *The Finishing School.*

Frye, Joanne S. "Beyond Teleology: *Violet Clay* and *The Stone Angel.*" In her *Living Stories, Telling Lives: Women and the Novel in Contemporary Experience,* pp. 109-42. Ann Arbor: University of Michigan Press, 1986.

Provides analysis of alternative narrative strategies employed by Godwin in *Violet Clay* and Margaret Laurence in *The Stone Angel* to portray female autonomy and the process of self-definition.

Lyons, Gene. "Plot and Counterplot." *Newsweek* (12 September 1983): 80.

A tempered review of *Mr. Bedford and the Muses.*

Mickelson, Anne Z. "Gail Godwin: Order and Accommodation." In her *Reaching Out: Sensitivity and Order in Recent American Fiction by Women,* pp. 68-86. Metuchen, NJ: Scarecrow Press, 1979.

Examines male-female relationships, female independence, and narrative presentation in Godwin's fiction, particularly in *The Odd Woman.*

Seidel, Kathryn Lee. "Gail Godwin and Ellen Glasgow: Southern Mothers and Daughters." *Tulsa Studies in Women's Literature* 10, No. 2 (Fall 1991): 287-94.

A comparative study of female characters and Southern literary themes in the fiction of Godwin and Ellen Glasgow.

Additional coverage of Godwin's life and career is contained in the following sources published by Gale: *Contemporary Authors,* Vols. 29-32R; *Contemporary Authors New Revision Series,* Vols. 15, 43; *Dictionary of Literary Biography,* Vol. 6; *DISCovering Authors Modules: Popular Fiction and Genre Authors;* and *Major Twentieth- Century Writers.*

Graham Greene

1904-1991

English novelist, short story writer, essayist, dramatist, screenplay writer, travel writer, autobiographer, and critic.

The following entry presents an overview of Greene's career through 1994. For further information on his life and works, see *CLC*, Volumes 1, 3, 6, 9, 14, 18, 27, 37, 70, and 72.

INTRODUCTION

A prolific and widely popular literary figure, Graham Greene is recognized as one the finest English novelists of the twentieth century. Best known for his engaging thrillers, distinguished for their masterful plotting, moral complexity, and suspenseful themes of pursuit and detection, Greene attained rare prestige as a critical and commercial success. His literary reputation rests primarily on his "Catholic" novels—*Brighton Rock* (1938), *The Power and the Glory* (1940), *The Heart of the Matter* (1948), and *The End of the Affair* (1951)—and his Cold War political novels, including *The Quiet American* (1955), *A Burnt-Out Case* (1961), *The Comedians* (1966), and *The Honorary Consul* (1973). A champion of the underdog, the irreverent, and the aggrieved, Greene portrays the human tendency toward corruption and the possibility of redemption. His preoccupation with religious and political topics, colored by his affinity for Catholicism and communism, is a prominent and controversial feature of his fiction. A consummate storyteller noted for his realistic style and idiosyncratic ethical perspective, Greene is considered among the most accomplished writers of his generation.

Biographical Information

Born in Berkhamsted, Hertfordshire, England, Greene was one of six children of Charles Henry Greene, headmaster of Berkhamsted School, and Marion R. Greene, a relative of Robert Louis Stevenson. A precocious introvert and sensitive soul, Greene endured a miserable childhood at the hands of his moralizing father and boarding school brutes. At age sixteen he suffered a nervous breakdown and briefly fled home, leading to a period of psychoanalytic treatment. Greene's unhappy adolescence, punctuated by intense boredom and flirtations with suicide, informed much of his early writing and iconoclastic sentiments. Upon graduating from Berkhamsted School, Greene attended Balliol College, Oxford, where he studied modern history and earned an undergraduate degree in 1925. While at Oxford, Greene briefly joined the Communist Party and met his future wife, Vivien Dayrell Browning, whom he married in 1927. Shortly before their marriage, he converted from Anglicanism to Roman Catholicism. Greene worked as a sub-editor for the *Times* of London from 1926 until the publication his first novel, *The Man Within* (1929), after which he became a full-time writer. Weak sales of his next two novels prompted him to write *Stamboul Train* (1932), the first of many popular thriller's subtitled "entertainments," including *A Gun for Sale* (1936), *The Confidential Agent* (1939), *The Ministry of Fear* (1943), and *The Third Man* (1950). His first volume of short stories appeared as *The Basement Room and Other Stories* (1936). During the 1930s, Greene wrote film criticism for *Night and Day* and *Spectator*, collected in *The Pleasure-Dome* (1972). He also travelled to Liberia and Mexico to gather experiences for his fiction, recorded in the travelogues *Journey Without Maps* (1936) and *The Lawless Roads* (1939). The novels *It's a Battlefield* (1934) and *England Made Me* (1935) illustrate his lifelong leftist sympathies, which later were distinguished by notorious associations with Soviet spy Kim Philby, Fidel Castro, and Ho Chi Minh. Greene produced the first of his "Catholic" novels with *Brighton Rock* (1938), followed by *The Power and the Glory* (1940), *The Heart of the Matter* (1948), and *The End of the Affair* (1951)—among his best

-known works. After serving with the British Foreign Office in Sierre Leone during the Second World War, Greene witnessed political upheavals in Indochina, the Belgian Congo, Haiti, and Cuba as an freelance journalist. The post-war novels *The Quiet American* (1955), *Our Man in Havana* (1958), *A Burnt-Out Case* (1961), and *The Comedians* (1966) reflect his interest in international affairs during the Cold War. Greene adapted many of his novels and "entertainments" into screenplays. He also published additional volumes of short stories, including *Nineteen Stories* (1947) and *A Sense of Reality* (1963). Greene also wrote several plays, notably *The Living Room* (1953), *The Potting Shed* (1957), and *The Complaisant Lover* (1959). His other late novels such as *The Honorary Consul* (1973), *The Human Factor* (1978), and *The Tenth Man* (1985) were well received. Among his many distinctions and honorary degrees, Greene was named Companion of Honour in England (1966), Chevalier of the Legion of Honor in France (1967), Companion of Literature by the Royal Society of Literature (1984), and received the British Order of Merit (1986). Greene died in Vevey, Switzerland, at age eighty-six. His personal experiences are documented in two autobiographies—*A Sort of Life* (1971) and the sequel *Ways of Escape* (1980).

Major Works

Greene's enormous popularity and critical recognition is based largely upon his "Catholic" and political novels. Though variously classified as "entertainments" and novels proper, each reflects his serious preoccupation with aspects of spiritual edification, moral turpitude, ideological commitment, and the potential for salvation in the modern world. Drawing upon the narrative conventions of crime and spy fiction, Greene's novels often involve exotic international settings and alluring depiction of murder, adultery, political intrigue, suicide, assassination, and pursuit. The protagonists are typically fallen or hapless characters whose moral failings, both innate and socially conditioned, reflect a broad range of corruption and suffering, especially as caused by extremes of disengagement and orthodoxy. Greene's four "Catholic" novels—*Brighton Rock, The Power and the Glory, The Heart of the Matter,* and *The End of the Affair*—offer insight into the theological concepts of mortal sin and atonement, drawing attention to the paradoxical virtues of vice itself. Set in the working-class neighborhood of a seaside resort town, *Brighton Rock* features Pinkie Brown, a teenage thug who exacts vengeance on a newspaperman for betraying his gang. Pinkie marries Rose, a naive waitress, to stonewall testimony against him. Ida Arnold, a local matron and unlikely investigator, eventually takes up the case and hounds Pinkie to his death. The Catholic theme comes to the forefront when Rose consults a priest about Pinkie's damnation. *The Power and the Glory* is set in Mexico during anticlerical persecutions of the 1930s. The protagonist is a renegade Catholic priest who continues to carry out his ecclesiastic duties despite official sanctions that have driven away all other priests. An unrepentant though self-loathing sinner—he is an alcoholic and father of an illegitimate child—the "whiskey priest" is tracked by a "mestizo," or half-caste, and eventually captured by the police. His martyrdom is complicated by the contradictory facts of his charity and unsaintly indulgence. *The Heart of the Matter,* which takes place in Sierra Leone, involves Major Scobie, a Catholic policeman and devout husband whose tragic vice—pity—leads him to betray his wife, religion, and profession in an extramarital affair and diamond smuggling scheme that drives him to suicide. Among his most overt religious novels, *The End of the Affair* involves an English woman whose passionate love for God is mistaken for an adulterous affair by her jealous husband and former lover. Greene's political novels—*The Quiet American, A Burnt-Out Case, The Comedians,* and *The Honorary Consul*—are set against the backdrop of contemporary Third World trouble spots in Asia, Africa, and Latin America. Though drawing attention to the sociopolitical circumstances of each locale, the religious concerns of earlier novels persist in the overarching theme of moral ambiguity. *The Quiet American* is set in Vietnam during the turbulent 1950s. Noted for its anti-Americanism, Greene juxtaposes the practical hedonism of Thomas Fowler, a cynical English journalist, with the puritanical innocence of Alden Pyle, an idealistic American whose naive and self-righteous assumptions about Indochinese culture lead to his demise. *A Burnt-Out Case* involves a leprosarium in the Congo where Querry, a disillusioned doctor, grapples with his lack of compassion for human suffering by engaging in a futile battle with the mutilating disease, drawing parallels between the ravages of leprosy and a life without faith. *The Comedians* takes place in Haiti during the dictatorship of Francois Duvalier. The story revolves around the experiences of Brown, a lapsed Catholic and hotel owner engaged in a doomed affair with a diplomat's wife, the Smiths, an American couple committed to vegetarianism, and Jones, a con-man, as they are drawn into revolutionary activities. Brown's view of God as a "practical joker" underscores his indifference and the absurdity of the appalling violence and exploitation under Duvalier. Set in Paraguay, *The Honorary Consul* centers upon Eduardo Plarr, a doctor of English-Paraguayan descent who aids a Paraguayan guerrilla group. Among the rebels is Rivas, Plarr's former classmate and an ex-priest. Plarr becomes entangled in an ethical dilemma when the guerrillas kidnap an elderly ambassador, Charley Fortnum, whom Plarr is called upon to care for. Fortnum's young wife is also Plarr's mistress, further complicating his moral obligations. *The Human Factor* involves an international espionage scandal caused by Castle, a minor British intelligence officer who leaks information to the Soviets to aid black South Africans, among whom is his wife. When the security breach is discovered, another agent is mistakenly murdered before authorities close in on Castle and he flees for Moscow, leaving his wife and child behind.

Critical Reception

Greene is considered one of the most outstanding British novelists of the century. Widely praised for his superb narrative abilities, vivid cinematic descriptions, and compelling fusion of religious and political themes, he is regarded as a master craftsman and formidable moralist. Though critics discern the literary influence of Henry James and Joseph Conrad in his work, Greene confesses an equal debt to adventure writers such as H. Rider Haggard, John Buchan, and Stanley Weyman. Credited with redefining the modern suspense novel, most critics contend that Greene's melodramatic plots and sensational depiction of violence and sex belie a complex synthesis of theology, world politics, and existential psychology that elevate his popular thrillers to the level of high literature. Critics agree that Greene's "Catholic" and political novels are his masterpieces and constitute the central achievement of his large oeuvre, particularly *Brighton Rock, The Power and the Glory,* and *The End of the Affair.* Critical attention is frequently directed toward Greene's distinct religious perspective, controversial left-wing rhetoric, and recurring themes of pursuit and moral equivocation in his novels. While some of Greene's detractors find fault in his preoccupation with Catholicism, cited as a narrow obsession that confines his novels to sectarian eschatology and Manichean divisions, others assert the universal significance of such themes as they relate to problems of moral obligation and political commitment. As many critics note, Greene's sympathetic sinners, criminals, and double agents symbolize the degradation of the individual and necessity of moral compromise amid the hellish realities of violence, corruption, and poverty in the modern world. An international best-selling author, Greene's fiction is acclaimed for its entertainment value and provocative examination of sin, moral relativism, and problems associated with spiritual faith in the contemporary world.

PRINCIPAL WORKS

The Man Within (novel) 1929
The Name of Action (novel) 1930
Rumour at Nightfall (novel) 1931
Stamboul Train [also published as *Orient Express,* 1933] (novel) 1932
It's a Battlefield (novel) 1934
England Made Me [also published as *The Shipwrecked,* 1953] (novel) 1935
The Basement Room and Other Stories (short stories) 1936
A Gun for Sale: An Entertainment [also published as *This Gun for Hire,* 1936] (novel) 1936
Journey Without Maps (travel writing) 1936
Brighton Rock (novel) 1938
The Confidential Agent: An Entertainment (novel) 1939
The Lawless Roads [also published as *Another Mexico,* 1939] (travel writing) 1939
The Power and the Glory [also published as *The Labyrinthine Ways,* 1940] (novel) 1940
The Ministry of Fear: An Entertainment (novel) 1943
Brighton Rock (screenplay) 1946
Nineteen Stories [enlarged edition published as *Twenty-One Stories,* 1955] (short stories) 1947
The Fallen Idol (screenplay) 1948
The Heart of the Matter (novel) 1948
The Third Man (screenplay) 1949
The Third Man: An Entertainment (novel) 1950
The End of the Affair (novel) 1951
The Living Room: A Play in Two Acts (drama) 1953
Loser Takes All (novel) 1955
The Quiet American (novel) 1955
The Potting Shed: A Play in Three Acts (drama) 1957
Our Man in Havana: An Entertainment (novel) 1958
The Complaisant Lover: A Comedy (drama) 1959
Our Man in Havana (screenplay) 1960
A Burnt-Out Case (novel) 1961
A Sense of Reality (short stories) 1963
Carving a Statue: A Play (drama) 1964
The Comedians (novel) 1966
The Comedians (screenplay) 1967
May We Borrow Your Husband? and Other Comedies of the Sexual Life (short stories) 1967
The Collected Essays (essays) 1969
Travels with My Aunt: A Novel (novel) 1969
A Sort of Life (autobiography) 1971
The Collected Stories of Graham Greene (short stories) 1972
The Pleasure-Dome: The Collected Film Criticism, 1935-40 (essays) 1972
The Honorary Consul (novel) 1973
The Human Factor (novel) 1978
Doctor Fischer of Geneva; or, The Bomb Party (novel) 1980
Ways of Escape (autobiography) 1980
Monsignor Quixote (novel) 1982
Getting to Know the General: The Story of an Involvement (memoir) 1984
The Tenth Man (novel) 1985
The Captain and the Enemy (novel) 1988
Yours etc.: Letters to the Press, 1945-1989 (letters) 1989
The Last Word and Other Stories (short stories) 1990

CRITICISM

Gary P. Storhoff (essay date Spring 1984)

SOURCE: "To Choose a Different Loyalty: Greene's Politics

in *The Human Factor*," in *Essays in Literature*, Vol. 11, No. 1, Spring, 1984, pp. 59-66.

[*In the following essay, Storhoff examines Greene's portrayal of the conflicting interests of political action, personal morality, and institutional order in* The Human Factor. *"For Greene," writes Storhoff, "religion should not take one out of the political world; instead, it should provide one with a coherent moral vision and profound scope that the secular world cannot offer."*]

In Graham Greene's story **"Under the Garden"** (1963), the ancient Javitt, instructing the young protagonist on how to succeed in the world, says, "If you have to earn a living, boy, and the price they make you pay is loyalty, be a double agent—and never let either of the two sides know your real name." Javitt's wisdom is adopted by Maurice Castle, the double agent in ***The Human Factor,*** which Greene also wrote in the 1960s but put aside because of the defection of his friend, Kim Philby. The figure of the double agent wreaking confusion in the State places ***The Human Factor*** well within the orbit of Greene's preceding political novels—***The Quiet American, The Comedians, The Honorary Consul***—for like these other books, he sets in motion the interactions between political ideology, social commitment, personal morality, and the moral qualities of the State.

Greene's use of the spy thriller to communicate political themes reveals his indebtedness to Joseph Conrad, whose *The Secret Agent*, like ***The Human Factor,*** accentuates the vast discrepancy between our romanticized conception of the secret agent and his dull reality. Indeed, Greene makes his debt explicit by the allusion to Conrad's mad Professor—"A man in love walks through the world like an anarchist, carrying a time bomb"—and by the implicit comparison between Conrad's Winnie and his character Sarah, who "had learned not to probe too far." Beyond narrative similarities, however, Greene dramatizes the Conradian vision that human beings are divided in their fundamental needs. On the one hand, they would like to make their world routine and predictable, stable and orderly. Thus, each character loves his placid bourgeois existence: Hargreaves, his estate; Daintry, his apartment and cheese and tin of sardines; Castle, his comfortable domestic life with Sarah. Yet counterpoised against this fundamental need for order is the craving for the mysterious, transcendent, and enigmatic—a more expansive and majestic universe where justice is finally meted out. Thus Hargreaves laments the loss of nineteenth-century Africa, with its "chiefs and witch doctors and bush schools and devils and rain queens"; Castle nostalgically remembers his childhood fairy land, where loyalty to imaginary dragons was possible; and Davis apes the romantic James Bond. Greene's characters, then, are caught up in irreconcilable conflict, for commitment to one world means loss of the other.

The double agent, because he is at once committed *and* independent and therefore ambivalent toward the political order, best incarnates this paradoxical condition. As a double agent, Castle's role is to "right the balance," to ensure justice will be done in spite of the manifest failures of politics. In his famous essay **"The Lost Childhood,"** Greene attributes to Marjorie Bowen's *The Viper of Milan* the philosophical vision that was to inform his career: "Anyway she had given me my pattern—religion might later explain it to me in other terms, but the pattern was already there—perfect evil walking the world where perfect good can never walk again, and only the pendulum ensures that after all in the end justice is done." This oft-quoted passage reflects Greene's preoccupation with sin, evil, and loss; but critics have seldom emphasized the final, more optimistic clause of his sentence: "*only the pendulum ensures that after all in the end justice is done*" (emphasis mine). Like many of Greene's protagonists, Castle is unwilling to wait for the pendulum's final swing, and the central problem of the novel is how to translate his humanitarian concern into action, given the failure of institutional politics.

The British Secret Intelligence Service symbolizes the individual's involvement in the impersonal political world. Microcosmic, the SIS is a vast network of connections and communications, where messages nevertheless become "mutilated" and incomprehensible; where men appear to trust each other but do not hesitate to betray one another to serve personal ends. Although ostensibly dedicated to a single purpose of maintaining British order and comfort, the SIS actually mirrors the private obsessions of the characters. In it, Hargreaves sees the salvation of English Liberalism; Percival, the ascendency of the technocratic state; Daintry, a safe job with a pension. The fact that none of these characters is entirely wrong only compounds Greene's irony. For Greene, the "State" is no independent abstraction, but rather the sum total of all people's actions, evolving without malice or beneficence or a single motivating force. The political world operates chaotically, with no concern for justice, its trellised actions originating in individual quests for meaning.

In Davis's murder—one of the few purely political acts in the novel—Greene dramatizes the delusion that the State, with its clearly defined hierarchy and rational organization, can never bring about a just world. "C" knows that the SIS harbors a "mole," an informer who has leaked insignificant information on Africa to the Soviet Union. The information does not endanger national security except that it would embarrass the SIS; the management recognize that their own fragile order is threatened, for they would appear foolish and incompetent to the Americans, who are themselves concerned about their image. In identifying the mole, they overlook Castle because he has a wife and a cousin in the government, and they kill Davis, whose flashy life is belied by a desire for a quiet, monogamous life with Cynthia, a secretary. The novel begins, then, with a breach of justice, arising out of a quest for personal, not national, order.

Davis's murder measures the chaos of political mismanagement. No one really gives the order to kill him; his death "just happens." Hargreaves is later troubled that Davis is killed, for he is unwilling to acknowledge his complicity in the affair. Percival, wrongly assuming Hargreave's authorization, plots the murder and carries it out, but will not acknowledge Davis's humanity—he prefers to compared Davis to "an enormous trout." Castle knew that transmitting more information to the Russians might mean Davis's death, but he transmits it anyway. Even Cynthia, as she realizes later, could have been kinder to Davis. All are in some way implicated, but no one is responsible. Throughout the book, Greene emphasizes how people, institutions, and nations constantly work at cross-purposes; thus, every event—like Davis's murder or Castle's escape—is composed of acrimonious divisions rather than unified, coherent effort. Greene's meaning is clear: to except justice from the State is to be tragically deluded.

Into this highly politicized world Greene places his protagonist, Maurice Castle, who resolutely proclaims, "I have no politics." Wishing to remain untroubled by the ambiguities of political commitment to either England or the Soviet Union, he prefers his tranquil, domestic life with Sarah, who says, "We have our own country. You and I and Sam. You've never betrayed that country, Maurice." Castle tacitly confirms her naive sense of divisibility between home and nation, a division he has taken great pains to secure. Yet his retreat into bourgeois security is balanced by his own sense of responsibility and his idealized vision of an orderly, just world—he "could seldom resist a call of distress"—that his own action might bring about. His lost childhood, characterized by a dragon and the mysterious forest, recalls a world of moral absolutes where defense of the weak is imperative and justice is certain.

Castle believes he is actuated by "gratitude" to Carson for helping Sarah escape South Africa. His mother ascribes his gratitude to his deep insecurity: "You always had an exaggerated sense of gratitude for the least kindness. It was a sort of insecurity . . . ." Certainly Castle, like the other characters, wants the stability that middle-class existence should ensure: he assiduously invests even his simplest habits with great meaning, not merely to deflect the suspicion of his superiors but to protect himself from the absurd. His name implies that he is his own bastion; also, the name suggests "castling," a protective chess move. Undoubtedly Castle's insecurity is a partial explanation of his motives. However, insecurity does not fully explain his willingness to risk himself for others. His "exaggerated sense of gratitude" is really congruent with his need for affirming human bonds. He responds with gratitude because he needs to believe that people, unlike institutions, do not act haphazardly or without good cause. His gratitude, then, affirms a world of significance, where an individual's actions have genuine meaning. His function in the SIS, to receive and decode messages, is appropriate for someone who takes human connections so seriously. Ironically, it is Castle's "gratitude," his need for human connections, that severs him from his community.

Greene clarifies Castle's political dilemma by introducing two foils, Mr. Halliday and Daintry. The first is an ideologue whose devotion to Communist principles is not linked to a passion for individual justice; the second understands personal suffering but lacks the courage to choose another's welfare above his own. Shrugging off Stalinist brutalizations as "little things," Halliday has lost his own humanity, for he is afraid to examine his own "silence of pain and doubt." He is like Castle because he attributes his idealism to a troubled childhood, but his commitment to abstract political ideals has robbed him of his humanity. Greene neatly dramatizes the incongruity of his noble idealism and his sordid actions with his expedient decision to kill Buller, whose faithfulness parodies Percival's confidence in Castle, and Castle's in the KGB. Halliday's high-minded goals are made even more unreachable by his disregard for individuals.

In contrast to Halliday, Daintry is sensitive to the needs of others, but his pathetic life is wholly circumscribed by his function in an office that proscribes significant communication. He is just another alienated State employee, and his misery emphatically conveys the illusory comfort a "secure" world provides. Daintry has the opportunity to defy his superiors politically when he discovers that Castle is the mole, yet Judas-like he betrays Castle to Percival. Like so many other characters in the novel, Daintry suffers deeply from wounds inflicted in childhood. And in adulthood, regularity has taken precedence over his humanity, so that even though he remembers his friendship with Castle, he is unable to act upon it. In Halliday and Daintry, then, Greene defines the dangers, yet the necessity, of political commitment.

"Where freedom is absent," writes Irving Howe in a different context, "politics is fate." Castle, thinking he had fulfilled obligations to the Communists, stumbles on Operation Remus, a plan whereby the West would equip South Africa with nuclear weapons to deploy against a Black revolt. Suddenly he is propelled into a world of choice, and Greene makes Castle's choice necessary and sympathetic: Castle chooses "a different loyalty," as Percival puts it. But Percival misunderstands Castle's true loyalty. Moved by the remembered image in Africa of a "dying child and the vulture," Castle commits himself not to the Soviets but to his own wider, far more inclusive sense of humanity that knows neither nationalistic nor racial boundaries. Although he cannot believe in Christ, his Christ-like mission to "right the balance" is inspired by Carson, the "secular priest" who represents the moral and political ideal. Carson, Castle says, "survived Stalin like Roman Catholics survived the Borgias," an analogy that confers on Carson the stature of spiritual *and* secular hero. The selfless commitment of both Carson and Castle points to the Christian cast of Greene's politics: dedicated effort to relieve individuals, coupled with a sense of human community, reflects God's love for man. Through politics, man can give witness to Christian faith.

On the novel's surface, we have a sense of Castle's inevitable failure, and after his escape the settings shift rapidly to enhance our sense of political disappointment. Castle is first brought to a hotel that reveals the Westernization of all the grandeur Africa used to represent. A bizarre duplication of the tropics, the "Starflight Hotel" with its "artificial sky" and "innumerable pinpoint stars" is, appropriately, the place Castle acquires his fake identity. A make-up man who himself is nameless and faceless deprives Castle of his identity in a few minutes, dismissing his uniqueness as a person with ideological dogma: "The human visage is infinitely adaptable. That is a good argument against the importance of heredity." Significantly, the new identity Castle acquires is that of a blind man, a symbolic culmination of the theme of political blindness running throughout the novel. There is only one character who sincerely appreciates the meretricious elegance of the Starflight Hotel: Blit, an American whose name suggests his spiritual vacancy. In Blit, Greene repeats his motif of comfort and simple desires in a purely comic mode: "Smart idea, this joint," says Blit. "Just like the Virgin Islands. I'd put on my Bermuda shorts if I had them."

Castle's final alienation occurs in Moscow. Here, from the barren isolation of his room, Castle gazes out at the red star on Christmas night: "There was a certain beauty in the view as there is in all cities at night. Only the daylight was drab." The passage implies that Moscow is like any other city of man: well-lit, superficially gay, meretriciously beautiful; but, in the daylight of truth, empty of meaning. Russia is depicted as a frozen land where entombed, spiritless bodies—like the statues of Lenin, Marx, and Engels at the University Library (which itself parodies a decayed church)—appear and disappear, leaving no impression except for footprints in the "merciless, interminable, annihilating snow, a snow in which one could except the world to end."

Ironically, Castle moves from his own country where he was free to talk but couldn't to a nation where not only is he not at liberty to say what he wishes but where he does not even know the language. When he does have an opportunity to talk—with Ivan, Boris, or the defector Bellamy—the topic is usually what previously was closest to his heart, his own personal comfort, secured for him by a seemingly solicitous State. But like his adopted son Sam, Castle is, so to speak, "a Ward in Chancery," a prisoner of a nation. Greene makes this point emotionally powerful with the concluding scene of the book, in which Sarah speaks for the last time with Maurice: "She said, 'Maurice, Maurice, please go on hoping,' but in the long unbroken silence which followed she realized that the line to Moscow was dead."

Castle, like Fowler at the conclusion of ***The Quiet American,*** needs "someone" to talk to—"someone" who can understand the seriousness of Castle's political gesture and therefore give it meaning. The implication at the end of the book is that God—and God alone—endows human action with meaning; to be human necessarily involves commitment, but men must choose God before any other choice is meaningful. At first reading, the novel seems to stress the failure of individual politics, and Greene seems to share Joseph Conrad's skepticism of political action. Yet the world of ***The Human Factor*** is somewhat better because of Castle's action: Operation Remus is exposed, and in Greene's fictive world this act is significant because, presumably, other humanitarian individuals will share Castle's repulsion. Merely because justice is only partly done, we cannot therefore dismiss private action as meaningless: although the ultimate consequences of Castle's choice are unrevealed, Greene rejects a world made of neatly labeled boxes, the metaphor that Percival finds so fetching, in favor of a more complex, integrated world, where Castle's private decision has consequences at an international level. Political engagement is not absurd; presumptively it has some redemptive power.

Even on a more personal level, Castle's sacrifice is redeemed from the absurd. Though he consciously associates his own mission with Christ's, he denies Christ as "that legendary figure whom he would have liked to believe in." There is, however, the strong suggestion that Castle will recover his lost faith. In Moscow he finds his own situation reflected in *Robinson Crusoe,* whose protagonist desires personal comforts but also understands the nature of desolation. Crusoe, though, undergoes a conversion in his loneliness and discovers the consoling power of God: "That he could fully make up to me, the Deficiencies of my Solitary State, and the want of Humane Society by his Presence, and the Communications of his Grace to my Soul, supporting, comforting, and encouraging me to depend upon his Providence here, and hope for his Eternal Presence hereafter." Greene's allusion to *Robinson Crusoe* makes the book open-ended, mitigating the seemingly despairing conclusion with the suggestion that Castle's sacrifice—purposeless though it may initially seem in the chaotic world of international politics—has meaning in a transcendent moral sphere. On his island, Crusoe attempts to synthesize his actions with his religious convictions; he tries to accept his place in the world with equanimity, having faith that the universe is ultimately just. Castle has sacrificed himself for his moral principles, but to make his own action meaningful, he must envision his life within a religious context. For Greene, religion should not take one out of the political world; instead, it should provide one with a coherent moral vision and profound scope that the secular world cannot offer. Without faith in God, Greene implies, man cannot properly value his fellow man.

The allusion to *Robinson Crusoe* and the character of Carson imply Greene's alternative to complacency and nihilism: what Greene calls "empirical Marxism." Empirical Marxism for Greene is a Marxist but nondogmatic commitment to revolution, a commitment that ensures justice for the individual as the highest political value. Revolutionary politics must be conjoined with Christianity's emphasis on individual salvation. In an interview with Fidel Castro in 1966 (presumably about the time ***The Human Factor*** was being written), Greene argues ". . . for the possibility, not of a mere chilly co-existence, but of cooperation between Catholicism and Communism." This same view is indirectly presented in ***The Human Factor,*** but indirection is Greene's aesthetic for political novels: "If anyone has anything direct to say about society or politics, let him say it as journalism," he said in an interview with Philip Toynbee. In Carson, whose commitment to an ideology is not an obstacle to his individual charity, Greene symbolizes the Marxist-Christian; and Castle, though he sees his life as nonpolitical, fashions his political identity when he takes Carson as his model. Both Carson and Castle, of course, have as their spiritual model the selfless love and charity of Christ.

As a writer, Greene sees himself playing a political role, the significance of which he communicates throughout the novel by means of his literary allusions. He posits literature as a possible means of realizing, if not a more humane State, at least a wider sense of fellowship. Trollope, Tolstoy, Browning, Balzac, Dickens, Defoe, Richardson, even Rider Haggard—all these writers mentioned in the novel performed in Greene's estimation a political service, for in some way they extended our emotional life to others, showing us we are not unique in our search for meaning and order. In his famous letter to V. S. Pritchett, Greene contends that the obligation of the writer is to be "grit" in the machinery of the State; the writer must resist the State's attempt to restrict our sympathy so we are easier to control: ". . . one of the major objects of his craft . . . is the awakening of sympathy. Now the State is invariably ready to confuse, like a schoolmaster, justice with retribution, and isn't it possibly the story-teller's task to elicit sympathy and a measure of understanding for those who live outside the boundaries of State sympathy?" In ***The Human Factor,*** Greene successfully accomplishes this task. In our sympathy for Castle, we are made to abolish easily acquired loyalties to envisage a more profound division of loyalties in the human spirit. In so doing, we extend our emotional world to accommodate what Greene celebrates: the fusion of the religious and the political.

Doreen D'Cruz (essay date Fall 1987)

SOURCE: "Comedy and Moral Stasis in Greene's *The Comedians,*" in *Renascence: Essays on Value in Literature,* Vol. 40, No. 1, Fall, 1987, pp. 53-63.

[*In the following essay, D'Cruz identifies the "comedian" as a chameleon-like figure whose emotional disengagement represents an adaptive behavior to cope with reality in a tragic modern world.*]

One of the major imperatives in the fiction of Graham Greene is the need to divulge the nightmarish and horrifying quality of reality. Greene depends on sensational and melodramatic detail to authenticate the terrifying excesses of the real world. In his subsequent fiction, having established his universe, Greene studies the screens men create to shelter themselves from reality. The abstract mind proved to be the greatest betrayer of reality. Those with a penchant for abstraction wear the guise of naive idealism, childishness, or an unthinking dogmatism. In ***The Comedians,*** as in the earlier novel ***Our Man in Havana,*** Greene finds a new disguise for the character so woefully disjoined from his world. He is the comedian, caught in a facile role, a mere cardboard figure on the world's stage. As melodramatic material defined reality for Greene, so comedy indicates the separation from that reality and the consequent emotional sterility.

In Greene's didactic framework the comedian stands in antithesis to the tragic figure. Greene identifies tragedy with reality, not simply because the world wears tragedy's dark colours, but also because the genuine extremities of nightmare, terror, grief, and pity, tragedy's emotions, disallow the masks the comedian can so easily assume. The force of extreme feelings does not allow the comedian's vacillation from one superficial role to another. Rather, such emotional depth demands and exacts unambiguous commitment, as with Fowler in ***The Quiet American.*** The comedian's trademark is an absence of dedication, a dislike for involvement.

In ***The Comedians*** Greene gives immediate focus to his comic theme, finding in the comedian an explicit exemplar of the disengaged man. The chameleon serves as an appropriate symbol for the comedian who, like the chameleon, demonstrates an astounding adaptability to his immediate environment. He is perennially Protean and flexible because of his limited capacity for emotional involvement. In a horrifying and calamitous universe he reveals a consistent equanimity. His disjunction from horror reflects an emotional blindness and in his equanimity we see an insuperable egoism. His misguided imagination conjures up a convenient world, obviating the need for commitment. Since flux depends on one's emotional vitality the comedian is always in stasis. The improbable names in the novel—Brown, Jones and Smith—suggest the assumption of the chameleon's camouflage; the man seeking anonymity would find in such common names convenient disguises. They are, therefore, not unexpectedly the appellations proliferating on life's stage.

Greene identifies in his comedians a tendency towards a Berkeleyan mode of idealism which emerges in the insistence upon a congruence between the self's vision and the world. The comedian as a result denies the validity of other vision and other realities. For instance, in the imagined world that Brown constructs out of his jealousy, Jones is assumed to have seduced Brown's complaint mistress. Martha, Brown assigns Martha a wanton temperament and an unquenchable libido, needing outlet in the arms of Jones, her husband Luis, and Brown himself. Each plays the part Brown's jealousy assigns; like a novelist, he creates a dependent and private world, refusing to acknowledge a reality beyond his private vision to Jones, Martha, or Luis. Thus he epitomizes in life an insuperable idealism, worthy of Berkeley, inviting Martha's vehement but astute comment:

> You're Berkeleyan. My God, what a Berkeleyan. You've turned poor Jones into a seducer and me into a wanton mistress. You can't even believe in your mother's medal, can you? You've written her a different part. My dear, try to believe we exist when you aren't there. We're independent of you. None of us is like you fancy we are.

Obviously Green, like Martha, seems to abjure the Berkeleyan assumptions of "eese est percipii" and other attendant forms of idealism. In this respect, Green's moral vision may be seen to have a profound impact on his fictional mode. His career as a novelist spans some fifty odd years. He is partly contemporary with such innovators of literary form as Virginia Woolf and James Joyce. But Greene is curiously traditional in form and makes no bones about his antipathy for Woolf's mode of fiction, which dispenses with the social fabric of the world for the tortuous and winding reaches of consciousness. Greene shows scarcely concealed aversion for the Berkeleyan bent in Woolf. In his ***Collected Essays,*** Greene asserts with some vehemence:

> The visible world for him [the novelist] ceased to exist as completely as the spiritual. Mrs. Dalloway walking down Regent Street was aware of the glitter of shop windows, the smooth passage of cars, the conversation of shoppers, but it was only a Regent Street seen by Mrs. Dalloway that was conveyed to the reader: a charming whimsical rather sentimental prose poem was what Regent Street had become: a current of air, a touch of scent, a sparkle of glass. But, we protest, Regent Street too has a right to exist: it is more real than Mrs. Dalloway, and we look back with nostalgia towards the chop houses, the mean courts, the still Sunday streets of Dickens.

Greene saw the characters of Woolf and Forster as wandering "Like cardboard symbols through a world that was paper-thin."

Notwithstanding his admiration for Henry James, in another essay in the same volume, Greene acknowledges Woolf as an heir of the Jamesian reach for the "pure" novel. But while James strove towards capturing the dizzying and tortuous patterns of the mind he did not totally lose sight of an objective visible world in his fiction. For instance, one could read the growth of Strether in *The Ambassadors* as an attempt by the subjective mind to understand and assimilate objective reality. Greene ascribes a visible world to James's fiction:

> This, then was his visible universe: visible indeed if it faced him daily in his glass: the treachery of friends, the meanest kind of lies, 'the black and merciless things,' as he wrote in the scenario of *The Ivory Tower,* that are behind great possessions.

What Greene sees as James's visible world is akin to the objective reality of Greene's own fiction. Greene paints an undeviatingly gray world, replete with betrayal, treachery, moral commitment shorn of moral satisfaction, and unbounded egoism. In his later fiction, through his use of comedy and his distaste of Berkeley, we realize the philosophical basis for Greene's unremitting insistence on the authenticity of the physical world. The ability to grasp concrete physical reality serves as the best palliative to subjectivism and its attendant egoism.

Greene's distrust of comedy replete with its private vision may indeed be a conscious, not an accidental, rebuttal to Virginia Woolf. Mrs. Woolf in her famous essay conjures up three fictional characters, who rise up to entice the intending novelist: Brown, Smith, and Jones. These are the very names of Greene's comic characters in ***The Comedians.*** By eschewing the egoistic, subjective vision, with its capacity for denying an objective world whose horrors reach melodramatic proportions, Greene affirms the seriousness of life. Indeed, to his mind, life is death's anteroom, and there one cannot allow banalities. The comedian's role is grimly inappropriate.

The narrator of ***The Comedians,*** Brown, manages to justify his comic role by positing a divine comedian at the helm of the universe, who plays fast and loose with his creation. Once Brown had believed in the Christian God and life, he thought, was a serious affair. The divine tragedian dominated a world of genuine tears. In time, Brown lost faith and God became a comedian. The comic world had forfeited the intensity of tragedy. Even its tears were not genuine, but rather the result of laughter: "I laughed till the tears came." Comedy can never guarantee reality, as tragedy and nightmare can; the light-hearted mask can conceal horror and unabated violence. Given Greene's "seedy" universe, the insulation from tragedy and its accompanying emotions of terror and pity create a falsely gay picture of reality.

The three comedians on a Dutch ship, with its incongruous Greek name, *Medea*, steer towards reality as they approach Haiti. The real approximates melodrama and finds its clearest crystallization in Haiti's institutionalized violence. Greene's view of the universe has not deviated since the entertainments, when he enshrined its horror in melodrama. Haiti is not an exception to the human condition, but rather reveals in stark detail its calamitous flaw. Brown compares cruelty to a searchlight: "It sweeps from one spot to another. We only escape it for a time." The searchlight is on Haiti at the moment, but Greene's searing vision had already visited in succession the nightmares and tawdry realities of Mexico, Sierra Leone, and Vietnam.

Brown best exemplifies the comedian's invulnerability to the real world. Even when the rest drop their comic masks, Brown keeps his to the end. It almost seems as if destiny had intended him for the comedian's part. His birth in Monaco renders him "a citizen of nowhere." Fate had pre-disposed him to be totally uncommitted. Despite opposing influences and the combined lure of faith and vocation, Brown opts for the gambler's life. He would pick a living here and there, change his chameleon's color with the wind, and be ruled by roulette. Brown, unable to sink roots anywhere, accurately diagnoses that "transience [is] my pigmentation; my roots would never go deep enough anywhere to make me a home or make me secure with love."

Brown, endowed with the gambler's instinct and blessed with few scruples, is not above underhanded necessities. He graduates from a waiter in a Soho restaurant to the Trocadero, using forged references. Then he assumes an entirely new camouflage as an adviser to a firm dealing in educational publications. An accomplished comedian, he occupies a desk in the Intelligence Department during the war, supervising propaganda to Vichy territory. Finally, he pushes the comedian's luck to the extreme, peddling the works of an art student as the productions of imagined masters, as the gambler finds his victims among his kind. Brown's trick reflects a Berkeleyan mind in action. He foists on others an insubstantial world, located only in his imagination.

Brown, by some less than fortunate meshing of circumstances, assumes his mother's comic legacy. Genetic inheritance, or pure coincidence, contrives a repetition of the comic role into the second generation despite the contrary influence of the Jesuits. Brown sees in his mother a veteran of the comic craft. As if roulette were the secret symbol of comedians, in his mother's China pig-bank Brown finds a five franc roulette token, similar to the one which led to his expulsion from the Jesuits when he dropped it in a chapel collection. Her extravagant title, "Comtesse de Lascot-Villiers," and her shocking red hair seem to be the accoutrements of a consummate actress. She manifests the "tart's" facility for picking a living. Taking the short-cut to wealth she inherits the Hotel Trianon under dubious, though strictly legal, circumstances. Finally, this irrepressible woman makes even love comedy's prey. She implores her black lover, Marcel, "Pretend that I love you like a mistress. Pretend that you love me like a lover. Pretend that I would die for you and that you would die for me." Love is a game of pretence. But Marcel refuses to play the game when he kills himself for love. As Brown points out, "Death is a proof of sincerity."

The deepest and holiest connections disintegrate before the comedian's levity. Even between the mother and son only a chimera of what should be exists. At her death, Brown hopes that her likability had been passed to him, calculatingly observing its advantage to business. As for his father, Brown has no knowledge of him, not even whether his name be "Brown." Worse, he possesses no curiosity about his father; only a hollow resides in place of the curiosity. His parentage had thus equipped Brown for the comedian's part.

Nevertheless, commitment and the attraction of a vocation emerge on the horizon as dim temptations. Here, as in ***Brighton Rock,*** a struggle at the very periphery of consciousness receives focus and portrayal through symbols. Music is the dominant motif of conflict in ***Brighton Rock.*** In ***The Comedians*** the inaccessibility of water implies the comedian's distance from commitment. Water is an ambiguous symbol. It is at once Pilate's means of relinquishing responsibility and a symbol of faith through the drops of baptism. To Dr. Magiot, water represents the divesting of oneself from all commitment. He associates it with that long-ago act of the Roman Governor of Judea, carved into Christianity's memory. But the novel predominantly identifies water with belief and involvement. In ***The Comedians*** water commands the intensity, fervor, depth, and insight associated with the sea in ***Brighton Rock,*** where the sea serves as a portent of eternity.

The first of the water symbols in ***The Comedians*** is the seagull, which ushered in Brown's happy loss of virginity. Before the roulette had enchanted Brown's life along its uneven, unpredictable, and dissembling course, before he had donned the comedian's garb, in that vulnerable moment of first sex a seagull flew in. He found himself "as firm as a man" and he took the woman "with such ease and confidence." It was a triumphant moment. The affair lasted only a few minutes, but they crystallized a perfection he never reached afterwards. Before the jealous lover, the comedian's offspring, had overtaken him, this was the only affair he ever had containing no pain or regret.

Just before his mother dies, a death hastened by her unquenchable sexual appetite, Brown dreams of water. He awakens from the dream to the commotion of his mother's death. Madame la Comtesse had been a comedian to the end. She had taken her pretense of passion for Marcel to death's door, unashamed and unaware of the incongruity of mixing comedy with the tragic seriousness of death. As this consummate comedian plays her final role the dream reinforces her son's comic legacy. In the dream he is an altar-boy on the side of a lake, drawn by the water's magnetic force. But a wind rises above the lake and draws the water away from him until it becomes a thin line on the horizon's edge. In its wake only a desert of pebbles remains. The altar-boy's vestments symbolize vocation, faith, commitment. In the withdrawing water one sees the retreat of faith. The spoilt priest must now put on a comedian's costume.

In yet another dream Brown's spoilt priesthood takes the form of explicit liturgical symbols. His dream shows him as a boy at the communion rail in the chapel at Monte Carlo. The priest passes Brown by, refusing him the bourbon biscuits he places in the mouths of the other communicants. Brown stubbornly retains his place, but is refused a second time. He then leaves the rail walking down the aisle, which had become an aviary of parrots chained to their crosses. The exclusion from communion obviously ranks Brown among the undedicated and uncommitted. The transformation of the congregation into parrots perhaps serves as Brown's comment on the religious. He probably equates religiosity with ritualistic repetition. Being a comedian he is not privy to more than a superficial observation.

The comedian's sterile, desert existence invades his actual relationships too. For a short span of time in the Trianon, Martha and Brown find peace and the rare intimacy of conversation, which exceeds even the intimacy of caresses. The promised land of milk and honey seems to lie before Brown. He could imagine "the taste of milk on her breasts and the taste of honey between her thighs . . . ." But the momentary hope evaporates. The promised land always stands at a tantalizing distance, leaving Brown in the barren desert where love cannot bloom.

Brown's affair with Martha is a banal indulgence in levity when juxtaposed against the seriousness life demands. Indeed Brown refers to his nightly rendezvous with Martha, by the statue of Columbus, as an act belonging to "the theatre of farce." An hotelier cuckolding a diplomat, in a cramped Peugeot amidst the tangle of limbs, is hardly a matter touching the sublime. Indeed, the overtones of immature, adolescent passion invite ridicule.

The tiresome relationship appears to function as a comic relief from the ongoing tragedy. The deaths of the minister, Dr. Philipot and Marcel interrupt the love affair and truncate the banality, lest the farcical obscure the weighty and serious. During their final meeting the gravity of Dr. Magiot's death casts ridicule on their frivolous affair. By careful juxtapositions, and through intimations of the dignity, intensity, and solemnity invested on our lives through death, Greene discredits the comedian's role. In death's anteroom, decorum not flippancy, intensity not frivolity should supervene.

Greene emphatically denies that jealousy enjoys any validity in love's domain. Rather, the comedian's egoism produces the jealous lover. He is intent not so much on loving, as on counting the ways in which he is loved. The true lover, on the other hand, squanders his love in abandonment. The comedian is incapable of reckless love inasmuch as he is incapable of commitment. He merely plays the lover's role. But he applies the wrong test of love, seeking proof in jealousy rather than in an abandoned generosity. Jealousy is the only intensity in Brown's world. A true son of his mother, he can only flit from role to role. He demonstrates his mother's frivolity in the face of death by keeping a paper weight bearing R.I.P. for non-urgent mail. Death invites neither seriousness nor urgency.

Jones, too, is a comedian. According to his own estimation, he is a "tart," having forfeited the "toff's" respectability and choosing instead to live by his wits. He acquires all the appurtenances of one on stage; his unmitigated role-playing does not reveal the man behind the performer, although it is evident that the performer is not the man. He speaks an out-of-date slang, as though he "had studied it in a dictionary of popular usage, but not in the latest edition." He introduces himself as Major Jones, but the military title sits uneasily on him, lacking authenticity. Even Brown, born in Monaco, citizen of nowhere, invites the black steward's conspiratorial whisper "I'm a British subject, sah." The steward makes no such claims to Jones. The comedian's alienation from country, belief, and principle is visible in Jones.

He regales Brown, and whoever else he has for audience, with his soldierly exploits, seeking to validate his role in their eyes. He talks of having fought in Burma during the war, carries a cocktail case from Asprey's which, he claims, dates from his Burmese days, and boasts of what he could do with an army of fifty Haitians. A gambler, Jones, too, in a symbolic sense, belongs to the clan whose sign is the roulette token. He plays for big stakes in Haiti, but loses eventually. He had at least once before gambled heavily in Stanleyville. Like Brown, he changes colour with the ease of a chameleon.

Jones, unlike Brown who had not learned "the trick of laughter," is an entertainer. He fits one's conventional notions of a stage comedian. Jones has enough tricks up his sleeve to make Tin-Tin, the prostitute he had slept with, laugh. She liked him for the hilarity he provided. His metaphorical identity as a comedian is brought to literal realization when he disguises himself as a woman to escape from the *Medea*. This is not the first time he had had to disguise himself. But now, the comedian manages to find an appreciative audience in Martha Pineda. She laughs delightedly and uncontrollably at Jones in his elaborate female attire. Despite his ambiguous background, and despite the fact that nobody trusts him, Jones has the gift of winning friends. Curiously, Jones the "tart" and habitué of saloon bars, brings into Martha's home an air of domesticity.

The novel seems to suggest that Jones, despite his considerable talents, is a reluctant comedian. He speaks enviously of the "toffs" who have "reason, intelligence, character" on their side. A flat foot had prevented Jones from pursuing his vocation as a soldier. He asks Brown, "You can feel a vocation, can't you, even if you can't practice it?" Brown has had his chance at vocation, faith and commitment, but he has turned his back on such a life. Jones never had the chance. He sees in the committed vegetarian, Mr. Smith, a father he would have liked to have.

Jones's dim yearning for commitment is subtly symbolized by water. He boasts of being able to sniff water a long way off. He seeks the baptismal waters, not Pilate's symbol. The comedian's domain appears inimical to the smell of water. Jones claims that grease paint drowns the smell of water. Under pouring rain, Jones is driven to his last assignment to join the rebels. In this final adventure he divests himself of the comedian's attire. His death as a soldier and leader attests to his sincerity. Among the surviving rebels, he was remembered as someone who could smell water a long way off. Indeed, Jones had followed his smell to the utmost limits, finding there both death and his vocation.

Jones does not attempt, like Brown or his mother, the incongruous mixing of death's seriousness with the comedian's levity. Hiding in the cemetery, with death as an imminent threat, Jones reveals to Brown the truth about himself. The game had turned serious. Obviously, comedy cannot prevail in the gray universe.

The last of the improbably named three, Smith, happens to be a "toff." He has faith and commitment, even though only in vegetarianism. The sincerity of his ambitions and motives precludes role playing. Smith is not an actor; but by virtue of an idealism little influenced by concrete reality he falls heir to the comedian's Berkeleyan vision. Smith had been a Presidential Candidate in 1948. His name had appeared on the ballot in Wisconsin where he ran on the vegetarian ticket. This gentle, simple idealist, however, uneasily plays the politician's role. Brown observes, "I could imagine him a homespun poet or perhaps the dean of an obscure college, but never a politician."

Smith's idealism bears an incongruous relationship to the nightmare of Haiti. He brings his gentle, peace-loving vegetarian philosophy to that spot where cruelty's searchlight is especially brilliant. What is damnable, however, is that he fails to discern Haiti's horror and the absurdity, perhaps even frivolity, of his ambitions there: he wants to build a vegetarian center with a restaurant, theatre, and cinema. Perhaps the center might eventually produce a school of vegetarian dramatists. Obviously, his subjective vision bears no relation to the objective reality.

Smith had been a freedom rider in the cause of black rights. His embracing of the black cause and his sincere love for blacks prevent him from accepting their necessary human flaws and proneness to evil. Confronted with Haiti's excesses, he feels it necessary to explain that colour is not accountable for the cruelty. After all, white-skinned Hitler had done worse. In Smith's need to absolve the blacks we see that he has not transcended his white world. Despite his best intentions the blacks are still a cause to be championed by the idealist, not individuals whose colour is immaterial and who demonstrate, like everyone else, the entire spectrum of moral obliquity. His extreme idealism recalls Greene's best known fictional American, Alden Pyle. Both are deeply immersed in their subjective world. Both think in large abstract categories. Smith's ideals speak of "Mankind, Justice, the Pursuit of Happiness." But Greene had stacked all his cards against Pyle. It seemed an accomplished fact that Pyle would never touch reality or feel compassion. Idealism had seduced and neutralized his sensitivities. Smith, however, still retains his sympathy and kindness. Perhaps foolishly, he intervenes in the senseless and cruel world of Haiti, imagining he can right its wrongs and grossly underestimating the relentless nightmare "Papa Doc" had inflicted on his domain.

Finally, in Duvalierville, Smith's eyes open. The death of Dr. Philipot, the obstruction of his funeral, and the blatant cruelty of the Tonton Macoutes had not penetrated Smith as the hopeless aspect of Duvalierville, Haiti's answer to Brazilia. Only then does he relinquish the comedian's role (since Greene evidently intends comedy of a kind in Smith's gross, incongruous disjunction from reality) to reach heroic proportions in his sincere, and now realistic, commitment. Brown attests to Smith's heroism.

The comedian's resilience and fidelity to his role meets its greatest threat from horror and nightmare. Haiti divests not a few of its comedians of their costumes. Dr. Philipot's nephew, the young Henri Philipot, gives up his decadent imitations of Baudelaire and his efforts at parading as a poet for the serious and sincere attempt at revolution. Martha dissociates herself from comedy. Her love for her child Angel is sincere and represents her best part. Even in the area of sexual love she writes like one who has known a generous abandoned love, not its chimera, crystallized in jealousy. In a letter to Brown, Martha says,

> Perhaps the sexual life is the great test. If we can survive it with charity to those we love and with affection to those we have betrayed, we needn't worry so much about the good and the bad in us. But jealousy, distrust, cruelty, revenge, recrimination . . . then we fail. The wrong is in the failure even if we are the victims and not the executioners.

But Dr. Magiot best exemplifies the committed individual, the comedian's diametric opposite. He is the adherent of a faith, Communism, claiming for it a *mystique* and a *politique* as in Catholicism. He implores Brown not to lose all faith even if he has lost faith in Catholicism. The novel ends with an urgent emphasis on the need for faith. In the memorial service for the rebels the priest insists that even violence supersedes indifference. Violence, at least, can be an expression of love; indifference expresses nothing. The rebels, as Philipot assures Brown, never lacked water, the symbol of faith and commitment.

Eventually, Haiti enforces commitment. In the discovery of a vocation Jones and Philipot discover themselves, though Brown remains the notable exception. At the end, he musters a weak *apologia* for the uncommitted, claiming that the rootless and faithless in their inaction demonstrate the greatest commitment—a commitment to "the whole world of evil and of good, to the wise and to the foolish, to the indifferent and to the mistaken." They are "rolled round on Earth's diurnal course, with rocks and stones and trees." Brown's deep stasis is manifested in claiming oneness with the passive; he has in effect exchanged his humanity for the deathlike immobility of a rock, stone, or tree. His death-in-life finds expression in his new career as a mortician. The novel ends with Mr. Fernandez, his partner, summoning him to his first assignment.

The Comedians reiterates under the symbol of comedy Greene's concern with the rootless, faithless individual. In his late phase, after having written his Catholic novels, Greene defines rootlessness in religious language, that is, the spoilt priest, the failed vocation, the eroded faith. They are all ingredients of one who dons the comedian's attire in a tragic universe.

David Pryce-Jones (review date 23 January 1989)

SOURCE: "Graham Cracker," in *The New Republic,* January 23, 1989, pp. 28-31.

[*In the following review, Pryce-Jones criticizes Greene's political loyalties and offers unfavorable assessment of* The Captain and the Enemy.]

Within living memory, broad-chested and vigorous John Bull has become the skulking and down-at-heel Englishman who feels sorry for himself. How was it possible to have engineered poverty and called it socialism? How was it possible to have turned one's back on millions of needy people abroad and called it decolonization? Graham Greene is not answerable for developments of this kind, but as the most prestigious and long-living writer of his generation, he did more than his fair share to generate the atmosphere that seemed to justify decay and doom. He has uniquely romanticized failure. A future Gibbon will quarry Greene's collected works for *The Decline and Fall of Great Britain.*

To feel sorry for oneself is perhaps a natural failing in whoever supposes that he is losing status and power. In Greene's best years, it is true, defeatism stalked the land. Still, it was never necessary to accept this as the one and only reality of the time, appeasing rather than resisting. Self-pity of Greene's variety is objectionable on account of the plea for privilege contained within it; the self-pitier begs for allowance to be made for his circumstances, to be excused the consequences of his actions, to be held unaccountable for any generalizations from his views, to be left to enjoy exemptions and double standards.

Greene's popularity arose from the skill and single-mindedness with which he made special pleas for those failures that are easy to identify with emotively: unhappy childhood, love that has soured, a sense of being hemmed in or hunted by a bully, a society in which the powers that be are indifferent or brutish. His characters fall into two narrow ranges. There are the tormented boys and persecuted underdogs, and the unscrupulous adults from a genuine or would-be upper crust. The latter are the agents and patients of a society that cannot help producing cruelty, and to which allegiance could not possibly be due. Of course, those who are comfortable and safe are enormously flattered to see themselves as victims. Evelyn Waugh, who preferred the hard road of reality that might end in a masterpiece, kept a close eye on Greene, and was the first to note the strategy of his rival: "His early books are full of self-pity at poverty and obscurity; now self-pity at his successes."

Poverty and obscurity were alike imaginary, without significance. Brewers since the 18th century, the Greene family was lodged securely at the top of British society. (In 1984, to celebrate Greene's 80th birthday, the family brewery marketed 100,000 bottles of a light ale bearing his name.) Greene's father was headmaster of Berkhamsted, an ancient public school, and close relations included senior and respected civil servants. His mother's first cousin was Robert Louis Stevenson. At Balliol, one of the most distinguished Oxford colleges, Greene's contemporaries included Cyril Connolly, Peter Quennell, and Harold Acton, destined all to take their place in the establishment.

In memoirs and diaries of the day, Greene crops up in the company of his peers, in Jamaica with Noel Coward, in Capri with Gracie Fields, at a lunch in the Greek Embassy in honor of Queen Frederika of Greece, staying in country houses with the rich and titled. Following the publication of his first novel in 1929, Ottoline Morrell wrote to congratulate him, and to take him up. Waugh proposed him for White's Club, a stronghold of the landed aristocracy, and Greene gladly accepted his election. For years he lived in Albany, the most famous and exclusive building of its kind in central London, and had a house in Italy. In 1966 Greene moved to France, to the fashionable Boulevard Malesherbes in Paris, and to Antibes.

These rewards and graces accord deservedly with Greene's standing and industry. ***The Captain and the Enemy*** is his 23rd novel, almost his 50th book, coming after travel books, plays and film scripts, children's books, short stories, a biography, critical essays, much and varied journalism spread over the past six decades. Here (and in huge sales worldwide in all major languages) is proof of what can be achieved by a professional who does his thousand words a day. He has received the Order of Merit and the Companion of Honour. Is it victimization to have been denied the Nobel Prize? A member of the Swedish jury is rumored to be particularly obstructive.

The interplay of underdogs and bullies provided "the usual Left-wing scenery," as George Orwell long ago summarized Greene's fiction. Greene's characteristic division between a "good" side and a "bad" side comes straight from the Age of Dictators. The cold war offered the ideal context in which to enlarge "the usual Left-wing scenery." Greene exploited it tirelessly to project a long series of admirable and stalwart underdogs, often (though not exclusively) Marxists, always wrongfully persecuted by an equally long series of American bullies, with here and there a chinless British wonder. Some of the American bullies are especially destructive because they do not have the wit to perceive what they are doing.

Throughout the years Greene has been one of the most voluble critics of the West, seizing upon what he takes to be evidence of folly and wickedness in the democracies and publicizing it in books and articles and interviews (or, *faute de mieux*, by means of a barrage of letters to the press). No writer outside the Communist Party has led such a campaign against the West, or found such justification for the Soviet Union. Greene is sincere. His projection of the cold war years is pure melodrama, but he has come to believe it absolutely. He supposes himself to be on the run, defending the good from the bad, an innocent who is right to feel sorry for himself.

At Oxford in 1922, under the influence of Claud Cockburn, Greene joined the Communist Party, only to leave it for the Catholic Church. Catholicism inhibited him from romancing either side in the Spanish Civil War. He began his political tourism, instead, in Mexico. First-hand experience of the persecution of the Catholic Church there led to ***The Lawless Roads*** in 1939. In that idiosyncratic book of reportage, he described local anti-clerical and Communist barbarities, and a day came when he hated the Mexicans. Changes of regime, he saw, would not mean changes of heart. A culture was at work in which a few fought to give orders, and everyone else obeyed: "In Mexico there were always other generals." The democratic alternative, as exemplified by passing American tourists or businessmen, might even be worse, "just the drugstore and the Coca-Cola, the hamburger, the sinless empty graceless chromium world."

Had that limited and melodramatic characterization in any way approximated the reality of democracy, the Second World War might have gone hard indeed. Was Nazism (or Communism) to be resisted for Coca-Cola? Once more, Greene's disparagement amounts to self-pitying regret that what he held to be unattractive was so visible before his fastidious eyes. Afterward, in London as the war was beginning, he published an essay to proclaim that life under German bombing was just and poetic. "The innocent will be given their peace, and the unhappy will know more happiness than they have ever dreamed about, and poor muddled people will be given an answer they have to accept. We needn't feel pity for any of the innocents." To be deprived of the empty chromium world was really a stroke of luck. This was another typical, patronizing measurement of reality by standards of artifice and romance.

For the rest of the war, Greene was away in Sierra Leone, as a member of MI6, the foreign branch of the Intelligence service. He rose in MI6 to become a friend and subordinate of Kim Philby, then not yet suspected of being a traitor. With the onset of the cold war, the British establishment had to rethink its position; the balance of power had shifted against it. Much influential opinion maintained that America was seeking a historic revenge by deliberately supplanting the British presence in the world. Some refined the proposition to argue that the British presence had become an anachronism, and ought to be brought to an end no matter what the consequences. Finally a few believed that exquisite British pink was best deepened on the map into progressive Soviet red. (Philby was a displaced power-hungry imperialist of that type.) No sort of thinker, Greene borrowed according to his mood from all these reactions to political flux.

British and French measures of defense against Communist or nationalist insurgents seemed foolish to Greene. Written with the added authority of someone once on the inside, ***Our Man in Havana*** and ***The Human Factor*** are novels celebrating the bankruptcy of British intelligence in its efforts at defense. Such efforts were a waste of energy, evidence only that the innocent were persecuted and the upper crust unscrupulous. In Malaya, Greene found himself feeling sometimes "a measure of compassion" for the Communist guerrillas, who apparently overcame their sexual passions in the jungle and wrote poetry. Colonialist planters, by contrast, drank and attended Scottish dinners with "A Wee Bit Haggis." In Kenya during the Mau Mau disturbances, Greene caricatured British attitudes toward the Kikuyu with the words, "It was as though Jeeves had taken to the jungle," while Dedan Kimathi, who bound his followers to him with ceremonies of blood-letting and bestiality with goats, was smoothed away with the observation that "over and over again one was moved by the simplicity of this savage enemy." In Vietnam, it was embarrassing to lunch with the French General de Lattre de Tassigny, who was a loser, and clownish enough, besides, to inquire whether Greene was still a spy. What a pleasure it was, therefore, to take tea not long afterward with Ho Chi Minh, who was a winner, and to congratulate himself on having in his pocket a small silver cocktail shaker from Asprey's.

The fellow traveler must be selective in what he reports and admits. If the Soviets have actually done anything that can be criticized, he must maintain that the West has done the same to an even more harmful degree, and therefore that the Soviet fault is excusable. Greene is a master of these false equations. What he likes to call "British tortures" in Ulster, for example, seem to him on a footing with Stalinist show trials, "which we had been so quick to condemn." In 1968, in a preface to Philby's memoirs, Greene likened him to a Catholic in the reign of Queen Elizabeth I, as if the Tudor religious wars somehow resembled Stalinism. In the Soviet Union in 1986, Greene thanked his hosts in the *Literaturnaya Gazeta* of September 10 for "the warm welcome I have received in the U.S.S.R." and went on to enthuse over his old friend Philby. "I personally feel a great admiration for him, for the consistency with which he came to his new convictions and defended them in the struggle against fascism." Struggling against fascism, yes, in the years when the Soviet Union was fighting Hitler; but in fact Philby was betraying his own democratic, anti-fascist country.

In Prague early in 1948, Greene depicted the Soviet coup as a farce, during the course of which he was obliged to sleep on a sofa and to scrounge food with diplomats in a hotel basement. He asks now, "Who could have foretold on that fantastic night the Slansky trial, all the Stalin horrors, the brief spring, and then Dubcek and Smrkovsky dragged as prisoners to Moscow?" The answer is, anybody sober and unromantic enough to have taken the trouble to look at Soviet reality. Nor was it any bother to visit Poland as the guest of Pax, the front organization erected by the Communist Party to try to control the Catholic Church; or to state in public that East Berlin was preferable to West Berlin. He summed it all up in a letter to the London *Times* in September 1967: "If I had to choose between life in the Soviet Union and life in the United States, I would certainly choose the Soviet Union."

Freedom, tolerance, pluralism, wealth are things Greene takes for granted for himself; the airplane ticket in his pocket permits him to turn his back safely on totalitarianism. Analysis consists, for Greene, in outburst. He has no understanding of the political or historical processes that have led the United States to occupy its position in the world. His criticism of America is, at bottom, aesthetic. It expresses a superior distaste, a revulsion at people who do not know the correct forms of behavior.

Americans, as Greene put it in ***The Quiet American,*** are "big, noisy, boyish and middle-aged." One of this type proved "an emblematic statue of all I thought I hated in America." That particular novel helped to cast over American action in Vietnam a taint, an air of superciliousness, which became widespread. (The character of certain American actions helped, too.) The Communist victory led to persecution, and eventually to the boat people, which was as predictable as the events in Czechoslovakia. In 1971 Greene could write, "South Vietnam has suffered under the Japanese and the French, it has suffered under President Diem and his successors. It has suffered under the Americans, but when has it 'once' suffered under communism?" Reproved by a critic, he replied that the Communists had merely been fighting a civil war, adding defensively, and with the fellow traveler's usual glibness, "Why do supporters of the Pentagon always write of men, women, and children being 'butchered' in a communist offensive, and yet the poor victims of an American offensive become merely 'casualties'?"

For some years now, events in Latin America have dominated his writings. The perception that in this culture "there were always other generals" has been put out of mind. Greene takes particular pride in "my friend Fidel Castro," giving accounts of meals and audiences with him in Havana, pointing out to admiring interviewers which pictures in the Antibes apartment were gifts from Fidel. "I'd still fight for Cuba," he was declaring in 1969. Cuban intervention in Angola, he asserted, was not Soviet-sponsored, but an independent and justified initiative of Castro's.

His advocacy of the Sandinistas, in particular, is passionate and unqualified. As with the Czechs in 1948, then with the Vietnamese, so now he doubts whether the Sandinistas are Marxist-Leninists. Once again he finds no reason to foresee (at this late date, no reason even to speculate) that the future might bring horrors. In 1986 he wrote that "the key positions of foreign affairs, health and education and culture are all held by Catholic priests." The Archbishop is opposed to the Sandinistas, to be sure, but "the church does not belong to the Archbishop, it belongs to the Catholic people. . . . There are Marxists in the Government, yes, but Marxism is an economic theory not a heresy."

One pronouncement after another reveals his distance from reality. "I would have thought that Nicaragua was the first Latin American country under authoritarian rule (Somoza supported by the United States), to have reverted by revolution in the direction of democracy." And there is no persecution of churchgoers in Nicaragua because "I have attended Mass in Managua and I have seen religious celebrations in the streets of León and Catholic posters along the main roads." Speaking little or no Spanish, Greene nonetheless knows that the Miskito Indians were removed by the Sandinistas for their own good: a Maryknoll nun told him so. She may have been the only American whose word was good enough for Greene.

The lengths to which Greene goes to quarrel with American representatives are childish, provoking the authorities, for example, to refuse him entry visas, resigning from the American Academy of Arts and Letters, and so on. Under the Freedom of Information Act, he obtained his file of 45 pages, of which 16 had been inked out. This the great dissenter sold at public auction. Once again masking the truth about recurrent and very tangible royalties, he wrote to the London *Times* to wonder "whether it might be worth my while to obtain a second installment and later a third one, a good means of earning a livelihood in old age."

"To be praised was agony . . . the excitement, was overshadowed by the knowledge of failure. . . . I belong on the side of the victims." Culled at random from his autobiographical writings, phrases like these fly by the score in the face of truth. On the side of the victims, in Antibes? Knowledge of failure, with royalties paid from all over the world in a country with tax concessions for writers, in White's Club?

Greene's self-serving fantasies were evident in ***J'Accuse,*** a pamphlet he published in 1982 about a private family matter. Greene's long-standing companion had a daughter married to a young man now accused of being a small-time local crook. Greene claimed that in the divorce proceedings of this couple, and then in custodial arrangements for their children, the authorities had conspired at a miscarriage of justice. Once he had supposed that the CIA might murder him in Central America; now he intimated that he might be gunned down on the Riviera. For this, Zola's title! (Later Greene inveighed in the press against the purchase by an American publishing house of his publishers in London, whose chairman was his nephew. On the side of the victims, browbeating his own relative in the correspondence columns?)

Greene's recent novels have been built upon fantasies too large and too improbable to sustain a narrative: the wrong man appointed a monsignor; a bank manager caught up in the travels of his aunt with a war criminal in Latin America; a man who pays another to go in his stead before a firing squad; a millionaire who tests his dinner guests by placing on their plates crackers with expensive gifts inside, with the exception of one containing an explosive device. ***The Captain and the Enemy*** also has no contact with observable life.

The new book is, not surprisingly, a document of self-pity. A 12-year-old boy is at the mercy of unscrupulous adults. At his English public school, this boy is confronted by a stranger, the Captain, who is an aging and inept confidence trickster. The Captain explains that he and the boy's father have played backgammon, and that the boy is the reward for the winner. Listening without demur, the boy leaves school to settle for years in a dim basement with the Captain and his mistress. The book's detail—currency, architecture, conduct—derives from pre-1914 England. ***The Captain and the Enemy*** evokes not another nightmare from childhood, but anachronism. As though by means of a time machine, the scene switches to contemporary Panama, where the Captain is now flying guns to the Sandinistas. "The Enemy" are the Americans and their stooges, who have a hand in the Captain's death as he crashes his aircraft onto Somoza's bunker in Managua. The boy, ostensibly aged 22 at this point, is left to conclude, "I'm on my own now."

Unfortunately, local changes have caught Greene on the hop. Where it was once right for the Panama of Torrijos to resist America, it is wrong for the Panama of Noriega to do the same. (The writer Lee Langley has noticed Greene's attempt to reverse out of another bind of a similar sort. In ***Brighton Rock,*** published in 1938, when anti-Semitism was all the rage, the criminal character was "a small dark Jew with a neat round belly" and had "Semitic features." In post-war editions of the novel, however, this has been amended to "a small dark man" whose features have become "Italianate.")

The Captain says of himself that he had been a prisoner of war of the Germans. Apparently he had nothing more than a dictionary to read at the time, as a result of which words like "fuliginous" and "glabrous" feature in his vocabulary. This heavy-handed joke is all there is to humanize the character, to support the complete reversal of role whereby this rather miserable liar and cheat somehow acquires an aircraft, as well as the skill and the determination to fly it to a heroic death. Nor can the Enemy be considered particularly outrageous in wanting to keep tabs on this weird figure in their midst.

Panama and its politics, in short, have been grafted onto a fiction of an antique England in the attempt yet again to match "bad" bullies against "good" underdogs. Melodrama, again, is the result of this willful ordering of the world. It seems that even the slightest evocation of an English boyhood leads Greene's imagination directly to the wicked wilds of the CIA. By now America has been distorted to serve as a superior force, or more to the point, as a horrid father figure, in whose light he can justifiably feel sorry for himself.

If Graham Greene had lived in the heyday of British power, he might have had confidence in his gift for story-telling. As things were, he claimed the privileges customary to wealth and freedom while feeling free to ignore the customary responsibilities. In this respect, he spoke for many in Britain and elsewhere who believed that they should be allowed to continue enjoying their ease and safety without paying the price for them. A view of himself and of the world emerges in Greene's work which finds virtue in surrender. Nobody expressed with more literary force the longing to escape painlessly from the totalitarian realities of the '30s and the cold war. Greene's appeasing instincts provided the melodrama upon which his reputation has been built, but those same instincts also ensured that even in his lifetime his work would become a period curiosity.

Bruce Bawer (essay date October 1989)

SOURCE: "Graham Greene: The Catholic Novels," in *The New Criterion,* Vol. 8, No. 2, October, 1989, pp. 24-32.

[*In the following essay, Bawer examines Greene's Catholic conversion, his personal faith, and the significance of Catholicism in* The Power and the Glory, The Heart of the Matter, The End of the Affair, *and* A Burnt-Out Case.]

In his long and celebrated literary career—which I began to examine in the last issue of *The New Criterion*—Graham Greene has written some three dozen novels, "entertainments," plays, essays, memoirs, short story collections, and travel books. But it is those books which, for want of a better term, we may call his Catholic novels (***The Power and the Glory, The Heart of the Matter, The End of the Affair,*** and ***A Burnt-Out Case***) and his later political novels (***The Quiet American, The Comedians, The Honorary Consul,*** and ***The Human Factor***) that are generally acknowledged, for better or worse, to comprise the nucleus of his oeuvre. Though there are other works by Greene that have scattered and enthusiastic support, critics who speak of Greene's literary mastery tend almost exclusively to cite some or all of the books on this list as evidence of that mastery; and it is the Catholic novels that are mentioned most frequently of all. This being the case, it seems necessary to devote special attention to those books, and to ask certain questions in connection with them, namely: How did Greene come to Catholicism? In what form did Catholicism, in turn, come to enter his work? What does religious faith mean to him, and what role does it play in his fiction?

Considering that Graham Greene is one of the world's most respected Catholic writers, the story of his introduction to the Roman Catholic faith is somewhat less than inspiring. In 1925 Greene met and fell in love with a Catholic girl named Vivien Dayrell-Browning, who declared that she would not marry him unless he converted to her faith. He did so within the year, although Norman Sherry's account, in his recent biography of Greene, shows no evidence of a real conversion, and Greene (in his memoir ***A Sort of Life***) is oddly vague and noncommittal: "I can only remember that in January 1926 I became convinced of the probable existence of something we call God, though I now dislike the word with all its anthropomorphic associations and prefer Chardin's 'Omega Point.'" Greene's references to Catholicism in his letters of the period are flippant, as is his reminiscence of his Catholic instruction: "Now it occurred to me, during the long empty mornings, that if I were to marry a Catholic I ought at least to learn the nature and limits of the beliefs she held. It was only fair, since she knew what I believed—in nothing supernatural. Besides, I thought, it would kill the time." (To "kill the time" has, of course, always been an important end for Greene.) For the most part, then, Greene seems to have looked upon his conversion to Catholicism in the same way that he looked upon his youthful association with the German embassy and his entry into the Communist Party—namely, as a means to other ends, in this case marriage to Vivien.

Though the time came when Greene found it useful to place Catholic doctrines and characters at the center of his work, true Catholic piety and reflectiveness have continued to seem alien to him. He has often described himself, paradoxically, as a "Catholic agnostic." Certainly he has never made any bones about his distrust of orthodox Catholic theology, his utter lack of curiosity about the intellectual underpinnings of the Church. One cannot help but connect him, in this regard, with Henry Pulling's dotty, lawless Aunt Augusta in ***Travels with My Aunt,*** who, upon being asked if she is really a Roman Catholic, replies, "Yes, my dear, only I just don't believe in all the things they believe in." For Greene, intellectual assent to a set of doctrines prescribed by somebody else has little or nothing to do with being a Catholic; he has always felt free to accept or discard various elements of Roman dogma as he sees fit, and to contort Catholic precepts beyond recognition in order to suit his own psychological needs.

At times, indeed, Greene seems to have disposed of so much of Catholicism that there would appear to be no particular reason to call it Catholicism and not something else. Like Maurice, his protagonist in ***The End of the Affair,*** he "find[s] it hard to conceive of any God who is not as simple as a perfect equation, as clear as air." Greene much prefers a primitive religion to a doctrinaire, over intellectualized one; he obviously shares the feeling of Dr. Colin, the African-based leprosy specialist in ***A Burnt-Out Case,*** when he comments that "it's a strange Christianity we have here, but I wonder whether the Apostles would find it as difficult to recognize as the collected works of Thomas Aquinas. If Peter could have understood those, it would have been an even greater miracle than Pentecost, don't you think? Even the Nicaean Creed—it has the flavour of higher mathematics to me." At one point Querry, the book's protagonist, goes so far as to say that "it would be a good thing for all of us if we were even more superficial."

In this connection, it should be observed that Catholicism served Greene for many years as the locus—the essentially arbitrary locus—of something that he called "faith." A remark that Greene made in a 1986 interview with the *Literaturnaya Gazeta* is of interest. In the interview, he nonchalantly politicized the story of his conversion for the Soviet editors: "The nearer fascism came to us, and the more it spread all over the world, the more necessary it was to oppose it by building moral obstacles to it in the consciousness of the masses. It is here that I opted for faith. . . . I felt it necessary to make faith the symbol of resistance." Patently dishonest though this anti-fascist version of Greene's conversion may be, there is a truth at its center: namely, that Catholicism has generally functioned, in Greene's personal metaphysics, as a sort of escape hatch from the cold-eyed realism of which he is so proud; despite his professed loathing of romanticism, and his much-vaunted "realistic" attitude toward the Western world, the capitalistic system, and the United States, Greene's "faith" has provided him with a means of holding what are basically romantic views of certain aspects of life—in particular of Marxist ideas, exploits, and leaders. As the narrator remarks in ***The Heart of the Matter,*** "[I]f romance is what one lives by, one must never be cured of it. The world has too many spoilt priests of this faith or that: better surely to pretend a belief than wander in that vicious vacuum of cruelty and despair."

In its emphasis on faith, on the individual's personal relationship with God, and on a vigorous suspicion of prescribed doctrine, Greene's personal version of Christianity might seem to some observers more Protestant (if anything) than Catholic. Yet time and again Greene has gone out of his way to belittle Protestantism in general and the Anglicanism of his birth in particular. At times, indeed, he writes as if it were agreed by the whole world that Catholicism were the only real religion—the only one, that is to say, which can truly inhabit a soul and bring a communicant closer to God—and Anglicanism nothing more than a social club, a collection of pompous, empty rituals whose participants give no thought to virtue or sin or the deity. "You are an Englishman," a Portuguese captain says to Scobie, a colonial policeman, in ***The Heart of the Matter.*** "You wouldn't believe in prayer." Scobie counters, "I'm a Catholic, too." Later in the novel, Scobie reflects that his mistress, Helen, has it good: since she's not a Catholic, "[s]he's lucky. She's free." The implication here—and elsewhere in Greene's oeuvre—is that non-Catholics are innocents of a sort, bound by no moral code and free of the dark and difficult knowledge that Catholics share. Catholicism, in short, is serious; Anglicanism is vain and frivolous. And yet Greene's easy dismissal of orthodox Catholic thought, his audacious distortion of its precepts to suit his own purposes, and his facile fictional use of such concepts as eternal damnation may well strike some readers—Catholic, Anglican, or otherwise—as the very height of vanity and frivolity.

How did a young man who had been brought up in the Church of England end up such a fervent—if iconoclastic—Catholic? The question brings us back, I think, to Greene's childhood at the Berkhamsted School and to his headmaster father's stern sexual precepts; for the more closely one examines Greene's attitude toward religion, the more strongly one feels that conversion to Catholicism must have seemed, to the young Greene, a perfect way of rejecting his Anglican father, even while, in a sense, he was (consciously or not) perpetuating the old man's moral domination over him. For however much of Catholic doctrine Greene chose to leave out of his personal version of the religion, he certainly retained—and, it might be argued, blew out of all proportion—Catholicism's strict views on sex and marriage. In the process he managed to make of the Catholic Church (at least in terms of its sexual teachings) a veritable replica of the Berkhamsted of his youth. The Catholic protagonists in several of his novels, after all, agonize over the sin of fornication in a way that would have been far more familiar to a tormented Victorian (or, in Greene's case, Georgian) public school boy than it would be to even an unusually devout modern-day Catholic. And so many of his autobiographical protagonists prove to have been educated at seminaries or Jesuit schools that one gets the impression Greene regards such institutions as rough equivalents of Berkhamsted—at least, that is, when it comes to the attitudes toward sex and sin that these schools have inculcated into the souls of their alumni. It is almost as if the young Greene, feeling irrationally guilty as he broke his childhood ties to family and school, found it necessary to replace Berkhamsted with the Catholic Church, and his father with God—and, in the process, also found it necessary to make certain adjustments in Catholicism so that it might more nearly approximate, in temper and teachings, the institution in which he had been raised.

There are other likely reasons for his attraction to Catholicism. Given the fact that Greene, even in his early youth, was a master of suicidal boredom and misanthropic despair, he must surely have seen Roman Catholicism, with its reverence for suffering, as a way of legitimizing his veritable fetishization of misery. Time and again, his Catholic novels equate suffering with life, seriousness, wisdom. "As long as one suffers," he writes in ***The End of the Affair,*** "one lives." And in ***The Heart of the Matter*** "Despair is the price one pays for setting oneself an impossible aim. It is, one is told, the unforgivable sin, but it is a sin the corrupt or evil man never practices. He always has hope. He never reaches the freezing point of knowing absolute failure. Only the man of good will carries always in his heart this capacity for damnation." The epigraph to ***The End of the Affair*** is from Léon Bloy: "Man has places in his heart which do not yet exist, and into them enters suffering in order that they may have existence." Too often, alas, Greene's fixation on suffering seems masochistic, morbid; certainly the notion that religion should be nothing but suffering is as distasteful as the notion that it should be nothing but sweetness and light.

There is one additional factor in Greene's attraction to Catholicism whose importance cannot be underestimated. Norman Sherry's biography mentions only one aspect of Catholicism that genuinely appealed to Greene at the time of his conversion: the belief in hell. As Greene said at the time, "It gives something hard, non-sentimental and exciting." Hard, non-sentimental, and exciting: he might, one cannot but notice, be describing one of his own entertainments. And indeed it seems to have been not so much hell itself but the *melodrama* of hell, and of Catholicism in general, that captivated the young man. To the thoroughly English Greene, Catholicism must have seemed exotic and Latin, must have appealed not only to his personal sense of alienation but to the thrillermeister's love of the sensational. His Catholic novels, in any event, make it clear that Greene cherishes the drama of sin and eternal damnation; one thinks, for example, of the scene in ***The Heart of the Matter*** in which Scobie, taking communion in a state of mortal sin, is "aware of the pale papery taste of his eternal sentence on the tongue." What other religion could provide higher drama?

Traces of Greene's distinctive view of Catholicism—or of its development—appear in virtually all of Greene's novels. But it reaches its apotheosis in four of them: ***The Power and the Glory, The Heart of the Matter, The End of the Affair,*** and ***A Burnt-Out Case.*** Taken together, these books almost seem to have been designed as a set of Greenian Articles of Faith. The chief tenets of this faith—among them the notion of experience as the road to metaphysical knowledge, of prodigious sin as the path to saintliness—are explored tirelessly in these books; if various other Greene novels convey the idea that it is important to have some kind of faith or to take a stand on one side or the other of a given contest, these four novels spell out Greene's specific brand of faith with considerable precision. Each of them contains a major character who is a sinner, whose central conflict is his struggle with faith, and whose struggle ends in death; invariably, the assumptions upon which the conflict takes place, the terms in which it is presented, and the conclusions which are drawn from its outcome derive entirely from Greene's own iconoclastic version of Catholicism.

For instance, ***The Power and the Glory*** (1940), set in socialist Mexico in the 1930s, takes as its protagonist a cowardly alcoholic priest who has married one woman and fathered a child by another. This "whiskey priest" (whose name we never learn) is the last Roman Catholic cleric remaining in a province where it's been declared a crime to say Mass; like many a Greene hero, he spends much of the book on the lam from the authorities. This simply structured novel is dense with evocations of rural poverty and with pronouncements about various spiritual topics—good and evil, love and lust, experience and innocence—from which Greene typically doesn't distance himself at all. "[O]ur sins have so much beauty," the whiskey priest declares at one point. "I'm a bad priest, you see. I know—from experience—how much beauty Satan carried down with him when he fell. Nobody ever said the fallen angels were the ugly ones." It is his corruption, the priest says, that has brought him close to God: as a "comparatively innocent" young man, he was "unbearable." (In Greene's novels, of course, innocent men are invariably unbearable.) And indeed we are meant to understand, at the book's conclusion, that for all his sin the priest may well be something of a saint.

Though Greene does not depart radically here from the brisk, lucid manner of his early novels and entertainments, he does—rather like Hemingway in *For Whom the Bell Tolls*—attempt to modify his characteristic precision and simplicity in the direction of a certain austere stateliness, and thereby to give his "whiskey priest" a magnitude, and even a kind of coarse nobility, that his previous heroes didn't have. As in Hemingway's novel, however, the results of this stylistic modification are questionable. For one thing, the frequent appearance of colons between strings of independent clauses ("The squad of police made their way back to the station: they walked raggedly with rifles slung anyhow: ends of cotton where buttons should have been: a puttee slipping down over the ankle: small men with black secret Indian eyes") seems to have no *raison d'être* other than the author's affectation; for another, the novel's plainness of style ("He hustled them out: one by one they picked their way across the clearing towards the hut: and the old man set off down the path toward the river to take the place of the boy who watched the ford for soldiers") feels strained and phony in the way of the most self-parodic Hemingway.

Patently, Greene seeks to convey in this novel a solemn, intense vision of the human condition—a vision in which there would appear to be little room for the humor that helps (occasionally, at least) to relieve the darkness of his earlier books. But it's less a vision, really, than a contrivance, a repetitive and deliberate hammering away at the irony of the priest's position as "a damned man putting God into the mouths of men." The priest constantly flagellates himself, and we're plainly meant to be moved by his distress; but because that supposed distress is, for the most part, simply reiterated, rather than being reflected in a serious effort to change his ways, it's hard to take it very seriously. It's hard, for that matter, to believe that *Greene* takes it seriously: for the novel shows every sign of having been built less upon a passionate devotion to the idea of God than upon a view—at once glib, sentimental, patronizing, and upper-crust-Protestant—of swarthy, dirt-poor, Romance-language-speaking Catholics as close to the earth and, *ipso facto,* close to the Almighty.

The sinner at the heart of ***The Heart of the Matter*** (1948), which takes place during World War II, is Major Scobie, the middle-aged assistant police commissioner in a British colonial town on the West African coast. Described by his superior as "Scobie the Just," by a Syrian trader as "a just man," by a local MI5 agent named Wilson as "too damned honest to live," and by his wife, Louise, as "the typical second man . . . [t]he one who always does the work," Scobie has been stationed in this town for fifteen years—"too long to go," as he puts it—and he has a rare understanding of and compassion for the natives. He also is a Catholic (he married into the faith) and a loyal husband, and has the sort of less-than-rosy outlook of which Greene approves: "It seemed to Scobie that life was immeasurably long. Couldn't the test of man have been carried out in fewer years? Couldn't we have committed our first major sin at seven, have ruined ourselves for love or hate at ten, have clutched at redemption on a fifteen-year-old death bed?"

Love, sin, and redemption are, as it happens, the principal concerns here; and the first intimation of peril comes when Wilson becomes infatuated with Louise. But Scobie's true downfall begins when he encounters a boatful of shipwreck survivors, falls swiftly in love with one of them—a young widow named Helen Rolt—and commences to break his marital vows while Louise is away: "God can wait, he thought: how can one love God at the expense of one of his creatures?" During his affair with Helen, Scobie is insufferable—although Greene doesn't seem to *intend* for him to be insufferable—about the threat of perdition hanging over his head. "If you believe in hell," Helen asks him, "why are you with me now?" Good question. And after Louise's return, Scobie finds himself in a spiritual bind: if he doesn't take communion with Louise, she'll know he committed a mortal sin; if he does take it with the taint of his adultery on his soul, he will (he believes) be irredeemably damned. In the end, he chooses the latter; and, after taking communion ("O God, I offer up my damnation to you"), whining to Helen about it ("I'm damned for all eternity . . . What I've done is far worse than murder"), and wallowing for a while in self-pity ("This was what human love had done to him—it had robbed him of love for eternity"), he commits suicide—which, we've been told, "puts a man outside mercy." For those who haven't caught the irony here, Greene has already spelled it out: "Only the man of good will carries always in his heart this capacity for damnation."

With its solemn (if often highly dubious) aphorisms about love, damnation, and eternity, its consistently elevated tone, its sweltering and exotic African setting (whose purpose is perhaps to suggest at once the intensity of Scobie's passions, the extremity of his spiritual crisis, and the torment of hell), and its unyielding focus upon a man's relentless march toward his own everlasting doom, this novel seems to insist, with every sentence, on its own greatness. And many readers, over the years, have agreed that it *is* great. But is it? For a man who believes that adultery is a path to hell, Scobie certainly doesn't seem to put up much of a struggle against temptation—which makes it hard to take all the rhetoric about God and sin and damnation very seriously. Nor does he try very hard to escape his doom after sleeping with Helen; he presents himself in the confessional, to be sure, but since he can't promise to avoid seeing Helen, the priest can't guarantee a valid absolution. It's absurd: if Scobie truly believes his soul is on the line, why doesn't he do everything in his power to avoid Helen? Or at least, for heaven's sake, skip communion till the romance blows over? His behavior is so irrational, so preposterously gentlemanly, so *English;* to read about his fate is to feel that a real Catholic could never have invented such a character, a man who would sacrifice his eternal soul to avoid creating a scene.

What Greene has manufactured here is a public school heroic fantasy which has no relevance whatsoever to the real world, Catholic or otherwise; in the person of Scobie, Greene brings together a rigid Catholic faith (which might be found in a certain kind of man) with a readiness to commit adultery (which might be characteristic of another, very different sort of man); combining the two traits, however, results not in a portrait of a complex, full-blooded individual but in an unbelievable concoction that reflects only its creator's obsessions. It may be that the only way one can easily understand Scobie, in real-world terms, is as a man who has for years been waiting for a good reason to kill himself. Certainly his thoughts are full of the subject: he ponders the fact that "[d]eath never comes when one desires it most"; he reflects of his long-deceased daughter that she "was safe now, for ever" (like many Greene characters, he considers death a sanctuary). If ***The Heart of the Matter*** is effective, it is largely as a demonstration of the ability of emotionally disturbed individuals to twist religion into a tool of self-destruction.

The End of the Affair (1951), like ***The Heart of the Matter,*** depicts a fatal romantic triangle. Set in London and its environs, the novel is described by its narrator and protagonist, a writer named Maurice Bendrix, as "a record of hate far more than of love." As the novel opens in January of 1946, Bendrix learns from his friend Henry Miles, a high ranking member of the government, that Henry's wife, Sarah, may be having an affair; Bendrix is hurt, for unbeknownst to Henry, he had enjoyed a three-year liaison with Sarah himself until, a year and a half earlier, she broke it off inexplicably and Bendrix "began quite seriously to think of suicide." Now, desperate to know the truth, Bendrix engages a detective; the man pinches Sarah's diary, and it is from this document that Bendrix learns why she separated from him. One day, thinking him dead in an air raid, she had prayed to God: "Let him be alive, and I *will* believe. . . . I'll give him up for ever, only let him be alive." When Bendrix indeed proved to be alive, Sarah kept her word to God, and ever since has been engaged in a struggle with the idea of God, resenting Him, seeking advice from a financial anti-religionist, and pouring her heart into her diary: "I want Maurice. I want ordinary corrupt human love. Dear God, you know I want to want Your pain, but I don't want it now." Bendrix refuses to take God seriously as a rival, and seeks to revive their affair. But he succeeds only (though an unfortunate happenstance) in bringing about Sarah's death—and learns afterward that she had been taking instruction in Catholicism, a faith into which (though she never knew it) she had been baptized as a child.

In many ways ***The End of the Affair*** is one of Greene's best books. It is exquisitely shaped and paced, the people and their relationships seem real, and both the passion and the bitterness ring true; though plenty of abstractions are brought into play, one does not constantly have the feeling that the characters serve merely as symbolic tokens. Yet, reading Sarah's diary account of her discovery of faith, one does want to ask the question: why Catholicism and not Anglicanism? Why must belief in a Creator necessarily lead, in the world according to Greene, to belief—as Sarah puts it—in "the whole bag of tricks" of the Catholic Church? The revelation of Sarah's childhood Catholicism suggests that Greene wants us to see her recent enthusiasm for the faith as some sort of mystical event, a reclaiming of Sarah, as it were, God; but this reading, it seems to me, cheapens the book, turns it into a kind of religious thriller. (Do even pious Catholics believe that God plays such games?) One prefers to think that Sarah chooses Catholicism because it is the one Christian faith that would flatly forbid her to divorce Henry and marry Maurice—an act against which her sense of guilt about the affair rebels. To posit such a reading is not to deny the sublimity of religious faith, but merely to acknowledge the importance—to life, to literature, and even perhaps to God—of human character and psychology; what makes ***The End of the Affair*** more successful than ***The Power and the Glory*** and ***The Heart of the Matter*** is its greater appreciation of that importance.

A Burnt-Out Case (1961), the last of Greene's explicitly Catholic books, is in some ways a departure from its predecessors. It begins, with the mysterious arrival of Querry, a world-famous church architect, at a small Central African leper hospital on a remote tributary of the Congo. Querry has come to the hospital—which is run by Catholic priests and by one Dr. Colin, and which is crowded with "burnt-out cases" (patients, many of them disfigured and impaired, from whose systems the leprosy infection has totally disappeared)—to finish out his life away from civilization. Why? Because in his own way Querry is a burnt-out case, too; or so, at least, he tells everyone who's ready to listen. Yes, he's perfectly scrupulous, well-functioning: "You are a whole man as far as one can see," says Parkinson, a sleazy reporter who tracks him down to the hospital. But Querry knows better: he's lost his faith. In contrast to his parents' simple, instinctive religion, he had constructed an edifice of logical proofs of the existence of God; but his realization that he didn't truly accept those proofs has caused an emotional crisis. He realizes he's been deceiving himself: he's never really loved ("Perhaps it's true that you can't believe in a god without loving a human being or love a human being without believing in a god"), never built a church for love of anything but himself ("To build a church when you don't believe in a god seems a little indecent, doesn't it?"). He'd always thought himself dedicated to God, but knows now that "anything he had ever done must have been done for love of himself." If Sarah, in ***The End of the Affair,*** longs for the suffering that will mark her as a true Christian, Querry is past all that: "I suffer from nothing. I no longer know what suffering is. I have come to an end of all that. . . ." (One of the novel's epigraphs comes from Dante: "I did not die, yet nothing of life remained.")

Over the next few months, Querry assists the priests and helps them plan a new hospital. Ironically, when he saves a man's life he is celebrated as a saint by the ignoble Parkinson, the innocent Father Thomas, and the intellectual M. Rycker (a local factory manager and former seminarian);

yet when he is falsely accused of having an affair with Mme. Rycker, those who declared him a saint are the first to condemn him. Interestingly—in what seems to be something of a move away from Greene's earlier concentration on faith, and toward a doctrine of good works—Querry's staunchest ally (and the most sympathetic and level-headed character in the book) is Dr. Colin, who "had long ago . . . lost faith in any god that a priest would have recognized," but who, despite his atheism, we are manifestly supposed to admire for his tireless dedication to the sick. Likewise, we're supposed to admire the priests (except for Father Thomas), who "would much prefer to talk about turbines" than about canon law, and who are "too busy to bother themselves with what the Church considered sin (moral theology was the subject they were least concerned with)."

And we *do* admire them. But it's hard to admire Querry. Though he's a decent enough chap, his enthusiasm for his own suffering is wearisome in the extreme; it comes across as the manifestation not of a crisis of faith (as Greene would have us believe) but of severe neurosis. Querry keeps insisting upon his inability to love and to believe, but it's all just words, words, words: his torment is never dramatized, just endlessly proclaimed. And to a large extent, it's simply too weird and too abstract to identify with: he can't make love anymore, he says, because sex should be an enacting of God's love for his people and he can no longer believe in God. We're apparently meant to see all this soul-searching as part of a sacred struggle, but for the most part it seems merely solipsistic, selfish; and it seems especially so because at the *léproserie* he is surrounded by people—among them many small children—who have a much more visible reason than he does to bewail their fates. Yet not even the sight of armless babies can take Querry out of himself for very long, and Greene doesn't seem to intend the irony: to him, as to Querry, the leprosy patients are basically set decoration, their physical disfigurement a metaphor for Querry's spiritual mutilation. Likewise, when Querry compares his own late, lamented intellectual Catholicism with his parents' "simple and uncomplex heart[s]," Greene doesn't seem to want us to find him arrogant—but of course we do. Even Dr. Colin regards Querry as a privileged character; when a priest suggests that publicity for the hospital might attract funds that could help hundreds of lepers, Dr. Colin rejects the idea because it wouldn't be good for Querry. "Limelight," he says, "is not very good for the mutilated."

There are logical problems with the book, too. The idea of a church architect as celebrity is a bit difficult to buy. And then there are certain questions of motivation: Querry claims to have come to the *léproserie* in order to escape the world, the Church, *labéte humanine*; yet, if this is the case, how did he happen to end up as a veritable social worker in a part of Central Africa that seems to contain more Catholics than the Vatican? And why, if he didn't want reporters to track him down, did he give everyone along the way his real name? Greene shows no sign of doubting Querry's motives. Then, as in ***The Heart of the Matter,*** there's the suicide angle. "A man can't live with nothing but himself," Dr. Colin says; "[s]ooner or later he would kill himself." Yes, Querry replies, "[i]f he had enough interest." Like Scobie, he seems essentially to be a suicide in search of a catalyst.

For the most part, indeed, all of Greene's so-called Catholic novels seem ultimately to have less to do with religion, *per se,* than with psychopathology—and, one might add, with melodramatic artifice; as I've suggested in connection with ***The End of the Affair,*** it might even be more nearly correct to call them religious thrillers. To be sure, they have been treated very respectfully by critics and readers, and it is true that their deeply afflicted protagonists, their solemn metaphysical utterances, their grand abstraction, their richly symbolic settings, and their tragic endings tend to enforce the impression that Greene is a serious—perhaps even a profound—laborer in the fields of spiritual allegory. Yet to read these books in sequence is to become increasingly aware of the overly manipulated characters, the windy rhetoric, the author's glib misreading of the human heart. There are so many immense abstractions planted so closely together here that few of them have room to grow into life; but then it would be virtually impossible for *any* story to bear the weight of meaning that Greene seeks to impose on these tales. All four books, furthermore, are informed not only by the extreme notion—as expressed in the Charles Péguy quotation that Greene used as an epigraph to ***The Heart of the Matter***—that "[t]he sinner is at the heart of Christianity," but also by Greene's even more extreme corollary that the greater one's sins are, the closer one is to God, and the more likely one is to be a saint. While this may sound like clever theology, in practice it's simply offensive: if we are to believe such things, then how are we to feel about Hitler? In this and other such pronouncements by Greene, one hears the voice not of a serious moral philosopher but of the melodramatist, the author of thrillers out for sheer effect.

Elliott Malamet (essay date Winter 1991)

SOURCE: "Graham Greene and the Hounds of *Brighton Rock,*" in *Modern Fiction Studies,* Vol. 37, No. 4, Winter, 1991, pp. 689-703.

[*In the following essay, Malamet discusses elements of detection, pursuit, and evasion in* Brighton Rock. *Contrary to critical interpretations that emphasis the conflict between Ida and Pinkie, Malamet contends that "the metaphysical hunt is the more fundamental tension for Pinkie, and it is centered around his connection to the past, and his relationship with Rose Wilson and the invisible hand of God."*]

The narrative of Graham Greene's ***Brighton Rock*** gains force through the presentation of two conflicting impulses continually at war with one another. The text describes not only the literal pursuit of Hale, and then the hunt for Pinkie, but also abounds with the metaphoric terminology of detection, containment, and capture, from Rose's yearning to seal Pinkie's words on a recording to the snapshot of an unaware Spicer that hangs outside a photographer's kiosk for all the world to peruse. Yet concurrent with these attempts by characters to "pin down" one another, are the dark pockets of incomprehensibility that stubbornly thwart and even mock human perception. Pinkie best exemplifies this enigma: "You couldn't tell if he was scared; his young ancient poker-face told nothing." Determined to foil any surveillance of his inner being, he has "an air of removing his thoughts, like heavy bales and stacking them inside, turning the key on all the world." He utterly rejects any attempt to categorize or define him; when he is criticized by a former member of his gang, he aligns himself with Christ as the paradigm of the misunderstood figure prone to the subjective fancies of others: "The picture Cubitt drew had got nothing to do with him: it was like the pictures men drew of Christ, the image of their own sentimentality. Cubitt couldn't know." Although the limited accessibility of Pinkie's inner self to outsiders may be attributable to the notion formulated by Terry Eagleton that he and Rose "belong to a metaphysical elite," it is also true that Ida Arnold, whom no one might accuse of an alienating religious philosophy, is as hard to pierce as the darkest Jansenist: "Her large clear eyes . . . told nothing, gave away no secrets. Camaraderie, good nature, cheeriness fell like shutters before a plate-glass window. You could only guess at the goods behind . . . ."

The tension in the novel between detection and evasion, the vast emotional spaces separating the characters and the fiercely dogged pursuit intended to annihilate that gap, centers around Pinkie. Perhaps because of his very reticence, he does not lack for pursuers; he is the magnet for various kinds of detection, and nearly everyone and everything in the novel eventually comes to hunt him. Critical studies of the novel have long focused on the philosophical opposition between Ida and Pinkie, but in the following I argue that Ida is but one in a series of "hounds"—Colleoni, the police, his childhood, Rose, God—each representing a different threat to Pinkie. Yet for all of his pursuers, and despite the novel's constant emphasis on the use of messages, photographs, recordings, signs, witnesses—all forms of tracing an individual—Pinkie emerges as profoundly indecipherable.

One of the central ironies in ***Brighton Rock*** is that although Pinkie is constantly watched or hunted by these antagonists, Greene seldom places him in a position of physical danger or of needing to escape an actual threat. Despite a few instances of actual pursuit—Colleoni's men tracking Pinkie after the racetrack incident or the race at the end of the novel to stop the killing of Rose—much of the action, from a strictly conventional point of view, is rather static. The characters all know where they can find one another; in fact, Pinkie is adamant that he will never leave Brighton:

> He stared straight out towards France, an unknown land. At his back beyond the Cosmopolitan, Old Steyne, the Lewes Road, stood the downs, villages, cattle round the dewponds, another unknown land. This was his territory, the populous foreshore, a few thousand acres of houses. . . . It had been Kite's territory, it had been good enough for Kite, and when Kite had died in the waiting-room at St Pancras, it had been as if a father had died, leaving him an inheritance it was his duty never to leave for strange acres.

The repeated mention of such locales as The Cosmopolitan, Snow's, and Frank's Place enhances the presence of gang rivalry in ***Brighton Rock,*** as if this were a story of conflict over "turf."

The rigidity of boundary division pertains to various levels of meaning and is an obstacle to sophisticated detection. If Pinkie is ill at ease in the posh interiors of the Cosmopolitan Hotel, Ida is presented as being still more out of place with Catholic ideology. Intent on obliterating the notion of limited access that territorial division implies, she lies to gain entry into Rose's new home at Frank's Place, which she soon dominates: "She said, 'Come in, dear, and shut the door behind you,' as if it were *her* room." But her inability to persuade Rose to "cross over" to the world of Right and Wrong bespeaks frontiers that cannot be penetrated simply through willfulness. Their dispute is rife with the rhetoric of territory and space, both in a logistical and a metaphysical sense:

> "You ought to go home" [said Ida].
>
> Rose clenched her hands in defence of the brass bed, the ewer of dusty water:
> "This is home."
>
> "I know one thing you don't" [said Ida]. "I know the difference between Right and Wrong. They didn't teach you *that* at school."
>
> Rose didn't answer; the woman was quite right: the two words meant nothing to her. Their taste was extinguished by stronger foods—Good and Evil.

For Ida, the dynamic of Right and Wrong and the sanctity of Life in its most reductive form is the guiding philosophy of detection: "She didn't believe in heaven or hell, only in ghosts, ouija boards, tables which rapped and little inept voices speaking plaintively of flowers. Let Papists treat death with flippancy: life wasn't so important perhaps to them as what came after: but to her death was the end of everything . . . ." "The end of everything" means that Ida's pursuit is entirely contained within this side of the boundary between heaven and earth. Greene therefore uses Ida's penchant for questioning only as a superficial means of framing the issues of detection in ***Brighton Rock.*** Ida's quest for satisfaction extends to other areas besides death or justice; her determination is also unwavering when it comes to sexual desire and, as with the ouija board, her outlook is predetermined by what she wants: "She was shaken by a Bacchic and a bawdy mood. In every word either of them uttered she detected the one meaning." Given this singlemindedness, it is not surprising after Ida's terrifyingly casual references to an "eye for an eye," "fair play," and the thrill of the hunt, that she eventually loses sight of the point of origin of pursuit: "Poor old Fred—the name no longer conveyed any sense of grief or pathos. She couldn't remember anything much about him now . . . The hunt was what mattered."

Ida's loss of perspective regarding her first motives for detection is paralleled by Pinkie's bewilderment over the uncharted and unexpected domain towards which his crimes have led him: "It was as if he were being driven too far down a road he only wanted to travel a certain distance." The proliferation of crimes is such that the initial act turns out to be not the central deed of the novel but a preliminary to an ever spreading wave of events—this is an intrinsic element in the modern thriller. Raymond Chandler's *The Big Sleep* is the scene of no less than six murders, each one as it were overlapping with and diverting attention from the last; the sense of *growing* evil colors the overall tone of the narrative. Every movement forward—that is, each successive criminal act—leads the narrative further away from its original impetus. Hence the structure of this kind of story almost guarantees the loss of origins that Pinkie feels; as ***Brighton Rock*** progresses, Greene concentrates on Pinkie's recognition of that loss and his unspoken awareness that the way of return is closed:

> He felt that if he could concentrate enough, it would be possible to eliminate every sign of her . . . everything would be just the same as before . . . before he entered Snow's and felt under that cloth for a ticket which wasn't there and began the deception and shame. The whole origin of the thing was lost; he could hardly remember Hale as a person or his murder as a crime—it was all now him and her.

The irony of Hale, the man whose livelihood as Kolley Kibber is contingent on his leaving "signs" of himself that will allow for his identification—"It was his duty to-day to be spotted"—is that his end is traceless; he literally drops out of sight and is promptly cremated, his ashes becoming "part of the smoke nuisance over London." As later in ***The Power and the Glory*** and ***The Heart of the Matter,*** Greene unveils the action through the eyes of a peripheral character. Hale is but the outer edge of a thread that keeps unraveling until we reach the darkest core of the novel, and perhaps does not end even then, as Rose walks off to the "worst horror of all."

Any discussion of detection in ***Brighton Rock*** cannot be limited to the conflict between Ida and Pinkie. In some respects she is Pinkie's least worrisome foe, for she represents only one facet of pursuit, the detective who maintains the criterion of the conventional morality of "justice." She is echoed in this by the mobster, Colleoni; his desire to squeeze Pinkie out of business is grounded upon material considerations and the universe of the tangible. Greene's portrait of the racketeer associates him with Ida: "he looked as a man might look who owned the whole world, the whole visible world that is, the cash registers and policeman and prostitutes, Parliament and the laws which say 'this is Right and this is Wrong.'" The world view embodied by Ida and Colleoni harries Pinkie in the area of his physical well-being and challenges his twisted criminal pride. But the notion of Hale as a "beginning" that becomes lost, a vanished *starting place,* has implications for Pinkie that are far graver than Ida's doctrine of vengeance. As ***Brighton Rock*** develops, Greene draws on other levels of Pinkie's experience to construct a series of pursuers that hound him in a way that Ida cannot. This metaphysical hunt is the more fundamental tension for Pinkie, and it is centered around his connection to the past, and his relationship with Rose Wilson and the invisible hand of God.

Pinkie's recollections of childhood are terse and frightening:

> The Boy crossed over towards Old Steyne walking slowly . . . Every step was a retreat. He thought he had escaped for ever by the whole length of the parade, and now extreme poverty took him back . . . The Salvation Army Citadel marked with its battlements the very border of his home. He began to fear recognition and feel an obscure shame as if it were his native streets which had the right to forgive and not he to reproach them with the dreary and dingy past . . . His home was gone: a flat place among the rubble may have marked its hearth; the room at the bend of the stairs where the Saturday night exercise had taken place was now just air. He wondered

with horror whether it all had to be built again for him; it looked better as air.

His old neighborhood, like Hale, is a destroyed point of origin. The past is a dark hole; to detect innocence one must "go back a long way further . . . innocence was the ugly cry of birth." His childhood neighborhood duplicates that of Rose's, and the oppressive atmosphere of her parents' home in Nelson Place reminds Pinkie of the awful grip of the past that he has endeavored to outrun: "He looked with horror round the room: nobody could say he hadn't done right to get away from this, to commit any crime." The depiction of the ramshackle house metaphorically reinforces the diminished avenues open to him in his own life: "there wasn't really much choice of direction: there was only one door . . . ." The gutted remains of their roots leaves Pinkie and Rose with a "common geography" both physically and spiritually, and while Ida is most often put forward as Pinkie's chief nemesis, it is Rose who unwittingly bears down on him with the dread of the past: "He thought he had made his escape, and here his home was: back beside him, making claims." Pinkie's musings that she is "something which completed him" cannot remove the fact of his anxiety over her knowledge and his deeper fear of being possessed by her. Ida forces Pinkie to deal with the law, but Rose's pursuit of him drives Pinkie into confronting hideous corners of his self.

Rose's role as a saint or a "holy fool" has been well documented, but her function as a kind of detective is also consistently marked by Greene from early on in the novel. "'I always look at you close,'" she tells Pinkie, and then adds almost apologetically, "'the customer, I mean.'" Her acute and artless focus is as relentless as Ida's; she immediately suspects that it is Spicer, and not Hale, who has left one of the Kolley Kibber cards, a recognition for which Pinkie could hang:

> "Who was your friend?" she asked, peering into the darkness.
>
> "He don't matter," the Boy said.
>
> "I thought somehow—I couldn't see properly"
>
> "He don't matter," the Boy repeated. . . .
>
> "I've got a memory for faces."

Although Pinkie contemptuously taunts her—"you don't know anything"—he learns that underestimating her is his biggest mistake when she assures him that it was Spicer "'who left the card.'" Only her love for Pinkie compromises her detective skills; her sudden and infrequent displays of self-assertion are easily converted into "a blind willingness to be deceived." The intimidating spectre of Pinkie's life feels, at times, like a foreign country: "she stumbled hopelessly in an attempt to convey the sense she had of the territory in which he moved: a place of accidents and unexplained events, the stranger with a card, the fight on the course, the headlong fall." But although she will follow him anywhere, Rose is intuitive to at least some part of his emotional life; her "detection" of his virginity enrages him: "'You're my first,' she said. 'I'm glad.' When she said that, he began again to hate her." Gradually, Pinkie becomes keenly aware of her as an adversary: "He'd got to close her mouth one way or another."

When contrasted with Ida's "experienced eyes," Rose's innocence would seem a welcome respite for Pinkie, and their initial date is filled with his confident scorn: "'You're innocent. . . . You're green . . . .'" But the same qualities that are meant to illustrate Rose's goodness become for Pinkie akin to the closing door of a trap. He grimly interprets her love and devotion as but another mask covering possessiveness, and her naïveté puts him on guard more than any policeman can: "Could one ever be safe with someone who realized so little how she had got mixed up in things?" His life is defined by "a series of complicated tactical exercises," and he employs a multifaceted plan to stave off Rose's particular threat of curiosity, stifling domesticity, and seemingly unwitting ingenuousness. He delicately oscillates between a strategy of steely confrontation, intended to defuse preemptively any memories or questions that still linger in her mind about the fact that she saw Spicer leave Hale's card on the day of the murder, and an alternate path of appeasement should the former tactic fail. Their conversations can suddenly veer into a zone of dangerous insecurity for Pinkie, as when Rose unexpectedly decides to strike back at him:

> He said, "Talk, can't you? Say something."
>
> "You wanted to be quiet," she retorted with a sudden anger which took him by surprise. He hadn't thought her capable of that. "If I don't suit you," she said, "you can leave me alone. I didn't ask to come out . . . If I'm not grand enough—your car and all—"
>
> "Who said—"
>
> "Oh," she said, "I'm not that dumb. I've seen you looking at me. My hat—" It occurred to him suddenly that she might even get up and leave him, go back to Snow's with her secret for the first comer who questioned her kindly he had to conciliate her, they were walking out, he'd got to do the things expected of him.

Rose, despite her ostensible simplicity, tenaciously clings

to "the secret, the memory still lodged securely in her skull." Greene implies that the raw material of Rose's detective skills—her natural tendency to store past information—is actually caused by her very lack of worldliness; a paucity of social experience leads her to seek excitement and life from the dreams inside her head: "She had an immense store of trivial memories and when she wasn't living in the future she was living in the past"

The mixture in Rose of understanding and ignorance, self-deceiving innocence and shrewd perceptiveness, reflects a character who thinks and operates on different levels of awareness at different moments, and provides a difficult problem for Pinkie. His assessments of Rose contradict one another when they are added up and examined; it is as if he would like to think that she can be easily managed but finds himself stung into a grudging re-evaluation of her character because of something she will do or say, as when she urges him to make a recording of his voice and he rebukes her: "For the second time he came up against her sudden irresponsible resentment. She was soft, she was dumb, she was sentimental—and then suddenly she was dangerous. About a hat, about a gramophone record. 'All right,' she said, 'go away. You've never given me a thing.'" Pinkie feels assured of her simplicity and lack of imagination, but is astounded later on when he finds that not only has she figured out his link to the murder of Hale, but that she is a willing, if passive, accomplice to his acts:

> For a moment he was amazed. Then he laughed softly with infinite contempt and superiority at a world which used words like innocence. "Why," he said, "that's rich. You knew all along. You guessed. And I thought you were so green you hadn't lost the eggshell. And there you were"—he built her up in the mind's eye that day at Peacchaven, among the harvest wines at Snow's—"there you were, knowing."
>
> She didn't deny it: sitting there with her hands locked between her knees she accepted everything. "It's rich," he said. "Why, when you come to think of it—you're as bad as me."

Her undetectability is stressed by Greene just as strongly as is Pinkie's; the sense of her own enigmatic core is deeply expressed even in the midst of an apology for her outburst over the record: "'Something came over me,' she said, avoiding his eyes with an expression he couldn't read, obscure and despairing."

Thus Robert O. Evans's assertion that Rose is "far too innocent, doubtless that is why she is called Rose," does not account for enough complexity in her; Greene displays her "knowledge" in her rejection of Ida: "[Ida] could tell her nothing she didn't know about these [Good and Evil]—she knew by tests as clear as mathematics that Pinkie was evil—what did it matter in that case whether he was right or wrong?" At first, living in Frank's Place and adjusting to her married status is bewildering for her:

> . . . in the hall a ball of paper scuffled under her feet. She smoothed it out and read a pencilled message: "Lock your door. Have a good time." She didn't understand it: it might as well have been in code—she assumed it must have something to do with this foreign world where you sinned on a bed and people lost their lives suddenly and strange men hacked at your door and cursed you in the night.

But the significance of this new environment is that it entails a change in Rose; she is now privy to the adulterous secrets of Frank's wife—"'You won't tell anyone you saw us, dear, will you?'"—and she has begun to share, if only on a trivial scale, Pinkie's world of crime: "With her fingers on the lid of the soap-dish she waited—somebody was coming down the passage: it wasn't Judy and it wasn't Dallow—perhaps it was the man they called Frank. The footsteps passed; she lifted the lid and unwrapped the half-crown. She had stolen biscuits, she had never stolen money before. She expected to feel shame, but it didn't come—only again the odd swell of pride." Like one of Greene's secret agents Rose has "joined the other side now for ever. The half-crown was like a medal for services rendered. People coming back from seven-thirty Mass, people on the way to eight-thirty Matins—she watched them in their dark clothes like a spy." This is comic in the same way as Raven—the embittered young criminal of ***A Gun for Sale*** whom Greene calls "a first sketch for Pinkie" (***Ways of Escape***)—peeks at a shop window Jesus and interprets the crucifixion as a kind of gang war. The analogies in both cases seem humorously disproportionate, but one senses that Greene is only half joking, and that through her relationship with Pinkie, Rose has become a kind of outsider spying on "ordinary" lives: "And *she* stood now where Pinkie had stood—outside, looking in."

Pinkie decides that his only recourse to secure her absolute loyalty lies in his ability to "sidetrack her mind." Although he consistently returns to his position that Rose accepts "deception with such hopeless ease that he could feel a sort of tenderness for her stupidity," Greene reveals the underside of the dynamic with an image of finality at the moment when Pinkie realizes that he will have to marry her: "Some day he would be free again. He put out his hands towards her as if she were the detective with the cuffs . . . ." The handcuffs are a symbol in his mind of what he sees as Rose's unrelenting pressure to detect and possess him, a feeling which heightens just after they are married: "They walked a foot apart along the pavement. Her words scratched tentatively at the barrier like a bird's claws on a window-pane. He could feel her all the time trying to get at him: even her humility seemed to him a trap. The crude quick ceremony was a claim on him." His "furious disgust at the made bed," an unhappy symbol of the domestication of their relationship, turns to total fear at the unexpected thought that their alliance could produce a child: "He watched her with terror and disgust as if he were watching the ugly birth itself, the rivet of another life already pinning him down. . . ."

The sequence that charts Pinkie's hesitant and evasive path towards the wedding bed—interrupted by scenes of being refused accommodations at The Cosmopolitan, the recording of his horrifying message, buying sticks of Brighton rock under the pier, a trip to the movies—not only illustrates his dread of sexuality but prefigures the last third of the novel, which concentrates on how Pinkie's world closes around him in a tightening web. At the same time that Greene stresses the self-contained, hidden, and often undetectable nature of characters such as Pinkie, Rose, and Ida, and the distances and boundary divisions which separate them, he also integrates the reverse impulse into the plot and language of the novel by utilizing images of aggression that connote an enormous desire to catch and clamp down upon one's quarry. Seemingly random references to an owl, described as "swooping low . . . on furry and predatory wings," or the sight of "a mousetrap by a hole . . . [where] the bait had been stolen and the trap had snapped on nothing at all," are part of a deliberate imagistic pattern meant to convey the desperate sense of detection and pursuit that imbues the novel. Pinkie's surprised conclusion that he and Rose are somehow spiritual twins, that "there's not a pin to choose between us," is interestingly reflected in the careful matching of his feeling of being handcuffed with his own persistent and aggressive attack on her wrists, beginning with their first night out together:

> "You don't know anything," he said, with contempt in his nails.
>
> "Oh no," she protested. "I know a lot."
>
> The Boy grinned at her, "Not a thing," pinching the skin of her wrist until his nails nearly met. "You'd like me for your boy, eh? We'll keep company?"
>
> "Oh," she said, "I'd love it." Tears of pride and pain pricked behind her lids. "If you like doing that," she said, "go on."

Rose's uncomplaining submission to her pain and her enduring love for Pinkie allow for the plausibility of the piercing of her wrists as a mock crucifixion. Pinkie's efforts to exert his will over her reach a bizarre climax when Rose nearly commits suicide: "She put the gun up to her ear and put it down again with a feeling of sickness—it was a poor love that was afraid to die . . . She felt his will moving her hand—she could trust him."

Pinkie's relationship with her is but a small part of his overall desire for control: "His breast ached with the effort to enclose the whole world." But his ambitions to encircle the world are ironically countered by Ida, experienced by Pinkie as a clinging animal: "The Boy looked across the tea-room and the empty tables to where the woman sat. How she hung on. Like a ferret he'd seen on the Down, among the chalky holes, fastened to a hare's throat." Even a light-hearted citation by Prewitt, upon being disturbed by a noisy neighbor, to Polonius' spying and subsequent murder in *Hamlet,* is transformed by Greene into an allusive backdrop for Pinkie's anxiety about Ida's intrusion into his affairs:

> "How now? A rat?" Mr Prewitt quoted. The house shook as a heavy engine pulled out. "Polonius," Mr Prewitt explained.
>
> "Polony? What polony?"
>
> "No, No," Mr Prewitt said. "The rank intruding fool, I mean. In Hamlet."
>
> "Listen," the Boy said impatiently, "has a woman been round here asking questions?"

The most powerful example of the kind of claustrophobic pressure that Pinkie feels is brought out at the conclusion of ***Brighton Rock***; as he drives in a rainstorm with the hope that soon he will be rid of Rose, the image of predatory wings is repeated, this time to haunt him with the active, almost nightmarish intervention of God's presence:

> An enormous emotion beat on him; it was like something trying to get in; the presence of gigantic wings against the glass. Dona nobis pacem. He withstood it. . . . If the glass broke, if the beast—whatever it was—got in, God knows what it would do. He had a sense of huge havoc—the confession, the penance and the sacrament—and awful distraction, and he drove blind into the rain.

This is but one of many places in Greene's work where a tension is articulated between two forces separated by some form of wall of division. At times this divider acts like a funhouse mirror, creating a grotesquely altered perspective that causes one side to view the other improperly, as Greene notes about the novelist Frederic Rolfe and those who misperceived him: "Mr Pirie-Gordon and the partners of

Chatto and Windus beckon and speak like figures on the other side of a distorting glass pane. They have quite a different reality, much thinner reality, they are not concerned with eternal damnation. And their memories of Rolfe are puzzled, a little amused, a little exasperated . . . ." (***Collected Essays***).

Often there is a great force that strains against this door; in ***Journey Without Maps,*** Greene writes of the "earliest dream" he can remember, a dream "of something outside that has got to come in . . . a force exerted on a door, an influence that drifted after me upstairs and pressed against windows." The presence willing itself to break through the glass—this is the God as Intruder that constitutes Pinkie's terrifying moment. But the barrier of the window is one that Rose also encounters, and it relates to a deep wish which she feels may never be fulfilled, if what she suspects regarding Pinkie's final intentions turns out to be true:

> She put a hand on him and felt his instinctive withdrawal: for a moment she was shaken by an awful doubt—if this was the darkest nightmare of all, if he didn't love her, as the woman said . . . The buses passed them going downhill to the town: little bright domestic cages in which people sat with baskets and books: a child pressed her face to the glass and for a moment at a traffic light they were so close the face might have been held against her breast.

The child inside this cage of domesticity comes within arm's length of Rose, but it is a world in a moving bus, soon to be gone. After Pinkie pulls the car to the side of a cliff, he spots a light "behind a stained-glass door," with its clear intimation of a church. Greene brings to life the lure of the unknown "other," and also the intangible struggle between detection and hiddenness, through the visceral image of something or someone pushing against glass, seeking to find an elusive reality on the other side.

Thus the sense of being hunted rears up and haunts Pinkie at every turn; the most insidious part of the feeling is the fear of not knowing precisely *who* is following him, and also a lack of assurance about when the chase will end and what its ultimate consequences will be: "Not a single false step, but every step conditioned by a pressure he couldn't even place: a woman asking questions, messages on the telephone scaring Spicer. He thought: when I've married the girl, will it stop then? Where else can it drive me, and with a twitch of the mouth, he wondered—what worse?" The suggestion that the pressure Pinkie feels ultimately derives from something other than an earthly source is one that Greene constantly circles around. He punctuates the narrative in several places with the picture of an old man stooping, searching among stones for food or clothing, and then translates the image of the old man into a metaphor for the divine detective: "It was almost dark along the beach; the edge of sea was like a line of writing in whitewash: big sprawling letters. They meant nothing at this distance. A shadow stooped with infinite patience and disinterred some relic from the shingle."

In his well-known essay on François Mauriac, Greene analyzes the monitoring of a character by God: "The ungainly clergyman [in a Trollope novel] picking his back-booted way through the mud, handling so awkwardly his umbrella, speaking of his miserable income and stumbling through a proposal of marriage, exists in a way that Mrs Woolf's Mr Ramsay never does, because we are aware that he exists not only to the woman he is addressing but also in a God's eye" (***Collected Essays***). This is a point Greene returns to repeatedly in his writing: man is made visible, given form, by the detection and even prosecution of heaven. Writing of Somerset Maugham, Greene observers: "He cannot believe in a God who punishes and he cannot therefore believe in the importance of a human action . . . Rob human beings of their heavenly and their infernal importance, and you rob your characters of their individuality" (***Collected Essays***). ***Brighton Rock*** goes one step further than Trollope's benign heavenly observer; the passage depicting Pinkie's drive through the rain strikingly recalls "The Hound of Heaven," a poem which Greene held in high esteem, and Pinkie's rush to avoid God's grace echoes [Francis] Thompson's opening lines: "I fled Him down the nights and down the days; / I fled Him, down the arches of the years; / I fled Him, down the labyrinthine ways / Of my own mind . . . ." The God who confronts the narrator at the end of the Thompson poem assumes a knowing paternal air: "All which I took from thee I did but take, / Not for thy harms, / But just that thou might'st seek it in My arms." No such reconciliation is allowed in ***Brighton Rock***; in a novel where the images of containment and capture are manifold, it appears that there is something within Pinkie that is even more overwhelming than the pursuit of God: "he couldn't experience contrition—the ribs of his body were like steel bands which held him down to eternal unrepentance."

In the novel's final chapters it seems as if God chases Pinkie, but in an earlier scene, after he escapes the knifing at the racetrack, it is Pinkie who years, "with a faint nostalgia for the tiny dark confessional box, the priest's voice, and the people waiting under the statue, before the bright lights burning down in the pink glasses, to be made safe from eternal pain." He eludes Colleoni's men by ducking into an empty garage, that actually is a kind of "potting shed." Greene's later play of the same name suggests that the potting shed is a place of potential rebirth, a setting which is connected to the saving and even miraculous power of God. But the other aspects of the potting shed—its darkness, its status as a place of refuge, the whole connotation of something buried beneath the earth—calls attention to the themes of crime and hiddenness in ***Brighton Rock,*** and the idea of a detective's quest is further magnified by the "marks" left by the owner of the shed:

> Whoever the owner was, he had come a long way to land up here. The pram-wheelbarrow was covered with labels—the marks of innumerable train journeys—Doncaster, Lichfield, Clacton (that must have been a summer holiday), Ipswich, Northampton—roughly torn off for the next journey they left, in the litter which remained, an unmistakable trail. And this, the small villa under the racecourse, was the best finish he could manage.

The description of the trial that eventually ends, foreshadows Pinkie's own trek; the only possible "detour," that of repentance, is rejected in light of his "dim desire for annihilation . . . the vast superiority of vacancy." Pinkie's demise is deliberately constructed to parallel the path of Hale that begins the novel. Hale concentrates on being spotted, only to be reduced to "indistinguishable grey ash"; Pinkie, in turn, purposefully leaves clues of his whereabouts as part of his alibi: "He planted his information pedantically, as carefully as he had had them lay Fred's cards along the route—for later use." He usurps Hale's role as a "distributor of signs," as he consistently demonstrates in his relationship with Rose; not only does he imprint a scalding outburst of hate in the recording booth, but he converts a message of love from her into a tool of power: "He held it up into the grey light and read—with difficulty. 'I love you, Pinkie. I don't care what you do. I love you for ever. You've been good to me. Wherever you go, I'll go too.' . . . He crumbled it in his fist: a dustbin stood outside a fishmonger's—then he held his hand. An obscure sense told him you never knew—it might prove useful one day." He uses the note to prod her into giving up her life—"He took his hand out of his pocket and laid on his knee a paper she recognized. He said, 'You mean that—don't you?'"—and attempts to complete the process of elimination through yet another scrap of paper that will explain the "suicide": "She said, 'I wrote what you wanted.'" Pinkie's alibi for these events is contingent on a carefully fabricated trail: "The Boy had left too many signs behind him—the message at the shooting-range, at the car-park: he wanted to be followed in good time, in his own time." Given his struggle to control and manipulate the use of signs, Pinkie's end is as ironic as Kolley Kibber's, as though once again all the traces of a life simply vanish into a blank void:

> He looked half his size, doubled up in appalling agony: it was as if the flames had literally got him and he shrank—shrank into a schoolboy flying in panic and pain, scrambling over a fence, running on.
>
> "Stop him," Dallow cried: it wasn't any good: he was at the edge, he was over: they couldn't even hear a splash. It was as if he'd been withdrawn suddenly by a hand out of any existence—past or present, whipped away into zero—nothing.

The trail of ***Brighton Rock*** ends with Pinkie's disappearance from the map, and for all the clues and signs that the novel discusses, Pinkie is not so much "detected" as chased out of the world; he remains an unexplainable mystery, an unsolved case. As Greene indicates, Pinkie's end is a "zero," a circular line that revolves round and round with no discernible start or finish. Pinkie is the zero or the undetectable life; despite the sociological chronicle of a loveless and poverty filled childhood, Pinkie's origins cannot fully account for him and, moreover, the theological ambivalence implicit in the priest's advice to Rose that one cannot conceive of the "strangeness of the mercy of God," thereby implying the possibility of Pinkie's salvation, means that in a Greeneian universe we cannot be sure of Pinkie's final status either. The novel contrasts Ida's smug satisfaction with the outcome—"'He's not on my conscience anyway'"—with the priest's sense that the verdict may not have been sealed on Pinkie: "'But we must hope,' he said mechanically, 'hope and pray.'" But neither Ida's inclination to close the case nor the dim spark of grace that the priest believes may yet be available can help illuminate the darkness that shrouded Pinkie in "this life." In a discussion of the postmodernist novel that is suggestive of the problem of Pinkie, Michael Holquist surmises that "if, in the detective story, death must be solved, in the new metaphysical detective story it is *life* which must be solved." At best, Pinkie's pursuers—God included—are only able to partially detect him, and Greene emphasizes the corruption of a sign as Rose walks off to the horror of Pinkie's recording, as though with all the goodwill in heaven, Pinkie has the last word on knowability here on earth.

Martin Lebowitz (review date Autumn 1991)

SOURCE: "The Uncynical Disillusion of Graham Greene," in *The Southern Review,* Vol. 27, No. 4, Autumn, 1991, pp. 946-48.

[*In the following review, Lebowitz discusses Greene's moral and religious vision in* The Last Word and Other Stories.]

Many years ago, T. S. Eliot remarked that wisdom consists largely of uncynical disillusion and that uncynical disillusion is essential to religious understanding as well. For Graham Greene, as for Eliot, detective fiction is a parable or paradigm of thoughtful disillusion. In the stories included in this thin volume, reflective of this disillusion is the tone of affective neutrality or realism that has become Greene's trademark. It is distinct from both pessimism and optimism and evokes a sense of reality which is causal and definitive rather than idealistic and emotional. Greene's realism is aseptic in that it is free of both preconceptions and strict implications. Of course, one might reply that objectivity is itself a hypothetical ideal that a writer may approach perhaps but never actually achieve. Nevertheless, in a manner reminiscent of Santayana in *The Realm of Matter,* Greene appears to champion the objective ideal by identifying God with a type of intellectual perception of matter. Indeed, one might conclude that God in Greene's vision provides an ideal limit of perception rather than a practicable goal.

The best story in the collection is the first and title story. It portrays a deranged and impecunious old man dying a slow, agonizing death in a squalid room in the mordant and moribund world of the future; unified despotically, this world has transcended nationalism and nationalities and is marked above all by squalor, anhedonia, and a crippled and ruthless purposiveness. The old man is the last pope in a society destitute of religion and indeed of any ethos, spirit, or mystique. The temporal ruler of this society mercifully executes the old man, ending his misery, and the reader is left with an intimation that this society, a sort of apotheosis of impersonality, is expected to enjoy the same fate. But what is one to make of the story's concluding question: "is it possible that what this man believed may be true?" The contrast between Greene's professed beliefs in Catholicism and the "objectivity" or tenor of his literary technique here and in his other work may make the question of true belief insoluble.

Another characteristic of Graham Greene—a result of the intensity of his moral preoccupation or soul-searching—is his pervasive ambiguity, reminiscent in some ways of Henry James. Thus the detective story, one of which is included in this book, is a paradigm of ambiguity, just as, in Kant, the Thing-in-Itself is an archetypal mystery. **"A Branch of the Service"** illustrates this ambiguity when a man patronizes a variety of restaurants for the ostensible purpose of evaluating for a magazine their food, service, and facilities, while he is more seriously concerned in observing some diners exchange incriminating information. The moral irony here is self-evident.

Religious consciousness as a subject for soul-searching is an identifying theme of Greene's work. Thus, in an **"Appointment with the General,"** the revolutionary mystique of Latin American countries has an ambiguous relation to politics as such since, more so than in developed countries, revolution there consists above all in the pursuit of power. Thus an ambiguity in this story is that the General dreams obsessively of death, a symbol not simply of his own demise but of the vacuity and hopelessness of his endeavors for his country. That his interviewer in the story is an attractive French woman might suggest a moral contrast between the French Revolution and revolution in Latin America.

In a brilliant story called **"The Lottery Ticket,"** Greene describes with an anthropologist's perception a small, tropical, almost inaccessible state in Mexico—primitive, backward, and violent, although a "democracy," in its poverty and in its politics. This town epitomizes the human condition in all its desperation and hopelessness. The story's hero has bought a lottery ticket in Vera Cruz and when he wins the lottery, he wants to donate the money to improving the condition of life in the destitute, benighted region. The lottery ticket becomes a symbol of the capitalism that has been repudiated there. Greene seems to be saying that all societies create symbols of indeterminacy that they may or may not identify with religion; but their human or psychological significance is religious nonetheless. Thus capitalism itself may be viewed as a transcendental myth subordinating human nature to a higher reality whose workings are, in the end, inscrutable. The indeterminacy of existence is a metaphysical datum from which philosophy, politics, ethics, religion, and even science necessarily derive.

The dismal squalor that comprises the milieu in which Graham Greene's fiction usually occurs is redeemable, if at all, only by religion, whether religion is viewed as literal truth or as mythic and poetic moral vision. I would suggest that, of these two views, the first is facile and uninspiring, while the second is Promethean and heroic.

Trevor L. Williams (essay date Spring 1992)

SOURCE: "History Over Theology: The Case for Pinkie in Greene's *Brighton Rock,*" in *Studies in the Novel,* Vol. 24, No. 1, Spring, 1992, pp. 67-77.

[*In the following essay, Williams draws attention to the sociopolitical context and value of* Brighton Rock. *According to Williams,* "Brighton Rock *remains one of Greene's most ambitious achievements for its ability to encapsulate an historical movement, namely the collapse of the British economic power in the 1930s with the consequent paralysis and the poverty that crept like a cancer across the normal social boundaries."*]

Brighton Rock (1938), reprinted countless times, remains one of Greene's most intriguing novels, eminently teachable in the classroom, mixing as it does the detective novel genre with adolescent sex hang-ups, and complicated by the claims of religion. It is also a period piece, evoking with the starkness of a black and white movie the feel of the 1930s in England, a country already in decline even before World War

Two finally pushed it off the center of the world stage. Part of Greene's attraction as a writer always is that, having been in the right place at the right time, he is then able to chronicle with documentary fidelity the fall of some corrupt regime or other. ***Brighton Rock,*** a consistently symbolic and allegorical novel, does not, despite its fidelity to the "lower" Brighton of the time, chronicle the fall of *England* precisely, but seems (with the benefit of fifty years' hindsight) to hint at the much larger literal and figurative fall that the world war eventually brought. At the same time, the heavy emphasis on the "Roman" religion, criticized even, or especially, by Catholic critics over the years, now seems anachronistic, as much imposed from above as the obligatory unsullied working-class hero in works of socialist realism of the same period. I hope in this essay to direct attention away from the dated moral abstractions (is anyone seriously interested in an ethical league table where Good comes in first and Right a distant second, and where Evil is somehow preferable to "mere" Wrong?) and to concentrate more on the sociopolitical value of the novel. Greene's catholicism, too, rather than being taken at its own valuation, can be inserted into a sociopolitical context.

A young man who joins the Communist Party for four weeks in 1926 and later the same year is received into the Roman Catholic Church is clearly in need of a belief-system. These initiations were also ways of declaring contempt for an upper-class establishment (Tory and Anglican) which between 1914 and 1918 had sent a generation into the trenches of the Western Front and which now presided benignly over an economically stagnant Britain. The General Strike of 1926 was the nearest Britain came to a violent revolution in this century and the strike only failed because of the irresolution of trade union leaders (nor should it be forgotten, here, that many of Greene's fellow students at Oxford helped keep the trains running, thus playing their own minor part in preserving the political *status quo*). With the failure of social democracy to seize the moment of revolution, the Communist Party was, and remained throughout the 1920s, a natural haven for a few sensitive upper middle-class students alienated by the incompetence and corruption of their (own) ruling class. (Philby, Burgess, Maclean, Blunt: the names chronicle the history of spying in Britain.) To join the Communist Party or to spy for the forerunners of the K.G.B. was not, I would assert, an act of solidarity with the Soviet system, but a calculated attack designed to undermine a ruling class which had betrayed or was continuing to betray, through economic mismanagement and political indifference, the interests of the country as a whole. Greene himself is quite specific about this in ***The Human Factor*** (1978) where Castle, the Communist spy, is "innocent" (committed as he is to love, human rights, and the well-being of his own country) when compared to the morally loathsome representatives in the novel of the country's ruling class, for whom the "foreign country" to be subjugated is the democratic Britain outside the establishment enclave of London clubs and country houses. It was logical then that Greene would be drawn to so "principled" a spy as Philby, a voluntary exile in Moscow as much as Greene himself in Antibes.

In the English-speaking countries, to join the Communist Party, in 1926 as much as in 1990, is to marginalize oneself from the mainstream of party political life, though often the ideas generated by the Party later become, with circulation, received opinion in the middle ground of politics. Similarly, to join the Catholic Church in 1926 was also an act of marginalization, if socially safer and demographically more comforting. If in 1960 the religion of the president of the United States, a country where Catholics were a larger percentage of the total population than in England, was an issue, it is easy to imagine the kind of shadow status that Catholicism occupied in Britain in 1926. For the Catholic convert here was a war to wage. And, as everyone knows, Greene regularly inserts a Catholic character or a discussion of Catholic doctrine into his fiction, as if, it sometimes seems, to demonstrate his fidelity to a "party line" (of his own making). In a novel like ***The Power and the Glory*** (1940) the demonstration is integral to the theme and so is not a distraction. In ***Brighton Rock,*** however, where Pinkie and Rose are powerful characters, but extremely marginalized socially, the catholicism distorts, gets in the way of, what frequently seems like a socialist critique struggling to emerge. It's as if Greene, committed emotionally to both "-isms," catholicism and socialism, could not decide which theology to work with in describing the fallen world of Brighton.

So, while ***Brighton Rock,*** like many Greene novels, has the virtue of verisimilitude (in this instance to the "feel" of the 1930s British seaside resort, not much changed in its basic structure to this day), the novel does not quite feel right, it does not quite "come off." Perhaps (and T. S. Eliot's famous "objective correlative" explanation for Hamlet's "failure" will help here) Greene was not in total control of his material. We recall that Milton set out to justify the ways of God to man, but instead produced a Satan whom all succeeding generations found sympathetic. Greene creates a Satan in Pinkie whom he tries to condemn through repellent descriptions, but while Milton's Satan became sympathetic *despite* the poet's best efforts to turn the party line against him, Greene actively intervenes on Satan's behalf by suggesting constantly that Pinkie's dedication to evil is superior to Ida's obsession with right and wrong. The intervention fails (and accounts for one of the weaknesses in ***Brighton Rock***), because, I would suspect, few readers of the novel have ever found it possible to sympathize with Pinkie merely on the ground that he was a "Roman" and therefore in touch with something eternal called Evil. Rather, the average reader might well be prepared to accord Pinkie some sympathy on the ground that he was socially deprived and thus as a character to be subsumed under the more mundane problems of the here and now represented by the "Right and Wrong" position in the novel incarnated in Ida. Just as, following the marxist view that social being determines consciousness, Hamlet cannot escape being a product of a corrupt court but must somehow escape that contamination and rise heroically above and beyond the court, so Pinkie is trapped in a contradiction of his author's making. While Pinkie's consciousness is "produced" in the slums of Brighton, his author would have us believe that he escapes that social determination and is derived, uncontaminated by the merely social, from some theological infinity of pain.

Of course, this notion of the absolution of Evil is not unique to Greene amongst twentieth century authors, nor is it necessarily the product of a "Roman" view of the universe. It raises its head in Conrad, can be seen in the character Loerke in Lawrence's *Women in Love,* and is a major theme in early T. S. Eliot. Early in *Heart of Darkness* Marlow rejects the moral flabbiness of the Manager and other lesser mortals than Kurtz, preferring the latter's single-minded dedication to Evil, invoked, vaguely, in "the horror, the horror." Eliot picks up this distinction in "The Hollow Men" whose epigraph recalls this mysterious description of Kurtz's death. This fascination with "the horror" is really a theological evasion, an attempt to mystify what is totally explicable by the action of men pursuing, in all instances, goals which are economic even before they are political. The evasion is perpetuated even in a brilliant movie such as *Apocalypse Now,* where the madness committed on behalf (ultimately) of American *economic* goals is accounted for by the "evil" of a single individual. Ironically, Greene himself clearly saw this evasion in Vietnam, and exposed it in ***The Quiet American*** (1955), which thirty years after its publication became required reading as Americans began to analyze the horror they had just lived through.

In ***Brighton Rock,*** however, Greene's determination to impose a Catholic framework on the fallen world of Brighton proves a distraction, even though Greene is careful to delineate the social rottenness and even to draw attention to the almost universal poverty, both material and spiritual. Unfortunately, this fallen world is too easily ascribed to the weakness of Protestantism as a religion, simplistically leaving only the "Roman" faith as the superior vehicle for dealing with the eternal verities. Even then Greene gets it wrong, since his suggestion that the trials and tribulations of Pinkie and Rose will be rewarded in the next world is no more nor less than what Protestant divines were holding out to the working class throughout the nineteenth century. Poor but honest, the oppressed classes could rest happy in their confident inheritance of the Kingdom of Heaven. Greene further sentimentalizes Pinkie's evil by suggesting at the very end that Rose may already be carrying Pinkie's child within her, which will somehow compensate for the final horror when she puts on the record and listens to Pinkie's words of "love."

Despite the distortions caused by the imposed Catholic framework, ***Brighton Rock*** remains one of Greene's most ambitious achievements for its ability to encapsulate an historical moment, namely the collapse of British economic power in the 1930s with the consequent paralysis and the poverty that crept like a cancer across the normal social boundaries (Mr. Prewitt the lawyer is a brilliant illustration of the latter). Greene's ability to analyze social conditions through the symbolism of fiction contrasts starkly with some of the myths erected by historians about that phase of British history. The summer of 1990 saw the patriotic 50th anniversary celebrations of the "Dunkirk spirit" and the heroism of "the Few." Though the heroism was genuine, the truth, as Clive Ponting has heretically pointed out, was that the wartime cabinet, meeting on August 22, 1940, had to decide whether to sue for peace with the Nazis or whether to pay the price demanded by the United States for its economic co-operation, namely liquidation of Britains's imperial assets. In May/June 1940 two views of the way ahead dominated debate in the cabinet: "peace now" urged by the foreign secretary, Lord Halifax, a leading appeaser, or "let's wait" (to see if Hitler will give us better terms, the view of the new prime minister, Churchill). Clearly, these are not differences of philosophy. Either way, the English ruling class was prepared to preside over a fallen country, and Greene, with his connections to the intelligence community, would have ample cause to know that the country had been betrayed over many decades by its own upper class.

While Greene throughout his career carefully singles out various ruling elites as the source of betrayal, this, despite his consistently leftish philosophical stance, does not make him a socialist. He clearly shows sympathy for the lower class characters in ***Brighton Rock*** caught in a hell not, mostly, of their own making, and gratuitously introduces two upper-class "hearties" who, sizing up Rose's sexual potential, mockingly reify her in the pub, yet no characters, other than Rose, no matter what their class, escape Greene's criticism. An interesting example of this generalized criticism of "fallen England" occurs at the beginning of Part 4, where the people who pour into Brighton for the Bank Holiday are described as a "migration of insects." Bosch-like in its detail, the panorama includes a blind man's band (whom Pinkie, unaware they are blind, will later push roughly off the kerb) and some rich hockeying schoolgirls well above the "plebeian procession, those whom the buses wouldn't hold, plodding up the down, kicking up the dust, eating buns out of paper bags . . . It was as if the whole road moved upwards like an underground staircase in the dusty sunlight." The vision, in its entirety, is truly "underground." It also includes, remarkably, a disproportionately long description (ten lines in the Penguin text) of a "negro" sitting on a bench in the "Pavilion garden" smoking a cigar. He has "great teeth gleaming like an advertisement" and "cushiony lips," and the children playing nearby back away from him "uneasily." Why does Greene, drawing a composite picture of "Brighton," allow so much space to this black person, especially when blacks in the 1930s formed such a minuscule part of the total British population (let alone of Brighton's)? Why indeed does Greene reproduce the typically "white" view of a black person's physiognomy? I can only speculate that the narrative's "political unconscious" has tapped into the racist fear and loathing of the foreign, of the outsider who would intrude and gnaw away at the nation's entrails, threatening the livelihood of the nation's youth, a fear not specific to England, of course. This non-specific, all-inclusive (Catholic?), criticism of the fallen Protestant world is, or would be, a weakness insofar as it purports to represent Greene's own imposed Catholic ideology (and of course Greene's total oeuvre is ample evidence of the frequent indivisibility of Greene and the omniscient narrator), but insofar as ***Brighton Rock*** reflects the "condition of England" the inclusion of this xenophobic undercurrent is realistic (and one that will not easily go away from English life).

Interestingly, in the Collected Edition of ***Brighton Rock*** (1970) Greene seems to have regretted this xenophobic note, even to the extent of silently omitting several anti-semitic references glaringly there in the first edition (and chronicled in the footnote that follows). Clearly these are post-Holocaust emendations, yet the anti-semitic references to rich Jews are an essential, even if racist, echo of 1930s history and their omission weakens slightly the force of Greene's social critique. The xenophobia emerges also in the character of Colleoni, the smooth man building a monopoly on organized crime in Brighton, a Jew in the first edition but an *Italian* gangster after 1970. Colleoni belongs to a well-established literary tradition, especially in spy fiction, of the suspicious foreigner (even more suspicious if Jewish) who does indeed turn out to be a spy. Whenever Pinkie sees or thinks of Colleoni it is as if over an immense divide of ownership. As Colleoni pads through the Metropole or relaxes in a limousine, he forcibly reminds Pinkie how much he is deprived of ownership in his own city. This is especially the case when Pinkie himself tries to book a room in the Metropole on his wedding night. He is refused a room purely on class grounds.

I want now to shift the argument to the question of ownership as such, for it is here that one can make the case (the case that Greene tries to make on purely theological grounds) that Pinkie and Rose are indeed superior to the other characters. To begin with Colleoni:

> His old Italian face showed few emotions but a mild amusement, a mild friendliness; but suddenly sitting there in the rich Victorian room, with the gold lighter in his pocket and the cigar-case on his lap, he looked as a man might look who owned the whole world, the whole visible world that is, the cash registers and policemen and prostitutes. Parliament and the laws which say "this is Right and this is Wrong."

Even though Colleoni may own only the "visible world," this still remains a powerful vision of complacent ownership, the assertion of a universalized (again the word "Catholic" comes punningly to mind) power to control every facet of political, economic and social life. Pinkie will notice only the outward manifestation of this ownership (on his wedding day he remembers a "gold cigarette case"), the fetishized commodity, but the reader is probably more aware of the total overall control that Colleoni exercises, Colleoni here being no longer the small-time gangster but the representative figure for a rapacious owning class. The novel as a whole demonstrates that Colleoni uses violence quickly, surgically and treacherously, but normally Colleoni is "respectable" and respected within the Metropole Hotel, that emblem of effortless wealth and power. For much of the novel he is barely visible, yet his control is pervasive. This above all is the triumph of Greene's realism, for surely this is indeed most people's experience of the way power works in a society: very rarely does a democratic society have to resort to violence to ensure the stability of the *status quo* but if it must it will.

But how *is* such power exercised non-violently? Or, the same question: how do people consent to have such power exercised over them? One answer (the easy one, it now seems in retrospect) was given by Althusser two decades ago, when he coined the term "ideological state apparatuses." He meant the institutions of government, education, the churches, the military, and the large corporations (especially media corporations)—all these institutions may countenance change (that is, they are not irredeemably conservative—but they will ensure that they maintain control over the *content* of change. Where radical divestiture of power occurs (as in Gorbachev's Soviet Union) uncertainty, to put it mildly, occurs. A world governed by "Colleoni" cannot brook uncertainty. But the search for a theoretical answer to the problem of "consent" must take us further back than Althusser, to the Marcuse of *One-Dimensional Man,* which remains, a generation later, one of the most brilliant analyses of, and attacks upon, the thought-system underlying both advanced capitalism and Soviet communism. Marcuse there refers to "the closing of the universe of discourse," the tendency in advanced industrial society for only one view of the world to dominate, all others, though "allowed," being relegated to the margins. Thus a massive "consensus" of the center will effectively close off meaningful debate about radical alternatives, the latter being dismissed as "utopian," always forever unattainable. The "consensus" then becomes the common sense way of viewing reality and is reinforced daily in the way Althusser described. (Gorbachev's Russia is, again, a dire warning of what happens when the consensus is allowed to break down—and, significantly, no Western country has yet shown that kind of appetite for democratic dismantling of its constituent parts.) And how does this relate to Greene? I would argue that Ida (or rather "Ida") represents this massive assertion of common sense, of the one-dimensional mentality, the closing of the universe of discourse. Ida's ouija board comes up with the letters "FRESUICILLEYE" and, like Ida, we can extract meaning to suit our own purposes, so that this "one-eyed" view becomes a form of moral and intellectual "suicide" in which "freedom" is threatened.

To put it allegorically, "Colleoni" needs "Ida" to help keep "Pinkie" and "Rose," the lowest segment of the non-owning classes, marginalized. Together, though in separate spheres, Colleoni and Ida seek to exclude Pinkie (and, inevitably, Rose) from ownership of their own lives, their souls even. Ida would take away the last vestige of choice from Rose, reducing her to an animal passivity. Ida represents that vast petty bourgeoisie and respectable working class who by their silence give consent to actions carried out, nominally, on their behalf and thus give legitimacy to this "fallen world." Greene remembers to include them: they are the London girls whom Hale tries to pick up, they are the waitresses at Snow's, the desk clerk at the Metropole, and, memorably, they are the Mr. Prewitts.

If Pinkie deserves sympathy it's not on the Greene ground that he belongs to a superior religion and may yet, despite his evil, be saved; it's because he comes from the same destitute background as Rose and carries it as a "visible scar," a place where love is suffocated "among the lavatory smells." Thus Greene does emphasize Pinkie's social being (even if he weakens this insight constantly by referring to Pinkie's Satanic origins). Since both Pinkie and Rose come from the same social background, though one is "evil" and the other "good," it is clear that a simplistic sociological (base/superstructural) explanation of moral development is inadequate. But Greene's "theological" explanation is itself reductive, especially when he has the 17-year old Pinkie declare, "Credo in unum Satanum." To reduce Pinkie like this to something unique, *sui generis,* a high school dropout who speaks perfect Latin, is to distract attention from those moments when Greene *does* allow the social complexity of Pinkie's being to come through. The most notable moments of course are those when Pinkie expresses extreme distaste for marriage and sexuality: "To marry—it was like ordure on the hands" and (love-making) "seemed to him more like death than when Hale and Spicer had died." As "explanation" the text focusses on Pinkie's enforced Saturday night witnessing of his parents' copulation, but Greene is here making it easy for the reader to mutter something about adequate housing and proper privacy. The underlying materialist explanation for Pinkie emerges clearly near the end:

> A brain was only capable of what it could conceive, and it couldn't conceive what it had never experienced: his cells were formed of the cement school playground, the dead fire and the dying man in the St. Pancras waiting-room, his bed at Frank's and his parents' bed.

This seems much more to the point than "Credo in unum Satanum." For Pinkie "life" is "gaol, it's not knowing where to get some money. Worms and cataract, cancer . . . children being born. It's dying slowly." It is this materialist underpinning of the novel (always Greene's strength, anyway) which allows Pinkie to be human and vulnerable, as when he weeps under the influence of some sentimental film-music: "it was like a vision of release to an imprisoned man. He felt constriction and saw—hopelessly out of reach—a limitless freedom: no fear, no hatred, no envy." He also weeps under the razor attack by Colleoni's gang and he recalls weeping when being caned at school. Terry Eagleton argues that the novel "detaches (Pinkie) from any natural locality and so renders his evil less environmentally explicable." It is true that we don't see Pinkie "operate" in his own environment, but enough description occurs (particularly during the visit to Rose's parents) for a materialist or "environmental" explanation to be supplied by the reader.

I should like to return finally to the unresolved tensions which lie at the heart of ***Brighton Rock.*** As Eagleton points out, Pinkie "embodies a kind of true negation, (yet) Pinkie's view of experience is time and again confirmed by the novel itself." A fundamental opposition exists not so much between theological views as between the political choices available to the actors in world history: either this world's "not a bad old place," as Ida frequently claims, or it's a place where you die "slowly." Ida's view entails accepting the *status quo.* Going with Pinkie entails entering a dark night, not knowing how it will end, a revolutionary step. History shows that revolutions can be either reactionary or progressive, or even have both tendencies simultaneously. Any revolution associated (symbolically) with Pinkie would probably be fascist, but one associated with Rose would almost certainly be progressive (a point I would like to return to). This irresolution, at the "political" heart of the novel, is not, I would argue, a weakness, but rather a realistic reflection of political reality in 1930s Britain. This was the time of appeasement, of coalition government, the broad consensus, and it was also a time of extreme economic marginalization for the Pinkies and the Roses. Being neither an avowed socialist nor a proletarian novelist. Greene does not need to resolve the issue one way or another. If anything, his ending is, in political terms, "reformist": despite the horror of Pinkie's recorded voice awaiting Rose, the last page points to a vaguely "better" future, the cliché of birth and renewal and redemption. Again (and always at the level of symbolism) this is historically "accurate": Pinkie's voice is the voice of fascism leading to war, on the other side of which is the social democratic future.

But still the political problem remains. Isn't Ida's the voice of the people and doesn't Greene dismiss this voice as a source of salvation? Clearly Greene (not just the "narrator") despises Ida for her devotion to the things of this world, the here and now, to justice, fair play and a satisfying glass of Guinness. The narrator maintains a persistent sneer whenever Ida looms into view, but I'm sure I'm not alone in asserting that the reader's natural inclination, even if one stops short of "identifying" with Ida, is to resist being seduced by that sneer and to hope that Ida will indeed track down Pinkie, not because, any more than Ida, we want Hale's murder avenged, but because we are disturbed that such evil is *abroad* even, let alone that it should remain "unpunished." The majority of readers perhaps are on Ida's side as she follows Pinkie and saves Rose with "merciless compassion." However, by the end of the novel, the "hunt" or detection element is probably less fascinating than the final suspense over whether Rose will commit suicide, or to put it in Greene's terms, whether Good will submit to Evil.

Pinkie and Rose do seem superior to Ida, finally, but not because Catholic absolutism is about to overcome the Protestant consensus. Rather, what seems admirable in the final pages about these social outcasts is their deliberate choice of a fate, damnation, whose finality would shame those Protestant pursuers, "showing them they couldn't pick and choose." To choose one's fate, to make (as far as possible) rational choices, is morally and politically superior to drifting with the tide of Ida's modern history, yet an immediate caveat must be entered: Pinkie does *not* choose suicide, since he never intends to carry out his part of the pact, and Rose's choice is forced upon her (though her instinctive rebellion against the act shows that had she in fact committed suicide it would ultimately have been out of a deliberate and conscious choice. Damned already, Pinkie chooses to intensify the damnation that already awaits him). Even so, the end of the novel is important simply for raising the issue of choice at all. Though Greene is asking a theological question, a much deeper social and political question seems to be posed at the level of the novel's political unconscious: given that this Brighton, this England, this world even, is utterly "fallen" ("why, this is Hell nor are we out of it"), do we have to recognize that fact and *change* it, as Marx urged, or do we go along with Ida and raise our glasses to this imperfect world which nonetheless allows us a modicum of happiness as we float by? It is at this deeper structural level that one makes a case for admiring Pinkie and Rose as against Ida, Prewitt, Colleoni and all the other corrupt and fallen characters. However minimally, Pinkie and Rose make a choice, an act of resistance, and briefly step on to firm ground out of a sea of false consciousness. But the birth of new consciousness will involve endless struggle.

Christine De Vinne (essay date October 1993)

SOURCE: "Truth and Falsehood in the Metaphors of *A Burnt-Out Case*," in *English Studies*, Vol. 74, No. 5, October, 1993, pp. 445-50.

[*In the following essay, De Vinne discusses the metaphorical significance of children and childhood in* A Burnt-Out Case. *According to De Vinne, "childhood corresponds with falsehood while adulthood symbolizes truth" in the novel.*]

A Burnt-Out Case is Graham Greene's narrative of a disillusioned architect who seeks spiritual and emotional peace among burnt-out lepers deep in the Congo. There, in a primitive world far removed from the distractions of civilization, its characters confront the essential questions of life. The rhetoric of the novel too is stripped of anything extraneous; Greene makes clear that the story is based on two simple, straightforward metaphors. The first and most obvious establishes leprosy as a symbol of the disillusionment from which Querry suffers. Like a leper whose disease has spent itself after eating away fingers and toes, this afflicted man confesses to Dr. Colin, 'I am one of the mutilated.' Numbed by leprosy both mental and spiritual, he is senseless to joy as well as to pain. The distance he travels to find a home in his suffering suggests Greene's second metaphor, that of journey. The outward journey Querry makes into the heart of Africa, as far as river and road can take him, corresponds to an inward journey of the man's heart. The inner journey must parallel the outer one to the leprosarium, for only by coming to know himself, by reaching 'the furthest point' of self-knowledge, can he be cured.

Given Greene's two basic metaphors, it is easy to see why references to disease and journey abound in the novel. However, those two symbols do not account for its numerous allusions to childhood and children, particularly in a text where none of the major characters are minors. Their presence in the work of an author as economical in style as Greene suggests that a third metaphor is operative, one for which childhood or youth must be the vehicle. While an obvious conclusion in a search for the tenor of such a metaphor might be to identify childhood with truth or innocence, the novel's journalist offers his own caution against such a simplistic explanation: 'It's a funny thing about metaphors—they never really follow through.' In fact, a careful examination of the roles of the characters reveals that ***A Burnt-Out Case*** rests on a surprising premise, that in Greene's topography childhood corresponds with falsehood while adulthood symbolizes truth.

The central character for all of the novel arrives in the Congo well into adulthood, a figure in his late fifties. He is Querry, a soul on quest who asks questions of life and a hunted man who is pursued by fame and fortune, as the 'querry' 'quarry' wordplay underlying his name suggests. His character is as ambiguous as his name. It would seem that he wishes to leave all the trappings of adulthood behind him—the sophistication of Europe, the practice of his profession, even the pleasure of sex. And yet he faces in Africa questions of personal identity and metaphysical truth that only an adult can answer. Querry stands between two worlds, the world of adulthood and the world of childhood. He scorns the childish 'innocence and immaturity' of the fathers' cardgames and likewise disdains the stuffy sophistry of Rycker's adult discussions. Although, as Daphna Erdinast-Vulcan notes, he claims biological parenthood, he maintains that his children have 'disappeared into the world a long time ago,' presumably grown, and he declines any adult responsibility for them. He longs for the simple joys of the Pendélé that his servant Deo Gratias, a deformed leper, seeks in the bush, yet he has the sophistication to recognize that he can never find it. Querry the character must learn what Greene the author has learned by the time he composes his autobiography at the age of sixty-seven, that an adult should return to the experiences of 'the distant time' and 'feel them, as [one] felt them then,' not to revert to childhood but to bring order and truth to adult life.

The close identification between adulthood and truth in Querry's quest is best seen in contrast with the child figures and their inherent dishonesty in ***A Burnt-out Case.*** The most obvious of these is Marie, the wife of Rycker, whom Querry mistakes for his daughter rather than his spouse. All Greene's descriptions of this character emphasize her youth: she appears to be a 'girl' with an 'unformed face'; she is afraid of moths, lizards, cardgames and everything she does not understand; she speaks in stilted copybook phrases; she giggles with the easy amusement of the young; and she writes in a schoolgirl script. Narcissistic and immature, she is an arrested adolescent, her development frozen at the time she left her family home and convent school to wed the man old enough to be her father, suggests K. C. Joseph Kurismmootil in his analysis of this character. Even Querry is deceived by her apparent innocence; on the night which will condemn him, he visits her room under the delusion that '[t]his one [is] too young to be a great danger.' But Marie is far from innocent. As child in Greene's Congo she typifies falsehood and poses the gravest threat to Querry's life. With the 'transparent honesty of a child who has prepared a cast-iron lie' she convinces herself, her husband, and the community of the leprosarium that Querry has slept with her and she now carries his child. 'God preserve us all from innocence,' proclaims the cornered Querry, for it is the false innocence of Marie's childhood which costs him his life.

Marie's husband, André Rycker, is as much a child as she is. He boasts of his extensive experience, both secular and religious, but he remains just as selfish and false as the other child figures in ***A Burnt-Out Case.*** He uses people like he uses religion, to create his own false world. Patronizing and patriarchal, he cultivates a childish dependency in his wife, telling her how to behave at parties and lisping her name as the babyish 'Mawie' for a term of endearment prior to lovemaking. An architect of delusions, he constructs a false image of love based on theology rather than affection and a false image of Querry based on illusion rather than truth. Initially he insists that the newcomer is a man of faith and intellect even when Querry denies both appellations; later he converts to an equally mistaken but far more dangerous belief, that Querry is an adulterer who has violated his marriage. In killing Querry, Rycker epitomizes all that is wrong with the child in Greene's burnt-out world: he acts out of false beliefs. He hunts Querry down because he believes the man has seduced his wife and he shoots because he believes Querry is laughing at him.

The religious analogue to the coarse, self-seeking Rycker is the immature, self-centered Father Thomas. Despite his position as ordained priest and director of the leprosarium's schools, Father Thomas remains 'doomed to a perpetual and unhappy youth.' He has never outgrown his childhood fear of the dark or accepted adult responsibility for his physical and psychological limitations, his poor eyesight and his inability to adjust to mission life. Doubting himself and his vocation, he seeks to make of Querry a sainted model for overcoming all his imperfections. He talks to the Superior about Querry's rescue of the lost Deo Gratias and muses aloud, 'I hope I would have done what he did, going out at night into the bush looking for a servant, but I doubt . . . .' He watches Querry help carry the feverish Parkinson ashore and says in admiration, 'We could all learn from you.' Like Rycker, Father Thomas prefers his false sanctified version of Querry to the truth, and like Rycker the priest condemns the man as quickly as he canonizes him. Another victim of Marie's lies, Thomas hears of her accusations against Querry and dissolves in childish disappointment and tears. Just like the Ryckers, the self-centered Father Thomas has used Querry for his own purposes and chosen the false security of a make-believe world rather than the adult fact of the real one.

The child as metaphor for falsehood lies at the core of one other character in ***A Burnt-Out Case,*** the journalist Parkinson. This vulgar opportunist exhibits a childishness more covert than the other characters'. Hints of it are evident, however, when he arrives from Luc, lying in a boat, naked, helpless, and unable to communicate. His choices, moreover, clearly mark him as child. He prostitutes his profession at the price of truth. He falsely credits 'Stanley and his little band' with exploration of the leprosarium area, ascribes quotations to spurious sources, and uses his camera to create visual lies. Like Marie, Rycker and Thomas, he produces his own false image of Querry, as 'The Recluse of the Great River,' and 'The Saint with a Past,' but his guilt exceeds theirs on two counts: he is conscious of the falsehoods he perpetrates, and he promulgates them far and wide for his own gain. He deliberately fabricates the scenario of the wronged husband out of adjoining rooms, powder-smudged towels and coded journal entry on Querry and Marie's ill-fated trip to Luc. For his own childish gain he has forsaken his art and turned to scandal and falsehood on a personal and professional level.

Once the Ryckers and Thomas and Parkinson have invaded what Richard Kelly calls Querry's 'Garden of Eden,' there is no such thing as childhood innocence. There is still adult truth, however, and Querry's insistence on truth identifies him as one of Greene's heroes. The man constantly 'worries over truth' while he 'searches for peace,' writes D. J. Dooley. He is honest with himself in claiming to have reached 'the end of desire and the end of a vocation.' He is equally honest with others; to all who will listen he proclaims that any good acts he performs spring not from faith or altruism but boredom and disillusionment. He is honest with Rycker in asserting that he is not an intellectual, with Marie in asserting that he is not a lover, with Thomas in asserting that he is not a saint, and with Parkinson in asserting that he is not a hero. The problem is that these characters reject the straightforward truth, weave their own mystique around him, and then condemn him when their self-made vision crumbles. Querry's 'mistake' is to cling tenaciously to the truth; he chooses an adult solution in a world of children. Inevitably, when he has faced the final truth about himself, that he is cured, he dies at the end of Rycker's own version of a juvenile cops-and-robbers game.

Querry's cure is dependent on his recognition of truth, for it requires that he rediscover the reserves of goodness and meaning his life still holds. His physician and guide in the essential lesson of adulthood is the forthright Dr. Colin, modeled after Docteur Michel Lechat of the Yonda leper colony, to whom Greene dedicated the book. The doctor's fervent affirmation of life and truth clearly marks him as adult. A pure scientist, he searches for empirical truth. He pores over his secular Bible, the 'Atlas of Leprosy,' dreams of living 'to see leprosy in retreat,' and rages against the unnecessary suffering of a disease science should be able to prevent. He takes on Querry as one of his patients and insists that, for a man without feeling, the only hope for life lies in sharing others' pain: 'A man can't live with nothing but himself. . . . Sooner or later he would kill himself.' Ironically, in Greene's hands Colin's cure of Querry is inextricably bound to his death. He takes his first step out of his solitary world when he agrees to drive to Luc for the doctor's new equipment; there he meets the Ryckers, and Marie later allows that she at once fell in love with him (228). Likewise, he undertakes his last visit to the city, the trip on which Marie accompanies him, in order to return with medicines and supplies. Colin cures Querry by teaching him the truth that one cannot live like a burnt-out leper, feeling and caring for nothing, in the adult world. Rather, one must reach out to the other, and the pain of the embrace, even when it means death, is the surest sign of life.

A second adult character who collaborates in Querry's cure is the unnamed Superior of the leper colony. Naive in the ways of the world, he mistakes bidets for footbaths, but he possesses real insight into matters of the soul. His world is that of religious truth, not the heady, theological doctrine that gratifies Rycker, but the lived truth that enables him to preach to the lepers on the real 'Klistian' love. For him the divine truth is that everyone is redeemed, and this truth sets him free to offer friendship to the atheist Colin, support to the doubt-torn Thomas, and encouragement to the searching Querry. With him Querry discusses not faith but maturity. He describes the child-like dreams of Pendélé that captivate him and listens reflectively when the father counters, 'People have to grow up. We are called to more complicated things than that.' His wisdom is missed most keenly at the moment of crisis, when all the 'complicated things' in the lies of Marie and Rycker and Parkinson converge, and even the self-important Father Thomas exclaims. 'How I wish the Superior were here.' When he returns, the truth that he sees is bigger than all their lies, and he refuses to judge or condemn. Like Colin, his secular counterpart, he has outgrown the childish urge to divide the world into 'good guys' and 'bad guys,' saints and sinners, and he can live with the ambiguity of the adult world.

The complex adult world that Greene's characters occupy requires thoughtful analysis on the part of his audience. In 'Graham Greene's Rhetoric,' Gransden suggests that readers can best understand Greene's tone and structure by looking carefully at his style, particularly his use of catalogue and simile. What Gransden says of these tropes could well be extended to metaphor by virtue of its close association with simile:

> These two figures occur so often in Greene that they go beyond mere mannerism. They do much to control and formalise his realism, and indeed in a sense to undermine it, for they show that a world whose surface is intensely realistic moves uneasily beneath the surface into fractured and divided images which reflect profound psychological, moral and social tensions.

By extension, Gransden's essay, although limited to Greene's earlier novels, suggests a model for ***A Burnt-out Case*** as well, especially for the allegory of the jeweller which the story contains. In the light of his interpretation, this bedtime fable assumes rhetorical as well as dramatic importance. While many critics analyze the piece as a confession of Greene's own disillusionment or a commentary on the tension between faith and despair, it is just as much an extended metaphor of childhood and adulthood. The jeweller grows from a trusting boy to a disenchanted adult, one who attempts, as does Querry, to fight the myths that have grown around him. He loses his belief in people not because they ridicule his art but because they falsely overrate it. He loses his belief in the King not because of intellectual arguments but because the vision of him which he learned in childhood, the promise of blissful reward or painful punishment, proves false in light of adult reality.

Once the jeweller, himself a thinly-masked metaphor for Querry, has 'discovered that there was no such king' and he has reached 'the end of his vocation,' Querry returns from storyline back to fictive reality, but the larger metaphor is still operative. In response to the story's inconclusive ending. Marie asks, 'So then?'; Querry replies, 'I told you, didn't I, that it's just as difficult to leave a profession as to leave a husband,' and follows with a catalogue of all the difficulties she would face in attempting to break away from Rycker. She is right, he tells her at the beginning of the fable, to believe that both of them are 'much too old for fairy-stories,' and he is wrong to believe in the false sense of child-like trust that a bedtime story can engender in teller as well as listener. As Marie sleeps he too succumbs to childish fantasy and in the coolness of dawn reflects that '[p]erhaps he had found here a country and a life.' In Greene's metaphor of childhood, however, such peace can only be deceptive. The truths about life and love and faith which the fable contains are no match for the wiles of the 'child' who falls asleep deriding her husband and giggling, 'I could almost say to him, couldn't I, that we'd spent the night together.'

The story of the jeweller, like the broader story of Querry's life in ***A Burnt-Out Case,*** is a fable in which the adult must come to recognize the deceptions of childhood and grow past the resulting disappointment. Appropriately, then, Greene reserves what A. A. DeVitis terms 'the final, choric commentary on the story's action' to the doctor, who, with the Superior, best represents mature truth. Their very adulthood, in Greene's logic, guarantees their honesty, and so their words can be trusted. They first tell the truth about Querry, the doctor pronouncing that 'he had been cured' and the priest avowing that he had found for his life 'a happy ending.' Even more, since they are adults, they reveal the truths of their own lives. The Superior quotes Pascal in his belief that the 'man who starts looking for God,' like the one who has looked for love, 'has already found him'; Colin returns to his dispensary to meet yet another victim of leprosy and insist, 'I can promise you that there will be no mutilations.' Both will continue to search out the painful truths that hide like leprosy below the surface of life, for they know that only if they do so can they help anyone grow to adulthood.

Greene, too, has been true to his purpose in this final scene. The two adults, metaphors for truth, together examine Colin's latest patient, a child of three. Both recognize the symptoms of incipient leprosy in the boy, whose outward appearance gives a deceptive impression of health. On a literal level, this child carries the potential for death, just as the novel's figurative children have been instruments of death. Hope remains, however. In the scientific truth that the doctor seeks, in the religious truth that the priest pursues, lies the promise of life. And in the metaphorical truth that the author presents, the reader who probes beneath the surface will find Greene's authentic message of life.

Elliott Malamet (essay date Summer 1994)

SOURCE: "The Uses of Delay in *The Power and the Glory,*" in *Renascence: Essays on Value in Literature,* Vol. 46, No. 4, Summer, 1994, pp. 211-23.

[*In the following essay, Malamet examines the narrative function and symbolic significance of delay, hesitation, and suspense in* The Power and the Glory.]

Just past the midpoint of ***The Power and the Glory,*** as the whisky priest is being led to jail, Graham Greene reiterates the feelings of resignation and fear that have hitherto haunted him: "He knew it was the beginning of the end—after all these years. . . . When would they discover who he really was? When would he meet the half-caste, or the lieutenant who had interrogated him already?" As in a number of Greene's preceding works, such as ***A Gun for Sale*** and ***Brighton Rock,*** a sense of inevitability hangs over the main pursuit of the novel; the priest broods over the fact that he must eventually be hunted down. In an earlier passage, he nervously awaits in his home village the arrival of the lieutenant and his men: "Was this the end at last, he wondered? . . . If they were so careful, they must know beyond the shadow of doubt that he was here. It was the end." Yet on both occasions his anxiety is premature; the lieutenant fails to recognize him although they face each other. We are repeatedly invited to share the priest's point of view that there is no way out. The first time he is arrested, he thinks, "Everything now seemed irrevocable," and yet Greene heightens the suspense and then allows the priest to evade capture. After being released in the morning from the cell, the priest is prevented from going to wash with the other prisoners: "'We've got other plans for you,' the sergeant said." This vaguely threatening statement is followed by a trivial inquiry as to how the priest has slept in the night, which only furthers his anxiety about "how much longer all these preliminaries" will take. When he is subsequently recognized by the half-caste, who is also in the prison, it seems "as if God were deciding . . . finally." But the dichotomy between recognition and capture becomes ironically complete at this stage. The police have unknowingly arrested the man they have been seeking, but the lieutenant fails to identify him, while the half-caste recognizes but chooses not to implicate him.

The priest's musings about "preliminaries" and "God deciding" are, on one level, apt metaphors for the author's manipulation of the text. Greene's use of deferral bears clear links to typical devices of movement and suspension found in most mystery stories, where

> that state of more or less pleasurable tension concerning an outcome, which we call suspense, depends on something not happening too fast. In other words, the detective story formula offers a remarkably clear example of the crucial narrative principle of "deliberately impeded form." ([Dennis] Porter)

But Greene's handling of the pursuit narrative is also marked by certain essential differences and resists narrow genre categorization. R. W. B. Lewis is correct in his surmise that by the time of ***Brighton Rock*** "the unsolvable mystery of the human condition . . . has become Greene's obsessive subject," and that a central weakness in the earlier novels is "rooted in a failure to disentangle the *mystery* of the mystery, to separate it out from the contingencies of melodrama and the staged surprises of the brain-twister," but his statement requires a fuller account. In what follows, I explore the purpose for which Greene employs such thriller devices as pursuit and delay in ***The Power and the Glory.*** Delay operates on many levels in the novel, from the text's hesitation in identifying the priest—including his own reticence to reveal himself—to the suspension of his capture. Ultimately, Greene alternates the hindrance of the lieutenant's goal of the priest's arrest with a different vision of deferral, one that can be seen within the religious context of a winding quest toward an unspecified, and never fully confirmed, future redemption.

The familiar materials of the thriller form are all present in ***The Power and the Glory***: the pursued man, the threat of violence, the shadow of betrayal. From the motto taken from Dryden denoting the hunt to the use of delay to create suspense, the novel is suggestive of the techniques and narrative structure of a fast-paced crime story. But these elements are clearly wedded to a deeper purpose; for R. W. B. Lewis, ***The Power and the Glory,*** along with such books as ***Brighton Rock*** and ***The Heart of the Matter,*** is "a mystery story, in the popular sense, that functions ably as a trial run for a mystery drama in a more ancient theological sense." This thought is echoed by Grahame Smith, who points to the novel's structure "of an elemental pursuit; the simple outlines of this are obvious. But, as well as being the hunted, the whisky priest is also a hunter in quest of what is presumably life's most important object, its meaning. For him this can be found only within not just a religious, but a Catholic, context." The fabrication of suspense for its own sake is thus not Greene's final goal in this novel; as he asserts in a review of Livingstone's travel writings, "the plot of the novel catches the attention, but the subject lies deeper." With this quotation in mind, Gwenn Boardman wisely cautions against a simplistic reading of the text:

> Too often, criticism of ***The Power and the Glory*** focuses on its pursuits by secular and divine "hounds" while missing the novel's deeper subject . . . . in ***The Power and the Glory,*** there is the "map" of the plot, an exciting and sometimes terrible narrative. There are also special marks—the allusions to Catholic teaching and the very title of the novel.

These "special marks"—the priest's journey to self-realization and the earthly restoration of the power and glory of God—constitute for Boardman the novel's essence.

But this assessment, while accurate, verges on establishing too rigid a dichotomy between form and content in the story, between the employment of pursuit and suspense and the depiction of the priest's development as a man of God. "The hunt," if rather limited as a strict plot device, is fertile as a metaphor; it is a means of gaining access to and understanding this deep subject. For Greene's fiction does not take the divine presence for granted; Tennyson's acquiescence that "I still believe, though I cannot see. And I have faith that God will be waiting for me when I have crossed the bar" ([J. Hillis] Miller) is accelerated by Greene into an active process of looking for grace in a world considered to be "a burning and abandoned ship" (***The Power and the Glory***). The notion of abandonment presumes an Abandoner, and pursuit in the novel is both an indispensable narrative tool and a symbol by which Greene evokes the sense of something missing, of an *absence.* That the police hunt is subsumed within the search for God is indicated by the priest's initial decision not to head north to safety, but to travel "in the actual track of the police . . . . he wasn't ready yet for the final surrender . . . Jogging up and down on the mule he tried to bribe God with promises of firmness." In this sense Greene interestingly reverses the traditional detective novel sequence whereby a puzzle precipitates a search; in ***The Power and the Glory,*** it is the search for the priest, who is temporarily at large, that calls attention to the more mysterious gap between man and God.

The novel begins, appropriately enough, with the language of searching: "Mr Tench went out to look for his ether cylinder, into the blazing Mexico sun and the bleaching dust. A few vultures looked down from the roof with shabby indifference: he wasn't carrion yet." The image of the vultures occurs throughout the first chapter, an overt symbol for the machinery of the state that converges on the lone priest, and it also embodies the designation of the Church as a parasitical entity feeding on the poor that composes the core of the lieutenant's plea to the priest's village neighbors: "You're fools if you still believe what the priests tell you. All they want is your money." The hunt for the priest is already underway at the outset and spans the entire length of the text, but Greene slowly reorients the meaning of the novel's chases. The priest's dream in the crowded jail cell distinguishes between genuine and illusory pursuits:

> His eyes closed and immediately he began to dream. He was being pursued; he stood outside a door banging on it, begging for admission, but nobody answered—there was a word, a password, which would save him, but he had forgotten it. . . . His feet had gone to sleep and he knelt outside the door. Then he knew why he wanted to get in: he wasn't being pursued at all: that was a mistake. His child lay beside him bleeding to death and this was a doctor's house. He banged on the door and shouted, "Even if I can't think of the right word, haven't you a heart?"

The underlying direction of the priest's experience is the attempt to "see the doctor"; he must bang on the door and find the "right word" that leads to God. One of the main objects of the novel's deferrals and postponements, therefore, is to allow the priest to forge a more profound bond with his faith. Delay works as a thriller technique but it also contains Christian significance, as Patricia A. Parker writes:

> The time between First and Second Coming is itself a respite or "dilation," an interval in which the eschatological Judgment is held over or deferred, a period of uncertain duration when the "end" already accomplished in the Advent is, paradoxically, not yet come. . . . The deferral of the promised end is, in the phrase of Alanus de Insulis, the "dilatio patriae," the delay of the coming of the Sabbath which is the extended interval of time itself.

The Power and the Glory is ironically structured around the various "comings" of the lieutenant; his failure to perceive the priest the first two times they meet necessitates a delay in judgment and the priest's predetermined end is thus briefly stayed. Greene's incorporation of deferral as a thematic component in the novel's Christian content is also exemplified by the priest's sermon to the peasants about heaven:

> We deny ourselves so that we can enjoy. You have heard of rich men in the north who eat salted foods, so that they can be thirsty—for what they call the cocktail. Before the marriage, too, there is the long betrothal . . . . the beating you always get from the jefe because you are too poor to pay, smallpox and fever, hunger . . . that is all part of heaven—the preparation. Perhaps without them, who can tell, you wouldn't enjoy heaven so much.

Here life resembles a dilatory quest that culminates in heavenly fulfillment, but this tribute to what lies ahead is subverted by the insistent and immediate pursuit of the lieutenant close at hand:

> It was not easy to concentrate: the police were not far away. . . . A voice whispered urgently to him, "Father."
>
> "Yes?"
>
> "The police are on the way. They are only a mile off, coming through the forest."

The juxtaposition of a speech that promises something that can only be fully tasted in the future, and a Mass which can brook no delay—"Were they on horseback or on foot? If they were on foot, he had twenty minutes left to finish Mass and hide"—sharply denotes the novel's tension between movement and suspension.

The plot of a thriller is consumed by its forward motion, by the spectre of the chase and capture that is always ahead, but the classic detective story, as Dennis Porter notes, "is a genre committed to an act of recovery, moving forward in order to move back." In ***The Power and the Glory,*** the priest is the focal point for these two competing narrative patterns. One is the prospective view: what is likely to happen next given the unfolding action? The other, the retrospective impulse, continually refashions meanings of the past as plot developments lead to a new understanding of prior events. This is what Robert Coover refers to as

> a tension in narrative, as in life, between the sensation of time as a linear experience, one thing following sequentially (causally or not) upon another, and time as a patterning of interrelated ex-

> periences reflected upon as though it had a geography and could be mapped. It is, in a sense, the tension between future time, which, with its promise of death and its intransigent sequence of days and nights, bears down upon us remorselessly, and time past, which if it can be said to exist at all, exists only in cranial space, in that sprawling, multilevel and often chaotic house of our memory.

This duality infuses ***The Power and the Glory.*** Even as his doomed fate chases and passes by the priest several times before finally ensnaring him, the novel's pattern of delay grants him several opportunities to uncover and reexamine memories of complacency and greed in his past: "somewhere they accumulated in secret—the rubble of his failures." While the lieutenant, at least on the surface, is content with simply finding and executing his man, the priest, in being forced to flee, gains a sharpened perception of his previous behavior—"the fat youngish priest who stood with one plump hand splayed authoritatively out while the tongue played pleasantly with the word 'Governor'"—and deepens his sympathy for others.

There are few clues to the priest's past life; one is a scrap of paper left over from a dinner given at Concepción in his honor that he carries with him "as a charm," a reminder of a time when he had envisioned that "a whole serene life lay ahead—he *had* ambition. But in the night spent with the mestizo, his ambitions come back to him as "something faintly comic." His life as a fugitive has brought with it the gradual surrender of the signs and objects of the priesthood:

> feast days and fast days and days of abstinence had been the first to go: then he had ceased to trouble more than occasionally about his breviary—and finally he had left it behind altogether at the port in one of his periodic attempts at escape. Then the altar stone went—too dangerous to carry with him.

But the loss of his chalice or the breviary—the signs of his vocation—does not displace the priest's hermeneutic frame of reference; he interprets humanity itself as a series of traces of divine presence: "God was the parent, but He was also the policeman, the criminal, the priest, the maniac and the judge. Something resembling God dangled from the gibbet or went into odd attitudes before the bullets in a prison yard or contorted itself like a camel in the attitude of sex." The novel expresses the difficulty in experiencing God's connection with man, as the Indian woman's futile prayer for her child indicates: "Did she expect a miracle? and if she did, why should it not be granted her, the priest wondered? . . . The priest found himself watching the child for some movement. When none came, it was as if God had missed an opportunity." But the priest never questions the *truth* of presence and takes as his underlying assumption that God, while transcendent, is surely an everpresent reality; after he is let out of prison, he notes, "God had decided." This is what Thomas J. J. Altizer speaks of as the "clear and radical distinction between an unknowability which is the consequence of the presence of a transcendent or mysterious identity and an unknowability which is the consequence of the absence of all identity as such." Thus the priest also looks to the unfolding of events as a symbol of divine intention; before he is let out of jail, he strikes

> yet another bargain with God. This time, if he escaped from the prison, he would escape altogether. He would go north over the border. His escape was so improbable that, if it happened, it couldn't be anything else but a sign—an indication that he was doing more harm by his example than good by his occasional confessions.

The text initially concentrates on the police search, but the priest's blurred photograph on the police-station wall symbolizes the difficulty the police have in identifying him. The Chief of Police notes that the priest "can pass as a gringo," and the drive to hunt down the priest is carefully thwarted by Greene through many devices, including the blurring of identity. The lieutenant admits that the priest "looks like all the rest," a situation that proves frustrating: "If only, he thought, we had a proper photograph—he wanted to know the features of his enemy." Even the mother of his child has difficulty in spotting him when they reunite after a six-year absence:

> "Ah, Maria," he said, "and how are you?"
>
> "Well," she exclaimed, "is it you, father?"
>
> He didn't look directly at her: His eyes were sly and cautious. He said, "You didn't recognize me?"
>
> "You've changed." She looked him up and down with a kind of contempt.

While the police are facing difficulties in their forages at capture, the priest is coming to terms with an identity that he initially tries to leave fuzzy, like the hard-to-decipher photograph. At first, the priest embraces anonymity. Like a shadowy criminal in this watchful universe of Tabasco, he must be guarded in his initial conversation with Mr Tench:

> The stranger said, "I was expecting to see someone. The name was Lopez."
>
> "Oh, they shot him weeks ago," Mr Tench said.

> "Dead?"
>
> "You know how it is round here. Friend of yours?"
>
> "No, no," the man protested hurriedly. "Just a friend of a friend."

The technique of introducing the priest as an unidentified presence is repeated often in the novel. Several times he is described as "the stranger," and when he re-enters the town of the opening chapter he is simply depicted as the "man in the . . . drill suit." Daphna Erdinast-Vulcan points out what she views as the thematic function that this hiddenness serves: "[in Part I] we recognize the protagonist as a priest only by the circumstances which surround him and not by any essential, identifiable quality in himself. . . . The author seems to tell us in this way that the man is not yet worthy of his role as a priest, a father of his people." But even after he is designated "a priest," he is still forced to adopt various disguises. Pressed for a name by the lieutenant in the village confrontation, he uses that of Montez, the man who has been shot earlier in Concepción as part of the lieutenant's hostage-taking plan. And his conversation with the mestizo is couched in denials:

> "Won't you say a prayer, father, before we sleep?"
>
> "Why do you call me that?" he asked sharply, peering across the shadowy floor to where the half-caste sat against the door.
>
> "You *are* a father, aren't you?"
>
> "I have a child," the priest said, "if that's what you mean."

Finally, however, the priest relents to the mestizo's incessant probing:

> A voice said, "You *are* the priest, aren't you?"
>
> "Yes." It was as if they had climbed out of their opposing trenches and met in No Man's Land among the wires to fraternise.

The priest's shifting guises indicate not only how he is seen by others but also mark his faltering progress toward self-recognition and connection with God. One of the central ironies of the novel is that the priest eludes capture often, and yet at the same time he betrays his identity repeatedly through the compassionate embodiment of his calling. The mestizo, noting the priest's refusal to beat his mule, comments, "You talk like a priest," a phrase that is repeated word for word by a murderer in the prison cell in response to the priest's gentle admonition that "It's a terrible thing to kill a man." ***The Power and the Glory*** traces the growth of the priest's self-scrutiny and draws a parallel between this and his deepening understanding of God and the subsequent desire, in the prison, to drop his various masks and be seen for what he is. Greene reflects this picture of the intertwined reality of man's relation to himself and his communion with God in the description of the vandalized cemetery in Carmen:

> One image of the Mother of God had lost ears and arms and stood like a pagan Venus over the grave of some rich forgotten timber merchant. It was odd—this fury to deface, because, of course, you could never deface enough. If God had been like a toad, you could have rid the globe of toads, but when God was like yourself, it was no good being content with stone figures—you had to kill yourself among the graves.

Just as ridding oneself of God here is said to require self-destruction, then to seek for and find God entails the search for oneself.

The pattern of the priest's initial hesitation but ultimate admission of his vocation is most powerfully expressed in the prison, where he is touched by "a sense of companionship which he had never experienced in the old days when pious people came kissing his black cotton glove." His encounter with the pious woman juxtaposes his past reactions to such meetings with a new awareness: "He was more out of touch with her kind than he had ever been; he would have known what to say to her in the old days, feeling no pity at all, speaking with half a mind a platitude or two." His feelings of helplessness form the beginnings of a true integrity; he is unwilling and unable to substitute the easy rhetoric of the past for the genuine difficulty of present communication. His self-revelation to the prisoners is preceded by Greene's reminder that the priest has a secret life. An old man in the cell relates that he has an illegitimate daughter, which he does not realize reaches deep into the heart of his listener. This poignant irony, combined with the subsequent story, approvingly told by the pious woman, of priests who took away the man's child, prompts the priest to break the shield of anonymity and bare his identity: "He said after a moment's hesitation, very distinctly, 'I am a priest.'"

The parallel structure of police pursuit and the priest's growing wish to make himself known continues to be purposefully interlinked. The priest remains invisible to his police pursuers; they still cannot identify him despite the fact that on his photograph someone has "put a ring round his face to pick it out." The photograph records something that has since altered; formerly, his was "a buffoon's face, good enough for mild jokes to women, but unsuitable at the altar-rail. He had tried to change it—and indeed, he thought, indeed I have succeeded, they'll never recognize me now . . . ." Though Greene asserts that "the priest, for all his recollections of periods in his life when he was different, never changed" ([Marie-Francoise] Allain), the priest attributes his undetectability in the eyes of the law to a new internal reality:

> The priest stood not far from his own portrait on the wall and waited. Once he glanced quickly and nervously up at the old crumpled newspaper cutting and thought, It's not very like me now. What an unbearable creature he must have been in those days. . . . Then, in his innocence, he had felt no love for anyone; now in his corruption he had learnt . . .

The termination of the hunt, it becomes clear, is contingent on the priest's final "return." Part III of ***The Power and the Glory*** describes the priest's brief, tranquil stay with the Lehrs, but the visit is intended as a kind of temporary interlude, an illusion of peace. Lured away by the mestizo to attend to the dying American gangster, Calver, the priest quickly forgets the Lehrs: "the other world had stretched a hand across the border, and he was again in the atmosphere of flight." The story is fashioned so that we accept the reality of flight and the priest's eventual capture as the unavoidable conditions of the text. After the priest leaves the Lehrs' comfortable haven (thereby confirming his ultimate commitment to divine service), the strands of the narrative converge methodically. The priest himself announces that the suspension of the story will no longer be necessary: "'Now,' the priest said briskly, 'we won't delay any more,' and he started down the path, with a small sack slung over his shoulder." But this statement, which seems perfectly supported by the subsequent hastening of plot developments—the priest's capture and execution—is still undermined by Greene in the remainder of the story. For delay continues to plague the narrative; even the self-assured and end-oriented lieutenant, who is "in a hurry to get home," is befuddled and thrown into doubt by what he perceives as the confusing, duplicitous course of the priest's arguments: "You never talk straight. You say one thing to me—but to another man, or a woman, you say, 'God is love.'" The ending is further delayed by the lieutenant's assent to the priest's wish for a confessor; Padre José's hesitation, and the argument with his wife over the matter, conflicts with the lieutenant's desperate desire to progress to an ending:

> "Perhaps, my dear," José said, "it's my duty . . ."
>
> "You aren't a priest any more," the woman said, "you're my husband." She used a coarse word. "That's your duty now."
> The lieutenant . . . said, "I can't wait here while you argue. Are you going to come with me?"

If the fear of nonresolution haunts the lieutenant—"You have such odd ideas . . . Sometimes I feel you're just trying to talk me round," he tells the priest—then the hollow ring of closure seems to deflate his former zeal for the hunt: "He looked back on the weeks of hunting as a happy time which was over now for ever. He felt without a purpose, as if life had drained out of the world."

As the novel works its way to a close, Greene inserts a "fictional" analogue to the real story of the plot, with the tale of a saint that Luis' mother reads him:

> "Reaching the wall, Juan turned and began to pray—not for himself, but for his enemies. . . . He raised the crucifix at the end of his beads and prayed that God would forgive them . . ."
>
> "Had they loaded?" the boy asked.
>
> "What do you mean—'had they loaded'?"
>
> "Why didn't they fire and stop him?"
>
> "Because God decided otherwise."

The reverent fictional treatment of the death of the priest is parodic in its simplicity, but the parallel runs deeper than this, for the mother's narrative is also *delayed* in comic fashion:

> "Now the moment had come, the officer gave the order to fire, and—" She had been reading too fast because it was past the little girls' bedtime and now she was thwarted by a fit of hiccups. "Fire," she repeated, "and . . ."
>
> The two little girls sat placidly side by side—they looked nearly asleep—this was the part of the book they never cared much about . . .
>
> "Fire," the mother tried again . . .

Finally the mother blurts out the remaining narrative and quickly ushers a close to the bedtime story: "'And now,' the mother went rapidly on, clapping her hands, 'to bed.'" Like a microcosm of the detective action of the novel, the woman's recitation of pious stories to her children features a delayed ending until, in the last chapter, the man of God is shot.

Almost all fiction operates on some principle of delay or suspension, but the use of *peripeteia*—especially in the ordinary detective story—is absorbed by the reader in a spirit of confident anticipation of an ending to the text which will establish order and grant explanatory meaning to the preceding narrative. This is what Frank Kermode refers to in *The Sense of an Ending* as a "disconfirmation followed by a consonance; the interest of having our expectations falsified is obviously related to our wish to reach the discovery or recognition by an unexpected and instructive route. It has nothing whatever to do with any reluctance on our part to get there at all." Greene's suspensions, his twists in the narrative path, are not absorbed or given full relief by the ending of his novels, but it is not just that his books contain "open" endings characteristic of many modernist works which refuse to seal the illusion of a fully rounded life that is now poised and ready for evaluation ([Marianna] Torgovnick). Critical interest in Greene often focuses on what follows the last page; speculations abound in the reader's mind as to the status of Pinkie, or the whisky priest, or Scobie. What is their post-narrative fate? ([Albert] Sonnenfeld). The Lehrs' Bible contains explicit directions for theological problem solving:

> If you are in trouble read Psalm 34.
> If trade is poor Psalm 37. . . .
> If you desire peaceful slumbers Psalm 121.

But the priest's astonishment at these "over-simple explanations" perhaps reflects Greene's own sense of wonder about the metaphysical realm.

The Power and the Glory ends with the ultimate repudiation of the lieutenant's pursuit, and of the teleological drive of the thriller, with the resurrection of the priesthood:

> "If you would let me come in," the man said with an odd frightened smile, and suddenly lowering his voice he said to the boy, "I am a priest."
>
> "You?" the boy exclaimed.
>
> "Yes," he said gently. "My name is Father—" But the boy had already swung the door open and put his lips to his hand before the other could give himself a name.

Thus the text's "speechless" conclusion is particularly skillful in its conflation of a realistic narrative requirement—the obscuring of clerical identity is vital in an atmosphere of persecution—with a deeper metaphor which is at work here, the silence of ineffable mystery.

FURTHER READING

Criticism

Bawer, Bruce. "'Baseless Dreaming': The Novels of Graham Greene." *The New Criterion* 8, No. 1 (September 1989): 17-33.

Provides an overview of Greene's fiction, literary career, and recent critical studies of his life and work.

Chatman, Seymour. "Who Is the Best Narrator? The Case of *The Third Man*." *Style* 23, No. 2 (Summer 1989): 189-96.

Examines the role of the narrator in *The Third Man* and the significance of Greene's choice to use different narrators in the film and book versions.

Craig, Randall. "Good Places and Promised Lands in *The Comedians*." *Renascence: Essays on Value in Literature* 39, No. 1 (Fall 1986): 312-24.

Explores the significance of public and private environments and elements of theatricality in *The Comedians*.

Diemert, Brian. "The Pursuit of Justice: Graham Greene's Refiguring of the Detective Story in *It's a Battlefield*." *Papers on Language and Literature* 30, No. 3 (Summer 1994): 285-308.

Examines Greene's reformulation of popular detective fiction and thriller conventions in *It's a Battlefield*.

Dogan, James. "Memory and Automythography in Graham Greene's *Under the Garden*." *Literature and Psychology* 40, Nos. 1-2 (Spring-Summer 1994): 81-107.

Discusses autobiographic allusions to Greene's adolescent breakdown, psychoanalysis, and recovery in the short story "Under the Garden."

Macleod, Norman. "'This Strange, Rather Sad Story': The Reflexive Design of Graham Greene's *The Third Man*." *Dalhousie Review* 63, No. 2 (Summer 1983): 216-41.

Examines Greene's self-referential authorial presence in *The Third Man* as evident in elements of parody and duality.

Schafer, Elizabeth. "Shakespeare in Greenland: A Note on *The Heart of the Matter*." *Journal of Modern Literature* XVII, No. 4 (Spring 1991): 588-91.

Examines the significance of literary quotes and intertextual references to Shakespeare in *The Heart of the Matter*.

Smyer, Richard I. "*The Tenth Man:* Graham Greene's French Connection." *Essays in Literature* 15, No. 2 (Fall 1988): 193-206.

Explores the influence of French literature and culture reflected in Greene's moral, political, and religious perspective in *The Tenth Man*.

Stannard, Martin. "In Search of Himselves: The Autobiographical Writings of Graham Greene." *Prose Studies* 8, No. 2 (September 1985): 139-55.

Examines Greene's self-conception as revealed in *A Sort of Life, Ways of Escape,* and other autobiographic writings.

Walker, Ronald G. "World Without End: An Approach to Narrative Structure in Greene's *The End of the Affair.*" *Texas Studies in Literature and Language* 26, No. 2 (Summer 1984): 218-41.

Examines the narrative progression, formal divisions, and spatio-temporal presentation of *The End of the Affair.*

Interview

MacArthur, John R. "Last Words from Graham Greene." *The Progressive* 55, No. 6 (June 1991): 25-8.

Greene comments on his writings, literary career, and current political affairs in Latin America and the Middle East.

Additional coverage of Greene's life and career is contained in the following sources published by Gale: *Authors in the News,* Vol. 2; *Concise Dictionary of British Literary Biography,* 1945-1960; *Contemporary Authors,* Vols. 13-16R, 133; *Contemporary Authors New Revision Series,* Vol. 35; *Dictionary of Literary Biography,* Vols. 13, 15, 77, 100, 162; *Dictionary of Literary Biography Yearbook,* Vol. 91; *DISCovering Authors; DISCovering Authors: British; DISCovering Authors: Canadian; DISCovering Authors Modules: Most-Studied and Novelists; Major Twentieth Century Writers; Something About the Author,* Vol. 20; and *World Literature Criticism.*

Ernst Jünger
1895-1998

(Also transliterated as Ernst Juenger) German novelist and essayist.

The following entry presents an overview of Jünger's career through 1994.

INTRODUCTION

Jünger began his career as a soldier and philosopher, but he was also an accomplished natural scientist, a novelist, and an essayist. Although Jünger was never a formal member of the Nazi Party, many Party members considered him one of the intellectual fathers of Nazism. His relationship with the Party was complicated due to his close alliance with many Nazi officials, but he is one of a few writers who criticized Nazi leadership, denied membership in the party, and survived.

Biographical Information

Jünger was born in Heidelberg, Germany, in March 29, 1895. At 16 he fled his home and joined the French Foreign Legion. His father and the local authorities tracked Jünger down and sent him home. In 1914 he enlisted in the German Army. He was wounded seven times during World War I and received the *Pour le Mérite,* Germany's highest military honor. After the war, Jünger's father encouraged him to publish a book based on the journal he kept during the war. The result was *In Stahlgewittern* (*Storm of Steel;* 1922) which recounts his war experiences. Jünger developed an interest in natural science and attended the University of Leipzig to study philosophy and zoology. He studied biology at the University of Naples in the 1920s and became an expert in the field of entomology. Jünger's early writing was political in nature, and from 1918 to 1933 he dabbled in the political arena. His activities included editing a magazine for the *Stahlhelm,* a militant veterans' group in the 1920s. Jünger dropped out of practical politics when Hitler rose to power because he disagreed with what he considered the Nazi Party's subversion of true totalitarianism. Even though he kept himself away from practical politics since 1933, he did have influential friends. These friends enabled him to get away with more than most writers under the Nazi regime, including publishing his *Auf den Marmorklippen* (*On the Marble Cliffs;* 1939), which is critical of the Nazi Party. In 1939 Jünger resumed his military career, serving on both the Eastern and Western fronts during World War II. Jünger served in Paris for part of the war, acting as a liaison between Nazi Party officials and French intellectuals. He was discharged in 1944 for being unfit to serve, but the real reason was due to his suspected involvement in the plot to assassinate Hitler. His son died in the final days of fighting on the Italian front, and this left Jünger bitter and disillusioned with war. After World War II Jünger published an essay he wrote in 1942, *Der Friede* (*The Peace;* 1945), which called for world peace and was dedicated to his son. After the fall of the Third Reich, Jünger refused to undergo an Allied denazification procedure, asserting that he was never a Nazi.

Major Works

Jünger's earlier work is in journal form and includes nostalgic reminiscences of his time as a soldier. *Storm of Steel,* in addition to other early journals, celebrates war. His article, *Die totale Mobilmachung* (1931) glorified a society permanently mobilized for total war. Jünger's next essay, *Der Arbeiter* (1932), outlined Jünger's idea of the new modern society. Jünger called for a depersonalized type, militant and radical, to replace the bourgeois individual and to usher in the new order. Jünger's controversial *On the Marble Cliffs* focuses on two brothers who settle in a fertile valley after a lost war. The area is filled with hard-working peasants and shepherds, and the forest is ruled by the Chief Ranger who uses his inhuman followers in attempts to conquer the peasants. There are several small factions who oppose the Chief Ranger, but they do not have the strength or unity to defeat him. The conclusion forecasts a triumph by the Chief Ranger, but there is allusion to hopes that out of the ashes new life will arise. After World War II, Jünger again turned to journal form in his *Strahlungen* (1949) to relate his experiences during the war. At this point in his career, Jünger's work becomes more mystical and explores the isolated individual threatened with destruction by impersonal technical forces. *Heliopolis* (1949) tells the story of two hostile rulers and the people who are the victims of their struggle for power. Another futuristic novel, *Eumeswil* (1977) is composed of the anecdotes and thoughts of a young night steward in the household of The Condor, the ruler of the fictional Eumeswil. The government of Eumeswil is dictatorial, and the book explores personal identity in the face of conformity. Common to Jünger's novels is his combination of the scientific and the magical, and his dystopian rather than utopian vision of the future. In *Aladin's Problem* (*Aladdin's Problem;* 1983), Friedrich Baroh is a member of an aristocratic German family who defects to the West. He takes a position in his uncle's funeral parlor and conceives of an idea to build a mausoleum which will guarantee eternal rest. The business is an international success, but there are questions of Baroh's ultimate happiness as he ruminates on philosophical questions. Jünger has also written several travel essays about his extensive journeys around the world. Some of Jünger's work, including *Annaeherungen* (1970), explores the roles of intoxication and drug use in enhancing human thought.

Critical Reception

Much of the critical commentary on Jünger's work has surrounded his political beliefs and his relationship to Nazism, rather than his merits as a writer. His earlier conservative politics would appear to put him in sync with the Nazi Party, which caused several reviewers to dismiss his work and his books to be banned in Allied occupied Germany. Most critics, however, assert that *On the Marble Cliffs* is a thinly veiled attack on Nazism and Hitler's rise to power. Although Jünger himself has denied this supposition, it is generally accepted. Many reviewers are impressed with Jünger's intellectual capabilities, but some reviewers complain that his philosophical and intellectual pursuits effect the nature of his fiction. They claim that his overriding philosophical intentions lower his novels' quality of storytelling. Marcus Bullock says, "His narratives do not invite one to identify with the action or the figures who carry it. His novels do not hold up a mirror to the familiar domain of human life, but clearly and deliberately go exploring beyond it." Many reviewers point out the phases of Jünger's career, asserting that Jünger abandoned his glorification of war for more humanistic pursuits. Despite the changes in his work, Ian Baruma asserts that "it was the irrational that attracted Jünger all his life: the intoxication of drugs, of revolution, of war."

PRINCIPAL WORKS

Der Kampf als inneres Erlebnis (history) 1922
In Stahlgewittern: Aus dem Tagebuch eines Strosstruppfuehrers [*Storm of Steel: From the Diary of a German Storm-Troop Officer on the Western Front*] (journal) 1922
Das Waeldchen 125: Ein Chronik aus den Grabenkaempfen 1918 [*Copse One Hundred Twenty-Five: A Chronicle from the Trench Warfare of 1918*] (journal) 1925
Feuer und Blut: Ein kleiner Ausschnitt aus einer grossen Schlacht (history) 1925
Das abenteuerliche Herz: Aufzeichnungen bei Tag und Nacht (short stories) 1929; published as *Das abenteuerliche Herz: Figuren und Capriccios,* 1938
Die totale Mobilmachung (essay) 1931
Der Arbeiter: Herrschaft und Gestalt (essay) 1932
Blaetter und Steine (essay) 1934
Afrikanische Spiele [*African Diversions*] (journal) 1936
Auf den Marmorklippen [*On the Marble Cliffs*] (novel) 1939
Gaerten und Strassen: Aus den Tagebuechern von 1939 und 1940 (journal) 1942
Der Friede: Ein Wort an die Jugend Europas, ein Wort an Die Jugend der Welt [*The Peace*] (essay) 1945
Sprache und Koerperbau (essay) 1947
Ein Inselfruehling: Ein Tagebuch aus Rhodes (travel journal) 1948
Heliopolis: Rueckblick auf eine Stadt (novel) 1949
Strahlungen (journal) 1949
Ueber die Linie (essay) 1950
Der Waldgang (essay) 1951
Der gordische Knoten (essay) 1953
Am Sarazenenturm (travel journal) 1955
Glaeserne Bienen [*The Glass Bees*] (novel) 1957
Subtile Jagden (memoirs) 1967
Annaeherungen: Drogen und Rausch (nonfiction) 1970
Die Zwille (novel) 1973
Eumeswil (novel) 1977
Siebzig verweht (journal) 1980-81
Aladin's Problem [*Aladdin's Problem*] (novel) 1983
Eine Gefuehrliche Begegnung [*A Dangerous Encounter*] (novel) 1985

CRITICISM

Louis Clair (review date 27 March 1948)

SOURCE: A review of *On the Marble Cliffs*, in *The Nation*, Vol. 166, No. 13, March 27, 1948, pp. 357-58.

[*In the following review, Clair asserts that Jünger's* On the Marble Cliffs *"is an anti-Nazi document, but it is also one of the most beautiful novels of imagination of modern Germany, an allegory in the grand symbolist manner of the death of a civilization."*]

Somewhere in a mythical landscape, high above the marble cliffs, on the edge of a fertile valley, two brothers—retired army officers—have settled after a lost war. Below in the peaceful countryside an industrious and quiet people tills its fields; farther on lives a rude yet hospitable tribe of shepherds, closely following traditional ways of life. Still farther away, in the thicknesses of the dark and impenetrable forest, the Chief Ranger, a demoniac figure, rules over the marshes with the aid of his cruel, inhuman underlings and plans to conquer the peaceful world of the peasants and shepherds outside his dark domain.

This is the setting. Juenger describes the methods, of cunning maneuver combined with brute force, which the Chief Ranger uses to achieve his goal.

On the Marble Cliffs is *a roman à clef*, an attack on Nazism only thinly veiled by the extraneous allusions, the strange locale, and the romantic style; but it is also a work of art in its own right. Juenger is a masterly stylist, who likes to experiment with the rhythmic possibilities in sentence structure and takes a sensuous pleasure in the quality of words and the shades of meaning. (The translation, if somewhat stiff, has succeeded in conveying much if not all of the dense brilliancy of Juenger's style.) Literary German suffered considerably from the barbarian language of command that the Nazis introduced in all media of communication, but Juenger is one of the few whose style not only kept its earlier purity but also gained in power and richness.

The book appeared in German shortly after the outbreak of the war and immediately achieved a considerable success, though the *Völkische Beobachter* and other Nazi papers attacked it violently and succeeded for a time in having it withdrawn from circulation. The ostensibly unpolitical story, set in a region outside time and space, in which demons consort with human beings, and primitive and highly civilized peoples live side by side, where the real and the unreal are constantly mixed and ironically inverted, was an unmistakable attack upon the regime. No German could miss the allusions to the terrorists who "wore the mask of order," to the man "who hated the plow, the corn, the vine, and the animals tamed by man, whose heart was only stirred when moss and ivy grew green on the ruins of the towns," and of whom the narrator could say, "Fear enveloped him, and I am convinced that therein far more than his own person lay his power. Only when things had begun to totter from their inherent weakness could he exercise his might." Though Juenger used that "slave language" which has been employed many times to cloak a political message against a hated tyranny, his meaning could hardly have escaped the censor. The reasons for the opposition of the Nazis are obvious; it is much less clear how the book could appear at all.

In fact, no author but Juenger would have dared to publish it: it would have been difficult to suppress the work of a man who had been one of the intellectual fathers of Nazism. To be sure, Juenger himself had never belonged to the Nazi Party, but among the young intellectuals who later became devoted Nazis he played a much more important role than the fussy prophets of blood and soil. Juenger had achieved fame as the author of books which hailed the "cosmic experience of war," as the prophet of the "total mobilization," that is, the total annihilation of the personality in the meshes of the all-embracing, all-pervasive state. Juenger had hailed the emergence of a new depersonalized type, the "worker type," destined to replace the bourgeois individual and to express the complete functionalism of the war society; he had written that morality now had become an unnecessary luxury and that the "worker" type must develop a sort of "color blindness toward values." Juenger was looked upon as a deviant yet basically dependable ideologist of the regime, though he had kept aloof from things political since 1933. Overt action could not be taken against the work of such a man, especially since he was backed by some influential army circles.

Moreover, ***On the Marble Cliffs*** is by no means a call to action. The brothers chronicle the gradual success of the forces of evil but abstain from any attempt to halt its progress. When they finally flee *to the country that has been their enemy in the last war*, they listen to a song from the shore: "Since no man then can give us aid, We turn to God in our great need." However, if Juenger chronicles the progress of evil, he refuses to participate in it. The narrator says: "I took an oath that I would rather fall in loneliness with the free men than go in triumph among the slaves."

Juenger showed great courage in publishing the book at the time he did, for it is a balance sheet of the depravity, the nihilism, and the destruction of all moral values that were the Hitler regime; it marked, moreover, the author's complete break with his past. It is an anti-Nazi document, but it is also one of the most beautiful novels of imagination of modern Germany, an allegory in the grand symbolist manner of the death of a civilization.

H. F. Peters (essay date Spring 1958)

SOURCE: "Ernst Jünger's Concern with E. A. Poe," in *Comparative Literature,* Vol. X, No. 2, Spring, 1958, pp. 144-49.

[*In the following essay, Peters discusses the theme of terror in the works of Jünger and Edgar Allen Poe.*]

Frequent references to E. A. Poe in the works of Ernst Jünger, particularly in those written during and after World War II, raise two questions: First, what is it that attracts Jünger and Poe? And second, has Jünger's interest in Poe influenced his own writings? This paper addresses itself to the first question. Concerning the second, let me simply say that I do not think it is possible to trace any direct influences of Poe on Jünger. Undoubtedly Jünger sees in Poe more than the expert craftsman of grotesque tales and romantic fantasies, although the role of the romantic element in Jünger's work should not be underestimated. The relationship of the two authors is one of affinity rather than dependency, an affinity rooted in their common concern with one major literary theme—the theme of terror.

Terror, as a literary theme, is as old as literature itself. The Greeks considered it an essential element of tragedy. In German literature the romantic poets, notably E. T. A. Hoffmann, were past masters at it—so much so that, when the theme began to appear in Poe's writings, he was accused of plagiarizing the Germans. He defended himself against this charge by protesting that, "if in many of my productions terror has been the thesis, I maintain that terror is not of Germany but of the soul."

It is surely no accident that Poe's terrors of the soul find an echo among contemporary writers. The ever-increasing complexities of our technological civilization, the threat of total destruction which hangs over us in the shape of mushroom clouds, give rise to deep-seated fears. We may dismiss such fears and refuse to talk about them; they are present nevertheless. For, as Jünger says:

> . . . was uns im Innersten beschäftigt, entzicht sich der Mitteilung, ja fast der eigenen Wahrnehmung. Da gibt es Themen, die sich geheimnisvoll durch die Jahre hindurch fortspinnen, wie etwa das der Auswegslosigkeit, die unsere Zeit erfüllt. Sie erinnert an das großartige Bild der Lebenswoge der asiatischen Malerei, auch an den Malstrom von E. A. Poe.

This entry in Jünger's war diary, ***Strahlungen,*** is dated Paris, November 18, 1941. The reference to Poe's "A Descent into the Maelström" is instructive. To understand its significance the reader must recall the events of the war winter of 1941. These were the months when Hitler's armies suffered their first serious reverses in Russia. Under the impact of an unusually severe winter, they reeled back before Moscow. To Jünger, the author of the subtly anti-Nazi novel, ***Auf den Marmorklippen,*** it meant that the end was in sight, the revolution of nihilism drawing to a close. "Wir haben in diesen Wochen den Nullpunkt passiert," he noted in his diary. "Dennoch ist es merkmürdig, daß mich im tiefsten Grunde Zuversicht belebt."

The narrator in Poe's story also passes through the "zero point" and is saved. Salvation from the jaws of death is one aspect of the terror theme. Jünger's image of the wave of life which carries man beyond destruction is exemplified by the manner in which Poe's hero is carried through the maelström and cast back into life. His brother is drowned because he lacks faith in the uplifting power of the waves. Paralyzed by terror, he clings to the ring bolt and is sucked down into the abyss.

The moral of Poe's story is that it is fatal to panic in the face of death. Terror is a test of character. If you succumb to it you are lost. It is a lesson that Jünger learned in two world wars. He feels it has a special meaning in our age. Are we not all standing at the brink of a maelström that may destroy us if we lose heart? That is why he says in a letter to me, dated January 9, 1957: "Der Malstrom erschien und erscheint mir noch als eine besonders gelungene Diagnose und Prognose unserer Zeit. Ihre Tendenz ist auf die knappste Formel gebracht."

An entry in an earlier diary, ***Gärten und Straßen,*** August 19, 1939, gives a clue to the nature of Poe's diagnosis as Jünger interprets it: "Die beste Schilderung des voll automatisierten Zustandes enthält die Erzählung 'Hinab in den Maelstrom' von E. A. Poe." Man's fate in a world of vast and terrifying mechanical forces that seem to be beyond human control is one of Jünger's major concerns. He thinks that Poe anticipated such a state and therefore deserves the epithet, "der erste Autor des zwanzigsten Jahrhunderts," which the Goncourts bestowed upon him. Poe's image of the maelström is to Jünger a symbol of our age.

He gives a similar symbolic interpretation of Poe's story, "The Pit and the Pendulum."

> Die Wassergrube gibt uns das Bild des Kessels, der immer dichteren Umkreisung, der Raum wird enger und drängt auf die Ratten zu. Das Pendel ist das Sinnbild der toten, meßbaren Zeit. Es ist die scharfe Sichel des Chronos, die an ihm schwingt und den Gefesselten bedroht, doch ihn zugleich befreit, wenn er sich ihrer zu bedienen weiß.

"Kessel" refers here to the great battles of encirclement, the *Kessel-schlachten* of the war in Russia, the classic example of which is Stalingrad. Jünger, the author of ***In Stahlgewittern,*** continues to think in military images. But there is this difference—while Jünger in his earlier books glorified war, his concern in his later books is with the isolated individual threatened with destruction by impersonal technical forces.

> Die immer künstlicheren Städte, die automatischen Bezüge, die Kriege und Bürgerkriege, die Maschinenhöllen, die grauen Despotien, Gefängnisse und raffinierten Nachstellungen—das alles sind Dinge, die Namen bekommen haben und die den Menschen Tag und Nacht beschäftigen.

These themes also occupied Poe. He anticipated many of the mechanical horrors that have become reality in our time. But the real significance of Poe's nightmarish visions is that he analyzed them and uncovered the strange ambivalence of the soul, which can be fascinated by what terrifies it. In "The Imp of the Perverse" he lays bare that streak in man which makes him seek out the very dangers that threaten to destroy him. "There is no passion so demonically impatient, as that of him, who shuddering upon the edge of a precipice, thus meditates a plunge." Modern psychologists call this fascination with terror the death wish of the soul. It is a theme that often occurs in Jünger. "Der Schwindel vor dem kosmischen Abgrund ist ein nihilistischer Aspekt," he writes with reference to Poe's essay "Eureka," and asks: "soll man, und sei es auch nur geistig, die äußersten Gewässer aufsuchen, die Katarakte, den Malstromwirbel, die großen Abgründe?" He answers yes. "In unserer Lage sind wir verpflichtet, mit der Katastrophe zu rechnen und mit ihr schlafen zu gehen, damit sie uns nicht zur Nacht überrascht." Like Hölderlin ("wo aber die Gefahr ist, wächst das Rettende auch") Jünger believes that the greater the dangers the better the chances of salvation. "Bei großen Gefahren wird das Rettende tiefer gesucht werden, and zwar bei den Müttern, und in dieser Berührung wird Urkraft befreit. Ihr können die reinen Zeitmächte nicht standhalten."

The difference between Jünger and Poe lies in their attitude towards "das Rettende," which may perhaps be interpreted as Providence. In Poe's stories salvation is usually the result of a rational act on the part of the threatened. Lashing himself to the water cask was such a rational act which saved the narrator of "A Descent into the Maelström." Jünger too believes in the saving power of courageous action, but courage alone is not enough. Something else is necessary, the support of a transcendental force, a wholly irrational power of salvation. While Poe is fundamentally a rationalist who knows the irrational yearnings of the soul, Jünger has been tending more and more towards mysticism. Rationalism, he thinks, leads to mechanism and mechanism to torture.

> Zahllose leben heute, welche die Zentren des nihilistischen Vorganges, die Tiefpunkte des Malstromes passiert haben. Sie wissen, daß dort die Mechanik sich immer drohender enthüllt; der Mensch befindet sich im Inneren einer großen Maschine, die zu seiner Vernichtung ersonnen ist. Sie mußten auch erfahren, daß jeder Rationalismus zum Mechanismus, und jeder Mechanismus zur Folter führt, als seiner logischen Konsequenz. Das hat man im 19. Jahrhundert noch nicht gesehen.

Nor, we might add, did Jünger see it in his earlier writings. This difference in attitude towards salvation in Poe and Jünger accounts for the different emphasis in their treatment of terror. For Poe it is the fascination with terror that leads him back to the same theme time and again. Jünger's emphasis is on salvation from terror. While in Poe's stories unrelieved terror often prevails, producing a melodramatic effect, Jünger imparts to his readers a sense of man's ultimate conquest of the powers of darkness. In a rather mystifying entry in ***Strahlungen,*** dated Paris, January 15, 1942, Jünger draws this distinction between himself and Poe. He quotes a letter he received from a friend concerning his "schwarze Fürstin": "Ich meine, daß Ihre Fürstin etwas vom 'Untergang des Hauses Usher' beeinflußt ist. Doch wird hier der Weg zur Heilung gezeigt. Das ist gut. Poe zeigte nur den Untergang."

In a letter to me, January 9, 1957, Jünger explains that this entry refers to his story **"Der Hippopotamus,"** published in ***Das abenteuerliche Herz.*** The heroine of his capriccio, as he calls it, is that unhappy Brunswick princess who was queen of England at the time of Napoleon. She was a victim of severe mental depressions, and the story deals with a method of treatment. As in Poe's "The Fall of the House of Usher," the narrator in Jünger's story faces a strange and threatening situation. He finds himself in the presence and at the mercy of a person who is obviously going mad. But, while in Poe's story madness finally overwhelms everything, with the narrator fleeing aghast from a scene of horror he has been unable to alleviate, Jünger presents a cure. It combines scientific and magical elements. Scientific are the prescriptions of sleeping drugs, magical the incantations the princess is to use when she feels the approach of her illness. This combination of scientific and magical elements is a distinguishing feature of Jünger's prose. It has given rise to the expression "magischer Realismus."

Scientific and magical elements also intermingle in Poe's work. But Poe saw in magic mainly a destructive force, a dark demonic power that both terrifies and fascinates the soul. To Jünger the magical forces in life are those that uplift man, carrying him beyond destruction. The mediaeval distinction between black and white magic might perhaps be applied to Poe and Jünger. The latter's concern is with man's ascent from the dark realm of demons. To his wife, who was living amidst the terrors of aerial bombardment, he wrote in June 1943: "Was Dich betrifft, so fühle ich mit Gewißheit, daß Du unbeschadet dem großen Malstrom entrinnen wirst; verliere das Vertrauen zu Deiner eigentlichen Bestimmung nicht." Poe did not have such faith to counterbalance the terrors of his soul.

Jünger is interested in Poe's world because it gives him insights into the "dark mathematics" of fate.

> Im Malstrom Edgar Allan Poes besitzen wir eine der großen Visionen, die unsere Katastrophe vorausschauten, und von allen die bildhafteste. Wir sind nun in jenen Teil des Wirbels abgesunken, in dem dic Verhältnisse in ihrer dunklen Mathematik, zugleich cinfacher und faszinierender, sichtbar werden.

Both Poe and Jünger know that there are powerful and irrational forces that urge man to seek his own destruction. This knowledge terrified Poe and he communicates to his reader a sense of doom: "And my soul from out that shadow that lies floating on the floor / Shall be lifted—nevermore!" Jünger sees a challenge to rise above it, not merely through resolute action but through faith in God's saving grace. At the end of ***Auf den Marmorklippen,*** when after a night of terror the powers of darkness seem firmly established, the sound of an organ is heard and the words:

> Weil denn kein Mensch uns helfen kann
> Rufen wir Gott um Hilfe an.

It should be noted in conclusion that Jünger's religious position, as reflected by writings cited in this paper, has puzzled many readers of his earlier works. They are not convinced that the former champion of "total mobilization," the herald of the front soldier, the author of ***Der Arbeiter,*** has undergone a genuine conversion. They feel that his metaphysical speculations are forced and his dreams, visions, and belief in magic are at best a substitute for religion. Jünger himself has noted that an age of terror inevitably gives rise to "Ersatzreligionen von unabsehbarer Zahl."

I would suggest that these critics ponder the significance of the maelström image which occupies such an important place in Jünger's later books. In its dual aspect of death and rebirth it symbolizes the human condition as all the great teachers of religion have taught us to see it. Like many writers of his generation in Germany and elsewhere—T. S. Eliot is a case in point—Jünger descended into the maelström, embraced nihilism or, as he put it, was for a time a fellow traveler of the "Mauretanians." But he did not stay there.

> Tatsächlich war, als ich diese Fabel ["Der Hippopotamus"] vor einem Besuch bie Kubin konzipierte, die Sehnsucht nach dem Aufstieg aus den dunklen Dämonenreichen des Malstroms in mir besonders stark. Man muß derartiges auch als Prognostikon betrachten, denn die erfundenen Figuren eröffnen den Schicksalsreigen, sie tanzen ihm bald lächelnd, bald schauerlich voran, und Dichtung ist unsichtbare, noch ungelebte Historie.

Amidst the terrors of a world in chaos Jünger found "Das Rettende." That, it seems to me, is the heart of the matter.

John K. Cooley (essay date Autumn 1958)

SOURCE: "The Adventures of Ernst Jünger," in *Books Abroad,* Vol. 32, No. 4, Autumn, 1958, pp. 365-68.

[*In the following essay, Cooley traces the place of adventure in Jünger's life and work.*]

Ernst Jünger's career as an author has been built around the search for adventure. With Germany, he found what he sought in war, and was finally appalled by the consequences. With her, too, he has struggled with the spirit of nihilism, both in the acute political form to which the German people fell prey between 1918 and 1945, and in the private realm of his own life. From his later books it appears that he feels both struggles to have been successful, at least temporarily.

Jünger may fairly be viewed as a more purely German writer of prose, just as Stefan George was a purely German poet, whereas Hesse and Rilke would be artists with a more European outlook who simply happened to be born to the German language. Jünger's career before 1945, at least, was in fact bound up inextricably with Germany's fate. In this year appeared his own formal break with the past, the pamphlet ***Der Friede.*** Whether his own rejection of nihilism and violence, and his recent quests for new experience in travel and metaphysics are part of a German trend is still uncertain.

Jünger's early life stands under the sign of Mars. Born in Heidelberg in 1885, he went almost directly from school to the battlefields of World War One. Wounded fourteen times, he received the *Pour le Mérite.* His book ***In Stahlgewittern*** celebrates the military virtues with unabashed fervor. In the same warlike vein were ***Der Kampf als inneres Erlebnis, Das***

Wäldchen 125, Feuer und Blut, and the first version of ***Das abenteuerliche Herz.***

If war was Jünger's first formative experience, natural science was his next. In far-flung studies and travels he discovered the worlds of zoology, botany, mineralogy. They reappear vividly in such descriptions as those of the Naples aquarium in ***Das abenteuerliche Herz,*** or the herbarium in ***Auf den Marmorklippen.*** His scientific training helped to model his prose into its hard, polished forms; precise, yet rich in suggestion and meaning, with a powerful inner rhythm which reached its heights in ***Auf den Marmorklippen.***

Politics was Jünger's third and certainly his most perilous adventure. In the years after 1918 he flirted seriously with the Right wing, ultranationalistic groups that badgered the Weimar Republic. For a time he even edited a magazine for the *Stahlhelm,* the militant veterans' group of the Twenties. He militated in the ranks of the new *Reichswehr,* the semi-secret *Führerheer,* or "army of leaders," that subverted the military clauses of the Versailles Treaty, thus playing into the hands of the Nazis, the "street rabble" which their snobbish aristocrats professed to despise.

Jünger's later regrets about this period are revealed in his work. Here the nationalist groupings are usually identified as the mythical order of Mauretania, upon which Max Bense commented at length in his absorbing study *Ptolemäer und Mauretanier.* "Instead of remaining at my studies," Jünger confesses in a revealing passage of ***Das abenteuerliche Herz,*** "I enlisted in the ranks of the Mauretanians, those subaltern polytechnicians of power."

Power and technics in their widest implications became Jünger's next preoccupations. In an imaginative, yet sociologically profound study entitled ***Der Arbeiter,*** he dissected the emotional structure of the modern worker and compared it with that of the soldier. In this light he examined the terrible dilemmas which total mobilization and total automation present for the human race.

When did Jünger, now grown taciturn in public life, decisively turn away from his earlier gods of power? It is hard to say exactly, but it is interesting that his next book, appearing less than two years after Hitler seized power, was ***Blätter und Steine,*** a delightful collection of rather whimsical essays. His fanciful ***Afrikanische Spiele*** were based on a brief experience with the French Foreign Legion before World War One and continued the "escapist" line in many respects. So did the second, self-censored version of ***Das abenteuerliche Herz,*** a remarkable short volume of scientific or pseudo-scientific sketches, allegorical fantasies, dream sequences, and poetical renditions of existential philosophy, from which much of the blood and gore of the earlier edition was missing.

Jünger promptly answered the call to the colors again in 1939 and served on both Eastern and Western fronts. All the available evidence suggests that this time his enthusiasm was greatly diminished. With some astonishment, Germany witnessed the somewhat tardy withdrawal from circulation, apparently on Gestapo orders, of the allegorical novel which may prove to be the finest of his career, ***Auf den Marmorklippen.*** It is this book which many of Jünger's present admirers contend places him among the ranks of the "inner emigration," the writers who stayed inside the Nazi pseudo-society but uttered veiled protests against it.

The plot, if it could be called one, is wholly removed from any single real setting; it is *zeitentrückt, "removed from* time," as the Germans like to say. The "Chief Forester," a villainous, backward ruler with an insatiable lust for power and destruction, preys, from the depths of his dark forest, upon the serene, time-ripened community which stands on the Marble Cliffs, overlooking the sea. In the idyllic civilization of the Marble Cliffs, the conservative European values are symbolized in the gardens and herbarium of the narrator, who finally flees the encroaching hordes of the barbarian enemy with the oath that "for all the future it was better lonesomely to fall with the free, than to go forward in triumph with the serfs."

Though the orthodox interpretation of this book outside Germany has been that it was anti-Nazi allegory, Jünger himself has appeared to deny this in his next book. This was ***Strahlungen,*** a collection of wartime diaries which, due mainly to French curiosity about Jünger's period of service with the occupation in Paris, was first published under French license in the French occupation zone of Germany (despite the fact that Jünger himself had not yet been pronounced "de-Nazified"). Commenting on an article about ***Auf den Marmorklippen*** by the Swiss critic Naef, Jünger writes, "If an intelligent critic like him, who can have no doubts about the real situation in Germany, relates the contents of this book to our political circumstances, then carelessness, if not malice, must have played a role."

Yet the book is certainly allegory on the total plight of Western civilization in this century, even if not specifically meant to deal with the German situation. And in the same book, ***Strahlungen,*** does not Jünger contemptuously refer to Hitler as "Knièbolo," a mad tyrant, and does he not tell with obvious approval what he knew of the unsuccessful officers' conspiracy to kill him during the summer of 1944?

Ernst Jünger, as he all but admits, was probably in considerable danger himself. His protector, General von Stülpnagel, the German commander in Paris whom Jünger calls "one of the last knights," killed himself to avoid the "lemurs," as Jünger calls them, of the Gestapo. Bitter, too, are his thoughts on the useless death of his son, Ernst, in some of the late fighting on the Italian front. And by the time he came to describe, at the book's end, the entry of American tanks into Kirchhorst in April, 1945, he had realized that, "From such a defeat, one does not recover as once after Jena or Sedan. This means a turning point in the life of the nations, and not only innumerable men, but also much that lies in our innermost, must die during such a transition." With many of his countrymen come to this realization very late indeed, Jünger gazes into the ashes, hopefully looking for the Phoenix of a new Germany.

Heliopolis continues this search and projects further some of the prophetic themes suggested in ***Auf den Marmorklippen.*** It is roughly comparable to some of our better science fiction. Somewhere in a southern civilization of the future stands Heliopolis, the seat of two hostile rulers. One is the aristocratic "Proconsul," in whose cause Lucius, Jünger's hero, serves. The other is the "Landvogt," who commands the power of the masses and the street. Caught between the two and reminiscent of the Jews in Nazi Germany, are the "Parsees," a persecuted race. Space ships, televisors, power rays are matter-of-fact accessories.

In the end, Lucius, recognizing the hopelessly Utopian nature of the Proconsul's desire to preserve the old culture through enlightened despotism, leaves his service to answer a mysterious summons from the "Regent." The latter is a third, remote and apparently all-powerful ruler who may be God, or the ideal state, or both. In any case, though Lucius hopes to return as a harbinger of the Regent's universal peace, the author recognizes the futility of this hope for the present: "But these days are far removed from us."

This futility is, doubtless, for Jünger as for so many of his European contemporaries, one reason for his postwar preoccupation with metaphysics, and especially the philosophy of existence. It could hardly have been coincidence that his book ***Der Waldgang*** appeared in the same year and under the same publisher's imprint as Martin Heidegger's *Holzwege,* or that other philosophical essay of Jünger's, ***Über die Linie,*** a postscript to Nietzsche which professed to see a way out of nihilism at last.

It is probable that Jünger had long been familiar with Heidegger's "Being and Time," and the philosopher's influence on him seems to have grown through the years. A figure appearing repeatedly in his books, imparting to him dreamlike admonitions and communications, is the "teacher" Nigromontanus, or *Schwarzwäldler* in German. This "Black Forester" is none other than Heidegger himself, who comes from the Black Forest. In ***Das abenteuerliche Herz*** and other books he warns his disciple to look behind the veils which cover the "authenticity of things" and discover his true nature, as well as that of death. He presents the existentialist dogma of first acknowledging the inevitable fact of one's own eventual death and then beginning one's life anew.

Jünger sees three main roads to "authentic existence": dream (*Traum*); intoxication (*Rausch*); fortune (*Glück*). At the end, however, actually lies death, the supreme contact with Being and Reality. On the "lonesome march" to this final encounter, says Jünger in ***Das abenteuerliche Herz,*** "one is like a soldier who will regain his rank" after he has halted before the gates of death "as before a lonely customs house in the highest mountains, where the coin of memory is exchanged for gold" and where the dying man perceives that no one is at his heels, not even the Devil, but that "on the contrary, he exchanges fear against security."

Jünger differs from Heidegger in that to him animals and plants are examples of real "beings" in the "authentic" state, whereas for Heidegger they are merely *vorhanden,* "present in the world," unable to participate in "authentic" existence, which is reserved to the human individual alone. Jünger, however, sees this reality in all living creatures: in a woodpecker by the Bodensee, in a black codfish twitching its life away in a Norwegian fish market, in a rare scarab he turns up under a rock near Casablanca. This insistence that a human being, in order to be whole and healthy, must develop an awe and respect for other creatures, reappears in all his recent travel books, which, like ***Ein Inselfrühling*** and ***Am Sarazenenturm*** are mainly records of his very German fascination with the Mediterranean.

In his latest book, ***Gläserne Bienen,*** Jünger returns to his earlier preoccupations with the power of technology and the technology of power. The hero, Rittmeister Richard, a former cavalry officer stemming from the ordered society before World War One, is faced with the choice of starving or seeking employment with Zapparoni, an industrial magnate who produces all types of mechanical toys and robots which can readily be adapted as weapons. Again, the themes of Germany's defeat and possible redemption are suggested. Jünger sees some kind of *modus vivendi,* perhaps an armed truce, between the individual and the dehumanized world of technology as the only program for survival. In this book, he is on warmer, easier terms with the human personality than he has been before.

It is a fair conclusion, I think, from the body of his work thus far, that Jünger, after having grown thoroughly familiar, during all his adventures, with the worst and most demonic sides of man's nature, now entertains hopes for the triumph of his better side. In the final episode of ***Das abenteuerliche Herz,*** the narrator walks the streets of Ponta Delgada, in the remote Azores, where "the eye beholds the flowers of a new world." Suddenly he spots a fish dealer who, in crying out his wares to windows closed tightly against the noonday sun, seems to add something in a mumble, softly to himself:

> And so we walked through the hot alleys to offer fish which no one wanted at noon. And long I listened to his two voices, the loudly echoing, exuberantly soliciting cry, and the soft, despairing monologue. I followed him with an eavesdropping lust, for I marked well that here it was no longer a question of fish, but that on this lost island I was hearing the poem of man—at once his loud bragging and his soft, imploring song.

Arthur R. Evans, Jr. (essay date 1978)

SOURCE: "Ernst Jünger's *Auf den Marmorklippen:* a sketch toward an interpretation," in *Symbolism and Modern Literature,* edited by Marcel Tetel, Duke University Press, 1978, pp. 26-43.

[*In the following essay, Evans, Jr. discusses the plot and philosophy behind Jünger's* Auf den Marmorklippen, *and asserts that Jünger believes "in the power of civilizing energies to overcome evil."*]

Ernst Jünger's allegorical novel depicts a model of world harmony, a cosmos destroyed by brutish, anarchical forces. It opens on a nostalgic note, evoking the poignant memories of a way of life founded on fraternity, civil order, the rhythm of nature, and a respect for the traditional pieties. The mood is autumnal and, appropriately, reference is made to the festivals celebrated once upon a time in conjunction with the yearly harvests. The new wine is tasted, nuts are eaten, there is time for bird shooting, and crowds congregate along the shores of the Grand Marina to carouse and joust with one another in displays of wit. At early morning the sun rises over Alta Plana, situated to the south, beyond the waters of the Marina, just as the sun will set, at the end of the novel—to rise again, we know—upon the prosperous homestead of Ansgar up on the mountains of Alta Plana. On a bright day the eye can see all the way to the borders of New Burgundy where the high-born family of Sunmyra, representative of the declining aristocracy, lives and farms its estates. On their way home at dawn from the fall feastings, the two brothers now and then catch a glimpse of some startling scene or image having the power to call up, but only for a moment, the archaic, preternatural spirit of the land, fecund yet terrible in its promise of unnamed menace.

There were celebrations, too, which usher in the spring equinox. Here the brothers and townspeople of the Marina, dressed up as clowns decked out in bird feathers, join in the merriment by attaching themselves to the guild of the woodpeckers. Meanwhile, the crowd sets up in the old marketplace the traditional tree of fools. In mocking, discordant accompaniment to the general festivity are the shrill call and answer of the authentic birds of the area. Their ominous cry is to the rites of spring what the chilling images of nature's secrets are to the winemaking holidays: a sign of foreboding amidst the general air of abundance and well-being.

The narrator and Bruder Otho live in the Rue Cloister (*Rautenklause*). To get to their home from the Marina one passes through the Cock Gate, from which on the left loom up the Marble Cliffs, the cloister itself being situated on the edge of the cliff in close proximity to long stretches of grapeland. During the spring the hyacinth blooms and in fall the wild cherry, but all year long the silver-green rue bushes give off their pungent odor. *Ruta,* herb of grace in the lore of flowers, possesses powers against evil spells: formerly, a branch of rue was used to sprinkle holy water in churches, and the ancients, according to Pliny, believed that the plant not only improved the physical strength of the eye but bestowed, as well, an inner vision, a second sight. The Rue Cloister consists of a library, which opens onto the garden where the golden lily is in flower, and, on the second floor, an herbarium. Here the brothers are engaged, with the aid of Linnaeus' *Systema Naturale,* upon a lifetime's labor of collecting and classifying the flora of the region. Living with the two of them is Lampusa, who acts as a housekeeper and tends the kitchen placed in the lower recesses of the Marble Cliffs, and Erio, the illegitimate child of the narrator, whose mother is Silvia, daughter of Lampusa. The boy and his grandmother have been brought to the Cloister by Bruder Otho who has the knack of winning people's confidence, a gift for bringing out the best in them. Lampusa is the Terrible Mother, a telluric force, one who knows the dark, generative—and destructive—secrets of nature. She entertains Belovar, the just herdsman, in her cliff cellar but at the same time is on good terms with the *Oberförster's* ruthless huntsmen. Lampusa communicates with the lancehead vipers who dwell in the crevices of the Marble Cliffs and, at sunset, descend to the court of the cloister to drink the milk which she sets out for them. Distinguished from the rest by her brass-burnished scales and jewel-like green head is the leader of the viper train, Griffin, who becomes the special pet of Erio, the divine child or *puer senex,* a model of strength and purity whose presence invigorates the brothers while at their work. Whenever these serpents join company with Erio, they gather about him in the form of a sun disk.

Hard by the Rue Cloister, on the southern, Marina side of the Marble Cliffs, stands the monastery of the Falcifera, dedicated to Maria Lunaris. She, in the words of Bruder Otho, combines on a higher plane the virtues of Fortuna and Vesta and must be seen as a beneficent counterforce to the baleful charms of Lampusa. The monastery houses the eminent botanist Father Lampros, who, as a specialist on the symmetry of fruits, can help the brothers currently at work on a study of how plants, in their growth, form a circle around an axis. Obedient to nature's ways, as is indicated by his other name Phyllobius, he who lives with leaves, and by the motto engraved on his cornelian ring, "meyn geduld hat ursach" (patience is my strength; i.e., I bide my time), Lampros has been initiated into the nutritional, curative, and integrating properties of plant life. First met by the brothers with a gladiola in hand (*Siegwurzrispe*) and light streaming from the transept window on his white mantle, this priest is the great force for good, for the sustaining recreative virtues of spirituality in the face of the destructive powers unleashed by the *Oberförster.* Lampros and Maria are, respectively, the solar and lunar principles at work, a *hieros gamos* or union of the blazing sun of science and the twilight of imagination and mystery. Both the Rue Cloister and the monastery, then, are fully achieved centers of being, for at the brother's house it is they who represent the conscious, rational mind, whereas Lampusa incarnates infrarational, chthonic drives. The force joining and transcending the two realms, and the link between cloister and monastery—in his messages to the brothers, Lampros will entrust their dispatch only to him—is Erio, the mystic, heroic child. And the configuration of the sun disk formed by the serpents under Erio's spell—"coiled into a circle, [the serpent] symbolizes the self-sufficiency and oneness which are associated with God's preservative power"—finds its parallel in that mysterium revealed in the monastery garden by Lampros to the two brothers, the green circlet of leaves and the vibrant, radiant center of the otherwise quite inconspicuous plantain, *Plantago major.* Coiled snake and plantain, like Bruder Otho's golden lily and the gladiola of Lampros, are thus mandalas, Indian circular images signifying, in modern psychoanalytic terms, that wholeness which the human personality strives to attain. The contemplative stillness of the monastery enclosure, the bright blue sky and strong sunlight which are the atmospheric setting for the disclosure of the hidden, restorative virtualities of the plantain flower, form a pastoral landscape, a *locus amoenus,* lying at the extreme opposite to the horrible forest clearing of Köppelsbleek with its instruments of torture and perversion, lost in mist, and haunted by the mocking cry of the cuckoo bird and the whispering of bats.

This place of infamy, the source from which terror will spread out over the land—"die üble Küche, aus der die Nebel über die Marina zogen"—lies to the north of the Marble Cliffs, on the far side of the Campagna, just beyond the marshlands where the domain of the *Oberförster* begins. On days when the brothers are pleased with the progress of their research, they will climb to the summit of the Cliffs and enjoy the sublimity of its panoramic view. At other times, tired and depressed, the two will set out on botanical excursions in search of a new specimen. One such field trip, undertaken to find a variety of Linnaeus' *rubra*—the woodland orchid (*Rote Waldvögelein*)—brings them deep within the Campagna, past the three poplars and the obscene image of the Red Steer, to the sickle-shaped Flayers' Copse (the depraved antitype of Mary's cloister, the Falcifera, "sickle-bearing," "sickle-shaped"). To their delight they discover the flower—but at the same time, too, the ghastly spectacle of Köppelsbleek with its stakes and hooks, rattling skulls, and singing dwarf hard at work. Terrified, the impulse is to flee the place, but catching hold of themselves, they are reminded of their obligation as scientists to enter a description of the woodland plant and its natural setting in their journal. Here again the flower functions as a mandala, an image of the potentialities of the self. In the juxtaposition of orchid and skull, beauty in its vital growth and radiance resists the destructive power of evil.

Linked with the mandala as a conserving, integrative force are the lamp and mirror of Nigromontanus (necromancer), used at the discretion of Bruder Otho, the pure blue flame of which acts as a caustic burning objects down to their very essence. In the "time of troubles" which has overcome the land of the Marble Cliffs, the brothers must be ready at any moment to set fire, as eventually they will, to herbarium and library. Nigromontanus' mirror with its device, "Und sollte die Erde wie ein Geschoss zerspringen / Ist unsere Wandlung Feuer und weisse Glut" (And were the earth to explode like a shot / In our transformation we have become fire and a white glow), is assurance that their painfully acquired spiritual acquisitions will not fall prey to base powers, but instead be preserved in a higher order. If the mandala is an expression of the organic, curative virtues of nature, then the mirror translates the transforming power of art in its victory over the forces of destruction. These agents of conservation gather to themselves a whole series of such efficacious symbols. At moments of fatigue and discouragement, the narrator and Bruder Otho close the doors of the cloister, drink wine, breathe the fragrance of stored-up leaves and flower petals, light the pure-grained candles of the Provençal knight Deodat, which call to mind the sunset hour in Rhodes; they will page through the books of trusted authors and browse among old letters from cherished friends. These varied, intimate sensations and nostalgic musings nourish an idealizing memory which shores up the fragments of the past and protects them against the erosion of time. The brothers are fond, too, of composing gnomic couplets or doggerel lines which sum up, in their pithiness, nature's laws. Scribbled down on slips of paper, they serve in the evening as points of departure for serious conversation, after which they are discarded. These sibylline jottings join mandala and mirror and the various stimulants to memory as steps in a contemplative ritual dedicated to moral order, heightened awareness, and the effort to discern a pattern in the manifoldness of nature.

The present course of events occurs some seven years after the war against Alta Plana to which the brothers ascribe the ills that have ever since slowly infected the land. During the war they were enrolled in the Purple Riders, an elite squadron of the order of the Mauretanians, and it was here that they knew and frequented the company of the *Oberförster,* who was for a time commander of all Mauretania. Prior to their enlistment, the brothers were living at loose ends; distracted and jaded by a way of life which had no meaning for them, they joined this far-flung order dedicated to the pursuit of power for its own sake. The Mauretanians are cool, disabused realists, the managerial strategists of Jünger's ***Der Arbeiter.*** Disciplined, endowed with keen practical intelligence, these men are committed to a ruthlessly detached view of political power. The philosophy of action which they espouse is a peculiarly abstract, efficient one intent only upon the manipulation of tangible forces: *a priori* values and inherited loyalties count for nothing in its calculations. These ascetics of the will, with their single-minded vision, exercise a strong attraction on the brothers wandering about feckless and apathetic.

Thus the Mauretanian order and the regimen of the Rue Cloister lie at opposite poles from each other, yet their extremes meet. The Rue Cloister:

> Vielleicht war es *die starke Luft der Rautenklause,* die unserem Denken eine neue Richtung gab, gleich wie im reinem Sauerstoff die Flamme steiler und heller brennt (The new direction which our thought took was no doubt owing to the bracing air of the Rue Cloister, just as in pure oxygen the flame burns higher and brighter).

And the Mauretanians:

> Bei den Mauretanieren . . . herrschte unberührte Stille wie im Zentrum des Zyklons. Wenn man in den Abgrund stürzt, soll man die Dinge in dem letzten Grad der Klarheit wie durch überschärfte Gläser sehen. Diesen Blick, doch ohne Furcht, gewann man in *der Luft der Mauretania,* die von Grund auf böse war (An undisturbed stillness as in the center of a cyclone prevailed among the Mauretanians. When we plunge into the abyss, we see things in their highest degree of clarity, just like looking through a sharply focused lens. This is the kind of vision, but without fear, that one attained to in the air of Mauretania which [nevertheless] was evil from the ground up).

The discipline of each of these separate ways of life, active and contemplative, calls for lucidity of outlook and the strict dedication to an ideal. The common denominator is an ethic which will both concentrate and liberate vital energies. Something of the element of play in its detachment and gratuitousness, its release of powers within very fixed limitations, enters into both spheres. Each of these styles is radically set apart from the normal, commonplace routines of life and demands from its initiates the virtues which we normally associate with solitude: a freedom from distraction, perseverance, and a steady reliance upon one's own moral resources. Given, then, the factors common to these two pursuits, the conquest of power, on the one hand, and the search for truth, on the other, both by nature radically alien to a bourgeois existence, though directed to entirely opposite ends, it is not surprising that they should appeal to the two brothers at different periods in their life, just as, indeed, they have to Ernst Jünger himself, warrior and contemplative, the author and actor of ***In Stahlgewittern*** and ***Subtile Jagden.*** On the level of biography, of *la vie romancée,* an essential though not, of course, the most important vantage point from which to read our novel, the campaign in Alta Plana with its sorry aftermath is a near-literal translation of Ernst and Friedrich Georg Jünger's engagement in the First World War and their subsequent conviction, never in doubt, that Germany's series of humiliating setbacks in the twenties must be seen as a result of the fatherland's disastrous defeat and the succeeding injustices of the Versailles Treaty. The boredom with life as it is felt by narrator and Bruder Otho transcribes fictionally the Jünger brothers' disdain for the Weimar Republic's experiment in parliamentary democracy, with its assumed concessions to mass opinion, as well as their fear of the growing rationalization and vulgarization of all areas of life in contemporary Germany. Even such a detail in the story as the magnanimity shown by the brothers towards Ansgar, the enemy soldier, finds its real-life counterpart in Jünger's gallant attitude and gestures towards his English enemies on the western front during the Great War and in his desperate efforts generally to imagine some kind of chivalry in even the bloodiest moments of trench fighting.

Yet for all the points of similarity between the way of the Cloister and that of Mauretania, it is the differences which are crucial and must be stressed. The latter has as its purpose self-aggrandizement achieved through means which depend upon aggression, domination, and exploitation; the other, to which the brothers have become converted, calls for a renunciation of self, an openness to natural laws and processes which transcend the individual person and serve to integrate him in an indivisible order, at once physical and spiritual. The grandmaster of the Mauretanians is the Chief Ranger—the *Oberförster.* His extraordinary presence, alluded to in the very first pages of the novel, shadows the entire narration without his ever once making an actual appearance. We hear his trumpeting laughter at the moment when he unleashes Chiffon Rouge and the bloodhound pack, and can envision the ilex-leaf pattern of his coat as he rides with arrogant assurance through his domains. He is the prince of darkness, "der Geist, der stets verneint." From his various strongholds deep within the forest interior, he sends forth his "glowworms," huntsmen, and mercenaries to spread suspicion, pick quarrels, aggravate troubled situations, abet corruption, and perpetrate acts of terrorism. Since the days of Charlemagne the Marina has often been invaded and occupied by foreign troops; but manners, customs, and even the physical setting of the area have changed very little. It is only now with the end of hostilities against Alta Plana that a perceptible deterioration has come about in the quality of life and the general look of things. The time-honored ways of the vintner, poet, and philosopher are despised in favor of the raw, boisterous behavior of the Campagna herdsmen. Once the privilege of heros, the sacred funeral rites of *elegeion* and *eburnum,* severely set forth and devoutly attended to, have become profaned, being now nothing better than raucous wakes to which any common bootlicker is entitled. One-time citizens of the Marina, who as refugees from justice have fled to the bogs and meadows of the Campagna, keep up connections with the homeland, thus making possible a continuous intrusion of alien, questionable practices. Progressively, the constabulary of the local police chief, Biedenhorn, himself open to corruption, has been infiltrated by bullies and criminal types dispatched from the "back of the beyond." For life in the Campagna, too, has degenerated. Because of the sinister influence of the *Oberförster,* the native, barbaric elements have become unruly, prone to yield to the darker, vicious sides of their nature. The kind of rude but fundamentally decent code of social behavior as represented by Belovar and his son Sombor, who stand for the older, authentic morality of the Campagna, is fast disappearing. A debilitating fever, a general failure of nerve paralyze the whole area, from the confines of the Campagna down beyond the Marina's shore to the holiday islands of the Hesperides where in happier times people used to row over, during the autumn, to enjoy the festivities of St. Peter's Fish and to delight in the sight and fragrance of the roses which bloom all year. Only the Rue Cloister and the Convent of Maria Lunaris, both close by the Marble Cliffs and oases of the spiritual life, remain immune against this corrupting malaise. Yet even here the menace is very real: Lampusa's ambiguous presence inhabits the lower depths of the white peaks.

During their tour of duty with the Mauretanians, the narrator and Bruder Otho would, on occasion, drink and ride with the *Oberförster.* His grand manner and the charismatic authority which he wielded fascinated them. His person, if somewhat ridiculous, possessed a genuine compelling force, all the more dominating for standing out in such contrast to the inertia of the times. Here was a creature possessed by some daemonic power, capable, one feared, of appalling acts; yet demanding from us, however grudgingly and qualified, our admiration. As the brothers remark upon listening to the ruthless exploits of the Capitano, who was later to introduce them to the *Oberförster* and to Mauretania: "Lieber noch mit diesem stürzen, als mit jenen leben, die die Furcht im Staub zu kriechen zwingt" (Better to fall with this fellow than to live with those whom fear brings to their knees in the dust). Nor do the brothers question the rightness of the war they engage in against the Alta Plana. For them it is a matter, in the last resort, of doing their duty—and duty is itself a source of order, of inner strength. Nevertheless, they sympathize with these people who were defending their freedom against foreign oppression. It is perhaps the encounter with Ansgar and the mercy they show him that first prompt a decisive change of heart. From their present point of view, absorbed in the life of the Rue Cloister, they see that the two of them could have risen high in the ranks of Mauretania were it not for their sense of outrage at its repressive measures against the suffering and the weak. The fundamental inhumanity of the order was intolerable to them and they had to leave. That change of heart brought on by the meeting with Ansgar in the treacherous mountain passes of the Bergland is steadily reinforced and brought to a firm resolution in the close association with Pater Lampros. They have renounced the use of force and put off forever the way of the Mauretanians. This is apparent in the brothers' refusal, after momentarily weighing their decision, to join Belovar in ridding the area through violent means of the *Oberförster*'s terrorist gangs. Aided by Lampros' example, they are determined to resist the present tyranny by remaining unswervingly devoted to a life of study and contemplation.

The choice they have made is summed up in the meeting with Braquemart (short, broad-bladed sword) and Sunmyra (he who does not speak). Each of the two is only half a person: the first, the epitome of the Mauretanian outlook, is a technician of power but with no feeling for the affective, infrarational bases of our existence; the other a sensitive, noble spirit but without the force to act upon his fine impulses. The two, nihilist and aristocrat, have come together to challenge in his very seat of authority the despotic rule of the *Oberförster.* Their well-intentioned, futile, and ultimately tragic union points to the deep, seemingly irreconcilable divisions in contemporary Western culture between a conservative humanism which has lost confidence in itself and is powerless to shape the dynamic forces released by contemporary civilization, and an arrogant, runaway technocracy, heedless of spiritual values and revealing itself in certain of its grander conceptions to be grimly antihuman. "Tout ce que nous savons, tout ce que nous pouvons," Valéry writes, "a fini par s'opposer à tout ce que nous sommes." As the two men walk up the Marble Cliffs, the Prince of Sunmyra scarcely pays attention to the magical lance-head vipers, while Braquemart contemptuously steps aside from their path. Head and heart have been severed from each other, and the "two cultures" go blindly each its own way. The pathetic, frustrated efforts of Sunmyra anticipate with astonishing foresight the deliberations and abortive attempts of the German aristocracy, such men as Claus von Stauffenberg, Count Helmuth James von Moltke, Peter Yorck von Wartenburg, and Adam von Trott zu Solz, to resist and overcome Hitler. It had been Jünger's forlorn hope, often commented upon in his journals of the World War II years, that the aristocracy, the Prussian landed gentry, would provide the moral leadership for a "conservative revolution" against the modern ideologies of capitalism and communism, thus preventing the rise to power and consolidation of National Socialism. Lampros' intercession on Sunmyra's behalf and the preservation of the latter's head in the petal-strewn amphora represent Jünger's sympathies with the traditional values of the German nobility, the bearers of that "Third Force," so called from the vantage point of the political right. Hearing on May 1, 1945, of Hitler's death, Jünger remarked—referring to Stauffenberg's abortive attempt at assassination the year previously—upon his own early awareness that any serious try on Hitler's life would have had to be made by one born of the old aristocracy and that, paradoxically, the dramatic and spiritual effect of such an act would lie only in its failure. "I pointed this out in detail with the figure of Sunmyra in 1939."

Sunmyra is scarcely twenty years old, yet already stooped in body and world-weary in mind. He shows interesting resemblances to and differences from the thaumaturgic child Erio, wise far beyond his years and a never-failing source of joy. When the narrator sets out on his perilous search for the young prince, he takes with him the reassuring smile of Erio. It is the brother's hope, disappointed by events, that Sunmyra can come under the care of Father Lampros, for they are confident that this counselor of souls can restore to the tired scion of an old Burgundy family the faith, purpose, and resolve to check the disorders raging all about and to build anew. They do join each other in spirit, priest and dreamer, in the spectacular scene of apotheosis capping the catastrophic events which overtake the Grand Marina. While the Cloister of Maria Lunaris goes up in flames, the brothers hold aloft to Lampros amidst the wreckage the embalmed head of Sunmyra; the hierophant, as a sign of consecration, returns this invocatory gesture by raising his hand with the cornelian ring (bearing the motto, "I bide my time"). The nobleman's sacrifice has been made wholly acceptable, a pleasing gift. The large rose window in the transept, where the brothers first met the priest, falls in upon Lampros, its green tracery reproducing in outline the wondrous plantain flower of the monastery garden. The prince's head, purplish in cast from its preservative of wine and roses, and the glowing stained-glass window complete the series of mandalas and thus set a seal upon the exchange of sacred gestures. In the general holocaust which sweeps the country, the young Sunmyra's death is an offering in prayer for a new beginning.

Braquemart is Jünger's embodiment of a specifically modern form of evil, rootless, without allegiance, scientifically trained but one-dimensional; contemptuous of sentiment, resentful by instinct, he is bent upon destruction—even if it means, as by the logic of his character it must, self-destruction. He belongs, like Koestler's Gleitkin, to the race of the Neo-Neanderthals. In the play of forces, ideological and psychological, Braquemart sides with the *Oberförster*, though there are important differences between them. As the principle of evil, the Chief Ranger belongs, mythologically, to an ancient heritage which includes the various personifications of Satan as well as the archvillains of the Gothic novel and the Romantic imagination. A creature of the twilight, he has a wisdom of the ways of beast, wind, and rain. He is the dark, gnostic power of all the many versions of a Manichaean view of life (cf. his countertype, Lampros, the Greek word for "brilliant," "effulgent"). However real his menacing presence, there is, as a creation of myth, something fanciful and literary about him. Though both men are possessed by a frenzy to destroy, Braquemart is a different matter. He is a peculiarly modern phenomenon, conceived and analyzed imaginatively in Dostoevski's novels, heralded in Nietzsche, and realized in the revolutions and wars of our century. His nihilism is the product of a dehumanized rationalism which thrives in our modern age of capitalist enterprise, vast urbanized conglomerates, relentless technocratic advances, bureaucratization, and sophisticated advertising. The complexity and nervous rhythms of today exasperate his sensibilities and turn him inward, creating a mood of sullenness and self-hate. Hence Braquemart's urge to make *tabula rasa* of everything: his natural climate is the desert, just as the forest is the habitat of the *Oberförster*. Jünger insists upon the fact that *der Alte* of the forest is a man of action, whereas Braquemart is a theorist. In any confrontation the modern city-bred nihilist is no match for the anarchist from the deep, primeval interior; the former, as the inheritor of all the dark secrets of the *selva oscura*, is simply too old in experience to be outdone by such a latecomer. And so, quite predictably, the latter's joint expedition with Sunmyra ends in disaster. Upon the arrival of the pair in the evening at the Rue Cloister, the Japanese lilies have opened up, displaying in their flawless beauty six slender stamens set in a circle about the pistil; when they take leave of the brothers at dawn, the lily's purity has been flawed: night moths have done it violence, and as the narrator makes this discovery, he detects in the distance the cuckoo bird's call, its mocking sound not having been heard since that horrendous afternoon at Köppelsbleek.

This ghoulish site serves at the end of the novel as the meeting ground for the deadly struggle between Belovar and the *Oberförster*, the autochthonous forces of the Campagna pitted against the barbarous anarchy of the forest. Here, in the natural scheme of things, the contest is more evenly matched, and it is only because of greatly superior numbers that the Chief Ranger is finally able to rout his opposition. Their savage encounter engages the two dog packs, the Molosson mastiffs of Belovar led by Leontodon and the *Oberförster*'s red-and-black Cuban bloodhounds with the dreaded Chiffon Rouge at their head. The dog of story and legend, Anubis, Cerberus, Xolotl, has been traditionally associated with death and the underworld, and these dogs of the *Marmorklippen* are hellhounds. Their tearing at each other, in this Night of the Long Knives, is the final, convulsive release of all the pent-up fury and agitation, intrigue and suspicion which have been plaguing the country. The discharge of brutish force, of hot blood, must be seen as setting off the general destruction by fire which sweeps the entire area. The war between the Campagna and Forest, in which the narrator takes part almost in spite of himself—dedicated as he has been to the pursuits of peace—is a psychomachy, a death struggle between the powers of good and evil which explodes into holocaust. From the top of the Marble Cliffs where the narrator had been given in privileged moments of the past a vision of world harmony, he sees, laid out in front of him as far as the eye can reach, a view of total conflagration. The old order of things has gone up in smoke, and together with it the Rue Cloister, consumed by the flame of Nigromontanus' lamp, and the Convent of Maria Lunaris.

In Chiffon Rouge's deadly pursuit of the narrator, it is Erio who comes to the latter's aid. Lampusa, in league with the *Oberförster,* scorns to give help to the oppressed, while Bruder Otho, preoccupied with mirror and lamp, is lost in thought and not to be distracted by any concern for his brother's physical safety: these are witch and scientist transfixed by their own obsessive concerns and closed to any call from outside. The narrator leaps over the garden wall, falling in the lily bed, whereupon at a signal from Erio the lance-head vipers, Griffin in the lead, descend the steps of the Marble Cliffs. The bejeweled serpent strikes at Chiffon Rouge, who drops dead among the lilies, while the remaining vipers, in describing a golden circle about the feeding bowl, move out in stately, martial rhythm and strangle in a flash both bloodhound and men. The boy leaves then, smiling at the narrator, and we never hear from him again. Erio, like Lampros, has acted as a psychopomp for the brothers, initiating them into the mysteries. Griffin (*Greifin*), the name of the magnificent queen of the vipers, is an allusion to the mythical beast of antique and medieval lore (m. Greif) whose twin nature, lion(ess) and eagle, binds together in a single whole earthly and celestial energies. The rich, complex symbolism adhering to this serpent makes her a figure of harmony, and thus a salvific force. With the extermination of the hellhound Chiffon Rouge, the sinister powers released by the *Oberförster* have been brought under control, and life can now begin anew on the Grand Marina. As an emphatic sign of resurrection, Bruder Otho restores to its former dignity the sacred ritual of the *eburnum* while participating in funeral services for Sunmyra at the old family chapel. Yet if there are hesitant steps toward a return to normality and hope, the dangers to existence persist: Biedenhorn, the sycophantic police captain, always alert to which way the wind is blowing, has run up over the town fortress the flag of the red boar's head, an emblem, like night moth, dog, and cuckoo bird, of the *Oberförster*'s menacing presence.

Our parable's schematic alignment of good and evil forces finds its metaphoric counterpart in the studied use of narrative moments rendered antithetically in light and dark: the smile of Erio and Lampusa's surly glance; the gold lily and the shimmering bodies of the lance-head vipers as contrasted with the blood-stained, weathered imagery and dark fauna of Köppelsbleek; the periods of joy in scientific study accompanied by excursions to the summit of the cliffs, followed by intervals of depression and the outings into the grey Campagna marshlands. Appalled by the sight of the decapitated Sunmyra, the narrator falls into a trance, a traumatic seizure in which his right arm is paralyzed; it is in such a state that he participates in the great regenerative destruction by burning and sees the gardens of the Rue Cloister, while being chased by Chiffon Rouge, as in a magical, metallic light. It is only when the serpents have assumed the mandala shape just prior to their attack that the narrator is roused from his dream and his arm quickened to life. Indeed the two principal centers of action, symbolic poles in this fable, are conceived in terms of *chiaroscuro:* the gleaming Marble Cliffs and that heart of darkness, the forest lair of the Chief Ranger. The motif of light as a symbol of harmony is complemented by a strong if discreet colorist sense which presents in rich array efficacious objects and phenómena. Their virtuality for good is mirrored forth in vivid, pleasing color. Consider only the dramatic moment of the ruin by fire of Rue Cloister and Maria Lunaris late in the novel; chromatic values and hues are set off against each other with rich yet restrained effect: lilies and roses, the white of Deodat's candles and the wine-purple trophy of Sunmyra's head, Lampros' vestments and cornelian ring placed in the green setting of the cloister window, and the pure, steady, resonant blue of Nigromontanus' lamp. These colors burst forth, then, and are burned out in the awesome incandescence of the final, apocalyptic fires which sweep the country.

The purging holocaust brings with it the hope of a new life. The Alta Plana for which the brothers set sail succeeds, as a spiritual landmark, to the Marble Cliffs of the Grand Marina, just as Ansgar *père et fils,* who welcome them to their farmstead, now replace Belovar and his son Sombor. The barns, stalls, and family dwelling are all, within the shadow of the live oak, set together in one complex—the image of a unitary, organic scheme of life, and similar in this singular grouping to the brothers' family house in the north where the sword of chivalry lies. As in a spiraling climb, like that about the margin of the White Cliffs, we have come back to a point from where we started but on a higher level of ascent. In moments of deep contentment, narrator and brother are in the habit of climbing the marble peaks to watch the sun play upon sea and countryside.

> Wenn wir vom hohen Sitze auf die Stätten schauten, wie sie der Mensch zum Schutz, zur Lust, zur Nahrung und Verehrung sich errichtet, dann schomolzen die Zeiten vor unserm Auge innig ineinander ein. Und wie aus offenen Schreinen traten die Toten unsichtbar hervor. Sie sind uns immer nah, wo unser Blick voll Liebe auf altbebautem Lande ruht, und wie in Stein und Ackerfurchen ihr Erbe lebt, so waltet ihr treuer Ahnengeist in Feld und Flur (When we look out from high places upon the abodes of man, and consider how they have been erected in his honor and for his enjoyment, protection, and sustenance, then before our view all time fuses into a single moment. And the dead step forward, invisible, as though from open shrines. They are always close to us wherever our eye rests, full of affection, upon the land cultivated from old, and just as their inheritance lives in stone and furrow, so the true ancestral spirit presides in field and meadow).

From this privileged prospect, the different periods of the past merge into a single span, and time is seen under the sign of infinity, *sub specie aeternitatis.* "I live in the leaf" (which buds and withers), says Lampros for whom all scientific theories have their validity because each one, in turn, brings its contribution to the great mystery of genesis. Disintegration and reintegration, the recurring cycle of cosmos and chaos, catastrophe and rebirth, in individual lives as well as among nations and civilizations, define the underlying pattern of historical enactment which Ernst Jünger studies from the top of the Marble Cliffs. Individual fate functions as type and symbol, while the single occurrence in time is charged with depth and gravity, being conceived as the manifestation of a supratemporal order of recurrence. In this allegorical meditation on world harmony, the vision of which is gnostic, mythic, and archetypal, Jünger belongs squarely to the tradition of German romanticism: his *Naturphilosophie,* with its organicism, Platonic resonances, and delight in symbol and faraway incident, makes him a *frère spirituel* of Goethe and Novalis.

"Dreieinig sind das Wort, die Freiheit und der Geist" (The Word, Freedom, and Spirit are triune). This solemn, trinitarian affirmation occurring in the very middle of our narration gives witness to Jünger's credo in the power of civilizing energies to overcome evil—an act of faith nourished by a perennial philosophy which equates order with *logos.* Hence the studied, disciplined care with which the novel is composed, Jünger assuming, in the manner of his master, Nietzsche, a prophetic, monumental, apodictic tone. Archaisms and exotic touches reinforce the timelessness of this fable in which automobiles make their way through feudal settings. Sentences are deliberately weighed against each other to assure a full, steady, cadenced effect, while a telling image or an aphorism of gnomic import rounds off the individual paragraphs unanimated by any conversation and, in their unremitting gravity of mood, giving the semblance of marble stelae. Ritual, choice artefacts, beautiful natural forms, contemplative leisure, and scientific research—in a word, all of the ingredients and values of a classic, high culture—are celebrated in a book completed on the eve of Hitler's invasion of Poland and just a few weeks before Jünger himself, resignedly, will report for military service as a captain in the *Wehrmacht.* His aestheticism and detachment, which have been strongly criticized and do at times lapse into a cold preciosity, are intended to serve as charms which ward off malign forces threatening to overwhelm philosophic composure and the rule of reason.

Marcus Bullock (essay date Fall 1986)

SOURCE: "Ernst Jünger: Literature, Warfare and the Intoxication of Philosophy," in *Mosaic,* Vol. XIX, No. 4, Fall, 1986, pp. 107-19.

[In the following essay, Bullock explores Jünger's ideas about the use of drugs and intoxication in intellectual thought.]

When the editors of Mircea Eliade's *Festschrift* of 1969 at the University of Chicago Press asked Ernst Jünger to contribute an essay on the use of drugs as an agency in the exploration of human consciousness, their choice reflected the general recognition of a place to which he has long held undisputed claim in Europe. He is without doubt the most solidly established and authoritative literary voice on that continent to continue the tradition of Baudelaire, E. T. A. Hoffmann, Poe and Coleridge by making the experience of drugs and intoxication central to the world he investigates. The association between Jünger and Eliade had, of course, been active for many years before then. In 1959 they founded the journal *Antaios* together, brought out in Stuttgart by Jünger's publisher Klett-Cotta. The precise nature of this association, illustrated by the focus of interest to which their journal is dedicated, reveals a great deal about the particular way Jünger carries on that tradition. It also indicates some very important differences between Jünger's approach to this issue and that which has become established in the English-speaking world. Through these differences, one can not only account for the striking lack of familiarity with his name and work among British and American audiences—in dramatic contrast to his success and influence in France—but also show something very specific about the German tradition which he represents.

The record of interests and accomplishments by the two editors of *Antaios* gives a clear sense of how it cuts across the customary dividing line between disciplines of objective knowledge and the realm of literature. Eliade, the Rumanian cultural anthropologist, achieved international renown as a scholar and researcher into the esoteric religious traditions and occultic folklore of both East and West. He is also the author of several works of fiction. Ernst Jünger is known primarily as a novelist and as the writer of some of the most remarkable accounts of experience in the trenches of World War I, but his copious output extends far beyond literary fiction and reminiscence. Not only is his range of interests astonishingly broad, but he has also been quite influential in the most diverse areas. In 1932, for example, he published ***Der Arbeiter,*** a hotly debated analysis of the political consequences of twentieth-century technology and mechanized warfare, for which he represents a radical right-wing perspective on the contemporary situation and prospects for the future. In 1950 he contributed a philosophical essay, ***"Über die Linie"*** **("Across the Line")** to a collection in celebration of Martin Heidegger's sixtieth birthday. Heidegger responded with a discussion of that work he entitled *"Über 'die Linie'"* ("On 'the Line'") in a collection to celebrate Jünger's sixtieth birthday. That essay was later reprinted, with minor additions, as *Zur Seinsfrage.*

While philosophy and political speculation both lie within the domain of the pen as close neighbors of literary fiction, there are yet further extensions of Jünger's concerns that, even to a superficial glance, suggest an unusual combination of interests and talents. As a young man after the war, he studied biology, including a period in the twenties at the University of Naples. This itself was the expression of a passionate curiosity from his earliest years about the phenomena of nature, and it developed later into a real expertise in entomology. Jünger's scientific work on insects, specializing in beetles, earned him a measure of international standing seldom accorded an amateur in our age. His discoveries are reflected in the fact that three species bear his name.

The tradition in which he carries on this research, which he refers to as "the subtle hunt," is not that of conventional natural science, but is rooted in the same kind of metaphysical speculation that underlay Goethe's scientific work. Goethe's attempt to overturn the Newtonian theory of color with his own ideas in the treatise *Die Farbenlehre,* or his efforts to argue the existence of a primal plant form, *die Urpflanze,* are not generally taken very seriously by English commentators. Literary critics have tended to take their cue on these matters from the established scientific world, where, of course, those hypotheses have been completely rejected. Even the genuine and scientifically recognized discovery of the intermaxillary bone in the human skull credited to Goethe, and therefore the speculative method which led him to it, is often dismissed as a fluke. The methodological debate at that time concerning restrictions in the definition or conception of objective knowledge is continued today in a figure like Jünger, and in the project carried on by the contributors of *Antaios.* Through his work, one can identify a great deal of that which is represented very strongly, though by no means exclusively, in the German tradition, and stands distinct from epistemological criteria predominant for generations in the Anglo-Saxon and French rationalist view of knowledge. The contrasting approach one finds in Jünger's thinking is therefore very useful in opening up an understanding of the different ways in which the divisions of knowledge are brought about, as well as the different ways in which the content of normal and altered modes of experience is interpreted.

What we think of as the practice of rational scientific investigation is based on the idea of bringing as much of the world as possible into the singular plane of critical observation and causal explanation. Historically this springs from the Enlightenment, and this in turn is usually associated with the socio-historical development of bourgeois power and influence through the rationalized relations of the market economy. Without wishing to probe these propositions too carefully, one can still say with confidence that Germany did not pass through any such historical process as unambiguously as did Britain and France or, via the export of their institutions, North America. Germany, politically fragmented into a patchwork of, in many cases, quasi-feudal states until these were progressively absorbed by Bismarck's Prussia in the nineteenth century, was not a conducive background for a philosophical vision of transparent, rational unity on a single, naturally articulated plane. This simple and positive picture does not seem to reflect the truth of a German's rather more complex, frustrating and contradictory experience in the world. German thinkers, accordingly, show a tendency again and again to have to resort to a further dimension. They look for another level of being from which a speculative or metaphysical unity may be derived.

For Goethe, this was a hierarchical order of nature. For Hegel, the *Weltgeist.* By the later part of the nineteenth century, the subsequent versions of such entities were becoming increasingly identified with that which was peculiar to German history and, more specifically, foreign to the conditions in its more "advanced" rivals. By the same token, emphasis on such elements as the foundation of Germany's identity meant suspicion and dislike of those alien characteristics which Germany was inevitably coming to adopt more and more as it progressed in its efforts to compete with foreign rivals. Thus, these philosophical outlooks came to be set in radical opposition to the evolving social realities accompanying increased urbanization, industrialization and liberalization. Friedrich Nietzsche's will to power was one of these. Another, less well-known to the outside, but probably more subtly influential within Germany, was Wilhelm Dilthey's "philosophy of life." In his essay "On some Motifs in Baudelaire," Walter Benjamin remarks:

> Since the end of the last century, philosophy has made a series of attempts to lay hold of the 'true' experience as opposed to the kind that manifests itself in the standardized, denatured life of the civilized masses. It is customary to classify these efforts under the heading of a philosophy of life. Their point of departure, understandably enough, was not man's life in society. What they invoked was poetry ['Dichtung'], preferably nature, and, finally and most emphatically, the age of myths. Dilthey's book *Das Erlebnis und die Dichtung* represents one of the earliest of these efforts. . . .

The concern of these nineteenth-century German thinkers is to shift the criterion of truth and significance away from that which is central to rationalist and pragmatic ways of thinking, to shift the center of "reality" to a new locus in a "depth" separate from the surfaces of material or social human phenomena. Jünger most certainly stands in that same tradition. His writing, from his earliest work portraying the battles and slaughter of the war, has striven to identify and reveal an inner dimension of experience in violence and conflict which runs diametrically counter to any rational revulsion toward and rejection of those aspects of human existence. His studies in entomology consider the insect world as a kind of hieroglyph by which nature reveals its fundamental patterns, which likewise prove to flow through an equality of creation and destruction quite indifferent to rational desires for a productive stability in the world. The mythic stratum of life which enters and transforms the ordinary domain of existence, therefore, is opposed to the pragmatic considerations of advantage and security. It breaks into that domain disruptively and rapturously. In contrast to the pedestrian values of the "civilized masses," it is an ecstasy and an intoxication.

The fundamental idea behind the interpretation of enraptured, ecstatic and intoxicated states, in a tradition which turns toward a hidden mythic or elemental level for its truth, is that this alteration of consciousness is a break with the singular level of a unified world. It is not a more fluid, swifter, less inhibited movement through the articulations of one continuous reality, like a renewed melody in a single key, but the sound of new notes from a quite different key, one with a deeper and more universal tone. In **"Drugs and Ecstasy"** Jünger expresses this as the difference separating mythic and historical time:

> If we compare the triumphs of Alexander and Dionysos, we touch upon the difference between historical and elemental power. Success in history, as the conquest of Babylon, for example, shows, is fleeting and tied to names. The moment does not return in the same form; it becomes a link in the chain of historical time. But if we consider changes in the elemental world, neither names nor dates are important and yet changes take place time and again, not only below historical time, but also within it. They burst forth like magma from its crust.
>
> But let us stay with wine. Alexander was forced to retreat from India, while Dionysos even today reigns as a nameless host. Wine has changed Europe more forcefully than has the sword: even today it is considered to be a medium of cultic transformation. The exchange of new poisons and ecstasies, and also of new vices, fevers and diseases, lacks the kind of definite dating by which coronations or decisive battles are remembered. Such exchanges remain in the dark, in the entanglement of the roots. We can surmise the events, but we can neither know their extent nor penetrate their depth.

Considered from this aspect, the boundaries between different disciplines which make up the various territories of the "horizontal" plane of objective or historical knowledge are transcended by their relation to the depth of the elemental and the mythic representations by which we attempt to grasp it. All branches of learning in this light begin to resemble the compositions of poetry. They are metaphors or translations of something both separate from them, yet perhaps alive in the spirit which animates them. This is clearly visible in the contributions which make up the journal *Antaios*. Here, the results of research by archaeologists, psychologists and linguists appear alongside essays by philosophers and literary scholars, by art historians and ethnologists. What characterizes almost all of them, and indeed makes the journal absorbing reading, is that each is willing to surrender the autonomy of his or her own field—from which only a limited surmise of deeper understanding is possible—and struggle toward an exchange of knowledge which cannot appear to a singular and complete view. The horizontal distribution in a mosaic of knowledge is made relative to a more obscure vertical dimension toward which all pitch their labors.

Jünger's own essays illustrate that same approach to a wide range of his own interests, from speculations on the nature of language in ***"Sprache und Körperbau"*** in 1947, or on the nature of Orient and Occident in ***"Der Gordische Knoten"*** in 1953. What is no less important, though much more commonly misinterpreted, is the effect this approach has on his literary fiction. It turns his focus away from the portrayal of individuals pursuing the motives which are evident in the ordinary experience of daily life. It turns him away from what one expects to find as "character development." His narratives do not invite one to identify with the action or the figures who carry it. His novels do not hold up a mirror to the familiar domain of human life, but clearly and deliberately go exploring beyond it.

For this reason many critics have castigated him for his "coldness." George Steiner, for example, in an article on Jünger's novel ***Auf den Marmorklippen*** writes that "Reading [Jünger's] work, one experiences what Emily Dickinson termed 'a zero at the bone.'" That which for Jünger himself is a deliberately chosen path, a fundamental shift in the place where the star is sought by which the voyage to truth should navigate, appears to Steiner simply a failure. He accuses Jünger of writing as he does out of incapacity to hold on to the familiar dimension of experience: "Jünger makes a virtue of what is, essentially, a grave defect of consciousness, an atrophy at the vital center."

J. P. Stern, in what is still the best book on Jünger in English, attacks him for what he calls the "abstraction" of his language. He sees this, moreover, as a quite general feature of German writing in our time: "In this sense, then, twentieth century German is invaded by abstraction, for it responds to the events in the world not directly, in the language of common discourse, but imperfectly, in semi-philosophical, semi-sociological, 'learned' and set terms, which are committed neither to the events nor to fundamental doctrine."

It is clear from these two sources that the problem lies in the inability of one tradition to find correct terms and criteria to account for the concerns in another. Each of these critics sees only the negative movement, the deviation from that standard mode of consciousness whose "vital center" Steiner cannot find represented in Jünger's writing. If Jünger has chosen an alternate center about which true experience is to orbit, one which does not lie within what Stern recognizes as the reality of "events" or a tenable and plausible "fundamental doctrine," then this would have to produce a division between two mutually incomprehensible domains. And if the language which represents Jünger's "truth" seems to the alternate view "abstract" or without life from one side, this begins, as Benjamin pointed out in relation to that enterprise he dates from Dilthey, with exactly the same response from the other.

Similarly, the living experience pursued in each of these two directions, and the validity of their esthetic achievements, will appear hollow and bogus to the other. But this is inevitable with any situation where there are two mutually exclusive ways of making meaning out of the world and the human condition in it. As Benjamin observes in his essay on Surrealism: "The dialectics of intoxication are indeed curious. Is not perhaps all ecstasy in one world humiliating sobriety in that complementary to it?"

Opinions on Jünger's work generally, on the quality of his writing, and especially on the "ecstatic" or "intoxicated" elements of the experience he portrays, vary according to the way the commentator identifies his own position relative to the tradition represented there, and the validity of a "mythic" stratum of being. Helmut Kaiser, for example, in his book *Mythos, Rausch und Reaktion,* which is written from the East German ideological perspective, refuses to acknowledge any genuine esthetic achievement in such work. Commenting on what is intended to be a moment of epiphany in the contemplation of a particular plant described in ***Auf den Marmorklippen,*** he observes: "One has to take his word for it that he was, as he himself says, pierced 'by lightning' at the sight of the plantain; he does not show it in the text."

Like Stern, he objects to the deliberate, and, for him, false efforts to create symbols which are as dead in conception as the world they are meant to signify is abstract and void of reality: "What the reader finds in his symbols are robots, perhaps spiritual symbols, but these are always defunct, paper fruits which were dead before they were born. Thus Jünger lacks precisely that on which art depends: a portrayal of the human sphere." This, Kaiser argues, reflects Jünger's retreat into the sterile isolation of private fantasy. He cannot accept it as a separate order of experience, for with these images "this meeting takes place in great solitude, mostly in dreams or in intoxications produced by particular alkaloids."

Such criticism of Jünger is clearly tied very closely to the perception that he stands in a line of development which includes Fascism. Benjamin actually concludes his comment on Dilthey by tracing that line through Klages to Jung who, he says, "made common cause with Fascism." Although Jünger in fact distanced himself from the Nazi party before it was established in power, and his political sympathies did not ally him with any very specific entity or policy among the actual choices, there is no doubt that in his *theoretical* positions he can be located very close to a fascistic or fascistic ideology. Indeed, in 1930, Benjamin wrote an article entitled *"Theorien des deutschen Faschismus"* on a volume Jünger edited, and in which he included the radically imperialist and militarist essay, ***"Die totale Mobilmachung."***

Jünger's supporters, like Eliade, have often been simply indifferent to the question of ideology. In other cases—like the comments of the novelist Alfred Andersch, who was distinctly left-wing politically, and had a scrupulously anti-Fascist record—the connection between any occasional ideological lapses and the esthetic quality of his literary work is denied in plain terms. More recently, the very thorough, detailed and scholarly book on Jünger's work by Karl Heinz Bohrer, *Die Ästhetik des Schreckens,* has attempted to connect this particular approach to writing with that of a non-German, and politically more defensible tradition: French Surrealism.

The essential idea of this is not new. Many critics have referred to similarities between the two perspectives: their emphasis on the imagination, enraptured states of mind, the use of intoxicants to transform the shape of experience and the fascination with highly charged, shocking or even violent imagery. One will find that connection made repeatedly in Gerhard Loose's commentaries, to name just one. The special contribution of Bohrer's long and ambitious study is that it does not rest with enumeration of surface parallels, but endeavors to show that there is a deeper necessity running through the developing histories of each manifestation.

This argument takes the form, in part, of tracing their origins back to an anti-Enlightenment ancestry in figures of the late eighteenth century, including the Marquis de Sade on the French side, and J. G. Hamann in Germany. Commenting on remarks in the first (1929) version of Jünger's book ***Das abenteurliche Herz*** which mock the pallid lifelessness of the Enlightenment, Bohrer notes: "He probably took his philosophical support for this from Hamann, whose statement that 'thought' is the 'garment of the soul' he recalls. Hamann had put forward the priority of sensual cognition over philosophy in such a manner in 'Aesthetica in Nuce' that Aragon, had he known this text, would have felt an absolute identity with it." Bohrer's enterprise is taken severely to task by subsequent commentaries like Wolfgang Kaempfer's 1981 book on Ernst Jünger for having blurred a number of essential concepts and distinctions in order to establish his position.

It is true that Surrealism represents one instance of a repeating pattern in French culture of phases where a strong attraction for mythic, metaphysical or esoteric modalities recurs. Frequently this manifests itself in some enthusiasm for German culture, such as Baudelaire's response to Wagner, and indeed one might see the same thing at work in the current enthusiasm in France for Jünger's work. Nevertheless, there remain real distinctions here which it is quite wrong to overlook. Certainly nothing of this apparent parallel history mapped out by Bohrer through late Romantic pessimism and nineteenth-century estheticism accounts for the strong commitment to social revolution and political justice which André Breton and Louis Aragon espoused after the Moroccan War of 1925.

This difference can also be drawn into line with the distinction between the conception of intoxication to which they held, and that of the tradition represented by Jünger. What they hoped to release by the use of drugs may indeed have been a kind of antipodes to the experience of regular life in the bourgeois sphere, but it was by no means so distant an opposite as the elemental realm to which Jünger refers. On the contrary, the Surrealist understanding of the subconscious clearly posits it as still only an extension of the human sphere, not an alternative to it. Jünger's violent and harshly demanding mythic domain is one where the person not only transcends the narrow and bogus values of bourgeois individuality but also frees himself from all the desires of security, comfort, pleasure and happiness which animate the familiar experience of everyday life.

For the Surrealists, the subconscious was merely the home of a more vivid, vibrant and unfettered version of those desires. Thus although there is a real difference between the desire uncovered by revelation of subconscious contents of the mind and personality and that of the bourgeois domain, that difference does not involve breaking out into a realm which disrupts the integrity of the desiring subject. Surrealism simply subverts the false limits constructed about the enfeebled and conventionalized image of the bourgeois individual as defined by the relations and demands of a competitive economy and administrative structure.

Benjamin, in his essay on the Surrealists, notes how their emphasis on ecstatic experience as an opposition to that domain of purposes does indeed dissolve away the idea of the self determined by it: "In the world's structure dream loosens individuality like a bad tooth." Yet he sees an important dialectical element in their procedure here: "This loosening of the self by intoxication is, at the same time, precisely the fruitful, living experience that allowed these people to step outside the domain of intoxication." This is all-important to Benjamin, for, writing in 1929, the aspect of their work and their movement which strikes him as embodying its principal value is its place in the political awareness and struggle of socialist resistance to the rising threat of Fascism. The dialectical step beyond intoxication which is reached by entering into it is the beginning of a new realm of purposes, now directed toward the revolutionary transformation of social reality. This means that the intoxicated rapture of poetry must be carried over beyond the limited space of a momentary ecstasy, and sustain a renewed sense of the rights and potentials to be redeemed in all levels of actual human life.

Benjamin has hopes for their project to "win the energies of intoxication for the revolution," but he has doubts too. He wonders whether they are "successful in welding this experience of freedom to the other revolutionary experience that we have to acknowledge because it has been ours, the constructive, dictatorial side of revolution? In short, have they bound revolt to revolution?"

Their task is to step beyond the imaginative rejection of things as these make themselves known under the conditions of bourgeois knowledge, a rejection pursued into the alternative domains of art, literature, the occult and drug-induced raptures, and bring this exterior perspective to bear on the irrational self-contradictions of an ideology which insists on calling itself rationalism. The danger to which the are subject and which threatens their ability to complete this task lies in the "pernicious romantic prejudices" which lead to fascination with those alternatives as objects of desire and pursuit for their own sake. They are emphasized *instead* of the renewed possibilities of consciousness in political reality. They are a place of flight and complacent illusion. Understanding this is the key to all Benjamin has to say about the dialectic of intoxication:

> Any serious exploration of occult, surrealistic, phantasmagoric gifts and phenomena presupposes a dialectical intertwinement to which a romantic turn of mind is impervious. For histrionic or fanatical stress on the mysterious side of the mysterious takes us no further; we penetrate the mystery only to the degree that we recognize it in the everyday world, by virtue of a dialectical optic that perceives the everyday as impenetrable, the impenetrable as everyday. The most passionate investigation of telepathic phenomena, for example, will not teach us half as much about reading (which is an eminently telepathic process), as the profane illumination of reading about telepathic phenomena. And the most passionate investigation of the hashish trance will not teach us half as much about thinking (which is eminently narcotic), as the profane illumination of thinking about the hashish trance.

The validity of exploration of such altered states of consciousness depends on the capacity to overcome that romantic attribution of separate reality which enthralls the mind and "takes us no further." That in turn depends on the understanding that the subject experiencing an altered state of consciousness remains in principle the same; the consciousness is essentially that of the same person, and the content of consciousness, the ideas and dreams, are those of the same person also, albeit revealed at a heightened level of intensity by the removal of inhibiting agencies and habits of mind. Although the Surrealists distanced themselves from Baudelaire's posture of religious and moral condemnation of drugs, their sense of how opium or hashish affected the economy of the mind was similar to his as expressed in *Les Paradis artificiels,* just as he followed De Quincey on the psychology of intoxication.

Baudelaire affirms, as does his English forerunner, the closeness of the intoxicated state to the norm which reigns in the drug-taker's life: "*Dans ses* Confessions, *De Quincey affirme avec raison que l'opium . . . n'excite* [*l'homme*] *. . . que dans sa voie naturelle, et qu'ainsi, pour juger les merveilles de l'opium, il serait absurde d'en référer â un marchand de boeufs; car celui-ci ne rêvera que boeufs et pâturages.*" It is on this basis that Benjamin can demand that the revelations of ecstatic visions be made subject to the same criteria of knowledge as those of a sober state, just as the conventions of conformist ideology must be treated to the same skepticism as one applies to raptures and dreams.

Once again, he is highly suspicious of the excesses of Surrealism in its disregard for the seriousness of an objective knowledge. He cites a declaration by Appolinaire and Breton that "The conquests of science rest far more on a surrealistic than on a logical thinking" and rejects it because "such integration is too impetuous." The estheticism of this position has its equivalent in the pose of moral Antinomianism to which they likewise yielded too readily: "The seduction was too great to regard the Satanism of a Rimbaud and a Lautréamont as a pendant to art for art's sake in an inventory of snobbery." Nevertheless, there is a dialectical aspect in that apparent romantic fecklessness: "If . . . one resolves to open up this romantic dummy, one finds something usable inside." And that bears out the positive position adopted regarding the political currents of the time, for "One finds the cult of evil as a political device, however romantic, to disinfect and isolate against all moralizing dilettantism."

The estheticism, the antirational epistemology, and the cultivation of intoxications are all, therefore, directed away from the thinking which reigns in the established ideological domain, and yet remain close enough to the sphere of concrete life, the material issues of politics, that they may be drawn on in their behalf in a positive sense. Benjamin's response in *Theories of German Fascism,* on the other hand, finds absolutely no such positive aspect in Jünger's estheticism, which he regards solely as a rejection of human life and an abandonment in favor of mythic phantasm of the tasks imposed by the realities of concrete existence: "The most rabidly decadent origins of this new theory of war are emblazoned on their foreheads: it is nothing other than an uninhibited translation of the principles of *l'art pour l'art* to war itself." And he quotes his friend Florens Christian Rang on the confused otherworldliness behind Jünger's glorification of purposeless destruction, and the flight from reality into bogus ideal realms in this:

> [The] horrible world-view of world-death instead of world-life . . . is made lighter in the philosophy of German Idealism by the notion that behind the

clouds there is after all a starry sky. This fundamental German spiritual tendency in its depth lacks will, does not mean what it says, is a crawling, cowardly know-nothingness, a desire not to live, but also a desire not to die either. . . . For this is the German half-attitude towards life—to be able to throw it away when it doesn't cost anything, in the moment of intoxication, with those left behind cared for, and with this short-lived sacrifice surrounded by, an eternal halo.

This "starry sky" in its crisp clarity which justifies the blurry and abysmal vision of real life is given incomparably greater command over all things to deny and contradict them than the "Surreal" is given over the things of the "real." It does not just loosen individuality "like a rotten tooth," it completely dissolves away the particularity of the subject and his claims to a real place in the world.

The separateness of this ideal or "true" domain from the sphere of ordinary human interests and human life can be detected in that aspect of the psychology of intoxication where it would seem Jünger comes closest to agreeing with Baudelaire and De Quincey. In ***Annäherungen,*** the book of reminiscences and speculations about drugs which he put together in 1970 as a direct result of the train of thought begun by "Drugs and Ecstasy" and taking that essay as its first chapter, he refers directly to the observation in *Les Paradis artificiels* on cattle merchants and intoxicants. The idea that drugs do not add anything, but only potentiate the ordinary circulation of thoughts and impressions also occurs elsewhere—for example in comments written in 1940 in response to a book on E. T. A. Hoffmann. The difference from either Baudelaire, or De Quincey, or the Surrealists is that he is concerned neither with new ways of living in the same world, nor new knowledge about it.

He compares Baudelaire's position here with a poem on a similar theme by Goethe, "*Die Schatzgräber.*" He rejects Goethe's admonition against vain efforts to dig for treasure one would not know how to possess. The objective is not to gain something new brought into one's possession from another dimension, but rather to transform one's existence by engaging in life focused on another center altogether. He writes: "Digging is never in vain, if it goes deep enough. Every point is equidistant from the center, wherever we put our spade to the earth. Every step leads nearer to the goal; that is also true for steps backward."

His agreeing with Baudelaire on the point that no new insight or knowledge is gained in intoxicated states does not imply that Jünger also concurs with Baudelaire's insistence that states of consciousness altered by drugs fail to break the singular dimension of common reality. The reason for this is that Jünger does not consider the issue here to turn on questions of knowledge. The order of transformation he envisages is not restricted to the elemental entering the mind in the form of anything so objective as a specific insight. Acquiring such insights in the modality of knowledge would mean that the knowing subject remained in essence unchanged. As a mere object, the elemental dimension would then be no more than an extended content in a vessel which might accept and hold it, but without undergoing transmutation of its own substance—an abstract enlightenment as opposed to vital participation. The alternative world of experience Jünger depicts is the transmutation of life itself as an expression of the elemental domain.

This may be seen most distinctly in the way he regards the experiences he went through as a front-line soldier in the First World War, especially as these are portrayed in his 1922 book ***Der Kampf als inneres Erlebnis.*** Here he is concerned with unveiling the esoteric forces which manifest themselves in warfare, entirely unconnected with the apparent political and economic purposes the means of war are intended to attain. War is therefore a world unto itself, in the creation of which it is the other aspects of life that are secondary, and only means. The vision and experience of war are an intoxicating fever pitch of life. Only that which matches the overwhelming fury in the flood of impressions it sets loose is worthy of desire and worthy of being considered real.

In the chapter entitled *Eros,* he starts with an explanation of the double meaning of the soldier's hard and brutal pursuit of sex. It is both "the urge of life to express itself at the height of intensity once more, and flight into the thicket of intoxications so as to become oblivious in lust to the dangers that threaten." Sexuality figures at this stage as a much more intriguing counterpart to concrete reality than the simpler stimulation and oblivion produced by that other agency used to shift the accent of consciousness at the front, alcohol. It involves a more elaborate set of circumstances and a different kind of human context removed from the trenches, but the role it plays is not that of the tender restoration of personal existence in a relationship of love. The sexual encounter becomes a rare and separate point of vantage at which one kind of elemental experience sweeps through another. Love is transformed into an impersonal force, one that is more powerful than death, and therefore capable of obliterating the soldier's personal fear of death: "When his breath died away in the whirlwind of love he was so freed from the self, so entwined in the whirl of life, so infused in the eternity of all things, that for this moment Death appeared to him in its true aspect: small and contemptible. It was left behind, far below, when the curve of feeling shot steeply up beyond thinking."

It is significant that this is the point at which death is said to appear in its *true* guise, rather than the temporary disguise in which ecstatic erotic pleasure might be thought to veil it. The full implications are still not always articulated at this stage, for the idea still seems half lost in the rhetorical flourish of a mind fascinated by its own triumph over fear. He writes, in this vein: "Then, though only as a gift granted to those with the best blood, there came the intoxication at the spectacle of one's own daring." It is still an ecstasy, a fiery moment in which the heat of feeling lifts a spirit beyond the light of thinking. He ranks it together with other conventional figures of this experience: "And one last thing: ecstasy. This state of the saint, the great poet and the great love is also granted to great courage."

Such an experience does, however, have two phases. First it is a liberation, a breaking free of an ordinary place cramped among the oppressive desiderata of individual existence: "That is an intoxication beyond all intoxications, an unleashing that bursts every bond." But it is also an experience which brings the soldier into another sphere, uniting him with a larger reality: "Then he is melted together with the universe . . . it is as though the wave had glided back into the ocean's surge."

The abandon of wild ecstatic courage is a self-abandonment. It breaks away from the despised brief life of an individual and the enclosed, fragile existence he knows, to hatch out for flight through an experience beyond bounds. The things of the narrow world therefore undergo a reduction in significance. Their meaning in themselves is also abandoned; they must become indifferent as ends. Nothing may be desired for its part in the texture of ordinary human life. This ecstasy of self-forgetting weakens the links of consciousness to a domain of rational purposes and breaks loose from an identity anchored there. Consequently strength accumulates in the reality and attraction of what lies beyond, even though it may strike the person looking on from outside as strangely abstract and nebulous.

Yet for the soldiers this may grow beyond mere glimpses of a realm manifesting itself through those elements which fret and strain the tissue of the regular order of things. The war may supplant that order. A new and dangerous mythic reality takes form in its place. Out of the tormented fragments of such an existence, a fearful ideology takes shape. Those elements begin to take on a single meaning—as doorways to pass through into this fire: "All being blazed for them from *one* source, whether that was in a full glass, the raging eyes of the enemy or in the yielding smile of a girl."

This intoxication is the construction of a unified world where there is no unity in the reigning order of things. That is also why, beyond the particular experience of warfare, it becomes possible to subsume all the different fields of knowledge represented in Jünger's wide-ranging interests and writings under his singular view of the ideal or mythic stratum of being. In the same way, all the different areas of special knowledge represented in the contributions to the journal *Antaios* can be brought together as indications of a deeper, hidden knowledge to which they are all relative. In politics, that might appear to give the right to one tyrannical power to subjugate the varieties of human existence before a single expression of the mythic entity. Such was the ideological basis on which the Fascist movements were able to draw adherents from the ranks of "romantically" enthralled intellectuals nostalgic for life imbued with elemental meaning. In Jünger's case, however, any political engagement along these lines was always restricted to theoretical positions. Though he was intrigued by all violent and absolutist expressions of power, including those of Bolshevism as well as the Right, they also disgusted him in their actual reality.

No particular manifestation of political order could ever be an adequate or true representation of the Idea he traced into the darkness at the root of all things. But at the same time, the attitude of *l'art pour l'art* applied to the normal disciplines of understanding asserts an indifferentism between discourses. It produces an equality between fiction. *Dichtung,* and all attempts to claim truth in the rational pursuit of knowledge. Therefore, in the spirit of Dilthey and the *Lebensphilosophie,* it raises up the practice of poetry, as it does the idea of "Nature" and the "Age of Myth," to a degree of significance which completely distorts the role and function of fictional representation in language, and this, in turn, is a damaging affliction of the different fields of rational knowledge. It is not a dialectical development of consciousness through them, but rather leaves them lame, just as Jünger describes himself in his Paris journals as lamed by the image of Hitler, and, as he makes clear in those journals during the last year of the Second World War, incapable of taking any part in the resistance to him.

Russell A. Berman (essay date 1989)

SOURCE: "Written Right Across Their Faces: Ernst Jünger's Fascist Modernism," in *Modernity and the Text: Revisions of German Modernism,* edited by Andreas Huyssen and David Bathrick, Columbia University Press, 1989, pp. 60-80.

[*In the following essay, Berman discusses the fascist representation of Leni Riefenstahl's film* Triumph of the Will *and the fascist modernism of Jünger's* The Worker.]

If the will triumphs, who loses? *Triumph of the Will,* Leni Riefenstahl's cinematic account of the 1934 Nazi Party convention at Nuremberg, is one of the few aesthetic monuments of German fascism that have attracted serious critical scrutiny. In scene after scene one finds evidence of the ideological self-understanding of National Socialism: Hitler's descent from the clouds, the cathartic applause welcoming the charismatic leader, the visions of the medieval city, the presence of the unified folk including contingents of peasants in their traditional costumes, the rough-and-tumble life in the encampment, the mass chorus of the Work Front, the demonstration of the Hitler Youth, the celebratory display of banners, torchlight processions, and a soundtrack that mixes Wagnerian strains with patriotic songs and martial anthems. The list could be extended, and each item could be decoded and explained within the constellation of the right-wing populism, the *völkisch* ideology, on which German fascism thrived. That sort of investigation can have a compelling explanatory value in regard to the political content of the film. However, I should like to eschew the ideological-critical stance and investigate the rhetorical grounding of Riefenstahl's énonciation, an investigation that can shed light on a politics prior to ideological contents, that is, the politics of fascist representation. It is this rhetorical politics that will concern me later when I turn to Ernst Jünger's construction of a fascist modernism, and it is the examination of rhetoric that may allow me to answer the question posed initially: if the will triumphs, who loses?

Triumph of the Will begins, like most films, with script, with words on the screen, but this opening gesture takes on particular importance within fascist rhetoric. Elsewhere titles name the individual work, give credit to individual artists, and, perhaps, locate the precise historical setting. Here, by way of contrast, the writing on the silver wall invokes the history that has passed—history, or historiography, the writing of history, as past—in order to introduce the agent of its supersession: in the cloudy heavens emerges an airplane, the paradigmatic modernist vehicle, bearing the body of the divine leader, the guarantor of national resurrection, whose arrival on earth signifies the miraculous incarnation of the will triumphant, Henceforth history is overcome, and the jubilant folk rejoices in a redeemed present provided by the presence in flesh and blood of the visible savior. The point is not that Hitler lands in Nuremberg; the point is that Hitler lands in Nuremberg and is seen. "Wir wollen unsren Führer sehen" (We want to see our leader), cries the crowd, and the film, *Triumph of the Will,* defines itself as the proper medium of a fascist privileging of sight and visual representation. The will triumphs when it becomes visually evident, and it triumphs over the alternative representational option, cited at the commencement of the film, writing and an associated culture of verbal literacy. When the will triumphs as image, it is script that is defeated: the verbal titles of the cinematic preface, henceforth displaced by Riefenstahl's shots; the written signatures of the "November traitors"; the Versailles Treaty, denigrated as just so much paper; and the volumes that disappeared in the conflagrations of May 1933.

Triumph of the Will defines a fascist rhetoric as the displacement of verbal by visual representation: the power of the image renders scripture obsolete. This contention may be tentatively, although not conclusively, confirmed by two pieces of evidence. I draw the first from the folklore of fascism, the infinitely repeated vernacular attribution of Hitler's success to the unique power of his eyes that allegedly fastened his interlocutors and fascinated the captivated masses, as if the force of fascist rhetoric depended less on words than on the energy of vision (cf. the parallel claim that no one ever "read" *Mein Kampf*). I return to the film for the second piece of evidence, the self-effacing signature of the director. After Hitler's triumphal arrival and the evening demonstration outside his window, the cinematic narrative proceeds to the next morning, crack of dawn in Nuremberg—sleeping streets, the city walls, the ancient bridges—and for a brief moment one catches a glimpse of the shadow cast by the photographic apparatus. Note: not a glimpse of the apparatus itself (technology is excluded) but its shadow projected onto the wall as a metaphor of the cinematic screen. The signature announces the age of the film and the priority of visual representation as the rhetorical practice of fascism. Hitler turns out to be precisely the enigma described by the subtitle of Hans-Jürgen Syberberg's cinematic investigation of National Socialism: "a film from Germany."

Much more could be said about the specifically rhetorical problems posed by *Triumph of the Will,* especially with regard to the status of speech in the film: the political speeches at the convention, Hitler's several addresses, and the text of the mass chorus. Briefly, I would argue that its verbal character is always secondary to the visual spectacle and the image of the present speaker, and that it therefore differs fundamentally from the initial script, the writing whose author is necessarily absent. A considerably more difficult problem involves the role of radio and loudspeakers in National Socialist Germany, an obvious case of disembodied speech, on which the power of the regime indisputably depended. Rather than pursue these matters, however, I will conclude these introductory observations, having used Riefenstahl's film in order to isolate a crucial conflict between visual and verbal representation, in particular the insistence on the priority of image over writing as a stratagem of fascist power. I call this a crucial conflict because it turns out to be the central rhetorical principle in Ernst Jünger's formulation of fascist modernism as described in his 1932 volume ***The Worker,*** bearing the telling subtitle *Herrschaft und Gestalt,* which I render inadequately as *Domination and Form.* For it is visual form that will, in Jünger's modernist account, displace an obsolete culture of bourgeois writing and guarantee the authority of fascist domination.

Jünger's proximity to the problematic isolated in Riefenstahl's film is evident in the first paragraph of the 1932 preface. I will cite it now and later comment on its rhetorical self-positioning, its claims regarding competing modes of representation, rather than on its ideological contents, that is, the significance of his terminology, such as "worker."

> It is the plan of this book to make the Gestalt of the worker visible, beyond all theories, all parties, and all prejudices—to make it visible as an effective mass, which has already intervened in history and imperiously determines the forms of a transformed world. Because this is less a matter of new thoughts or a new system than of a new reality, everything depends on the sharpness of the description, which demands eyes capable of a complete and unclouded vision.

It is nearly unnecessary to underscore Jünger's insistence on the urgency of visual representation. The project of his book amounts to a making visible (*sichtbar zu machen*) of a form (*Gestalt*); this in turn leads to a presentation that demands eyes (*die Augen voraussetzt*) with an unclouded vision (*denen die volle und unbefangene Sehkraft gegeben ist*). The desideratum of sight and form, the image of images, pervades the text, which consequently defines its rhetorical mode as *descriptio*—to be understood less in terms of the etymology pointing toward writing (*be-schreiben*) than as a project of visualization to be carried out by writing. Imagistic vision is then set in contrast to an alternative constellation of theories, parties, and prejudices, a domain of ideas, defined as mere ideas, that is, separate from reality. The descriptive representation of Gestalt has powerful practical consequences (*die bereits mächtig in die Geschichte eingegriffen*), as opposed to the ultimately powerless ephemera of "new thoughts or a new system." "System"—a standard Nazi pejorative for the Weimar Republic; Jünger is suggesting in 1932 that a new order of power, structure, and form will replace an anachronistic amalgam of empty theories, political parties, and effete idealism. This paraphrase points out the underlying diachronic presumption, the transition from a bourgeois age of subjective interiority, the site of literary culture, to a postindividualism of visible power. This transition is central to Jünger's political ideology, his hostility to democracy, and his totalitarian preferences. It is, moreover, central to his aesthetics; the disparagement of a powerless culture of idealism and the advocacy of artistic formations (*Gestaltung*) with life-practical ramifications are homologous to the terms of the modernist attack on the bourgeois institution of autonomous art such as Peter Bürger has presented in his *Theory of the Avant-Garde.*

In ***The Worker,*** Jünger undertakes myriad permutations of these themes, but the overriding concern remains the Gestalt, the visual form or structure: "The Gestalt contains the whole, which encompasses more than the sum of its parts and which an anatomical age could never achieve." Here Jünger borrows from a reactionary strain in German romanticism running through Wagner and Langbehn that denounced the analytical intellect and the individuation of bourgeois society; in the Gestalt, Jünger discovers synthetic power. "It is the sign of an imminent epoch that one will again see, feel, and act in the thrall of Gestalten." Again Jünger declares an epochal transformation and emphasizes the practical ramifications (*handeln*) of the Gestalt. "In politics too everything depends on bringing into battle Gestalten and not concepts, ideas, or mere illusions." The force of the Gestalt is set in contrast to the forms of subjective consciousness, denounced for their irrelevance. Thus the Gestalt is capable of totalization, it is practical, and it is therefore superior to the verbiage and concepts of autonomous culture. The visual Gestalt displaces the terms of writing. The fascist Gestalt displaces the bourgeois who was never a Gestalt but only an individual, a mere part, in an "anatomical," which is to say, analytic or atomistic age. It is finally the heroic Gestalt, the will incarnate, plain for all who have eyes to see, whom Riefenstahl brings to Nuremberg, to wipe away the writing and everything that writing represents.

Before proceeding with my discussion of ***The Worker*** and the particular character of the descriptive rhetoric of fascist representation, I want to explore some aesthetic and aesthetic-historical aspects of the problem of fascism and modernism. Fascism and modernism—that is a touchy combination. Postwar criticism, at least in the West, was eager to exclude from serious discussion literature complicitous in fascism. A conservative humanism attempted to escape the political turbulence of the twentieth century by turning its gaze toward the values of an unimpeachable occidental tradition with which one could hope to overcome the political catastrophes of the present. The same exclusionary move could of course be repeated on the left, for example, Sartre's reading Céline out of the French literary tradition. A further case that makes the issue clear: the efforts by the defenders of Ezra Pound to separate his poetic from his political imagination in order to canonize the former while relegating the latter to the domain of insanity, as if modernist innovation were necessarily separate from or even opposed to fascist totalitarianism. Meanwhile, during the first postwar decade in Eastern Europe, when the Lukácsian paradigm held sway (before the Hungarian Revolution of 1956), an association of modernism and decadence tended to lead to a collapsing of modernism and fascism *tout court.* That may overstate the case and do the critic Lukács some injustice, but it certainly corresponds to widespread political judgments associated with the aesthetics of socialist realism in that period. Classical critical theory, anxious to develop a general account of fascism, did little better in formulating a specific account of fascist aesthetics, although it provides a wealth of insights and comes close to an answer in the exchange on surrealism.

Recent critical work has begun to move beyond both the

absolute separation of fascism and modernism and the thorough identification of fascism and modernism. Several preliminary points can be made. First, against efforts to prohibit a thematization of fascism within literary criticism, one notes that a considerable number of authors, whose works are irrefutably embedded in modernism, were drawn to various models of fascism: Marinetti, Céline, Maurras, Pound, Lewis, Hamsun, Benn, and Jünger. Second, against (socialist realist) efforts to collapse fascism and modernism, one notes the plethora of clearly modernist authors to whom it is patently absurd to ascribe an association with fascism: Brecht, Kafka, Mann, Döblin, Proust, Sartre, Joyce, and Woolf. Therefore if one were to endeavor to set the poetics of the modernist authors attracted to fascism in some resonance with their political proclivities, then the resulting model (or models) would not be adequate as accounts of modernism in general. A fascist modernism would have to be distinguished from competing versions that, as also modernist, are likely to display certain affinities or homologies, but that will be clearly distinct variations of the modernist problematic. Finally, the aesthetic profile of models of a fascist and a leftist and a liberal modernism ought to highlight aesthetic features and not concentrate on the political deeds of the historical individuals. Writers near political movements may always tend to be eccentric figures, outside of the inner circle of institutionalized political power. The proper question for literary critical inquiry has to do with the extent to which the political imagination of the author or the text (which may be extraordinarily eccentric when measured against the standard of the established political power) contributes to the construction of an aesthetic project and, in particular, one that can be labeled characteristically modernist.

In order to describe three competing models of modernist aesthetics—all of which are initiated by political motivations—I begin by limiting the term to its normal usage, parallel to the connotation of the term "modern art," that is, the radical aesthetic innovation that commences around 1900. Whether the proper dating begins somewhat earlier (with Heine and Baudelaire) or later (the generation of 1914) is less important than distinguishing this sense of the "modern" from the larger usage of a postmedieval modernity suggested by the German term *Neuzeit.* In his *Theory of Communicative Action,* Habermas works with this second, epochal model and, drawing on Weber and one strand in Adorno's thought, describes the differentiation of a particular aesthetic value-sphere undergoing a linear progress of autonomization. More sensitive to the vagaries of aesthetic representation in the twentieth century, Bürger insists on a rupture in the trajectory of autonomization produced by the historical avant-garde movements. In this context, I cannot even attempt a critique of Bürger's analysis of that rupture and I cite him only in regard to his insistence on the distinction between, on the one hand, an aesthetic culture of the eighteenth and nineteenth centuries, and, on the other hand, one of the avant-garde and modernism (I will also bracket a discussion of the exaggerated distinctions between modernism and the avant-garde).

These reflections on the theoretical construction of a category of modernism indicate the need for a nonmodernist foil, a countermodel of bourgeois culture against which one indeed finds all the aesthetic innovators of the early twentieth century railing: the art of the Victorian or the Wilhelmine establishments is regarded as just so much philistinism, historicism, sentimentalism, ornamentalism, and so forth. The key features of that countermodel include: (1) a developmental teleology, especially in the linear narratives of the Bildungsroman as well as in the bourgeois drama; (2) a thematics of identity-construction for the bourgeois subject undergoing the development; (3) an aesthetics of fictionality guaranteeing an autonomy, that is, a separation of the work of art from immediate life-practical concerns. It is this third point that Bürger underscores, singling it out as the object of attack by the historical avant-garde movements in order to sublate art and life-practice. That attack also leads, I contend, to a revision of the other aspects of the model—teleology and subjectivity—and all three aspects are lodged in an ostentatious antibourgeois gesturing that often induced an explicit politicization, particularly in the context of World War I and its aftermath. The moment of modernism was marked by the belief in the confluence of aesthetic and political change. The optimistic and perhaps self-serving assumption of modernist writers was the claim that literary innovation stood in some easy correspondence with political innovation. Hence the political motivation behind the competing modernist models.

Modernism was constituted by what it perceived to be the bourgeois aesthetics of autonomy, that is, teleology, identity, and fictionality. I identify three ideal types of German modernist aesthetics—fascist modernism, epic leftism, and liberal modernism—each of which proposes homologous alternatives to the terms of autonomy aesthetics. In place of bourgeois teleology, fascist modernism operates with iteration, a perpetual repetition of the same, suggesting the eternal return of a cyclical history. In place of identity-construction, it offers the spectacle, unnuanced and unquestioned, the authoritative presence of Jünger's aestheticized battlefields; in place of fictionality, it denounces escapism and claims for its texts a curious pseudodocumentary status. Hence Dinter footnotes his *völkisch* novels with alleged proofs, and Jünger prefers the memoir; he does not turn to the novel form until the mid-1930s, when, as in the case of Benn and Heidegger, a disappointment with the reality of the fascist revolution began to induce minor revisions of the positions held earlier.

Epic leftism replaces development with static examples of false consciousness (Döblin's Biberkopf), identity with dialectical constellations (Brecht), and fictionality with an operative aesthetics of documentary literature (Ottwalt). For liberal modernism, the corresponding features are seriality (Mann's *Doctor Faustus*), ambivalence (Broch's *Bergroman*), and the objectivity afforded by essayism (Musil). This map is of course only a map and would need extensive elaboration. I mention it in order to locate a fascist aesthetics within the modernist field next to alternative versions of German modernism. This is a necessary task, since Jünger himself underscores only the diachronic component, fascist aesthetics as a critique of an obsolete autonomy aesthetics, and does not recognize simultaneous but alternative critiques of the same autonomy aesthetics. Nevertheless this map has in fact only placed modernism as a catalogue of aesthetic categories. It has not yet led us much closer to the answer to the question that I began to examine before regarding the rhetoric of fascism: is there a specifically fascist politics of representation? Now I add an additional question: how does fascism subvert its own claim? Do immanent contradictions erode the flaunted stability of fascism? To find the answers, it is necessary to return to ***The Worker*** and to investigate a rhetorical micropractice in Jünger's text.

In the second part of ***The Worker,*** sections 58-67 bear the title "Art as the Formation (*Gestaltung*) of the World of Work." Since the whole book is devoted to the project of producing form as visually evident, the question of representation is not at all restricted to these passages. Everywhere the grand theme is the imposition of contours and the description of surface structures. There is no longer any inside and outside; there is no longer any above and below but only a ubiquitous constellation of power as form. Therefore the whole book enters a plea for the projection of the categories of art onto everyday life, an "aestheticization of politics," to use Benjamin's designation of fascism. In sections 58-67, Jünger consequently does not articulate a separate aesthetics, describing instead the separation of a sequestered aesthetic realm as itself anachronistic. Autonomous art is an expression of the obsolete bourgeois world view, that is, in place of an explicit aesthetic theory, Jünger provides a fascist version of the end-of-art theorem.

For Jünger, bourgeois conceptions of aesthetic autonomy are corollaries to the modern, that is, postmedieval (*neuzeitliche*), constructions of individuality. Despite the fragmentation of the universalist claims of the Catholic Church and a sweeping process of secularization, bourgeois individuality remains grounded in the tradition of the Christian soul. The constitutive categories of the autonomous personality recur in the autonomous work of art as the discourse of the individual genius: "The history of art appears here above all as the history of the personality, and the work itself as an autobiographical document." As the bourgeois individual loses legitimacy—Jünger counterposes him to the soldier in his war memoirs of the twenties and to the worker in 1932—so does the bourgeois understanding of art. In the era of total mobilization, autonomy in no field can be tolerated. To the extent that bourgeois culture still plays a role, it merely provides an escapist refuge for a privileged few, while impeding the urgently necessary decisions in the ongoing state of emergency. Jünger has nothing but contempt for the manner in which the Weimar state draped itself with signs of culture, the portraits of writers and artists on stamps and currency, as compensation for its inability to master the political crisis. "It is a kind of opium that masks the danger and produces a deceptive sense of order. This is an intolerable luxury now when we should not be talking about traditions but creating them." Bourgeois autonomy has run its course and can no longer claim the allegiance of the generation of the trenches: "Our fathers perhaps still had the time to concern themselves with the ideals of an objective science or an art that exists for itself. We however find ourselves clearly in a situation in which not this or that but the totality of our life is in question"—thus the fascist version of the modernist hostility to the culture of the philistine nineteenth century. In place of philistinism and autonomy aesthetics, Jünger advocates a postautonomous, postmodern culture that structures life-experience within an overriding Gestalt of authority. He identifies public practices likely to organize the masses and abolish private identity: film, architecture, urban planning, *Landschaftsgestaltung*—practices that are inimical to the victims of fascist modernism: subjectivity, privacy, and writing.

I turn now to a passage that I consider particularly important, not only because it again repeats the critique of autonomy aesthetics—such repetition corresponds to the iterative aspect of fascist modernism—but because it does so with a phrase that will allow me to unravel the textual web and explore the politics of fascist representation. Jünger first identifies a parasitic artistry (*schmarotzendes Artistentum*) that, like standard bourgeois art, sets itself apart from life-practice but that, in addition has lost the genuine values of earlier generations. Clearly the object of attack is contemporary innovative art, which, for Jünger, is not only bourgeois (which would be bad enough) but epigonic as well.

Jünger then proceeds to associate these degenerate artists with the advocates of an aesthetics of autonomy. Recall that, for Jünger, the insistence on the autonomous status of art represents an impediment to resolving the political emergency. He therefore accuses the proponents of autonomy of treason in a remarkable turn of phrase: "Therefore in Germany one meets this artistry with dead certainty (*tödlicher Sicherheit*) in close connection with all those forces on whom a hidden or overt treasonous character is written right across their faces (*denen ein verhüllter oder unverhüllter verräterischer Charakter ins Gesicht geschrieben ist*)."

Why does the accomplished stylist Jünger choose this phrasing? Whose faces does he envision and what is written across them? And what does this figure of speech tell us about the status of writing in fascist rhetoric?

Let me first complete the recapitulation of the passage in order to indicate the importance of the matter for the history of fascism and the status of literature within it. Jünger goes on to predict or, better, to look forward to the wrathful retribution these treasonous aesthetes will soon meet:

> Fortunately one finds in our youth a growing attention for these sorts of connections; and one begins to understand that in this domain even just the use of abstract thought is tantamount to a treasonous activity. A new sort of Dominican zeal has the nerve to regret the end of the persecution of heretics—but have patience, such persecutions are in preparation already, and nothing will hold them back, as soon as one has recognized that for us a factual finding of heresy is called for on the grounds of the belief in the dualism of the world and its systems.

Clearly Jünger is not, as he has recently claimed in retrospect, merely describing an objective historical process but rather applauding the impending initiation of a new inquisition in order to purge Germany of the heresy of dualism, that is, the claim that autonomous dimensions of human activity might operate outside the structure of power. The general heresy exists in several versions; he speaks of materialist and spiritualist positions that appear to be mutually exclusive. He must be referring to Marxist materialism and conservative idealism, the twin opponents of fascism that the Nazis would name with the crude alliteration of "Rotfront and Reaktion." Despite their apparent antagonisms, Jünger insists that both have a fundamental hostility to the survival of the German Reich: November treason in art. Both are implicated in an ultimately bourgeois discourse of an emancipatory narrative; both propagate the enervating nihilism of dialectical thought, shattering the totality into an endless series of antinomies; and both are blind to the *Gestalt* of *Herrschaft.*

The passage, especially the description of opponents with treason written right across their faces, immediately suggests several points. Recall that their crime involves the advocacy of autonomy, that is, the separation of art and, more broadly, all representational practices of culture from life-practice. Jünger's image denounces that belief by reducing the distance between writing and the body to nil. The body of the text is transformed into the body as the text, as if Jünger were already preparing to tattoo the victims of the emerging Dominican zeal. Jünger metes out a punishment fit to the crime: the proponents of bourgeois idealism learn about the materiality of language, as script branded in their flesh, across their faces.

In addition to this corporealization of writing, homologous to the appearance of Gestalt and the incarnation of the will in the body of the leader, the passage betrays a simultaneous hostility to particular identity. The victims are guilty not simply of treason but of having treason written across their faces, thus rendering them identifiable. Because they emerge as particular, they are fair game for particular persecution. Jünger does not like *their* faces because he does not like faces, that is, the representation of an individual personality, at all, especially those that are constituted by writing. The vision of persecution to which he looks forward anticipates the book-burnings of 1933, which can be considered not only as political demonstrations but as literary acts, the fascist realization of the generally modernist posture of iconoclasm toward a literary culture deemed traditional.

Beyond these explicit ramifications of Jünger's figure of the inscribed physiognomy, the passage is implicated in fundamental aspects of fascist representation. I want to isolate three points and comment on each of them: (1) the moment of recognition and the priority of vision (sight and the faces); (2) the perception of particular identity through a characteristic marking (writing as scar); and (3) the antipathy toward a symbolic order and the imaginary desire to escape writing.

1) Throughout Jünger's oeuvre, a series of descriptions defines the dimension of sight and its counterpart, physiognomy, in both negative and positive versions. The sentimental bourgeois, with sight clouded by emotion, is out of place in the age of total warfare, for "it is not the time to read your 'Werther' with tearful eyes." Eyes trapped in the darkness of bourgeois interiority cannot provide the clarity of vision demanded at the outset of ***The Worker.*** Moreover it is writing, a founding text of German bourgeois culture, *Werther,* that leaves its traces on the cheeks, traces that mark the individual as such, while they simultaneously distort his vision.

The positive *Doppelgänger* of the lachrymose bourgeois stares out from under the *Stahlhelm,* a physiognomy devoid of literacy or emotions but toughened by modern warfare into a calloused clarity:

> [The face] has become more metallic, its surface is galvanized, the bone structure is evident, and the traits are clear and tense. The gaze is steady and fixed, trained on objects moving at high velocities. It is the face of a race that has begun to develop in the peculiar demands of a new landscape, where one is represented neither as a person nor an individual but as a type.

The right-wing critique of bourgeois individuality could not be more explicit; it announces the end of interiority and the emancipation of vision. The new man has unimpaired sight, just as the contours of his face take on the sharp and clear lines of Gestalt. Yet no lines of age deface the complexion of the eternal youth invoked by fascism. Ambiguity disappears. The face of the hawk-eyed soldier is the diametrical opposite of the image of a spectacled intellectual, a rigid mask without nuance.

Jünger's moment of recognition privileges the clear image of the soldier and then doubles the point by attributing to it a clarity of vision. Conversely, the bourgeois, who cannot see through his tears, is embedded in a literary culture of writing. Hence the treason of those whose faces are marked by writing: they disrupt the presence of the image with the mendacity of words. Jünger's fascist modernism promises to liberate the imaginary from the Jacobin tyranny of the symbolic order. It draws on a long-standing reactionary tradition, a Wagnerian formulation of which can help us identify Jünger's traitors. Polemicizing against the actor Josef Kainz, Wagner writes: "One's impression is as though the Saviour had been cut out of a painting of the Crucifixion, and replaced by a Jewish demagogue." It is not Christ but Christ's image that concerns Wagner, but the point is moot since Christ as the visible incarnation is image and is threatened by the Jew as language and the people of the Book. Based on the Old Testament prohibition of graven images, the aporetic construction of Wagnerian anti-Semitism contrasts the visible Gestalt with an alternative defined as verbal and hence inimical to visual appearance. Wagner's logic is perversely consistent when he continues: "A race whose general appearance we cannot consider suitable for aesthetic purposes is by the same token incapable of any artistic presentation of its nature." Because their God is invisible, Wagner denounces the visible appearance of Jews and considers them a threat to any representative images. The legacy of Wagner's anti-Semitism recurs in Jünger as the contrasting physiognomies and the agonistic confrontation of Gestalt and writing. Figures with writing in their faces are Jews: "And thou shalt bind them for a sign upon thy hand, and they shall be for frontlets between thine eyes" (Deuteronomy 6:8). The phylacteries, the sign of treason, have become the mark of Cain by which the fascist modernist recognizes the enemy. The French racial anthropologist and fascist collaborator Georges Montandon entitles a pamphlet *Comment reconnaître le Juif?* Jünger's answer must be: by signs of writing.

2) Signs of writing in the face mar the image and make it particular. The scar produces identity, be it the wound received by Rotpeter in Kafka's "Report to an Academy" or the vernacular understanding of the significance of the tattoo, as expressed in an advertisement: "Who you are / What you stand for / On your skin / If you like—forever." Scarring the face in the ritual dual, the *Bestimmungsmensur,* a key element in German student culture, survived despite an imperial prohibition of genuine duels in 1883, various papal encyclicals, and the agitation of the Deutsche Antiduell-Liga, founded in 1902; if the social function of the *Schmiss* had to do with the production of the signs of an elite, its expressed purpose involved the preservation of individual honor and the strengthening of the participant's personality. Jünger could recognize treason "written right across their faces" because that writing, the scar, produced individual identity, which was anathema, as we have seen, for fascist modernism.

This connection is confirmed by the discussion of the scar of Odysseus in the first chapter (written in 1942) of Erich Auerbach's *Mimesis.* When Odysseus returns to Ithaca, the servant Eurykleia, who had nursed him as a child, recognizes him by a scar on his thigh, as if the marking on the body were the locus of the personal identity that Jünger detests. Auerbach describes how Homer interrupts the narrative at the moment of recognition in order to recount how young Odysseus, visiting his grandfather Autolykos, received the scar. The wound marks the body and marks the rite of passage from a preliterate infancy to a symbolic maturity associated with writing and language. This suggestion goes beyond Auerbach but is compatible with his argument that the interpolated incident does not heighten suspense; instead it testifies to the mimetic impulse in the Homeric text to encompass the world with language and to omit nothing from the verse. The scar on the body that grants Odysseus identity and personal language also generates the expansive agility of poetic language.

Auerbach juxtaposes the story of Odysseus' return with the sacrifice of Isaac in order to contrast Homeric and biblical narration. Critics have however pointed out the fundamental similarity, the thematic concern with the production of male identity in barely hidden practices of ritual scarring. When Jünger denounces the marked bodies of his opponents, he participates in a sublimated anti-Semitism by articulating a displaced critique of circumcision. His critique of identity is a fascist critique of *male* identity. Patriarchal culture depends on the symbolic order of law and language; fascist anti-patriarchy, which is always implicitly an attack on the patriarch as Jew, is an attack on the practices of writing in order to resurrect the imaginary as Gestalt, the visible body without stigmata, descending from the clouds over Nuremberg.

3) "Written right across their faces"—the scar in the face is a long-standing topos of the writer. It is because of a scar of irresolution that Montaigne, in his essay "Of Presumption," chooses a private life of writing and abjures the courtly public where kings are represented in portraits. The writer Jünger abhors that bourgeois privacy and casts con-

stant aspersion on "the desks of Europe" where the culture of literacy takes place. The fascist modernist denounces identities constituted by language, while expressing a desire for the image freed from verbal mediation. Of course both this denunciation and this desire are themselves lodged in language. Jünger's prose searches for the Gestalt, which is outside of language, by means of language. Its descriptive *parole* is committed to the abolition of *langue*. Similarly Jünger hopes to be able to recognize the new post-bourgeois type who, by definition, can have no identifying features. This slippery rhetorical situation can be analyzed through the parameters of the trope of ekphrasis.

Ekphrasis was the primary technical option in the speech of praise (epideixis or panegyric) that, during the Roman Empire, overshadowed the other two objects of classical rhetoric, judicial and deliberative speech. It profoundly influenced the poetry of late antiquity and the Middle Ages. For Ernst Robert Curtius, ekphrasis is above all laudatory description, accounts of beautiful persons and landscapes, leading to the topos of the *locus amoenus,* in the tradition of which the sensuous spectacles of Jünger's battlefields have to be placed. However, as a description of beautiful objects, ekphrasis has a somewhat more precise usage, which Leo Spitzer articulates with reference to the definition of the trope provided by Théophile Gautier, "'une transposition d'art,' the reproduction through the medium of words of sensuously perceptible *objets d'art* (ut pictura poesis)." Classical examples include the descriptions of the ornamental shields of Achilles and Aeneas and of various cups, garments, and sculptures. The term is occasionally extended to include descriptions of poetic renderings, e.g., the interpolated narrations included in the *Metamorphoses,* although this usage certainly goes beyond the limits suggested by Spitzer. In either the limited or this extended sense, ekphrasis has to do with the verbal representation of aesthetic representation. It functions either to interrupt the course of the narrative (like the account of Odysseus' scar which is ekphrastic only if one accepts my suggestion that the scar is an instance of writing or aesthetic marking) or as an allegorical interlude: Achilles' shield reproduces the cosmos and Aeneas' shield predicts the future. "Its images of Roman history chart the course of destiny in which the hero must play his inevitable role and illumine the similarity between his own deeds of violence and those of his descendants." The proximity to Jünger's military fatalism is evident.

However, the connection between this aspect of classical rhetoric and fascist modernism is not merely thematic. Jünger's descriptivism and his fascination with the visible Gestalt are ekphrastic in a new and revealing manner. The authors of antiquity devote special attention at particular moments to works of art, as if art were already a relatively autonomous sphere, separate (no matter how integrated) from the rest of the narrative, to which the author would return at the conclusion of the aesthetic description. For Homer the whole world and all its details can of course be mastered by poetic representation, and Auerbach could therefore contrast the Homeric text with the sparse abstraction of the biblical epic. This does not mean that the Homeric cosmos is always aestheticized in advance or that the work of art is indistinguishable from all other dimensions of human activity. Yet this is precisely the case for fascist modernism where the aporia of bourgeois autonomy is sublated through a universal aestheticization. The writer approaches a cosmos that is only art, and he can only recount its aestheticized Gestalt. Ekphrasis becomes the sole option of a literature that takes the classical admonition to an extreme: ut pictura poesis.

I have tried to demonstrate the ekphrastic character of Jünger's rhetorical stance not only to identify the continuity of certain topoi—from the shield to the *Stahlhelm,* from *locus amoenus* to *Langemarck*—but to investigate the politics of representation in fascist modernism. Ekphrasis necessarily implies a double dialectic: it invokes as present a missing object, and it appropriates speech to produce a visual image. Each of these points is worthy of consideration with reference to Jünger's writing.

Ekphrasis conveys the desire for an absent object, which Jünger attempts to redeem as Gestalt, just as the Gestalt of Hitler arrives in Riefenstahl's Nuremberg as the vehicle of national resurrection. A regenerative aesthetics pervades much of European fascist ideology: the object that is missing has to be retrieved from death. Jünger's writing constitutes an extended project to overcome the mass death of World War I. In ***The Worker*** he asks: "What kinds of minds are these that do not know that no mind can be deeper or wiser than that of any of the soldiers who fell on the Somme or in Flanders?" Jünger, the intellectual, is prepared to sacrifice intellectual identity in order to revivify the anonymous cadavers of the war. Ekphrastic writing becomes an exchange, a sacrifice of atonement as payment for the absent bodies. Because bullets have robbed them of their subjectivity, Jünger makes a career of denying his own and repressing his pain. This self-denial and repression account for the banality of his contributions to the controversy around his receipt of the Goethe Award: a fundamental inability to give serious consideration to the consequences of his fascist advocacy. Reminiscent of Hannah Arendt's Eichmann, Jünger's mental blockage is due to the trauma of the trenches. He is marked by the guilt of the survivor who cannot account for his having escaped death. When asked by an interviewer if he was sad to have survived 1914, he only objects to the coarse phrasing and adds that he "agrees with the ancient Greeks: those who fall in war are honored by men and gods. That would have been a good ending." He refers to his refusal to flee into a bomb shelter during a British air raid on Paris in 1944 (the incident is described in ***Strahlungen***) as a "toast with death" (*ein Bruderschaftstrinken mit dem Tode*). Similarly when critics complain that he did not resist the Nazis adamantly enough after 1933, his testy response that opposition would have led to execution in a camp has all the earmarks of a classical psychoanalytic denial: as if he knew he should have acted differently and had met his death long ago.

His ekphrastic rhetoric is therefore both a desire for the absent object and a desire for the absence of the author. Jünger simultaneously undertakes resurrection and enacts his own death. In this gruesome exchange, the idealized physiognomy of the new man is the *facies hippocratica:* for Benjamin a critical tool to pursue the mortification of the artwork with an eye to redemption, for Jünger a prescription for the aestheticization of life as death mask without transcendence.

Jünger's version of the death of the author can be treated as one item in the history of German intellectuals responding to the catastrophes of war and holocaust. It is also implicated in the second dialectic of ekphrasis, the effort to appropriate language in order to surpass it with the production of image. This tension is a constitutive moment of the trope but comes to the fore in the ekphrastic rhetoric of fascist modernism. It corresponds to the displacement of writing by image in *Triumph of the Will* and to the emphatic prescription of ***The Worker*** where "it is no longer a matter of a change of styles [i.e., modes of literary expression] but rather of the becoming visible of another Gestalt (*das Sichtbarwerden einer anderen Gestalt*)." Fascism as the aestheticization of politics transforms the world into a visual object, the spectacular landscapes of industry and war, and this first renders writing solely descriptive only to proceed to the denigration of writing as not-visual. The author's hatred for identities constituted by the presence of writing in their faces is also a self-hatred of the author as writer. It is a writing trying to escape writing. In fascist modernism, the imaginary rebels against the symbolic order of language where the author, dependent on language, is necessarily at home. It is literature at the moment of the auto-da-fé, always about to go up in flames along with the identity of the writer. If Jünger's military thematics recall Virgil's account of Aeneas' shield, his constitution of a self-subverting writing is closer to the Ovidian version of ekphrasis, the perpetual destruction of the second-order narrators in the *Metamorphoses:* Jünger's decimation of his own subjectivity repeats the slaying of Marsyas, the death wish of the descriptive poet, fleeing language.

Fleeing language, the fascist rhetorician also flees time. The classical ekphrasis interrupted the linear progress of the surrounding narrative, drawing attention to a particular *locus* apparently impervious to the vagaries of temporality. In fascist modernism, ekphrastic representation resonates with the antiteleological bias that all versions of modernism share in their rejection of traditional bourgeois culture. I want to conclude with a remark on the organization of time associated with autonomy aesthetics and its critique at the moment of the modern.

Horkheimer and Adorno's account of Odysseus and the Sirens in the first chapter of *Dialectic of Enlightenment* describes the moment of birth of bourgeois aesthetic culture. It is a process of autonomization, insofar as the local myth, still embedded in primitive religious cult, is subjected to the force of enlightenment secularization and robbed of its apotropaic power: the song of the Sirens becomes the song of art. Henceforth art has no life-practical consequences, although the nonoperative character is experienced in different manners by the opposed classes in heteronomous society. Art is simply denied the slaves whose ears are plugged with wax, while the bourgeois adventurer can partake of aesthetic expression only at the price of binding his hands to the mast. This cultural autonomization is located meanwhile within the context of a victory over space: Odysseus, the first hero in the age of discovery, navigates unknown seas and subdues them, while his body, which is separated from art, also escapes danger. Mastering the globe, he lives to tell the tale, and this is the birth of history, the victory over the lyric entreaties of forgetfulness, which allows the constructions of narratives of teleological practice.

Because historical memory and aesthetic autonomy are consanguineous, the modernist attack on autonomy aesthetics begins to pull apart the intricacies of the Odyssean nexus. The distance between body and text is radically reduced, and experience undergoes a respatialization: Odysseus could traverse every dangerous terrain, while Jünger's hero remains in the field with neither personal past nor individual future. The optimistic temporality of linear progress is frozen, but each version of modernism records the end of history in a different way. Liberal modernism, as a rhetoric of irony, critiques structures of representation and explores the immobility of the present. Epic leftism, with its anticipatory hopes of radical revolution, operates as prolepsis and explodes the continuum of history. The ekphrasis of fascist modernism asserts the immutable presence of Gestalt and exalts the luminous positivity of visible power that will shine for a thousand years, uncorrupted by the infectious nihilism of writing. It glows with the light of the image; "the fully enlightened earth radiates in the sign of disaster triumphant."

David Ohana (essay date 1989)

SOURCE: "Nietzsche and Ernst Jünger: From Nihilism to Totalitarianism," in *History of European Ideas,* Vol. 11, 1989, pp. 751-58.

[In the following essay, Ohana analyzes how "the modern Jüngerian vision of technology led towards a new political form of totalitarian nihilism."]

The aesthetic-nihilistic revolution in western culture initiated by Nietzsche in the nineteenth century was transformed by Ernst Jünger into a modern vision of technology and a new political pattern of totalitarian nihilism. Over and above 'nihilism' and 'totalitarianism' as such, there is an additional dialectical phenomenon, namely a synthesis of both concepts: the nihilist mentality, whether from inner compulsion or immanent logic, is driven to acceptance of totalitarian behaviour which is characterised by its extreme dynamism. The structure of the essay reflects the emergence and crystallisation of what I call 'nihilistic-totalitarian syndrome' from its philosophical basis to a fully-developed intellectual current in the form of a new and total consciousness expressed in Jünger's early writings.

Nietzsche used history as the starting point of a reorientation of traditional Western philosophy. According to Nietzsche, modern man, in the genealogy of his basic concepts, has discovered that the idols which he shaped with his own hands—God, morality, reason, truth—are a broken reed, a golem which turned on its creator. Nietzsche was the genealogist of Western culture who found that its values were bereft of any significance whatsoever. For him, they were no more than superstructures, narcotic drugs or energy-pills which injected taste and purpose into a world without taste or purpose. Modern man has discovered that his God is an image which man formed with his own hands in self-protection, reason is a delusion and a fraud, morality, all in all, is institutionalised habit, and objective truth is an impossibility. Nietzsche looked at the nihilism of this epoch and diagnosed it in all its nakedness. Modern man was totally naked, a leaf tossed in the wind. Disillusioned with theology and disappointed with progress, he was suddenly aware of the vast abyss which threatened to swallow everything up, nihilism lieth at the door.

Nietzsche's method of exposure was to destroy prevailing illusions, those fictions which, useful for existence, hide the meaninglessness of existence. Nietzsche stripped the masks off, one by one, religion, politics, nationality, ideology. 'Nihilism stands at the door' and Nietzsche explained its appearance by invoking the inner logic of European history until that time: the cultural development of Europe with its Christian morality and rational philosophy. Secularism opened up a chasm: until that time Christian morality had served as a fictive defence against nihilism by endowing man with a definite value in face of the arbitrariness of the forces of creation and destruction. Morality, in short, had given a purpose to life and a significance to man. What, then, was the significance of nihilism as an opposing movement, or, to be more exact, as a movement opposed to itself? The answer is: 'the uppermost values become valueless'. Morality, which served as a degenerate instrument for the continuation of existence and a distorted will-to-power, prevented man from perceiving the depths of nothingness. But, at the same time, morality contained the very truths which worked against itself: morality was revealed as an illusion and turned against itself, the golem turned upon its maker.

Likewise, the belief—in the Christian and the Platonic version alike—that this world is an illusion, and that consequently the next world must be regarded as the real one, was also revealed as fictive. Nietzsche's analysis is the most radical possible: nihilism sprang logically and inexorably from the European-Christian tradition. In other words, Western culture was bound to end up in nihilism.

Nietzsche indicated two forms of nihilism. 'Active' nihilism was the starting point of modernism because it uprooted the old or normative values and institutions by denying objectivity, promoting subjectivity and individualism, and regarding the world as a totality and a work of art. Nietzsche's modernism recognised nihilism as a path to aesthetics: the value of the objective world being nullified, man made his private world into an aestheticism. 'Tired' or 'Passive' nihilism, on the other hand, consisted of 'attempts to escape nihilism without revaluating our values so far'. This was a reaction of fear before the chaos which opened up. What did this mean in practice? The liberation of man from religious beliefs led to an uprooting of man from his world. Man continued to search for something to hold onto outside himself, a supernatural authority.

Modern man looked for a new authority in something else: the rule of reason or the tyranny of history. In a different context, Nietzsche had said: 'extreme positions are not exchanged for moderate positions, but for contrary positions'. The man who lost his higher authorities succumbed to despair, but the supernatural authorities were not the contrary of this self-despair: they were its other face. In either case, man denied his own authority and projected it onto a dominating external entity: the religious tyranny of God, the intellectual tyranny of historicism, political religions, or self annihilation. External tyranny and self-negation are two facets of alienation, or, in other words, man's flight from himself.

The modern concept of alienation appeared only in the post-kantian world. Only when man had created his world according to the patterns of his consciousness did he ask himself why he had become enslaved to the world of his creation. According to Nietzsche's analysis, a nihilistic consciousness is the Archimedean point in the encounter between enslavement and freedom. A nihilistic consciousness is the guarantee of true freedom: modern man's awareness of his internalisation of the values of society leads to the uprooting of all values.

But Nietzsche went beyond the analysis of historical or functional nihilism—that is, beyond comprehending nihilism as a value—to metaphysical nihilism. As Heidegger said: 'Nothing and nihill . . . are concepts of being and not of value'. Nihilism is part of existence, and must be seen as it is, without searching for a transcendental refuge. Metaphysical nihilism is to be found here and now, and its meaning is not the denial of morality, the denial of the meaning of the universe, or eternal recurrence in the manner of the Stoics or Ecclesiastes. It is a terrified glance at existence as nothingness. In Nietzsche, 'things' do not exist: The 'Rausch' is dominant. The world is 'without form and void', and, if there is no A or B, then there cannot be any relationship between them, and words such as 'value', 'purpose' and 'truth' are meaningless. Seen in this perspective, 'active' nihilism affirms the reality of existence over its irrationality and disharmony.

It is illuminating to compare Nietzsche's grasp of the meaninglessness of existence with that of Albert Camus and Meister Eckhardt. In Camus, it is the absurdity of existence which is dominant, but Camus did not invalidate the material world, only the significance of that world. For Eckhardt, the mystic, this world also had no meaning, but he hoped to be 'swallowed up in God' and to lose his personality in some transcendental entity. Camus could have said: 'My kingdom is this world'. Eckhardt could have said: 'My kingdom is the kingdom of heaven'. Nietzsche agreed with Camus that there is no kingdom of heaven, and with Eckhardt that there is no kingdom of this world. For Nietzsche, there was no 'this world' and no 'next world'. Nihilism was integral to being, and yet, for all that, Nietzsche affirmed existence over meaninglessness.

The will-to-power was not a late manifestation of Nietzsche's philosophy which evolved as a counter-reaction to nihilism. The concept of the will-to-power was integral to Nietzsche's unmethodical method. The nihilistic consciousness and the will-to-power dwell together side by side, and both are the very essence of existence. 'This, my Dionysian world', said Nietzsche, 'of the eternally self-creating the eternally self-destroying.' The Nietzschean therapy of radical diagnosis lay in the existence of the will-to-power as a counterweight to nihilism. After having stripped off the masks of deception, illusion and preconception, Nietzsche concluded that the will-to-power, as the ultimate reality, constituted the fundamental condition of the world. Nietzsche conferred on the cosmos, purposeless and undefined, an immanent explanation in the form of an ontological-monistic factor, the will-to-power, and in this he may be regarded as the last of the pre-Socratics.

Among the other interpretations of the question that have been offered, I suggest that it is worth while to consider the conclusion reached by Nietzsche's positivist philosophy: namely, that beyond nihilism, there is either scepticism which denies everything, or freedom which affirms everything. It is precisely the meaninglessness of the universe which gives rise to the affirmation of destiny. Eternal recurrence is the most extreme form of nihilism. Zarathustra was the personification of the myth of eternal recurrence, and yet he showed the way to the superman. Spinoza's *amor dei* (love of God) was replaced by Nietzsche's *amor fati* (love of fate). Nietzschean nihilism adopted an absolute position concerning the rejection of objective values. Nihilism was the rejection of everything which deserved to be rejected, and this rejection paved the way for the affirmation and intensification of the will-to-power. The theory of eternal recurrence stripped all values of their value; the theory of the superman was an affirmation of all beings. The superman is both the person who says yes to the disharmonious universe and affirms fate as it is, and who says no to the value of values and to the very existence of a scale of values. The will-to-power and the nihilistic consciousness are the two faces of the superman.

The Nietzschean superman is a sovereign individual who confirms himself in his destiny. In other words, the superman, in his nihilistic consciousness, is committed to building up his will-to-power. Moreover, the greater his nihilistic consciousness is, the stronger is the basis of his will-to-power. Conversely without a nihilistic consciousness, no will-to-power can exist. A weak man lacking nihilistic consciousness, and with an effete will-to-power, joins his fellows and together with them creates a herd society. The superman fuses the critique of pure nihilism (nihilistic consciousness) with the critique of active nihilism (the destruction of dominant illusions), and this establishes the will-to-power. The superman beholds the naked reality and affirms it just as it is.

In his 'Who is Nietzsche's Zarathustra?' Heidegger analysed what he called Nietzsche's 'metaphysical thinking' and wrote: 'Nietzsche's thought of the eternal recurrence of the same is a fantastic mysticism, it would seem that the present age should teach us to know better: assuming, of course, that thought destined to bring the essence of modern technology to light. What is the essence of the modern dynamo other than one expression of the eternal recurrence of the same?'

In the Feschtschrift for Jünger's sixtieth birthday, Heidegger wrote: 'Your work ***Der Arbeiter*** provides a description of European nihilism in the stage which succeeded the First World War. "Die totale Mobilmachung" is derived from your study; ***Der Arbeiter*** belongs to the stage of active nihilism'. Heidegger connected Jünger's modern technological vision with Nietzsche's metaphysics. As he said: 'The being in its entirety appears to you within the light and shade of the will-to-power, which Nietzsche interpreted as a doctrine of values'.

Ernst Jünger saw the First World War as the most concrete manifestation of Nietzsche's existential, aesthetic and nihilistic outlook. In his early writings, Jünger depicted the war as an existential moment, a mystical experience, an earthquake which overtakes a man unawares. His ***In Stahlgewittern*** (***The Storm of Steel***), described the war as a beautiful, overwhelming modern experience. He aestheticised the experience of battle: 'I watched the slaughter. . .' . he said, 'as if I were in the loge of a theatre'. In ***Der Kampf als inneres Erlebnis*** (***Battle as an Inner Experience***), the Jüngerian new man was 'the storm pioneer, the elite of central Europe. A wholly new race, intelligent and full of will, that emerges here in battle . . . Tomorrow he will be the axis around which life will revolve faster and faster'. The Nietzschean superman was distorted by Jünger into nationalist, elitist, powerful figure which found as existential significance in the First World War.

In his article, **'Die totale Mobilmachung'** (**'Total Mobilisation'**) which inspired Walter Benjamin's thesis on the aesthetiation of politics, Jünger glorified a society permanently mobilised for a total war. This total mobilisation was pure pleasure, something completely purposeless, a work of art: the battlefield was described as a 'spectacle', a 'volcano', a 'landscape'. Total mobilisation typified the new war and the modern society, whereas partial mobilisation characterised the nineteenth century. The First World War was a watershed point which witnessed a 'growing transformation of life into energy'. Work and war as manifestations of energy for energy's sake were metaphorical actions deriving from the metaphysics of the will-to-power. Man's metaphorical mastery of the universe was made possible by modern technology. Man's mastery of technology had no purpose except mobilisation for its own sake; the result was total mobilisation, in work or war. It represented an active nihilism, or a nihilistic will-to-power.

Technology had now superseded nature, but, in fact, as Jünger said in ***Der Arbeiter,*** 'technology and nature are not opposites'. The machine, as an act of will, imposes order on the modern chaos, and in this Jünger's nihilism reaches its climax, because his technology is entirely amoral: it has no rational or functional content. Here we have a revaluation of the idea of the machine and technology: once regarded as a functional matter of technique or utility, it had some to be considered the very essence of modern man. In ***Feuer und Blut,*** Jünger invoked Nietzsche to provide a legitimation for his nihilistic technology: 'Yes, the machine is beautiful', he said. 'It must be beautiful for him who loves life in all life's fullness and power. The machine must also be incorporated into what Nietzsche (who, in his renaissance landscape, still had no place for the machine) meant when he attacked Darwinism. Nietzsche insisted that life is not only a merciless struggle for survival but also possesses a will to higher and deeper goals. In the technology of the First World War, Jünger's superman made his appearance as 'homo mechanicus'. The idea, of this 'man of war' was to turn his body into a 'steel object' or a 'social machine': what Klaus Thewelit called 'the conservative utopia of the totally mechanical body'. The man-machine holism was well exemplified in the relationship between the soldier and the technology of war: 'We have to transfer what lies inside us onto the machine'.

The front-line soldier as the new man had two aspects: on the one hand, he typified the chaos of battle (to use J. P. Stern's expression), and on the other hand, 'total mobilisation'. Jünger's 'new men' comprised the Jüngerian order, which also had a dual character, or, in the words of Walter Struve, was characterised by quiet anarchy within a very rigid order'. A characteristic distortion of the Nietzsche ideal of the superman as a creature who creates himself may be found in Jünger's concept of the individual. He saw the '. . . individual as a means, not an end, as the bearer of power as well as freedom. The individual develops his higher power, develops domination in general where he is in a position of service . . . The deepest happiness of man lies in the fact that he will be sacrifice . . .'

In the ***Der Arbeiter*** Jünger's 'worker' is neither nationalist nor socialist, neither democratic nor revolutionary, but a technician: a member of the 'hierarchical state', the 'new order' or the 'work-state'. The 'worker' is a standardised creation who wears a uniform and is not a private individual but a type. Jünger used the term 'worker' to designate the type of the new man who supersedes the citizen (Burger) of bourgeois society and the 'class' with its Marxist consciousness. The 'worker' and the 'bourgeois' are not classes but a Gestalt. What is this Gestalt? Jünger wrote: 'Gestalt must be visible beyond the will and beyond history; it must also be visible beyond values. It does not presuppose any quality'. Technology is mobilised through the 'Gestalt of the worker', which Jünger saw as a holistic instrument for creating a new way of relating to the real world. Gestalt was for Jünger what myth represented for Georges Sorel, a passage from the physical to the metaphysical: 'In the Gestalt' he said 'lies the whole, which encompasses more than the sum of its parts.

Jünger's axiom 'from mathematics to metaphysics' found a paramount expression in work. His cosmological vision of work accorded the worker an ontological status, and related to work as *energos,* in the original sense of the Greek term as a manifestation of the energy in the universe which is found in man. Work effects a synthesis of human actions and natural energy by means of technology. War is no longer an end in itself, but a manifestation of the general phenomenon of work. The worker-soldiers no longer fight spontaneously but are systematically 'called up for work'. In the society mobilised for work and total war there is no longer any distinction between the civilian and the soldier between the front and the rear, between war and peace. In the state of the future war and work become identical concepts.

As Heidegger pointed out in his series of seminars on Jünger which he gave from 1936 to 1940 and from 1940 to 1946, Jünger's 'worker' is to be understood first and foremost as a metaphysical prototype which emerged from the modernism of the beginning of the twentieth century. This prototype was influenced by Nietzsche's Zarathustra, an embodiment of the metaphysics which prepared the way for the new man, in the same way as Rilke's angle, Trakle's stranger, Spengler's barbarian, Sorel's syndicalist, Wyndham Lewis's vorticist, and the Italian and Russian futurist. Jünger wished to depart from traditional European history; unlike Max Weber, he did not regard work as an expression of the Protestant desire for acceptance by God, and, unlike Marx, he did not consider it an expression of freedom or alienation. Jünger's 'worker' created the myth of the modern world. The essence of modernity was for him the total mobilisation of the worker as an existential style, and the metaphysical nihilistic consciousness as a normal condition.

Jünger evoked the memory of the first mechanised war in order to create a technological myth in which technology was no longer a function of man, but, on the contrary, directed, guided and moulded man and his role in the new hierarchical society. What the modern Jüngerian vision of technology has taught us is not how totalitarianism used technology for its own purposes, but how technology influenced the totalitarian and nihilistic conception of man. In other words, the modern Jüngerian vision of technology led towards a new political form of totalitarian nihilism.

E. Keller (essay date May 1992)

SOURCE: "A German-French Encounter: Ernst Jünger and Rimbaud," in *AUMLA,* No. 77, May, 1992, pp. 56-63.

[*In the following essay, Keller traces the influence of Rimbaud's "Le Bateau ivre" on Jünger's work.*]

Looking back to the First World War, Jünger documents his enthusiasm for Rimbaud's 'Le Bateau ivre' in recalling a visit of two fellow officers, to whom he read Rimbaud's poem, which, as he notes, occupied him greatly at that time. One of these officers was Werner von Fritsch who, twenty years later, rose to celebrity in the so-called Fritsch-Krise, as one of the first prominent opponents of Hitler's aggressive policies and one of the politician's first victims within the military. According to his surviving, unnamed fellow-visitor, Fritsch summed up his view of Jünger's recitation with the sentence: 'This man would do well to retire', a judgement which Jünger considered both well-intended and entirely apposite.

The time alluded to here was the year 1919, when Jünger was stationed in Hannover in the Mittelstrasse 7a, in quarters traditionally popular with officers in service there. Thus he points out that one of his predecessors in the flat he was occupying then was none other than the old Paul von Hindenburg, the same man who had presented the coveted 'Pour le mérite' to him, with the sobering commentary that the awarding of such a high distinction had rarely been beneficial for a young officer. Jünger's proximity to the past and future leaders of the German army demonstrates how much he himself was part of this establishment at that time. However, in conjunction with Jünger's own comment that the classification 'Reader' in a personal file hardly constituted a recommendation for a successful military career, Fritsch's suggestion clearly indicates Jünger's position as an outsider in this circle.

The encounter with Rimbaud's 'Le Bateau ivre' occurs at an important point in Jünger's life—at a time when he ceases to be a soldier and begins to become a writer. On the advice of his father, he had begun to write the first version of the account of his experiences in the First World War, published at his own expense in 1920 under the title ***In Stahlgewittern.*** More than fifty years later Jünger would describe this venture, in striking agreement with the most recent commentaries on this period of this life, as an attempt to come to terms with an 'overpowering, indeed deadly experience', by means of writing—suggesting at the same time that this attempt might not have been entirely successful. In order to complete the transition which according to his own judgement fifty years later, the 'Bateau ivre' had 'almost' brought about in Jünger's life, a new attempt had to be made. This attempt resulted in the publication in 1929 of ***Das abenteuerliche Herz,*** which once and for all broke with the description of the wartime experience. Here, the choice between Bellona and Athene, which Jünger mentions later, has finally been decided in favour of the latter. It is worth noting that here too reference is made to Rimbaud's poem.

In his choice of Rimbaud as representative of the longing for a life beyond the confines of middle class existence, Jünger hardly had a claim to originality. Before the First World War Rimbaud had played this role in the works of Trakl and Heym, and after it, in those of Brecht and Klaus Mann. It is the attraction to this particular poem of this poet, and to the motif of shipwreck, which makes the case of Jünger special.

The theme of shipwreck that constitutes the central motif of Rimbaud's poem had been one of the favoured topics of European Romanticism. Its importance in the works of Eichendorff and Brentano has been demonstrated by Bernhard Blume, who shows that in both cases, shipwreck is seen in terms of a failure, whose consequences only could be overcome by divine intervention. However, Jünger never mentions these two writers in his works and diaries. The impact of Rimbaud's 'Le Bateau ivre' on Jünger in the early twenties seems to be based not only on the image of the shipwreck itself, but also on Rimbaud's reinterpretation of it as 'the end of an experience and the beginning of another', as a recent critic of the poem put it. The concept of failure implicit in this symbol is not seen, as Eva Riedel points out, as a termination, but as the precondition for a new existence.

An overview of Jünger's works from ***In Stahlgewittern*** to ***Eine gefährliche Begegnung*** shows how central for him was this metaphor in which he later saw a key for understanding our time. The survivor of the First World War uses it in various ways to describe the situation in the barrages of the Battle of the Somme, and his diary entries during the Second World War show that this metaphor has lost nothing of its attraction for him. This fascination is expressed in his often lengthy reflections on the collection of works on shipwrecks which he made during those years, as well as in his remarks on E. A. Poe's 'A descent into Maelström', a work in which he sees 'eine besonders gelungene Diagnose und Prognose unserer Zeit'. In his later readings of such events, the emphasis shifts from the problem of sheer survival to the idea of a new beginning, emerging out of adversity. This is evident, for example, in his diary entry of December 29, 1944. The same principle is also applied in a more general context.

In his comments on Isaiah, it is elevated in accordance with his neo-platonic world-view to a cosmic plane, whereby the prophet's apocalyptic vision of destruction and new birth is explained as 'eine Art Dreifelderwirtschaft. . . : irdischer Aufbau, Brache, geistige Frucht'. The same principle also underlies the biography of Lucius de Geer, the hero of his novel ***Heliopolis,*** in which he sums up the experience of his war years. The disaster which strikes de Geer becomes the basis for his elevation to a higher social and spiritual sphere. And it is certainly not fortuitous that the point of change is marked by a close call at sea.

These examples explain to a certain extent Jünger's enthusiasm for 'Le Bateau ivre'. They do not explain why this particular poem was selected by him at this point in his intellectual biography, and only then. Here, a look at the circumstances in which this poem was conceived, as well as those in which it was received, might help. Rimbaud wrote 'Le Bateau ivre', when he was about to break with his way of life in Charlesville, a fact to which considerable significance is attached by most critics commenting on this poem and this period of Rimbaud's life. Jünger encountered Rimbaud at a time when he was in the process of dealing with his First World War experience and was considering a career as a writer. More than fifty years later he describes his situation in those days in the following terms:

> Es kommt mir vor, als ob er (namely, Ernst Herhaus, whose diary *Der zerbrochene Schlaf* Jünger comments upon here, [EK]), sich in ähnlicher Lage wie ich vor fünfzig Jahren befände: ein Übermächtiges, ja tödliches Erleben ist durch Autorschaft zu bewältigen. Gelingt es nicht, so droht Versandung und Wiederholung . . . So schilderte ich den Ersten Weltkrieg im Erleben von vier Jahren, dann eines Monats, endlich eines Tags.

In either case, this change to a new way of life could not be achieved at once. Rimbaud made several attempts to flee from Charlesville, before he finally joined Verlaine in Paris in September 1871. Following in the footsteps of his father, Jünger at first tried the career of a natural scientist with his studies in Leipzig, abandoning them in favour of the role of political activist and commentator. After the disastrous failure of his 'Schließt Euch zusammen'-appeal in 1926, he finally settled for the existence of a nonpolitical writer with the publication of ***Das abenteuerliche Herz*** in 1929. Three recent critics of Jünger's life and work, of such different persuasions as Gerda Liebchen, Hans-Harald Müller and Julien Hervier, agree that this work marks a new stage in Jünger's development as a writer.

It may be mentioned here that reference is made in two ways to Rimbaud in ***Das abenteuerliche Herz,*** in both cases, to underpin Jünger's idiosyncratic world view. Thus, he quotes these lines of 'Le Bateau ivre':

> 'Ich wollte, die Kinder hätten mit mir all die
> Arten
> Goldener und singender Fische gesehn'

as testimony for a view of nature opposed to the purely instrumental perspective of science or commerce. Besides Rimbaud, Dürer and Matthias Claudius are also referred to as typifying this view. The second reference to the French writer occurs in the opening paragraph in ***Das abenteuerliche Herz.*** This demonstrates the proximity of Jünger's concept of writing to that of Rimbaud, as formulated in his *Lettres du voyant.* Rimbaud had expressed his view thus: 'Car Je est un autre . . . Cela m'est évident: j'éclosion de ma pensée: je la regarde, je l'écoute . . .' . Jünger, justifying his interest in his own personality as a starting point for writing says: 'Einmal besitze ich das bestimmte

Gefühl, einem im Grunde fremden und rätselhaften Wesen nachzuspüren'.

But here the similarity ends. Whereas Rimbaud proceeds to describe the transfiguration of the poet into a visionary, Jünger settles for the concept of the writer as a witness, and continues:

> 'Dann aber weiß ich auch, daß mein Grunderlebnis, das, was eben durch den lebendigen Vorgang sich zum Ausdruck bringt, das für meine Generation typische Erlebnis ist . . .'

The formal consequence of this decision is the choice of the diary as Jünger's favourite form of literary communication—one to which he adhered to both in his first work, ***In Stahlgewittern*** and in ***Das abenteuerliche Herz,*** as well as in ***Strahlungen*** and ***Siebzig verweht.***

Once this period of transition from the soldier to the writer, from the chronicler of the war experience to the commentator of broader cultural issues, had been completed, Jünger's attitude to Rimbaud took a different turn. Where he still refers to him, it is in the context of cultural history, using Rimbaud's work as a marker for particular literary trends. Reflecting on Rimbaud in this way, he wavers between seeing him as one of the last representatives of nineteenth-century poetry, on the one hand, and, on the other, as one of the first precursors of modernity. This reflects a similar dichotomy in French literary criticism. Regarding Rimbaud's poetry as 'ein letztes Fanal . . . der kopernikanischen Dichtung', namely of traditional poetry, in ***Blätter und Steine*** as well as in ***Strahlungen*** he seems to share René Etiemble's opinion of Rimbaud's poetry, namely as inspired by the practices of 'les parnassiens'. In 1970 this view changes and Rimbaud is seen in accordance with the judgment of André Breton and Roland Barthes as one of the 'Kirchenväter der Moderne'. As far as Jünger's own readings at that time were concerned he seemed to prefer Verlaine's poetry to that of Rimbaud, noting that his copy of Verlaine's verses was among his most thumbed books. Verlaine, for whom, not unlike Jünger, writing was a means of stabilizing his existence, seemed at that time closer to him than the poet who fell silent at the beginning of his twenties.

Looking back to Jünger's beginnings, we note, however that together with Huysmans, Rimbaud is one of the French writers with whom he began his life-long dialogue with French literary figures, amongst whom the diarists had a particularly favoured position. It is a dialogue which might well have made its contribution to that 'humanistische Wende' which separates the early works of Jünger from his later ones. The encounter with Rimbaud's 'Le Bateau ivre', a work embodying many of Jünger's preferred motifs, appears in retrospect as that event which marked for him the début of his career as a writer, as well as providing one of those jolts which helped him in the end to abandon 'Bellona' for the sake of 'Athena'.

Eils Lotozo (review date 22 November 1992)

SOURCE: "A Booming Necropolis," in *New York Times Book Review*, Vol. 97, November 22, 1992, p. 24.

[*In the following review, Lotozo praises Jünger's* Aladdin's Problem.]

He has been recognized as one of the great figures of 20th-century German letters, yet after more than 70 years and 50 books the work of Ernst Jünger—who is still writing at the age of 97—remains largely untranslated into English. A political philosopher who is difficult to categorize, Mr. Jünger is best known for his futuristic novels, including ***The Glass Bees, Eumeswil, Heliopolis*** and ***On the Marble Cliffs,*** which was published in 1942, while its author was serving as a captain in the German Army. An allegorical attack on the Nazi Government, ***On the Marble Cliffs*** somehow eluded the censors and went on to become an international best seller.

In ***Aladdin's Problem,*** a novel that was published in German in 1983, Mr. Jünger sticks to the present and offers more metaphysics than politics. The narrator is Friedrich Baroh, a 37-year-old East German Army deserter who has fled to the West. Employed as a funeral director in a prosperous firm owned by his uncle, Baroh—with the help of his friend Kornfeld—dreams up a bizarre but wildly successful venture: Terrestra, a vast, international, ecumenical necropolis located in Turkey, which offers graves guaranteed for eternity. To his surprise, Baroh discovers that he has aroused a "primal instinct," a desire for some sense of permanence amid the planet's endless upheavals. Very soon, business is booming.

Baroh tells his story in a digressive, allusive, ironic monologue that combines autobiographical details—touching, for example, on his increasingly distant marriage and his aristocratic roots—with musings on such topics as nihilism, the ahistorical modern world, U.F.O.'s, the myth of progress, the absence of angels and the death of the gods, funerary rituals as emblems of culture and the problem of "power with its delights and dangers." (Think of Milan Kundera without the eroticism and you've got an idea of Mr. Jünger's aphoristic style.)

Despite his success as a capitalist, all does not seem to work out for Baroh. In fact, as the novel progresses it appears that he may be going mad. ("Given the sinister way in which our world is changing," he remarks, "almost everybody ought to be familiar with this mood, in which one begins to doubt rationality.") Then again, Baroh might be in the midst of a transforming spiritual experience, heralded by an otherworldly messenger called Phares.

A scholarly afterword by Martin Meyer suggests that Mr. Jünger has been heavily influenced by the philosophy of the Swedish mystic Emanuel Swedenborg. But you needn't bone up on Swedenborgian notions of spirit and matter to enjoy the wry humor and tersely poetic language in Joachim Neugroschel's graceful English translation of ***Aladdin's Problem.*** Readers will be stirred by its persistent and intriguing questions about the conflicts between nature and technology, the individual and the state, and by its examination of humanity's place in this wasteland of a world that we are rapidly creating.

Thomas McGonigle (review date 7 February 1993)

SOURCE: "Witness to the Century," in *Washington Post Book World,* February 7, 1993, p. 11.

[*In the following review, McGonigle discusses Jünger's* Aladdin's Problem *and asserts that "through the power of fiction and the authority of a long life's experience, Jünger makes us take with appropriate seriousness his observations about the modern world."*]

At 97, Ernst Jünger is both Germany's and Europe's oldest and most distinguished writer. Unfortunately he is little-known in the United States. But in a long and adventurous life Jünger has been able to fulfill two-thirds of the famous prescription of Baudelaire: "There are but three beings worthy of respect: the priest, the warrior and the poet. To know, to kill and to create."

Even before the First World War, Jünger had already run away from his conventional middle-class family and served in the French Foreign Legion. During WWI itself he fought, for Germany, an entire four years in the front-line trenches; was seriously wounded seven times and was awarded the German equivalent of the Congressional Medal of Honor. Two of his books about his wartime experiences have been translated as ***The Storm of Steel*** and ***Copse 125.*** The first of these is a celebration of the exhilaration that Jünger experienced during combat while leading a unit of shock troops. "It was," he writes, "a good and strenuous life and the war for all its destructiveness, was an incomparable schooling of the heart."

After the war Jünger studied biology and pursued entomological research, publishing a number of books foretelling the rise of an inhuman technological society and the death of both the individual and of personal heroism.

Recalled to the army at the outbreak of the Second World War, he served notably in Paris where he was a sort of unofficial liaison between the German army and French intellectuals. After the war, the novelist refused to submit to any Allied denazification procedure on the grounds that he had never been a Nazi.

In the years since then Jünger has published a shelf of books: a series of visionary novels, an extensive diary that is a perennial bestseller in France, entomological research papers, volumes of travel writings, and even a book of recounting his experiences under LSD (administered by his friend, the inventor of the drug, Albert Hofmann).

Hitherto Jünger has been best-known in this country for two novels: the anti-Nazi parable ***On the Marble Cliffs,*** published originally and astonishingly in Germany in 1938, and the futuristic novel ***The Glass Bees*** (translated by poet Louise Bogan). In the newly translated ***Aladdin's Problem,*** first published in 1983, Friedrich Baroh, disguised scion of an aristocratic German family, delivers a monologue about the aftermath of the Second World War in Poland: Baroh is drafted into the Polish army, rises quickly and then defects to the West where he goes to university, marries and takes a position in his uncle's funeral parlor. After a visit to the cemetery at Verdun, Baroh conceives the idea of a vast mausoleum, to be built in Turkey, to provide a resting place for all the world's restless dead.

Such a bald description does little justice to the epigrammatic plot of ***Aladdin's Problem.*** However, the author himself provides, in the final section, another summary:

> So far, my story is a statistical matter, under the subheading: Personal success after difficulties in war and civil war. These ascents occur not only in business, but also in art and science. Like a winning lottery ticket, they presuppose an enormous number of losers. Nor do I consider unusual that stage of nihilism in which I abide as in a waiting-room, half bored, half expecting the warning bell. Individuals become passengers, and it is surprising that the waiter still takes their order? Given the sinister way in which our world is changing, almost everybody ought to be familiar with this mood, in which one begins to doubt rationality. Perhaps the whole thing is a ghostly dream.

By having carefully delineated the rise of his hero, Jünger is able to conflate that story with his own personal history.

Moreover, through the power of fiction and the authority of a long life's experience, Jünger makes us take with appropriate seriousness his observations about the modern world: "Culture is based on the treatment of the dead culture vanishes with the decay of graves or rather: this decay announces that the end is nigh."

And finally, Aladdin's problem? Jünger reminds us, "Aladdin's lamp was made of pewter or copper, perhaps merely clay." Through its power "he could put up palaces or wipe out cities overnight . . . The lamp guaranteed dominion as far as the frontier of the traveled world—from China to Mauritania. Aladdin preferred the life of a minor despot. Our lamp is made of uranium. It establishes the same problem: power streaming toward us titanically."

Ian Buruma (review date 24 June 1993)

SOURCE: "The Anarch at Twilight," in *The New York Review of Books,* Vol. 40, June 24, 1993, pp. 27-30.

[*In the following review, Buruma traces Jünger's political and intellectual thought throughout his career and in his novels* Aladdin's Problem *and* A Dangerous Encounter.]

Ernst Jünger will be ninety-eight this year. He was smaller than I imagined. But he looks fit and still remarkably handsome. His head is crowned with thick, white hair, brushed forward, giving his rather hawkish face the sculpted air of a marble Roman senator. Jünger begins each day by jotting down his dreams. Then he takes a cold bath. He recently had a dream about Hitler.

He told me about it at his house in Wilflingen, a pretty Swabian village built around the Stauffenberg castle, which belongs to relatives of Count Claus Schenk von Stauffenberg, the man who tried to assassinate Hitler. Jünger's study is that of a German aesthete in the 1930s: fine Persian carpets, leather-bound volumes of Byron, Wilde, Poe, Hölderlin, Montherlant, the Russians. Recalling his Hitler dream appeared to give him intense pleasure. His watery eyes twinkled and he finished his story with a barking soldier's laugh: "Hah!"

This was clearly part of Jünger's repertoire for foreign visitors, part of the Ernst Jünger show, for he produced a sheaf of recent newspaper articles about himself in French and Italian, several of which had the Hitler dream in their headlines. He also showed me the latest addition to his diaries, published in a German literary magazine. And sure enough there it was: "A crash landing at night because of a pilot error. Hitler was there too, the first time he appeared in my dreams—nothing special about him. . . ."

"Nothing special. . . ?"

"Nothing special. Hitler, you see, was just a product of his time. Like Napoleon, really, except that he had an even greater potential. He did what we all wanted, and promised so much more: he wiped out the humiliation of Versailles and got rid of unemployment. Then he ruined everything. The problem was his character. A negative character."

And yet Hitler had spared Jünger more than once. When a top Nazi functionary named Bouhler—who made his name promoting involuntary euthanasia—complained to Hitler about him in 1939, Hitler said: "Leave Jünger alone." Bouhler killed himself in 1945, but after the war, Jünger was threatened again, this time by German Communists, and Brecht used Hitler's exact words: "Leave Jünger alone."

A German writer who could annoy Nazis and Communists, yet enjoy the support of Hitler and Brecht, must have had something special going for him. Perhaps Brecht and Hitler realized something that simpler believers did not: that Jünger could be useful as a fellow enemy of bourgeois liberalism. Or maybe they were simply fascinated by Jünger's mystique. If so, they were not the only ones. On Jünger's ninetieth birthday Francois Mitterrand paid a special visit to Wilflingen, together with Helmut Kohl. "Mitterrand was sitting right where you are now," said Jünger, pointing at my chair. "And Filipe Gonzales sat in this chair," said Jünger's wife, who was sitting on my left. She is referred to in Jünger's diaries as "the little bull." I could see why. She looked tougher than he did. I was asked to admire some photographs of Jünger and his various distinguished guests. In one of them, Jorge Luis Borges could be seen, dressed impeccably, leaning on his stick. "A gentleman!" barked Frau Jünger, a *Herr.*

Part of Jünger's interest is his age. He must be one of the very few people still writing who was already alive during the Dreyfus affair, and fought in both world wars. Such longevity is as fascinating as a brilliant life cut short: Ernst Jünger and Wilfred Owen, the two ends of a romantic scale. Jünger always did cut a romantic figure. I have in front of me a picture taken during the Great War, of Jünger in uniform: dark and slender, one delicate hand wrapped round a pair of leather gloves, the Iron Cross pinned to a finely cut tunic, the greatcoat casually undone: the perfect image of the brooding soldier-poet, master of the exquisite phrase and the unflinching kill. Jünger was a Hemingway with the beauty of Rupert Brooke; or perhaps not Hemingway, for Jünger was the real thing: he was a legionnaire in North Africa, a thrice-wounded commando officer in France, and the youngest lieutenant to receive the *Croix Pour le Mérite.*

Jünger's love of the military life has prompted speculations about his love life. Both he and his wife were scornful of a

German writer who had recently said that Jünger was afraid of women. "He wrote that," snorted the little bull, "because he thinks Ernst Jünger had no experience with women before becoming a soldier. Well, that's not at all my understanding." Jünger gave his wife a roguish look. "Hah!" was all he said.

Jünger has a prose style to match his soldier-poet image. It is highly polished, elegant without being perfumed. Bruce Chatwin described Jünger's most famous book, ***On the Marble Cliffs,*** an allegory about a Hitlerian tyrant, published in 1939, as "the prose equivalent of an art nouveau object in glass." One is reminded, occasionally, of Nabokov, without the jokes. Thomas Mann wrote in 1945, after dismissing everything published under Goebbels as "stinking of blood and shame," that Jünger's German was "much too beautiful for Hitler's Germany."

Jünger was, however, not the only literary dandy, or poet-soldier of his time, and if his reputation had rested solely on his rather absurd essays about blood, war, and the new machine age, or on such cut glass curiosities as ***On the Marble Cliffs,*** his fascination would have faded, and neither Mitterrand not Kohl would have bothered to congratulate him.

No, there is something else about Jünger which made his mystique more lasting, especially in France, where his star shines more brightly than in Germany. The received opinion on Jünger, at least among his admirers, is that he changed his mind in a dramatic way. From being a glorifier of war and a radical nationalist who saw fit to send Hitler a copy of his essay ***Fire and Blood,*** inscribed to "our national leader, Adolf Hitler," Jünger turned into an anti-Nazi dissident. Comments in his diary, kept during his stint in occupied Paris as a Wehrmacht officer, are cited as evidence. And much is also made of a document sent in December 1944 by Roland Freisler, the "hanging judge" of the *Volksgericht,* to Martin Bormann. In this letter, Freisler informs the *Reichsleiter* that Hitler wished the plan to prosecute Jünger for high treason to be dropped. Clearly, Bormann and Freisler were keen on snaring Jünger, on the grounds of spreading defeatism (involvement in the assassination attempt on Hitler could not be pinned on him, even though he was on friendly terms with officers in the plot), and just as clearly Jünger's skin had been saved by his Führer once again.

That Jünger was a fascistic thinker in the 1920s and 1930s is beyond much doubt. Which is not to say he was a Nazi. Like many nationalists and conservatives (Carl Schmitt, Gottfried Benn, Heidegger) he sympathized with the Nazi movement, but (unlike Heidegger) he never joined the party. It is sometimes hard to classify Jünger's ideas as right or left; he was in that sinister region where the two extremes met. His mentor in the 1930s was Ernst Niekisch, leader of the "Prussian Communists," whose ideology, promoted in Jünger's inimitable prose, was a mixture of Bolshevism and aristocratic reveille. Together with the new breed of hard, heroic workers, the noble veterans of Langemarck and Verdun would destroy the flabby bourgeoisie and struggle toward a world state.

The battle of Langemarck, a disastrous enterprise at the beginning of World War I costing 145,000 lives, played a large part in Jünger's political fantasy life, as it did in Hitler's. Both men had fought there. At Langemarck (in Hitler's words) man fought against man and heroes died with the *Deutschlandlied* ringing in their ears. At Langemarck (in Jünger's words) a cosmic battle took place, in which the "individual, representing all that is weakened and doomed" was crushed by the "steel laws" of the mechanical age. But out of this cosmic baptism by fire "a kind of vanguard would arise, a new backbone of fighting organizations—an elite one could also describe as an order."

Postwar Jüngerians (including Jünger himself) have tended to interpret these phrases as purely descriptive, prescient visions of the world to come. The least one can say is that the spectacle of mass society, rootless, restless, and spiritually adrift, filled him with ambivalence. In his essay **"Total Mobilization" ("Die totale Mobilmachung")**, written in 1930, Jünger describes the "wonderful and terrifying spectacle" of totalitarian states mobilizing every man, woman, and child from the moment they are born toward total industrial war. Individual freedom ("always a questionable concept anyway") becomes meaningless, elections a sham. Humanistic values dissolve in a mechanized, abstract world, in which entire cities disappear in bombings and peoples are wiped out by poison gas. Descriptive, indeed; prescient, certainly. But then one gets to the final paragraphs of the essay, which take us straight back to Langemarck:

> In the depth of its craters, this war had a meaning, which no amount of arithmetic could possibly quantify. One could already hear it in the cheering of the army volunteers, who sounded the voice of the formidable German demon, a voice which combined weariness of old values with longing for a new life. Who could have thought that the sons of a materialist generation could have greeted death so ardently? . . . Just as the real fulfillment of an honestly lived life is the gain of one's own, deeper character, so the result of this war cannot be anything but the recovery of a deeper Germany. . . .
>
> Deep under the areas where the dialectics of war aims are meaningful, the German met with a superior force: he encountered himself. And so this war was for him above all a way to realize him-

> self. Our rearmament, therefore, in which we have long been engaged, must be a mobilization of the Germans—and nothing else.

This is not the voice of a cool, aristocratic detachment (that would come later). This is the cheering of an enthusiast. Jünger often uses the word *Rausch,* intoxication, to describe his war experiences. He used the same word in the title of a book about his experiments with drugs: ***Annäherungen, Drogen und Rausch*** (***Approximations, Drugs and Intoxication***). Jünger began taking ether during World War I, then he experimented with opium, cocaine, hashish, LSD, as well as mushrooms of various kinds. He liked LSD, but hashish, he said, made him feel aggressive. It was fascinating and distinctly odd to hear the old soldier describe his trips, while the little bull offered me some more coffee and cake. I asked him whether the intoxication of battle was like being high on drugs. "Yes, yes," he said, "but modern warfare has destroyed all that. A real old cavalry charge, that was something! Hah!"

Even though Jünger is said to have coined the term "total mobilization," he was not a very original thinker. The meaninglessness of post-religious life came from Nietzsche; the celebration of the state from Spengler; and the deep *Geist* of the Germans from just about everyone right of center. The idea that human events are the result of cosmic forces came from Heidegger, who characterized the Nazi movement as a meeting of technology, destined by the planets, and the new man. The contempt for materialism and liberal democracy was as thick in the air as oxygen at the time, and visions of brave (or wicked) mechanical worlds were shared by many intellectuals, some of whom—H. G. Wells, for example—were more extreme than Jünger. In fact, it is in France that Jünger's spiritual ancestors can be found, perhaps more readily than in Germany. Maurice Barrès, one of the patriarchs of fascism, had already come up with the phrase "machinism" to describe the modern age, before the turn of the century. And his idea that "what gives the individual or a nation its values is that its energies are tensed to a greater or lesser degree" could have been written by Jünger himself. I was interested to note the complete works of Barrès on Jünger's bookshelf.

Fascists, as well as the revolutionary socialists, were obsessed by the twin ideas of mass movement and self-elected elites—fighting vanguards to replace the aristocracy of the *ancien régime.* Before the Great War, the French syndicalist leader Emile Pouget believed it was the duty of a small elite to lead into action the mass of "human zeros," as he so charmingly put it. Democracy, he said, was not only "vulgar," but it would gum up the revolutionary works. Henri de Man (Paul's uncle) began as a socialist writer and ended as a collaborator of the Nazis. He believed in heroism, sacrifice, collective action, and . . . "a superior class." He wrote that "no society is possible without an aristocracy." Jünger thought so too. In ***"Der Waldgang,"*** an essay published in 1951 (!), he observed that democracy inevitably leads to mob rule (*Pöbelherrschaft*). What was needed was a new nobility (*Ritterschaft*), to overcome the leveling forces of a new collectivist age. But Jünger set his standards high. In a reversal of (Groucho) Marx's maxim, he once famously said he was so elitist that no elite was good enough for him. His ideal is what he calls the Anarch, the spiritual aristocrat, lifted by his noble spirit far above the mob to a higher sphere of absolute freedom and autonomy.

This is a constant theme in fascistic or anti-liberal thinking: a hatred of bourgeois individualism on the one hand, and a yearning to stand above the masses on the other. In his prewar writings, Jünger flirted with the ideal of a militarized elite, something between the *Freikorps* and the SS, a vanguard of hard, technical warriors. At the same time, he was a more traditional German intellectual of the type that Thomas Mann portrayed in his *Reflections of an Unpolitical Man,* the high-minded aesthete, whose purity would be sullied by the merest whiff of practical politics. When Hitler allegedly offered Jünger a seat in the Reichstag in 1927, Jünger is said to have turned it down, with the remark that the composition of one verse was of more value than representing sixty thousand "idiots" in parliament.

So when during the 1930s Jünger finally recoiled in disgust at what Hitlerism had caused, he retreated into two towers of the finest ivory: the disengaged world of letters and the higher echelons of the Wehrmacht. Jünger spoke of a select *Ritterschaft* within the army, which remained aloof from Hitler's terror. And Gottfried Benn said that joining the German army was tantamount to "inner immigration." A doubtful view, if one thinks what this fine body of men did on the Eastern Front. But it might have been true in Paris, where the poet-soldiers, or at least the more cultivated officers, were sent to flatter the French intelligentsia into submission. Jünger adored Paris, the jewel saved from the wreckage. Indeed, the Paris of Jean Cocteau and General von Stülpnagel was perfect for him. He was far more at home there than in coarse and thuggish Berlin. In Paris he could buy fine antiquarian books, fill his diary with elegant aphorisms, and indulge in little jokes at the Hotel Raphael about those ghastly Nazis.

Quite when he turned against the brown tide, and why, is not easy to pinpoint. Not before 1938, at any rate. Or at least not openly. In an interview with *Der Spiegel* in 1982 (when he received the Goethe Prize), Jünger said he still absolutely agreed with the annexations of Sudetenland and Austria. ***On the Marble Cliffs*** is usually seen as the first public expression of his distaste. It became a best seller, and was much admired by Stephen Spender, among others. Thousands of German soldiers carried it in their knapsacks. Spender visited Jünger in 1946 and had his copy signed. The novel is indeed full of disgust for the violence and destruction unleashed by the Chief Ranger and his barbaric Mauretanians. This Hitler-like tyrant and his brown-shirt-like hordes are out to destroy the fair land in the Grand Marina, descriptions of which are reminiscent of the Blood and Soil (*Blubo*) literature of the time: ". . . as if the graves had opened, the dead rose up invisibly. They are always near to us when we look upon a land we love, in which an ancient culture has its roots. . . ."

But more interesting in the light of Jünger's subsequent career is the behavior of the narrator and Brother Otho. The narrator is an entomologist, like Jünger himself. A visit to Jünger's house includes a tour of his impressive collection of rare beetles, all neatly pinned down in wooden drawers. Jünger once said he hated power stations, because they destroyed insect life. Brother Otho, like Jünger's brother, the poet Friedrich Georg, composes phrases in light meter, aiming "to fix a fragment of this world's mosaic like a stone mounted in metal." As these two aesthetes reflect upon the meaning of life, high up on the marble cliffs, the lands down below are threatened by the Mauretanians: "The time was ripe for terror. In this respect man-made order is like the universe—from time to time it must plunge into the flames to be born anew."

It is a fine poetic sentiment to be sure, but there is something repellent about such musings, even as millions are killed. Why on earth *must* the universe plunge into flames from time to time? And was retreat into higher spheres really the proper response? Was it truly so noble to be above it all? But then there is something Neronian about Jünger. In his Paris diary there is a famous description of Jünger, in May 1944, standing on the roof of the Hotel Raphael, a glass of burgundy afloat with strawberries to hand, watching Paris burning in a bombing raid. The beauty of the spectacle inspires him to compare Paris to "a flower impregnated with deadly pollen." Still, Neronian or not, there could be little doubt about Jünger's disdain for the Nazis. As with many cultivated Germans, this was partly a matter of class, in the British as well as the American sense of the word. The Nazis were so terribly vulgar.

The wonderful diaries of Friedrich Percyval Reck-Malleczewen are a perfect illustration of this attitude (even though "Reck" was by no means as aloof from the world as Jünger). Like Jünger, Reck deplored the collapse of the old order, although, unlike Jünger, he had never applauded the new one. He was no democrat either. And he, too, was a sworn enemy of materialism and a believer in aristocracy, "our little phalanx." But sprinkled among his fits of rage at the terrible deeds of the Nazi thugs are sniffy remarks about Hitler's resemblance to a headwaiter, or Goering's shocking taste, only to be expected in "the son of a Rosenheim waitress," or Goebbels as "the limping haberdashery salesman." Hitler, wrote Reck, rising to his theme, was a "middle class antichrist."

But it would be unfair to Jünger to ignore remarks in his Paris diaries that showed he was more than a snob. He did say, on June 7, 1943, that he felt ashamed to be in uniform, after seeing Jewish girls wearing the yellow star in the Rue Royale. This was after he had enjoyed a stimulating conversation with Paul Morand about American literature over lunch at Maxim's.

Jünger tended to shy away from the out-and-out *collabos* in Paris. According to his diaries, he bumps into Drieu La Rochelle from time to time, but finds him tiresome. Henri de Man puts in an appearance, but Jünger thinks him a corrupted apparatchik. Of Marcel Déat, rabid ideologue of the Action Francaise, he observes that too much striving for power at any price "coarsens the skin." And Robert Brasillach, the Nazified journalist, does not appear in the diaries at all. I asked Jünger about this. "Well," he said, "one didn't read the newspapers, and I disliked the man. Because of his bad table manners, chiefly."

Jünger felt more at home with aesthetes like Montherlant and Cocteau, with whom he could discuss de Quincey's opium dreams. Some of his Parisian friends, such as Jean Paulhan, even had connections in the resistance. But, says Jünger, "One never mentioned that, of course. We only spoke of literary matters." Was this circle his idea of a *Ritterschaft?* "Indeed it was. A true elite is never active. It exists for cultivated conversations in exclusive drawing rooms."

So, disdain, disgust, and elegant retreat, yes. But did Jünger's political views really change? I think less so than some of his admirers would have us believe. It is a sign of honesty as well as consistency that he included all his prewar writings in postwar anthologies. Well, all but one article, published in 1930, entitled **"Nationalism and the Jewish Problem,"** of which, quite properly, he felt ashamed. All the rest he continued to regard as important. If one compares the postwar novels and essays with the older work, one finds that Jünger's vision of the world remained essentially unchanged. He is still obsessed with the mechanical "titanic" age, which wiped out the old order, with all its values and virtues. A loyal disciple of Nietzsche and Heidegger to the end, he still frets about the nihilism of modern man. And he continues to loathe the leveling vulgarity of liberal democracy. When a plan to name a school in Germany after Heidegger came to nothing, Jünger wrote a letter to congratulate his old master on the absence of his name. "If we lived in 'normal times,'" he wrote, "the school would have borne your name." One shudders to think what normal times would be in a Jüngerian Germany.

There is, however, one difference between Jünger's post-war and prewar writings: what could still inspire occasional bursts of enthusiasm before the war—the new orders of technical samurai, etc.—filled him with despair after the war was over. He has an explanation for this, given in his *Spiegel* interview. He compared his earlier enthusiasm to being in a football match where you get carried away by the excitement, even if football does not interest you in the least. "The same thing happens," he explained, "when I step into a political system. I have a weakness for systems of order, the Jesuits, for example, or the Prussian army, or the court of Louis XIV." The thing about his prewar writing is, however, that he took a certain aesthetic pleasure in the spectacle of collapsing orders too.

But Jünger has also offered another explanation for his apparent change of attitude. Memories of Langemarck had still offered him visions of old-fashioned heroism. As he put it in his *Spiegel* interview: "The last real war was the First World War." Then he still believed that man was stronger than matter. But now we know that "the technician has won and the old grades have dissolved." The soldier, in Jünger's view, ceased to be a warrior. Heroism no longer had a place in the "titanic wars" fought by industrial armies of technical workers. "When I'm called a glorifier of war," Jünger said, "I do not disagree. Homer, after all, was a glorifier of war too, as were thousands after him."

War as a destroyer of what Edmund Blunden called "degree" is a fearful thing to any conservative. Blunden wrote an elegiac book about England called *Cricket Country* in 1944. War, he worried, would damage the "harmony of life." by which he meant the "principle of grades of society. . . ." Jünger was concerned about this too, but the main source of his anguish was the loss of soldierly virtue, of honor. Jünger not only hates nuclear power for its threat to his beloved beetles. He hates it because it has removed the last vestiges of chivalry from war. The atom bomb, he has argued, erroneously alas, made obsolete "real wars," where man fights man, and heroes die with the *Deutschlandlied* ringing in their cars.

One would expect this nostalgia for manly wars to appeal mostly to conservative romantics—Winston Churchill shared Jünger's regret about the bomb. In fact, however, this side of Jünger also appealed to the Communist playwright and Brecht devotee Heiner Müller. Müller quoted Jünger in his argument that we must "restore meaning" to war. War "is the last refuge of what we call human." The bomb, like capitalism, is a product of rationalism, resulting in nihilism and industrial death. Like Jünger (and Nietzsche, Heidegger, T. S. Eliot, etc.). Müller is haunted by the idea of a spiritual void in modern man. Communism provided an answer. But since the iron curtain disappeared, "man has been delivered defenseless to the machine world."

This theme runs through everything Jünger has ever written, during the Weimar Republic, during the war, and ever since. Müller's (and Brecht's) liking for Jünger is no accident. For Jünger is intellectually, or perhaps one should say spiritually, much closer to the Communists than to the mostly liberal writers of the Federal Republic. Even his utopianism has a familiar Bolshevist ring. In his essay **"Peace"** (**"Der Friede"**), written during the war but published after 1945, Jünger constructed a blueprint for the future world state. National democracies, he said, would be "overcome." Technical problems—industry, housing, transport, trade—would be solved by an authoritarian world state. But the state would be inspired by a higher faith, transcending materialist concerns, a faith whose seeds were sown by the sacrifice of soldiers, and whose spiritual reservoir was still to be found in the nobility and *Geist* of the German people. In this essay, Jünger makes the rather astonishing remark that it took "courage to remain a German" during the war, a great deal more courage, that is, than was shown by the likes of Thomas Mann or Marlene Dietrich, who stood on the other side as German cities were flattened. (That such writers as Alfred Döblin and Lion Feuchtwanger had no choice in this matter, Jünger tactfully leaves unsaid.)

Living in the Federal Republic of Germany for almost fifty years has dulled Jünger's taste for Utopia, and his novels more and more read like elegies. But his line on machinism, titanism, and the spiritual void has never wavered. ***Aladdin's Problem,*** published in English for the first time last year by Marsilio Publishers, proves this point. Aladdin's problem is the vacuousness behind the absolute power of modern man. Aladdin is the ultimate *Arbeiter*, omnipotent and without soul.

The hero of the story is a man rather like the author himself: Friedrich Baroh, a melancholic old soldier of aristocratic pedigree (four ancestors received the *Pour le Mérite*), disillusioned with the emptiness of modern materialism. He served in the East German army, a grim experience only made tolerable by his friendship with a like-minded young captain, whose build and demeanor were those of a proud horseman who could only regret the day the cavalry dismounted. Their conversations are rather like those Jünger recorded in his Paris diaries, between the author and von Stülpnagel, say, or the causeries of the narrator and Brother Otho in ***On the Marble Cliffs:*** cultivated, detached, above it all. Baroh defects to the West but not because he believes in freedom—"I am no liberal—at least not in the sense that people have to get together and vote on the matter." A man "with a good mind will realize his potential in any regime." A doubtful view, but one that might occur from the perspective of a very high ivory tower. Like all Jünger's heroes, Baroh is an Anarch.

Westward, at any rate, he goes, there to get married and find employment in his uncle's funeral business. The business grows into a huge, international enterprise, a bizarre caricature of modern corporate life. The fact that the nature of the business is death leads to a philosophical paradox which opens the way to much Jüngerian musing. For the business itself is meaningless, even nihilistic, but at the same time, "Culture is based on the treatment of the dead; culture vanishes with the decay of graves. . . ." In a sense, then, Baroh's business—of building a gigantic necropolis in Turkey—is God's business. But we live in an age when

> titanic forces in mechanical disguise are supplanting the gods. Wherever Zeus no longer rules, crown, scepter, and borders are becoming senseless; with Ares, the heroes are making their farewells; and with Great Pan, nature is dying.

There is really only so much of this one can take, however polished the prose, for Jünger pushes his line with the drilling insistence of an old club bore. And he has done so in book after book after book. At one point in the story Friedrich Baroh observes that 1888, the Year of the Three Emperors, marked "the onset of the labor pains of Titanism, the a historical era. That year, Nietzsche decided to build his work 'toward the catastrophe.'" It is in precisely that year that the second novel under review, [***A Dangerous Encounter***], first published in Germany in 1985, is set.

Paris, 1888. The machine age is upon us. The main, aristocratic characters are exhausted, out of harmony with the world, at the end of their tether, born a century too late. Captain Kargané, a naval officer who believed that "something irretrievable had been lost with the sailing ships," is trapped in a loveless marriage with a bored and voluptuous countess, who amuses herself with young actors. The captain seeks solace in the Levant, but there too, "the last hour had unmistakably sounded; the triumphal march of universal platitude could no longer be checked."

Ducasse, the decadent scion of an old family, "would have been more at home in the previous century, as the friend of princes who reveled before the deluge." Now, in the soulless age of steam and light, he is reduced to being a mischievous arbiter of elegance at the doubtful tables of rich strangers. He contrives to arrange a tryst in an exclusive house of pleasure between the bored countess, mentioned above, and Gerhard, a young German dreamer sent to Paris to complete his sentimental education. A horrible murder follows and Inspector Dobrowsky enters the scene, a technical man, an *Arbeiter,* who "wore suits from the rack, impossible neckties, shirts and collars upon which the lye from laundries had tested its causticity." Dobrowsky "had one of those faces which have become more common since the invention of the railroad: many faces leave their traces in it and become anonymous."

This seemed an odd sentence: many faces leave their traces. . . . So I checked the German original. What it really says is "many races leave their traces. . . ." Quite a difference. And it only shows, yet again, how at the core of Jünger's melancholy philosophy lies the monumental snobbery—social, intellectual, racial—of the Anarch. Naturally, the mongrel Dubrowsky turns out to be the only winner in the story. It is his age, after all.

But the novel ends with a minor restoration of harmony. A duel is arranged between the captain and the German dreamer. Gerhard's second is a drunken *Rittmeister,* who, like the others (except the mongrel detective of course), was born a century too late. But the duel restores some of his old pride, the prospect of honorable death revives him: "He had shaved and for the first time in a long good while felt good about himself again." But, alas, the duel is prevented at the last minute by the clever inspector, who arrives with a fire engine with clanging bells. Kargané then saves his honor by shooting himself through the heart.

Culture is based upon the treatment of the dead. It would perhaps have been more Jüngerian to say it is based upon the way we choose to die. Like a true veteran of Langemarck, Jünger always remained faithful to the dead cult of his youth. As one of the official celebrators of that battle said: "Happiness lies only in sacrificial death." It is a ghastly philosophy, which has done untold damage to mankind. Blinded by his *Angst* of the spiritual void, Jünger, and many people like him, has missed the most important point about machines: it is not machines that threaten life, but the crazy beliefs of the men who operate them. Skepticism is far less corrosive of honor than a surfeit of irrational faith.

Yet it was the irrational that attracted Jünger all his life: the intoxication of drugs, of revolution, of war. This does not mean he was responsible for the rise and *Rausch* of the Third Reich. But neither can one say, as he continues to do that his prewar works merely reflected the times, like a literary seismograph. For Ernst Jünger was one of the people who helped to shape those intoxicating times. I asked him what had been his proudest achievement. He answered that some people felt satisfied with their work, but that he was not one of them. "All my works are but approximations of the highest, of the sublime. What I mean to say is, my books are approaches to the absolute." Another word for the absolute is death.

E. Keller (essay date May 1994)

SOURCE: "Wrestling with an Old Trauma: Ernst Jünger's Changing Perception of Destructiveness," in *AUMLA,* No. 81, May, 1994, pp. 21-31.

[In the following essay, Keller discusses the place of destructiveness and compassion in Jünger's work.]

Destructiveness is one theme which is ever present in the work of Ernst Jünger from ***In Stahlgewittern*** to ***Eine gefährliche Begegnung.*** It dominates the first of these texts and is critically assessed in the latter, indicating that division in Jünger's work at which he had hinted in his diary entry of 16 September 1942. There he had made the less than modest remark that he considered his books on the First World War, ***Die totale Mobilmachung, Der Arbeiter*** and sections of his essay ***Über den Schmerz,*** as his 'Old Testament'. It was that part of his work which was dominated by the theme of aggressiveness and which had made his name notorious. His account of the First World War was such that some critics expressed doubt that what he produced could still be considered literature, while others could see Jünger's rendering of his war experience in psycho-pathological terms only. Unlike Henri Barbusse, for whom the experience of the First World War had been the basis for a passionate plea for pacifism in his novel *Le Feu,* Jünger saw in it the redemption from the constraints of an over-refined culture. For him war was not so much an aberration of humanity as a revelation of its true face. In this respect he was in agreement with Freud who, during these war years, had enlarged his view of humanity to include a concept of destructiveness which he described in strikingly similar terms to those of Jünger. Yet, whereas Freud registers these developments with concern, Jünger seems to welcome them. When looking at the combatants of the First World War Jünger does not visualize the average conscript, as Barbusse with his 'poilus' had done, but concentrates rather on the 'wenigen Erlesenen', who actually thrived in this situation.

These 'Stahlgestalten' are for him—as the 'Urmenschen' are for Freud—the living proof that the sources of war are to be found 'tief in unserer Brust' and that 'Die Sucht, zu zerstören, ist tief im menschlichen Wesen verwurzelt [. . .]'. Such figures reveal their relationship to their primeval ancestors, particularly in their disregard for the life of their fellow-men, a point on which both Jünger and Freud agreed, and one which Jünger elaborated on by referring to this exalted breed of warriors as 'prächtige Raubtiere'. Jünger sifts through his knowledge of history to locate precedents to an attitude which links the exploits of the battlefield with an excessive life style, regarded by him as characteristic of his princes of the trenches. These he finds in the actions of figures like Tamerlan and the asiatic despots whose morality Jünger describes thus:

> Sie handelten, wie es ihrem Wesen entsprach. Töten war ihnen Moral, wie den Christen Nächstenliebe. Sie waren wilde Eroberer [. . .] Man kann Genuß an ihnen empfinden wie an bunten Raubtieren, die mit kühnen Lichtern in den Augen durch tropische Dickungen brechen. Sie waren vollendet in sich.

The mercilessness advocated here would also form the prominent feature of a state run by such princes of the trenches; a state whose blueprint Jünger had presented in ***Der Arbeiter.*** Here Jünger had noted that in this state the notion of 'der sehr alten Wissenschaft der Entvölkerungspolitik' would be revived. The attitude of 'désinvolture' so often advocated by Jünger and described in his essay ***Über den Schmerz*** as that 'angemessene Kälte [. . .] des Zuschauers, der von den Rängen des Zirkus aus das Blut fremder Fechter verströmen sieht [. . .]' would be the adequate position from which to confront the obduracy of the world that is revealed in these works.

The concepts which dominated the first part of Jünger's career as a writer, and which were often bitterly attacked by critics, continued to play their role in the second, as narratives such as ***Auf den Marmorklippen, Heliopolis, Die Zwille*** and ***Eine gefährliche Begegnung*** demonstrate. In all of these works the theme of destructiveness is still present, but is counterbalanced by a reflective questioning of its appropriateness and by the introduction of the idea of compassion, an idea completely missing in the works of the earlier period.

Looking at figures such as the Oberförster in the ***Marmorklippen,*** the Landvogt in ***Heliopolis,*** Teo in ***Die Zwille*** and Kargané in ***Eine gefährliche Begegnung*** we note that all share some of the qualities of the 'Stahlgestalten' and of the 'Raubtiere' extolled in the earlier work. Like them they are linked with death, destruction and excess. This much is obvious in the case of the Oberförster as the destroyer of the Marina, and the Landvogt as the persecutor of the Parses in ***Heliopolis,*** but these elements are also present in figures like Teo or Kargané. Teo, like his forbears in ***Der Kampf als inneres Erlebnis,*** is introduced to us as a hunter of men, as are the Oberförster and the Landvogt, and like them he is driven 'zu Dingen, die verletzend, gefährlich, tödlich sind'. He shares with the Oberförster and the Landvogt the measured use of terror to achieve his ends. Kargané, the fourth discernible member of this group, fits a similar pattern. Described as 'intelligent, präzis, tapfer, [. . .] gewiß auch brutal', he is presented to us as a 'Freibeuter' and an exemplary representative of that type of man with whose help colonial empires were created in the space of decades.

Aggressiveness and disregard for the suffering of others link these figures with their predecessors of Jünger's 'Old Testament', as do the nature of their excesses, in which they almost slavishingly follow the pattern set by the oriental despots conjured up in ***Der Kampf als inneres Erlebnis.*** The 'Asiatischen Partien' of the Oberförster bear witness to this as do the 'Orgien' of the Landvogt or the activities Kargané conducts in his Transylvanian castle. It is likewise made clear that the inclinations of the precocious Teo tend in the same direction.

It is one of the features of Jünger's later works that the opponents of these figures of aggressiveness are not entirely set apart from them. It is made plain to us that they have important features in common which they, however, strive to overcome. In the case of the ***Marmorklippen*** this is related in the autobiographical account of the two brothers who, among other things, admit that they themselves enjoyed the destructiveness of warfare, appreciated, for a period in their lives, the social contact with the Oberförster, as well as holding membership of the power-seeking order of the Mauretania. Similarly the hero of ***Heliopolis,*** de Geer, who associates concentration camps with the domain of the Landvogt, is confronted in the laurel night dream with a scene in such a camp, presented to him with the commentary 'Das bist du!'. For all his innocence Clamor, the hero of ***Die Zwille,*** nevertheless shares with his deadly aggressive counterpart Teo a morbid fascination with crime. Gerhard von Busche, more passive bystander than anything else in the crime committed in ***Gefährliche Begegnung,*** nevertheless contemplates whether he himself rather than Kargané should not be considered the culprit, and ultimately concludes: 'Im Abgrund waren die Menschen nicht verschieden; sie schmolzen wie Zinnfiguren ineinander ein'. In formulating his view of the situation in this way Busche alludes to an idea which seems to underlie all previous stories and which is made most explicit in ***Die Zwille.*** There the idea that even the most innocent share a common tie of human aggressiveness, or as Jünger likes to call this, share our fateful Cainitian heritage, is imparted to us by the reflections of the Superus, who, while the father of Teo, is however in character as in his inclinations very much closer to Clamor. While reflecting upon the differences between his own gentleness and the aggressiveness of his son Teo and the company Teo attracts, he comes up with an insight similar to that of von Busche, when he states:

> Dort unten, wo ich allein bin, sind Teo und Clamor mir ähnlich, [. . .] da beginnt es schon zu verschmelzen, doch noch ein Stockwerk tiefer, und sie werden identisch mit mir. Wie soll ich da urteilen?

Brigitte Reitenbach in her study on ***Die Zwille*** has demonstrated that the idea formulated here by the Superus is symbolically expressed in the form of that particular type of sling-shot (= Zwille), around which this narrative is constructed. Taking the stem of 'die Zwille' to symbolise a common heritage, the Superus draws an analogy between the two branches which fork from this stem and the two different types of conduct under discussion: one branch representing the aggressiveness of Teo, and the other the gentleness of Clamor.

What differentiates these two lifestyles from one another is the idea of compassion, a concept alien to Jünger's 'Old Testament'. To delineate the scope of this concept it might be useful to recall the definitions of both Theodor W. Adorno, who analysed the concept against the background of the German catastrophe, and Arthur Schopenhauer, a philosopher, whom Jünger knew well. Adorno notes the 'Perhorreszierung des Mitleids' by the 'faschistischen Herren der Welt' and later defines compassion as 'das Gefühl der Solidarität mit den [. . .] quälbaren Körpern'. With this conception of compassion Adorno comes close to the view of Arthur Schopenhauer, who explains it as the

> ganz unmittelbare, von allen anderweitigen Rücksichten unabhängige *Teilnahme* zunächst am *Leiden* eines andern und dadurch an der Verhinderung oder Aufhebung dieses Leidens

coming in the end to the conclusion that

> Dieses Mitleid ganz allein ist die wirkliche Basis aller *freien* Gerechtigkeit und aller *echten* Menschenliebe.

The application of these concepts of compassion to the four works under discussion seems to present difficulties for the reader only in the case of the ***Marmorklippen.*** It would appear that the admission of the two brothers that they lacked the gift to perceive the sufferings of the weak and nameless 'wie man vom Senatorensitze in die Arena blickt' is an allusion to Jünger's statement in his essay ***Über den Schmerz,*** and is one of the first of many similar revocations of his earlier attitude. However does this change of mind also translate into compassion in ***Marmorklippen?*** The critics dealing with this question are divided. Gerhard Loose, who believes that compassion is evident in this work, points to the brothers' chivalrous care for women and children, an episode which Marian McQueen disparages as 'a showy, almost gratuitous, act of chivalry' by the two brothers carrying little weight 'given their previous abandonment of the Marina to its own military defense'. To this negative vote in regard to the practice of compassion in ***Marmorklippen*** can be added the concerns of Hansjörg Schelle, who points critically to the way the narrator forsakes both his lover and his son. So whereas the ***Marmorklippen*** is perceived to represent a break with previously held positions, as is argued for instance by Karl Heinz Bohrer, it also demonstrates the difficulties its author had in successfully integrating this new concept of compassion into his work.

Such difficulties no longer seemed to apply to ***Heliopolis*** and the works leading up to this novel. Its hero, Lucius de

Geer, notes disapprovingly that 'Tötung des Mitleids in der eigenen Brust' is the prerequisite for acquiring a position of power, 'gewollte Macht' as he puts it. His attitude towards the persecuted and the tortured fulfils Adorno's definition of compassion to the letter. His commitment to compassion, moreover, which he places above military efficiency, becomes in the end the reason for his fall and subsequent reorientation. In ***Die Zwille*** Clamor shows compassion for the downtrodden as well as for the animals who become the victims of Teo's destructiveness, and, when expelled from the school, finally becomes an object of compassion himself, when a benevolent teacher is prepared to take charge of him in his father's stead.

Not unlike Lucius de Geer in ***Heliopolis,*** Rittmeister von Goldhammer in ***Eine gefährliche Begegnung*** disregards all conventions of his social standing and risks ostracism by his colleagues in his determination to prevent the duel between Kargané and von Busche from taking place, because he sees it as a 'Zugriff auf einen, der sich nicht wehren konnte'. Compassion for the defenceless is the driving force behind his action.

Ernst Jünger had travelled a long way from his 'Stahlgestalten' of the twenties to these figures of mercy of the seventies and eighties. To have accomplished this journey was, considering its beginnings, no mean achievement.

Thomas McGonigle (review date 1 May 1994)

SOURCE: "Deadly Details and Rules for Living," in *Chicago Tribune,* May 1, 1994, p. 6.

[*In the following excerpt, McGonigle asserts that in* Eumeswil *"Jünger is concerned solely with attempting to answer the question: How is one to live?"*]

. . . Ernst Jünger's ***Eumeswil*** is the distillation of its author's search for a basis upon which to build a life of integrity so as to survive the ever-present totalitarian temptations.

Still little known in America, Jünger, who will be 100 years old next year, may be Europe's most important living writer. Bringing the authority of his career and life to everything he writes, he has been able to fulfill two-thirds of the famous prescription of Baudelaire: "There are but three beings worthy of respect: the priest, the warrior and the poet. To know, to kill and to create."

During the First World War, Jünger fought in the frontline trenches, was seriously wounded seven times and awarded the *Pour le Merite,* the German equivalent of the Congressional Medal of Honor. ***Storm of Steel,*** a memoir based on his wartime experiences, may be the greatest, and the most disturbing, war book ever written—for it is not a complaint against war's futility but rather a celebration of the exhilaration Jünger felt in the heat of combat.

After the war Jünger was involved in irregular conflicts that lasted into the early 1920s. He studied biology and pursued entomological research as well as publishing a number of books that predicted the rise of an inhuman technological society and the death of both the individual and personal heroism. Astonishingly, in 1938 in Germany he published a popular and biting anti-Nazi parable, ***On the Marble Cliffs.***

Recalled to the army at the outbreak of the Second World War, Jünger served in Paris, where he was an unofficial liaison between the German army and world of French intellectuals. He was implicated in the plot against Hitler's life, but a letter has come to light, signed by Hitler himself, forbidding any harassment of Jünger by the Gestapo. After the war Jünger refused to submit to the Allied de-Nazification process on the grounds that he had never been a Nazi. The communist playwright Bertolt Brecht, in a neat act of symmetry, wrote a letter in Jünger's defense.

Since the war Jünger has published a series of visionary novels (three of which have appeared in translation, ***The Glass Bees, Aladdin's Problem*** and ***A Dangerous Encounter***), an extensive diary that is a perennial bestseller in France, entomological research papers, volumes of travel writings and a book recounting his experiences under LSD administered by his friend Albert Hofmann, the inventor of the drug.

There are no books in the American literary tradition like ***Eumeswil,*** which only by default can be described as a novel. Foregoing plot, Jünger is concerned solely with attempting to answer the question: How is one to live?

Composed, we eventually learn, of the secret writings of a young night steward in the household of The Condor, the ruler of Eumeswil, a decaying authoritarian city-state, the book is a compilation of overheard anecdote, ruminations on the different types of despotism and reflections on a wide range of interests—from the decay of language, to the relations between the sexes and right on to the ideal diet:

> I am unconcerned with how people judge me; but how shall I stand the test of my self-criticism? It is hard when a man summons himself to the bar. . . . It makes no difference to me whether Eumeswil is ruled by tyrants or demagogues. Any man who swears allegiance to a political change is a fool. . . . The most rudimentary step toward freedom is to free oneself from all that.

Jünger pulls the reader into his book with the disquieting power of anecdotes:

> Once in Peru, I participated in a ritual fiesta that involves the sacrifice of a condor. It always takes place in February. These people are truculent; though worshipping the bird as a god, they slowly torture it to death. More than anything else, however, the condor is kept for a bullfight. First, they let it starve for a week; then they tie it, like a rider to the back of the bull, which has been stabbed bloody with lances. The populace is thrown into a paroxysm while the condor with outspread wings rips the mighty animal to pieces.

By entrusting the narrative to a 29-year-old, Jünger avoids any easy dismissal of his work as being the thoughts of a grumpy old man. The impersonation of the earnest informed young voice allows us a sympathetic identification.

Reading ***Eumeswil*** one wonders whether Jünger's imagination will give way to some sort of cheap science fiction resolution. But readers of this book will find that it finally brings them face to face with cold objective actuality: The fact that "At bottom, everyone is solitary, poor, and 'only' in the world."

FURTHER READING

Criticism

Barnouw, Dagmar. "Opening and Closing the Past in Postwar German Literature: Time, Guilt, Memory, and the Critics." In *Legacies and Ambiguities: Postwar Fiction and Culture in West Germany and Japan,* edited by Ernestine Schlant and J. Thomas Rimer, pp. 227-48. Washington, D.C.: The Woodrow Wilson Center Press, 1991.

Discusses Jünger's Utopian novels and how they were received by critics.

Biro, Matthew. "The New Man as Cyborg: Figures of Technology in Weimar Visual Culture." *New German Critique,* No. 62 (Spring/Summer 1994): 71-110.

Analyzes how technology figures into the history of the Weimar culture, specifically looking at the work of Raoul Hausmann, Fritz Lang, and Ernst Jünger.

Kater, Michael H. "Anti-Fascist Intellectuals in the Third Reich." *Canadian Journal of History* 16, No. 2 (August 1981): 263-77.

Discusses the question of why anti-Fascist intellectuals were not more vocal about their opposition to Hitler.

Mandel, Siegfried. "The German Novel: In the Wake of Organized Madness." *Contemporary European Novelists,* edited by Siegfried Mandel, pp. 69-125. Carbondale, IL: Southern Illinois University Press, 1968.

Traces the history of the German novel since World War II.

Additional coverage of Jünger's life and career is contained in the following sources published by Gale: *Contemporary Authors,* Vols. 101 and 167; *Contemporary Authors New Revision Series,* Vols. 21 and 47; and *Dictionary of Literary Biography,* Vol. 56.

John Cowper Powys

1872-1963

English novelist, essayist, poet, and critic.

The following entry presents criticism on Powys's career through 1995. For further information on his life and works, see *CLC*, Volumes 9, 15, and 46.

INTRODUCTION

John Cowper Powys is considered one of the great modern English Romantic authors. A prolific writer of poetry and essays on philosophy, religion, and literature, as well as his remarkable *Autobiography* (1934), he is best known for his highly original novels. These fall into three categories: the twentieth-century stories of his beloved southwestern England, his "Wessex romances"; historical romances of ancient Wales; and his smaller science fantasies written after 1952. His masterpieces include *A Glastonbury Romance* (1932), *Owen Glendower* (1940), and *Porius* (1951). Typically Powys's novels are massive in size and complexity, with interconnected plots, strong characters, and vivid detail. He probes his characters' psyches by embodying modern psychology in Celtic mythology and natural settings. His themes of reconciling individual strife with cosmic forces, and sexual urges with mystical redemption reflect his own struggle for self-understanding. Critics have compared his novels to the works of William Shakespeare, Thomas Hardy, Walter Scott, James Joyce, and D. H. Lawrence.

Biographical Information

Born a parson's son, Powys was the eldest of eleven children and brother of two other notable writers, T. F. Powys and Llewellyn Powys. He was raised in the Dorset-Somerset countryside, the setting of his future "Wessex romances." His father claimed descendancy from a Welsh lord, and his mother's family tree included poets John Cowper and John Donne. Powys cultivated a certain eccentricity during his schooldays, although he was later renowned for his graciousness and amiability. He attended Sherbourne and Corpus Christi College, Cambridge, and became a lecturer in literature. Hoping to build a career from his poetry, he published his first volumes in 1896 and 1899. However, an estrangement from his wife and the need to support an only son led to a public speaking career in America in 1910. Speaking engagements took him to scores of public halls, colleges, and universities including public debates with Will Durant and Bertrand Russell. While lecturing set his reputation as a keen interpreter of literature and philosophy, he published prodigiously, including his first novel *Wood and Stone* (1915) and eleven other books and articles from 1915 to 1923. In 1929 he gave up public speaking, due to poor health, for full-time writing. He lived in upstate New York with his life-companion Phyllis Playter and published, among other important works, his first masterpiece *A Glastonbury Romance* (1932). Although Powys claimed his years in America were his best, he longed for Wales, his ancestral home. In 1936 he moved to Blaenau-Festiniog in North Wales and produced two more masterpieces *Owen Glendower* (1940) and *Porius* (1951). Powys wrote his last full-length novel in 1960 as he approached the age of ninety.

Major Works

Powys's finest philosophic writing includes his best-seller *The Meaning of Culture* (1929), *A Philosophy of Solitude* (1933), and *The Art of Happiness* (1935). His *Autobiography* (1934) is considered incomparable for its candor, its self-denigration, and its humor. *One Hundred Best Books* (1916), *The Pleasures of Literature* (1938) (published as *The Enjoyment of Literature* in the United States), *Dostoievsky* (1946), and *Rabelais* (1948) represent his best literary criticism. His poem *Lucifer* (composed in 1906, published in 1956) is considered his most eloquent. Powys's first novels *Wood and Stone* (1915), *Rodmoor* (1916), and *Ducdame* (1925) introduce the use of natural elements as forces driving the actions of his characters. His first "Wessex romance" *Wolf Solent* (1929) establishes him as an author of esoteric interest. It concerns Wolf's return home to Dorset and his ordeal of writing an "underground history" of the community that emphasizes its evil. In contrast to this single-character study, *A Glastonbury Romance* (1932), the second "Wessex" piece, is a tour de force that rolls back the centuries to connect multiple characters in modern-day Glastonbury with the Holy Grail and the First Cause. *Weymouth Sands* (1934) and *Maiden Castle* (1936) complete this series. Powys's first historical romance *Owen Glendower* (1940) chronicles Owen's ill-fated push to free Wales from English rule during the fifteenth century. In the second, *Porius* (1951), a Welsh prince prepares to take over his father's throne in a world of giants, Mithraic cults, and Arthurian legend after the fall of Rome. Toward the end of Powys's life, his interest turns increasingly to fantasy, evident in his novels *Atlantis* (1954) and *The Brazen Head* (1956).

Critical Reception

As a young man, Powys had many friends among the leading writers of the day in Wales and America, and devoted readers throughout the world, but only an insistent minority of critics to praise him. Since his death, however, critical assessment of his literary canon has become increasingly widespread and positive. Yet questions remain concerning the size and complexity of his novels. Among these, *A Glastonbury Romance, Owen Glendower,* and *Porius* are considered masterpieces because they best illustrate Powys's gift for blending high drama with intuitive insight into the human psyche. But some reviewers have been put off by their epic proportions in terms of the number of words and pages, the number of characters and plots, and the layers of allegory that seem to intrude on each other and cause confusion. Critic Jerome McGann believes that the problem lies not with Powys's works, but rather with the reader's expectations. He compares *Porius* to Joyce's *Finnegan's Wake,* arguing that, like Joyce, Powys was moving his writing to a "new order and level." According to McGann, *Wolf Solent* was Powys's last "novel," and *A Glastonbury Romance* was one of the "first of the unique prose inventions [Powys] sometimes called 'romances' [which attempt to] incorporate the novel back into its romance origins . . . the exact reverse of Scott's move . . . to accommodate romance fiction to the novel." Renowned critic G. Wilson Knight nominated Powys for the Nobel Prize in Literature in 1959. He has compared Powys to Shakespeare for his "visionary penetration and mastery of the concrete." Angus Wilson likens him to Dickens for his "genius for comedy and crowd, for larger-than-life characters. . . ." George Steiner sees in *Wolf Solent* as in no other English fiction "that realization of the meshing of human and natural presences which marks Tolstoy," and in *Owen Glendower,* Powys's remarkable ability to make the past into the present.

PRINCIPAL WORKS

Wood and Stone (novel) 1915
One Hundred Best Books (essays) 1916
Rodmoor (novel) 1916
Ducdame (novel) 1925
The Meaning of Culture (essays) 1929
Wolf Solent (novel) 1929
A Glastonbury Romance (novel) 1932
A Philosophy of Solitude (essays) 1933
Autobiography (autobiography) 1934
Weymouth Sands (novel) 1934
The Art of Happiness (essays) 1935
Maiden Castle (novel) 1936
The Pleasures of Literature (essays) 1938
Owen Glendower (novel) 1940
Dostoievsky (essays) 1946
Rabelais (essays) 1948
Porius (novel) 1951
Atlantis (novel) 1954
The Brazen Head (novel) 1956
Lucifer: A Poem (poem) 1956

CRITICISM

G. Arnold Shaw (review date June 1915)

SOURCE: A review of *Visions and Revisions* in *The North American Review,* Vol. CCI, June, 1915, pp. 923-25.

[*In the following review of* Visions and Revisions, *Shaw praises Powys's gift for literary criticism, but pans his indulgent view of great writers.*]

Mr. Powys is a critic of astonishing brilliancy and insight. Among modern writers upon literature there are few who approach him in the power of perfectly identifying himself with the spirit of the writer whom he describes; there is hardly one who so often gives the reader occasion for a kind of inward shout of joy. A hatred of shallow creeds and narrow dogmas gives vigor and point to his style; a serious and profound feeling for life as a whole lends fervor to his appreciation of strong thoughts and beautiful imaginings. And about the greatest of the writers of whom he treats—about Shakespeare, about Goethe, about Dante, about Dickens—he is in the main tremendously right. There can be no question of his power to guide and almost miraculously to deepen appreciation.

This, in fact, is all that he professes to do. He disclaims philosophic narrowness, and simply relates the adventures of his own soul. And yet he has a philosophy—of course. "If there is any unity in these essays," he writes, "it will be found in a blurred and stammered attempt to indicate how far it may be possible, in spite of the limitations of our ordinary nature, to live in the light of the 'grand style.' I mean that we can live in the atmosphere, the temper, the mood, the attitude toward things which 'the grand style' they [the great writers] use, evokes and sustains." And the users of the 'grand style' are those who have learned that the most important thing in the world is to realize to the fullest limit of their consciousness what it means to be born a Man. All this "has nothing to do with 'right' or 'wrong.' . . . The whole thing consists in growing vividly conscious of those moods and events which are permanent and human as compared with other moods and events which are transitory and unimportant."

This approach to criticism is immensely attractive, in the first place just because it gives a superior significance to the great writers, defying the curse of philistinism and reconciling one's moral with one's esthetic feelings; in the second place, because it suggests the possibility of finding a noble and satisfying way of life outside the narrow confines of any moral system or religious creed—in human nature itself as found at its strongest and freest in great literature.

As one reads on, one discovers that nothing annoys Mr. Powys so much as a shallow optimism. In this feeling one is inclined to join. Nothing *is* more annoying than a shallow optimism. If there is much in this world that is unaccountably good, there is much also that is unaccountably evil, and to profess disbelief in the latter smacks of ignorance or hypocrisy. Mr. Powys, moreover, shows no exclusive preference for those writers who begin with the thesis that "life is a tale told by an idiot," and end with it. Nevertheless, his pessimism goes deep. One begins to see, moreover, that he recommends not merely courage and resignation to the will of the gods, but almost any form of esthetic *escape* from the inconsistency and cruelty of life which a kind of fundamental decency permits. Thus he commends somewhat extravagantly the epicureanism of Pater, the poses and caprices of Charles Lamb, deepening these attitudes toward life to profundity and exalting them to heroism.

Just what this point of view may ultimately mean may be best seen in that passage in which Mr. Powys describes his manner of instructing "the Innocents" in regard to the philosophy of Walter Pater. "I try to explain," he informs us, "how . . . it is our right to test every single experience that life can offer, short of those which would make things harder, narrower, less easy, for 'the other person.' And if my Innocents ask—as they sometimes do—Innocents are like that!–'Why must we consider the other person?' I answer—for no *reason,* and under no threat or danger or categorical imperative; but simply because we have grown to be the sort of animal, the sort of queer fish, who *cannot* do the things 'that he would.' It is not, I try to indicate, a case of conscience; it is a matter of taste. . . ."

In opposition to the point of view so consistently and successfully applied to criticism by Mr. Powys, it is possible to urge that the great writers are not, after all, "the Law and the Prophets"; that the untutored mind may without them discover the way of life through religious intuition; that what the untutored mind really lacks and what the great writers teach is tolerance, catholicity, that power of imaginative sympathy which makes man feel less lonely and gives a touch of dignity to his poor estate. And if one may be permitted to emulate a certain comfortable brusqueness of speech in which Mr. Powys sometimes indulges, one may suggest that to call the sense of right and wrong a "matter of taste" is perhaps quite as much damned foolishness as are some other things; that it is, possibly, to quote the words of Manson in *The Servant in the House,* "both foolish and damned."

Lawrence Gilman (review date September 1916)

SOURCE: "The Immortals and Mr. Powys," in *The North American Review,* Vol. CCIV, September, 1916, pp. 457-60.

[*In the following review, Gilman discusses some of Powys's surprising choices for inclusion in his* One Hundred Best Books.]

As soon as we encountered Mr. John Cowper Powys's ***One Hundred Best Books, With a Commentary and An Essay on Books and Reading,*** we proceeded to follow the habit of Emerson (or was it Lamb or Hazlitt!—we have looked it up repeatedly, but we always forget). That is to say, coming upon a new book, we turned away and read an old one; but in this case, the old one was also by Mr. John Cowper Powys. It was his share of a volume called ***Confessions of Two Brothers,*** and our hope was that we should find there some information as to the equipment of this adventurous and greatly-daring author. We found what we had hoped to find: a light that flooded the secret chambers of Mr. Powys's soul, disclosing the ways of his mind and the nature of his taste.

We had known that Mr. Powys was *arbiter elegantiarum* to those dear ladies, avid of aesthetic fertilization, aflame with spiritual passion, who compose the audiences at lecture-courses in those fountains of American culture, our women's clubs and our church "parlors." We knew that Mr. Powys was one of the best beloved of the interpreters and priests of beauty who are privileged to minister unto those ardent and eager souls; that he was a lecturer prized and quoted, wearing with grace and majesty, we doubted not, the splendid mantle of intellectual authority. We knew that he had published critical essays in which the *Kansas City Star* found "a semblance of the Grand Style." Also, we knew, he had published a novel which moved the *Philadelphia Record* to exclaim of it that "every page is a joy," and caused the *Press* of that incomparable city to note that "Mr. Powys's style is the style of Thomas Hardy"—we paid small attention to the characteristically cloistered observation of the *Nation* that it was "a book of distinctive flavor," detecting in that unhandsomely reticent estimate a soul inimical to sweetness or to light. We knew, finally, that Mr. Powys was famous, was International. Nevertheless, we felt it our duty to explore the ***Confessions,*** in order that we might be prepared to approach ***One Hundred Best Books*** with some preliminary knowledge, authoritatively derived, as to the qualities of mind and heart which the author must have brought to the conduct of his high and consecrated task.

The first thing we learned (and we beg the reader not to object, in haste, that the point is irrelevant)—the first thing we learned was communicated to us in this passage, on the opening page of the ***Confessions:*** "It came over me yesterday that the whole secret of my being, of my happiness and my misery, was to be discovered in my *hands.*" It seems that when Mr. Powys is quiescent, or engaged in quotidian pursuits (eating or bathing or tieing a shoe-string or posting a letter) his hands are dead hands—clumsy, helpless, inert: "They are out of reach of the electricity of my being. My consciousness does not penetrate to where they hang." But when Mr. Powys is lecturing, a miracle occurs: "My hands change completely and my consciousness flows through them to the tips of my fingers. . . . I feel them as I speak; and between them and the waves of my thought there is a direct magnetic connection. Under ordinary conditions my hands are the hands of a dead body. When I am lecturing, they are the hands of a lover; of a lover caressing his darling." Fascinating as this is, we were still unsatisfied; but the ***Confessions*** led us further: they took us from those inspired and amorous hands inward, upward, and downward. We found, according to Mr. Powys, that his exterior appearance "gives an impression of power and formidableness that is altogether misleading": for beneath his "Roman Despot look" he conceals a shrinking timidity, "the soul of a slave." Traveling still further inward, we ascertained that Mr. Powys is dowered with a mind that is "singularly clear, fluid, and nimble"; yet we learned, with a brief sigh for the inescapable carnality of our kind, that, for Mr. Powys, the earth-breath is dangerously seductive: "I live," he tells us, "a double life. I live in my mind, which is eternally restless, mobile, and light as air; and in my sensations, which are heavily-weighted, earth-bound. . . ." As to his creed: "I believe everything and—nothing; and I pass from sensation to sensation like a moth from bush to bush." In his tastes, Mr. Powys prefers blue to yellow, satin to velvet, horse-hair sofas to cushioned couches.

Concerning his quality as a critic, we were cheered to find that for once the encomium on the publisher's wrapper is correct. Mr. Powys, says the wrapper, "is without a peer in his particular field: that of telling rapt audiences the adventures of his soul among masterpieces"; and this is corroborated by the candid admission of Mr. Powys himself: for he tells us in the ***Confessions*** that he is "an eloquently impassioned critic" ("not even my enemies could deny my right to that title," says he). Indeed, he is prepared to rate himself as "the very acme and apogee of a born critic" ("I do not regard it as an outrageous claim," he observes). Gifted with an "abnormal and insatiable receptivity, a sort of sensual voluptuousness in the intellectual world," it is easy to understand by what path he has climbed to his apogee. Finally, and we shall do well to remember the caution, Mr. Powys utters this warning: "I am much cleverer than my enemies suppose"; though how so genial and confiding a soul as Mr. Powys could have incurred any enemies we find it impossible to perceive.

You now have, perhaps, an outline of Mr. Powys, from the mystical sentience of his hands and the duality of his inner life and the shape and texture of his mind, to his taste in sofas and his affinity with the moth. And so we come to the ***Hundred Best Books.***

Clearly it was rare sport for Mr. Powys to compile this scrupulously heterodox catalogue. In selecting his list he was actuated, he tells us, by "shameless subjectivity"; and he realized that his choice of books would be "a challenge to the intelligence perusing it." The claims of venerated reputations have not annoyed him. He glories in the "essential right of personal choice"; and "the great still images from the dusty museum of standard authors" can go hang for all he cares. So it would never do to demand of him indignantly why he omits George Eliot and includes Mr. Gilbert Cannan; for that would be merely playing into his hands: that is precisely what he wants you to do. He rejoices in his contempt for the "well-read" philistine, the worshiper of orthodox excellence. He is the tameless urchin of criticism, and he makes his outrageous racket with his stick on your front fence in order that you may be teased to come out and swear at him.

You find a list which begins soberly enough (it is, no doubt, intended as a decoy) with the Psalms of David, the *Odyssey,* The *Bacchæ* of Euripides, Horace, Catullus, the *Divine Comedy,* Rabelais, *Candide,* Shakespeare (with *Troilus and Cressida, Measure for Measure,* and *Timon of Athens* preferred for special mention), Milton, Sir Thomas Browne, Cervantes, Goethe, Emerson: you find this list, which starts off with such sweet and classic reasonableness, abruptly presenting you with Sudermann and his *Song of Songs,* Hauptmann and *The Fool in Christ,* Ibsen's *Wild Duck,* Mr. Edgar Lee Masters and his *Spoon River Anthology,* and—Mr. Oliver-Onions: whereby you know that Mr. Powys is off at last, clattering happily with his ribald stick along your decorous palings.

Thereafter, the fun progresses according to Mr. Powys's uncompromising schedule. Artzibasheff with his *Sanine* is yoked with Lamb and his *Elia;* Mr. George Bernard Shaw, costumed as John Tanner, flees in panic from Jane Austen; Mr. Chesterton, spouting conciliatory paradoxes, walks arm-in-arm with Emily Brontë. Ruthlessly Mr. Powys assembles them. You do not know whether to ponder more over those who have been invited to the party or over those who have been ignored. Here is Oscar Wilde; but where is Plato! You are delighted to welcome *Alice in Wonderland;* but where is Maeterlinck! Mr. W. Somerset Maugham is here, and so is Mr. Vincent O'Sullivan; Mr. Arnold Bennett chats amicably with his rival trilogist, Mr. Onions; and Anton Tchekov broods gently by himself, perhaps wondering why Tolstoi was omitted from the list of guests—a slight which he must bear in common with the authors of the Book of Job, Ecclesiastes, the Song of Solomon, the New Testament, Aeschylus, Sophocles, Chaucer, Webster, Marlowe, Fielding, Flaubert, Hawthorne, Defoe, the *Upanishads,* the *Arabian Nights,* and a host of other disconsolate immortals and abandoned masterworks.

We like Mr. Powys. We like his *gamineries,* his charming assurance, his cosy confidences, his exuberant atrocities. He is indeed, as he says, an acme and an apogee.

Mary Ross (review date 19 May 1929)

SOURCE: "Beyond the Beckoning Waters," in *New York Herald Tribune Books,* Vol. 5, No. 35, May 19, 1929, pp. 1-2.

[*In the following review, Ross commends Powys for the powerful narrative and fresh imagery of* Wolf Solent.]

The old Quaker's observation that every one but thee and me is a little mad, and thee is not quite above suspicion, might serve as a smug comment on the magnificent story of ***Wolf Solent.*** But its smugness would be untrue to the spirit of Wolf and his creator. Those aberrant impulses that lure us toward the bright circle of lunacy except no man, though many of us are too fearful to admit them to even our most secret thinking. But Mr. Powys looks wonderingly, without blinking, at the shuttles of shame, ecstasy, glory and degradation which cross and recross to weave the unique and mysterious pattern that is a human life. He grasps the shuttles with firm and sensitive hands, and the fabric of his book is rich and strange. It is at once as natural and as eerie as the phosphorescent wake of a ship breasting the waters of a midnight sea.

Externally ***Wolf Solent*** is the story of a man of thirty-five, who took refuge in the Dorset village of his forefathers when he had been rasped past the limit of his endurance by a schoolmaster's life in middle-class London. Chance and family influence had got him a post as secretary to the obscene old squire of Ramsgard to write a chronicle of the Dorset that was known to the bedposts in brothels, to the counters of barrooms, the butlers' pantries in old houses and the muddy ditches in old lovers' lanes. In Ramsgard he found love, marriage, friends, a home and a means of livelihood.

Below that current in deeper and more troubled waters runs the real course of the book. Wolf Solent was a sick man, harried by the demands that life made upon him. Into his sensitive and troubled soul experience intruded like the crash of a stone in a millpond, stirring up mud and debris, bespattering the water lilies. As he rode to Ramsgard in the train there floated between him and the green masses of the trees the phantom face of a man whom he had glimpsed on the steps of Waterloo Station—an English face, but also a Chinese face, a Russian face, "just the face of a man, of a mortal man, against whom Providence has grown as malignant as a mad dog."

Wolf himself knew the bite of the mad dog. He had had to leave London, because, two months before, in the midst of an innocent discourse on the reign of Queen Anne, some dam in his own mind had suddenly given away, and before his astonished pupils he danced what he called his "malice-dance," pouring out a torrent of wild, indecent invectives on every aspect of the modern world.

As he looked out the window again there hovered before him a monstrous apparition of invention, a whole round world pierced and sullied by iron-clad motors like colossal beetles, its waters ravaged by the throbbing prows of relentless vessels, its air shot through by the stinging assault of airplanes. From this intolerable assault of noise and motion he had made himself a retreat. This obtrusive world could lay no finger on him. He had no urge to action, to literary or intellectual achievement. "He hid, deep down in his being, a contempt that was actually *malicious* in its pride for all the human phenomena of worldly success. It was as if he had been some changeling from a different planet, a planet where the issues of life—the great dualistic struggles between life and death—never emerged from the charmed circle of the individual's private consciousness."

When the stones became too troublesome he could sink still further below the waters of that pond, into a stillness where nothing could pierce, where his mind could unfold like the giant leaves of some fabulous tropic vegetation. This was his mainstay, his "life-illusion," the "reality" by which he lived, the refuge which the world so far had not been able to violate. That way lies poetry, and if one follow it far enough, madness.

The sore spot in Wolf Solent was a talisman whereby he felt—and suffered—the phantoms that pursued those other souls in Ramsgard who, there as everywhere else, pursued their courses in essential isolation, glimpsing only now and then the common sun over them and the earth under their feet. Deny the village he could not; for its tentacles had sunk deep into him in the remote halcyon days of his childhood. Short of his own dissolution, they could not be dislodged. Bit by bit he realized and accepted them: first the elemental realities—the rain-drenched lanes and hedges; the Arthurian hills across which be plunged, alone or with the beautiful Gerda; and ominous Lenty Pond, which becomes the symbol of his struggle.

It was a legend of the village, which floated before him elusively for months, that each generation of the squires of Ramsgard had caused a young man to drown himself in Lenty Pond. The beautiful boy who had preceded him as secretary to the squire had died in bed, of double pneumonia, but it was believed that his spirit still walked the lanes, and his white face would float under the waters of the pond till another came there to take his place and let him rest in peace.

The Dorset village was like an old garden grown in on itself, roots intertwined under the soil, branches twisted grotesquely to reach the sun between overhanging leaves and stone wall. As Wolf for a time became aware only of the grotesqueness of the clasp of root upon root, it was a garden of malign ghosts. Beyond lay only the beckoning waters of Lenty Pond. The octopus of reality touched his "life illusion," grasped it, squeezed it dry and flung it aside. He was empty, defenseless, to himself degraded beyond all hope of rebirth.

But gradually from those roots he began to draw life. The phantoms faded and he saw that it was his own spirit that had painted them on the air. The people about him—the delicate and amazingly distinct gallery which Mr. Powys summons in the figures of Wolf's gallant mother; his lovely wife, Gerda; his "true love," the wraith-like Christie Malakite; the old squire, Jason; the poet, Darnley Otter and the rest; became not monstrous outgrowths, but natural and separate flowerings of forces which involved them all.

There was a night when Wolf Solent came near to slipping quietly into Lenty Pond to fulfill the destiny that seemed to be pressing in upon him. Then there came a day when he realized that his body had saved him, that the disease was in his own mind, and that that mind was what he had to reckon with. He would take as the talisman of his day 'endure or escape.' He had made peace with the world. Lenty Pond no longer could frighten him.

Possibly some such struggle as this is a universal price of an artist's existence. But beyond that, differing only in the richness and intensity of its nature, it is a common experience that lies unrecognized in less conscious spirits, one price of honest life and growth. In its reach and its grasp ***Wolf Solent*** transcends the reefs of mere self-pitying aesthetic agony on which many a lesser vessel of exploration has been wrecked. Will Durant calls the book "an organized 'Ulysses.'" In the beauty and freshness of its imagery and the sustained interest of its narrative its power is without question. Its prose often rises to the cadence of poetry. And beyond beauty, it sinks shafts through the unique personalities and provincial setting with which it deals, to a core of truth which is the stuff of human experience, whether in a cottage in Dorset or a furnished room on Manhattan Island.

Henry James Forman (review date 10 November 1929)

SOURCE: "Mr. Powys Inquires Into the Meaning of Culture, in *New York Times Book Review,* November 10, 1929, p. 2.

[*In the following review of* The Meaning of Culture, *Forman discusses Powys's "working substitute" for religious faith.*]

It is not for nothing that Mr. Powys in the book under review addresses himself primarily to the young. The maturer consciousness, the character that is already formed and set, how tolerant so ever it may be, must nevertheless constantly rebel at any one else's idea of what culture should be. For culture is one of those elusive attributes in the individual at least as difficult to define as what makes a gentleman. Indeed, both of those words and their definitions are what sensitive people shy away from and seldom bring forward if they can help it. Mr. Powys himself, being a sensitive artist and a man of an exquisite culture, may be presumed to have drawn back more than once until, with something of grimness in his determination, he finally decided to speak to the young upon this difficult subject that so many a lesser and perhaps a greater than he would shrink from as from a violence. Was it Titus who upon entering the Holy of Holies, which moved an integral and obstinate people to endless devotion, found it empty? One may imagine Mr. Powys facing his particular arcanum and finding nothing to inventory save his own soul and mind. And no man of Mr. Powys's attainments could have found that an easy task. The more credit to him for producing under these circumstances a book at once full and cogent and worthy anybody's perusal.

Let it be said at once that with culture in the sense of a *kultur,* the culture of a nation or a continent, Mr. Powys has nothing to do. His primary aim, indeed, is to save the individual in face of the mass, the machine, the turbulent chaotic present. To use his own words:

> What is aimed at here is to find in the instinctive and rationalized habits of human culture itself a sort of working substitute for the simpler religious faith of the past, for its heroic synthesis of so many human activities and emotions, something, in fact, that shall at once awaken us to the magic of life, so overlaid and vulgarized by modern conditions and calm us and steady us in our intelligent enjoyment of it.

There is a physical beauty and a moral, Cardinal Newman once said, when speaking to somewhat similar purpose: "There is a beauty of person, there is a beauty of our moral being, which is natural virtue; and in like manner there is a beauty, there is a perfection of the intellect." The intellect, the soul, the spirit—it is to the beautification of these that Mr. Powys aims, not, as he tells us, by means of "bitter onslaughts upon stupidity and obscurantism," but rather by the building up, "fragment by fragment, a new emotional and mental synthesis." And the very attempt to build up such a synthesis today is already an achievement.

But, indeed, this is much more than an attempt. The analysis of the true nature of what culture is, as set forth in the first five chapters, though it may not square with every one's idea of the content of a rounded culture, must nevertheless enter somehow into that idea. However imperfect the counsel, no man has ever been the worse for being counseled to perfection. Mr. Powys is urgent that we read metaphysics; that we should mold and achieve a philosophy of our own in preference to splitting hairs upon the great philosophic schools of thought. Better read Plato, Montaigne, Goethe, Wordsworth, Emerson, Pater, Proust, than Hume, Kant, Spenser or Whitehead. To read and appreciate Doughty's "Arabia Deserta" and Sir Thomas Browne's "Urn-Burial" is "a convincing proof that one's esthetic sophistication is an authentic thing."

Does the mature reader imagine that the reviewer is trying to be humorous? Remember, Mr. Powys is speaking to the young. Better they be told thus baldly than not be told at all. Surely some one must tell them that they may, if they wish, admire Aldous Huxley, T. S. Eliot and Ernest Hemingway and still enjoy Homer and Plato and Goethe and Rabelais. It may be news to some that they need to be told. But Mr. Powys comes in contact with great numbers of seekers after culture on his lecture tours and should have a very clear knowledge of what they lack.

> Und was mir fehlt, du Kleine,
> *Fehlt manchem im deutschen Land.*

once sang Heine, and our own lacks are just as plentiful. If a boy or girl is surrounded by an irksome home or economic atmosphere,

> sink into your own soul! [urges Mr. Powys]. Use your imagination and your senses upon the few simple elements of the Eternal that surround us all and the few undying books that you can lay your hands on, and create a new soul of awareness under the surface of your quotidian submission.

Now, clearly, neither Professor Dewey, nor Santayana, nor Whitehead probably need this advice, but many there be who do. They need it the more because, as Mr. Powys points out, culture today comes with exceeding difficulty. The tabloids, the noise, the radio, the movies, the jazz–"the wonder grows that any human beings are left in these places whose debauched wits retain the least resemblance to old-fashioned human minds."

Mr. Powys set out to make no bitter onslaughts upon stupidity and obscurantism. But flesh and blood can hardly resist the impulse in face of the conditions that surround most of us.

Nothing but an extreme and an almost misanthropic individualism can save us from the ubiquitous atmosphere of all this psychic vulgarity. We must accept the situation. We must harden our hearts against social-mindedness. We must welcome proudly all accusations of priggishness and pedantry. The worst prig in the world is a less despicable animal than these besotted slaves of a "sense of humor," these flunkeyish lickspittles of folk-foolery, these gesticulating Robots. A facetious popularization of the old mythologies has become a modern craze; and while the real poetry connected with Helen of Troy is a forbidden affectation, the story of the woman herself lends itself most horribly well to a comic Freudianism!

Mr. Powys, notwithstanding his early resolve, has much to say of these present-day obstacles to culture. And who shall gainsay him that there are many? One of his very best chapters is the one entitled **"Culture and Nature."** It is hardly possible to quote any of it without quoting all of it. But his own love for nature and the balm that it can bring to the soul, whether directly of itself or through some of the great poets, such as Homer, Virgil, Wordsworth, these are something that the modern young city person should take to his bosom. There are chapters upon **"Culture and Love," "Culture and Human Relations," "Culture and Destiny."** There is much that is readable and interesting in all of these. But the one entitled **"Culture and the Art of Reading"** will perhaps prove nearer to a *vademecum* for the young than any of the others. For reading is, after all, the least strait of all the gates.

Leonard Woolf (review date 3 January 1931)

SOURCE: "Much Ado About Nothing," in *The Nation & Athenaeum*, January 3, 1931, pp. 461-62.

[*In the following excerpt, Woolf pans* In Defence of Sensuality *for its prolixity.*]

One must begin a review of this book by taking one's hat off to and acknowledging Mr. Powys's obvious sincerity. His book contains so much quackery and gush, such an enormous k of words for so small a kernel of matter, that it would be easy to make a great mistake and think that the author must be posturing. That is clearly not the case; Mr. Powys is terrifically in earnest and believes every word that he says. But sincerity is not enough. The youth of seventeen who discovers that moonlight is romantic and, under the influence of the discovery, writes many thousand lines of sentimental verse, may be quite sincere. That, however, does not prevent us recognizing that he is suffering from a well-known youth disorder, a kind of emotional measles of which one symptom is a rash of bad poetry. Sincerity is not enough. You may be a sincere inquisitor, a sincere bore, a sincere quack, the sincere writer of a bad book, as bad a book as this of Mr. Powys's.

Mr. Powys has really written a really bad book. Even its title is bad. Everyone reading the title would think that Mr. Powys was writing about sensuality in the ordinary sense, and his excuse and that of his publisher for using a title so completely misleading is a very bad one. His book contains his "philosophy of life," and the matter which goes to it is so exiguous that he could have said all he really has to say in ten pages. The rest of the book is a flood of (perfectly sincere) gush and endless repetition. For instance, Mr. Powys thinks—and I am disposed, or was disposed when I began reading his book, to agree with him—that if a "beggar" in the street asks you for sixpence, you should give it to him. I do not know how many times Mr. Powys does not come back to this point and repeat all his old arguments for giving the sixpence. The result in my case was that, though I agreed with him the first time, when I heard his argument for the hundredth time, he had driven me to such desperation that I have discovered convincing reasons for refusing two old women selling matches, and one ex-Service man singing hymns, the pence that they otherwise might have got from me. I doubt whether now even my favourite beggar who used to haunt High Street, Kensington, accompanied by a strange black and white cur ornamented with a kind of saddle of red and blue flannel on which sat two large white rats, could extract a copper from me. And I shall have to invent some argument which is not Mr. Powys's to allow myself the pleasure of giving sixpence to the melancholy lady who tinkles so faintly and sweetly on the harp on Saturday evenings.

Mr. Powys would say that I am trying to be humorous and that humour is a bad thing. There is a certain amount of truth in his attack upon humour, and here again when he said it the first time, I agreed with much of what he said. But when he had said it all over again for the hundredth time, one felt that he had got it all out of proportion, that he was making a terrible to-do about nothing, and that he was merely showing, by his lack of humour, that humour after all is of some importance. And so it is with all that he has to say. There is a good deal of truth in the little kernel of matter which he has embedded in all these highfalutin' words. It is true that the happiness which comes through the senses and the memory is an important ingredient of life, and one which the modern bourgeois form of society underestimates. It is true that much can be said in favour of loneliness, and that the modern world, both in its pleasures and its economic organization, is too gregarious. It is true that, because you have a respectable collar and an account or overdraft at the bank, you have no "cosmic" (I borrow a favourite word of Mr. Powys's) reason for thinking that you are thereby a better man than the next beggar you meet in the street. It is probably true that you should not form a habit of refusing beggars in the street, though I doubt whether it is true that you should, like Mr. Powys, form a conscious and somewhat Pecksniffian habit of giving them coppers and cups of coffee.

I cannot see that the kernel of truth in Mr. Powys's book is any more extensive or more important than what I have extracted in the previous sentences. He wraps it up in voluminous swaddling clothes of sentimentalism, mysticism, and honest quackery of the kind which is extremely fashionable these days. Mr. Powys has all the paraphernalia of modern, anti-rationalist mysticism with which we are already familiar in Keyserling, Steiner, Spengler, and a number of minor constellations. He is not content with saying that what he calls sensuality is a very good thing. He calls it "the secret of life" and "the purpose of life." How does Mr. Powys know what the secret of life is? How does he know that there is a secret of life? Of course, Mr. Powys never condescends to answer such questions—he covers up his traces by continually talking about such things as "the ichthyosaurus-ego" and the "First Cause," with which or whom he seems to be on terms of enviable intimacy. And "the purpose of life"! How can Mr. Powys or any other human being imagine that they know what "the purpose of life" is? It is almost inconceivable that an intelligent man like Mr. Powys can really delude himself into believing that the purpose of life—in this inhuman universe of icy space and flaming suns—is the "arrangement of thought," the pleasure of lying in bed in the morning or of remembering a windy warm day on the Downs. Mr. Powys—and all of us—know just about as much about the purpose of life as a tapeworm, and we do not conceal the fact by draping our ignorance in the vague and pretentious language which Mr. Powys is so fond of. "In loneliness," says Mr. Powys, "a human being *feels himself backward,* down the long series of his avatars, into the earlier planetary life of animals, birds, and reptiles, end even into the cosmogonic life of rocks and stones." The use of the words "avatar," "planetary," and "cosmogonic" in this sentence does not save it from being pure, unadulterated nonsense. "The soul feeds on dreams like a great immortal ox on sweet grass," writes Mr. Powys. As far as truth and meaning go, he might just as well have written (and more grammatically): "The soul feeds on dreams as a small mortal cow on soya bean cake." But that, of course, would have given the show away. One way of not giving the mystical show away is, apparently, to call everything cosmic. The following is a list of things to which Mr. Powys applies the usually irrelevant and meaningless adjective "cosmic" and the list is certainly not complete: philosophy, emotions, reality, mutations, scepticism, sense, ecstasy, gestures, happiness.

Mr. Powys, as we have said, has the modern mystics' fashionable contempt for reason. Truth, of course, is revealed not by reason, but by some operation of the soul which has nothing to do with the intellect or the laws of logic. If this be really the case, it is legitimate to inquire why Mr. Powys should waste his and our time by writing 287 pages in which he never ceases to argue with us, to use reason and logic to convince us (unsuccessfully) that what he believes and says is true? Even in the mystic, cosmic regions to which he invites us, it appears that the laws not only of reason but of arithmetic work: otherwise why does he write like this: "What we call the First Cause is the necessary centre of all these universes; and back and down into the First Cause every living soul can descend. When, however, two identities are linked together in this mystic-sensuous embrace, it is a double soul that thus sinks down; and a double anger against the evil it finds there, and a double gratitude for the good it finds there, floods this pair of conscious beings." It is quite a relief to find that in this cosmic region, though a plural subject can take a verb in the singular, at any rate "twice one equals two" applies to souls and their emotions.

Mary Ross (review date 27 March 1932)

SOURCE: "A Cosmology For Hero," in *New York Herald Tribune Books,* Vol. 8, No. 29, March 27, 1932, p. 7.

[*In the following excerpt, Ross compares* A Glastonbury Romance *to* Wolf Solent, *and faults the former for its lack of coherence.*]

> At the striking of noon on a certain March 5 there occurred within a causal radius of Brandon railway station and yet beyond the deepest pools of emptyness, between the uttermost stellar systems, one of those infinitesimal ripples in the creative silence of the First Cause, which always occur when an exceptional stir of heightened consciousness agitates any living organism in this astronomical universe. Something passed at that moment, a wave, a motion, a vibration, too tenuous to be called magnetic, too subliminal to be called spiritual, between the soul of a particular human being who was emerging from a third-class carriage of the 12:19 train from London and the divine-diabolic First Cause of all life.

Thus, in its first paragraph, Mr. Powys sets the key for ***A Glastonbury Romance.*** Through nearly 1,200 large and closely printed pages its tentacles reach out in a determined effort to connect the infinitesimal and the infinite.

Its visible scene is the town of Glastonbury in modern times. Its visible people include a Mayor, a manufacturer, a doctor, a landed proprietor, a philosophical anarchist, a would-be writer, an elderly aristocrat, a vicar and his son, laborers, farmers and so on, with their wives, sweethearts, children, friends and the like; a prefixed list of "principal characters" enumerates forty-six persons. Its action, as the dust cover declares, "embraces no less than six major love affairs, one murder, three births and two deaths." Its thinking includes the establishment of a commune in a modern English town of ancient lineage, all of which the author declares in a foreword to be "pure invention." In fact, he insists categorically that "not a single scene, or situation, or character, or episode in this book has been drawn in any respect, or in any sense whatsoever, from real life." On closing what undoubtedly is one of the longest novels of all times, one feels that unfortunately this is true in a sense which the statement did not intend to imply.

Behind the kaleidoscope implied in this summary of the volume's vital statistics there lies layer upon layer of allegory, as below the Glastonbury land on which Philip Crow set his modern dye works there lay buried remains that traced back through the British kings to Arthur and beyond to the ancient peoples of the lake village, lost in the mists of antiquity. Only mysticism can bridge the span that Mr. Powys has set himself between the railway clock (assuming that I am correct in my reading of "causal" in that first sentence) with the creative silence of the First Causes. A vision hovers over this modern Glastonbury in the unpardonable sin of a Welsh antiquary, the religious fervor of the former secretary-valet of a late canon, who at the time of the story has become the rich Mayor; in the perversity of John Crow, the cancer of Tittie Petherton, the madness of Bet, the naturalism of Mother Legge, a procuress; in the simplicity of the country people. In it, as in a mirage, one sees the gleams and stains of the Arthurian legend, even to the Grail which appears to the Vicar's son in a coal barge. Behind this shadow play lurk still deeper reaches of ancient myth, to which Christian symbolism is only a recent sheath. At the kernel apparently (it is far from clear to me) lies that First Cause. Mr. Powys's preoccupation with mysteries seems to have permeated even the blurb writer of the jacket, who asserts cryptically that "his creation is more than a book."

The author's preceding novel, ***Wolf Solent,*** seemed to me a moving and vivid portrayal of the strange, often incomprehensible, currents that govern the life of one man. In the present story, however, it is not a person but a cosmology that is the hero. Varieties of human experience seem less important for what they are in themselves than for their bearing on the unrolling of some universal plan. Patiently, laboriously, sometimes brilliantly, the author puts his finger on some quality in the relationship of two persons, and then tries to trace it out in universal terms, back again to the First Cause. Or starting from a conflict of ambivalence, he works forward. "The mind of the First Cause was twofold—self-contradictory, divided against itself. The multifarious minds that stir up the chemistry of matter today are all descended from the First Cause and share its dualistic nature, its mingling of abominable cruelty with magnanimous consideration." This purpose involves pondering the contradictions of thought and feeling, and especially in this book the varieties of experience that spring from some manifestation or aberration of sex.

The symbol of *t'ai chi,* the interlocked yang and yin which from remote times have represented the antithesis of day and night, heat and cold, male and female, might well stand as the goal of ***A Glastonbury Romance.*** But in the tone of the story one feels not the sense of balance, of complement, which the symbol implies, but a conflict, a striving for unity (despite the author's repeated avowal that none exists), from which has ensued this enormous and to me inchoate volume. This conflict—this thirst for an *explanation,* a cosmology, if you will—is in direct antithesis to that creative realization of a moment in the flow of time out of which is born what we call consciousness and in another form art. As a by-product of his central purpose, Mr. Powys has given this book beautiful sentences, occasional gleams of imaginative realization that are wholly satisfying. But the struggle in which it is rooted seems to me to bring confusion and an alien purpose.

Percy Hutchison (review date 20 November 1938)

SOURCE: "Adventures Among Masterpieces," in *New York Times Book Review,* November 20, 1938, p. 2.

[*In the following excerpt, Hutchison favorably reviews* Enjoyment of Literature.]

For upward of forty years Mr. Powys has traveled widely in the realms of gold, and his individualistic and penetrating appraisals of their States and goodly kingdoms have won him the confidence of hosts of readers. The present book embodies the maturity of Mr. Powys's thinking; in it he reviews his literary adventures among the masterpieces of the world. The pages flame with what is almost a religious ardor of passionate love for these masterpieces. And because Mr. Powys has the power to communicate his own buoyant pleasure in reading he is the adventurer who infects others with the high spirit of the quest. In consequence this book is out of the ordinary in its field; the gigantic effort of a truly critical mind that is strongly buttressed by imagination and deeply imbued with a sense of spiritual values.

Significant of this is the fact that Mr. Powys devotes his first two chapters to the Bible as literature, although the Bible, certainly the New Testament, does not antedate the Iliad and the Odyssey. But from these two testaments to eternal truths, so the thesis would run, emerged forces which were destined to shape a great deal of the thought and the imagination of the world for centuries to come. Homer, by elevating men above the cheap and vulgar, was to deepen human consciousness. But not even the mighty Greek, who was on familiar terms with heroes and with gods alike, could give other than secular stirring to the Christian mind. And the Greek tragic dramatist, virtually unknown to the Western world for centuries, had little influence on Western though. Yet Powys finds today the influence of Sophocles and Aeschylus great indeed. Dostoievsky, Hardy, Eugene O'Neill, he finds stemming back to the ancient tragedians of Athens. One should know these antique play-wrights better, would be Mr. Powys's admonition.

Enjoyment of Literature proceeds in the main chronologically, but it is not to be concluded, therefore, that Mr. Powys is engaged on literary history, for that is the very thing on which Mr. Powys is not engaged. But he is convinced by the evidence that there is in literature a subterranean "river of tradition," not only as to the kind of subject but even the kind of treatment of that subject, "that will strike deepest into what is universal and unchanging." Hence, although each of the chapters in this book appears to be an independent study, each is but a wave in one same strong stream.

It is Dante who is taken up next, and with the great Florentine Western literature moves definitely into the Christian path. Refusing the Greek idea of fate, Dante reaffirms to the world the concepts of good and evil, gives to them tragic recognition as forces to make or mar. Yet Mr. Powys feels that there has been an overemphasis on Dante as a moral guide. For him, Dante's stress upon endurance as the greatest of human virtues is what renders him supreme. Many, of course, will dissent from this and will cling to Dante, as others will cling to Milton, for something akin to guidance. But Powys is never so happy as when he can be provocative.

Rabelais, Montaigne and Cervantes follow in order. And we are not sure but that we should recommend the chapter on Rabelais as an introduction to the mind of Mr. Powys, because in its seeming paradoxes, which are not paradoxes at all, but are all beautifully, even wittily, resolved, we find this adventurer and critic at his supreme best. Rabelais, although just emerged from the censor's ban and not yet on the library's free shelves, held a commanding position in the literature of the Renaissance. And although Mr. Powys is willing to say that he cannot stomach all of the muddied outpourings of the ex-monk, he places him higher than Plato, Cervantes or Montaigne, ranging him beside Homer and Shakespeare because of his "cosmic optimism," his "Cyclopean drollery." And, rejecting a conventional interpretation of Rabelais, that he uses his extravagant humor as a mask to placate authority, Mr. Powys rises to indignant heights. For him that humor is the man's complete philosophy; while he has managed to retain "the mystical quintessence of medieval piety," he has also a vein of unctuous, homely piety that has something of the best of Protestantism in it.

With a book so large as ***Enjoyment of Literature,*** and ranging so widely, a reviewer can but be eclectic. Hence, we shall move on to the moderns, only noting by the way that Mr. Powys recommends those who read Montaigne in their youth to reread him in their later years for his great help in integrating one's essential personality, and Cervantes both for his irony and for the livingness of the story. Mr. Powys's study of Shakespeare we shall leave for the reader to take in relation to his study of the Greek dramatists, and the study of Milton with the chapter on Dante. Also the keen and delightful analysis of the humor of Charles Dickens in connection with the humor of Cervantes and Rabelais.

Coming to America, although Mr. Powys gives a few paragraphs to Emerson, the Sage of Concord does not get an entire chapter; and Longfellow and Whittier receive no mention. Whitman has a niche by himself, and Melville and Poe share one together.

Stating the fairly obvious fact that the striking characteristic of Whitman's poetry is an astounding optimism which is entirely heathen and profane, Mr. Powys, with his ability to show how in an individual mind there can be reconciliation of opposites, also gives Whitman credit for a metaphysic while he staggers the rational mind with the vast scope of his "mystical pluralism." Whitman, of course, has been almost as fiercely debated as Rabelais, and, earlier at least, with as bated breath. Mr. Powys's sane and discerning probings here should go far to bring him into clearer perspective. Say what you will, he sums up, Whitman's poetry "offers a triumphant response to the natural heart's desire of the natural man."

Poe is valued by Mr. Powys for his metrical virtuosity; and Melville (with this critic we are ever getting back to philosophy) for "his dark, satanic mysticism." And Powys finds the first as much underrated in the twentieth century as the latter was during the nineteenth. For Mr. Powys, "Moby Dick" is the greatest of all novels of the sea, more profoundly significant than the particularized stories of Joseph Conrad.

Essays on Goethe, Wordsworth, the neglected and unappreciated Matthew Arnold, Nietzsche, Proust, Dostoievsky and Hardy, complete the generous contents of this book, with Mr. Powys's highest encomiums reserved for the last two. Indeed, he says of Dostoievsky that he is as much greater than all other novelists as Homer and Shakespeare than all other poets: "For he is superior to the rest in all the main essentials of fiction. He is a greater artist, a greater psychologist, a greater prophet, a greater thinker." And Mr. Powys refuses to except even Thomas Hardy, his Dorsetshire neighbor, although, clearly, he places the man whom in his youth he called "Promethean," only second to the Russian. Hardy's strength, for Powys, lies in his arraignment of the ways of God to man, quite the reverse of justification. Does Powys exhibit rather too marked a preference for the dark, the satanic, the pessimistic in literature? If so, how can he call his writings "enjoyment of literature"?

That these apparent contradictions may be seen as not incompatible is the achievement of this book. It is not a perverse achievement. Mr. Powys does not delight in pessimism as a child delights in rubbing a bruise to experience the hurt. But, with the Prophets of Israel, with the Greek tragedians, Rabelais, Hardy, Dostoievsky, he looks life squarely in the eyes and says that life is not good. But the countenance of life, as reflected by the mirror of art—one can enjoy the reflection and derive from it a sustaining power. ***Enjoyment of Literature*** is a profound excursion into literature, an adventure ennobling and inspiring of mind and imagination.

Mary Ross (review date 26 January 1941)

SOURCE: "Vast Novel of Medieval Wales" in *New York Herald Tribune Books,* January 26, 1941, p. 4.

[*In the following excerpt, Ross gives a mixed review of* Owen Glendower.]

Many motives, presumably, may underlie the writing of a historical novel. There may be a desire to escape from one's own time to an era where, at least in retrospect, the brave were braver and the fair more fair and all more picturesquely dressed. There may be a desire, as in Elizabeth Page's "The Tree of Liberty," to see the longer perspective of distant-period forces which illuminate our own; or as in L. H. Myers's remarkable trilogy, "The Root and the Flower," the author may choose a remote time and place in order to free his readers from their own immediate preoccupations and associations so that they will be the more able to examine some particular problem around which the story is woven. More simply, the desire may have been an extension of the curiosity which underlies most fiction, a desire to clothe in living flesh and so to see and feel the events which formal history has recorded in a succession of names and dates.

This last, I should guess, was the compelling motive for the writing of Mr. Powys's vast novel of Wales at the beginning of the fifteenth century. In contrast to many of his other books, he makes relatively little use of subjective symbolism and mysticism. It is rather as though, steeped in the songs, legends and chronicles of his native land, he has set himself the task of making a living whole out of the fragments preserved by the antiquarians. More than half the persons of the story bear names known to history, while the central figure, Owen Glendower, is the national hero who in 1400 led his countrymen in their last and most formidable uprising.

In an **"Argument"** prefaced to the story Mr. Powys points out that the beginning of the fifteenth century found Europe in the seething unrest of transition. In an era of "degenerate faith and degenerate chivalry." John Wycliffe, whose sermons had set people to questioning the social and moral, as well as the theological, conventions of the time, had died in 1384. The turn of the century found "an age of unscrupulous individualism but also an age when *national self-consciousness* under independent rulers superseded the old feudal ideal of a united Christendom under Emperor and Pope." The years of the story—1400 to 1416—saw "the beginning of one of the most momentous and startling epochs of *transition* that the world has known: the transition from the more or less federated Christendom of the Middle Ages to the turbulent evolution of our modern sovereign states."

Owen Glendower was a man in his middle years when first he led his people in revolt, a scholar as well as a soldier with, in Mr. Powys's interpretation, strains of the mystic, the charlatan and the demagogue. The immediate cause of his taking up arms was a personal quarrel with his English neighbors, the Greys of Ruthin, but once the turmoil was started, his followers rode with the cause of Welsh independence to victories through most of a decade. Owen made an official treaty with the French, openly styled himself Prince of Wales and called a parliament. The Battle of Harlech, in which his wife, daughter and grandchildren were taken captive, saw the end of the power of a man whose remarkable personality, exploits and cultivation are attested by history as well as by legend.

The figure of Owen dominates Mr. Powys's story, and is the center about which the scores of lesser characters and the hurly-burly of episodes revolve. Secondary only to Owen is his young kinsman and secretary, Rhisiart ab Owen, whose love for Owen's daughter Catharine and for Tegolin, the fictional maid who rode with Owen's men into battle, occasions the continuing thread of action in the book. Rhisiart, a young law scholar just up from Oxford, is more nearly attuned to the oncoming changes than his chieftain, who could lead his people up to, but not into, the newer ways; in Rhisiart, moreover, Norman blood helped temper Welsh ardors. But just as these times had meant the dissolution of the unity of old faiths and old loyalties, so for Rhisiart, even when he had become Judge Rhisiart, there was success neither in love nor in politics.

As its great length might suggest, ***Owen Glendower*** is written with Mr. Powys's characteristic exuberance, which gives vigor to its portraits of both historical and fictional characters. This exuberance, however, and the very breadth and intensity of Mr. Powys's concern for his subject tend to diffuse interest to an extent that is often confusing, the more so in a realm of strange names, customs and legends. The wealth of material that has gone into this novel makes it at points more dazzling than clear, a fault that becomes serious as one progresses through nearly a thousand closely printed pages, at least to a reader who has no background of national loyalties into which to fit Mr. Powys's synthesis and extension of old stories.

Owen Glendower is like a tapestry, many parts of which delight, though others will startle, any who love romance. From the standpoint he expresses in the prefatory **"Argument,"** however, the author might have attained his objectives more nearly had he given less. In mood ***Owen Glendower*** is less exalted—if you will, hysterical—than some of Mr. Powys's earlier books, notably than his other very long novel, ***Wolf Solent.*** Possibly because of this greater objectivity, it lacks, on the whole, the sustained emotion and intensity of his work at its best. For the same reason, it probably will be more generally liked, especially by readers who bring to it a prior concern that all these things have "happened in their beauty and in their pain."

Jane Spence Southron (review date 26 January 1941)

SOURCE: "Mr. Powys Writes of Ancient Wales," in *New York Times Book Review,* January 26, 1941, p. 7.

[*In the following review, Southron commends* Owen Glendower *for its faithfulness to early Welsh tradition.*]

Any one not Welsh who, like this reviewer, has lived in Wales and so become more than casually acquainted with the Welsh people of both north and south knows that the outstanding characteristics of the race are an inherent poetical quality, an ineradicable mysticism, an innate aristocracy of soul and a hard, stiffening core of realistic perception. No one alive today could be more fitted and qualified to interpret his people and country to the modern world than John Cowper Powys, himself descended, on his father's side, from ancient princes of mid-Wales and with William Cowper and John Donne in his mother's family tree. Mr. Powys's own distinctive contribution to modern literature elsewhere and in these volumes is, both in inspirational essence and uncompromising realism, in direct continuity with early Welsh tradition.

Owen Glyn Dwr, hero of insurgent Wales in the first decade of the fifteenth century, when Henry IV of Lancaster, "the usurper," was King of England, is of all historical Welshmen the one most representative of his countrymen. The story of his general acclaim as "Prince" of Wales to lead an insurrection of the common folk, supported by great Welsh lords determined to deliver their land from English rule, is one vouched for by history.

In Mr. Powys's hands the story of the war becomes a saga depicting the blind adventuring of mortal man, with fate working out the issue inexorably. He has treated it selectively as to incidents, throwing those that were of final importance into prominence, stressing details of vital and integrating significance, suppressing what savored of routine and blending all into a whole of rare beauty by creational interpretation.

All the main actors in the historical drama are here—forty three of them, French, English, Welsh; poets, clerics, Lollards, harpist, the English King and young Prince Hal—supported by a cast of about half their number listed by Mr. Powys as "unmentioned in history." Although the nonhistorical people, connected closely, save for one or two, by family, tribal or community ties to the others, illustrate period vagaries more than do those who carry most of the history on their shoulders, there is no definite line of demarcation.

Rhisiart ab Owen, for instance, Owen's secretary and chief of the young gallants of the saga, is historical; but Tegolin, one of the two women he loved, is fictional. Abbot Cust and Prior Bevan are fictional but no less essentially of the story and time than the historical Archbishop responsible, with Henry, for the burning of heretics, one of whom, the historical Walter Brut, Rhisiart's friend, only escapes the slow torture at death by fire through a tragic ruse. Gilles de Pirogue, one of the two fictional Ambassadors to Owen's court, is as typical of degeneracy in early fifteenth-century France as the historical Patrouillart de Trie, who stormed a castle alone, is of its chivalry. In both groups the cruelty and the tenderness of the age, its idealism and its earthiness, its superstitious ignorance and it straining after beauty and spirituality are rendered with equal, antiphonal effect.

Owen is, here, a realistic mystic who, in a later age, might have been a great astronomer. He is a capable administrator who conceives and, had fate willed, might have carried into actuality a workable system of law and government for his country. His strategy at Bryn Glas proves him to have been, naturally, an able soldier. A lack of ultimate hardness in advance of his period prevents him risking the destruction of his men by a forlorn and desperate push through hostile country; but, more than all else, it was his essential Welshness, hindering him from believing in the value of material success, that defeated him.

In all or nearly all of this Mr. Powys is in line with history or historical possibility. On one point, however, he notably diverges, sublimating the careless sensuality, bearing, then, no intolerable stigma, with which report tagged Owen ("father of many bastards") into a solitary incident steeped in the romance of self-denial.

This is a book into which you plunge and lose yourself; led back through the centuries and ages by the oldest of all enchantments, that of the gifted word.

Harry Thornton Moore (review date 14 April 1941)

SOURCE: "Mystics and Rebels," in *The New Republic,* Vol. 104, No. 15, April 14, 1941, p. 509.

[*In the following excerpt, Moore extols* Owen Glendower *for its drama and "evocation of the past," but takes exception to its disproportionate size and style.*]

We all know Glendower through Shakespeare, who presents the Welsh hero as a strutting and irascible star-gazer: Owen was politically in the wrong camp and, besides, Shakespeare liked to kid the Welsh. John Cowper Powys' two-volume novel gives us a different Owen—mystic, with a power of letting his spirit float away from his body, but in the main a practical and brilliant leader of an oppressed minority. Owen could whip the armies of Henry IV so long as the Welsh kept fighting a nuisance war, but he could never establish a peaceful, independent Welsh nation. At the end, Mr. Powys gives him a dramatic and impressive death scene in the traditionally magic Welsh mountains.

The story of Owen's revolt is presented through a thick broth of Cowper-Powysian prose. The central consciousness is sometimes Owen's, but oftener it is that of his kinsman on the illegitimate side, Rhisiart ab Owen. At the end of the book Rhisiart is a famous English lawyer, far removed from the youth of Welsh and Norman blood who had left Oxford for Welsh to become Owen's secretary. Rhisiart is easily the most oversexed character in all the hectic literature of today: "He had the feeling that his fate was advancing upon him in the form of a vast pair of dusky feminine breasts, each with a crater where the nipple should have been out of which proceeded fire and smoke!" Rhisiart's entire approach to the sexual is like this; he sets a new record even for a Powys hero by having erotic inclinations toward almost every character in the book. Rhisiart is irrevocably bound to two girls, but his sexual impulses run on beyond them to every girl in the story, and even to old women, pages and dwarfs. Owen, historically a noted libertine, is shown as a renouncer of temptation, at least in one big self-denial scene. As in the previous novels by this author, the motives of behavior are not easy to understand: here the obscurity is more in keeping with the background, and helps to suggest the world of Celtic fable and of dark old chronicles. The book is frequently effective on the atmospheric side: the guerilla Owen, moving from place to place in wild Wales, keeps a stately court in ruined castles, where his retinue are to be seen mostly by torch-light—savage hillmen, a mad friar screaming that King Richard still lives, the old seneschal who cherishes a famous ancient sword, the bards, bowmen, sorceresses, the flamboyant Hotspur and all the rest, in vivid costumes amid the shattered mystic castles—all these have the medieval flavor.

Yet there is another aspect of the book to be considered before the reader hazards the 963 pages. It is bad in so many ways that one wonders how it ever got published in its present state. The story is disproportionate, wind-baggy, and loaded with references to legends that only a Cymric specialist would know; it is lumpishly written, and full of stylistic ineptitudes. But if the book is read it will be for the unquestionable power of its dramatic moments, and for its evocation of the past. At least one can say for it that it is a most unusual combination of the impressive and the goofy.

Henry Miller (review date January 1963)

SOURCE: "The Immortal Bard," in *A Review of English Literature,* Vol. IV, No. 1, January, 1963, pp. 21-24.

[*In the following review, Miller gives a brief account of Powys's life, and praises his* Autobiography *and* A Glastonbury Romance.]

My admiration, love and reverence for John Cowper Powys began when I was in my twenties and has continued ever since, which is to say for a period of almost fifty years. Some thirty years or more after I first heard him lecture I had the rare good fortune to visit him at his home in Corwen, Wales. I found the same wonderful being whom I had idolised in my youth, only he had grown younger, healthier, gayer. There he was, remote from the world, living on a pittance, writing faithfully each day as ever, and, though seemingly cut off from the world, in communication with an ungodly number of friends, compeers and 'true believers'.

The secret of his joyous wisdom may be found in his little books which deal with life and art, with everyday philosophy and the cultivation of the sensual nature. In these works he takes us by the hand, as it were, and leads us through the cultural labyrinth in which most of us grope and stagger aimlessly. With his guidance the virtue and blessing of simplicity are rediscovered.

For thirty years this fascinating torch-bearer roamed far and wide over the vast wilderness which is America, giving his lectures with the same fervour whether addressing an audience of a dozen or a thousand. He spoke with the eloquence of a prophet always—on art, life, love, literature—using as models such classic figures as Homer, Dante, Rabelais, Goethe, as well as the leading spirits of the modern age, such as Blake, Nietzsche, Dostoievsky. During these thirty years of hopping from town to town, village to village, he found time to write some of his major works: ***Wolf Solent,*** the ***Autobiography*** and ***A Glastonbury Romance.***

The ***Autobiography*** I still believe to be the greatest, the most magnificent, of all autobiographies. I say this, having read most if not all of the celebrated works in this category. Reading it, one feels that he has lived life to the fullest. A rare and mighty spirit breathes, or rather blows, throughout. As for ***A Glastonbury Romance,*** I repeat what I have said time and again, that it is unique in the whole of English literature. It took me almost a year to read it. I read only a few pages at a time, savouring and re-savouring every single morsel, every tiniest crumb, and dreading to come to the end. How this great work can be so neglected, so almost unknown, is a mystery to me. Or rather it would be, did I not know from sad experience that the truly great works of literature usually reach us fifty or a hundred years late.

Were I to seek a single adjective by which to summarise the wizardry of this author I should fasten on 'mantic'. It is a dark word which covers a multitude of things. An astrologer would probably make much of his Neptunian and Uranian qualities. For this author has not only the ability to sound the innermost depths, he can also reach beyond the stars. He has a polarity and a gamut which is almost terrifying.

The soul of virtue, he has no fear of exploring the dark, inchoate realms in which good and evil are drowned. Pagan that he is, he has no compunction about soiling his hands. Naturally, he prefers the Old Testament to the New. He is on the side of the great Jehovah rather than that of the sickly Saviour whom the Christian world professes to worship. He is for the gods, really, rather than for God. And, like the ancients, he invests his gods with monstrous as well as sublime qualities.

His literary gods, all of universal spirit, are out-sized, superabundantly endowed, overflowing with life, and givers of life. Each year he re-reads his Homer, Dante, Goethe—Whitman too, if I am not mistaken. These are his boon companions, as well as the daisies, the little creatures, the village idiots, the wastrels, the snails and toads, the leviathans and behemoths, the nonconformists, the rebels. (And why, in his ***Autobiography,*** does he dwell with such gratitude and affection upon the Jews and the Negroes? He knows whereof he speaks.) Though his compassion embraces the despised and the downtrodden, it is the anomalous ones, the antipodal beings, more especially the defiant ones, to whom he is drawn. Despite the wide range of his embrace he is never the Buddha. Nor would he ever wish to be a Buddha.

His philosophy is a living, everyday philosophy, free of all the metaphysical abstractions which characterise both Eastern and Western thought. If anything, it derives from Laotse and Heraclitus. The lucidity with which he pierces life's problems lays bare the primordial darkness in which we are eternally wrapped; it never seeks to explain it away. He takes his stand before Abraham, before all that has a name was named. That is why he can speak so knowingly and intimately of the slug or any creature of the primal ooze. He is at home everywhere, even with dullards. How rare among creative spirits is this gift of participation and identification! What use the brotherhood of man, he seems to say, if it does not include all that lives and breathes? They are there in his books, these creatures whom we exclude from our dubious brotherhood. He makes them talk and act. He is never the entomologist, the botanist or the horticulturist; he entomologises, botanises, horticulturises. Put him in a cell or dungeon, isolate him from the world of men and women, and he would find as rich a life as in any high place. Perhaps a richer life, for not only does he know how to crawl, cling, slither, suck and sting, he knows also how to vanish into thin air, find his way in the star drift, live not only in myth and legend, in muck and glory, but in fraud and phantasy, in doldrums and ecstasies.

A remarkable fellow, quite. Of this world and the next. Of worlds unborn. Friar John is his moniker. Suits him to a T. Can neither be frocked nor defrocked. Is of no denomination, no caste or creed. Human, all-too-human.

Nostalgia for the ancestral haunts of the bards drove him back to the land of his forbears. He had served a long, long term in the American wilderness. He watered it faithfully. One may still find flowers which testify to his quondam presence there. Here and there a meadow lark will recall his passage and make to sing. Here and there, in the swamps, an occasional bull frog, like yours truly, endeavours to croak his paean at mention of the magic name.

He was my first living idol, John Cowper Powys. And he remains one to this day. In my youth I had many idols. Some I could never reconcile with the others. Some had been dead for centuries; others, like Vivekananda, had hardly turned cold. Friar John was on speaking terms with them all. So comfortably and securely niched was he in this strange pantheon that not even an earthquake could shake him loose. Of them all, only he possessed the universal tongue. Only he could turn his head full circle.

If there was a guiding spirit which gave inspiration and direction to the Master, I would imagine it to be Arthur's. *There* was the mantic sovereign of all the worlds which dreamers dreamed, yet none had seen or lived. King Arthur, light of the Western world. It was out of this world that I like to believe Friar John was born and to which he will return. The heraldic world which never fades because it alone is real and true.

Douglas Robillard (essay date October 1968)

SOURCE: "Landscape with Figures: The Early Fiction of John Cowper Powys," in *Studies in the Literary Imagination,* October, 1968, pp. 51-58.

[*In the following essay, Robillard gives a detailed overview of Powys's early fiction, including* Wood and Stone, Rodmoor, Ducdame, Wolf Solent, *and* A Glastonbury Romance.]

The present critical reputation of John Cowper Powys (1872-1963) can be illustrated by the surprise with which his name was mentioned in a recent piece in the *New York Times Book Review.* In reviewing George Steiner's *Language and Silence,* the writer took note of the value Steiner seemed to place upon Powys's work; and, indeed, Steiner, who is a welcome champion of Powys, had said that ***Wolf Solent*** is the only novel in English to rival Tolstoy. Such are the extremes that a small, insistent minority praises and even risks over-praising their man while the majority simply ignores him. But the quality of scholarship and criticism which have appeared since his death is indisputable. We have the excellent, complex, and demanding critical study of the fiction by G. Wilson Knight, *The Saturnian Quest;* the biographical and critical overview of all the work by H. P. Collins, *John Cowper Powys: Old Earthman;* Derek Langridge's *John Cowper Powys: A Record of Achievement,* which contains a large amount of valuable bibliographical information; and Kenneth Hopkins' biography, *The Powys Brothers.* That Powys is now attracting such an amount of attention indicates the durability of his appeal and the likelihood of further critical revaluation.

It is given to some writers to be so energetic and productive that their writings spill into a number of channels and cannot readily be classified. As the author of more than fifty volumes, Powys might well be considered a poet, with five volumes and ***Lucifer,*** a lengthy epic, to his credit; a critic and biographer, whose works include volumes of essays and book-length studies of Dorothy Richardson, Rabelais, and Dostoevsky; a writer of fiction, who produced fifteen novels; or, quite apart from all this, a keenly intelligent author of numerous volumes of philosophy and commentary. Nor does this categorizing quite exhaust his potentialities. The published letters to Louis Wilkinson reveal him as a vigorous, readable correspondent, and the existence of large caches of unpublished letters at Yale, Syracuse, and elsewhere promises well for the future of his reputation. He is too massive a subject to be treated briefly, and I mean to advance only tentative statements about his early fiction in order to attract readers to him. It is likely that readers may need enticement; Powys wrote long, substantial novels, and one may be put off by the two volumes of ***Wolf Solent*** or the more than eleven hundred closely packed pages of ***A Glastonbury Romance.***

When Powys began writing novels, he was already in his early forties and had a lengthy career as writer and lecturer behind him. His earlier work had been poetry, and as a lecturer he had ranged throughout England, Europe, and America. A good part of the time he had spent writing a book on Keats, a long-term project that worried him but never reached publication. When his American lecture agent, G. Arnold Shaw, set up as a publisher in 1914, Powys was in a singularly excellent position to contribute to the venture. He had read widely, had thought hard about literature and talked often about it, and wanted to shape his thoughts into critical essays. He wanted to continue his interrupted work as a poet, although, by this time, nearly two decades after a promising beginning, he suspected that he could never become what he confesses he wanted so badly to be, a major poet. And, in addition, the persistent writing of fiction over a period of years by T. F. Powys, his younger brother, must have been a stimulus to him to attempt work in the novel. He found that he had a model ready to hand in the novels of his much admired neighbor, Thomas Hardy. Powys's first novel, ***Wood and Stone*** (1915), is dedicated to Hardy, though one hardly needs the dedication or the weak prefatory disclaimer of influence to see the print of Hardy upon the work.

Powys had chosen his master wisely, for Hardy's philosophical position matched his in many ways, and his own predilection was always to move Nature into the arena usually reserved for human characters and make a landscape a moving force in the fortunes of his characters. It is the quality of the countryside that forces upon the people the chief characteristics of their lives, much as it does in Hardy's novels. In some ways, Powys moves beyond Hardy, giving Nature an even more important role, animating and personifying it till it has life and movement of its own. In ***Wood and Stone,*** the dominant influence is that of the stone quarries of Dorset. Besides being a natural element in the composition of the tale, stone is a symbol for the power, cruelty, and selfishness of the times before the self-sacrifice of Christ upon the wood of the cross. The themes of the novel are worked out in this play of the two impulses, power and perverted sadism, and the gentleness and quietness of apparently ineffectual self-sacrifice. Powys conceives many of his fictions in just such a dualism, with the landscape reflecting the struggle fully as much as the people do. In the twenty-first chapter, **"Caesar's Quarry,"** all the elements of plot, setting, and character join to build to a powerful scene of confrontation. Innocence is trapped there but rescued when madness, in the person of James Anderson, a stonecutter, breaks into the scene with demented shouts and gestures before he walks blindly off a cliff to his death. Putting one of his theses into the mouth of a character, Powys observes that the forces which move men are elemental, destructive, and powerful; they are as much natural catastrophes as earthquakes, floods, and avalanches.

The dramatic contention of good and evil plays its part against other landscapes as well. The second novel, ***Rodmoor*** (1916), shifts the scene from the western mountains to the fishing villages and open, low country of East Anglia. But this landscape plays as much upon the people as does the other, for it shapes their lives, their ways of thinking, and their feelings. Because the land is low, the seas encroach upon it and the inhabitants are constantly driven from their land and left rootless and without tradition. The land that their ancestors worked has been lost to the sea; even the churches have had to be moved at frequent intervals and, as a result, the people themselves are said to have a reputation for impiety and perversion. Likewise, this steady destructiveness finds its ethical equivalent in the philosophical view that destruction is the essence of life. But the sea is not the only feature of the landscape that affects the lives of the inhabitants of the village of Rodmoor. Inland are the fens, which cast upon much of the novel the atmosphere of solitude, flatness, wildness, and terror. It is a dreary area, so much alike in its whole expanse that one can lose hope and die in it. The pattern of events in the novel is to be found in the pattern of the seasons and they, too, play their part in shaping character and event. The summer heat and the damp and heavy air of Rodmoor create an atmosphere of madness and abnormality, where the self-annihilating madness of Adrian Sorio, artist and philosopher, are most in evidence. The final scenes of the novel take place in November and are heavily freighted with the atmosphere of death, so that we are prepared for the madness, death, and suicide that bring the tale to its conclusion.

Powys's third novel, ***Ducdame*** (1925), has less in it of the strongly etched landscape and more interest in the people who inhabit the place. It is a defect of the first novels that Powys creates characters who are not adequate to the world that surrounds them. They are not nearly as strongly conceived or as individual as the landscape, the natural elements, and the seasons. Instead, as is so often the case in fiction that leans heavily upon scene for character and treats it as though it is a living presence, the people tend to be types representing forms of behavior that the author wants to get into his fiction in order to illustrate his ideas. Thus, in ***Wood and Stone,*** power is personified by Mortimer Romer and sadism by his daughter Gladys. The good and innocent in humanity are represented in the character of the unfortunately named Lacrima Traffio, who is all too good, and equally in Maurice Quincunx, who is all too ineffectual. Madness, like sadism, is an especially fascinating subject for Powys, and he manages to put a madman near the center of each of his first three novels. In ***Wood and Stone,*** the madness of James Anderson is directed inward because of his essential gentleness. In ***Rodmoor,*** madness is manifested in the life and work of Adrian Sorio, and here it is a more complex element, for Sorio's madness is made to express one of the major themes of the novel, the drift toward annihilation. The artist first preaches death, and then dies in the midst of his madness. In ***Ducdame,*** it is part of the character of William Hastings, a vicar who sees the struggle between opposing forces that Powys so likes to portray as one between life and death. Like Sorio, he is madly intent upon writing out his obsession into a book. And, while he believes that the two forces are inextricable, that man can germinate life or destroy it, he is insistently on the side of the death force. That he plunges out into a stormy night at the climax of the novel, his madness in full possession of his spirit, and kills Rook Ashover just at the moment that Ashover's wife is bearing a child, illustrates both his view and that of Powys. Man, who can create, has an irresistible urge to destroy.

It should be noted that, unlike younger first novelists, Powys does not show much uncertainty of intention or execution in these early works. Even from the first, his novels have a shape and firmness of outline that make them well worth reading. But, in a way, the first three books are a preparation for two much finer works, ***Wolf Solent*** (1929) and ***A Glastonbury Romance*** (1932). If it was necessary for Powys to gain practice as a novelist, he should have had it by the time he turned to the writing of these novels. Starting late, with a fund of skill already at his disposal, he had given about fifteen years and three novels to whatever apprenticeship that might be necessary.

The basic premise of ***Wolf Solent*** is the treatment of the individual life and its development, the careful chronicling of the single character and all the influences that work upon him. Wolf Solent is the not-quite young man returning to the home ground that has been dishonored by his father. He knows the entire history of the town and of most of the people who live there, although he has no personal experience of either. The job that brings him home will take in the entire surrounding countryside, the past and the present, good and evil; for it is the writing, in collaboration with Squire Urquhart, of an "underground history" of Dorset which will emphasize the perversion and evil of the territory. Urquhart himself is an embodiment of the evil that so fascinates him, another in the portrait gallery of cruel and sadistic figures that Powys is always attempting to draw. The secondary characters add to the life of the novel and at the same time reflect or throw light upon Wolf's character. Thus we have the poetic temperament and awkward unsociability of Jason Otter, whose poems depict the neighborhood and at the same time cut into the psychological nature of the problems of good and evil; Malakite, the bookseller, another of the men of evil; his daughter, Christie, who represents the elusive spiritual element that satisfies in some part of the needs of Wolf, busy yearning for both the spiritual and the sexual in women. That he courts and marries Gerda, who is all physical, and then misses the comforts of Christie, is an expression of his divided nature.

It is, finally, the concentration upon the one personality that unifies the book, giving it richness and fullness that are satisfying; but, irritatingly, the novel is at times prolix and tedious. In a way, Powys is providing a fictional synthesis of his own life and opinions. He always leaned toward the confessional side of writing; one of his earlier efforts had been the collaboration, with his brother Llewelyn, upon ***Confessions of Two Brothers*** (1916). It is significant that while Llewelyn's portion of the book is a rather slight gathering of diary jottings, John took advantage of the created form to pour out his thoughts and feelings about poetry and personality, his paradox of assuming his own sadistic and self-destroying nature. If one has his biography in mind, it is easy to see how much of his own person, self, opinions, and feelings he puts into each of the characters of the early novels. Traits of this one personality overflow into several of the characters, men and women alike, in each novel, as if the novelist recognizes that characters have to be stylized and that complexity has to be hinted at while the people themselves can represent only one or two traits; the recognition that all the subtlety and variety of a single human personality cannot be presented in one created character. The realization must have been frustrating for Powys, who thought constantly about his own rich and variable personality. He was to make a large-scale attempt to present all the turns and twists, the variables, the dark spots, the quirks of his own personality in his ***Autobiography*** (1934). And, because of the intensity of his effort, the book is a remarkable and intensely readable record. In ***Wolf Solent,*** he was, so to speak, offering a fictional trial run at presenting a whole personality. Wolf is undeniably John Powys, with all his weirdness and all the weirdness he imagines he possesses, a victim of his own sadism, sentimentality, talent, and sensuality.

In spite of its length, ***Wolf Solent*** gives the impression of being a small-scaled novel because of its focus upon a single character. In ***A Glastonbury Romance,*** Powys returns to the panoramic kind of novel he had attempted in ***Wood and Stone*** and ***Rodmoor,*** the full treatment of an entire locale that is ripe with history, myth, scandal, and the powerful burden of the present. For all that it looks traditional and is not shaped in any experimental manner, the novel is more of the generation of Lawrence and Joyce than it is of the generation of Bennett and Galsworthy, both of whom might be claimed as more nearly Powys's contemporaries than the later writers. It has some elements of the pageant about it; the two major scenes are worked out in a crucifixion and a deluge. It is full to the brim with characters who are so fully developed as to compete vigorously for the attention: John Geard, Will Zoyland, Philip Crow, Sam Dekker, Owen Evans. Powys's men are almost more interesting and impressive than his women. There are so many plots being developed at once, with crossings as the characters encounter one another and begin influencing other lives, that it is often difficult to keep all the parts separated and clear in the mind. And, running below the level of plot and character is a complex mythic substructure that makes the whole unwieldy machine work.

One strand of the myth is the Grail quest, with the attempt to found a new religion that will compound the religious and the anciently pagan. John Geard, "Bloody Johnny," is the center of this movement, a demonic presence with apparently magical powers to heal the sick and revive the dead. His powers are opened to public exhibit in the "religious circus," the mystery play and pageant that he organizes for Midsummer Day. It combines, religion, legend, history, and paganism; all the figures of the Arthurian story are present except Merlin, who, for all his absence, is a kind of center for the whole novel, and the pageant reverses chronology in the interests of symbolism, working from most recent times to the distant past in presenting the Arthurian Cycle, the Passion of Christ, and the ancient Cymric Mythology.

One of Powys's excellences as a writer is his ability to describe large, impressive, panoramic scenes, full of people, movement, contrast, and color. Both ***Wood and Stone,*** with its election scene and ***Wolf Solent,*** with its fairs, are distinguished for their use of these large structuring devices, placed at strategic points in their development. Powys uses such scenes as focal points for the meeting of opposing forces and ideas, for the confrontation of friends and enemies, and for the dramatic exposition of theme. Here, the pageant grows in a chapter of some seventy pages, a long, carefully worked out, complex scene that draws together all the major characters with their fears and ideas and lets them grate upon each other.

The perceptive remarks on the novel by G. Wilson Knight emphasize the sharp contrast between the pagan and the Christian elements, presented as though they are in conflict. In ***Wood and Stone,*** the two opposing forces had been represented by the two materials of the title, the wood for the cross, crucifixion, and self-sacrifice, stone for the granitic hardness of the ancient doctrine and the sadistic cruelty of its human practitioners. Here, the doctrine of Bloody Johnny Geard is opposed by the saint-like turning of Sam Dekker, who moves from the self-abuse of sensual love to a simpler life as Holy Sam, the laboring man who takes care of an infirm old man and an idiot boy. His holiness leads him to a great vision:

> When the vision appeared, and it came sailing into the midst of the bleeding darkness that was Sam's consciousness, healing everything, changing everything, each detail of what he saw he saw with a clearness that branded it forever upon his brain. He saw a globular chalice that had two circular handles. The substance it was made of was clearer than crystal; and within it there was dark

water streaked with blood, and within the water was a shining fish.

On the contrary, for John Geard, hell is the cave at Wookey Hole. Philip Crow, owner of the property, has been conducted to these lower regions before by Persephone Spear, who is both lover and goddess of the darkness and the underworld. As Geard stumbles about under the electric lights that have been mounted to make the Hole a tourist attraction, he finds himself under the stone figure of the Witch of Wookey:

> Here Bloody Johnny awkwardly disembarked, feeling, though he knew nothing of Dante, very much what that medieval Harrower of Hell felt, when he, still a man of flesh-and-blood, moved among the infernal wraiths. He advanced under the precipitous wall of the vast cavern, his feet sinking, as he walked, in the loose shingle of that Acherontic shore.

When the Deluge comes, it is almost inevitable that it will take the life of John Geard, for it is the wrathful recompense of an angry God for his blasphemies as the founder of a newer, or perhaps older, set of religious ideals. It does not detract from the achievement that the scene of the deluge comes at the end of an already very long book. Powys is not always a consummate stylist; he often sputters, gets long-winded, becomes entangled in his own visionary rhetoric, and loses his way. But he knows how to rise to a great occasion and a great theme, and the rhythm of his prose matches the quality of his subject:

> The great waves of the far Atlantic, rising from the surface of unusual spring tides, were drawn, during the first two weeks of that particular March, by a moon more magnetic and potent as she approached her luminous rondure than any moon that had been seen on that coast for many a long year. Up the sands and shoals and mudflats, up the inlets and estuaries and backwaters of that channel-shore raced steadily, higher and higher as day followed day, these irresistible hosts of invading waters. Across the far-stretching flats of Bridgewater Bay these moon-drawn death-bringers gathered, stealing, shoaling, rippling, tossing, waves and groundswells together, cresting billows and unruffled curves of slippery water, rolling in with a volume that increased its momentum with every tide that advanced, till it covered sand-wastes and sand-dunes, grassy shelves and sea-banks, that had not felt the sea for centuries. Out of the misty western horizon they came, rocking, heaving, rising, sinking, and beneath them were shoals of unusual fish and above them were flocks of unusual gulls. There was a strange colour upon them, too, these far-travelled deep-sea waves, and a strange smell rose up from them, a smell that came from the far-off mid-Atlantic for many days.

It is possible to see Powys taking new turns in his life and career after expending large energies upon ***A Glastonbury Romance.*** He turned sixty and, symbolically, set forth his ***Autobiography.*** After a lifetime, almost, of traveling to lecture on life in the United States, he turned again to England, but only briefly. His last move, to Wales, and his residence there for the final twenty-eight years of his life was symbolic too, for there he could nourish his obsessive Welshness, which must have been more imaginative than real and work out the materials for his later novels: the historical in ***Owen Glendower*** (1940) and ***The Brazen Head*** (1956); the legendary in ***Porius*** (1951) and ***Atlantis*** (1954); and fantasy and a sense of the grotesque in the other novels. A wider avatar of life is to be glimpsed in these later books, as Powys reached the point where, in the words of H. P. Collins, "his desire to escape the present in magnificent fantasy began to counterpoise his passion for deeper psychological reality." The earlier narratives, as we examine them, seem more fixed in time and place, their characters more human and more susceptible to the weight of experience and landscape.

David A. Cook (essay date Summer 1972)

SOURCE: "John Cowper Powys' *A Glastonbury Romance:* A Modern Mystery Play," in *Contemporary Literature,* Vol. XIII, No. 3, Summer, 1972, pp. 341-60.

[*In the following essay, Cook explores the themes and characters of* A Glastonbury Romance, *and compares its style to the novels of Dostoevsky.*]

> The psychic history of a place like Glastonbury is not an easy thing to write down in set terms, for not only does chance play an enormous part in it, but there are many forces at work for which human language has at present no fit terms.

John Cowper Powys' first important work, ***Wolf Solent*** (1929), is a novel which follows a fairly simple course of narrative development through the experience of a single center of consciousness to a predictable conclusion. It is like a swollen brook running through the plains of Dorsetshire without variation or divergence to the sea. ***A Glastonbury Romance*** (1932), Powys' second major novel, is like that vast and chaotic sea itself—a book whose centers are myriad and multiform and whose circumference is an awesome authorial omniscience aspiring toward the cosmic consciousness of God. That the novel has a localized setting at all is an accident of form. Its true setting is the cosmos itself, upon whose vertical axis Glastonbury is but a single if important coordinate; and it is the vertical axis which matters here ultimately. For all the panoramic sweep of Powys' descriptions, evoking not merely Somersetshire but Wessex and England, for all his intricate patterning of spatial and temporal relationships, helping to make the book the longest undivided novel in our language, it is a reality transcending these which provides the motive force of ***A Glastonbury Romance***—that is, the Holy Grail (for, Christian or pagan, it is preeminently holy in Powys), "that fragment of Beyond-Time fallen through a crack in the world-ceiling upon the Time-Floor" (p. 789). The function of each entity trapped upon the Time-Floor in the vicinity of Glastonbury is to come to terms with this sacred object, and so the novel has no plot in a conventional sense. Rather, significant action occurs on a spiritual plane.

On the level of character this response involves a choice between the pagan and the Christian Grail (which manifests itself in terms of Arthurian legend as a choice between Merlin and Arthur, and in terms of the Nietzschean dichotomy which is everpresent to Powys as a choice between Christ Dionysus and Christ Apollo); for the Isle of Glastonbury is above all a center of spiritual warfare where the exiled heathen deities of the Tor (rising from the Somerset plane like "the phallus of an unknown god") battle fiercely with the Christian divinity of the Abbey for ascendancy over the soul of Wessex. Which grail our characters choose to follow and the intensity with which they pursue it determines the nature and degree of psychic integration that they will be permitted to achieve in the course of the novel; but personal salvation is conceived to depend in part upon an agency beyond the self and its volitions. It is as if, having stabilized self in ***Wolf Solent,*** Powys now seeks to attune it with some eternal principle or godhead which promises cosmic as well as psychological wholeness.

In this and other respects ***A Glastonbury Romance*** resembles the novels of Powys' acknowledged master Dostoevsky. Indeed, what Marc Slonim has called Dostoevsky's "psychological clairvoyance and ideological profundity" are qualities which pervade ***A Glastonbury Romance,*** and so too are Dostoevsky's crudities of construction and style. The formal eclecticism of *The Brothers Karamazov* as characterized by Slonim, for instance, exactly parallels that of Powys' novel: "Straight exposition . . . is followed by dramatic scenes or long dialogue; dynamic narrative full of suspense and action is interrupted by forensic speeches quoted *in extenso;* flashes of violence follow disquisitions on Christianity; sarcastic hints and humorous character sketches alternate with descriptions of death and hallucination." Furthermore, the critical charges leveled against both books have been precisely the same–"lengthy dialogue, distracting sub-plots, the melodramatic piling up of incidents and coincidences, the high-pitched tone of the narrative, which often jars and exhausts the reader." Yet it is a testament to the genius of both artists that their immense spiritual vitality has enabled them to triumph absolutely over absurdities of plot and clumsiness of narrative technique, creating novels whose strength and unity of vision render their technical flaws irrelevant. The visions are ultimately dissimilar, it is true; and Powys may have failed to grasp the overriding importance of Dostoevsky's Christian orthodoxy and political conservatism, so antithetical to all orthodoxies were his own views; but his numerous studies of Dostoevsky reveal that Powys felt his way into the great Russian's soul as few men have done before or since. The affinity between the two is one of temperament rather than intellect, for both were great undisciplined mystics who understood intimately and instinctively, as Powys wrote of his mentor in 1916, "*the depravity of the spirit,* as well as of the flesh, and the amazing wantonness, whereby the human will does not always seek its own realization and well-being, but quite as often its own laceration and destruction." But unlike Dostoevsky Powys seeks redemption upon a larger scale than the merely human, and his conception of salvation extends to the earth itself. As one character in ***A Glastonbury Romance*** puts it: "Matter must be redeemed; and only Christ can redeem it. *Christ,* I say; not Jesus. *Verbum caro factum est.* . . . It's the Thing Outside breaking into our closed circle. And every atom of Matter feels it. Matter is no longer separate from Spirit. It has become the living flesh of Spirit" (p. 265). This is why G. Wilson Knight can write with a kind of absolute justification, "***A Glastonbury Romance*** is less a book than a Bible." It is a novel too, however, and while it may be the sacred text of the Powys canon, ***A Glastonbury Romance*** shares certain thematic concerns with its more secular fellows.

Like ***Wolf Solent, A Glastonbury Romance*** opens with the return of a native to his homeland after long absence. John Crow, our "human norm" in the novel's animistic universe, arrives in East Anglia from a fifteen-year sojourn in Paris to attend the funeral of his wealthy grandfather, the Canon William Crow of Norfolk. There he meets for the first time since childhood his anima-like cousin Mary Crow and immediately recognizes his destiny to merge with her spiritually *and* physically (p. 19), exclusive, however, of sexual intercourse. To even suggest such a union in a modern context is remarkable enough; to actually depict it without embarrassment or absurdity is next to impossible. Yet Powys does exactly this in the second chapter of the novel where John and Mary come together in a finely realized act of symbolic intercourse in a rowboat on the Wissey River:

> The prolonged struggle of these two with the boat and with the water became in a very inti-

> mate sense their marriage day upon earth. By his saltasting sweat and by her wrought-up passion of guiding, these two "run-down adventurers" plighted their troth for the rest of their days. . . . They clung to each other with a grim, vicious, indignant resolve to enjoy a sensuality of oneness; a sensuality of unity snatched out of the drifting flood of space and time. It was not directed to anything beyond itself, this desire of theirs. It was innocent of any idea of offspring. It was an absolute, fortified and consecrated by the furious efforts they were making, by the diamond-bright sparkles upon the broken water, by the sullen clicking of the rowlocks.
>
> John had begun to count now. "I'll stop after twenty more strokes," he thought. But when the last of the twenty came, and he found in the beating pulse of his exhaustion an undreamed-of nerve of renewal, he did *not* stop. The dazzling spouts of water drops which followed his oars, each time he drew them from the water, mingled now with a renewed counting. "Ten . . . eleven . . . twelve . . . thirteen . . . fourteen . . . fifteen . . ." Those rhythmic, up-flung splashes of dancing crystal, stirred and subsiding amid the long emerald-green weeds, became the thudding reverberation of his own unconquerable heartbeats. (pp. 64-65)

John's coalescence with this feminine projection of his very soul secures for him a degree of ontological stability unparalleled by his counterparts in Powys' other novels. For this reason he becomes less a participant in the great spiritual drama to be enacted at Glastonbury than a spectator to it, and his role as central figure is usurped by other characters as the novel unfolds. More significant, perhaps, he has certain congenital limitations which preclude full response to the "aura" of this ancient island fastness.

Powys will repeatedly make the point that the Norfolk-born Crows—even the most sensitive among them, like John and Mary—are descendants of the conqueror race which rode roughshod over the sacred mythologies of Celtic Britain during the Invasion and, as such, are aliens to Glastonbury and its awful burden of Mystery. It is not that they are immune to the influence of the Grail (for no one is) but rather that the blood of their forthright and pragmatic Norman ancestors prejudices them against the Unseen in favor of the palpably material and causes them to hold the legend-steeped Glastonbury in contempt as an evasive, feminine, and irrational presence—all of which it is. Thus, John and Mary will live and work in Glastonbury for the duration of their relationship, but "rooted in fen-mud and vicious heathenism," they remain temperamentally indisposed to its atmosphere. Even after John has been granted a vision of Excalibur on Pomparlès Bridge, he will persist in his skeptical attitude toward the Glastonbury *mythos*. Indeed, the intense spirituality of the place discomfits these "healthy-minded" Crows to such an extent that, however benevolent their resolve, they all end by becoming its enemies.

John's cousin Philip possesses this racial attribute in its most extreme form. A grasping industrial magnate who bears unmistakable kinship with Lawrence's Gerald Crich, and the foremost entrepreneur in Glastonbury, Philip Crow has come to Norfolk hoping to inherit the better part of his grandfather's estate in order to electrify and mechanize his tin mine at Wookey Hole, Somerset, formerly a sacred cave of the Druids. Though Philip is included in Powys' comprehensive "Tolstoyan sympathy," he is easily the least humane character in the novel, hating Glastonbury and all it represents, and admitting at one point: "It would be a good thing if the Glastonbury people would simply die off. . . . How these Christs and Buddhas . . . ever reached the point of feeling that it was worth their while to save the human race is more than I can understand. . . . If I could cut off the heads of all the poor of Glastonbury and fill their houses with a picked set of men and women who could really work I'd do it tomorrow" (pp. 776-77). Driven by an insatiable desire to subdue both man and nature to the will of the machine, Philip Crow is the great antagonist of the Grail and all that is holy in the human spirit and the world. But myth and religion are formidable opponents for a mere capitalist, and Philip soon learns that his grandfather's money has been bequeathed to a professional exponent of the Unseen, Johnny Geard, nonconformist preacher *cum* Powysian mystic and the strangest defender the Grail has ever found.

This remarkable personage is one of Powys' greatest creations. Known to the townspeople of Glastonbury as "Bloody Johnny" (owing to his frequent invocation of the Blood of Christ), Geard is the very type of thaumaturgic field preacher—half-charlatan, half-Dionysian Messiah—which Powys conceived himself to be in his American lecture tours. Bloody Johnny has reached the conclusion that the Western world stands upon the brink of a great spiritual renaissance whose center, with a little intelligent promotion, will be Glastonbury itself. He seems truly to believe that, with Jerusalem, Mecca, and Rome, Glastonbury is one of the few "reservoirs of world-magic on the whole surface of the globe" (p. 291), and he hopes ultimately to establish the site of Chalice Well near the Tor as a nonsectarian shrine on the order of Lourdes, fully sanctified by miracles which he will himself perform. For the present, however, his purpose holds to inaugurate a Midsummer Religious Festival at Glastonbury climaxed by a spectacular Passion play which will attract international attention to the place. During his tenure as curate to Canon Crow, Geard has apparently inspired this orthodox clergyman with the same fantastic notion; and the old priest leaves Bloody Johnny a small fortune with which to prosecute the unlikely scheme. The Canon's erstwhile legatees are outraged that this unctuous, brandy-swilling son of the lower middle classes should thus inherit the family wealth, but the will is airtight; and the Crows grudgingly remove themselves to Glastonbury where for one reason or another they all temporarily reside.

In Glastonbury we are introduced to a large new cast of characters (the author claims forty-eight principle figures in all), most of whom, as Roland Mathias has remarked, "are not products of society, but foci of intellectual, genealogical, geological, and vegetable processes." By far the most important of these figures are Owen Evans and Sam Dekker, who represent respectively the two aspects of Apollonian Christianity that Powys finds most dangerous to the human spirit and yet most fascinating to the creative mind—guilt and renunciation. Mr. Evans is an itinerant Welsh scholar and crypto-sadist engaged in writing a definitive biography of Merlin (in which he hopes to explicate the sorcerer's Nirvanic translation to the mysterious "Esplumeoir") when he is not grappling strenuously with his monstrous fantasies of cruelty and the agonizing guilt they engender. Indeed, he martyrs himself daily to this cerebral perversion, which he believes to be the "Unpardonable Sin," and, like the ghastly, tortured Christ of Calvary, assumes the bloodguilt of the race in the process (p. 95). His remorse is so great in fact that Evans allows himself to be literally crucified in the Glastonbury Passion Play and almost dies of asphyxia. Yet it is less a physical yearning for mayhem that afflicts Owen Evans than a Dostoevskian *mal d'esprit.* He believes in evil as a constitutive force generated exclusively by man—"man the cruel, man the bloodfiend, man the voluptuous tormentor, man the rejoicer in pain, man the inventor of pain, man the pain-be-getter, the pain-eater, the pain-drinker, the pain-devil" (p. 642)—but his own victims are all phantoms, so that neither his crimes nor his guilt are subject to material restraints:

> His mind seemed . . . absolutely balanced on a taut and twanging wire between two terrible eternities, an eternity of wilful horror, and an eternity of bleached, arid futility, devoid of all life-sap. He could feel the path to the horror, shivering with deadly phosphorescent sweetness. He could feel the path to the renunciation filling his nostrils with acrid dust, parching his naked feet, withering every human sensation till it was hollow as the shard of a dead beetle! The nature of his temptation was such that it had nothing to redeem it. . . .
>
> . . . And his imagination . . . settled itself like a dung-wasp upon the nature of his conscious life if he *did* yield to it. He saw his soul in the form of an unspeakable worm, writhing in pursuit of new, and ever new mental victims, drinking new, and ever new innocent blood. (pp. 254-55)

The ultimate horror in the Powysian universe is not sadism but solipsism run wild; and Mr. Evans more than any other character in Powys' novels bears its stigmata.

If Evans is a Stavroghin *manqué,* Sam Dekker stands somewhere between Prince Myshkin and Alyosha Karamazov. He is the awkward but well-intentioned son of the Reverend Matt Dekker, Vicar of Glastonbury; he has for some time conducted an affair with the beautiful (and married) Nell Zoyland, whom he loves dearly. But Sam also loves the lean and ascetic Christ of Glastonbury Abbey, who requires awful sacrifice of his worshippers; and after a spiritual struggle of some magnitude, he renounces his near perfect relationship with Nell to become "Holy Sam," saintlike hermit of the Glastonbury water meadows whose *Imitatio Christi* makes him the laughingstock of the town. Though the religious quests of Evans and Sam come to completely different ends, both are initially grounded in the joyless (and, for Powys, wrong-headed) assumption that man's sinfulness can only be redeemed through pain and self-denial. Theirs is the tragic, suffering Christ of the Crucifixion who dies for a race which, as Sam tells Evans, is "all scales, scurf, scab, on the same twisting, cresting dragon of the slime" (p. 856).

Far different is Johnny Geard's Messiah who, if He has an orthodox equivalent at all, must be said to be the Christ of the Incarnation and the Resurrection. For Geard, Christ's Blood is not the substance shed on Calvary but an ichorous fluid which streams in the firmament at sunset and dawn, the sap which rises daily in every living thing to produce new life, and the great tidal billow of the sea. Redemption comes not through fastidious renunciation but unqualified acceptance of everything in the cosmos from excrement to ether. The heretical Easter Mass that Geard celebrates for his Saviour in his wife's garden is wholly characteristic:

> He sank down on his knees in the presence of a little square patch of grass, a few privet bushes, and a tiny round bed with three dead hyacinths in it, and in this position began, with a sort of ravenous greed, tearing open the loaf and gobbling great lumps of crumb from the centre of it. These mouthfuls he washed down with repeated gulps of port wine. . . .
>
> "Christ is risen! Christ is risen!" muttered Bloody Johnny, with his mouth full of the inside of his loaf. "Christ our Passover," he went on, "is sacrificed for us; let us therefore keep the Feast!" (pp. 422-23)

> The image he evoked in his imagination did not resemble in the least degree the tortured Figure of Pain worshipped by Sam Dekker. . . . (p. 456)

Later, Sam himself will note the extreme contrast between his god and Geard's:

> How different was Sam's Christ from Mr. Geard's! Mr. Geard's Christ was a Power to be exploited. In his weird gnostic dialogues with *his* Master, [Geard] addressed Him like a friend, almost like an equal. He was [his] great magician, his super-Merlin, by whose strength and support he became strong. Never once had it crossed the threshold of Mr. Geard's consciousness that it was his duty to live a life of self-sacrifice. (pp. 950-51)

Geard's Christ, then, is a benevolent Anarch, much closer to the chthonian deities of the Tor than to the hieratic divinities of the Abbey; and through the medium of Bloody Johnny He becomes a living presence in Glastonbury, succoring the same downtrodden contingent of humanity—the sick, abnormal, and disenfranchised—that Powys himself championed during his American lecture tours.

Like Powys, Geard is a spiritual communist who believes that all life is holy and, as his influence in Glastonbury grows, he becomes a material communist as well. When he manages to have himself elected mayor of the town by an unlikely coalition of Liberals, Laborites, and Bolsheviks, Geard sets about at once to reorganize Glastonbury as a socialist commune in order to implement his religious revival. His constant refrain in the early days of his crusade has been that he will restore the town and its historic ruins (held in trust by the state) to "the People." The Normans, he contends, "Brought the Devil with 'em . . . and the Devil's gentlemen" (p. 287) and still hold the rightful property of Saxon and Celt alike in thrall. Now, from his new position of authority, Geard convinces the town council to municipalize Glastonbury's industry, largely the property of Philip Crow, and distribute the shares among the populace (exactly how remains unclear—and unimportant: critics who carp at the novel's political improbabilities forget the most emphatic word of its title). In thus forcing Crow out of business and dividing his wealth among his natural enemies, Geard is only fulfilling the manifest destiny of the Glastonbury people to cast out the Invader and usurp the centuries of illegitimate authority which has attempted to rule them since the Battle of Hastings; and Powys leaves no doubt as to the people's ultimate allegiance:

> They were lean and lanky men, descendants by centuries of inbreeding of those heathen aboriginals of the Isle of Glastonbury who resisted St. Joseph, St. David, St. Indractus, St. Gildas, St. Patrick, St. Dunstan, St. Benignus and St. Bridget, in their attempts to spiritualise them, who were forever revolting against both church and state, who seemed inspired in their rebellions by the old chthonian divinities of Tor Hill, . . . and whom nobody but Bloody Johnny seemed able to manage. (pp. 966-67)

On a symbolic level this rebellion is figured in the return not of Arthur but his Celtic prototypes, Uther Pendragon or Urien, and a whole succession of vanquished Fisher Kings:

> The sturdy northeastern invaders—the ancestors of Philip and John—beat back more than Mr. Evans' people when they swept the Celts into South Wales. They beat back with them their thaumaturgic demigods, the Living Corpse, for instance, of Uther Pendragon, the mysterious Urien, King of yr Echwyd, the Land of Glamour and Illusion, the Land whose vapours are always livid blue, that mystic colour named by the bards *gorlassar,* and Arawn, King of Annwn, they beat back, together with those weird protectors of the heathen Grail, the Fisher King Petchere and the Maimed King Pelles. . . . And along with Mr. Evans' people, and their dark chthonian gods, these healthy-minded invaders had driven back the very *dreams* of these Cymric and Brythonic tribes. (p. 788)

Geard's "new religion" is based precisely on the restoration of this exiled mythology, for like Jung he believes that man has become spiritually impoverished through the loss of his unconscious symbols, or archetypes (p. 1124). Indeed, Owen Evans believes that Geard has recovered *yr Echwyd* in Glastonbury itself:

> Few Glastonbury people realise that they are actually living in *yr Echwyd,* the land of Annwn, the land of twilight and death, where the shores are of Mortuorum Mare, the Sea of the Departed. This place has always been set apart . . . from the earliest times . . . Urien the Mysterious, Avallach the Unknown, were Fisher Kings here . . . and for what did they fish? . . .
>
> . . . What they sought . . . what the Fisher Kings of my people sought, and no other priests of no other race on earth have ever sought it . . . was not only the Cauldron and the Spear . . . not only the sheath and the knife, not only the Mwys of Gwyddno and the Sword of Arthur, but that

which exists in the moment of timeless time when these two are one! (pp. 771-72)

It is the heathen Grail, then, which the Merlinesque Geard through the medium of his weird evangelical mysticism will offer Glastonbury; but other citizens of the town are less confident of its miraculous properties than the jittery, guilt-ridden Mr. Evans.

The professional classes of Glastonbury continue to regard Geard as a degenerate fraud even after his Midsummer Pageant brings the prosperity and renown he has forecast for the town. Philip, of course, would like to see him hanged; and even John, who now works for Geard in a public relations capacity and harbors a certain grudging admiration for him, is frequently revolted by the Mayor's "new Revelation" ("What the devil am I doing in this muggy hole, selling my soul and swallowing all this tosh?" [p. 707]). Various other middle-class characters are alternately affronted and appalled by Geard's ability to converse with congenital imbeciles, heal the incurably ill, and resolve complicated crises with Joycean gibberish while apparently drunk on port or brandy. Indeed, a straightforward account of Geard's exploits would tax the faith of the most credulous reader. Yet Powys describes them, like so much else in the novel, with such energetic brilliance, such sustained and vibrant intensity, that we readily overlook the absurdity of the particular situation. Witness, for example, the Glastonbury Miracle, Geard's exorcism (for it cannot be called a cure in any known medical sense) of Tittie Petherton's breast cancer at Chalice Well:

> Straining every nerve of his nature, body and soul together, he forced himself to envisage that cancer as something towards which he was directing arrow after arrow of blighting, withering, deadly force. "The great thing is to *see* it," he said to himself, while his black eyes now alight with their most burning fury, stripped the poor woman of every stitch of clothing.
>
> His arrows of thought now became a spear—the Bleeding Lance of the oldest legends of Carbonek—and with an actual tremor of his upraised, naked arms, he felt himself to be plunging this formidable weapon into that worst enemy of all women! "I've done it," he repeated, for the second time, as he saw Tittie's eyes begin slowly to close.
>
> And then Mr. Geard shivered and his teeth began to chatter.
>
> Perhaps he wouldn't have succeeded after all if there hadn't come into his head at that moment an actual vision of one tiny living tendril of that murderous octopus under the sleeping woman's flesh. With one terrific upheaval of the whole of his massive frame, its gastric, its pulmonary, its spinal, its phallic force, and even lifting himself up on tiptoe from the gravel at the bottom of the fount, he plunged that Bleeding Lance of his mind into the half-dead cancer.
>
> Then he bowed himself forward, like the trunk of a tree in a great storm, till his forehead touched the surface of the water. From that surface he proceeded to gulp down, in long, panting, gurgling gasps, enough water to satisfy the thirst of the Questing Beast. "Blood of Christ!" he spluttered; and it was the first time during this great struggle that his favourite expression had crossed his lips. (pp. 739-40)

In passages like this one Powys does not ask us to suspend our disbelief; he forces us to suspend it through the sheer inundative power of his prose.

Geard, however, continues to encounter opposition at every level of society. Local Bolshevik leader Red Robinson, for instance—less a character than a diagrammatic representation of virulent class "atred"—despises the Mayor officially for his tempering the Revolution with religion and, more accurately, for his simple good fortune. But Geard has the temporary fealty of the proud and rebellious townspeople and, more important strategically, the patronage of his old friend Henry Zoyland, tenth Marquis of P., who collects the land rents on most of Glastonbury and its environs. It is in fact on a visit to the Marquis' hunting lodge at Mark's Court, by local tradition the site of Merlin's last earthly appearance, that Geard consolidates his vision of the heathen Grail.

After a terrifying but victorious midnight struggle with the spirit of the sorceress Nineue, the fatal anima-sprite who imprisoned great Merlin forever in her crystal cave, the Mayor of Glastonbury is confirmed in his *tao:*

> For a thousand years the Grail has been attracting thought to itself, because of the magnetism of Christ's Blood. The Graïl is now an organic nucleus of creation and destruction. Christ's Blood cries aloud from it by day and by night. . . . I know now what the Grail is. It is the desire of the generations mingling like water with the Blood of Christ, and caught in a fragment of Substance that is beyond Matter! It is a little nucleus of Eternity, dropped somehow from the outer spaces upon one particular spot! (p. 473)

Geard (and Powys) believes that in its descent this sacred fragment of Beyond-Matter has left a corridorlike rift in the fabric of time through which the spirit of all Matter must pass for its redemption. Matter is not evil in itself, as Mr. Evans claims (p. 264); rather, it becomes so by imprisoning something which struggles to escape into the shaft of atemporality created by the Grail. This is the "secret of the Inanimate" so crucial in Powys, that matter, like man himself, contains a soul which labors toward release—a simple enough concept for cosmic seers like Geard and Merlin, or Sylvanus Cobbold in the later ***Weymouth Sands*** (1934), but one that is lost upon the anthropocentric consciousness of humanity at large. The Powysian Grail vision, then, requires for its fulfillment a recognition of the Christ in matter as well as in man; and this is precisely what Sam Dekker achieves when he finally surrenders the oppressive burden of human misery he has chosen to bear and turns from the crucified Man-God of his father's theology to a more animistic image of redemption not far removed from Geard's.

Sam had earlier agreed with Evans as to the essential baseness of matter, telling him at one point: "I feel that the whole Creation is on the wrong track. . . . What Christ has to do is to deny the whole thing, root and branch" (p. 857). But as he stands alone one evening on the banks of the Brue with the whole of mystical Glastonbury stretched before him, Sam gazes upon an aged post embedded in the river mud and is plunged into ecstatic communion with the created matter which surrounds him: "He began to realise that the soul of the inanimate, the indwelling breath of life in all these ancient lifeless things, whereof the town was so full, was really moving towards him" (p. 978). Solid matter suddenly becomes porous, and Sam, caught out of himself, realizes its "life-essence" as a vibrantly animated World-Fish "passing through the primeval watery element that existed in all things" (p. 980). Then, without a second's warning the earth, water, and darkness crack, and Sam is brutally ravished by the great Dionysian godhead which has brooded over Glastonbury for centuries awaiting its moment of annunciation:

> It was as if the whole of Sam's consciousness became the hidden darkness of his inmost organism; and when this darkness was split, and the whole atmosphere split, and the earth and the air split, what he felt to be a gigantic spear was struck into his bowels and struck *from below*. . . .
>
> . . . He had become a bleeding mass of darkness. His consciousness was a dark surface of water; and up through this water, tearing it, rending it, dividing it, turning it into blood, shivered this crashing stroke, this stroke that was delivered from abysses of the earth, far deeper than the bottom of the Brue. (pp. 981-82)

The pain subsides, and Sam is granted his vision of the heathen Grail: "He saw a globular chalice that had two circular handles. The substance it was made of was clearer than crystal; and within it there was dark water streaked with blood, and within the water was a shining fish" (p. 982).

The following morning, still dazed, Sam attempts to evaluate his incredible experience and realizes, with Johnny Geard, that a new revelation has been made at Glastonbury: "Christ is in the Stones and in the Water; it is Jesus who is dead and buried. There's something in Nature that has turned against Nature and is escaping from Nature. There's a Christ in matter that is nearer the Grail than the Christ of the Church" (pp. 986-87). But the true identity of this new Messiah remains obscure to Sam until later in the day when he is giving a constipated octogenarian an enema and the significance of his recent vision breaks full upon him:

> As he struggled with his task, bending over the old gentleman's rear, the tension of his spirit brought back with a rush the miraculous power of the vision he had seen. The two extremes of his experience, the anus of an aged man and the wavering shaft of an Absolute, piercing his own earthly body, mingled and fused together in his consciousness. Holy Sam felt, as he went on with the business, a strange second sight, an inkling, as to some incredible secret, whereby the whole massed weight of the world's tormented flesh was labouring towards some release. (p. 991)

In this quintessentially Powysian moment Sam recognizes that "his living tortured Christ was now changed to something else" (p. 991)—specifically, the all-accepting, wholly irrational, and ecstatic Christ of Johnny Geard. Like Wolf Solent's similar discovery of the transfiguring mantle of romance behind a foul-smelling pigsty, Sam Dekker's excremental realization of an indwelling spirit in all that is brings with it a supreme moment of integration, unifying a heretofore divided self:

> "I have seen it! I have seen it!" the heart within him cried; and in a vague, delicious, dreamy reverie he became aware of an important psychic change in his inmost self-consciousness. This change was nothing less than a coming together of his body and soul. Although his soul still felt independent of his body, and free of his body, it no longer felt contemptuous of his body. It had ceased to utter its mandates in the tone of a slave-driver. Its mere presence within his body at this moment seemed to make Sam's flesh feel porous and transparent, as if large, cool, undulating waves were sweeping through it. (p. 998)

Sam's, however, is an extraordinary case. He has been

singled out for spiritual greatness from the earliest chapters of the novel, and his true vision of the Grail is all but inevitable. Other upshots of the new tide of mysticism sweeping Glastonbury are less beneficent.

Owen Evans, for example, is not so fortunate in his Grail quest as Sam. After his crucifixion in the Pageant—a magnificently rendered agony in which Powys literally attempts to recreate the subjective experience of Christ on the Cross—Evans is granted no rectification of the will but driven with ever-increasing fervor to actually witness some sadistic act. When he discovers that the crazed imbecile Finn Toller plans to murder John Crow on Glastonbury Tor by crushing his skull with an iron bar, Evans secretly arranges to watch this latter-day reenactment of the "Dolorous Blow" which Malory's Balin gave the Fisher King Pelles, bringing years of pestilence and famine upon three realms and creating the Waste Land. On the appointed day, however, Evans' wife, the ingenious Cordelia ("Cordy") *née* Geard, senses that her husband is about to embark upon some ruinous pursuit and provokes him into an act of oral intercourse which successfully defuses his volatile passion ("Not for nothing was this brave girl the child of Geard of Glastonbury" [p. 1083]), even as he remembers "how more than once he had dressed up that pillow of his in his own vest and shirt and had pounded it with the poker from the fender while an orgasm of terrible ecstasy dissolved his very soul" (p. 1074). In the event, moreover, Toller bludgeons by mistake Tom Barter, John's boyhood friend (and lover); and Evans, who has exhaustedly repented of his evil intention and set out to warn the party, arrives moments late upon the scene to discover the battered corpse. Viewing thus the grisly result of his insane passion for violence permanently debilitates Evans, and he spends the rest of his days in impotent seclusion without ever broaching Merlin's great secret.

Following the murder on the Tor, we sense that something has gone seriously amiss with the Glastonbury Revelation. An atmosphere of dissolution settles over the land (pp. 1080-81), suffusing those mysterious blue Somersetshire vapors with a faint odor of decomposition. The townspeople become restless; sexual perversions are rife. John and Mary Crow return to Norfolk with their old friend's body, determined to remain there, far from the "morbid-legended fields" of Glastonbury. Philip Crow believes that his adversary's power is on the wane; and Geard himself, like many another spiritual leader before him, is disturbed to find his flock riven with factionalism and petty doctrinal dispute:

> In place of one great final outpouring of the Spirit, obliterating all divisions, all quarrels, all maliciousness, and setting him free, they were back again in the old wrangling human arena, Celt against Saxon, Capitalist against Communist, and every Philip against every John! Mr. Geard had come . . . in the mood of Elijah when he was transported to Heaven in a chariot of fire. But now he began to feel that his Lord had forsaken him and left him alone with the false prophets. (p. 1141)

It is young Paul Trent, however, the gentle philosophical anarchist come to town from the Scilly Isles to observe Geard's socialist experiment in action, who puts his finger on the source of the Glastonbury malaise: "A feeling stole over him as if all the way down its long history Glastonbury, the Feminine Person, like Mary at the feet of the Master, had been waiting for the fuss to cease, for the voices to subside, for the dust to sink down" (p. 1046).

Like the Grail itself—Cauldron of Ceridwen or vessel of Christ's Blood—Glastonbury is a feminine presence, and she is deeply mistrustful of all the bustling, goal-directed human activity which the "new Revelation" has engendered in her womb. Murder is as nothing to Glastonbury, for she has experienced a multitude of such crimes in her long history; but she does fear rational human industry and has spent all her centuries of inscrutable calm resisting the wedge of purposeful behavior which men have attempted to drive into her bowels. Since the Midsummer Festival and the miracle performed at Chalice Well, Bloody Johnny has become a figure of legendary reputation, attracting hordes of wealthy pilgrims to his shrine from all over the world; and, ironically, Geard's bid to revive Glastonbury's ancient Mystery threatens her more than Philip Crow's concerted effort to destroy it. For the Grail can never be killed, but it may be comprehended; and Glastonbury above all does not wish to be grasped, even by her most devoted admirers. Indeed, she must remain beyond what even Powys can elucidate; and so, in "a trance of mindless passivity" (p. 1046), the Feminine Emanation of Glastonbury calls down upon herself a deluge to sweep away the ordered madness of humanity and return her great mystical body to the aboriginal chaos from which it issued.

For two ominous weeks in March the flood moves inland from the sea with the slow and terrible inevitability of some ancient prophecy fulfilled, bringing memories of "far-off mysterious disasters" and awakening in the low-lying Somerset vales "feelings that had not come to the population of those places for many a long year" (p. 1118). Yet there is no suggestion of divine retribution in the Glastonbury inundation as there is in the flood which concludes *The Mill on the Floss* (F. R. Leavis to the contrary notwithstanding). The rising of the waters is as purely natural and volitionless as a dream of god in the mind of man, or the sleeping thoughts of Glastonbury herself, "floating on its softly upheaving sea-surface of feminine breasts" (p. 779). It is simply element calling to element across the leagues of cultivated silt that separate the island-city from the sea. The winter-wasted land itself cries out for healing inundation:

> Liberated from the frost and ice of winter, a thousand unfrequented backwaters, bordered by dead, wind-swept rushes, clammy with salt-smelling marsh-lichens and thick-stalked glaucous-grey weeds, seemed actually calling out to the sea to come and cover their brackish pools. Salt amphibious growths, weeds of the terraqueous marshes, they seemed to be yearning, these neutral children of the margin, for the real salt sea to rush over them and ravish them. (p. 1115)

But the proud people of Glastonbury, preoccupied with exciting public events and their own newfound prosperity, go about their business heedless of the saltlike pungency of the air and the cries of gulls drawing ever closer. Bloody Johnny alone seems to realize the destructive magnitude of the approaching deluge and this only in the most personal sense. He has told his followers: "What matter if Arthur never *does* return. *I* am here" (p. 1142). But Geard's secret conviction is that when the flood waters pour through the streets of town, his work there will be finished and that like Glastonbury herself he must return to the element which gave him birth. Death presents itself to Geard as a completely natural function of his life, and the thought of suicide does not enter his mind. It is simply that his Master has called him to Himself and, as always, Johnny Geard obeys.

The deluge comes and is absolute, devastating both Philip Crow's industrial empire and the expensively designed paraphernalia of the Mayor's new religion; but most of the townspeople are saved (a bit miraculously, as all things happen in Glastonbury) by the intervention of the civil authorities. Bloody Johnny, however, has willed to die; and this resolve is only strengthened by his casual contact with the drowned corpse of a local beauty:

> No sooner had his hand encountered that ice-cold exposed bosom than he left it there, lying like a heavy horse-mushroom on the girl's breast. And with his hand resting there his face took upon itself the very expression of this dead woman. His eyes closed. His jaw fell open. His nostrils grew pinched and thin. Certain lines disappeared from his face altogether and certain completely new ones showed themselves. (pp. 1150-51)

Through that mystical sympathy with all created things which has characterized his life, Geard's death-change has already begun; and after rescuing Philip Crow from the half-submerged wing of his downed aeroplane, Bloody Johnny drowns himself rather clumsily on the site of the old Lake Village, the settlement of an early people who predated the Celts. His death agony is horrible because he has not allowed for the unnatural coldness of the water or the awful spasmic pain of suffocation; but when his body at last collapses and his grotesque struggling subsides, Geard achieves an "unbelievably delicious calm" and, dying to intenser life, sees the Grail:

> In calm, inviolable peace Mr. Geard saw his life, saw his death, and saw also that nameless Object, that fragment of the Absolute, about which all his days he had been murmuring. . . . It was as if he had ceased to belong to our world of looking-glass pantomime wherein we are driven to worship we know not what; and had slipped down among the gods and taken his place among those who cast their own mysterious reflections in the Glastonbury of our bewilderment.
>
> . . . In his dying moments, Geard of Glastonbury did actually pass, consciously and peacefully, into those natural elements that he had always treated with a certain careless and unaesthetic aplomb. (pp. 1170-71)

It is wholly appropriate that Johnny Geard should pass into the Grail (or perhaps into the mysterious "Esplumeoir") on this eminently pre-Christian and pre-Celtic spot; for as Powys has told us all along the great Mystery of Glastonbury precedes the Virgin Mary and Her Son, precedes Ceridwen and *Pair Dadendi,* the Cauldron of Rebirth, precedes even the Lake-dwellers themselves, reaching back beyond time to the uncreated chaos which existed immeasurably before there were ever men to dream of gods.

A Glastonbury Romance is itself a prose inundation corresponding to the torrential deluge that overwhelms the town; and just as floods do not end but subside, so the novel does not conclude with Geard's death but tapers off into a strangely beautiful epilogue invoking "the great goddess Cybele, whose forehead is crowned with the Turrets of the Impossible" (p. 1172). Though her name belongs to an earth-goddess of Asia Minor, Cybele has no specific mythological equivalent here. She is rather an incarnation of that in the cosmos which answers to the deepest spiritual yearnings of man, the "Unknown Dimension" from which the Grail proceeds; and her presence moves in darkness "from cult to cult, from shrine to shrine, from revelation to revelation," pre-existing and outlasting them all. But the end is not yet, for the "ribs of our ancient earth are riddled with desperate pieties" (p. 1173), and while man continues to aspire beyond the limits of the possible, she will sustain him in his faiths, mad and frantic though they be:

> For She whom the ancients named Cybele is in reality that beautiful and terrible Force by which the Lies of great creative Nature give birth to Truth that is to be.

> Out of the Timeless she came down into time. Out of the Un-named she came down into our human symbols.
>
> Through all the stammerings of strange tongues and murmurings of obscure invocations she still upholds her cause; the cause of the unseen against the seen, of the weak against the strong, of that which is not, and yet is, against that which is, and yet is not.
>
> Thus she abides; her Towers forever rising, forever vanishing. Never or Always. (p. 1174)

This enigmatic conclusion is perfectly consonant with the rest of the novel, for ultimately ***A Glastonbury Romance*** is a book which refuses to reduce itself to easy formulas. It does not so much defy analysis as evade it, disliking to be held; and perhaps because it is essentially a book about the wellsprings of our religious instincts whose major symbol is "older than the orbits of the stars," Powys did not intend that we should fully comprehend it. As he wrote in the "Preface" to the 1955 edition of the novel: "Its heroine is the Grail. Its hero is the Life poured into the Grail. Its message is that no one Receptacle of Life and no one Fountain of Life poured into that Receptacle can contain or explain what the world offers us."

G. Wilson Knight (review date February 1973)

SOURCE: "John Cowper Powys as Humorist," in *Contemporary Review*, Vol. 222, No. 1285, February, 1973, pp. 78-83.

[*In the following review, Knight highlights humorous excerpts from the works of Powys.*]

We could say that there are three main myths in modern Europe: the Faust myth, the Don Juan myth and the Prometheus myth; the first covering evil and tragedy, the second sex and comedy, and the third something ahead of us, Nietzsche's superman, an extension of human consciousness. Powys's fictions cover the first two, his philosophical books, ***In Spite Of*** especially, lay foundations for the third. Here I discuss, primarily, the play of humour suffusing, and at times dominating, his writings.

His letters are rich with it. It is usually a humour turned against himself, as when he imagines a publisher saying: 'Oh, that terrible heavy-weather John Cowper—What I say is, he's the only one of these buggers I know who has the gift of combining Risquéness and Dullness' (***Letters to Louis Wilkinson,*** June 23, 1936). His range of half-denigratory phrases applied to himself is unlimited, both in the letters and the ***Autobiography.*** He calls himself a charlatan, a zany, a clown. He likes clowns. In a letter to me of December 11, 1956, he said that he was 'a born actor but I suspect more still of a born Circus clown and lets hope *at my best* a born (Shakespearean or not) *Stage Clown*!'. There is an argument in ***A Glastonbury Romance*** as to whether they shall have a clown in the passion play, countering the Christ-story, with 'wild Rabelaisian gags' (XVII, 538 or 518.) A clown, sympathetically handled, is a well-developed personality in ***Weymouth Sands.***

Together with this pervading humility there is a corresponding courtesy to the reader. It would be an error to regard it as self-abasement. He knows his importance; he knows that he is a great genius; but this genius is one with his importance as clown, as outsider, almost as anarch. But within the anarchy is fun.

In the stories his humour is of the kindly sort. I once, writing of Byron's *Don Juan* in *Poets of Action* (page 259; originally *The Burning Oracle,* page 284), drew a distinction between (i) sympathetic and (ii) derisive humour. The first, which I regard as good, tends to dissolve all conventional valuations in what I called a 'golden centre'; the other, which is bad, wills to bring conventional critical judgements drawn from morality or religion to bear on this centre. Provided we remain serious there is no harm in this; moral satire has its place. The point is, we should not be amused during the process: moralistic humour is, for me, a contradiction in terms. The golden centre is not to be too precisely defined; it is common-sense; reality, things-as-they-are; above all, it is *sexuality.* Good humour is an approach to joy.

I offer an example of this dissolution of conventional appearance in the golden centre. In ***Wolf Solent*** (XIV, 300-2 or 284-6) the respectable Squire (who is also a Gothic monster), Squire Urquhart, and the disgruntled and unhappy poet, Jason Otter, are suddenly transformed by the sight of two village boys swimming naked in Lenty Pond. Of Otter's face we hear that 'Every trace of nervousness passed out of it and every shadow of misery. It seemed to be illuminated by some soft inner light. . . .' The Squire calling out 'Well done, Weevil! Well done!' as he watched 'the flexible muscles and slim back of the swimmer' is also transfigured:

> The Squire had the air of an innocent, energetic schoolmaster superintending some species of athletic sports. Jason had the look of an enraptured saint, liberated from earthly persecution and awakening to the pure ecstasies of Paradise.

Such was the effect on these two of 'the classic nakedness of the two youths'. A phrase that follows, 'the purged and almost hieratic look', is a key: we have watched a purgation, or *catharsis.*

This may be said to be an example less of humour than of what all good humour is, or should be, *for;* but it is also, at least where Squire Urquhart is concerned, extraordinarily amusing, to us, as we read. The respectable appearances that so torment humanity are dissolved into, not an obvious, certainly not a *respectable,* good, but an instinct. There is a radiant result. The incident is left undeveloped, or it might have ruined the book.

We find something similar, with a sharper play of actual humour, in an incident in ***Weymouth Sands*** (XIII, 488-9 or 469-70), where a girl, entranced by the bodies of boys bathing, asks the philosopher, Richard Gaul, if it is wrong of her? He replies:

> It seems to me, Peggie, what you represent at present is the third rung of the philosophic ladder to the Contemplative Ecstasy. When you have reached the ninth rung you will find—you will lose—I mean you will gain—

He is, perhaps fortunately, interrupted. All the idealisms of the race are gently toppled over by Gaul's hesitancy.

It need not be a matter of '*voyeur*' instincts, though these were, as we know from the ***Autobiography,*** strong in Powys. Central to Powys is the frank revelation of his own sexual secrets throughout the ***Autobiography.*** This conditions equally his humility before the reader and his humour.

Powys's scheme of things accepts a 'multiverse' in place of a 'universe'. He does not like things tidied up and mind-dominated into a system. The sign for 'universe' is 3, expressing the Trinitarian unity; the sign for a 'multiverse', signifying chance and the play of imponderables, is 4 (Whitman's 'square deific'). This means much to Powys and any conflict between the two views is to him important. And yet there is a speech in ***Porius*** where this conflict is, to me at least, rendered very amusing.

A fanatical Christian is speaking of Myrddin Wyllt, or Merlin:

> Oh, how that unholy, huddled-up monstrous toad hates the very name of the Blessed Trinity! He has even dared to declare, as Christ's poor servants in Caerwynt and Caerlleon and Caerloyw and Caerlyr have told me, that one of the worst of these devils in human flesh that those thrice-accursed Greeks called 'Philosophers', a prize-devil, a master-devil, a dragon-tailed devil, a great ramping, roaring, ram's-horn devil called Pythagoras, swore that the number *four* and not the number *three* was the secret of God's most holy cosmos! (XXI, 482)

Supervening on the genuine interest of the philosophic conflict adumbrated, there is a grand humour; and that humour suggests the provisionality of *all* philosophic argument.

That is why Powys was so fascinated by Rabelais, and wrote a study of him in the volume ***Rabelais,*** in which he, perhaps for the first time in world-literature, explains the nature and purpose of great, and often obscene, humour. Rabelais stands for life-worship against all religious and sexual taboos. He is 'the humorous prophet of the new Federation of the World' (VII, 359). His wisdom is variously defined: it is pre-eminently a child's wisdom; it comes from below rather than from above; it involves obscenities. He points the way to a multiverse of unsystematised possibility. He would liberate the 'unfathomable well-spring of creative force' within us (IX, 385).

Rabelais is a redeeming, purifying, power. In a poem called **"The Classic Touch"** (included in the Selection of Powys's poems edited by Kenneth Hopkins), Powys writes of himself in misery in a 'crowded town', repellent and ugly. Then his eye falls suddenly on 'a patch of ancient wall':

> And there an indecent sketch
> Limned by some laughing boy—
> O lovely and obscene wretch!—
> Swept from me all annoy.
>
> And the hideous iron place
> With its monstrous crowds and cars
> Was whirled into outer space
> And diffused among the stars.
>
> And alone by the fire with you
> I sat and read Rabelais—
> Rue des Beaux Arts, *mon loup*!
> And my soul was once more gay.
>
> And the old great shades returned,
> And the large sweet thoughts flowed free,
> And my heart within me burned,
> And that town was nothing to me!

It is natural that ***Rabelais*** should appear as a contrast to the sadistic horrors of ***Morwyn,*** that Sadists' Hell, to deliver a gospel of frank enjoyment of all sensual pleasures, provided that they contain no 'cruelty' (Part V, 313).

Here we come up against a crux. What if the sexual centres themselves are entwined with cruelty, with violence? Do they not cease to be golden? And does this not let in the whole range of taboos, moral and religious?

Well, Powys is not only our greatest—if not our only—authority on obscene humour, but he is also, very certainly, our first authority on evil. Both involve the sexual instinct. He knows in himself, and admits, a sexual-sadistic instinct. Powys does not of course claim to answer the problem of evil, since that cannot be done; but he does probe it, especially in that fearful study of Mr. Evans, the sadist, in ***A Glastonbury Romance.*** Mr. Evans has, and wrestles with, an ingrained compact with the Devil, his sadistic instinct, even more surely than Doctor Faustus. Suffering as he does from the ultimate evil within the First Cause he has insight into mysteries unknown to others. He is passionately concerned with what he takes to be the 'basic Secret of Life', as expressed in the ancient poem *The Harrying of Annwn* (XXV 843-4 or 807-9). He is here in a company of people discussing the formation of a Commune in Glastonbury, and is suddenly struck with some nameless absurdity:

> He suddenly burst into a spasm of suppressed laughter which had an extremely disconcerting effect upon the ears of his hearers. Mr. Evans was evidently on the edge of a shameless and vociferous laughing-fit caused by some interior vision which struck his mind as a monstrous Rabelaisian jest. . . . It was as if he had suddenly been permitted by a special dispensation of Providence to catch a glimpse of the monstrous cosmic joke, abominable, heroic, megalomaniacal, into which the whole creation resolved itself! (XXV, 843-4 or 808)

What that 'cosmic joke' is, is not defined; but when he quiets down, he urges that it is not 'money or position in life that makes the difference between happiness and unhappiness. It's something else . . . and when I think of how unimportant all these questions are in comparison with . . . I could . . . I would . . . ' (XXV, 845 or 810). He breaks off.

> His face which at this moment was a mixture of Don Quixote, the Devil, and Dean Swift, broke into certain deep wrinkles, evidences of another laughing-fit, which contorted it considerably, while he controlled and prevented the outburst.

Don Quixote, for Mr. Evans' battling with the evil; the Devil, for the evil nevertheless inextricably rooted in him; and Swift, for the scorn which this dual knowledge brings to bear on all social planning. The humour is derisive, but we should note that it attacks the superficialities in the name of a deeper reality; our reading of Powys's humour holds good. What Mr. Evans's outburst appears to signify is the appalling necessity of our uncovering and facing the 'basic Secret of Life', with a view to some kind of liberation. If he is thinking of his own ingrained evil, and he surely is (see XXV 847-9 or 811-813), sexual instinct is involved. This we must face, honestly, in all its perverted and obscene aspects, and, as far as may be, accept it, as a means to purgation. The implications of such an acceptance I have discussed elsewhere, in *The Saturnian Quest* and *Neglected Powers.* In Mr. Evans's hilarious outburst we have an extraordinary and probably unique impingement of the comedic on the tragic.

The tendency of Powys's later work favours the Rabelaisian gospel. In ***Atlantis*** Zeuks as humorist is certainly favoured as against his natural rival, the prophet of the mysteries, Enorches. Ajax, at the point of death, recounts how he had once looked for a 'laughing man' at the bottom of some mysterious hole, which seems to prefigure the tunnel of life, and now: 'A power tells me, you laughing one, that you are my dream come true' (VIII, 279, 281). Zeuks' humour is as a golden prize beyond, or within, the darkness.

In the important collection of Powys's letters to Nicholas Ross (Bertram Rota, 1971), Powys acknowledges his debt to Charlie Chaplin:

> What I am primarily and by nature is a mixture of a born clown and a born story-teller, and this was evidently clear to Charlie Chaplin when we met, for he taught me more of this art of combining clownery with oratory and with drama in my quarter of an hour with him, than I have learnt from any other person save Rabelais his wone self. (September 24, 1955)

Again:

> Yes, I am a born Clown and therefore just suited to write fairy stories as I have done since I was ten years old. . . . (February 9, 1960)

This relation of clowning to fairy stories is very interesting. Powys's last books were given a fairy story structure and planning. In them fantasy, which is a brand, or branch, of humour, is unfettered and possibilities unlimited, as in the essentially child-like quality and fairy-tale grotesquerie which Powys so loved in Rabelais.

Powys believed in children, and even solicits this belief to challenge the sadistic horrors. Writing to me on February 6, 1957, after urging that 'sex-maniacs' should 'use their imagination on themselves and not on others', he continues:

> I bet if Gilles de Retz had been ready to learn from me, from *Jack the Imaginary Ripper,* his 250 victims would have descendants still alive! But notice the proof that the wisest people in the world are children—I must not add old rogues in their *second childhood*!—and what are the wisest books in the world? Not the Bible or the Koran or the Vedanta but *Grimm's Fairy Tales* and *Mother Goose,* tales including *Blue Beard* in their

> scope. Jesus was right there. We grown-ups have no idea of what children see and know. . . .

Profound issues are involved.

In Powys's last stories, ***Up and Out, The Mountains of the Moon*** (published in ***Up and Out***) and ***All or Nothing,*** a children's fairy-tale manner is fused with space-fiction to bear on the deepest problems of Powys's life and work. These are reduced to simplicity and concretely expressed. Time and Eternity appear disadvantageously in ***Up and Out,*** and the people take a leap into another dimension to enjoy a spiritualistic existence for a while before dissolution. Space retains more honour, as ultimately the most real thing we know (***The Mountains of the Moon,*** 192). In ***Up and Out*** God himself engages in a friendly discussion as to the mess he has made of creation and whether he should have another try, and if so, what it should be like; and he comes again, in ***All or Nothing,*** as a Newt. ***All or Nothing*** uses a symbolism of creation and its opposite, 'Everything' and 'Nothingness' (VI, 40). In ***The Mountains of the Moon*** we have the delightful Terrestrial Milestones (152), objects from Earth's history collected on the Moon: the core of Eve's apple, a piece of the Ten Commandments, the heel of Achilles, a string from Nero's lyre, one of King Alfred's burnt cakes; most attractive of all, the Black and White Feathers from the Raven and Dove of the Ark, whose conversation is wonderful and whose union after long separation symbolises a union of dark and light. That these stories do indeed house much of Powys's most cherished wisdom may be supposed from the part played by giants in ***All or Nothing.*** The Cerne Giant, for so long a dominant power, actually comes to life, on the star Vindex, and delivers, in simple words, and for the first time in Powys's public writings, Powys's masturbatory doctrine (XXVII, 192).

All this can only be received if we respond to the story and its humour, as a child would. This is not to say that all the elements contained would appeal to a child, any more than in *Gulliver's Travels;* what the stories offer is a child-like approach to the profundities. Powys in old age saw himself as, in part, a child. On January 14, 1947, he wrote to me that he was thinking of composing

> something in praise of *Second childhood* for if *theirs* is the kingdom of heaven what about doubling 'theirs' with the dotage of a *second go* at that 'Something far more deeply interfused'?

And on February 27, 1957:

> I'd love to write a book entitled *Second Childhood* wherein I shall show the weird strange curious mysterious magnetic psychic *understanding* that exists between *really* old people such as I am now—much older than I was when I wrote ***The Art of Growing Old***—and Babies and Toddlers and *all children* up to 41 It is a most interesting thing. A week ago I went to see a Doctor . . . and in the Surgery waiting room we were about a dozen *adults* or even 15 and one tiny child of about 2. *It* and *I* sat gravely in the circle. Then very gravely I waved to it. And with equal gravity it waved back at me. It was just as if we had both said to each other: 'Lord! What fools these grown-up mortals be!'

On October 12, 1957, he told me that old age was 'the happiest of all the epochs of my life, the one I am enjoying now—which I know I am being absolutely correct in calling second-childhood.' He tells how he waves from his window to 'tiny toddlers between one and three-and-a-half', and they wave back.

Folly has become wisdom and wisdom folly: 'Lord! What fools these grown-up mortals be!' The clown and the child hold the secret. It is as old as the New Testament, and repeated by Blake, Wordsworth, Shelley and throughout Nietzsche's *Thus Spake Zarathustra,* with its progress from Camel, through Lion, to Child (I.i). It is also very modern. Powys is modern. He belongs to the age of the *Theatre of the Absurd* and the 'permissive society'. In a pluralistic and directionless universe of unlimited possibility these point, provisionally, ahead; to the change of consciousness of the Aquarian age adumbrated by Powys's books ***Obstinate Cymric, Rabelais*** and ***In Spite Of;*** which corresponds to Shelley's description (*Prometheus Unbound,* IV, 370-423) of the liberation of Prometheus.

George Steiner (review date 16 May 1975)

SOURCE: "The Problem of Powys," in *Times Literary Supplement,* No. 3819, May 16, 1975, p. 541.

[*In the following excerpt, Steiner discusses the reception of Powys's works in England and elsewhere.*]

There is, of course, a Powys problem. For G. Wilson Knight, perhaps the noblest of our critics, John Cowper Powys is a writer whose powers, whose visionary penetration and mastery of the concrete are, not in any loose metaphoric sense but by virtue of closely argued analogy and estimate, Shakespearean. Angus Wilson finds in Powys a novelist whose genius for comedy and crowd, for larger-than-life characters shaping and being shaped by the animate agencies of the environment is the rival of Dickens's. To a faithful circle of British readers, Powys is not only a supreme artist, but the great seer after Blake and a companion for life. No less than during his career as a charismatic lecturer—with members of the audience often following him from city to city—Powys continues to command an American and Canadian following. North American scholars, critics and bibliographers generate a growing body of Powys studies. The early novels—***Rodmoor, Ducdame***—have lately been translated into French and he is *au programme* both in the Sorbonne and among a devoted circle of younger scholars (of the publication, last year, of a remarkable Powys number in the review *Granit*). Powys's fiction and philosophy, his essays on literature and the meaning of human experience, are highly valued in Germany where he received the only major literary award given to him in his long and prodigal life. There are passionate Powysians in Japan.

A lecturer in English at Swansea, on the other hand, declares Powys to be an "old third-rate windbag". (the author of this remark is, to be sure, the most brutal of F. R. Leavis's imitators). More significantly the experiment undertaken by Penguin in issuing ***Wolf Solent***—an experiment whose success might have led to the publication in the same format of the other major works—proved abortive. The negative view taken at the time by V. S. Pritchett, a humane reader of wide sympathies, seemed to crystallize general indifference or distaste. An attempt to obtain an honorary fellowship for Powys on the occasion of his ninetieth birthday was rebuffed by Corpus Christi College, Cambridge, with the utmost arrogance; so far as he was remembered at all, the sometime member was a source of vague embarrassment. In his own country John Cowper Powys remained essentially unknown and unhonoured (there is a substantial growing archive at Churchill College).

This gap between Powys's place at home and abroad gives a clue. Though a proud descendant of Donne and Cowper, though "of the earth earthy" in Somerset and Dorset, Powys was, in certain crucial respects, alien to the British climate. It is not only that he wrote a number of his greatest books in upper New York State, and that he revelled in the spacious energies of the American way; nor is it a question of his persistent, eloquently proclaimed indebtedness to such Continental masters as Rabelais, Goethe, Nietzsche and Dostoevsky (though both these "alienations" matter). It is a central issue of personality, of register, of life-style. Wanderer, magus, rhetorician, John Cowper Powys did not feel himself to be a part of modern England, but rather a Celt with enigmatic "Jewish-Scotch" atavisms or, as he preferred to put it, a "Brython" of Immemorial strength and strangeness.

But these distances, in part literary and self-dramatizing, in part contingent (he spent many years in America because he could find no suitable work in England), cannot account for so drastic a disagreement in critical judgment. To some Powys is, beyond any question, a genius, a teacher of moral and philosophic values unique in the modern context and, together with Thomas Hardy and D. H. Lawrence, the greatest of British novelists in this century. To others he is either a bore, a charlatan, or both. Despite the notorious instability and modishness of literary "placements", particularly where the achievement of a recent figure is concerned, a split of opinion so wide and, apparently, uncompromising is, in fact, exceedingly rare. There is, customarily, a qualifying middle ground, an agreement over the range of useful disagreement which will lead, often fairly rapidly, to consensus. Over Powys there is, on both sides, a sense of exasperation or blank puzzlement. In such a case one had best state one's convictions.

I believe ***Wolf Solent*** to be one of the very great novels in the language, challenging comparison with *Middlemarch* by virtue of its intelligence of the range of its social comprehension, and comparable, as is perhaps no other English fiction to that realization of the meshing of human and natural presences which marks Tolstoy. ***Weymouth Sands*** (or ***Jobber Skald***) is a flawed composition, uneven in its distribution of narrative levels, but containing a wealth of characterization and landscape, of humour and symbolic incident which justify the parallels often drawn between it and the work of Dickens. There are excesses of style, of dimension, of incantation in ***Owen Glendower;*** at moments that black devil of sadism which Powys feared and exposed himself to so intensely, almost mars the fabric, the organic unfolding of the book.

But, choosing my words with extreme care, I would say that no other work in our literature, with the specific exception of Shakespeare's histories, themselves so creatively at hand in Powys's imagination, can match ***Owen Glendower*** in making a past present. Here, more than in Scott, the power of a writer to "dream backward", to furnish our sensibilities with felt remembrance of remote but formative experience, is tested and made tangible. The ***Glastonbury Romance*** defies any concise or confident valuation. The early chapters of erotic infatuation—with their physical candour so much fiercer, so much more charged with risk than were the guarded tactics of Lawrence—and the famous chapters of flood and apocalypse which complete the novel, are like nothing else in our prose. Again, certain characters are Shakespearean in their prodigality of being, of personal idiom, in the capacity they possess to lodge in our minds. But there are also grey stretches in this enormous design, loose ends and metaphysical-psychological soliloquies so insistent as to spill over into melodrama or idiosyncrasy.

Porius is a novel one attempts, retreats from, returns to with a deepening sense of magic and authority. Here size has become utter density, and philosophic speculations are fully embodied. The difficulties are extreme, not only because of the time and locale chosen (the marches of Arthurian Britain), or because of the incisiveness of mythological reference on which the narrative depends. They stem from a combination of violent incident with the subtlest introspection. The effect is, in the truest sense, uncanny, as if Rabelais's genius for physical action, for the enormity of matter, were shot through with a Jamesian focus on motive and nuance. It sounds absurd, but there it is.

Look at the scene in which Merlin crosses the river, in which Merlin's ambiguous nature and numinous motion literally metamorphose light and air, the pulse of identity in the animals and men who watch his coming, and you will experience a flash of vision ("flash" is wrong—it is more like light spreading across live waters at once rapid and stately) which no other writer has surpassed. And, to give that suggestion its entire vulnerability, let it include Shakespeare and Blake. ***Porius*** stands foremost, I think among Powys's novels. The book on Rabelais is the best of his literary philosophic criticism or, rather, "presentations"—for Powys was a presenter of other men's works more often than he was a judge. The ***Autobiography*** is a masterpiece, Coleridgean in its introspective scruple, but also of a lyric breadth, of a delight in the absurdities and wonder of self which recall *The Prelude.*

Why is it that these convictions will, even to many unbiased readers, seem bizarre? Why should it be that the case of John Cowper Powys offers no shared idiom for collaborative dissent?

Part of the answer, at least, is straightforward. There is so much more to Powys than the clutch of great novels and the autobiography, and the addenda are of a kind almost to destroy, to make endlessly irritating all but the best work. Starting late in life, driven by volcanic energies, he wrote far too much. There are in the books which come after ***Porius,*** and in such experiments as ***Maiden Castle*** and ***Atlantis*** remarkable pages, but too much of the continued outpouring was just that—garrulous, self-indulgent, rhetorical. The instinct for myth from which Powys drew his radical strength came to betray him. What had been illumination and a Shakespearian understanding of the life of imagery and symbolic act, turned into a farrago of Arthurian, Emersonian-transcendentalist and even Meredithian invocations and gestures (the line to Meredith would repay study).

Insights into the subconscious, once acute and unsparing, a genuine apprehension of the play of free forces around strong personalities and natural sites, turned into a tedious, vaguely bullying parapsychology. The man would preach with the relentless loquacity and sing-song innocence of a village saint. (Though even here embarrassment or scorn may be too facile a reflex: was Powys wrong when he insisted that men would find no cure for cancer or other major diseases so long as they tortured animals and practised vivisection in the name of medical research?)

The sense of silliness, of faddish obsession, of private cult, has been reinforced by the publication, over these past years, of Powys's correspondence with various intimates. Reasons of piety and economics (the books are not large) may explain such publication, but the effect has been disastrous. The idiom is one of tremulous homo-eroticism. This is, in part a matter of style, of Powys's personal roots in the world of Pre-Raphaelite and *fin de siècle* expression. But it points also to that enigmatic, partly autistic, partly encompassing sexuality (the current jargon would be "polymorphic") which lies at the centre of Powys's achievement, but around which there is to this day a barrier of silence or giggly allusion. (Wilson Knight's approach being the robust exception). In short Powys and Powysians have made it difficult for those who want to enter their world and discover the major books in their integrity.

These major books, moreover, are of a tonality and dimension wholly at odds with current habits of speech and of reading. For motives too complex, too serious to be casually enumerated, the climate of British feeling over recent decades has favoured ironic constraint, sparsity of idiom and shape. The normative posture is one of wary thrift or ironic deflation, in respect of style, theme, personal investment. The grand motion, the orchestral, the "copious", to borrow a term used by Donald Davie, are distrusted. These attitudes militate against a number of major artists. They have, until very recently, kept the work of Sir Michael Tippett from the pivotal, pre-eminent place which belongs to it in modern British music. They have, so far, prevented widespread response to the stature of David Jones. They may, in some measure at least, have inhibited the formation of that critical, corrective yet also collaborative circle of attention and discrimination which might have disciplined the gifts of Lawrence Durrell. What is certain is that Powys's writings, like those of the masters of Jacobean and baroque prose, demand an ear for the richness, for the cumulative sonorities, for the "drama" of the language of a kind which nothing in our present habits cultivates. Much of his work, like that of Carlyle and Ruskin, asks to be read aloud, so that the "swing of the sea" (Hopkins was yet another "aural" craftsman) or the rushing voices of wind and forest which give it its magic can be realized. ***Wolf Solent, A Glastonbury Romance, Owen Glendower, Porius*** call for patience, for a suspension of disenchantment, for a delight in the sheer prodigality of English speech as Shakespeare, Sir Thomas Browne, Melville or Ruskin used it. One must yield to the great music of these books, or they will remain closed. But the prerequisites of leisure, of "inner space", of trust and communal (Powys would have said "racial") pride which this act of reading, of audition depends on are precisely those currently in short supply.

This poses problems of tactics, of priority. Powys's letters to Iorwerth C. Peate, poet, writer, first curator of the Welsh Folk Museum, do not come under the damaging rubric of other marginalia. ***Letters 1937-1954*** shows Powys at his most characteristic; humorous, modest, voracious for new knowledge, engaged—for the benefit of ***Owen Glendower*** and ***Porius***—in transmuting himself into a true and obstinate Cymric. The letters show his wondrous isolation from the world (he had not heard of Albert Schweitzer until late 1944). They give clues to his bizarre politics: "I'm an *odd* Tory since my favourite poet is Walt Whitman." They document his fierce distrust of the brand of punitive Christianity and cultural reaction which he sensed, with unerring speed and directness, in the tracts and critical pronouncements of T. S. Eliot and C. S. Lewis ("these sly ones"). But publications of this type *are* marginal and, it may well be, a luxury at this stage in Powys's fortunes.

Is there not a case, indeed an urgent case, for the production of a compendious anthology, containing essential biographical and bibliographical information, together with generous selections from the major novels related, shown to be logically and organically interwoven, by a critical commentary? Objections to such a scheme are obvious ("how can one fairly select from books so densely put together, etc"). But it was precisely a *vade mecum* of this design, Malcolm Cowley's *Portable Faulkner* which, in the 1940s, broke through the esoteric status of Faulkner's work and made of it a main feature in the landscape. It is, in the meantime, good news that ***Wolf Solent*** is again in print and that the Village Press will reissue ***Porius.***

The question of biography is also a vital one. The ***Autobiography*** is a deliberately allusive, masked statement. It conceals or allegorizes far more than it declares. It is an intricate work of art, not a chronicle of the facts. But it is these we need to know. We need a life of John Cowper Powys, not merely glimpses of the Powys clan, telling us of the circumstances, locale, chronology which surround his writings, and informing us—within proper bounds of taste and respect for the sensibilities of the living—about what we ought to know of his passions and erotic convictions if we are to make good sense of the novels. Only a serious, full-scale biography can rescue John Cowper Powys from the cult-groups and whispering indirections of the Powysians, whose labours and enthusiasm have done a tremendous lot to keep the flame bright, but who have also, in fact, set barriers of initiation between Powys's genius and a general public.

Denis Lane (review date Fall 1981)

SOURCE: "The Reemergence of John Cowper Powys," in *The Antioch Review,* Vol. 39, No. 4, Fall, 1981, pp. 422-30.

[In the following excerpt, Lane favorably reviews Powys's major literary works in light of renewed interest in England.]

Pause at the bookstall of any airport or railway station in England and you are almost sure to find numerous handsome Penguin or Picador editions of the works of John Cowper Powys. Once a newsmaker in the United States, a popular figure of the lecturing circuit for almost twenty-five years, Powys is now largely unknown in America, except among a coterie of devoted scholars and those readers of novels who can remember the original publication of his works here in the twenties and thirties. All of this is likely to change. Should the planned serialization by British television of his vast ***A Glastonbury Romance*** result in its being imported by the American educational networks (a strong possibility in view of the present popularity of many televised versions of the English classics), then there will be a veritable resurgence of interest—such as has been seen in England over the past ten years—in the life and work of this extraordinary man.

John Cowper Powys (pronounced Poe-iss) was born in Shirley, Derbyshire, on 8 October 1872, but his formative years were spent in the Southwest of England, first at Dorchester, and then at Montacute in Somerset, where his father, the Reverend Charles Francis Powys, had been appointed vicar in 1885. All of this may seem unremarkable in itself, but John Cowper was the first of eleven children, most of whom went on to achieve distinction in one way or another. In addition to John, the brothers Theodore and Llewelyn became writers of note; Philippa was an essayist and poet, Gertrude an artist, while Marian, who subsequently emigrated to America, established herself as an authority on lace, which she appraised for the U.S. Customs Service. Seven of the eleven children, in all, were to publish books.

The self-insulating world of this late-Victorian family, "private and tribal," as one critic has described it, had enormous impact on Powys the writer. The shadow of the father looms large in Powys's early work, and although his ultimate, essentially humanistic viewpoint amounts to a stinging rejection of his father's staunch Christianity, it also represents an acceptance of the benevolent and sensitive spirit that accompanied it. Then too, Powys's love of nature, which can be found on every page of his novels and which invests them with their fibrous richness, was an inheritance from the father for whom, in Powys's words, nature was "part of his passionate—but totally subjective—romance of life." His early attachment to literature Powys acquired from his mother, a somewhat timid and enduring woman (portrayed lovingly by Llewelyn in his *Skin for Skin*) who was herself descended from the English poets Cowper and Donne. Though the family atmosphere was far from oppressive, there was nevertheless an inward orientation—a sense of separateness—that left a distinct imprint on some of the children, particularly when it came to establishing contacts in what was for them an "outside" world. Theodore, for instance, seems to have been claimed quite early in life by a sort of mental morbidity that he was unable fully to shake loose, while John, although subsequently renowned for his graciousness and amiability, was given at public school and university (Sherbourne and Corpus Christi, Cambridge, respectively) to the deliberate cultivation of bouts of mania and eccentricity.

It was in America that Powys was able to channel these neuroses in a positive direction, and it was in his novels—many of which carry figures of self-portraiture—that he submerged them. Powys first came to America in 1905, but it was an estrangement from his wife of fourteen years and the need to support an only son that in 1910 led him to pursue on a permanent basis the lucrative territory of America in his career as a public speaker. For almost a quarter of a century Powys crisscrossed the country, familiarizing himself with its cities and towns and, on endless walks ("one of my chief life-exigencies"), its suburbs and waysides. He traveled incessantly by train, knew the great railroad termini (few airports then) and the grand hotels of the day; spoke at such various places as the old Lincoln Center in Chicago, Cooper Union and the Labor Temple in New York, and at scores of colleges and universities throughout the South and Midwest. He debated publicly the likes of Will Durant and Bertrand Russell; secured the adoration of Isadora Duncan, the friendship of Theodore Dreiser, and the admiration of Henry Miller. On the platform, Powys was by all accounts a masterly performer, a truly magnetic personality who could command the attention of vast and varied audiences. In this, it seems, his striking physiognomy—a noble head dominated by searching eyes and topped with a mass of curly hair—served him well. Will Durant's 1931 portrait of Powys in *Adventures in Genius* provides an unforgettable description of the fantastic lecturer in high form: ". . . tall, thin, ungainly, angular . . . long arachnid legs, long simian arms, long, restless, pseudopodian fingers, the Word made not flesh but bone and naked nerves; the stooping carriage of a solicitous giant. . . . the trembling mouth of the poet . . . the eyes startled and piercing, hunted and hunting, tossed and pulled about with things vividly seen, haunted with mystery and frightened with understanding. . . ." This was the speaker who caused Ariel Durant, hearing Powys for the first time in New York, to rush home to Will to exclaim that she had just "seen Shelley plain."

Powys's subject was "culture"—in short, literature and philosophy—but it also included forays into political theory and social organization. He was a subtle analyst of capitalism and the capitalist frame of mind, as can be witnessed in print in his 1936 essay **"Farewell to America"** and in the characterization of the industrialist Philip Crow in ***A Glastonbury Romance.*** As a lecturer, his style and viewpoint were not to everyone's liking, however. His detractors called him a charlatan, a term that Powys, who was a genuine maverick and natural self-publicist, embraced with pride. "I am a born actor," he would frequently declare, adding that he was one who had "rebuked the mighty and exalted the leper."

This much is the public memory of John Cowper Powys—proselytizer, lecturer, ardent individualist—but along with this Powys was gradually building in America another reputation: that of writer. Typically, the output was prodigious, particularly when one considers the rigorous speaking schedule he was following at that time. In one eight-year period, 1915 to 1923, he produced no less than twelve books—novels, poetry, philosophy, autobiography, and literary criticism—together with countless articles in magazines and newspapers (the *Dial, Forum,* and *Scribner's* were favorite outlets). As Kenneth Hopkins notes, by 1917 Powys's public stature was sufficient to allow him to appear for the defense at the prosecution of the *Little Review* in connection with its publication of James Joyce's *Ulysses.* He was also an early defender of Dreiser when he too came under attack. Although Powys's own work never encountered difficulties of this type, it was some few years before it was accepted with anything approaching widespread admiration. The turning point occurred in 1929 with the appearance of two books: first, his powerful and unusual novel, ***Wolf Solent,*** the forerunner of what can be considered his major novels, and then, the highly successful ***The Meaning of Culture,*** the first of a series of books of popular philosophy consisting of eclectic and personal formulas for independent living, prototypes of which had appeared earlier in the Little Blue Books series of the Haldeman-Julius Company.

By this time Powys had reached the age of fifty-eight, a late start for a writer but one that he seized with relish, especially now that, having retired from lecturing because of ill health, he had taken up residence "deep in the land of the Mohawks," at a Dutch cottage near Hillsdale in upstate New York. "I have what I've never had before," he wrote to one of his brothers, "*real time* to write in, hours and hours of time. I can shuffle time, like you shuffle snow, in a great wooden spade." It was there, and in North Wales, where he finally settled in 1935, that Powys produced the five or six novels that are his masterworks, and where also he was to write the work entitled ***Autobiography*** (1934), that astonishing piece of self-revelation that J. B. Priestley justly describes as "one of the greatest autobiographies of the English language."

While Powys was to celebrate his energetic years in America ("incomparably the best years of my life") in both the autobiography and the essays of the period, America nowhere appears in his central novels. That world remains, in surface texture at least, the world of his childhood, of Dorset and Somerset, and in two later novels the historic world of the Powyses' ancestral Wales. The westcountry wanderings of the eponymous Wolf Solent, for instance, clearly replicate those of Powys's own younger days, as is reflected in his 1961 preface (written, with amazing clarity, when he was eighty-nine): "***Wolf Solent*** is a book of Nostalgia, written in a foreign country with the pen of a traveller and the ink-blood of his home." Yet to say that Powys's novels center upon Wessex is to define only partly the world they inhabit, for his vision is so copious and so extensive that ultimately their true setting is nothing less than the cosmos itself. In brief, they debate the nature of the universe and man's place within it. Like later novels, the seminal ***Wolf Solent*** reveals Powys's belief in the transforming powers of the human will and the human imagination, and his belief—so germane to us today—that every man and woman has the creative potential to shape a future of happiness and self-fulfillment, irrespective of the particular circumstances under which he or she labors. Thus all of his novels exist as imaginative efforts to reconcile this faith in individual creativity with the reality of human experience. From Wolf Solent, his first major figure, to Porius, his last, he maintains a long line of characters bound up in a state of "deep contemplative tension," each calling upon his will's "unbounded power," and each in his own manner fulfilling the Powys credo that the universe is "always capable of being further discovered and further created."

On the surface, Powys's philosophy, as espoused in novels and essays alike, appears to argue against the cultivation of ordinary contacts with human society—a communion with nature, for instance, is always depicted with prominence as a saving grace in life—and there is no doubt that collectively they abjure the modern world, just as they implicitly question modern religion and modern philosophy. Yet they remain deeply human. They concentrate primarily upon individual dramas, dramas seen less in relation to the present than to the past, but that nevertheless combine trenchant insights into social, sexual, and familial relations in modern life. The climax of ***Wolf Solent,*** a study of emotional evolution in a young man of severely introspective habits, occurs behind a pigsty—a typically Powysian metaphor of the modern world—when Wolf's mental turmoil is finally put to rest in a vision that replaces his previously complacent idealism with the realism inherent in a life based upon perpetual renewal and endurance. Such a note of psychological pragmatism, embodied in a novel of eloquence and descriptive beauty, led Theodore Dreiser to comment that it "holds speculations so intense, so searching and ennobling as to suggest little less than revelation—at their lowest ebb high poetry."

If ***Wolf Solent*** was to establish Powys's reputation, then his next novel, ***A Glastonbury Romance*** (1932), served to confirm it. The binding element in this huge, labyrinthine chronicle—estimated by one critic to be the longest undivided novel in the English language—is the mystical and spiritual ethos of Glastonbury, whose impact Powys tests upon his characters. The focus, wide and all-inclusive, falls now upon numinous rather than emotional awareness. We are here truly in the domain of the Powys novel: characters are many and Dickensian in variety (the front matter lists forty-seven "principal" characters alone); events encompass the dramatic and the miraculous (a crucifixion, a devastating flood, a murder, even an exorcism); mood is intense and quickened by the spiritual presence of figures of myth and tradition; a rich iconography interweaves the ancient with the modern, the historical with the legendary. The novel is the outgrowth of Powys's lifelong interest in religious and philosophical creeds. Thematically, it deals with the religious response to life. It is a searching examination, conducted by means of exempla and personal experience. The stories of John Crow, Sam Dekker, and "Bloody Johnny"—John Geard, the street-corner revivalist turned provincial guru—all contribute in various ways towards a definition of what is religious in life and to an explanation of the origins of religious instinct. In the course of his investigations, Powys questions many systems of values, even at times his own, and it may be these episodes (by their presence if not their substance) that are the most significant and the most telling. Some critics have suggested that in this way Powys deserts the reader, by providing no positives, no definitive answers, but such is exactly his intention. "I try to advocate," he wrote in the preface to a 1955 edition, ". . . an acceptance of our life in the spirit of absolutely undogmatic ignorance," and he would argue that a book is worthless that pretends to solve life's mysteries with a system. Despite its underlying tone of philosophical circumspection, ***A Glastonbury Romance*** stands as a wonderfully human document. Panoramic in design, charged with scenes of great vividness, and informed by its author's quizzical vitality, it is nothing less than a giant of a novel. Its style is unmistakably Powys's own: a sweeping, stirring prose, rich in elemental imagery and archetypal symbol. There is no doubt that it will make superb television; indeed, it would be a fine instance of poetic justice, for tragically Powys himself never made a penny from the novel—its royalties being swallowed up by a disastrous libel suit brought by a westcountry landowner.

There followed two more novels with Wessex settings. The first, ***Weymouth Sands*** (1934)–"my seaside tale," as Powys fondly called it—was the last product of his American years. Its integration of separate narrative episodes into an all-inclusive mixture of humor and pathos makes ***Weymouth Sands*** the most innovative, the most compact, and, for many readers, the most enjoyable of his novels—"a happy book" is how G. Wilson Knight describes it. Its message concerning the triumph of perseverance over despair is worked out through a series of streams of consciousness, overlaid by, or set against, the cumulative metaphors of the book: the sea, the sands, the rocks, and the settlements of the Dorset coastline. In short, ***Weymouth Sands*** is a novel of the margins, its sands the margins of consciousness, where the psychic residua of its characters are confronted and laid bare. The Weymouth area was, interestingly, the final resting place of John Cowper Powys, for it was at Chesil Beach, one of this novel's central locations, that his ashes were scattered following his death in 1963. After ***Weymouth Sands*** came ***Maiden Castle*** (1936), a moral fable about the negative powers of presumption. Here, in a novel written during a year's stay in England, Powys broke new ground as he began to give full rein to his mythopoeic genius. Set in and around the great neolithic earthwork of Maidun, near Dorchester, the novel presents a fascinating study of human relationships, of their fruition and decline, within a close circle of what Powys called "enemy-friends," and of the abrasions and incompatibilities that can result from close and repetitive contacts. These difficulties are heightened by the claim of one of the characters to powers of reincarnation, a claim that Powys, though judicious in his depiction of the reactions of other characters, did not entirely diminish. At the novel's core are considerations of pain and cruelty, death and the past, a combination that caught the eye—not surprisingly perhaps—of the late Dennis Wheatley, whose works explore these murky areas.

The homecoming to Wales marked Powys's final phase, but his energies were by no means depleted: two of his best novels and a cluster of fantasies, the products of extreme old age, were yet to come. Wales, never far from the center of Powys's imagination (his family traces its descent from the ancient Welsh princes of Powysland), consumed it entirely when he made his eventual move there in 1935. Thinking of himself then as an "Aboriginal Welshman," Powys renewed his lifelong interest in the history and literature of Wales and in later years even learned to read and write Welsh, a feat of considerable proportions in view of the acknowledged difficulty of the language and his own advanced age. This deep-rooted interest in the culture and traditions of his adoptive home was poured lavishly into the work of his last twenty-five years. Where Powys had moved gradually into the past with the historic associations of the ***Romance*** and ***Maiden Castle,*** in ***Owen Glendower*** (1940) and ***Porius*** (1951) he broke with the present entirely to re-create, in fifteenth-and fifth-century settings respectively, two panoramic episodes in Welsh history. ***Owen Glendower,*** following in its broadest outline the known facts of its hero's great rebellion against the English, is a marvelous blend of historicity and vision, of mythology and romance, and for this it has won high praise from such eminent voices as those of Angus Wilson and George Steiner. Essentially, the novel is a restatement of Powys's earlier theme of self-determination, only this time in terms of national rather than individual significance. ***Porius,*** however, is a world unto itself just as, equally, it is the summit of Powys's achievement. Eight years in the writing, ***Porius*** is in fact a mythic rendering of Powys's personal creed and his candescent belief in the existence of "an old human vitality . . . that will yet make *man,* rather than any Man-God, or God-Man, the creator of man's future." The novel's brilliant and teeming action, couched in an atmosphere that is both elemental and regressive, is too complex to summarize. But this much can be said: that for all its atavism of mood and setting, ***Porius*** is nonetheless a manifestly twentieth-century novel, and it is so because it presents a doctrine that finds philosophical solace in variety rather than in any ultimate or absolute theory. It speaks to an age that, like the Dark Ages in which it is set, is fraught, in Powys's words, "with the terrifying possibilities of human disaster," but it does so in terms that iterate the power of diminishing such possibilities and stress the view that good, whether in "fellow-feeling" or "kindness," is capable of increase. It was perhaps this work more than any other that spurred G. Wilson Knight to nominate Powys for the Nobel Prize in Literature in 1959. (Although Powys did not win the Nobel—the honors that year went to Salvatore Quasimodo—he had the previous year been the recipient of the Plaque of the Academy of Arts of Hamburg, a distinction granted previously to only one other novelist, Thomas Mann.)

It is upon the six novels that I have mentioned and the autobiography that future interest in John Cowper Powys will undoubtedly center. These works represent a unique and impressive achievement. Their concerns are as wide as they are profound. They attempt to find or portray an actual, valid, and preeminently practical interpretation of the universe. For some readers they offer alternate values to those held by the twentieth century; for others they offer pragmatic advice on living one's life in a spirit of courageous acceptance. Collectively, Powys's novels are a forceful antidote to the Age of Anxiety. They are written out of an affirmative spirit, capturing with richness and with vision man's organic desire for peace and happiness, yet they do so without blinking at ultimate problems of human perversity, suffering, and death. A reasonable optimism is how we might best characterize the moral legacy of John Cowper Powys.

A. N. Wilson (review date 22 April 1995)

SOURCE: "Strangest of Geniuses," in *The Spectator,* Vol. 224, No. 8702, April 22, 1995, pp. 32-33.

[*In the following review of* Petrushka and the Dancer, *Wilson credits Powys's companion Phyllis Playter for her inspirational support.*]

It would be interesting to know how these diaries would strike a reader who did not know the four great novels of John Cowper Powys: ***Wolf Solent, A Glastonbury Romance, Weymouth Sands*** and ***Maiden Castle,*** or his magnificent collection of essays, ***The Pleasures of Literature;*** or his superb essay on **"The Art of Happiness,"** or his ***Autobiography,*** which deserves to be placed on the shelf beside Saint Augustine and Rousseau. In the period covered by these journals, all these great books were produced.

Powys is one of those authors who is omnipresent in his work. To read his novels is to be confronted with his extraordinary personality—his 'manias', his pantheism, his vivid empathy for the sorrows and joys of women (springing from what he called his lesbianism), his passionate love of the Wessex of his childhood, his preoccupation with domestic trivia, his Homeric sense of the blank human tragedy. While becoming engaged with the lives and struggles of his characters, we are perpetually aware that he is there too, both as the narrator, and—for he is one of the greatest of clowns and play-actors in the history of literature—as most of the characters in the books.

In ***Weymouth Sands,*** for example, it was perfectly obvious to me (though I knew next to nothing of his biography when I first read it) that Powys 'was' the diffident teacher of Latin, Magnus Muir, obsessed by his 'crush' on the promiscuous Curly Wix, and by the brooding presence in that seaside resort of his dead father. Equally obvious was the fact that the author 'is' the crazy figure of Sylvanus Cobbold, the madman who 'prays' to his bit of rope with the frequently repeated mantra, '*Caput anus, caput anus*', and who has an 'unsuitable' but passionate relationship with the sylph-like, just-pubescent daughter of the Punch and Judy man.

In this diary, we discover that this peculiar relationship—one of the most touching in all modern fiction—was suggested to Powys by his life-companion Phyllis Playter, known in the diary as the T. T.—the Tiny Thin:

> She thinks all the time. And now she has thought out a wonderful idea for my book—about making Sylvanus Cobbold into a revivalistic preacher with a little idiot or subnormal girlfriend.

She it was, incidentally, who gave Powys the name of his most vigorous male character in the book—Jobber Skald. Inspired! We could not have guessed, unless we had read these diaries, what labours, imaginative and intellectual, the T. T. expended on helping Powys with his creations—reading drafts, being brave enough to condemn as well as to praise, and seeing into the life of this strangest of geniuses. She does almost emerge from the diaries as his co-author.

But, for that large proportion of the reading public who have never read these novels, these great novels, these greater by far than D. H. Lawrence or James Joyce novels, these novels which are of a world class, and whose neglect by the British reading public is one of the weirdest mysteries, to this unread majority, how will these diaries appear? They tell the story of a strange old man, (57 when the book starts) sharing a small flat in New York with his little sylph, the Tiny Thin, their doll Olwen and their dog, sometimes called the Black, sometimes called the Old. Powys earns a living as a hack lecturer, going from town to town in the United States to hold forth on varied literary topics. He was preoccupied in almost equal measure by the huge tribe of his English relations and their shared childhood in Sherbourne and Weymouth, and by the hellish consequences of his duodenal ulcer. His rigid diet of milk, eggs and bread and butter, and the inevitable resultant constipation, is one of the diaries' most repeated themes:

> This morning—for I took three Pills last night—my stiff and obdurate Bowels worked all right & dung hard as Owl Pellets or Ichthyosaurus turds were driven out of my throbbing bum-gut.

On many mornings, he was less fortunate:

> It was as if through my bum-gut I was giving birth to a Cannon-ball. I could not make it go out nor could I draw it back.

His fumbling adventures with the enema—he was so clumsy that the T. T. eventually took to 'helping' him with it—take up almost as much diary-space as his literary reflexions. ('The T. T. doesn't like too much space in my diary devoted to Number 2!'. One knows how she felt.)

The diaries, like everything else he wrote, were designed to be read first and chiefly by her. 'Shakespeare led a life of allegory; his works are the comments on it', wrote John Keats. The same is true of John Cowper Powys, which is what makes this diary so remarkably revealing a document, for in its pages we feel that we are close to the very heart of his creative process. His love for his little 'sylph', their complicated and difficult life-pilgrimage—from New York City to Phudd Bottom in New York State; from Phudd Bottom to England, where they lived first in the wilds of Dorset (where the T. T. was wretchedly miserable) and then in a poky flat in Dorchester—are turning themselves all the time into those magisterial and peculiar and endlessly readable novels.

The most powerful evocation of their relationship is probably to be found in ***Maiden Castle,*** where the ineffectual Dud Noman's inability to satisfy the emotional needs of Wizzie leads to one of the most dramatic emotional dénouements in English fiction. (Why has it never been taken up by the feminists?) When she read ***Maiden Castle,*** which she did, chapter by chapter, aloud to the author, the T. T. was bitterly upset. 'Is this the result of our 15 years' life together?' The mistake she made, Powys adds,

> was not taking into account the maniacal convolutions of my reserves! As I left out my mother from my ***Autobiography***, so in dealing with Noman & his girl I dodged and avoided any introduction of the precious and indescribable pleasures of every sort that I myself have got from living with the T. T.

That it was a love-match of the deepest kind cannot be in question. After their tiff about ***Maiden Castle,***

> in the morning after breakfast I made love to the T. T. . . . in the Passage! And this pleased me; for this immorality christened, as it were, our dwelling.
>
> It is extraordinary how our emotional imaginations are identical—'the T. T.'s' and 'The Man's'. It is a mystery considering how, when she came in that big young-girl-of-24 hat with a brim I caught her wrist as my white slave for purely wicked reasons—never did I know (when I wrote her name in the dust) how our emotional nervous imaginations were destined to display absolute identity.

This being the case, Powys's diary is not merely the egotistical ravings of a self-proclaimed genius. It is a moving tribute to the woman who helped to fashion him as a writer. None of the books which he wrote before he met her were any good. And I think one finds the clue to what is so memorable and exciting about the novels in this entry:

> After breakfast the T. T. talked with extraordinary eloquence about that experience of life—that thick, rich feeling of life made up of a vast number of tragic experiences or experiences observed in others or just intuitively grasped even if you live in one place all your days. This deep life-feeling she says is the chief thing! Shakespeare & Dostoievsky have it & Dickens a little too but not Balzac. Tolstoy has it. She says I spoil it in my books by Propaganda.

It is really the case that in the four great novels, Powys, almost alone among the English prose writers, achieves this quality of felt life which one discerns in Shakespeare. Equally, we can salute the T. T.'s good judgment in despairing of his mad preacher, or bardic wizard side. Not that she was any more sensible than he was. Their shared whimsy, their devotion to their doll Olwen, for example, will not please every reader. (In one strange entry, Powys achieves an erection merely by stroking Olwen). The belief that the Powyses were ancient kings of Wales, and their move to that Principality for the last 28 years of their shared life marked the change in his writing from modern romance to Welsh history and mythology. (There are some ludicrous photographs, one of which depicts Powys in bardic robes and a mitre, with the T. T. wearing a sinister-looking papier-maché mask.)

It was the T. T. who urged all this upon him, encouraging him, for example, to write ***Owen Glendower,*** which must be a masterpiece which has defeated all but the most ardent Powysians. Ditto the impressive, but at 900 pages surely the most unfinishable Dark Age Romance, ***Porius.*** Yet greater pens than mine—Angus Wilson's and Irish Murdoch's, for example—have expressed admiration for these works.

Will this diary, punctiliously edited and cut down to manageable size by the admirable Dr Krissdottir, lead to a Powys revival? Will those who enjoy the novels of Martin (or come to that Kingsley) Amis see the point of making the great imaginative journey through ***A Glastonbury Romance*****?** It took the foolish things of the world to confound the wise, and the weak things of the world to confound the strong. I fear that John Cowper Powys's extreme oddness (which made his schooldays at Sherbourne such torture, and which isolated him socially from all but his enormous family and his close circle of friends) will put people off.

The point to grasp about Powys is that while much of what he thought and wrote is profoundly eccentric, he is in fact one of the great mainstream European writers, who tackles the themes of love between men and women, and the peculiar manner in which societies cohere. His characters confront the Nature of Things with a baldness and raw vivacity which makes comparisons with *King Lear* seem quite reasonable. He tried to do for the novel what Homer did for the epic. When we read these diary accounts of domestic trivia, lavatory agony, money worries and correspondence with unsympathetic publishers and agents, and of the poor T. T.'s repeated gloom and despairs, we can only marvel the more that out of such strange earthen vessels such glory sprang forth.

John Bayley (essay date 19 May 1995)

SOURCE: "A Seer of the Flesh," in the *Times Literary Supplement,* No. 4807, May 19, 1995, pp.3-4.

[*In the following excerpt, Bayley praises* Petrushka and the Dancer *and* The Letters of John Cowper Powys to Frances Gregg, Vol. 1 *(edited by Oliver Marlow Wilkinson and Christopher Wilkinson).*]

It seems unlikely that the critics will ever resolve the question of John Cowper Powys's status as a novelist. There is no version of the canon, or the "hundred best novels", in which his inclusion is taken for granted; he is not a standard author in any series, or regularly revived in paperback, like most classics. But in a sense this absence is itself his status. It seems to keep him absurdly, disconcertingly alive, while the *oeuvre* of James Joyce, say, becomes more purely monumental by the year. The Joyce industry works on the monument like the restorers on the Albert Memorial; whereas the Powys cottage industry goes on in its own slightly dotty way, disputing his philosophies, teasing and worshipping in equal measure, losing faith and regaining it. Even D.H. Lawrence, for all his aliveness (and Powys was a passionate admirer of the Lawrence letters), does not reach, as it were, this extraordinary gusto of ongoing literary instability.

Powys's diaries are as compulsively readable as Lawrence's letters; they are so clearly the groundwork, in both authors, of all their other writings; and with the same kind of personality informing them, very different as the two personalities are. Powys was a natural diarist, like Kilvert, inhabiting the daily form with the same clumsy ease with which his cast of characters inhabit the novels. Only in his ***Autobiography***—a form in which Powys never seemed quite at home—and in some of his didactic and philosophical works, does the Powys personality lose its magical feel of closeness and elusiveness and appear ordinarily self-centred, cranky and prosaic. Of course, even when he is at his most mesmeric it is never difficult for his reader—his "dear far off reader wherever you are" as he calls him in the diary—to "see through" Powys, just as nothing is easier than to see through Lawrence. But then, as the great writer Elias Canetti once more or less remarked, seeing through great writers gets you nowhere.

Selected and skillfully edited by Morine Krisdóttir, doyenne among Powys scholars and devotees, the diaries begin on June 1, 1929, with Powys leaving New York, and his usual gruelling round on the American lecturing circuit, for his annual holiday with relatives and friends in England. He is fifty-six. Both he and his younger brother Llewelyn ("Lulu") have become well known as lecturers in America. His last novel, ***Wolf Solent*** is selling well, and so is ***The Story of Philosophy.*** He is beginning to write ***A Glastonbury Romance*** and ***The Meaning of Culture.*** As Arnold Bennett had found (both Powys and Phyllis Playter, his companion, were great admirers of *Clayhanger*), a novelist who was well known or becoming well known in those hopeful days of idealisms and urges towards learning could greatly increase his earning power by turning out, between novels, books on the hundred best books, with titles like ***The Pleasures of Literature, The Art of Happiness, A Philosophy of Solitude,*** and even ***In Defence of Sensuality,*** although Powys's publisher, Mr. Schuster, was a little worried about that one.

Back in England, Llewelyn is living on the Dorset coast, between recurrences of his tuberculosis, with his wife Alyse Gregory and his mistress Gamel Woolsey, now pregnant by him and about to have an abortion, after which she will decide to leave him and to marry Gerald Brenan. Alyse always treated Gamel, at least in public, with great kindness and consideration, and if her husband tried to bully his elder brother (they were in fact a very close pair), she would shake a finger at him and say "Mr. Powys shouldn't do that". John Cowper's enormous shrewdness and innocence entered with relish into this 30s world of "indescribable intrigues and cross-currents of all these conflicting personalities", as he happily called them. ("Lulu came to see me in bed, and as he went downstairs he said 'some people love me, but others think—'".) They all engage together in a complex idyll, hunting flints and fossils in the cliff ("I begged them to desist from this tiresome antiquarian pursuit"). Then Lulu, Gamel and Alyse are all busy downstairs cooking haddock for John Cowper, "because it is my favourite fish"; and Lulu bathes and runs naked along the shore. "Turned to meet him and embraced him all dripping and drenched with sea-salt—watched him rejoin Alyse and Gamel. Contemplated their three figures . . . Lulu naked, the two women clothed—like Epicurus with Leontion and Ternissa. Like Odysseus with Calypso and Nausicaa."

Two Powys sisters, Gertrude, a painter, and Philippa, a poet, are also living near by—Marian, another sister, had emigrated to New York where she runs a successful lace shop—and John Cowper leaves to visit his own wife and son in Sussex. He has never lived with his wife, but as she is very religious he has never divorced her, and their son Littleton, christened after the second oldest Powys brother, has become an Anglican priest.

> Had a *very* happy breakfast with my son and heard him defend the art of dissimulation and diplomacy . . . how surpassingly beautiful his face does become at times—his complexion like a sea-shell and his eyes glaucous and luminous. He has sometimes an *angelic beauty.* He said he felt a gentle diffused amorousness to girls. . . . His sweet-natured tact between two such eccentric and selfish devils as his mother and me is beautiful and touching to see. He told me he would like to be a farm labourer–"old Father Powys"—and sometimes be allowed to say Mass by the parson. I think he is *very* like Alyosha.

Powys was a ritualist in his own way, a one-man Shaman or "super-ritualist" as he called himself; and yet these processes involved an absurdity of freedom and humour which liberated every mystical or mumbo-jumbo act. His phrase for what was quintessentially personal in himself, or in anyone else—our "Life Illusion"—aptly shows the whole ambiguous but unharmful gusto of his being: what we live by is not an "illusion", because it *is* what we live by, but the word "illusion" expresses both the absurdity and the necessity of being oneself; and this extraordinary diary seems to sum up the whole essence of that self-generating being. Nothing in his Life Illusion can be described in any other way than the way that he does it, as a poem can only in its own words be itself. "Tao" or "Zen" become totally inert terms if they are invoked in this context; and yet they are, of course, related to it. When Wolf Solent, in the novel of that name, sees the root of an alder diving inconspicuously into the dark river water, the act it tells him of is not that of Wordsworthian nature but a sudden and intense enhancement of his own Life Illusion. And the commonplaceness of such moments is part of their joy, as is in the diary an inconspicuous, almost unnoticeable reference to sheep passing "thro' the shadows of the ash-tree whose roots by the wooden palings I look at".

In a luminous introduction, Dr. Krisdóttir comes as close as one can do to conveying the remarkable qualities of the diary. Powys's fascination, as she notes, "lies in his ability to pass through boundaries as if boundaries did not exist. For him there was no demarcation between the outer world and the inner, no gap of desire between the self and the not-self. He clasps 'some extremely provocative embracing trees that I call the Lesbians', and the embracing trees are . . . identical with his body." In a sense and if Wordsworth should be in question, Powys lived all his life in the state whose withdrawal from Wordsworth himself is recorded in the Immortality Ode.

It is the total lack of "mysticism" in any ordinary sense that appeals so strongly in the daily record here, with an appeal like Kilvert's, but, of course, far more shameless and explicit than anything personal in Kilvert's themselves sometimes surprising paragraphs. To quote Dr. Krisdóttir again: "the world that is Powys is displayed in the Diary matter-of-factly, dispassionately—his self-centredness, his sadism, his sexual fantasies, his sicknesses, his shamanistic rituals, blandly poured out for the reader. In our world of carefully created borders this antic eccentricity, this elliptical off-centredness, is either violently rejected or passionately accepted."

I would not quite agree that one needs either to accept or reject Powys, still less that there need be anything violent or passionate in the process. To paraphrase Canetti again, either to worship or to write off a great phenomenon and a great literary identity like Powys gets you no further than "seeing through it" would do. Communion is the point; and communion with him through the diary, or in the earlier novels, can be as effortless as it is intimate and undignified, involving no sense of our interrogating another person. Instead, we are with Powys, say, on the train which carries him on his last extended American lecture tour, a *via dolorosa* of dyspepsia from his ulcer in town halls and pretentious hotels. It was preceded by a public debate at Utica between himself and Bertrand Russell on whether marriage was or was not a good thing. Powys, faithful all his life, after the rapid failure of his own marriage, to his odd companion Phyllis Playter, thought it was. Russell dryly disagreed. Outside the hotel in Pittsburgh, he has an experience similar to that of Wolf Solent with the miserable man on Waterloo Steps; and it makes him feel he has "the soft fussy egotistic coward soul of an Archdeacon". Then he is back in the train at Racine, seeing the light on the cold lake. "Very hostile to me all whiteness except the girl's body I love. I don't like the idea of the Beatific Vision being whiteness. I like it to be green or sometimes blue. Dyspepsia bad and a long long lunch. A wild reckless lecture on Dostoevsky."

The vanished world of the American lecture circuit, in which Powys was Ancient Mariner and Don Quixote, Moses with his tables and the old man of the sea, made strenuous demands on those who panned its gold for their livelihood. "Once on this accursed tour my stomach was so upset that I dreamt of nothing else but going to look for places where I could *shit* in peace." He feels he has become like his own father, the patriarchal rector of Montacute, "an old lonely deep *animal*", "some savage constipated panther like my father when my mother was dying; and he cried out 'Can't I even have my breakfast in peace?'"

In the summer of 1930, he and Phyllis Playter—known in the diary as the T. T., the "Tiny Thin", the "Tao", or the "terminals"—retired thankfully to a little house at Phudd Bottom (superlatively Powysian name!) near Hillsdale in upper New York State. There the diary takes on its characteristic and absorbing density, recording walks with the black spaniel "the Old", progress on ***A Glastonbury Romance,*** ulcer pains and enemas, often administered by the T. T. and necessitated by his peculiar diet. Occasionally they are distracted by a visit from Edna St. Vincent Millay, who lives not far away with her husband, and he needs a little whisky then to calm his nerves after the social gin-drinking. There is the stove problem, and the cold of the winter. But the most real, and as it seems involuntary, achievement of the diary is the gradual creation of the two characters, himself and his beloved, and the way in which their two personalities emerge quite separately, and as it were laboriously, from the vivid but disjected prose, like creatures with wings slowly uncrumpling from a chrysalis. The apparition of the T. T.—her kindness, her irritation, her pining for town life, her house-proudness and her menstrual troubles—brings to life a person who is whole and complete in herself, and in no way dependent on the patronage of masculine shaping or viewpoint. Especially alive is the T. T.'s American seriousness, which Powys revered, and himself took very seriously as the utterance of an inspiritive muse."

> After breakfast the T. T. talked with extraordinary eloquence about that *experience* of life—that thick rich feeling of life made up of a vast number of tragic experiences or of experiences observed in others or just intuitively grasped even if you live in one place all your days. This deep life-feeling she says is the chief thing! Shakespeare and Dostoevsky have it and Dickens a *little* too but *not* Balzac. Tolstoy has it a little. She says I spoil it in my books by propaganda.

As the editor points out, the techniques employed in the diary "are more deliberate and complex than its seeming artlessness and hap-hazardness at first suggest". For its author it was, as he says, "one of those things you are proud of doing just because it was difficult to do". His ***Autobiography*** was probably much easier, since he presents himself there by conventional means, which seem actually to invite the reader to "see through" him; a process which soon becomes tedious and uninteresting, just as—one cannot help feeling—Powys himself would soon have become tedious if actually encountered in the flesh. The diary holds and retains the mystery of creation, an absorbing secret which does not seem to present the portrait of a self and a loved one, but the T. T.'s "thick rich feeling intuitively grasped", by a clumsy and groping but strangely thrilling seer of the flesh, to whom Hardy had once said: "Your fate is in the lap of the gods, Powys."

The spell remains unbroken even by some characteristically comic outcry—a disillusionment that might belong to anyone, more specifically to any disappointed author.

> ***Glastonbury*** is a *failure*. Only 4000 copies sold. . . . This is a Serious Blow, to which I must adjust myself when I had been secretly hoping for I know not what terrific Kudos including the Noble [*sic*] Prize & being knighted by my Sovereign & receiving the acclamation of Europe & seeing the book translated into all languages—& best of all sold at the entrance to the Ruins in Glastonbury itself! Well I must resign myself to its being a failure.

Touching indeed, though human, all too human; and this comparative lack of interest in the Powys novels in 1932 has continued to the present day. Powys rejected with horror an approach from Hollywood which would probably in any case have come to nothing and, if it had come off, could only have resulted in a travesty. But what he felt here as failure was one of the reasons which eventually persuaded them to leave Phudd Bottom and return to Europe, setting first at a Dorset cottage near his brothers Theodore and Llewelyn, afterwards, and for good, in North Wales, Powys dying in 1963 and Phyllis Playter surviving him for many years. Although Wales was a tremendous source of inspiration in his later years, it could be argued that it diluted Powys's true subject—his own Life Illusion—and that we find him at his most original and most characteristic not in ***Porius*** and ***Owen Glendower,*** and in the later mythological fantasies, but in his early novels like ***Wood and Stone*** and ***Rodmoor,*** as well as in ***Wolf Solent*** and ***Weymouth Sands.*** It is in these works that the spirit of the diary nestles and is tabernacled, as it were, converting itself into his liveliest, most humorous and most compelling fiction.

The present selection of the diary ends with the death from tuberculosis of Llewelyn Powys in 1939, when, in the editor's words, "the war and death of loved ones gave it 'a sense of ending'"; but the diary itself continues for many years after that. Although Powys hoped it would eventually be published, he realized it would have to be edited, a task he hoped to carry out with the T. T., but they never got around to it. So we take leave of this extraordinary couple, the dancer and her Petrushka, as Powys sometimes wrote of them, living in a tiny Welsh cottage, with the T. T.'s mother and aunt (Powys describes his lover as the most loving and obedient of daughters) installed in another one down the road. On January 1, 1940, he records the deaths of so many in his big family, and quotes from Hardy's poem "He Resolves to Say No More"—never a possible decision for Powys—while talking about "the beginning of the end of all of us" and "the T. T.'s future life when Petrushka be the ghost on the roof".

In 1912, Powys met Frances Gregg, who came up to him after one of his American lectures and presented him with a poem called "Perché". That was the start of a remarkable series of letters from him to her which were discovered in a sack at Plymouth dockyard, where she had a wartime job scrubbing floors in the canteen, and which have now been beautifully edited by her son Oliver Wilkinson. His mother had put the letters in the sack on the night she and his grandmother were both killed by a German bomb. Powys and Frances were in love for years, but since he could not and would not divorce his wife, she married his great friend Louis Wilkinson, who was to write under the name Louis Marlow. The marriage was the cause of great jealousy to Powys, and appears in various guises in his novels.

The letters themselves are almost as fascinating as the diary, and exhibit the same elemental feelings—love, jealousy, possessiveness—transmuted into the characteristic humour of the Powysian Life Illusion. Although he remained close to Louis Wilkinson and Frances after they were married, the Powys comedy of tensions remained; and so did his gladness, as he puts it in an earlier letter, "that fate would have me fond not only of receiving humiliating blows from hands I care for, but for having set up on the walls of my palace scrolls that no one—no! *No one* is able to read! . . ." The couple he had brought together (and who remained devoted to him, Frances especially) teased him by calling him "an Inflexible Toad", but oddly enough he reserved his sharpest jealousy for Ezra Pound, who Frances was also seeing a great deal of. The letters are irresistible; and for everyone interested in Powysiana, Oliver Wilkinson's extensive and charming annotation of the several characters who figure in them will be of great practical value.

FURTHER READING

Criticism

Anderson, John Redwood. "John Cowper Powys's *Lucifer,* An Appreciation." *The Dublin Magazine* XXXII, No. 3 (July-September 1957): 37-43.

Compares this "great poem" to Milton's *Paradise Lost* and Shelley's *Prometheus Unbound.*

Bullett, Gerald. Review of *Ducdame* by John Cowper Powys. *Saturday Review* 140 (22 August 1925): 214-15.

Faults *Ducdame* for its trite ideas, poor paragraph construction, and prolixity.

Coombes, Harry. "John Cowper Powys: A Modern Merlin?" *The Southern Review* XI, No. 4 (October 1975): 779-93.

Contrasts the writing styles of John Cowper Powys and his brother Theodore, claiming Theodore as the superior writer.

Duncan, Ian. "The Mythology of Escape: *Owen Glendower* and the Failure of Historical Romance." *Powys Notes* 8, No. 1 (Spring-Summer 1992): 53-81.

Discusses *Owen Glendower*'s shortcomings as a historical romance.

Jones, Ben. "Exile and Presences: Powys's Nihilism." *Powys Notes* 7, No. 1 (Spring-Summer 1991): 4-20.

Examines nihilism in Powys's novels *Ducdame, Wolf Solent,* and *A Glastonbury Romance.*

Lewis, Joan L. Review of *Rabelais* by John Cowper Powys. *Ethics* LXII, No. 1 (October 1951): 76.

Commends Powys for his fine translation and insightful interpretation of Rabelais' philosophy.

Priestley, J. B. "The Happy Introvert." *A Review of English Literature* 4, No. 1 (January 1963): 25-32.

Draws on excerpts from the *Autobiography, A Philosophy of Solitude,* and *In Spite Of* to provide understanding of Powys's personality.

Reynolds, Horace. "Stimulation to Good Reading." *Christian Science Monitor* XXXI, No. 45 (18 January 1939): 12.

Commends Powys's *Enjoyment of Literature* for its catholicity, vivid expression, and perceptiveness.

Additional coverage of Powys's life and career is contained in the following sources published by Gale: *Contemporary Authors,* Vols. 85-88; *Dictionary of Literary Biography,* Vol. 15; and *Major Twentieth-Century Writers.*

Adrienne Rich

1929-

American poet, essayist, and drama writer.

The following entry presents an overview of Rich's career through 1998. For further information on her life and works, see *CLC,* Volumes 3, 6, 7, 11, 18, 36, 73, and 76.

INTRODUCTION

An important poet of the post-World War II era, Rich writes highly crafted lyrics which explore socially relevant topics—including feminism and lesbianism—and criticize patriarchal societies and institutions. She also is an influential essayist whose prose works have advanced theories of feminist criticism. As an early proponent of societal changes that reflect the values and goals of women, Rich articulates one of the most profound poetic statements of the feminist movement in the United States. Her development of a relaxed form of free verse combined with formal diction has been seen by many critics as revolutionary and distinctive in American poetry. "Adrienne Rich's poetry has always raised important, difficult questions about the cultural uses of poetry and the ideology of poetic and critical tradition," according to Alice Templeton. "For over forty years her work has provided the occasion for critics to comment on the art of poetry, its political significance, the character of poetic tradition, and the value of poetry as a critical and creative cultural activity."

Biographical Information

Born May 16, 1929, in Baltimore, Maryland, Rich was home-schooled until the fourth grade, but she showed an early interest in writing and availed herself of her father's extensive Victorian literature collection. Rich graduated from Radcliffe College in 1951, the same year she published her first poetry collection, *A Change of World,* which garnered the Yale Series of Younger Poets award. She accepted a Guggenheim Fellowship in 1952 and traveled to England and throughout Europe. When she returned the next year, she married Harvard University economist Alfred H. Conrad. Upon the birth of her first son in 1955 Rich published her second poetry collection, *The Diamond Cutters,* but by 1959, Rich was the mother of three sons and had little time for writing. However, the publication of *Snapshots of a Daughter-in-Law* in 1963 marked her poetic breakthrough to national prominence, particularly because of its overt delineation of female themes. In 1966 Rich moved with her family to New York City, where she became active in the civil rights and anti-war movements. During that time she produced the poetry collections *Necessities of Life* (1966), *Leaflets* (1969), and *The Will to Change* (1971). By 1969 she was estranged from her husband, who committed suicide the following year. During the early 1970s Rich devoted much time to the women's liberation movement and gradually identified herself as a radical feminist. She won the National Book Award in 1974 for *Diving into the Wreck* (1973), but she refused it as an individual and instead accepted it on behalf of women whose voices were silenced. Rich came out as a lesbian in 1976, at which time she advocated a female separatist philosophy in her subsequent poetry collections *Twenty-one Love Poems* (1977), *The Dream of a Common Language* (1978), and *A Wild Patience Has Taken Me This Far* (1981). She displayed a similar philosophy in *The Fact of a Doorframe* (1984), as well as in the essays collected in *Of Woman Born* (1976) and *On Lies, Secrets, and Silence* (1979). During the 1980s Rich broadened her audience by addressing such diverse issues as poverty, violence, and racism in *Your Native Land, Your Life* (1986), *Blood, Bread and Poetry* (1986), and *Time's Power* (1988). Throughout her writing career Rich has honed her feminist, lesbian aesthetic by lecturing at American universities, most notably as professor of English and feminist studies at Stanford University from 1986 to 1992. Since then Rich has received numerous accolades, including the Robert Frost Silver Medal for Lifetime Achievement in Poetry and the William Whithead Award of the Gay and Lesbian Publishing Triangle for Lifetime Achievement in Letters. Following her award-winning poetry collections *An Atlas of the Difficult World* (1991) and *Dark Fields of the Republic* (1995), Rich also earned a 1997 National Medal of the Arts, but declined the award stating that "the very meaning of art is incompatible with the cynical politics of [President Clinton's] Administration."

Major Works

Rich's poetry is often divided into discrete phases that reflect the evolutionary nature of her art as well as the changing consciousness of women in general during the latter half of the twentieth century. The formal lyric structures and representations of alienation and loss in *A Change of World* and *The Diamond Cutters* evince Rich's early affinities with modernist poets. The poetry of *Snapshots of a Daughter-in-Law,* considered her first transitional work, departs from the formalism of her previous art by using free verse and speaking to women's themes. The title poem, for instance, expresses a young woman's anger and frustration at her banal, limited existence in a male-dominated society. *Necessities of Life, Leaflets,* and *The Will to Change* comprise the second phase of Rich's career. Confrontational in tone, these works focus on the relationship between private and public life, openly reject patriarchal culture and language, and reflect her growing dissatisfaction with contemporary society and her increasingly complex personal and political beliefs. These works also feature Rich's experiments with various means of communication as alternatives to traditional poetic methods; for example, "Images for Godard" and "Shooting Script" incorporate such techniques of New Wave filmmakers as rapid successions of images, freeze frames, and jump cuts. *Diving into the Wreck,* Rich's second major transitional work—considered by many as her finest collection—stands as a radical feminist critique of contemporary society. Many of these poems assert the importance of reinventing cultural standards in feminist terms and point to women's need for self-determination. The poems of *The Dream of a Common Language, A Wild Patience Has Taken Me This Far,* and *The Fact of a Doorframe* lend a historical perspective to the idea of "woman" and celebrate the accomplishments of women both individually and collectively. They represent, for instance, the achievements and hardships of such historical figures as Emily Dickinson, Susan B. Anthony, Marie Curie, and Ethel Rosenberg as well as Rich's own grandmothers. Other poems, such as "For Julia in Nebraska," "The Spirit of Place," and the sequence *Twenty-one Love Poems,* emphasize the value of a distinct community of women and frankly present lesbian sexuality and relationships. Although subsequent works expand Rich's feminist ideals, they also address new issues. The long sequence "Sources" in *Your Native Land, Your Life,* for example, confronts the poet's Jewish heritage and the effect of the Holocaust on her life and work. "Living Memory" from *Time's Power* focuses on the consequences of time and aging and also meditates on the poet's bond to the American landscape. Through first-person narratives and dogmatic language, the poems in *An Atlas of the Difficult World* concern such themes as poverty, the Persian Gulf War, and the exploitation of minorities and women in terms of Rich's own personal experiences. *Dark Fields of the Republic* continues to broaden the poet's themes, focusing on the promise and failure of the American dream, class and gender struggles, and racial inequality. Rich's prose work explores similar feminist concerns. *Of Woman Born* studies the contemporary concept of motherhood, while *On Lies, Secrets, and Silence* furthers Rich's feminist aesthetic, most notably in "When We Dead Awaken," which clarifies Rich's call for female self-determination. *Blood, Bread, and Poetry* examines lesbian issues and addresses questions of racial identity and racism. The essays of *What Is Found There* (1993) contain meditations on politics, poetry, and poets in relation to larger themes of social, ecological, and political crises of the United States.

Critical Reception

Rich's poetry has not always been described as "feminist," especially her early poems. W. H. Auden, for instance, in his foreword to *A Change of World,* found that her poems "are neatly and modestly dressed, speak directly but do not mumble, respect their elders but are not cowed by them, and do not tell fibs." Since the publication of *Diving into the Wreck,* however, most critics have analyzed Rich's writings as artistic expressions of feminist politics. Although many reviewers have admired her formal versatility, others have complained about the didactic tone of her work or have perceived an anti-male bias. Critical commentary has reflected the polemics of her poetry: critics who adhere to Rich's politics often commend her work unconditionally, while those who dissent from her radical feminism usually disavow her writings. A conclusive appraisal of Rich's canon has remained elusive, despite several attempts since the early 1990s—a testament perhaps of the poet's continuous revision of her views and approaches to contemporary issues. Nonetheless, the general consensus among critics recognizes Rich's intelligent, imaginative, and innovative portrayals of women in her poetry as significant contributions to the feminist movement. "There is no one whose poetry has spoken more eloquently for the oppressed and marginalized in America, no one who has more compassionately charted the course of individual suffering across the horrifying and impersonal growth of recent history," David St. John has said, adding that Rich's works "continue to be essential writings in the ongoing feminist struggle in [the United States] and throughout the world."

PRINCIPAL WORKS

Ariadne: A Play in Three Acts and Poems (drama and poetry) 1939
Not I, But Death, A Play in One Act (drama) 1941
A Change of World (poetry) 1951
The Diamond Cutters, and Other Poems (poetry) 1955
Snapshots of a Daughter-in-Law: Poems, 1954-1962 (poetry) 1963; revised edition, 1983
Necessities of Life: Poems, 1962-1965 (poetry) 1966
Selected Poems (poetry) 1967
Leaflets: Poems, 1965-1968 (poetry) 1969
The Will to Change: Poems, 1968-1970 (poetry) 1971
Diving into the Wreck: Poems, 1971-1972 (poetry) 1973
Poems: Selected and New, 1950-1974 (poetry) 1975
Of Woman Born: Motherhood as Experience and Institution (essays) 1976
Twenty-One Love Poems (poetry) 1976
Women and Honor: Some Notes on Lying (essay) 1977
**The Dream of a Common Language: Poems, 1974-1977* (poetry) 1978
On Lies, Secrets, and Silence: Selected Prose, 1966-1978 (essays) 1979
Compulsory Heterosexuality and Lesbian Existence (essay) 1980
A Wild Patience Has Taken Me This Far: Poems, 1978-1981 (poetry) 1981
The Fact of a Doorframe: Poems Selected and New, 1950-1984 (poetry) 1984
Blood, Bread, and Poetry: Selected Prose, 1979-1985 (essays) 1986
†*Your Native Land, Your Life* (poetry) 1986
Time's Power: Poems, 1985-1988 (poetry) 1989
An Atlas of the Difficult World: Poems, 1988-1991 (poetry) 1991
Collected Early Poems, 1950-1970 (poetry) 1993
What Is Found There: Notebooks on Poetry and Politics (prose) 1993
Dark Fields of the Republic (poetry) 1995

*This work includes *Twenty-One Love Poems.*
†This work includes the chapbook "Sources," which was first published in 1983.

CRITICISM

Kevin McGuirk (essay date Spring 1993)

SOURCE: "Philoctetes Radicalized: 'Twenty-one Love Poems and the Lyric Career of Adrienne Rich," in *Contemporary Literature,* Vol. 34, No. 1, Spring, 1993, pp. 61-87.

[*In the following essay, McGuirk situates* Twenty-one Love Poems *in "a context of poetics as ideology," exposing "the ideological limitations of a poetic mode" and theorizing a method of "reading lyric in general and Rich's lyric in particular."*]

As Willard Spiegelman points out, among the major poets of the English language in this half century, Adrienne Rich is alone in making of lyric a medium adequate to the task of propounding a politics. ***The Dream of a Common Language*** (1978), a watershed volume in this development, achieves moments of high lyrical poetry—centered in subjective experience, yet confident in the transcendent presence of otherness to the self—but a poetry that also insists on a relational, not unitary, subjectivity—social, gendered, historical: a politicized lyric self.

Given the tendency in some current criticism to regard lyric as a belated poetic mode and to employ it critically as a rather inert concept, reading a contemporary in relation to lyric might seem a regressive activity. It is my contention that a better theorized lyric—not a new apology for lyric, but a reading that inserts lyric in the world as an ideological practice—will provide leverage for understanding the development of a highly politicized poet like Rich, whose work traverses the line between lyric expression and rhetorical act. Theorizing lyric in terms of a lyric self alone will be unhelpful here, if not misleading. For Paula Bennett, Rich, along with Emily Dickinson and Sylvia Plath, would seem to write a purified lyric—a medium that does not mediate—in which these women were able to throw off "self-alienating masks," to speak "directly from the unacceptable core of their being" and so to attain "the crown or lyric 'I' they knew was theirs." This conception of lyric as transparent window on the individual woman's being is inadequate to Rich's work for two related reasons.

First, although Rich's work can be situated within a poetics of the lyric derived from romanticism, her work shows strong affinities with the rhetorical tradition as well. Her dream of a common language, her sense of a common world of women and a readership of women, finds a gloss in Hans-Georg Gadamer's note that the basis of the rhetorical tradition lies in "an art of common speech, the language of our common sense, our *sensus communis,*" that "rhetoric . . . demands that one know for whom one is speaking." Rhetoric, then—and this is the sense in which I will use the term—as language disposed toward others, whether overt in direct address or implicit in stances that reflect an awareness of a broad, socially conceived audience. Second, lyric is not simply a site for the expression of a given content. While Rich's experience as a woman is obviously the primary context and motive of her later work, the ideological practice of lyric remains both a condition of and an impediment to the project of making the love between women the basis of "a whole new poetry."

Rachel Blau DuPlessis has noted that in the 1970s, "the act of cultural criticism became [Rich's] central lyric act," and a number of writers have made similar claims placing Rich's work in this terrain between lyric and rhetoric. Joanne Feit Diehl has written of the oscillation in ***Dream*** between intimate address (associated with lyric) and assertion (associated with rhetoric), while Charles Altieri and Spiegelman have remarked on the presence in Rich's work of the period of both lyrical and discursive elements. I aim simply to contribute to this general perception by adjusting the critical focus. If lyric is not to remain finally a romantic quality or tendency which is somehow united in Rich's work with discursive, cultural, and political activity, it needs an ideological identity. Rich's political art, I think, attempts to insert lyric into an ideological field. The resulting changes demand our notice. Ideology, according to Louis Althusser's influential definition, is the representation of an imaginary relationship of the subject to her conditions of existence. Like the aesthetic in general, romantic lyric presents itself as "ideologically innocent"; its ideological power resides in this very "innocence," which is achieved on the one hand by miming the exact structure of Althusser's trope of ideology—"I address myself to you"—and on the other by suppressing signs of its address to readers. Obviously it is produced for public consumption, yet lyric's inward focus is such that in addressing itself to no one in particular, or to a "you" that is socially unconditioned, any awareness of audience remains concealed. Thus—to transpose Theodor Adorno's terms—in reading romantic lyric, "Precisely that which is not [ideological] in a poem should become its [ideological] aspect."

As a whole, ***The Dream of a Common Language*** conveys through its affirmations of identity and community—of the "*primary presence of women to ourselves and each other*"—the strength of a faith won in struggle. The highest expression of this faith is **"Phantasia for Elvira Shatayev,"** an account by the leader of a women's climbing team of its members' growing strength and love and interdependence as they prepare for the climb on which they eventually die. Speaking from a transcendent afterlife, Shatayev declares, "if in this sleep I speak / it's with a voice no longer personal (I want to say *with voices*)." In contrast to these women "stream[ing] into the unfinished," the poem's addressee, Shatayev's husband, comes alone to find the bodies: "with your love your loss / . . . / You climbed here for yourself / we climbed for ourselves." Surpassing her husband, a figure for the solitary male poet as well as men in general, Rich's Shatayev affirms the greater transcendence possible when women bond together in communal enterprise.

Twenty-one Love Poems, however, presents a more conflicted negotiation between identity and difference, poetry and the world. Like the **"Phantasia,"** it seeks to place the individual lyric poet in a wider human context, but here this means opening the intimate space of the love lyric to social and literary contexts, contexts that challenge rather than support the poet's desire for woman-to-woman bonding. As such it offers an occasion for examining both the problematic relations between lyric and the rhetorical dimension, and the local dialogue of lyric and rhetoric that occupies the poetic center of Rich's later work. In this essay I have three entwined tasks: to situate Rich's work in a poetic context—a context of poetics as ideology; to present a reading of the ***Love Poems*** as a trial of the ideological limitations of a poetic mode; and to attempt provisionally to theorize reading lyric in general and Rich's lyric in particular.

Philoctetes Radicalized

I want to begin with an allusion Rich makes that will stand as a trope of the career that preceded her feminist work of the seventies. In the eighth of the ***Twenty-one Love Poems,*** the poet remembers herself "years back . . . / hurting with an infected foot, Philoctetes / in woman's form, limping the long path"—she is above a cliff, pondering suicide, "nursing, measuring that wound." The story of Philoctetes, the Greek archer bitten by a venomous snake on the journey to Troy and abandoned by his fellows on the uninhabited island of Lemnos, receives a reading apposite to the case of Rich in Edmund Wilson's "Philoctetes: The Wound and the Bow," the famous title essay of a book published, and reprinted numerous times, around mid-century and surely known to Rich. According to one commentator, Wilson "sought to read the [play] *Philoktetes* as Sophokles' universal statement on the role of the artist in society: wounded, outcast, lacking some inner quality that might permit him or her to engage in the mundane events of life." But Wilson really constructs this reading by grafting onto Sophocles' work the symbolist play of the same name by André Gide. Gide's Philoctetes tells his would-be rescuers, Odysseus and the youth Neoptolemus, that during his years alone, "I came to understand that words inevitably become more beautiful from the moment they are no longer put together in response to the demands of others." For Wilson, this "anchorite" who claims that his "only care is to be" is "a literary man." Odysseus, in contrast, is a practical man and, not incidentally, a skillful rhetorician, a counterfigure to Gide's hero, who refuses the world of action and allows the intruders to steal his magic bow. Sophocles' hero goes on to the Trojan War, but only after he is liberated from his bitter personal isolation by the sympathetic understanding of Neoptolemus.

The figure of Philoctetes evokes a number of intersecting relations: relations between self and world; self-love, personal love, and love or duty in community; between the poem as self-reflexive utterance (the symbolist ideal) or self-complete dramatic object (the New Critical ideal) and the poem as a rhetorical practice closely linked to political change, which is to say, the poem as an activity of the self grounded in ethos. Adrienne Rich is a poet who, though she continues to write from the lyric "I," becomes in the seventies increasingly active in the rhetorical dimension, producing a lyric that moves from the pole of pathos—a concept that has virtually defined lyric since the romantics—closer to the pole of rhetoric and ethos. Since the romantics, and until recently, lyric has been considered a rhetoric-free realm. That is, the relation of poem to audience has been treated as accidental rather than substantial. But lyric has, of course, had a rhetoric. Jerome McGann calls it "a rhetoric of displacement" in which "the audience is not addressed directly." The lyric *norm,* then, as Northrop Frye puts it, echoing John Stuart Mill, is for the poem to be "preeminently the utterance that is overheard." One important consequence of the norm, McGann writes, "is the illusion of freedom which it fosters—as if the reader were not being placed under the power of the writer's rhetoric." In other words, since the reader of lyric need not be aware of herself or himself *as* reader, since the deictics of the poem remain general and the speaker nameless (and typically genderless), the mechanism of identification that powers lyric is relatively simplified. The reader, merging with the poet, becomes the passive consumer of the poet's experience.

My argument here is that by the time of ***The Dream of a Common Language,*** Rich has "unfictionalized" a mode of discourse theorized by the New Critics in terms of dramatic propriety and "embodied" meaning, as opposed to a propositional or rhetorical meaning. Margaret Atwood's comment, that "Rich's poems do not demand the willing suspension of disbelief. They demand belief," gestures in this direction. Rich, in short, radicalizes the lyric mode in the service of a feminist poetics and politics that would erase the ideological lines drawn between the male figures: the political Odysseus, Philoctetes the "literary man," and the sympathetic or emotional Neoptolemus.

Rich's first two volumes, ***A Change of World*** (1951) and ***The Diamond Cutters*** (1955), are characterized by a will to passivity expressed in claims like, "We had to take the world as it was given." A typical gesture is the measured retreat from a chaotic, threatening world that can only be suffered, and held at bay only by artistic form. James Breslin writes of **"Storm Warnings"**—in which the poet, closing up a house against a storm, declares, "the wind will rise, / We can only close the shutters"—that it is "both an expression of Rich's yearning for the well-made autotelic poem and a revelation of the psychological needs such poetry serves." In other poems, the human is virtually identified with passive suffering, while "inhuman" art consoles or redeems by transforming suffering into pathos. "A too compassionate art is half an art," the poet argues in **"At a Bach Concert":** "Only such proud restraining purity [as Bach's] / Restores the else-betrayed, too-human heart."

The root sense of the term *pathos* is, of course, "to suffer." The literary sense of the term is exemplified and epitomized in Rich's early work, where pathos is suffering displaced to a poetic plane, or "suffering made literary"—universal, necessary, part of the human condition. Sharon Cameron has noted that "Lyric speakers . . . do not have names." Here, in addition to simplifying identification, the absence of name—like the absence of gender—helps to persuade us of the universality of what is a particular experience. For example, the alienation felt by the protagonist of **"The Tourist and the Town,"** whose experience issues in the banal generalization, "To work and suffer is to be at home," is in fact the quite special sensation of a sensitive, young, upper-class American woman touring Europe after college graduation. Rich confirms this reading in changing the pronoun of the poem, in a later selection of her work, from "he" to "she," because, she says, the poem was really about herself. "When the poem was written," she explains, "a notion of male experience as universal prevailed which made the feminine pronoun suspect, or merely 'personal.'" Counterpressures appear throughout these volumes, in poems like the well-known **"Aunt Jennifer's Tigers,"** which portrays a woman whose hands embroider prancing tigers while burdened by "The massive weight of Uncle's wedding band"; but the poet remains determinedly among those "who," in her own phrase, "know limits." The reader of these poems, passive first in merely overhearing—or merely *suffering*—the poems, is doubly dyed in pathos by sharing the perspective of a poet who, finally, chooses to suffer the world.

If Rich's later project is primarily, as Altieri puts it, "a matter of ethos," if she seeks to situate the lyric self in the political world, this means replacing the pathos of the private lyric self with the "woman-centered," "woman-identified" experience of ethical community. At the center of such experience for Rich, as critics have noted, is the love relationship between two women. The love poem or poem of relationship has, however, been a constant in her work, and as such it may provide a reference point for any account of changes in her career.

In the fifties, Rich's love or marriage poems typically present a wife- or lover-poet maturely propounding the wisdom of accepting limits. **"An Unsaid Word"** untypically foregrounds gender difference, but in a manner embarrassingly determined to approve a relation permitted only by a sexist ideology:

She who has the power to call her man
From that estranged intensity
Where his mind forages alone,
Yet keeps her peace and leaves him free,
And when his thoughts to her return
Stands where he left her, still his own,
Knows this the hardest thing to learn.

Though the poet is determined, the indirections of this poem betray a resistance to straightforward advocacy of a sexist position. The negative—"unsaid word"—indicates that there is in fact "a word" held in abeyance, while the hypothetical mode of the poem suggests an inability finally to accept the imperative the poem apparently takes as a given. In the end, **"An Unsaid Word"** leaves the impression of personal will and identity reined in by ideological will, by prosodic skill and syntactic control.

In the sixties, Rich discovers that "The world breathes underneath our bed," and that the well-wrought lyric poem cannot accommodate her present experience of the world. Throughout the decade, she increasingly employs more fragmented forms, collage techniques that depend as much on the juxtaposition of statement and image as the control of a single speaker. While the influence of Charles Olson, who decried "the lyrical interference of the individual as ego" and advocated "composition by field," is evident, the field of Rich's action is never, as in Olson's "Objectism," merely phenomenal but always political: the poet is not an object among other objects, but a subject among other subjects. Rich's career as a political poet begins with ***Leaflets*** (1969). "I want this to reach you," she writes in the title poem, "who told me once that poetry is nothing sacred / . . . / I want this to be yours"—poetry, then, as leaflets, "scraps of paper" dispersed into the broad community, performing, Rich hopes, an ethical task. One measure of her growth as a rhetorical poet in the last two decades is the **"Dedications"** poem of her recent sequence "An Atlas of the Difficult World." Knowing now that her poetry reaches people, she recites a litany Whitmanian in its confidence: "I know you are reading this poem / late, before leaving your office / . . . / I know you are reading this poem in a waiting-room / of eyes met and unmeeting, of identity with strangers / . . . / I know you are reading this poem listening for something, torn between bitterness and hope." It is in the seventies, with the development of a positive feminism and an alternative order to the bourgeois marriage and well-wrought poem, that Rich begins to break a path that will lead beyond the lyric of pathos to a rhetorical lyric practice.

Rich's influential and widely suggestive essay **"When We Dead Awaken: Writing as Re-Vision"** (1971) marks the early phase of an overt feminism. There Rich speaks compellingly of the need to discover "ways . . . in which the energy of creation and the energy of relation can be united." Perhaps it is in response to this need that the trope of address comes to govern much of her work, since in address the poet does not turn away from relation, as does the poet of the inward meditative lyric, but sustains or creates relation as she shapes her poem. For Rich, forging the poem is forging relation. In addition, address to historical women can serve a communal function, linking the lyric self to ethical community, for it uses apostrophe's seeming power to raise the dead and to bestow subjectivity in order to bring distant or historical women into the imaginative life of contemporary readers. It thus contributes to the development of a feminist ethos which needs, like any ethos, vivid exemplary figures and a historical dimension.

The Philoctetes of Gide, it is clear, would be anathema to the feminist Rich. The old Rich, the ancestor she alludes to in the Philoctetes poem, was a woman who established herself as a poet in the New Critical fifties and survived the anguished sixties and the interval of anger and sense of victimization that preceded the affirmations of ***The Dream of a Common Language.*** Now she tells her lover, "The woman who cherished / her suffering is dead . . . / I want to go on from here with you / fighting the temptation to make a career of pain." Philoctetes' own career of pain, in Sophocles' play, ended in a return to practical and communal activity—the Trojan War. Rich's return is significantly different. If the figure of a solitary, (emotionally) wounded woman on a cliff, contemplating suicide, evokes Ovid's Sappho, who threw herself from a cliff in despair of the love of a man, then, in her will to go on with a woman, her battle a matter of sustaining a self in relationship with an other, Rich at once rejects her own flirtation with suicide, the figure of the self-destructive woman in literature, and embraces the historical Sappho who chose to love women, and to sing not epics of war but lyrics of relation.

The Sequence of Love Poems

When we come to the sequence of love poems, however, relation loses the relatively clear lines of definition it possesses in the public sphere. With an intimate relationship already in place, the ongoing, potentially endless character of the form tends to release the poet from the work of forging relation in order to meditate on love, on his own responses, and on the discourse of love itself. The result is often the transformation of the addressed lover into a merely voiceless figure—a mirror—by which the poet establishes and explores his or her identity. But meditation on the discourse of love can also probe and question its own conventions. Thus Rich, in poem VII of the ***Twenty-one Love Poems***:

Is all this close to the wolverines' howled
signals,
that modulated cantata of the wild?

or, when away from you I try to create you in
words,
am I simply using you . . .

These questions articulate a problematic that seems endemic to the lyric mode, which I want to address here: is this natural, spontaneous (and therefore innocent) song, or is it a ruse that serves only to establish my identity?

Addressed by a woman-poet to an unnamed woman-lover, ***Twenty-one Love Poems,*** in Diehl's words, "seek[s] to combine a self-consciousness associated with establishing an alternative poetic ground based on a lesbian relationship, a world without men, and an attempt to convert a specific intimacy into a paradigm that maps the possibilities of such a relationship for a radically alternative poetics." This account, with its professionalizing "seek to" and "an attempt to," emphasizes the nature of the sequence as trial, a trial both of the poet's political project and of the possibilities of the love sequence for woman-to-woman relationships. The love sequence is on trial because it is a form that has embodied specific gender relations. The very conventions Rich seeks to overcome operate not just in the poem's content but in the very *materia* of her discourse. Thus the questions I cited above are not an instance only, as Jan Montefiore argues, of the poet "worr[ying] lest the inevitable gap between the text she produces and her lived, shared experience, may make her risk reducing her lover to a prop in her own poems' linguistic drama": they *exemplify,* as well as question, the problematic at the heart of romantic lyric, for although they literally direct themselves to an addressee, they remain "rhetorical" (in the conventional sense), impelling a monologue forward rather than initiating a dialogue. They thus verge upon "using" their addressee as "prop" themselves, exerting, in effect, an ideological force upon her. Nevertheless, in articulating a problematic, they raise it into critical view, and thus direct us toward the poetic center of the issues the sequence explores.

In an essay on "the rhetorics of sexuality," Margaret Homans outlines a figurative strategy Emily Dickinson employs to rewrite the romance plot of male desire for a distant woman. Unable to translate his desire into action, the Petrarchan lover-poet only displaces it to a figurative plane where he constructs his absent beloved as a tissue of metaphors of his own making. Stimulated by these—usually visual—metaphors, he gazes upon her image. She becomes a mirror of his desire that, however, merely perpetuates his desire, creating a very *mise en abîme* of pathos. In contrast, Homans argues, Dickinson, relying principally on metonymy, which is based on contiguity rather than absence, represents "a female sexuality (privileging touch) that is also a female textuality (privileging metonymy)." Jane Hedley offers an account of Rich's revision of the romance plot in the same terms. Rich celebrates contact: waking in her lover's bed, traveling together, lovemaking and desire expressed as touch, not gaze. As Hedley notes, when Rich goes beyond the merely literal description of her lover's hands—"precisely equal to my own— / only the thumb is longer, larger"—by asserting that "in these hands / I could trust the world," she is using metonymy: "Hands become a figure for the power of women as it might be exercised along various dimensions." This metonymic textuality echoes the sexuality Rich represents in the unnumbered **"Floating Poem":**

the live, insatiate dance of your nipples in my
mouth—
your touch on me, firm, protective, searching
me out, your strong tongue and slender fingers
reaching where I had been waiting years for you
in my rose-wet cave—whatever happens, this is.

Touch, contact, mutuality, the presence of two lovers to one another—these replace the gaze of desire dominant in the male tradition.

Homans argues that "a poem's rhetoric is dialectically bound up with its subject matter"; its particular use of figures, like metaphor and metonymy, is ideological. Ethical revision, however, one might argue, begins with the character of the lover-poet, "a woman sworn to lucidity," as Rich puts it in an earlier poem—active, questioning, determined to make love not an escape but a way of being in the world. Intimate I-you discourse tends to exclude the world of third persons, so that the drift into "a *solitude à deux,*" as DuPlessis notes, has to be consciously resisted. So strong is the drift, and so strong is Rich's determination to resist it, that she immediately defends against it: her first act is to declare the need to live in the patriarchal city and to understand "our" lives as part of that city:

Wherever in this city, screens flicker
with pornography, with science-fiction vampires,
victimized hirelings bending to the lash,
we also have to walk . . . if simply as we walk
through the rainsoaked garbage, the tabloid
cruelties
of our own neighborhoods.
We need to grasp our lives inseparable
from those rancid dreams, that blurt of metal,
those disgraces[.]

She does not, in Breslin's terms, yearn for the well-made autotelic poem, and she is determined to resist the psychology such poetry serves. These lovers will not live in "sonnets, little rooms," like those Donne envisioned canonized in his poem canonized by the New Criticism. Indeed, as Hedley points out, the absence in the opening poem of the pronoun "I" emphasizes Rich's aim to ground the lovers' life and the sequence itself in literal contemporary history. Moreover, it works rhetorically to invite us as readers into the poem and posits our collective experience as the context for the individual lovers' experience. The sequence then attempts to negotiate, for an "I" and a "you," a space that touches on one side the absolute collectivity represented by "we" and, on the other, the isolation of "I" alone, the only pronoun in the final poem.

Unwilling to accept a symbolist or romantic isolation freed from ethical concern, the poet must invoke contexts; but since, as she says, "No one has imagined us"—that is, lesbians, in art and literature—she must repeatedly invoke texts from the masculine tradition. The result is that, in first allowing these texts presence, and perhaps even priority, in order to deny their pertinence, the poet must employ largely negative ways of defining the lovers' life together. This is in striking contrast to the rest of a volume characterized by affirmation. It is as if here, at the center of her project, in the intimate space of "two lovers of one gender," she is most vulnerable and therefore most embattled. The allusion to Philoctetes is a complex example of simultaneous invocation, revision, and negation. In another poem, the poet figures the lovers' life together as a journey by car through an uncharted territory where the signal their radio picks up is "neither *Rosenkavalier* nor *Götterdämmerung* / but a woman's voice singing old songs / with new words, with a quiet bass, a flute / plucked and fingered by women outside the law." Later, as the relationship falters, she warns that "*Tristan und Isolde* is scarcely the story, / women at least should know the difference / between love and death. No poison cup, / No penance." And in a poem I will deal with in some detail further on, her lover's passive response to the end of the relationship is "in fugue" with the pathos of Matthew Arnold's "To Marguerite," a poem in which the speaker attributes the "severance" of two lovers to the ruling of "a God."

What such negations and countering affirmations reflect is an imbalance and the consequent difficulty which, as Diehl writes, the sequence "so starkly articulate[s]: the difficulty of reinventing names for experience, of placing the female self at the center of the mimetic process." The male texts are actual and specific; neither the women musicians nor the songs have specific existence. Not surprisingly, when the poet imagines what the lovers' experience might provide for others, her vision is notably generalized:

> Merely a notion that the tape-recorder
> should have caught some ghost of us. . . :
> . . . .
> this we were, this is how we tried to love,
> and these are the forces they had ranged against
> us,
> and these are the forces we had ranged within
> us,
> within us and against us, against us and within
> us.

Perhaps the poet wishes by such generalities to avoid mythologizing the relationship. Nevertheless, the need for "reinventing names," given the lack of suitable objects in the existing culture, often leads Rich to attempt to name the lovers' experience by identifying them with an equally generalized nature:

> We want to live like trees,
> . . . .
> our animal passion rooted in the city. (I)

> Your eyes are everlasting, the green spark
> of the blue-eyed grass of early summer,
> the green-blue wild cress washed by the spring.
> (III)

> Sleeping, turning in turn like planets
> rotating in their midnight meadow (XII)

> —tender, delicate
> your lovemaking, like the half-curled frond
> of the fiddlehead fern in forests
> just washed by sun. (**"Floating Poem"**)

Rich's commitment to ethos, however, to situating the poem within the existing social order, forestalls the potential for pathos in such identifications. Indeed, the social texts with which Rich has framed her experience can only undermine, or at least compromise, the identifications with nature. From the opening lines, the sequence rejects the notion of a "green world" outside the problematics of patriarchy, whether for women-lovers or a feminist lyric poet. Even the unnumbered **"Floating Poem"** is "simultaneously give[n] and denie[d] its inviolability" by the poems around it.

Consider in this connection the questions of poem VII. The first—"Is all this close to the wolverines' howled signals. . . ?"—links naturalness of speech with naturalness of being, pondering whether the discourse of the love poems possesses the naturalness attributed elsewhere to the lovers themselves. The second—"when away from you I try to create you in words, / am I simply using you. . . ?"—ponders an opposite view: that this poem is language, signs not signals, the scheme of a linguistically constituted "I," a means of self-definition in relation to others—and an inescapably social activity. In the first question, the poet's "cantata of the wild" looks to be a green world within discourse and the "I" itself an unconditioned subjectivity of natural process. But if Rich's project is in part to take the lyric "I" beyond romantic pathos to participate in ethos, there must be found a means of making the transcendent world it appears to inhabit contingent, and of making the reader's experience of the poem ethical too, more than a vicarious experience of the pathos of unconditioned subjectivity. The second question points to such a means, in a direction I want to begin to follow now.

"I am Adrienne"

Emile Benveniste's argument that subjectivity is established in uttering the pronoun "I" can be brought to bear on lyric discourse in obvious, but limited, ways. The conversational model Benveniste employs—where the positions "I" and "you" are exchanged by individuals in dialogue—is only partly fulfilled by the monologic lyric. The polarity of "I" and "you," Benveniste writes, "does not mean either equality or symmetry: 'ego' always has a position of transcendence with regard to *you*." This describes a linguistic condition for ***Twenty-one Love Poems*** that is complicated, however, by the poems' eventual deployment of the relationship between enunciation and enounced. As the utterance that is overheard, lyric normally suppresses the distinction between the two, compelling us to read a poem as if it were transparently the utterance of a single speaker when in fact the writer/enunciator and the enounced, or *represented* "I," are not the same. While transparency can be made translucency by different formal and rhetorical strategies that highlight enunciation (address to the reader, overt artifice, disjunctive syntax, and so forth), such remain exceptions to general practice. The "prosody of natural speech," as Antony Easthope points out, has been normative in English poetry since the Renaissance.

One effect of the "prosody of natural speech" is the immediate sense of voice that lyric produces. Voice, or the strong impression of the presence of a speaking "I," and not character, class, or gender, is the principal feature of lyric poetry. To say that voice always predominates over situation in lyric is another way of saying that the "I" always holds a position of transcendence. It is easy to see, then, why lyric has been valorized as a mode that expresses and enlists wide sympathies—a mode that convinces the reader of its universality simply by "suturing" him or her into the subject position of the represented, and usually unnamed, speaker.

In an interview published in 1977, shortly after the publication of ***Twenty-one Love Poems*** as a chapbook, Rich recalled her response to two heterosexual women friends who, as she says, "wrote to me about reading ***Twenty-One Love Poems*** with their male lovers, assuring me how 'universal' the poems were. I found myself angered, and when I asked myself why, I realized that it was anger at having my work essentially assimilated and stripped of its meaning, 'integrated' into heterosexual romance. That kind of 'acceptance' of the book seems to me a refusal of its deepest implications." Montefiore suggests that while Rich's anger at her friends' insensitivity is just, it is not fully informed in the matter of her poetry, for although the lesbian content of the poem must be acknowledged, "it does not follow that the language or form of the poetry is specifically female: there is nothing intrinsically gendered about free verse"; "injection of new experiential content is not in itself a transformation of poetry." More pertinent, I would argue, is the generally displaced rhetoric of the poems. Only a refusal to read a lyric poem can evade the pressure of the powerful operation that allows us no perspective except that of the represented speaker while seducing us, as McGann notes, with an illusion of freedom from rhetorical constraint. Lyric, in short, insists that we experience the poem principally through identification. So it should not be surprising that a sympathetic, and careless, reader, invited to identify with the poems' speaker, should call the poems "universal."

The sequence, however, increasingly works against such simple identification—and against the step up to universals. The mechanism of identification is complicated by the accumulation of various deictics for the poem that compete with the generalized deictics of lyric (*here, there, then, now, I you*) for dominance. The range of reference in ***Twenty-one Love Poems,*** both literal and literary, counters the inward drift of love lyric, as well as our tendency to read the protagonists as timeless fictions. Though Rich does at moments rather blandly insist on the ordinariness of things transformed ("the early light of spring / flashing off ordinary walls, the Pez Dorado, / the Discount Wares, the shoe store"), references like these establish a literal setting for the poems' action. The name of the friend, "Kenneth," who "tells me he's been arranging his books / so he can look at Blake and Kafka while he types," bears no discernible symbolic trace; such detail serves to remind us of the literal, social identity of the speaker—she's not just a lover—and to impede simple identification by the reader with the speaker. The climax of the sequence occurs when the poet gives the most central literal detail, her own name. "Now you're in fugue," she tells her lover,

> across from what some I'm sure
> Victorian poet called the *salt estranging sea.*
>
> Those are the words that come to mind.
> I feel estrangement, yes. As I've felt dawn
> pushing toward daybreak. Something: a cleft of
> light—?
> Close between grief and anger, a space opens
> where I am Adrienne alone. And growing colder.
> (XVIII)

Obtruding the literal poet upon the fictional "I" of the sequence, this passage betrays the lyric promise of identification. Remember Sharon Cameron's observation that lyric speakers do not have names, and the New Critical principle that, for the purposes of reading and criticism, poets are extraneous to their poems. A recent objection to Rich's self-naming comes from a different critical quarter which, however, shares that emphasis on fiction.

Margaret Homans's discussion of ***The Dream of a Common Language*** in *Women Writers and Poetic Identity* is mainly concerned with showing the advantages of **"Phantasia for Elvira Shatayev,"** which offers romantic transcendence of nature to women, over **"Transcendental Etude."** The latter poem concludes with the vision of a woman who in weaving together the small scraps of nature at hand becomes "one with her body." Her "composition" has nothing to do with "mere will to mastery." Homans finds in this rejection of the high values of art, and the identification of the woman with nature, a reductive vision for women and a poetic that is "poetically terminal," because it tries "to make an end to figuration." This high investment in figuration and transcendence is reflected in the tenor of Homans's all too brief response to Rich's literal self-naming:

> When Rich says ". . . I am Adrienne alone" . . . that particular personal "I" differs greatly from the sense of self that underlies much of Romantic poetry. Wordsworth, egotist though he is, does not name himself Wordsworth; "creative soul" and "Poet" are names that enlarge the self, where explicit naming would diminish it. . . . The unmasked and reductive "I" is only a further function of that belief in the literal, that it can be expressed and have literal effects. The new "I" [of feminist poetry] has nothing to do with creative power; its purpose is to make poetry approximate as closely as possible a personal, spoken communication.

Homans's critique misses the mark, I think, because it assumes that what lies before a woman poet is an either/or choice between transcendence and literal identifications. In my view, Rich's project has more to do with articulating a relationship between transcendence and history, and that relationship comes down, in lyric poetry, to a relationship between the "I" itself and the social text of the world.

Rich may align the lovers with that social text through allusion to the masculine tradition in art and reference to the world outside their door, but these strategies do not touch the "I," which is, as in all lyric, the center of the poems. However much the poet might attempt to make that identity a political and contingent one, the "I" cannot ever refer outside the poem, since the pronoun "I" has no referent in the way that "tree," for example, has; "its task is to indicate the person uttering the present instance of discourse that contains the 'I'." "I" is inescapably transcendent with respect to any other aspect of a lyric poem.

The problem for ***Twenty-one Love Poems*** that follows is this: the sequence contains two incompatible propositions about the relation between the poet and her world, two ideologies. The first is the declared one: "we have to grasp our lives inseparable from those rancid dreams"—of the literal urban setting, patriarchal history, the masculine tradition in poetry. The second is embedded in the discourse of an "I" addressing a "you." It says that "I" and "you" are the only real presences in the poem. Or, to put a finer point on it, it suggests that only "I" is really present, since "you" remains without speech and never occupies the center of discourse.

In naming herself, however, the poet becomes a *third* person, someone who is called Adrienne, and thus radically compromises her privileged position as transcendent "I." She no longer speaks from the position of the represented "I," or enounced subject, but from a position of enunciation. Rich acknowledges, in effect, a double position: she is inescapably transcendent "I" *and* a person with a name given by history; hers is an act of recognition, specifically that "'I' is ideological." Her lover meanwhile "turn[s] aside from pain" and succumbs to Arnoldian pathos.

If Rich recognizes that "'I' is ideological," she will not therefore cease to write from her subjectivity. It is in part the wish to escape the ideological condition of language that leads to a poetics of pathos—like that represented by Gide's symbolist Philoctetes—which includes rhetoric in its vocabulary only as a term of disparagement. Rich is pragmatic, if nothing else: to be politically efficacious, to be ethical, means to engage the "oppressor's language." Moreover, it is only the full experience of transcendence in freely uttering the pronoun "I," an experience long denied to women, that allows one to intervene in the ideological field which is history. Saying "I am Adrienne," then, does not erase the transcendent "I" of the lyric poet but balances it, across the copula, with the contingent identity given by history.

Lyric/Rhetoric

In firmly dividing poetry from rhetoric, Mill expressed a growing prejudice of his age: "Eloquence is *heard,*" he wrote, "poetry is *overheard.* Eloquence supposes an audience; the peculiarity of poetry appears to lie in the poet's utter unconsciousness of a listener." That Frye followed Mill in his influential account of the modes and genres suggests that the prejudice still has currency. "Can anyone but a philistine . . . talk about lyric poetry and society?"—that is the question Adorno anticipates as he approaches his topic; lyric, it is understood, has exclusively to do with private experience. Closer to our time, Jonathan Arac notes that even in the most recent and sophisticated work to be published on lyric, the anthology *Lyric Poetry: Beyond New Criticism,* "The most common sense among those who have used the notion is that lyric expresses pure subjectivity."

Postmodernist criticism has sought to release poetry from the equation with romantic lyric implicit in statements like Mill's, but lyric itself remains unregenerate. The opposition of lyric to rhetorical concerns, to ethos, still structures our thinking and prevents us from understanding lyric historically as a flexible mode that moves back and forth—through historical periods, or within the body of a poet's work—between inward meditation, address to a "you" with awareness of a wider audience, and direct address to a broad community by the literal poet.

In this essay, I have largely assumed the opposition, taking "lyric" to mean "romantic lyric" and allowing it to structure my argument. ***Twenty-one Love Poems*** is exemplary in this regard. It begins by addressing a thematic opposition—lovers/city—which it seeks to dissolve, or transform, but moves crucially to address the related discursive opposition of poetry and rhetoric. In doing so, ***Twenty-one Love Poems*** serves to prepare the more radical move in later volumes to a nonromantic lyric.

I want to make this clearer. If Rich in a sense "unfictionalizes," it is not to move lyric toward the confessional mode, but to bring it into the realm of ethos. To appreciate her work, then, we need a notion of lyric capacious enough to comprehend the rhetorical dimension and criteria beyond, in Donald Wesling's words, the merely "singable, and the personal." Marjorie Perloff, judging it a "curious twist," suggests that while "Rich regularly writes in the lyric first person," she is "a notably impersonal, didactic poet." She complains further that Rich "is so anxious to *teach* and to *persuade* that she tends to forget that form is itself a political statement." All that Rich offers, in Perloff's view, is the thin poetic gruel of teaching and persuading. The problem here is that Perloff's critical assumptions—chiefly, that the form/content dichotomy represents the sum of what is poetically relevant—cannot comprehend a poetry that conjoins lyric and rhetoric, integrating formal effect and personal detail with a rhetorical purpose.

In ***The Dream of a Common Language,*** part of that purpose is to urge on (women) readers the value of identification among women: "The drive / to connect," Rich tells us, is of "the true nature of poetry." But the connection, as I've been arguing, is not simple. Lyric's mechanism of identification becomes demanding and specific, since the poet is no longer the passive, nameless, genderless, or timeless self of her early work but instead is active, named, gendered, and historical. Rich's assumption of a female audience, one that is not a ghetto, in a manner that is not embattled, is a rhetorical move both politically and poetically significant. Politically, the lyric norm is a resource: to begin with, the norm invites readers into identification with lyric speakers; in Rich's poetry, identification is demanding but a source of strength as well—as, for example, the **"Phantasia"** seeks to make clear. Poetically, the assumption of a female audience has to change the way we read lyric poetry. It is not only Philoctetes, the poet, who has been radicalized: Rich's poetry radicalizes the reading of lyric, for women directly, secondarily for men, by challenging the gender complacency that goes with conventional interpretation. Reading lyric becomes an ethical practice. Instead of passively consuming the experience of an unconditioned lyric "I," we are challenged by difference, and by awareness of the enunciating poet behind the "I" of the poem.

As Rich moves away in the eighties from the emphasis of the seventies on woman-identified, potentially transcendent experience and further from romantic ideals generally, the mechanism of identification is less critical. We are more likely to encounter poems addressed to literal named people and poems self-consciously about Rich's personal and historical existence as poet and citizen. Hence the title of a 1986 volume, ***Your Native Land, Your Life.*** The "I" of these later volumes is, then, even more explicitly constructed rhetorically and ethically, rather than by virtue of a displaced rhetoric and private pathos that permit the illusion of transcendence. In **"Sources,"** an autobiographical sequence of twenty-three poems dated 1981-82, Rich addresses her long-dead husband:

> I have resisted this for years, writing to you as if you could hear me. . . . I've had a sense of protecting your existence, not using it merely as a theme for poetry or tragic musings; letting you dwell in the minds of those who have reason to miss you, in your way, or their way, not mine. The living, writers especially, are terrible projectionists. I hate the way they use the dead.
>
> Yet I can't finish this without speaking to you, not simply of you.

Here is a poet fully cognizant of the problematics of address. Like ideology—remembering Althusser's trope, "I address myself to you"—address creates a listening subject by, paradoxically, subjecting it to the speaking "I." Rich affirms it nevertheless as a mode of relationship in poetry that she is unwilling to do without—a rhetoric, which makes the lyric poem more than the "musings" of the poet to herself. If she is to use the dead, or living, in poetry, her risk will at least be underwritten by her own contingency and responsibility. Once explicitly named in ***Twenty-one Love Poems,*** Rich no longer speaks as the enounced "I" of a discourse that presumes its ideological innocence, but writes from the position of an enunciating "Adrienne."

Elissa Greenwald (essay date Fall 1993)

SOURCE: "The Dream of a Common Language: Vietnam Poetry as Reformation of Language and Feeling in the Poems of Adrienne Rich," in *Journal of American Culture,* Vol. 16, No. 3, Fall, 1993, pp. 97-102.

[Below, Greenwald explains the effect of Rich's feminist consciousness in her poetry of the Vietnam era, highlighting her empathy with "the Enemy" and her appeal for a subjective version of the truth about war.]

The presence of the Vietnam War in the poetry of Adrienne Rich must be considered in the context of her own presence at peace demonstrations and protests against the war throughout the 1960s and early 1970s, and her continuing leadership in the antiwar, feminist, and civil rights movements through the present time. During the Vietnam War, Rich's poetry was her public means of political protest, at a time when poetry was less divorced from the public realm than it is now. That Rich's and other poets' continuing cries against war, most recently in concerted protests against the Gulf War, have not had the public impact of earlier protests against the Vietnam war, is only testimony to the deformation of language and politics that is the legacy of the Vietnam war and its successors, the U.S. wars of the 1980s and the Gulf War. For Rich, the effects of the war in Vietnam included a corruption of language. In her poetry, then, the attempt to imagine and bring about peace especially takes the form of forging a new language and new poetic forms, seeking in subjectivity and improvisational form a new mode of truth-telling to counteract the distortions of official language during the war.

The fragmentary mode that has become the *modus operandi* of the 1980's and 1990's is seen in Rich's poetry as a consequence of living for nearly a decade in a nation at war, though one experienced by non-combatants in this country at a distance, through television imagery rather than directly. The consequences of being constant perpetrators of a brutal war include, for people in the United States, dislocations of both consciousness and morality. In Rich's poetry, by recovering meaning in language, the poet can provide a voice of public as well as private morality. Throughout her work, she seeks to validate her own language and subjectivity as a truthful counter to the public lies of official policy in Vietnam. Rich interweaves two themes in her poems about the war: the desire to identify and empathize with "the Enemy," the people of Vietnam, and the need to forge a new language that will reflect a subjective rather than "official" version of truth.

For Rich, the war invades personal as well as public interactions and even deforms the self. She seeks the reality behind the evasive official language of war in order to make the horrors of war vivid and so to accept moral responsibility for them. Through exploration of a subjectivity that counters official "facts," Rich also begins to forge a feminist consciousness, using military metaphors to describe her own consciousness (as in **"Planetarium"** [1968], *ARP*):

> I am bombarded yet   I stand
>
> I have been standing all my life in the
> direct path of a battery of signals
> the most accurately transmitted most
> untranslatable language in the universe. . . .

As the poem indicates, a position of seeming vulnerability can become one of power; the "untranslatable language," when translated, will put her in tune with forces that permeate the universe. While she initially identifies with the "enemy" as victim, seeing the female body as the site of "wounds," ultimately a female and feminist consciousness becomes a source of power to defeat the forces of war.

Similarly, in her poems about Vietnam Rich translates the "burning" of her own anger and desire into an external force, a revolutionary fire of consciousness which unites her with others. In **"The Burning of Paper Instead of Children,"** she links the burning of children by napalm in Vietnam with the burning of Jewish victims of the Holocaust. Her heritage as a Jew (she is the child of a Jewish father and a Christian mother) provides her with both a means to empathize more fully with the "enemy" or victim in Vietnam and a history and moral legacy to counteract the destruction of the past that characterizes the war. In this and other poems, Rich makes "burning" the sign of a purgative moral anger and protest, a passion which remakes language and reality.

Rich's poems about Vietnam appear chiefly in three volumes, ***Leaflets: Poems 1965-1968, The Will to Change*** (1971), and ***Diving into the Wreck*** (1973), though her concern with peace continues to be a prominent concern throughout her poetry. In ***Leaflets,*** the war appears more often as imagery or background than as direct subject. But the poems convey the reality of life in wartime, when images of violence are never far from one's consciousness. In many poems in this volume, Rich undercuts the tendency towards violence by showing how the notion of the "Enemy" demonizes human beings; she seeks to understand and love the other by forging a subjectivity that internalizes the pain of others to chasten but strengthen the self.

In **"The Demon Lover,"** the lover who seems to elude and frustrate her may also be a symbol of Death itself. For their lack of communication and pleasure takes place under the sign of war, at a time when the world is characterized by "something piercing and marred." Nonetheless, **"The Demon Lover"** celebrates the power of sexuality and language in a world characterized by destruction. She deconstructs the notion of the Enemy (who in this poem may be the loved one himself) by showing how clearly such notions are projections of anxieties within the self, results of a failure to love. In this poem, the war comes home to both community and personal relationships.

In one image, the poet dreams that she is actually under attack, in a fulfillment of the worst anxieties of people in the United States during the war in Vietnam: "I dreamed about the war. / We were all sitting at table / in a kitchen in Chicago. / The radio had just screamed / that Illinois was the target. / No one felt like leaving, / we sat by the open window / and talked in the sunset." This image of careless disregard for imminent danger is also one of freedom and language-making in the face of destruction. For, as Rich affirms, "Only where there is language is there world." Language at once mediates and creates reality for us. Though the harsh and distorting language of war may deform the world, the poet's words help to restore it: "Death's in the air, / we all know that. Still, for an hour, / I'd like to be gay. / . . . We are our words, and black and bruised and blue. / Under our skins, we're laughing." The knowledge or experience of violence and death has not destroyed the human capacity for language as celebration.

Nonetheless, the war cannot be exiled from one's consciousness. In **"Nightbreak,"** Rich shows how war has been internalized, imploded into love relations, as she portrays love as a beleaguered battleground. Rich takes on the guilt of U.S. violence in Vietnam by making herself the enemy, identifying with the Vietnamese as she pictures her own body as the site of war. **"Nightbreak,"** with its dream-like images, translates the battlefield of war into the landscape of everyday life. The imagery of burning ("Into the oildrum drops / the ball of fire") and of enemy raids—images with which people in the United States were bombarded during the Vietnam War—has become internalized, so that nightfall in her bedroom recapitulates nightbreak on the battlefield.

The poet depicts her own body as what is broken or wounded, as the force of destruction is localized to her bed, which may be a place where broken pieces are also joined. On one level, her descriptions here may be seen as two views of heterosexual sex, as either healing ("the rifts fill") or "wounding." On another level, the images indicates Rich's personification of the war in her own body, as she takes on the wounds of Vietnam: "In the bed the pieces fly together / and the rifts fill or else / my body is a list of wounds / symmetrically placed / a village / blown open by planes / that did not finish the job."

Rich shows the absurdity of describing people as "the enemy" by showing that in effect there is no enemy: "the enemy has withdrawn / between raids become invisible / there are / no agencies / of relief." Here, as she becomes the "shaken target" who eventually succumbs to sleep, the estranged and distant lover becomes a version of the enemy. In a more metaphysical sense, the withdrawal of the enemy symbolizes the lack of real agency, the impersonal machinery of war.

Rich here indicates the capacity of love or of her own creative imagination to make "the pieces fly together." The world that remains here is deeply "cracked" and scarred, but nightbreak is "Time for the pieces / to move / dumbly back / toward each other." The image of two lovers reconciling applies as well to the two countries which are enemies, to the attempted union of fragments. In this poem, as in Eliot's "The Waste Land," Rich seeks usable fragments of history or language to "shore against my ruins." Poetry is seen as an act of healing, of overcoming the division between the self and an "enemy" which may be imaginary.

In **"The Burning of Paper Instead of Children"** (also written in 1968), in ***The Will to Change,*** Rich more fully connects public war and private disturbance. This poem explores the capacity of language to elucidate or obscure moral truth. It begins with a neighbor's protest against her son's burning of a book, which the neighbor says reminds him of Hitler. As Rich also recalls the recent destruction of written draft records by Daniel Berrigan in Catonsville, Maryland, she realizes that the real parallel to the Nazis is in the burning of children by napalm in Vietnam. The moral status of language itself is unclear, as the poem's epigraph, a quotation from Berrigan, suggests that he was driven to action to evade the ambiguities of language: "I was in danger of verbalizing my moral impulses out of existence." The imagery of burning spreads to connect the Berrigans' destruction of draft records with Hitler's book-burning and the burning of villages and countryside with napalm in Vietnam. Ultimately Rich honors both her neighbor's memories of the Holocaust and her son's innocence by distinguishing the burning of paper from the burning of children, while understanding the historical link between the two in the Holocaust.

Rich begins by evoking a library, a storehouse of records that preserves the past (while the draft office attacked by the Berrigans contained records destined to deliver young men to death). Even her library contains books that evoke images of death and burning: *The Book of the Dead, The Trial of Jeanne d'Arc.* Rich identifies with Joan of Arc in both her heroism and her martyrdom: "I dream of her too often // love and fear in a house / knowledge of the oppressor / I know it hurts to burn." Burning becomes internal as well as external, the expression of faith and protest as well as suffering. Hatred of the "oppressor" causes both Rich and Joan of Arc to burn; Rich links hatred of the public "oppressor" (of patriarchy, of a war-waging government) to the private oppression she experiences "in a house," the "love and fear" she may feel for a lover seen as another kind of oppressor.

The lover is the subject of the poem's second section, in which the cultural pursuits of the neighbor mentioned at the poem's beginning (science and art) are translated into a description of sexual love, seen as "a time of chemistry and music." In a moment of heightened intimacy, the poet is at once delivered from the necessity of using language ("relief // from this tongue this slab of limestone") and yet in need of it, in order to communicate with another human being: "knowledge of the oppressor / this is the oppressor's language // yet I need it to talk to you." The lover then becomes not himself the "oppressor," but only another victim, forced to use the "oppressor's language" in order to communicate. Language becomes at once the enabler of and the barrier to private communication and love.

Language itself must be purged, for the oppressor's language deliberately distorts or deletes the fact of oppression: the disorder of poverty, the aggression of war. In seeking "the fracture of order / the repair of speech / to overcome this suffering," Rich quotes one of her students at the City University of New York, whose somewhat fractured yet eloquent prose reveals the sufferings of poverty.

This imperfect expression is, for Rich, far more eloquent than most books in her library, because it reflects and depicts social and political reality. She finds literature largely inadequate as a guide to life and especially to love. For literary experience does not necessarily clarify feeling; one must burn through (not burn up) language to reach the truth it at once embodies and conceals: "so on that page / the clot and fissure / of it appears / words of a man / in pain / a naked word / entering the clot / a hand grasping / through bars . . . / *burn the texts* said Artaud." In Artaud's revolutionary formulation, only by destroying accepted texts can the meaning hidden in language be released from its imperfect embodiment, so that a revolution in feeling as well as politics can occur.

In the final section of the poem, Rich connects her private voice with the public speech of protests, such as that of the Berrigans and even her own political speeches: "I am composing on the typewriter late at night, thinking of today. How well we all spoke." In extemporaneous verse, Rich provides a different kind of language, more personal and improvisational than the received wisdom of the official, oppressor's language.

For Rich, here language can only reflect the poetry-killing reality of the war and other forms of suffering. Suffering can be articulated only briefly and in glimpses, as, echoing her student's words, she notes: "Some of the suffering are: it is hard to tell the truth; this is America; I cannot touch you now." Finally, Rich is unable to overcome the numbness that comes from years of watching American brutality in Vietnam: "The burning of a book arouses no sensation in me." The Berrigans' protest and what it is protesting are linked, as the fires of her own anger and faith become the fires of oppression which neither she nor her poetry can escape: "I know it hurts to burn. The typewriter is overheated, my mouth is burning, I cannot touch you and this is the oppressor's language."

In this poem, Rich has tried to use the literature of the past as a resource, but only finds herself consumed by the burning within and outside of her. Clearly, the war has come home ("there are flames of napalm in Catonsville, Maryland") and though she wishes to protect her son, she must also face the necessity of seeing her own numbness passed down to her child, who thus may lose a sense of morality. Yet in the final conflagration of **"The Burning of Paper Instead of Children,"** Rich succeeds at least in questioning the certainties of language (an important effort since, as Berrigan writes, he was in danger of "verbalizing my moral impulses out of existence") and virtually burning through language itself, attempting to escape its falsifying potential to provide a medium that reflects suffering and feeling.

While the poet's voice becomes almost literally self-consuming in **"The Burning of Paper Instead of Children,"** it is more detached and analytic in **"The Phenomenology of Anger"** (1972), from ***Diving into the Wreck.*** Here, as the title implies, the poet steps back from her anger to depict the horrors of war with an almost documentary precision, rather than the tumultuous agglomeration of events and images with which **"The Burning of Paper Instead of Children"** concludes.

In this poem, written in the same year as **"Diving into the Wreck"** (1972)—a poem in which Rich sorts through the detritus of history to recover the history of women—, she sorts through a series of frightening emotions: forms of anger and "Madness. Suicide. Murder." The sometimes flat tone reflects the terror and numbness of a time near the end of a seemingly endless war, which Rich describes as "Time without a taste: time without decisions."

In this poem, Rich longs for burning as a release from stasis. Just as she initially envies "the freedom of the wholly mad," she longs for fire—for passion, for emotion—which she cannot kindle. Even on a literal level, she cannot start a fire from logs, though she welcomes the "warm sweet simmer of the hay." She differentiates the burning of natural passion from the artificial destruction of war. Her vision of "the enemy" here is as the opposite of what burns: something frozen, "shrouded / in a snowy blur, abominable snowman." While the language of war would see the Vietnamese people as the enemy, here the enemy is a hypostatized villain, sub- or superhuman, that has no country. The enemy is the personification of war itself, of the kind of thinking that dichotomizes and polarizes countries and people:

"at once the most destructive / and the most elusive being / gunning down the babies at My Lai / vanishing in the face of confrontation. // The prince of air and darkness / computing body counts, masturbating / in the factory / of facts."

The poet directs her pain and rage not inward, towards madness and suicide, but in a focused attack on the beast of war itself:

> . . . When I dream of meeting
> the enemy, this is my dream:
>
> white acetylene
> ripples from my body
> effortlessly released
> perfectly trained
> on the true enemy
>
> raking his body down to the thread
> of existence
> burning away his lie
> leaving him in a new world; a changed
> man

The "true enemy" is not the Vietnamese people but the war machine and patriarchy itself, and Rich sees herself as using the heat of her voice, her passion, and her body to strip away the "lie" of those institutions and to make the world anew.

Yet the distortions of personal life that are caused by or parallel to the distortions of war remain. Against the background of her protests against the war, Rich sketches the picture of an alienated personal life, in which her lover withdraws from her into activities hauntingly reminiscent of the war. A simple domestic gesture—the spreading of a pesticide, perhaps, or the burning of crops to make them grow more—takes on sinister overtones, as the lover becomes a version of the enemy who attacked "the babies at My Lai," who takes refuge from emotional issues in artificial destruction: "you are out there burning the crops / with some new sublimate. . ."; "Last night, in this room, weeping / I asked you: *what are you feeling? / do you feel anything?* // Now in the torsion of your body / as you defoliate the fields we lived from / I have your answer." Rich suggests that the deformation of private feeling is not just a consequence but the cause of war, the source of the capacity to become detached from feeling which enables atrocities like the one at My Lai to occur.

Against the background of this unnatural destruction, Rich longs for a life at one with nature, a landscape which begins to sound not unlike that of Vietnam: "I would have loved to live in a world / of women and men gaily / in collusion with green leaves, stalks, / building mineral cities, transparent domes, / little huts of woven grass / each with its own pattern— / a conspiracy to co-exist with the Crab Nebula, the exploding / universe, the Mind—." The consciousness with which the poet seeks to place herself in harmony is that of the universe itself, an almost God-like intelligence or at least a natural governing order.

But this image of Utopian cities composed of natural structures is only a dream. In reality she sees "how we are burning up our lives" as the poem concludes with a Dantesque vision of a city with subway riders apparently "asleep or drugged." Nonetheless, the burning of passion and anger within her is present in others as well, even those who seem numbed. Finally, in this poem she is not consumed by that passion but gains from it a revolutionary stance, a new form of consciousness which, unlike the fire of "defoliation" or the "new sublimate," burns with a purgative force:

> others sit
> staring holes of fire into the air
> others plan rebellion:
> night after night
> awake in prison, my mind
> licked at the mattress like a flame
> till the cellblock went up roaring
>
> Thoreau setting fire to the woods
>
> Every act of becoming conscious
> (it says here in this book)
> is an unnatural act

In wartime, the revolutionary, what deviates from accepted wisdom, is seen as unnatural, yet it is in reality the most natural of all, as she implies by invoking Thoreau, naturalist and revolutionary.

While, in **"The Burning of Paper Instead of Children,"** the poet and poetry are virtually consumed from within, in this poem the poet's analysis of her anger as phenomenon allows the fire to be expressed in condemnation of the most horrible atrocities, and to forge a new language and consciousness. Rich's "dream of a common language" depends first of all on the capacity to create a new subjectivity which avoids the threats of "madness" and "suicide," to refine anger to an "acetylene" intensity and focus, and then to share that new consciousness with others who "burn" similarly under the weight of oppression. In poems like **"Nightbreak,"** where her body becomes the Vietnamese village, or **"Planetarium,"** where she similarly becomes the receptacle for radio signals, Rich takes the status of victim into her own consciousness and even her own body. She forges a new, feminist subjectivity based on the rejection rather than imposition of oppression, the identification with rather than opposition to "the enemy."

Such identification means for Rich exploring a particularly female capacity to overcome the difference between self and other, which she sees as a "source of power" (**"Three Conversations"** [1974], *ARP* 115). The subjectivity which for Rich begins as a site or result of wounding becomes ultimately a way to heal and remake reality. The use of sexuality as the ground on which language and love rather than aggression must be founded enables her to connect a feminist consciousness with the female body. In her poetry, her subjectivity becomes a new mode of truth.

Through Rich's symbolism and her innovative, seemingly improvisational, forms, her most private experience (as depicted in the poetry) becomes the foundation for a feminist consciousness that is a political as well as a personal force. In **"A Valediction Forbidding Mourning"** (1970), she notes her desire, in the face of meanings that elude her, "to do something very common, in my own way." In **"Implosions"** (1968), the poet notes that "I wanted to choose words that even you / would have to be changed by" and asks the anonymous "you" to "Take the word / of my pulse." That language, founded in the body, borne along the blood, becomes in **"When We Dead Awaken"** (1971) an elemental force, the blue vein of her pulse translated into a vein in bedrock:

> Here in the matrix of need and anger . . .
> . . . never have we been closer to the truth
> of the lies we were living, listen to me:
> the faithfulness I can imagine would be a weed
> flowering in tar, a blue energy piercing
> the massed atoms of a bedrock disbelief.

In poems like **"Planetarium"** (1968), her individual quest for wholeness and linguistic expression becomes a communal one:

> I am an instrument in the shape
> of a woman trying to translate pulsations
> into images for the relief of the body
> and the reconstruction of the mind.

Here it is not only her own body that she seeks to relieve nor her own mind that she tries to reconstruct. From the depths of her own subjectivity, Rich forges a new, woman-centered consciousness in which individual perception becomes part of a common understanding and common good. This common language is one her poetry at once exemplifies and helps to create.

Rich's feminist consciousness was forged in the fires of Vietnam, in protests against the war and sometimes against the protesters as well. The necessity of linking feminism and pacifism so forcefully underlined by Rich in prose (***Of Woman Born; On Lies, Secrets, and Silence***) as well as poetry was made clear again as fires burned in Iraq and Kuwait during the Gulf War in 1991. For only when feminism continues to critique militarism can both peace and women's freedom have a chance.

Alice Templeton (essay date Fall 1993)

SOURCE: "Contradictions: Tracking Adrienne Rich's Poetry," in *Tulsa Studies in Women's Literature,* Vol. 12, No. 2, Fall, 1993, pp. 333-40.

[*In the following essay, Templeton provides an overview of the major trends and themes of criticism in Rich's poetry.*]

Adrienne Rich's poetry has always raised important, difficult questions about the cultural uses of poetry and the ideology of poetic and critical tradition. For over forty years her work has provided the occasion for critics to comment on the art of poetry, its political significance, the character of poetic tradition, and the value of poetry as a critical and creative cultural activity. Ranging in tone from eulogistic to condemnatory, prescriptive to paternal, these critical statements comprise a narrative that divulges part of the use to which Rich's poetry has been put; and like an exemplary exercise in dialogical discourse, the narrative implied by Rich criticism contains contradictory claims whose meanings modulate as new contexts and statements arise.

In 1951 W. H. Auden praised Rich for the craftsmanship and modesty in the poems in her first volume, ***A Change of World,*** published in the Yale Series of Younger Poets. Though Auden greatly underestimated Rich's role in reshaping the modernist tradition, the two issues raised in his introduction continue to interest critics of Rich's work: the question of whether Rich manages the "detachment from the self and its emotions without which no art is possible," and Rich's place in poetic tradition, especially her development from a "modest" participant in modernism to a radical critic of the solipsism and sexism often implied in a modernist aesthetic. The artistic standing of Rich's poetry and its resistant relation to the dominant poetic tradition preoccupy critics throughout every stage of Rich's work, from the early formalist poetry in her first two volumes, through the woman-centered, feminist writings culminating in the seventies with ***The Dream of a Common Language*** (1978), to Rich's postmodern feminist critique of a range of subjects, including her personal heritage, the legacies of historical and national location, and ideologies of time and aging in the volumes since ***A Wild Patience Has Taken Me This Far*** (1981).

Seven books of criticism published in English in the last twenty years express contradictory evaluations of Rich's work as they illustrate the challenges that her poetry presents to academic criticism. In 1975 Norton issued a critical edition [*Adrienne Rich's Poetry*], edited by Barbara Charlesworth Gelpi and Albert Gelpi, which includes selected poems, excerpts from Rich's prose and interviews, critical articles, and reviews. Published on the heels of Rich's first overtly feminist volume of poetry, ***Diving Into the Wreck*** (1973), the Norton critical edition collects pieces that reveal the tension and contradiction characteristic of Rich criticism in the sixties and seventies. While Robert Boyers condemns Rich's work for having become "charged . . . with the nauseous propaganda of the advance-guard cultural radicals" and urges the poet to abandon the "will to be contemporary" for higher, aesthetic ground, Wendy Martin praises the poetry for organizing "an intricate and complex cluster of perceptions which comprise the reality of the modern woman." Certainly Rich's enfranchisement of the female reader partly accounts for the threat some critics perceive to aesthetic excellence: Boyers even charges that Rich appeals to readers who "are nothing but contemporary and who therefore can have little sense of the proper gravity of the poetic art." Two apparently contrary critical impulses emerge in the Gelpis' edition, sometimes manifested, as with Helen Vendler, in the same critic: the defense of poetry as a nonpolitical, universal, aesthetic enterprise and the appreciation of Rich's oppositional stance, particularly her articulation of the complications of contemporary feminist thinking. The criticism in the Gelpis' first collection portrays a poet who has been admitted into the academic canon but on probationary terms.

Nearly ten years after the Norton critical edition appeared, Jane Roberta Cooper edited an anthology of criticism entitled *Reading Adrienne Rich* (1984), which includes articles on the poetry (all written by women), reviews from 1951-1981, and studies of Rich's prose. As Cooper puts it, the critical essays "interpret Adrienne Rich's work on the terms she has chosen in the last decade," while the reviews are included "for their historical value." Among the reviews Cooper finds a "decisive split" between "feminist and patriarchal understandings of poetry, criticism, and gender"; those written before ***Diving Into the Wreck*** "betray the blind spots of masculine literary culture" by failing to acknowledge the poetry's specific focus on women's experience, while those written after 1973 are more likely to read Rich's work from a feminist perspective. The themes discussed in the essays remain constant concerns in Rich's poetry and in the criticism: the connection between poetry and political change, Rich's reading and writing of women's history in her poetry, language as both a liberating and constraining cultural legacy, the poet's engagement in a radical feminist discourse, Rich's feminist ethics, her place in American poetic tradition, and the poetry's intertextual resonances with the work of other poets. What is most apparent about these essays now is their determination to apply Rich's own feminist terminology and way of reading, as gleaned from her prose, lectures, and the poems themselves, without introducing extrinsic or nonfeminist critical paradigms. The essays are both valuable for their sympathetic hermeneutic, especially as we gain historical distance from that time, and limited to the level of expository analysis because of it.

Also in 1984, Myriam Diaz-Diocaretz, Chilean poet and translator of Rich's work, published three essays as a book under the title *The Transforming Power of Language*. To explain Rich's development of a feminist poetic discourse that emphasizes the communicative function of poetry over its expressive value, Diaz-Diocaretz analyzes Rich's unique author-position, the centrality of the reader in the poetry, and the constant inclusion within Rich's poems of "alien texts" that clarify and complicate the poet's stance. For example, the allusions to canonic English poetry in **"Snapshots of a Daughter-in-Law"** reveal the speaker's sense of cultural betrayal even as they express her knowledge of high culture; and the lines from Susan B. Anthony's diaries and the echo of Matthew Arnold in **"Culture and Anarchy"** establish a complex historical context for contemporary women's activism that is at once nurturing and conflictual. For Diaz-Diocaretz, as for Adrian Oktenberg in Cooper's book, Rich's radical feminist discourse is epitomized in ***Twenty-One Love Poems,*** the cycle of lesbian lyric poems that reinvents as it subverts the tradition of heterosexual love sonnets. Though the book lacks careful editing, Diaz-Diocaretz's use of continental critical concepts, specifically Michel Foucault's "author-function" and Julia Kristeva's "intertextuality," makes her feminist analysis more suggestive for the present reader than much of the criticism that depends solely on close readings and critical paradigms intrinsic to Rich's writing.

In *Translating Poetic Discourse* (1985), Diaz-Diocaretz expands her analysis of Rich's radical poetic discourse by discussing the particular ideological and linguistic difficulties of translating Rich's poems into Spanish. In the case of Rich's poetry, translating worlds is as crucial as translating words: the translator must not only communicate with the reader steeped in the norms of the Spanish world but also find equivalents in that world for the cultural icons and texts that Rich constantly incorporates as a means of defining her iconoclastic, "homosocial" stance in relation to dominant culture. The book continually offers examples of the ways in which Rich's use of language, not just her themes, challenge heterosexual cultural assumptions. It provides not only a systematic semiotic reading of Rich's work, but also insight into the ideological, creative work of translation and its importance in shaping literary history. Diaz-Diocaretz is one of the few critics of Rich's work who, without qualifications, embraces Rich's radicalism, locating it in her use of language rather than in themes alone.

In *The Aesthetics of Power* (1986), Claire Keyes frames her chronological reading of Rich's poetry through ***A Wild Patience Has Taken Me This Far*** (1981) with American feminist concepts, including Elaine Showalter's "wild zone," Judith Kegan Gardiner's definition of female identity as a process, and Tillie Olsen's insistence on the usefulness of art. Keyes traces Rich's development of a specifically "female" aesthetics as the poet attempts to resolve the "dilemma of power" that her identity as both poet and woman raises: the "artist's ability to shape her forms does not necessarily translate to her ability to shape her environment or gain control over her life." According to Keyes, Rich eventually conceptualizes a "beneficent female power—both personal and political—predicated upon her own experience as woman and poet." Yet Keyes concludes that in ***A Wild Patience*** Rich's beliefs take precedence over poetry, so that "truth" is not discovered in the process of making the poem, but is preordained. Like many critics of Rich's work, even sympathetic ones, Keyes finally abandons the crucial question raised by her own analysis and by Rich's poetry—i.e., the connection between poetic and literal power—and retreats in her conclusion to the comfort of rather standard aesthetic criteria. Keyes worries that Rich too often strays outside the boundaries of the poetic enterprise to write documentary disguised as poetry. The present reader might value the book more if Keyes had examined in theoretical terms the assumptions behind her aesthetic judgments and the antagonism she finds between the aesthetic and pragmatic powers of poetry.

The most recently published full-length study of Rich's work, Craig Werner's *Adrienne Rich: The Poet and Her Critics* (1988), offers readings of Rich's poems in the context of her entire poetic project while it examines other critics' approaches, many of which ignore the process-oriented poetics Rich espouses. Even as he defends Rich's own process as the primary context for evaluating individual poems, Werner offers very close, formalist readings and analyses of prosody of single poems. In this way he not only argues for the organic integrity of Rich's canon, but also answers those critics, including Helen Vendler and Cary Nelson, who find aesthetic flaws in much of Rich's politically engaged work. Werner describes the contradictions within Rich criticism as a "clash" between academic critics who, rather than actually engaging in Rich's process, dismiss her feminism as mere orthodoxy and Rich's feminist aesthetics, which works against the "cultural solipsism" and isolated subjectivity that literary study has traditionally privileged. Unlike most criticism that analyzes Rich's poetic career as a self-conscious process of personal and communal transformation, Werner's study is organized primarily by themes, and only secondarily by chronology.

Werner closes his book with a chapter that places Rich in the context of American poetry, a task that compels critics of all leanings. Several critical books that attempt to define poetic tradition devote a section or chapter to Rich's work. Suzanne Juhasz's *Naked and Fiery Forms* (1978), Deborah Pope's *A Separate Vision* (1984), Wendy Martin's *An American Triptych* (1984), Alicia Ostriker's *Stealing the Language* (1986), and Paula Bennett's *My Life a Loaded Gun* (1986) all place Rich's work in a continuum of American women's writing. David Kalstone's *Five Temperaments* (1977), Cary Nelson's *Our Last First Poets: Vision and History in Contemporary American Poetry* (1981), Charles Altieri's *Self and Sensibility in Contemporary American Poetry* (1984), and Walter Kalaidjian's *Languages of Liberation: The Social Text in Contemporary American Poetry* (1989) evaluate Rich's unique contribution to American poetry by comparing her vision and poetics to those of male contemporaries. Rich's formal training and self-conscious participation in poetic tradition demand that her work be understood in the context of mainstream American poetry; yet her position since the early seventies as a radical political poet who challenges the very terms of academic literary debate makes her a resistant, uncooperative figure in conventional discussions of poetic tradition. As Anne Herzog has commented, it is impossible to assimilate Rich's political poetry fully into "a tradition which exonerates instead the formally-interested, politically 'disinterested,' 'complete' and controlled personal lyric." Certainly, though, in the present climate of politicized criticism, it is now impossible for critics either to take the claims of such a tradition at face value or to ignore the political implications of the personal lyric, no matter what disclaimers come with it.

The emphasis in Rich's feminist writing on the communicative value of poetry also places her work within the American poetic tradition but sets it against the American formalist critical tradition. Helen Vendler notes that like mainstream, "plain-style" American poets who resist elitist aestheticizing in favor of engaging an "ordinary" audience, Rich "asks to be judged on effectiveness, rather than on conventional ideas of 'beauty.'" Cary Nelson explains, with some regret, that Rich's poetics, which values poems more as a means to effect change rather than as aesthetic ends in themselves, disrupts the authority of externally imposed aesthetic standards: "The criterion for value becomes the degree to which the poem participates in the developing poetic. A particular poem may be of interest . . . even when it is not very good." As Oktenberg has said, unlike most contemporary poets who produce "an accumulation of poems," Rich has created a self-contextualizing, self-referential "body of work" that alternately satisfies and disappoints formalist critical strategies. Perhaps no American poet is as convinced as Rich is of the liberating potential of literary experience yet at the same time as systematically skeptical of the ideological machinery on which literary study rides.

That fact makes the Gelpis' latest version of the Norton critical edition [*Adrienne Rich's Poetry and Prose* (1993)] a welcome but somewhat disquieting newcomer to the party of Rich criticism. It is long overdue, since the original edition (1975) has been outdated as a textbook for some time. The new edition represents Rich's writing more fully by reprinting selected poetry through ***An Atlas of the Difficult World*** (1992) and selected prose published since the earlier edition. It retains three of the critical essays from the earlier version (by W. H. Auden, Albert Gelpi, and Helen Vendler), includes some feminist essays from Cooper's book (by Judith McDaniel, Adrian Oktenberg, Olga Broumas, and Margaret Atwood), and also adds more recent critical pieces by Charles Altieri, Terrence des Pres, and Willard Spiegelman that valuably analyze Rich's distinct poetic strategies, especially in the context of American poetry and of "political" poetry. A timeline of critical poses unfolds: the early formalist criticisms and reviews with their reserved praise of Rich's promise, the feminist essays that appreciate the poetry for its focus on social and personal transformation, and the newer brand of essentially formalist essays that grant rather than resist the political coloring of Rich's lyric pose as they discuss primarily aesthetic issues. The political awareness in the recent essays especially reveals the difference that work like Rich's has made in critical standards, yet alongside the tones of formalist caution and feminist commitment, they also suggest a new, subtle level of tension between the poet and the critical establishment. Now, instead of displacing the antagonistic or overly accommodating critical attitude, perhaps the challenge for Rich's writing as it seeks to invite the reader into cultural participation will be overriding the current nonchalance about poetry's political value, an attitude that can easily trivialize the costs and rewards of Rich's poetic project even as it acknowledges them.

The Gelpis' book stands as a reminder that even as the poet lives and writes, the historical grit that irritated her into writing poetry is already being ground to a smooth textual surface (by history? by critical overdetermination? by changes in cultural values?), whose rough geology will have to be composed by the reader's historical imagination. Rich's poetry demands the jagged, painful terrain of engaged memory, not just the soothing continuity of order. Like most retrospective collections of selected works and critical essays, the new Norton edition by its nature implies a continuum in the poetry and the criticism that obscures the risks involved in each of Rich's own writings and the turbulence her work caused among critics—difficulties that the collision of different kinds of texts, not just academic essays and reviews, might convey. If it were not for the poetry itself, the new Norton critical edition would make it easy to forget that Rich was ever, and ever is, on probation, if no longer obviously with the critical establishment, then with her own creative and political conscience.

Because Rich's poetry constantly puts the practice and use of literary art under suspicion, almost no critic of Rich's work can avoid discussing the paradoxes and politics within the criticism itself; however, along with weaving its own self-reflexive narrative, criticism also needs to account for the cultural currency of Rich's work outside the academy. Feminist-informed cultural critics are likely to focus more on the participatory role of the reader in Rich's writing, noted by Diaz-Diocaretz, Patrocinio Schweickart, and others, to determine the pragmatic effects of Rich's poetry as it works to transform the reader from a passive cultural receptor into an active cultural participant.

Future criticism promises to be more eclectic in its uses of theory both to reflect the insights of postmodern feminism and to address Rich's extension, in her latest three volumes, of feminist analysis to ideological systems other than sexual difference. Rich's most recent volume ***An Atlas of the Difficult World,*** which concerns individual and communal uses of monuments and icons of all kinds, clearly calls for more acute discussions of the relations between aesthetic value and existential effect, and demands further critical examination of our ways of reading and using cultural icons, including poems and poetic tradition. As Rich continues to search for "a reader by whom I could not be mistaken," the critic of Rich's work will aspire to be that reader. Both will find qualified fulfillment because, fortunately, like the constantly changing narrative composed by Rich's critics, the poetry will not keep still for either the writer or the reader.

Langdon Hammer (essay date Winter 1995)

SOURCE: "Art and AIDS; or, How Will Culture Cure You?," in *Raritan,* Vol. 14, No. 3, Winter, 1995, pp. 103-18.

[In the essay below, Hammer meditates on various aspects of the relation between "culture" and "AIDS"—between aesthetics and sexuality—by comparing Rich's "In Memoriam: D. K." and James Merrill's "Farewell Performance."]

This essay will address the question in my title through a reading of two poems. One is by Adrienne Rich, the other by James Merrill; both are elegies for the literary critic David Kalstone. In each case, Kalstone's death in 1986 from AIDS-related causes provokes a troubled meditation on the relation between culture and AIDS. *Culture* is Rich's word for the high art of Mozart and Keats, and I will use it in that restricted, old-fashioned sense, since it is exactly the high-art forms of the ballet, opera, and lyric that are in question for Rich and Merrill. Culture is seen in their poems as powerless to help people with AIDS, so removed is it from the material realities of disease and death. Yet culture also seems strangely involved in the suffering caused by HIV, as if it were itself infected. The instability of the relation between culture and AIDS in these poems—the feeling that high art is alternately remote from the catastrophe "AIDS" names *and* deeply implicated in it—structures the unstable, ambivalent relations between these poets and their friend. Those relations include in each case erotic longing and erotophobic dread. At issue for both poets is the connectedness of grief and fear—grief that they have been separated from their friend, and fear that they may be reunited with him.

The pairing of Rich and Merrill, the political poet and the esthete, may seem an unlikely one, but there is a precedent for it in *Five Temperaments,* Kalstone's critical study of Lowell, Bishop, Merrill, Rich, and Ashbery, published in 1977. Although set forth in Kalstone's characteristically modest, nonpolemical prose (or just for this reason), *Five Temperaments* helped to define and secure one of the canonical formations in postmodern American poetry. Kalstone's practice in *Five Temperaments*—his focus on individual poets, the informal elegance of his style, his reliance not on any kind of theory but on his own taste and discrimination (his own "temperament")—reflects the virtues he sees in the poets he writes about. The group they constitute in his book is imagined less as a movement or school than as a coterie. That it is a homosexual coterie goes without saying—literally, since Kalstone does not explicitly discuss lesbian and gay sexuality, although only one of the "five temperaments" he studies—Robert Lowell's—is straight. Kalstone simply assumes, rather than argues, the paradigmatic status of homosexual writing; queer poems are the norm in his work. In a sense, the question of sexuality is sublimated in his criticism in the same way that he sees sexuality sublimated in the poems he discusses. The word *temperament* is important. Borrowed from Balanchine's *Four Temperaments,* it calls attention to Kalstone's faith in the value of the individual sensibility. Both essential to the making of art and itself the outcome of esthetic experience, sensibility for Kalstone is created through a tempering process by which the poet moves beyond the passions and losses of lived experience—seen, in Kalstone's chapters on Rich and Merrill, as specifically sexual fires—toward a distinctive, formalized self. Ballet is a suggestive model for this process: its way of using the natural body, which it turns into a stylized esthetic form, is analogous to the way these poets recreate their lives in and through art. The result in *Five Temperaments* is an ethical criticism centered on the question of what kind of life poetry makes available to poets and readers. Near the end of his book Kalstone writes: "we learn from the best of these poets what writing can and cannot do for their lives."

Given this emphasis in his criticism on poetry's value for living, it is perhaps not surprising that a number of poets have written about Kalstone's death, asking, in effect, what art could or could not do for Kalstone himself. These poets include, in addition to Rich and Merrill, Henri Cole, Alfred Corn, Anthony Hecht, Richard Howard, J. McClatchy, and Mona Van Duyn. They are poets strongly identified with the high-art traditions I am calling *culture*; and when they ask what art could or could not do for Kalstone, they are also asking what it can or cannot do for themselves and their readers. Kalstone is recalled in their poems as a beloved friend whose cultivation, sensitivity, and wit give moving proof that devotion to art can sustain and elevate a life. But they also suggest how AIDS threatens this idealization of the life-enhancing powers of art. In particular, these poems link anxieties about male homosexuality with anxieties about the effects of art. Although the connection between HIV-transmission and gay male sex is only contingent, male homosexuality and AIDS are indissolubly bound in the imaginative constructions of our society. This is the case in the nuanced literary texts I will be discussing no less than in the tabloid fantasies of mass culture. For Rich and Merrill, the sublimation of sexuality in esthetic experience seems to transfer the threat of infection from the realm of sexuality to that of art, leading both poets to wonder whether there is not something potentially unhealthy, even contaminating about art—above all, about art's effects on the way one lives. Kalstone makes such a compelling subject for poetry because his life and death both affirm and challenge the humanistic ideal of a cultured life, an ideal that is crucial not only to poetry that Kalstone particularly admired, but to most poetry written in America today.

Rich's poetry is not an exception, although her feminism makes her critical of the universalizing terms in which culture is usually defended. She began her career as a formalist poet writing in the same mode as Merrill. When she redefined herself as a feminist poet, Rich repudiated the elitism, as she saw it, of her early work. But this development was not a rejection, as much as an extension, of an assumption Rich shared with Kalstone: that culture can and should help people live. So when, in the middle of her poem **"In Memoriam: D. K.,"** Rich asks Kalstone, "How will culture cure you?," Rich is asking him the kind of question he asked in criticism, and that she has always asked in poetry. In the poem's opening paragraph, Rich speaks of her friend in the third-person as if he were ill but still alive and walking on the street. In the second paragraph, Rich addresses Kalstone in the second-person, asking him how he thinks culture is going to help him in his illness.

> And what good will it do you
> to go home and put on the Mozart Requiem?
> Read Keats? How will culture cure you?
>   Poor,
> unhappy
> unwell culture what can it sing or say
> six weeks from now, to you?

It is possible to hear these questions as mocking ones.

Heard in this way, they ironically, aggressively separate Rich from the culture-lover, the male critic who, infected by HIV, returns home to a sheltered space of esthetic reflection and listens to Mozart or reads Keats. In this setting, the contemplation of art is a means of thinking about dying that does not oblige the person with AIDS to take action or to connect his condition with that of less privileged people out on the street—to whose fate, however, his own remains bound. Bitterly, Rich's poem seems to ask of the dead man, What good does your refined temperament do you now? In another sense, though, Rich is asking Kalstone about the limits of her own ability, as a poet, to help him, as if she were saying, What good does my refined temperament, my culture, do you now? That guilty question is close to the surface of the poem when Rich shifts her attention to culture itself, which, as if sympathetically, seems as "Poor, unhappy," and "unwell" as the person with AIDS. In its incapacity to cure, culture has come to seem contaminated—elite, decadent, ineffectual.

There is also an implication that, before it can cure, culture itself must be cured; which is to say, culture must be disassociated from death, or more exactly, from a certain morbid construction of desire. Of course, the deathliness of desire and the desirability of death are familiar ideas in Romantic art. In her elegy for Kalstone, Rich is consciously writing against that tradition and its identification of beauty with morbidity. That is the polemical force of the striking and deliberate echo of Keats in Rich's last paragraph. Here is Keats's famous fragment, "This living hand," followed by the closing lines of Rich's poem:

> This living hand, now warm and capable
> Of earnest grasping, would, if it were cold
> And in the icy silence of the tomb,
> So haunt thy days and chill thy dreaming nights
> That thou would wish thine own heart dry of blood,
> So in my veins red life might stream again,
> And thou be conscience-calmed. See, here it is—
> I hold it towards you.

> Give me your living hand If I could take the hour
> death moved into you undeclared, unnamed
> —even if sweet, if I could take that hour
> between my forceps tear at it like a monster
> wrench it out of your flesh dissolve its shape in quicklime
> and make you well again
>   no, not again
> but still. . . .

"This living hand," Keats writes, extending it to the reader in a gesture that promises not so much to save the dying poet as to draw the reader into the text's odd, unliving afterlife. "Give me your living hand," Rich replies, speaking to her friend as if to Keats in an imaginative move that promises to reverse the deathly spell of the Romantic text and place Rich's poem safely, unambiguously on the side of life (where the poem appears, like the elegy by Merrill, in the anthology of AIDS poetry edited by Michael Klein, *Poets for Life*).

When I told a friend, a poet, I was working on Rich's elegy, he said, "I *hate* that poem! It's like Kalstone read Keats, got sick, and died." I don't hate Rich's poem—I admire it, but my friend was right about what it means to read Keats in this case. In the poem's first paragraph, death has "its music," as autumn does in Keats's final ode, and music somehow carries death within it. That opening paragraph makes us feel that reading Keats, or listening to Mozart, is like looking at beautiful flowers, and that these are both sexually exciting and potentially dangerous acts.

> A man walking on the street
> feels unwell has felt unwell
> all week, a little Yet the flowers crammed
> in pots on the corner: furled anemones:
> he knows they open
> burgundy, violet, pink, amarillo
> all the way to their velvet cores
> The flowers hanging over the fence: fuchsias:
> each tongued, staring, all of a fire:
> the flowers He who has
> been happy oftener than sad
> carelessly happy well oftener than sick
> one of the lucky is thinking about death
> and its music about poetry
> its translations of his life

The man on the street "feels unwell," "Yet the flowers" call him out of himself; he looks on them as a consolation, if not a cure, for disease. But they signify something more like the cause of the man's illness, since the poem allows one to feel that it was the carelessness of his happiness, the false sense of immunity that came with being "one of the lucky," a man privileged by temperament and culture, that exposed him to infection to begin with. Rather than making sexuality seem as innocent as esthetic contemplation, the implicit analogy between them makes esthetic contemplation seem as highly fraught as sexuality. The flowers arouse in Rich's friend a desire to penetrate them, or to offer himself for penetration in the same way that the flowers seem to, these brilliantly colored, "furled" anemones that open ("he knows") "all the way to their velvet cores." The "tongued" and "staring" blooms are a line-up of boys, "all of a fire," as beautiful and threatening as the death-bound young man who reaches out to the reader in Keats's fragment.

Because death and desire are linked in this way here, when Rich tries, in the last paragraph, to remove death from her poem, she must also try to remove sexual desire. "If I could take the hour / death moved into you," Rich begins, envisioning death as a force that comes from outside the self, and specifically as a penetrating sexual partner. The metaphor fixes the "undeclared, unnamed" origin of infection in a moment of "carelessly happy" sex—what Rich refers to as the fatal "hour / death moved into you." She calls that hour a "a monster" not so much although, as because, it was also a "sweet" time: the horror Rich expresses arises both from the irreversibility of HIV infection and from the sexual form of its transmission. The irreversibility of HIV and its sexual transmission connect infection, in this case, with human conception—only it is death, not life, that gay male sex breeds. That is the underlying fantasy, I think, at the end of the poem. When the poet wishes she could extract death from the sick man's body, the tool that Rich imagines using, forceps, evokes childbirth and surgery at once, and she becomes a midwife bringing forth a monster born of desire and disease.

The man in the first line of Rich's poem, "walking on the street" like anyone else, confronts us with the "oxymoronic image of a healthy sick person," as Peter Bowen, in another context, has described the paradoxical status of HIV-infected people who are asymptomatic. The image is confusing, Bowen explains, because, "in addition to raising the frightening possibility that anyone . . . could be infected and not show it," it "complicates the rigid binary division that categorizes people as either healthy or sick, living or dying, and, to some extent, innocent or guilty." Rich moves to resolve this confusion of categories at the end of her poem when she reestablishes the difference between the living and dying, healthy and sick, by imagining the removal of death from the body of her friend. But Rich's fantasy only restates the confusion of categories she began with, and it points to her own implication in death. When Rich returns to "the hour / death moved into you," she is not reversing, as much as repeating, the penetration of the body that signifies death in this poem. For Rich's desire to enter her friend's body retraces the path death took there, putting her in contact with it. There is also a sense that, when she imagines her removal of death as a form of childbirth, Rich is placing the gay man with AIDS in the position of a woman. That gesture draws Kalstone away from the risks of gay male sexual practice evoked earlier in the poem, and it interprets Rich's relation to him according to the model of nurturant relations between women Rich has elsewhere called "the lesbian continuum." But the gesture works in the opposite direction too by emphasizing the poet's identification with her friend and drawing her closer to his unhealthy condition. That is, if the feminizing of the gay man with AIDS makes him like the poet, and therefore alive and well, it also makes her like him, which means infected and dying.

The danger Rich's identification with Kalstone conveys is reinforced by the ghostly presence of Keats's fragment. Recall the reciprocity Keats evokes: "if it were cold / And in the icy silence of the tomb," the speaker's outstretched hand would "So haunt thy days and chill thy dreaming nights / That thou would wish thine own heart dry of blood, / So in my veins red life might stream again." For the reader Keats addresses, the desire to exchange fluids with the dead—"red life"—will be motivated by a disturbed conscience, rather than sympathy. In the age of AIDS, "This living hand" speaks to the sexual guilt of survivors, and it proposes a kind of erotic sacrifice as a means of discharging that guilt (through a vampire fantasy long associated with same-sex desire: you will have to give up your own life, in the form of your blood, to satisfy the dead, the contamination of whose blood has killed them). Rich does not speak of such a terrifying exchange of fluids. Breaking off before completing her final sentence, the one that begins "if I could," Rich stops short of specifying what she would do, or give up, in order to bring her friend back to life. But Keats's proposition haunts Rich's incompleted one, which ends abruptly, but eloquently enough, in silence.

Rich's wish in this poem is to take hold of AIDS and "dissolve its shape in quicklime," but it is AIDS that takes hold of her poem and dissolves it. That is the powerful effect of the final fragmentary lines. Throughout the poem, Rich arranges her free verse with double-spacing within the line. These caesuras create a small but notable break within each line (suggesting an internal threat perhaps like that of the virus itself). At the end of the poem, Rich's lines break apart. This breaking occurs when Rich constructs the penultimate line by dropping a half-line down from the one above it ("and make you well again / no, not again") and then ends with a two-word phrase and ellipsis: "but still. . . ." These lines push Rich's poem to the edge of inarticulateness: Rich appears unsure of what she has "to sing or say" to her friend now that she has relinquished the fantasy of healing him. Admitting culture's incapacity to "cure" AIDS, to make the person with AIDS "well again," Rich claims for her poem only the power of make-believe—the power to speak to Kalstone as if he were not dead "but still" alive and uninfected. The final ellipsis enacts a falling away, then, that acknowledges that the hand Rich wishes to grasp is no longer living. There is grief in this conclusion. But there is also relief: the moment at which she is separated from her friend, when it becomes impossible to speak to him any longer (to go on pretending), the poet is also released from the threat the dead hand represents. At the end of the poem, Rich, not Kalstone, is restored to life.

. . . . .

Merrill's elegy for Kalstone is a suggestive complement to Rich's, because it explores the same confusion of categories hers does, but comes to a different conclusion. Rich's effort to place art on the side of life is consistent with the distrust of artifice, virtuosity, and performance she has shown throughout her career. In contrast, Merrill has always been dedicated to exactly these dimensions of esthetic experience. The title of his elegy, "Farewell Performance," declares that stance archly and sadly. But like Rich, Merrill is skeptical about culture's power to console. His poem, inscribed *for DK,* begins with an account of an evening at the ballet. It is perhaps a memory of the New York City Ballet performance of *Mozartiana* that Suzanne Farrell dedicated to Kalstone, her friend and admirer, two days after his death.

> Art. It cures affliction. As lights go down and
> Maestro lifts his wand, the unfailing sea change
> starts within us. Limber alembics once more
> make of the common
>
> lot a pure, brief gold. At the end our bravos
> call them back, sweat-soldered and leotarded,
> back, again back—anything not to face the
> fact that it's over.

"Art. It cures affliction." Merrill can only take this truism seriously by forgetting about his subject. But then that is just the cure art seems to offer, a temporary forgetting. Merrill has come to the ballet in memory of Kalstone, the balletomane, but the evening allows Merrill to forget his grief for a while, even as the account of it postpones, until the start of the third stanza, Merrill's acknowledgment of his friend's death: "You are gone." "At the end, our bravos / call them back," Merrill says of the dancers. The audience urges them "back, again back," with a will "not to face the / fact that it's over," implying that the need to defer this moment had compelled the audience's pleasure in the dance from the beginning. In this sense, art is no cure at all.

In fact, it might be seen as a cause of disease. This is the possibility Merrill goes on to explore, in a move strikingly like Rich's, when he compares esthetic experience to infection. This is Merrill's story of his own role in the performance of a private ceremony—the release of Kalstone's ashes in Long Island Sound.

> You are gone. You'd caught like a cold their airy
> lust for essence. Now, in the furnace parched to
> ten or twelve light handfuls, a mortal gravel
> sifted through fingers,
>
> coarse yet grayly glimmering sublimate of
> palace days, Strauss, Sidney, the lover's
> plaintive
> *Can't we just be friends?* which your breakfast
> phone call
> clothed in amusement,
>
> this is what we paddled a neighbor's dinghy
> out to scatter—Peter who grasped the buoy,
> I who held the box underwater, freeing
> all it contained. Past
>
> sunny, fluent soundings that gruel of selfhood
> taking manlike shape for one last jeté on
> ghostly—wait, ah!—point into darkness
> vanished.
> High up, a gull's wings
>
> clapped. The house lights (always supposing,
> caro,
> Earth remains your house) at their brightest set
> the
> scene for good: true colors, the sun-warm hand
> to
> cover my wet one. . . .

"You'd caught like a cold their airy / lust for essence," Merrill jokes, as if to explain the simple fact that "You are gone." Is there a sense in which Kalstone is dead *because* he loved the New York City Ballet? To answer that question, we need to remember that the dancers' transcendental drive is a lustful one, and that this lust can be "caught" like a cold. In "Matinees," a sonnet sequence that is also dedicated to Kalstone, Merrill makes the same set of associations. These lines come near the end of the sequence.

> When Jan Kiepura sang His Handsomeness
> Of Mantua those high airs light as lust
> Attuned one's bare throat to the dagger-thrust.
> Living for them would have been death no less.
>
> Or Lehmann's Marschallin!—heartbreak so
> shrewd,
> So ostrich-plumed, one ached to disengage
> Oneself from a last love, at center stage,
> To the beloved's dazzled gratitude.
>
> What havoc certain Saturday afternoons
> Wrought upon a bright young person's morals
> I now leave to the public to condemn.
>
> The point thereafter was to arrange for one's
> Own chills and fever, passions and betrayals,
> Chiefly in order to make song of them.

Grand opera, not ballet, is the art form in question here. The soprano's thrillingly "high airs" operate like "lust" to open the poet's own throat to receive a deadly, sexual "dagger-thrust." In this theater of queer desires, where Merrill and Kalstone are both at home, art triumphs over nature, and the body opens itself to overwhelming, transforming passions. The self forged in this theater is a cultivated temperament, what "Farewell Performance" calls the "grayly glimmering sublimate of / palace days, Strauss, Sidney, the lover's plaintive / *Can't we just be friends?*" But the passage through fire "Farewell Performance" concerns is not metaphorical; Merrill is discussing the cremation of his friend's body and the scattering of his ashes. "Matinees" (where the opera audience is a "furnace roaring praise") was written twenty years before "Farewell Performance." Viewed from the perspective of the later poem, the plan to arrange "for one's / Own chills and fever, passions and betrayals," is provocative. Someone might want to ask: Did David Kalstone kill himself? But the real question is: How can Merrill avoid that suggestion—and its homophobic charge—without also renouncing the desire for deathlike raptures?

Leo Bersani and, more recently, Tim Dean have addressed the general implications of that question by using the psychoanalytic concept of the death drive to locate a self-destructive moment in gay desire that is not simply an internalization of the murderous will of the so-called general population. I will not try to summarize their complex arguments, but I want to take from Dean, in particular, Lacan's reformulation of the death drive as the expression of an internal psychic conflict. In Dean's view, "Perhaps the greatest psychic horror of AIDS for a culture that always segregates and shifts death elsewhere is the way AIDS intertwines death with life—and with what is generally assumed to be the life force: the sex drive." This is the horror we see in Rich's elegy for Kalstone. For Dean, that horror is essential to *jouissance,* the notoriously untranslatable term Lacan uses to define the pleasure beyond the pleasure principle that is at the heart of human sexuality. Among American critics, *jouissance* has often been identified with a certain uncritical celebration of sexuality. Dean wishes to restore to it the negativity the term conveys in Lacan. "In its combination of sex and death," Dean explains, "*jouissance* is like AIDS"; and in this sense, the intertwining of sex and death in AIDS can be seen as a paradigm, not a perversion, of sexual desire. The idea is important because it breaks down the binary division between the living and the dead, and it gives us a theoretical model for "the oxymoronic image of a healthy sick person." With Dean's argument in mind, we can understand the "confusing" image of the person who is at once HIV-infected and asymptomatic as an image of the confusion of life and death that, in Lacan as in Freud, structures psychic life in general. The point is not that there is no difference between those who are infected with HIV and those who are not, but that the special "horror" of AIDS—its linking of sex and death—cannot be confined to the gay man with AIDS.

I think the final stanzas of "Farewell Performance" work toward the same idea. At first, Merrill seems to accept his severance from Kalstone when Peter, his lover, places his "sunwarm," living hand on Merrill's wet one. Peter's gesture recalls the poet to life, drying and warming the hand that released the dead man's remains into the underworld. But it is not easy to let go of the dead, and the question of the poet's relation to his dead friend returns when the dancers return to the stage for a last bow.

Back they come. How you would have loved it. We in
turn have risen. Pity and terror done with,
programs furled, lips parted, we jostle forward
eager to hail them,

more, to join the troupe—will a friend enroll us
one fine day? Strange, though. For up close their magic
self-destructs. Pale, dripping, with downcast eyes they've
seen where it led you.

Here Merrill recovers, not his friend, but the dancers his friend loved, who are also figures for his lovers. From the beginning, there is an interesting vagueness about the dancers. They are simply *they*—a pronoun that gives their bodies an indistinct, spectral quality, allowing them to float free of personality and gender, even as the poet emphasizes their physicality. "Sweat-soldered," when we see them in the second stanza, the dancers are fused together by glistening traces of the "sea-change" that was their performance. It is over, but they return, esthetic forms—stylized bodies—that triumph over time. Yet "up close their magic / self-destructs." "Self-destructs," because their sweat is a sign of human labor: their magic is dispelled by the same force, the body, that created it; their sweat reveals the bodily effort necessary to produce the transcendent effect of their effortlessness. For the audience as well as the dancers, it is a moment of desublimation that brings to consciousness the sexual intensities submerged in, and yet animating, the performance. In this sense, Merrill's verb "self-destructs" seems more pointed, suggesting not only that the magic of the dance destroys itself, but that it impels those under its influence to do the same. Perhaps the excitement of esthetic experience, like sexuality, is self-destructive in a way that Lacan's concept of the death drive is intended to describe.

"The aggressivity that interests Lacan," writes Richard Boothby, a valuable expositor of Lacan and Freud, "is not a defense of an ideal unity of the self but a rebellion against it. Aggressivity is a drive toward violation of the imaginary form of the body that models the ego." The aggressivity that Boothby speaks of works like the dancers' "airy / lust for essence": it uses the body to speak on behalf of the inexpressible desires excluded by the social ego, that is, everything in subjectivity that lies beyond representation. Expressing the inexpressible, the dancers' mastery of the body extends to the point of its violation and unmaking. This is the point arrived at in the middle of Merrill's poem when the dead man's ashes momentarily cohere in the "manlike shape" of a dancer—before they vanish into ocean darkness. From their own "sea-change," Merrill's dancers return to the stage "pale" and "dripping," as if drained or drowned. I would like to think that Merrill's language here, reinforced by his decision to write in Sapphic meter, is intended to recall Sappho's second ode, perhaps the most famous lyric expression of same-sex desire and one of Longinus's examples of the sublime. Sappho's poem breaks off at the moment when, bearing her toward the woman she wants, passion drives the poet toward death: "Cold sweat pours off me; shivering grips me all over; I am paler than grass; I seem near to dying" (in Neil Hertz's translation). Like disease, desire seizes Sappho with a force she cannot contain—no more than the dancers can stop themselves from sweating. The fluids their bodies release (like tears, like cum, like night sweats) enact a radical dissolution of self.

The complexity of Merrill's relation to his dead friend is made clear in those closing stanzas. Wishing he could share the encore with Kalstone (and so call *him* back), Merrill is drawn to the stage in an erotic flurry ("lips parted") with the rest of the audience; perhaps Peter is included in the "we" Merrill describes. Merrill finds himself desiring not simply to hail the dancers in their other world, but to join them there. Feigning a giddy naiveté, Merrill wonders aloud, "will a friend enroll us / one fine day?" The troupe Merrill speaks of is an elite company of artists, like that of *Five Temperaments,* as surely as it is the spectral society of the AIDS dead. Heard as a question about sexually transmitted disease, the answer to Merrill's query is, Yes indeed, a friend may enroll you; maybe he already has. It must be this recognition that determines the poet's sudden sense of alienation ("Strange, though"), his abrupt recoil from the self-destroying magic of the troupe. It is hard not to hear a homophobic moral in Merrill's last sentence: "with downcast eyes they've / seen where it led you." That phrase "led you" evokes art's power to seduce those who live for it, with the pejorative meaning of "lead astray"; and there is no question but that the poet's friend has been led to death. Yet any sense in which Merrill may be felt to stand apart from his friend at the end of the poem, immune to art's magic, is qualified by the "downcast" eyes of the dancers. "Downcast" is an exceptionally rich word in this context. It implies mourning, regret, and shame; it is an English version of the Greek word "catastrophe"; and it reminds us that at this moment the dancers' eyes meet those of the audience below them. The magic of the dance led David Kalstone to the lip of the stage where James Merrill now stands in his place. The scene restages the scattering of Kalstone's ashes, when Merrill's own eyes were downcast, watching as his friend—with "one last jeté"—vanished in the waters below him. Now, the dancers look down on Merrill, who looks up at them. Who is in the underworld and who is not?

Culture cures no one in Merrill's poem. What it does do—what esthetic experience does—is break down the boundary between people on stage and in the audience, between people who suffer and those who observe them. Art, in this specific sense, communicates AIDS. At the end of Merrill's poem, in that final stanza, the dead and living recognize each other—or recognize themselves in each other—with a feeling of complicity I want to call love.

Betty S. Flowers (essay date 1995)

SOURCE: "Wrestling with the Mother and Father: 'His' and 'Her' in Adrienne Rich," in *Private Voices, Public Lives: Women Speak on the Literary Life,* edited by Nancy Owen Nelson, University of North Texas Press, 1995, pp. 54-63.

[*Below, Flowers ponders the significance of Rich's substitution of the "experiential, subjective, personal" feminine pronoun* she *for the "analytical, objective, universal" masculine pronoun* he *in her poem* "Afterward," *elucidating the consequence in relation to both feminist criticism specifically and literary criticism in general.*]

On a summer Texas day twenty years ago, a footnote to a poem shifted the geography of my mind. I have been wrestling with the issues this footnote raised ever since. The poem was Adrienne Rich's lyric **"Afterward":**

> Now that your hopes are shamed, you stand
> At last believing and resigned,
> And none of us who touch your hand
> Know how to give you back in kind
> The words you flung when hopes were proud:
> *Being born to happiness*
> *Above the asking of the crowd,*
> *You would not take a finger less.*
> We who know limits now give room
> To one who grows to fit her doom.

The footnote simply said that "her doom" was originally "his doom." Rich explained this change in a note to **"The Tourist and the Town":**

> The pronouns in the third part of the poem were originally masculine. But the tourist was a woman, myself, and I never saw her as anything else. In 1953, when the poem was written, some notion of "universality" prevailed which made the feminine pronoun suspect, "personal." In this poem, and in **"Afterward"** in ***A Change of World,*** I have altered the pronouns not simply as a matter of fact but because they alter, for me, the dimensions of the poem.

What Rich was saying to me is that she took a poem that was originally universal ("his") and simply by changing one pronoun ("his" to "her") made it "merely" subjective, personal, and political. When the pronoun is masculine, "We who know limits" is all humankind; when the pronoun is feminine, "We who know limits" are the other women now giving room "To one who grows to fit her doom." With "his" now "her," would the poem last beyond the feminist politics of the times within which it was written? Had Rich limited the long-term impact of the poem—its life?—by packing it in the fiery passion of the political moment rather than the salt and ice of the universal human condition?

More to the point: would I, in my role as teacher and literary critic, ever make such a "his" to "her" move, knowing how it would limit the impact of my voice? It seemed unthinkable, for I had worked most of my life to move out of the circumscribed realm of the mother, with its swamps of subjectivity and endless round of chores and dependencies upon the male, into the rock-like realm of the father, with its clear, cool, dispassionate atmosphere (so I imagined) and its world of books rather than babies. What hard labor it had cost to fly out of "her" nest and up into "his" tower. And once in the tower, what dangers of falling were all around.

I remember during my first semester as an assistant professor, one of my colleagues asking me how I felt knowing that I had taken a job that might otherwise have gone to a man who had to support a family. I remember considering submitting articles under non-gendered initials—except that I had the misfortune of having "B. S." as those initials. I remember . . . but these sorts of things happened to many of us who lived through this time.

Some dangers were more subtle. My first semester, a number of female graduate students asked me to help found a consciousness-raising group. In the heady early days of feminism, these CR groups formed the living cells of what became a new body of thought leading to action. Small and without media scrutiny, intimate and honest, these groups did just what they were called—they raised consciousness. We discovered that our most private fears were shared, that, for example, we all felt we had gotten into graduate school by some kind of fluke and that we would sooner or later be unmasked as the charlatans that we were. But I was not in graduate school any more, I was the one professor in a group of students who might take a course from me. Feminist solidarity?—or conduct unbecoming a professional? What would it mean for my academic reputation that my female students were hearing my most intimate fears as a woman? Soon I observed that my male colleagues were "Dr. Smith" and "Professor Jones," and I was "Betty Sue."

Other dangers were more subtle yet. As a five-year-old, sitting in the front row of the Methodist Church in Abilene, Texas, I whiled away the sermons of Dallas Denver Denison (some names are worse than "Betty Sue") by looking at the stained glass windows. My favorite was the one of Mary and Martha. Mary, the attentive student, was sitting at the feet of the Lord, and Martha was standing in the doorway holding a tray. I could almost hear her complaint because it echoed what my mother would say to my father: "Why don't you tell her to come help me in the kitchen?" And then the words of the Lord: "Martha, Martha, thou art careful and troubled about many things: But one thing is needful: and Mary hath chosen that good part, which shall not be taken away from her."

I was determined to choose the "good part," not the serving tray—the world of teachers and students, which I identified with the master in the living room (fathers) and not the mothers in the kitchen.

> Nervy, glowering, your daughter
> wipes the teaspoons, grows another way.
> (from Rich, **"Snapshots of a Daughter-in-Law"**)

But in my first year as an assistant professor, I was appointed to seventeen committees as the "token woman." And I spent countless hours counseling female students, including three who were suffering sexual harassment (as we later learned to call it) from senior professors in my college—what to do? I quickly realized that the job of female literature professor involved so much counseling that I needed to know more about psychology and so began a formal study of the subject. And then one day the associate dean of my college said, "Every minute you spend with a student is a minute you're not spending doing your research." And I was told that seventeen committees was fifteen more than my assistant professor colleagues had been asked to serve on. I was not so different from my mother after all, "careful and troubled about many things." And what was "that good part" that would not be taken away from me? My research leading to tenure? Should I turn away all the young women who were trying to find their voice so that I could write feminist literary criticism? So I could find my own voice of authority? So I could forget "her" problems and enter "his" universal world? What was my work in the world?

And what was the world in which I was working? I was in the same department as my male colleagues—but we seemed to be in utterly different worlds.

Which was the "real world" of a literature professor in a large, research university? What did it mean to teach human beings, especially women, and not just texts? What was the function of criticism: Knowledge for its own sake? To lead readers to a greater appreciation of a poem? To make students better readers and writers and so more effective as workers and citizens and leaders? To increase the capacity for joy through art? To serve my university by enhancing my reputation as a critic, thereby adding to the reputation of the university? Was the best thing I could do as a professor to close my door and read and write? After all, that is what had drawn me to the profession in the first place.

> There must be ways, and we will be finding out more and more about them, in which the energy of creation and the energy of relation can be united. But in those earlier years I always felt the conflict as a failure of love in myself. (Rich, **"When We Dead Awaken"**)

Now, here, in the middle of this article, I also am wrestling with the mother and the father. The energy of relation moves me in the direction of service—I want what I am saying to be of some use to you. I'm afraid I haven't said enough about Adrienne Rich's poetry, to share my admiration for her work and her life. I feel I should go to the kitchen and make some literary criticism and come back with a tray of it for you. In our profession, the mothers serve the fathers in us all.

But the voice that speaks with this desire is not the voice of the professional critic. The professional critic was not invited to this party. Instead, as the editor of this book says, "each woman is concerned with telling how the pursuit of literary study has, in a real sense, shaped her perceptions of her self and her work."

So what happened when I pursued the poetry of Adrienne Rich, the poet who changed "his" to "her"? First I went **"Diving Into the Wreck":**

> I am she: I am he
>
> whose drowned face sleeps with open eyes
> whose breasts still bear the stress
> whose silver, copper, vermeil cargo lies
> obscurely inside barrels
> half-wedged and left to rot
> we are the half-destroyed instruments
> that once held to a course
> the water-eaten log
> the fouled compass
>
> We are, I am, you are
> by cowardice or courage
> the one who find our way back to this scene
> carrying a knife, a camera
> a book of myths
> in which
> our names do not appear.

Yes, that was what I was up to—plotting a new course, asserting my identity apart from the old myths, uniting the male and female within:

> if I come into a room out of the sharp misty light
> and hear them talking a dead language
> if they ask me my identity
> what can I say but
> I am the androgyne
> I am the living mind you fail to describe
> in your dead language.
> (from Rich, **"The Stranger"**)

The image of the androgyne was compelling, for it seemed to offer a way beyond the polarized dualities of creation and relation that so plagued my work. True there was no androgynous pronoun to take the place of the polarized "his" and "her"; true there was no history or literature of androgyny to speak of and so nothing to ground it in. The androgyne was the vision of a future, not a clue to what had shaped us. No wonder female writers like Virginia Woolf and Adrienne Rich were drawn to it.

But then Rich moved more fully into "her," repudiating the androgyne in both her poetry and her prose:

> There are words I cannot choose again:
> *humanism androgyny*
>
> Such words have no shame in them, no diffidence
> before the raging stoic grandmothers: their
> glint is too shallow, like a dye
> that does not permeate
> the fibres of actual life
> as we live it, now . . .
> (from Rich, **"Natural Resources"**)

As Rich put it, "The very structure of the word replicates the sexual dichotomy and the priority of *andros* (male) over *gyne* (female)" (**"The Kingdom of the Fathers"**).

I could see Rich's point about androgyny, but I only half agreed with her about the raging grandmothers. I could not join with enthusiasm the more separatist feminists who were trying to find a new female voice, because the voice I knew when I honored the grandmothers was a voice of relation. At that point I began a long journey, a dialogue between the world of the past and the world of the future, mediated by whatever fullness of consciousness I could gather in the present. I could see my profession through that dialogue, knowing that whatever it would be in the future could not be a mere continuation of the past. Certain freedoms began to emerge.

One had to do with polarization, the tendency of the mind to turn difference into opposites. I began to emerge from the world of duality when I read a simple story in Irene de Castillejo's *Knowing Woman* about a woman who dreamed of her soul as a young girl. De Castillejo, a Jungian analyst, was familiar with Jung's dictum: "If, therefore, we speak of the *anima* of a man we must logically speak of the *animus* of a woman, if we are to give the soul of woman its right name." But what de Castillejo saw was that the female psyche was not set up as the mirror image of the male psyche—that difference was not opposition in spite of what our child minds might have concluded. I once was talking with a six-year-old nephew about a boxer we had seen on TV. He said, "Boys are strong, aren't they?" I said, "Yes." And then he added, "Girls are weak, aren't they?" I could see his thought process at work, its primitive logic: if boys are opposite from girls, and boys are strong, it follows that girls are weak.

We see this oppositional "logic" in much of literature: if men are logical, women are emotional; if men are logos, women are love. The left brain that writes is fascinated by the mystery of the Other. "Until we can understand the assumptions in which we are drenched," says Rich, "we cannot know ourselves" (**"When We Dead Awaken"**).

Understanding "the assumptions in which we are drenched"—that has come to be the passion that motivates my life as a literary critic. I say it a slightly different way—understanding the myths that have made us, the stories we tell about who we are. Like Rich, I have come to see this activity as a combination of poetry and politics. Deconstructing the stories we tell about who we are is political, for it involves wrestling with both the mother and the father of our culture. Seeing the new stories that might be emerging—or helping to give birth to them—falls into the realm of poetry, of mythos. Analysis is useful in the destruction of the old; but mythos holds the energies of vision that create the new.

At one point in the recent feminist re-visioning of early history, it was popular to speak of early matriarchal societies. The archeological evidence for such early cultures has been shown to be problematic—but one image from that conversation about "the matriarchy" has remained with me as a vivid and useful one. It was said that the reason we couldn't find unequivocal evidence of a period of matriarchy was that we were looking for cultures in which queens reigned instead of kings. But that's a polarized, patriarchal way of looking—it's not that a matriarchy would be the polar opposite of a patriarchy, with a queen on the throne instead of a king, but that it would be a different paradigm altogether, one of co-rulership.

With this complex image as a background, I asked the question: what would a methodology look like that was not simply a replacement of "his" by "her"? What if the move to replace the analytical, objective, and universal by the experiential, subjective, and personal is simply a move along the same continuum, like replacing "king" with "queen"? What would an entirely new methodology look like, one that lay outside this bipolar construct?

I have no immediate answer to this question—simply two responses. The first is represented by this article, which, like the other essays in this book, is written in an experiential, subjective, and personal mode. So little has been done from "her" end of the continuum that we have a limited idea of the possibilities or of what new ways of seeing might arise out of this more subjective practice. Even where the methodology has been "objective," as in much feminist criticism, the very act of looking at literature through feminist eyes has led us to put quotation marks around "objective" and "universal." Probably, were we to explore the subjective and personal in greater depth, we would be led to add quotation marks around those adjectives, also. For example, if we remained conscious that "the personal is political," we would be tempted to say "personal," adding the quotation marks to highlight our awareness of the always, already existing interconnectedness of the self with others.

In other words, a methodology that highlights "her" *within* the bipolar construct changes the nature of the poles. I came to appreciate the more separatist aspects of Rich's feminism through understanding this principle.

> . . . and we still have to reckon with Swift
> loathing the woman's flesh while praising her
> mind,
> Goethe's dread of the Mothers, Claudel vilifying
> Gide,
> and the ghosts—their hands clasped for
> centuries—
> of artists dying in childbirth, wise-women
> charred at the stake,
> centuries of books unwritten piled behind these
> shelves;
> and we still have to stare into the absence
> of men who would not, women who could not,
> speak
> to our life—this still unexcavated hole
> called civilization, this act of translation, this
> half-world.
> (from Rich, ***Twenty-One Love Poems***)

But my second response to the question of methodology is to suggest a different model, one that lies outside current bipolarizations but takes the tendency toward bipolarizations into account. My name for it at the moment is "dialogue," and I mean by this, putting disparate elements into a "working community" with each other and seeing what happens. I'm still groping towards this, but my experiments on the edge of the discipline lead me to feel there is treasure in the area, even if I have not found it in a usable form.

Let me give an example. One of the major assumptions in which we are drenched, to use Rich's phrasing, is what might be called "the economic myth." Material reality is bottom-line reality, and we look at history and literature through the lenses of class and power. We have great difficulty, for example, reading religious literature from within its own assumptions. But what if we consciously created an economic myth—a story about the future of the world, say, which was held as a fiction but used in planning?

Two years ago I joined a team of twenty people, most of them economists, to write global scenarios—the future of the world for the next thirty years. The project was sponsored by a multinational corporation as part of its planning cycle. What made it interesting to a literary critic experimenting with methodological boundaries was the fact that we were to create two equally plausible fictions about the future. These fictions would then be disseminated to company managers worldwide as a way of holding the corporate culture together—but also as a way to think about the future in common without falling under the illusion that we could know what that future might be.

During the time I was writing these stories, the company also sponsored scenario-building for the future of South Africa. Participants in South Africa came to the table to work on "fictions" who had never worked on politics together, and the four stories they created led the participants to adopt a common vision for change. Meanwhile, back in London, three of our team members began talking about the changes that occurred in their thinking about reality from working with the stories. To put it too simply, but briefly: they began to see that while the scenarios we had created were equally plausible, enough people "believing" in one could push events toward that story's conclusions. The dialogue of economic fact and narrative fiction began to result in a view of reality that was much more pliable and that reflected more of the "subjective" mind that looked "out" upon it than the team members had originally thought possible.

"This book is about desire and daily life," says Rich in the preface to ***What is Found There: Notebooks on Poetry and Politics***:

> I began it because I needed a way of thinking about poetry outside of writing poems; and about the society I was living and writing in, which smelled to me of timidity, docility, demoralization, acceptance of the unacceptable. In the general public disarray of thinking, of feeling, I saw an atrophy of our power to imagine other ways of navigating into our collective future.

"To imagine other ways"—that to me is the power of literature, the essence of the dialogue between readers and poets. Even when literature seems to reflect our experience almost exactly, we are led to see that we are not alone in our sorrow or joy—and in seeing that community of experience, we are seeing "another way."

But I think there are other ways of imagining our roles as literary critics, also. What if our dialogue were not only *with* literature but *from* literature—looking through literature at culture? What if we taught our students and our culture to hold the stories we tell about who we are *as* stories rather than as beliefs? Perhaps we could learn how to listen to each other and how to welcome different stories while searching for common threads. And perhaps as we wrestle with the bipolar categories of mother and father, creation and relation, that have shaped our thinking, we can begin "to imagine other ways of navigating into our collective future."

David St. John (review date 25 February 1996)

SOURCE: "Brightening the Landscape," in *Los Angeles Times Book Review,* February 25, 1996, p. 5.

[*In the following glowing review of* Dark Fields of the Republic, *St. John admires Rich's poetic style for its blending of personal details with broad public concerns.*]

During the past 40 years as a poet, essayist and political activist, Adrienne Rich has stood as a reminder of what an engaged political life coupled with a supreme poetic gift can offer to a starved culture. Given the bleak landscape of what seems to be our national political and social agenda, Rich's new collection of poems takes on a prescient resonance.

It would be hard to overstate Rich's influence as a cultural presence. There is no one whose poetry has spoken more eloquently for the oppressed and marginalized in America, no one who has more compassionately charted the course of individual human suffering across the horrifying and impersonal graph of recent history. Rich's extraordinary essays continue to be essential writings in the ongoing feminist struggle in this country and throughout the world.

The title of Rich's new collection, ***Dark Fields of the Republic,*** is drawn from the book's epigraph, a passage from *The Great Gatsby* that reflects the author's ongoing concern with the promises made by and failures attendant to the American dream. The realities of class and the disappointments that many have suffered in their hope for true equality in racial and gender issues seem mitigated for Rich only by the belief that the struggle for social good indeed continues, even in those—in our—"dark fields."

The poems therefore continue to be works of meditation, harsh reckoning, occasional despair and perpetual hope. Typically, Rich weaves deeply personal, even intimate, details of experience across a larger public tableau. In the poem **"To the Days,"** she writes, "Whatever you bring in your hands, I need to see it." And later in the same poem, "To smell another woman's hair, to taste her skin. / To know the bodies drifting underwater. / To be human, said Rosa—I can't teach you that."

The invocation here of Rosa Luxemburg, the social activist and one of Rich's longtime models, is a way for Rich to enlarge the private world with what she sees as the public resonance of each personal choice. That is why the poem, in addressing a "you" that becomes simultaneously a lover, the reader and a historical time, echoes at its end what the speaker has acknowledged at the poem's opening: "I want more from you than I ever knew to ask."

Yet other questions and demands inevitably blossom throughout ***Dark Fields of the Republic,*** as many of these poems confront the tension and conflict the poet feels from experiencing a great individual peace and even an intimate satisfaction with her companion, while still feeling the wrenching anguish of the world's daily events.

The book revolves around several powerful sequences of poems. The first, **"Calle Vision,"** is one of Rich's most deeply personal poems, examining the mirrored nature of love and suffering, echoing the transience of any body, any landscape, any history (even the most private). With her familiar defiance, Rich instructs herself and us, "never forget / the body's pain / never divide it."

The brief but troubling sequence, **"Then or Now,"** is an astounding meditation on the idea of political "innocence" or "guilt" among, Rich says in a note, "artists and intellectuals like myself in the United States." The final part of the poem, entitled **"And Now,"** serves as a candid, even explicit, apologia about a life in art and politics:

> I tried to listen to the public voice of
> our time tried to survey our public
> space as best I could—tried to
> remember and stay faithful to details,
> note precisely how the air moved and
> where the clock's hands stood and
> who was in charge of definitions
> and who stood by receiving them when the
> name of compassion was changed to
> the name of guilt when to feel with
> human stranger was declared obsolete.

Constellated around Rich's longer sequences are many wonderful individual poems, including **"From Pierced Darkness."** The poem sketches the urban purgatory of New York City in December, though the nearing holidays seem to bring little sense of generosity to the landscape or its figures. One passage notes:

> Her pierced darkness. Drag queen
> dressed to kill
> in beauty
> drawing her bridgelit shawls
> over her shoulders. Her caves ghosted by foxes.

She has also provided the poem **"Late Ghazal,"** a witty and moving *ars poetica* meant to echo poems from an earlier period in her career. It concludes:

> I took my body anyplace with me.
> In the thickets of abstraction my skin ran with
> blood.
> Life was always stronger . . . the critics couldn't
> get it.
> Memory says the music always ran ahead of the
> words.

Yet it is in the book's final sequence, **"Inscriptions,"** that we find again the remarkably complex braiding of the personal and public (or historical) that Rich perfected in the title poem of her previous collection, ***An Atlas of the Difficult World.*** Though more compressed than that poem, **"Inscriptions"** stands as one of the most powerful works of Rich's career.

"Inscriptions" asks: What is the progress of a sensibility—political, artistic or otherwise? How does one grow able to stand as an individual within any community of larger belief, that is, a belief larger than any individual? Rich's words are themselves inscriptions in a diary of lifelong political and social involvement, replete with intimate reflections and shrewd character sketches of fellow travelers.

The triumph of this poem is that its power resides, as with all of Rich's finest poems, with the delicacy of its details. It resists at every turn the question Rich asks throughout. "Should I simplify any life for you?" It is the poem of one lover for another, yet of a lover who also loves the larger world.

All poets know that there is nothing more difficult than melding a political conscience with a lyric speaking voice. Rich's poetry instructs us about the importance of finding a way. To summon any comparable literary accomplishment we need to look to the passionate work of the great Chilean poet Cesar Vallejo or to the luminous precision of the remarkable Polish poet Zbigniew Herbert. In this country, Adrienne Rich has no peer.

Denis Donoghue (review date 21 April 1996)

SOURCE: "Poetic Anger," in *The New York Times Book Review,* April 21, 1996, pp. 32-3.

[*In the review below, Donoghue faults the themes and tone of* Dark Fields of the Republic, *claiming that "each of the poems is interesting mainly because* [Rich] *wrote it."*]

Adrienne Rich publishes a new volume of her poetry every three or four years and, less frequently, books of prose on major concerns, especially themes *ad feminam.* Her readers treasure these books, I imagine, as a series of journals or notebooks, leaflets—evidence of Ms. Rich's desiring, thinking and feeling, her distinctive ways of being alive. As she wrote in ***The Dream of a Common Language,*** "The story of our lives becomes our lives."

It hardly matters, then, except to the history of American poetry, that few of her new poems achieve the autonomy of a work of art, floating free of their autobiographical contexts. Each of the poems is interesting mainly because she wrote it: the words return to their speaker and document her public life. I find her new poems hard to memorize; they slip in and out of my mind as many of her earlier poems don't, the poems that generations of readers continue to recite for pleasure and companionship. My short list of those includes **"Ideal Landscape," "The Middle-Aged," "Holiday," "Necessities of Life," "In the Woods," "The Roofwalker," "Face to Face," "Like This Together," "Open-Air Museum," "Two Songs," "The Demon Lover," "Night Watch"** and **"After Dark."**

Ms. Rich's first book was ***A Change of World*** (1951). In his foreword to it, W. H. Auden said that "poems are analogous to persons" and that "the poems a reader will encounter in this book are neatly and modestly dressed, speak quietly but do not mumble, respect their elders but are not cowed by them, and do not tell fibs." Since then, Ms. Rich has exercised her will to change. The poems in ***Dark Fields of the Republic*** are not notable for modesty of dress, they never mumble but they do not always speak quietly, they repudiate their elders as if on principle, and if they do not tell fibs they sometimes say things that are not true.

It is not true, for instance, as Ms. Rich says in **"Food Packages: 1947,"** that "Europe is trying / to revive / with the Jews somewhere else." That is not what Europe was trying to do in 1947. It is not true—or at least not adequate to a complex truth—that there was a moment in American public life

> when the name of compassion
> was changed to the name of guilt
> when to feel with a human stranger
> was declared obsolete.

Declared by whom? I wish the poet would name names instead of resorting to the diffuse incrimination of the passive voice. Nor is it true of "our country" that it has "its own ways of making people disappear." Ms. Rich well knows that "disappear" is an emphatic word in the vocabulary of state-enforced murder, and not only in Latin America. "Our country" is not justly to be compared with China, the Soviet Union, Chile, South Africa, Guatemala, Bosnia or any other state that has effected the disappearance of millions. But perhaps a poet is not on oath when she is angry, as Ms. Rich regularly is.

Over the course of many books, she has been turning her life into poetry, her poetry back into her life. She has written of herself as child, daughter, wife—the woe that is in marriage, "this sin / of wedlock"—and mother. "Mother I no more am, / but woman, and nightmare."

She has interrogated the values of home, homelessness, homesickness and shelter. She has also written of the body in pain, of living in a bad world ("a land-mass / puffed up with bad faith and fatigue") and of sundry fears oppressive in "turbid America." In many poems and essays, too, Ms. Rich has been reflecting on her most insistent theme, "the naked and unabashed failure of patriarchal politics and patriarchal civilization." Writing of these difficult ordinary matters, she has become a heroine to many, a representative woman—feminist, socialist, lesbian. Readers who do not share these avocations and commitments still like to have them articulated: it is a matter of conscience. Ms. Rich's poems in ***Necessities of Life*** (1968), ***Leaflets*** (1969) and ***Diving Into the Wreck*** (1973) keep us alert to feelings we may no longer otherwise hold. Her more recent books are not as pointed as those, though each of them has fine poems. As a poet, Ms. Rich has had difficulty coping with the fact that it is no longer 1968 or 1974: the exacerbations are different now and not quite answerable to the rhetorical means she devised for those gone occasions. The dark fields of the republic—F. Scott Fitzgerald's phrase in *The Great Gatsby*—are sufficient grounds of dismay, but not of anger immediate enough to hurt Ms. Rich into her most telling poetry. As in previous books, she is determined to be glum, but the engaged poems of the new book haven't found enough to be engaged by; they are abstracted from detail no longer there in the old way. Ms. Rich says of the new sequence **"Then or Now"** that "the poems owe much . . . to the continuing pressure of events," but she hasn't made us see the events or feel their pressure.

It is not surprising that the themes of the new book have not impelled Ms. Rich to mine all the resources of the language. She has long chosen to speak directly and simply, though she knows that "obscurity has its tale to tell." She has put her language on a thin diet, as if she associated the plenitude of her old music with triviality and corruption. I can't reconcile myself to the loss, and I read aloud **"The Loser"** to remind myself of poetic pleasures Ms. Rich has now largely disavowed. In this poem from ***Snapshots of a Daughter-in-Law*** (1963), a man speaks of the woman he once loved:

> Your wedding made my eyes ache; soon
> the world would be worse off for one
> more golden apple dropped to ground
> without the least protesting sound,
> and you would windfall lie, and we
> forget your shimmer on the tree.

"Windfall lie" may echo the "leafmeal lie" of Gerard Manley Hopkins's "Spring and Fall." But that is not a flaw, the stanza moves to its own rhythm. In another early poem, **"Continuum,"** Ms. Rich speaks of someone

> whose voice
> I may never hear, but go on hoping
> to hear, tonight, tomorrow, someday,
> as I go on hoping to feel
> tears of mercy in the of course impersonal rain.

Ms. Rich is mindful of a degree of the pathetic fallacy in "tears of mercy," but mindful also of the due claim of that hope: she respects the feeling just as much as her vigilance in guarding against its presumption.

I have quoted these passages to indicate the sacrifice Ms. Rich has made in securing the thin lines of her recent poetry. She has elected to do without copiousness, ambiguity, historical weight and density, "the old masters, the old sources," humor, wit, the play of word upon word. "We are our words, and black and bruised and blue," she wrote in **"The Demon Lover."** But in ***Dark Fields of the Republic*** it is hard to feel that the words are black and bruised and blue when they appear for the most part self-protected, insured against catastrophe as against joy:

> I was telling you a story about love
> how even in war it goes on speaking its own
> language
>
> Yes you said but the larynx is bloodied
> the knife was well-aimed into the throat
>
> Well I said love is hated   it has no price
>
> No you said   you are talking about feelings
> Have you ever felt nothing?   that is what war is
> now
>
> Then a shadow skimmed your face
> Go on talking in a normal voice   you murmured
> Nothing is listening.

One of the attractions of Ms. Rich's poems has been the sense that they are conversations from which you and I are not excluded; but I wouldn't want to take part in this one. The fluency of the poem is gained by making its words weightless: war and love are not experiences burdened with particular fear, actual pain; they are notions between which the speakers glide. I don't believe in the knife, the larynx or the throat: they, too, are mere notions. Nor do I believe the fib that war has become nothing. It is not nothing to those who suffer it, or return home, homeless, destroyed by it.

Sylvia Henneberg (essay date Spring 1997)

SOURCE: "Rich's 'Autumn Equinox,'" in *The Explicator,* Vol. 55, No. 3, Spring, 1997, pp. 169-72.

[*In the following essay, Henneberg identifies the feminine and masculine positions in the early poem* "Autumn Equinox" *in terms of the primary concerns of Rich's later poetry: "the dream and the limitations of a common language."*]

Adrienne Rich's semiautobiographical narrative poem **"Autumn Equinox"** (1955) anticipates two central concerns of her "coming-out" volume of poetry, ***The Dream of a Common Language*** (1978), and her subsequent poetry: the dream and the limitations of a common language.

"Autumn Equinox" presents a middle-aged female speaker reflecting on her marriage. In the poem she is portrayed raking autumn leaves in the yard, while her husband, a professor, remains in the house reading Dryden. The atmosphere is one of resignation and silence; and a sense of the speaker's patient anticipation of death, paralleled by autumn's calm move toward winter, pervades the lines. Lyman, the husband, and his wife do not communicate with each other. When the speaker wants to know why he, "that least acidulous of men," reads satires, she does not ask him directly but instead attempts to clarify her perplexity by browsing through his book "[w]hen he [is] gone." She talks more with her neighbor Alice Hume than with Lyman. Though she calls these chats the "dry philosophy of neighborhood," they surpass her exchanges with her husband, for it is in connection with Alice and never with Lyman that the verbs "to say" and "to talk" appear.

A long flashback follows, in which the speaker admits that Lyman has never been the man of her dreams, that she joined him out of "[a] woman's need for love of any kind." She thinks back to her wedding day, which was perfectly acceptable in the eyes of all the other participants but terrifying to her. Reminiscent of Sylvia Plath's "The Disquieting Muses," the passage describes how the speaker's "aunts . . . nodded like the Fates," signaling that "nemesis was accomplished." The speaker and Lyman are only the "semblance of a bride and groom," and the wedding, to her, is not the blissful climax of her life but a "dry immutability." She never clearly states that babies were born, but if we assume that her children are the "angular young [who] took up their bats and shouted / Throughout the afternoon," then that is all they have been to her: angular youths playing and shouting all afternoon. She makes no endearing mention of them.

The speaker becomes aware of her dissatisfaction with her married life and decides to attempt her first act of resistance: She "change[s] the parlor curtains / To ones the like of which were never seen / Along our grave and academic street." These she hangs up "in defiance." Next, she admits to herself that she despises the way her bond to her husband has kept her distant from experience and from all the "marvels of the world." Marriage has made impossible the access to such treasures as "The Pyramids" and "Cologne Cathedral"; they have been reduced to pictures, literally locked away in frames of black oak. The speaker soon gives signs of her unhappiness, weeping at night and voicing that she "thought life was different than it is." But she cannot explain what she means and thus lets her feelings drift into silence.

Because the poem's speaker is unable to communicate with her husband, Alicia Ostriker has concluded that hers is "'the unsaid word' of a wife in loyal stasis while her husband ranges" and that she "goes down to old age mildly, unprotesting." Silence, unsaid words, unprotesting attitudes, however, are not necessarily an absolute nothing, and they certainly do not have to indicate loyalty. As Michel Foucault states,

> Silence itself—the thing one declines to say, or is forbidden to name, the discretion that is required between different speakers—is less the absolute limit of discourse, the other side from which it is separated by a strict boundary, than an element that functions alongside the things said, with them and in relation to them within over-all strategies. There is no binary division to be made between what one says and what one does not say. . . . There is not one but many silences, and they are an integral part of the strategies that underlie and permeate discourses.

Foucault argues that there exist different ways of "not saying things," and I would suggest that for the poem's speaker, such acts as hanging up loud curtains and admitting to herself that she is utterly unhappy are ways of "not saying things." Above all, however, the poem itself, five pages worth of reflections, represents an important discourse that runs parallel to her silence.

Returning to the present, to the autumn of the year and of her life, the speaker tries to convince us and herself that at some indeterminate point in life she ceased to be dissatisfied and began to live out her marriage—society's dream of the common language—contentedly. The final image of the poem seems to support such assurances of contentment: She has "raked three bushel baskets full of leaves— / Enough for one September afternoon." However, her apparent satisfaction, like her silence, is undermined by an eloquent narrative that does nothing but question, doubt, and criticize the past and the present. Moreover, the activity of working outdoors until three baskets are filled with leaves suggests her need to let out frustration, to counteract Lyman's stasis in the house, to express herself.

Her seeming resignation and passivity are, in other words, not real. Though she gives the appearance of patiently acquiescing to a doomed life of matrimony with nothing left to hope for but death, a very real resistance to that fate pervades the whole text. The poem is appropriately set during the autumn equinox, the time of year when night, which might be associated with the female speaker, and day, representing her husband Lyman, are of equal length and strength. From this point on, night will be longer, thus represented more strongly. As surely as autumn equinox will give way to longer nights, the wife will succeed in changing the terms of her marriage: the dominance, privileges, and priorities that have hitherto always worked to her disadvantage will be altered. When she claims, "We finish off / Not quite as we began," she is expressing confidence in this change, rather than what at first sight may be taken to be pessimism and resignation.

The poem's attack is not primarily directed against man/Lyman but against marriage, the institution that, according to Rich, brings unhappiness to both individuals involved. "Young lovers," both male and female, who "talk of giving all the heart / Into each other's trust" use a "rhetoric" that "Won't stand for analyzing." Rich recognizes that there are necessarily and always differences between individuals and sees the danger of attempting to ignore those differences through the union of marriage. If marriage is the common language, then the common language is too limited; a language of difference that acknowledges the individuality of identities is preferable by far.

Although Rich focuses on connection and distance between women in ***The Dream of a Common Language*** and her subsequent book of poetry, ***A Wild Patience Has Taken Me This Far*** (1981), the recognition that differences between individuals, whether they be heterosexual or homosexual, cannot always or entirely be effaced by a common language is as central to her later poetry as it is to **"Autumn Equinox."**

FURTHER READING

Criticism

"Thanks Anyway." *Time* (21 July 1997): 83.

Brief notice that Rich declined the 1997 National Medal of the Arts because "the very meaning of art is incompatible with the cynical politics of [Clinton's] Administration."

Additional coverage of Rich's life and career is contained in the following sources published by Gale: *Contemporary Authors,* Vols. 9-12, rev. ed.; *Contemporary Authors New Revision Series,* Vols. 20, 53; *Dictionary of Literary Biography,* Vols. 5, 67; *DISCovering Authors Modules: Poets; Major Twentieth-Century Writers;* and *Poetry Criticism,* Vol. 5.

Quentin Tarantino

1963-

(Full name Quentin Jerome Tarantino) American director and screenplay writer.

The following entry presents an overview of Tarantino's career through 1998.

INTRODUCTION

Among the most successful American filmmakers to emerge in the 1990s, Quentin Tarantino is best known for his offbeat, darkly satiric gangster films *Reservoir Dogs* (1992), *Pulp Fiction* (1994), and *Jackie Brown* (1997). Earning large box office receipts and cult adoration as a new renegade force in Hollywood, Tarantino is distinguished for his signature aesthetic (including a penchant for extraordinary, but sometimes humorously rendered) violence, long sequences of dialogue in which characters examine subjects such as cheeseburgers and pop songs in exhaustive detail, and a glorification of popular culture in general and B-movies in particular. Aside from the qualities of his movies themselves, Tarantino is noted for the fact that he achieved success outside of the Hollywood mainstream as a video store clerk-cum-independent filmmaker who cobbled together $1.5 million to make his first picture. As such he has offered an example to other aspiring cineasts, and his enormous financial and critical success—*Pulp Fiction* won the Palme d'Or at the Cannes Film Festival, an Academy Award for Best Screenplay Written Directly for the Screen, and other awards—has gained the attention of Hollywood. Thus Tarantino has emerged, as he observed somewhat derisively in a 1997 interview with *New York Times Magazine,* as "an adjective": "Every third script out there," he said, "is described as 'Tarantino-esque.'"

Biographical Information

Tarantino was born in Knoxville, Tennessee, in 1963, and was reportedly named after a Burt Reynolds character on television. In 1965, when he was two years old, his mother Connie left his father and moved to California, bringing Tarantino with her. Still a teenager, Connie, who later became a corporate executive, settled in Harbor City, a middle-class neighborhood that bordered on rougher areas. Among the latter was the town of Carson, which included a theatre where Tarantino regularly attended movies. Though he was a bright child, he suffered from hyperactivity, and did poorly in school. Finally, having failed several grades, he dropped out of the ninth grade when he was fifteen or sixteen years old. He went to work as an usher at a pornographic movie theatre and studied acting, but except for a bit part as an Elvis impersonator on the television show "Golden Girls" in 1990, achieved little success as an actor. At age twenty-two, he went to work at Video Archives, which he has referred to as "the best video store in the Los Angeles area." The job, which he held for five years, gave him important exposure to a wide variety of films, and he and coworker Roger Avary—another future filmmaker—would often see four movies a day. In 1990, Tarantino and Avary went to work with producer John Langley, a regular video store customer, and moved to Hollywood. There they began developing the all-important contacts, most notably with producer Lawrence Bender, necessary in the world of filmmaking, and raised $1.5 million. In film terms, it was a shoestring budget at best; but it was enough to make *Reservoir Dogs,* which grossed many times that sum. With the release of the film two years later, and the resulting critical attention, Tarantino was propelled to stardom on a level seldom enjoyed by the people behind the camera. Though he has acted in a number of movies, most of these are roles either in his own films, or cameos in those of others. Director Tony Scott bought one of Tarantino's early screenplays, which became *True Romance*

(1993), and a story by Tarantino became the basis for Oliver Stone's *Natural Born Killers* (1994). Tarantino and Stone disagreed over the latter picture, however, and Tarantino disclaimed all involvement in the resulting film, even delaying release of *Pulp Fiction* until later that year in order to further establish his distance from it. As for *Pulp Fiction,* Tarantino again managed to make a film on a relatively small budget, $8 million, and this time enjoyed even greater critical and commercial success. Along with his emerging notoriety, Tarantino began to establish himself as a Hollywood businessman. Having formed A Band Apart, his production company, in 1991, he later formed commercial and music subsidiaries, and in 1995 established Rolling Thunder, a specialty distribution company. During the mid-1990s, he played small roles in the making of several films, including an uncredited rewrite on Scott's *Crimson Tide* in 1995. He also worked with Robert Rodriguez, another independent filmmaking sensation whose *El Mariachi* was remade for U.S. audiences as *Desperado* (with a cameo by Tarantino), on *From Dusk Till Dawn* (1995). In 1997, Tarantino released his third movie as writer and director, *Jackie Brown,* based on the novel *Rum Punch* by Elmore Leonard.

Major Works

Just as Tarantino's films are peppered with references to other directors' movies, *Reservoir Dogs* appears to be modeled on Stanley Kubrick's *The Killing* (1956), a dispassionate post mortem on a robbery. The storyline of Tarantino's film is simple: an aging crime boss gathers a group of criminals, who are given colors (e.g., Mr. Blonde, Mr. Pink, etc.) instead of names in order to protect their identities, and plans a jewelry-store heist. But one of the men is a cop, and the robbery—which itself is never depicted—goes terribly wrong. The film plays tricks with time, shifting backward and forward, for instance from a long scene in a pancake house before the heist to a short vignette of a horribly wounded gangster just after it. After a series of temporal disjunctions, the action ultimately returns to a warehouse where the robbers have gathered to square off against one another in an attempt to find the traitor. As notable as the temporal shifts are the film's stylistic touches: the brutal violence against the 1970s musical soundtrack, the use of matching anonymous black suits by the color-designated robbers, and the long quasi-philosophical discussions which take place in the stage-like warehouse. *True Romance* similarly involves a crime, or series of crimes, that have gone wrong; but whereas *Pulp Fiction* takes place in a world of men, without benefit of female characters, at the center of *True Romance* is, as its name implies, a love story. The central figures, Clarence and the prostitute Alabama, are thrown together by circumstances, and when Clarence kills Alabama's pimp and steals a bag containing a fortune in cocaine, they are forced on a cross-country race against federal agents and a crime boss. Like *Reservoir Dogs, True Romance* ends in a bloodbath, but with a twist. *Pulp Fiction,* in contrast, actually begins with a standoff, or rather with events leading up to a standoff; but in a "Tarantino-esque" inversion of time sequence. The viewer will not return to the opening scene, and thus know what comes next, until the end of the movie. *Pulp Fiction* is comprised of several plots, most of them surrounding a drug lord named Marsellus. There is a subplot involving two hit men employed by him; one centering on Marsellus's alluring wife, who suffers a near-fatal heroin overdose while out on the town with one of the hit men; as well as a sequence involving a boxer who double-crosses Marsellus and flees for his life, only to find himself in a position to save the man who wants to kill him. In the final scene, one of the hit men makes a decision to leave his life of crime; already the audience has seen a segment that takes place later in time, in which the other henchman confronts the results of his own refusal to do so. "The Man from Hollywood," Tarantino's section in *Four Rooms* (1995), for which he and three other directors made segments, is much simpler, and revolves around an attempt to reenact a hair-raising scene from an Alfred Hitchcock television show in which Steve McQueen bets Peter Lorre his little finger than he can get his lighter to light ten times in a row. In *From Dusk Till Dawn* Tarantino presents an unusual combination of a straightforward bank robber getaway story with a tale of Mexican vampires. His next film, *Jackie Brown,* uncharacteristically features a female protagonist. The title character and heroine is an underpaid flight attendant who earns extra money by helping an arms dealer, Ordell, launder money. When she is caught by the police, Ordell, fearing that she will turn him in, wants to eliminate her. On this backbone of plot are formed numerous other subplots, most notably ones involving a tender-hearted bail bondsman who comes to Jackie's rescue, and the federal agents who goad her into helping them. All her adversaries underestimate Jackie, as a sequence surrounding the transfer of a bag containing money serves to illustrate. More complex than *Reservoir Dogs* and *Pulp Fiction* in terms of character development, *Jackie Brown* also follows an essentially linear progression of events that relies upon fewer temporal shifts to move the story along.

Critical Reception

Reviewers have been as quick to praise Tarantino for aspects of his style as they have been to condemn what many consider his excessive use of violence. As critics note, one of the most memorable parts of *Reservoir Dogs* is a gruesome scene in which Mr. Blonde cuts off a police officer's ear while the 1970s hit "Stuck in the Middle with You" plays in the background. Likewise, *Pulp Fiction* features a brutal S&M homosexual rape scene, along with a large body count. His penchant for violence and degradation has prompted some reviewers to compare Tarantino's early work to French dramatist Antonin Artaud's Theater of Cruelty. However, as critics observe, *Jackie Brown* is relatively restrained with regard to bloodshed. This has led several reviewers to suggest that Tarantino is mellowing, and many have noted signs of maturation with regard to character development and his treatment of love. Whereas *Pulp Fiction* takes place entirely in a man's world, *Jackie Brown* includes a touching, unconsummated relationship between the bail bondsman and the title character. Though Tarantino has proven less likely to exploit bloodshed or sex in his latest film, he has, as critics observe, maintained another aspect of his style: an attitude towards pop culture, including B-movies, old TV shows, and other paraphernalia of mass media, that wavers between veneration and satire. The opening scene of *Reservoir Dogs,* in which Mr. Brown (played by Tarantino himself) offers a memorable exegesis of Madonna's 1985 hit "Like a Virgin," and the long discussion about cheeseburgers between the two hoodlums in *Pulp Fiction* are frequently cited as emblematic of his style. Tarantino's contributions to *True Romance* and *Four Rooms* were panned by most reviewers, and *From Dusk Till Dawn* received mixed assessment. While Tarantino's detractors dismiss his work as derivative, sensational, and nihilistic, others praise his films for their eccentric humor, wit, and unpretentious democratic perspective. As Tarantino commented in a 1997 interview with *New York Times Magazine:* "I don't believe in elitism. I don't think the audience is this dumb person lower than me. I am the audience."

PRINCIPAL WORKS

Reservoir Dogs (film) 1992
True Romance (screenplay) 1993
Pulp Fiction (film) 1994
Four Rooms [with Alexandre Rockwell, Allison Anders, and Robert Rodriguez] (film) 1995
From Dusk Till Dawn [with Robert Rodriguez] (film) 1996
Jackie Brown (film) 1997

CRITICISM

Kenneth Turan (review date 23 October 1992)

SOURCE: "'Reservoir Dogs,' Tarantino's Brash Debut Film, Announces a Director to Be Reckoned With," in *Los Angeles Times,* October 23, 1992, pp. F1, F14.

[*In the following review, Turan offers qualified evaluation of* Reservoir Dogs. *While praising Tarantino's "undeniable skill," Turan objects to his preoccupation with "operatic violence."*]

Like it or not (and many people will have their doubts), writer-director Quentin Tarantino has arrived, in your face and on the screen. His brash debut film, ***Reservoir Dogs,*** a showy but insubstantial comic opera of violence, is as much a calling card as a movie, an audacious high-wire act announcing that he is here and to be reckoned with.

Strong violence is Tarantino's passion, and he embraces it with gleeful, almost religious, fervor. An energetic macho stunt, ***Reservoir Dogs*** (selected theaters) glories in its excesses of blood and community, delighting, in classic Grand Guignol fashion, in going as far over the too as the man's imagination will take it.

Tarantino does have the filmmaking flair to go along with his zeal. Though ***Reservoir Dogs***' story line of what happens when a well-planned robbery goes wrong is a staple of both B pictures and pulp fiction, Tarantino's palpable enthusiasm, his unapologetic passion for what he's created, reinvigorates this venerable plot and; mayhem aside, makes it involving for longer than you might suspect.

Tarantino's background is as an actor and he has a gift for writing great bursts of caustic, quirky dialogue, verbal arias that show off not only his facility with scabrous, tough guy language but also the abilities of his performers. And it was that script that attracted excellent actors like Harvey Keitel (who also signed on as co-producer), Tim Roth, Michael Madsen and Steve Buscemi to the film.

Tarantino's writing style is clear from ***Dogs***' opening set piece, focused around a table in a Los Angeles coffee shop where a group of seven nondescript men are just finishing up what looks to be a hearty breakfast. Tarantino (who cast himself as Mr. Brown) starts things off with an exaggeratedly profane exegesis on what Madonna's "Like a Virgin" is really all about, followed by a cranky riff by Mr. Pink (Steve Buscemi) on why he doesn't believe in tipping.

Almost immediately after this meal, there is a sudden cut to the bloody interior of a late-model car, where Mr. Orange (Tim Roth), shot so badly he seems almost to be drowning in his own blood, holds tight to the hand of a frantic Mr. White (Harvey Keitel) as he heads the car toward a prearranged rendezvous spot.

For five of those original seven breakfasters, each named (for security reasons) after a color and all identically dressed in black suits, white shirts, thin black ties and sunglasses, turn out to be participants in a robbery of a diamond wholesaler planned by the other two, Joe (Lawrence Tierney) and his son, Nice Guy Eddie (Chris Penn).

None of this is immediately obvious, coming into focus in bits and pieces, for Tarantino has broken his story up and told it non-chronologically. Energetic scenes of the shootout alternate with quiet flashbacks to the planning as well as the emotionally unstable situation at the rendezvous spot, as the surviving gang members scream bloody murder at each other, trying to figure out how an easy job turns into a fiasco while Mr. Orange swoons in his own blood on the floor.

This is definitely not the Gang That Couldn't Shoot Straight, but rather a group of genuine hard guys, criminal professionals and proud of it, who know everything from how long the police take to respond to alarms, to which parts of the body are the most painful to be shot in. The type of crowd that follows the question of "Did you kill anybody?" with a perfectly natural. "Any real people or just cops?"

Part of the appeal of ***Reservoir Dogs***' (R-rated for strong violence and language) is the way it makes all this feel terribly authentic, a veracity that is a tribute to the skill of its actors. Though it seems a shame to pick favorites in one of the year's most cohesive ensembles, three performers do stand out.

Steve Buscemi, also featured in the upcoming "In the Soup," is deadpan funny as the cranky Mr. Pink; veteran Lawrence Tierney, with a voice like a tow-truck winch, is gruff as they get as the gang's rapacious boss; and Michael Madsen, a veteran of "Thelma & Louise," plays the unforgettable Mr. Blonde, the mellow sadist who loves 1970s music and provides ***Reservoir Dogs*** with its most talked-about moments of gory violence.

Though it's impossible not to appreciate the undeniable skill and elan Tarantino brings to all this, it is also difficult not to wish ***Reservoir Dogs*** weren't so determinedly one-dimensional, so in love with operatic violence at the expense of everything else. The old gangster movies its creator idolizes were better at balancing things, at adding creditable emotional connection and regret to their dead-end proceedings. As Tarantino makes more films (and his dance card is already quite crowded), perhaps he will see his way clear to going that one step beyond what he's accomplished here. You could even, in the spirit of things, call it something to shoot for.

Manohla Dargis (essay date November 1992)

SOURCE: "Who's Afraid of Red, Yellow, and Blonde?," in *Artforum,* Vol. 31, No. 3, November, 1992, p. 11.

[*In the following essay, Dargis examines the depiction of male violence in* Reservoir Dogs.]

> *Let me tell you what "Like a Virgin"'s about. It's about this cooz who's a regular fuckin' machine. I'm talkin' mornin' day night afternoon dick dick dick dick dick dick dick dick dick.*
>
> *Then one day she meets this John Holmes motherfucker and it's like, Whoa baby. I mean this cat is like Charles Bronson in* The Great Escape: *he's diggin' tunnels. All right, she's gettin' some serious dick action and she's feelin' somethin' she hasn't felt since forever. Pain. Pain. It hurts, it hurts her . . . just like it did the first time. You see the pain is remindin' the fuck machine what it was once like to be a virgin. Hence, "Like a Virgin."*
>
> —Mr. Brown (Quentin Tarantino) in ***Reservoir Dogs,*** 1992
>
> *Why? Because it feels so good.*
>
> —Benny (Warren Oates), on shooting a man already conspicuously dead in Sam Peckinpah's *Bring Me the Head of Alfredo Garcia,* 1974

Quentin Tarantino's ***Reservoir Dogs*** opens in a diner with eight men telling stories and talking trash around a table. As the camera prowls from face to face, a man named Mr. Brown theorizes about Madonna's song "Like a Virgin": "Pain. Pain," he says, teasing out the words. Later, as the group is paying the bill, a Mr. Pink refuses to tip. The off-screen waitress' service, he complains, wasn't special. "What's special," asks Mr. Blue, "take you in the back and suck your dick?"

Reservoir Dogs is the story of a well-planned heist turned bloody. It is loosely based on Stanley Kubrick's 1956 *The Killing,* but that film unfolds like a blueprint—a cool, precise analysis of a robbery. In perverse contrast, Tarantino skips the crime itself. His point isn't the heist but the players: the film is an anatomy less of a crime than of men choosing lives of violence.

A history of American cinema could be traced on the bruised, besieged male body, from westerns to gangster sagas to male weepies to war films, from Red River to Brian De Palma's *Scarface,* from Nick Ray's *Bigger Than Life* to *Rambo.* Feminist theorists have made much of the sadism visited on women in film, but male-on-male violence probably drives more movies. It's violence characterized as much by masochism as by sadism: film after film features men at risk (physically, emotionally, spiritually) who can only find redemption through pain, theirs or someone else's. Even the newest revisionist Clint Eastwood western, *Unforgiven,* though it works overtime to show gun-slingers as sociopaths, in the end leaves no option but brutality.

In truth, isn't ritual sacrifice usually at the expense of the marginal—women, children, captives, animals? Yet male directors embrace male sacrifice. The stakes have never seemed higher than during the last twenty years, as '70s prodigals like Francis Ford Coppola, Brian De Palma, and Martin Scorsese know well. Certainly it's no accident that since the early '70s—years of emergent feminism and black power—the neogangster film has become the essential American genre. In the outlaw zones of the goodfellas and the new jack "gangstas," violence runs amok, delivered from messy ("politically correct") accountability into a hyperbolic masculinity.

Cut to a man screaming in the back-seat of a car, his white shirt blossoming red. The screamer is Mr. Orange (Tim Roth); the driver is Mr. White (Harvey Keitel), his comforting words working a feeble counterpoint to agony. As the film progresses, Mr. Orange's blood tracks the story. Its slow and steady flow brackets the plot like a parody of Aristotelian poetics, making literal the structural "violence" of classical narrative. In the beginning, through, there's nothing but Orange's pain—clear, distinct, pure.

Apparently the robbery has turned into a massacre. The details surface only as retold by the robbers at a warehouse rendezvous, trickling out through verbal and visual flashback. The effect is less the *Rashomon* point about rival truths than something akin to psychoanalysis: like the therapeutic process, ***Reservoir Dogs*** tells a story, is *about* telling stories, and depends on stories for its own creation. Down to the coloristic aliases, the film posits a male identity that must tell itself stories to exist.

If this is film as riddle, built on an action that is absent, another absence is equally self-evident: female characters. In so many films women are decoys in a male struggle between Eros and Thanatos. Here they exist only in jokes, smutty asides, and yet more stories. If they're the fulcrum of masculine bad faith, it's because of the male unconscious, not because of anything they initiate themselves. When White takes a comb to Orange's gore-slicked hair, the gesture is both desperate and patently feminine. The ties that bind these men in masculinity are raw and crushing in part because women, like the crime, have no present reality; both are blanks, screens for uncontradicted fantasy.

Brought together as cogs in a larceny machine, the men are tied in a fragile union of professionalism and gender. Their connection can make for moments of uncommon kindness, as when White comforts the dying Orange with words and embraces ("touched for the very first time"?). But the bond is perilous, even irrational. Having launched the massacre at the heist, Mr. Blonde (Michael Madsen) makes the rendezvous with a policeman stashed in his car trunk. Left temporarily in charge, he tortures his hostage with slowed and chilling exactitude—and with pleasure. Blonde flips on the radio—the '70s hit "Stuck in the Middle with You," by Stealer's Wheel—pulls out a straight-edge, and begins a snaky, sensuous little dance. Eyebrows up, mouth curled, he plays the blade in front of the cop, darting and slicing like a matador.

It's a lethal number, for the captive audience onscreen as well as off. Then the camera cuts to an empty corner of the warehouse. There's no spectacular squirt of gore, no bloody "money shot" (the cum shot that authenticates sex in porno movies), only a kind of embarrassed retreat. In one gesture Tarantino severs the camera and us from the scene, stripping the moment of its voyeuristic pleasure, though not of its sadism.

Reservoir Dogs only feels like one of the most graphic features to hit the big screen lately. What makes the violence hurt isn't some outrageous, literally deadening body count but the way Tarantino decelerates pain, squeezing it out drop by anguished drop. When men go into fatal slo-mo freefall in a Peckinpah movie, or in the work of Hong Kong's John Woo, their agony is itself heroic; though Tarantino too slows down agony, he keeps it in real time. In ***Reservoir Dogs*** some men kill for business, others because, as Warren Oates explained, "it feels so good." As Freud writes of the death instinct, "Even where it emerges . . . in the blindest fury of destructiveness, . . . the satisfaction of the instinct is accompanied by an extraordinarily high degree of narcissistic enjoyment."

Through stories, the men in ***Reservoir Dogs*** teach each other to be men. When the lessons are learned, they kill each other. It's a world in which the only alternative to business is death, and male violence is as inevitable as it is irrational. In this world, getting it up means never having to say you're sorry, Just Make my day.

Stanley Kauffmann (review date 23 November 1992)

SOURCE: "Blood Lines," in *New Republic,* November 23, 1992, pp. 30-1.

[*In the following review, Kauffmann offers tempered praise for* Reservoir Dogs.]

How happy the human race must be these days. Photography and cinematography have done so much to further our age-old appetite for the sanguine. It's as if, after many centuries of waiting, those of us who do not actually hack or bludgeon now have the chance to *see* the hacked and bludgeoned. The latest *Granta* has a piece by Luc Sante—part of a new book called *Evidence*—that consists of police-file photographs of murder victims with his critical comments on them. In his aesthetic study of these pictures, "a style announced itself, deliberate and inimitable."

But never mind police files. Killing is in full flood around the globe—see tomorrow's newspaper—and we can all savor it in detail. Out of Vietnam, T.V. created the Living-Room War; now we have the living-room world slaughter. Every morning, along with the orange juice, blood; every evening, along with the nightcap, blood. Who could ask for more?

We could. Real blood is not enough. We want more. Thus many kinds of films, from the fantastic to the factual, pour out to slake us.

When the subject of film violence is raised, there's one predictable response: violence is sanctified by its antiquity in drama, from the children of Atreus to the present. Of course, without violence (and the other equally dominant theme, sex), drama wouldn't exist. What this means is that, from the start, the drama recognized that almost all human beings are basically, ultimately, xenophobic and homicidal.

Then why raise the subject again? First, to inquire whether the argument from antiquity covers every case. Second, to try to find out whether I'm going insane. Adjustment to changing values is the prime law of the twentieth century, but once in a while a film comes along that makes me imagine that everyone has a mental compass on the subject of violence and that I must tap mine to make sure it's not stuck.

Perhaps what I'm saying is that 1992 is not 1969. In 1969 we got Sam Peckinpah's *The Wild Bunch,* which outraged many with its bloodletting but which struck me as an exemplary Artaudian work of art—even if Peckinpah had never heard of Artaud. In "The Theater and Cruelty" Artaud wrote that he wanted the theater to focus on, among other things, "atrocious crimes" in relation to "the terrible lyricism" of mankind's prevailing myths. This is precisely what Peckinpah's film did. It took the Western out of its false sentimental precincts (even as used by the genius of Ford) and brought it into ancient, profound continuities.

Now comes a gangster film called ***Reservoir Dogs*** (Miramax), crammed with murders, which has little relation to anything but itself. With a considerable heave, this might be seen as postmodernist, but even if true, it would be an afterthought. The immediate effect of ***Reservoir Dogs*** is to make us tap that mental compass. It's not the most violent picture ever; what film could aspire to that title? But it's so well made, the violence is so gratuitous, and the general reception has been so delighted, that attention must be paid.

It's a first film, written and directed by Quentin Tarantino, who also plays a small role. Almost from the start, we see blood. After a diamond robbery, two members of the robber gang are fleeing in a car; one is the driver and the other is a man in the back seat, gut-shot, who is blood-drenched and hysterical about dying. The driver knows he can't take the wounded man to a hospital or a doctor, so he speeds to the warehouse that is the gang's rendezvous and deposits him on the floor with empty words of reassurance.

In this empty warehouse, as on a stage, most of the film is played out. Other gang members turn up, all of them certain that their caper was tipped to the police; hence the shoot-out through which they had to escape with their loot. There is a fink in the gang, apparently. The film's bloodbath goes on, especially through flashbacks that explain what led these various men to this warehouse. One arrival brings in a hostage policeman, who is tied to a chair and eventually tortured to make him identify the fink. At one point the torturer makes jokes with the cop's severed ear.

A good deal of ***Reservoir Dogs*** (a title I don't understand) was difficult for me to watch. The razor stuff, especially, made me avert my eyes. But, cinematically speaking, it's plainly the debut of a talent. The opening sequence under the credits, in which the camera very slowly keeps circling the gang sitting around a restaurant table discussing sex and ribbing one of the gangsters for refusing to tip the waitress, alerts us immediately. The way Tarantino sees this sequence and his tap-dance, snare-drum rhythms of dialogue promise that this filmmaking will be better than most, especially most first films. The promise is kept; yet at the end I was left with a kind of despair.

Yes, Tarantino has a sense of dramatic disposition and, with his imaginative cinematographer Andrzej Sekula, he lights and frames every scene as if he were sculpting it. Yes, the very last moments of the film quite consciously take the multiple killings and the torrential gore into the edges of satire. What depresses is that a director of Tarantino's cinematic gifts should have chosen this particular film for his debut. It has so little plot—the search for the fink is its only thread—that it clearly was made just for the sake of its making, the application of style to sheer slaughter. Indulging the so-called critical fallacy of trying to decipher an artist's intent, I'd hazard that Tarantino wrote this script because he thought it would be relatively easy to get it financed. Is this to accuse him of cynicism? Well, what god hovers over this film but the classic deity of cynicism?

Which does not let us, the audience, off the hook. Whatever Tarantino's reasons for writing his screenplay, financiers would not have backed it unless they thought they could rely on us to see it. Filmmaking affects society much less than society affects filmmaking; and as one of the audience, I become particularly aware from time to time of what filmmakers take for granted about me. I'm still tapping that mental compass.

The actors all do well enough—notably Lawrence Tierney as the granitic gang chief, Harvey Keitel and Michael Madsen as two of his mob—but it's difficult to be impressed by the acting of gangster roles. They are almost our equivalent, in conventions, of Noh drama. No doubt that at the Pearly Gates, the Guardian asks an American actor: "I know, I know, gangster roles. But what else?"

Jonathan Romney (review date 8 January 1993)

SOURCE: "Partners in Crime," in *New Statesman & Society*, January 8, 1993, pp. 34, 36.

[*In the following review, Romney offers favorable assessment of* Reservoir Dogs.]

Who said the devil doesn't have all the best tunes? In 1971, A *Clockwork Orange* shocked everyone rigid because its droog Alex liked to choreograph his ultraviolence to a Beethoven soundtrack. Twenty years on, things are a little more flip. In Quentin Tarantino's ***Reservoir Dogs*** (on general release), Michael Madsen's psycho gangster Mr Blonde tortures a policeman to Stealer's Wheel singing "Stuck In The Middle with You".

It's a deeply unsettling scene to watch, not just for the violence itself, but also for Madsen's jokey, debonnaire little dance—a gruesome flirtation with the victim, *and* with the audience. It works horribly well. I saw the film at a late-night public preview and the general atmosphere was nervy, to say the least; there were uneasy titters throughout, but the weirdest thing was the way one man shouted out "Sexy!" when Mr Blonde produced his can of gasoline with obvious, ominous intent.

What's scary is that you actually want to see him use it—you realise this as the scene develops, and catch yourself doing an anxious double-take. ***Reservoir Dogs,*** the debut by a young director whose *noir* literacy is evident in every detail, is about the glamour of violence, but it's not quite sure whether to analyse it or relish it. A gang of hoods retreats after a failed heist: as one member (Tim Roth) lies copiously bleeding, another (the superb Steve Buscemi) goes supernova pernickety, and a third (Harvey Keitel, authoritative but uncharacteristically muted) tries to hold the whole thing together. That the characters are all casual killers is a given fact. The drama starts from that ground, working your reactions in a way it never could if killing were presented as some antisocial anomaly.

Reservoir Dogs is a thoroughgoing example of Theatre of Cruelty, in a quite literal sense. It's more like stage drama than most filmed versions of stage-plays; where the latter try to hide their origins by "opening-out", Tarantino makes his film stagy by closing in.

The stage is an abandoned warehouse in which characters are carefully positioned to face the audience and for maximum bodily interaction. Long takes emphasise the rhythm of words and gestures, and foreground acting skills to a remarkable degree.

The film's point is that the life of crime is entirely about acting. The chief hood (bulb-headed veteran Lawrence Tierney) allots names—Mr Pink, Mr Orange, Mr White—to gang members who quibble over their parts, then get into them like Method trainees, erasing their own identities. Play a part well enough, the film seems to say, and action becomes an act, and morality simply what's beyond the proscenium arch. The problem is, the same applies for the audience as well.

The film's ambivalent achievement is that it makes violence more alive and more seductive than any other film I can remember. It reinvents violence as spectacle, and effectively as *live* spectacle: something practically unthinkable in cinema. Tarantino uses a startling array of distancing techniques—voice-overs, flashbacks, fractured chronology, jovially naff 1970s soundtrack and discreet trickery like the moment in the torture scene where a shaky camera suddenly cuts away and steadies itself, staring in rigid shock at a corner of the room. But all these ways of highlighting the violence as funky guignol allow you to dig it all the more.

Reservoir Dogs demystifies as well as glamorises; but it's hard to say which it does more. Maybe that can only be determined by whether or not people are moved to shout "Sexy!" However, it does undercut the most obvious expectation of exploitation movies by having an all-male cast: significantly, the only woman I can recall in it appears briefly, to fire the shot that starts the action off.

It's an odd film, involving while it's on, but not leaving any real traces once you leave the cinema.

Kenneth Turan (review date 10 September 1993)

SOURCE: "Gunfight at the Hokey Corral," in *Los Angeles Times*, September 10, 1993, pp. F1, F8.

[*In the following review, Turan offers negative assessment of* True Romance.]

It is hard to say what is more dispiriting about ***True Romance,*** the movie itself or the fact that someone somewhere is sure to applaud its hollow, dime-store nihilism and smug pseudo-hip posturing as a bright new day in American cinema.

In truth this latest example of Hollywood's growing fascination with Bad Boy Chic (the kind of films where the men are violence-prone misfits and the women gasp and coo) has all the originality of a paper cup. A derivative dead end that pushes familiar genre themes way past absurdity. ***True Romance*** is anything but truthful and not even remotely romantic.

Starring Christian Slater and Patricia Arquette as lowlifes in jeopardy and in love, ***True Romance*** also features cameos by Dennis Hopper, Gary Oldman, Christopher Walken, Brad Pitt and Chris Penn, actors with a gleeful affinity for sadistic beatings, sullen gunplay and other over-the-edge antics.

The light for all these moths is screenwriter Quentin Tarantino, the poet laureate of Bad Boy Chic, whose brassy debut as a writer-director, ***Reservoir Dogs,*** brought so much spirited energy and enthusiasm to its blood-soaked violence that casually dismissing it couldn't be done.

Tarantino, however, is not the director here. Tony Scott is, and one of the few things ***True Romance*** (rated R for strong violence and language and for sexuality and drug use) does well is provide a strong argument for writers being put in charge of their own material.

A celebrated director of commercials, Scott has had major box-office successes ("Top Gun" and "Beverly Hills Cop II") as well as embarrassments ("The Hunger" and "Days of Thunder"), but a sensitivity to the written word and a grace with actors have never been his trademarks. ***Romance***'s clumsy, treatment of Tarantino's idiosyncratic lines will be obvious to anyone who has seen ***Reservoir Dogs,*** and its considerable violence feels piled on and excessive in a way that picture managed to avoid.

In fairness, though, ***Romance,*** apparently the first thing Tarantino ever wrote and sold, is not the most compelling of narratives. With its erratic plot turns and showoff sequences, it has the feeling of a "Hey, notice me" spec script, written to impress anyone who read it with how clever its creator is. And its inclusion of sappy plot twists better suited to "Free Willy" does not speak well for its thematic integrity.

Clarence Worley (Slater), mild-mannered comic-book store employee and major fan of Asian fighting hero Sonny Chiba, is first glimpsed at a bar, trying to pick up an understandably bored floozy by rhapsodizing about Elvis and his own personal "live fast, die young and leave a good-looking corpse" philosophy.

Hanging out at his favorite action theater, Clarence makes a connection with Alabama Whitman (Arquette), a bimbo with a heart of gold who keeps falling out of her fluorescent clothes and has a weakness for fake leopard-skin outfits.

Though no signs of it are visible on screen, Clarence and Alabama immediately develop such a passion for each other that his and hers tattoos can't be avoided. Next, after some business with the nasty Drexl Spivey (Oldman, over the top even for him) gets taken care of, the love birds head out for California in a large purple Cadillac, determined to make their fortune and avoid the evil forces that have ended up on their trail.

In its focus on star-crossed lovers on the run, ***True Romance*** tries to be a kind of post-modern homage to the lonely hearts of film noir. Unfortunately, without a sense of style that extends below its trash-loving surface, its extremes of behavior are tedious and cartoonish and its attempts at wit little more than smug.

Unable to get the emotional effects it is after, ***True Romance*** ends up, like a defiant teen-ager, striking what it thinks are the appropriate poses and hoping nobody will notice the difference. The film also displays an almost religious veneration for on-screen violence, a blanket reverence for guns and blood as gee-whiz swell that is both childish and off-putting. Nothing is more irritating than a dumb film that thinks it's hip, and ***True Romance*** is this year's model.

Richard Alleva (review date 22 October 1993)

SOURCE: "Smut in Your Eye: Scott's 'True Romance,'" in *Commonweal,* October 22, 1993, pp. 22-4.

[*In the following review, Alleva offers unfavorable evaluation of* True Romance.]

Want to feel like a fool? Go see ***True Romance.*** That will do the trick.

For starters, there's the fictional company you will have to keep. The hero is an Elvis-obsessed, moronic piece of white trash named Clarence Worley who, when he's not clerking in a comic-book store (where he reverently samples the product), doesn't get out of his apartment much, although he always treats himself to a Kung-fu triple feature on his birthday. And, get this, his favorite chop-socky star isn't the dynamic Bruce Lee or the endearing Karate clown, Jackie Chan, but the bestial Sonny Chiba, who tears off the gonads of his opponents and holds them up to the camera for our delectation. Clarence's latest such excursion rewards him with the company of Alabama Whitman, a bubble-headed tart sent to the lad by his employer as a birthday present. Alabama is the sort of girl who thinks that having one's life controlled by a pimp isn't so bad, though, come to think of it, hers did spend some time recently stomping on the stomach of one of the other whores in his stable. A few scenes later, Alabama learns that Clarence, seeking to avenge her honor or, more likely, assuage his own jealousy, has just murdered both her pimp and another gangster. To which she can only gush, "You are so-o-o romantic."

If these characters aren't repulsive enough for you, then be warned that they are played by Christian Slater and Patricia Arquette. Both of them struck me as nonentities when I first saw them (Slater in *The Name of the Rose,* Arquette in *Ethan Frome*), but I now see that that was only because they were unfairly burdened with roles requiring intelligence and charm. Here, as violence-loving turnipheads, they attain visibility, Slater by doing a third-rate imitation of Jack Nicholson and Arquette by emulating the naive vivacity of Melanie Griffith. Their performances aren't exactly good but they meet this movie's requirements by being sufficiently animalistic.

Now I'm certainly not suggesting that characters have to be subtle or likable to be compelling. The quite similar protagonists of Terence Malick's *Badlands,* played by Martin Sheen and Sissy Spacek, were even more psychotic than this current duo. But Malick managed to conduct the viewer into the dreams and aspirations of his delinquents. He made you see their self-images as well as their frightful deed and so you enjoyed bifocal vision: whenever Sheen murdered, you shuddered at the action but you were also gripped by the self-deluding fantasies that propelled him to his crimes.

In ***True Romance,*** the strategies of writer Quentin Tarantino and director Tony Scott are the opposite of Malick's. They don't reveal anything about their main characters that you haven't known from the start. Slater's eyebrow-arching frenzy and Arquette's baby doll gurgling are what you're stuck with for the entirety of the movie. It's true that Clarence has a couple of daydream colloquies with his idol, Elvis Presley, but in these scenes the ghostly rock star merely urges Clarence on to do what he would do anyway. And isn't Presley an inappropriate choice as pop Mephisto to Clarence? Presley's persona both as singer and actor was that of a good ol' boy, sexually potent but also honest, tender, and even socially responsible (remember "In the Ghetto?"), ready to use his fists in defense of women and children but otherwise nonviolent. Why would the spirit of this redneck Galahad urge his fan on to homicide and drug dealing?

For drug dealing is indeed the mission as Clarence and his inamorata, with a suitcase loaded with cocaine taken from the dead pimp, drive from Detroit to L.A. to sell the dope to Hollywood executives. What they don't know is that the mob is in pursuit and, later, some L.A. cops are conducting a sting. All these mobsters and detectives and Hollywood shysters are portrayed as just so many comic monsters equal to one another in greed and viciousness, and they display Tarantino's greatest writing talent: his knack for serving up comic-sinister dialogue which is not only funny but which registers the stirrings of violence as a Geiger counter detects the presence of radiation. Tarantino can't write a father-son reconciliation or a truly interesting love scene but he is a whiz at capturing the profane mockery and excitement of detectives listening on headphones to a drug deal. And he is also good at pushing the comic-sinister into sheer horror, as when an assassin admits to a victim that he used to be sickened whenever he killed but now does it just to see the expressions on his victims' faces change.

The supporting players, abetted by Tony Scott's galvanizing staging, have such a field day that they easily nudge aside the leads. There are four stand-outs. Gary Oldman astonished me as a white pimp trying with considerable success to look and sound black. The actor charges the air around him with nearly palpable menace. Saul Rubenick (the dime novelist of *Unforgiven*) is deliciously loathsome as a self-bedazzled movie producer; Christopher Walken, though patently miscast as a Sicilian mafioso, manages once again to use his cobra magnetism to elicit both laughs and chills. But best of all is Bronson Pinchot as a profoundly luckless go-between memorably named Elliot Blitzer. Pinchot endows this craven would-be actor, producer's toady, and police informant with so much humor and (relative) sanity that Blitzer becomes the single truly human presence in this cast of maniacs. Solicitude for one's own skin may not be the noblest of emotions, but when Pinchot, trapped between the ranks of mafia and police, suggests that everyone hold their fire until he slips out since "all this is really none of my business," he expresses the only emotion in this movie untainted by the malice Tarantino shows for both his characters and his audience.

For an example of that malice, take the scene in which gangsters led by Walken interrogate Clarence's father (Dennis Hopper) in order to learn our hero's whereabouts. Hopper defies his tormentors and provokes them into killing him before he breaks under torture. All very noble, but note how Tarantino taints this act of heroism. Hopper, learning that Walken is Sicilian, taunts the elegant hoodlum with the fact that Moors raided Sicily centuries ago and impregnated the women. Therefore, concludes this well-read security guard, all you Sicilians are "part nigger." Granted, the speech does have a certain nasty humor and Walken's bemused reactions to it are hilarious. I also grant Bernard Shaw's insight that people don't have their virtues and vices in neat separate packages but have them all messed together. A brave and loving father *can* be a bigot too, or at least talk like a bigot in order to inflame his enemies. What bothers me about the speech is that its sole aim is not to reveal character under pressure but merely to shock. No, not even to shock but just to give us yet another dirty little dig in the ribs.

The "true romance" of the title is similarly subverted. In this movie's world of violence and greed, we are meant to see that the lovers, at least, are pure in their passion. But why is the first sex scene preceded by Clarence reading a violent comic book to his girl? And why is a later sex bout accomplished in a phone booth while Clarence calls a pal who is sitting on the toilet. Whatever Tony Scott and Quentin Tarantino feel about true romance in the abstract, they certainly mock it in their characters.

And consider the treatment of violence. Clarence and Alabama often watch glitzy, ridiculous crime shows on TV before and after launching into some violent encounter of their own. An ironic juxtaposition? Fantasy violence vs. the sting of reality? But though the violence undergone by the lovers is considerably more graphic than what they watch, it is just as unbelievable, just as much without real consequences. Lengthily stomped by the pimp, Clarence dashes through the rest of the movie without so much as a stitch in his side. Alabama, beaten nearly into jello by an assassin, feels fine after Clarence dabs her face with Kleenex. Why these instantaneous recoveries? Comedy? No, for they aren't done with the clean exaggeration of comedy which makes us laugh. Satire? No, for satire has a moral purpose. A sort of Brechtian distancing device? No, for the violence is so lovingly savored by the camera that we can't be distanced from it a moment later by a bit of unreality.

No, there is some other underlying emotion at the core of this movie, and I'll venture a guess as to what it is.

Under the squeal of brakes and the bursts of firepower, I seemed to hear someone in the theater's darkness muttering, "It's a joke, see? Everything's a joke. Movies are a joke, and what people will settle for from the movies is a joke. And you are a joke for watching this movie." I think it was Tarantino himself I was hearing sniggering whenever viewers flinched, sneering whenever they began to be interested in what he had helped to put on the screen.

Nihilistic laughter in the dark.

David Denby (review date 3 October 1994)

SOURCE: "A Thugfest," in *New York,* October 3, 1994, pp. 96-9.

[*In the following review, Denby offers favorable evaluation of* Pulp Fiction.]

It's not hard to see why actors have been eager to work with the young writer-director Quentin Tarantino. A bad-boy entertainer, "dark" but playful, Tarantino writes an American gutter rant—golden arias of vituperation interlaced with patches of odd, hilarious formality (the formality functions like an outbreak of classical movement in the middle of a modern-dance concert). His latest, ***Pulp Fiction,*** which won the Palme d'Or at Cannes last spring and just opened the New York Film Festival, is an ecstatically entertaining piece of suave mockery. Tarantino serves up low-life characters and situations from old novels and movies, and he revels in every manner of pulp flagrancy—murder and betrayal, drugs, sex, and episodes of sardonically distanced sadomasochism. But the language pours forth with a richness never heard in conventional pulp, and he plays havoc with our expectations. There are three overlapping stories in ***Pulp Fiction,*** and the structure is bound with words—anecdotes, debates, rococo profanities, biblical quotations. Amazingly, the complex of overturned expectations gets set right by the end.

Like Altman and Scorsese twenty years ago or Godard a decade before that, Tarantino, 31, has quickly become an international film-festival celebrity. At the moment, he's an avatar of American hip, perhaps the only one in the movie business. (Jim Jarmusch's stylized ennui has come to look like artistic and personal enervation.) Tarantino, commercial yet intransigent, is the hero of those who long to be produced, those who have daring ideas but no way of realizing them. Like the earlier movie men, Tarantino is immersed in cinema; he even comes garlanded with a myth comparable to Scorsese's asthmatic, movie-enriched childhood. A sort of Southern California swamp-mall creature, he rises, unschooled, from a clerk's position at a video store with thousands of films in his head and grand ambitions in his heart. Having seen and digested everything, he understands the logic and secrets of movie genres, the hidden strength of their conventions; therefore, he can play, he can mix cruelty and formal inventiveness (sometimes the formal play is itself cruel), teasing, undermining, subverting, while telling a story at the same time.

Pulp Fiction is about Los Angeles crum-bums—gangsters, a boxer ordered to take a dive, molls, a pair of sadists. The movie is not meant to be sincere. In a Scorsese movie like *Mean Streets* or *GoodFellas,* the characters, as much as lovers in an opera by Verdi, suffer and die. But Tarantino's gangsters are not "real." ***Pulp Fiction*** is play, a commentary on old movies. Tarantino works with trash, and by analyzing, criticizing, and formalizing it, he emerges with something new, just as Godard made a lyrical work of art in *Breathless* out of his memories of casually crappy American B-movies. Of course Godard was, and is, a Swiss-Parisian intellectual, and the tonalities of his work are drier, more cerebral. ***Pulp Fiction,*** by contrast, displays an entertainer's talent for luridness. It's a very funky, American sort of pop masterpiece, improbable, uproarious, with bright colors and danger and blood right on the surface. And yet the movie is not heartless like ***Natural Born Killers;*** and for all its joking, ***Pulp Fiction*** is not a put-on. Tarantino gives us the great pulp theme without its attendant clichés. It's a movie about loyalty.

What a jump forward! I can't say I was a fan of Tarantino's 1992 debut film, ***Reservoir Dogs.*** The movie was like a nihilistic film-school exercise—a malignant gloss, perhaps, on Stanley Kubrick's early heist picture, *The Killing*. I enjoyed the virtuoso cursing, the grotesque ironies, but Tarantino depended on blood and sadism so thoroughly that the genre tease lost its wit. (Being bullied by hipness is the same as being bullied by anything else.) Apart from enjoying one baroquely nasty scene between Christopher Walken and Dennis Hopper, I also hated ***True Romance,*** a movie that Tarantino wrote but Tony Scott directed. A commercial hack like Scott working on Tarantino's material revealed what trash unredeemed by irony might look like. ***True Romance*** was all processed, violent thrills, with cocaine dust for glamour.

Pulp Fiction isn't nihilistic, and it certainly isn't stupid. If the theme is loyalty, the basic dramatic unit is the couple—men and women and men and men. Two petty thieves sitting in a diner, played by Tim Roth and Amanda Plummer, skinny and intense, mated like rabbits, rise from their seats and announce a stickup. Lightweights, thrill-seeking amateurs, they pull out their guns—and the episode breaks off. That's the beginning of the movie, and we return to them at the end, though what appears in the interim isn't all flashback. Some of it takes place before that moment, some *after.* The chronology of the three stories is daringly skewed so we can see people in the midst of different yet connected actions. Call it *collateral* narration. What goes around comes around.

The two principal characters are hit men in black suits, white shirts, and black ties. John Travolta, overweight, puffy, with long hair falling from a knot in strands (at times, in his black suit, he looks like a Hasid), and Samuel L. Jackson, lean, curly-haired, with a mean tongue, work for a local crime boss (Ving Rhames). That morning, on the way to the job (killing yuppie punks who have taken something that belongs to their boss), the two hit men have a long conversation about a man who massaged the feet of the boss's wife and was tossed out the window. Is massaging a woman's feet an offense worthy of death, like adultery? The conversation goes on and on, with perfect seriousness—the two thugs could be disputatious monks in the late Middle Ages. The movie is less about crime than about what happens before and after crime—the shadows and echoes of an act rather than the act itself.

Tarantino has pushed to an extreme the pleasures of pulp, which are, of course, the pleasures of sensation and cheapness, and moods of shallow, voluptuous despair. Pulp fiction, especially in its aesthetically and intellectually respectable *noir* forms (the books of Dashiell Hammett and Raymond Chandler, the movies of John Huston, Howard Hawks, Robert Siodmak, Robert Aldrich, et al.), is a disillusioned, dark-shadowed urban poetry of losers, chippies, meatball thugs. But so much has been accomplished in the *noir* tradition, you can't do it straight anymore. So Tarantino works in banal daylight, on the L.A. streets, and we never do find out why the hit men kill the punks or what's in the stolen briefcase. And what had seemed incidental—the conversation about tending the boss's wife—turns out to be the essence of the first story.

Travolta is himself given the job of entertaining her for the evening. Witchy in dark hair, bangs, and matching ruby lips and nails, Uma Thurman's predatory moll has the lacquered beauty of those only-in-the-movies women (Veronica Lake, Jane Greer, Gene Tierney, et al.) from the forties. She takes Travolta to a glowing retro-fifties restaurant that features tables placed inside long-finned cars and a headwaiter imitating Ed Sullivan—the period references dance around deliriously. Afraid of his boss (if he sleeps with the wife, he'll die), Travolta walks on eggshells until the instant that Uma snorts heroin by mistake and the scene turns toward black comedy with moments so appalling you can't take your eyes off the screen even as you are close to nausea.

Most of the behavior onscreen is outrageous, yet each character feels justified in what he does and engages in long tirades of rational discourse when anyone disagrees. Samuel L. Jackson's blistering rant draws on the traditions of black street preachers and con artists; the rhetoric of insult and indignant, high-voiced hyperbole propels the language beyond Scorsese's tough-guy repetitions into a new movie poetry—Jackson dominates the screen. The movie is not so much a set of stories as a way of life and a habit of consciousness. Tarantino may be saying that Scorsese's kind of sincerity is no longer possible: These people know they are playing a role. Gangsters imitate movies and movies imitate gangsters in an endless chain. That situation could produce a stale, literary "postmodernist" cinema, but ***Pulp Fiction*** stays wild. The genre situations are invaded by weirdness, mess, coincidence. People talk much longer than you expect.

The second story begins with a stoic Hemingwayesque

loser—a boxer, played by Bruce Willis, who has been paid by the crime boss to take a dive, and who refuses to go down. Holed up in a motel room with his kittenish French girlfriend (Maria de Medeiros, who could be Maria in the sleeping bag from *For Whom the Bell Tolls*), Willis realizes he has to return home to retrieve a family heirloom, a watch his father once stored up his ass in a Vietnamese prison camp. A sacred treasure! What follows, as Willis runs into the angry crime boss, and they both wind up as prisoners in an S&M dungeon, is so startlingly funny—so far out yet logical—that Tarantino seems to be goosing the entire solemn history of action cinema. And the last sequence, in which the two hit men, with a dead body on their hands, require the services of a gentleman hood, the Wolf (Harvey Keitel), also seems a kind of preposterous valedictory. The dead bodies must be disposed of. Farewell to pulp fiction! As we return to the diner, and the two rabbity amateurs from the opening scene, the executioner played by Samuel L. Jackson movingly resigns from crime.

Tarantino has himself expressed his desire to make other kinds of movies. In the roundelay of violence and comedy that is ***Pulp Fiction,*** he has hilariously summed up an immense genre and gloriously achieved his exit from it. Life beckons from beyond the video store.

Peter Travers (review date 6 October 1994)

SOURCE: "Tarantino's Twist," in *Rolling Stone,* October 6, 1994, pp. 79-81.

[*In the following review, Travers offers high praise for* Pulp Fiction.]

Now that Quentin Tarantino's ***Pulp Fiction*** has won the Palme d'Or at Cannes, opened the New York Film Festival and made the former video-store clerk a name to suck up to big time in Hollywood, you're probably thinking the writer-director of ***Reservoir Dogs*** has sold out his renegade ass. Think again. The proudly disreputable ***Pulp Fiction*** (cost: a measly $8 million) is the new King Kong of crime movies. It's an anthology that blends three stories and 12 principal characters into a mesmerizing mosaic of the Los Angeles scuzz world. The acting is dynamite: John Travolta and Bruce Willis can consider their careers revived. Buoyed by Tarantino's strafing wit, the action sizzles, and so does the sex. ***Pulp Fiction*** is ferocious fun without a trace of caution, complacency or political correctness to inhibit its 154 deliciously lurid minutes.

That said, Tarantino's twist on the pulp genre is also damn near a work of art. At 31, he shows a disdain—rare among his peers—for flashy style and lofty pretension. His passion is for storytelling that allows the most outrageous characters to reveal their feelings in long takes and torrents of words, poetic and profane. Tony Scott's glossy direction blurred the Tarantino script for ***True Romance,*** and Oliver Stone obliterated Tarantino entirely in ***Natural Born Killers.***

Pulp Fiction proves that Tarantino is the ideal director, for preserving the verbal rhythm and wicked playfulness of his scripts. He revels in pop culture, especially that of the 70s, and he's no snob: The French New Wave or blaxploitation, *The Wild Bunch or The Brady Bunch*—it's all grist. Unlike other raiders of Hitchcock, Howard Hawks and Sam Fuller, Tarantino has found his own voice.

He has also found censure. The ear-slicing scene in ***Reservoir Dogs,*** his stunning 1992 debut film about a jewel heist, made him the whipping boy for film violence. A graphic adrenalin shot to the heart in ***Pulp Fiction*** will raise more hackles. Such hand wringing only blinds audiences to Tarantino's underrated and powerfully suggestive gift for language. Do yourself a favor with ***Pulp Fiction.*** Don't just watch, listen.

Take an early scene between Travolta's Vincent Vega and Samuel L. Jackson as his hood partner, Jules Winnfield. Decked out Dogs style in dark suits, they are about to bust in on some preppy amateurs who stole something belonging to their bad ass boss, Marsellus Wallace (the excellent Ving Rhames). But before the job, they talk—casual stuff, but it's how they define themselves. Jules can't figure why Marsellus tossed a buddy off a balcony for giving Marsellus' bride, Mia (Uma Thurman), a foot massage. "It's laying hands on Marsellus' new wife in a familiar way," says Vincent. "Is it as bad as eatin' her out? No, but you're in the same fuckin' ballpark."

The debate on sexual etiquette is hilarious; they could be two pals driving to work, except their work is crime. "Let's get into character," says Jules, before he and Vincent bust in on the preps. Vincent radiates silent cool, while Jules raves on about "furious anger." It's a coldblooded thing he says for effect. The source isn't a movie; it's the Bible—a sly irony that spills over into sinister when Jules suddenly shoots one boy for effect. The victim isn't a disposable Hollywood bad guy; he's a scared kid. We are staggered. But not Jules and Vincent. They have turned murder into performance art. It doesn't touch them. Or does it? Jackson's astounding portrayal reveals that Jules is developing a conscience.

It is Tarantino's considerable achievement to show what it takes for these men to play their roles as killers. For Vincent, it's drugs. Marsellus orders Vincent to take Mia out for dinner while he's out of town. To calm his nerves, Vincent stops off to score heroin from Lance (Eric Stoltz), a dealer with a wife (Rosanna Arquette) who has pierced her body with studs in 16 places, even her tongue.

Vincent needs help getting through the night. Mia takes him to Jack Rabbit Slim's, a diner filled with '50s movie memorabilia. Vincent orders a Douglas Sirk steak, while Mia hits the ladies' room to powder her nose with coke. Cinematographer Andrzej Sekula and editor Sally Menke show dazzling craft, but ***Pulp Fiction*** is an actors' show. The usually glassy Thurman is marvelous here, seductively scrappy as she teases Vincent for gossiping with Jules ("You're worse than a sewing circle"). Best of all, she gets him to the dance floor for a twist contest. Travolta is doughier than in his *Saturday Night Fever* days, but even playing a junkie reptile he exhibits amazing grace. His slow dance with Mia to a Chuck Berry oldie exudes down 'n' dirty eroticism and unexpected romantic longing. Travolta makes a spectacular comeback with this brilliant, intuitive performance.

Willis, as boxer Butch Coolidge, also digs into his tastiest role in years. Marsellus sends Vincent to kill Butch for refusing to take a dive. But the mean palooka, reformed by his love for a French chatterbox, Fabienne (Maria de Medeiros), has skipped town. Almost. Butch risks returning for a gold watch. His late father had that watch hidden up his ass in a Nam prison camp, according to Dad's buddy (Christopher Walken). Going back gets Butch involved with Marsellus and two hillbillies who tie them up for a bout of buttfucking.

Suffice it to say, the revenge isn't pretty. Neither is the mess when Vincent accidentally blows the head off a guy in the back seat of the car Jules is driving. The cleanup, supervised by a courtly mob facilitator called the Wolf (Harvey Keitel in peak form), takes place in the garage of Jules' pal Jimmie (a memorably miffed Tarantino), who wants these gangsters out before his nurse wife Bonnie comes home. "The Bonnie Situation" is the film's comic high point, as tough guys are reduced to frightened boys at the prospect of a woman's wrath.

But Tarantino is after more than laughs. Near the end, Jules—sitting in a coffee shop with Vincent—enjoys a "moment of clarity" about changing his life. Unfortunately, two small-time crooks played by Tim Roth and Amanda Plummer choose that moment to rob the place. Chaos ensues, though Tarantino never loses his film's moral center. He refuses to patronize, glamorize or judge his band of outsiders. Instead, he lets us see the glimmers of humanity that emerge when they drop their masks of control. It's Tarantino's compassion that deepens the film and sets it apart from trendy, pud-pulling, cinematic nihilism. It also sets Tarantino apart as a major filmmaker, worthy of comparison to early Godard (*Bande à Part*) and Scorsese (*Mean Streets*). There's a special kick that comes from watching something this thrillingly alive. Pauline Kael calls it "getting drunk on movies." Whatever you call it, ***Pulp Fiction*** is indisputably great.

Jonathan Romney (review date 8 October 1994)

SOURCE: "A Real Hamburger of a Movie," in *New Statesman & Society,* October 8, 1994, p. 29.

[*In the following review, Romney offers unfavorable assessment of* Pulp Fiction.]

I don't have that much to say about Quentin Tarantino's ***Pulp Fiction,*** but that's OK, because it has plenty to say for itself. Watching it is like sitting in a diner for hours on end while the guy opposite you simultaneously gabbles away, stuffs his face and juggles balls. Sort of how you'd imagine a dinner date with Tarantino to be.

I loved ***Reservoir Dogs.*** Loved the suits, loved the pace, loved the bloodshed, loved the shock of alarm when the film suddenly made you realise *how much* you loved the bloodshed . . . Apart from the endless opening waffle about Madonna, which reminded me horribly of my days as a rock critic, ***Reservoir Dogs*** was cool. And since being for Tarantino or *against* him seemed overnight to become a yardstick of social hipness, I guess that made me cool too.

Pulp Fiction, though, leaves me cold. Even more than ***Reservoir Dogs,*** this is a film that you can't just like—you have to subscribe to it. It doesn't try to seduce or persuade you, nor does it clam up and cut to the chase, as *Reservoir Dogs* did. It just asks whether or not you can buy into a code of nerd-chic values largely determined by Tarantino's own obsessions. If you accept that B-movie in-jokes, veiled allusions to *Charlie's Angels,* knowing the difference between Jayne Mansfield and Mamie Van Doren, and caring about the International language of junk food is, like, as serious as your life, then this movie's for you. If you can't, then you're out of the game. ***Pulp Fiction*** bombards you with constant excess—of information, of narrative, of violence, of pop-culture trivia, of smart-ass high-banality backchat, flings it all in your lap like a warm ketchup-heavy cheeseburger, and demands that you either swallow it or sling it out.

On paper, ***Pulp Fiction*** offers plenty of incentive to join its club—a devious triple-layered, false-bottomed narrative structure, jolt after nerve-jangling jolt, and a brace of punchy, charismatic performances: John Travolta as flabby, slow-witted nice guy Vincent, who happens to be a ruthless hitman, Samuel Jackson as his fearsome Bible-spouting buddy Jules, who has "Bad Motherfucker" embroidered on his wallet, Harvey Keitel being the dapper elder statesman, and Bruce

Willis finally putting his oxen lunkishness to good use as a boxer on the skids.

But before you can enjoy these pleasures, there are considerable obstacles to get past. ***Pulp Fiction*** opens with a diner conversation as rambling and one-note as the Madonna debate in ***Dogs***—and if you don't buy the notion that Tim Roth and Amanda Plummer, as lovebird felons, are compelling company to hang out with, then you're going to be bored until the surf music kicks in over the credits. Then, after a burst of Kool and the Gang, cut to Travolta and Jackson en route to a hit, lost in a colloquy on European burger bars and the erotics of foot massage. Again, if you couldn't care less that the French call a quarter-pounder with cheese a *burger royal,* then you might already be wondering whether this film's for you. Every film entails a match or mis-match between its concerns and the viewer's, but few assert such a singular or fastidious set of obsessions.

The same applies to the Tarantino sense of humour and the way it works itself out in the violence. ***Reservoir Dogs***' cruel ironies resolved themselves in the way that the violence came both randomly and inexorably. Here, though, the brutality is laid on as a succession of one-shot gags, *Road Runner* style. Mostly, these are at the expense of the little-league minor players who get blown away because they're not so cool—like the college boys who are the first to face Jules' Old Testament vengeance.

Then there's the gruesome misogyny in the first story, in which Vincent goes out on the town with the boss's wife (Uma Thurman). Dressed up as a jokey dire warning about hard drugs, what happens to Thurman's Mia is no more than an excuse to see what a B-film vamp looks like when she gets real messed up. ***Pulp Fiction*** does indeed look like the director's book of imaginary dates—a whole succession of dream babes drop into the narrative almost at random, and only Thurman gets much to do. (Tarantino's beginning to look like the studio head's son in *The Player,* ordering starlets from the casting catalogue.)

Pulp Fiction isn't too choosy about who gets it in the neck—just about all our favourite characters suffer some humiliation along the way, sometimes in outrageously cavalier fashion. But the narrative twists aren't as tight as you'd like—Tarantino's characters keep wilfully strolling into hell, but they nearly always stroll out again, mopping their brow with a whistle of relief. Pandora's box is opened only to be safely shut again. The film never puts us on the spot or makes us fear that we're going to find ourselves in a tight corner with its characters.

The blood-letting is pure joke-shop violence, designed to shake you out of your seat. But there's nothing behind the jokes, which are rather less funny and certainly less ironically biting, than the various Acme appliances that blow up in the Coyote's face in *Road Runner.* The murderous efficiency of ***Dogs*** has vanished. Here, Tarantino has the time and the budget to do what he likes, and he does everything that comes into his head. But you miss that cold fast sleazy hit that the title promises. This isn't pulp fiction so much as a big flabby airport paperback with a flashy embossed cover.

David Wild (essay date 3 November 1994)

SOURCE: "Quentin Tarantino," in *Rolling Stone,* November 3, 1994, pp. 76-78, 80-1, 110.

[*In the following essay, Wild discusses Tarantino's films, career, and artistic influences.*]

Quentin Tarantino, madman of movie mayhem, has a mother. How's that for a shocker? She has seen ***Reservoir Dogs,*** the 1992 heist film that made a cult sensation of her writer-director-actor son and raised the stakes on movie gore with a 10-minute torture scene featuring the severing of an ear. "That happens to be my mother's favorite scene," says Tarantino, 31, a high-school dropout who has gone from video-store clerk to genius auteur du jour in just a few feverishly busy years. Mom has just checked out ***Pulp Fiction,*** a wildly ambitious and darkly comic crime anthology about Los Angeles lowlife that won the Palme d'Or at Cannes, opened the prestigious New York Film Festival and put her son in the hot-contender line at next year's Oscars. Although the film includes shootings, stabbings, S&M, homosexual rape and a drug-overdose sequence that leaves audiences reeling. Mom doesn't flinch. Tarantino's West Hollywood, Calif, bachelor apartment is another matter. "That's not particularly my decorating style," she says with a laugh.

Chez Tarantino is hardly the sort of glitzy home in the Hills one might imagine to house a ballsy, Generation X-rated triple threat on the verge of becoming his own one-man genre. Rather the homey—OK, messy—pad looks like a kitschy pop-culture Valhalla. Movie posters, videos, laser discs, albums, fanzines, books and assorted film artifacts fill every available inch. Along with memorabilia from his own movies—including that razor used in the infamous ear-slicing scene—there's a frighteningly lifelike head of B-movie diva Barbara Steele, a pack of genuine *Texas Chainsaw* chili, a *Zorro* knife given to him by Jennifer Beals, a Robert Vaughn doll, cases by the dozen of bottled Pepsi and what is undoubtedly one of the world's most impressive collections of film- and TV-related board games.

"I've been collecting all this shit for years," says Tarantino, who is wearing a Racer X T-shirt today. "Then I finally decided I wanted to start collecting something new. At first I chose lunch boxes, but they really rape you on lunch boxes. They're just too fucking expensive. And as for dolls, well, you can't have much fun with them! You have to keep them in the box. So, I started with board games." Proudly, he shows off his collection, which he has broken down by genre. *The Dukes of Hazzard,* he reports, is a particularly fine game. Two of his most impressive acquisitions are *Dawn of the Dead* and *Universe,* which he claims is "the closest they ever came to an official *2001: A Space Odyssey* game." The bedroom is dominated by a personal collection of tapes large enough to open a video store of one's own. The fare here ranges from art-house classics to *Ma Barker's Killer Brood* and a healthy number of vintage blaxploitation flicks.

You also can't help noticing the shrine to John Travolta above the ledge of Tarantino's fireplace. Certainly part of the satisfaction of making ***Pulp Fiction*** for Tarantino came from the opportunity to work with Travolta, a k a Vinnie Barbarino, head Sweathog on one of Tarantino's TV faves from the '70s, *Welcome Back, Kotter.* The movie helps restore the 40-year-old actor's stardom to its prior luster after a string of less than challenging roles. In a film of standout performances from Bruce Willis, Samuel L. Jackson, Uma Thurman, Tim Roth, Amanda Plummer, Christopher Walken, Harvey Keitel and Tarantino himself, Travolta scores a stunning comeback as the henchman, hot dancer and heroin junkie Vincent Vega. Tarantino will happily expound for hours on the "total brilliance" of the actor's work 13 years ago in Brian De Palma's *Blow Out.* "John's a real sweetheart, and we became friends," he says. "I just gave John a role like the ones he used to do, and I took him seriously. But getting to know John, I can sort of see why he did all those *Look Who's Talking* baby movies, because that character is kind of similar to who he is in real life—he's this kind of goofy, charming kind of guy."

Travolta was similarly charmed. "I've been doing this for 20 years now, and I've never seen anyone have more fun on a movie set than Quentin," he says. "And it's contagious. You think, 'If this guy can get off as much as he does, then I *definitely* want to get on board this boat.' His knowledge of film is acute. His joy of film is acute. Just the pure wattage of Quentin as a human being is extraordinary. And his willingness to accept criticism as well as admiration and not get introverted by it just floors me. I'm so envious of it. I can't find his fear."

So what did Travolta make of Tarantino's deep appreciation of his past work? "How can you *not* respond to that?" Travolta says. "It was swiftly and clearly articulated to me what I meant to him growing up and what I meant—in certain performances—to a whole generation." Travolta lets out a small chuckle, then adds, "I realized that Quentin represents how a lot of people feel about me, only now it's OK to say it."

All this mutual admiration begs a question: When Tarantino first met with Travolta before casting him, did he mention that he had a shrine to the actor above his fireplace? "No, I didn't tell John about the shrine," Tarantino says. "But I *did* bring along my Vinnie Barbarino doll so he could sign it for me."

The success of ***Pulp Fiction*** tastes sweet to Tarantino. Not so long ago, the most high-profile credit this engagingly intense wanna-be could boast was playing one of three Elvis imitators on an episode of *Golden Girls.* He made his first splash with ***Reservoir Dogs,*** an existential heist film with an unseen heist, and returned a year later as the writer of Tony Scott's underrated ***True Romance.*** More recently, Tarantino was in the public eye for writing the story that, shall we say evolved into Oliver Stone's controversy-raising ***Natural Born Killers.*** Somehow he even found the time to briefly help out pal Julia Sweeney (who has a cameo in ***Pulp Fiction***) with the now-you-see-it-now-you-don't movie *It's Pat.*

But for all this activity, Tarantino is definitely *not* your average Hollywood careerist. Extremely confident yet decidedly unpretentious, he remains very much a fan—one with strong and exceedingly far-flung tastes. Talking with a *Rolling Stone* writer, the tall, lantern-jawed Tarantino makes a point of addressing the nonburning issue of how *Perfect,* a movie that starred Travolta as a *Rolling Stone* writer, was woefully underappreciated. He's the guy who loved Kevin Costner's megaflop *Wyatt Earp.* An avowed *Baywatch* watcher, Tarantino is happy to ponder the frankly frightening issue of David Hasselhoff's big-screen potential. He's also the rare and brave aesthete able to make the qualitative judgment that *Look Who's Talking Too* represents the creative apex of that cinematic Travolta trilogy.

Tarantino's pop-culture-freak status has even informed his own performances. In ***Reservoir Dogs*** he made a memorable appearance as Mr. Brown, arguing passionately with Mr. Pink (Steve Buscemi) over the true meaning of Madonna's "Like a Virgin." Mr. Brown insists that the lyric is "a metaphor for a big dick," while Mr. Pink rather more romantically suggests that the song is about love. For the record, Her Blondness eventually settled the matter. "Madonna liked the movie alot, but she said I'm not right," says Tarantino. "She signed my *Erotica* album, 'Dear Quentin, It's about love, it's not about dick. Madonna.'" In the current *Sleep With Me,* Tarantino nearly steals the show with a cameo as a partygoer lecturing passionately on the homosexual subtext of *Top Gun.*

Even the Tarantino kitchen—with its apparent life-time supply of Yoo Hoo prominently displayed next to a big box of Captain Crunch—suggests a sort of gleefully arrested development. But after some years where he had trouble getting arrested in Hollywood, Tarantino has established himself as a mature and much in demand talent. Still, it wasn't long ago that Tarantino was just a clerk toiling at Video Archives, a *cinéaste*-run video store in Manhattan Beach, Calif. "People ask me if I went to film school," he says. "And I tell them, 'No, I went to *films.*'"

The clerk Christian Slater played in ***True Romance*** was based on Tarantino's younger days living near the Los Angeles airport. "All day long he just sees people taking off and leaving," says Tarantino. "And he's going nowhere. I'm not that guy anymore. That guy is someone who's never had a girlfriend, he's very inexperienced and naive. He's only had failure in his life." In the hands of director Tony Scott (who also happened to direct *Top Gun*), the film became a hyperviolent but highly romantic theme-park ride. "Tony did a great job," he says admiringly. "The movie was really cool. Of course, the whole thing was bizarre for me to see—like watching a big-budget feature of your home movies."

Admiring would *not* be the word to describe Tarantino's feelings regarding what became of his ***Natural Born Killers*** screenplay, which Oliver Stone ultimately chose to substantially rework with his collaborators. Tarantino declined script credit, taking responsibility only inasmuch as the movie was based on a story by him. In fact, bringing up ***Natural Born Killers*** is the single easiest way to quiet this otherwise affable chatterbox. Asked if he has seen the film, Tarantino turns strangely silent.

"No," he says finally.

According to Tarantino, he was invited to a preview screening of ***Killers*** but declined, saying he would catch it in the theater. "It's just kind of out there, and it doesn't have *anything* to do with me," he says after being coaxed to elaborate. "I think people pretty much know that I have distanced myself from the film. I don't think I'll get much credit, and I don't think I'll get much blame. I'm definitely not looking for either. If you like it, then that's Oliver. If you *don't* like it, that's Oliver, too."

In fact, the release date of ***Pulp Fiction***—a film substantially closer to his heart—was pushed back by Tarantino, producer Lawrence Bender and Miramax Films partly to distance it from ***Killers.*** "At first we were going to open it in August, which is the perfect time for sleepers," he says. "Then we heard ***Killers*** was coming out in August, and at first my attitude was, fuck it, let's open it the same day. But in the end, I don't want that association. I could just see all those double reviews in *Rolling Stone, Time* and *Newsweek.* You know, a photo from it next to a photo from ***Pulp.*** We'd be forever linked."

Pulp Fiction began with a 500-page first draft. For Tarantino "the only strange thing about writing ***Pulp*** was that for once, I knew what I was writing was going to get made," he says. "It's not so ethereal anymore. And if it's going to be made, it ought to be worth making. That's a harsh magnifying glass. Certainly, Tarantino bit off a lot with the intricately plotted ***Pulp,*** a film he early on described as "an anthology about a community of crooks." In writing ***Pulp Fiction,*** he says he was influenced by the writings of J. D. Salinger: "When you read his Glass family stories, they all eventually add up to one big story. That was the biggest example for me." Some writer pals advised Tarantino that he might have difficulty following up his ***Dogs*** debut. "Callie Khouri, who wrote *Thelma and Louise,* and Richard La Gravenese, who wrote *Fisher King,* both told me I was going to have trouble writing the next one," he recalls. "Fortunately, it really wasn't *that* difficult."

Even having the ***Pulp*** script put in turnaround by TriStar ended up helping Tarantino to make the film for a lean $8 million at Miramax—part of the reason the movie's already out of the red in presales. "I enjoyed making ***Pulp*** even more than ***Dogs*** because this time I sort of knew what I was doing." Tarantino says. "Back when we were making ***Dogs,*** Lawrence and I used to joke that we were the least experienced guys on the set. Because we *were.* This time around, we'd been there and done that, which made the whole thing a lot more fun." Tarantino has nothing but raves for all the cast, including Keitel, who makes a dramatic appearance—alongside Tarantino—as the Wolf, a resourceful Mr. Fix-It. This seems to be typecasting, since Keitel proved a savior when he helped kick start Tarantino's career by signing up to be a reservoir dog.

To hear Tarantino tell it, the hardest part since ***Pulp*** is getting down to work with all the Hollywood distractions. "A lot of young directors get a little success and turn into phone junkies," he says with a slight tone of disgust. "All they do is *talk.* My attitude is, *fuck* all these phone calls, forget all these meetings, you have work to do! Eighty percent of the people calling you in this business, their *job* is to make phone calls all day. But that's not *our* job."

On a sunny Hollywood afternoon, Quentin Tarantino is in his natural habitat: the movies. Lately, making movies can get in the way of watching them, but this isn't one of those days. This afternoon he's one of the few nonsenior citizens attending a lunchtime screening of *Mad Love* at the Los Angeles County Art Museum. "I think most of the people here must have seen it when it came out in 1935," he says, checking out the crowd.

Mad Love—later adapted as *The Hands of Orlac*—is a nicely twisted Karl Freund film starring Peter Lorre as a crazed physician who's driven by love to undertake some rather misguided surgery. Tarantino is psyched to finally see it. Somehow he has always missed the film, but he's already well versed in its lore. "The director was the cinematographer of *Metropolis,*" he explains excitedly. "And in Pauline Kael's famous essay 'Raising Kane,' she claims that this was the movie cinematographer Gregg Toland did before *Citizen Kane* to try things out for *Kane* later." With that, he sits back and smiles as the theater darkens.

After the movie lets out, Tarantino walks out into a blindingly sunny L.A. day. Over lunch at nearby Johnnie's, a no-frills diner that served as a ***Reservoir Dogs*** location, he's asked if it's unusual for him to be coming out of a film in the middle of a beautiful day. "Not at all," he says. "I go to movies *whenever* I can. I mean, I've done a few interviews where people have said they want to hang out with me on an average day and do what I do. And I always think they're waiting for me to take them horseback riding or something. They've definitely got the wrong guy. I go to movies, sometimes more than once a day, and I watch TV with friends. Occasionally, I go to coffee shops. That and I work. *That's* what I do."

This state of affairs is not a recent development. It has pretty much been the same routine since Tarantino grew up in L.A.'s South Bay in the shadow of the Los Angeles International Airport.

His parents had already split when a 2-year-old Quentin and his mother, Connie, moved west from Knoxville, Tenn., where she had been a student. According to Connie, who later remarried, Quentin was already demonstrating an insatiable appetite for movies. "Some people describe me as a permissive mother," she says. "I took Quentin to every movie I saw. I didn't censor his material." Soon, the young auteur's bedroom was beginning to resemble his current apartment. "I kept a pretty tight rein on Quentin in the rest of the house," she says, laughing.

"My mother worked very hard to supply me with a nice house to live in," Tarantino recalls. "We lived in Harbor City, which is middle class but a little rough." Connie describes the area as upper middle class—"even if that doesn't fit in with the rags-to-riches story some people want to tell about him." But she adds that "even early on, Quentin was drawn to some rough neighborhoods." The attraction, it goes without saying, was the movies.

Young Quentin—who both mother and son agree hated school—had found his refuge. "See, Harbor City's positioned between Torrance, which is an OK neighborhood, and Carson, which is rougher," he explains. "I spent a lot of my time in Carson because that's where the Carson Twin Cinema was. That was the theater that showed all the kung fu movies and the Allied International movies like *The Van.* The first time I met Danny De Vito, I said, 'Oh, yeah, Danny, you were in *The Van* and *Pom-Pom Girls.'* There was also the Del Amo Mall theater, where all the real Hollywood stuff played, and I went there, too. Basically, I spent my life at the movies.

"I grew up going to the grind houses and to the art houses and loving them both equally," Tarantino adds. "That sort of defines my aesthetic. I mean, it's not like I'm some arty guy just getting off on myself. I think studios are afraid of one thing, and that is someone's going to make a boring movie. My stuff may not be obvious, but it's not esoteric, either. I'll never write a movie about sheep herders contemplating God and life."

Tarantino broke into movies professionally as a teen-ager by ushering porn watchers at the Pussycat Theater in Torrance. He'd already tried his hand at writing his first screenplay, penning something called *Captain Peacbfuzz and the Anchovy Bandit.* At 22—around the time he started shooting a never-completed 16mm film called *My Best Friend's Birthday*—he got a much more satisfying and educational job working at Video Archives, a relatively small operation that Tarantino proudly calls "the best video store in the Los Angeles area." It was there that he met up with like-minded movie freaks such as fellow clerk Roger Avary, for whose recent directorial debut, *Killing Zoe,* Tarantino served as an executive producer. "Now Video Archives is like L.A.'s answer to the *Cashiers du Cinéma,*" Tarantino says with a laugh. "At William Morris they'll be telling agents, 'You've gotta check out the scene at that video store."

"I basically lived there for years," he continues. "We'd get off work, close up the store, then sit around and watch movies all night. Other times Roger, our friend Scott and I would take a Friday and plot things out so we could see all four new movies we were interested in. We always took whatever we got paid and put in right back into the industry."

"Quentin was *always* a great talker," Avary recalls. "The only difference now is that everybody's listening." At first there was some tension between the two. "We were a little competitive about who knew more about movies," says Avary. "Eventually, though, we realized that despite being very different people, we had the exact same tastes. It was kismet." Avary—who contributed to the story of ***Pulp Fiction***—sees himself and Tarantino as part of a whole new out-of-the-stores-and-onto-the-screens movement. "Film schools have become *completely* franchised," Avary says. "There's a fresh generation of filmmakers, and they're coming out of the video stores. All of us have the advantage of a data base of thousands of movies."

Unsurprisingly, then, a few naysaying critics have called Tarantino's work derivative. Some saw ***Reservoir Dogs*** as borrowing heavily from earlier movies, including Kubrick's *The Killing.* "Generally, I've been treated really well by the press," says Tarantino, who still regrets that famed *New Yorker* critic Pauline Kael—"one of my biggest influences, my Kingsfield," he calls her—retired before ***Reservoir Dogs*** came out. "But a few critics have said, ironically enough, that ***Dogs*** felt like a film-school movie—that it's a film more about movies then about life experiences. I don't agree. I think one of the strengths of the film is that it is realistic. It does give you a glimpse into the criminal life. But I also like the idea of my films commenting on film itself. A lot of directors I love have done that." Suddenly, Tarantino grins wildly. "And the fact of the matter is, the shots I actually *did* rip off no one has caught yet.

"Part of the fun of making movies is that you're on ground that's been covered before," he says, "and you can use that as a jumping-off point for all the weird places you want to go. I'm trying to make a combination of a movie movie and a real movie. I want to make movie movies with *real* consequences."

One real consequence of the artful brutality that has marked the movies Tarantino has made thus far is the reputation it has earned him—like Peckinpah before him—as the thinking-man's poet of violence. Some audiences still may be having flashbacks to the ear amputation scene in ***Reservoir Dogs,*** which Tarantino—a pop-music lover of extremely catholic tastes—played out to the cheerful strains of Stealers Wheel's '70s classic "Stuck in the Middle With You."

"It never bothered me when people walked out," Tarantino says. "It just meant that scene *worked.* Go to a video store and nine out of 10 films in the action-adventure section are more graphic than mine. But I'm not interested in making a cartoon. I'm interested in making the violence *real.*"

Still, when Tarantino showed the film early on at a horror festival in Spain— where it followed a splatterfest called *Brain Dead*—he figured that he had found an audience that wouldn't be thrown by the sadism on display. "So we show the movie, and, like, 15 people walk out during the torture, including [cult horror director] Wes Craven and [horror special-effects artist] Rick Baker," says Tarantino. "Wes Craven—the guy who directed *Last House on the Left,* for God's sakes—walked out of *my* movie. Stuart Gordon—the guy who did *Re-Animator*—was one of the judges, and he was burying his head in his hands. It was hysterical." Tarantino later ran into Baker, who told him: "Quentin, I walked out of your movie, but I want you to take it as a compliment. See, we all deal in fantasy. There's no such thing as werewolves or vampires. You're dealing with real-life violence, and I can't deal with it."

Pulp Fiction offers no shortage of scenes for its exhausted but exhilarated audience to talk about on the way out, including that memorable male-on-male S&M rape scene. "Well, *Deliverance* did it," he says. "*American Me* did it, too. There's like *three* butt-fucking scenes in *American Me.* That's definitely the one to beat in that particular category!"

As it turned out, nobody beat ***Pulp Fiction*** at Cannes. The victory of the Palme d'Or surprised many observers but not Tarantino himself. "I thought it was in the realm of possibility," he says, smiling. "Basically, it was like no one knew about our movie, then it was like *boom*! It's like people who really shouldn't know what the Palme d'Or is, they all of a sudden knew that and I won. I guess it's sort of like *sex, lies and videotape* just coming out of nowhere. After Cannes was over, I went to Paris to chill out. Let me tell you, when you win the Palme d'Or, *don't* go to Paris to chill out. Cannes is their Oscars, so everyone was coming up saying, 'You're the American who won the big award.'"

Today, Tarantino—who doesn't have a girlfriend at the moment and who has apparently failed to develop the habit of having torrid affairs with his actresses—says that he wants to take a break. "I've got to take some time to have a life," he says. But a few weeks later, word comes that Tarantino's going back to work. In October he'll star as Jimmy Destiny in director Jack Baran's Las Vegas-set *Destiny Turns On the Radio.* After that, he'll direct one segment of an anthology movie called ***Four Rooms,*** which will also call on the talents of Allison Anders, Alexandre Rockwell and Robert Rodriguez.

Tarantino, who was thanked by Kurt Cobain in the liner notes for *In Utero,* seems to be on the verge of turning into a cinematic slacker icon. But his mother—who is boycotting ***Natural Born Killers*** out of respect for her son—says success hasn't spoiled him yet: "No, I haven't seen any change in Quentin. He's just as self-confident as he's always been."

In terms of the long run, Tarantino explains that he simply wants to stay on the treacherous career path that he has set for himself. "When you look at a career in Hollywood, it seems like there's two roads," he says as he sits back happily among the meaningful clutter of his home. "There's the studio-hack career or the art-film career. They're *both* dangerous roads. Nobody wants to turn into a back. But the art-film trip is just as bad because you get lost and start disappearing up your own ass. But there is another road, I think, where the budgets of your film depend on what type of movie you're making, where you're making a movie you really want to make and that someone might really want to see.

"All I have to do is stay on that road."

T. J. Binyon (review date 11 November 1994)

SOURCE: "Hot Shot," in *Times Literary Supplement,* November 11, 1994, p. 26.

[*In the following review, Binyon offers favorable assessment of* Pulp Fiction.]

Quentin Tarantino's latest film, ***Pulp Fiction,*** opens and closes in a Los Angeles coffee shop. In the prologue, a young couple, Pumpkin (Tim Roth) and Honey Bunny (Amanda Plummer), are contemplating over breakfast a change in business methods: robbing coffee shops instead of liquor stores. Two and a half hours later, the epilogue returns to the same place at the same time. Drawing their 32s, Pumpkin and Honey Bunny leap on to the coffee-shop tables to put theory into practice. Within this circular frame three stories are loosely woven together; the narration glides from one to another, slips backwards and forwards in time. The stories are connected by the presence in each of a Mr Big of organized crime, Marsellus Wallace (Ving Rhames), a shadowy figure—for most of the film we only see the back of his neck. In the first story, two hitmen, Vincent Vega (John Travolta) and Jules Winnfield (Samuel L. Jackson), retrieve Marsellus's suitcase from a bunch of amateur young crooks and end up picking bits of skull and brains off the back seat of a 1974 Chevy Nova; in the second, Vincent, on Marsellus's instructions, takes the latter's wife, Mia (Uma Thurman), out for an evening. They go to a 1950s diner, Jackrabbit Slim's, where they eat in a booth made from a red 1959 Edsel, are served by a Buddy Holly lookalike, and win a trophy in a twist contest. In the third, boxer Butch Coolidge (Bruce Willis), paid by Marsellus to take a fall in the fifth, wins the fight and cleans up in bets, but instead of leaving town post-haste with his French girl-friend Fabienne (Maria de Medeiros), stays to retrieve a gold watch that belonged to his great-granddaddy, and by chance is able to rescue Marsellus from a couple of redneck sodomites.

Quentin Tarantino is Hollywood's hottest property at the moment. ***Reservoir Dogs*** (1992) has achieved cult status, both here and in the States; ***Pulp Fiction*** won the Palme d'Or at this year's Cannes Film Festival, and Travolta has been tipped for an Oscar. Two of Tarantino's earlier scripts have been snapped up and made into films: ***True Romance*** by Tony Scott and ***Natural Born Killers*** by Oliver Stone—though Tarantino has removed his name from the credits of the second. The script of ***Pulp Fiction*** has been published and will shortly be followed by that of ***Reservoir Dogs.*** No newspaper has seemed complete without a Tarantino profile; BBC1's *Omnibus* devoted a recent edition to his life and work. He has been acclaimed as the first post-postmodernist, and the analysis of Madonna's "Like a Virgin" ("all about a girl who digs a guy with a big dick") given by Mr Brown (Quentin Tarantino) in ***Reservoir Dogs*** has been described as "an anti-intellectual demystification of Madonna's much chewed-over status as a postfeminist icon".

Pulp Fiction, thank goodness, takes itself much less seriously: indeed, is often hilariously funny. Tarantino has developed the method of wringing humour from the most unlikely situations with which he experimented in ***Reservoir Dogs.*** The episodes themselves are not structured as comedy. The laughs come sometimes from the contrast between dialogue and action: Jules chewing on a victim's Big Kahuna Burger and pronouncing it "the cornerstone of any nutritious breakfast" before blowing the man away; Vince objecting to the instructions given to him by Mr Wolf (Harvey Keitel) on how to get rid of a headless corpse and a blood-spattered car because they are not accompanied by "please". Sometimes they are purely sight gags: Butch weighing up the merits of a hammer, a baseball bat and a chainsaw as anti-redneck weaponry before settling for a Samurai sword; Mia galvanically restored to life after a drug overdose when Vince stabs her in the heart with an adrenalin syringe.

The film's title, assisted by a publicity still showing Uma Thurman curled up on a couch with a 35-cent paperback called *Harlot in her Heart* (a scene which does not occur in the film), has fed the idea that ***Pulp Fiction*** is a homage to pulp magazines of the 1930s and 40s, such as *Black Mask,* and to the writers who contributed to them, such as Hammett, Chandler, and the lesser-known Jim Thompson, David Goodis and Cornell Woolrich. But this interpretation seems mistaken. Tarantino is the ultimate film freak, a man who, in Monte Helman's words, "lives, breathes, eats and sleeps cinema", who worked for years in a video store and can, at the drop of a hat, give you the entire cast list of *Attack of the Crab Monster* and recite verbatim most of its dialogue. His characters share his knowledge and his tastes: Freddy, in ***Reservoir Dogs,*** remembers being interrupted when viewing a video of *Lost Boys* ("Vampiric bikers corrupt innocent teenagers", *Halliwell's Film Guide*); Butch wakes up to find Fabienne watching a film on television in which a bunch of Hell's Angels are taking on the entire Vietnamese army and immediately identifies it as *The Losers;* while cleaning up the car, Vince warns Jules that he won't take any more abuse: "I'm a race-car and you got me in the red. *Redline 7000,* that's where you are"—a reference to the Howard Hawks film about stockcar racing, *Redline 7000.* Jules replies with two more filmic comparisons: "Every time my fingers touch brain I'm 'Superfly TNT', I'm the *Guns of Navarone.*"

It is films, not fiction, which provide the raw material for Tarantino's work; but at the same time it is fiction, not films, which provides him with the methods for manipulating this material. ***Pulp Fiction*** is an extraordinarily literary film, put together more as a novel than as a film script. The circular form, the dislocated time sequence, the non-linear narrative, the weaving together of several disparate stories: all these are literary, not cinematic devices. As he himself remarked in one interview, "I think I've taken on an established genre like the pulp thriller and made it challenging to myself and the audience". Though there may be no connection between Raymond Chandler's books and Tarantino's films, this remark, oddly enough, closely echoes Chandler's summing-up, in a letter to his literary agent, of his achievement: "To accept a mediocre form and make something like literature out of it is in itself rather an accomplishment." Perhaps it is as yet a little early to decide whether Tarantino's claim is as justified as Chandler's.

Stanley Kauffmann (review date 14 November 1994)

SOURCE: "Shooting Up," in *New Republic,* November 14, 1994, pp. 26-7.]

[*In the following review, Kauffmann offers unfavorable evaluation of* Pulp Fiction.]

By now everybody knows that Quentin Tarantino is the happiest man in the world. Not so many years ago he was a clerk in a California video store, devouring film film film. Then he tried to break into filmmaking himself, first by writing scripts. It took years to get in. But those video days and the buff-dom of his boyhood sustained him, and now he is where he dreamed of being. He is making the films that will stock those video stores. Some younger aspirant will sell Tarantino tapes.

About his grit and passion, no question. About his achievements so far, some doubts. His first film was ***Reservoir Dogs,*** which drew particular attention because of its tidy frame and its offhand violence, but which seemed to me shrewdly opportunistic—a subject and style carefully chosen by a man who wanted to get into filmmaking, who had tried various keys in the lock and had at last picked the right one. Then, along with other work, he wrote a story that Oliver Stone used as the basis for ***Natural Born Killers.*** (Composers often write virtuosic variations on simple tunes.) Now comes his much-trumpeted second film.

Pulp Fiction (Miramax) is ***Reservoir Dogs*** rewarded. Because of the first film's success, the second had a larger budget, thus has greater length, more stars, more lavish production, more violence—and certainly more room for the blackish humor that was visible in Tarantino's first. But, like the first film, ***Pulp Fiction*** revels in an underworld of menace and violence, of crime as cosmos, of sleaze. Tarantino of course wrote his own screenplay, and he tries to license his moral locale with an opening title that quotes two dictionary definitions of pulp. The first one is literal; the second is the figurative usage, derived from magazines of the past that were published on cheap pulp paper and specialized in lurid fiction of several genres.

He interweaves three stories. The film opens in a diner. A pair of petty crooks, played by Amanda Plummer and Tim Roth, after some dejected conversation decide to change their luck by robbing the very diner in which they are sitting. Just as they pull their pistols, we shift to the second story. John Travolta and Samuel L. Jackson are hit men for a drug czar, on their way to a hit. They converse casually, like telephone repairmen on their way to a routine job. They arrive where they're headed and do their killing.

That evening Travolta, under orders from his boss, escorts the boss's wife for the evening—dinner and dancing. The wife is Uma Thurman in a black wig. (A reference to Louise Brooks? Jeanne Moreau in *The Bride Wore Black?*) Thurman's greed for drugs complicates Travolta's evening with her.

The third story concerns a boxer, Bruce Willis. That same drug czar, Ving Rhames, apparently a heavy bettor, orders Willis to take a dive in the fifth round of an upcoming fight. Willis double-crosses him. This leads to his pursuit by the czar, more killing and the capture of both the boxer and the czar in a homosexual S&M den. (By now—no, before this—we are ticking off the film sources that Tarantino has been remembering.)

A further episode involves several of the above people—and Tarantino himself, passable in a small role—with Harvey Keitel, who repeats his performance in an earlier film as an efficient clean-up man for hit men in trouble. The picture closes at the diner where it began. Travolta and Jackson arrive just as Plummer and Roth stick it up. (There's a time bend here—one of the picture's better gimmicks. We already know the fate that awaits Travolta elsewhere.)

At the center of most of the action—actually, it's just off-center—is a black attaché case, highly valuable for some unrevealed reason. Whenever it's opened, it lights the face of the person looking in. (Derived, perhaps, from the mysterious box in Buñuel's *Belle de Jour.*)

In one tangential way, Tarantino resembles recent Woody Allen: almost every one of his characters is a (presumably deliberate) cliché. The exception is in a flashback, a Marine officer just returned from Vietnam—and he's not really a character, just one long deadpan comic speech, laid in like a mosaic by Christopher Walken. All the others are familiar: the portentous gang chief, the workaday hit men (one of whom quotes the Bible), the pug with a streak of sentiment and so on.

Some of the action strains belief in a picture that dwells mostly in the naturalistic realm. On her night out, Thurman takes a life-threatening overdose of heroin, is revived at someone's house with a jolt of adrenalin straight to the heart, then is taken home by Travolta and dropped off as if it had been an ordinary date. I suppose there's meant to be some burlesque edge to this sequence, but even so, it's pretty farfetched. More matter-of-fact glitches: guns are fired in residential areas, and no neighbors seem to hear them. Willis kills a man, wipes the gun free of his fingerprints and then puts his prints on a doorknob. During the diner holdup, a couple of dozen people are ordered to lie on the floor. Not one of them makes a sound or a move—they become cardboard cut-outs—during long conversations among the principals.

Travolta, only seventeen years after *Saturday Night Fever,* has lost his looks but not his appeal: he is still quietly, modestly engaging. Jackson grows as he goes, a solid actor. Willis proves again that, when he has something other than an action-film dummy to play, he can act. Thurman is better as this tough cookie than as her usual Miss Winsome; still, it's hard to believe that she's an object of desire. Rhames, her husband, has taciturn depth. Plummer and Roth are beneath comment.

The designer, David Wasco, gave the settings the right gloppy postcard look, which Andrzej Sekula's camera exploits. Karyn Rachtman's music track buzzes the picture along very helpfully. And there's no doubt that director Tarantino's long film immersion has given him the eye and ear to do what he wants to do here—not only to pack the punch of the good Hollywood crime directors but to tease out the backhand sting that some of them had. Perhaps in the future he'll emulate other kinds of directors and films.

Meanwhile, however, what's most bothersome about ***Pulp Fiction*** is its success. This is not to be mean-spirited about Tarantino himself; may he harvest all the available millions. But the way that this picture has been so widely ravened up and drooled over verges on the disgusting. ***Pulp Fiction*** nourishes, abets, cultural slumming.

So much of what inundates us these days—in film, in various kinds of pop music— is calculated grunginess, of climate and temper. So much of what goes on in (what I hear of) rock music revels in the lower end of every kind of spectrum, grungy ideas and diction delivered by grungy people. So much of modern film seems to compete in grunginess. Very little of this stuff seems to have anything to do with the lives actually lived by its avid public. Most of it seems designed as guided tours of an underworld for people otherwise placed—career-oriented students, job holding others. Escapism always has been one function of theater and film, and for ages it was cloyingly pretty-pretty. Boy, has the pendulum swung.

Richard Alleva (review date 18 November 1994)

SOURCE: "Beaten to a Pulp," in *Commonweal,* November 18, 1994, pp. 30-1.

[In the following review, Alleva offers favorable evaluation of Pulp Fiction.]

Maybe you have to be able to see through Quentin Tarantino before you can enjoy him. Like all his previous movies, ***Pulp Fiction*** is packed with violent larcenies, shootouts, drug deals, mob executions, gangland politicking, and (a Tarantino specialty) heavy-duty, sadistically gloating speeches made by hitmen to their victims just before the bullet to the brain is dispatched. No wonder that this latest Hollywood *wunderkind* has been labeled the "hot high priest of film ultra-violence," "the Sultan of Sadism," and so forth.

Yet ***Pulp Fiction*** has about as much to do with actual criminality or violence as *Cyrano de Bergerac* with the realities of seventeenth-century France or *The Prisoner of Zenda* with Balkan politics. I make these comparisons respectfully, for this movie gives us precisely what the title of an earlier Tarantino script promised (however ironically) but didn't deliver: true romance.

Any romance must have an element of sham in its make-up. It comes with the territory and helps make the territory a tourist attraction. The gangsters of ***Pulp Fiction,*** taken as criminal studies, are strictly factitious. Their tough talk is wise-guy literate, media-smart, obscenely epigrammatic. Tarantino gangsters must be couch potatoes and video fiends when they're not slaughtering each other: they use the Fonz and the cute pig from "Green Acres" as reference points and can spot the difference between Marilyn Monroe and Mamie Van Doren impersonators. I can't imagine one of these hoods reading anything as workaday as a racing form, but I bet all of them subscribe to *Variety.*

In short, Tarantino gangsters are actors in the flimsiest of underworld disguises. No Frank Sinatra heist flick (*Oceans 11,* say, or *Robin and the 7 Hoods*) was so flauntingly unauthentic. The conversation of these hooligans may be spiked with the argot of Hollywood players and hustlers, but their lives are utterly devoid of the grunginess, boredom, pettiness, and the close attention to shady economics that you find in the memories and histories of real criminals. If gangsters really had this sort of wit, they'd be writing screenplays.

But the sham of romance serves the truth of romance. *Cyrano de Bergerac* may not be a believable portrait of a poet-soldier in the age of Richelieu, but he is a truthful embodiment of a chivalric ideal. Tarantino's gangsters are mere marionettes of violence but their dance is gripping because it's performed in the Theater of Destiny that is Tarantino's vision of life. When the hit men Jules and Vincent (Samuel Jackson and John Travolta) saunter out of a restaurant at the film's conclusion, we know that one of them is doomed and the other saved. Whence the doom? Whence the salvation?

In ***Pulp Fiction,*** significance saves. Refusing to see the significance of events, dismissing all circumstance as happenstance, refusing to believe that you are undergoing your own destiny can doom you. (So you have a destiny anyway—a horrid one!) Of course, the web of one's destiny always gets tangled with the webs of others, and a good part of the romantic excitement of ***Pulp Fiction*** lies in the way Tarantino lets us have a bird's-eye view of overlapping fates.

The movie is told in five chapters and a prologue:

Prologue: A husband-and-wife stick-up team (Tim Roth and Amanda Plummer) sit in a restaurant and discuss over coffee the best sorts of places to rob. The wife proposes that the very place they're in would be ideal. The husband agrees and they spring into action. End of prologue; the credits roll.

Chapter 1: Two hit men (Jackson and Travolta) murder some drug dealers who have cheated their boss, a drug lord named Marcellus. Then something happens to these killers that makes them return to headquarters. The pair look bemused, wrung-out, almost slaphappy. What happened? We don't find out until chapter 4.

Chapter 2: Travolta is ordered to chaperone Marcellus's sexy wife (Uma Thurman) while the boss is away on business. Travolta and Thurman are mutually attracted and mutually wary; then a near-catastrophe makes sex impractical and unthinkable.

Chapter 3: After accepting a bribe from Marcellus to take a dive, boxer Bruce Willis bets big money on himself to win and proceeds to massacre his opponent. He flees Marcellus's vengeance, then recklessly returns to his apartment to recover his dead father's watch. As a result, the boxer brushes up against death three times, once at Travolta's hands.

Chapter 4 brings us back to the hit men at the end of chapter 1. It is now shown that Travolta and Jackson were almost killed at the conclusion of their assignment, but their lives were spared. Jackson decides to reform his life, Travolta shrugs and is determined to go on as before.

Chapter 5: The two hoods have taken their philosophical argument to a restaurant which may look strangely familiar. Suddenly, Tim Roth and Amanda Plummer spring into action. We are back in the prologue! And soon Roth is moving toward Jackson for his money or his life. Jackson cocks a pistol under the table. But can he really kill a man now that he's promised God to turn over a new leaf?

The effect all this time-hopping has on our sympathies is both discombobulating and exhilarating. Travolta, for instance, is a killer in part 1. But in part 2 he's at the center of the action, is in peril, and, willy-nilly, we feel for him. But in part 3, Travolta is a killer again and this time . . . hey! he's trying to rub out *this* episode's hero, Bruce Willis. Then, in parts 4 and 5, Travolta is again in trouble, but he seems sullen and clownish compared with Jackson who is undergoing a spiritual conversion. And besides, because 4 and 5 take place *before* the events of chapter 3, we know how Travolta is going to behave toward Willis. How deeply can we sympathize with this young man? How thoroughly can we detest this young killer?

The script is put together with a jeweler's precision and makes the writing of every American film I've seen in the past year—even *Quiz Show*—seem like so much child's play. A couple of examples of Tarantino's canniness:

Chapter 3 opens with a flashback of Bruce Willis as a boy receiving his dead father's watch from a soldier who suffered with the father in a Viet Cong prisoner-of-war camp. The officer explains why he's been so zealous in delivering the father's bequest: "When you're together with someone in a pit of hell, you owe something to that person." Later, Willis will find himself in his own "pit of hell" with his worst enemy, Marcellus, as fellow prisoner. Willis gets a chance to escape and leave Marcellus to suffer a slow, horrible demise. Why can't he bring himself to leave? Then the words come back to us just as they are probably coming back to him: ". . . you owe something to that person."

That's a compassionate moment but a more typical example of Tarantino's scabrousness immediately follows. Willis looks for a weapon to use against the serial killers. He's in a pawnshop, so there are several choices. He finds a hammer and hefts it. Not bad. But he exchanges it for a baseball bat. Better. Then he picks up a chainsaw. Better and worse. The audience starts to titter nervously. But wait, Willis has spotted something else on a high shelf and reaches for it. Samurai sword. The horrified laughter this sequence gets from the audience is the kind of reaction Oliver Stone tries to evoke repeatedly in ***Natural Born Killers*** (which is a drastic rewrite of a Tarantino script) with scant success. Tarantino achieves it time and again with fiendish accuracy.

Tarantino is a deft director of actors but for the most part he succeeds by getting his well-cast players to tread familiar ground. The exception is Samuel L. Jackson. He's played tough guys before but this one he takes to a higher plane. He makes Jules an almost Shakespearean reservoir of strength, cruelty, righteousness, intellectual showiness, loyalty, sadism, and compassion. He is titanic.

Tarantino is also adroit with the camera. Jackson and Travolta arrive outside an apartment only to discover that they're too early to execute a hit. "Let's hang back," Jackson says, and they do, literally, by walking away from the camera down a hallway. In long shot, they carry on a innocuous, funny conversation. Finally, it's time for the kill. "Let's get into character." They walk into close-up and are once again frightening.

Or at least as frightening as gangsters can be in a Tarantino movie. The cinematic flourishes, the pop references, the movie-movie in-jokes, the glamour of the performers, the self-conscious hipness of the dialogue—all this cushions the violence, makes it bearable, and, yes, even glamorizes it.

"Let's get into character." Indeed. These are actors being popped, not characters of substance. Go see *Menace II Society* or *Good Fellas* if you want the grime of crime. In Tarantino's hands, pulp fiction becomes sheer romance.

Dennis Cooper (essay date March 1995)

SOURCE: "Minor Magic," in *Artforum,* Vol. 33, No. 7, March, 1995, pp. 63-6, 110.

[*In the following essay, Cooper discusses the appeal of Tarantino's dialogue and cinematic presentation.*]

There should be a dozen youngish American filmmakers as inspired as Quentin Tarantino. Then it would be easier to designate him a quirkily brilliant minor director, which is what he is. But even with his rather glaring limitations—stagey archetypal characters, short- and long-term memory problems, a lazy visual sense—there's so much finely tuned energy in his films compared to most of his contemporaries. Tarantino really is one of the few post-Martin Scorsese directors capable of bona fide cinematic magic. He isn't in a class with, say, *serioso* experimentalists like Jon Jost and James Benning, but, like them, he is fascinated by Scorsese and *his* obsessions (the intricacies of male angst). Scorsese is deep, and his best films are girded with emotional and spiritual scars. Tarantino gives terrific surface, but in a Ted Kennedy kind of way—he makes you feel like you're in the presence of greatness, even if the charisma is essentially inherited.

Tarantino can do great scenes, and his films' residual narrative drift is busy and clever enough to keep the momentum going. His forte is exquisitely rendered horror: the young drug dealers blown away and Uma Thurman's OD and lifesaving adrenaline shot in ***Pulp Fiction;*** the cop torture scene in ***Reservoir Dogs*** (1992), Dennis Hopper's execution by Christopher Walken in the Tarantino-scripted (but not directed) ***True Romance*** (1993), the slaughter in the diner that opens Oliver Stone's semi-Tarantino-scripted ***Natural Born Killers*** (1994). Before he became overly enamored of emptily gorgeous spectacle, Bernardo Bertolucci constructed similarly mind-boggling mid-film epiphanies, albeit scenes less triggered by literary games than by massively repressed homosexual longing, almost always by a man for a boy: the adolescent junkie's seduction by a father look-alike in *Luna* (1979), a child's spontaneous shooting of his pedophile suitor in *The Conformist* (1971), the upper-class boy's horrendous murder by his working-class molester in *1900* (1977). Bertolucci's films have a strong political outlook, are versed in 20th-century philosophy, and are obsessively concerned with and painfully befuddled by their characters' hidden motivations. By comparison, Tarantino's films are pointedly thrill-seeking and apsychological.

Tarantino does one thing with absolute brilliance: he boxes talky, neurotic, bright but half-articulate, schlumpy characters into parallel orbits around an agreeable, slightly flammable, usually trendy topic—Madonna, TV chat shows, kinky sex, etc. The conversations he constructs are so superficially systematic that when one character grows frightened of a commitment to the interchange, separates, and unleashes some private insanity on his or her companion, the effect is nightmarish. In Tarantino's view, contemporary humans are something on the order of walking-talking issues of *Details* magazine, addicted to MTV chat and tabloid trivia. A verbal scrim unites his characters but quarantines the aspects of their psyches they cannot articulate—sexual attraction, emotional involvement, spiritual interests, etc. As a result, his characters are continually jittery, but the psychological reasons for their jitters are never specified, probably because Tarantino is afraid to know them.

While it's easy to recognize his characters' transgressive impulses—which are more savvily up to the minute than authentically personalized—their transgressions have no resonance. In fact the violence in his films would have a pornographic effect if it wasn't for the way he manipulates the viewers' morality. This moralistic fascination with the amoral, which is shared by David Lynch among others, may be the main reason why, apart from their poetic gift of the gab, Tarantino's films are more compelling than, say, neorealistic "streetwise" TV series like *NYPD Blue,* but less absorbing than a docuaction series like Cops, which focuses, with similar irony but less agenda, on a similar social register (disenfranchised lower middle class).

The thing is, Tarantino is such a talented writer, and his neuroses feel unusually emblematic of the general cultural malaise circa the early '90s. His p.o.v., frequently attacked for its cheap shots at the powerless, is actually, albeit *selectively,* compassionate—strangely innocent and guileless. Tarantino tends to rescue and recontextualize unintentionally sublime scenes from the skid row of B-movie history, like some post-Modern Florence Nightingale with a soft spot re cultural trash.

Tarantino's writing is so pure in its own weird way that it misfires when he isn't in the director's chair. If it weren't for the prettiness of its script, ***True Romance*** would be a misshapen and aimless action flick for the MTV set. Its ugliness is too ugly, its cleverness too paved over by technical competence, its p.o.v. too blandly disapproving of its protagonists. ***Natural Born Killers,*** which Tarantino partially scripted and now disowns, has its technical charms, but Stone's cinematographic overdrive flattens the dialogue's obsessive machinations. Tarantino isn't such a great director either (or not yet anyway)—he's just a carefully skillful, sincere one. But it's hard to imagine a better look to go along with his scripts. He may be an artist on the order of songwriter and fellow ironist Randy Newman, whose complex yet simply crafted songs function only in his own clunky, amateurish renditions. Both men's talents are just a little too idiosyncratic and fueled by unconscious drives to survive an out-of-body experience.

Tarantino's possibly doomed to be an imperfect maverick filmmaker, not what some would like him to be—the new Robert Towne or Paul Schrader, pre-directorial pretensions. While the hype around his skimpy, samey output may strike some as too much too soon, it's not especially surprising. Two or three films down the road, Tarantino's little tricks could well be schtick; in fact I'd lay money on it. For now, though, his peculiar talent feels real, and obviously life is short.

Gary Indiana (essay date March 1995)

SOURCE: "Geek Chic," in *Artforum,* Vol. 33, No. 7, March, 1995, pp. 63-6, 104, 108.

[*In the following essay, Indiana discusses the depiction of black experience, violence, and masculinity in Tarantino's films.*]

Like O.J. Simpson and Newt Gingrich, Quentin Tarantino has become one of those cosmically disseminated mirages that even the most resolute ascetic living in a hole somewhere becomes aware of "through the media." For us ordinary folks who consume magazines and TV programs haphazardly, he—like O.J., like Newt—has acquired the pull of a vortex into which all conversation eventually spills. Edgy from coffee nerves, verbally diarrheic, a study in hip geekiness or geeky hipness, Tarantino's personality is on display in dozens of print interviews and talk shows, and it's the same one he gives all his characters. Like them, he's fond of crunchy breakfast cereals, cartoons, obscure movies, and disco hits of the '70s; like them, he favors the verbal tropisms of the "interesting" digression, the aria of cultural trivia, the self-consuming monologue. More than with most American directors, he and his films seem like the same thing.

Tarantino locates hipness in the same unlovely products of American pop culture that so many foreign teenagers find endlessly marvelous. His ideal character is the kind of American who beats a path to McDonald's when visiting Paris, someone whose frame of reference instantly assimilates the Other into its own obstinately lowbrow schema—anything reachier would be pretentious. At the same time, this character comes stuffed with the most arcane erudition, permissible, one supposes, because erudition is essentially unintelligent. Like the Jim Jarmusch of *Stranger Than Paradise* and *Mystery Train,* Tarantino is an intellectual who enjoys playing dumb, who pumps up the assertive dumbness embedded in hipness. This gives him the kind of aerial view associated with satire, though it would be hard to say what Tarantino's satirizing other than his own saturation by old movies.

Tarantino flirts with the belief that energetic posturing will make his skin turn black, a delusion shared by white entertainers like Sandra Bernhard and Camille Paglia. In its most exacerbated form, this sentimental tic of the white hipster locates all "authenticity" in the black experience, against which all other experience becomes the material of grotesque irony. To be really, really cool becomes the spiritual equivalent of blackness, and even superior to it: there are plenty of square black people but not one square cool person. For the Tarantino of ***Pulp Fiction,*** blackness is a plastic holy grail, a mythic substance with real effects and its own medieval code. It becomes "pulped" in a number of extremely cool ways, some of them literal (the black accomplice whose brains accidentally get splattered, the Mr. Big who dominates most of the white characters' lives yet gets fucked in the ass by a psychopathic redneck). Tarantino is goofing on coolness and white ideas about blackness, pushing them over the top. But within that goof is a have-it-both-ways determination to be the coolest of all filmmakers, which costs him something in credibility.

Tarantino's subject is maleness: by repicturing cinema's rituals of masculinity in wildly exaggerated forms, he has achieved a more daring deconstruction than even directors like Martin Scorsese and Francis Ford Coppola. Unlike them, though, he has trouble depicting women in more than one dimension—in the movies he's directed he has barely tried. ***Reservoir Dogs*** is an all-male, all-macho, *grindingly* homoerotic film, deliberately hobbled by Tarantino's refusal to picture the anal intercourse that all its characters yearn for (albeit with a firearm rather than a penis), either as recipients or givers. In Tarantino's realm of anal longing, women are almost beside the point. Mia, in ***Pulp Fiction,*** is a charming cartoon of Anna Karenina; like the magic animal in a fairy tale, her narrative function is to test Travolta's loyalty to her husband, his boss. Male fealty, of course, wins out. All ***Pulp Fiction***'s other females orbit the "active" males they're paired with as if attached by Crazy Glue, in one case requesting "oral pleasure" with the languid coquettishness of a teenage catamite.

It's this director's genius to toss incompatible ingredients like a salad. His movies are formulaic but the formula is unique, a wild collision of things—the rupture of narrative time, rougher and more radical than Godard's; the layering of quotations from other movies; the characters besotted by their own eloquence; the Mexican standoff; the petty conversation carried on during horrendous violence. Tarantino can invest a cliché with breathless energy. However sketchy his people look, he makes sure they register onscreen in some indelible way—they may not have depth but they have presence. Tarantino is immersed in movies he's seen on video, which may explain why their appropriation seems somehow weightless: they're two steps removed from the primary creative process. One is always inside an artifact cobbled from other artifacts rather than from any profound experience of life. (In this, Tarantino resembles, of all people, Jorge Luis Borges, a writer entirely produced by what he'd read, whose talent was best applied, with ample irony, to genre—detective fiction, the parable, the fairy tale.) But this is also Tarantino's strength: he has an almost Buñuelian fluency with film—"has movies in his fingertips," like the hero of Alexander Kluge's film *The Blind Director.* This becomes especially obvious in ***Natural Born Killers*** and ***True Romance,*** two surprisingly trite movies made by other directors from Tarantino's scripts. These films only come alive during the scattered moments when Tarantino's writing survives molestation.

"Alive" may be too strong a word, though, even in Tarantino's own movies. Tarantino's set pieces—bursts of operatic violence scored to brilliantly incongruous soliloquies and other business (I'm thinking of Michael Madsen's song, dance, and razor routine in ***Reservoir Dogs***)—produce an amphetamine rush that often leaves a tinny aftertaste. We are thrown into a world whose particular deity extends compassion only to the hip and the violent, never to the "asshole" victims. This may pump us up with a certain Nietzschean elation, but can only be followed, sooner or later, by a bewildered sense of depletion, as if we'd been talked into robbing a liquor store or running over a dog. The director can credibly claim that the violence in his films is "unreal"—an aperçu he cribbed from Godard ("It isn't blood, it's *red*")—but it has to be added that an excessive display of unreal violence has the same adventitious quality that wall-to-wall singing had in the old MGM musicals, which gets us not very far from "a wax museum with a pulse."

I have the feeling that ***Pulp Fiction*** looks as good as it does partly because, its formidable virtues aside, studio pictures have become more idiotic, rebarbatively predictable, and smug. A wild card like Tarantino, versed in everything that still works in the Hollywood mold and at the same time graced with idiosyncrasy, stubbornness, and uncanny energy, can deliver the goods to an audience starved for nuance but allergic to "art." It was the mistake of former wunderkinder like David Lynch to imagine the audience wanted "art" (along with some sideshow touches), or a signature style, or a lot of other things extraneous to sitting in the dark with a tub of popcorn. (*Blue Velvet* worked mainly because its audience had never seen Kenneth Anger's *Scorpio Rising.*) The best thing about Tarantino's movies is that they aren't "art," they just go where art goes, without being overly fastidious about how they get there.

Robin Wood (essay date March 1995)

SOURCE: "Slick Shtick," in *Artforum,* Vol. 33, No. 7, March, 1995, pp. 63-6, 110.

[*In the following essay, Wood discusses elements of satire, violence, and homophobia in* Reservoir Dogs *and* Pulp Fiction.]

American culture generally enjoys cleverness: it is so much easier to grasp than real intelligence, so much less challenging and dangerous. Cleverness doesn't disturb, it keeps people happy, gives them "kicks," it's all slick fun. And Americans are supposed to be happy—isn't this the land of equal opportunity, so if you're *not* happy it's your own fault, there must be something wrong with you. Cleverness helps you to forget that things might be different, might be better, that a struggle for change might be desirable and necessary: sure the culture's shot to pieces, but it's still good for a laugh if you look at things in the right, the *clever,* way.

Cleverness feeds on and nurtures cynicism and nihilism. ***Pulp Fiction*** is a work of phenomenal cleverness and no intelligence whatsoever.

Cleverness assumes a special function in an age of economic collapse and moral, emotional, and psychological confusion and desperation. In the land of the free and happy, despair cannot be ideologically countenanced. There are two antidotes: an abrupt swing to the right, involving the restoration of the Good Old Values (capitalism, patriarchy, the nuclear family), underpinned by a revival of the more debased forms of religion; and, as an alternative refuge, the resurgence of cynicism. The one offers the comforting sense that if you follow the Bible you'll go to Heaven, and people who don't will go to Hell; the other offers the equally comforting sense that if everything is hopeless and change is impossible, all you can do is have as much fun as possible.

How long will Quentin Tarantino (and the Tarantino craze) last? ***Pulp Fiction*** and its companion piece, ***True Romance,*** which Tarantino didn't direct but wrote, do not strike me as representing the kind of creativity that can sustain itself for long. A brief blaze followed by an abrupt fizzle, like those other comets of post-'70s critical hysteria David Lynch and the Coens brothers? Lynch has already sunk below the horizon, and the Coens are sinking even as I write. Creativity cannot survive for long on a diet of cynicism and nihilism, even with the support and encouragement of contemporary critical "taste." ***Pulp Fiction*** has given critics exactly what they wanted in 1994, just as *Blue Velvet* did in 1986, and Tarantino will doubtless thrive briefly on their adulation—until the next comet appears.

But the issue may not be quite so simple. I have not yet mentioned ***Reservoir Dogs,*** and ***Reservoir Dogs,*** although discernibly by the same artist as ***Pulp Fiction,*** is another matter. The essential difference between the films is epitomized in the two, superficially similar torture scenes: that in ***Reservoir Dogs*** is genuinely appalling, while that in ***Pulp Fiction*** is clearly offered as funny. (The entire Bruce Willis episode in ***Pulp Fiction,*** Christopher Walken's brilliant monologue aside, strikes me as the low point of Tarantino's career so far.) The earlier film's relative modesty and discipline, combined with its force, tautness, and precision, suggest an underlying seriousness of purpose—an underlying *intelligence* that ***Pulp Fiction*** fritters away in adolescent self-indulgence.

The distinction of ***Reservoir Dogs*** lies not merely in its formal perfection (the intricately nonchronological narrative structure) and the single-minded rigor with which its thesis ("reservoir dogs" end up eating each other) is worked out, but in its very particular relation to the contemporary crisis of "masculinity." The threat to masculinity represented by the growing emancipation, independence, and activeness of women has evoked a range of responses in the culture that are mirrored in Hollywood cinema. There has been the attempt (almost invariably compromised and recuperative) to depict strong, "liberated" women, and the corresponding attempt to define a new version of "Mr. Nice Guy," the sensitive and caring male. The alternative response is the hysterical overvaluation and exaggeration of masculinity represented by Schwarzenegger, Stallone, and Norris (often spilling over, at least in the case of the first two, into knowing but uneasy parody that allows us sophisticates to indulge ourselves while not taking it all too seriously). ***Reservoir Dogs*** carries this almost to the point of a kind of mass psychosis, the characters (not one of whom remains alive at the end) destroyed by the very drives that make them so destructive.

Women scarcely appear in the film, and are violently treated when they do. The references to them in the dialogue define them exclusively as sex objects. The men's inability to relate to women on any other level has two inevitable consequences: the total repression of their own femininity, and the constantly lurking threat of homosexuality. Tarantino's films, and for that matter his interviews, are shot through with homoerotic reference, and sometimes by its converse, homophobia; see, for instance, his celebrated riff on *Top Gun* in his cameo appearance in *Sleep with Me.* This becomes most explicit—indeed, to the point of obsession—in ***True Romance*** (which was directed by Tony Scott, the director of *Top Gun*): within the first five minutes we are regaled with the hero's fantasy of fucking Elvis Presley, and from there the references recur pervasively.

The men of ***Reservoir Dogs,*** conditioned not to love women, are evaluated in terms of their ability (or in most cases their inability) to love each other. The poles are represented by Michael Madsen's Mr. Blond and Harvey Keitel's Mr. White. The former is the film's explicitly psychotic character, incapable of relating to anyone except by violence. When he slices off the cop's ear with a razor, his immediate taunt defines the act's essentially sexual nature: "Was that as good for you as it was for me?" The moment is "answered" at the end of the film by the erotic tenderness with which Keitel cradles the wounded undercover man (Tim Roth), who responds to this sudden and intense intimacy by confessing his identity—whereupon Keitel shoots him. It's the one moment in Tarantino's work so far where he discovers a sense of the tragic; it's also the climactic moment of the film, its culmination and its "point." Keitel provides ***Reservoir Dogs*** with the moral center that ***Pulp Fiction*** so conspicuously and disastrously lacks.

When ***Pulp Fiction*** appeared, a few reviewers, while frothing at the mouth with enthusiasm, expressed a fear that Tarantino might be "spoiled" by such swift success. To me, the film seems the work of someone already spoiled, but reseeing ***Reservoir Dogs*** gives me pause: a far more distinguished debut film than those of either Lynch or the Coens, it suggests (as theirs do not) a kind of creativity that might survive and develop. In fact there are areas of interest in Tarantino's work out of which creative development might be possible. One would entail confronting and resolving the implications of the obsessive homoerotic references. Another, which might at first glance appear contradictory, arises out of the commitment to a wildly romantic *amour fou* that is the main impetus of the screenplays for both ***True Romance*** and ***Natural Born Killers.*** After all, Gregg Araki fused the two in *The Living End,* an even more remarkable debut than ***Reservoir Dogs.***

Jack Mathews (review date 25 December 1995)

SOURCE: "'Four Rooms' No Showcase for Quartet of Filmmakers," in *Los Angeles Times,* December 25, 1996, p. F12.

[*In the following review, Mathews offers negative assessment of* Four Rooms.]

Alexandre Rockwell, who came up with the idea for the anthology comedy ***Four Rooms,*** says of the characters in his segment, "They are walking the line, and when you walk the line, sometimes you fall into hell and sometimes you trip into heaven."

Moviegoers run the same risk every time they plunk down the price of a ticket, and those who do so for this film will soon feel the heat of Satan's breath.

It's not enough to say that ***Four Rooms*** is a bad movie. It's four bad movies rolled into one, the sum being even worse than the parts. It's an embarrassment for its quartet of respected independent filmmakers, and an object lesson for investors suffering Sundance Syndrome, that bandwagon urge to throw money after talent unveiled at festivals.

It was on the film festival circuit where Rockwell ("In the Soup") and his collaborators Quentin Tarantino (***Reservoir Dogs***), Allison Anders ("Gas Food Lodging") and Robert Rodriguez ("El Mariachi") got to know one another, and it's no surprise they all went for his idea, which was for each to write and direct a segment about a nervous bellhop manning a rundown Los Angeles hotel by himself on New Year's Eve.

The surprise comes in the quality of the work they turned in.

After a credit sequence that is a reasonably wacky knock-off of those done for the "Pink Panther" series, ***Four Rooms*** introduces the bellboy Ted (Tim Roth), who is left alone as the hotel—a chintzy version of the purgatory setting of "Barton Fink"—fills up with weirdos, and endures a nightmarish string of adventures in four of his guests' rooms.

In Anders opening episode, "The Missing Ingredient," Ted delivers room service to a coven of witches—Madonna, Valeria Golino, Sammi Davis and Ione Skye among them—and sticks around to donate sperm for an annual body fluids ritual. In Rockwell's "The Wrong Man," he walks in on, a couple (David Proval, Jennifer Beals) enacting a dangerous game of bondage and is mistaken by the gun-toting husband for his bound and gagged wife's lover. In Rodriguez's "The Misbehavers," Ted is asked to look in on a pair of kids watching television while a corpse rots in the mattress beneath them. And in Tarantino's "The Man From Hollywood," the bellboy is offered $1,000 by three drunks (Tarantino, Bruce Willis and Paul Calderon) to wield the hatchet in a reenactment of an episode of "Alfred Hitchcock Presents."

Sounds better than it is.

Rodriguez's story is by far the best, something like a C-minus to the others' Fs. For one thing, it has Antonio Banderas, in the film's *only* restrained performance, playing a menacing Latino who offers Ted a $500 baby-sitting fee so he and his wife can go out on the town. For another, Ted isn't in it that much; it's mostly about the two kids playing "Home Alone," drinking champagne, smoking, playing darts with a syringe and blaming the corpse's odor on each other's feet.

We can only wonder what was on Tim Roth's mind when he got a fix on his character. It's as if he's doing an impression of Jim Carrey doing an impression of Jerry Lewis in "The Bellboy." Whatever you think of Carrey and Lewis, Roth's physical comedy skills are dwarfed by their genius. It is a gutsy performance, a blur of facial ties and weaselly stammers, but we've slept in hotel rooms that are funnier.

It is either ironic or fitting that Rockwell's episode is the most pointless. ***Four Rooms*** has been cut by 26 minutes since its ridiculed premiere at the Toronto Film Festival. They might have been wiser to simply jettison this entire segment.

Anders' "The Missing Ingredient" is an aimless mess, with the witches wandering around moaning, a couple of them decorously topless, as they try to call up the spirit of their goddess, a '50s stripper named Diana, from the bridal suite's whirlpool bath.

But it is Tarantino's contribution that is the most disappointing. The least we'd expect from the creator of ***Reservoir Dogs, True Romance*** and ***Pulp Fiction*** is some brittle dialogue and an engaging character or two. There's nothing of the sort here.

Tarantino, still fancying himself an actor, is "The Man From Hollywood," a drunken spendthrift determined to reenact the "Alfred Hitchcock" episode where Peter Lorre gets Steve McQueen to bet his little finger that he can get his cigarette lighter to work 10 straight times. It's a shaggy-dog story, again with no point, unless you want to bet how many times Tarantino can scream the F-word in 10 minutes.

You may feel like screaming it a few times yourself as you walk out of the theater, but at least you'll have a good reason.

Jack Mathews (review date 19 January 1996)

SOURCE: "Add Horror, Drama, Robbers, a Biker Bar; Blend on High," in *Los Angeles Times,* January 19, 1996, pp. F1, F8.

[*In the following review, Mathews offers unfavorable assessment of* From Dusk Till Dawn.]

As both a veteran video store clerk and movie junkie, Quentin Tarantino knows that "The Desperate Hours" belongs in the drama section and "Night of the Living Dead" in the horror. So where, if he had his old job, would he rack Robert Rodriguez's ***From Dusk Till Dawn,*** which, in the blink of an eye, shifts from the first genre to the second, all in the name of comedy?

Tarantino wrote ***From Dusk Till Dawn*** in 1990 for a reported fee of $1,500. It was undoubtedly one of those projects he hoped to get made for the price of a used Acura, and maybe garner a few kind words in Fangoria magazine. But something called ***Pulp Fiction*** happened, and a script that would—*should*—still be collecting dust has become a major motion picture.

From Dusk Till Dawn is a film nerd's fever dream, a Frankenstein's monster of used movie parts, deliberately mismatched styles, and deliriously implausible characters. For a full hour, it is the story of a pair of murdering, bank-robbing brothers, holding a family hostage while making their escape into Mexico. Then, after they arrive at a topless biker bar in the middle of nowhere, it becomes a chaotic, bloody, nonstop battle with ancient Aztec vampires.

Something like that.

For ***Pulp Fiction*** fans, that first hour has its moments. It's pure-blend Tarantino, comic violence and deadpan dialogue, and the brothers Gecko—played by the commanding George Clooney, from TV's "ER," and an uncharacteristically restrained Tarantino—are riotously evil. Clooney's Seth is the rational one, the tough-talking boss with just the faintest hint of a conscience, and Tarantino's Richard is a paranoid schizophrenic, detecting a conspiracy or a come-on with every twitch of a hostage.

The brothers have left a trail of bodies from Missouri to Texas when they decide to commandeer the motor home of the vacationing Fuller family—the ex-parson Jacob (Harvey Keitel, with a scruffy beard and a New York Texan twang), his daughter Kate (Juliette Lewis; the desert wouldn't be the same without her), and son Scott (Ernest Liu). With his children's lives on the line, Jacob agrees to drive the Geckos across the border and to the nightclub where they are to rendezvous with fellow gang member Carlos (Cheech Marin).

This club looks like a Hell's Angels Fourth of July celebration in the Twilight Zone. There are feather-clad "hairwarts" sitting at every table, and beautiful naked women dancing all around them. No sooner have the brothers and their hostages arrived when one of the dancers morphs into a lizard-faced monster and the bar fight of the century is on.

Rodriguez, whose $7,000 "El Mariachi" made him a legend of independent film, relishes bloody cartoon violence and he had the budget here to create about 40 minutes of frantic mayhem. From Tarantino, we get a plot twist where the bad guys are suddenly the good guys. From Rodriguez, we get enough graphic carnage—decapitations, exploding bodies, flying limbs, splashed blood, staked hearts—to fill a thousand EC comics.

The fight sequence is an astonishing feat of craftsmanship, if not of taste, logic or anything else you might recommend. Rodriguez hews to a shovel-it-all-in philosophy, where anything done in a previous monster movie is worth multiplying here, and he has choreographed and edited it into a kaleidoscopic *danse* macabre. But as much as you may admire the effort that went into it, and its sheer energy on screen, the sequence extends a half-hour beyond the point of wretched excess.

From the moment the bar fight begins, the characters created by Clooney, Tarantino and the others cease to exist. The actors are there, but only as human faces contrasted with the monsters, and there is no further reason to wonder what will become of them.

The conceit of the movie's tone and plot switch is likely to be appreciated only by audiences who share Tarantino's and Rodriguez's pack-rat aesthetic, where every character, event and line of dialogue exists as a spoof of old genre movies.

It was a fresh trick in ***Pulp Fiction*** and "El Mariachi," but it's road kill now, and no matter how many genres they take on at once, it's likely to smell old.

Lyall Bush (essay date January-February 1996)

SOURCE: "Doing Brando," in *Film Comment,* Vol. 32, No. 1, January-February, 1996, pp. 83-8.

[*In the following essay, Bush examines the persona of violent male characters in Tarantino's films, especially as derived from earlier crime genre films and performances by Marlon Brando.*]

Back in the early Fifties, a solid decade before Quentin Tarantino was born into Knoxville, Tennessee poverty, Marlon Brando, young and still hard, was re-surveying the horizon of passion for postwar American men. He carved out low swales of improvisatory naturalism, and shaped patches of dark mumbling where rash and grievous outbursts could feel at home with the new Beat preference for the raw over the cooked. Brando made something of a new Eden of, and for, men. But it was a dark and vexed place mostly, the little light there was fighting through to bowers of mossy sex—a subject that Brando (according to Peter Manso's biography, *Brando*) apparently knew about in spades. Most of the significant male actors who arrived in Brando's wake took up his landscaper's mission, laying down the fresh sod of a transition from David Niven and Cary Grant, actors defined by their wit and charm, to stew-fed and unschooled Nixon and Eisenhower loners, dirty cowboys in white T-shirts and baby smiles: Warren Beatty, Jack Nicholson, Robert De Niro, even, God help us, Sly Stallone and Mickey Rourke—every one of them Brando-ized. All incomprehensible shrugs and gestures, they let inward turns and conscious animal eyes do their speaking for them.

Yet, having made the world, Brando withdrew. He became the éminence grise of male expressivity, with Stanley Kowalski's scream in *A Streetcar Named Desire* its primary reference point. In *Streetcar* ('51), Brando grafted the toughs from *Scarface* ('32) onto images of troubled men—Montgomery Clift and Frank Sinatra types, both frail oddball misfits in films like *From Here to Eternity* and *The Man With the Golden Arm.* (When Sinatra and Brando met in 1955 on the set of *Guys and Dolls,* the two stars bristled. Manso records one anecdote in which Sinatra, asked by Brando to go over lines together, is reported to have replied, "Don't give me any of that Actors Studio shit.") In the parts he played, Brando often made characters who combined hard shells with disconnection and daydreaming. From these general attributes, he invented a poetry of checked speech and body language whose apotheosis came in *The Godfather* ('72), a film in which, it's no accident, he played a numb-faced gangster who likes to garden. (Eighteen years later, in *The Freshman,* he would parody the role, compressing the Don's deliberate menace into those knuckly, walnut-crushing hands.)

The heat of the Brando image made its impression in the most unlikely places. Al Pacino's gay bankrobber in *Dog Day Afternoon* owes as much to Brando as his Michael Corleone does. Robert De Niro's work from *Taxi Driver* on seems a jigsaw of Brando parts; his Jake La Motta in *Raging Bull* takes us to palookaville hell and ends the bum boxer portrait that Brando's Terry Malloy, in *On the Waterfront* ('54), first made fine. The whole notion of the character who is driven by excess rather than control, heat rather than cool reserve, is almost impossible to imagine before *Streetcar.* Valentino, his heat all veils and wide eyes, hardly counts.

The male stuff Brando tapped into and made gush also made Martin Scorsese's career imaginable. The back alleys of sexual anxiety and bullies' rage in Scorsese come from the vein Brando started on, even when spliced and bypassed to suit Scorsese's Mulberry Street memories. When De Niro stands in front of that mirror in *Taxi Driver,* improvising the encounter that always ends with the tilted neck, the cracked smile and "You're dead now, fuck," the bailing twine of rage that twists around the performance is rooted in Brando, whose Mona Lisa smile, and what Norman Mailer once called his "muted animal voice," lends Travis Bickle's its sick promise.

Quentin Tarantino, whom no one can get enough of now for mostly good reasons (despite the recent predictable backlash), has made two films about disturbed talkaholics whose crimes crank up the male anger Brando made important from boiling to steam heat. ***Reservoir Dogs*** and ***Pulp Fiction*** tend to stick fury and humor in the same corner and let them knock each other out: each film sutures audiences into the characters' un-grown-up pain a little in the way Brando in, say, *The Wild One* ('54) inveigled viewers into his world of hurt. But Tarantino does it with a funny little mash of elements that jams dangerous male-bonding bits from Peckinpah and Scorsese together with weird monologues out of Tennessee Williams and Sam Shepard, and ultimately with something all his own: something hilarious and theatrical and wholly new that brings Godard out of avant-garde turnaround, sits him down with a five-dollar shake, and overhauls his overbearing Sartrean revulsion at the consumer world. The resultant combo platter of sampled storylines, guru sophistication, and something kin to personal obsession began seriously carrying away audiences at the 1994 Cannesfest with the force of intoxication.

Tarantino has said, over and over, that with ***Pulp Fiction*** he wanted to take "the oldest stories in the book" and push at them until they became something else. Taking his lead, critics have invoked Salinger and Faulkner as well as the *nouvelle vague*'s penchant for spooning absurdity over Hollywood B films of the Forties and Fifties. But these explanations sound a little like apologies, cooked-up reasons for people to sit in good conscience through the wrench of violence that roots the films (a violence that is also at the core of ***True Romance,*** the Tony Scott film Tarantino scripted, and of ***Natural Born Killers,*** the Oliver Stone film based on a Tarantino script). So, what gives? Discard the notion that his films have huge cultural resource, and what's left to account for the big box office returns? A good part of the reason for the films' success has to be the talk. Tarantino writes characters who dress in suits discarded from *Mean Streets* but who might have spent their youth with alternative comics and high-sugar cereals: his men yak like Ritalin-starved talkaholics. Guns holstered or in hand, they go on at the mouth, more intelligent than they have any right to be. Yet, speech hooked to speech, all the words line up like cars in a train that's directed to the end-punctuation of automatic gunfire.

What a lot of this talk sounds like is Brando, unlaced and undone. Listen to John Travolta's Vincent Vega in ***Pulp Fiction*** and you can hear echoes of a mobile Brando speech pattern under the surface. It's a mumble all right, but a mumble let off the leash, equal parts Barbarino and barbarian. It says, Nothing deep here; it's the voice of a killer who suspects that goofing around is the other half, if not the better part, of valor. Vincent, a well-mannered killer who also shoots heroin, will pee on anything once, just to see. But the kind of talk just to talk is the foundation of Tarantino's new take on the thieves-like-us genre. Characters say *everything* that's on their minds, usually in pairs as in avant-garde theater, and anything's worth a dialogic divagation from the main road too—no exchange has too many slow-downs or S-patterns for him. Potbellies, Fonzie, miracles, grace, Netherland french-fry garnish—when ***Pulp Fiction*** is finished, what Sinatra called Brando's "Actors Studio shit," the inarticulate rage that transformed two generations of male behavior on and off the screen, is pulled down, like a tent-trailer in a hailstorm. Forty years after Brando wrote the lexicon for the rock'n'roll actor's every hunted look and ambiguously cocked head, Tarantino has smashed it, made all that improvisation, all that Jackson Pollock gesture, Stella Adler breathing, and Lee Strasberg memory a collection of museum pieces. And he's done it through long exchanges of dialogue that sound like O'Neil on a heroin bender. But that's cool: the first rockin' actor, Brando didn't give a damn for the theatrical tradition that came before him either: he ripped it up. (In a career review for *The New Yorker,* Harold Brodkey called Brando's animal quality his "shitting-on-you wildness.")

But killing Brando—that is, killing the idea that there's anything worth hearing behind the aphasia and the half-thoughts, killing the myth that masculine silence is rippling with something to say—is part of a larger guerrilla attack on outworn models of dangerous men that's been creeping up on us for a few years now. Real-life mass killers (the ones Tarantino's are cashing in on, kind of) have become crosscultural celebs with long, detailed biographies that do the speaking for them; and the kind of death we imagine they manufacture has taken hold in the public imagination as something that belongs to us, and that maybe some parts of some of us belong to, too.

Yet with real differences. The recent killers served up by film culture—from the real-life cretin that Joe Pesci plays in *GoodFellas* to Hannibal Lecter and the pseudo-documentary serial killers in ***Natural Born Killers,*** are always shadow and light refractions of the real ones. Shadow and light because, steeped in sprayed gore, they are shocking, but also kind of *ironical,* as though what they do with human bodies and what they do in mind- and word-games with each other were A and B sides of the same hot single. No character in the culture is more mythological right now than the enigmatic random killer, but his profile—loner, rebel, quiet—was first forged in *The Wild One,* which made *enigma* one of the central requirements of a film about masculine violence. But where Brando's Johnny only wanted to rebel against a vague whaddyagot, killers now, impulses before anything else, all reactive nervous tissue, are the central symbols of American experience this side of the mainstream. They are Raymond Carver characters grown tired of fishing slime from Yakima swimming pools.

Until recently, the killer's onscreen personality had fewer options. The culture's central psycho, the Brando of killers, is Norman Bates. But Norman's nuttiness follows an Oedipal plot about the corkscrew turns mother love can take that now seems almost dopey. Bonnie and Clyde were maximally mixed-up kids; so, essentially, were the thrill killers, Leopold and Loeb. Killers seem most understandable as explainable versions of ourselves gone wrong, and for particular reasons.

In the late Sixties and into the Seventies and Eighties, the killer evolved. Instead of detailing the lives of misunderstood heroes (*Thieves Like Us*) or unraveling the minds of derailed crazies (*Psycho*), films like *In Cold Blood, Honeymoon Killers, Taxi Driver, Texas Chainsaw Massacre, Badlands,* and *Henry: Portrait of a Serial Killer* began to offer portraits of incomprehensible drifters, disenfranchised garbage collectors, and disconnected vets. "I ain't got no plan," Martin Sheen's Kit says halfway through his spree in the brilliant *Badlands,* saying something about the wild peripheries of the democratic experiment. The killers in these films are not us, they're not even close—they're spectacularly damned figures out of Baudelairean poetry, literary weirdos who arrive in a bolus of strikingly fine, maze-y American films late in the decade of assassination when the romance of the American century seems to be drying up. In *In Cold Blood,* Richard Brooks, taking a cue from Truman Capote, refused to assign meaning of any sort to Richard Hickock and Perry Smith, who sweep into a small Kansas town in night air and put death on a Norman Rockwell family like handprints on a rifle. A roadside sign in front of the motel where the two criminals are caught has burned-out letters, making the sign read an ominous vacancy of OOM. But that's about as deep as things got. In a similar sort of way, *Badlands* shows us Kit standing on a cow carcass, telling his girlfriend he sees visions and dreams of things he can't name. The films are fascinating because these scenes often precede or follow blackly humorous ones. In *Badlands,* Kit speaks into a rich man's Dictaphone during a respite in his crosscountry killing; what he says has no reason to be as comic as it is, except that it has come from him. "Consider," he says, his voice flat, "the minority point of view. But when the majority is known, try to accept and live with it." It's funny because it isn't entirely foolish.

A decade and a little later, these episodes give way to more terrifying combinations of humor and rage. John McNaughton's *Henry: Portrait of a Serial Killer,* the brilliant low-budget and documentary-like film about Henry Lee Lucas's spree of murders in the Seventies, uses a humor so baleful that it is possible to feel a little afraid of your own impulse to laugh. In one sequence, Henry and his partner Otis ambush a middle-class couple and their teenage son in their own home. We watch the three family members struggle on the floor, their shoes slipping on the wall-to-wall carpeting. Through the struggle, even after he has snapped their necks, Otis laughs as though he is only rough-housing. But a cut resituates the murders: we now see that this episode is past, is on video, that Henry and Otis have been watching this all with us (having taped it with a stolen camcorder), drinking beer and staring quietly, hours or days later. And it's a *relief* to be away from the screams of violated bodies, from the awful voyeurism. And it's then you can understand what a dark, dark comedy this is about the human impulse to watch.

Rémy Belveaux's *Man Bites Dog,* a rainy black-and-white faux-documentary about a charming sociopath who heaves victims' bodies into a quarry pond and converses animatedly before and after, over demitasse cups of espresso, about architecture, morality and women, is only a little less alarming than *Henry.* More deliberately *funny, Man Bites Dog* maps out the oppositionality in a killer's consciousness, his simultaneous remoteness and proximity. But the film's final image of conscious life is that of a mechanically absorbed gaze: When unseen shooters strike down the killer and crew, the camera becomes the last "living" witness. Fallen on its side, the last few feet spool out recording the fall of dust in an abandoned warehouse. It's an image of cinematic as well as human disintegration: the film is aborting its attempt to "do" the killer.

Stand-Up Killers

Tarantino's films come out of some of the same moiling for gold that you see in *Man Bites Dog* (Tarantino has said he admires Belveaux's work) and, most simply put, that is their postmodern face. That is, the films revel in laying down for viewers what comes next, yet announce their suspicion about telling crime story narratives founded on a "what comes next" aesthetic. Different from the big, loaded crime-spree movies produced between 1967 and 1974, Tarantino's films don't regard planlessness and plotlessness as significant, nor do they troll off-ramps exemplifying the absence of meaning and hope or a government gone mad. Tarantino characters are more upbeat, they find it hard to stay serious, and their attention spans are so fretted by television time that their stories seem unable to sustain the cultural meaning you might want to find in them. Paying attention to money as well as honing their wit, to killing and keeping an eye fixed on trivia, makes wandering from the point difficult to avoid.

Consider a useful contrast. *Taxi Driver*'s Travis Bickle logs a lot of television time, too. But TV is not his friend; it seems to breathe out toxic messages about the world that confirm his sense of himself as an avenging angel. When one day, falling asleep, he kicks over the set and destroys it, the backward crash becomes a metaphor of his isolation and dementia; tipped back with a cracked white-noise smile, the TV is both dead and alive. Tarantino's characters mostly know what they know via mediation. They know things as they relate to American pop culture of the past twenty years, and they like to surf the detritus of their memories of marginal films and buried rock'n'roll and drug culture. That's how they understand things, and that's how they feel real. At one point in ***Reservoir Dogs,*** a film known mostly for ten or fifteen minutes of abject bloodletting, two connoisseurs of minutiae, Mr. Pink (Steve Buscemi) and Mr. Orange (Tim Roth), supposed to be memorizing the details of a jewel heist, try instead to remember the star of *Get Christie Love!* In the backseat of a car they snap their fingers trying to spark a memory. Watching, it's easy to get giddy. Everything about them, aside from the handguns, says carpool.

There's something else, too, something quick-witted and alive in what they say, that carries their talk outside the junk culture they live in, makes them kin to Sam Beckett or David Mamet, smart deconstructors of conversation. Way, way inside the culture, on intimate terms with its vital organs and main arteries (and unafraid to tickle them or stick them until they gush), these new psychos resemble trivia-mad New York intellectuals playing out manic sandbox dreams of guns and bigtalk, remembering and dismembering to the crack of doom.

Brando Redux

Reservoir Dogs, much disliked and even despised by the country's tonier reviewers for the smile it stamped on its in-your-face Niagara of bloodletting, was quickly embraced by students and film addicts looking for the next thing, or bored by Jim Jarmusch's abstractions and Woody Allen's last decade of finger exercises. What was new was the humor that marbled the violence, as in the defining Tarantino scene of the mutilation of a policeman. Mr. Blonde (Michael Madsen) frugs to Stealer's Wheel's "Stuck in the Middle With You," with more charm than a young, thickset sociopath has any right to possess, flips open a straight razor, and, with the slightest discernible shift from dancing to destruction, lays his big body on the cop and saws off his ear.

This is nobody's idea of fun, which the camera acknowledges by quietly lifting away from the scene to stare at the far wall of the warehouse where the thieves have arranged to meet. When the camera comes back to Mr. Blonde, he is holding the ear between thumb and forefinger, smirking in a sulky, wise-ass Brando kind of way. Then, refusing to be either shocked or warmed by his deed, he performs some improv that has nothing to do with the Stanislavski method. "Hey," he whispers into the ear, the cop screaming, "What's goin' on?" The atrocity, for those moviegoers who have fallen hard for this film, is jump-started into humor by that moment—and it is weird how appealing Madsen is in the scene, down to the way, dancing, he dips his head and moves his arms. In this context the brutality, so rattling, is transformed: Mr. Blonde, talking to the deaf ear afterwards, seems to recognize his absurdity. He's been talking to deaf ears all his life.

Groping to express the film's vitality, critics have called on Greek and Jacobean tragedy, describing the systemic geometry of the slaughter of each of the principals. But Tarantino's masters aren't ancient. In fact, for all the sadism in the new narrative order, the film in many places seems wrapped in Saran.

Things, situations, characters feel secondary, and much of the violence seems deferred. Speaking into the ear, Michael Madsen's Mr. Blonde crosswires James Dean's smile with Robert Mitchum's demented preacher in *Night of the Hunter.* Follow that smile further, as far as cinephilic Tarantino may have, and you might see how Madsen has boosted an expression from the Dean-esque Kit in *Badlands.* Certainly Tarantino knows how to tickle the collective memory: ***True Romance*** rips off *Badlands*' flat voiceover narration along with its Satieish score.

There's a hothouse quality to the performances, too. In ***Dogs***' most original sequence, Tim Roth, an undercover cop infiltrating the band of jewel thieves, is told by his partner: "Undercover cop's got to be Marlon Brando. You got to be a great actor, you got to be naturalistic." So Tim Roth, the English actor, plays an Angeleno cop who plays a lowlife thief whose true story we have watched him rehearse and perfect to seamless perfection. It's hard to remember a more inspired recent directorial choice, and ***Reservoir Dogs*** plays the idea hard. As Roth lays out his bogus story to Joe Cappa, Lawrence Tierney, Christopher Penn, and Harvey Keitel, we are placed in a flashback of the central scene as it "occurred." Watch Tim Roth being "Brando" in a men's room in a flashback of a made-up story—the episode is a perfect example of cinematic vertigo: truth wrapped around falsehood wrapped around truth, and so on.

If ***Reservoir Dogs*** has Tim Roth's single set-piece story, ***Pulp Fiction*** is more or less composed of them, scenarios lifted from some primordial ooze of Prohibition- and Depression-era pulp writing. Begun, sort of, in situational clichés before their engines rev, the stories have deep and jarring laughs built into them. Spree-crime lovers coffee up and plot the stickup of a huge diner; a boxer is bribed to throw a fight, then doesn't; a sensitive thug steps out with the boss's wife. Tarantino claims he crabbed the story ideas from old semi-porn magazines, but they're more like riffs on old movies, and even then not really. In the longest storyline, a pair of professional killers talk at length before they shoot their victims, then talk some more, always with the slightly insane politeness of Laurel and Hardy. One of the killers worries what will happen when he takes out the boss's wife; there's a rumor that another man has gone through a window for giving her a foot massage. It's something he understands.

Wandering as elastically in its way as *Slacker,* ***Pulp Fiction*** nevertheless has a Wellesian bigness. Speeches take off like jet planes and seem to do the work for Tarantino that improvisation and violence do for Scorsese—it's shtick that gravitates to savagery. Yet where Scorsese mythologizes the secrets and silences of men, usually composing a scene in each film that is a freezing take on male rage, Tarantino prefers messier and goofier probes, like the exchange between Vincent and Jules about pig filth versus dog filth that Scorsese might have pushed in another direction. As in ***Reservoir Dogs,*** characters persist in finding it difficult to judge whether a .38 in their face or the bark of someone's order is more annoying. To them, it's all a matter of words, and they grab at them the way Woody Allen characters used to, riveted by tones and sounds more than by anything happening outside their heads. For all the violence, ***Reservoir Dogs*** and ***Pulp Fiction*** are closer to *My Dinner With Andre* than to *Raging Bull.* Jules, for example, doesn't care if Vincent just blew off someone's face by accident; it matters more that Vincent accept his proposition that minutes before God deflected bullets aimed at them, and it *matters* that Vincent be convinced. It's key to a lot of Tarantino's characters: they go half-crazy trying to explain nuances to each other.

Stone Alone

As a measure of how Tarantino uses the violence in his stories to do damage to older ways of making meaning, look at ***Natural Born Killers,*** Oliver Stone's grievous take on the world of celebrity killers. Pinned pretty accurately by many reviewers as Stone's latest parable of the American fall, with a stick-in-the-mud moral stance about killers as media celebrities, the lapel-grabbing crosshatch of films stocks and cutting (Anthony Lane of *The New Yorker* called it "*Bonnie and Clyde* in a blender") manages only momentarily to divert the old-fashioned explanation that Mickey and Mallory's guncraziness is directly traceable to abuse and dysfunction. Wild on the surface, ***NBK***'s creakily dated message is that socially responsible programs could have saved the killers. Even *Texas Chainsaw Massacre,* which points to the shutdown of the town's slaughterhouse as the indirect socioeconomic source of the killers' desire for new skins to make new selves from, has a funny, self-reflexive scene in which the father sees the chainsaw damage on the front door and yells, "Look at what you've done!" That's what Stone needs a little of; *JFK,* almost the same film, was better because almost everyone outside Kevin Costner seemed to have dropped from the land of Diane Arbus. (Plus, in the Kennedy assassination lore about big and small plots Stone caught a wave that started way, way down in the American psyche.)

Since *JFK* it seems Stone has spent more time in the black-spine, True Crime isle of the bookstore where he bought *Crossfire.* True Crime's roots lie in the same partly true and partly fiction Prohibition pulp prose that Tarantino draws on, and that exploits our collective fears that killers like Ted Bundy and John Wayne Gacy and Charles Manson ("the king" in ***NBK*** terms) are, like Soviet moles of Cold War fiction, potential behind every slightly odd smile. More than other story forms, crime-spree stories beg big answers. Is it possible that child abuse, in some combination with a sensation-mad media and ruinous voodoo economics, manufactures killers? It's tempting to believe it, especially since the alternative choice is to believe that natural-born killers exist as surely as three-legged babies. The first theory suggests its own solution (fix the system), but the second, which supposes a pattern of genetic damage as predictable as the flight of swallows, holds out none.

Murder and Transcendence

Back in 1957, in the first decade of Brando, the year they caught Ed Gein, the Wisconsin cannibal and cross-dresser (and original for Norman Bates), Norman Mailer published an essay called "The White Negro" that argued, "The psychopath murders—if he has the courage—out of the necessity to purge his violence, for if he cannot empty his hatred then he cannot love." Mailer caught hell for writing "if he has the courage," for giving the time of day to the thought that homicide might in some cases be a form of personal growth. It didn't help when years later he helped release the killer-writer, Jack Henry Abbott, who was out of prison less than two weeks before he stabbed a waiter to death for—shades of *Taxi Driver*—looking at him. ***Pulp Fiction,*** new as a penny, mines a White Negro vein in wondering if madmen and brutes might be looking for salvation, just mostly in the wrong places and with the wrong methods and opening gambits. "Who you lookin' at?" Butch (Bruce Willis with a brushcut) asks Vincent. "You, palooka," Vincent replies, cuffing a Terry Malloy type with a Joe Bazooka line. "You, punchy."

What sets Tarantino apart is that he's smart enough to know how to manage any of his labyrinthine exchanges of looks. Near the end of ***Pulp Fiction,*** Jules and Vincent talk about God and miracles in the Hawthorne Grill. Jules believes God has interceded that morning when the bullets fired from a few feet away flew either past or through them. Now, over pancakes, he says he will leave the gangster life "to walk the earth, like Caine in *Kung Fu.*" Vincent, mouth full of bacon and still chewing on Jules's opinion that pork is filthy, announces, "I'm gonna take a shit." With the best cursing since *Glengarry Glen Ross* and the most original characters in American cinema since the early Seventies (think of *Chinatown* and *The Godfather*), Tarantino seems to be blazing a new trail in the Hollywood movie. And, as it looks right now, he's doing it as an insider, one whose dialogue is—Mailer's old word—hip enough to begin with God and end with excrement, and whose major characters exit at the end into light. With Harvey Keitel, the eldest and most enigmatic character in both ***Reservoir Dogs*** and ***Pulp Fiction,*** the exception to the rule, his characters are all post-Brando: their speech lives large, comes packing.

Lynn Hirschberg (interview date 16 November 1997)

SOURCE: "The Man Who Changed Everything," in *New York Times Magazine,* November 16, 1997, pp. 112, 114-5, 117.

[*In the following interview, Tarantino discusses his films and the Hollywood movie industry.*]

Quentin Tarantino, in shorts and a T-shirt, is padding around his palatial mansion in the Hollywood Hills on a Sunday afternoon in late October. He has lived here less than a year, and the previous occupant, the pop singer Richard Marx, left most of his overstuffed furniture behind. Tarantino has added some touches: movie posters are strewn everywhere; there are bronze sculptures of characters from ***Reservoir***

Dogs, his first movie, and ***Pulp Fiction;*** a goldfish, a gold lamp and Tarantino's screenwriting Oscar for ***Pulp Fiction*** (also gold) are carefully arranged in front of a picture window. "Feng shui," Tarantino explains.

Piled on the living-room floor are videocassettes of scenes from Tarantino's new movie, ***Jackie Brown,*** which is scheduled to open Christmas Day. Based on the Elmore Leonard novel "Rum Punch," ***Jackie Brown*** stars that 70's blaxploitation icon Pam Grier as a stewardess embroiled in an elaborate money-laundering/drug-pushing/gun-running scheme. The film also stars Samuel L. Jackson, Robert De Niro and Robert Forster, who is best known, if he is known at all, for playing Banyon on the NBC show of that name during the 70's. "That's one of the best things about ***Pulp Fiction*** being successful," Tarantino says. "It gives you the power to cast Robert Forster."

Beyond casting, ***Pulp Fiction*** really changed everything. The movie, a critical and commercial hit (grossing $250 million world-wide), established Miramax as a mini-studio, jump-started John Travolta's ailing career, reignited a sort of independent spirit among film makers and made a star out of Tarantino. At first he appeared to be a type: the video geek who lived and breathed movies, classifying them in his own way (a-bunch-of-guys-on-a-mission movies, revenge movies, two-guys-and-a-girl movies and so on) and savoring them. (He would show prospective girlfriends "Rio Bravo," and if they didn't like it, their days were probably numbered.) But Tarantino was not as childlike as his movie-nerd image might have suggested. He not only studied movies, he studied the careers of directors and producers, and he knew what to expect and what he wanted. His goal was simple: Tarantino was interested in posterity, a body of work that would endure.

Pulp Fiction made Tarantino famous in a particular kind of way. He seemed brilliant and accessible—through the movie, he tapped into the collective unconscious that is pop culture. Thirty-four now, hip but not intimidating, Tarantino could be that cool pal you always wanted. He has created a world and the audience wants to live there.

"People think they know me," Tarantino says. They honk at him when he drives. They follow him down the streets of L.A. with posters and photos to sign. When he drinks in a bar, a steady stream of fans approach his table. "Thank you," he'll say, taking a girl's hand. "You're so nice."

The fame brought to him by ***Pulp Fiction,*** and then his wish to act in movies as well as direct, has created something of a journalistic backlash in the last two years. "They want four more ***Pulp Fiction***s," says Tarantino, who has no intention of pleasing anyone but himself. "But why would that be interesting?" Instead, ***Jackie Brown,*** which was shot in the South Bay, Tarantino's childhood turf in Los Angeles, is more of a character study than a pop opera. "It's a quiet film," Tarantino says, smiling. "But my idea of quiet may not be anyone else's."

[*Hirschberg:*] *Do you think movies are getting worse?*

[Tarantino:] No. I've never thought that. There's always enough good movies that come out at the end of the year to justify everything—studio-wise and independents. If you can get one masterpiece a year, do you have any right to expect more than that? We're talking about a masterpiece that will live on for all time. And sometimes you get two or three or four. If you get one, that's enough.

Three years ago, you were the one. **Pulp Fiction** *was a huge success, and it changed the world of independents. How did that affect you?*

I think I was mentally prepared for success. I always though that through a body of work, I'd get to a place where I'd be respected. My work would matter, and I'd have my place in film history. I always figured I would make a splash. I just didn't think I'd get to where I wanted to go in two movies. But I always wanted success. And the more success you have, the more power you have. I don't need to talk a hot actor into doing my movie to get my movie made. And that's true power—if you don't need Tom Hanks or Tom Cruise to say yes to your movie to do it. Which isn't to say I wouldn't want those guys, but it would be my choice. I want *me* to be enough. That's the power I have.

But it happened very quickly, and that was a surprise. I became an adjective sooner than I thought I was going to.

An adjective?

Every third script out there is described as "Tarantino-esque."

Right after **Pulp Fiction,** *you acted in the "Tarantino-esque" "Destiny Turns On the Radio," and then in* **Four Rooms.** *People went crazy. I think that the public felt you shouldn't act, you should just direct.*

The main thing people took shots at was that I didn't make another movie right away. And I'm never going to be the director that makes a movie a year. I don't see how directors do that and live a life.

Did that backlash get to you?

I don't think it has any effect on my work, but it's sort of affected my life. Journalists can't conceive that the things they wrote in Entertainment Weekly or Movieline don't really affect my life. I was made fun of and kicked around a little. I learned pretty early on to stop reading that stuff.

But you felt press was critical to the success of **Pulp Fiction.**

That's true. The reason I'm popular overseas is because I spent a solid year overseas with ***Reservoir Dogs*** doing the talk shows and interviews. I would arrive in a country unknown and I would leave known. So when it came time to sell ***Pulp Fiction,*** they knew exactly who I was. I walk in Tokyo and they recognize me. In Communist countries and everything. We showed ***Pulp Fiction*** in China. The Government sanctioned it, and I've never seen a more enthusiastic response. When I went to introduce the movie, it was more like a rock concert than a movie. It was like freedom, a night of freedom.

But as far as America is concerned, I did the talk shows and magazine articles and profiles and all, and people started writing that "Quentin Tarantino is a master of self-promotion." That was a big thing: *master of self-promotion.* And I didn't do anything different than an actor does. I didn't do *one more interview* than an actor does. I just did the publicity rounds.

Do you think it was crucial to the success of the movie?

Nah. That much press doesn't really sell a proportionate number of tickets, but it does make you famous. I actually don't think that this article in People or this article in Us sells a ticket. But it does make you famous.

You could take 30 percent of my fame away and I'd be just fine. It's not that I don't want to be famous, but 30 percent less would be great. I used to like to walk and be in my own head, and I can't really do that now. If I was trying to pick up a girl every night, it would be the greatest thing in the world, but I'm not. That's really easy now, but I don't want to do that.

Did Miramax ever pressure you to get back to work?

Never, never, never, never, never.

You're seen as Mr. Indie Guy Success Story, but you actually wrote **Pulp Fiction** *for a studio, Tri-Star.*

They said no right away, so there was no problem. And Harvey Weinstein of Miramax got it like, *bam!*—in the second breath. Tri-Star never saw it until I was finished with it. It said on it, "Last Draft." They knew, This is it. I said, This is what I'm prepared to make.

Were you worried they'd say yes?

What I was worried about was that they wouldn't be into it and they'd do it anyway because it was so cheap. But they were scared of it. And they didn't think it was going to be funny. Mike Medavoy, the head of Tri-Star then, was the guy who put the kibosh on it. He actually had just come back from Washington, where Clinton had done this big thing about how Hollywood has to be more responsible and all this stuff. He'd just come back and we threw ***Pulp Fiction*** in his lap. I was very disillusioned when he turned it down because I thought he was a studio guy with guts and he was just scared of the material. At the same time, I have to give him a little credit for some honesty. He didn't lie. He answered questions I'd always wanted to know.

Like what?

Well, they knew they weren't going to be able to control me. They had to buy me hook, line and sinker or forget it. It said on there, "Last Draft"—they knew I wasn't going to change it. But I gave him a cast list. It read like, for, say, the role of Pumpkin, "This role will be offered to Tim Roth"—who ultimately played it. "If Tim Roth turns it down, this role will be offered to the next person on the list and so on." There were no maybes about it. It was how it is. And Medavoy read the list, and we had a big meeting about it and he goes: "Tim Roth is a very fine actor, but Johnny Depp is also on your list. I would rather offer the part to Johnny Depp. And if he turns it down, we should go to Christian Slater. That would be my order."

And then I got to ask him the question I'd always been dying to ask. I said, "Do you actually think that Johnny Depp, in the role of Pumpkin, who's only in the last scene and the first scene, do you actually think that would mean a dollar's worth of difference at the box office?" And he goes, "It won't mean a dime, but it will make me feel better."

There's nothing else to be said after that. That says it all. I don't want to make movies that way. But that doesn't make Medavoy a crooked bastard. It makes him very honest.

Tri-Star had paid you a million dollars for that script. Weren't you nervous about breaking the deal?

No. I had heard all the stories about projects sitting on the shelf. There was every chance, in fact, in all likelihood, a studio would not want to make ***Pulp Fiction.*** If any studio would have done it, it would have been Tri-Star. Mike Medavoy had run Orion, which functioned like an independent.

You and Miramax sort of grew up together.

Oh, yeah—I'm their Mickey Mouse. I always joke with them that three years ago, at any major event or anything—

like, if all the studio people had Thanksgiving—Miramax would have had to sit at the kids table. Now, not only is Miramax sitting at the big table, but everyone's watching what they're eating.

Do the big studios ever tempt you?

After ***Reservoir Dogs,*** I got a ton of offers from actors with production companies. And some things came my way. "Speed" was offered to me. "Speed" was originally supposed to be an independent-type action film. It's hard to believe that now, but they used ***Reservoir Dogs*** and "Bad Lieutenant" as examples of the direction they were headed. It was supposed to be the same market. Then the other real big movie offered to me was "Men in Black." I never even read it.

If I'd been offered "Hero," I would have done "Hero." That would have been my Capra movie. It would have been smaller. I would have cast Travolta. The screenwriter, David Peoples, wrote a great script. Stephen Frears, the director, took "Hero" as a job—I can tell. The movie is hitting its head on the ceiling of his talent, where the script wants to go to the moon. I've seen that a few times now.

Do you think studios mess up movies?

No. It's totally the director. I've never gone through the whole big-studio experience, but . . . I have. That's a lie. Miramax is a studio. There are no two ways about it.

But people are crazy about Miramax.

When ***Pulp Fiction*** came out, I didn't realize the resentment toward Miramax throughout the industry. When the movie came out, there was a big think piece published in Variety questioning the sense of Miramax releasing what is definitely viewed as an "art film" so wide—1,000 screens. How foolish they were. And that they were overspending on advertising.

Then, if you remember, we were in 1,100 theaters, and "The Specialist," starring Sharon Stone and Sylvester Stallone, was in, like, 2,300 theaters. We were No. 1 and no one believed it. And then, came Week 2, we killed them. At the end of the day, the studios don't like these intruders coming into the business. In a weird way, Harvey and Bob Weinstein kind of remind the studios where they all started. They're the real W.B. I call them the Brothers Weinstein. The B.W.'s.

Do you still think about budget?

Yes. ***Jackie Brown*** only cost $12 million. You can't lose. You absolutely, positively can't lose. And you don't have to compromise. After ***Reservoir Dogs,*** all the studios thought: Wow—that's good film. This guy is a very exciting film maker. And you could tell they were thinking, If we match this guy with more commercial subject matter, he can bat it out of the park. And they'd be right, by the way. At one point, it was a major consideration for Scorsese to do "Dick Tracy." And that's right up his alley. If I used bigger actors, made action movies, I wouldn't be selling out. De Palma did not sell out when he did "The Untouchables"—it was a marriage made in heaven. And I love "Mission: Impossible." To me, that's a $100 million movie made with the integrity of an artist. And the more I've seen it, the more I love it. I own a print of it. If I go and do "The Man From U.N.C.L.E.," I'm going to make it with Warner Brothers. That's what Warner Brothers does. That would be the logical place. But not because I'm standing on a stepladder reaching for commerciality. I don't have to prove anything as far as audience is concerned.

Your confidence is impressive, but neither **Reservoir Dogs** *nor* **True Romance,** *which you wrote the script for, was a hit. Didn't you ever worry?*

During preproduction on ***Pulp Fiction, True Romance*** came out and it didn't do well. That scared me. I thought, Maybe there isn't a big audience for what it is that I do. But the example that gave me confidence was Jane Campion. That year, she had her big breakout hit with "The Piano." There was nothing to suggest in her previous work that she would ever find a large audience. But her doing what she does with the right film and the right story did find that audience. And now there are these insane $100 million expectations on ***Jackie Brown,*** which is a smaller, character-based movie with a female lead. Well, I'm not in this for a couple of movies. I'm in this for a lifetime.

Do you watch movies while you're shooting?

During ***Jackie Brown,*** I would watch one side of the laser disk for "Carlito's Way." My cinematographer and I watched two movies: "Hickey and Boggs," which was directed by Robert Culp and was shot in the 70's—it's a really good movie. And then we watched "They All Laughed," by Peter Bogdanovich. Both were perfect for ***Jackie Brown.*** "They All Laughed" is a masterpiece, I think. It captures a fairy-tale New York. It makes New York look like Paris in the 20's. It makes you want to live there. And we kind of used it. And then we watched "Straight Time," one of the best L.A. crime movies ever. But I wanted ***Jackie Brown*** to look more like a movie than that. "Straight Time" is too gritty.

How about casting the movie?

You actually have to cast your own movie. By that I mean, on ***Reservoir Dogs,*** they wanted us to cast a bunch of made-for-video actors, a bunch of semi-on-the-rise B-level guys thrown together without any thought of whether or not they would work well together. They wanted us to use these medium names on the rise. We wouldn't do it.

The hardest part to give up in ***Jackie Brown*** was Ordell, who is played by Samuel L. Jackson. I *was* Ordell. It was so easy to write Ordell. I was Ordell for the year I was writing the script. I had to really work hard in letting go of Ordell and letting Sam play him and not being a jerk about stuff. Sam was him for 10 weeks; I was Ordell for 52 weeks.

Ordell was all my mentors as a young man growing up. Ordell was who I could have been. It was interesting writing the film because that all kind of came back to me, and that persona of who I could have been at 17 if I didn't have artistic ambitions. That was it. If I hadn't wanted to make movies, I would have ended up as Ordell. I wouldn't have been a postman or worked at the phone company or been a salesman or a guy selling gold by the inch. I would have been involved with one scam after another. I would have done something that I would have gone to jail for. But I picked my path. And luckily, I was able to deal with all those things about me through my work.

And Robert De Niro is in the movie. Lately, it seems, his talent is taken for granted.

Definitely. De Niro's work in "Heat" is amazing. And he's amazing in "Casino." He was robbed of a nomination on either of those films. De Niro is a major supporter of me acting. We're going to do a movie together.

Critics have taken potshots at me for acting. I don't think they think I'm as serious about acting as I am. But I have had nothing but support from other actors. So who am I going to listen to? Am I going to listen to J. Hoberman or Robert De Niro? Am I going to listen to Caryn James or Nic Cage?

Nic Cage is about to play Superman. Which super-hero would you want to be?

That's tough. [*long pause*] I think I'd be Luke Cage, the black super-hero. Nic Cage took his name from Luke Cage. Luke Cage was a blaxploitation comic-book hero. He's my favorite character. Luke Cage was framed for heroin possession and he was in jail, and a doctor did an experiment on him and he busts out of jail and he ends up with super strength. The doctor's chemical bath gave him steel-hard skin. His skin is bulletproof. He changed his name and rented himself out: Luke Cage, Hero for Hire. Everyone thinks he's dead, but he's always on the run. He's a superhero version of "Shaft." He's a great character.

You've always had a great love of mainstream, pop stuff. You're like a collector.

I don't believe in elitism. I don't think the audience is this dumb person lower than me. I am the audience.

Do you ever think about how you would change the movie business?

Well, I have a big problem with the stars getting $20 million. I think it's just greed, it's a greed that will ultimately kill the business.

Do you say that to John Travolta, who gets $20 million a picture?

I have said that to him. He says, That's the going price. And I understand that. If *I* was going on the market, and the going price for directors is $6 million, I could get $10 million with the right project. And I would start to care about kicking it up.

But I don't want to. It's not right. My hero when it comes to taking care of himself and owning his stuff is Clint Eastwood. That's who I pattern my entire business after. He takes short money when he works for Warner Brothers, brings the movies in for a price and, goddamn it, when they make money, he gets paid. He's my hero.

Do you ever get scared? Are you always in such a doubt-free zone?

Why should I be scared? You do the work and that's what is important. It sounds big, but I've built my whole career on courage. This whole thing is about when I'm an old man and I'm not doing anything anymore. It ain't about the moment. I'm not making films for right now—I'm making films for 40 years from now.

Todd McCarthy (review date 22 December 1997)

SOURCE: A review of *Jackie Brown,* in *Variety,* December 22, 1997, pp. 57-8.

[*In the following review, McCarthy offers tempered criticism of* Jackie Brown.]

Facing the daunting task of making a third feature that could measure up to ***Reservoir Dogs*** and ***Pulp Fiction,*** not to mention one that would disarm the detractors ready to pounce on him no matter what, Quentin Tarantino treads turf that is both familiar and fresh in ***Jackie Brown.*** Unquestionably too long, and lacking the snap and audaciousness of the pictures that made him the talk of the town, this narratively faithful but conceptually imaginative adaptation of Elmore Leonard's novel "Rum Punch" nonetheless offers an abundance of pleasures, especially in the realm of characterization and atmosphere. Down-and-dirty pic looks to find its most ardent fans among cinephiles and black viewers, with mainstream critics and audiences more likely to harp on its obvious indulgences. B.O. prospects are OK in urban areas, less so elsewhere.

Enshrined as Hollywood's golden bad boy after ***Pulp Fiction,*** Tarantino was clearly in a position to do anything he wanted as his next film, and took more than three years to do it. Superficially sticking to his roots in violent crime stories and paying homage to '70s blaxploitation pics through his offbeat casting of Pam Grier in the title role, writer-director also uses the occasion to expand his range promisingly in more emotional and nuanced directions. This development may be lost on genre fans expecting heavy mayhem and gunplay, of which there is some, but it augurs well for Tarantino one day venturing into other types of stories.

As it is, ***Jackie Brown*** is an arguably too fulsome examination of deceit, treachery, cunning, stupidity, mistrust, risk and daring among a group of small-timers. Transferring the action from Leonard's Miami to his own South Bay area of L.A. and changing the leading character from white to black, Tarantino has adhered closely to the plot of the celebrated authors 1995 bestseller but has given it a distinctive tang through his patented touch with contempo street dialogue and highly personal use of source music and pop culture artifacts.

Film takes its own sweet time setting its gears in motion, with the emphasis on sweet when it comes to amusingly establishing its characters, but to the detriment of pace.

Ordell Robbie (Samuel L. Jackson) is a very smooth and lethal arms dealer operating out of a Hermosa Beach pad he shares with blond and always stoned surfer girl Melanie (Bridget Fonda). Hanging out with his longtime partner, Louis Gara (Robert De Niro), who has just been released from the slammer after serving four years for bank robbery, Ordell critiques the various assault weapons he can deliver while announcing that he intends to get out of the illicit gun business after stashing away another 500 grand down in Mexico.

But Ordell, whose nearly every phrase contains the n-word, must first deal with an errant associate, Beaumont (Chris Tucker), a fast-talking hustler who has violated his parole. In a sequence that typifies Tarantino's taste for combining outrageous comedy with startling violence, Ordell sweet-talks his manic friend into climbing into his car trunk in order to surprise an adversary, then, in a boldly protracted long shot, casually shoots him when they arrive at a vacant lot.

More trouble lands on Ordell's doorstep when stewardess Jackie Brown (Grief) is busted at LAX by ATF agent Ray Nicolette (Michael Keaton) and cop Mark Dargus (Michael Bowen) while smuggling money into the country for him. Facing a prison term and meager future prospects upon her release, the sharp-looking lady in her mid-40s knows she'll get off easy if she helps the authorities nail Ordell, who bails Jackie out but is thwarted in his attempt to do to her what he did to Beaumont.

In a story featuring several relationships in which trust and mutual suspicion perform a continual balancing act, the most significant is the one carrying the least narrative weight. Bail bondsman Max Cherry (Robert Forster), a resolutely solid, middle-class and middle-aged man whom Ordell uses to spring his friends, picks Jackie up at jail.

His function in the plot would end there except that, in a moment conveyed with great wit through the music, he falls hard for Jackie the moment he sees her, takes her for a relaxing drink and eventually sets this woman with few options on a path that will see her bravely playing the authorities and Ordell against each other.

The quasi-romance between these two unlikely partners, both of whom are at midlife crossroads, provides a quiet emotional undercurrent beneath the yarn's otherwise more extreme eruptions. Laying low for a while Louis takes the flaky Melanie up on her invitation to have sex, then berates Ordell for trusting her. Admitting to Ordell that she's had to cooperate with the cops, Jackie convinces him that she's going to put one over on them by staging an intricate money exchange in which she'll actually return to Ordell nearly all of his $500,000.

In a mild, but nonetheless highly effective, echo of his ***Pulp Fiction*** structural experimentation, Tarantino, in a 20-minute set piece, stages this exchange three times from different points of view, each one revealing key aspects of the daredevil maneuver. As the main participants urgently pursue their interests in the bloody aftermath, half of the major characters bite the dust, leading to a mutedly upbeat finale.

The action indisputably flags during the long midsection, but the film's longueurs are inseparable from its strengths in that they stem from the same fact: Tarantino works his scenes for all they are worth, extracting from them the maximum values of drama, humor, color and character. For him, there are no small or insignificant sequences, nothing to be thrown away.

The results of this approach are scenes that, individually,

play wonderfully well but, when laid end to end, tend to flatten out. Pic suffers not only from overlength, but from a lack of dramatic peaks and valleys, of punctuation, something that was alleviated in the equally long ***Pulp Fiction*** by the audacious dovetailing structure and more outrageous incidents.

Ultimately, despite the flavorsome aspects of all the elements, it can be argued that a genre piece of this kind has trouble supporting such extended treatment, even when the characters and situations are deepened as far as Tarantino takes them. In this light, the director's courage in scouting the outer reaches of this sort of material can be regarded sympathetically, even if the approach ultimately reveals the form's limitations.

Tarantino's knack for imaginative casting and extracting unusual, unexpected notes from actors is in full flower here. A true icon of the '70s, Grier, who has aged beautifully, may not have the widest range, but her tremendous poise, visible at once in the opening shots of her arriving at LAX, serves her exceedingly well, and she does have two or three big moments to sink her teeth into.

Jackson, sporting a flowing hairdo and martial-arts-inspired chin hair, is superb as the charming, loquacious, ultimately malevolent gunrunner who uses people as pawns. Forster, another thesp Tarantino has resurrected, lends a wonderfully lived-in quality to the bail bondsman who's seen it all and has a special appreciation for what Jackie is going through.

Fonda brings an irreverent spunkiness to her amoral beach girl, and Keaton manages to inject some honest emotion into his efficient federal agent. De Niro plays a seedy, relatively uninteresting sideline character for most of the way, only to erupt in the late going in ways that are both insanely violent and touchingly honest and loyal.

The enormously entertaining soundtrack is loaded with soul and funk hits, some from vintage blaxploitation hits. Technically, the film is evocative of mostly dingy locales where the characters live and operate, and pointedly avoids a slick look.

Kenneth Turan (review date 24 December 1997)

SOURCE: "Tarantino Lets Attitude Show in 'Jackie,'" in *Los Angeles Times,* December 24, 1997, pp. F2, F12.

[*In the following review, Turan offers unfavorable assessment of* Jackie Brown.]

Unlikely as it sounds, ***Jackie Brown*** is Quentin Tarantino's idea of a nice film. Not that it's everyone's idea of nice: This hotbed of industrial-strength profanity isn't headed for the Disney Channel any time soon. But motivating the writer-director here is not his usual impulse toward outrageousness but what has to be called a sweet desire to pay tribute to two key influences in his creative life, writer Elmore Leonard and star Pam Grier.

This is Tarantino's first film since ***Pulp Fiction*** won the Palme d'Or at Cannes 31/2 years ago, a long enough time for numerous imitators to have clogged cinemas worldwide with rip-offs of his cascading blood and brain matter style.

However, those expecting Tarantino to pick up where he left off will be disappointed in ***Jackie Brown.*** Instead of rearranging audience's sensibilities, he's taken the typically twisty plot of Leonard's "Rum Punch" and run it through his personal Mixmaster. The result is a raunchy doodle, a leisurely and easygoing diversion that goes down easy enough but is far from compelling.

A fan of Leonard for years, Tarantino also realized that by changing the race of "Rum Punch's" female protagonist he could also turn this film into a tribute to Grier. For those with short memories, she's the no-nonsense star of over-the-top 1970s blaxploitation films like "Coffy," "Foxy Brown" and "Sheba Baby" the director is an unabashed fan of.

This decision gives ***Jackie Brown*** a poignant feeling at times, especially in a closing close-up of Grier's face that is in an unnerving way reminiscent of the celebrated shot of Garbo at the end of "Queen Christina." But tribute is a hard act for someone with Tarantino's sensibility to master, and ***Jackie Brown*** casts doubt on whether he's the right director to make "nice" an involving quality.

For one thing, at 2 hours and 40 minutes, ***Jackie Brown*** plainly takes longer than it should to unfold. Along with that too-leisurely pace goes a lack of immediacy, a sense that this is the kind of thing that Tarantino not only might have done in his sleep but in fact has.

Helping keep people awake is Tarantino's trademark wall-to-wall profanity, which can be spell-binding but this time around is so dependent on casual usage of the N-word that fellow writer-director Spike Lee was moved to complain publicly about it.

Most of the hard talk comes from Samuel L. Jackson as Ordell Robbie, introduced in an apartment in Hermosa Beach showing a video called "Chicks 'n' Guns" to the very different Louis Gara and Melanie Ralston.

Melanie (Bridget Fonda) is Ordell's girlfriend, a kittenish

surf bunny whose ambition doesn't seem to extend past getting high and watching TV. Louis (Robert De Niro) is an old pal of Ordell's who's just gotten out of prison and is looking for a situation.

Ordell himself is a gun dealer, proud of his merchandise ("the AK-47, when you absolutely positively got to kill every [expletive] in the room") but ruthless and menacing to his employees when he needs to be.

One of those workers is Jackie Brown (Grier), a stewardess with a fly-by-night airline that shuttles between L.A. and Mexico. The government, in the person of Alcohol, Tobacco and Firearms agent Ray Nicolette (Michael Keaton), puts pressure on her to turn Ordell in. But Jackie, aided by been-around bail bondsman Max Cherry (Robert Forster) would rather play both sides against each other and get a crack at liberating Ordell's half-million-dollar stash.

Though it's Jackson who provides whatever energy ***Jackie Brown*** can manage, it is a treat to see Grier, who has the intimidating physicality of a sexy linebacker, be "too cool for school" and face down any troubles the script throws her way.

While Leonard's original novel was set in the Miami area, Tarantino moved it to L.A., which means lines about Roscoe's Chicken & Waffles and key scenes are set in the Del Amo Fashion Center. Tarantino feels at home in the South Bay, maybe too much so. He's relaxed so much he hasn't given this film more than attitude, and even attitude can wear thin after a while.

Todd F. Davis and Kenneth Womack (essay date January 1998)

SOURCE: "Sheparding the Weak: The Ethics of Redemption in Quentin Tarantino's *Pulp Fiction,*" in *Literature-Film Quarterly,* Vol. 26, No. 1, January, 1998, pp. 60-6.

[*In the following essay, Davis and Womack explore themes of moral development and spiritual conversion in* Pulp Fiction. *According to the critics, "Beyond the hazy lens of Tarantino's deliberately dark gangland tableau . . .* Pulp Fiction *proffers a fictional universe where miracles still happen, where love can still make a difference."*]

Although a number of critics in the popular press laud Quentin Tarantino's ***Pulp Fiction*** (1994) for its non-linear narrative, quirky performances, and oddly resonant dialogue regarding such issues as hamburgers, television pilot episodes, and foot massages, critics in other circles such as Anthony Lane (*The New Yorker*) and Tom Whalen (*Literature/Film Quarterly*) deride Tarantino's creation for its extreme violence and lack of moral clarity. In "Degrees of Cool," Lane maligns the film for the director's over-arching reliance upon pop-cultural minutiae and its "black morality and wicked accoutrements," while in "Film Noir: Killer Style," Whalen argues that ***Pulp Fiction*** functions upon a cinematic tableau devoid of meaning and further suggests that the characters who populate Tarantino's oeuvre live in a world that operates beyond the strictures of morality. Whalen writes, "Greed and drugs, chance and what wits these characters have left after their ears have been deafened by the gun blasts are what they live by." Such critical assessments of the film, however, neglect to account for the remarkably palpable elements of metamorphosis involved in the redemption of the character who functions largely as ***Pulp Fiction***'s moral axis, Jules Winnfield (Samuel L. Jackson). His dramatic struggle with the notion of divine intervention in the film's final reel—in addition to the ethical crises that confront Butch Coolidge (Bruce Willis) as he maneuvers through ***Pulp Fiction***'s labyrinthine middle-third—belies any rudimentary evaluation of the film as a morally vacuous vehicle that emphasizes Tarantino's lust for the flashy entrails of pop culture over the sublime qualities of artistic substance.

By using the interpretive strategies established by the ongoing project of ethical criticism, promulgated by such figures as Wayne Booth, Martha C. Nussbaum, and J. Hillis Miller, we will reveal the manner in which Tarantino utilizes the otherwise mundane moments of conversation and reflection in the lives of gangsters—perennially employed as mere plot devices in the annals of American cinema, but rarely depicted as fully realized characters engaging in workaday human experience—as a means for exploring ethical and philosophical questions regarding faith, morality, commitment, and the human community. In his prodigious volume, *The Company We Keep: An Ethics of Fiction,* Booth advocates a form of criticism that examines a work of art in order to discover and make explicit the moral sensibility informing that work. If we are to accept the proposition that narratives reflect human experience while at the same time they affect human experience, that narratives are both a product of the social order and help establish and maintain that social order, it becomes clear that—in its desire to examine the moral and ethical nature of a work of art—ethical criticism establishes an important bond between the life of the narrative and the life of the reader. Patricia Meyer Spacks contends that while fictional narratives offer opportunities for ethical reflection, they are not imperatives for behavior; rather, according to Spacks, "paradigms of fiction provide an opportunity for moral playfulness: cost-free experimentation." While the conditions of the visual experience inherent in film underscore the remarkable power of narratives to impinge upon human experience, or what Spacks calls the "experience of agency or its illusion," those experiences acquired through cinematic representation—although powerful and affecting—may be understood as activities that afford experimentation, the trying on of new possibilities without the finality or consequences of life beyond the comforting walls of the cineplex.

Although ***Pulp Fiction***'s detractors might balk at the very notion of "cost-free experimentation" within the nefarious context of the gangster milieu, as Michael Wilmington remarks, ***Pulp Fiction*** "*doesn't* feel like the usual high-tech, nasty blood-and-guts thriller, those mercenary super-trash studio hits pumped out by Arnold Schwarzenegger, Sylvester Stallone, or Steven Seagal." In fact, Tarantino's film produces a mere six on-screen corpses in comparison with the nameless and faceless thousands who perish for the sake of box office dollars and "money shots" in such films as Stallone's *Rambo: First Blood II* (1985), Jean- Claude Van Damme's *Cyborg* (1989), or Seagal's *Marked for Death* (1990). Instead, surprising images of community built upon individual struggles with faith, loyalty, pride, and—perhaps even most remarkably—love resonate long after the final, accidental report of Vincent Vega's (John Travolta) 45. As Tobin Siebers notes in *The Ethics of Criticism,* "The heart of ethics is the desire for community"; throughout ***Pulp Fiction*** Tarantino seeks to establish a community not only among his fictional characters but with his viewing audience as well. The witty repartee that many critics praise as the film's singular strength in fact affords its audience with a pop-cultural inroad into Tarantino's fictive world—a universe rendered even more tangible through its myriad representations of shared cultural ephemera such as the ethics of five-dollar milkshakes and the French translations of McDonald's fare that oddly but inevitably lead to larger ontological discussions concerning the existence of God and the veracity of miracles. The uncanny ease with which Vincent and Jules traverse such topics despite their ignoble vocation finds its roots in the heritage of their (and our own) shared experiences; and, as Nussbaum notes, the search for the good human life invariably includes "joke telling, hospitality, friendship, love itself."

These moments in their fictional representation afford Vincent and Jules with the trappings of verisimilitude, rendering them into fully realized human characters, rather than mere gangland caricatures. In short, we discover ourselves laughing with them while viewing Tarantino's film because—aside from the weapons and drugs that mark their world—many of their thoughts and concerns seem not so different from our own. According to Jorge Luis Borges, this cognitive phenomenon—*dédoublement,* the process through which we recognize ourselves within the margins of a dramatic presentation—disconcerts us because of its implicit suggestion that we might be characters within someone else's fiction. Tarantino's vision finds its power in the conversations between Jules and Vincent, and with each casual connection we find ourselves caring for the inner lives of those we might ordinarily find reprehensible. For this reason, the conversion from hired killer to man-of-faith that we witness in Jules, contrasted with Vincent's unwillingness to invest in any relationship or activity that fails to satisfy his own desires, impacts us even more profoundly. At the same time, we empathize with Vincent and his id-driven desires for personal satisfaction and pleasure. Although we might recoil from the chilling scene in which the smiling, drugged Vincent drives through the darkness on his way to meet Mia Wallace (Uma Thurman), his sudden death later in the film still possesses the power to shock and sadden us. As Lane notes, despite his narcissistic behavior, Vincent nevertheless "reminds us of the pleasures of inactivity, the deep need to hang out"—moments evinced by "the rather endearing shots of him sitting on the toilet reading *Modesty Blaise*."

While Vincent possesses considerable on-screen charm in ***Pulp Fiction,*** his abiding narcissism in fact precludes his ability to experience sustained human relationships without the benefit and security of emotional distance. In *Tales of Love,* Julia Kristeva contends "that the narcissist . . . is precisely someone incapable of love"; and for this reason, in ***Pulp Fiction*** Vincent must irrevocably reposition the mirror in an effort to reflect his own needs, deflect the desires of others, and gaze fully upon his own image. The emotional distance that Vincent's narcissist fosters inevitably problematizes his ability to foment human interconnection, as demonstrated by Tarantino's depictions of Vincent's behavior in interpersonal relationships. In short, Vincent lacks the "desire for community" of which Siebers speaks. In the first of the film's three interwoven, achronological stories, "Vincent Vega and Marsellus Wallace's Wife," Vincent engages in friendly banter with his drug-dealer friend Lance (Eric Stoltz), yet their conversation never truly moves beyond the explicit reason for their meeting—a drug transaction to satisfy the cravings of Vincent's addiction. The pride that motivates Vincent's narcissistic behavior permeates the entire scene with Lance, as revealed by the bravado that Vincent evidences in his blustery descriptions of the European drug trade—"Remember, I just got back from Amsterdam"—and in his later, caustic remarks about the revenge that he imagines for the vandal who damaged his prized Chevrolet Malibu: "I just wish I caught em doing it, ya know? Oh man, I'd give anything to catch em doing it. It'a been worth him doing it, if I coulda just caught em, you know what I mean?"

Vincent undertakes a transaction of another sort in his dealings with Mia, the wife of his mob superior, Marsellus Wallace (Ving Rhames). When the mob boss travels to Florida on business, he orders Vincent to spend an evening with his wife during his absence. Vincent's principal concerns during his evening with Mia find their roots in his instinctive proclivities for satisfying his personal desires and ensuring his self-preservation. During their visit to the nostalgic 1950s-style restaurant, Jackrabbit Slim's, Mia and Vincent amuse themselves with the same brand of playful banter that characterizes all of Vincent's relationships. As the evening unfolds, the "couple" share a contest-winning dance and Mia penultimately invites Vincent in for a night-cap. The deliberately unhurried pace of their "date" allows Tarantino to infuse the scene with the archetypal cinematic expectation—for both the characters and for the audience—of sex. While Mia glides in the living room to the strains of Urge Overkill's acerbic version of Neil Diamond's "Girl, You'll Be a Woman Soon," Vincent retires to the bathroom for an anxious moment of ethical reflection. Literally staring at his own image in the bathroom mirror, he reminds himself of the inherent dangers awaiting him in the other room:

> One drink and leave. Don't be rude, but drink your drink quickly, say goodbye, walk out the door, get in your car, and go down the road. It's a moral test of yourself, whether or not you can maintain loyalty. Because when people are loyal to each other, that's very meaningful. So you're gonna go out there, drink your drink, say "Goodnight, I've had a very lovely evening," go home, and jack off. And that's all you're gonna do.

Despite his comments about the "meaningful" nature of fidelity and friendship, Vincent's loyalty finds its motivation not in his affection and esteem for Marsellus, but in his fears about the mob boss's possible retaliation for such a personal indiscretion.

As if to over-dramatize Vincent's narcissism, Tarantino concludes their "date" with Mia's accidental heroin overdose—an incident that requires Vincent to save her life (and his own) by stabbing Mia in the heart with an injection of adrenaline at the home of his drug dealer—rather than with the anticipated sexual encounter. At no time during this scene are we convinced that Vincent's manic drive to save Mia's life represents anything more than his interest in self-preservation. In fact, when he calls Lance on his cellular phone his initial comments concern his own perilous dilemma, rather than Mia's more immediate, tenuous plight: "Lance, this is Vincent, I'm in big fuckin' trouble man, I'm on my way to your place." Later, while attempting to convince the drug dealer to assist him in resurrecting Mia from her drug-induced stupor, Vincent appeals to Lance's own desires for self-preservation: "This fucked-up bitch is Marsellus Wallace's wife. Now if she fuckin' croaks on me, I'm a grease spot. But before he turns me into a bar [of] soap, I'm gonna be forced to tell'im about how you coulda saved her life, but instead you let her die on your front lawn."

In contrast to Vincent's over-arching, ethically fractured drive for self- preservation, Butch's moral sensibilities emanate from his fidelity and respect for his late father, his genuine affection for his girlfriend, Fabienne (Maria de Medeiros), and the humanity that he discovers within himself when confronted with the power to decide the fate of his mortal enemy. In ***Pulp Fiction***'s second tale, "The Gold Watch," Tarantino constructs an elaborate flashback—delivered in a protracted monologue by Captain Koons (Christopher Walken)—to reveal both the way that Butch, as a five-year-old, learns about the strange history of his family's most sacred heirloom, a gold wristwatch, as well as to underscore the roots of Butch's undying loyalty to his father's memory. Koons relates to Butch the inordinate difficulties that three generations of Coolidge men, as well as Koons himself, endured in successive wars in order to preserve the watch for their descendants. Played to deadpan comic relief, but essential for Butch's understanding of his precursors' remarkable physical sacrifices in his family's name, Koons divulges the method of rectal transport necessary to return the watch to Butch from Vietnam.

A professional boxer by trade, Butch's devotion to his family's name endures a moral test *sans pareil* after Butch agrees to throw a boxing match at the behest of Marsellus. Although Butch diverges from their agreement and wins the fight—literally killing his opponent in the process—before he and Fabienne can escape from Marsellus's henchmen and establish a new life together in a remote locale, Butch discovers that Fabienne has mistakenly left his father's watch in their old apartment. After Butch erupts in a fury of anger at Fabienne's forgetfulness, he tells his frightened girlfriend, "Fabienne, that was my father's fuckin' watch. You know what my father went through to get me that watch? I don't want to get into to it right now but he went through a lot." Upon discerning her fear, Butch attempts to comfort Fabienne after he determines that such odious behavior—"too crudely unloving and self-absorbed," in Nussbaum's words—diverges from the genuine compassion and love that he feels for her. Thus, he assumes responsibility for the incident: "If you did leave it at the apartment, it's not your fault. I had you bring a bunch of stuff. I reminded you about it, but I didn't illustrate how personal the watch was to me. If all I gave a fuck about was my watch, I should've told you. You're not a mind reader." Determined to retrieve his father's watch, Butch—making the ultimate sacrifice that love demands—risks his life in a daring attempt to preserve his family's legacy. While Butch safely recovers the watch from the apartment—and, in the process of making his escape, kills Vincent with the gangster's own machine gun—he confronts his most challenging ethical test when he must decide whether or not to spare Marsellus from sodomy and certain death at the hands of two hillbilly sadomasochists. Although he had intended to kill Marsellus himself only moments before, as Tarantino writes in his screenplay for ***Pulp Fiction,*** "Butch decides for the life of him, he can't leave anybody in a situation like that." He simply cannot abandon his community.

Like Butch's, Jules's metamorphosis leads to spiritual redemption, and, ultimately—after accepting the possibility of miracles in a postmodern world—to his disavowal of "the life." Remarkably, Whalen describes the landscape of ***Pulp Fiction*** as "a cartoon world, two-dimensional characters in a two-dimensional universe," while comparing Jules's metamorphosis unfavorably with the metaphysical dimensions of Wile E. Coyote's cartoon experience, which, Whalen claims, possesses "more conflict (and truth and meaning)." Yet Whalen neglects to consider the fact that in the film's final tale, "The Bonnie Situation," Tarantino devotes particular narrative attention to Jules's spiritual awakening, his protracted and difficult struggle to understand the veracity of his own rebirth. Jules's dramatic conversion occurs while he and Vincent carry out a professional hit for Marsellus; before they complete their errand, however, one of their targets ambushes the gangsters and empties his gun in their direction. Miraculously, they remain unscathed. Although their survival astonishes both men, Vincent refuses to acknowledge the event as anything more than a freak occurrence, while Jules views it as the product of divine intervention: "If you wanna play blind man, then go walk with a Shepherd," Jules remarks to his skeptical partner, "But me, my eyes are wide fuckin' open." Because Jules embraces the providential nature of their good fortune, he tells Vincent that he intends to retire from their iniquitous profession. In this manner, he undergoes a "cataleptic impression"—a cognitive, philosophical phenomenon that, according to Nussbaum, "has the power, just through its own felt quality, to drag us to assent, to convince us that things could not be otherwise. It is defined as a mark or impress upon the soul." For Jules, things can simply never be the same again.

After such revelations, according to Nussbaum, ethical figures discover "the feeling that the other life would just not be comprehensible as a life for a human being with human virtues and human heroism." In this way, Jules realizes that he must instead quest for some other life beyond the underworld in order to test and make use of his new, transformed value system. At breakfast later that morning, Jules and Vincent pursue a philosophical debate unusual for a film of this nature, but apropos of the kind of narrative that Tarantino wishes to achieve in order to highlight, through dislocation, Jules's complex and mysterious conversion. Jules understands the power of the miracle that he witnesses because, unlike the insular, self-motivated Vincent, he possesses the ethical faculties to heed—indeed, to "listen" to—the transformational power of their experience. As Booth notes, in such an instance the "quality of life in the moment of 'listening' is not what it would have been if we had not listened." Jules's recognition of the miracle, then, like the cognitive power that enables him to enjoy his cataleptic impression, affords him a "moment of clarity": virtually unavailable to the ethically vacant and emotionally deaf Vincent. As Jules remarks to Vincent, "It could be God stopped the bullets, he changed Coke into Pepsi, he found my fuckin' car keys. You don't judge shit like this based on merit. Whether or not what we experienced was an according-to-Hoyle-miracle is insignificant. What is significant is I felt God's touch. God got involved." But for all his self-assurance that God indeed became involved, Jules himself remains perplexed about the nature of his calling.

For this reason, Jules engages in the act of what Miller refers to as the "ethics of reading." "At such moments," Miller writes, "an author turns back on himself, so to speak, turns back on a text he or she has written, re-reads it." As the de facto author of his own life, Jules reflects upon his past experience as text, attempting to interpret its meaning before his conversion, while seeking to decipher the text that has yet to be written. But the abrasive and unsettling terrain of ***Pulp Fiction*** does not allow Jules the opportunity for the ease of quiet, personal reflection, When the restaurant robbery—concocted spontaneously by Pumpkin (Tim Roth) and Honey Bunny (Amanda Plummer)—interrupts his contemplation, Jules thwarts their plans by holding Pumpkin at gun point: "Now this is the situation," he tells the amateur thieves. "Normally both of your asses would be dead as fuckin' fried chicken. But you happened to pull this shit while I'm in a transitional period." Before releasing the thieves, Jules reflects upon—indeed, "re-reads"—the text of Ezekiel 25:17, a passage that he appropriated during his gangster days as a trademark conclusion to his professional hits:

> The path of the righteous man is beset on all sides by the inequities of the selfish and the tyranny of evil men. Blessed is he who, in the name of charity and goodwill, shepherds the weak through the valley of the darkness. For he is truly his brother's keeper and the finder of lost children. And I will strike down upon thee with great vengeance and furious anger those who attempt to poison and destroy my brothers. And you will know I am the Lord when I lay my vengeance upon you.

Previously employing the passage as a means for delivering death, after the advent of his conversion Jules reinterprets the passage and discovers the horrible truth about his past existence. For the first time, Jules realizes the value of human life, and his own ability to sustain it. "The truth is you're the weak. And I'm the tyranny of evil men," he tells the thieves. "But I'm tryin'. I'm tryin' real hard to be the shepherd."

The redemptive act of re-reading the text of his life, then, allows Jules to glimpse for the first time the prospects of faith, hope, and love—possibilities that the stasis of his past life, in its devotion to death, could never offer. As Jules unveils his intentions to leave "the life," Vincent recoils in horror at the mere notion of existence without the comfort of material possessions: "Jules, you're gonna be like those pieces of shit out there who beg for change. They walk around like a bunch of fuckin' zombies, they sleep in garbage bins, they eat what I throw away, and dogs piss on 'em. They got a word for 'em, they're called bums. And without a job, residence, or legal tender, that's what you're gonna be—a fuckin' bum!" Yet Jules finds solemnity in his decision. He will simply walk the earth—"You know, like Cain in Kung Fu. Just walk from town to town, meet people, get in adventures"—and, although he pledges himself to the promise of spiritual redemption, he realizes nevertheless that such a commitment necessitates faith in the intensity of his cataleptic impression, and in the unknowable ways of God: "If it takes forever, I'll wait forever," he tells Vincent. In this way, Tarantino establishes Jules as the moral center of his film, and, for this reason, ***Pulp Fiction***'s achronological narrative takes on greater ethical force when Jules spares Pumpkin and Honey Bunny in the film's final moments. If the thieves confront Jules in the film's opening sequence, before he experiences divine intervention, they would surely meet with his wrathful, original reading of Ezekiel 25:17. Instead, Tarantino offers Jules's act of contrition, his desire to shepherd the weak. By sparing the lives of the thieves, Jules sustains the life of the community. The power of Jules's metamorphosis lies in the risk that faith demands and his discovery of what Nussbaum calls the "various and powerful" forces of love, "forces making for danger, the urgent need for protection and self-sufficiency, the opposite and equal need for joy and communication and connection." Beyond the hazy lens of Tarantino's deliberately dark gangland tableau—beyond the greed, drugs, and gun blasts that Whalen so laments—***Pulp Fiction*** proffers a fictional universe where miracles still happen, where love can still make a difference.

Peter Travers (review date 22 January 1998)

SOURCE: "Return of a Foxy Mama," in *Rolling Stone,* January 22, 1998, pp. 61-2.

[*In the following review, Travers offers high praise for* Jackie Brown.]

Sorry to disappoint those who longed to see Quentin Tarantino fall on his famously flashy ass, but the overlong, overindulgent ***Jackie Brown***—the Q man's first feature as a writer and director since ***Pulp Fiction,*** in 1994—scores a knockout just the same. Loaded with action, laughs, smart dialogue and potent performances, ***Jackie Brown*** is most memorable for its unexpected feeling. Tarantino adapts Elmore Leonard's 1992 crime novel, *Rum Punch,* without losing the author's compassion for compromised characters who defy the reduced options that come with age.

What's this—the graying of ***Reservoir Dogs,*** raunch tinged with rue? A little bit. But before you get medieval on Tarantino's ass, consider the insinuating premise: Jackie Burke, the book's white stewardess, is now Jackie Brown and played by that icon of'70s blaxploitation films, Pam Grier (*Coffy, Foxy Brown, Sheba Baby*). Tarantino was just 10 years old back in 1973 when Grier, now 48, played Coffy, a nurse at war with the drug lords who hooked her 11-year-old sister on smack. Coffy seduces one drooling pusher by letting her breasts slip alluringly from her blouse; she then blows his head off with a shotgun.

Moments like these clearly had a profound effect on young Quentin. His affection for Grier, and the maverick spirit she brought to films most critics wrote off as gory junk, fill every frame. Jackie is still a looker, but a low-paying job flying shuttles between Los Angeles and Mexico has removed some of her sparkle. Things turn for the worse when the LAPD and ATF agent Ray Nicolet (a twitchy Michael Keaton) arrest Jackie for smuggling in money and a bag of cocaine for gunrunner Ordell Robbie (Samuel L. Jackson).

And where is Ordell when his courier is facing prison? He's in the apartment of stoner Melanie Ralston (Bridget Fonda), a past-her-prime surfer girl who gives Ordell attitude for showing chicks-with-guns videos to ex-con Louis Gara (Robert De Niro). Of the virtues of the AK-47, Ordell tells dimbulb Louis, "When you absolutely, positively gotta kill every muthafucker in the room, accept no substitute." Ordell won't accept Jackie sitting in jail, so he arranges for bail bondsman Max Cherry (Robert Forster) to spring her. That way Ordell can kill Jackie before she rats on him to the feds to save her ass.

Tarantino lets these characters play out their destinies against an atmosphere of seductive B-movie sleaze that is deftly evoked in the cinematography of Guillermo Navaro. Jackson is perfection, combining charm and menace with uncanny brilliance. And Fonda keeps springing surprises. Playing bad liberates her. Tarantino, the screen's leading foot fetishist since the death of Luis Buñuel, has Melanie wiggle her toes to entice Louis. "Wanna fuck?" she asks. "Sure," he says, THREE MINUTES LATER, a title card announces, and they're done. De Niro's performance is one finely calibrated slow burn as Louis withers under Melanie's sarcasm. "How'd you ever rob a bank, Lou-*is*?" she says, putting a hiss in that final syllable each time she says his name, which causes Lou-*is* to blow.

The glory of the film resides in the unlikely romance between Jackie and Max. He hears music when he first sees her—it's '70s soul, of course. And she introduces him to the Delfonics. "How do you feel about getting old?" Jackie asks Max, who admits he bought a wig when his hair started to fall out. "My ass ain't the same," Jackie grudgingly confesses. "Bigger?" asks Max, smiling. "Nothin' wrong with that."

Forster (*Medium Cool,* TV's *Banyon*) broke into movies in 1967 as an object of lust for both Elizabeth Taylor and Marlon Brando in *Reflections in a Golden Eye.* Now, at 56, he brings off a personal triumph as a hard case stirring long-buried emotions. Is Jackie using Max in an elaborate scheme to steal $500,000 from Ordell—Tarantino stages the sting in a shopping mall and milks the money exchange for maximum suspense—or is it true love? Max is afraid to look too closely, which gives Forster's scenes with Grier a heartbreaking intensity.

And Grier, a babe for the ages, is a sensation. Jackie can press a gun to Ordell's dick and stare down a cop with the same icy cool. "Are you afraid of me?" Jackie asks Max. "A little bit," he answers. Jackie is scared, too. Driving toward a new life she can't define, Jackie sings along with Bobby Womack's "Across 110th Street" on the car radio. It's a '70s song about busting out of ghettos. Tarantino knows that drill. In this transitional film, he acknowledges his debt to the elegant crime fiction of Elmore Leonard and the crude vitality of blaxploitation. For Tarantino and his protagonist, ***Jackie Brown*** crackles with the fear and exhilaration of moving on.

FURTHER READING

Criticism

Bowman, James. "On the Q.T." *American Spectator* 29, No. 11 (November 1996): 72-3.

Discusses Tarantino's negative influence on other filmmakers.

Denby, David. "The Good Enough Mother." *New York* (20 September 1993): 64-5.

A negative review of *True Romance.*

Gallafent, Edward. "Geek Makes Good." *Times Literary Supplement* (16 February 1996): 21.

Discusses Tarantino's films and career through review of Wensley Clarkson's *Quentin Tarantino: Shooting From the Hip,* Jami Bernard's *Quentin Tarantino: The Man and His Movies,* and Jeff Dawson's *Tarantino: The Inside Story.*

Lyons, Donald. "Scumbags." *Film Comment* 28, No. 6 (November-December 1992): 8-9.

Discusses *Reservoir Dogs* and Harvey Keitel's role in the movie.

Additional coverage of Tarantino's life and career is contained in the following source published by Gale: *Contemporary Authors*, Vol. 171.

James Thurber
1894-1961

(Full name James Grover Thurber) American dramatist, essayist, short story writer, cartoonist, illustrator, memoirist, and author of children's fiction.

The following entry presents an overview of Thurber's career through 1994. For further information on his life and works, see *CLC,* Volumes 5, 11, 25.

INTRODUCTION

One of the most popular and respected humorists of the twentieth century, James Thurber was often called the Mark Twain of his era. Among his admirers were Ernest Hemingway and T. S. Eliot. Along with E. B. White, Robert Benchley, and other writers under the tutelage of *New Yorker* editor Harold Ross, Thurber set the standard for sophisticated humor and prose style for a generation of American readers and writers. His stories, essays, and drawings combine the mundane and the absurd to create characters and situations at once strange and familiar that continue to fascinate and amuse his audience.

Biographical Information

Thurber was born in Columbus, Ohio, in 1894, the second son of Charles and Mary Fisher Thurber. His parents, a not very successful father and strong-willed mother provide the apparent models for the "Little Man" and the domineering woman characters that populate much of his writing. As a youth, Thurber suffered a severe eye injury while playing a game of William Tell with his older brother. This accidental blinding in one eye is believed to have contributed to the gradual loss of sight in the other eye, and Thurber was completely blind by 1951. A good student and writer for his high school newspaper and literary and humor magazines at Ohio State University, Thurber nonetheless struggled in college, taking a year off in 1914-15 and leaving without a degree in 1918. Excluded from military service by his blindness, Thurber worked as a code clerk for the U. S. State Department in Washington and then at the U. S. Embassy in Paris. Upon his return to Columbus in 1920, Thurber became a reporter for the *Columbus Dispatch.* In 1922, he married Althea Adams. His only child, Rosemary, was born in 1931. During the mid-1920s, Thurber began writing humorous fiction in his spare time. In 1925, he took a position as a rewrite man for the Paris edition of *The Chicago Tribune.* Returning to New York in 1926, he worked for the *New York Evening Post* and continued his freelance writing. The following year he met E. B. White, who landed him a job on the fledgling *New Yorker* magazine. Thurber left the *New Yorker* in 1933, but continued to be a regular contributor to the magazine until his death in 1961.

Major Works

Thurber and the *New Yorker* were perfectly suited to each other, and his "Talk of the Town" column soon made him a celebrity. He and White collaborated on *Is Sex Necessary?* in 1929. His short, humorous pieces from unusual perspectives provided the material for *The Owl in the Attic* (1931), *The Seal in the Bedroom* (1932), and *My Life and Hard Times* (1933). These works gave him a solid and enthusiastic audience, and he left the *New Yorker* in 1933. After half a dozen collections of stories, essays, and drawings, and a successful play–*The Male Animal* (1940), written in collaboration with his college friend Elliot Nugent—Thurber turned to children's books, publishing *Many Moons* (1943), *The Great Quillow* (1944), *The White Deer* (1945), *The Thirteen Clocks* (1950), and *The Wonderful O* (1957) while also producing seven collections of stories, essays, drawings, and fables for his loyal adult audience. Thurber's most famous story, "The Secret Life of Walter Mitty," appeared in *My World—and Welcome to It* (1942), along with another popular story, "The Catbird Seat." Thurber's own favorite, and that of his long-time friend White, was the decidedly serious reflection on the human penchant for war—*The Last Flower: A Parable in Pictures* (1939).

Critical Reception

Since its earliest appearance, Thurber's work has been highly acclaimed. Critics have appreciated his precise, fluid style, his apt phrasing, and the understated caricatures in his drawings. Hemingway called him the best writer in America, and T. S. Eliot thought his works would endure as "documents of his age." Though his writing style and type of humor has become somewhat dated, his early essays, his "casual" pieces, and the drawings from his years at the *New Yorker* continue to delight and provoke readers and critics alike. In recent years, some observers have pointed out the misanthropy and bitterness of many of his characterizations and the personal unhappiness of his final years. However, Robert D. Arner calls Thurber's art an accurate documenting of the Depression era. To prove his point, Arner quotes author E. B. White: "it [Thurber's work] is not merely a criticism of manners . . . but something more profound. His writings and also his illustrations are capable of surviving the immediate environment and time out of which they spring. To some extent, they will be a document of the age they belong to."

PRINCIPAL WORKS

Is Sex Necessary?; Or, Why You Feel the Way You Do [with E. B. White] (essays) 1929
The Owl in the Attic and Other Perplexities (essays) 1931
The Seal in the Bedroom and Other Predicaments (essays, drawings) 1932
My Life and Hard Times (memoir) 1933
The Middle-Aged Man on the Flying Trapeze (essays) 1935
Let Your Mind Alone! and Other More or Less Inspirational Pieces (essays) 1937
The Last Flower: A Parable in Pictures (fable, drawings) 1939
Fables for Our Times and Famous Poems Illustrated (fables, drawings) 1940
The Male Animal [with Elliot Nugent] (drama) 1940
My World–and Welcome to It (short stories, drawings) 1942
Men, Women and Dogs (short stories, drawings) 1943
Many Moons (fairy tale, drawings) 1943
The Great Quillow (fairy tale, drawings) 1944
The Thurber Carnival (essays, short stories, drawings) 1945
The White Deer (fairy tale, drawings) 1945
The Beast in Me and Other Animals (essays, drawings) 1948
The Thirteen Clocks (fairy tale, drawings) 1950
The Thurber Album (reminiscences, drawings) 1952
Thurber Country (reminiscences, sketches, drawings) 1953
Thurber's Dogs (essays, short stories, drawings) 1955
Further Fables for Our Time (fables, drawings) 1956
The Wonderful O (fairy tale, drawings) 1957
Lanterns and Lances (essays) 1961
Credos and Curios (essays, sketches, reminiscences) 1962
A Thurber Carnival (essays, short stories, drawings) 1962
Thurber and Company (essays, drawings) 1966
Selected Letters of James Thurber (letters) 1981
The Night the Ghost Got In (short stories) 1983
Collecting Himself (essays, short stories, drawings) 1990

CRITICISM

Nathaniel Benchley (review date 25 November 1962)

SOURCE: "If There Is No Human Comedy, It Will Be Necessary to Create One," in *New York Herald Tribune Books,* November 25, 1962, p. 3.

[*The following positive review considers Thurber's* Credos and Curios *in relation to the author's whole body of work.*]

Reviewing a book by James Thurber is something like describing the Taj Mahal; what can possibly be said that hasn't been said before? His twenty-fifth book is a collection of some of his last pieces and some not so recent, and it demonstrates, as though the point hadn't already been made, the wide range of Thurber's subjects and moods. There is none of the wild comedy of the early, or ***My Life and Hard Times,*** Thurber, nor any of the quick satire of the ***Fables for Our Time***; this book shows the brooding, sometimes bitter Thurber, alternating with flashes of warmth and sentiment that are all the more welcome for being unexpected.

The things that troubled Thurber were well worth brooding about, such as bigotry, Babbittry, and the decline of humor, to say nothing of the future of mankind and the cult of burgeoning stupidity. These he attacked in a number of ways, sometimes in the short-story form, sometimes in parable, and sometimes in the form of a two-man monologue (or, if you prefer, a one-man dialogue) in which he and a straight man discussed a subject from as many angles as possible, in the end leaving it torn and bloody on the rug. In one piece, called **"The Future, If Any, of Comedy, or, Where Do We Go From Here?"** he said: "I even remember when we wrote about the bright human spectacle, and the human comedy. If there is no human comedy, it will be necessary to create one. How long can the needle of the human gramophone stay in the rut of *Angst* without wearing out and ending in the repetition of a ghoulish gibbering? . . . Life at the moment is a tale told in an idiom, full of unsoundness and fury, signifying nonism." And if there was anything that Thurber hated (and there were several things) it was nonism.

On the other hand, there are seven pieces about friends or acquaintances: Mary Petty, E. B. White, Elliott Nugent, Robert Benchley, F. Scott Fitzgerald, George S. Kaufman, and John McNulty. They are all written about people he admired, and the warmth that glows through the McNulty piece makes a fond and fitting conclusion to the book. Describing his friend, he said, "He was small, I guess, measured by physical height and weight, but I have a tendency to look up when I think of him, for to me he was nine feet tall. That was the stature, at any rate, of his unflagging comic spirit. . . . There was nothing of the literary elf about McNulty, who once said to me, 'Only people with Vincent for a middle name write about leprechauns.'" And he quotes the last letter McNulty wrote him, a one-sentence message shortly before McNulty's death saying simply: "I think that maybe threescore years and ten is subject to change without notice."

All of the pieces, both the bitter and the gentle, have one thing in common, and that is Thurber's love and mastery of words. Thurber could juggle words like a circus acrobat, flinging them high in the air, bouncing them off similar and dissimilar words, breaking them up into their component parts and juggling *them* for a while, then reassembling them all into a sentence or paragraph that sang like a brook. His similes were incomparable ("He is as menacing as a flung knife." "Falling back on journalism is like falling back full-length on a chest of carpenter's tools"), and his ear for the sound of a sentence was flawless, as when he described *Ross* as "a Borglum figure out of the deep tangled wildwood of the Far West, a brilliant and restless man of distinguished profanity and articulate gesture." He could make words do anything he wanted (who else could write a book without using the letter "O"?) and what he wanted was nothing but the best.

Frank Getlein (review date 22 December 1962)

SOURCE: "Thurber's Last Collection," in *The New Republic,* Vol. December 22, 1962, pp. 24-5.

[*In the following review the critic deems that Thurber's posthumously published essays and sketches in* Credos and Curios *are a representative summary of Thurber's career.*]

My introduction to graduate studies consisted, in part, of a mournful account, by a seminar director, of how the next of kin of practically all literary figures were permitted to lay ignorant hands on whatever papers were lying about and, even more unthinkably, were permitted to throw them into the trash barrel or the fireplace in the name of cleaning the place up for the realtor. The seminar director felt, very strongly, that law should protect all papers for the eventual arrival of the graduate student to count, collate, and publish what in his lifetime the subject himself had not published.

On the other hand, I know a lady in Milwaukee who has a long-standing agreement with her next-door neighbor: whichever of them dies first, the other is pledged to rush into the house, empty the bureaus and desks, and burn everything.

Both attitudes have been evoked by the posthumous publication of Thurber's last collection of short pieces with a foreword by Mrs. Thurber, which at first gives the impression of being a conventional memorial. The fact, however, seems to be that ***Credos and Curios*** was planned, and titled, by Thurber himself and is not a sweeping up of manuscripts left lying around. Moreover, all of the 21 pieces were previously published in a wide variety of magazines or books. The present selection is his own and clearly represents an assembled statement he felt worth repeating.

"Credos" in the title is an alarming word and it may have been the cause for the alarm some reviewers have expressed about the book. In the last decade of his life Thurber's gloomy pronouncements about modern times caused a lot of people to sigh for the carefree life in old Ohio, where football players were transported to the state university on scholarships, where electricity was thought to leak from empty light sockets, and where a memorable Thurber uncle was cut down in his prime by the Dutch Elm disease.

Thurber himself suffered the diminishing of faith and the lack of prudence to state publicly that McCarthy, in addition to his other crimes, had pretty well killed comedy. In this Thurber was wrong. He had himself taken on McCarthy—and bested him—a good decade and a half before McCarthy became a menace. There is no single character in the show to correspond directly with the late Senator, but the whole spirit of bumbling evil that is the antagonist of ***The Male Animal*** is the spirit of the times that made McCarthy, incredibly, a formidable figure.

Yet the evidence of the book is not that the Ohio days represent the golden youth of the writer, with gloom and doom closing in with the closing years, or, for that matter, with the closing in of eyesight. On the contrary, the earliest piece in the book, dated 1928, is a lot gloomier than anything that comes from more recent times.

A good part of Thurber's credo is expressed in the form of tributes to his friends—Benchley, McNulty, Elliott Nugent, George S. Kaufman. They all behaved professionally in the way Thurber regarded as ideal. They had the gifts of sharp observation and precise phrasing which he had himself. To a man they were and still are underrated. Thurber was writing for all of them and for himself, though not deliberately, when he wrote, "The heavier critics have underrated Benchley because of his 'short flight,' missing his distinguished contribution to the fine art of comic brevity. He would thank me not to call him an artist, but I think he was an artist who wouldn't give up to it, like a busy housewife fighting the onset of a migraine headache."

Probably the most beautiful of the many beautiful drawings in the book is the one on the jacket, "Thurber and his Circle," which shows the author, arms aloft, talking enthusiastically to a roomful of slumbering men, women, dogs and pictures on the wall. The core of the book seems to be a series of pieces about talk, or of talk. Sometimes they are stories of people talking about talking in one context or another. Throughout the section, Thurber is enchanted by what can be done with words and appalled by what is being done to them by forces as different as television, psychoanalysis—another old opponent, early bested—and the national determination to get to the moon. Or are these topics all that different? Possibly Thurber, at the risk of being denounced as a senile punster, is, besides getting off a steady stream of word-play, seriously defending language itself from the encroachments of barbarian hordes who have in common only their ignorance of language and their easy assumption that they own it.

The Atlantic Monthly (review date December 1962)

SOURCE: "Three of a School," in *The Atlantic Monthly*, Vol. 20, No. 6, December, 1962, pp. 170, 172.

[*In the following brief review, the critic laments that Thurber's* Credos and Curios *is likely his last work.*]

When a writer has entertained us so well for so many years as James Thurber did, it is difficult to pick up his latest book and believe it will be the last, as the posthumous ***Credos and Curios*** may very well be, unless, please God, there is more uncollected Thurber lying around. The loss is all the more painful when we notice that the most recent pieces here collected show that the incomparable humorist retained every bit of brilliance and verve to the very end.

Most of these pieces, I suppose, might be labeled "casuals," though in the literal sense of the word Thurber never wrote anything casual in his life. His style was a product of intense concentration, and few writers of our time could pack more into a single page or paragraph. Much of his comic effect depended upon the ability to bring his entire point of view—really a weird kind of common sense—to bear upon the apparently trivial points his terrier mind could root out of the human confusion around us.

In his last years he turned more and more frequently to pieces of personal reminiscence, like his wonderful memorial to Harold Ross, where the humor became more affectionate than biting. The present volume includes a number of fine personal portraits and tributes: to Robert Benchley, Scott Fitzgerald, E. B. White, and others. The most moving of these—and, fittingly enough, it is placed at the end of the book—is a salute to his dear departed friend John McNulty, which maintains so wonderfully the tone of hail and farewell that one finds oneself wishing Thurber were around to say the last words about himself.

Charles E. May (essay date Fall 1978)

SOURCE: "Christian Parody in Thurber's 'You Could Look It Up,'" in *Studies in Short Fiction*, Vol. 15, No. 4, Fall, 1978, pp. 453-4.

[*This essay views Thurber's baseball short story "You Could Look It Up" as an "ironic, modernized retelling" of a biblical tale.*]

A basic characteristic of James Thurber's short fiction is that many of his stories are ironic treatments of established literary conventions, fables, and tales. Thurber imposes his own brand of satire on the adventure story in **"The Secret Life of Walter Mitty,"** the perfect crime story in **"The Catbird Seat,"** and the American success story in **"The Greatest Man in the World."** ***Fables for Our Time*** represents a sustained effort in the ironic, modernized retelling of ancient stories and tales. Several critics have noted Thurber's technique of transferring the basic plot line of such legends and conventions to a modern milieu and then cluing the reader to what he is doing by scattering puns and allusions to the original story throughout his retelling.

Usually the story behind the story is quite obvious and easily pointed out. However, no one has ever noted this basic Thurber device in his Lardner-like idiomatic baseball story, **"You Could Look It Up,"** where the legend beneath the legend is more subtly embedded. Anthologized in, among several other collections, Warren and Erskin's best-selling *Short Story Masterpieces,* the story has surely been read by enough students and teachers for someone to have spotted the game Thurber is playing here; yet, as far as I can tell, his joke has remained private.

Thurber once said that history and legend are so close in his world that he often walks with one foot in each. Consequently, the reader who tries to follow the repeated suggestions of Doc, the narrator of **"You Could Look It Up,"** and look up the story behind the story might, after failing to find it in history, try legend. An analysis of the plot and central characters of the story as well as the many puns and allusions throughout suggests that Thurber wants us to "look it up" in the New Testament. The story is an Americanized retelling of the scapegoat Christ story. In a country where baseball is the national sport, followed religiously every weekend, the record books of the game might easily parallel the Bible for those true believers who can quote scores and name players the way some preachers can quote scripture.

The plot of the story is quite simple. The manager of a baseball team in a slump signs a midget that no one can pitch to. However, the midget loses an important game by bunting (which, given his size, is the only kind of hit he can get) into an unintentional sacrifice play; his sacrifice and subsequent disappearance bring new spirit into the team. At first glance, this might seem a poor parallel to the coming of Christ whose sacrifice infuses a new spirit into mankind. However, the many puns and allusions throughout the story suggest that this is indeed Thurber's intention. The midget, Pearl du Monville, pops up "outa nowheres," a mysterious freak that the manager Squawks Magrew must touch to find out if he is real. Of no determinate sex ("Most people name of Pearl is girls," says Doc, "but this Pearl du Monville was a man, if you could call a fella a man who was only thirty-four, thirty-five inches high.") and of no determinate age ("He might 'a' been fifteen or he might 'a' been a hundred, you couldn't tell."); Pearl's name suggests who he is.

Pearl is the Pearl of Great Price, a metaphor that many Biblical commentators see as a prefigurative reference to Christ. Furthermore, Pearl is du Monville, that is, of the City of Man. Magrew introduces him as a "monseer," i.e., "man seer," of the "old, old school." Doc's favorite malapropism, repeated several times throughout the story, is "Bethlehem broke loose"; the phrase takes on added significance at the climax of the story when Pearl makes his sacrifice play: "Bethlehem broke loose on that ball field and in them stands. They ain't never been nothin' like it since creation was begun." This broadly comic scene symbolically enjambs both the birth and the death/ascension of Christ, as Pearl toddles toward first base "yelping like a stuck sheep" and Magrew sends him flying high into the air toward center field where the center fielder pulls him down "like he was liftin' a sleeping baby from a cradle."

Just as Christ "fails" in a literal sense while on earth, yet "succeeds" when he sacrifices self and ascends, so does Pearl lose the game, yet, after vanishing "into the thin of the air," truly "win" for the ball club by infusing a "new spirit" into them, thus ending their slump. Thurber's ironic game in this story then is not only to satirize the "golden days of the national pastime," but also to retell within a modern American myth and idiom, the story of the golden days of the Christian religion.

Wes D. Gehring (essay date Winter 1979-80)

SOURCE: "The Comic Anti-Hero in American Fiction: Its First Full Articulation," in *Thalia,* Vol. 2, No. 3, Winter, 1979-80, pp. 11-14.

[*In this essay, Gehring identifies Thurber's work for the* New Yorker *in the 1920s as one of the first instances of a new twentieth-century literary figure, the comic anti-hero.*]

The comic anti-hero, who tries to create order in a world where order is impossible, is the dominant type in American humor today. Terms associated with anti-hero frustrations have entered our vocabulary, from Joseph Heller's "catch-22," from the book by the same name, to Kurt Vonnegut's "and so it goes," from *Slaughterhouse-Five.*

America's favorite cinema clown—Woody Allen—is based on the anti-hero mold, just as America's favorite cartoon character is—Charlie Brown. In today's American literature, the important comedy artists also draw equally from this mold, from Philip Roth and John Barth to the aforementioned Vonnegut and Heller. In fact, a Nobel Prize in literature has recently been given to one of the most distinguished creators of anti-heroes, Saul Bellow.

Credit for the full blossoming of the anti-hero in American humor is usually given to the early *New Yorker* magazine (1925-30s): "The magazine which was more responsible than any other medium for the rise of a new type of humor . . . " More specifically, this meant four writers—Clarence Day, Robert Benchley, James Thurber, and S. D. Perelman. Walter Blair has noted:

> . . . though they did not entirely break with the past—no humorist is likely to do this—they wrote humor based upon assumptions quite different from those of older humorists and employed techniques contrasting with older techniques.

The real significance of the *New Yorker* was that it allowed the American comic-anti-hero to come to center stage. Though he was not new to American humor, few comedy figures ever are, he had generally played a secondary role (when he appeared at all) to the more capable figures of the 19th-century American humor, such as the practical New England Yankee or the crafty frontiersman of the southwest (both capable crackerbarrel figures). A sustained articulation of the contrast between the two types of heroes is to be found in *The Biglow Papers* of James Russell Lowell. These letters juxtapose Yankee Hosea Biglow against anti-heroic Birdofredum Sawin. The complete stupidity of Birdofredum underlines the capabilities of the Yankee Hosea Biglow.

It should also be noted that even the capable 19th century figure—the crackerbarrel type—could sometimes display anti-heroic characteristics. Norris Yates has labeled such case examples of the "wise fool":

> . . . the humorous writers frequently made the country-store philosopher expound unwelcome truths behind a protective mask of character deficiency or of linguistic, logical or factual error . . . Thus Huck Finn notices that the hogs have the run of a certain country church, and he says, "Most folks don't go to church only when they've got to; but a hog is different."

Secondary characters like Birdofredum Sawin or "wise fools," such as Huck Finn, mark 19th century predecessors for the 20th century anti-hero. However, these anti-hero ancestors existed in a comedy world still considered to be rational. Thus, the dominant comedy type continued to be the capable, reasoning crackerbarrel philosopher. Yates implied just that when he noted that " . . . one important difference between them [the crackerbarrel philosophers] and the Little Man [the comic anti-hero] is that the latter is not certain of his identity."

As American comedy tastes began to find an increased affinity with the anti-hero, early in the 20th century, the anti-hero as well as anti-heroic traits became more visible in our comedy culture, from the cartoon strips of George Herriman ("Krazy Kat") and George McManus ("Bringing Up Father") to vaudeville comics like Joe Cook and Ed Wynn. Yet it still remained for the aforementioned *New Yorker* writers to create the first full articulation of the anti-hero.

A close analysis of this *New Yorker* work reveals five distinctive characteristics of the comic anti-hero. Each characteristic also constitutes a break with what was then still the dominant character type in American humor—the capable figure. Particular attention will be paid to the work of Benchley and Thurber, because it best exemplified the anti-hero and because they were most productive during this period.

First, the comic anti-hero of these *New Yorker* writers generally tends to have time on his hands. The use made of this leisure time is probably most often associated with Thurber (thanks to his **"The Secret Life of Walter Mitty"**) and his protagonist's fantasy daydreams of bravery and high adventure. It is the free time fate of this figure to be a "hero" only in dreams:

> . . . Captain Mitty stood up and strapped on his huge Webley-Vickers automatic. "It's forty kilometers through hell, sir," said the sergeant. Mitty finished one last brandy. "After all," he said softly, "what isn't?" The pounding of the cannon increased; there was the rat-tat-tatting of machine guns . . .
>
> Something struck his shoulder. "I've been looking all over this hotel for you," said Mrs. Mitty. "Why do you have to hide in this old chair?"

Secondly, the *New Yorker* anti-hero virtually never seems to have the opportunity or the inclination to foster an interest in politics. His is a non-political but frustrating domestic life, occasionally punctured by an equally frustrating sortie to the store, or a small social gathering. These minor domestic chores must take first priority for him to maintain some hold on reality. This hold, which is slipshod at best, is put at a precarious imbalance by world events and political figures. Thus, when a comic anti-hero makes one of his very rare excursions into the political arena, reality begins to swirl down the drain:

> Mussolini seemed to be a good man to interview; so I got an interview with him. "Mr. Mussolini," I said, "as I understand your theory of government, while it is not without its Greek foundations, it dates even farther back, in its essence to the Assyrian system."
>
> "What?" asked Mussolini.
>
> "I said, as I understand your theory of government, while it is not without its Greek foundations, it dates even farther back to the ancient Assyrian system. Am I right?"
>
> "Assyrian here seen Kelly? K-E-double-L-Y. That was a good song, too," said Il Duce.

"A good song is right," I replied. "And now might I ask, how did you come by that beard?"

"That is not a beard," replied the Great Man.

"That is my forehead I am smooth shaven, as a matter of fact."

"So you are, so you are," I apologized. "I was forgetting."

We both sat silent for a while, thinking of the old days in Syracuse High.

The third characteristic of the *New Yorker* comic anti-hero is constant frustration. Any attempt to lead a rational life is destined to fail; it is an irrational world for him, and any attempt to bring order to it results in total frustration. The frustrations themselves, however, can be lumped into two main danger areas.

Women represent the first category of these potentially severe frustration spots for the man. The secret to this female power can be found in Thurber's **"Destructive Forces in Life."** Near the beginning of the story he pens a drawing of an unhappy man and smiling wife, entitling it "A Mentally Disciplined Husband with Mentally Undisciplined Wife." This domestic mugshot leads to the sad story of one more frustrated male. But the key at this point is the conclusion of the tale: " . . . the undisciplined mind [that of the woman] runs far less chance of having its purposes thwarted, its plans distorted, its whole scheme and system wrenched out of line. The undisciplined mind, in short, is far better adapted to the confused world in which we live today than the streamlined mind [the disciplined mind—that of the man]. This is, I am afraid, no place for the streamlined mind."

To have an "undisciplined mind" merely means that one can cope with life, make decisions, and proceed with living. This often invites eccentricity in the anti-hero woman. In a sense, this is an offensive maneuver—what better way is there to deal with an irrational world than by being irrational? Probably Thurber's best example of such a woman is his grandma:

> who . . . lived the latter years of her life in the horrible suspicion that electricity was dripping invisibly all over the house. It leaked . . . out of empty sockets if the wall switch had been left on. She would go around screwing in bulbs, and if they lighted up she would hastily and fearfully turn off the wall switch . . . happy in the satisfaction that she had stopped not only a costly but a dangerous leak.

But the point remains that, as eccentric as Grandma Thurber may be, she makes decisions and does things—and then gets on with living. Meanwhile, the male attempts to make sense of it all (both women and the world) and goes near crazy in the process of trying. Moreover, he cannot proceed without understanding and since there is no understanding. . . .

Machinery represents the other category of these potentially severe frustration spots for the comic anti-hero—something Thurber captures quite nicely in a story whose title says it all: **"The Car We Had to Push."** Yet, for the best capsule definition of the dangers of mechanization, one must turn to Perelman's attempt to put together a moth-proof closet known as the Jiffy-Cloz—"The shortest, cheapest method of inducing a nervous breakdown ever perfected."

It should be kept in mind, moreover, that the frustrations of the anti-hero, be they precipitated by females, machines, or other irritants, are often seen in physical terms. As has been the case with earlier American schools of comedy, what is generally funny about the *New Yorker* anti-hero's predicament are descriptions of physical frustration, frequently displayed through physical discomfort. A glance at some typically anti-heroic titles underlines this: "The Dog that Bit People," "The Night the Bed Fell," "The Calf in the Closet," and "How to Break 90 in Croquet." Moreover, this visual sense is accented by the celebrated drawings of Thurber, the delightful caricatures by Gluyas Williams that grace the Benchley stories, and the cartoons of Day.

The fourth characteristic of the *New Yorker's* anti-hero is the fact that he is portrayed as a childlike figure. This is most effectively shown in the eight stories comprising **"Part One: Mr. and Mrs. Monroe"** of Thurber's ***The Owl in the Attic***—especially in **"Mr. Monroe and the Moving Men."** In this story, once the wife leaves, the husband is helpless. This helplessness occurs despite the fact that before she left" . . . little Mrs. Monroe had led her husband from room to room, pointing out what was to go into storage and what was to be sent to the summer place . . . " But now, "little Mrs. Monroe was away, unavoidably away, terrifyingly away," and he cannot remember where things should go and what she had said. And he certainly has no ready answers for the moving men's questions. The names they use to address him progressively indicate a loss of respect for him, and range from "chief" and "mister," to "buddy" and "pardner," to the child nickname of "sonny." By the end of the story, he is reduced to tears.

The fifth and final characteristic is that the anti-hero is an urban dwelling animal. In fact, the *New Yorker* was founded literally on an attack against the old value system—as a "magazine which is not edited for the old lady in Dubuque

. . . a magazine avowedly published for a metropolitan audience . . ." Thus, the *New Yorker* focuses on the city. Yet, what is written about metropolitan living hardly constitutes a love letter.

The trials of city living are nicely sketched by Benchley. He has a poor sense of direction and the complex modern city only compounds this—in "Spying on the Vehicular Tunnel," he becomes lost on a walking tour of the Holland Tunnel. When he attempts to leave the driving to someone else (especially on formal dress occasions) by taking a taxicab, he invariably enters a musty vehicle that more closely resembles " . . . the old sleigh which used to stand up in the attic at Grandpa's barn in Mullbury" than an automobile. Moreover, there are so many people squeezed into the city that he must stand in long lines for everything. For Benchley, this is best exemplified by the post office—"It has been estimated that six-tenths of the population of the United States spend their entire lives standing in line in a post office."

Ironically, despite the fact that the *New Yorker* anti-hero is based in the city, he is a loner, either playing by himself or hiding. The city is full of eccentric people and he wants to avoid them. Yet, despite the fact that he avoids them, and possibly *because* he avoids them, his behavior also takes on something of an eccentric nature. For Benchley's hero this eccentricity might be diagnosed as seeing little animals, while Thurber's has a tendency to hide in boxes or let his mind wander a bit too far. Despite the fact that these visions become plausible when explained as merely momentary harmless regressions to childhood or as typical fleeting daydreams, they are dangerous if too much time is spent in these *nether* conditions, for they might lead the hero to be institutionalized. Thus, like Thurber's **"A Unicorn in the Garden"** (where a wife tries to get her husband committed for seeing this mythical animal, but is committed herself), the anti-hero must be careful to whom he relates these phobias.

These, then, are the five main characteristics of the *New Yorker* comic anti-hero. Though each one was not necessarily new to American humor, as a group they represented a distinct break with the more traditional (and capable) figure of American humor, such as the Yankee crackerbarrel philosopher. There is no easy explanation as to why the transition, from capable hero to incompetent, has taken place. Yet, if a consensus were necessary, it would no doubt focus on Wylie Sypher's statement: "The comic now is more relevant, or at least more accessible, than the tragic."

In a world that seems every day more irrational, the anti-hero is fated to be forever frustrated. He is frustrated because he tries to create order (as his 19th century comedy counterparts did) in a world where order is impossible. But the scope of today's crises goes beyond the common-sense platitudes of any updated crackerbarrel philosopher. The anti-hero is " . . . incapable of inventing homespun maxims about hundred-megaton bombs, or of feeling any native self-confidence in the face of uncontrollable fallout." He eventually deals with this frightening outside world by not dealing with it at all. Instead, he focuses: "microscopically upon the individual unit . . . that interior reality—or hysteria . . . In consequence, modern humor deals significantly with frustrating trivia." Thus, the non-political, domestically frustrated anti-hero comes to represent that old cartoon of the ostrich with his head in the sand. Initially the audience laughs at him (instead of with him, as was the case with the capable hero) both with a feeling of *superiority* and with *surprise* (that anyone could be so incompetent)—embracing two classic comedy axioms. Yet, at heart, it is an audience that is only too aware of the closeness, even parallels, existing between the anti-hero's frustrations and their own lives—frustrations that are often mere microcosms of greater fears.

Anti-heroes help us cope (through laughter) with this absurd modern world. where our only good defense seems to be a humor founded in absurdity.

Roderick Nordell (review date 14 December 1981)

SOURCE: "Laughter Improves Everything," in *Christian Science Monitor*, December 14, 1981, pp. B1, B3.

[*This review of* Selected Letters of James Thurber *warmly appreciates the substance of the volume but comments unfavorably on the selection criteria for which letters are included.*]

James Thurber deftly took care of the whole business of collecting authors' letters when he reviewed an imagined volume of his own correspondence. "A certain Groping, to be sure, is discernible," he wrote, "but it doesn't appear to be toward anything." Used as a Foreword to this book of actual Thurber letters, his critique demonstrates in spades the vision of humor that glints through the following pages—a vision undiminished by the impaired eyesight that looms large in the letters but not without an edge of humorous perspective, too.

"Laughter need not be cut out of anything, since it improves everything." Thurber writes. "The power that created the poodle, the platypus, and people has an integrated sense of both comedy and tragedy." He goes on to give an example of taking humor seriously, as all good humorists must, even while fighting the impulse to take themselves too much so.

"[Robert] Benchley once said, 'Only a humorist could take humor apart, and he has too much humor to do it.' Serious definition of a free-lance writer: One who gets paid per word or per piece. Benchley's humorous, hence perfect, definition: 'One who gets paid per word per piece or perhaps.' Which is the more serious, the utterly serious, or the partly humorous?"

Hence, no doubt. Thurber's regard for research, for getting things right as well as funny, When, for instance, he writes his celebrated book about editor Harold Ross and the *New Yorker,* he fusses in letters about not being able to set down everything that he would like to. The letters add to the Thurber legend of hard writing making easy reading, the man whose first drafts "sound twelve years old." whose supple prose is the product of multiple rewrites.

Yet Thurber is, or lets himself appear as human as the characters in his humor. He admits to being depressed when, amid all the lines attributed to *New Yorker* writers, "something of my own, of which I was fond, was never repeated to me by anyone." It was when someone asked him to draw new illustrations for *Alice in Wonderland* and he replied, "I tell you what let's do, let's keep the Tenniel drawings and I'll rewrite the book." He also rather liked the sign he put up at the office when partitions were being constantly changed: "Alterations going on as usual during business."

The word "selected" really means something in the title of this volume. We're left wanting more missives to editor Ross; for instance, who gets fewer pages than Thurber's eye doctor. We wish we could see the omitted letters, of which there were tantalizing glimpses in Burton Bernstein's biography of Thurber. There is a lot of white space in addition to the still incomparable Thurber drawings.

But the selected morsels are often hilarious or touching. Here is the comic technician debating getting extra mileage from cartoons by finding new captions for them. Here is the friend concerned with matters far from the printed page, whether or not the correspondents are writers, too, like Katherine and Andy (E. B.) White.

Thurber admires Sinclair Lewis for being nice to his secretary's elderly mother. He delights in being able to write "that hardest of all things, a letter to a girl six years old" (if only one of those were included!). He defends John O'Hara's small-boyishness, for unless artists "can remember what it was to be a little boy, they are only half complete as artist and as man."

"Every time is a time for humor, especially now," he writes to Andy White in the early 1950s, "because the Communists set out long ago to knock it off, and writing it is doing battle in one small corner of the field."

Thurber's corner has turned out to be not all that small and it is good to have these letters, so congenially edited by Helen Thurber and Edward Weeks, to fill it a little fuller.

David Montrose (review date 5 February 1982)

SOURCE: Review of *Selected Letters of James Thurber,* in *New Statesman,* Vol. 103, No. 2655, February 5, 1982, p. 24.

[*This brief review faults the editors of this volume of letters for their selection criteria, calling the compilation disappointing.*]

Thurber was an inveterate letter writer from college days until his death in 1961. When his appalling eyesight became blindness in 1947, he simply resorted to dictation; even afterwards, friends still received occasional notes in his big scrawl. That the letters provide a valuable biographical source was amply recognised by Burton Bernstein, whose *Thurber* (1975) frequently resembles a collection of letters interspersed with commentary. This being so, devotees of—Twain perhaps excepted—America's greatest humorist will approach this selection with much anticipation, especially as they have waited 15 years since their last fix: the posthumous ***Thurber and Company.*** They are liable to be disappointed.

The editors cannot be blamed for the familiarity of these letters, nearly all of which were included, along with many others in ***Thurber,*** they *can* be blamed for their eccentric selection methods. The earliest letter dates from August 1935, by which time Thurber was 40, had published three books (a fourth appeared later that year), and had already left the *New Yorker.* All very curious until one recalls that Thurber married Helen, his second wife, in July, 1935. So it seems that, for some reason, Mrs Thurber has used her editorial position to eliminate letters predating the marriage.

The selection remains puzzling even if this peculiar arrangement is overlooked. The letters to Harold Ross are drawn exclusively from 1947-49, and there are only five of them: a derisory morsel from a relationship that spanned four decades, from 1927, when Thurber joined the *New Yorker,* until Ross's death in 1951; the two sets of letters to E. B. White are separated by an unexplained 'lost decade': one set is from 1936-39, the other from 1950-61; there are no letters to Elliott Nugent, Thurber's collaborator on ***The Male Animal*** and a friend since their Ohio State days; the editors have deliberately chosen brief letters, despite Thurber's preferences for long rambling missives. Above all, the selection is just too slender—a fragment of a voluminous archive—with little sense of connection or continuity between individual letters. Each letter wastefully begins on a new page, so the book contains many white blanks.

The letters that *are* included are a mixed lot: inconsequential chatter to friends; numerous bulletins on Thurber's eye condition (one section comprises letters to his ophthalmologist); business letters to editors about works-in-progress (a section deals with the composition of his memoir, ***The Years with Ross***); some nice anecdotes and reminiscences. Tactfully, the editors have omitted the 'raving' letters Thurber tended to write during his final years when his mental health—always troubled—was exceptionally fragile.

Selected Letters of James Thurber is, then, an incomplete and unbalanced compilation. Thurberphiles might better look to Bernstein's book, which features a larger and wider selection of letters and enables them to be seen in perspective and in context.

Marilyn Underwood (essay date Summer 1982)

SOURCE: "Thurber's 'The Catbird Seat,'" in *The Explicator,* Vol. 140, No. 4, Summer, 1982, pp. 49-50.

[*In this brief essay, Underwood offers a previously overloooked explanation for the events of Thurber's classic story.*]

Critics of James Thurber's **"The Catbird Seat"** invariably refer to his humorous tone, his control of language, and his effective characterization in this tight-plotting short story. But this is not all; one needs to dig deeper to unearth what devices Thurber uses to make this story the success it is. One device in particular has been overlooked by critics. A biologist would not have been so negligent: he would have looked at the catbird's *seat* and would have seen an instant correlation to the events and characters in Thurber's story.

Anyone who picks up a copy of Peterson's *A Field Guide to the Birds of Texas* (Boston: Houghton Mifflin, 1963) will find on page 182 a description of the catbird. This bird is unobtuse, "skulks in undergrowth," and is hard to rile. However, upon being disturbed, it will come out from the underbrush, where it meshes with its environment because of its drab coloring, and will flare its tail feathers, showing a rusty tuft of seat (or "under tail-coverts") to the cause of its disturbance.

This description is significant to understanding Thurber's short story. Consider who is first "sitting in the catbird's seat" or "sitting pretty"—Mrs. Ulgine Barrows, an upstart, a new-comer, a defiler, an intruder in the territory of Erwin Martin. That her name sounds much like *sparrows* is equally significant. Note the imported sparrow's characteristics: a little gray bird that takes territory away from the domestic bird by "setting in" noisily, eating the seeds of the domestic, and making, literally, a mess of the former domestic bird's habitat. The sparrow, with its conical-shaped short bill, is quick and effective in pecking away the foundations of the former owner's home. Soon only sparrows inhabit the territory, the take-over complete.

Mrs. Ulgine Barrows is "sitting in the catbird's seat," flaunting her tail (if you will) in the face of everyone in the office of F & S. She is an import, having been brought in by Mr. Fitweiler. She "eats the seeds" of the employees at F & S, taking from them the sustenance, the employment that has been theirs for years. Aggressive as an efficiency expert, she has several fired; others just quit. If she is not stopped, the very foundations of F & S will crumble. Mr Martin, astute as he is austere, comprehends this eventuality, but, like the catbird, remains quiet and unobtuse—until she invades his territory.

Consider now Mr. Martin and the connotations inherent in his name. The martin is a member of the swallow family, a small gray bird with long wings, a forked tail, swift and graceful flight. *Swallowtail* is a term for *cutaway,* a man's formal coat with tails. Indeed, it is easy to imagine Mr. Martin clad in a cutaway, as he is precise in nature, impeccable in character, and haughty in his regard for his occupation and position.

Mr. Fitweiler innocently brings Mrs. Barrow to his firm—as if in a *fit* (defined as "a sudden, acute attack" and "a highly emotional reaction") to the F & S *weiler* or *hamlet.* Also innocently, he allows her to quack and bray commands, yell and bawl obscenities, and chip and pick "at the foundation stones" of F & S. Thurber's descriptive terms of Ulgine Barrows are similar to the terms used to describe the calls of yet another bird—the cuckoo-burro—which is distinguished by a raucous, braying, laughing call that approximates the ass for which it is appropriately named (as is apparently Mrs. Barrows).

Barrows' asininity does not concern Mr. Martin, though it bothers him; but her invasion of his territory does, to the extent that he plans his strategy, which he changes at the last minute. Instead of "rubbing her out," he flaunts his tail jauntily by being obnoxious, by exhibition of characteristics not his own. In short, he shows a color heretofore covert. When the deed's done, he very unobtrusively returns to his underbrush, the W20 file, "wearing a look of studious concentration," while his antagonist is removed from the coveted "catbird's seat."

Robert D. Arner (essay date Summer/Fall 1982)

SOURCE: "'The Black, Memorable Year 1929': James Thurber and The Great Depression," in *Studies in American Humor,* Vol. 3, Nos. 2 & 3, Summer/Fall, 1982, pp. 237-52.

[In this essay, Arner discusses the first ten years of Thurber's writing career and his humor's relation to the Depression era.]

The first ten years of James Thurber's career coincide almost exactly with the decade that historians have generally agreed to call the Great Depression, 1929-1939. Although Thurber had been working for and contributing to the *New Yorker* since March of 1927, his first book, a collaboration with E. B. White entitled ***Is Sex Necessary? or Why You Feel the Way You Do,*** did not appear until November 7, 1929, about two weeks after Black Thursday. Other collections of casuals and cartoons followed in quick succession: ***The Owl in the Attic*** (1931), ***The Seal in the Bedroom*** (1932), ***My Life and Hard Times*** (1933), ***The Middle-Aged Man on the Flying Trapeze*** (1935), and ***Let Your Mind Alone!*** (1937). Thurber's final book of that despairing decade, ***The Last Flower*** (1939), appeared shortly after the invasion of Poland on September 1, 1939, and, in its haunting, poignant parable in pictures about the collapse of civilization before the brutal onslaught of war, it clearly reflects the success of Hitler's blitzkrieg and most of the other anxieties of the modern age as well. Together with the pieces that Thurber eventually gathered into **"Fables for Our Time"** in ***Fables for Our Time and Famous Poems Illustrated*** (1940) and that had already begun to appear in the *New Yorker* in 1939, ***The Last Flower*** reveals, among other things, that the humorist could no longer afford to shut his ears "to the ominous rumblings of the dynasties of the world moving toward a cloudier chaos than ever before." As early as 1933, in **"Preface to a Life,"** Thurber had indicated an awareness that playful humor was to be a casualty of the Depression, political collectivization, and fascism—abroad and at home. But this awareness accelerated during the decade.

If Thurber's attentiveness to the world at large had changed during the decade on matters like "the menaces of empire" (***TC,*** 174), on one issue it seems to have remained the same. In the middle 1950s, he was to tell George Plimpton and Max Steele of the *Paris Review* that the Depression had had a permanent impact on American humor, "Much worse than Hitler and the war," but in the writings and cartoons that actually appeared during that time there are at most a scant half dozen direct references to the Depression itself as a woeful fact of American life, and all of these are very brief, with the exception of an uncollected piece entitled **"Mr. Hoover or Mr. Coolidge"** (1932), which spoofs the Republican effort to comprehend the true nature of the economic issues at stake in the upcoming Presidential election. Perhaps his most important acknowledgment of the plight of the nation while the Depression was still the main problem of Americans is the opening line of **"Pythagoras and the Ladder"** in ***Let Your Mind Alone!*** from which I have taken part of the title of this paper. "It was in none other than the black, memorable year 1929," Thurber writes,

> that the indefatigable Professor Walter B. Pitkin rose up with the announcement that "for the first time in the career of mankind happiness is coming within reach of millions of people."

Thurber's irony, it seems to me, aims not only at the disjunction between the historical moment and the glad tidings proclaimed by an accomplished American huckster of happiness, but also at the American's preoccupation with being happy, with happiness as the goal of life, as if in perverse misapplication of the most famous line in the Declaration of Independence. Unhappiness is un-American, we seem to believe, and becoming happy is something in the nature of a patriotic duty for all of us. Thurber's remark also takes in, I believe, most of the politicians of the period, from men like Herbert Hoover, who offered only genial assurances that prosperity was just around the corner, to men like Franklin Roosevelt, whose plan of action Thurber seems generally to have approved but who came to power at the Democratic Convention of 1931 with the premature announcement that happy days were here again. It is not hard to hear in such assertions, at any rate, the familiar ring of an authentically American confidence game.

Thurber's most extended comments on the Depression appear in a piece that could be termed a retrospective, since it was written and published more than a year after Pearl Harbor. Entitled **"The Secret Life of James Thurber"** (1943), this casual takes off from the high price of Salvador Dali's *The Secret Life of Salvador Dali,* which reminds Thurber that his own "autobiography," ***My Life and Hard Times,*** had gone for just $1.75 back in 1933. "The publishers explained," says Thurber,

> that the price was a closely approximated vertical, prefigured on the basis of profitable ceiling, which in turn was arrived at by taking into consideration the effect of diminishing returns of the horizontal factor. (***TC,*** 30)

"In those days," Thurber explicates this explanation, "all heads of business firms adopted a guarded kind of double talk . . . because nobody knew what was going to happen and nobody understood what had . . . [O]ur civilization was in greater danger of being turned off than of gradually crumbling away" (***TC,*** 31). But now, he says, "with the world in ten times as serious condition as it was in 1933" (***TC***, 31), Dali's publishers want six dollars for his life story. His own mistake, Thurber concludes, lay in not baring enough facts of his secret life to justify a higher price.

Thurber's chief mode of participating in the Depression was his running battle with Leftist writers and critics. Given the infrequency and brevity of Thurber's comments on the Depression, together with the *New Yorker*'s unmistakable ambience of affluence with its ads for Packard and Pierce-Arrow, Brooks Brothers and Bonwit Teller, it is small wonder that Leftists viewed his writing with distrust and dismay. Thurber's assessment of the complaint against *New Yorker* writers in general, that "we don't attack communism but we don't go for it, head over heels" (Bernstein, 229), greatly understates the true animosity involved in this particular literary controversy. Certainly it oversimplifies the issues. Like most other modernists, Thurber maintained throughout that he was simply defending art from contamination by life. Art was inescapably autobiographical, to be sure, as he told Malcolm Cowley: "[O]ur own lives must always be the subject for our writings, come what may" (Bernstein, 230). But the achievement of art required distance from life, as he wrote to Max Eastman at about the same time. "Humor," he said, "is a kind of emotional chaos told about calmly and quietly in retrospect." In this version of Wordsworth's dictum, calm and quiet are clearly needed to transmute the raw materials of experience into art. The mistake of the Leftists, in Thurber's opinion, was that they were at once too conscious of being literary people and too involved in politics to practice the patience that art requires. This first point he made, once again, in a letter to Cowley, condemning the contributors to Granville Hick's *Proletarian Literature in the United States* as "a bunch of writers" who speak to each other and not to the worker in a language workers can understand:

> Those writers really want to be writers, making money, laying lovely women and handsome men. . . . [T]hey don't really want to be out suffering with the worker (after all, they remember Waldo Frank and his broken head and that it wasn't the police or the strike-breaker who broke it). (Bernstein, 235)

In a more comic vein, Thurber tried to make his point about the Leftists' use of a language alien to their intended audience in a piece entitled **"What Are the Leftists Saying"** (1937), in which he "defines" for the uninitiated the meaning of terms like "escapism" and the practice of unmasking ideologies. His second point, that the Leftists try to live their lives as though life were literature, is the main theme of **"How to Write a Long Autobiography"** (1937), in which Thurber produces the following sentence from Joseph Freeman's *An American Testament:* "'It was my idealistic, religious, artistic bias which made me blind to pragmatism'" (***LYMA***, 219). "That is the topic sentence of a letter which somehow does not sound like a letter to a friend at all," writes Thurber. "It sounds more like an essay written to save in a file and someday print in a book" (***LYMA***, 219).

> Communist intellectuals are the most facile and articulate of all writers, and words come out of most of them like water from a faucet, so I can't say for sure the letters were rewritten; I just say they sound rewritten. (***LYMA***, 220)

Thurber also wrote another piece, **"Notes for a Proletarian Novel"** (1934), in which he laments the fact that he has no deep knowledge of the plight of the worker and so cannot hope to produce writing that will please critics like Granville Hicks.

The Leftists, for their part, countered Thurber's laughter with the charge of triviality and detachment from life that has stuck with Thurber ever since. Reviewing a book by Franklin P. Adams in the *New Masses* in 1934, Robert Forsythe (the pen name of Kyle Crichton) found Adams' "mild jousting at minor evils," insignificant though it was, a relief when compared with the work of "such other humorists as James Thurber, Frank Sullivan, E. B. White, and S. J. Perelman . . . "

> They are so resolutely turned away from anything in life that what they write has the quality of a fantasy, something written on and about the island of Atlantis. At first glance it seems a mystery how they maintain their seclusion from contemporary ideas, but it is not so much that they fail to know things are happening as that they feel any upsurge of emotion is not quite civilized. Obviously what one must have to be a success with the *New Yorker* is an ability to make even the most transcendental event trivial. The trick is never to raise the voice, never to become excited in the face of disaster, always to drink the old-fashioned to the last orange peel despite the revolution without.

Thurber and his colleagues, Crichton concluded, were but the "court jesters for their decaying betters," displaying all the prejudices of "young men who are at last accepted on Park Avenue" (24).

Although he found himself in distinguished company on Crichton's list, Thurber took strong exception to these remarks. They were in fact, the proximate cause of his review of Hicks' anthology of proletarian writing, in which Thurber stated: "[W]hat some of these proletarian writers need to learn is simply how to write, not only with intensity, but with conviction, not only with a feeling for the worker but a feeling for literary effects." But he was not content to criticize them only in such direct ways. To demonstrate what he meant about a lack of feeling for literary effect, for example, he wrote **"Bateman Comes Home"** (1936), a parody of Erskine Caldwell. Caldwell's work appeared with some regularity in the *New Masses,* and Thurber obviously took him as the prototype of the proletarian writer who confuses life with art. **"Bateman Comes Home"** consists of three pages of insane dialogue in grotesquely rendered dialect capped by a single sentence: "If you keep on long enough it turns into a novel" (*TC,* 99). So much for Caldwell's sense of form and the Leftists' claim that their writing represents reality unmediated by art. Insofar as it draws the reader's attention to the conventions of literary discourse, parody is a doubly effective weapon for combating the proletarians' contention that what they write is taken directly from life rather than from literary tradition. It neutralizes what Thurber called their "added advantage of writing sloppily and mushily just because whatever they have to say is so significant it doesn't make any difference how they say it . . . " (Bernstein, 231).

Thurber's remarks about the sloppiness of proletarian writing were not aimed at Caldwell, however. His chief target was William Saroyan, whose short story "The Daring Young Man on the Flying Trapeze" and subsequent collection of stories under the same title were hailed by Leftist critics as a major literary event of 1934. Both the story and Saroyan's writing in general appalled Thurber. "I have been working for weeks on a Saroyan parody," he told Cowley. "I get so mad I spoil it and have to let it dry."

> It seems to me significant that this man, who can not write and in admitting it really boasts that he can, should have caught whatever fancy it is that he has caught. Is he a proof and sign of the fact that if your writing deals with poor people out of work, etc. it is now bound to sell, no matter how bad it is?

Saroyan, Thurber concluded, "writes a whole lot like Jack Johnson . . . would write if he could" (Bernstein, 230). Apparently Thurber never cooled down sufficiently to complete his Saroyon parody. The writing of parody requires at least some measure of sympathy with the intended target. Thurber had none for Saroyon. Thurber took his revenge in the title of his next collection of *New Yorker* pieces, ***The Middle-Aged Man on the Flying Trapeze*** (1935), which acknowledges Saroyan's presence on the literary landscape only to reject in the volume every major Leftist premise about the forms, themes, and proper subjects of literature. The title illustration shows an awkward, obviously out-of-place fellow, pince-nez perched precariously on his nose, who has let go of his trapeze prematurely only to discover with some astonishment that the woman on whom he had counted to catch him has no intention of doing so. She is suspended supinely in the classic pose of sexual receptivity but faces the wrong way and wears an enigmatic smile. What foolishness about the proper role of males could have tempted Thurber's male up there in the first place? The drawing ironically makes use of the rhythmical surge and swing of the trapeze as a metaphor for sexual intercourse, in this case *coitus interruptus,* and spoofs the Freudian symbolism of flight. Possibly for autobiographical reasons—his marriage to Althea Adams ended in divorce on May 24, 1935 (Bernstein, 246)—this is perhaps Thurber's bleakest book, though also one of his best; but the central theme of miserable marriages nonetheless works well with the title as a critique of Saroyan-style realism even as it also underscores Thurber's simultaneous criticism of the middle-class illusion of romantic love.

For Depression-weary Americans, Thurber's title would also have summoned up two other social myths besides Saroyan's, both of them somewhere near the conservative end of the political spectrum. One of these myths recalls post-Civil War America and the small town and rural society which Thurber had already treated comically in ***My Life and Hard Times*** and would later celebrate in ***Thurber Country*** (1952). This is the world in which the song "The Daring Young Man on the Flying Trapeze" originated in the first place, a world where, as Thurber described it in **"Return of the Native"** (1950), "There was a lot of picnicking and canoeing and cycling, and going for hikes in the woods on Sundays in spring, the men in boaters and bright blazers, and the women in shirtwaists and skirts." Its virtues were self-sufficiency, contentment, modest economic competence, and a kind of wide-eyed innocence before the outside world. There are, Thurber suggests, no daring young men any more, only worn out and ludicrous middle-aged ones who make themselves look even more foolish by placing themselves in situations into which only daring young men should enter. But there are, alas, plenty of P. T. Barnums left in Depression-ridden America, and there are still more suckers born every minute.

The second social myth entangled in Thurber's allusive title is, like the first one, a myth of a better, communal world. The song "The Daring Young Man on the Flying Trapeze" was, as it happens, very popular in 1935, owing entirely to its resurrection in *It Happened One Night,* a movie that had won four Academy Awards the previous year. The film was directed by Frank Capra, whose overriding purpose in this and other films has been described by historian Robert Sklar as a "desire to revitalize the nation's old communal myths." Capra's film starred Clark Gable and Claudette Colbert and handily defeated for best movie of the year such competitiors as King Vidor's *Our Daily Bread,* a film that focused Marxist social philosophy and nostalgia for the rural past upon the problems of contemporary America. *It Happened One Night* is noteworthy for its portrait of some American capitalists as phony stuffed shirts whose effete nature has caused all the trouble in the nation, while others are fatherly, kindly, and understanding men like Colbert's father.

Thurber's controversies with the literary Leftists of the 1930s left him with deep scars. Thurber never did live down the charge of triviality first leveled against him in the *New Masses*. Though he bitterly assailed the Communist-hunting activities of Senator McCarthy and his cohorts in the late forties and early fifties, he never quite forgave such former friends as Donald Ogden Stewart and Dorothy Parker. As late as 1960 when he wrote **"The Case of Comedy,"** they were very much on his mind. The Leftists, he said, are continuing their "concerted attack on humor as antisocial, antiracial, antilabor, [and] antiproletarian. . . . [T]hey have left no stereotype unused in their attack, from 'no time for comedy' to the grim warnings that humor is a sickness, a sign of inferiority complex, a shield and not a weapon." Those final metaphors belong to Dorothy Parker, and they originally appeared in the *New Masses* during a debate already nearly a quarter century old when Thurber penned his words.

II

Had the Depression inspired only such pieces as **"How to Write a Long Autobiography," "What Are the Leftists Saying?,"** and the parodies of Caldwell and a few other writers, that would indeed have seemed to justify Kyle Crichton's claim that politics for Thurber was largely a matter of personal preference and class prejudice and that he wrote in a social vacuum. But there are, in fact, numerous other pieces not so purposefully or narrowly political which show Thurber as an acute observer of his times; these works clearly grow out of the Depression broadly considered as a psychological if not an economic and political phenomenon. Perhaps the most cynical story Thurber ever wrote, for example, **"The Greatest Man in the World"** (1931), belongs equally in time and temperament to the Depression era, when disillusionment with the American dream was rampant. The extravagance of the title tells us that this is a story about the carny hype and hoopla of the popular press, which affixed such hyperbolic labels to the latest hero as a mere matter of course. The term carries no historical force; it is unabashedly superlative because it does not really intend to invite comparison with other great men but simply to promote the most recent and, therefore, the "greatest" one. It belongs to the world of P. T. Barnum, to circus showmanship and spectacle, and is not something with which responsible journalism would have anything to do.

But, Thurber implies, in the 1930s no journalism was responsible. It is one measure of the depth of his cynicism that the story is told from the perspective of 1950, as if only in the future could Americans hope to gain a clear view of events supposedly taking place in 1937 but actually being written and read about in 1931. The effect of this tactic is ultimately ironic in the extreme, for in the context of the story the narrator's claim that Lindbergh and Byrd were true heroes cannot be given credence. It is impossible to reveal the "true" story about one hero without in some measure calling into question the pedigree of all heroes, Lindbergh and Byrd included. Perhaps, after all, these men were only more pliable than Jackie "Pal" Smurch, more malleable beneath the pressure of the press and the wishes of the President. The future stretches far beyond 1950, at any rate, and tomorrow or tomorrow may bring new facts to light about the "real" Byrd and Lindbergh. Moreover, a story in which newspapermen distort facts both to sensationalize them and then to cover up a murder, in effect rewriting the life and death of Jackie Smurch, inescapably raises questions about the motives of this anonymous reporter who reports the facts from the future. What purposes of the "present" does this view of the "past" serve? What does the narrator expect to get out of telling the story? The net effect of Thurber's "futuristic" strategy—that is, of publishing a story in 1931 about events in 1937 told about by a narrator in 1950—is to highlight the theme of fiction at the expense of historical fact. There is, perhaps, no ascertainable truth inherent in any moment of history; there are only the stories that men see fit to tell.

Still, there are both benign and sinister fictions. So far as the reader can tell, the entity entitled **"The Greatest Man in the World"** falls into the first category, while the reconstruction of the events of Smurch's life and death within the story falls into the second. The murder of Smurch is motivated by yet another fiction, the myth of the American hero, which is believed most by those most responsible for creating it. Not the smallest irony in a story of many ironies is that Smurch's accomplishment is actually substantial, just as the circumstances of his humble, Western origins could be made to fit the outlines of an approved American myth if only he would cooperate. A tinkerer and mechanic by trade, like the Wright Brothers or like Lindbergh himself, Smurch represents not so much a parody as a reduction to the lowest common denominator of the "heroic" American virtues of individualism, initiative, resourcefulness, and self-reliance. He has all of these but nothing more, and in his vulgarity he reveals that such "virtues" are in reality only other names for antisocial acquisitiveness, egotism, and simple greed. He unmasks the myth of the American hero, just as his intractable behavior will at last unmask American officialdom. Smurch has at least the saving grace of understanding and admitting that there is money to be made by becoming a celebrity, but the myth denies such motivation and attempts to ground American heroism instead on rural innocence and altruism. In this regard, I think it likely that **"The Greatest Man in the World"** was written, at least in part, to satirize through Jackie Smurch the simplistic view of Will Rogers, whom Thurber actively disliked (Bernstein, 237), that aviation would provide America with her next generation of heroes and restore society to those frontier values now deeply buried beneath consumerism and bureau "bunk." Thurber would have agreed with the diagnosis, but the man who wrote in 1929 that aviation and sex had been greatly overemphasized by our civilization would have viewed the popular infatuation with flight, which the popularity of Will Rogers did much to promote, as just another form of bunk.

In many ways, **"The Greatest Man in the World"** hearkens back to the Roaring Twenties, the decade that invented public relations and mass consumption to begin with and that perfected hero worship as a fine and essential American art. It is the decade that gave America the public symbol of Silent Cal and the rural boyhood of Herbert Hoover so wonderfully satirized in Grant Wood's painting, "The Birthplace of Herbert Hoover." Thurber's story also constitutes a critique of the hypocrisy of prohibition, which offered Americans the heavy drinking Warren Harding as the candidate of the "dries" and defined the average American as a criminal if he or she drank while largely ignoring the evidence of corruption that finally became public as the Teapot Dome scandal. The mass adulation of Lindbergh, Thurber sensed, arose in large part out of the moral morass that American government had become and continued to be. Americans ascribed to the aviator precisely those virtues from which they most feared they had departed, thereby re-assuring themselves that they still valued what they did not. Thurber's story comprehends as well the notion that hero worship in the twenties and the thirties measured the failure of the average American's life, his or her fall into mere statistical existence and anonymity at the hands of mass marketeers. In the exploits of Lindbergh or Ruth or even Al Capone, Americans could vicariously experience the success that had eluded them, the celebrity that they would never share.

III

As Americans during the Depression sought to relieve the dullness and dreariness of their lives, they turned to movies for their heroes and for escape. One promotional blurb for a major studio put the matter perfectly, attempting to obscure the profit motive of film production behind the genial guise of public service: "There's a Paramount picture probably around the corner. See it and you'll be out of yourself, living someone else's life." In this context, I think it is significant that two of Thurber's major fictions, **"The Remarkable Case of Mr. Bruhl"** (1930) and **"The Secret Life of Walter Mitty"** (1939), literary fantasies of escape, practically enclose the decade of the Depression and abound in images drawn from the popular media, including not only movies but also adventure fiction and tabloid journalism. In these stories, I believe, Thurber touches the mentality of the Great Depression most intimately.

"The Remarkable Case of Mr. Bruhl" perhaps lacks the historical resonance of **"The Greatest Man in the World,"** but as Thurber's earliest excursion into the world of fantasy it commands our attention for its handling of a theme that was to become increasingly important to Thurber over the years. Its frame of reference, as allusions within the story make clear, is to be found in books like *Al Capone* and *10,000 Public Enemies* and in movies like *Alibi* (1929), reminding us that in 1931 "Hollywood stars and Chicago mobsters topped the list of best-known personalities on the American scene; as a life choice, stardom and grand-scale crime loomed equally out of reach for the average man," who nevertheless would gladly have exchanged his banal existence for a moment of glory. One of the major surprise hit movies of 1935, *The Whole Town's Talking,* worked this fantasy to perfection, Edward G. Robinson plays both a notorious gangster and an accountant whose one distinction is that he looks exactly like the gangster. Encouraged by the police to play a part to entrap the public enemy, the accountant begins to take on aspects of the gangster's assertive identity and to learn the argot of the underworld. The point of the movie, according to one historian of American crime movies, is that "in every milquetoast there beats the secret heart of a mobster" (Carlens, 141).

But Thurber got there first. His character, Samuel O. Bruhl (the acronym of Bruhl's initials perhaps hints equally at an identity buried deep beneath Bruhl's conventional self and at the pathos of Bruhl's life), is "just an ordinary-looking citizen, like you and me, except for a curious, shoe-shaped scar on his left cheek, which he got when he fell against a wagon-tongue in his youth" (***TC,*** 143). So far Bruhl's biography is explicable. That scar, however, marks him out for a strange destiny, for it completes an otherwise vague resemblance to George "Shoescar" Clinigan, a notorious gangster. When a gang war erupts and Clinigan is severely wounded, Bruhl begins to fear for his own life. He begins to slink around and to dodge imaginary enemies, although on this point the narrator seems to wish us to understand that someone may actually have begun to follow Bruhl. Gradually, Bruhl's personality changes. His wife discovers books about gangsters hidden in the recesses of his closet, an analogue for the inaccessible spaces of his mind, and soon he starts lounging about the house in red pajamas, like Al Capone, and speaking in hardboiled "gangsterese." Eventually, he is assassinated at a small inn in the Catskills, but, true to the code of *omerte* he refuses to describe who has shot him. "'They never talk,'" says the New York City Police Commissioner who has been brought to the scene to question him, and Mr. Bruhl, hearing this, "smiled, a pleased smile, and closed his eyes" (***TC***, 148).

So far as the historical placement of this story within the general emotional milieu of the Depression is concerned, the most important elements of Thurber's portrait of Mr. Bruhl are set before us in the opening paragraph. Samuel O. Bruhl, we are told, "had a good job as treasurer for a syrup-and-fondant concern, a large, devout wife, two tractable daughters, and a nice home in Brooklyn."

> He worked from nine to five, took in a show occasionally, played a bad, complacent game of golf, and was usually in bed by nine o'clock. The Bruhls had a dog named Burt, a small circle of friends, and an old sedan. They had made a comfortable, if unexciting, adjustment to life. (***TC***, 143)

If boredom is indeed the absolutely indispensable precondition for fantasy and the fantastic that critics have claimed it is, then Mr. Bruhl has clearly been set up for a total reversal of the plot line of his life. Possessed already of the outward signs of the American dream, or at least the minimal middle-class version of it, Bruhl lacks any inner substance; he is, in fact, a void, a mere "case" (the pun lurks in Thurber's title, of course), and the identity of Shoescar Clinigan easily moves into the vacuum within. Up to a point, we are not witnessing a fantasy at all but a genuine psychosis of a kind reported fairly frequently in psychoanalytical literature: Mr. Bruhl has become the thing he most fears.

But not entirely so. It is not Clinigan whom he fears after all, but rather the gangsters and police who have sworn to get Clinigan. Thus he has objectified his existence as a victim of bureaucratic manipulation by transforming himself into the subject of a massive police manhunt, even as he has given expression to an unstated wish to be somebody else, someone exciting, by becoming a desperado. What remains fantastic in the story is not Bruhl's transference of identity but rather his ability to make his inner world visible upon the page, to summon up before our eyes the gangsters who shoot him down. Their rigorously maintained silence as they ritualistically assemble their guns links them at once and simultaneously with the inner, silent world of Bruhl's fantasies—the narrator is incapable of invading Bruhl's consciousness—and the external world of gangster lore, in which they seem, however, like Hemingway's gangsters in "The Killers," both themselves and caricatures or parodies, that is, literary versions, of themselves—and creatures of Mr. Bruhl's cliche-ridden imagination.

It is this familiarity of the gangsters' bearing and being that links them most closely to the world of the uncanny. How strange yet how predictable are the truths of personality that may lie beneath conventional existence? This theme is driven home by Thurber's relentless use of cliched expression to register the narrator's inability and unwillingness to penetrate into Mr. Bruhl's interior. When we think about it, what untranslatable worlds of mystery beyond our comprehension are simultaneously held at bay and yet acknowledged by our word "coincidence" and by such commonplace expressions as "oddly enough" and "quite by accident" or by subjunctive structures. These are the structures and transitions that move Thurber's story forward, the small change of daily speech revealed at last as a language that admits the fantastic and uncanny into life. In the silence beyond such phrases Thurber's story really happens.

One key allusion in the **"The Remarkable Case of Mr. Bruhl"** brings home the boredom of Bruhl's daily life while at the same time relating it to the inexplicable. A man of "colorless comings and goings" whose dreams are of "small stature" (***TC***, 143) indeed, Bruhl reminds the narrator of "the sort of average citizen that observers of Judd Gray thought Judd Gray was" (***TC***, 143). Readers in 1930 would have no difficulty remembering the murder of Albert Snyder by his wife, Ruth, and her lover, Judd Gray, in 1927 and the sensational Snyder-Gray murder trial of the same year, with all its strange disclosures about secret personalities, its journalistic hoopla, and its bizarre fascination for the American public. Villains to hiss and boo, it seems, are just as necessary to people uncertain of their own morality as are heroes to a populace losing individual identity amidst increasing throngs of the faceless, and Ruth Snyder and Judd Gray, in turning so entirely on each other and trying to blame each other for plotting and carrying out the murder, played the role of villain to perfection. Gray was unmanly, the papers said, in not protecting his former lover even under such circumstances and in trying to save himself by accusing her; Ruth Snyder was the "Clytemnestra of Long Island," as Elmer Davis of the *New Yorker* saw things, and Gray was but a featureless Aegisthus. To John Kabler, looking back on the crime ten years later, Gray was "the Caspar Milquetoast who never quite rates the better high-school secret societies" and his murder of Albert Snyder symbolized "the frenzy of the little man . . . renouncing his littleness, avenging a lifetime of inferiority and frustration." The key to it all, Kabler implicitly agreed with Thurber, was that the American Dream had become a nightmare of meaninglessness and pointlessness, even for Albert Snyder and his wife before Gray ever entered the picture:

> They came to Queens, that dead-level Canaan of the white collar worker, where addresses run dizzily into five digits and uniform clap board houses jammed cheek by jowl, row upon row and block after block, stretch into limitless monotony; where a radio enlivens every other home and existence is placid, routine, inexpen-

> sive—until revolt against tedium explodes without warning. (9)

Although Thurber thought highly enough of his story to include it in two major anthologies, ***The Middle-Aged Man on the Flying Trapeze*** and that showcase of the very best of Thurber, ***The Thurber Carnival,*** critics have had very little to say about it except that Bruhl, like Walter Mitty, demonstrates the self-destructive powers of fantasy. Perhaps so. But Thurber's placement of the story next to **"The Luck of Jad Peters"** in ***The Thurber Carnival,*** an autobiographical reminiscence which is also concerned with the strange coincidences by which Fate rides men down, indicates that both this theme and the historical character of Judd Gray held a special fascination for Thurber. The mode of **"The Remarkable Case of Mr. Bruhl"** is somber, hardly comic at all, unless we define comedy very broadly as aiming at some clarification of the mystery of our lives—a definition that will also do for tragedy as well. Next to this piece, **"The Secret Life of Walter Mitty,"** though disquieting, seems almost lighthearted.

"The Secret Life of Walter Mitty" is so well known and has been discussed so frequently in criticism that I want to add at this point only a caution to those who see Mitty as a version of Thurber—and their numbers are legion—that this piece, too, is best viewed in a cultural context that includes the Depression and the mounting crisis in Europe. There are oblique allusions to heroic films like Howard Hawks' *The Dawn Patrol* (1930), as Walter Blair and Hamlin Hill have pointed out, and the world of Perry Mason does not lie far away, but the only important historical allusion is to the Waterbury trial of 1938, which Mitty, typically, gets all wrong. The newsboy's shouting about the trial precipitates Mitty into a fantasy in which he is on trial for murder, but the actual Waterbury trial involved large scale and high level graft and corruption. Thurber uses the allusion to add a subtle touch to his characterization of Mitty and to enlarge the frame of reference of his story to include other characters who, like Mitty, have led secret and prohibited lives. It may also be worth remarking that the same year in which Walter Mitty was invented saw the debut of Superman, a character who is able to solve apparently unsolvable problems and whose secret life is lived as a Walter Mitty-ish fellow named Clark Kent. The disjunction between his real and his imaginary self reverses the comic split in Walter Mitty, but it is worth pondering if this at first unlikely pairing of Mitty and Superman does not lead to the same point at the end: in every Superman there lurks unrecognized a man like Walter Mitty, inadequate to history and inept at personal relationships both with bosses and with women. The widespread popularity of both Walter Mitty and Superman throughout the 1940's suggests that they spoke to something in American experience, and I suggest that that something is identical for each.

IV

This overview of Thurber in the thirties has necessarily scanted or ignored entirely important aspects of his writing in order to concentrate on those works most closely tied to the Depression or to states of mind engendered by the Depression. Thurber's last attempt at fantasy before turning to the fairy tale in the middle 1940s came in **"The Lady on 142"** in 1943, a piece which clearly demarcates the dream from the reality by enclosing the fantasy—a spoof of Alfred Hitchcock thrillers and *The Maltese Falcon*—within a framework of reality. If Thurber, somewhat paradoxically, found more freedom for his imagination in the bound motifs and preformed literary material of the fairy tale and the fable, the reason, I believe, has something to do with an altering national mood. If this paper has demonstrated anything, however, it is that the standard approaches to Thurber that emphasize the war between men and women, the essential sameness of the Thurber male and female, or even the theme of melancholy as the key to Thurber's humor, are inadequate to explain his fiction and cartoons. Despite the recent appearance of a new study, we badly need a re-reading of his work. Such a reappraisal would emphasize Thurber's themes and forms in relation to particular historical moments, popular culture, and the like. Only then, I believe, will we fully appreciate the wisdom of T.S. Eliot's assessment of Thurber's comic genius. "Unlike so much humor," Eliot said of Thurber's work,

> it is not merely a criticism of manners . . . but something more profound. His writings and also his illustrations are capable of surviving the immediate environment and time out of which they spring. To some extent, they will be a document of the age they belong to.

As we have seen, Thurber's work does indeed document the Depression years, and I believe that his humor in general will finally be recognized as documenting the age in which it was written.

Melvin Maddocks (essay date Fall 1985)

SOURCE: "James Thurber and the Hazards of Humor," in *Sewanee Review,* Vol. XCIII, No. 4, Fall, 1985, pp. 597-601.

[*This rapid overview of many of Thurber's most famous works aims to dispute Thurber's critical reputation as the foremost American humorist of his time.*]

While he was still alive, James Thurber was judged to be

the best humorist since Mark Twain—if not something more. After calling him his "favourite humorist," T. S. Eliot weightily pronounced Thurber's writing and illustrations to be "a document of the age they belong to." Ernest Hemingway appeared on Thurber dustjackets, declaring that here was the "best writing coming out of America."

Nothing kills a soufflé like praising it in terms of a roast-beef dinner. The pleasures of Thurber are still there for the rereading, but one savors them moderately. The superlatives applied by Thurber's colleagues and contemporaries seem excessive to the point of embarrassment today, especially when applied to his essays. In retrospect the essays of *New Yorker* humorists—those famous "casuals"—come across as group representatives of a journalistic genre. Frank Sullivan, Russell Maloney, E. B. White, Thurber—there is something institutional and anonymous, something interchangeable, about the way these writers and others domesticated madness into mere whimsy and clothed it in the finest English-tweed prose native Americans could produce.

In fact Thurber's first success was a collaboration with White, in which the authorship of chapters is nearly impossible to spot. ***Is Sex Necessary?*** was published just weeks after the 1929 stock-market crash. The book sold 50,000 copies in that first dark year and still remains in print. The titles of the chapters are self-explanatory: **"A Discussion of Feminine Types," "What Should Children Tell Parents?", "Frigidity in Men," "The Sexual Revolution: Being a Rather Complete Survey of the Entire Sexual Scene."** Thurber and White had their sitting target—the sexpert, even then filling the air with solemn jargon that reduced passion to a clinical exercise. The two satirists made up extravagant case histories, inventing names like Lt. Col. H. R. L. Le Boutellier, C. I. E., Schlaugenschloss Haus, King's Byway, Boissy-Le-Doux sur Seine.

Thurber first served as illustrator in this volume, tamely and realistically by later standards. A typically literal cartoon bore the caption: "Occasions arise sometimes when a girl presses her knee, ever so gently, against the knee of the young man she is out with." This is clearly superior college humor, but it does not wholly escape the category of lampoon; and there is a sense that the brilliant bumbler Robert Benchley, clearing his throat and waving a pointer at his charts, had mocked The Authority more wittily before. Benchley was the original for the *New Yorker* humorists who followed.

When an ambitious case is being made for Thurber, ***My Life and Hard Times*** (1933) almost invariably gets nominated as his masterpiece. The comparison with Mark Twain is a little too glibly justified by this fanciful autobiography, pitting a boyhood in Columbus, Ohio, against a boyhood in Hannibal, Missouri. "I suppose that the high-water mark of my youth in Columbus, Ohio, was the night the bed fell on my father," Thurber began, and the hyperbole flowed freely from there.

Thurber was not a subtle inventor. When he set out to invent confusion, he invented chaos. When he set out to invent a character, he invented an eccentric. The chaos verged on slapstick humor; the eccentric verged on a comic-strip cartoon. Take first-cousin Briggs Beall, apparently a total fabrication. Beall kept a glass of camphor by his bed from fear that he might suffocate in his sleep one night without the aid of this pungent reviver. Instead he almost suffocated from the camphor.

The "night the bed fell" is neatly bracketed with the "time I fell out of the gun room in Mr. James Stanley's house," an anecdote Thurber introduces in the last chapter and then coyly evades. But the general pattern remains constant. Our raconteur is a man to whom the oddest people, the most personable dogs, and the orneriest automobiles are attached. There is a charm to Thurber's manner—offhand and meandering, setting up one tall tale after another by making a virtue of the non sequitur. In effect he is a snob of the comic disaster, taking every mishap as "one of those bewildering involvements for which my family had, I am afraid, a kind of unhappy genius." The more fantastic, the more grandly muddled, he makes his Columbus and his people, the more he is able to love them.

Thurber's short stories share the same simple if not simplistic outline of his essays and autobiography. His most famous short story, **"The Secret Life of Walter Mitty,"** is a single joke ingeniously sustained. The Caspar Milquetoast, dreaming of heroic deeds as a navy commander or a surgeon while waiting meekly for his wife to finish shopping, is the raw material of a *New Yorker* cartoon. Thurber stories provide few second insights. A rereading of **"Walter Mitty"** only makes Thurber seem excessively tender and indulgent toward the Small Boy he treasured in men—and found threatened by Thurber women.

"The Breaking Up of the Winships" explicitly treats the war between the sexes as an absurd escalating argument over the merits of Greta Garbo and Donald Duck as cinematic geniuses. Thurber maintains an evenhanded position through most of the story, before tipping the balance against the wife at the end.

"The Catbird Seat" measures, even more starkly than his cartoons, Thurber's animosity and fear toward women. The discrediting of poor Ulgine Barrows, the office efficiency-expert, is savage revenge beyond any reasonable provocation within the story.

Even in a memoir of his days in France, the unmistakably

menacing Thurber woman appears, "large and shapeless and possessed of an unforgettable toothiness. Her smile, under her considerable mustache, was quick and savage and frightening, like a flash of lightning lighting up a ruined woods."

"Jim had it in for women," E. B. White, perhaps his closest friend, conceded.

Whatever emotion Thurber's short stories possess derives from two chief plots: men harassed by women; and men abandoned by women, like the protagonist of **"One Is a Wanderer,"** drinking himself into a fit state to retire to sleep in his lonely hotel room.

When all is said and done, Thurber may have loved only his dogs and his idealization of writing-men-in-groups, Our Crowd at the *New Yorker.* And the latter were totally safe in his affections only when dead. He praised John McNulty posthumously thus: "The angel that writes names in a book of gold must long ago have put McNulty down as one who delighted in his fellow man." Robert Benchley also brought out heavenly choirs from the otherwise skeptical Thurber. He quotes a Benchley friend saying of the angels: "They're going to have to stay up late in heaven now." Then Thurber goes on to top even that tribute: "Yes, they're staying up late, I know, and, what is more, they must be having the time of their infinities. Lucky angels."

The self-perception of *New Yorker* writers, especially the humorists, is a fascinating subject. Benchley condemned himself because he failed to become a scholarly critic of English poetry, as he presumed his Harvard professors intended him to be. S. J. Perelman hung a portrait of James Joyce on the wall of his study, signaling him as the exemplar for his own surrealistic prose. To those readers simply after a good laugh, E. B. White announced that humor "plays close to the big hot fire that is Truth." Thurber spoke so often of Lewis Carroll and Henry James that a reader could take these allusions as self-referrals.

The connection between what Thurber was writing and what he thought he was writing is not always clear. In his preface to ***My Life and Hard Times,*** after providing ballast with a passage from Benvenuto Cellini, Thurber mused characteristically about the destiny of the humorist: "This type of writing is not a joyous form of self-expression but the manifestation of a twitchiness at once cosmic and mundane. . . . To call such persons 'humorists,' a loose-fitting and ugly word, is to miss the nature of their dilemma. . . . The little wheels of their invention are set in motion by the damp hand of melancholy."

Toward the end of his life Thurber wrote more and more pieces with titles like **"A Farewell to Speech"** and **"The Decline and Fall of the King's English."** His preoccupation with language became fastidious to the point of being cranky. An insomniac, he counted words the way other men counted sheep, winding up with lists of words beginning with "P, the purloining letter, the stealer of sleep." He struck the posture of a Minister of Culture in a very small republic.

The social critic Otto Friedrich accused Thurber of becoming obsessed with trivia. Thurber did not deny it, but huffily defended himself with his latter-day loftiness: "Trivia Mundi has always been as dear and as necessary to me as her bigger and more glamorous sister, Gloria."

He called anger "one of the necessary virtues," but he seemed to get angry about less and less. His life became a litany of gripes. A reader found Thurber besieged and beleaguered by rock music, radio news broadcasts, junk mail, and unwanted phone calls. Everything shoddy flourished, while worthy institutions, like the railroad, went to hell.

Thurber constantly complained about the decline of humor, even in the *New Yorker* ("the magazine is turning grim and long"). But while criticizing glumness in others, he wrote, "I cannot confine myself to lightness in a period of human life that demands light."

The allusions to Henry James went up and up. Within a few pages he used the same tag from Horace twice. "He was pompous and unbelievably humorless when he decided that he was a man of letters," his longtime friend Ann Honeycutt complained.

His prose fell into a new richness. He referred to aging as suffering "the silent artillery of time," and to his insomnia as "the white watches of the woeful night." ***The Last Flower,*** his obvious and sentimental fantasy about future world wars, became his favorite work.

"The Last Clock"—a **"Fable for the Time, Such As It Is, of Man"**—holds up far better today. This less ambitious (and less famous) fairy tale of an ogre who eats up all the clocks in his castle and then in his town plays lovely variations on the conquest of time. It reads as if it were being told—improvised.

Was Thurber ever quite the writer he and his contemporaries took him to be? As a writer Thurber generally slaved over his revisions. He had a penchant for clean copy, and he was forever typing his pages, again and again. For Thurber as an artist there was serendipity from the start when he drew one of his most celebrated illustrations of a seal on the headboard of a bed because he was having difficulty drawing a seal on a rock.

The proof of Thurber's minor genius as an artist may be

shown by the success of his illustrations to some of poetry's most tired warhorses in "Famous Poems Illustrated." In "The Sands o' Dee" Charles Kingsley wrote: "The creeping tide came up along the sand"—and what a "creeping tide" Thurber drew, all baleful eyes and round paws—a hopelessly overweight, waddling puppy of a tide.

Young Lochinvar, swinging his grumpy and plump "fair lady" aboard his charger, is a sight to see. But it is the Thurber charger, wide-eyed and apprehensive at his double load, that carries the scene.

When he came to Longfellow's youth, bearing through an Alpine village the "banner with the strange device—Excelsior!", Thurber had the inspiration to draw an Ivy Leaguer with a bow tie, carrying the sort of pennant waved by undergraduates on the fifty-yard line.

In a childhood accident Thurber was blinded in one eye by his brother's arrow. As he slowly went blind in the other eye, he was left to his dark fancy, and he summoned up the vividly rounded blurs of his inner vision. His response was an act of courage and imagination.

When Thurber cultists who admired his art threatened to turn his head by overblown comparisons, mostly to Matisse, E. B. White sensibly told him: "If you ever got good you'd be mediocre." A reconsiderer of Thurber almost a quarter of a century after his death might extend White's clever observation to argue that Thurber "got good" as a writer, and became as other writers. But as an artist he remained blessedly unimproved, and today his squiggled lines still say witty, quirky, and revealing things beyond the power of his words.

Edward Sorel (review date 5 November 1989)

SOURCE: "The Business of Being Funny," in *New York Times Book Review,* November 5, 1989, p. 36.

[*This brief review finds most of the works included in* Collecting Himself *not worth a new anthology but nonetheless appreciates a few of Thurber's more insightful essays.*]

I somehow assumed that James Thurber's literary bones had been picked clean long ago. After all, posthumous collections had been published in 1962 and 1966 (Thurber died in 1961), and even then there was not enough new material to fill the books—both included work from previous collections. How, then, can there be at this late date unanthologized Thurber worthy of yet another volume?

Well, there can't. The fact is that although ***Collecting Himself*** contains many drawings never before published—reason enough to buy it—only some of the writing deserved to be resurrected. Several parodies are dated and no longer amuse, and many of the "casuals" (The *New Yorker*'s term for informal fiction and nonfiction articles) are too precious, too ephemeral. The book's editor, Michael J. Rosen, can certainly not be blamed for wanting to bring more of the humorist's work to light—he knows we Thurber addicts will take whatever we can get—but judging by this collection, there is not much choice Thurber left.

Whatever the book lacks in vintage material, however, It does give us Thurber working in a lot of different literary forms. We have book and theater reviews, essays on a wide variety of subjects, letters, reminiscences, satires, gag cartoons and a scathing polemic aimed at a professor of psychiatry who considered *Alice in Wonderland* too unwholesome for his children. Mr. Rosen, the literary director of the Thurber House—a writers' center in Thurber's Columbus, Ohio, boyhood home—has wisely avoided any attempt at arranging the pieces chronologically. Had he done so, the book would have been too light at one end (Thurber's early copy for *The Columbus Dispatch*) and too heavy at the other (tendentious, angry letters from his last years).

When both Thurber and *The New Yorker* were young, they enjoyed poking fun at anything that seemed staid or pretentious. A fine example of the irreverent Thurber is **"Recollections of Henry James,"** which appeared in *The New Yorker* in 1933. That year Thurber had overdosed on autobiographies that contained reminiscences of James, and he determined to offer his own, undeterred by the fact that he had never met the illustrious novelist. Written in the serpentine style that distinguishes James's prose, this piece gets my vote for the best parody of the much-parodied James, as well as being a marvelous spoof of the reverential memoirs that, praise be, are no longer fashionable. Here, at least, is an example of Thurber in top form.

Still, it is the serious, somewhat bitter essays that Thurber wrote late in his life that most hold one's attention. Many of these sober ruminations are, oddly enough, about the nature of humor and the business of being funny. He gave much thought to what constitutes humor and the different forms it takes. Once, while being interviewed on television by Edward R. Murrow, he extemporized what became a classic definition: "The wit makes fun of other persons; the satirist makes fun of the world; the humorist makes fun of himself."

Thurber himself was all three, but it was as a humorist

mocking his youth in a fictive Columbus that he most endeared himself to Americans. When ***My Life and Hard Times*** was published in 1933, it turned everyone from Ernest Hemingway to T. S. Eliot into a Thurber enthusiast. From that time on he was constantly being compared to Mark Twain, favorably as a rule. Like Twain, Thurber had his dark side (see Burton Bernstein's superb biography), and he shared with Twain a low opinion of his fellow man. There is no better example of Thurber's misanthropy than **"Thinking Ourselves Into Trouble"**—a dark piece, written in 1939, with such an unrelenting sense of doom for the future of man that I would never have taken it to be by Thurber, except that no one else could have written about the cosmos in quite this way.

> "It is surely not going too far, in view of everything, to venture the opinion that Man is not so high as he thinks he is. It is surely permissible to hazard the guess that somewhere beyond Betelgeuse there may be a race of men whose intelligence makes ours seem like the works of an old-fashioned music box. The Earth, it seems to me, may well be the Siberia or the Perth Amboy of the inhabited planets of the Universe."

If ***Collecting Himself*** has done nothing more than resurrect this anguished, long-forgotten essay, it will have been worth all Mr. Rosen's determined rummaging.

Anthony Quinn (review date 15 December 1989)

SOURCE: "Laughter in the Dark," in *New Statesman and Society,* Vol. 2, No. 80, December 15, 1989, p. 37.

[*In contrast to unenthusiastic responses to Thurber's* Collecting Himself, *this review finds the collection a "luminous delight."*]

Trying to explain the mechanics of humour can be a dispiriting business. Analyse a poem and one's appreciation might be enriched; analyse a joke and something quite different happens, delicate ironies and clever nuances evaporate before your eyes, punch lines wither and die. "Humour can be dissected, as a frog can, but the thing dies in the process and the innards are discouraging to any but the pure scientific mind," was E B White's sage observation.

One fancies that a professional humourist would always guard the "secret" of his art, but White's friend and colleague James Thurber seemed genuinely interested in its disclosure, and arrived at a conclusion that touches us all on the raw: "Human dignity, the humourist believes, is not only silly but a little sad. So are dreams and conventions and illusions. The fine brave fragile stuff that people live by. They look so swell, and go to pieces so easily."

An eloquent diagnosis, perhaps, but it hardly explains why this new compendium of Thurber's essays, reviews, cartoons, articles and letters is such a joy. I have never come across anyone who has properly elucidated the essence of Thurber's gift—I'm not sure I want to. Michael Rosen has corralled these loose bits and pieces into rough clumps of categories, reasoning that they have never been collected between hard covers before and together offer a coherent body of opinion on style, or, as the book's sub-title promises, "on writing and writers, humour and himself". All we have to do is sit back and enjoy the ride.

Thurber wrote and drew for the *New Yorker* in its heyday, sharing space with the likes of Dorothy Parker, Benchley, Woollcott and White, and battling with the editorial eccentricities of Harold Ross. These were evidently something of a trial to a writer whose natural facility for language was constantly trammelled by Ross's pedantry and fastidiousness. He quotes this example of editorial "lunacy"—"You have the word 'make' on galleys 3, 9 and 11", and his own exasperated response—"For God's sake, Shakespeare used 'to be' twice in one line and 'tomorrow' three times in one line. Where were the *New Yorker* editors then?" Realising that language should take precedence over "house style", Thurber gives grammar a thorough medical, slicing open sentences with the brisk confidence of a surgeon to check for sclerotic commas or inflammation of the syntax. He lights the way towards clarity with a civilised grace and wit.

He grew progressively blinder during his lifetime, though as the essays and book reviews here bear out, his critical gaze was undimmed. In a funny and trenchant piece on Thomas Wolfe he takes a sidelong swipe at the glib extravagance of book reviewers: "At least twice a month, as all readers of book reviews know, a new genius emerges and sets an all-time all-American tidemark with a vital and all-embracing picture of American life that is haunting and unforgettable and filled with a unique power and a strange and moving beauty." The observation has worn all too well. Elsewhere parodic shafts expertly pin down writers both admired and loathed, either deflating the splendour of Henry James's interminable periods, or skewering the pretentious twaddle of Gertrude Stein. Chekhov's lugubrious tug and Eugene O'Neill's tortuous psychodrama are sent up in miniatures of teasing affection.

Collecting Himself is a valuable reminder of Thurber's everyday brilliance, and a tonic in the midst of present-day drabness. These writings and drawings present a world view less jaundiced than that of Parker and Perelman but one that is no less perceptive, despite—or maybe because of—his waning eyesight. For him it may have been laughter in the dark; for us it's a luminous delight.

William Joyce (review date 25 November 1990)

SOURCE: "A Thimbleful of Thurber," in *Los Angeles Times Book Review,* November 25, 1990, p. 25.

[*In this review, Joyce, a writer of children's books, welcomes the republication of three of Thurber's books for young people.*]

I had forgotten that James Thurber had written any children's books. Or rather, I never knew it, or at least I never knew I knew it. I'd read his books as a child, but I took no notice of who'd written them. Like most kids, all I cared about was the story. Did the prince save the girl? Did the bad guy get what was coming to him? Did everything work out in the end, and most important, did I enjoy the whole rigamarole?

With Thurber's books the answer was a definite "yes" when I was a child, and that opinion still holds true now that I'm supposedly all grown up and pay attention to authors' names. With the reissue of three of Thurber's books for young people—***Many Moons, The Wonderful O,*** and ***The Thirteen Clocks***—we now have the fun of rediscovering some of this great man's best work.

The Wonderful O, first published in 1957 and reissued now in a fascimile edition, is an allegorical story of the tiny "Island of Ooroo." Poor "Ooroo" is invaded by treasure-seeking pirates whose leader has a bitter dislike for the letter "O" and so bans any and all use of the offending vowel for the duration of his occupation.

This wreaks considerable havoc. Not only is the name of their beloved island reduced to one measly consonant, but there are now "cabins without logs . . . , mantels but no clocks . . . . , keys without locks, walls without doors, rugs without floors. . . . A fellow named Otto Ott, when asked his name, could only stutter and poor Ophelia Oliver now being Phelia Liver can't get a date, and saying 'Hello' at church will get you in trouble." You don't have to be a Rocket Scientist to see where all this is headed. Suffice it to say that everything ends happily; though the plot is a little musty and heavy on the message, there's still great fun in this handsome edition.

Many recent reissues of children's classics have been marred by implanting new, more "contemporary" illustrations in an attempt to update the look of the book. This is a shame. Quite often, the "colorization" of these books, with new artwork that reeks of cute, tampers with our memories and, even worse, weakens the appeal of the volume. So hats off to the publishers for retaining Marc Simont's simple, witty illustrations, a worthy accompaniment to Thurber's whirligig prose.

The Thirteen Clocks, also reissued in its original format with Simont's illustrations, is a fairy-tale romance with a traditional genre story line—a stalwart prince is out to rescue a beautiful princess from the clutches of an evil duke. There are spies, monsters, betrayals, hair's-breadth escapes, spells to be broken and all the usual accouterments, but Thurber gives the proceedings his own particular deadpan spin.

The evil duke is so evil he whiles away his mornings "placekicking puppies and punting kittens." The ever-handsome prince, bored with his royal trappings, travels foreign lands in rags, looking for the "maiden of his dreams, singing as he goes, learning the life of the lowly, and slaying a dragon here and there." It all makes for a rousing concoction of adventure, humor and satire that defies any conventional classification.

Of the Thurber works being reissued, however, my favorite is ***Many Moons,*** the story of Princess Lenore, who is bedridden from imbibing too many raspberry tarts. "If I can have the moon, I will be well again," she confides to her father the King. The Lord High Chamberlain, the Royal Wizard, and the Royal Mathematician are all urgently consulted, but despite their vast knowledge, none can deliver the much-needed moon. The wily Court Jester is the only one level-headed enough to save the day.

Avoiding the pratfalls of most reissues, this edition with new full-color paintings by Simont has been produced with obvious thought and care. It is a worthy reinterpretation, though it can't eclipse the glories of the 1943 original (which is still in print, and carries Louis Slobodkin's Caldecott Award-winning pictures).

Simont's work brings a pleasing unity to this new deluge of Thurber, and his efforts in ***Many Moons*** couldn't be better. His watercolors are airy, bold and witty. His Court Jester, a sprawling, gangling youth, is an inspired departure from Slobodkin's serene, more adult counterpart—and he even includes a caricature of Thurber as one of the King's advisers.

So James Thurber has returned to young readers, not only in word but in likeness. His style of rowdy pixilation will exert anew its cheerful influence on readers young and old.

Anthony Kaufman (essay date Spring 1994)

SOURCE: "'Things Close In': Dissolution and Misanthropy in 'The Secret Life of Walter Mitty,'" in *Studies in American Fiction,* Vol. 22, No. 1, Spring, 1994, pp. 105-10.

[In the following essay, Kaufman disputes the consensus that Walter Mitty is an everyman to be sympathized with. Instead, he proposes that the story is a critique of Mitty's inability to cope with his life.]

"The Secret Life of Walter Mitty" is quite possibly the best known American short story. "Walter Mitty" as a character type has penetrated the popular imagination: we speak of a person inclined to day dreaming as a "Walter Mitty." Mitty, by consensus, represents the American little man, comfortably suburban, but bored to death with a middle-class, middlebrow life. Clearly his life is severely conventional, and it is obvious that Thurber is suggesting that American middle-class life offers little in the way of opportunities for romance, heroism, "a life full of passion, poetry, and hate," as a song written eight years before "Mitty," "As Time Goes By," puts it. The story has become folksy—Mitty is seen as endearing, the amiable little man, who dreams his dreams like all of us, and who triumphs in his dreams over the dull, gray world of suburban (and for that matter urban) America. The feature film made of the story in 1949 presents him thus; and two generations have seen him as a character rather like Dagwood Bumstead: the American middle-class everyman, presented to us with a wry but friendly smile.

But the story itself, and the story when set within the context of Thurber's life and career, can be read quite differently and, I think, in terms truer to Thurber's comic imagination. Mitty's rejection and withdrawal from the world are more radical than can be denoted by the idea of "daydreaming." In fact, we witness the descent of Mitty into ever increasing preoccupation with his fantasy life and increasing rejection of the so-called real world. His withdrawal is symptomatic not of mild-mannered exasperation with a trivial world, but of anger and misanthropy.

Although the story is charming, critics have not done justice to what lies below its surface laughter: clearly Mitty is gradually withdrawing into his daydreams, into an interior reality progressively stronger and more satisfying. The so-called real world becomes increasingly distant and unavailable for Mitty: "things close in." A note of unjustified critical optimism is found, for example, in the introduction to the story in a popular anthology of short stories: The editors suggest that Walter Mitty "is a changing character," in the process of change. In his own way, he is coming to grips with the real world." This is misleading. Yes, Mitty is in the process of change, but it is to misanthropy, withdrawal, and final dissolution. Mitty's feelings of insignificance, his awareness of his own negligibility, his bitterness towards the world, lead him to covert aggression which must be expressed indirectly, or in a hidden manner.

Thurber himself made claims for the essential seriousness of his stories: "In anything funny you write that isn't close to serious you've missed something along the line." The most powerful claim for the seriousness of Thurber's humor came from T.S. Eliot, who called Thurber his favorite humorist and said:

> It is a form of humor which is also a way of saying something serious. There is a criticism of life at the bottom of it. It is serious and even somber. Unlike so much of humor, it is not merely a criticism of manners—that is, of the superficial aspects of society at a given moment—but something more profound. His writings and also his illustrations are capable of surviving the immediate environment and time out of which they spring. To some extent, they will be a document of the age they belong to.

This is well illustrated in **"The Secret Life of Walter Mitty,"** where the daydreams are seen not merely as momentary escapes from a dull reality into exciting fantasy, but also as an index to Mitty's anger, desperation, and willingness to escape permanently into the more satisfying dream world of his imagination. In his interview with George Plimpton and Max Steele, Thurber remarked that in **"The Secret Life of Walter Mitty"** he had "tried to treat the remarkable as commonplace." What is finally remarkable are not the little man's dreams of glory, but what they say about him, about his mental situation.

Bored and suffering from feelings of inadequacy, Mitty compensates and defends himself through fantasies. Within the fantasies there is an element of revenge: against his wife, who is replaced by the lovely dark-haired girl of the courtroom drama; against Dr. Renshaw, who in the operating room fantasy becomes distraught and haggard; against the many petty authority figures that surround and scrutinize Mitty, watchful for signs of deviant behavior. Seemingly his only defense against the scrutiny and tyranny of the world, the fantasies are entirely humorless from Mitty's perspective; Mitty does not use them as a mockery of the real world, but as a means of escape.

That the fantasies are risible in themselves is obvious: they derive from period Hollywood films and popular fiction and are manifestations of the mass American culture that has formed Mitty but not sustained him. Mitty's fantasies may reveal a longing for the heroic, but much of the delight of the story comes from our perception of how formulaic, superficial, and false to life they really are. Thurber has great fun with the conventional situations and dialogue of popular movies and fiction. The point is that the little man dreams the little man's fantasies—he is not creative enough, not sufficiently individual enough to create his own—and in that sense he is representative of the American middle-class everyman: someone more singular would have more singular fantasies. Given Thurber's constant privileging of the creative imagination in his fiction, the comedy must be directed at Mitty, a middle American devoid of creative imagination, who must take even his inner life from pop fiction and the moviemills of Sam Goldwyn and Jack Warner. Thurber's satire is thus directed partly at the thinness of popular art as well as its product, Walter Mitty.

Thurber had ambivalent feelings about American popular art; he seems to have relished such entertainments, and at the same time to have been contemptuous of them. This may be sensed in Mitty's fantasies: hilariously familiar and predictable, they are the prime source of the story's laughter, and it seems clear that Thurber had some affection for the tinpot dramas of Hollywood. Clearly Mitty's fantasies are cardboard, predictable, synthetic; one need only compare them to the glorious fantasy of the man who sees a unicorn in the garden to see a contrast between a creative (although deluded) imagination, and the reliance of the dull little man, Mitty, on pasteboard fantasies. In Thurber's earlier **"Unicorn in the Garden,"** the fantasy is unique; and as the figure of the unicorn suggests, rich and strange. Here the little man is opposed by his dominant, hostile wife, but triumphs over her, first through his experience of the beauty and rarity of his vision, and second through his wit in denying his vision. Mitty's fantasies are comic-book stuff—the humor in them is not his, but that of his creator, Thurber, who parodies the formulaic and cliche-ridden format to perfection.

There are thus strong limits on our ability to sympathize with Mitty. The thinness, the prefabricated quality of the fantasies, are hardly seen as superior to the real world, but as childish and badly made. Moreover, he accepts *passively* the absurdity of the popular movies and fiction; lacking a critical sense, he passively lives out in his fantasies the nonsense of bad art. This latter is important, for Thurber suggests here the insidious and subversive quality of popular culture—all-pervasive, ever present, attacking us from many strong sources: movies, fiction, radio (and of course even more so today through television). Mitty is the product of this culture: passive, withdrawn, resentful, anxious. Defeated by life, damaged in self-esteem, he is a receptive target for the fantasies of the group mind.

Mitty, representative of a certain social condition, has a dreadful choice: the real world, Waterbury, known for the manufacture of clocks, and thus suggestive of the routinized, quotidian life, or the fantasy world supplied him by incompetent and venal "artists" through the agency of highly competent distributors like Goldwyn and Warner, advertising people, radio executives, and so on. In short, Mitty can choose the pointless and unsatisfying tick-tock of everyday life, or the sound and fury of popular culture. Mitty shuttles between the two worlds, drawn from one to the other largely through chance and opportunity: a newsboy's cry draws him into the world of courtroom drama; the fantasy is interrupted by a chance remark of a passerby. Mitty feels himself under scrutiny: his wife, Dr. Renshaw, the passerby, the traffic cop, the parking lot attendant, all watch him, ready to note his deviance, his incompetence, his withdrawal.

The degradation and humiliation that lead eventually to his dissolution, the dissolving of his already tenuous identity, are represented by the inglorious parcels he carries through the streets of Waterbury: overshoes and puppy biscuit. In his outward life he is almost inarticulate; Mitty doesn't say anything other than "I was thinking" or "puppy biscuit" or "oh gee." And the silent little man—his thoughts are inward—doesn't act, except to plod forward on his degrading errands. His resentment of his wife's treatment of him, his own sense of negligibility and feelings of inadequacy, are covert, but there. About to be dismissed by Mrs. Mitty as she leaves the family car (reminding him to wear the hated gloves—"You're not a young man any longer"), Mitty "raced the engine a little." He takes off the inglorious gloves as soon as he pulls away from her, only to put them back on hurriedly when snapped at by a traffic cop. Later, in the operating room drama they will again appear, transformed into symbols of his competence and authority, as the surgeon's rubber gloves. Near the end of the story, Mitty rebels once more; to Mrs. Mitty's barrage of irritating questions, Walter snaps: "I was thinking . . . Does it ever occur to you that I am sometimes thinking?" Mrs. Mitty is the foremost and most formidable of the many petty authority figures Walter must put up with forever: the cop, the parking-lot attendant, the garage mechanic—and of course there are many more offstage. Mitty's plea for some recognition of his inward life, his being, is ignored by his wife as a matter of course. And even the revolving doors of the hotel "made a faintly derisive whistling sound" when Mitty meekly follows his wife from the hotel to the parking lot.

It would be possible to regard Walter Mitty as another example of a thousand henpecked hubbies, the very stuff of popular humor. But the order of the story's events goes beyond simply portraying the little man and his dominant wife. A strong suggestion in the story is that Mitty is slowly withdrawing from life, living more and more in his tinseltown fantasies. This is apparent at the abrupt conclusion of his first day-dream, when he is drawn away from his huge, hurtling eight-engined Navy Hydroplane by Mrs. Mitty: "'Not so fast. You're driving too fast.'"

> "Hmm?" said Walter Mitty. He looked at his wife, in the seat beside him, with shocked astonishment.

> She seemed grossly unfamiliar, like a strange woman who had yelled at him in a crowd (p. 47).

It is clear even in this first fantasy that Mitty has withdrawn to the point where his return to reality is shocking, unfamiliar, and unsatisfactory; he return to everyday life slowly and with regret, "the roaring of the SN202 through the worst storm in twenty years of Navy flying fading in the remote, intimate airways of his mind."

As the story proceeds, we note a pattern of suggestion that he has become strikingly withdrawn; this is apparent to the casual observer as well as Mrs. Mitty: "'You're tensed up again,' said Mrs. Mitty: 'It's one of your days. I wish you'd let Dr. Renshaw look you over.'" The garage attendant looks at him closely; the passerby in the street is amused by the abstracted Mitty, and notes, "that man said 'puppy biscuit.'" Near the conclusion Mrs. Mitty looks hard at her husband and says "I'm going to take your temperature when I get you home." This suggestion of progressive withdrawal is seen in the fantasies and increasingly he becomes preoccupied with loss of control and death. Each successive fantasy places Mitty in greater peril and possessing less control. Yet death is always delayed; before the climax of each fantasy, the dream is intruded upon by the outside world and destroyed.

In the first fantasy, Commander Mitty, the "Old Man," guides the eight-engined SN202 at 8500 rpm through a hurricane of ice in full dress uniform. Here, despite the danger and threat of death, Mitty is entirely in control; "the old man ain't afraid of Hell," the crew knows the Commander will bring them through. In the second, Dr. Mitty is asked to take over the difficult operation on the millionaire banker Wellington McMillan ("and close personal friend of Roosevelt") who is suffering from "obstreosis of the ductal tract. Tertiary." Later, we learn the case worsens, "coreopsis has set in." In both fantasies, Mitty's competence with machines, his grace under pressure, are associated with life—with saving the lives of his crew, then the life of the millionaire banker.

In the third fantasy, Mitty is no longer entirely in control. On trial for murder, defendant Mitty is badgered by the DA. He remains cool, calmly acknowledging (and thus compromising his defense) that "this is my Webley-Vickers 50.80," and calms the bickering attorneys by pointing out that he "could have killed Gregory Fitzhurst at three hundred feet *with my left hand*" ("With any known make of gun"). Mitty now is on the defensive, threatened with imprisonment and death—although we are to assume in accordance with the conventions of pop fiction that Gregory Fitzhurst had it coming and Mitty will be acquitted, vindicated, and rewarded with the "lovely dark-haired girl."

In the fourth fantasy, RAF Captain Mitty must fly "forty kilometers through hell." Here, however, the implication is that he may not survive. Captain Mitty's war-weary tragic whimsy is impeccable: forty kilometers through hell? "After all, what isn't"—a line to which Ronald Colman or Richard Burton could do justice. As the sound of the cannon, machine guns ("pocketa-pocketa-pocketa"), and the new flame-throwers grows louder, Mitty, who holds his brandy well and needs to now, turns to the door of the dugout: "He turned and waved to the sergeant. 'Cheerio!'" This cheerio may be his last; the situation seems hopeless. The last fantasy shows Mitty the Revolutionary passive, defenseless, on the point of death. Always the hero, he handles his imminent death with stiff upper lip—"To hell with the handkerchief"—but from the rifles of the firing squad there seems to be no escape. And here at the conclusion of the story there is no interruption and return to life—instead, there is the suggestion that Mitty will ultimately withdraw, irrevocably, into his interior world.

The fantasies portray, then, a progressive lack of control: from "the Old Man will get us through" and the hopeful request that Doctor Mitty will save the wealthy patient; to Mitty as defendant, questioned on the stand, warding off the sneering DA; to Captain Mitty going out to face death; and finally, the last fantasy, where the only control he has left is seen in the stiff upper lip. That the fantasies all have to do with loss of control and death seems to indicate his increasing withdrawal from the real world in favor of his fantasies, and his longing for death as the ultimate escape. "Things close in," says Mitty "vaguely," sunk in the big leather chair in the lobby, where he has hidden himself. Mitty is gradually withdrawing from an unsatisfactory life to the solace and fulfillment of his dreams.

Certainly we can sympathize with Walter Mitty; like his, our world is made up of traffic cops, garage mechanics, parking lot attendants, and the dulling quest for Kleenex, Squibb's toothpaste, razor blades, "bicarbonate, carborundum, initiative and referendum"—the very rhythm of the mundane life in the Clock City. But Mitty's fantasies, inadequate and shabby, suggest that Mitty himself is the primary target of Thurber's satire. Certainly the story implies a bourgeois America, where opportunities for heroic action are nonexistent, a world of overshoes and puppy biscuit. And Thurber's anger, later in his career to become obsessively misanthropic (with a special vein of misogyny), is clearly present here, as directed primarily toward the officiously mothering wife as well as the surrounding host of petty authority figures.

The final lines of the story are ironic. Rather than validate Mitty because we understand that by means of his dreams he conquers the unsatisfactory world, the final lines ("Walter Mitty the Undefeated, inscrutable to the last") diminish and ridicule him. Mitty is all too scrutable: not the amiable little man, conquering the bullying stupid world through his guilelessness, but very much the failure he and the world think him. Even so accomplished a critic as Tobias sees Mitty as one of those Thurber heroes who "can conceive of a larger order than a simple formula." But Mitty's ability to conceive the heroic is negligible; his fantasies are on the order of those dreadful radio adventure shows like "Captain Midnight" that Thurber mocks in the story **"Thix."** Many critics have seen Mitty's fantasies as a triumph of affirmation. Robert E. Morsberger suggests that through his fantasies Mitty triumphs over a "sense of inadequacy and a nagging wife," and Charles S. Holmes suggests that in fantasy, Mitty finds "the means to reshape outer defeat into inner victory." Robert H. Elias maintains that beginning with "Mitty" in 1939, Thurber enters a period of "a humanistic affirmation." Mrs. Mitty stands as an enemy of the imagination, but, says Elias, in the fantasies Mitty achieves a victory, even if qualified, "that contributes to self preservation." But Mitty's fantasies are hardly works of the creative imagination, rather those of an imagination derivative and sterile. Far from leading to self-preservation, Mitty's fantasies indicate his increasing withdrawal into the silence of his interior life. Thurber's implication is that Mitty and those like him are not the victims of "the world"—unsatisfactory as it may be—but of a fatal passivity, a lack of courage and imagination. Mitty's failure is the failure to accept the world, and live his life in it, even knowing his own unimportance in it. Thurber does not want us to sympathize with Mitty's neurosis, for such a condition is not in itself pitiable or inevitable in modern life. Mitty is an adult; he should use such resources as he has to live out his life.

That Mitty is made into a comic character by the shabby quality of his fantasies, fantasies understood as the means of withdrawal and covert means of aggression, would seem confirmed by a glance at three analogous stories by Thurber: **"The Lady on 142," "The Catbird Seat,"** and **"The Curb in the Sky."** The first of these, another story set in wartime, again presents the little man's Hollywood fantasies. Here, while waiting for a local train in rural Connecticut, the protagonist and his wife overhear a chance telephone message from the stationmaster from the train, number 142, from New York. "Conductor Reagan on 142 has the lady the office was asking about." On this slender basis, the little man projects a Hollywood fantasy of spies. He tells his wife he is convinced that the woman on 142 is a spy and that the FBI has hunted her down. His wife dismisses such bizarre stuff, suggesting the alternative that the woman has simply been taken sick on the train. She wittily deflates the little man's fantasy.

The fantasy of spies in Connecticut is made ludicrous, as are the fantasies of **"The Secret Life of Walter Mitty,"** by its clichéd quality, and the comic appeal is to our recognition of these threadbare formulas of popular movies. The little man of **"The Lady on 142"** creates through his unoriginal imagination a sappy fantasy, peopled by figures who look too much like characters in a B movie. Although his fantasy is funny, it is not the product of a creative imagination and the conscious mockery of a threadbare entertainment, but a stale recreation of such second-rate stuff.

There is more to be said about this B Film fantasy. The little man falls asleep and his fantasy of espionage continues as a dream. The dream ends with the husband about to be executed—he knows too much—but as in "Mitty," the dream is interrupted by the outside world before its climax; the little man returns to consciousness. There is a dogged and resentful quality in the little man; awake he holds on to his fantasy tenaciously—it is not private, as is Mitty's; instead he insists upon its reality to his wife and her friend. We are not to see this little man as insane, or progressively withdrawing; awake he is self-consciously projecting a fantasy situation to amuse himself in a boring situation and to once again irritate his wife. They know each other too well; each possesses a laugh known to annoy the other, and clearly they are longtime antagonists. To insist on the absurdity—spies on the clunky little local—is to annoy his spouse in that indirect but effective manner that Thurber's marriage partners use to perfection. The fantasy is a means of aggression.

"Mitty" is further clarified by a second interesting contrast: Thurber's famous story of **"The Catbird Seat."** This story portrays the colorless life of the head of the Filing Department at F & S, a seemingly mild-mannered little man whose life is routinized to the point of absurdity. Unlike Mitty however, Martin is supremely *happy* with his situation: he does not dream of glory; he is entirely fulfilled within the offices of Fitweiler. This satisfaction with the ghastly routine of his life, his satisfaction in the dignity of his position, makes him a figure of fun, as suggested in Mr. Fitweiler's quite serious praise: "Man is fallible but Martin isn't."

He, like Mitty, is opposed by a large or large-seeming woman, Mrs. Barrows. She represents a threat to his place, identity and dignity. Everything Ulgine Barrows is threatens Mr. Martin's sense of his world: she is loud, vulgar, incompetent—a circus horse he calls her, and moreover, one with "a quacking voice and braying laugh." But unlike Mitty, Martin is able, through an odd quirk of imagination, through a bizarre use of fantasy, to oust Mrs. Barrows and regain the serenity of his once threatened position. His fantasy, that he is a drinking, smoking druggie, he plays out to the destruction of his enemy.

This story also begins within the matrix of popular fiction: in this case, the detective story. The little man plots and will execute the perfect crime. This conventional scenario is discarded by Martin midway through its enactment, as he realizes that there is a much better way to destroy Mrs. Barrows. By creating and acting out a fiction, a wild-man persona, he can discredit Mrs. Barrows in the eyes of the Boss. Mr. Martin is aware that he has created a fantasy. Playing it out—"I'll be cooked to the gills when I bump that old buzzard off'—Martin acts to secure his position. That the fantasy is the machinations of a dim, unadventurous little man is part of the joke, but Martin is in a sense admirable; beneath the typical look of studious concentration lurks not Mitty, the passive little man, but the ruthless desperado. Here the fantasy is clearly a means of aggression, and is not used as an escape, but to secure Mr. Martin's sense of himself as confirmed in his real life. In both **"The Secret Life of Mitty"** and **"The Catbird Seat,"** the little man struggles to maintain a sense of self-value. Martin fights to keep the sense of himself inherent in his position at F & S, which he finds of supreme value; his anger turns outward towards the despicable Ulgine. Mitty attempts to create and sustain some sense of power and value in himself in his increasingly more profound withdrawal into fantasy; his anger turns inward and becomes sterile. Martin creates and acts; his unoriginal detective story compromises our estimation of his imagination, but his spontaneous ability to create a marvelous trick to oust his antagonist makes his triumph admirable.

A story less well known perhaps, but one of Thurber's best and one that is illuminating in its parallels to **"Mitty,"** is **"The Curb in the Sky."** Here Charlie Deshler, dashing, widely traveled, and experienced, a great story teller—just the opposite of Mitty—is reduced to despair and finally incarceration in a mental hospital by his wife, a perky, vivacious woman with the annoying, indeed infuriating, habit of finishing people's sentences for them. Charlie's friends look on with resignation as he, characteristically impetuous, marries Dorothy; they know that the outcome will be Charlie's decline and fall. She begins to interrupt his favorite stories, correcting them, and finally taking over and telling the story herself. Charlie realizes what is happening to him, and after two years of this begins to defend himself by recounting to his guests one of his own *dreams*, knowing that his wife cannot correct and preempt these flights of a singular imagination. His fantasies are to save his sanity: "They became the only life he had that was his own" (p. 79).

He tells a bizarre dream of his flight to the moon in an airplane "made out of telephone wires and pieces of old leather." He is stopped by "a man who looked like Santa Claus, only he was dressed in the uniform of a customs officer." This figure tells Charlie that "'you can't go to the moon, if you are the man who invented these wedding cookies.' Then he showed me a cookie made in the shape of a man and woman being married—little images of a man and a woman and a minister, made of dough and fastened firmly to a round, crisp cookie base" (p. 79).

But Charlie's device is futile; the narrator tells us that "any psychiatrist will tell you that at the end of the way Charlie was going lies madness in the form of monomania. You can't live in a fantastic dream world, night in and night out and then day in and day out, and remain sane. The substance began to die slowly out of Charlie's life, and he began to live entirely in shadow" (p. 79). Worn and desperate, Charlie begins to tell obsessively this one story of the interrupted flight to the moon over and over, and after a month or two, "Charlie finally had to be sent to an asylum." Apart from Dorothy, Charlie seems to improve, but when the narrator visits Charlie in the asylum, he finds Dorothy seated beside her husband's bed, "bright-eyed and eager." "I was somehow surprised to see her there, having figured that Charlie had, at least, won sanctuary from his wife. He looked quite mad" (p. 80). Charlie tells his story, only to be—inevitably and fatally—interrupted and corrected by his wife. "'So I pulled over to a curb—' 'No. You pulled over to a *cloud*,' said Dorothy. 'There aren't any curbs in the *sky*. There *couldn't* be. You pulled over to a cloud'" (p. 80).

Charlie is finished. The once vital male is reduced to despair and madness. His hope to find room for his imagination and story-telling skills, to dominate and please, is futile. Seemingly concerned and helpful, but effectively domineering and egotistical, the wife triumphs. Fantasy involving hostility toward the wife, obsessive living within fantasy, fantasy leading to withdrawal and passivity, these are analogous to the story of Walter Mitty. The comparison suggests that finally Mitty's fantasies (far less imaginative and creative than Charlie's) will be similarly futile and will lead finally to a similar fate.

Although **"The Lady on 142," "The Catbird Seat,"** and **"The Curb in the Sky"** are delightful stories, **"Mitty"** appears to be the more profound: the secret inner life, a defensive and aggressive tactic at the same time, the suggestion of Mitty's universality, but also of his progressive dissolution and increasing awareness of death, carry the story beyond the others. The mockery of the impoverished imagination formed by an inadequate culture, and the failure of Mitty's will to act, cause Mitty to be more memorable than the protagonists of the other stories. Mitty is not simply the little man, representative of our desire to dream of glory in reaction to a dull world, but suggestive of a situation far more troublesome: one may see in Mitty misanthropy—his disgust with the banality of his everyday life is unbearable. Traditionally, the misanthrope figure withdraws: Timon of Athens to the wilderness; Gulliver to his stable; Alceste of *Le Misanthrope* to the "desert," in three classic versions. Mitty is no less a misanthropist; his disgust and bitterness emerge again and again in lines of fantasy dialogue: "'It's forty kilometers through hell, sir,' said the sergeant. Mitty finished one last brandy. 'After all,' he said softly 'what isn't?'" But he is the misanthrope demystified and made middle-class; obviously the suburban man can neither imagine nor afford the drama of a retreat into the wilderness. Mitty's retreat is inward, to the remote, intimate airways of his mind.

James Idema (review date 10 July 1994)

SOURCE: "From the Thurber Trove: Good Humor, Good Always," in *Chicago Tribune Books,* July 10, 1994, p. 6.

[*The following review finds the previously uncollected works in* People Have More Fun Than Anybody *equal to any of Thurber's more celebrated and familiar writing and cartoons.*]

It's possible that people of a certain age would find examples of writing and drawing that made them laugh out loud in their younger days just as amusing today. It's possible also that they would find the material disappointing and dated. Why did this stuff seem so funny 50 years ago?

The fact that the 100 or so essays and drawings in ***People Have More Fun Than Anybody*** were previously uncollected raises a more direct question about durability. Until now were these pieces of James Thurber's that the editor says he culled from "the crumbling pages of early *New Yorkers* and defunct magazines like *PM* unworthy of preservation between hard covers?

The evidence at hand strongly suggests no. Even the skeptical will find most of these samples to be vintage Thurber, illustrating the enduring relevance that T. S. Eliot detected in Thurber's work in 1951. In the preface Eliot is quoted from a *Time* cover story of that year.

> [Thurber's work] is a form of humor which is also a way of saying something serious. There is a criticism of life at the bottom of it. It is serious and even somber. Unlike so much humor it is not merely a criticism of manners—that is, of the superficial aspects of society at a given moment—but something more profound. His writings and also his illustrations are capable of surviving the immediate environment and time out of which they spring.

Eliot here is pretty "serious and even somber" himself. Recalling his scholarly mien one hopes that, encountering Thurber, he too laughed out loud. It's possible to get too serious about things like this. Surely one of the endearing qualities about Thurber's work is its delightful, uncomplicated silliness. When aficionados trade recollections of their favorite Thurber cartoons or essays, they don't ponder their social significance. They just laugh and recall others.

Remember the seal in the bedroom, they say, the owl in the attic, the day the bed fell and the electricity leaked. Remember that drawing of the woman confronting the hippo-like beast, beside which lie a shoe, a hat and a cold pipe, and demanding: "What have you done with Dr. Millmoss?"

Those pieces from previous collections are no more entertaining than the material in ***People Have More Fun Than Anybody,*** subtitled "A Centennial Celebration." They're just more familiar. The fun in the new book (for some of us) is recognizing a long-forgotten cartoon or bit of writing that we might not have ever seen again.

A drawing from a 1936 *New Yorker* cover, for example, epitomizes a frequent leitmotif of Thurber's. In the near background a smilingly confident woman is racing through the woods, led by a dog on a leash. In the foreground, just out of her sight, a man cowers behind a tree. We realize he is doomed because the dog has obviously already spotted him. **"My Day (With Apologies to Eleanor Roosevelt),"** from the same year, is a takeoff on the first lady's popular newspaper column. Good to have this gentle parody preserved.

The familiar inhabitants of Thurber land are all accounted for here—those dogs, the ambling as well as the contemplative; those terrible women, the immensely glowering and the smugly obdurate, the startlingly athletic and the frighteningly glacial; those men, the cringing and haunted husbands, bewildered fathers, bland psychiatrists, ferocious fencers. And the stories and fables are small masterpieces of contemporary comment.

It is surely sobering to those of us who recall fondly the Thurber of ***Men, Women and Dogs, Lanterns and Lances*** and ***My World—and Welcome to It*** to realize that Thurber would have been 100 years old next December. This quote from ***Lanterns and Lances*** seems particularly fitting:

> "Many things, or rather people and ideas, are dealt with here in what I hope is a humorous vein, for, as I keep pointing out, humor in a living culture must not be put away in the attic with the flag, but should be flaunted, like the flag, bravely.

Craig Seligman (essay date Fall 1994)

SOURCE: "The Cottage of Smugness," in *The Threepenny Review,* Vol. XV, No. 3, Fall, 1994, pp. 26-8.

[*In the following mixed assessment, Seligman finds that*

some of Thurber's work retains a peculiar charm but that most of it is overwrought and dated, the product of a talent that never achieved its potential.]

In reviewing these skeptical reflections on the centenary of James Thurber, I find there is an aspect of his output that I've tended to slight, and so I had better acknowledge it up front: his charm. I can't deny Thurber's charm. His work is full of it; his silly drawings, especially, are rife with it. You have probably encountered the story, told in many places, of how in the late 1920s E. B. White retrieved some of his friend's doodlings from the floor of the office they shared at *The New Yorker*, inked in the penciled squiggles, and submitted the results to Harold Ross, the magazine's founding editor. Ross was skeptical; so was Thurber. But Thurber's drawings, like his stories and essays, have taken their place in the pantheon of American humor. They are disarmingly unforced and, technically, disarmingly primitive. "If you ever got good you'd be mediocre," White told him astutely. The fact that he never got good is probably the reason that his artwork now seems so much more idiosyncratic and so much less dated than most of his prose: the naïveté that Matisse achieved by overcoming his artistic training Thurber attained by never having had any. I don't draw the contrast out of the blue; it was made in Thurber's heyday, and not altogether preposterously. White, in fact, came to regard the drawings as his friend's greatest work. I don't agree, because they have none of the power of the writing. But they also have none of the problems: they treat the same themes that in Thurber's stories make me want to leave the room, and yet they feel whimsical, painless—fantastic.

Thurber's writing is not fantastic. Even when it takes the form of fables or fairy tales, its homely, quotidian detail (which is often an intentional deflating device) keeps it down to earth. And while at its loveliest, as in **"The Catbird Seat"** and **"The Unicorn in the Garden,"** it, too, is beautifully unforced, you certainly couldn't call it primitive. Some of the essays amount to writerly attempts at doodling—bagatelles whose aimlessness is largely the point. But they never attain the purity of the drawings, because they've been too painstakingly hammered out, and labor is the surest way to kill a joke.

Thurber died in 1961, the year of Hemingway's suicide, and three decades later his name is practically as resonant. If Hemingway gave voice to a native fixation on manliness and self-reliance, then Thurber, in some odd way his counterpart, came to enunciate a native emasculation. Any reader who has perused more than a few of his stories or leafed through the many drawings of harridans and meek little men knows how transfixed he was by the vision of male ineptitude before female assurance and strength. His caricatures could make the conflict funny, pathetic, or ugly, but in every case his discomfort—his terror—is evident. One reason that **"The Catbird Seat"** and **"The Unicorn in the Garden"** stand out among Thurber's stories is that the meek little men in them prevail, which is such a rarity in his universe that they seem more like fairy tales than his fairy tales do. Much more often, almost too often to enumerate, the little man is crushed. (The Bert Pendlys and Walter Mittys retreat into the only available refuge, neurosis and fantasy.) Thurber's fear of women runs so deep that it teeters on the verge of feminism, since his women are the equals—no, the betters—of the weaklings who are supposed to dominate them. But it never occurred to him to explore this paradox by questioning the scheme of things. If the women weren't subservient, then there was something the matter with the men.

You don't have to dig to unearth the evidence of Thurber's insecurity. It isn't buried. The mortifying moment in **"The Thin Red Leash"** when he is walking his pert little Scottie and a "huge steamfitter" addresses him, "What d'y' say me an' you an' the dog go somewheres and have tea?" is typical. His only major fight with Harold Ross erupted after Ross called him "a sis." "Jared L. Manley," the pseudonym he took for the "Where Are They Now?" series he worked on for the magazine in the 1930s, was a reference to "the manly art of self-defense"—an art that the delicate writer, blind in one eye (and in later years in both), could never practice himself. But he loved the idea of using his fists. When Dorothy Parker declared, "Humor is a shield, not a weapon," he bristled. "Humor is as big a fist as any other form, or maybe bigger," he protested to White. And when a reader wrote *The New Republic* complaining that a review by Thurber had been "a slap in the face," he snapped back triumphantly, "I didn't realize my hand was open."

Strength, virility, dominance is Thurber's running subtext—his running text. His marriage tales (stories like **"Am I Not Your Rosalind?," "The Breaking Up of the Winships,"** and **"The Case of Dimity Ann"**) presage and sometimes rival the venom of *Who's Afraid of Virginia Woolf?*, which owes a great deal to them. When it comes to character, though, Thurber isn't much of a psychologist; his defensiveness (and he never claims to be a disinterested observer) keeps him from getting very far beneath the surface of others. There is only one character he is really interested in probing, and the spectacle of his self-exposure can be riveting. On a few occasions—as in **"Teacher's Pet,"**—he takes it to frightening lengths.

Kelby, the fifty-year-old protagonist of **"Teacher's Pet,"** has never gotten over his eighth-grade humiliation at the hands of a bully. Thirty-seven years later his cowardice still preys on him. Near the end of the story, he happens upon two boys repeating the same ugly, age-old scenario; incensed, he chases off the bully. Then he turns to the sniveling victim, whose name is Elbert, and suddenly he flips:

> "Shut up!" shouted Kelby. "Shut up!" But the boy kept on. Kelby looked at his quivering lower lip and at the convulsion of his stomach. Elbert was fighting to gain control of himself, but he lost the battle and began to weep unrestrainedly. Kelby was suddenly upon him. He grabbed him tightly by the shoulders and shook him until his head bobbed back and forth. He let go of the boy's left shoulder and slapped him on the cheek. "You little crybaby!" sobbed Kelby. "You goddam little coward!"

A few paragraphs later, the story is diminished by a neat, ironic close. But the rawness of the self-loathing that breaks through at this climax is almost sickening. For the brief moment that you see clearly into Thurber's torment, you can sense the power that he had at his disposal—or might have had, if his gaze had always been so unflinching.

But even when he flinches he's revealing. ***The Male Animal,*** the 1940 comedy he wrote with Elliott Nugent, is probably the work that lays his anxieties most cruelly bare. The central figure is a milquetoast academic whose wife nearly leaves him for his former rival, a onetime football hero who has returned to the campus for a big game. Professor Tommy Turner displays his moral fiber in a fight for academic freedom against a redbaiter on the Board Trustees. But his moral fiber doesn't give off much of a sexual scent, and the academic-freedom side of the story, which was Nugent's contribution, fades before the more elemental conflict between the physically timid male and the strapping, confident one, which was, naturally, Thurber's. Thurber often does what he can to shore up his morale by making his strong men stupid, but he can't ignore their seductiveness. The play's title comes from a speech in which a sloshed Tommy proclaims that a man has to fight when his mate is lured away:

> The sea lion knows better. He snarls. He gores. He roars with his antlers. He knows that love is a thing you do something about. He knows it is a thing that words can kill. You do something. You don't just sit there . . . . A woman likes a man who does something. All the male animals fight for the female, from the land crab to the bird of paradise. They don't just sit and talk. They act.

Tommy's wife, Ellen, represents one of Thurber's few attempts to set forth a woman who's not a caricature. She doesn't stand 6'6" or look ready to wrestle, but she turns out to be, in her primped, demure way, as ruthless a castrating bitch as any of the viragoes in the cartoons. (Olivia de Havilland read the role perfectly in the 1942 movie, in which, opposite Henry Fonda's Tommy, she gave one of the hardest performances of her career.) Of course, Tommy finally proves that he's a "scrapper"—which is the same word Thurber uses in **"The Thin Red Leash"** to defend his little dog. But the way he prevails is so corny, so equivocal, and so lacking in conviction that it does much to explain why both the play and the movie have been forgotten.

Though Thurber got out of Columbus for good when he was thirty, it stayed with him; later on he could never quite decide whether he was a man-about-town or a hick at heart. He despised the narrowness and philistinism of the place ("Millions for manure, but not one cent for literature" was a barb he was fond of quoting). In 1951 Ohio State, his alma mater, offered him an honorary degree right on the heels of issuing a gag rule subjecting all campus speeches to prior scrutiny—weirdly paralleling the outrages he and Nugent had thought up a dozen years earlier for ***The Male Animal.*** He declined it in disgust.

And yet he stayed loyal. You would never know from any of his written recollections how much he looked down on his boyhood home. What mockery he does indulge in is fond: he treats Columbus as the norm—heartland America, unsophisticated but honest and practical. He devoted two very different books to recollections of Ohio, and both of them are, in their own ways, sugar-coated. ***My Life and Hard Times*** (1933), the source of some of his most widely anthologized stories (including **"The Night the Bed Fell"** and **"The Night the Ghost Got In"**), reorganizes his troubled childhood into a comic idyll, depicting the Thurbers as wildly eccentric but at the same time solidly normal—a prototype for the zany-but-healthy families that would infest TV sitcoms a couple of decades later. The America of these pseudo-memoirs is the same picket-fence Eden that the Hollywood studios hawked to their audience; and in both cases a public enchanted by the sweetness of the vision let itself be conned into nostalgia for something that had never been.

Thurber's second Ohio book, ***The Thurber Album*** (1952)—fifteen portraits of family pillars, local eccentrics, college teachers, and other early mentors—is far less antic than ***My Life and Hard Times,*** but no tougher. The crinkly smiles do give it a lovely surface, though. Thurber's gift for candying the past stood in inverse proportion to his prudishness and priggishness about the present, and the ***Album*** made an ideal setting for his bumpless prose. The same gift put satire beyond him: his best humor is whimsical, not satiric. The typical pattern is for an artist to learn from one or more mentors, pull away, and finally—in some fashion, at least—repudiate them. But Thurber was never able to put anybody behind him; he was fatally easy on his memories and his ideals. He soft-pedaled the flaws in the people he wrote about (and still got howls of protest from his family), and what criticisms he did offer were so gentle they amounted to caresses, even in the case of one professor who at an advanced age took up fascism. He was no scrapper—there was something fundamentally passive in his nature. He was a born protégé, which is what made him putty in the hands of Harold Ross and E. B. White.

Thurber, of course, had a large part in creating *The New Yorker,* and it had a larger part in creating him. The man and the magazine split rather bitterly in the years after Ross's death, but by then they were destined, like Rogers and Astaire, to be remembered as a couple. Thurber arrived on the premises when he was thirty-two, an advanced age for a writer to fall under someone else's shaping influence. But there can be little doubt that it was Ross who set the stamp on his output. By all accounts Ross had the true editor's genius for finding people who could give him what he wanted—a genius he demonstrated in hiring White and Thurber, whose previous careers had not been stellar and whose later ones probably wouldn't have amounted to much without him, either. *The New Yorker,* so the story goes, saved Thurber from the demands of journalistic topicality and from the intimidation of the larger forms. Working in the smaller ones, he could let his restless imagination swing like a weather vane, toward cartoons, stories, essays, sketches—whichever way the wind was blowing. He was the consummate doodler, and in letting him doodle, *The New Yorker* made Thurber possible.

That, at least, is the standard version. But isn't there another possibility: that the sparks that flash intermittently from his hundreds and hundreds of pages are just hints of his genius? When lightning strikes in Thurber, it mainly illuminates the surrounding expanse of flat terrain. Granted, **"The Catbird Seat"**—to take the story he acknowledged as his best—is perfect, on its small scale. But it isn't *For Whom the Bell Tolls,* and if you gather up all the scattered flashes of Thurber's brilliance, they still don't add up to a *For Whom the Bell Tolls.* A stale scent of disappointment wafts out from between the covers of his many books. They're charming, they're *fine,* but when you come upon a lethally powerful story like **"A Couple of Hamburgers"** or **"Teacher's Pet,"** you get a sulfurous whiff of what *might* have been. Taste, decorum, and good humor were always dangers for *New Yorker* writers, and in Thurber they neutralized something that was ugly but potentially great: the rage, which wasn't so much controlled as suppressed.

It did eventually surface, poisoning his personality (which had never been very pleasant), but by that time it had corroded into resentfulness. In his later work, he abandoned humor for grandstanding and turned into a windbag. "How many years will it take to convince people that I'm not a clown?" he demanded the year he died. His last books make grotesquely unpleasant reading: the misogyny grew rancid, and the attempts at satire dissolved into angry carping, aimless word games, and a generalized geriatric bitterness.

But in his prime he suppressed that anger. His prose is so held in that it practically aches. Thurber's humorous writing too often carries you for long expectant periods in a state of pre-laughter, waiting for the sneeze of hilarity that never comes. And though he wasn't a one-note writer, he sounded one note at a time. There's not much ambiguity in Thurber: when he's breezy, it's unalloyed, as it is when he's touching or cruel or pensive, but he seldom brings conflicting responses into play, and a single piece almost never demonstrates his range. That's a trap for the writer of casuals; and Thurber, whose youthful attempts at a novel and later forays into dramatic writing after ***The Male Animal*** all came to nothing, was always conscious of his failure in the larger forms. The locus classicus of this discomfort is his preface to ***My Life and Hard Times,*** in which he bemoans the plight of "writers of light pieces running from a thousand to two thousand words":

> The notion that such persons are gay of heart and carefree is curiously untrue. They lead, as a matter of fact, an existence of jumpiness and apprehension. They sit on the edge of the chair of Literature. In the house of Life they have the feeling that they have never taken off their overcoats: Afraid of losing themselves in the larger flight of the two-volume novel, or even the one-volume novel, they stick to short accounts of their misadventures because they never get so deep into them but that they feel they can get out. This type of writing is not a joyous form of self-expression but the manifestation of a twitchiness at once cosmic and mundane. . . . To call such persons "humorists," a loose-fitting and ugly word, is to miss the nature of their dilemma and the dilemma of their nature. The little wheels of their invention are set in motion by the damp hand of melancholy.

Prose that fresh and delicately balanced is a peculiar medium for a message of such insecure gloom, but that's Thurber—and, of course, the passage really has nothing to do with other "writers of light pieces." Instead it's a frank evaluation of his own artistic (and personal) limitations, something close to a confession of failure.

And yet none of his contemporaries would have dreamed of calling him a failure—he was a household word, the most celebrated luminary on Ross's celebrated staff. (Auden and Eliot were among his fans.) Nor would he have called himself a failure, though the defensiveness and pugnacity of his later years suggest a self-doubt that he never honestly owned up to. He couldn't: failure was anathema. He *had* to be on the winning team. At Ohio State he had been a nobody until Elliott Nugent, five years younger but already a campus mover, took him under his wing, got him into his fraternity, and buoyed his confidence so effectively that

Thurber went on to become a honcho in the drama society and to edit the college newspaper and the literary magazine. Later on, when he had the good fortune to be invited onto *The New Yorker*, it was the same story writ bigger. Belonging was everything; sometimes his clubbiness about the place is enough to set your teeth on edge. Hence his feeling of loss in the late 1930s when he returned to the office after a long absence in Europe. He was incensed at the changes, and he bitched and grumbled about them to his dying day, convinced that everyone who had a hand in shaping the magazine after he did was taking it in the wrong direction. It was no longer *his* club.

Thurber had opinions on all the controversies of the era and was always readier than White was to dive into the fray. Ross didn't take him seriously as a critic, though—a light that shows that his famous instinct could sometimes fail him. Thurber's book reviews for *The New Republic* and other magazines exhibit a contemplative appealingly confident side that's very different from the glib, ironic voice of the stories and casuals. Like White, Thurber considered himself an average Joe and narrowed his eyes at theory. His jabs at psychoanalysis suggest that above all he thought Freudians took everything (including themselves) too solemnly. And as for Marxists, "Why, in God's name," he demanded of Malcolm Cowley, "can't they have one or two likeable, genial, humorous, natural human beings to espouse their cause?"

Much more than White, he loved playing the litterateur. He never got over his infatuation with Henry James; during the course of his career he made several attempts to imitate his style that are too affectionate, and too dull, to qualify as parody. But as he always acknowledged, the decisive turn in his career came when Ross, shortly after Thurber's arrival at *The New Yorker*, put him in a tiny office with White (who was, like Nugent, five years his junior). Thurber said later that he "learned discipline in writing from studying Andy White's stuff"; it helped him escape the involuted rhythms of James and the other florid models he had come of age on. "I would use 'in fine,' 'as who should say,' and the like. . . . The precision and clarity of White's writing helped me a lot, slowed me down from the dog-trot of newspaper tempo and made me realize a writer turns on his mind, not a faucet."

Of course, as Charles S. Holmes points out in his excellent 1972 study, *The Clocks of Columbus*, one of the principal reasons Thurber was able to learn so rapidly from White was that they were so much alike to begin with. They brought, a curiously parochial voice to *The New Yorker*'s sophistication, reflecting and amplifying Ross's own suspicion of anything highfalutin. They believed in good writing, certainly—good and plain; fancy thought and fancy verbiage made them wary. Thurber, though, had loftier ambitions and a grander, if wobblier, self-image. There can be no doubt that White—the same White who later, in *The Elements of Style*, would declare flatly, "The approach to style is by way of plainness, simplicity, orderliness, sincerity"—helped Thurber get rid of some youthful excesses. White's cleanness is a relief after the curlicued journalism that preceded it, and you can't deny its purity even if you find it (as I do) placid. But what may not be so apparent at first glance, and may never have been apparent at Ross's *New Yorker*, is that it's also a highly personal style. It fit White as neatly as complications and involutions fit James; but it was a style designed to simplify, and Thurber was anything but simple. Here was a man who would get soused and bully his friends, who pursued women and then couldn't perform with them, who broke down and cried at his own wedding, who missed his daughter's birth because he was out on the town with an old girlfriend—a volatile, self-destructive, complicated, *sloppy* man. (If Burton Bernstein's sour 1975 biography demonstrates anything, it demonstrates that.) Yet he cramped his antic imagination into the bland, inhibited, moderate-to-a-fault Yankee manner that had been perfected by White and sanctified by Ross. The unruffled, unruffling tone may have suited the teacher's pet who yearned to please; but it denied, or tried to deny, the sociopath who was spoiling to bloody every psyche in the room—the creepy, not-nice but not-dull side of Thurber, the side where all the powder was stored.

The White style works best for Thurber in the reportorial pieces, like the five-part series on soap opera that was reprinted in ***The Beast in Me.*** And that's what it remains best for. Years after the passing of Ross, a writer as eccentric and strong-willed as Truman Capote could be cowed by the aura of *The New Yorker* into sacrificing his peculiar voice for the neat, spare White style when he reported *In Cold Blood* for Ross's successor, William Shawn. We owe Ross a debt of gratitude for some of the century's best reporting, but his ideas about literature were modest: witness the rise, under the tutelage of Katharine Angell (another instance of his knack for locating people who could put his vision into practice), of the understated, under-plotted prose form that was to become known as the *New Yorker* story. Modesty, though, didn't become Thurber; he was an egomaniac, a braggart, and a messy, oversized talent, born, like so many of his tormented generation, to go too far. But he never went far enough.

Hemingway, to be fair, had it easier. He could inhabit his macho men with such unwavering, aching conviction because he was giving form to a cultural ideal; the culture was behind him all the way. Thurber didn't have the wherewithal to challenge the ideal, but he knew that he didn't live up to it, and he could look around him and see that not many others did, either. His work is all about getting pushed around, and about how the pushed-around shuffle through their lives deprived of conviction and self-respect. And that's why, for all the smugness and the simmering nastiness, he is still so resonant (more resonant, in the sense that he deals with the ground-down actual, than Hemingway): he enuciated the resignation, the deflation, the dull gray tragedy of American manhood. But *funny*?

The "mannerisms, tricks, adornments" that White warns the young writer against, given time and nurture, can grow into profound expressions of personality, as they did with James or, in a very different fashion, with Hemingway. The *New Yorker* style carried Thurber to fame, but it left him there, stranded down below the heights there is every indication he could have scaled. Did Ross and White give him the means to climb them, or did they hold him back? Or did he *let* them hold him back when, breaking away, he could have ascended beyond their view? If *The New Yorker* made Thurber possible, it also bound him down to the dismal earth. He had the talent but he lacked the nerve. The road of modesty led to the cottage of smugness.

FURTHER READING

Bibliographies

Bernstein, Burton. *Thurber: A Biography.* New York: Dodd, Mead and Company, 1975: 517-20.

List of primary and secondary critical sources for the definitive Thurber biography.

Bowden, Edwin T. *James Thurber: A Bibliography.* Columbus: Ohio State University Press, 1969.

A comprehensive bibliographic source of Thurber's works and criticism.

Biographies

Bernstein, Burton. *Thurber: A Biography.* New York: Dodd, Mead and Company, 1975.

A definitive work on Thurber's life, unflattering but disinterested.

Grauer, Neil. *Remember Laughter: A Life of James Thurber.* Lincoln: University of Nebraska Press, 1995.

A sympathetic view of Thurber's life.

Criticism

Appelbaum, Judith. "Paperback Talk." *New York Times Book Review* (12 December 1982): 34.

Positive notice of the publication of *Selected Letters.*

Baldwin, Alice. "James Thurber's Compounds." *Language and Style* III, No. 2 (Summer 1970): 185-96.

A discussion of Thurber's innovative and idiosyncratic word compounding.

Dunning, Jennifer. "Paperback Talk." *New York Times Book Review* (30 October 1977): 57.

Brief review of the reissue of Thurber's children's book, *The Thirteen Clocks.*

Review of *Credos and Curios. New York Times Book Review* (13 March 1983): 28.

Positive note on the reissue of the 1962 collection.

Review of *Thurber's Dogs. New York Times Book Review* (13 May 1984): 38.

Brief, appreciative notice of the reissue of Thurber's 1955 volume.

Stafford, Jean. Review of *The Great Quillow. New Yorker* 51 (1 December 1975): 178.

A very brief review of the reissue of one of Thurber's lesser known children's stories.

Additional coverage of Thurber's life and career is contained in the following sources published by Gale: *Contemporary Authors,* Vols. 73-76; *Contemporary Authors New Revision Series,* Vols. 17, 39; *Concise Dictionary of American Literary Biography, 1929-41; Discovering Authors; Discovering Authors: British; Discovering Authors: Canadian; DISCovering Authors Modules: Dramatists, Most-Studied Authors,* and *Novelists; Dictionary of Literary Biography,* Vols. 4, 11, 22, 102; *Major Authors and Illustrators for Young Adults; Major Twentieth-Century Writers; Something about the Author,* Vol. 13; and *Short Story Criticism,* Vol. 1.

□ Contemporary Literary Criticism

Indexes

Literary Criticism Series
Cumulative Author Index
Cumulative Topic Index
Cumulative Nationality Index
Title Index, Volume 125

How to Use This Index

The main references

Camus, Albert
1913-1960 . . . . **CLC 1, 2, 4, 9, 11, 14, 32, 69; DA; DAB; DAC; DAM DRAM, MST, NOV; DC2; SSC 9; WLC**

list all author entries in the following Gale Literary Criticism series:

BLC = *Black Literature Criticism*
BLCS = *Black Literature Criticism Supplement*
CLC = *Contemporary Literary Criticism*
CLR = *Children's Literature Review*
CMLC = *Classical and Medieval Literature Criticism*
DA = *DISCovering Authors*
DAB = *DISCovering Authors: British*
DAC = *DISCovering Authors: Canadian*
DAM = *DISCovering Authors Modules*
DRAM = *dramatists;* ***MST*** = *most-studied authors;* ***MULT*** = *multicultural authors;* ***NOV*** = *novelists;* ***POET*** = *poets;* ***POP*** = *popular/genre writers;* ***DC*** = *Drama Criticism*
HLC = *Hispanic Literature Criticism*
LC = *Literature Criticism from 1400 to 1800*
NCLC = *Nineteenth-Century Literature Criticism*
PC = *Poetry Criticism*
SSC = *Short Story Criticism*
TCLC = *Twentieth-Century Literary Criticism*
WLC = *World Literature Criticism, 1500 to the Present*
WLCS = *World Literature Criticism Supplement*

The cross-references

See also CA 89-92; DLB 72; MTCW

list all author entries in the following Gale biographical and literary sources:

AAYA = *Authors & Artists for Young Adults*
AITN = *Authors in the News*
BEST = *Bestsellers*
BW = *Black Writers*
CA = *Contemporary Authors*
CAAS = *Contemporary Authors Autobiography Series*
CABS = *Contemporary Authors Bibliographical Series*
CANR = *Contemporary Authors New Revision Series*
CAP = *Contemporary Authors Permanent Series*
CDALB = *Concise Dictionary of American Literary Biography*
CDBLB = *Concise Dictionary of British Literary Biography*
DLB = *Dictionary of Literary Biography*
DLBD = *Dictionary of Literary Biography Documentary Series*
DLBY = *Dictionary of Literary Biography Yearbook*
HW = *Hispanic Writers*
JRDA = *Junior DISCovering Authors*
MAICYA = *Major Authors and Illustrators for Children and Young Adults*
MTCW = *Major 20th-Century Writers*
NNAL = *Native North American Literature*
SAAS = *Something about the Author Autobiography Series*
SATA = *Something about the Author*
YABC = *Yesterday's Authors of Books for Children*

Literary Criticism Series Cumulative Author Index

Literary Criticism Series Cumulative Topic Index

This index lists all topic entries in Gale's *Classical and Medieval Literature Criticism, Contemporary Literary Criticism, Literature Criticism from 1400 to 1800, Nineteenth-Century Literature Criticism,* and *Twentieth-Century Literary Criticism.*

Topic Index

Contemporary Literary Criticism
Cumulative Nationality Index

Nationality Index

Nationality Index

Nationality Index

CLC-125 Title Index

ISBN 0-7876-3200-7

90000

9 780787 632007